Real and Per-Capita Data

Equals 15	Less 16	Equals 17	Less personal outlays			Equals 21	Percentage of disposable personal income			Gross domestic product		Disposable personal income		
			18	19	20		Personal outlays		24	25	26	27	28	
							22	23		Current prices	1987 prices	Current prices	1987 prices	
Personal income	Personal tax and nontax payments	Disposable personal income	Total	Personal consumption expenditures	Interest paid by persons	Personal saving	Total	Personal consumption expenditures	Personal saving	Per-capita dollars	Billions of dollars	Per-capita dollars	Billions of dollars	Year
Billions of dollars							Percent							
409.2	48.7	360.5	339.9	332.4	7.0	20.6	93.0	90.5	7.0	2,837	1,973.2	1,994	1,313.0	1960
426.5	50.3	376.2	351.3	343.5	7.3	24.9	93.1	90.7	6.9	2,891	2,025.6	2,048	1,356.4	1961
453.4	54.8	398.7	372.8	364.4	7.8	25.9	91.9	89.6	8.1	3,059	2,129.8	2,137	1,414.8	1962
476.4	58.0	418.4	393.7	384.2	8.9	24.6	92.9	90.5	7.1	3,190	2,218.0	2,210	1,461.1	1963
510.7	56.0	454.7	423.1	412.5	10.0	31.6	93.5	90.9	6.5	3,375	2,343.3	2,369	1,562.2	1964
552.9	61.9	491.0	456.4	444.6	11.1	34.6	94.3	92.2	5.7	3,624	2,473.5	2,527	1,653.5	1965
601.7	71.0	530.7	494.3	481.6	12.0	36.4	93.4	91.3	6.6	3,909	2,622.3	2,699	1,734.3	1966
646.5	77.9	568.6	522.8	509.3	12.5	45.9	93.5	91.4	6.5	4,090	2,690.3	2,861	1,811.4	1967
709.9	92.1	617.8	573.9	559.1	13.8	43.9	94.1	91.8	5.9	4,423	2,801.0	3,077	1,886.8	1968
773.7	109.9	663.8	620.4	603.7	15.7	43.4	93.1	90.7	6.9	4,729	2,877.1	3,274	1,947.4	1969
831.0	109.0	722.0	664.4	646.5	16.8	57.6	92.0	89.5	8.0	4,932	2,875.8	3,521	2,025.3	1970
893.5	108.7	784.9	719.3	700.3	17.8	65.5	91.7	89.2	8.3	5,274	2,965.1	3,779	2,099.9	1971
980.5	132.0	848.5	788.6	767.8	19.6	59.9	92.9	90.5	7.1	5,748	3,107.1	4,042	2,186.2	1972
1,098.7	140.6	958.1	871.9	848.1	22.4	86.2	91.0	88.5	9.0	6,368	3,268.6	4,521	2,334.1	1973
1,205.7	159.1	1,046.5	953.0	927.7	24.2	93.5	91.1	88.6	8.9	6,818	3,248.1	4,893	2,317.0	1974
1,307.3	156.4	1,150.9	1,050.4	1,024.9	24.5	100.4	91.3	89.1	8.7	7,343	3,221.7	5,329	2,355.4	1975
1,446.3	182.3	1,264.0	1,170.7	1,143.1	26.7	93.2	92.6	90.4	7.4	8,110	3,380.8	5,796	2,440.9	1976
1,601.3	210.0	1,391.3	1,303.1	1,271.5	30.7	88.1	93.7	91.4	6.3	8,973	3,533.2	6,316	2,512.6	1977
1,807.9	240.1	1,567.8	1,459.6	1,421.2	37.5	108.1	93.1	90.7	6.9	10,013	3,703.5	7,042	2,638.4	1978
2,033.1	280.2	1,753.0	1,629.3	1,583.7	44.5	123.7	92.9	90.3	7.1	11,062	3,796.8	7,787	2,710.1	1979
2,265.4	312.4	1,952.9	1,798.6	1,748.1	49.4	154.3	92.1	89.5	7.9	11,877	3,776.3	8,576	2,733.6	1980
2,534.7	360.2	2,174.5	1,982.1	1,926.2	54.6	192.4	91.2	88.6	8.8	13,178	3,843.1	9,455	2,795.8	1981
2,690.9	371.4	2,319.6	2,119.6	2,059.2	58.8	200.0	91.4	88.8	8.6	13,578	3,760.3	9,989	2,820.4	1982
2,862.5	368.8	2,493.7	2,324.7	2,257.5	65.7	169.1	93.2	90.5	6.8	14,551	3,906.6	10,642	2,893.6	1983
3,154.6	395.1	2,759.5	2,537.2	2,460.3	75.0	222.3	91.9	89.2	8.1	15,937	4,148.5	11,673	3,080.1	1984
3,379.8	436.8	2,943.0	2,753.2	2,667.4	83.6	189.8	93.6	90.6	6.4	16,900	4,279.8	12,339	3,162.1	1985
3,590.4	459.0	3,131.5	2,943.6	2,850.6	90.9	187.8	94.0	91.0	6.0	17,714	4,404.5	13,010	3,261.9	1986
3,802.0	512.5	3,289.5	3,146.9	3,052.2	92.3	142.6	95.7	92.8	4.3	18,683	4,540.0	13,545	3,289.6	1987
4,075.9	527.7	3,548.2	3,392.0	3,296.1	93.7	156.2	95.6	92.9	4.4	20,000	4,718.6	14,477	3,404.3	1988
4,380.2	591.7	3,788.6	3,621.6	3,517.9	101.6	166.9	95.6	92.9	4.4	21,231	4,836.9	15,313	3,471.2	1989
4,679.8	621.0	4,058.8	3,852.2	3,742.6	107.5	206.6	94.9	92.2	5.1	22,056	4,884.9	16,236	3,538.3	1990
4,833.9	616.0	4,217.8	3,995.8	3,886.8	106.8	222.1	94.7	92.2	5.3	22,419	4,848.4	16,693	3,534.1	1991
5,125.1	654.2	4,471.0	4,235.7	3,999.2	106.2	235.3	94.2	92.6	5.1	22,780	4,840.1	16,902	3,549.2	1992

Contemporary Macroeconomics

Eighth Edition

Milton H. Spencer
Professor of Economics, Emeritus
Wayne State University

Orley M. Amos, Jr.
Professor of Economics
Oklahoma State University

Worth Publishers

Contemporary Macroeconomics, Eighth Edition

Copyright © 1993, 1990, 1986, 1983, 1980, 1977, 1974, 1971
by Milton H. Spencer

All rights reserved.

Manufactured in the United States of America

Library of Congress Catalog Card Number: 92-61383

ISBN: 0-87901-615-9

Printing: 1 2 3 4 5—97 96 95 94 93

Development editor: Susan Seuling

Design: Malcolm Grear Designers

Art director: George Touloumes

Production editor: Barbara B. Toniolo

Production supervisor: Barbara Anne Seixas

Layout: Patricia Lawson

Photo researcher: Elaine Bernstein

Line art: Demetrios Zangos

Composition and separations: TSI Graphics, Inc.

Printing and binding: Von Hoffmann Press, Inc.

Cover and part opening art: Daniel Kraft

Worth Publishers
33 Irving Place
New York, New York 10003

For Darcy and Jeff; Robin;
Cathy and Scott
and
For Pam, Chris, and Holly

Contents in Brief

All parts, chapters, and chapter sections with substantial international content are indicated by a globe symbol 🌐.

Contents

CHAPTER 1

Economic Resources, Goals, and Institutions   20

CHAPTER 2

CHAPTER 3

The Ethics of Distribution   **76**
        Contributive Standard   76
        Needs Standard   76
        Equality Standard   76
        Conclusion: An "Optimal" Distribution?   77

The Business Sector: Organization and Size   **77**
        The Proprietorship   78
        The Partnership   78
        The Corporation   78
        Business Size and Problems of Bigness   79

The Foreign Sector: International Trade and Finance   **80**
        Enlarging the Circular-Flow Model   81
        How to Calculate Your Class's Gini Coefficient   85
TAKE A STAND *Income Distribution: Is It Fair?*   86

CHAPTER 4

The Public Sector—Government: Public Choice and Taxation   **88**

Economic Scope and Functions of Government   **89**
        Promotion and Regulation of the Private Sector   89
        Provision of Social Goods   89
        Conclusion: Achieving Efficiency Through the Market   90

Spillovers, Market Failure, and Public Choice   **91**
        Redressing Spillovers   91
        Dealing with International Spillovers   93
        Conclusion: Efficiency and Public Choice   93

Public-Sector Budgeting   **94**
        Public Overspending and Public Choice   94
        Scope of Government in Different Countries   96

Our Tax System   **96**
        Taxes on Income   97
        Taxes on Wealth   100
        Taxes on Activities   100
        An International Comparison of Tax Systems   100

Theories of Taxation   **101**
        Principles of Tax Equity   101
        Real-World Compromises:
        Three Classes of Tax Rates   102
        Tax Shifting and Incidence:
        Direct and Indirect Taxes   103

Completing the Circular-Flow Model   **104**

Origins: Government in the Economy   **104**
TAKE A STAND *Higher Education: Should Government Subsidize It?*   108

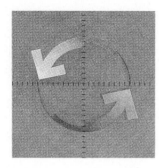

CHAPTER 7

**The Self-Correcting Economy:
Aggregate Demand and Aggregate Supply**   **156**

PART 3
Monetary Economics: Money, Banking, and Monetary Policy

CHAPTER 11

Central Banking: Federal Reserve Monetary Policy   246

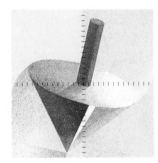

CHAPTER 14

**Income and Employment Determination:
Extending Macroeconomic Principles**   **316**

PART 5
Macroeconomics Today:
Ideas, Issues, and Policies — 375

CHAPTER 17

CHAPTER 20

International Macroeconomics: Recent Developments in the Global Economy   🌐 428

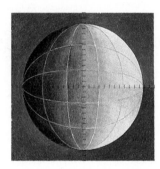

PART 6

International Economics and the World's
Economies   447

CHAPTER 21

International Trade: The Commerce of Nations   448

Preface

This is an exciting time to be studying economics. Communism and central planning have been rejected by many countries, now struggling to replace them with capitalism and free markets. The economic ties that nations are building with their neighbors are transforming the map into a jigsaw puzzle of regional trading groups. The explosive growth of global financial markets is having a dramatic impact on international money flows, business financing, and nations' banking systems.

At home, controversies abound over the size of the public sector, tax rates, economic stabilization measures, international trade and investment policies, and business-government relations. Policy recommendations pertaining to education, the environment, health care, family leave, welfare reform, the deficit, and other issues have the potential to affect us all. That is why, as his first order of business, President-elect Clinton convened an extraordinary 19-hour nationally televised teach-in on economics.

Now, more than ever, an understanding of economics is essential no matter what career path a student may choose.

About the Eighth Edition

The eighth edition has been thoroughly revised and updated to reflect current thinking in the field. As always, our main objective has been to provide a balanced treatment of economic theory and the real-world problems and policies it addresses. This edition has a co-author—Orley M. Amos, Jr., Robert S. and Grayce B. Kerr Distinguished Professor of Economics at Oklahoma State University. Professor Amos was introduced to economics as an undergraduate with the first edition of *Contemporary Economics,* and now he has enriched the eighth edition and its supplements with many creative ideas.

New Content

Current issues and perspectives are incorporated throughout the book to relate the study of economics to events of today. Of the numerous changes made, we point out the major ones here.

GDP and the New National Income Accounting

The eighth edition reflects the Commerce Department's recent change to gross domestic product as the measure of national income. Chapter 5 provides a comprehensive explanation of GDP and GNP and the relationship between them. The difference between the two measures is shown to be *net foreign factor income.* All subsequent chapters use GDP as the preferred measure.

Extensive Global Coverage

International examples and applications are integrated throughout the book, and full-color graphs and maps highlight global trends and patterns. Exhibits and features containing significant international material are highlighted with a globe symbol 🌐. In the overview chapters (Part 1), Chapter 1 develops an intuitive explanation of comparative advantage and opportunity cost and shows how they influence international trade. Chapter 3 introduces the foreign sector and foreign exchange markets. Chapter 4 discusses international spillovers and offers international comparisons of government spending and tax systems.

In the macroeconomics chapters, Chapter 5 provides global comparisons of aggregate income and output. Chapter 6 shows the international ramifications of business cycles. Chapter 9 looks at the influence of the Fed on the proposed European central bank. Chapter 11 examines the international effects of monetary policy. Chapter 19 includes a discussion of the meaning and implications of international indebtedness. And Chapter 20, a new chapter on International Macroeconomics, offers a current perspective on the rapidly changing global economy. Chapter 23 analyzes why past development strategies in some Latin American, Asian, and African countries have been ineffective or counterproductive. And Chapter 24, a new chapter on Transitional Economics, focuses on the principles and policies most likely to help former communist countries to implement market reforms successfully.

Productivity and Economic Growth

The goal of all nations is to achieve a rising standard of living. The methods of attaining that goal are the subject of Chapter 8. Rewritten almost entirely, this chapter explains the difference between partial and total factor productivity, the new phenomenon of growth convergence, the productivity slowdown, and prospective growth trends of the major industrial nations to the year 2020. The task of targeting growth is emphasized because of its implications for public policy. The classical theory of growth, explained through the contributions of Ricardo and Malthus, is related to today's advanced nations as well as to developing ones.

Monetary Economics

These chapters have been enhanced by the addition of new topics and new examples, including:

The Rapidly Changing Banking System In Chapter 9, the future role of banks is discussed in light of the financial services provided by major corporations, brokerage firms, and insurance companies.

Portfolio Management In Chapter 10, the revolution in portfolio selection theory and its impact on bank policies have prompted the inclusion of a substantial section on the concept of diversification.

Monetary Policy in an Open Economy In Chapter 11, foreign-exchange market intervention by the Fed is explained as a tool of monetary policy.

Loanable Funds Theory of Interest In Chapter 12, the complete theory is explained within an innovative framework of demand and supply graphs. The discussion emphasizes the use of the theory by the Fed and by Wall Street economists in forecasting interest rates. The logical equivalence of the theory to the liquidity preference explanation of interest used in Keynesian analysis is also pointed out.

Yield Curves and Forecasting with *P*-Star Chapter 12 shows how the Fed uses yield curves to determine its recommendations for monetary policy. The *P*-star equation is developed, and an exhibit demonstrates how the Fed relates money growth to the price level. A simple graphic model enables students to prepare their own price-level forecasts.

Deficits and Debt

Chapter 19 analyzes government budget deficits, today's issues concerning the national debt, the nature of trade deficits, and the meaning of international indebtedness. Topics include theories, evidence, and issues pertaining to: the debt neutrality (Ricardian equivalence) theorem, the *J*-curve, the inverted *J*-curve, trade-balance equations, foreign debt, inflationary impacts, and fiscal-monetary policies for reducing trade deficits and debt.

International Macroeconomics

A new chapter has been added to survey recent developments in the global economy. In Chapter 20, stages of economic integration, the emerging United States of Europe, potential world trading blocs, the new international banking and financial markets, and major trade policy issues are explained in detail with maps and analytical diagrams.

New Features

Anyone familiar with previous editions of this book will recall that it introduced many innovative features that, in true Schumpeterian fashion, have become standard in many economics textbooks. We introduce two new features in this edition—one on the development of economic thought, the other on current issues.

Origins

Economics has a rich intellectual history, and we have included highlights of it in sections called "Origins," which describe the contributions of major scholars to the development of key concepts covered in the chapters. Portraits and relevant biographical details are provided for context and human interest, but the emphasis is on economic thought, not biography. Among the topics covered are:

The Study of Markets Before Adam Smith (Chapter 2) The ideas of Thomas Aquinas and John Locke, both of whom influenced Smith and subsequent classical writers in widely different ways, are discussed.

How National Income Accounting Came About (Chapter 5) The systematization of national income accounting methods by America's Simon Kuznets in the 1930s and England's Richard Stone in the 1940s remedied the lack of appropriate economic data.

How the Keynesian Revolution Came to America (Chapter 16) The contributions of John R. Hicks, sometimes called "the other Keynes," and Alvin Hansen, nicknamed "the American Keynes," were essential to the dissemination of Keynesian theory although they are not widely known.

Take a Stand

Many chapters end with a rousing debate on a contemporary issue directly related to the chapter. First, the issue is explained, and persuasive affirmative and negative arguments are stated. Then, provocative questions encourage students to formulate their own opinions, to take a stand. These Take a Stand essays can be used for a structured debate, for class discussions, or for essay assignments.

Among the issues debated are:

- The Productivity Slowdown: Need We Worry? (Chapter 8)

- Banks: Can They Be "Too Big to Fail"? (Chapter 10)

- A Balanced Budget Amendment: Is It a Good Idea? (Chapter 15)

- Regional Trading Groups: Do They Promote Global Integration? (Chapter 20)

Pedagogical Improvements

Enhanced learning aids and organizational improvements have been incorporated to help students learn more economics and retain it longer.

Graphing Tutorial

Many students have difficulty with their economics course because they lack graphing skills. The introductory chapter remedies this deficiency with an extended graphing tutorial. Students learn how to construct, analyze, and interpret graphs, and how to measure and interpret slope. (*Graphics Tutorial* software and graphing exercises in the *Study Guide* offer additional practice.)

Extended Circular-Flow Diagrams

The circular flow of the economy is carefully developed in three stages. A simplified diagram in Chapter 1 offers a two-sector model of households and businesses. Chapter 3 extends the model to three sectors by adding the foreign sector and the foreign exchange market. Chapter 4 incorporates the government sector to produce the full, four-sector model.

Learning Aids

Longer or more technical chapters contain strategically located summaries, questions that students can use to test themselves, and thought questions. There are boxes containing interesting real-world concerns in many of the chapters. Examples include "Comparative Living Standards" in Chapter 1, "Business Cycles or Business Chaos?" in Chapter 6, "Is the Fed Too Independent?" in Chapter 11. In addition, current "Economics in the News" articles are included, many of which address international concerns.

Flexible Macroeconomics Organization

Monetary economics is covered before fiscal economics for two reasons: (1) Monetary policy has become the primary tool for economic stabilization; and (2) this order of topics makes for an easier transition to modern Keynesian analysis. However, the fiscal analysis chapters of Part 4 have been written so that they can be understood independently of the monetary analysis chapters of Part 3. This arrangement makes it easy to cover the topics in either sequence.

Keynesian-Cross Option Many economists are critical of the income-expenditure (Keynesian-cross) model because of its assumption of a constant price level. These critics favor the more modern income-price (*AD/AS*) model. Other economists believe that both models serve useful purposes. We have accommodated both points of view. Instructors who prefer not to cover the income-expenditure model can omit Chapters 13, 14, and 16 *without loss of the theory needed for policy analysis.* These instructors can move directly to Chapter 15 on fiscal policy, which is written within the framework of the income-price model. They can then skip to Chapter 17, which summarizes and integrates all of the main macroeconomic theories in terms of the income-price model. Completion of Chapter 17 will provide sound preparation for theory and policy discussions in all subsequent macro chapters.

Supplements for the Instructor

Enriched resources for the instructor include an expanded *Instructor's Resource Manual,* a revised and expanded *Test Bank* with software, and color transparencies.

Instructor's Resource Manual

Each chapter contains the following resources: Chapter Outline, Key Point Review, Learning Objectives, and Suggested Answers to Questions and Problems in the Textbook. In addition, co-author Orley Amos has prepared a large selection of handouts for each chapter, including:

- **Math Tool Kit** Step-by-step explanations of the basic algebra needed to understand economics.

- **Worksheet** Quantitative problems, based on a table of data, with an answer form and a separately printed solution.

- **Contemporary Analysis** Relevant news articles with analysis of the economic implications.

- **At Issue** Controversial topics for discussion, with arguments.

- **Cartoons** Satirical commentaries on current economic issues; useful as handouts or transparency masters.

Test Bank

Approximately 7,100 five-choice multiple-choice questions and 1,000 true-false questions are available in the two *Test Banks,* one for macroeconomics and one for microeconomics. Most of the questions require analysis, application, or interpretation of concepts or data. For macroeconomics, twelve ready-made examinations are provided, two for each part of the text.

Computerized Test-Generation Systems

The questions in the *Test Bank* form the database of three different computerized test-generation systems. CompuTest, a quick and easy system to use, is available for IBM PCs and true compatibles and for the Apple II family of personal computers. The Diploma IV system, from Brownstone Research Group, includes a number of options for instructors who wish to modify existing questions and add their own. It is available for IBM PCs and true compatibles. MicroTest III, from Chariot Software Group, is available for all Macintosh computers.

Color Transparencies

Full-color acetate transparency sets for macroeconomics and microeconomics include key graphs, charts, and diagrams with enlarged type for effective projection.

Supplements for the Student

Study Guide

The *Study Guide,* by Eric Blankmeyer and John W. Mogab (Southwest Texas State University), will help students at all levels of ability to learn, review, reinforce their understanding, and master the material in each chapter. Each *Study Guide* chapter contains the following:

- **Key Point Review** A thorough overview of chapter content.

- **Learning Objectives** The goals of the chapter. Each objective is keyed to questions in the *Study Guide* chapter and to page numbers in the textbook.

- **Key Terms** A matching exercise to help students verify and reinforce their understanding of the terms used in the chapter.

- **Objective Test Questions** A set of true-false and multiple-choice questions covering all important points in the chapter.

- **Problems and Applications** Several extended problems per chapter. These challenge students to apply quantitative and conceptual reasoning to their knowledge. There are tables to complete, graphs to draw and interpret, and exercises that help students consolidate their understanding of key ideas.

- **Questions to Think About** Far-reaching questions that encourage students to think critically about material they have learned.

- **Answers** Answers to key terms, questions, and problems and applications, along with page references to the relevant material in the textbook.

Contemporary Economics Graphics Tutorial

Interactive tutorial software, developed by Richard Alston and Wan Fu Chi (Weber State University), helps students to learn concepts, reinforce their understanding, and develop problem-solving skills. The software contains three programs:

- **Introduction to Graphing** Students learn how to read and construct graphs, including line graphs, pie charts, bar charts, and scatter diagrams. Over thirty annual and quarterly time series of major economic variables, such as GDP, price indexes, interest rates, and the money supply, are provided. Students can enter and save their own data to develop customized graphs.

- **Basics of Demand and Supply** The concepts of market equilibrium, price ceilings, price floors, elasticity, and changes in the determinants of demand and supply are reviewed and reinforced. These concepts are all presented graphically with running commentary, explanations, and hints for further learning. Students can use the programs to create new price and quantity equilibria.

- **The Global Economy** Dynamic graphs represent production possibilities, terms of trade, and the gains from trade. Examples of exchange rate determination give students experience with predicting the impact of the world's changing economic and financial situation.

Acknowledgments

It is a pleasure to acknowledge the help and cooperation we have received in the preparation of this book. Special thanks go to Timothy Tregarthen of the University of Colorado at Colorado Springs. A number of ideas, examples, and chapter-end discussion questions that he contributed to the seventh edition have been retained. We are also grateful to Andrew John of Michigan State University for sharing his ideas and expertise.

Over its life, this book has benefited from the advice of hundreds of dedicated teachers and scholars. While we cannot list them all here, nor the many students whose comments have helped to shape and improve the book, we are grateful for the suggestions of many people over two decades. We do want to thank those who reviewed substantial portions of this edition and shared their wisdom and their classroom experiences with us:

Jack Adams, *University of Arkansas-Little Rock*

Erwin Blackstone, *Temple University*

Eric Blankmeyer, *Southwest Texas State University*

Joe B. Copeland, *University of North Alabama*

Jack Inch, *Oakland Community College*

Andrew John, *Michigan State University*

Patrick Joyce, *Michigan Technological University*

Ruby Kishan, *Southwest Texas State University*

John W. Mogab, *Southwest Texas State University*

H. Richard Moss, *Ricks College*

Teresa Riley, *Youngstown State University*

Henry Ryder, *Gloucester County College*

Wm. Doyle Smith, *University of Texas, El Paso*

Abraham Usumang, *Bowling Green State University*

Mark Wilson, *The University of Charleston*

Milton H. Spencer
Orley M. Amos, Jr.

January 1993

Part 1

Overview: The Economic System

Getting Started in Economics

What Is Economics About?

Working with Theories and Models

Common Fallacies in Reasoning

The Language of Graphs

Extending Your Knowledge of Graphs

Making the Grade in Economics

Learning Guide

Watch for answers to these important questions

How is economics defined? What is the meaning of scarcity and how does it relate to the definition of economics?

Why are theories and models used in economics?

How are graphs constructed? How are they interpreted?

Economics is exciting and important. Anyone who thinks otherwise has failed to realize that economic ideas and practices have moved people to rebellion, and nations to war. The great issues that confront us today—among them international conflict, unemployment, inflation, poverty, discrimination, and environmental pollution—have economic roots. Even the small issues—the seeming impossibility of finding a parking space on most college campuses, the endless hours we seem to spend on "hold" on the telephone, the high price of books at the campus bookstore—are economic in nature. In order to analyze these problems, big or small, we must understand the economic forces that shape them.

What Is Economics About?

It will be helpful to begin our exploration of economics with a definition:

Economics is a *social science* concerned chiefly with the way society employs its *limited resources,* which have alternative uses, to produce goods and services for present and future consumption.

This definition of economics needs clarification of two points. First, why is economics a social science? Because it deals with the interactions of people, in particular, their interactions as they buy, sell, produce, and consume. Other social sciences, such as psychology and sociology, also deal with human interactions—

sometimes even economic interactions. But in economics, we study human interactions from a special standpoint and with special tools.

Second, what are resources, and what does it mean to say that they're limited? Resources comprise anything that can be used to produce goods and services. This includes human resources—labor and the skills workers possess—and material resources, such as machinery, buildings, and land. Resources are limited in the sense that, taken together, people want more goods and services than can be produced. This means that doing one thing with a resource requires giving up another. Because limited resources have *alternative* uses, economists call them *scarce*.

Thus, scarcity in the economic sense does not refer to quantity of a resource. The earth has a great deal of land, yet most of the earth's land is scarce because it has alternative uses. If land is used for a college campus, that same land isn't available for a shopping mall, a subdivision, or a park. The fact that doing one thing with land requires giving up something else tells us that land has alternative uses. Whether there is a lot of land or a little isn't the issue. *Scarcity* means that there are alternative uses for limited resources.

The Problem of Scarcity

The problem of scarcity confronts us constantly. Your time, for example, is scarce. If you decide to stay home and read, you can't use that time to go to the movies or to work out. If society decides to devote more resources to the construction of highways, it will have fewer resources for the construction of buildings. If a nation allocates more resources to the production of military goods, it will have fewer resources for the production of consumer goods.

Consider this book. The paper on which it was printed came from a tree that could have been used to make lumber for building houses. The ink was derived from petroleum that could have been used to make gasoline. The thread that holds the binding could have been used to stitch clothes. The fact that you have this particular copy of the book means someone else doesn't have it. Let's assume you're reading this book for a college course in economics. Your decision to go to college meant that you had to give up an alternative use for your time—perhaps a full-time job.

All societies confront the problem of scarcity and must choose among alternatives. The choices that a society makes, and the way it makes them, are determined by its economic system. An *economic system* is the laws, institutions, customs, and practices that determine how a society allocates its scarce resources. Two major types of economic systems are capitalism and socialism. The nature of these "isms," and comparisons between them, will concern us from time to time in this book.

"Micro" and "Macro"

Beginning courses in economics are traditionally divided into two components: microeconomics and macroeconomics. The two branches of economics contain some differences in viewpoint as well as some similarities.

Microeconomics is concerned with the specific parts or economic units that make up an economic system and with the relationships between those parts. In microeconomics, emphasis is placed on understanding the behavior of individual households, firms, and industries, and the ways in which such entities interact.

Macroeconomics is concerned with the economy as a whole, or with large segments of it. Macroeconomics focuses on such problems as the rate of unemployment, the changing level of prices, the nation's total output of goods and services, and the ways in which government raises and spends money.

Here is a convenient way of thinking about the differences and similarities between "micro" and "macro":

Microeconomics **tries to explain the trees, while** *macroeconomics* **tries to explain the forest. Both "micro" and "macro" are concerned with the construction of theories about economic behavior and the formulation of policies aimed at improving the economy's performance. These activities are the heart of economics.**

Working with Theories and Models

Economists, like other scientists, study phenomena by observing the world and collecting appropriate data. The goal of economists is to discover relationships between events or between quantities called *variables*. A variable is simply a measure that can take on different values. For example, economists may study the relationship between the price of automobiles and the number of automobiles purchased. The price and the number are the variables. From such a study, it may be possible to determine how changes in the price affect the quantities purchased. Ultimately, it may be possible to offer a good explanation for the relationship.

What Do Economists Do?

What will happen if Congress approves a 5 percent increase in personal income taxes? Will the increase in taxes take purchasing power out of the hands of consumers and thus cause them to reduce their spending? If consumers spend less, will prices fall? Will a decrease in production cause greater unemployment?

These questions—and many others in such areas as national defense, health, crime, the arts, poverty, transportation, etc.—are typical of the problems economists try to solve. Of course, in finding solutions, they become involved in formulating economic principles or theories which may then serve as a means for prediction and, hopefully, for control. For example, if economists can predict future changes of such variables as prices, employment, and spending, they can make recommendations to government officials, who in turn may use these suggestions as a basis for economic policies. Can you suggest some ways in which economists can be of use not only to the federal government, but also to state and local governments? To industry? To labor unions?

The questions that interest economists and the viewpoints they adopt are of great importance for society. Of course, economists don't always agree on the best way to implement policy decisions. In this respect, they are no different from most other experts. Engineers, for example, don't always agree on the best way to build a bridge; doctors are not always unanimous on the best way to treat a patient; and even in mathematics and physics, which people often think of as the most "exact" of all the sciences, the experts often disagree on the answers to advanced questions. But most economists, like scientists in other fields, are in remarkably close agreement on fundamental principles. [*Question:* Much of economics can be expressed in mathematical form. Does this make it more scientific?]

Hard Principles, Soft Policies

During a convention of the American Economic Association at the New York Hilton, several economists were lingering over cocktails in the hotel's lounge.

Concluding that the world was in a bad way, they started trying to find collective nouns to describe the people responsible. They agreed on an "exaltation" of liberals, a "petrification" of conservatives, an "hypocrisy" of politicians, and a "clutch" of business executives. "But how do we describe ourselves?" asked one of the economists. "Ah," said another, "we are a *confusion* of economists."

The story points to an ironic truth. When economists step out of the relatively secure realm of economic facts and theory, they enter a much less certain world of economic policy. This doesn't mean that their role as scientists ceases to exist. They simply shift their emphasis from "positive economics," which concerns what *is*, to "normative economics," which concerns what *ought* to be.

If you disagree with someone over positive statements in economics, you should be able to settle the controversy by logical argument and an appeal to the facts. But if you disagree over normative statements—statements about what is "good" and what is "bad," what is "right" and what is "wrong"—you may not be able to reach an agreement. This is because people's views are strongly influenced by complex mixtures of philosophical, social, and cultural factors.

A few examples of positive and normative statements illustrate the point:

Positive: Doctors earn more than school teachers.

Normative: Doctors ought to earn more than school teachers because doctors go through more years of training than school teachers.

The first statement is positive because it can be tested by empirical research. The second statement is normative because it expresses a value judgment.

Here are some more examples. Notice that the positive statements are objective and verifiable. Whether they are true or false is immaterial. The normative statements, however, aren't verifiable because they rely on subjective opinions or value judgments. These are emphasized by the underlined words.

Positive: Poverty can be cured by imposing higher taxes on the rich and redistributing the money to the poor.

Normative: No one <u>deserves</u> to live in poverty, and it isn't <u>fair</u> to expect anyone to do so. The rich <u>should</u> pay higher taxes which can be used to help the poor.

Positive: By building more public housing, government could provide shelter for millions of homeless citizens.

Normative: Everyone <u>needs</u> and is <u>entitled</u> to decent housing. It <u>ought</u> to be the responsibility of government to provide it.

In economic discussions, it pays to be on the lookout for words like "ought," "deserve," "fair," "should," "need," and "entitled." When you see them, you can be pretty confident that the user is making a normative (value) judgment.

Summarizing:

Positive economics consists of objective and/or empirically verifiable statements. Because it deals with "what is," not with "what ought to be," positive economics takes no particular ethical position and makes no value judgments. Economic principles are examples of positive economics.

Normative economics consists of subjective and/or unsubstantiated statements that lack positive knowledge or proof. Because it deals with "what ought to be," not with "what is," normative economics makes value judgments that reflect particular ethical views. Economic policies are often influenced substantially by normative considerations.

Most of economics deals with positive rather than normative matters because economics is concerned with developing and using fundamental principles. When the principles are applied to the formulation of policies, however, significant value judgments frequently arise that are the source of most disagreements in economics. These controversies often tend to be the most interesting and exciting parts of the subject.

Expressing Relationships

At one time, an explanation of a relationship between variables was called a *hypothesis* if there was no evidence to support it, a *theory* if there was some evidence, and a *law* or *principle* if it was certain. Scientists no longer emphasize these distinctions. They know that no hypothesis can be made about a subject of which one is completely ignorant. There must thus be at least some evidence before a hypothesis can be developed. Scientists know also that no scientific law is ever certain. Consequently, modern scientists tend to use the terms hypothesis, theory, law, and principle more or less interchangeably to express relationships.

A theory may be stated in the form of a *model*. A *model* is a representation of the essential features of a theory or of a real-world situation. A model may be expressed in the form of words, diagrams, tables of data, graphs, mathematical equations, or combinations of these.

Generally, a model is easier to manipulate than the reality it represents. This is because it is a simplification of reality. Only the properties of the reality that are thought to be relevant are included. A road map, for example, is a model. Unlike some other maps, which are also models, a road map doesn't show vegetation or climatic variation because these are not relevant to its purposes. But a road map will serve better than any other type of map to guide you across the country.

A theory or model usually fits the observed facts only approximately. It might have to be revised or even discarded as time passes and the facts themselves change. In recent years, some economic theories have been revised and have replaced older ones to provide better explanations of today's problems.

Common Fallacies in Reasoning

Like physicists and chemists, economists try to use observed, verifiable facts as stepping-stones to an understanding of how their portion of the world works. But physicists and chemists can usually discover rather quickly when they are in error. Typically, an experiment goes wrong; perhaps it causes an explosion. Economists cannot experiment in that way. They may labor for years under misapprehensions and may advocate policies that affect thousands or even millions of people. Consequently, it is important to discern at the outset whether economic arguments are rational. One way of doing this is to examine them carefully with the help of formal logic.

In common usage, the word "fallacy" denotes any mistaken idea or false belief. In a stricter sense, a fallacy is an error in reasoning or argument. This is what you should look for when you analyze economic ideas. Of course, an argument may be so obviously incorrect that it deceives nobody. For our purposes, however, we shall reserve the word "fallacy" for certain types of reasoning that, although incorrect, are nevertheless persuasive—a dangerous combination. Here are some typical fallacies of economic thinking. Understanding them will help you to pinpoint errors in other people's reasoning as well as in your own.

Fallacy of False Cause

Every science tries to discover cause-and-effect relationships. The *fallacy of false cause,* or *post hoc fallacy,* is often encountered in such efforts. (The latter name comes from the Latin expression *post hoc ergo propter hoc,* which means "after this, therefore because of this.") This fallacy is committed when a person mistakenly assumes that, because one event follows another or both events occur simultaneously, one is the cause and the other the effect.

It is common for a fallacy of false cause to be expressed in the form of an "if–then" argument:

> If A occurs, then B occurs.
> Therefore, A causes B.

Is this sufficient reason for concluding that *A* causes *B*? Not necessarily. There are other possible explanations:

- *B* may occur by chance.
- *B* may be caused by factors other than *A* (or by a third factor that is a common cause of both *A* and *B*).
- *B* may cause *A*.

Some possibilities are illustrated in the following examples:

> **Example 1**   Company *X* hired a new sales manager, and the firm's sales soared during the ensuing year.
>
> Therefore, the growth in sales was due to the new sales manager.

This argument, consisting of both the statement and the conclusion, is obviously a false cause or *post hoc* fallacy. It fails to point out that, although some of the growth in sales may be due to the manager's efforts, much or even most of it may be the result of other factors. These may be lower prices for the company's products, higher incomes of buyers, or an increase in the number of buyers in the market.

> **Example 2**   The severity of hay fever varies inversely with the price of corn. That is, the lower the price of corn, the greater the severity of hay fever, and vice versa.
>
> Therefore, corn prices affect hay fever.

It is true that the price of corn and the severity of hay fever are inversely related. But the fact is that ragweed is a cause of hay fever. The summer conditions that produce an abundance of ragweed—high temperatures and adequate rainfall—also produce an abundance of corn. This usually results in lower corn prices. Thus, it may seem as if corn prices affect hay fever. In reality, these factors are independent of each other, and a third factor is operating that is a common cause of both.

Fallacies of Composition and Division

Two additional fallacies are often encountered in economic arguments. The *fallacy of composition* occurs when one reasons that what is true of the parts of something is also necessarily true of the whole of it. The *fallacy of division* occurs when one contends that something that is true of the whole is also necessarily true of its parts taken separately.

The following arguments from microeconomics and macroeconomics illustrate these fallacies. Can you identify the fallacy and explain why the concluding statement in each case is fallacious?

- If the prices of new cars were to rise tomorrow by 10 percent, then automobile producers would experience higher profits. Therefore, if the prices of all goods and services throughout the economy were to increase tomorrow by 10 percent, all producers would experience higher profits.

The first statement is true; the second is false. Why? Here's a hint: What would happen to producers' costs if the prices of all goods and services were to increase tomorrow?

- If everyone cut down on their spending, the economy's income would decline and so too would people's saving. It follows that if you cut down on your own spending, then you would also experience a decrease in saving.

The first statement is true; the second is false. *Hint:* If you spend less of your income, what will happen to your saving?

Here are some more economic arguments, but without any hints. Can you explain why they are fallacious?

- If one family reduces its spending, then that family will increase its saving. It follows that if all families reduce their spending, then they will all increase their saving.

- Unrestricted trade between nations enriches everyone because it enables people to consume a greater quantity and variety of goods. Therefore, prompt removal of all international-trade barriers would immediately improve everyone's well-being.

- A family isn't better off if it has to pay higher taxes. It follows that the economy can't be better off if all families have to pay higher taxes.

The fallacies of composition and division are particularly relevant to the study of microeconomics and macroeconomics.

The fallacy of composition warns us that what is true of the parts is not necessarily true of the whole. Thus, generalizations of a microeconomic nature may not always be applicable to a macroeconomic problem. The fallacy of division warns us that what is true of the whole is not necessarily true of the parts. Thus, generalizations of a macroeconomic nature may not always be applicable to a microeconomic problem.

These ideas may seem obvious. However, the fallacies can be remarkably subtle when they occur in discussions of actual economic problems.

The Language of Graphs

A glance through the pages of this book should convince you that you'll be working with a great many graphs during this course. Graphs represent a kind of language. Therefore, you must master the language of graphs in order to master economics.

Happily, the language of graphs is a simple one to learn. There are a few "grammatical rules," and that's all. There are no irregular verbs, no conjugations, no tricky spellings, no problems with pronunciation. But if you haven't worked with graphs for awhile, you'll find it will take some time to master the language anew. So if you're at all rusty, now is the time to learn how to work with graphs.

Constructing Graphs

The idea underlying graphs is simple. Graphs show how things are related to one another. Because these "things" can have various values, we call them *variables:*

Graphs are diagrams that express relationships between variables.

To show relationships graphically, we draw two straight lines at right angles to each other on graph paper. These lines are called *axes*. As illustrated in Exhibit 1, one axis is horizontal, the other vertical.

The horizontal line is called the *x* axis, and the vertical line is called the *y* axis. The point of intersection is called the *origin*. These two lines divide the graph into four parts called *quadrants*. These quadrants are identified by starting with the upper right-hand quadrant and numbering them counterclockwise.

Notice that positive numbers on the *x* axis are to the right of the origin and negative numbers are to the left. Positive numbers on the *y* axis are above the origin, and negative numbers are below. We write the location of a point in the form (*x,y*), where *x* is the value on the *x* axis and *y* is the value on the *y* axis. These procedures for labeling and numbering are used in all branches of science.

Using this information, you can locate any point on the graph with two numbers—one for *x* and one for *y*—in much the same way as you would locate a ship at sea by its latitude and longitude. The two numbers are called the *coordinates* of the point. Thus, the coordinates of point *A* are (3,5), those of point *B* are

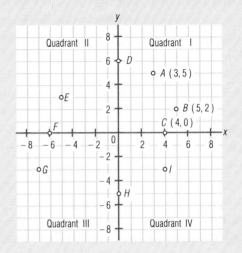

EXHIBIT 1

Constructing a Graph

The two intersecting straight lines divide the graph into four quadrants, which are numbered counterclockwise. Positive values are measured to the right along the *x* axis and upward along the *y* axis. Negative values are measured to the left along the *x* axis and downward along the *y* axis. Any point on the graph can be located by its coordinates.

(5,2), and those of point *C* are (4,0). The horizontal, or *x*, coordinate is always stated first and the vertical, or *y*, coordinate second. Can you give the coordinates of the remaining points?

Graphs such as these are used to show how one quantity varies in relation to another. In Exhibit 2, for example, the values of *x* and *y* are plotted from the data in the tables accompanying the graphs. In Figure (a), the points representing each pair of values of *x* and *y* are located and marked. The points are then connected with a smooth curve, in this case a straight line. Because the line slopes upward from left to right, the two variables are said to be *directly* related. As *x* increases, *y* increases; as *x* decreases, *y* decreases. In contrast, the line in Figure (b) slopes downward from left to right. Therefore, the two variables are said to be *inversely* related. As *x* increases, *y* decreases; as *x* decreases, *y* increases.

Using Graphs in Economics

In economics, the lines plotted usually fall entirely in the first quadrant. This is because the data on which the lines are based are almost always positive. Sometimes two or more lines are plotted on the same graph in order to examine the relationships between them. This is shown in Figure (a) of Exhibit 3. In order to distinguish between the lines, they may be labeled with different letters, such as *S* and *D*. Notice that the axes are also labeled with different letters, in this example, *P* and *Q*. In the accompanying table, each P_S value refers to the S curve, and each P_D value refers to the *D* curve. Can you read the coordinates of the points determining these lines? Try filling in the table.

Different scales and labels may be used on the horizontal and vertical axes to suit the particular purpose of the graph. An example of this is shown in Fig-

---

EXHIBIT 2

Direct and Inverse Relations

x	−3	−2	−1	0	1	2	3	4
y	−2	−1	0	1	2	3	4	5

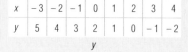

x	−3	−2	−1	0	1	2	3	4
y	5	4	3	2	1	0	−1	−2

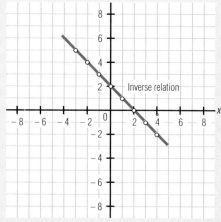

FIGURE (a) Direct Relation A line that slopes upward from left to right exhibits a *direct* relation between the two variables. As one variable increases, so does the other; as one decreases, so does the other.

FIGURE (b) Inverse Relation A line that slopes downward from left to right exhibits an *inverse* relation between the two variables. As one variable increases, the other decreases; as one decreases, the other increases.

EXHIBIT
3

Some Special Relations

Q	2	3		5	6
P_S	3			6	
P_D	7	6			

t	0	4	8	12	16
P					

Q		2		4		6	
C	110		30		30		110

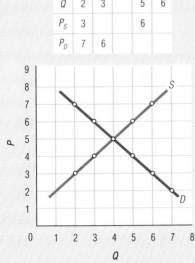

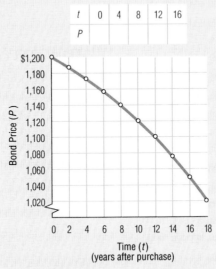

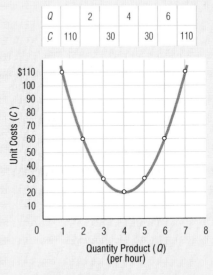

FIGURE (a) Two or more lines may be drawn on the same graph in order to study the relationships between them. Can you complete the table from the graph?

FIGURE (b) Scales should be chosen and axes labeled in the manner that best suits a particular problem. Can you use the graph to estimate the missing numbers in the table?

Note that the scaling of the horizontal axis is continuous (0, 2, 4, 6, 8, and so on), and thus the axis line is unbroken. The scaling of the vertical axis, on the other hand, jumps from 0 to $1,020, and moves thereafter in equal increments ($1,020, $1,040, $1,060, $1,080, and so on). The break in the scale between 0 and $1,020 is indicated by the break in the vertical axis line.

FIGURE (c) The points should be connected with care. Can you fill in the table from the graph?

ure (b). The vertical axis in this graph shows P, the price in dollars of a particular bond. The horizontal axis shows t, the time in number of years after the bond was purchased. The curve shows the relationship between these two variables. That is, it shows what happened to the price, P, of a bond t years after it was purchased. For example, the bond was initially purchased for $1,200, so at $t = 0$, $P = \$1,200$; and at $t = 2$ years, $P = \$1,190$. Can you fill in the table? Where necessary, try to estimate the numbers from the graph.

Finally, Figure (c) shows the unit costs, C, that a

certain firm experiences as a result of producing different quantities, Q, of a commodity. You should be able to fill in the table from the graph.

Extending Your Knowledge of Graphs

You now have enough background in graphing to interpret most of the graphs in this book. In a few instances, however, some additional graphic concepts will be introduced to provide a better understanding of particular economic ideas. These concepts will be explained now and reviewed again when the need arises.

Using Letters in Place of Numbers

In all the previous graphs, numbers were used in plotting the lines. But situations often arise when the numbers in a particular relationship are not known. Or the numbers are known, but it may nevertheless be desirable to express the relationship in general terms—that is, without using numbers. In such cases, it often proves helpful to use letters in place of numbers.

For example, sociological studies show that wealthier families tend to have fewer children than poorer families. This suggests that there is an *inverse* relationship between family income and birthrates. The relationship is illustrated in Exhibit 4. The relevant variables are expressed in terms of average income per family, shown on the horizontal axis, and average birthrate per family, shown on the vertical axis.

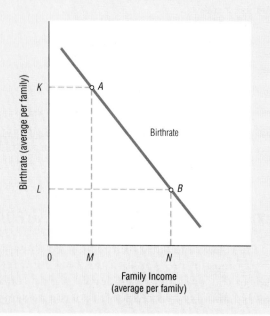

EXHIBIT
4

An Inverse Relationship

A relationship between variables can be expressed graphically even if the numbers representing the variables aren't known. In this example, the relationship between family income and birthrates is assumed to be inverse.

The points *A* and *B* on the curve associate a given income with a corresponding birthrate. Thus, at an income of *M*, the birthrate is *K*. At an income of *N*, the birthrate is *L*. It is important to notice that the line drawn this time is a straight one. We don't know in this case what particular shape it should have. If we had more information, we might find that the line is curved rather than straight.

Independent and Dependent Variables

When a relationship is graphed, there is often the implication that changes in one of the variables cause changes in the other. The variable that is believed to be causing the change is called the *independent variable,* and it is usually put on the horizontal axis. The variable that is presumably being affected by the other is called the *dependent variable,* and it is usually put on the vertical axis. The independent variable can thus be thought of as the cause, and the dependent variable the effect, in a particular relationship. Thus, in terms of Exhibit 4, for example, family income is believed to influence birthrates, not the other way around.

Keep in mind that the practice of associating an independent variable with the horizontal axis of a graph, and a dependent variable with the vertical, is a custom, not a rigid rule. As a result, you'll sometimes encounter graphs in economics (as well as in other subjects) in which the independent variable is shown on the vertical axis and the dependent variable on the horizontal.

Movements and Shifts

When we draw a graph showing a relationship between a dependent variable and an independent variable, we make certain assumptions. Among the most important is that *all other factors affecting the dependent variable remain constant.*

What are these "all other" factors? That depends on the particular relationship shown in the graph. For example, you don't have to take a course in sociology to know that, for the nation as a whole, birthrates depend on many factors. Among them are current family income, expected family income, family size, government policies (if any) toward population growth, cultural attitudes, religion, and a host of other conditions. In the birthrate graph drawn in Exhibit 4, we chose *one* of these variables, family income, as the independent variable. We thus assumed that all the other factors affecting birthrates were constant.

Movements Along the Curve

Looking back at Exhibit 4, you can readily see what happens when family income changes. Suppose that family income increases from *M* to *N*. The corresponding birthrate decreases from *K* to *L*. These changes are represented by a movement *downward* along the curve from *A* to *B*. Conversely, if family income decreases from *N* to *M,* the corresponding birthrate increases from *L* to *K*. These changes are represented by a movement *upward* along the curve from *B* to *A*.

This suggests a principle that you'll use frequently in economics:

In any graphic relationship, movements along a curve (whether upward or downward) are caused by changes in one of the two variables shown on the axes of the graph.

Shifts of the Curve

Suppose that instead of a change occurring in one of the variables on the graph, there is a change in one of the "all other" factors assumed constant when the graph was drawn. For example, suppose the government decides to pay families to have children—as some governments have done in order to encourage population growth. What would happen to birthrates?

You can probably guess the answer. At any *given* level of family income, families can now afford to have more children than they had before the government subsidy was granted. The results are illustrated in Exhibit 5. The old birthrate corresponding to a family income at *M* was originally at *K*. However, because of the government subsidy the new birthrate at the same income level *M* now turns out to be higher—at *H*. Similarly, at the income level *N* the old birthrate was initially at *L*. But as a result of the government's policy the new birthrate corresponding to the income level at *N* is now at *J*.

A change in government policy, one of the "all other" factors assumed constant when the curve was initially drawn, has thus caused the curve to shift to the right. This is emphasized by the arrows in Exhibit 5. What would happen if the government decides to rescind the subsidy and does not pay families to have babies? In that case the curve might shift to the left—back to its old position.

This suggests another principle that you'll use frequently in economics:

In a graph, shifts of a curve (whether to the right or to the left) are caused by a change in any of the fac- tors assumed constant when the curve is drawn. These factors are not shown on the axes of the graph.

Graphing Unrelated Variables

Can graphs be used to show *un*related variables? Is it sometimes useful to draw a curve that demonstrates the *absence* of a relationship? The answer is yes. One variable might be unrelated to another, and we may want to illustrate that.

As an example, suppose we want to show that the crime rate in Washington has nothing to do with the price of tea in China. To illustrate this graphically, we must demonstrate that, no matter what the price of tea in China, the crime rate in Washington remains the

EXHIBIT
5

Shifts of a Curve

When a curve is initially drawn, factors not shown on the axes of the graph that may influence the relationship are assumed to be constant. If a change occurs in any of these factors, the curve shifts to a new location.

Thus, if a government grants subsidies to families that have children, the initial birthrate curve for the nation as a whole shifts to the right. This means that, at any *given* level of family income, the new birthrate is higher than it was before the subsidy was granted. In view of this, what will likely happen to the curve if the subsidy is removed?

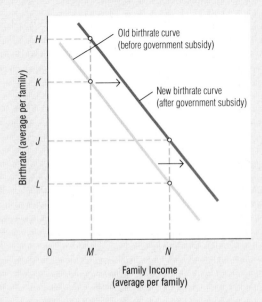

EXHIBIT
6

Illustrating the Absence of a Relationship

The horizontal line shows that, as the price of tea in China varies, nothing happens to the crime rate in Washington. That doesn't mean that the crime rate in Washington is a constant. It simply means that it is unaffected by tea prices on the other side of the world.

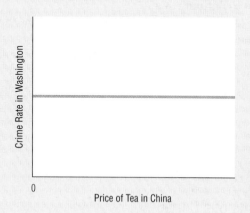

But we often like to know more about a relationship than that. For example, by how much would your grade point average increase if you spent more hours per week studying? How many fewer movies would you see each month if your income fell by half? These questions concern the *amount* of change that occurs in a dependent variable because of a change in an associated independent variable.

Let's look at the relation between body weight and calories consumed, and between body weight and exercise. The more calories you consume, the greater your weight is likely to be. Weight thus varies directly with calories consumed—a positive relation. On the other hand, the more exercise you do, the lower your weight is likely to be. Weight thus varies inversely with exercise performed—a negative relation.

But *by how much* will body weight change in relation to changes in these variables? Determining the answer involves a concept called *slope*. You can think of slope in the same sense as "steepness." Just as we refer to the slope (steepness) of a hill or a roof, so too we refer to the slope of a curve. The two diagrams in Exhibit 7, which demonstrate how slope is measured, illustrate these ideas. Both graphs are based on results of a 6-month weight-control study of overweight adults.

Figure (a) shows the relationship between body weight and calorie consumption. Slope is measured by the ratio of the change in vertical distance to the change in horizontal distance as we go from one point on the line to another. The change in vertical distance may be called the *rise* and the change in horizontal distance the *run*. So the slope is found from the formula

$$\text{Slope} = \frac{\text{change in vertical distance}}{\text{change in horizontal distance}} = \frac{\text{rise}}{\text{run}}$$

In Figure (a) the slope is 80 pounds per 1,000 calories. The slope therefore tells you that over the 6-month period of this study, a change in consumption of 1,000 calories per day resulted in a weight change of 80 pounds. The fact that the slope is positive—the curve is upward sloping—means that the relationship between the variables is *direct*. That is, an increase in calorie consumption results in an increase in body weight, and a decrease in calorie consumption results in a decrease in body weight. Both variables thus change in the same direction.

same. That doesn't mean that we think crime in Washington will never change, but that the price of tea in China won't influence it. We thus need a line showing that, at *any* price of tea in China, the crime rate in Washington is unaffected.

Exhibit 6 illustrates this type of graph. The price of tea in China (the potential "cause" variable) is placed on the horizontal axis and the crime rate in Washington (the potential "effect" variable) on the vertical. The horizontal line shows that, for each possible price, the crime rate remains the same. Thus, there is *no relationship*. That is, the price of tea in China has no effect on the crime rate in Washington.

Measuring Slope

When we look at a graph, we can tell whether the curve slopes upward or downward. If it's upward sloping, we know the relationship between the variables is direct, or positive. If it's downward sloping, we know the relationship is inverse, or negative.

EXHIBIT
7

Measuring Slope

A 6-month study of a group of overweight adults showed the extent to which body weight varies directly with calories consumed and inversely with exercise effort. The slope is measured by the ratio: rise ÷ run. It tells you the amount of change in the dependent variable (vertical axis) resulting from a given change in the independent variable (horizontal axis).

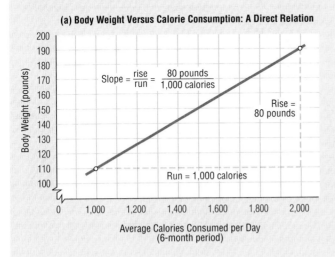

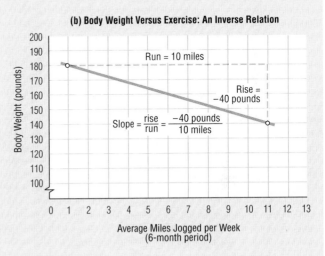

Figure (b) shows the relationship between body weight and exercise—the latter measured by miles per week of jogging. The slope is −40 pounds per 10 miles of jogging. This means that, over the 6-month period of this study, a change in distance jogged of 10 miles per week resulted in a weight change of 40 pounds. Because the slope is negative—the curve is downward sloping—the relationship between the variables is *inverse*. That is, they change in opposite directions.

Straight Lines and Curved Lines

One of the things you've noticed by now is that, when talking about graphs, lines are often called *curves* regardless of whether they're straight or rounded. This is common practice not only in economics but in all branches of science.

However, when talking about *slope*, a fundamental difference must be recognized between straight lines and curved ones. The distinctive feature of a straight line is that it has the same slope at each point. That's why the line is straight. A curved line, on the other hand, has a different slope at each point—which is what makes the line curved.

You can measure the slope of a straight line by dividing the rise by the run. The slope will be everywhere the same. But how do you measure the slope of a curved line if the slope is everywhere different? The answer requires you to recall some principles from high school geometry that are explained by three examples illustrated in Exhibit 8:

EXHIBIT
8

Measuring the Slope of a Curve at a Point

The slope of a curve at any point equals the slope of a straight-line tangent to the curve at that point. Slope is measured by the ratio: rise ÷ run.

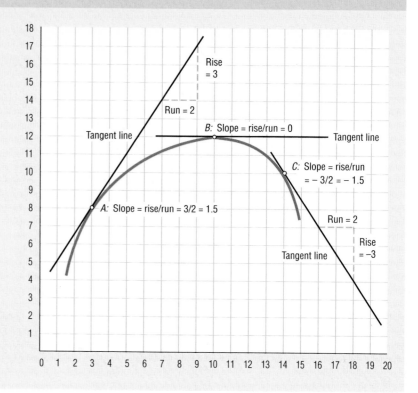

1.   Suppose you want to find the slope of the curve at a particular point, such as point *A*. The first step is to draw a straight-line tangent to the curve at that point. (A tangent is a point of contact.) It follows that the slope of the tangent, *which is the same at every point*, must equal the slope of the curve at the point of tangency. Thus, the slope of the tangent is the rise over the run, which equals 3/2 or 1.5. Therefore, the slope of the curve at point *A* is 1.5.

2.   You can find the slope of the curve at point *B* the same way. Because the curve's height is a maximum at this point, the tangent at *B* is a horizontal line. This means that the rise is zero for any given run. Therefore, the slope at point *B* is also zero. (*Question:* Suppose the curve were shaped like a U. What would be its slope at the minimum point?)

3.   The slope of the curve at point *C* is again equal to the slope of the tangent. Because the curve is downward sloping, the rise is a negative number. Thus, the slope of the tangent is −3/2 = −1.5. Therefore, the slope of the curve at point *C* is −1.5.

The slope of a straight line is the change in its vertical distance (or dependent variable) per unit of change in its horizontal distance (or independent variable). Slope is thus the ratio of rise ÷ run. A straight line has the same slope at each point, but a curved line has a different slope at each point. Therefore, to measure the slope of a curve at a point, draw a straight-line tangent to the curve at that point. The slope of the tangent will equal the slope of the curve at the point of tangency.

Time Series Graphs

We've been examining graphs that show the relationship between two variables. In many practical situations we want to depict a series of numbers over a pe-

EXHIBIT
9

Time Series Graphs

Two basic types of time series graphs are line graphs, as shown in Figure (a), and bar graphs, as shown in Figure (b).

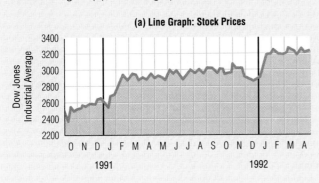

(a) Line Graph: Stock Prices

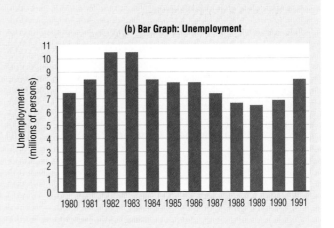

(b) Bar Graph: Unemployment

riod of time. A graph that does this is called a *time series graph*. You've seen many examples of such graphs in newspapers and magazines. Exhibit 9 provides some further illustrations. Here are several principles underlying them:

- The independent variable is "time." It's measured on the horizontal axis. The dependent variable, which varies with time, is measured on the vertical axis.

- The graphs may be drawn either as bar charts or as line charts. There are no hard and fast rules governing which type of chart to use. However, bar charts are normally employed to depict data covering specific *periods* of time. Line charts, on the other hand, are typically used to express data at specific *points* of time.

- The dependent variable changes over time. But this doesn't mean that time is the *cause* of the changes. Time is simply a substitute or proxy variable for the real factors that varied over time and are responsible for the changes.

Time series graphs are among the most common types of graphs employed in economics. You'll see many uses of them in this book as well as in newspaper articles dealing with economic topics.

Making the Grade in Economics

What steps can you take toward increasing your knowledge of economics and getting your desired course grade? There is a clear course of action.

Several studies have examined how the amount of effort students devote to their economics class affects their final grade. Exhibit 10 shows the results of one study. Let's look at Figure (a). On average, students who devoted only 10 hours to economics got a final exam score of 60. For students who devoted more time to the course, the final exam score did increase, but not by much. Those who studied for 30 hours averaged a final score of 65. At 60 study hours or more, scores on the final exam leveled off at about 70.

Attend Class; Don't Cram

Does this mean that no matter how much studying you do, you'll never get higher than a *C*? No. Class attendance and the avoidance of cramming are also important. Thus:

Figure (b) shows the relationship between the hours spent attending class and the final exam score. As class attendance increased from 10 hours to 40 hours, the final exam score rose from 60 to over 85. It's clear from the data that an important step toward

EXHIBIT
10

Effort and Exam Scores

The time you devote to your economics course can improve your final exam score up to a point. However, the type of effort you put in is more important than the total amount. Attending class more often leads to large improvements in final exam scores. Each extra hour of class lecture increases the final exam score by 1 point. Waiting until the last day before the final to study doesn't help. Students who cram the most before the final also receive the lowest grades.

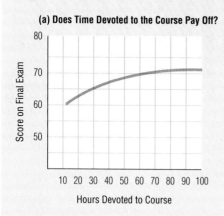

(a) Does Time Devoted to the Course Pay Off?

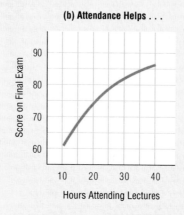

(b) Attendance Helps . . .

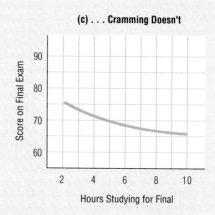

(c) . . . Cramming Doesn't

Source: Based on studies by Robert Schmidt of the University of Richmond, and Rendigs Fels and John Siegfried of Vanderbilt University.

getting a high grade in your economics course is to attend class regularly. The study of economics builds upon itself. Any class you miss limits your ability to understand material in later classes.

Figure (c) indicates a course of action to avoid. Don't cram for the final. Students who spent only two hours studying for the final actually received a higher final grade than those who spent 4, 6, or even 10 hours. Does this mean that you shouldn't study for the final? Not at all. It just means that you can't wait until the day before the final to learn the whole course.

Students who study most for the final are those who tend to study least during the rest of the course. The data suggest that those who keep up with assignments and attend class regularly will get the most benefit from their study time. So if you want to earn a good grade in economics, attend class and don't wait until the last minute to study.

Learn by Doing

Learning economics is like learning to play a musical instrument. *You have to practice.* Suppose you want to

play guitar. Even if you possess exceptional musical talent, study every book written on learning to play guitar, and watch experts play it, you won't become proficient without practice.

If you're like many students, one of the great mistakes you'll make in this course will be to spend a lot of time reading and watching economics. That is, you may study the text and your notes thoroughly (thus, reading economics) and pay undivided attention to your professor (thus, watching economics). But you won't become proficient in economics unless you practice what you're learning.

The way to practice any subject is by "doing it." Although no single method works best for everyone, here are some suggestions to help you make a strong beginning in economics:

1.   Buy a graph-paper notebook (either 4 squares or 5 squares to the inch) at your school bookstore. Take *all* your notes in that book. Economics notes consist of much more than expressions and sentences. They also include tables of numbers, graphs, diagrams, and some simple formulas. Using a graph-paper notebook will make it a lot

easier for you to write all your economics notes quickly, neatly, and correctly.

2. Whenever you see a graph in the text or on the chalkboard, get into the habit of sketching it. By doing that, you'll learn how to demonstrate the arguments you have studied. Graphs are very much a part of the language of economics, and you have to get accustomed to thinking in terms of them.

3. When you finish reading a chapter, review *all* the special terms and concepts listed at the end. These are defined within the chapter when they are first introduced. They are defined again in the Dictionary at the back of the book, so you can refer to them when the need arises. To an extent not found in other social sciences, economics has its own technical language. The Dictionary, when you use it, will help you learn that language.

4. If you're having trouble, *get help early!* Economic ideas tend to flow in a logical progression, building on previously learned assumptions, principles, and concepts. If you get behind in one part, chances are the next won't make much sense.

Finally:

Have fun! Economics touches virtually every aspect of human life. The revelations it yields about our lives are fascinating and often surprising. Learning economics may sometimes feel like hard work, but the work will pay rewarding dividends.

Summary of Important Ideas

1. Economics is a social science. It deals with aspects of human behavior—particularly how people earn a living and how societies produce goods and services.

2. The central concern of economics is scarcity. A resource is said to be scarce if alternative uses to that resource exist. This forces us to make choices among those alternatives.

3. The ways in which a society utilizes its resources are determined by its economic system. An economic system is the laws, institutions, customs, and practices that determine how a society allocates its scarce resources. Historically, capitalism and socialism have been the dominant economic systems.

4. Like all sciences, social or physical, economics uses theories and models to represent reality. These theories and models may need to be adjusted or even abandoned as facts change or as new facts come to light.

5. Several types of fallacies can be committed in economic reasoning. The most common are the fallacy of false cause and the fallacies of composition and division.

6. Graphs provide a visual way of expressing relationships between variables. Because economics relies heavily on quantitative variables, it makes intensive use of graphs. The concept of slope, or rate of change between variables, is at the heart of economics.

Terms and Concepts to Review

economics	*positive economics*
scarcity	*normative economics*
economic system	*model*
microeconomics	*slope*
macroeconomics	

Questions and Problems

1. A student said to her economics professor, "Water may be scarce in the Sahara desert, but it certainly isn't scarce over most of the earth. Most of the earth, after all, is *covered* with water." How do you suppose the professor responded?

2. Are yo-yos scarce? There's only one thing you can do with a yo-yo, so it doesn't have alternative uses and thus can't be scarce. What do you think?

3. Characterize the following statements as dealing predominantly with microeconomic or macroeconomic issues:

a. "The value of the nation's output of goods and services rose at a 3.4 percent annual rate in the last quarter. The increase was fueled by rising automobile production, increased exports, and a sharp rise in consumer spending."

b. "High gasoline prices lead to a greater demand for smaller, more fuel-efficient cars."

c. "With rising incomes and an older population, the demand for health-care services has increased sharply."

d. "Prices in some countries more than double in any given year, bringing the inflation rate above 100 percent."

e. "An important factor contributing to the divorce rate appears to be better job opportunities for women."

4. Look up the meanings of "fact" and "theory" in a good dictionary. Using what you've learned in this chapter, decide which of the following are statements of facts and which are theories. In what ways might you test each statement of theory?

a. The weather is muggier in Chicago than in St. Louis.

b. Germans drink more beer than Americans.

c. If an American Conference team wins the Super Bowl, stock prices will go down during the remainder of the year.

d. If the price of something rises, the quantity demanded in the market will fall.

e. Older people have higher incomes than younger people.

f. Wages rise with work experience.

5. "Everyone knows that the United States is one of the richest countries in the world. Therefore, economics as it is defined may be correct for poor countries, but certainly not for America. In America the problem is one of abundance, not scarcity." True or false? Explain.

6. Senator Jason is campaigning for a tax reduction. He argues that tax cuts in other major industrial nations have stimulated their rapid economic growth. Senator Blaine replies that what happens in nations thousands of miles away is no guide to what will happen here. Do you agree with Senator Blaine? Why or why not?

7. "A national minimum-wage law with no exemptions is a good thing. It assures that every worker receives at least a living wage." Is this statement positive or normative?

8. Positive economics permits the formulation of generalizations that can be used to make predictions. Therefore, positive economics is scientific. Do you agree?

9. "Any policy conclusion necessarily rests on a pre-

diction about the consequences of doing one thing rather than another, a prediction that must be based—implicitly or explicitly—on positive economics."

Milton Friedman, *Essays in Positive Economics*, 1962, p. 5.

What does this statement mean to you?

Identify at least one fallacy in each of the following:

10. "All rich nations have steel industries. Therefore, the surest way for a poor nation to become rich is to develop its own steel industry."

11. "The students who do best in economics have some working experience. Therefore, the surest way to receive a good grade in this course is to go out and get a job."

12. "To press forward with a properly ordered wage structure in each industry is the first condition for curbing competitive bargaining; but there is no reason why the process should stop there. What is good for each industry can hardly be bad for the economy as a whole."

The Socialist Union, *Twentieth Century Socialism*, 1956, p. 74.

13. "Each person's happiness is a good to that person, and the general happiness, therefore, a good to the aggregate of all persons."

John Stuart Mill, *Utilitarianism*, 1863, p. 48.

14. In a capitalist system, each business is free to set its own price on the product it sells. Therefore, there can't be anything wrong with all business owners getting together to agree on the prices of the products they sell.

15. Economics textbooks usually are long and dull, so we can't expect this one to be short and interesting.

16. "Roger Babson was best known for his predictions of the stock market. He once wrote an article in which he contended that gravity affects weather and crops, crops influence business, and business affects elections. He supported his thesis with an analysis of twenty-seven presidential elections [covering a period of more than 100 years]. In 75 percent of the cases, he said, the party in power remained in power when weather and business were good and was voted out when weather and business were bad."

Martin Gardner, *Fads and Fallacies in the Name of Science*, 1957, p. 97.

Exercises in Graphing

For exercises 1–3, sketch the graphs of the following relation-ships:

1.

x	1	2	3	4	5	6	7	8
y	1	2	3	4	5	6	7	8

2.

x	1	2	3	4	5	6	7
y	7	6	5	4	3	2	1

3.

x	−2	0	2	4
y	−8	−4	0	4

4. Sketch the following data on the same graph. Estimate the coordinates of the point of intersection of the two lines.

x	1	2	3	4
y	2	3	4	5

x	1	2	3	4
y	5	4	3	2

5. Sketch the graph of hog prices as a function of time:

time *(t)*	0	1	2	3	4	5	6	7	8
hog prices *(P)*	8	33	40	35	24	13	8	15	40

6. Which of the following interpretations of the graphs are correct, and which are incorrect? Explain why.

a. A reduction in the number of campus parking spaces available increases the number of minutes per day spent looking for space.

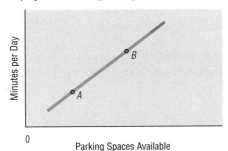

b. An increase in the nation's total income leads to more highway deaths per year.

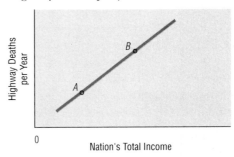

c. The more time students spend studying for their economics final examination, the lower their score.

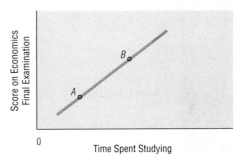

d. Spending on health care has no effect on the number of illnesses per year.

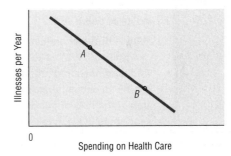

e. As family income rises, spending on food increases by decreasing amounts.

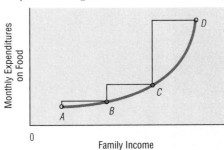

Chapter 1

Economic Resources, Goals, and Institutions

Learning Guide

Watch for answers to these important questions

What are the resources of our economic system? What kinds of payments are made for their use?

What goals do we want our economy to achieve? Can we trade various goals against one another? Are there costs of doing so?

Why is our economic system called "capitalistic"? What social, political, and economic institutions constitute the basis of capitalism? How can we depict the flow of goods and resources in a capitalistic system?

This evening it would be nice if you could read this chapter, do all your other course assignments, earn some money, engage in pleasant recreational activity, and go out for a leisurely dinner. But you can't do all these things. You'll have to give up one or more of them because they require *alternative* uses of your time. The existence of alternative uses indicates that time is scarce and that choices must be made concerning its use.

Economic systems also face the problem of scarcity. Our economy, for example, doesn't have unlimited human and material resources. Using a set of resources to produce one thing requires giving up something else. Resources thus have alternative uses. Accordingly, societies, like individuals, must make choices about the allocation of scarce resources. This chapter explores the nature of the choices that must be made in any economic system.

Resources of Economic Systems

Every economic system has various resources at its disposal to produce goods and services. These resources are of two broad types:

Material resources include such things as natural resources, raw materials, machinery and equipment, buildings, and transportation and communication facilities.

Human resources consist of the productive physical and mental abilities of people.

The Factors of Production

Economists often divide material resources into two subcategories—land and capital—and human resources into two subcategories—labor and entrepreneurship. These four types of resources are known formally as the *factors of production.* They are the basic components, or "inputs," that every society uses to produce goods and services, or "outputs." Thus, *the terms "resources" and "factors of production" are used interchangeably in economics.*

Land

The term *land,* in economics, means all nonhuman or "natural" resources. These are gifts of nature such as land itself, mineral deposits, timber, and water. Natural resources constitute the physical endowment upon which any civilization is built.

Although natural resources are helpful to economic activity, their existence doesn't guarantee an economy's prosperity. Some of the poorest nations on earth are blessed with huge endowments of natural resources, while some of the richest have very little. Mexico is a relatively poor country even though it is quite rich in natural resources. Japan is a relatively rich country even though it must import virtually every basic resource it uses.

Natural resources have little economic value unless a society is willing and able to develop them. Oil deposits were thought of as a natural nuisance until the 1850s. But technology and economic demand combined to find many uses for oil (among them fuel, lubricants, plastics, and chemicals). Oil therefore became a valuable natural resource.

Capital

Economists use the term "capital" differently from the way it is commonly used by people in business. In economics, *capital* is a manufactured good that is used to produce other goods. Therefore, capital may be defined simply as a produced means of further production. What "produced" indicates here is that capital is created by human resources working with material resources. Thus, timber is considered to be a natural resource, but lumber is capital. Some other examples of capital goods are tools, machinery and equipment, factory buildings, freight cars, and office furniture. All are economic resources that can be used to help produce consumer goods and services, such as food, cars, clothing, and health care.

It's important to note that capital, to the economist, means *physical* capital (goods used in production) and not *financial* capital (money). In the business world, *but not in economics,* people generally use the term "capital" to mean money—the funds used to purchase capital goods and to finance the operation of a business. For the economy as a whole, however, money is not a productive resource. If it were, nations could become rich simply by printing money. *Money's chief function is to facilitate the exchange of goods and services.* Money therefore serves as a lubricant rather than as a factor of production within the economic system.

Labor

To make land and capital productive requires labor. *Labor* is the efforts or activities of people hired to assist in the production of goods and services. In this sense, labor refers not to the workers themselves but to the service they provide by working.

In a broader sense, however, "labor" also means the services of everyone who works for a living. We often refer to the labor force of a nation—that is, all the people above a certain age who have jobs or are seeking jobs. The meaning of "labor force" and the notion of labor as a factor of production are different concepts in economics. The distinction between the two is generally clear from the context.

Entrepreneurship

For production of goods or services, the above three factors of production, land, capital, and labor, must be organized and combined. This is where entrepreneurship (sometimes called "ownership") comes in. "Entrepreneur" is a term coined by a nineteenth-century French economist, Jean Baptiste Say, to refer to someone who risks his or her money in a venture in hopes of making a profit.

Entrepreneurship means recognizing the opportunities to be gained from production, assembling the factors of production, raising the necessary funds, organizing the management, making the basic business policy decisions, and reaping the gains of success or the losses of failure. Some entrepreneurs act as their own managers; others hire people to serve as managers. But, regardless of who acts as manager, the *entrepreneurial function* is necessary to production.

Whether it is Henry Ford figuring out a new way to put cars together or Stephen Jobs inventing the personal computer, *entrepreneurs have been at the cutting edge of economic development.* **Perhaps more than any of the**

other factors of production, they account for the economic progress that capitalistic economies such as ours have enjoyed.

The Economic Problem: Scarcity, Choice, and Cost

People in any society want a wide variety of goods and services. Food, clothing, houses, automobiles, electronic products, education, and health care are only a few of the material things people desire. The response to the question, "Would you like a better car, a nicer place to live, or a vacation trip?" is likely to be yes.

Although people's desires for goods and services are virtually unlimited, the means of fulfilling those desires are not. The factors of production—land, labor, capital, and entrepreneurship—are scarce.

Scarcity

Remember that a resource is scarce if alternative uses for it exist. Because almost everything has alternative uses, almost everything is scarce. A good that isn't scarce is called a "free good." If a good is free, it's available in such sufficient abundance that it fills all our wants without reducing the amount available for someone else. Therefore, a *free good* is one that can be acquired without sacrifice—*without giving something up.*

There's more to this definition than is at first apparent. For example, is air a free good? Although everyone uses air to breathe, air has also become a convenient site to dump automobile exhaust. If society continues to dump more exhaust into the air, the air will be less satisfactory for breathing. Because alternative uses for air exist, air is a scarce resource.

What about sunshine? In most cases, sunshine is a free good. One person's decision to sit in the sun doesn't reduce the sunshine available for someone else. But there are some contexts in which even sunshine is scarce. Suppose, for example, that you put a solar collector on your roof. If your neighbor decides to grow a tall tree, it may shade the solar collector in the winter. Your neighbor's use of the sun to grow the tree is thus an alternative to your use of the sun to warm your house.

Sunshine is scarce in this instance because one use reduces the amount available for another. Indeed, the problem of alternative uses of the sun is sufficiently common that some states and localities have enacted zoning ordinances that specify which uses of sunshine will have priority.

Choice and Cost

Because resources are scarce, the decision to use them for one purpose necessarily precludes their use for another. *Choice thus entails costs.* For example, the cost of devoting more hours to your studies is the value of the time you are giving up. This value may consist of the income you would earn if you chose to work instead, or even the pleasure you would derive if you chose to loaf. The cost of producing more military goods is the forgone civilian goods that could have been produced. Can you think of some other illustrations?

These examples suggest a fundamental principle: *The cost of any choice is the value of the alternative forgone in making that choice.* In economics, we give a special name to this idea:

The value of the benefit forgone by choosing one alternative rather than another is called *opportunity cost.* This concept is also known as "alternative cost." It is measured by what an economic entity—such as a society, a business, a household, or an individual—is not doing but could be doing. *The opportunity cost of any decision is thus the value of the sacrificed alternative.*

Economic Systems

To best utilize scarce resources, nations organize *economic systems.* These consist of laws, institutions, customs, and practices that, taken together, establish the ways in which a society's scarce resources are allocated. Capitalism and socialism (and communism, which is a form of socialism) are economic systems. They differ from one another mainly in their forms of resource ownership and in their methods of resource use.

In a purely capitalistic system, both human resources and material resources—the factors of production—are privately (as distinguished from governmentally) owned. The owners of businesses and the managers they appoint decide how best to utilize the human and material resources at their disposal for purposes of making profits.

In a purely socialistic system, human resources are also owned by individuals, but material resources are owned by government, which represents society. Hence the name *socialism.* A government authority, normally a committee, manages the nation's human and material resources on behalf of society. The authority decides how best to utilize resources for purposes that do not ordinarily include profit making.

In the real world there are no purely capitalistic or socialistic systems. Instead, there are degrees of each.

Some material resources in capitalistic countries are governmentally owned, and some material resources in socialistic countries are privately owned. Whether a country is referred to as capitalistic or socialistic depends on the *predominant* characteristics of its economic system. Today, most countries are capitalistic, but more than one-fifth of the inhabited globe consists of nations that are predominantly socialistic.

Returns to Owners of Resources

Because resources are scarce, they can command a price in the marketplace. Therefore, people who own them don't generally give them away free. If you have a job, for example, you get paid for the services you provide. Similarly, other resource owners get paid for the services they provide. In economics, the payments that resource owners receive for supplying factors of production are given special names.

Those who supply land and other natural resources receive a payment called ***rent.*** Those who supply financial capital, the money that business firms borrow for the purchase of physical capital, receive a return called ***interest.*** Workers who sell their labor receive a payment called ***wages,*** which includes salaries, commissions, and the like. Finally, those who perform the entrepreneurial function receive, or at least hope for, ***profits.***

The yearly sum of rent, interest, wages, and profits for a country is the total annual income earned by all resource owners. This total is called ***national income.*** Exhibit 1 summarizes the factors of production and payments made for them.

Specialization and Division of Labor

Although the factors of production are grouped into four broad classes, there is generally a considerable degree of specialization within each class. Machines, for example, are designed to do specific jobs, and people are often trained to perform specific tasks.

Technically, ***specialization*** is the division of productive activities among people and regions with the result that no one person or area is self-sufficient. Specialization by workers is sometimes called ***division of labor.*** The result of specialization is an enormous gain in productivity, generally measured as output per worker.

These ideas have been fundamental to economic thinking for well over 200 years. They were first expressed in 1776 by Adam Smith, a Scottish philoso-

EXHIBIT 1

Classifying the Factors of Production

Resource or factor of production	Description	Payment
Land	Natural resources (e.g., land itself, including minerals, water, timber)	Rent
Capital	Produced resources (e.g., tools, factories, machines)	Interest
Labor	Physical and mental efforts (e.g., hired workers and professionals)	Wages
Entrepreneurship	Ownership function (e.g., organizing and financial risk taking)	Profit
Annual total		National income

pher who was the founder of modern economics. To generalize from Smith, specialization and division of labor increase production because they:

- Allow for the development and refinement of skills

- Eliminate the waste of time that is entailed in going from one job to another

- Simplify human tasks, thus permitting the introduction of labor-saving machines

Of course, specialization has its shortcomings. A repetitive, boring job can dull a worker's mind and can become little more than a naked means of subsistence. Accordingly, many companies continually seek ways to improve the quality of working life. In numerous manufacturing firms, for instance, assembly-line workers are being given larger shares of responsibility in the management of their work. And participatory decision making between workers and managers, once considered textbook theory, is becoming much more of a reality.

Specialization and International Trade

Just as specialization increases the productivity of labor and other resources, it also makes the countries of the world more productive. Countries tend to specialize in goods that they can produce at the lowest cost. This provides the basis for mutually beneficial trade among nations. A country *exports* goods that it produces at a low cost, then *imports* goods that other countries produce more cheaply. This is like a worker who specializes in one productive activity, then purchases other products with the income earned. Specialization and exchange allow nations to employ their scarce resources most productively. To see why let's look at an actual example of specialization and exchange.

Why doesn't the United States produce all of the scotch whiskey, woolen sweaters, and leather shoes it wants so that Americans don't have to import these goods from Britain? Likewise, why doesn't Britain produce all of the food, machinery, and chemicals it wants so that Britons don't have to import these goods from the United States?

Like all nations, the United States and Britain have limited resources or factors of production. Therefore, the resources can't be used to produce everything. Using them for one purpose precludes their use for another. The use that is precluded determines the sacrifice that is incurred—the *opportunity cost* of the decision.

Because nations have different quantities and qualities of resources, the United States and Britain will each want to use their limited factors of production in the least costly ways. This means that the two countries will produce those goods that entail the lowest opportunity cost and least sacrifice.

In America, the opportunity cost of manufacturing machinery is lower, and the opportunity cost of manufacturing sweaters is higher, than in Britain. In Britain, the reverse condition exists: The opportunity cost of manufacturing sweaters is lower than it is for manufacturing machinery. Therefore, compared to Britain, America has what may be called a *comparative advantage* in producing machinery and a *comparative disadvantage* in producing sweaters. Conversely, compared to America, Britain has a comparative advantage in producing sweaters and a comparative disadvantage in producing machinery.

It follows that, by *specializing* rather than generalizing, each country can make the goods in which it has a comparative advantage. The total output of machines and sweaters will therefore be greater. The two countries can then trade with each other for the goods in which they have a comparative disadvantage. In that way, both countries will be better off. They will be exporting goods that involve the lowest opportunity cost and least sacrifice to produce domestically. They will be importing goods that involve the highest opportunity cost and greatest sacrifice to produce domestically. As a result, each country can end up with more machines and more sweaters than if it tried to be self-sufficient and produce both. Thus:

Scarce resources are put to best use when nations specialize. Output is higher and global welfare is greater with international trade. Because of specialization, nations become increasingly dependent on one another for the goods they consume. This leads to growing integration of the world economy and, as a result, to global issues that affect all of us in our daily lives.

Goals of an Economic System

When we refer to an economy as a system, we imply that it has purpose and that there is order in its structure. What are the purposes of an economic system? What do we want an economy to do?

Four goals that are fundamental to all economic systems, capitalistic as well as socialistic, are *efficiency, equity, stability,* and *growth*. These goals are worth examining because they are universal standards used for judging economic practices and policies.

Efficiency: Full Employment of Resources

Because every society possesses only limited amounts of the various factors of production, every society wants to use them efficiently. What does this mean? In general, **efficiency** is the best use of available resources to attain a desired result. It is important to distinguish between two kinds of technical and economic efficiency.

Technical Efficiency

Engineers measure physical efficiency by the ratio of physical output to physical input. The greater the ratio, the greater the physical efficiency. If a motor, for example, uses 100 units of energy input to produce 75 units of energy output, the motor is said to be 75 percent efficient. If the motor produces 80 units of energy output for 100 units of energy input, the motor is 80 percent efficient.

A firm, an industry, or an entire economy is said to have achieved ***technical efficiency*** when it is producing maximum output by making the fullest possible utilization of available inputs. The available resources are then said to be *fully employed* in the most effective way. Therefore, no change in the combination of inputs can be made that will increase the output of one product of the system without decreasing the output of another.

This idea can be illustrated with an example. Suppose a farmer growing as much corn as possible with the available quantities of labor, capital, and land has achieved technical efficiency. Given these resources, it will be impossible for the farmer to increase the output of wheat (by transferring some resources out of corn production and into wheat production) without decreasing the farm's output of corn. Can you give a similar example for a manufacturing firm? For the producer of a service?

The concept of technical efficiency can be broadened from simple production systems to more complex ones, such as firms, industries, or an entire economy. An economic system, for example, is technically efficient if every producing unit in the system has attained technical efficiency—the greatest possible ratio of physical output to available physical input. *No change in the combination of society's resources can then be made that will increase the output of one product without decreasing the output of another.*

Economic (Allocative) Efficiency

Suppose a society has achieved technical efficiency and is making full use of its available resources. Would you give high marks to such a society if families who wanted a larger apartment had to wait 10 years before one became available? Would you think the economy efficient if people who wanted to buy meat for dinner had to spend all afternoon waiting in line outside the meat market? Most people would agree that an economic system ought to deliver the goods and services that people want and are able to pay for.

A useful standard in determining the success of an economy is ***economic,*** or ***allocative, efficiency.*** An economy is said to have achieved economic (allocative) efficiency when it is producing that combination of goods and services that people prefer, given their incomes. *No change can then be made in the combination of society's resources that will make someone better off without making someone else worse off—each in their own estimation.*

Technical and economic efficiency are related concepts. It is possible to have technical efficiency

without economic efficiency, but not economic efficiency without technical efficiency. Let's see why:

1. A society that has achieved technical efficiency is making full use of its available resources. But the society is not *economically* efficient unless it's producing the goods that people prefer to purchase with their existing incomes.

2. A society that has achieved economic efficiency has also achieved technical efficiency. That is, the society is not only producing the largest possible output with the available resources but is also satisfying consumer preferences. Economic efficiency is thus a general concept that includes technical efficiency.

Equity: Fairness or Economic Justice

Consideration of economic efficiency doesn't address the question of how a society's goods are shared. This is a matter of ***income distribution.*** It concerns the division of a society's output (that is, the income or value of what society earns from production) among its members. Because income distribution deals with the matter of who gets how much, it raises fundamental issues of equity, or justice. One of the major goals of our society is to achieve an equitable distribution of income. It's important to note that equitable means "fair" or "just," *not* "equal."

Equity is both a philosophical concept and an economic goal. There is no scientific way of concluding that one distribution of income is fair and therefore "good" while another is unfair and therefore "bad." Such judgments are normative, not positive. For example, in the United States a neurosurgeon may earn twenty times as much as a schoolteacher; in Britain, four times as much; in Israel, twice as much; and in Cuba, an even smaller ratio. Which ratio is considered equitable depends on society's prevailing rules or standards of income distribution. You will learn about such standards in later chapters.

Stability: Steady Average Price Level

A third economic goal of every society is to achieve stability of prices. This does not mean that *all* prices should be stable. That would be impossible in a society in which people are free to make economic decisions. However, it does mean that the general or *average* level of prices should be reasonably stable. This goal is important because the costs to society of a steadily rising average price level—inflation—are serious and pervasive.

Inflation does harm in various ways. It impairs efficiency by lowering incentives to produce. It redistributes income arbitrarily and inequitably by reducing many people's purchasing power by disproportionate amounts. Further, it greatly weakens the nation's ability to compete in world markets when prices at home rise faster than those in countries with which we trade.

Growth: Rising Output per Person

A fourth economic goal of every society is economic growth. By this is meant an increase in the quantity of goods and services produced per person—in other words, a rising standard of living.

Economic growth is related to the goals of stability, efficiency, and equity. By maintaining stability, an economy avoids substantial price fluctuations and is better able to encourage efficiency—continuous full employment of available resources. This, in turn, leads to a robust volume of economic activity and to steady economic growth. As a result, living standards are enhanced for all income groups in society because all of them benefit even if each receives a constant proportion of an expanding economic pie.

Establishing a Mix of Goals

The economic goals of efficiency, equity, stability, and growth are both *universal* and *all-inclusive.*

They are universal because they are pursued by all nations regardless of their economic systems. Nations may differ in the priorities they place on achieving the goals and on the means of attaining them. However, the goals themselves are never in question.

The goals are all-inclusive because they encompass all of the economic objectives that societies seek. In other words, any other economic goal you may be able to think of can be related to one of these four goals. For example:

■   Critics often contend that reducing environmental pollution should be a goal of economics. But economists can demonstrate that most forms of pollution are direct results of resource misallocation, and hence are problems of *efficiency.*

■   Policies that provide aid for the poor are matters of great social concern. But economists view the task of formulating such policies as a problem of *equity.*

These and other examples you'll learn about help reinforce this principle:

Economic problems and issues, and proposals for dealing with them, are always evaluated in terms of one or more of the four goals of *efficiency, equity, stability,* **and** *growth.*

As you will see, the goals are not easily attained. This is because their realization may involve certain sacrifices—for two reasons:

1. Free Choice Versus Governmental Direction

In a democracy, there is a close connection between political freedom and economic freedom. Citizens vote for legislators who influence government policy. Consumers choose the goods they want. Workers select their occupations. And holders of wealth employ their assets as they see fit. Government, of course, may impose certain restrictions that it believes are in the public's interest (or in the interest of some large voting bloc or effective pressure group). Also, discrimination may deprive some people of equal opportunities in employment. Nevertheless, freedom of choice in economic endeavors is an ideal of all democratic political and economic systems.

Unfortunately, freedom of choice may not always lead to the economic goals of efficiency, equity, stability, and growth. Or it may occasionally impede certain social goals. In these cases a society may decide to sacrifice some freedom of choice and to rely instead on government direction and control to try to correct the situation.

For example, legislation that outlaws smoking in certain public places deprives people of the freedom to smoke. However, allowing smoking in public places deprives other people of their right to clean air. One of the surprising things you'll learn in economics is that legislative prohibition isn't necessarily the best way of dealing with such problems. Other methods exist that can accomplish desired results while preserving freedom of choice.

2. Conflicting Goals

A second reason why sacrifices may be necessary is that goals can conflict with each other. For example, efficiency can conflict with stability if a high level of employment exerts upward pressure on prices. Similarly, economic growth can conflict with equity if a rising volume of output benefits some groups much more than others.

When such conflicts occur, government may try, through legislation or regulation, to promote the desirable goals while minimizing what is deemed unde-sirable. But even if such efforts achieve their declared objectives, they're likely to entail some costs. For in-stance, legislation that prohibits increases in wages and prices may very well succeed in curbing inflation. However, economics demonstrates that such legisla-tion will also limit freedom of choice for consumers, workers, and businesspeople alike—and may generate woefully inefficient outcomes.

Conclusion: Decisions Involve Trade-Offs

Every decision entails a choice between alternatives. If we are to make rational choices, we must understand the trade-offs. A trade-off is the cost of choosing one objective over another, or of formulating compro-mises between them. Thus, an overall challenge faced by every society is to establish a proper mix of goals. In doing so, a society—or a person, for that matter—can-not avoid trade-offs.

A nation's goals and the trade-offs it is willing to make vary according to its political and economic philosophies. For example:

History shows that most socialistic nations have justified rigid economic and political controls as nec-essary to achieve strong military preparedness along with high rates of efficiency and growth. Although their economic goals have not been realized, they have made substantial sacrifices of economic and political freedoms in pursuit of the goals.

Most capitalistic economies have achieved higher levels of efficiency and growth (and in some cases mil-itary preparedness) than socialistic economies without making substantial sacrifices of economic and political freedoms.

Summary Thus Far

1. Our economy's resources—the inputs it uses to produce outputs—are its factors of production. They are classified for convenience into four categories—land, capital, labor, and entrepreneurship.

2. Every society's factors of production are scarce—they have alternative uses. Societies establish eco-nomic systems to solve the problem of how their scarce resources will be used.

3. In a capitalistic system the factors of production are privately owned. Owners receive payments for their resources—rent for land, interest for capital, wages for labor, and profits for entrepreneurship.

4. Every society seeks to attain four economic goals: efficiency, equity, stability, and growth. However, the "mix" of goals that each society chooses depends on its economic system, values, and institutions.

The Great Questions: What? How? For Whom?

You've learned that, in economics, *scarcity* is the name of the game and *economizing*—combining resources ef-ficiently—is the way it is played. Individuals, as well as businesses and nations, "play" the game by deciding what will be sacrificed to get the things that are wanted. This requires making choices—a central problem of economics. Problems of choice arise be-cause scarce resources can be used to achieve differ-ent objectives.

How does an economic system achieve a particu-lar set of objectives? The answer is, by combining its *re-sources, wants,* and *technologies.* First, however, it must answer three fundamental and interdependent ques-tions.

What Goods and Services Should a Society Produce—and in What Quantities?

How should a society's scarce resources be allocated? Should some of them be taken out of the production of consumer goods (food, clothing, automobiles, and appliances) and put into the production of capital goods (tools, machines, tractors, and factories)? Would the reverse be better? For instance, by enlarg-ing its proportion of capital goods now, an economy will be able to produce more consumer goods in the future. It is necessary, then, to decide how much con-sumption should be sacrificed today to provide for in-creased output of consumer goods later.

A related question is: *How much* of each good will a society produce? How many automobiles? How much food and clothing? How many tractors, facto-ries, and so on? The values and priorities involved in making such decisions are extremely complex. Never-theless, in answering this question, a society is again choosing between present and future satisfactions. It is making a trade-off between the amount of con-sumption to be sacrificed today and the prospect of in-creased consumption at a later time.

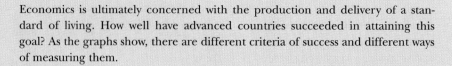

Comparative Living Standards

Economics is ultimately concerned with the production and delivery of a standard of living. How well have advanced countries succeeded in attaining this goal? As the graphs show, there are different criteria of success and different ways of measuring them.

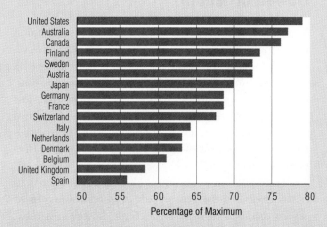

Standard of Living The United States ranks first, scoring 79%, on an index that rates the standard of living in sixteen wealthy nations.

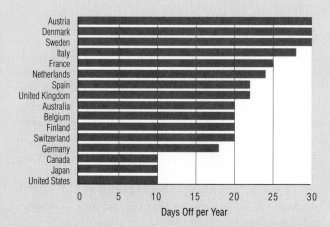

Vacation Time The world's most generous vacation benefits are found largely in Europe. Only the United States and Britain have no laws mandating minimum vacation days.

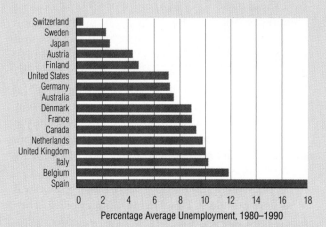

Jobs Unemployment is virtually unknown in prosperous Switzerland, but has been endemic in Spain's sluggish economy.

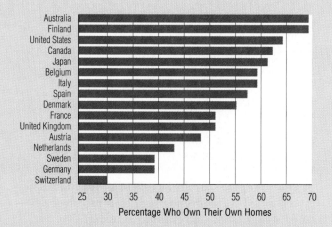

Home Ownership The percentage of households that own their homes tops 50% in eleven of sixteen industrialized countries. The U.S. rate trails that of Australia and Finland, where the government offers cash subsidies to home buyers and builders.

Selected Prices in Dollars

	Eden Prairie, Minn.	Pforzheim, Germany	Fukuoka, Japan
Gasoline (per gallon)	$1.33	$3.07	$3.80
Pantyhose (Christian Dior)	5.00	7.54	3.65
Compact disk	18.01	15.02	16.43
Daily newspaper	.35	1.10	.73
Big Mac	1.86	2.55	2.77
Movie ticket	6.00	6.96	11.68
Cup of coffee	.50	.70	1.83
Ground beef (per pound)	1.18	2.61	6.15
Six-pack of beer (domestic)	4.02	2.55	9.64
Eggs (per dozen)	.79	1.67	2.00
Red-leaf lettuce (per head)	.89	1.44	2.03

Consumer Prices The Japanese spend up to 420% more than their American and German counterparts on many consumer goods. That is in part because Japan restricts the number of large, cost-efficient stores that could force many mom-and-pop shops, which dominate Japanese retailing, to lower their prices.

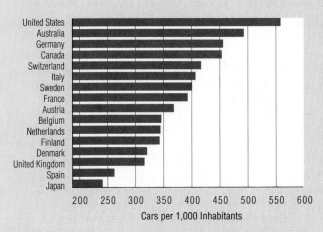

Cars per 1,000 Inhabitants

Automobiles The United States has far and away more passenger cars per 1,000 inhabitants than most major industrialized countries. Japan, the world's leading car manufacturer, trails the list.

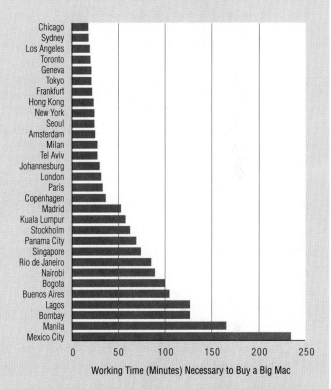

Working Time (Minutes) Necessary to Buy a Big Mac

Big Mac—The Earning Standard of the World McDonald's has infiltrated the global market to such a degree that now the Union Bank of Switzerland uses the Big Mac to compare earnings in cities around the world. By this measure, the best-paid workers are in Chicago, where it takes only 18 minutes to earn a Big Mac. The worst-paid are in Mexico City, where the average worker has to toil almost 4 hours to buy the burger. Union Bank doesn't include Moscow, where a Big Mac costs almost 2 days' pay.

Sources: All graphs except "Big Mac—The Earning Standard of the World" adapted from graphs and data in "A Look into Why We Still Live Best," *Money*, October 1991, pp. 88 ff. "Big Mac—The Earning Standard of the World" from *The Economist*, November 2, 1991.

How Should Resources Be Organized for Production?

Most goods can be produced in more than one way by using resources in different quantities and combinations. In the early days of the United States, for example, land was in abundant supply and labor was not. Therefore, labor was the limiting factor in producing agricultural commodities. In parts of the Far East, by contrast, land is relatively more scarce than labor. Consequently, large quantities of labor are applied to limited amounts of arable land.

Similarly, it's often possible to vary the combinations of resources in manufacturing. Automobiles, for example, can be produced from different combinations of such materials as steel, aluminum, or fiberglass, as well as with different combinations of labor and capital. Any society, therefore, decides how it will *organize* its scarce resources in order to use them efficiently.

For Whom Shall the Goods Be Produced?

Who is to receive what share of the economic pie? This question is of enormous significance—for two reasons:

1.   One of the criteria for judging the performance of an economic system is the way in which it distributes its goods and services. This is the goal of *equity.*

2.   The pattern of distribution determines our individual standards of living.

For these reasons, a significant part of economics is concerned with principles and policies affecting the apportionment of income among society's members.

Answering the Questions

The three great questions—*what, how,* and *for whom*—are fundamental in all societies. Each society answers these questions in different ways.

At one extreme is a **command economy.** This is an economy in which an authoritarian government exercises primary control over decisions concerning what to produce and how much to produce. It may also, but does not necessarily, decide for whom to produce. Socialist nations are examples of countries with *predominantly* command economies.

At the other extreme is the **market economy.** In such an economy, questions concerning what to produce, how much to produce, and for whom to produce are decided in an open market through competitive forces of supply and demand. The market economy embodies the idea of "pure" capitalism, also called "theoretical capitalism." It is an extremely useful model of what would happen in the absence of governmental direction. (The model's uses are examined in a number of later chapters.) It's important to note, however, that no countries with pure market economies exist.

Between the two extremes of a command economy and a market economy is the *mixed economy.* Here economic questions are decided partly by the workings of a free market and partly by governmental authority. Most developed nations are *predominantly* mixed economies. However, they vary in the degree of reliance they place on market mechanisms.

Society's Production Possibilities

Even a wealthy society can't escape the need for economizing. The process of economizing is complex, and must be simplified in order to focus on the basic concepts involved.

Let's begin by constructing a model of the economizing process for a hypothetical society. The model is based on four simplifying assumptions:

1.   **Two Goods** *The economy produces only agricultural products (such as crops and livestock) and capital goods (such as machines and factories).* The assumption of two goods allows us to analyze the problem using the language of graphs, and to derive principles for a simple economy. The principles derived, however, are applicable to a complex economy producing many goods.

2.   **Common Resources** *The same resources can be used to produce either or both of the two classes of goods and can be shifted freely between them.* This means that labor and other factors of production can be used to produce either food or machines, or different combinations of both.

3.   **Fixed Conditions** *The supply of resources and the state of technological knowledge are fixed.* In effect, this is an "all other things equal" assumption of the kind we always make when we draw a graph showing a relationship between two variables. Other conditions that may affect the variables are necessarily held constant when drawing the graph.

4.   Full Employment *Society's available resources are working in the most (technically) efficient way.* It follows from this assumption that the economy may be able to increase the production of one class of goods only by taking resources away from the production of another class of goods. However, the economy can't increase the production of *both* classes of goods because there are no excess resources available.

The model is depicted, in both tabular and graphic form, in Exhibit 2. The table is called a *production-possibilities schedule.* Notice that under production alternative *A,* the society would be devoting all its resources to the production of agricultural goods. It would thus be producing 14 units of agricultural goods and zero units of capital goods.

At the other extreme, alternative *G,* the society would be putting all its resources into the production

of capital goods. It would then be producing 6 units of capital goods and zero units of agricultural goods.

Realistically, a society operates somewhere between these extremes. If a society operating at point *A,* for example, tries to increase its production of capital goods by choosing among alternatives *B, C, D,* and so on, it must *sacrifice* some agricultural goods. The amount of sacrifice for each *additional* unit of capital goods is shown by the negative numbers in the fourth column of the table. The negative numbers represent the amount of agricultural goods the economy must give up to acquire one more unit of capital goods. Note that these negative numbers grow larger as the society moves from zero production of capital goods toward zero production of agricultural goods.

The information in the production-possibilities schedule can be transferred directly to the accompanying graph. The units of capital goods are scaled on

EXHIBIT
2

Society's Production-Possibilities Curve: Achieving Technical Efficiency

The table provides the data for the accompanying graph. A society that is producing a combination of goods on its production-possibilities curve has achieved *technical efficiency.* This means that the society has attained the largest possible output with available inputs. Therefore, no change in the combination of inputs can be made that will increase the output of one product without decreasing the output of another product.

However, the society will not have achieved *economic efficiency* unless it is producing the combination of goods that people prefer to purchase with their existing incomes.

Note: When sketching a production-possibilities curve freehand (that is, without basing it on a table of data), you should draw it smooth. A smooth curve is an idealization or model of a real situation and is easier to interpret than a jagged line.

Production-Possibilities Schedule

Production alternatives	Capital goods production	Agricultural goods production	Sacrifice of agricultural goods for capital goods
A	0	14	−1
B	1	13	−2
C	2	11	−2
D	3	9	−2
E	4	7	−3
F	5	4	−4
G	6	0	

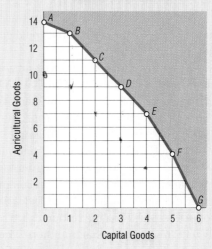

Production-Possibilities Curve

the horizontal axis and those for agricultural goods on the vertical axis. The line that connects the various production alternatives *A* through *G* is called a ***production-possibilities curve.*** It indicates all possible combinations of maximum total output for the society it represents.

Law of Increasing (Opportunity) Costs

Let's see how the production-possibilities curve is interpreted. In going from *A* to *B*, society gives up *one* unit of agricultural goods in order to free the resources needed to produce an additional unit of capital goods. In going from *B* to *C*, society gives up *two* units of agricultural goods in order to free the resources needed to produce an additional unit of capital goods. Traveling down the curve, a move from one point to the next tells you the amount of agricultural goods that the society must sacrifice to acquire one more unit of capital goods. *The slope of the curve at each point thus measures the cost of producing an additional unit of capital goods:*

At each point on the curve, the amount of agricultural goods sacrificed (measured on the vertical axis) may be thought of as the *rise,* and the amount of capital goods acquired (measured on the horizontal axis) as the *run.* The slope of a line at any point is measured by the ratio: rise ÷ run.

Thus, when going from *A* to *B*, the slope of the curve at *A* is –1/1 = –1. When going from *B* to *C*, the slope at *B* is –2/1 = –2. And so on. The slopes at various production alternatives are shown in the fourth column of the table. Because the curve is bowed out, it gets steeper as you travel down it. The numerical (absolute) values of the slopes thus become greater. In economic terms, this means that the costs (sacrifices of agricultural goods) increase as more capital goods are produced.

Why does an increasing amount of one good have to be sacrificed to obtain each additional unit of the other? The answer is that the economy's factors of production are not all equally suitable for producing the two types of goods. Fertile land, for example, is more suitable for crops than for factories, and unskilled farm workers are more adaptable to agriculture than to manufacturing. Even though an economy's resources may be substitutable within wide limits for given production purposes, the resources are relatively more efficient in some uses than in others. Thus, as society tries to increase its production of capital goods, it

must take increasing amounts of resources out of agriculture.

These points suggest the operation of an important law.

Law of Increasing (Opportunity) Costs   **As a society increases production of one good, it must sacrifice increasing amounts of an alternative good to produce each additional unit. The real cost of acquiring either good, therefore, is not the money that must be spent for it. The real cost is the amount of the *alternative* good that must be sacrificed. Increasing costs are reflected in the shape of the production-possibilities curve, which is bowed outward.**

Using Production-Possibilities Curves

A number of other ideas can be conveyed with production-possibilities curves. Exhibit 3 illustrates some of the more important ones.

Depicting Resource Underutilization—Unemployment

An economy that underutilizes its resources is producing at some point, such as *U*, inside its production-possibilities curve. This is shown in Figure (a). The economy is thus experiencing unemployment—inefficient resource utilization. Three of the moves that the economy can make to get back on the curve are to produce more capital goods *(horizontal arrow)*, more consumer goods *(vertical arrow)*, or more of both *(diagonal arrow)*. Any of these choices will increase employment, and therefore efficiency.

Illustrating Economic Growth

Increases in resources or improvements in technology will shift an economy's production-possibilities curve outward, as indicated in Figure (b). If the combination of capital goods and consumer goods being produced was initially at point *A*, the new combination might be at *B*, *C*, or *D*, as suggested by the arrows. Other combinations are also possible. The resulting expansion represents *economic growth*—a higher level of output per capita. Note from Figures (c) and (d) that the new curve need not necessarily be "parallel" to the old one. Changes in resources or in technology may bring about a greater increase in one type of output than in another.

Choosing Between Present Goods and Future Goods

A society that allocates more resources in the present to the production of capital goods than to the produc-

EXHIBIT
3

Applications of Production-Possibilities Curves

Production-possibilities curves can be used to depict resource underutilization [Figure (a)]. The curves can also be used to show economic growth [Figures (b), (c), and (d)], and the effects of choosing between "present" goods and "future" goods [Figures (e) and (f)].

Economic Growth

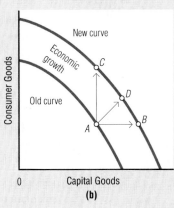

(b)

"Present" Goods or "Future" Goods

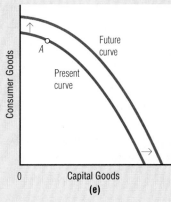

(e)

Resource Underutilization

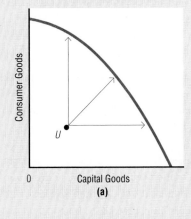

(a)

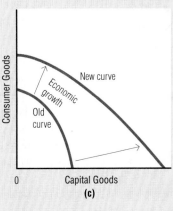

(c)

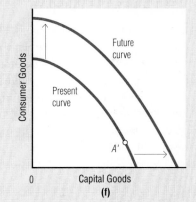

(f)

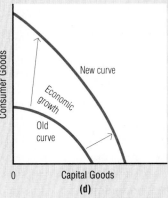

(d)

tion of consumer goods will have more of both kinds of goods in the future. In other words, the society will experience more economic growth. This is because consumer goods are used to satisfy present wants, whereas capital goods are used to satisfy future wants.

Figures (e) and (f) show how the degree of out-

ward shift of a society's future production-possibilities curve is affected by whether it chooses to be at point *A* (emphasizing consumer goods) or at point *A'* (emphasizing capital goods) on its present curve. Note that the outward shift of the curve in Figure (f) is greater than that in Figure (e).

Capitalism and Our Mixed Economy

The economic system of the United States and of many other countries is commonly known as "capitalism," "free enterprise," or "private enterprise." What does this mean?

Capitalism is a system of economic organization characterized by private ownership of the factors of production and their operation for profit under predominantly competitive conditions.

On what theoretical foundations does capitalism rest? Is our economy typical of theoretical (or pure) capitalism? The answers are best understood in terms of the institutions of our economic system.

Institutions of Capitalism

If you take a course in sociology, you will learn that social systems are often characterized by their *institutions*. These may be defined as those traditions, beliefs, and practices that are well established and widely held to be fundamental parts of a culture. Because capitalism is a type of social system—or more precisely, a type of *socioeconomic system*—it has its own particular institutions. The following are those on which a pure capitalistic system rests.

Private Property

The institution of *private property* is the most basic element of capitalism. It assures each person the right to acquire economic goods and resources by legitimate means, to enter into contracts concerning their use, and to dispose of them as desired.

This concept of private property was set forth in the writings of the late-seventeenth-century English philosopher John Locke. He justified private ownership and control of property as a "natural right" independent of the power of the state. This right, he maintained, provides maximum benefits for society as a whole. (In contrast, some socialist views prevailing since the nineteenth century have held that private property is a means of separating owners from workers and of exploiting the working class.)

The granting of property rights fulfills three important economic functions:

1. It provides owners with personal incentives to make the most productive use of their assets.

2. It strongly influences the distribution of wealth and income by allowing people to accumulate assets and to pass them on to others at the time of death.

3. It makes possible a high degree of exchange because people must have property rights before those rights can be transferred.

The social and economic consequences of these functions, as you will see, have been instrumental in the development of capitalism.

Self-Interest—The "Invisible Hand"

In 1776 a Scottish professor of philosophy, Adam Smith, published *The Wealth of Nations*. In this book, the first systematic study of capitalism, Smith described his principle of the **invisible hand**. This principle states that each person, pursuing self-interest without interference by government, will be led, as if by an invisible hand, to achieve the best good for society. In Smith's words:

> An individual neither intends to promote the public interest, nor knows he is promoting it. . . . He intends only his own gain, and he is led by an invisible hand to promote an end which was no part of his intention. . . . It is not from the benevolence of the butcher, the brewer, or the baker that we expect our dinner, but from their regard to their self-interest. We address ourselves not to their humanity, but to their self-love, and never talk to them of our necessities, but of their advantages.

Self-interest drives people to action, but alone it's not enough. People must understand the effects of their decisions and their actions on their economic well-being. *They must think rationally if they are to make the right decisions.*

The belief that people think rationally is at the heart of economics. It helps explain why economists long ago introduced the assumption that individuals, acting in their own self-interest, always attempt to obtain the greatest amount of satisfaction for the least amount of sacrifice or cost.

Forms of maximizing satisfaction are varied. They may consist of greater profits for a businessperson, higher wages or more leisure time for a worker, and greater pleasure from goods purchased for a consumer. They may also consist of totally unselfish and charitable acts by individuals. It can be argued that people engage in such acts because it makes them feel better and increases their own satisfaction.

Thus, even unselfish acts are performed out of self-interest.

Contrary to popular belief, self-interest is not unique to capitalism. Self-interest exists in other economic systems as well. But capitalism as a system thrives on its ability to guide individual economic decisions, motivated by self-interest, in directions that produce outcomes preferred by society.

Economic Individualism—Laissez-Faire

In the late seventeenth century, Louis XIV reigned as King of France. His finance minister, Jean Baptiste Colbert, asked a manufacturer by the name of Legendre how the government might help business. Legendre's reply was *"laissez nous faire"* (leave us alone). The expression, in slightly abbreviated form, has become a watchword and motto of capitalism.

Today we interpret **laissez-faire** to mean that the absence of government intervention leads to economic individualism and economic freedom. Under laissez-faire conditions, people's economic activities are their own private affairs. As consumers, they are free to spend their incomes as they choose. As producers, they are free to purchase the economic resources they desire and to use these resources as they wish.

Of course, laissez-faire doesn't imply a total absence of government intervention. With economic individualism and economic freedom go certain restraints imposed by society for the protection and general welfare of its citizens. Prohibitions against illegal economic activities such as force and fraud are examples. Can you see why, without such prohibitions, our economic system wouldn't work?

Competition and Free Markets

Capitalism operates under conditions of **competition.** This means that there is rivalry among sellers of similar goods to attract customers and among buyers to secure the goods that are wanted. There is rivalry among workers to obtain jobs and among employers to obtain workers. There is also rivalry among buyers and sellers of resources to transact business on the best terms that each can get from the other.

Ideal or theoretical capitalism is often described as a free-market system. A **free market** is one in which buyers and sellers can engage in transactions without restrictions imposed by government or any external force. Competition and free markets are closely related. In their most complete or purest form, free markets have two characteristics:

1. There are a large number of buyers and sellers, each with a small enough share of the total business so that no participant can affect the market price of the good.

2. Buyers and sellers are unencumbered by economic or institutional restrictions, and they possess full knowledge of market prices and alternatives. As a result, they enter or leave markets as they see fit.

Under such circumstances, the market price of a particular good is established by the interacting forces of buyers and sellers. Each buyer and each seller, acting in his or her own best interest as an economic agent, decides whether or not to transact business at the going price. No individual has control over the price because no one buyer or seller is large enough to exert any perceptible influence in the market.

In the real world, competition doesn't exist in this pure form. However, there are markets in which it is approximated in varying degrees. The closest we get to a *pure* free market is in organized exchanges such as the Chicago Board of Trade and the New York Mercantile Exchange. These markets, which are open to all buyers and sellers, deal in such standardized commodities as soybeans, grains, basic metals, lumber, and petroleum. Markets of this type (of which there are about a dozen in the United States) are studied in considerable detail in microeconomics and in some courses in finance.

Although the real world doesn't fully satisfy the assumptions of a *pure* free market, it appears to approximate them in varying degrees. Many people miss this point when they look at today's giant firms and argue that the U.S. economy is not as competitive as it once was. The opposite is the case; our economy is getting *more* competitive. As transportation and communication have improved, the arena in which firms compete is, to an increasing degree, a global one. In reality, many markets don't exhibit the two theoretical characteristics specified above. Nevertheless, most of the nation's largest corporations face far more world competition today than they faced a few decades ago.

To summarize:

A free market performs a number of important functions. Among them:

-   **It establishes competitive prices both for consumer goods and for the factors of production.**

-   **It encourages the efficient use of economic resources.**

The Price System

Who tells workers where to work or what occupations to choose? Who declares how many cars should be produced and how many homes should be built? Who specifies the predominant style of women's dresses or men's suits?

The greater the degree of competition, the more these matters will be decided impersonally and automatically by the **price system** or the *market system*. This may be viewed as a system of rewards and penalties. Rewards include profits for firms and people who succeed. Penalties include losses, or possibly bankruptcy, for those who fail. The price system is fundamental to the traditional concept of capitalism.

The price system basically operates on the principle that everything that is exchanged—every good, every service, and every resource—has its price. In a free market with many buyers and sellers, the prices of these things reflect the quantities that sellers make available and the quantities that buyers wish to purchase.

If buyers want to purchase more of a certain good than suppliers have available, its price will rise. This will encourage suppliers to produce and sell more of it. If buyers want to purchase less of a certain good than suppliers are prepared to sell, its price will fall. This will encourage buyers to purchase more of it.

This interaction between sellers and buyers in a competitive market, and the resulting changes in prices, are what most people refer to by the familiar phrase "supply and demand." But be careful about using this expression. As you'll soon discover, it has a much more precise meaning than is at first apparent.

Government: Rule Maker, Protector, Umpire

Capitalism has strong political as well as economic implications. According to the doctrine of laissez-faire, the functions of government in a capitalistic system are clearly identified. They include maintaining order, defining property rights, enforcing contracts, promoting competition, and defending the country. They also include issuing money, prescribing standards of weights and measures, raising funds to meet operating expenses, and deciding disputes over the interpretation of the rules.

Government, in this view, is essential to the existence of capitalism. When society's economic, social, or political values are violated, government, usually through its system of law, takes corrective action. When personal freedoms conflict, one individual's freedom must be limited so that another's may be preserved. In theoretical capitalism, government fulfills the roles of rule maker, protector, and umpire. Government does this, *in theory,* by imposing only those restrictions on personal freedoms that are necessary to protect the well-being of society, and by reconciling conflicts of values resulting from the free exercise of property rights.

Conclusion: Our Mixed Economy

Are the rule-making, protective, and mediating functions of government fulfilled in the U.S. economy? The answer is neither completely positive nor completely negative. Over the years, our economy has become increasingly complicated, and the role of government has expanded.

Through the use of legislation of various types, government has come to play a significant role as a protector and regulator of certain groups within the economy. For example:

Government has tried to promote the interests of agriculture, labor, and the consumer. It has controlled competition among such regulated industries as domestic transportation, communication, and power. It has sought to maintain effective competition in the unregulated industries that constitute the bulk of the business sector. Government has tried to keep the economy's total production and spending at a high level to achieve the long-run objectives of economic efficiency and growth.

Like many others, our economy is neither a pure market economy nor a pure command economy. It is a mixed but capitalistically oriented economy in which both private individuals and government exercise their economic influence in the marketplace. All countries today that call their economic systems "capitalistic" are actually mixed capitalistically oriented economies.

The Circular Flow of Economic Activity

How does a capitalistic system make products available to households and resources available to businesses? The answer is summarized in a simplified way in Ex-

EXHIBIT
4

The Circular Flow of Economic Activity: A Two-Sector Model

In this highly simplified model of an economy, households and businesses are linked through two markets: (1) the product markets, where goods and services are exchanged, and (2) the resource markets, where the factors of production are exchanged.

Questions of *what* and *how* to produce are answered in these markets. However, the question, *For whom?* is not directly apparent in this diagram. The answer depends on factor prices, which are determined in the resource markets, and on other considerations.

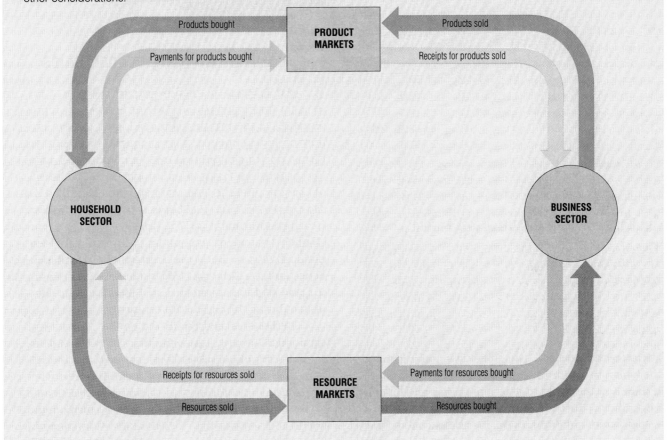

hibit 4. This model, the *circular flow of economic activity,* assumes that the total economy is divided into two sectors: households and businesses. (It neglects two other sectors, government and foreign, that will occupy much of our attention in coming chapters.) The model shows how the household and business sectors meet each other in two sets of markets: the product markets and the resource markets.

In the *product markets,* households buy the goods and services that businesses sell. Payments for these goods and services are represented by consumption expenditures that become the receipts of business. In the *resource markets,* businesses buy the factors of production that households sell. Payments for these factors of production are costs that become the money incomes of households.

All these transactions are accomplished in free markets by a price system that registers the wishes of buyers and sellers. In this system the product markets are the places where businesses decide *what* to produce, while the resource markets are the places where businesses decide *how* to produce.

One other feature of the diagram should be noted. The outer loop portrays the physical flow of goods and resources in one direction. The inner loop shows the corresponding flow of money in the opposite direction.

Every part of the circular-flow model (and, therefore, of the economy) depends ultimately on every other part. What happens in the market for vegetables will affect the wages paid to agricultural workers. Their wages, in turn, will affect their demand for housing. Their demand for housing will affect the price of lumber, which, in turn, will affect the wages of lumberjacks, and so on. Because the parts of the economic system are interdependent, what happens in one part ultimately has effects throughout the economy.

Limitations of the Circular-Flow Model

The circular-flow model is a simplified representation of an economic system. The chief function of the model is to illustrate several important economic relations. But, like any model, it is an abstraction from reality and therefore depicts only certain essential features. Among them:

Macroeconomic Relations The model says nothing about the behavior of individual buyers and sellers. Nor does it show how they react to determine prices and quantities in the product and resource markets. Hence, it is a *macroeconomic* rather than a microeconomic model.

Stable Flow The model assumes a steady, rather than a fluctuating, circular flow. It doesn't disclose the effects of variations in the flow on the economy's production and prices. Therefore, it says nothing about unemployment and inflation, which are problems of continuing concern.

Despite these limitations, the circular-flow concept provides many useful insights. They will become increasingly apparent as we seek to amplify the underlying ideas of the model in order to gain a better understanding of a modern mixed economy.

Adam Smith
(1723–1790)

Origins: The Founding of Economics

The year 1776 was marked by two great events in the struggle for emancipation. In North America, representatives of the British colonies adopted the Declaration of Independence. This eloquent statement set forth a doctrine of political freedom. In Europe, a former Scottish professor of philosophy at the University of Glasgow published a monumental book entitled *An Inquiry into the Nature and Causes of the Wealth of Nations.* Usually known simply as *The Wealth of Nations,* it is an eloquent statement expounding a doctrine of economic freedom. Both the Declaration of Independence and *The Wealth of Nations* stand as milestones in the Age of Enlightenment and Liberalism that blossomed during the eighteenth century.

The book earned Smith the epithet "founder of economics" because it was the first complete and systematic study of the subject. Smith argued that individuals know best what is good for them. If unrestricted by government controls or private monopolies, people will be motivated by the quest for profit to turn out the goods and services that society wants. Consequently, through free trade and free markets, self-interest will be harnessed to the common good.

Through his approach to economic questions and his organization of the science, Smith cast a mold for the main body of nineteenth-century economic thought. His views on public policy, which became the semiofficial doctrine of the British government, left their imprint on parliamentary debates and governmental reports. For these reasons, and because of his enormous influence upon succeeding generations of scholars, Smith's unique position in the history of economic thought is forever ensured.

An Adam Smith Sampler

Reading *The Wealth of Nations* today, one can see why the influence of this book reached out beyond the borders of economics. Like the Bible, Smith's treatise contains familiar concepts and well-worn truths on almost every page. As a result, "the shy and absent-minded scholar," as Smith was affectionately called, became the apostle of classical economic liberalism—meaning laissez-faire in his time. Today we tend to refer to such ideas as "conservatism."

The following quotations covering a wide range of topics convey the essence of Smith's beliefs.[*]

On Businesspeople

People of the same trade rarely meet together, even for merriment and diversion, but the conversation ends in a conspiracy against the public, or in some contrivance to raise prices.

On Free Trade

By restraining, either by high duties, or by absolute prohibitions, the importation of such goods from foreign countries as can be produced at home, the monopoly of the home market is more or less secured to the domestic industry employed in producing them.

To expect that the freedom of trade should ever be entirely restored, is as absurd as to expect that an Oceana or Utopia should ever be established. Not only the prejudices of the public, but what is much more unconquerable, the private interests of many individuals, irresistibly oppose it.

On Government Direction

The statesman who should attempt to direct private people in what manner they ought to employ their capitals would load himself with a most unnecessary attention. He would assume an authority, which could safely be trusted, not only to no single person, but to no council or senate whatever, and which would nowhere be so dangerous as in the hands of a man who had folly and presumption enough to fancy himself fit to exercise it.

On Human Nature

The uninterrupted effort of every man to better his condition is frequently powerful enough to maintain the natural progress of things toward improvement, in spite both of the extravagance of government and of the greatest errors of administration.

On Governmental Administration

The abuses which sometimes creep into the administration of a local and provincial revenue, however enormous they may appear, are in reality almost always trifling compared with the administration of the revenue of a great empire. They are, besides, much more easily corrected.

On Government Officials

It is the highest impertinence and presumption of kings and ministers to pretend to watch over the economy of private people, and to restrain their expense, either by sumptuary laws, or by prohibiting the importation of foreign luxuries. They are themselves always, and without any exception, the greatest spendthrifts in the society. Let them look well after their own expense, and they may safely trust private people with theirs. If their own extravagance does not ruin the state, that of their subjects never will.

There is no art that one government sooner learns from another than that of draining money from the pockets of the people.

On Public Versus Private Education

Those parts of education for which there are no public institutions are generally the best taught. When a young man goes to a fencing or a dancing school, he does not indeed always learn to fence or to dance very well; but he seldom fails to learn how to fence or to dance.

On the "Invisible Hand"

As every individual endeavours both to employ his capital in the support of domestic industry and to direct that industry so that its produce may be of the greatest value, every individual renders the annual revenue of the society as great as he can. He generally, indeed, neither intends to promote the public interest, nor knows how much he is promoting it. He intends only his own gain, and he is in this, as in many other cases, led by an invisible hand to promote an end which was no part of his intention. Nor is it always the worse that society was no part of it. By pursuing his own interest he frequently promotes that of the society more effectually than when he really intends to promote it.

[*] All quotations are from *The Wealth of Nations* (1776), except the last three. They are from a philosophical treatise by Smith, *The Theory of Moral Sentiments* (1759). Some quotations have been edited slightly to enhance readability by today's standards.

On Specialization

It is the maxim of every prudent master of a family, never to attempt to make at home what it will cost him more to make than to buy.

The tailor does not attempt to make his own shoes, but buys them of the shoemaker. The shoemaker does not attempt to make his own clothes, but employs a tailor. The farmer attempts to make neither the one nor the other, but employs different artificers.

On Exchange

Man is an animal which makes bargains. The propensity to truck, barter, and exchange one thing for another is common to all men, and to be found in no other race of animals.

Give me that which I want, and you shall have this which you want, is the meaning of every offer. It is in this manner that we obtain from one another the far greater part of those good offices which we stand in need of. It is not from the benevolence of the butcher, the brewer, or the baker, that we expect our dinner, but from their regard to their own interest. We address ourselves, not to their humanity but to their self-love, and never talk to them of our own necessities but of their advantages.

On Supply and Demand

When the quantity brought to market is just sufficient to supply the effectual demand and no more, the market price naturally comes to be either exactly, or as nearly as can be judged, the same as the natural price. The whole quantity upon hand can be disposed of for this price, and cannot be disposed of for more. The competition of the different dealers obliges them all to accept this price, but does not oblige them to accept less.

On Principal/Agent Relationships

The directors of joint-stock companies [corporations], being the managers of other people's money rather than their own, cannot well be expected to watch over it with the same anxious vigilance with which the owners in a private partnership frequently watch over their own. Like the stewards of a rich man, they are apt to consider attention to small matters as not for their master's honor, and very easily give themselves a dispensation from having it. Negligence and profusion, therefore, must always prevail, more or less, in the management of the affairs of such a company.

On Work and Leisure

Great labour, either of mind or body, continued for several days together requires to be relieved by some indulgence, sometimes of ease only, but sometimes too of dissipation and diversion. If it is not complied with, the consequences are often dangerous, and sometimes fatal.

On Colleges and Universities

The discipline of colleges and universities is contrived, not for the benefit of the students, but for the ease of the masters.

On Authoritarianism

Fear is in almost all cases a wretched instrument of government, and ought in particular never to be employed against any order or men who have the smallest pretensions to independency. To attempt to terrify them serves only to irritate their bad humour, and to confirm them in an opposition which more gentle usage might easily induce them to lay aside.

On Lotteries

The world neither ever saw, nor ever will see, a perfectly fair lottery, because the undertaker could make nothing by it. In the state lotteries the tickets are really not worth the price, yet the soberest people scarce look upon it as a folly to pay a small sum for the chance of gaining ten or twenty thousand pounds. In a lottery in which no prize exceeded twenty pounds, there would not be the same demand for tickets.

On International Relationships

In ancient times the opulent and civilized nations found it difficult to defend themselves against the poor and barbarous nations. In modern times the poor and barbarous find it difficult to defend themselves against the opulent and civilized.

On Human Equality

The difference of natural talents in different men is, in reality, much less than we are aware of. The difference between the most dissimilar characters, between a philosopher and a common street porter, for example, seems to arise not so much from nature, as from habit, custom, and education.

On Humaneness

No society can surely be flourishing and happy, of which the far greater part of the members are poor and miserable.

On Sympathy

To seem not to be affected with the joy of our companions is but want of politeness. But not to wear a serious countenance when they tell us their afflictions, is real and gross inhumanity.

On Happiness

What can be added to the happiness of a man who is in health, who is out of debt, and has a clear conscience?

Summary of Important Ideas

1. Society's resources are the ingredients of its production. The four classes of resources—labor, land, capital, and entrepreneurship—are commonly referred to as the factors of production. The returns received by the owners of these resources are wages, rent, interest, and profits.

2. Scarcity pervades our lives; virtually everything is scarce in at least some contexts. The existence of scarcity implies we must make choices. The cost of any choice is the value of the alternative forgone in making it.

3. Nations are more productive when they specialize. The concept of comparative advantage explains why countries specialize in the production of goods that they exchange in the global economy. Specialization and international trade increase output and improve global welfare.

4. Every economic system seeks to attain certain objectives. They are: (a) *efficiency* in the use of scarce resources, (b) *equity* in the distribution of income, (c) *stability* of prices, and (d) *growth* of real output per capita. In democratic capitalistic countries, these goals are sought within a framework of political and economic freedoms. Many countries vary, however, in the priorities they place on economic goals and the sacrifices to be made in attaining them.

5. Most economic problems are aspects of the three big questions that every society must answer. These are: (a) *what* to produce—and in what quantities? (b) *how* to produce? and (c) *for whom* to produce? The methods by which these questions are answered differ in mixed and in command economies.

6. In an economy characterized by technical efficiency (that is, by full employment of available resources), any increase in the output of some goods and services causes a reduction in the output of others. With given resources and technology, the production choices open to an economy can be summarized by its production-possibilities curve. The shape of this curve reflects the operation of the law of increasing costs. These costs are measured by their opportunity costs, the value of the sacrificed alternatives. The curve itself can be shifted outward through economic growth.

7. Capitalism is a type of economic organization in which the means of production and distribution are privately owned and used for private gain. All capitalistic countries today are, in varying degrees, "mixed" economies.

8. Capitalism rests on a foundation of certain socioeconomic institutions. These include private property, self-interest, economic individualism or laissez-faire, competition, and the price system.

9. The circular-flow model is a simplified representation of our economy. It focuses on aggregate relationships by depicting the flow of expenditures, goods, and resources that link major sectors and markets.

10. Adam Smith, a Scottish philosopher, was the founder of economics. His monumental treatise, *The Wealth of Nations* (1776), is one of the great classics not only of economics, but of philosophy and the social sciences as well. In this work he expounded the virtues of free markets, self interest, and minimum government involvement in the economy. If nations practiced these beliefs, he argued, competition would allocate society's resources to their most efficient uses as if guided by an "invisible hand."

Terms and Concepts to Review

factors of production
land
capital
labor
entrepreneurship
free good
opportunity cost
economic system
division of labor
efficiency
income distribution
equity
command economy
market economy
mixed economy

production-possibilities
    curve
law of increasing
    (opportunity) costs
capitalism
institutions
private property
"invisible hand"
laissez-faire
competition
free market
price system
circular flow of economic
    activity
product markets
resource markets

Questions and Problems

1. It is often asserted that Americans are wealthy because their nation is blessed with a generous endowment of natural resources. Yet American Indians, who had the same resources, barely existed at a subsistence level. Why did the colonists, and their descendants, become rich? Why were the Indians poor?

2. A professor posted the following sign over a stack of books he was trying to give away outside his office: "These books are not, of course, *free*. But you may have them if you wish, for no charge." What did he mean?

3. If you are not charged a price for the consumption of a good, the good must be a free good. True or false?

4. The cost of going to college is often greater for older students than for younger students, just as the cost of committing crimes is lower for young people than for older people. Why?

5. Would entrepreneurship exist in a purely communistic society in which all citizens live and work by the motto: "From each according to his or her ability, to each according to his or her needs"?

6. It is sometimes asserted that the act of exchange does not *create* wealth because it merely results in a redistribution of goods already in existence. Evaluate this argument.

7. Denmark produces some of the world's best butter. Yet most Danish butter producers use margarine in their homes instead of butter. Does this make sense? Explain.

8. The question, *For whom shall goods be produced?* is concerned with distributing total output among the members of society. Can you suggest at least three different criteria or rules for deciding who gets how much? Which criterion is best?

9. A conventional production-possibilities curve illustrates the law of increasing costs. Can you draw curves that illustrate (a) constant costs, and (b) decreasing costs? Define the meaning of each case.

10. Suppose that an economy produces only agricultural goods and capital goods. Using production-possibilities curves, illustrate the effect of a new capital-goods invention, assuming that it has *no direct impact* on agriculture (although it may have some indirect effects). Describe the possible adjustment paths that society may take as a result of the invention.

11. Distinguish between the concepts of *capital* and *capitalism*.

12. The "profit motive" is sometimes said to be one of the most fundamental features of capitalism. (a) What do you suppose is meant by the "profit motive"? (b) Why wasn't it explicitly listed in this chapter as one of the pillars of capitalism?

13. (a) "In a free competitive economy, the consumer is king." What does this mean? (b) "The producer, not the consumer, is king. After all, the producer is the one who advertises. Therefore, the producer is the one who creates wants and thereby influences what consumers will purchase." True or false? Explain.

14. "A shortcoming of a capitalistic society, as compared with a collectivist or socialistic one, is that people are not compensated in proportion to the usefulness and difficulty of their work." True or false? Explain.

15. If no pure market economy exists and no pure

command economy exists, why does economics, which purports to be a science and to deal with reality, bother with these concepts?

16. Comparative Advantage As you'll recall, a nation has a comparative advantage when it can produce a product at a lower opportunity cost, or sacrifice, than another nation can. Thus, suppose that both the United States and Japan can produce meat *(M)* and vegetables *(V)*, and that the output of the two products is measured in tons. In which products should the two countries specialize? To answer the question, let's assume the following conditions:

- In the United States, the opportunity cost of producing a ton of meat is 2 tons of vegetables. This means that the United States must sacrifice 2 tons of vegetables to produce an additional ton of meat. Thus, $2V = 1M$.

- In Japan, the opportunity cost of producing an additional ton of meat is 4 tons of vegetables. Thus, $4V = 1M$.

On the basis of these conditions, try answering the following questions:

a. In the United States, what is the opportunity cost of producing 1 ton of vegetables?

b. In Japan, what is the opportunity cost of producing 1 ton of vegetables?

c. Which country has a comparative advantage in meat production? Why?

d. Which country has a comparative advantage in vegetable production? Why?

e. According to the concept of comparative advantage, what should each country do in order to obtain the greatest benefit from trade?

f. Can a nation have a comparative advantage in all goods?

TAKE A STAND

Inefficiency: The Undoing of Communism?

Communism, one of the most influential ideas in the history of humankind, now appears discredited. Capitalism has been embraced by communist countries throughout the world, and most particularly in the countries of Eastern Europe and the former Soviet Union. Few countries are still avowedly communist; even China is experimenting with capitalist institutions. Private property, market exchanges, entrepreneurship and profit are being welcomed where once they were reviled. Ironically, communism was originally proposed in the nineteenth century as an inevitable successor to capitalism. Karl Marx argued that capitalism would eventually crumble, to be replaced first by socialism and, ultimately, by pure communism.

The collapse of the Soviet Union and the end of the Cold War were hailed by many, economists and noneconomists alike, as the vindication and victory of capitalism over communism. Many economists were not surprised by the downfall of communism because they believed that a communist economic system could never operate successfully or efficiently. *Did economic inefficiency bring about the fall of communism.*

Yes: Communism Ties the Invisible Hand

In a capitalist country such as the United States, an owner of a resource personally benefits from its sale and has every incentive to use that resource in the way that generates the highest possible return. Workers will try to sell their labor time to the firm that offers the highest available wage. City landowners will use their property for an office complex rather than an apple orchard. Investors will buy the stock of firms that they expect to prosper. The return from a resource is based, ultimately, on how much consumers are willing to pay for the goods that the resource helps to produce. Since consumers will pay more for goods that give them greater satisfaction, a private owner has the incentive to allocate resources to the production of goods that consumers want.

This allocation process is made possible in a capitalist society by the purchase and sale of goods in free markets. Free markets bring together buyers and sellers of goods and ensure that all mutually beneficial transactions are carried out. As a result, a market system, at least in its ideal form, can achieve an efficient allocation of resources: The invisible hand ensures that individuals seeking private gain act in the best interests of society as a whole.

In a communist system, by contrast, the invisible hand is tied. In the ideal of the communist system, all resources are owned collectively. Since individuals do not own resources, they cannot profit from their use and sale, and so have no incentive to allocate them in an efficient manner. Economic rewards in the system are unrelated to effort, so the farmer has no incentive to increase crop yields, the factory worker has no incentive to work hard, and the plant manager has no incentive to produce a usable product.

The result is an inefficient allocation of resources and a system that ultimately cannot provide for even the most basic needs of the population. Grain shortages, for example, were chronic in the former Soviet nations. Citizens of communist countries sometimes spent hours standing fruitlessly in line in the hope of purchasing meat or produce; the time wasted in such lines represented an extraordinary misuse of a valuable resource. It is no wonder, to an economist, that it was the Berlin Wall, and not capitalism, that eventually had to crumble.

No: It Was a Political Regime That Fell, Not an Economic System

The fall of the Berlin Wall was a triumph of individual liberty over totalitarianism and repression, not of capitalism over communism. In the nominally communist countries of the former Soviet Union and Eastern Europe, all resources, including human beings, were effectively owned and controlled by the government. This was not communism, but totalitarianism. In a truly communist society, individuals would collectively own resources and collectively decide upon their use. This system has not been tried.

Besides, it is misleading to evaluate communism using the assumptions of capitalist economics. A crucial assumption of economics is that human behavior is driven by self-interest; people act in selfish and greedy ways, and care primarily about personal gain. Supporters of communism believe that this is a narrow and unpleasant view of human nature. In a different and more humane social system, people would be motivated to work for the intrinsic pleasure of that work or for the satisfaction of serving society. Individuals would act in society's best interest simply because they wanted to. Goods would be allocated according to need, not as rewards for the accumulation of wealth and power.

Finally, anyone looking at the United States or other capitalist economies would surely question capitalism's supposed victory. It is true that the economic systems of Eastern Europe and the former Soviet Union failed in striking ways, but our own problems of poverty, crime, drugs, pollution, crumbling infrastructure, and decaying cities suggest that we are still far from a capitalist utopia.

The Question: Did Economic Inefficiency Bring About the Fall of Communism?

■ Some people believe that communism was destined to fail because collective ownership is inefficient. If goods are collectively owned, no one has the incentive to make sure resources are employed productively. Private ownership is needed for efficiency.

■ Others believe that the economic collapse of Eastern Europe was due to totalitarianism. Communism might not be inefficient; we don't know because it hasn't been tried.

Where Do You Stand?

1. The late British economist Joan Robinson wrote that "the invisible hand may work by strangulation." What do you think she meant?

2. Supporters of communism claim that it has never been tried. But if it's such a good idea, then why hasn't it been tried?

3. The musician and poet John Lennon wrote, "Imagine no possessions / I wonder if you can / No need for greed or hunger / A brotherhood of man." Can you detect a fallacy in this verse?

4. Did inefficiency cause the downfall of communism? Justify your stand.

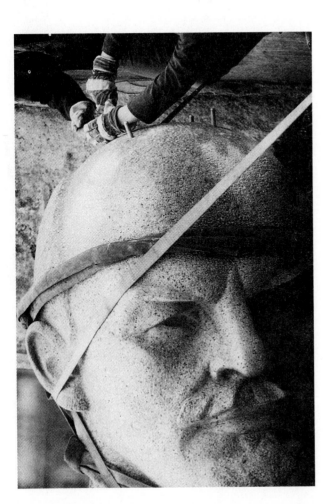

Chapter 2

The Laws of Demand and Supply: The Price System in a Pure Market Economy

What Do We Mean by Demand?

What Do We Mean by Supply?

Demand and Supply Together Make a Market

Two Kinds of Changes Involving Demand

Two Kinds of Changes Involving Supply

Combined Changes in Demand and Supply

The Market Economy: Is It "Good" or "Bad"?

Origins: The Study of Markets Before Adam Smith

Learning Guide
Watch for answers to these important questions

What are the "laws" of demand and supply? How do they affect the prices you pay for the things you buy?

What is a market economy? Why do we study it? How is a market economy related to a price system?

Are there advantages to a market economy? Disadvantages? How well does such an economy answer the questions, *What? How?* and *For whom?*

A parrot could answer many important economic questions correctly with just three simple words: "demand and supply." Here are a few examples.

Question Why are Rembrandt paintings expensive while water is cheap—especially since everyone needs water more than Rembrandts?

Answer Demand and supply.

Question Why is the cost of medical care rising faster than prices generally?

Answer Demand and supply.

Question Why are some luxury apartments vacant while there is a shortage of low-cost housing?

Answer Demand and supply.

Question Why do the prices of some goods fluctuate while the prices of others remain stable?

Answer Demand and supply.

Such simple answers to complex questions are not very illuminating. Nevertheless, it is true that much of economics is largely concerned with demand and supply. In this chapter, therefore, you will discover more about these concepts and the conditions that affect them.

46

What Do We Mean by Demand?

In economics, demand has a special meaning:

Demand is a *relation* showing the various amounts of a *commodity* that buyers would be willing and able to purchase at alternative prices during a given time period, all other things remaining the same.

The commodity, which may be a good or service, can be anything—hamburgers, shoes, VCRs, haircuts, labor time, steel, or any other item that is purchased in a market. Notice that demand is a *relation* between price and the amount of a commodity that will be bought during a given time period. In other words, demand isn't simply an amount. It's a "list" of amounts at various prices.

Let's take your demand for pizza as an example. If the price were $20 each, you might purchase only one per month. If the price were $10 each, you might purchase five per month. And if the price were $0—that is, if pizzas were available free—you might order a dozen per month. All of these possibilities constitute your demand for pizza.

Of course, prices of pizza are not the same everywhere. They often differ—even among sellers in the same market area. One reason why prices vary is that all pizzas are not identical. The same is true of automobiles, jeans, computers, and most other products you can think of. Each product is differentiated from its competitors and usually has its own distinct price.

But this isn't true of many undifferentiated goods. Examples are primary metals such as aluminum, copper, and tin; grain products such as corn, oats, and wheat; fibers such as burlap, cotton, and wool; and national currencies such as British pounds, Japanese yen, and U.S. dollars. Each of these and various other commodities is identical. As a result, *in a particular market, only one price exists for an undifferentiated product at a given time.* Prices of such products are reported daily in the business section of many newspapers.

You can best understand the "pure" operation of demand and supply by seeing it illustrated in terms of an undifferentiated good. Let's look at one of the above-mentioned commodities—wheat—as an example.

Demand Schedules and Demand Curves

Bread, cake, mayonnaise, peanut butter, and other packaged foods that you see on supermarket shelves are made by food companies. Some of the larger firms familiar to many Americans are General Mills, Kellogg, Nabisco, and Pillsbury. These companies and their many smaller competitors purchase agricultural commodities such as corn, oats, rye, wheat, and soybeans which they process into food products.

Suppose you've recently graduated from college and are working as a commodity buyer for a food company. What is your demand for a specific commodity, such as wheat?

According to the definition of demand, you must first ask, "At what prices?" Within a given period, you would be inclined to buy more wheat at a lower price than you would at a higher one. You could thus prepare a hypothetical list of the number of bushels of wheat you would buy at different prices during a particular period of time. Economists call such a list a *demand schedule.*

Exhibit 1 is a **demand schedule**. It is a list showing the number of units of a product that a buyer would be willing and able to purchase during a given period of time. The schedule in Exhibit 1 represents your demand for wheat over the price range shown. At $5 per bushel, you would buy 5 bushels per day. At $4 per bushel, you would buy 10 bushels per day. And so on.

EXHIBIT 1

An Individual Buyer's Demand Schedule for Wheat

A demand schedule is a list showing the number of units of a product that a buyer would be willing and able to purchase at various prices during a given period of time.

	Price (dollars per bushel)	Quantity demanded (bushels per day)
A	$5	5
B	4	10
C	3	20
D	2	35
E	1	60

If you wanted to, you could make the schedule more detailed by extending the price scale upward and by quoting the prices in dollars and cents instead of just dollars. But such detail isn't necessary. The schedule already gives you the highlights of your demand for wheat.

The information in the demand schedule can easily be presented in graphic form. The graphing process is done in three steps:

Step 1 Draw the vertical and horizontal axes of the graph and put the labels on both axes as shown in Exhibit 2. (For certain historical reasons, economists customarily measure price on the vertical axis and quantity on the horizontal axis.) The starting point or origin of the graph is always the lower left-hand corner, labeled 0 (zero).

Step 2 Plot the corresponding prices and quantities with dots. Then label them with the appropriate letters (*A, B, C, D,* and *E*) from the demand schedule in Exhibit 1. The letters help you to identify the points.

Step 3 Connect the points with a smooth curve.

You have just drawn a ***demand curve.*** It's the graphic equivalent of the demand schedule in Exhibit 1. The advantage of the curve is that it enables you to "see" the relation between price and quantity demanded. You can also read the values at a glance.

For instance, point *C* represents 20 bushels of wheat per day at a price of $3 per bushel. Would you agree that, at $1.50 per bushel, the quantity demanded is 45 bushels per day? Can you verify that, if the quantity demanded is 35 bushels per day, the *highest price* you would be willing to pay (called the ***demand price***) is $2 per bushel?

The Law of Demand

A look at the demand curve in Exhibit 2 will reveal its most fundamental property. *The curve slopes downward from left to right.* This characteristic illustrates the law of demand, which applies to virtually all goods. Here is a definition:

Law of demand **The quantity demanded of a good varies inversely with its price, assuming that other things that may affect demand remain the same. The most important of these are the buyer's income and the prices of related goods.**

(Note: In the definition, "inversely" means that when the price of a good decreases, the corre-

---

EXHIBIT 2

An Individual Buyer's Demand Curve for Wheat

A demand curve is the graph of a demand schedule. Each point along the curve represents a different price–quantity combination. A demand curve slopes downward from left to right, reflecting the fact that the quantity of a product demanded varies inversely with the price. This is called the *law of demand.*

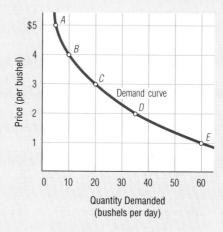

---

sponding quantity demanded increases. Also, when the price increases, the quantity demanded decreases.)

Why does the law of demand operate as it does?

1.   If the price of a good decreases, you are able to buy more of it if your income, tastes, and the prices of other goods remain the same. For instance, if you like steak but find it too expensive to buy frequently, a lower price might induce you to buy it more often.

2.   When the price of a product is reduced, you may buy more of it because it becomes a better bargain relative to other goods. Again, this is based on the assumption that your income, your tastes, and the prices of other goods remain constant. Thus, if the price of steak falls, you might buy more steak and fewer substitutes, such as hamburger or hot dogs. If the price of steak rises, however, you would tend to buy less steak and more substitutes.

3. Finally, the downward-sloping demand curve tells you that you would be willing to pay a relatively high price for a small amount of something. However, the more you have of it—other things remaining the same—the less you would care to pay for one more unit. Why? *Because each extra unit gives you less additional satisfaction or "utility" than the previous unit gave you.* For example, however crazy you are about ice-cream sundaes, there is a limit to the number you can eat in any given period. After the first few sundaes, your appetite, and the price you would pay for additional sundaes, would diminish rapidly.

No matter how much you like a product, your demand curve will slope downward for these three reasons. Do people in business believe that the demand curve is downward-sloping? Evidently, they do. Why else would they advertise bargains that encourage people to buy more goods at lower prices?

Market Demand Is the Sum of Individual Demands

If you were the only buyer of wheat in the market, your demand schedule would be the demand schedule for the entire market. But in reality there are many buyers. The total market demand schedule is obtained by adding up the quantities demanded by all buyers at each price. Exhibit 3 shows how this is done. This exhibit is based on the assumption that there are only three buyers—*X, Y,* and *Z.* However, the example can easily be expanded to include as many buyers as you wish.

EXHIBIT
3

Market Demand for Wheat, Assuming Three Buyers

The total market demand is obtained by adding all the quantities demanded by individual buyers at each price.

Price (dollars per bushel)	Quantity demanded (bushels per day)								Total market demand per day
	Buyer *X*		Buyer *Y*		Buyer *Z*				
$5	0	+	15	+	20	=			35
4	9	+	20	+	26	=			55
3	22	+	27	+	33	=			82
2	42	+	38	+	43	=			123
1	80	+	65	+	60	=			205

What Do We Mean by Supply?

You now have a basic understanding of demand and the behavior of buyers. The other half of the picture is supply and the behavior of sellers. Like demand, the term *supply* has a special meaning in economics.

Supply is a relation showing the various amounts of a commodity that sellers would be willing and able to make available for sale at alternative prices during a given time period, all other things remaining the same.

Compare this definition of supply with the definition of demand given near the beginning of this chapter. Note the similarities. Are there any differences?

Supply Schedules and Supply Curves

Each seller in the market has a **supply schedule** for a product, just as each buyer has a demand schedule. If you were a wheat farmer, Exhibit 4 might represent your individual supply schedule for wheat. This schedule indicates that, at a price of $1 per bushel, you would not be willing to supply any wheat at all. At a price of $2 per bushel, you would be willing to supply 21 bushels of wheat per day. And so on. Plotting these data on a graph gives the **supply curve** shown in Exhibit 5. What is your estimate of the quantity supplied at a price of $2.50 per unit? What is the *least price,* approximately, that will persuade you to supply 40 bushels per day?

In economics, the least price is more often called the **supply price.** This is the price necessary to call forth a given quantity. What do you estimate the supply price to be for 25 bushels per day?

An example of the supply schedules for three individual producers, *A, B,* and *C,* is presented in Exhibit 6. When the data are plotted, they yield the supply curves shown on the graphs. Note that the total market supply schedule is obtained by adding up the quantities supplied by all sellers at each market price. How does this compare with the way the total market demand schedule was derived earlier in Exhibit 3?

The Law of Supply

The supply curve as drawn has a distinguishing feature. Unlike the demand curve, the supply curve slopes *upward* from left to right. This feature reflects the law of supply:

EXHIBIT
4

An Individual Seller's Supply Schedule for Wheat

A supply schedule is a list showing the number of units of a product that a seller would be willing and able to make available for sale at various prices during a given period of time.

	Price (dollars per bushel)	Quantity supplied (bushels per day)
A'	$5	50
B'	4	42
C'	3	33
D'	2	21
E'	1	0

EXHIBIT
5

An Individual Seller's Supply Curve for Wheat

A supply curve is the graph of a supply schedule. Each point along the curve represents a different price–quantity combination. A supply curve slopes upward from left to right, reflecting the fact that the quantity of a product supplied varies directly with the price. This is called the *law of supply*.

EXHIBIT
6

Market Supply of Wheat, Assuming Three Sellers

The total market supply of wheat is obtained by adding all the quantities supplied by individual sellers at each price.

Price (dollars per bushel)	Quantity supplied (bushels per day)							Total market supply per day
	Seller A		Seller B		Seller C			
$5	52	+	56	+	60	=		168
4	46	+	49	+	50	=		145
3	36	+	42	+	40	=		118
2	26	+	28	+	26	=		80
1	0	+	15	+	10	=		25

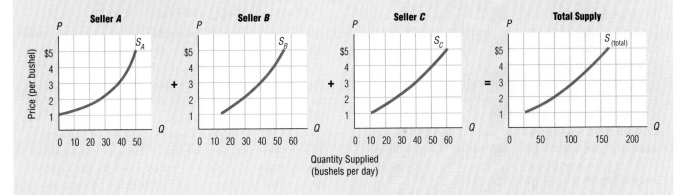

Quantity Supplied
(bushels per day)

Law of Supply **The quantity of a commodity supplied usually varies *directly* with its price, assuming that all other factors that may determine supply remain the same.**

(*Note:* As used here, "directly" means that the quantity produced and offered for sale increases as the price of the product rises and decreases as the price falls.)

Notice from the definition that the direct relation between quantity and price is *usually* true, but not always. The reasons for exceptions (which are few) are studied in microeconomics.

Why does the quantity supplied of a good normally vary directly with its price? A fundamental reason is the *law of increasing (opportunity) cost* explained in Chapter 1. As a firm devotes more labor, capital, and other resources to production, the opportunity cost of producing another unit of the good rises. In order to

cover these rising costs profitably, a higher price is necessary to call forth additional units.

Demand and Supply Together Make a Market

The forces of demand and supply determine prices in competitive markets.

A market exists whenever and wherever one or more buyers and sellers can negotiate for goods or services and thereby participate in determining their prices. A market, therefore, can be anywhere—on a street corner, on the other side of the world, or as close as the nearest telephone. *Competitive markets* consist of buyers and sellers so numerous that no single one can influence the market price by deciding to buy or not to buy, to sell or not to sell.

Demand and Supply at Work

A Russian Real Estate Market Emerges

By Andrea Rutherford
Staff Reporter of The Wall Street Journal

MOSCOW—In his search for an exciting career, Andrei Nikitin has tried everything from selling computers to working as a janitor in a maternity ward. The excitement picked up last year when Russia legalized private home ownership—Mr. Nikitin, 36 years old, became a real estate agent.

He suddenly is much in demand. "There's all this property out there, and it doesn't belong to anyone," he marvels. The message Mr. Nikitin gives his growing clientele is: buy now.

Real estate is one of the rare things that people can actually buy in Russia these days—for a steep price. A market for housing is taking shape after the national parliament legalized property ownership. It's still a seller's market, however, because of the maze of bureaucratic restrictions involved and an acute shortage of property on offer.

But the market in Russia got a boost when the republic's law making it easier to privatize state-owned apartments went into effect.

The Russian government reckons a private housing market will ease apartment shortages. It also wants people to start investing their extra rubles in real estate, helping to create a culture of property ownership deemed essential to the success of the market-oriented reforms.

Source: *The Wall Street Journal*, April 13, 1991, p. A11.

Buyers and Sellers in the Marketplace

By using the *total* demand and supply information derived in Exhibits 3 and 6, we can discover how the market price of a product and the quantity bought and sold are determined. The total market demand and supply schedules and their corresponding curves are reproduced in Exhibit 7. Note that the curves, labeled *D* and *S*, are identical with the total market curves graphed in Exhibits 3 and 6. The only difference is that both curves are now plotted in the same figure so that their interactions can be studied.

Observe that the demand and supply curves intersect at an *equilibrium* point. **Equilibrium** is a state of balance between opposing forces. Let's see what this means in terms of Exhibit 7.

Surpluses, Shortages, and Market Clearing

At any price above $2.50 per bushel, the quantity supplied exceeds the quantity demanded. (You can see this both from the table and the graph in Exhibit 7.) For example, at a price of $5 per bushel, the quantity supplied is 168 bushels per day, and the quantity demanded is 35 bushels per day. This means that, at the price of $5 per bushel, there is a *surplus* of $168 - 35 = 133$ bushels per day. **Surplus** is the amount by which the quantity of a good supplied exceeds the quantity demanded at a given price. Because sellers have made more wheat available than buyers want, sellers will compete with one another to dispose of their product and will thereby drive the price down.

At any price below $2.50 per bushel, the quantity demanded exceeds the quantity supplied. At $1 a bushel, for example, the quantity demanded is 205 bushels per day and the quantity supplied is 25 bushels per day. At this price, there is a *shortage* of $205 - 25 = 180$ bushels per day. **Shortage** is the amount by which the quantity of a good demanded exceeds the quantity supplied at a given price. Because buyers want more wheat than sellers will make available at this price, buyers will compete with one another to acquire the product and will thereby drive the price up.

At a price of $2.50 per bushel, the quantity demanded just equals the quantity supplied, 100 bushels per day. At this price there will be no surpluses or shortages. We refer to this price as the **equilibrium price** and to the corresponding quantity as the **equilibrium quantity.**

When the quantity demanded equals the quantity supplied, the market is in a state of *equilibrium.* The price of the product and the corresponding quantities

EXHIBIT
7

Equilibrium Price and Equilibrium Quantity for Wheat

The intersection of the demand and supply curves determines the equilibrium price of $2.50 per bushel and the equilibrium quantity of 100 bushels. Thus:

■ At any price below the equilibrium price, the quantity demanded exceeds the quantity supplied, and the price tends to rise.

■ At any price above the equilibrium price, the quantity supplied exceeds the quantity demanded, and the price tends to fall.

■ At the equilibrium price, the quantity supplied precisely equals the quantity demanded, and hence there is no tendency for the price to change.

Price (dollars per bushel)	Total market demand (bushels per day)	Total market supply (bushels per day)
$5	35	168
4	55	145
3	82	118
2	123	80
1	205	25

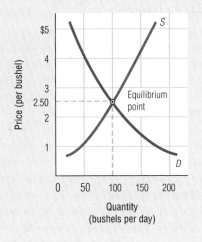

be changing. Then the market is in a state of *disequilibrium.*

The equilibrium price can be thought of as the *market-clearing price.* At that price there are no surpluses or shortages of the good. In general, when the price in a particular market is flexible, it fluctuates freely, thereby adjusting quickly to its market-clearing level.

Summary Thus Far

1. A downward-sloping demand curve means that buyers will purchase more of a good at a lower price than at a higher one. This illustrates the law of demand.

2. An upward-sloping supply curve means that sellers will offer more of a good at a higher price than at a lower one. This illustrates the law of supply.

3. The intersection of a demand and a supply curve for a good determines an equilibrium price and an equilibrium quantity. The equilibrium price can be thought of as the market-clearing price because it results in an absence of surpluses or shortages. If the price in a particular market is flexible, it adjusts quickly to its market-clearing level.

Two Kinds of Changes Involving Demand

Demand and supply curves have practical uses. You can employ them to answer many fundamental questions in economics. However, before doing so, it's important to note that there may be two kinds of changes involving demand. One is "a change in the quantity demanded," which is reflected in a movement *along* the demand curve. The other kind is "a change in demand," which is reflected in a movement of the demand curve itself.

Changes in the Quantity Demanded

Take another look at Exhibit 2. According to the law of demand, a downward movement along the curve in the general direction *A, B, C, . . .* signifies an increase in the quantity demanded as the *price is reduced.* An upward movement along the curve in the general direction *E, D, C, . . .* signifies a decrease in the quantity demanded as the *price is raised.* Any such movement along the curve, whether downward or upward, is

bought and sold are "in balance." That is, they have no tendency to change as a result of the opposing forces of demand and supply. However, when the quantities demanded and supplied at a given price are unequal or "out of balance," prices and quantities will called a ***change in the quantity demanded.*** Note that this expression refers to changes in the quantities purchased by buyers in response to *changes in price*.

Changes in Demand

The law of demand says that the quantity demanded of a good varies inversely with its price, assuming that all other things remain the same. What are these "other things"? What happens if they do not remain the same?

Among the "other things" that will influence the demand for a good are (1) buyers' incomes, (2) prices of related goods, (3) expectations of incomes and prices, and (4) nonmonetary conditions. All four of these will be explained shortly. But first, notice that these demand determinants are not measured on the axes of the graph and hence are assumed to be constant when you draw a demand curve. Therefore, a change in any one of them will cause a shift of the demand curve to a new position. When this happens, we say that there has been a ***change in demand***. The change may be either an increase or a decrease.

- An increase in demand can be visualized on a graph as a shift of the demand curve to the right. This is shown in Exhibit 8. The shift takes place from the old demand curve *D* to the new demand curve *D'*.

    What does this increase in demand tell you? It shows that, *at any given price, buyers are now willing to purchase more than they were willing to purchase before.* For example, the new curve indicates that, at a price of $30 per unit, buyers were previously willing to purchase 300 units per week. Now, after the increase in demand, they are willing to buy 400 units per week at the same price of $30 per unit.

- A decrease in demand can be visualized as a shift of the demand curve to the left, as shown in Exhibit 9. This time the graph illustrates that, *at any given price, buyers are now willing to purchase less than they were willing to purchase before.* Thus, at $30 per unit, people were willing to buy 300 units per week. Now, after the decrease in demand, they are willing to buy only 200 units per week at the same price of $30 per unit.

Test Yourself

1. An increase in demand means that, for any given quantity demanded, buyers are *now willing to pay a higher price* per unit than they were willing to pay be-

fore. Can you define a decrease in demand in a parallel way?

2. Look at Exhibit 8. What is your estimate of the highest price per unit that buyers were willing to pay for 300 units per week, before and after the increase in demand?

3. Look at Exhibit 9. What is your estimate of the highest price per unit that buyers were willing to pay for 200 units per week, before and after the decrease in demand?

4. Can you think of some actual examples that illustrate these ideas?

How do the changes in the demand determinants mentioned earlier (buyers' incomes, prices of related goods, expectations of incomes and prices, and nonmonetary factors) bring about a change in demand? In other words, how do these changes cause a shift of the demand curve to the right or to the left?

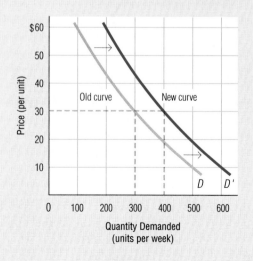

EXHIBIT 8

Increase in Demand

An increase in demand can be represented by a shift of the demand curve to the right. At any given price, people are now willing to buy more than they were willing to buy before.

Changes in Buyers' Incomes

The demand for most goods varies directly with buyers' incomes. This means the demand curves shift to the right when incomes rise and to the left when incomes fall. Products whose demand curves behave in this way are known as *superior goods*, or more popularly as *normal goods*. They are called this because they represent the "normal" situation. Examples include most food, clothing, cars, appliances, vacation trips, and other items that people typically buy.

For some goods, however, changes in consumption (prices remaining constant) vary inversely with changes in income over a certain range of income. Such products are called *inferior goods*. Typical examples are bread, potatoes, beans, and used goods, all of which are *relatively* inexpensive and are therefore bought in quantity by low-income families. As their incomes rise, these families can spend a larger amount on goods that are more desirable. Thus, they spend relatively less on bread and potatoes and more on fruits and vegetables, relatively less on beans and more

on meat and fish, relatively less on used goods and more on new goods.

Changes in Prices of Related Goods

The demand for any good is also affected by the prices of related goods. The strength of this relation depends on the extent to which consumers regard the products as competitive with, or complementary to, each other.

Some products are *substitute goods*—they are competitive with each other. The more people consume of one, the less they consume of another. An increase in the price of one leads to an increase in the demand for the other. Similarly, a decrease in the price of one leads to a decrease in the demand for the other. For example, if the price of Coca-Cola increases, cola drinkers will buy less Coca-Cola and more Pepsi-Cola. The market demand curve for Pepsi-Cola will therefore shift to the right. If the price of Coca-Cola decreases, people will be inclined to buy more Coca-Cola and less Pepsi-Cola. Then the market demand curve for Pepsi-Cola will shift to the left. What other substitute goods can you think of?

Some products are *complementary goods.* The more people consume of one complementary good, the more they consume of the other. An increase in the price of one leads to a decrease in the demand for the other. Conversely, a decrease in the price of one leads to an increase in the demand for the other. For example, if the price of cameras increases, people will buy fewer cameras—and therefore less film. The market demand curve for film will shift to the left.

Products that are neither substitutes nor complements are unrelated. The consumption of one does not affect the consumption of the other. Therefore, a change in the price of one does not cause a change in the demand for the other. Some examples are salt and pencils, chewing gum and paper clips, and thumbtacks and mustard.

But if a buyer's expenditure on a particular kind of good absorbs a considerable proportion of his or her budget, a change in its price may affect the buyer's demand for another product. This may be true even if the latter product is neither competitive with nor complementary to the former. One example is housing and entertainment. If the rent you pay for an apartment increases, you may decide to see fewer movies per month. Can you give some other examples? To generalize thus far:

If buyers' incomes remain constant, the market demand curve for a product will move in the same di-

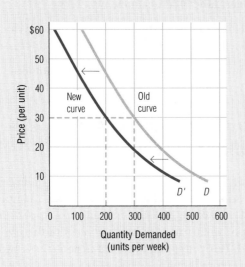

EXHIBIT 9

Decrease in Demand

A decrease in demand can be represented by a shift of the demand curve to the left. At any given price, people are now willing to buy less than they were willing to buy before.

rection as a change in the price of its substitute. Conversely, the market demand curve for a product will move in the direction opposite from a change in the price of its complement. This means that, for substitute products, the relation between a change in the price of one commodity and the resulting change in demand for the other is *direct*. For complementary products, the relation is *inverse*.

Changes in Expectations of Incomes and Prices

Changes in buyers' *expectations* of incomes and prices can also influence their demands for goods and services. If buyers expect higher incomes or higher prices in the near future, they may buy larger quantities of goods in anticipation of the increases. This causes the demand curves for those goods to shift to the right. If buyers expect lower incomes or lower prices, they may buy smaller quantities of goods and services. This causes the demand curves for those goods and services to shift to the left. For these reasons, economists often try to incorporate the effects of buyers' expectations into business forecasts.

Changes in Nonmonetary Conditions

Many conditions other than prices and incomes influence the demands for goods. These conditions include all nonmonetary determinants of demand, such as the age, occupation, sex, race, religion, education, and tastes of consumers, as well as the number of consumers. Changes in these conditions can affect the preferences of actual and potential consumers. However, economists customarily assume that, for large numbers of consumers, these nonmonetary conditions are stable—for two reasons:

1.   Nonmonetary conditions vary widely among people so their effects in the market tend to cancel out.

2.   Nonmonetary conditions change slowly because they are primarily the result of habit, demographic characteristics, and cultural traditions.

   Nonmonetary conditions affecting demand are assumed to remain stable in the short run. Because of this, economists always analyze demand in terms of prices and incomes.

Summing Up: Changes in and Movements of Demand

To reinforce what you've learned, let's review two essential ideas.

   Demand can be represented by a schedule or curve that reflects buyers' behavior at the time. Given the demand curve for a good, a change in price leads to a *change in the quantity demanded*, not to a change in demand. This means that there has been either an increase in the quantity demanded, as represented by a movement downward along the curve, or a decrease in the quantity demanded, as represented by a movement upward along the curve. The change is due to either a decrease or an increase in the price of the product (while all other demand determinants remain the same).

   A *change in demand* means that the schedule itself has changed. The demand curve has shifted either to the right, if there has been an increase in demand, or to the left, if there has been a decrease in demand. The shift is due to a change in any of the demand determinants that were assumed to remain constant when the curve was initially drawn.

   It's easy to commit errors in economic reasoning by failing to understand the important distinction between a change in the quantity demanded and a change in demand. These two ideas are of fundamental significance.

Test Yourself

Which of the following involve a change in the quantity demanded, and which involve a change in demand?

1.   People buy more bathing suits in the summer than in the winter.

2.   Consumer incomes fall, and the number of automobiles purchased declines.

3.   Honda reduces the prices of its motorcycles by 10 percent, and sales of Honda motorcycles increase.

4.   State College raises its tuition, and student enrollments decline.

Two Kinds of Changes Involving Supply

As with demand, so too with supply: *Two types of changes* may occur. One is called "a change in the quantity supplied"; the other is called "a change in supply." On the basis of what you now know about the theory of demand, can you guess the meanings of these two concepts before they are explained?

Changes in the Quantity Supplied

Look back at Exhibit 5. According to the law of supply, an upward movement along the curve signifies an increase in the quantity supplied as the *price is raised*. On the other hand, a downward movement along the curve signifies a decrease in the quantity supplied as the *price is reduced*. Any such upward or downward movement along the curve is called a **change in the quantity supplied**. Note that such movements are due exclusively to a *change in price*.

Changes in Supply

The law of supply says that the quantity supplied of a product usually varies directly with its price, assuming that all other things remain the same. The "other things" that may have an influence in determining supply are (1) resource prices or the costs of the factors of production, (2) prices of other goods, (3) suppliers' expectations, and (4) nonmonetary conditions If any of these determinants change, a new relation is established between price and quantity supplied. On a graph, this is shown by a shift of the supply curve to a new position, representing a **change in supply.**

- An increase in supply is represented by a shift of the supply curve to the right, as shown in Exhibit 10. *At any given price, sellers are now willing to supply more than they were willing to supply before.* For example, at a price of $30 per unit, sellers were previously willing to supply a total of 300 units per week. Now, after the increase in supply, they are willing to sell a total of 400 units per week at the same price of $30 per unit.

- A decrease in supply is represented by a shift of the supply curve to the left, as shown in Exhibit 11. *At any given price, sellers are now willing to supply less than they were willing to supply before.* For example, they were previously willing to supply a total of 300 units per week at a price of $30 per unit. Now, after the decrease in supply, they are willing to sell a total of 200 units per week at the same price of $30 per unit.

How will a change in any of the supply determinants listed above (resource prices, prices of other goods, suppliers' expectations, and nonmonetary conditions) bring about a change in supply?

EXHIBIT
10

Increase in Supply

An increase in supply can be represented by a shift of the supply curve to the right. At any given price, sellers are now willing to supply more than they were willing to supply before.

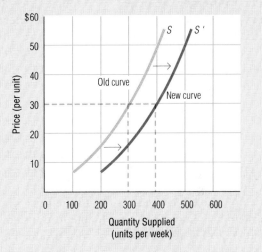

EXHIBIT
11

Decrease in Supply

A decrease in supply can be represented by a shift of the supply curve to the left. At any given price, sellers are now willing to supply more than they were willing to supply before.

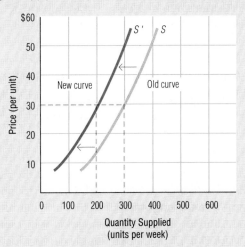

Changes in Resource Prices

Ordinarily, a decrease in resource prices (such as costs of materials) in a particular industry will reduce production costs and thus raise the potential for profits. Firms will then be likely to increase their output in order to capture more of these potential profits. This action will shift the total market supply curve to the right. Conversely, an increase in resource prices (such as wages) would tend to have the opposite effect, because it raises production costs and decreases profits. This encourages businesses in that industry to reduce their output. The market supply curve thus shifts to the left.

Changes in Prices of Related Goods

Business firms produce goods to earn profits. Changes in the relative prices of goods may change the relative profitability of those goods. This brings about changes in their respective supply curves. For instance, if the price of wheat increases relative to the price of corn, farmers may find it more profitable to transfer some land and other resources out of corn production and into wheat production. This would shift the market supply curve of corn to the left and the market supply curve of wheat to the right.

Changes in Expectations

Of course, changes in suppliers' *expectations* of prices will also influence their supply decisions. If some producers expect prices to rise, they may decide to hold back on their current output because they anticipate getting higher prices for their goods in the future and, therefore, earning higher profits. If other producers expect prices to decline, they may decide to increase their current output because they anticipate lower prices and earnings in the future.

Changes in Nonmonetary Conditions

Various conditions other than prices can affect the supply of a commodity. The most important are the state of technology and the number of sellers in the market. For example, the adoption of a new production method or a new machine can reduce the need for labor. This may improve efficiency and increase supply, shifting the market supply curve to the right. A decline in efficiency as a result of a failure to modernize can have the opposite effect. Similarly, an increase in the number of sellers in the market will result in a rightward shift of the market supply curve. A decrease in the number of sellers will cause a leftward shift of the curve.

Summing Up: Changes in and Movements of Supply

You've seen that supply can be represented by a schedule or curve that reflects sellers' attitudes at the time. A change in price leads to a *change in the quantity supplied,* not to a change in supply. An increase in the quantity supplied is indicated by a movement upward along the curve. Similarly, a decrease in the quantity supplied is indicated by a movement downward along the curve.

A *change in supply* means that the schedule itself has changed. That is, the curve has shifted to the right if there has been an increase in supply or to the left if there has been a decrease in supply. The shift is the result of a change in any of the supply determinants that were assumed to remain constant when the curve was initially drawn.

Thus, lessons learned from the study of demand are also applicable to supply. *You have to understand the important distinction between a change in the quantity supplied and a change in supply to avoid errors in economic reasoning.*

Test Yourself

1.   An increase in supply means that, for any given quantity supplied, sellers are now willing to accept a *lower price* per unit than before. Illustrate this with a graph. Define and illustrate a decrease in supply in a parallel way.

2.   Look back at Exhibit 10. What is your estimate of the lowest price per unit that sellers were willing to accept for a supply of 300 units per week, before the increase in supply? After the increase in supply?

3.   Look at Exhibit 11. What is your estimate of the lowest price per unit that sellers were willing to accept for a supply of 200 units per week, before the decrease in supply? After the decrease in supply?

Combined Changes in Demand and Supply

Demand and supply curves rarely remain fixed for very long. This is because the factors determining them, such as buyers' incomes, resource costs, buyers' and sellers' expectations, or the prices of related products, are continually changing. These changes cause the curves to shift. Because we are interested in learning about the behavior of prices and quantities in competitive markets, we must be able to analyze such shifts to evaluate their effects.

What happens when a demand or supply curve moves to a new position? The answer is that there may also be a change in the equilibrium price, the equilibrium quantity, or both. Some examples are presented in Exhibit 12. Let's see what the graphs tell us.

Note that in each set of curves in Figures (a) through (d), one of the curves shifted while the other remained unchanged. The effects on the equilibrium price and quantity in each case are depicted by the arrows. In Figure (a), an increase in demand resulted in an increase in both the equilibrium price and the equilibrium quantity. The opposite occurred in Figure (b) as a result of a decrease in demand. In Figure (c), an increase in supply resulted in a decrease in the equilibrium price and an increase in the equilibrium quantity. The opposite occurred in Figure (d) as a result of a decrease in supply.

Can you explain, using similar terms, what happened in Figures (e) and (f)?

The Market Economy: Is It "Good" or "Bad"?

In a competitive market, prices are determined solely by the free play of demand and supply. An economy characterized entirely by such markets would be a *pure market economy,* sometimes called a "competitive economy." The two expressions are often used interchangeably. They represent the "pure" model of capitalism.

What are the desirable features of such an economy? Does it have shortcomings? Is it realistic as a description of the capitalistic system? Answers to these questions can be expressed within the familiar framework of our society's four basic economic goals: efficiency, equity, stability, and growth.

Efficiency

In a competitive economy there is *consumer sovereignty.* That is, consumers "vote" by offering more dollars for some products and fewer dollars for others, depending on personal preferences. But preferences don't remain constant. They vary with changes in incomes and other conditions mentioned earlier. These variations cause shifts in demand curves. How do producers respond to these changes in demand? In general:

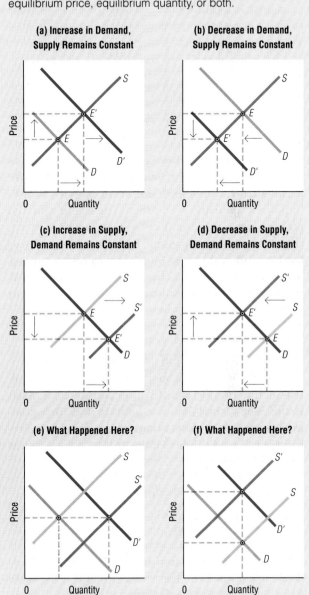

EXHIBIT 12

Changes in Demand and Supply

Shifts in the demand or supply curves will cause changes in equilibrium price, equilibrium quantity, or both.

(a) Increase in Demand, Supply Remains Constant

(b) Decrease in Demand, Supply Remains Constant

(c) Increase in Supply, Demand Remains Constant

(d) Decrease in Supply, Demand Remains Constant

(e) What Happened Here?

(f) What Happened Here?

In a pure market economy, resources will be used as efficiently as possible. This is true to the extent that demand and supply reflect all costs and benefits of production and consumption. The efficient use of resources occurs because firms in each industry compete for the dollar "votes" of consumers. As a result:

1.   Each firm, and the economy as a whole, achieves *technical efficiency* by making the fullest utilization of available inputs.

2.   The economy also achieves *economic efficiency*. It does this by fulfilling consumer preferences, that is, by producing the combination of goods that people are willing and able to purchase with their incomes.

In other words, a pure market economy achieves maximum output at the lowest prices consistent with existing costs, technology, and incomes. What is most important, perhaps, is that these results are achieved without direct intervention by government. Indeed, they come about through the free interactions of market demand and supply forces. These forces, as suggested by Adam Smith's "invisible hand," guide the allocation of society's resources to their most efficient uses.

Equity

A second feature of a pure market economy is that it distributes income in proportion to each person's contribution to production. If Wilson adds twice as much to the value of total output as Johnson does, then competition among employers and among suppliers of resources will tend to see to it that Wilson earns twice as much as Johnson.

The reason for this is not hard to see. No employer will pay either Wilson or Johnson more than the value that each contributes. And neither Wilson nor Johnson need accept less. Why? Because in a competitive economy, there would always be some other employer who would find it profitable to pay them what they are worth. The result is that the "invisible hand" of competition—the forces of demand and supply—guide Wilson and Johnson into the occupations that each performs best. In more general terms:

In a pure market economy, the factors of production tend to move into their most remunerative employments. This ensures that the entire income of society is distributed to the owners of resources in

proportion to their contribution to the economy's total output.

Can we conclude in any *scientific* way that this method of apportioning society's income is fair or equitable? Not really. Equity considerations are based on value judgments of right and wrong, good and bad. In such matters, your own opinion is not necessarily better or worse than someone else's. However, we will examine this matter in considerable detail at later points.

Stability and Growth

There are two other important features of a pure market economy. The first concerns fluctuations in prices, output, and employment, or the problem of economic *stability*. The second concerns the expansion of real output, or economic *growth*.

Stability   *A pure market economy maintains a level of total spending sufficient to sustain full employment (or full utilization) of society's available resources.* Of course, innovations and changes in production methods may cause lapses from full employment. However, such lapses tend to be temporary. Because of the competitive nature of both the product market and the resource market, the demands for and supplies of goods and the factors of production adjust quickly to changing economic conditions. As a result, the economy's output and employment tend to remain relatively stable. Prices, however, fluctuate around a long-run level corresponding to full employment.

Growth   *Part of the income received by the household sector is spent for consumption. The remaining portion—the household sector's savings—is borrowed by the business sector for investment in new production techniques, new plant and equipment, and the like.* The business sector thus borrows to engage in new investment. As a consequence, a society's holdings or stock of capital increases, and the production-possibilities curve shifts outward to the right. This means, as you've already learned, the society produces larger quantities of goods—that is, it experiences economic growth.

To summarize:

With respect to stability and growth, a pure market economy has two important characteristics:

1.   Prices fluctuate relatively more than output and employment to accommodate short-run changes

in the supplies of and the demands for goods and resources.

2. Economic growth takes place in response to new investment by entrepreneurs that seek better ways of improving production methods.

Some Real-World Imperfections

A pure market economy is the prototype of theoretical capitalism. But no actual economy can be considered a pure market economy. The ways in which modern, mixed capitalistic economies differ from the model are many and various. Although a pure market economy may achieve a high score when judged by the standards of efficiency, equity, stability, and growth, the report card on real-world capitalistic systems would, in varying degrees, be somewhat less glowing. Some of the more important criticisms may be described briefly.

Market Imperfections and Frictions

The market may not work as neatly in the real world as the theoretical model suggests. Imperfections and frictions, such as imperfect knowledge, resource immobility, and barriers to entering markets, impede the smooth functioning of the system.

For example, buyers and sellers of goods and resources do not usually have complete information about alternative prices, working conditions, and the like. Unemployed people frequently must be retrained before they can qualify for new jobs. And even when they are retrained, they may not be willing to bear the economic or psychic costs of moving long distances to accept employment.

Similarly, entrepreneurs and workers are often prevented from entering new industries because they lack the capital or the special know-how required. Or perhaps they cannot overcome monopolistic barriers, such as patent rights and apprenticeship requirements, that protect various business firms and unions from increased competition.

These and other obstacles retard the rate at which the factors of production shift out of declining industries and into expanding ones. As a result, imbalances in the form of shortages and surpluses arise in various product and resource markets. In a pure market economy, these imbalances wouldn't occur—or, if they did, they would be very short-lived.

Economic Inequity

In a market economy, incomes tend to be proportional to people's contributions to production. As we've seen, if Wilson adds twice as much to the value of total output as Johnson does, then Wilson's income will tend to be twice that of Johnson's.

This economic inequality can be further magnified by the right of inheritance. This fundamental institution of capitalism permits the accumulation of wealth within families. Such disparities in income and wealth can lead to economic and social inequities that are not based on people's contributions.

Technology and Large-Scale Production

The model of a pure market economy assumes that each industry comprises numerous small firms. Yet modern technology dictates that in many industries, such as automobile and aircraft manufacturing, firms must be very large if they are to make use of the most efficient means of production. In such industries, a few large firms are dominant.

Externalities

Another criticism is that the market system fails to reflect all the costs associated with production and consumption. As a result, there are side effects, or *externalities*. For example, production of some goods, such as steel, rubber, and chemicals, pollutes the environment and so contributes to *social costs*. Other goods, such as education, sanitation services, and park facilities, add to community satisfaction and so contribute to *social benefits*.

These externalities may not always be fully reflected in the prices of goods. To the extent that they are not, demand and supply curves fail to show *all* the costs and benefits of production. As a result, either too much or too little is produced, and resources are misallocated. You'll learn how this happens in some subsequent chapters.

Relevant Even If Not Realistic

For these reasons, the model of a pure market economy doesn't convey a perfect picture of the way in which the price system actually operates in a modern capitalistic society. Nevertheless, as you'll see later, the pure market model described in this chapter provides a useful framework for evaluating the performance of a capitalistic system. Hence, the model is relevant if not always realistic.

Origins: The Study of Markets Before Adam Smith

The modern study of economics dates from the publication of Adam Smith's *The Wealth of Nations* (1776). Yet centuries earlier, scholars and philosophers pondered the allocation of society's scarce resources. The formal study of markets had its origins in the philosophical inquiry of morals and ethics. Two early scholars who contributed to the analysis of market exchanges are Saint Thomas Aquinas and John Locke.

St. Thomas Aquinas: Scholastic of Early Capitalism

The period known as the Middle Ages covers approximately 1,000 years—from the fall of the Roman Empire in A.D. 476 to about 1500.

Modern capitalism took root in the last three of these ten centuries. Money and credit instruments gained wider acceptance in trade among European towns and cities. The ownership of tools of production became separated from their use. And a wage system emerged with the growth of urbanization and more centralized production.

The outstanding intellectual accomplishment of the late Middle Ages was the system of thought known as Scholasticism. The participants in this system are referred to as Scholastics or Schoolmen. Essentially, Scholasticism was an attempt to harmonize reason with faith. The method consisted of integrating philosophy and theology primarily on the basis of rationalism or logic rather than through science and experience.

Economic Beliefs

The greatest of the Scholastic philosophers was Thomas Aquinas, and his most famous work was the *Summa Theologica*. The English translation runs to some twenty volumes. In his writings on economic problems, Aquinas applied the principles of Aristotelian philosophy and logic to biblical teachings and canonical dogma. Thus, according to Aquinas:

St. Thomas Aquinas
(1225–1274)

- The individual's right to private property accords with natural law.

- Production under private ownership is preferred to production under communal ownership.

- Trade is to be condoned to the extent that it maintains the household and benefits the country.

- Sellers are bound to be truthful with their buyers.

- Fairness exists when goods are exchanged at equal values and at a "just" price that reflects the customary price.

- Wealth is good if it leads to a virtuous life.

- "Usury," which is defined as the charging of excess interest on loans, is among the most objectionable of trade practices.

Practical Rules

Aquinas and the Schoolmen were not in sympathy with many of the economic practices of their time. However, because they could do little to change the practices, they proceeded to make them as respectable as possible. This was done by establishing moral and ethical rules of economic behavior. Many of these rules are now an integral part of modern capitalistic philosophy.

For example, Aquinas decried usury. But he permitted the charging of *some* interest if a lender had to forgo an alternative investment that would have yielded an income. This was the principle of *lucrum cessans*—a concept similar to what is known as "opportunity cost" in modern economics. Aquinas also justified the idea that buyers on credit could pay more than the cash price and that discounts could be allowed on promissory notes. He also believed that many business transactions could entail special charges and payments.

Markets and Prices

Aquinas recognized that market prices were based on both the demand for commodities and their costs of supply. He argued that the "just price" of a good is the current market price that prevailed without fraud or control by a few powerful participants. He further contended that the just price was one established by the local market, rather than one imposed on the market by an outside ruler. The work by Aquinas formed a foundation for the modern study of markets and economics.

John Locke: Natural Rights

In the late 1600s, 100 years before Adam Smith, the great English philosopher John Locke considered the question of prices and market exchanges. His views on these matters were an integral part of his philosophy, which included the belief that people have natural rights and that governments are created to protect those rights. These ideas greatly influenced America's Founding Fathers. Locke's writings on the theory and functions of government formed much of the bases of both the *Declaration of Independence* and the *Constitution* that came a century later.

Economic Views

The period from 1500 to 1800 is known in economics as the age of mercantilism. This era was marked by the emergence of European nation-states from medieval feudal kingdoms. The economic philosophy of the time emphasized the cooperation between business and government. Business was seen as an extension of government, a relationship designed to promote more powerful nation-states. This was most obvious in international trade and in the exploration of the Asian, American, African, and Australian continents.

Locke contended, contrary to the mercantilist philosophy, that governments exist to preserve the

John Locke
(1632–1704)

natural rights of citizens. Predating Adam Smith's "invisible hand" by 100 years, Locke argued that society is better off if people are allowed to pursue life, liberty, and the acquisition of property. The natural pursuit of happiness and the enjoyment of private things, according to Locke, led to the common good.

Prompted by his desire to improve government, Locke developed sophisticated arguments on pressing economic problems. For example, he explored the fundamental nature of money and interest payments to argue that Parliament should not raise the legal rate of interest.

In his public-policy debates, Locke developed a theory of market-price determination that applied to all exchangeable goods. Although his analysis was simple by contemporary standards, it was remarkable for its time. Two centuries before demand and supply curves were drawn, he indicated that the quantity demanded of a good is inversely related to price and that the quantity supplied is directly related to price. He also expressed the idea that changes in price are due to changes in underlying demand and supply conditions.

On the Shoulders of Giants

"If I have seen farther than others, it is because I have stood on the shoulders of giants." So said Sir Isaac Newton, a contemporary of Locke and one the greatest mathematicians and physicists of all time.

It's often convenient to credit a single individual with the development of new ideas. In reality, the work of one is usually based on that of many predecessors. This is true of the study of markets. The exchange of goods through markets is a fundamental aspect of civilized society. It's not surprising, therefore, that scholars in fields other than economics have long questioned the nature and consequences of market behavior. It has been through their efforts that our contemporary understanding of markets is made possible.

Summary of Important Ideas

1. The purpose of studying demand and supply is to learn how a competitive or pure market economy works.

2. *Demand* is a relation between the price of a commodity and the quantity of it that buyers are willing and able to purchase at a given time. Other things affecting demand, such as buyers' income, prices of related goods, buyers' expectations of future incomes and prices, and various nonmonetary conditions, are assumed to remain the same. The law of demand states that the relation between price and quantity demanded is *inverse*—as the price rises, less is demanded. Demand curves slope downward from left to right.

3. *Supply* is a relation between the price of a commodity and the quantity of it that sellers are willing and able to sell at a given time. Other things affecting supply, such as resource costs, prices of related goods, suppliers' expectations of future costs and prices, and various nonmonetary conditions, are assumed to remain the same. The law of supply states that the relation between price and quantity supplied is usually *direct*—as the price rises, more is supplied. Supply curves typically slope upward from left to right.

4. The intersection of a market demand curve with a market supply curve shows the equilibrium price and the equilibrium quantity of a commodity. The equilibrium price is the market-clearing price because it results in an absence of surpluses or shortages. If the price in a particular market is flexible, it adjusts quickly to its market-clearing level.

5. Demand or supply curves may shift either left or right. The shifts occur as a result of changes in any of the determinants assumed to remain constant when the curves are drawn.

6. Movements along demand and supply curves result from changes in the price of the commodity while the other underlying determinants of demand and supply remain constant. Such movements are called either a change in the quantity demanded or a change in the quantity supplied. The distinction is important for an understanding of demand and supply.

7. In the real world, demand and supply curves are always shifting. A change in demand or a change in supply may result in a new equilibrium price, a new equilibrium quantity, or both, depending on the relative shifts of the curves.

8. A market economy is highly competitive. Prices and quantities are determined by numerous buyers and sellers through the free operation of demand and supply. Organized commodity markets, such as the New York Mercantile Exchange, or the Chicago Board of Trade, typify highly competitive markets. However, most of the markets in our economy differ from such competitive markets to varying degrees.

9. The study of market exchanges was undertaken by many scholars before Adam Smith. Two of the most noteworthy are St. Thomas Aquinas and John Locke. Aquinas was the great Scholastic of the thirteenth century. He applied some important economic ideas to religious teachings, especially that a "just" price was one established through the workings of a market. Locke, an eminent seventeenth-century scholar, applied the philosophy of natural rights to economic analysis. In particular, he developed a relatively sophisticated explanation of markets, including such essential ideas as demand and supply.

Terms and Concepts to Review

demand

demand schedule

demand curve

demand price

law of demand

supply

supply schedule

supply curve

supply price

law of supply

equilibrium

surplus

shortage

equilibrium price

equilibrium quantity

disequilibrium

market-clearing price

change in the quantity demanded	complementary goods
change in demand	change in the quantity supplied
superior goods	change in supply
normal goods	pure market economy
inferior goods	consumer sovereignty
substitute goods	externalities

Questions and Problems

In the following problems, draw graphs whenever possible to verify your answer.

1. Do the numerical quantities of a demand schedule describe buyers' behavior? If not, what is the fundamental property of a demand schedule?

2. Evaluate the following comments from newspaper editorials on the basis of what you know about the meaning of demand and scarcity in economics. (*Hint*: How meaningful are the italicized words?)

"Our community *needs* more schools and better teachers; after all, what could be more critical than the education of our children as future citizens?"

"The health of our citizens is uppermost in our minds. Ever since the rate of garbage pick-up in our northwest suburbs deteriorated to its present deplorable levels, it has been evident that our shortage of collection facilities has reached *emergency* proportions."

3. Some people would buy more of a good (such as jewelry or furs) at a high price than at a low price. This results in an upward-sloping demand curve. Would such a curve be an exception to the law of demand? Explain.

4. What would happen to the market demand curve for steak as a result of each of the following: (a) an increase in the average level of income, (b) an increase in the number of families, (c) a successful advertising campaign for veal and pork, (d) an increase in the prices of veal and pork, (e) a decrease in the prices of veal and pork?

5. What would happen to the demand for Pepsi-Cola if the price of Coca-Cola were doubled? Why would it happen?

6. Determine the effect on the supply of office buildings if each of the following happened: (a) the price of land rose, (b) the price of steel fell, (c) the price of cement fell, (d) a new and faster method of construction were adopted, (e) the number of firms that build offices declined, (f) rents for office buildings were expected to decline.

7. Analyze the following: (a) What would happen to the equilibrium price and equilibrium quantity of butter if the price of margarine rose substantially? (b) What would happen if there were an increase in the cost of producing butter?

8. "Wheat is wheat. Therefore, the price of wheat at any given time should be the same in Chicago as it is in Kansas City." Do you agree? Explain.

9. In organized commodity markets, buyers often become sellers and sellers often become buyers, depending on the price of the good. Examine the following schedule for five people: *A, B, C, D,* and *E.*

   a. Draw the market supply and demand curves, and estimate the equilibrium price and quantity.

   b. Show the effects on the market supply and demand curves if *C* drops out of the market.

10. How does St. Thomas Aquinas's view of a "just price" compare with the market equilibrium price? In what way is John Locke's philosophy of natural law consistent with Adam Smith's invisible hand?

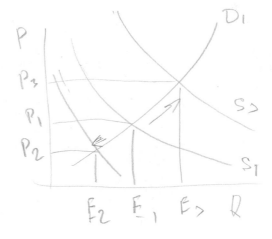

T A K E   A   S T A N D

Consumer Sovereignty: Do Consumers Rule?

In a capitalist, market-based economy, consumers get what they want. Or at least, so it is often claimed. The wishes of consumers, mediated by the competitive forces of a market economy, ultimately determine what goods are produced. Consumers purchase only the goods and services that they want; after all, nobody forces them to buy anything. If consumers decide that they like a brand of athletic shoe, a make of automobile, a type of cosmetic surgery, or some other good, the increase in demand for the good or service causes its price to rise. The market thus sends a signal to producers that this good is popular and profitable, and producers respond by increasing output. Goods that consumers don't want, by contrast, are left on the shelves of stores and supermarkets. Stores will not reorder such goods, and so firms will not find it profitable to produce them. The consumer rules.

A hard look at reality, however, casts doubt on this argument. If the consumer is sovereign, then why do you have trouble finding a comfortable pair of shoes? Why do stores sell eggs by the dozen when you want only two? Why do the networks always seem to cancel your favorite program? After all, you're a consumer. Perhaps the power of the purse is merely a convenient illusion. *Are consumers truly sovereign?*

Yes: Consumer Sovereignty Means Economic Democracy

Consumers are sovereign because, in a market economy, they get to decide how to spend their dollars. By their choices of goods and services in the marketplace, consumers transmit information about their likes and dislikes to producers. If producers want to stay in business, they have no choice but to respond to consumers' wishes. In effect, every dollar spent in the marketplace is like a vote. Goods that many consumers want get lots of votes, and so production of these goods continues. Goods that few consumers want get few votes, and so production of these goods is discontinued. Just as voter sovereignty makes for political democracy, consumer sovereignty creates economic democracy.

Of course, economic democracy does not mean that each consumer gets exactly the mix of goods and services desired, any more than political democracy means that we all get exactly the government that we want. But, in a market economy, the economic votes of all consumers do ensure that firms produce the goods that consumers, as a whole and on the average, want to purchase.

Contrast this scenario with a centrally-planned or command economy, where bureaucrats, not consumers, decide what is produced. Such an economic system prevailed to a greater or lesser extent in the communist countries of Eastern Europe and the former Soviet Union. In a command economy, consumers cannot use the marketplace to signal their preferences, and there need be no connection between what consumers want and what is actually produced. The competitive forces that compel firms to respond to consumers' wishes are absent in such an economy, and as a result shortages and surpluses arise. The history of command economies provides ample proof that they fail to satisfy consumers' needs and desires.

No: Consumer Sovereignty Is a Myth

First, it is deliberately misleading to call consumer sovereignty "economic democracy." In a democracy, the people rule. But in our economy, most of the wealth, and so most of the economic votes, are in the hands of a small fraction of the population. Donald Trump's preferences have much more influence on producers than yours or mine do. The appropriate political analogy for consumer sovereignty is not democracy, but plutocracy: government by the wealthy.

Second, the consumer sovereignty idea is based on an idealized pure market economy that exists only in theory. In the real world, many markets are not very competitive because a few large producers control production. You can probably name the dominant producers of automobiles or canned soup, for example; such producers are less prone to competitive forces and have more influence on the market than consumer sovereignty would suggest. The world also differs in other ways from the competitive deal. For one, consumers are not perfectly informed about the quality and prices of alternative products. A consumer may consistently select one brand of cheese over another regardless of price, unaware that both brands are manufactured identically by the same supplier. For another, the prices that consumers pay may not reflect the costs of pollution or other spillovers associated with production and consumption. Consumers might elect to drive less, for example, if they were forced to pay compensation for their contribution to deteriorating air quality. Markets in practice do not provide an ideal system for satisfying consumers' desires.

Consumers' choices are also limited to the goods that are actually out there in the marketplace; you cannot express a preference through the market for a good that doesn't exist. Finally, consumers' tastes may be influenced by advertising and social pressures. Through advertisements, firms persuade consumers that they want unnecessary and useless commodities. Consumers may appear to get what they want simply because they are trained to want what they get.

The Question: Are Consumers Sovereign?

- One view of a market economy is that it produces the goods that consumers want. Consumers indicate their likes and dislikes through their purchases of goods, and firms must respond to those wishes or go out of business.

- Another view is that inequalities of income and wealth, lack of competition, externalities, advertising, and other factors so distort the market system that real-world behavior travesties the pure market ideal. Consumer sovereignty is a myth.

Where Do You Stand?

1. Your local supermarket probably sells dozens of different breakfast cereals. Do you think this vindicates or contradicts the idea of consumer sovereignty?

2. Suppose that a market economy with given resources produces a given amount and mix of goods and services. A dictator in a command economy with the same resources could order the same levels of production, and could probably improve upon this allocation by compensating for externalities and other market imperfections. Therefore, a command economy must be better than a market economy. Do you agree? Explain.

3. Might consumers' tastes be manipulated in a command economy?

4. Are consumers sovereign? Justify your stand.

Chapter 3

The Private Sector—Household, Business, Foreign

The Household Sector: Income, Wealth, and Equity
The Ethics of Distribution
The Business Sector: Organization and Size
The Foreign Sector: International Trade and Finance

Learning Guide
Watch for answers to these important questions

What is meant by "income distribution"? Are there patterns or trends that enable us to compare the shares of income that different people receive?

How is income inequality measured? Why does income inequality exist? Are incomes more nearly equal today than they were several decades ago?

What standards exist for judging how income should be distributed? Is it possible to judge the fairness of such standards? Is there a "best" distribution of income for society?

How are businesses organized in our economy? Are some businesses too big? How big is big?

A nation's economy can be thought of as a huge pie. The pie can be cut into two large sectors—called private and public. Each of these, in turn, can be cut into smaller sectors. The word "sector" is used here to mean a segment or section of the economy—a slice of the pie. The *private sector* consists of households, businesses, and a foreign sector. The *public sector* consists of federal, state, and local governments.

This chapter explains some important aspects of the private sector. The next chapter deals with several essential features of the public sector.

You and I are part of the household sector. So too are some 90 million households. Households are the suppliers of the economy's inputs of human resources and the major purchasers of its outputs of goods and services.

Businesses, of which there are more than 15 million, make up a second group within the private sector. This group accounts for most of what the economy produces.

The foreign sector, which reflects the movements of goods, services, and financial claims into and out of the country, is the third component of the private sector. Because our economy plays a major role in the world economy, the foreign sector is of considerable importance to us and to other nations.

The Household Sector: Income, Wealth, and Equity

In the United States, concern with the distribution of income and wealth is as old as the nation itself. Alexander Hamilton believed that liberty without inequality of property ownership is impossible because "the inequality would unavoidably result from the very liberty itself." Thomas Jefferson remarked that the perpetuation of wealth through inheritance "sometimes does injury to the morals of youth by rendering them independent of, and disobedient to, their parents." And James Madison supported legislation that "would reduce extreme income and wealth toward a state of mediocrity and raise extreme indigence toward a state of comfort."

What constitutes an equitable or fair distribution of income and wealth among people? This question has been debated for centuries by economists, politicians, and social critics.

To begin, let's examine the facts. This is not easy, because there are different concepts of income and wealth. To most of us, income is simply money that people receive from various sources. Wealth is the value of the goods and property that people own. But a significant part of many people's income consists of more than wages and salaries. Income also includes money and nonmoney benefits such as subsidized education, welfare, subsidized health care, and expense accounts. Some of the money and nonmoney benefits are never reported to the tax authorities or to census takers. A similar problem affects the reporting of wealth. As a result, no government or private source provides complete and accurate information about the distribution of income and wealth.

With these deficiencies in mind, we can turn our attention to the available facts. First, however, we need two definitions:

Income is the gain derived from the use of human or material resources. It is a flow of dollars per unit of time. Thus, wages or salary is an example of income.

Wealth is anything that has value because it is capable of producing income either while it is owned or when it is sold. Thus, your car, stereo, securities, bank account, house or any other things of value you may own are examples of wealth. Wealth is a "stock" or accumulation of value, as distinct from a "flow" of income.

Functional Income Distribution

The study of income distribution is customarily divided into two parts—functional income distribution and personal income distribution.

Functional income distribution refers to the income payments made to the owners of the four factors of production. The four factors are labor, land, capital,

and entrepreneurship. The kinds of payments made to the owners of these factors are wages, rent, interest, and profit. Their annual sum is a measure of the nation's earnings and hence is called *national income.*

Exhibit 1 shows the shares of national income going to each class of resource owner. These proportions change very little from one year to the next. Therefore, it is more instructive to convey the highlights of the information over intervals of several years, as has been done in the graphs.

The titles in the exhibit are those used by the U.S. Department of Commerce. This agency compiles the data shown in the graphs. Note that Figures (a) and (b) both show wages as a share of national income. However, the U.S. Department of Commerce breaks wages into two categories: wages to individuals (which the Department calls "compensation of employees") and wages to proprietors (which the Department calls "proprietors' income"). Proprietors' income consists of wages earned by self-employed people and the profits of unincorporated businesses.

Compensation of Employees This category of income payments, shown in Figure (a), represents wages. It constitutes by far the largest share of national income—approximately 75 percent. The proportion has expanded steadily over the years, reflecting the growing importance of paid employment as the main source of people's income.

Proprietors' Income This class of payments, illustrated in Figure (b), has declined from almost 25 percent of national income at the beginning of the century to about 6 percent currently. The reason for the decline is that corporations have grown rapidly in importance during this century. As a result, they long ago replaced proprietorships as the economically dominant form of business organization and as a significant source of people's income.

Rental Income of Persons This component, shown in Figure (c), has been decreasing steadily for decades. Its share is now less than 2 percent of national income. One of the major reasons for the decline is that corporations, rather than individuals, have become the chief owners of rental property. Therefore, corporations are receiving an increasing proportion of rental income. This income becomes part of the income of corporations, which is shown in Figure (e).

Net Interest This item, illustrated in Figure (d), is the

EXHIBIT
1

Functional Distribution of National Income in the United States

Figures are decade averages, centered at the middle of each decade. Payments are shown as percentages of national income.

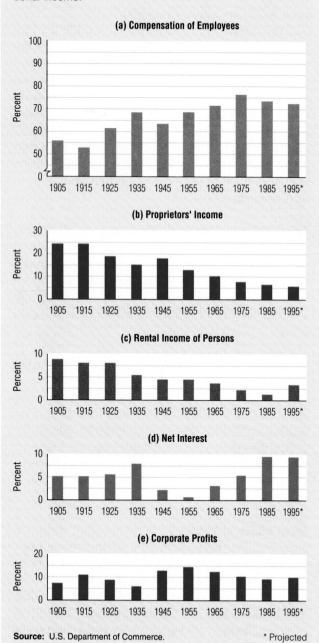

(a) Compensation of Employees

(b) Proprietors' Income

(c) Rental Income of Persons

(d) Net Interest

(e) Corporate Profits

Source: U.S. Department of Commerce.   * Projected

difference between what the business sector pays out in interest and what it takes in. For example, if you buy a Ford Motor Company bond, you are lending the company money for which it pays you interest. However, Ford Motor Company earns interest on financial claims (such as government bonds and consumer loans) that it holds against others. The same is true of many other firms. Net interest is thus the business sector's total interest payments to other sectors minus their total interest payments to the business sector. The trend of net interest payments is strongly affected by monetary and credit conditions. These are matters of fundamental concern in macroeconomics.

Corporate Profits This component of national income, shown in Figure (e), is what is "left over" after deducting corporate expenses from corporate gross income. Corporate expenses are largely contractual—they must be paid before corporate profits can be determined. Compared with the other payments (wages, rent, interest), therefore, corporate profits are the most variable. Because they are uncertain rewards for entrepreneurship (that is, for organizing and risk taking), corporate profits exhibit the greatest period-to-period fluctuations when measured in terms of percentage changes.

To summarize:

> Functional income distribution refers to the allocation of national income among the classes of resource owners. In recent decades, compensation of employees has averaged about 75 percent of national income. Proprietors' income, rental income of persons, and net interest have each averaged less than 10 percent. Corporate profits, which are the most variable because they are noncontractual and uncertain, have averaged about 10 percent.

Personal Income Distribution

How are personal incomes distributed in the United States? What percentage of families is rich and what percentage is poor? This is the problem of *personal income distribution*—the allocation of income among people.

The table in Exhibit 2 shows the relative share of total money income *before taxes* received by each fifth and the top 5 percent of all families in the United States. This table reveals three long-run characteristics:

EXHIBIT
2

Division of Income

The table shows the percentages of aggregate income (total money income before taxes) received by each fifth and the top 5 percent of families over the past five decades.

Figure (a) shows that in 1990, middle-income families constituted 54.7 percent of all families. Figure (b) shows that they earned about 40 percent of the nation's total family income. Bearing out the table, Figure (b) shows that the top-earning 20 percent of families garnered a 44.3-percent share of the total, while the lowest-earning 20 percent received a 4.6-percent share. Figure (c) shows that between 1975 and 1990, four-fifths of families saw their share of the total shrink by up to 1 percent, while the highest-earning fifth saw their share expand by 3.2 percent.

Income rank*	1950	1960	1970	1980	1990
Lowest fifth	4.5	4.8	5.4	5.1	4.6
Second fifth	11.9	12.2	12.2	11.8	10.8
Third fifth	17.4	17.8	17.8	17.5	16.6
Fourth fifth	23.6	24.0	23.8	24.2	23.8
Highest fifth	42.7	41.3	40.9	41.5	44.3
Top 5%	17.3	15.9	15.6	15.7	17.3
Ratio of top 5% to lowest fifth	3.8	3.3	2.9	3.1	3.8

* Because figures are rounded, the sum of the five fifths in each column may not add to 100. **Source:** U.S. Department of Commerce.

■ Low range   ■ Middle range   ■ High range

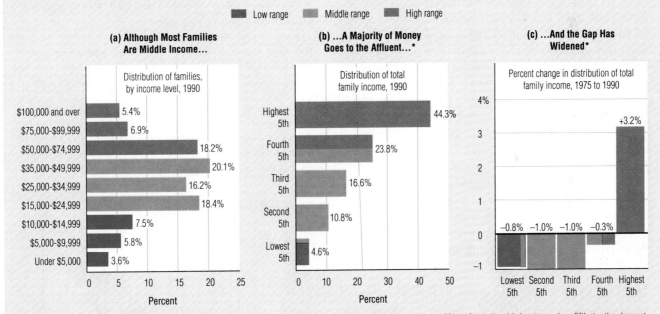

(a) Although Most Families Are Middle Income...

Distribution of families, by income level, 1990

$100,000 and over	5.4%
$75,000-$99,999	6.9%
$50,000-$74,999	18.2%
$35,000-$49,999	20.1%
$25,000-$34,999	16.2%
$15,000-$24,999	18.4%
$10,000-$14,999	7.5%
$5,000-$9,999	5.8%
Under $5,000	3.6%

Percent

(b) ...A Majority of Money Goes to the Affluent...*

Distribution of total family income, 1990

Highest 5th	44.3%
Fourth 5th	23.8%
Third 5th	16.6%
Second 5th	10.8%
Lowest 5th	4.6%

Percent

(c) ...And the Gap Has Widened*

Percent change in distribution of total family income, 1975 to 1990

Lowest 5th: −0.8% Second 5th: −1.0% Third 5th: −1.0% Fourth 5th: −0.3% Highest 5th: +3.2%

Source: Graphs are adapted from *Newsweek*, November 4, 1991.

*Figures (b) and (c) divide families by fifths, from the highest-earning fifth to the lowest-earning fifth. A small part of the lowest-earning fifth is classed with the midrange. About half of the next-to-highest-earning fifth is classed with the high range and about half is classed with the midrange.

1. The income received by the lowest fifth of families has averaged about 5 percent of total money income. (Money income is distinguished from non-money or in-kind income, such as food stamps, subsidized housing, and subsidized medical care.) The income received by the highest fifth has averaged more than 40 percent of total money income. This represents a long-run ratio of approximately 8:1.

2. The ratio of the share received by the top 5 percent to the share received by the lowest 20 percent declined substantially from 1950 to 1980. Since then it has increased. Over the period since 1950, the share of income earned by the richest 5 percent averages 3.5 times the share of income earned by the poorest 20 percent.

3. The distribution as a whole has remained fairly stable.

The graphs in Exhibit 2 provide some of the same information shown in the table, but in greater detail and from a somewhat different perspective.

Many observers believe that the pattern of income distribution will continue to remain about the same as it is now. Therefore, the question of whether or not incomes should be more nearly equal is a matter of continuing debate. The issues will be taken up later in the chapter.

Distribution of Wealth

The distribution of income has to do with who *gets* how much. The distribution of wealth has to do with who *has* how much. Wealth consists of assets that are capable of producing income—either while they are owned or when they are sold. Examples of wealth are stocks, bonds, savings accounts, land, and houses. Unfortunately, facts and figures about the distribution of wealth are limited and are not published periodically. As a result, we must rely on estimates from infrequent studies and reports.

These studies show, as you'll see shortly, that the concentration of wealth is considerably greater than the concentration of income. Further, the concentration of income-producing wealth is even more pronounced. For example, the top fifth of households owns the great bulk of stocks and bonds. However, this refers to direct holdings of securities. Indirectly, a large and growing proportion of the population owns stocks and bonds through retirement and pension funds, which invest heavily in such securities.

Measuring and Explaining Inequality in Income and Wealth Distribution

How can we illustrate and measure inequalities in the distribution of income and wealth? The most commonly used device is a type of graph called a **Lorenz diagram.** Such a graph is illustrated in Exhibit 3. Both the table and the graph show what percentage of people, ranked from the poorest to the richest, received what percentage of the nation's total income in a given year.

The graph is constructed by showing on the horizontal axis the number of income recipients—not in absolute terms but in percentages. Families, rather than individuals, are usually represented in a Lorenz diagram. The point marked 20 denotes the lowest 20

EXHIBIT 3

Illustrating Inequality with a Lorenz Diagram

(percentage of aggregate money income, before taxes, received by each fifth of families*)

Income rank	1990
Lowest fifth	5%
Second fifth	11
Middle fifth	17
Fourth fifth	24
Highest fifth	44

*Data are rounded to the nearest whole number for the accompanying graph.

Source: U.S. Department of Commerce.

The data from the table are used to construct a *Lorenz curve.* This curve shows the extent of departure between an equal distribution of income and the actual distribution of income.

From the curved line showing actual distribution, can you estimate the percentage of income received by the lowest 20 percent of families? The lowest 40 percent? 60 percent? 80 percent? 100 percent? Check your estimates against the data in the table to see if you are correct.

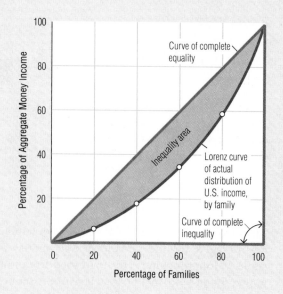

percent of the families; the point marked 40, the lowest 40 percent; and so on. The vertical axes measures percentages of total money income. Both axes have the same length and equal scales. Therefore, a diagonal line beginning at zero and sloping upward from left to right at a 45° angle represents the curve of complete equality.

Along this diagonal line of equal distribution, 20 percent of the families would receive 20 percent of total income. Similarly, 40 percent of the families would receive 40 percent of total income, and so on. This line is compared with the curve of actual distribution—called a *Lorenz curve*—derived from the data in the table. The area between the diagonal line of equal income distribution and the curved line of actual income distribution reflects the degree of income inequality. Thus, the more the curved line is bowed away from the diagonal, the greater is the inequality of income distribution.

How does the distribution of income compare with the distribution of wealth? The answer, given in terms of two Lorenz curves, is illustrated and explained in Exhibit 4.

Why Are Some People Rich and Others Poor?

What factors account for differences in income among households? There are many reasons. Among them:

1.   Differences in Wealth   Wealth is a significant source of income. Examples are income from real estate, income from financial investments, and income from interest. Therefore, a widely skewed (asymmetric) distribution of wealth is a major cause of income inequality.

2.   Differences in Earning Ability and Opportunity   People differ widely in education, intelligence, skill, motivation, energy, and talent. These differences translate into differences in earning ability. There are, moreover, differences in the opportunities that are available to people. Many people face job barriers because of their age, sex, or race. Legislation has made these barriers less formidable, but they are still responsible for some of the inequality in income distribution.

3.   Differences in Resource Mobility   The factors responsible for differences in earning ability and opportunity also make for differences in resource mobility. Many

EXHIBIT
4

Lorenz Curves of Income and Wealth Distribution

The distribution of wealth is considerably more unequal than the distribution of income. Inequality of wealth is both a cause and an effect of income inequality. High income leads to higher savings, which make possible further accumulation of wealth. This in turn engenders still higher income.

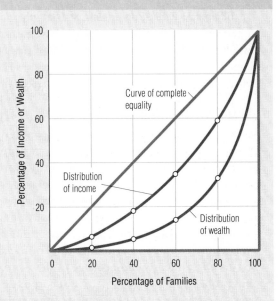

Source: Wealth data are from the Joint Economic Committee of the Congress, 1986. Studies of wealth distribution are done very infrequently.

people, for example, are prevented by a lack of information or a lack of financial means from moving into higher-paying occupations or locations. Consequently, low incomes and even extensive poverty may persist for years in some regions. This is true in certain parts of the United States, where share-croppers, migrant farm workers, and some factory laborers are able at best to earn only a substandard living.

4.   Differences in Luck A person born into a favorable environment and provided with opportunities to develop inherited potentials stands a greater chance of earning a higher income than one not so fortunate. This has been borne out by sociological studies of "vertical mobility"—the climb up the socioeconomic ladder.

5.   Differences in Age Young people who have recently entered the job market, and old people who have left it, have significantly lower incomes than those in mid-career.

6.   Differences in Human-Capital Investment Some people make heavier investments in their future earning capacity than do others. Sales clerks, for instance, may begin earning income immediately after graduating from high school. Most professionals, however, must spend many additional years in training. They often do this by living on borrowed funds. But in the long run they realize higher financial rewards for their investment of time and effort.

7.   Differences in Risk, Uncertainty, and Security Some occupations are more risky, and some have more uncertain futures, than others. These differences are reflected in earnings. Many people prefer security, in return for lower incomes, in the less risky and more certain fields of employment. For example, employees in relatively stable industries, such as civil service and banking, generally earn less than their counterparts in more unstable industries, such as manufacturing. Admittedly, lower incomes in some stable industries may be partly offset by nonmonetary factors, such as longer vacations, shorter working hours, and better fringe benefits. But the fact remains that coal miners earn more than road-construction workers, and window washers in skyscrapers earn more than dishwashers in restaurants. Similarly, most college professors earn less (but probably live longer) than most corporate executives. Clearly, the clash between risk, uncertainty, and security reveals itself in many ways.

These and other factors affecting people's in-

comes help explain why a Lorenz curve will always show some degree of inequality.

Measuring Inequality with the Gini Coefficient

Social scientists often express the precise degree of income inequality in terms of the *Gini coefficient of inequality.* (The concept is named after Corrodo Gini, an early-twentieth-century Italian statistician.) Look again at the Lorenz diagram in Exhibit 3. The Gini coefficient may be defined as the numerical value of the area between the Lorenz curve and the diagonal line divided by the numerical value of the entire area beneath the diagonal line. In simplest terms, the Gini coefficient is the ratio of the inequality area to the entire triangular area under the diagonal:

$$\text{Gini coefficient of inequality} = \frac{\text{inequality area}}{\text{triangular area}}$$

The value of the ratio may vary from 0 to 1. As incomes become more equal, the inequality area narrows relative to the triangular area under the diagonal. Thus, the Gini coefficient approaches zero. At zero there is no inequality—that is, all incomes are equal. As incomes become more unequal, the inequality area widens relative to the triangular area. Consequently, the Gini coefficient approaches 1. But the coefficient for any real-world society is always less than 1. A coefficient of 1 would indicate complete inequality, with one family getting all the income and the rest getting none.

Has the degree of income inequality become greater or less over the years? In 1950, the Gini coefficient of inequality for the United States was 0.38. Since then, the Gini coefficient of inequality has shown a gradual downward trend, decreasing to about 0.35 at present. The degree of income inequality thus appears to have declined slightly since the middle of this century.

Evaluating the Data: The Trouble with Lorenz Curves

As you've seen, income inequality is typically measured by a table of income distribution or by a Lorenz curve. The curve, of course, is derived directly from the table. The data in the table consist of what the U.S. Census Bureau (which compiles the figures) calls "money income."

Do money-income figures reveal all of the facts about income inequality? The answer is no—for several reasons:

1. Money Income Is Before-Tax Income It includes both personal income taxes and social security taxes. Payment of these taxes reduces income available for spending.

2. Money-Income Data Exclude Subsidies and Tax Advantages Many low-income families benefit from food stamps, low-cost housing, government rent supplements, and free medical care. Many middle- and upper-income families benefit from company-subsidized expense accounts and fringe benefits, and from favorable tax treatment of certain income and expenses. Because of these factors, money income and *equivalent* spending income can differ widely within income groups.

3. Money-Income Data Do Not Reflect Differences in Family Size A given amount of income can go further in a small family than in a large one. As a result, small families with low income may sometimes be better off than large families with greater income, depending on their relative *per capita* spendable income.

4. Money-Income Data Reflect Current Earnings, Not Lifetime Earnings The income of a schoolteacher and a professional athlete may be about the same over the course of their lifetimes. But the schoolteacher's income will be spread over a period of 40 years, whereas most of the athlete's income will be realized in less than 10 years. In any given year, therefore, the two incomes are likely to be highly unequal.

5. Money-Income Data Are Not Adjusted for Age Differences Among Income Groups To a large extent, income inequalities at any given time result from differences in the age and, therefore, in the earning power of the people in question. We don't ordinarily expect young people who have recently entered the job market, or old people who have left it, to have incomes as high as people in midcareer. The money-income data, however, do not distinguish incomes by ages and therefore reflect the inequalities across all ages.

6. Money-Income Data Are Not Adjusted for Regional Price Differences Prices in Mississippi, for example, are much lower than prices in Alaska. Similarly, incomes measured in money terms are much lower in Mississippi than in Alaska. The distribution of money incomes for the two states combined would thus be highly unequal. Correcting for regional differences, however, would result in a more equal distribution in terms of purchasing power of these incomes.

Conclusion: Be Wary of the "Facts"

Studies of income inequality are published frequently, and their results are reported in the news media. The studies are conducted by economists employed in universities, by research organizations, and by government departments. Sometimes these experts conclude that inequality has increased. At other times they conclude that it has decreased. Which assessment is correct?

It is essential to keep in mind that studies of income inequality are always based on very limited information. No one really knows how certain conditions such as subsidies, taxes, family size, and age differences affect inequality between income groups. Consequently, *judgments regarding changes in income inequality should always be regarded with skepticism.*

Income-inequality studies always fall short of accounting for all of the relevant facts. Because of this, conclusions based on such studies are likely either to overstate or to understate the true extent of income inequality. To be meaningful, estimates of income inequality should always be accompanied by explanations of the conditions that have been allowed for, and the conditions that have been neglected, in the measurement of income. Otherwise, the figures don't mean very much.

The Ethics of Distribution

The seventeenth-century English philosopher and essayist Francis Bacon remarked: "Money is like manure; not good except it be spread." But what criteria can be used for deciding how best to spread money? In other words, who should get how much? This is the age-old problem of economic justice—or what economists call "equity."

The problem can have no completely satisfactory solution because justice in any form is at best a tolerable accommodation of the conflicting interests of society. Nevertheless, a number of distributive standards have been proposed over the long history of discussions on the subject. Most of these standards derive from one of three criteria:

1. Distribution based on productive contribution

2. Distribution based on needs

3. Distribution based on equality

Contributive Standard

Most people would agree that a person should be paid what he or she deserves to be paid. This criterion, which fundamentally hinges on *merit*, represents one of the oldest concepts of justice.

Merit, however, is difficult to define and impossible to measure. How can we decide, in a manner acceptable to everyone, what each person merits or deserves? Surely, responsibility in a job is not the criterion, because air-traffic controllers earn far less than heart surgeons but hold more lives in their hands. Nor are years of formal education a criterion; most plumbers are more highly paid than schoolteachers. Certainly, the difficulty of a job is not the criterion, because difficulty depends on individual aptitudes and interests. Many more people can master advanced mathematics than can run a mile in 6 minutes. Almost all other standards of merit lead to similar contradictions. However, there is one measure of merit that is unique to capitalism:

The criterion of distribution in a capitalist society can be expressed by the phrase, "To each according to what he or she produces." This may be called a *contributive standard* **because it is based on the principle of payment according to contribution.**

How is one's productive contribution measured? The most objective way is measuring the value placed upon it in a free market. Here the prices of the factors of production are established by the interactions of demand and supply. The contribution to the total product made by a particular factor of production and the payment received for the contribution can then be measured. This is done by multiplying the price per unit of the factor by the number of units supplied. For example, if the market price of your labor is $10 per hour and you work 2,000 hours each year, your contribution to the total product and the payment you receive are both equal to $20,000. In reality, much more is involved in determining factor contributions and payments than is implied by this simple example. Nevertheless, the illustration emphasizes an important principle:

In a capitalistic or market economy, the payment received for a factor of production is the measure of its worth. This payment reflects the value of the factor's contribution to the total product. *It is determined by the impersonal pressure of market forces—not by the judgment of a central authority.*

Of course, society also recognizes obligations to its nonproducers: the aged, the disabled, the very young, the involuntarily unemployed, and so on. As a result, society employs some noncontributive criteria for apportioning income. But the contributive standard is the dominant one in a capitalistic economy.

Needs Standard

The distributive principle of pure capitalism, as we have seen, can be expressed by the phrase, "To each according to what he or she produces." In contrast, the distributive principle of pure communism may be described by the expression, "To each according to his or her needs."

The *needs standard* is not a distributive principle of communist philosophy only. This standard serves also as the criterion of distribution within most families. Further, in time of war or other emergency, some form of needs standard is often adopted by governments as a basis for rationing a severely limited supply of goods.

Distribution according to need has wide appeal. Upon close examination, however, its implementation poses two major difficulties:

1. "Need" is a normative term. No impersonal mechanism exists for measuring it. Thus, decisions to allocate goods according to need—whether such decisions are made within a family or on a national scale—must be based on someone's personal judgment.

2. Even if individual needs could be measured accurately, it is likely that allocating goods according to a needs standard would not precisely utilize the economy's entire output. There would be either shortages or surpluses, depending on whether the sum of needs was greater or less than the total product. (For example, people may "need" more cars than are produced, or the society may produce more cars than are "needed.") This is less likely to occur when output is distributed according to the contributive criterion of capitalism. Under such a system, market mechanisms tend to equate the incomes people receive with the value of what they contribute.

Equality Standard

A third criterion of distribution, proposed as far back as biblical times, is the *equality standard*. It is expressed most simply by the phrase, "To each equally."

The equality standard disregards the *inequality* of people's contributions. In view of this, is it a just standard? It may be considered so only if we assume that all individuals are alike in the *added* satisfaction or utility they receive from an extra dollar of income. In reality, an additional dollar of income may provide a greater gain in utility to some people than to others. In that case, justice is more properly served by distributing most of any increase in society's income to those who will enjoy it more.

However, there is no conclusive evidence that people are either alike or unlike in the satisfactions they derive from additional income. Therefore, the equalitarians (also called "egalitarians") argue that, because we cannot prove that people are unlike, we should assume that they are alike and distribute all incomes equally.

This conclusion, regardless of how plausible it may seem, illustrates a logical fallacy in reasoning. The fallacy is what philosophers call "argument from ignorance." It is committed whenever someone argues that a proposition is true simply because it has not been proved false, or that it is false because it has not been proved true.

In terms of the equality standard, this implies that we should go beyond the stage of theorizing about individual utilities and consider instead some of the realistic effects of an equality standard. Among the most important are the "motivational" ones:

An equal distribution of income would eliminate the incentive of rewards. There would be no economic motivation for people to develop or apply their skills, or to use economic resources efficiently, because there would be no commensurate return. The result would be declining economic progress and probable stagnation.

This argument assumes, of course, that economic progress attributable to inequality and material rewards is desirable. Some critics think it is not. We discuss this issue in later chapters.

Conclusion: An "Optimal" Distribution?

Is there some "ideal" degree of income inequality—a distribution that is not too extreme either way? What can be said about this hypothesis?

In a society characterized by a very unequal distribution of income, the economic surplus or savings of the rich minority can finance investment in capital.

The result is material and cultural advancement. This was true of such ancient civilizations as Egypt, Greece, and Rome. Their economies were based on slavery—the most unequal distributive system of all. But as a result, they were able to produce magnificent art, architecture, and other cultural achievements.

In a society whose limited income is distributed equally, virtually all income is likely to be spent on basic consumption goods. This leaves little if any savings with which to acquire capital goods. (Here we meet the familiar production-possibilities concept of earlier chapters. It involves the notion that every society makes choices between the proportions of consumption goods and capital goods it wishes to have.) Such a society, because of its equalitarian distributive policy, would tend to remain poor.

Every society seeks the best compromise—the "optimum"—between two extremes of income distribution. One of these extremes is substantial inequality; the other is complete equality. But each society's concept of the optimum depends on the society's goals and institutions. Therefore, there is no objective way of determining that a particular distribution of income is either "good" or "bad."

The Business Sector: Organization and Size

Business decisions and policies influence the nature, structure, and goals of our society. This makes the motives and actions of business firms the subject of ceaseless scrutiny and debate.

How are business firms organized? Why are some of them large and some small? Before we go on to answer these questions, a definition of a firm will be helpful:

A *firm* is a business organization that brings together and coordinates the factors of production—capital, land, labor, and entrepreneurship—for the purpose of supplying goods or services.

Firms may be classified in various ways. One way is to group them according to their products. Firms that turn out similar or identical products are said to be in the same *industry*. Thus, General Motors and Ford Motor Company are in the automobile industry. But General Motors also produces trucks, buses, and diesel locomotives, among other things. Therefore, it would be correct to say that General Motors is also in the truck industry, the bus industry, and the diesel-locomotive industry. Indeed, most large companies make more than one product. Can you name at least five industries in which General Electric is an important producer?

Another method of classifying firms is by their legal form of organization. Three types of organization are particularly common: the individual proprietorship, the partnership, and the corporation. More than 75 percent of all firms in the United States are proprietorships, about 10 percent are partnerships, and the remainder are corporations. Although the proportion of corporations is relatively small, this form of business organization accounts for most of our economy's total output.

The Proprietorship

The simplest, oldest, and most common form of business is the *proprietorship*. This is a firm in which the owner (proprietor) is solely responsible for the activities and liabilities of the business. Most of the firms you see every day, such as bakeries, hair salons, restaurants, gas stations, and television-repair shops are proprietorships. Why are proprietorships so common? Because they are relatively easy to establish. They usually do not require special business skills, experience, or large amounts of capital (although there are some exceptions). But proprietorships have some disadvantages too. They tend to lack stability and permanence, it is difficult for them to raise funds for expansion, and their owners are personally liable for all debts of the business.

The Partnership

A partnership is simply a modified version of a proprietorship. That is, a *partnership* is an association of two or more people to carry on, as co-owners, a business for profit. A partnership has the same kinds of advantages and disadvantages as a proprietorship—but on a somewhat different scale. For example, partners can pool their funds to establish a business and they can combine their talents to manage it. However, they are jointly and personally liable for all debts of the business.

The Corporation

The third form of business organization, and the most important from an economic standpoint, is the corporation. Here is a definition that will be amplified in the following paragraphs:

A *corporation* is an association of stockholders (owners) created under law but regarded by the courts as an artificial person existing only in an abstract legal sense. The chief economic characteristics of a corporation are (1) the limited liability of its stockholders, (2) stability and permanence, and (3) the ability to accumulate large sums of capital through the sale of stocks and bonds.

Some of the ideas in this definition may already be familiar to you. For example:

The ownership of a corporation is divided into units represented by shares of **stock.** A stockholder who owns 100 shares of stock in a corporation has twice as much "ownership" as a stockholder with only 50 shares. Stockholders may participate in the profits of the corporation by receiving **dividends** in the form of a certain amount of money per share. If the corporation doesn't earn a profit, there may be no dividends.

One of the distinguishing features of a corporation is the **limited liability** of its stockholders. The owners of a proprietorship or partnership can be held personally liable for the debts of the business. However, stockholders in corporations cannot be held liable for any of the firm's debts. For almost all practical purposes, the most that stockholders can lose if the business goes bankrupt is the money they paid for their stock.

The corporation has durability. Stockholders may come and go, but the corporation itself lives on. Indeed, some corporations in existence today were originally chartered hundreds of years ago. This permanence enhances the ability of corporations to finance their operations. They can raise large amounts of capital by selling stocks and bonds to the public. A **bond** is a promise to pay a certain sum of money, called "principal," a year or more in the future, plus interest at specified dates in the interim. Bonds may be thought of as *long-term* IOUs. Financial instruments that pay principal and interest in less than a year may be thought of as short-term IOUs.

Stockholders elect a board of directors, which is responsible for the management of the corporation. Each stockholder gets one vote for each share of stock owned. Some stockholders may thus elect themselves to the board if they own enough shares or if they can get the support of enough other stockholders. In large corporations, the board employs executives to manage the company and to report back to the board. In many corporations, one or more officers also serve as members of the board.

Business Size and Problems of Bigness

Most corporations in the United States are "small." Their assets (cash, buildings, equipment, inventories, and so forth) total less than a few hundred thousand, or perhaps up to a few million, dollars each. At the other extreme are corporations whose total assets run to tens of billions of dollars, and whose annual net profits after taxes exceed $1 billion. Some of these large corporations employ hundreds of thousands of workers and distribute profits to hundreds of thousands, or even millions, of stockholders. Together these companies control a large share of the nation's income-producing wealth. The names of most of the large corporations in the United States are already fa-

miliar to you. In fact, you're probably a customer for many of their products. Several of these firms are listed in Exhibit 5.

How big is big? By way of comparison, the annual sales of the largest companies shown in Exhibit 5 often exceed the value of output produced by many countries.

Bigness: Curse or Blessing?

Many observers look at the increasing role of giant firms in the economy and worry about the implications of such concentrations of power. The concerns typically expressed are these:

1.   Stockholders Are Not Managers A striking feature of most large corporations is the *separation of ownership and control.* This means that the stockholders who own the corporation may be so numerous that no single stockholder, or even small group of stockholders, may be able to control the firm. This can create a problem because it leaves the control over the firm's enormous assets to managers. The managers may, once in power,

EXHIBIT 5

Who's Who Among the Giants? America's Ten Largest Industrial Corporations Ranked by Sales, 1991	Company	Sales	Profits	Assets	Profits as a Percent of Sales	Profits as a Percent of Assets
		(in billions of dollars)				
	1. General Motors	123.7	(4.5)	184.3	(3.6)	2.4
	2. Exxon	103.2	5.6	87.6	5.4	6.4
	3. Ford Motor	89.0	(2.3)	174.4	(2.5)	(1.3)
	4. International Business Machines	64.8	(2.8)	92.5	(4.4)	(3.1)
	5. General Electric	60.2	2.6	168.3	4.4	1.6
	6. Mobil	56.9	1.9	42.2	3.4	4.6
	7. Philip Morris	48.1	3.0	47.4	6.2	6.3
	8. E. I. Du Pont de Nemours	38.0	1.4	36.1	3.7	3.9
	9. Texaco	37.6	1.3	26.2	3.4	4.9
	10. Chevron	36.8	1.3	34.6	3.5	3.7

Source: *Fortune,* April 20, 1992. ©1992 Time Inc. All rights reserved.

seek to further their own interests (with handsome salaries and benefits) rather than those of the company and its stockholders (with greater profits). To some extent, government regulations and laws have reduced the magnitude of this problem. But the chances of it arising still exist and will probably never be eliminated completely.

2.   Competing Versus Beneficial Interests   The separation of ownership and control thus contributes to what is known as a ***principal/agent problem.*** This consists of the relationships, which may be conflicting or cooperative, that arise when one party empowers another to act as a representative. In the case of a corporation, for example, the stockholders are principals who employ managers to act as agents. But as you've seen, the relationship between the two groups may be (1) mutually beneficial, or (2) at odds with each other. Because of such possibilities, the principal/agent problem can affect the outcomes of economic decisions. Various aspects of the problem will therefore be examined in later chapters.

3.   Market Domination   A large firm may be more than simply large; it may also be dominant in its own industry. Examples of important industries dominated by a few large companies include aluminum, telecommunications, aircraft engines, and cigarettes. The giants in these industries exercise varying degrees of power over the markets in which they deal. This *may* have several implications for such firms. For instance:

- They *may* be able to charge prices higher than would be charged were the industries more competitive.

- They *may* not improve their efficiency and productivity as much as they would were they subject to greater competition.

- They *may* have the power to influence some of the legislators and federal agencies responsible for regulating them.

While recognizing these negative possibilities, we should also take note of some positive considerations. The productive resources and scientific know-how of many of today's corporate giants are vital to the country in peace as well as in war. As some of the harshest critics of big business have acknowledged, these companies have been instrumental in providing us with the standard of living we now possess.

The Foreign Sector: International Trade and Finance

In addition to the household and business sectors of the economy, there is the foreign sector. This has gained in importance as the world's economies have become increasingly interdependent. A beginning course in economics would be remiss if it failed to take frequent and substantial account of the expanding role played by the foreign sector.

What is the foreign sector? In simplest terms, it's the "rest of the world"—everything beyond the boundaries of our national economy. While it's convenient to think of the foreign sector as a unified whole, in reality its participants are enormously diversified. The foreign sector has nearly six billion people, millions of private businesses, and more than 150 national governments in addition to thousands of local ones. This broad mix of participants embraces different cultures, pursues different goals, and interacts with our economy in varied ways. The interactions give rise to foreign-sector issues that you read and hear about almost every day:

- *Limit imports of goods?* Some foreign manufacturers are able to sell cars, computer chips, and various other products in this country at significantly lower prices than U.S. firms can. Should we impose limits on imports of these goods in order to provide more jobs for U.S. workers?

- *Prohibit exports of jobs?* Several thousand U.S. companies have shifted some of their manufacturing operations to low-wage countries like Mexico and Taiwan. Because this results in numerous U.S. jobs going to foreign workers, should legislation be passed prohibiting firms from "exporting employment"?

- *Prohibit immigration?* Immigration provides the U.S. economy with a source of labor. Much of it is cheap labor because many immigrants are willing to work long hours at low pay. Does this mean that immigration should be prohibited because, as many people believe, immigrants take jobs away from U.S. workers?

- *Limit foreign investment?* A number of foreign companies have invested in the United States by establishing production facilities and by acquiring American businesses. Sony, Toyota, Fuji Bank, British Petroleum, Royal Dutch/Shell, Seagram, Nestlé, and Bayer are among the numerous multinational firms whose neon signs light the skylines of many American cities. Should foreign investment in the United States be limited in order to prevent other countries from "buying up America"?

These issues do hardly more than suggest the increasingly important influence of the foreign sector on our economy. To gain further insight, it proves informative to look at the major types of products that the United States exports to the foreign sector. Among the chief ones are these:

Manufactured Goods   Machinery, transportation equipment, electronics, telecommunications, chemical elements, medicinals, pharmaceuticals, fertilizers, plastics, motor vehicles and parts, paper goods, fabrics, metals, scientific goods, and office equipment

Food Products, Mineral Goods, and Crude Materials   Meat, dairy, grains, fruits, vegetables, tobacco, coal, petroleum, soybeans, wood, textiles, and ores

Services   Banking, insurance, tourism (foreigners visiting the United States, thereby "purchasing" American scenery), education (foreign students attending American universities, thereby purchasing American training), and health care (foreign citizens coming to American hospitals to purchase special services)

This classification covers broad categories of products exported by the United States. Many specific goods and services within these categories are also imported by the United States. Adding together the values of all exports and imports yields a total that amounts to hundreds of billions of dollars annually.

Enlarging the Circular-Flow Model

In light of the importance of the foreign sector, it proves instructive to relate it to the other sectors of the economy that we've studied thus far.

In Chapter 1 you saw how a simple two-sector model consisting of households and businesses could be used to depict the circular flow of economic activity. That model can now be enlarged to include the foreign sector. Doing so brings us a step closer to obtaining a comprehensive overview of the entire circular-flow system. (The final step will be taken in Chapter 4 when we incorporate the government sector in the circular-flow model.)

The enlarged model is presented in Exhibit 6. It differs from the earlier one by the addition of several new flows to and from the foreign sector. Two important ideas conveyed by the illustration require particular attention:

1.   Imports and Exports Take Place Through Markets   The product markets and the resource markets are the links that connect households and businesses with the foreign sector. International trade takes place through these markets. Imports and exports of goods and services go through the product markets, and imports and exports of resources go through the resource markets. Thus, contrary to much popular belief, the activities of importing and exporting are carried on by private firms (not by the government) in response to consumer preferences. Therefore, the questions of *what* goods to produce and *how* to produce them, which are answered in the product and resource markets, remain relevant.

2.   Payments for Exports and Imports Are Made with Foreign Exchange   When goods are imported, they are paid for in the currency of the exporter. Thus, an American automobile importer sells U.S. dollars for Japanese yen in order to pay for Toyota cars. A British cereal company sells British pounds for U.S. dollars in order to pay for American corn. An American tourist visiting France sells U.S. dollars for French francs in order to pay for food and lodging. In general, national currencies (such as dollars, yen, pounds, francs, and pesos) used for making international payments are called *foreign exchange*. These currencies are bought and sold mostly by banks and dealers in a world market called the *foreign exchange market*.

Issues of international trade and international finance deal with some of today's most controversial economic problems. The problems exist because our economy is, in many ways, an integral part of the world economy. Therefore, it is essential that we understand our own as well as other countries' economic policies and activities because they often affect the well-being of the entire community of nations.

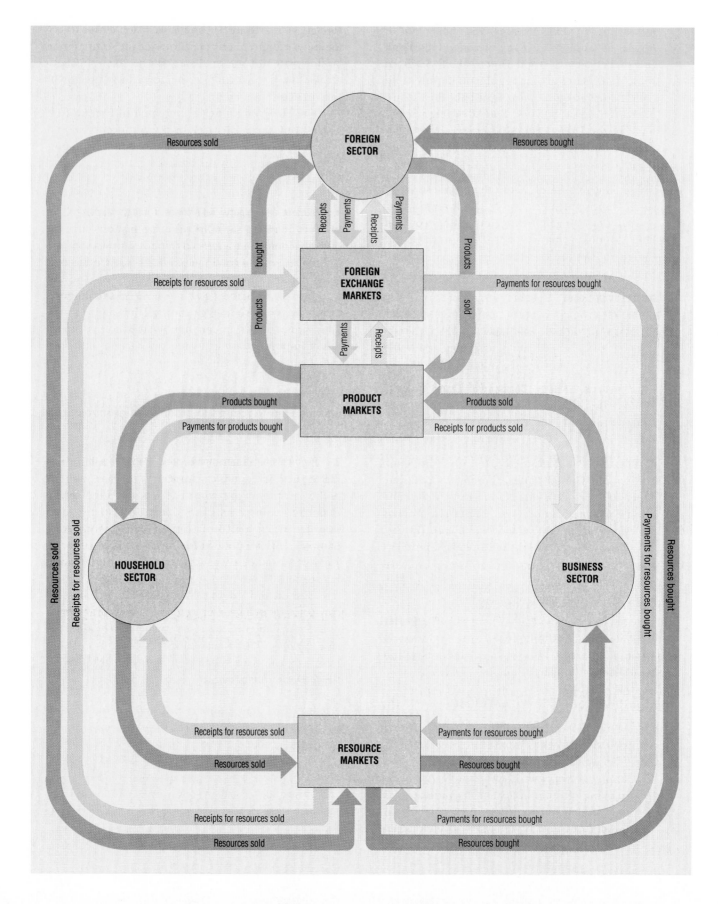

EXHIBIT
6

The Circular Flow of Economic Activity: A Three-Sector Model

The simple two-sector circular-flow model shown earlier used only households and businesses. These are now augmented by the foreign sector(see the model on page 82). Notice how this results in the addition of import and export flows through the product and resource markets, and in the addition of payment flows through the foreign exchange market.

Summary of Important Ideas

1. Income and wealth are among the chief measures of a society's well-being. Their distribution within society and the forces determining their distribution are of central concern.

2. The Lorenz diagram and the corresponding Gini coefficient are the most commonly used devices for measuring inequality in income and wealth. But they are only as reliable as the data and assumptions on which they are based. Therefore, the data and assumptions should always be analyzed with a critical eye.

3. There are many reasons for income inequality. Among the more important are differences in such factors as wealth, earning ability and opportunity, resource mobility, luck, age, human-capital investment, and occupational risk.

4. The degree of income inequality among income groups is affected by such factors as subsidies, taxes, and age differences. The net effects on inequality of some of these factors is not known with any degree of certainty. Therefore, any statements about increases or decreases in income inequality should always be regarded with some skepticism.

5. Ethical criteria exist for allocating income. Three major ones are (a) productive contribution, (b) needs, and (c) equality. The first is the primary standard of distribution in capitalistic economies. The second and third criteria are philosophical goals of pure communistic and of egalitarian societies—neither of which exist anywhere on a national scale.

6. Economic history indicates that the higher a nation's real income per capita, the more that nation tends to progress toward greater income equality. This is because only a rich nation can generate the savings needed to assist its poor. That is why low-income nations tend to have the most unequal distributions of income.

7. The business sector of the economy consists primarily of proprietorships, partnerships, and corporations. The number of proprietorships and partnerships greatly exceeds the number of corporations. However, corporations produce by far the largest proportion of the nation's goods and services. One reason is that corporations can raise large sums of money to finance expansion.

8. The consequences of business bigness are mixed. On the one hand, it has resulted in increased market power for some of the largest firms in various industries. On the other hand, many of the nation's largest firms have also been significantly responsible for some of the major advances in our standard of living and in our military preparedness.

9. The foreign sector, which consists of the households, businesses, and governments of other countries, can be incorporated in a circular-flow model. This augmented model depicts two sets of flows. They are: (a) physical imports and exports between our economy and the rest of the world, and (b) payments for imports and exports through the foreign exchange market.

Terms and Concepts to Review

private sector	*Gini coefficient of*
public sector	*inequality*
income	*firm*
wealth	*industry*
functional income	*proprietorship*
distribution	*partnership*
national income	*corporation*
personal income	*stock*
distribution	*dividends*
Lorenz diagram	*limited liability*
Lorenz curve	*bond*

separation of ownership and control

principal/agent problem

foreign exchange

foreign exchange market

Questions and Problems

1. What are the chief causes of income inequality among households? Would it be better if all incomes were equal? Explain.

2. Is it a necessary condition of capitalism that some people be rich and others be poor? Is it morally right for the government to tax the incomes of the rich and redistribute them to the poor? Defend your answer.

3. We cannot distribute goods according to people's needs because we do not know how to determine those needs. Therefore, why not solve the problem by (a) distributing *incomes* according to needs, and (b) permitting goods to be allocated through the price system, thereby preserving freedom of consumer choice?

4. "The principle of payment according to one's contribution to production (that is, contributive standard) assures that people get what they deserve. Therefore, it is more democratic than payment based on needs or on equality." Do you agree? Explain.

5. "If payments to individuals are based on needs or on equality, some people are bound to be exploited for the benefit of others." Is this statement true? What does "exploitation" mean? Explain.

6. "In a democracy, we do not allocate political votes in proportion to one's intelligence and ability to use them. Instead, everyone gets an equal vote. Therefore, the same should be true of dollar votes (income); everyone's should be equal." Do you agree?

7. "The value of a culture is measured by its peak accomplishments, not by its average level of achievement. Thus, a society of mud huts and one great cathedral is better than a society of stone huts and no cathedral. To put it differently, it is by the quality of its saints and heroes, not its common people, and by its masterpieces, not its domestic utensils, that a culture should be judged." What implications does this have for income distribution?

8. An eminent political scientist, Robert A. Dahl of Yale University, has challenged the assumption that stockholders should control the direction of a company. "I can discover absolutely no moral or political basis," he says, "for such a special right. Why investors and not consumers, workers, or, for that matter, the general public?" What implications does this statement have for the future of capitalism?

9. Can you suggest some advantages and disadvantages of "big" business?

10. What factors account for the long-run growth of our economy's foreign sector?

11. How would the growth of industrial sectors and the rise of living standards in poorer countries help and/or hurt the U.S. economy?

How to Calculate Your Class's Gini Coefficient

The Lorenz curve and the Gini coefficient are usually employed to express the degree of income inequality among families. But you can use these concepts to calculate the degree of *cash* inequality among the students in your class. Here's how to do it.

Step 1 Each student counts the cash in his or her possession, writes the amount on a slip of paper, and submits it to the instructor.

Step 2 The instructor may now ask a few students (depending on the size of the class) to analyze and tabulate the results. These are entered in columns (2) and (3) of the accompanying table. (The resulting table may be reproduced on the board so everyone can see it.) For illustrative purposes, it will be assumed that the class holds a total of $100, as you can verify by adding up the numbers in column (2).

Step 3 Complete columns (4) and (5) of the table. Then enter the letters *A* through *F* as shown in column (6).

Step 4 Construct a Lorenz diagram. *Connect the points with straight lines— not with a curved line.* (Straight lines will enable you to use a simple geometric approach that yields accurate results.) Note that, in this example, the lowest 20 percent of the students are holding 5 percent of the cash; label this point *B* on the Lorenz curve. The lowest 40 percent are holding 15 percent of the cash; label this point *C* on the curve. And so on.

Step 5 Decide how you will calculate the Gini coefficient of inequality. In order to do this, you must determine the inequality area. This is easily done by subtracting the entire area under the Lorenz curve from the large triangular area *AFG*. Here is the way to attack the problem:

First, note that the area under the Lorenz curve is equal to the sum of the separate triangular and trapezoidal areas beneath it. (A trapezoid is a four-sided figure with two parallel and two nonparallel sides.)

Second, to perform the necessary calculations, make use of the fact that the area *A* in terms of the base *b* and height *h* is found as follows:

for a triangle: $A = \frac{1}{2}bh$
for a trapezoid: $A = \frac{1}{2}b(h_1 + h_2)$

where h_1 and h_2 represent the heights of the left and right vertical sides.

Step 6 Now calculate the Gini coefficient of inequality, as follows:

a. Calculate the total triangular area beneath the diagonal (i.e., the area of triangle *AFG*).

Total area beneath the diagonal:
$\frac{1}{2} \times 100 \times 100 = 5,000$

b. Calculate the sum of the areas under the Lorenz curve (i.e., the sum of the small triangular area under *AB* and the four remaining trapezoidal areas under *BCDEF*).

Area beneath the Lorenz curve:
$50 + 200 + 450 + 800 + 1,500 = 3,000$

c. Subtract the answer in step **b** from the answer in step **a**.

Area between diagonal and Lorenz curve:
$5,000 - 3,000 = 2,000$

d. Express the result as a fraction of the total area in step **a**.

Gini coefficient of inequality:
$2,000/5,000 = 0.40$

(1) Percent of students	(2) Cash held	(3) Percent of cash held	(4) Cumulative percent of students	(5) Cumulative percent of cash held	(6) Point on Lorenz curve
0	$ 0	0%	0%	0%	A
Lowest fifth	5	5	20	5	B
Second fifth	10	10	40	15	C
Third fifth	15	15	60	30	D
Fourth fifth	20	20	80	50	E

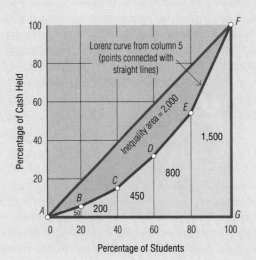

T A K E   A   S T A N D

Income Distribution: Is It Fair?

Economic justice is a basic goal of the economic system. A well-functioning economy not only produces the goods and services that people want, but distributes them in ways that people perceive as fair. In the United States, income and wealth are distributed quite unevenly. The richest 1 percent of the population now controls well over one-third of the nation's wealth. Yet, at the same time, our society has enacted many measures and policies designed to help the poor and promote equality of income. First, the federal income tax was constructed as a progressive system, meaning that those who earn higher incomes should pay a greater percentage of their income in tax. Second, the federal government has implemented a number of relief and income-equality programs, such as Medicaid, social security, and unemployment insurance. Has the United States done a good job of achieving economic justice? *Is the distribution of income fair?*

Yes: The System Rewards Talent and Hard Work

It is neither a surprise that incomes are distributed unequally in the United States and other capitalist economies, nor a problem. A capitalist economy, by its very nature, is one that rewards hard work and ability. Given two equally talented people, greater reward goes to the harder worker. Given two equally hard-working people, greater reward goes to the more talented.

Consider work effort first. People who work hard earn more than people who choose not to work as hard. Nothing could be fairer. It's just like working for a grade in your economics course. You can choose to work hard in pursuit of a higher grade, or you can choose to go to parties instead and risk getting a lower grade. You may make either choice and affect no one but yourself. However, if your professor chose to give everyone in the class the same grade, the outcome would certainly be unfair.

Now consider ability. A free-market economy rewards people according to how highly their skills and talents are rewarded by society. This, too, is fair and just. Movie stars and sports stars earn great incomes in large part because they have abilities that are rare and highly prized. The high incomes of these talented people reflect the high value that society places on their contributions. The same principle holds throughout the income distribution: Rewards received in the marketplace correspond to each individual's contribution to the production of goods and services that people are willing to pay for.

The distribution of income also reflects to some extent people's choices about their investment in human capital. Some individuals choose to get jobs straight out of high school. Others choose to sacrifice earnings early in life in order to go to college and get training that enables them to earn more later. Many professionals, such as lawyers and doctors, also must take many years of graduate training. The high incomes they earn when they qualify in their profession are a fair reward for their early sacrifices.

The free-market system of rewards is, therefore, not only fair, but also crucial to the successful functioning of society because it offers individuals the proper incentives to produce the goods that people are willing to pay for. Without these incentives, our economy would stagnate and everybody would lose. The progressive income tax and other attempts to change the distribution of income through taxation and the funding of social programs are harmful because they distort these incentives.

No: The Rich Are Simply Lucky

In a famous exchange between F. Scott Fitzgerald and Ernest Hemingway, Fitzgerald observed that "the rich are different from us." "Yes," replied Hemingway, "they have more money." The main reasons why the rich are rich and the poor are poor have little to do with effort and ability, and everything to do with inheritance and chance.

The American Dream is that anyone, no matter how poor, can achieve success and riches by dint of ability and sheer hard work. Rags-to-riches stories in the newspapers and on television remind us of this possibility. But the newsworthiness of such stories forces us to recognize that they are also rare. Most people who are born into rich families remain rich; most born poor remain poor. Studies suggest, for example, that close to 80 percent of all children born to parents in the bottom 5 percent of the income distribution will have incomes below the midpoint. Similarly, 80 percent of all children born to parents in the top 5 percent will have incomes above the midpoint. Thus, the role of wealth and circumstance in the distribution of income is undeniable. Inequalities persist through generations and are magnified by the fact that the wealthy also have most of the power in society. The children of the rich have access to the best schools and the best jobs. No wonder the rich stay rich.

The role of chance in the distribution of income is equally undeniable. A skilled worker earning a good wage one day may the next day be out of a job because new technologies have made her skills obsolete. An artist starving one year may the next year find his works fashionable and lucrative. These people

For example, if the rich are taxed at a higher rate, they may actually work harder in order to maintain their standard of living. And it's certainly hard to believe that movie and sports stars would abandon their careers to take jobs as checkout clerks if their taxes were raised. The current system is unfair, and we can use the tax system to make it fairer.

The Question: Is the Distribution of Income Fair?

■ Some believe that the economic system rewards hard work and ability, and that the distribution of income rightly reflects differences in effort and talent.

■ Others believe that incomes are unfairly distributed primarily because the economic system preserves existing inequalities, regardless of effort. If an individual's income does change, the change is usually due to random events completely beyond control.

Where Do You Stand?

1. The elderly are often among the poorer members of society. As the baby-boom generation ages, we might therefore expect to see greater inequality (as, say, measured by the Gini coefficient). Does this mean the distribution of income will become less fair?

2. The philosopher John Rawls (and others) suggested the following thought experiment for considering the justice of different economic and social systems. Suppose that, before you are born, you can choose the type of society in which you will live. You will be randomly assigned a place in that society, however. You might be the daughter of the richest person, or the son of the poorest, or anywhere in between. What sort of society would you choose? Would it resemble that of the United States?

3. If it is fair and just for the system to reward ability, are people who do not have abilities that society values not entitled to any economic rewards?

4. Is the income distribution fair? Justify your stand.

would find their income changing although there have been no changes in their work effort or talent. There is nothing fair or just about such arbitrary changes in fortune; they are random events not at all related to effort or ability.

To put the same point a slightly different way, there are probably children growing up in France or England who could be baseball or basketball superstars, but whose talent is never discovered because they don't get to play baseball or basketball. Equally, there are almost certainly American children who are natural rugby or cricket players, but whose ability will never be discovered or rewarded. Talents that could earn someone millions in the United States today would be worthless in other cultures or at other times, and vice versa.

Finally, our current system of rewards is not necessary for the economy to prosper. Studies suggest that changes in tax rates don't have a large effect on work effort. This makes sense.

Source: Gary Solon, "Intergenerational Income Mobility in the United States," *American Economic Review*, June 1992, pp. 393–408.

Chapter 4

The Public Sector—Government: Public Choice and Taxation

Economic Scope and Functions of Government

Spillovers, Market Failure, and Public Choice

Public-Sector Budgeting

Our Tax System

Theories of Taxation

Completing the Circular-Flow Model

Origins: Government in the Economy

Learning Guide

Watch for answers to these important questions

What is the role of government in our economy? How do we distinguish between the different types of goods that government provides?

Can government provide goods efficiently? What concepts can help us analyze and evaluate the provision of goods by the public sector?

How does the government raise money? How does it spend money? What methods can be used to achieve greater efficiency in budgeting?

What is the nature of our tax system? What principles are used to evaluate particular taxes and their effects?

Who was John Stuart Mill? What views did he have of the role of government in the economy?

One of the most remarkable trends in contemporary history has been the growth in the importance of government in economic life. As measured by government purchases of goods and services, the public sector bought 10 percent of the nation's total output in 1930. Today the public sector purchases approximately twice that percentage of the nation's total output. These facts raise many questions concerning the economic functions of government in our mixed economy. This chapter examines a few of the more important ones and provides some basic tools for understanding them.

Any serious discussion of government is bound to raise questions about taxes. Taxes, you may recall from your study of history, have sometimes been a major cause of wars and revolutions. Moreover, in our society today, taxes affect economic activity in many different ways.

When we speak of government, we ordinarily mean the federal government. But this chapter will also say some things about government at the state level and the local level. The local level includes counties, cities, villages, townships, school districts, and so on.

Economic Scope and Functions of Government

For centuries, political scholars have theorized about the purposes and functions of government. In *The Wealth of Nations*, Adam Smith said that government's role should be limited to national defense, the administration of justice, the facilitation of commerce, and the provision of certain public works. Many people today would agree with Smith, although some might add a few items to his list. For present purposes, the economic role of government can be considered to consist of two broad functions: (1) the promotion and regulation of the private sector, and (2) the provision of social goods.

Promotion and Regulation of the Private Sector

Government promotes and regulates the private sector in many ways. Sometimes it does this to the net advantage, and sometimes to the net disadvantage, of society as a whole. A complete analysis of the public sector's economic functions is impossible here. However, five major activities can be identified.

Providing a Stable Economic Environment Government facilitates the production, distribution, and consumption of goods and services. It does this by defining property rights, upholding contracts, adjudicating disputes, setting standards for weights and measures, enforcing law and order, and maintaining a monetary system. These activities are so fundamental to organized society that they existed even in ancient civilizations. The Code of Hammurabi (*circa* 2100 B.C.) and the later laws of ancient Egypt and Rome, for example, went into considerable detail in defining property rights and related matters pertaining to commerce.

Protecting the Public Welfare Government establishes health and safety standards in industry and regulates minimum wages for certain classes of workers. It also provides old-age, disability, sickness, and unemployment benefits for those who qualify. Of course, these social welfare measures are enacted primarily for humanitarian reasons. Nevertheless, some of the measures may be tacit admissions that the private sector has failed to fulfill human wants in a manner that society regards as equitable.

Granting Economic Privileges Through selective subsidies, tariffs, taxes, and other legal provisions, government favors particular consumers, industries, unions, and other segments of the economy. This elaborate network of privileges and controls results as much from political pressures as from economic logic. To a large extent, therefore, government privileges cause reduced efficiencies, higher prices, and misallocations of society's resources.

Maintaining Competition Specific laws forbid unregulated monopolies and unfair trade and labor practices. If government enforces these laws vigorously, it helps ensure the perpetuation of a strong private sector.

Encouraging Efficiency, Equity, Stability, and Growth Through appropriate tax, expenditure, and regulatory policies, government seeks to attain certain objectives. These include high employment, an equitable distribution of income, stable prices, and a steady rate of economic growth. The government's efforts are not always successful, however, for political reasons as well as for economic ones. Much of the study of economics is concerned with learning to understand these reasons.

This brief sketch of the economic activities of government leads to an important observation:

The promotional and regulatory activities of government are complex and widespread. Some of these activities are undertaken to correct for market failures. That is, they address the inability of the private sector, if left to itself, to achieve the goals of efficiency, equity, stability, and growth to the degree that society seeks. However, as you will see, the extent to which government activities contribute to the realization of these goals is often debatable.

Provision of Social Goods

All economic systems are concerned with the three fundamental questions: *What* will be produced? *How* will it be produced? and *Who* will receive the final output? In mixed capitalistic economies such as ours, these questions are answered primarily by the market system. But if certain types of goods and services are not, in the public's opinion, adequately provided by a free market, supplying them usually becomes a function of government. In this book we'll refer to such products as **social goods.** For present purposes, they may be classified into two groups—*public goods* and *merit goods.*

Public Goods

Public goods are sometimes called "collective" goods. Examples include national defense, street lighting, disease control, the administration of justice through the courts, air-traffic control, and public safety. An essential characteristic of public goods is that you cannot be excluded from receiving their benefits whether you pay for them or not.

Public goods can thus be distinguished from non-public goods. *Nonpublic goods* are private goods (such as food, automobiles, appliances, clothing, and services) that people buy in the market and certain social goods, known as merit goods, which are described below. Someone who doesn't pay for nonpublic goods can conceivably be excluded from using them. Therefore:

The distinction between public and nonpublic goods rests on what is called the *exclusion principle.* According to this principle, a good is nonpublic if someone who doesn't pay can be excluded from its use. Otherwise, it's a public good.

Merit (Quasi-Public) Goods

In addition to public goods, government provides **merit goods.** These are goods that government deems meritorious, or intrinsically worthy of production. Merit goods share, to different degrees, some of the properties of both public and private goods. Therefore, merit goods are also sometimes called "quasi-public goods." Some examples of merit goods provided by the federal and state governments are parks, public housing, and public hospitals. Some examples of merit goods provided by local governments are municipal libraries, tennis courts, golf courses, and museums.

In contrast to public goods, merit goods are subject to the exclusion principle, *even though the principle may not always be invoked.* Therefore, merit goods are not pure public goods. People could be charged for the use of merit goods instead of being given them "free" or at reduced prices. As you will see, this raises

interesting questions about efficiency and equity, problems that are among the fundamental concerns of economics.

Conclusion: Achieving Efficiency Through the Market

Throughout the nation's history, government has served as a rescuer, subsidizer, owner, and regulator of special interests. It has saved failing companies, financed roads and canals, subsidized industries, sheltered workers, protected consumers and businesses, stabilized credit, refereed competition, and regulated markets.

Government has also become the chief producer of social goods, both public and merit goods. Everyone receives the benefits of the former. The benefits of the latter are widely available and, in most cases, are provided at reduced prices. How does this affect the allocation of such goods?

In a free market, prices perform the allocative function. A resource is always allocated to its highest-valued use, as determined by the prices that buyers offer. But the situation is different with most social goods. Because many are made available "free" or at reduced prices, it is impossible to know the value people place on the goods. How, then, should government decide *what* and *how much* to produce?

A reasonable answer to this question is that government should seek ways of making more effective use of market mechanisms. This can be done through the use of special taxes, grants, and pricing strategies designed to test the demand for certain social goods. In this way, as you'll see below, officials can be guided in learning how to improve efficiency in the provision of these goods. Equally important, legislators can consider whether certain social goods might better be provided through the private sector.

Something to Think About

1. Radio and network television broadcasting are public goods. Why? What about cable television broadcasting?

2. In the United States (but not in most other countries), the great majority of radio and television broadcasts are provided by the private sector. Why do companies incur the costs of producing such goods if people can consume them without paying? Can you think of any other public goods that are provided by the private sector?

3. Are the government's postal services a public good? Why?

Spillovers, Market Failure, and Public Choice

Many social goods (as well as private goods) create "fallout" effects, or *spillovers.* These are external benefits or costs for which no compensation is made. Spillovers are also called *externalities*. The two terms are used interchangeably, so you should be familiar with both.

For example, in the public sector, air-traffic control at busy airports reduces noise for some nearby residents while increasing it for others. This is an unpaid-for benefit to the former and an uncompensated "cost" to the latter. In the private sector, similarly, a factory may provide income and employment to a community while polluting its environment. Thus, spillover benefits and costs exist with some private goods as well as with some social goods.

Spillovers are an indication of *market failure.* That is, their occurrence in a competitive free market is a sign that the market hasn't allocated its resources efficiently. As you will recall from your study of demand and supply, resource misallocation occurs if a good's costs and/or benefits are not fully reflected by its equilibrium price. When that happens, it is because the good's demand and supply curves do not incorporate the full value of society's sacrifices and preferences. The values that are not incorporated are externalities or spillovers. Their existence accounts for the failure of competitive free markets to provide outputs that are socially ideal.

Redressing Spillovers

What can be done to correct for the effects of spillovers? Because they are associated with private-sector market failure, corrective action to eliminate or offset them can come only from government. Two major approaches may be considered—market measures and nonmarket measures.

Market Measures: Internalizing the Externalities

One way of correcting for the effects of spillovers is to look for ways to incorporate them into a good's market demand and market supply curves. This is illustrated in Exhibit 1. Thus:

In Figure (a), any point on the normal market demand curve D expresses the **demand price.** This is the highest price that buyers are willing to pay for a given quantity of the good. The demand curve thus reflects only private benefits to buyers, not spillover benefits to nonbuyers or to society.

Similarly, any point on the normal market supply curve S expresses the **supply price.** This is the least price necessary to bring forth a given output. That is, it is the lowest price that sellers are willing to accept in order to supply a given quantity of the good. The supply curve thus reflects only private costs to producers, not spillover costs to anyone else.

The diagram assumes that *all* benefits and costs are incorporated in the demand and supply curves—there are no spillovers. Accordingly, the equilibrium quantity at Q is socially ideal because it represents an optimum allocation of society's resources. However, if all benefits and costs are not included in the demand and supply curves, then spillovers exist. The equilibrium quantity is not socially ideal. In that case, government can undertake either of two sets of policy measures to correct the situation:

Internalize Spillover Costs by Incorporating Them into the Market Supply Curve The effect of this approach is shown in Figure (b). It illustrates the case of an industry that pollutes its environment, thereby externalizing some costs of production to others. As a result, the supply curve S is "too low" because it does not include *all* of the costs of producing the product. Because of this, the equilibrium quantity is at Q rather than at Q'.

One measure that government can adopt to correct the situation is to require sellers to pay a *specific tax.* This is a per-unit payment on a good. That is, sellers would pay the tax T on each unit of the good produced. This would increase its costs of production by the amount of the tax, causing the supply curve to shift from S to S'. If the tax is large enough, it can compensate for any spillover costs that were not included in the original supply curve. The tax will thus reduce output from the level at Q to the socially optimum level at Q'. (*Question:* Can you show how the ideal output may also be achieved by imposing a specific tax on buyers?)

EXHIBIT
1

Spillover Effects in a Competitive Market

FIGURE (a) No Spillovers When the demand and supply curves include *all* costs and benefits, there are no spillover effects. The equilibrium quantity at *Q* is optimum, or ideal.

FIGURE (b) Spillover Costs Because some costs are externalized, resources are overallocated, and "too much" of the good (equal to *Q'Q*) is produced. To achieve the ideal output at *Q'*, government can impose a specific tax of *T* per unit on sellers. This will raise the supply curve from *S* to *S'*.

FIGURE (c) Spillover Benefits Because some benefits are externalized, resources are underallocated and "too little" of the good (equal to *QQ'*) is produced. Government can achieve the ideal output at *Q'* by giving buyers a specific subsidy of *U* per unit. This will shift the demand curve upward from *D* to *D'*.

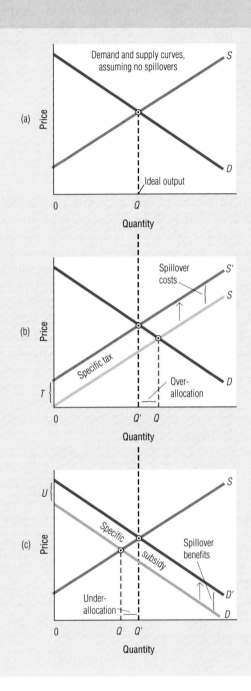

Internalize Spillover Benefits by Incorporating Them into the Market Demand Curve The effect of this approach is shown in Figure (c). It illustrates the case of an industry, such as private higher education, that externalizes some benefits by providing society with a more informed and concerned citizenry. As a result, the demand curve *D* is "too low" because it doesn't include *all* of the benefits obtained from the product.

Because of this, the equilibrium quantity is at *Q* rather than at *Q'*.

To correct this, government can bring about an increased output of the product by giving buyers a *specific subsidy*. This is a per unit grant on a commodity. As shown in the graph, buyers would receive the subsidy *U* on each unit of the good purchased. This would increase the consumption of the good, causing the demand curve to shift from D to D'. If the subsidy is large enough, it can compensate for any spillover benefits that weren't included in the original demand curve. Thus, the subsidy will increase output from the level at Q to the socially optimum level at Q'. (*Question:* Can you demonstrate that government can also achieve the ideal output by granting a specific subsidy to sellers?)

Nonmarket Measures: Government Regulation and Provision

In addition to the foregoing market devices, government can employ various nonmarket measures to influence output and resource allocation. This is accomplished by enacting appropriate legislation. For instance:

> Through government *regulation,* the outputs of some products (and by-products) for which spillovers are deemed to be undesirable can be reduced. Examples are industrial-waste disposal, smoke emission, and water pollution. In terms of Figure (b), in Exhibit 1, the purpose of such regulation is to shift the supply curve *upward* to achieve results similar to those attained by market measures (such as taxing sellers).

> Through government *provision,* the output of some goods for which spillovers are deemed to be desirable can be enlarged. You will recall that when government makes available such products, they are called "merit goods." Examples include public recreation, public housing, and public higher education. In terms of Figure (c), the purpose of such provision is to shift the supply curve *downward,* to achieve the same ideal output attained by market measures (such as subsidizing buyers).

> Thus, government regulation and provision, by their very nature, focus on influencing the supply of goods, not the demand for them.

Dealing with International Spillovers

National governments can address the domestic spillovers created by production within their own countries. But in many cases international spillovers occur. These result in external costs for some countries and external benefits for others.

Examples of international spillover costs are easy to find. Global warming, caused by heat-trapping gases belched out of power plants and cars, can melt polar ice caps, flood coastal cities, and turn farmland into deserts. Stratospheric erosion, caused by chemicals and gases that eat away Earth's protective ozone layer, may subject people to excessive ultraviolet radiation. Pollution of the oceans and destruction of rainforests can alter food chains and organic systems.

Examples of international spillover benefits are also apparent. National defense helps provide protection to neighboring friendly countries. Thus, Canada and Mexico are more secure when the United States is well-protected. Improvements in education make for a more enlightened world citizenry. And advances in disease control, technology, and information systems create benefits that accrue to all nations.

The ability to redress international spillovers lies beyond the scope and authority of a single national government. In view of this, is efficient resource allocation possible? The answer, in principle, is yes. Countries often join global agencies or negotiate agreements to deal with international spillovers. The United Nations is the most obvious example of a world organization established to address issues created by global externalities—including defense, disease prevention, and environmental pollution. Other examples include the North Atlantic Treaty Organization, the World Bank, the European Community, and the Association of Southeast Asian Nations.

Redressing spillovers is more difficult when they reach beyond national boundaries. However, the existence of international spillovers helps explain why national governments extend the scope of their activities into the global economy.

Conclusion: Efficiency and Public Choice

The analysis of spillovers leads to three important generalizations.

1. Referring back to Figure (b) of Exhibit 1, a competitive free market *overallocates* resources to the production of a good that has spillover costs. Consequently "too much" of the good is produced relative to its ideal output.

2. Referring back to Figure (c) of Exhibit 1, a competitive free market *underallocates* resources to the production of a good that has spillover benefits. Because of this, "too little" of the good is produced relative to its ideal output.

3. Government alters the outputs of many goods that have spillover costs and benefits. The alterations

are accomplished both by market mechanisms such as taxes and subsidies, and by nonmarket mechanisms such as regulation, provision, and international agreement.

The analysis of spillover costs and benefits is part of a larger branch of economics known as *public choice.* This may be defined as the study of nonmarket collective decision making, or the application of economics to political science. Public choice seeks to explain how and why government does what it does. The hope is that this will lead to developing ways of improving efficiency in the public sector—in the provision of social goods.

Public-Sector Budgeting

In the past few decades, the U.S. public sector has been characterized by a remarkable growth of expenditures at all levels of government—federal, state, and local. This means that a rising volume of the nation's output is being allocated by collective (rather than private) decision making. The long-run trends can be seen in Exhibit 2. There are four major reasons for the growth of government spending:

1. **Increased Demand for Social Goods and Services** The public sector has increased its expenditures on social goods, including education, transportation, social security, housing, and consumer protection.

2. **National Defense** A large part of the increase in federal spending can be attributed to expenditures on defense-related activities. These include both military personnel and military equipment.

3. **Interest on the Federal Debt** The last few decades have witnessed a huge rise in the interest payments made on our growing national debt. (The national debt is also called the public debt or the government debt.)

4. **Lagging Productivity of Government Employees** Productivity in the delivery of government services has frequently lagged behind rising costs. Consequently, government has found that the salaries and fringe benefits it pays its employees often grow faster than the efficiency of the services they perform.

As you might guess, any discussion of public-sector expenditures is bound to raise questions about public-sector revenues. The methods used by governments to manage their revenues and expenditures constitute

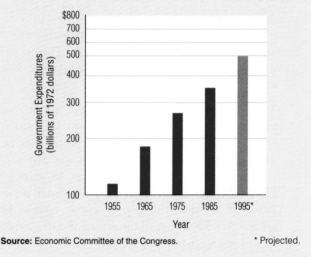

EXHIBIT 2

Growth of Government Expenditures

The size of the public sector, measured by government expenditures, has expanded steadily. Note that the vertical axis is expressed in constant dollars of a previous year. This removes the effects of inflation so that the data are not exaggerated by rising prices.

Source: Economic Committee of the Congress.   * Projected.

what is known as "public budgeting." Exhibit 3 describes and illustrates some trends of government budgets. It's important that you read the explanations accompanying the graphs in order to gain a better understanding of the role of government in our economy.

Budgeting for a government, like budgeting for a family, is an activity dealing with hopes and daydreams as well as hard facts. What is a *budget*? It is an itemized estimate of expected revenues and expenditures for a given period in the future. The federal budget covers a fiscal year. (A fiscal year is any 12-month period for which a business, government, or other organization plans the use of its revenues.) The budgets of some state and local governments cover a fiscal period that is longer than a year (typically 2 years).

Public Overspending and Public Choice

One of the notable trends that can be seen in Exhibit 3 is the persistent tendency of government outlays to exceed government receipts. Virtually all of the world's democracies have had similar experiences.

EXHIBIT
3

Federal, State, and Local Budgets: What Happens to Your Tax Dollars?

FIGURE (a) The government's total revenues and expenditures for any given year are rarely equal. When they are, the budget is said to be *balanced*. When total revenues exceed total expenditures in any given year, the budget is said to have a *surplus*. When total revenues are less than total expenditures, the budget is said to have a *deficit*.

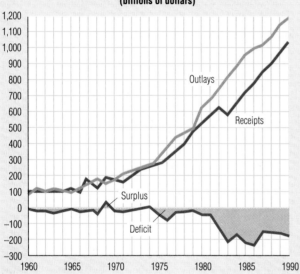

(a) Federal Budget Receipts and Outlays: 1960–1990
(billions of dollars)

FIGURE (b) For the federal government, *income taxes*, both individual and corporate, constitute the largest source of receipts. *Income security* payments, including social security benefits, unemployment compensation, public assistance (welfare), and federal employment retirement and disability benefits, constitute the largest category of outlays.

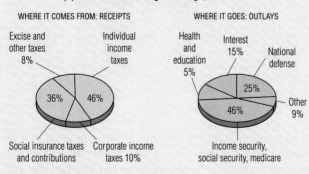

(b) Annual Federal Budget: Average, 1990–1992

WHERE IT COMES FROM: RECEIPTS

Excise and other taxes 8%
Individual income taxes 46%
36%
Social insurance taxes and contributions
Corporate income taxes 10%

WHERE IT GOES: OUTLAYS

Health and education 5%
Interest 15%
National defense
25%
Other 9%
46%
Income security, social security, medicare

Source: U.S. Department of Commerce preliminary data and estimates.

FIGURE (c) For state and local governments combined, *property taxes* (such as on land and buildings) and *sales taxes* make up the chief single sources of tax income. *Education* is the largest single category of expenditure.

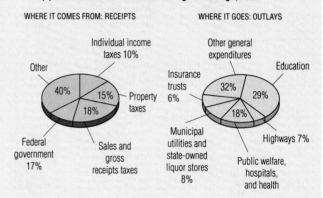

(c) State and Local Government Budgets: Average, 1990–1992

WHERE IT COMES FROM: RECEIPTS

Individual income taxes 10%
Other 40%
15% Property taxes
18%
Federal government 17%
Sales and gross receipts taxes

WHERE IT GOES: OUTLAYS

Other general expenditures 32%
Education 29%
Insurance trusts 6%
18%
Municipal utilities and state-owned liquor stores 8%
Highways 7%
Public welfare, hospitals, and health

FIGURE (d) Over the long run, state and local governments have received a rising percentage share of total tax revenues. In contrast, the federal government has received a declining percentage share. These trends reflect the need of state and local governments to finance their growing public functions.

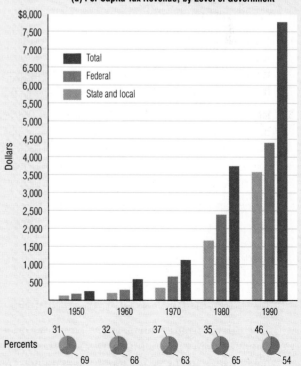

(d) Per Capita Tax Revenue, by Level of Government

They have found it nearly impossible to achieve long-run reductions in government spending, and they have found it equally difficult to raise taxes sufficiently to cover their spending. The result has been recurrent and, in many cases, mounting budget deficits. These occur because government (like many individuals) borrows in order to finance expenditures beyond its means.

Why has public overspending become chronic and seemingly uncontrollable? Public-choice experts offer an answer:

- Just as producers operate through the market system to satisfy consumers, elected politicians operate through the *voting* system to satisfy constituents.

- To an extent, politicians, as well as voters, act in pursuit of what they genuinely consider to be the "public interest." But also, to an extent, they act in pursuit of what they see as their own material interests. For most politicians these include enlarging their benefits and getting re-elected.

- Politicians therefore respond to voters by enacting spending programs that benefit constituents while refraining from enacting the tax legislation needed to finance the programs.

Public-choice scholars thus emphasize a fundamental distinction between public service and the public interest. The failure of society to recognize this distinction, they say, has been a major cause of the growth of big government.

What can be done to reverse this trend? Legislation is not sufficient, because history shows that political leaders can change the laws to fit their needs. Therefore:

According to public-choice experts, spending constraints must be imposed on politicians. The surest way of doing this is a constitutional amendment to balance the budget annually. This would require Congress to finance spending with taxes (rather than borrowing), thus making the public aware of the price it is paying for benefits received.

Scope of Government in Different Countries

Any discussion of government is likely to raise questions about its size. This in turn raises further questions about the cost to taxpayers of maintaining gov-

ernment, and its role in the economic system. History and experience show that, the larger the size of government, the more costly it is to maintain and the greater its involvement in the economy. Three measures—*size, cost,* and *involvement*—thus go hand in hand in reflecting the overall scope of government.

One way of measuring scope is to estimate government's tax revenues as a percentage of the value of the economy's total output. The result can then be compared with the same type of percentages estimated for other nations. This is done in Exhibit 4. It shows public-sector tax revenues as a percentage of total output for a number of countries. As you can see, in the United States tax revenues are approximately 30 percent of total output. But for the majority of other nations, tax revenues average between 35 and 50 percent of total output. Thus, by this measure of scope, the U.S. public sector isn't as large relative to the total economy as is the public sector in other major countries.

This suggests that, in other capitalistic nations, government involvement in the economy is considerably greater than it is in the United States. The evidence supports this belief. In Australia, Canada, New Zealand, and western European countries, partial or complete government ownership of industries deemed "essential" is common. Some of the major ones include airlines, railroads, television, communications, and health care. In Japan, South Korea, Taiwan, and other Asian capitalistic countries, private ownership prevails. However, selective government direction and assistance in the form of subsidies, tax favors, and import protection are frequently provided. And in Latin American, African, and some eastern European capitalistic countries, private ownership mixed with varying but substantial doses of government ownership, direction, and assistance are typical. Thus:

Government occupies an important position in all capitalistic economies. However, the U.S. government appears to play a relatively smaller role in the American economy than the governments of other capitalistic countries play in their economies.

Our Tax System

Government budgets deal not only with expenditures but also with revenues. Governments raise revenues through taxation. In view of this, we must ask: What is the nature of our tax system?

EXHIBIT
4

Scope of Government in Different Countries: Tax Revenues as a Percent of Output, 1990

Taxes collected by all levels of government in the United States average about 30 percent of the value of total output. This percentage is among the lowest of capitalistic countries, where tax collections average between 35 and 50 percent of output.

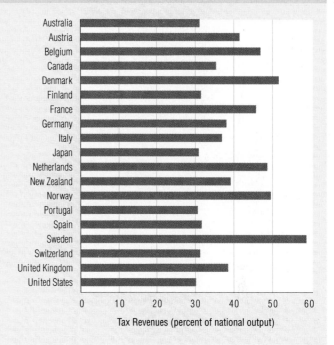

Source: U.S. Department of Commerce.

Tax Revenues (percent of national output)

A **tax** is a compulsory payment to government. Taxes can be levied and classified in many ways. In our own country and in many other nations, there are three principal types of taxes:

1. Taxes on income
   a. Personal income taxes
   b. Corporate income taxes

2. Taxes on wealth (including its ownership and transfer)
   a. Property taxes
   b. Death (estate and inheritance) and gift taxes

3. Taxes on activities (consumption, production, employment, and so forth)
   a. Sales and excise taxes
   b. Social security taxes

Some of these taxes are levied by the federal government, some by state and local governments, and some by all three. Although various other less important kinds of taxes exist, nearly all can be placed in one of the preceding three categories.

Taxes on Income

Income taxes are based on net income—what remains after certain items are deducted from gross income. The items that can be deducted and the tax rates that are applied are specified by law.

Personal Income Tax

In poetry, spring is a time when young people's fancies turn to thoughts of love. But in economics, spring is a much more mundane and certainly less romantic period. It is the season when millions of Americans begin to sort their previous year's income and expense records. As shown in Exhibit 5, this is the first step in determining your personal income tax.

In calculating this tax, you are allowed to take specific types of deductions and exemptions. Some deductions that may be made (within limits) from your income are donations to various nonprofit organizations such as the Red Cross, the Salvation Army, and your alma mater. You may also deduct (subject to certain provisions) some payments for doctor's bills, taxes paid to state and local governments, interest paid on some loans, and various other outlays. In addition, lim-

EXHIBIT 5

Structure of the Federal Personal Income Tax

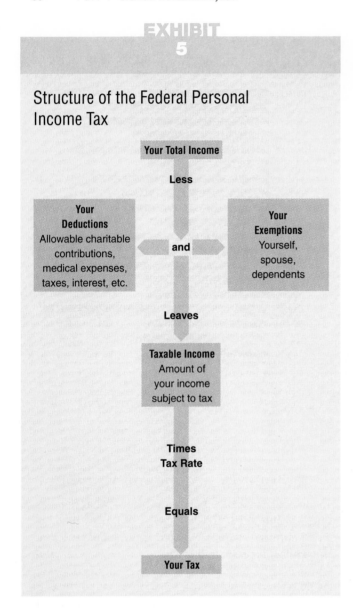

EXHIBIT 6

Federal Tax Brackets Change Frequently for Individuals

Income tax rates are based on *taxable income*, which is total income less deductions and exemptions.

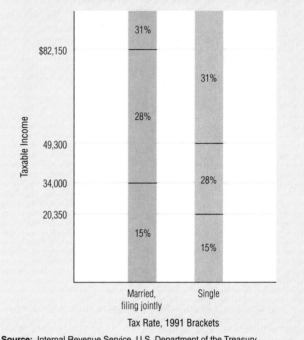

Source: Internal Revenue Service, U.S. Department of the Treasury.

Average Tax Rate   This is the proportion of total taxable income that you pay in taxes. That is:

$$\text{Average tax rate} \times \text{total taxable income} = \text{total personal income tax}$$

ited exemptions are permitted for support of yourself and your dependents. In this way, the government acknowledges that larger families require more funds than smaller ones do to meet their living costs.

The amount of income tax you must pay at a given income level depends on several things. These include whether you are single or married and what the particular tax rates happen to be at the time. The rates are usually revised by the government every few years, as you can see from Exhibit 6. Nevertheless, certain general principles underlying a tax-rate schedule never change. The most important involve a distinction between two types of rates—average and marginal.

Income, for tax purposes, is always expressed in annual terms. Thus, suppose you get a job at a salary which, after deductions and exemptions, leaves you with a total taxable income of $25,000 annually. If the tax laws are such that your average tax rate on that income is 20 percent, your total personal income tax will be $5,000.

In most cases we're more interested in the tax rate than in the amount of the tax. The *average tax rate* in the above equation can therefore be expressed by the formula:

$$\text{Average tax rate} = \frac{\text{total personal income tax}}{\text{total taxable income}}$$

Marginal Tax Rate If your taxable income increases, the amount of the increase is called "marginal income." But an increase in your taxable income will also result in an increase in the tax you pay—called "marginal tax." The *marginal tax rate* is the ratio of marginal tax to marginal income. Thus, suppose your total taxable income for a particular year increases by $4,000. If, as a result, you pay an additional tax of $1,000, your marginal tax rate is 25 percent. Stated in terms of a formula:

$$\begin{aligned} \frac{\text{Marginal}}{\text{tax rate}} &= \frac{\text{marginal tax}}{\text{marginal income}} \\[2mm] &= \frac{\substack{\text{change in total} \\ \text{personal income tax}}}{\substack{\text{change in total} \\ \text{taxable income}}} \end{aligned}$$

The marginal tax rate is the fraction, or percentage, of each additional dollar of income that is paid in taxes. However, because income tax rates are graduated according to income, the marginal tax rate is greater at higher income levels than at lower ones.

You can now see why two controversial aspects of the personal income tax are especially worth noting. They are incentives and loopholes.

Incentives The degree of graduation—or steepness—of the marginal tax-rate schedule undergoes frequent revision by Congress. These changes can have serious economic consequences. Rates must be high enough at all income levels to yield the desired amounts of revenues. However, rates that are too high at the upper income levels may discourage investment and risk taking. Correspondingly, rates that are too high at the lower income levels may reduce the incentive for taking on overtime work or second jobs. In view of this, is there a "best" or optimum tax-rate schedule for the economy as a whole? There probably is. But it changes as conditions change, reflecting political as well as economic circumstances of the times.

Loopholes Legal methods of *tax avoidance* enable many taxpayers to reduce their average rates. This is because our tax system contains various legal "loopholes" that permit relative tax advantages for people in almost every income class. For example, some types of income are exempt from taxes, such as income earned from certain types of financial investments. Similarly, some types of payments are deductible from income for tax purposes, such as interest paid on a primary home mortgage. Although changes in the tax laws have, over the years, closed many loopholes, it is not likely that they will ever be entirely eliminated. (By contrast, illegal methods of escaping taxes, such as lying about income or expenses, come under the general heading of *tax evasion*.)

Nearly all taxpayers, rich and poor alike, benefit from tax loopholes of one form or another. However, the greatest share of benefits from tax loopholes tends to benefit taxpayers with above-average incomes. Although many people do not realize it, this group also pays more than half the total personal income tax bill.

Corporate Income Tax

A significant source of revenue to the federal government is the corporate income tax. (Many states also tax corporate incomes, but at lower rates.) The corporate income tax is based on profit—the difference between a company's total income and its total expenses. The tax rate has varied over the years. During recent decades, it has averaged substantially less than 50 percent.

The corporate income tax raises some important issues. Among them:

- Some authorities argue that lower rates would leave corporations with more funds to use for expanding their operations, thereby creating more jobs. Others, however, contend that the rates should be higher, enabling government to reduce other taxes, especially personal income taxes.

- There is considerable controversy over who ultimately bears the burden of the corporate income tax. Some economists believe that the tax is shifted "forward" to consumers in the form of higher prices. Others contend that much of the tax is shifted "backward" to resource owners in the form of lower wages, rents, etc. Still other authorities believe that the tax is borne by the owners (stockholders) of the corporation because the tax is imposed on corporate profit. That is, the money the shareholders would receive as dividends is reduced because the corporation must pay income tax.

- The corporate income tax involves a form of *double taxation*. The corporation pays a tax on its profits, and the stockholder pays a personal income tax on the dividends received from those profits. Because of this multilevel impact of the corporate income tax, as well as its shiftability, it is widely believed to be both inefficient and inequitable.

There are no simple resolutions for these controversial issues. Each has valid aspects that are subject to frequent debate.

The remaining two categories that make up the structure of the American tax system are taxes on wealth and taxes on activities.

Taxes on Wealth

Property taxes are levied almost exclusively on land and buildings to help pay for public services. The taxes vary from relatively low rates in some rural areas to relatively high rates in localities with expensive public services.

Death taxes are levied, at the time of death, on estates by the federal government and on inheritances by some state governments. An estate is the value of everything that someone owns; an inheritance is an amount that someone receives. Like income taxes, death taxes exempt smaller estates and inheritances but tax the unexempt portions at progressive rates. Many wealthy people might try to avoid these taxes by distributing most of their property before death. Therefore, *gift taxes* are imposed on the transfer of assets beyond certain values. However, various legal devices, most notably trust funds, have enabled many people to lighten the burden of these taxes.

Taxes on Activities

Sales taxes are imposed by many state and local governments. These taxes are flat percentage levies on the retail prices of many goods and services. In some states or cities, food, medicine, and certain services are exempt from sales taxes. In other places, they are not. The federal government imposes no general sales tax on the final sale of goods. However, it does impose special sales taxes, called *excise taxes,* on the manufacture, sale, or consumption of specific commodities such as liquor, tobacco products, gasoline, and certain other goods.

Social security taxes are federal payroll taxes on wages and salaries. The taxes finance compulsory social programs that provide benefits to retired and disabled persons and to dependents of deceased workers. The taxes are imposed both on employees and on employers and are based on the incomes of the former. After a person has earned a certain amount each year, his or her income above that level is exempt from the tax.

An International Comparison of Tax Systems

The American tax system is a complex mixture of various types of taxes. Are they similar to those employed in other advanced nations? The answer is yes. All of the advanced countries rely primarily on four types of taxes—personal income, corporate profits, social security, and consumption. However, although the kinds of taxes employed are alike, the proportion of revenues that governments derive from each can differ considerably.

The proportions are shown for a number of advanced countries in Exhibit 7. As you can see, Canada, Sweden, and the United States rely relatively heavily on personal income taxes. Japan depends less on personal income taxes and more on corporate profits taxes. The governments of these four countries obtain

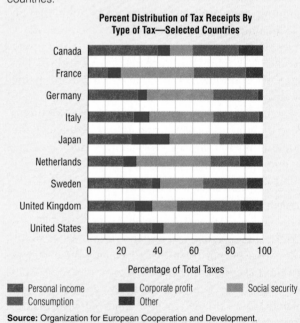

EXHIBIT 7

International Comparison of Taxes, 1988
(latest comparable data)

Nations finance most of their government expenditures with four kinds of taxes—personal income, corporate profit, social security, and consumption. The proportion of total tax revenues derived from each tax varies considerably between countries.

Percent Distribution of Tax Receipts By Type of Tax—Selected Countries

Canada
France
Germany
Italy
Japan
Netherlands
Sweden
United Kingdom
United States

0   20   40   60   80   100
Percentage of Total Taxes

- Personal income
- Consumption
- Corporate profit
- Other
- Social security

Source: Organization for European Cooperation and Development.

roughly the same proportion of their total revenues from personal income and corporate profits taxes together. In contrast, the governments of the other nations shown rely more strongly on social security taxes and on consumption taxes.

Why do these differences exist? Are there underlying principles that can account for the differences? Unfortunately, there is no simple answer.

In each nation, complex mixtures of tradition, culture, politics, and economics all play a role in influencing the types of taxes that are employed. As a result, it isn't possible to give any general reasons as to why certain types of taxes are relatively more important in some countries than in others.

Theories of Taxation

The power to tax is not only the power to destroy but also the power to keep alive.

So stated the U.S. Supreme Court in a famous case in 1899. Today hardly anyone would disagree. Because the power to tax is so weighty a matter, economists have developed several broad standards for judging the merits of a tax:

1. **Equity**   Tax burdens should be distributed justly.

2. **Efficiency, Stability, and Growth**   A tax should contribute toward improving resource allocation, economic stabilization, and growth in the total output of goods and services.

3. **Enforceability**   A tax should be adequate for its purpose and acceptable to the public, or else it will be impossible to enforce.

These criteria are simple and persuasive. But implementation, especially of equity, has caused much controversy. Let's see why.

Principles of Tax Equity

A good tax system should be fair. If people believe it is unfair—that too many loopholes benefit some people and not others—taxpayers' morale and the effectiveness of the tax system will deteriorate. Therefore, an ideal tax system imposes an equal tax *burden*—the "pain" of paying taxes—on everyone. To help achieve this objective, two standards of tax equity have evolved over the years.

Horizontal Equity   The doctrine of *horizontal equity* is that "equals should be treated equally." This means that people who are economically equal should bear equal tax burdens. That is, if people have the same income, wealth, or other taxpaying ability, they should pay the same amount of tax.

Vertical Equity   The doctrine of *vertical equity* is that "unequals should be treated unequally." This means that people who are economically unequal should bear equal tax *burdens*. That is, people with different incomes, wealth, or other taxpaying abilities should pay different amounts of tax so that everyone sacrifices equally.

Horizontal and vertical equity are standards for judging the fairness of a tax. Efforts to apply these standards have resulted in two fundamental principles of taxation—the benefit principle and the ability-to-pay principle.

Benefit Principle

The *benefit principle* holds that people should be taxed according to the benefits they receive. For example, the tax you pay on gasoline reflects the benefit you receive from driving on public roads. The more you drive, the more gasoline you use and the more taxes you pay. These tax revenues are typically set aside for financing highway construction and maintenance. Similarly, local governments pay for at least part of the construction of streets and sewers by taxing those residents who benefit directly from them.

What is wrong with the benefit principle as a general guide for taxation? There are two major difficulties:

- Relatively few publicly provided goods and services exist for which all benefits and beneficiaries can be readily determined. For many goods and services, the benefits would be impossible to determine. The entire nation benefits from social goods, such as public education, health and sanitation facilities, police and fire protection, and national defense. How can we decide which groups should pay the taxes for these things and which should not?

- Those who receive certain benefits may not be able to pay for them. For instance, it would be impossible to finance public welfare aid or unemployment compensation by taxing the recipients.

Ability-to-Pay Principle

The **ability-to-pay principle** states that the fairest tax is one that is based on the ability of the taxpayer to pay it, regardless of who derives the benefits from the tax. Therefore, the more wealth a person has or the higher his or her income, the higher the tax rate should be. This is based on the assumption that each dollar of taxes paid by a rich person "hurts" less than each dollar paid by a poor one. The personal income tax in the United States is structured on this principle.

There are two major difficulties in the use of this principle as a general guide for taxation:

- Ability to pay is a debatable concept—difficult to determine and impossible to measure. How can we really *know* that an additional thousand dollars a year in income means less to a rich person than to a poor person? The concept involves psychological and philosophical issues that economics is not equipped to explore.

- Even if we *assume* that certain taxes should be based on ability to pay, how can we distinguish between degrees of ability among different individuals? You may feel that a person who earns $50,000 a year is able to pay a higher tax rate than someone who earns $25,000. But *how much* higher? There is no simple answer, and no answer that is unarguably "just."

Real-World Compromises: Three Classes of Tax Rates

As a result of these difficulties, it has become necessary to adopt methods of implementing the benefit and ability-to-pay principles. The methods may not always be ideal, but they have proven to be practical.

Thus, three major classes of tax rates—proportional, progressive, and regressive—have evolved over the years. These types of rates differ from each other according to the way in which the amount of the tax is related to the **tax base.** This is the item being taxed. The value of property is the tax base for a property tax. Income is the tax base for an income tax. The value of goods sold is the tax base for a sales tax. When the total tax is divided by the tax base, the resulting figure, expressed as a percentage, is called the **tax rate.** Thus, a $10 tax on a tax base of $100 represents a tax rate of 10 percent. It follows that the tax base times the tax rate equals the tax yield to the government. This principle applies to all types of taxes.

Proportional Tax   A **proportional tax** is one whose percentage rate *remains constant* as the tax base increases. Consequently, the amount of the tax paid is proportional to the tax base. The property tax is an example. If the tax rate is constant at 5 percent, someone who owns property valued at $10,000 pays $500 in taxes. Someone who owns property valued at $100,000 pays $5,000 in taxes.

Progressive Tax   A **progressive tax** is one whose percentage rate *increases* as the tax base increases. In the United States, the federal personal income tax is the best example. The tax is graduated so that, theoretically, a person with a higher income pays a greater percentage in tax than a person with a lower income. We say "theoretically" because in reality certain loopholes in the tax structure reduce the progressive effect of the tax.

Regressive Tax   A **regressive tax** is one whose percentage rate *decreases* as the tax base increases. In this narrow, technical sense, there is no regressive tax in the United States. In practice, however, the term "regressive" is applied to any tax that takes a larger share of income from the low-income taxpayer than from the high-income taxpayer. Most proportional taxes, such as sales taxes, are considered to have regressive effects. For instance, a 6 percent sales tax is the same rate for everyone, rich and poor alike. But people with smaller incomes spend on average a larger percentage of their incomes. Therefore, the sales taxes they pay are a greater proportion of their incomes.

To summarize:

In the narrow, technical sense, definitions of proportional, progressive, and regressive taxes are expressed in terms of their actual tax bases. These are the things that are taxed, such as income, property, or value of goods sold. For *equity* purposes, however, the base chosen for comparison is always taxpayers' incomes—regardless of the actual tax base.

The *equity* distinctions among the three types of tax rates are illustrated with brief explanations in Exhibit 8. Take a few moments to study them before proceeding.

How do the foregoing principles and compromises apply to our tax system? Some of our taxes tend to lean more toward the benefit principle and others more toward the ability-to-pay principle. Social security, license, and gasoline taxes are some examples of the former; income, estate, and inheritance taxes are illustrative of the latter.

EXHIBIT
8

Proportional, Progressive, and Regressive Tax-Rate Structures in Equity Terms
(hypothetical data)

In equity terms, the structure of a tax is *always* evaluated by comparing the tax rate to the taxpayer's income—regardless of the actual tax base to which the tax is applied.

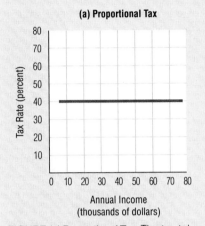

(a) Proportional Tax

Tax Rate (percent)

Annual Income
(thousands of dollars)

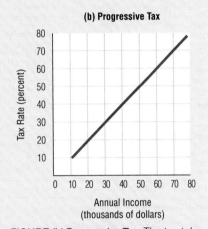

(b) Progressive Tax

Tax Rate (percent)

Annual Income
(thousands of dollars)

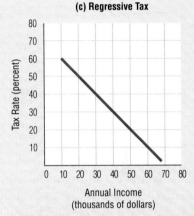

(c) Regressive Tax

Tax Rate (percent)

Annual Income
(thousands of dollars)

FIGURE (a) Proportional Tax The tax takes the same percentage of income from high-income taxpayers as from low-income taxpayers. In this example, the tax is 40 percent of a $10,000 income, 40 percent of a $20,000 income, etc.

FIGURE (b) Progressive Tax The tax takes a larger percentage of income from high-income taxpayers than from low-income taxpayers. In this example, the tax is 10 percent of a $10,000 income, 20 percent of a $20,000 income, etc.

FIGURE (c) Regressive Tax The tax takes a smaller percentage of income from high-income taxpayers than from low-income taxpayers. In this example, the tax is 60 percent of a $10,000 income, 50 percent of a $20,000 income, etc.

We can find examples of progressive, regressive, and proportional taxes in our tax system. Income and death taxes are progressive in both the technical sense and the equity sense because their percentage rates increase with the tax base. Property, general sales, and excise taxes are proportional in their technical structure because their rates are a constant percentage of the tax base. However, they also have the effect of regressive taxes because they consume a greater proportion of the income of lower-income taxpayers.

Tax Shifting and Incidence: Direct and Indirect Taxes

As you saw earlier in the discussion of corporate income taxes, the person or business firm upon whom a tax is initially imposed does not always bear its burden. For instance, a company may be able to *shift* all or part of a tax "forward" to its customers by charging them higher prices for its goods. Or it may be able to shift a tax "backward" to the owners of its factors of produc-

tion by paying them less for their materials and services. When a tax has been shifted, its burden or *incidence* is on someone else. In this connection, it is convenient to classify taxes into two categories: direct and indirect.

Direct taxes are those that are not shifted; their burden is borne by the persons or firms originally taxed. Typical examples are personal income taxes, social security taxes paid by employees, homeowners' property taxes, and death taxes. Taxes on corporate income are often considered to be only partly direct. Can you suggest why?

Indirect taxes are those that can be shifted either partly or entirely to payers other than the person or firm originally taxed. The most familiar example is the sales tax. Contrary to popular belief, this tax is imposed on sellers, not buyers. Sellers, however, typically shift the tax burden to buyers. Other examples of indirect taxes are excise taxes, taxes on business and rental property, social security taxes paid by employers, and probably, to a large extent, corporate income taxes.

In what direction will a tax be shifted, if it is shifted at all? This is a thorny problem in economic theory, and the experts do not always agree. In general:

Most taxes are like an increased cost to the taxpayer. Each taxpayer will try to pass them on to someone else. When an indirect tax is imposed, it tends—like lightning or water—to follow the path of least resistance through the markets in which the taxpayer deals. That is, the taxpayer tries to shift the tax by altering prices, inputs, or outputs according to the least degree of opposition encountered. This can have different effects on efficiency and equity from those initially intended.

Completing the Circular-Flow Model

The tax system, of course, is only one way in which the government sector is involved in the economy. Government affects the economy in other ways, as well. Some of these are diagrammed in Exhibit 9 with a complete version of the circular-flow model. Notice that the model includes three familiar sectors—household, business, and foreign. To complete the picture, the model now includes the government sector.

Government needs resources to carry on its operations. As Exhibit 9 shows, government acquires resources by purchasing factors of production (such as labor and equipment) in the resource markets. The factors that government purchases are used to produce social goods such as national defense, public education, public transportation, health care, and postal services. Government finances most of these social goods with taxes and fees imposed on the household and business sectors.

Some of the social goods produced by government are called "nonmarket goods, services, and grants." This is because these goods are given away free (that is, not sold directly) to the household and business sectors. Examples include national defense, public safety, and public health.

Other government-produced social goods are sold in both product and resource markets. Examples include postal services, public transportation, the goods provided by state-owned liquor stores, and the utilities provided by municipally owned electric companies and water companies. Some of these social goods are sold at below-cost or at subsidized prices. Others are sold at full cost or at above-cost prices. The receipts that government collects from the sale of social goods contribute to financing its operations. To summarize:

The chief functions of government are to (1) promote and regulate the private sector, and (2) provide social goods. To fulfill these functions, government participates in the resource and product markets, and finances most of its operations by imposing "charges"—mainly taxes—on the private sector. The ways in which government conducts these activities determine the role it plays and the influence it exerts in the economy.

Origins: Government in the Economy

Known equally well as a political philosopher and as an economist, the Englishman John Stuart Mill was the last of the major "mainstream" classical economists of the nineteenth century. His great two-volume treatise *Principles of Political Economy* (1848) was a masterful synthesis of classical ideas. The book became a standard text in economics for several decades. Numerous

John Stuart Mill
(1806–1873)

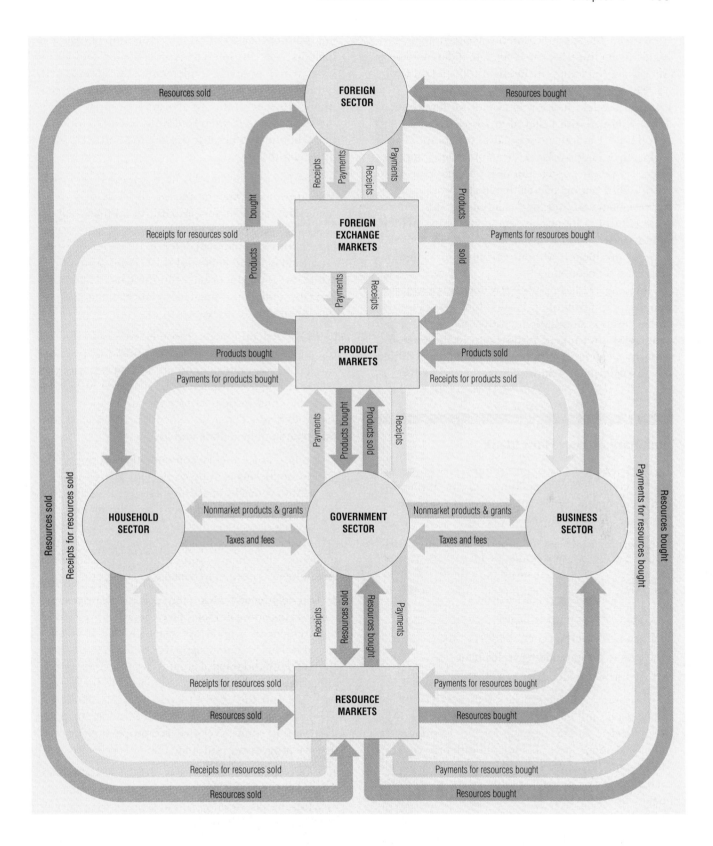

students in Europe and America learned about economics from this basic work. So, too, did a number of American presidents—including Abraham Lincoln.

Mill's major objective was economic reform. Government, he felt, had a role to play in the economy. Thus, although Mill believed in laissez-faire, he went beyond the "natural law of political economy." He did so by advocating worker education, democratic producer cooperatives, taxation of unearned gains from land, redistribution of wealth, shorter working days, improvements in working conditions, and government control of monopoly. These measures, Mill felt, would ensure workers the benefits of their contributions to production without violating the "immortal principles" of economics.

In an era of laissez-faire, it is easy to see why contemporaries of Mill often labeled him a socialist. But he believed too strongly in individual freedom to advocate major government involvement in the economy. By today's standards, Mill probably would be classified as a moderate conservative.

Summary of Important Ideas

1. The economic role of government may be considered to consist of two broad functions: (a) promotion and regulation of the private sector, and (b) provision of social goods.

2. Government promotes and regulates the private sector in many ways. For example, it

    a. tries to provide a stable economic environment

    b. performs social welfare activities

    c. grants economic privileges

    d. seeks to maintain competition

    e. tries to promote high employment

    f. redistributes income

3. Government provides social goods, which consist of public goods and merit goods. Public goods are those not subject to the exclusion principle. Examples are national defense, street lighting, and disease control. Merit goods are subject to the exclusion principle even though the principle is not always invoked. Examples are municipal libraries, national parks, and public hospitals.

4. Many social goods create "spillovers"—externalities in the form of benefits or costs. Methods for redressing spillovers consist of (a) internalization of costs and benefits, and (b) government regulation and provision. When properly implemented by government, these methods can contribute toward improving economic efficiency. Efficient allocation of social goods is more complicated when spillovers extend beyond national boundaries because the benefits and costs affect other countries.

5. The last several decades have witnessed a remarkable growth of expenditures at all levels of government. This has been due primarily to (a) increased demand for collective goods and services, (b) increased expenditures for national defense, (c) increased interest on the national debt, and (d) lagging productivity. While the government sector in the United States has been expanding, it is smaller—relative to national output—than other countries.

6. In the federal budget, income taxes, both individual and corporate, are the chief source of revenue. The main expenditure items are income security payments and national defense. In state and local budgets, the chief sources of revenue are property taxes and sales taxes. The main expenditure items are education and public welfare and health.

7. Public-choice theory contends that an important goal of politicians is to be re-elected. Therefore, they respond to voters by enacting spending programs that benefit constituents while refraining from enacting the tax legislation needed to finance the programs. The result is growing budget deficits. To reverse this tendency, the theory argues that a constitutional amendment is needed to balance the budget.

8. Our economy's tax structure consists of taxes on income, taxes on wealth, and taxes on activities. A chief requirement of a good tax system is that it be perceived as fair. Accepted standards of fairness are horizontal equity and vertical equity. Two principles of taxation that seek to apply these standards are the benefit principle and the ability-to-pay principle. However, these principles are often difficult to apply. In practice, we find some taxes that are proportional, some that are progressive, and some that are regressive.

9. Those upon whom a tax is levied are sometimes able to shift it forward or backward through changes in prices, inputs, or outputs. Thus, the burden or incidence of the tax falls on someone else. Such taxes are called indirect, as contrasted with direct taxes, which cannot be shifted.

10. All major nations finance most of their operations with four kinds of taxes—personal income, corporate profit, social security, and consumption. But the proportion of total tax revenues derived from each tax usually varies widely between countries.

11. John Stuart Mill was an eminent nineteenth century English philosopher and economist. A strong believer in laissez-faire, he nevertheless felt that government should adopt measures that would ensure workers the benefits of their contributions to production.

Terms and Concepts to Review

social goods	*property tax*
public goods	*death tax*
exclusion principle	*gift tax*
merit goods	*sales tax*
externalities	*excise tax*
market failure	*social security tax*
demand price	*horizontal equity*
supply price	*vertical equity*
specific tax	*benefit principle*
specific subsidy	*ability-to-pay principle*
public choice	*tax base*
budget	*tax rate*
average tax rate	*proportional tax*
marginal tax rate	*progressive tax*
tax avoidance	*regressive tax*
tax evasion	*direct tax*
double taxation	*indirect tax*

Questions and Problems

1. Public goods are not subject to the exclusion principle. How, then, do you explain the fact that some public goods are nevertheless provided by the private sector? Give some examples.

2. Spillover benefits and costs can be redressed in different ways. One approach was illustrated in this chapter with demand and supply curves. Using a similar approach, demonstrate the following propositions:

 a. Spillover costs can be corrected by imposing a specific (per unit) tax on buyers.

 b. Spillover benefits can be corrected by granting a specific (per unit) subsidy to sellers.

Do you see any equity implications in these approaches?

3. How can the costs of benefits provided by the government sector be reduced?

4. Which of the following are private goods? Public goods? Are any of them part private and part public? Why? (Be sure to focus on the definition of a public good in answering.)

 a. enforcement of laws

 b. a local government's garbage collection service

 c. elementary education

 d. parks

 e. highways

 f. television programs

5. Some economists and legislators contend that the present federal income tax reaches too far down into low-income brackets. Assume that you disagree with this contention, and offer arguments to defend your position.

6. If you were considering taking on an extra part-time job, would you base the decision on your average tax rate or on your marginal tax rate? Why?

7. The ability-to-pay principle of taxation may also be called the "equal-sacrifice principle." Can you explain why?

8. How can a market-oriented economy such as ours justify the large expenditures made by government on free public education?

9. Is the desire to maximize net social benefit a goal useful only to capitalistic economies, or does it apply to socialistic economies, too?

10. If you were advising a legislator on whether the government should spend an additional $10 billion on space exploration as opposed to public transportation, what approach would you use? What difficulties would you expect to encounter?

11. When the private costs of a decision are equal to its social costs, *all* the costs are borne by the decision maker. Do you agree? Explain.

12. What is wrong with using figures showing expenditures by government as a measure of the importance of government in our society?

T A K E   A   S T A N D

Higher Education: Should Government Subsidize It?

The United States devotes a large share of its resources to higher education. There are over 200 comprehensive research universities in the nation, and hundreds of other four-year and two-year colleges. These institutions are funded by a mix of tuition, grants, and government appropriations. Federal funds come in the form of guaranteed student loans, tax deductions for private contributions, and grants for academic research. State funds provide primary support; some states devote half their total appropriations to higher education. Students, particularly at public colleges, pay only a fraction of the total cost of their college education.

College graduates can expect significantly higher incomes than high school graduates, and those who take graduate degrees are likely to earn even more. How do we justify using government funds to subsidize the education of doctors, engineers, and other professionals who will earn salaries several times that of the average taxpayer? *Should government subsidize higher education?*

Yes: Education Is a Spillover Good

There is little doubt that students benefit from higher education. A college graduate can expect to earn $5,000 to $10,000 a year more than a person who only finished high school. The future monetary benefit of education is confirmed by the willingness of some students (or their parents) to pay $20,000 a year or more for four years at a private college. Better-educated workers earn more because they contribute more to production. Doctors, for example, earn more than the average taxpayer because they provide highly prized medical services.

Nevertheless, because government subsidies of higher education must be financed by taxpayers, the pertinent issue is whether or not they yield a corresponding benefit to society. In fact, higher education is a social good that provides significant spillover benefits, including technological improvements, better government, and fewer social problems. Educational subsidies contribute to technological improvement both by funding the basic research carried out by professors, and by helping to de-

fray the costs of educating the inventors and innovators of the future. Because better-educated people tend to keep themselves informed on current issues and to be politically active, educational subsidies foster improved government. And because, on the whole, better-educated people commit relatively few crimes and have little need for social services, subsidies reduce the drain on government resources. All of these spillovers benefit society. Therefore, in the interest of efficiency, government should pay some of the cost.

While serving the goal of efficiency, government subsidies to higher education also serve the goal of equality. If students had to pay the full cost of their education, only the wealthiest could afford college. The poor would be left in lower-paying jobs and the wealthy would continue to have the higher-paying jobs.

Finally, many foreign students take their degrees at U.S. colleges. When these students return to their native countries, the resulting "export" of education improves those countries and enhances international relationships. The entire globe benefits.

The spillover nature of higher education means that government subsidization is not misguided generosity, but an effective move toward efficiency and equality.

No: Subsidies Create Inefficiency

Government subsidies to higher education do not improve economic efficiency. Rather, they create inefficiency. Because government subsidies allow students to pay less than the cost of education, students consume too much education. Forcing students to pay the full cost would lead to a more efficient allocation of resources.

A free market provides the efficient quantity of a good because the price buyers pay is equal to the opportunity cost of providing the good. The opportunity cost is the value that society places on *other* goods that are not produced. When price equals opportunity cost, it is not possible to produce other goods that society values more.

When government subsidizes higher education, resources are wasted. Land and labor that should be used for the production of other goods are used instead to produce education. In particular, college faculty often undertake obscure researches funded by government subsidies, that provide no benefit to society.

The wasted resources include students. Many students earn degrees in arcane and socially useless subjects, then end up in the same job they would have had directly after high school, and with four fewer years of on-the-job experience.

The Question: Should Government Subsidize Higher Education?

■   One view is that government subsidies are needed because higher education provides spillover benefits to other members of society. If higher education were financed only by students, then not enough education would be produced. Economic efficiency requires government subsidies to higher education.

■   Another view is that government subsidies to higher education should be abolished. Because price is less than opportunity cost, too much education is produced. This wastes resources that could be used to produce other goods. Economic efficiency would be improved if government subsidies were eliminated.

Where Do You Stand?

Other students are simply not cut out for a college education and would be more productive in any of the myriad of jobs that don't require one. By reducing the cost of higher education to students, government simply encourages them to waste time attending classes.

Eliminating government subsidies would force colleges to be more competitive and efficient. If public colleges were forced to charge students the full cost of their education, then students would *demand* the best education possible. Colleges would not be able to slide by with incompetent instructors and useless required courses. Those colleges that gave the best "product" for the price would be most competitive. Those that didn't would be forced to leave the market. Higher education would be produced more efficiently and resources would be freed to produce other goods for society.

At the same time, no student with the desire and ability to pursue higher education need be denied the opportunity on financial grounds. Student loans guarantee even the most impoverished students access to higher education without shifting the burden of payment to the taxpayers. Eliminating government subsidies to higher education would thus improve efficiency without detracting from equality.

1.   Assuming that you (or your parents) currently pay only a fraction of the cost of your higher education, would you continue in college if you were forced to pay more? How much more would you be willing to pay before you decided not to obtain a college education? Would you be willing to pay more for a better education?

2.   Do you think your economics instructor would be better suited to the production of another good? Explain.

3.   If the reason for subsidizing higher education is to create more productive citizens, should public colleges be required to turn away the elderly and the terminally ill?

4.   Should government subsidize higher education? Justify your stand.

Source: James L. Payne, "Should Government Subsidize Higher Education?" *The Freeman,* May 1991, pp. 184–185.

Part 2

The Macroeconomy

CHAPTER 5

Measuring the Nation's Income: Gross Domestic Product and Gross National Product

GDP and GNP

National Income Accounting

Is GDP a Measure of Society's Well-Being?

Two Ways of Looking at GDP

Examining the Nation's Income Statement

Global Perspective: International Comparisons of
    Aggregate Income

Origins: How National Income Accounting Came About

Learning Guide

Watch for answers to these important questions

What is gross domestic product? What is gross national product? What do they do? How are they related?

How do we judge the nation's economic health? Are statistical measures available for evaluating the economy's overall performance?

What sorts of difficulties are encountered in estimating gross domestic product? Does it reflect society's well-being?

What is the relation between the economy's output and its income? Is the flow of expenditures on output equal to the flow of payments for income?

How does the value of the nation's output relate to the money that households actually have available for spending? Of what practical use is this information?

How do we compare the incomes of nations? What do the comparisons reveal about rich and poor countries?

In what period or era was national income accounting born? Why is this significant?

People are becoming increasingly concerned with their physical health. They are paying closer attention to their weight, pulse rate, blood pressure, and other measures of physical well-being. The same is true for those who are concerned with the nation's economic health. They are paying closer attention than ever before to statistical measures of the nation's output, unemployment rate, and prices. That is all to the good, for it helps make the public more aware of the nation's economic well-being.

The economy's level of activity—its state of health—is expressed in the form of data and graphs. These are published by the federal government and by various public and private organizations. Since the early 1930s, the U.S. Department of Commerce has been the nation's principal bookkeeper. It has been responsible for developing the majority of measures used to depict the economy's overall performance. Among the chief measures of economic performance are those known as "aggregate income statistics." In this chapter, you will learn about the most important types of aggregate income statistics.

GDP and GNP

Every nation's economy produces goods and services. Every society wants to know how well its economy is performing. The most comprehensive measures used for this purpose, and the ones that are quoted frequently in newspapers and business magazines, are *gross domestic product* (GDP) and *gross national product* (GNP).

GDP and GNP are close fraternal twins—very similar but not identical. For most practical purposes they may be thought of simply as the retail value of the nation's aggregate output. *Aggregate output* consists of the millions of different goods and services that an economy produces. A characteristic common to all these goods and services is that they have a money value. Therefore, GDP and GNP are always expressed in money terms. For the United States and some other major nations, gross domestic product and gross national product amount to trillions of dollars annually. In the United States, GDP and GNP are measured quarterly and annually by the U.S. Department of Commerce.

In any given year GDP and GNP are likely to differ from one another because each includes certain items that the other omits. The easiest way to see the differences is to begin with some definitions.

Gross domestic product is the total market value of all final goods and services produced during a year by *domestically located* resources. Whether the resources are American-owned or foreign-owned is immaterial. As long as the resources are located within the country, the value of the output they produce is included in U.S. GDP. For example, Toyota and Honda are Japanese corporations that manufacture some cars in the United States. The value of those cars, including the profits earned on them, is counted as part of America's GDP.

Gross national product is the market value of all final goods and services produced during a year by *domestically owned* resources. Whether the resources are located in the United States or abroad is immaterial. As long as the resources are owned by American nationals—individuals, firms, or government—the income that these resources earn for their owners is included in U.S. GNP. For example, Ford and General Motors are American corporations that manufacture some cars in foreign countries. The profits that Ford and GM earn on their foreign-made cars are counted as part of America's GNP. However, because those profits are not earned in the United States, they are not counted as part of America's GDP.

GDP and GNP are defined in terms of output. However, they are measured in terms of income.

Therefore, we need to know how output and income are related.

Aggregate Output = Aggregate Income

If aggregate output is the money value of what a nation produces, then aggregate income must be the money earned from what is produced. The reason is easy to see. The inputs, or resources, used to produce the nation's output are the four factors of production—labor, land, capital, and entrepreneurship. Of course, owners of these resources don't make them available for free. They receive payments in the form of wages, rent, interest, and profit. The sum of these payments is the nation's aggregate income.

The same idea can be looked at in a slightly different way. The total of what everyone spends is equal to the total of what everyone receives. This means that the public's total expenditure on the economy's aggregate output equals the total income received by the owners of the resources used to produce that output. As a result, the nation's aggregate output equals the nation's aggregate income. *Aggregate income* is the sum of wages, rent, interest, and profit—the money earned by the suppliers of the labor, land, capital, and entrepreneurship used to produce the aggregate output. By extension, gross domestic product can be viewed as *gross domestic income* (GDI), and gross national product can be viewed as *gross national income* (GNI). We can express the equality between aggregate output and aggregate income with two equations:

$$\textbf{GDP = GDI}$$
$$\textbf{GNP = GNI}$$

Both GDP and GNP are defined in terms of output produced. However, measuring them in terms of separate goods and services—cars, toasters, shirts, education, haircuts, medical care, and so on—would be unwieldy at best. The equality of aggregate output and aggregate income solves this problem by allowing us to measure GDP and GNP in terms of the income earned from production.

GDP and GNP differ only in certain items of income. The easiest way to see the difference is to look at the following equations:

GDP = income earned from domestic production   [1]

GNP = income earned from domestic production   [2]
     + net foreign factor income

GDP and GNP thus differ by the inclusion of "net foreign factor income." A more self-explanatory but longer name would be *net foreign income earned by owners of the factors of production*. Let's see what this means.

Understanding Net Foreign Factor Income

The term *net* refers to an amount remaining after deductions and adjustments are made. It usually arises whenever inflows and outflows are measured. For example, a company's net income is its revenues (money inflows) minus its expenses (money outflows). Similarly, a nation's net foreign factor income consists of factor income receipts from foreign sources minus factor income payments to foreign sources. Economists typically refer to foreign sources simply as "foreigners." The receipts from and payments to foreigners are included in the calculation of GNP.

GNP Includes Factor Income Receipts from Foreigners

Many U.S. households and businesses receive factor income from abroad. Some Americans earn wages and salaries in foreign countries, some Americans receive dividends on stock owned in foreign companies, and some Americans receive interest on bonds issued by foreign corporations and governments. Similarly, American multinational corporations earn profits on foreign operations. The recipients of these foreign incomes are U.S. nationals. Therefore, their income from abroad is counted as part of America's GNP. Conversely, that income is not counted in the GNP of the countries in which the income originated.

GNP Excludes Factor Income Payments to Foreigners

Many foreign households and businesses receive factor income from assets they own in the United States. Such assets include securities, real estate, and corporations. Because the owners of the assets are foreign nationals, the income they receive on their U.S. investments is excluded from America's GNP. However, that income is included in their own countries' GNP.

Keeping these two classes of income receipts and payments in mind, you can easily calculate America's net foreign factor income from the formula:

> Net foreign factor income   [3]
> = factor income receipts from foreigners
> − factor income payments to foreigners

As you saw in equation [2], net foreign factor income is included in gross national product. Therefore, GNP is concerned with who receives income—regardless of the country in which it originates. This isn't the case with gross domestic product. As equation [1] shows, GDP is concerned exclusively with the country in which income originates—regardless of who receives it.

GNP and GDP can thus be derived directly from one another, as the following equation shows.

> **GNP = GDP + net foreign factor income**   [4]

Exhibit 1 illustrates some international comparisons of GNP and GDP. The amount of difference between them depends on the influence of net foreign factor income on a nation's economy. For some countries the annual influence is considerable, and varies relatively widely from one year to the next. As a result, a nation's GDP may be significantly greater than its GNP in one year and significantly less in another.

Which Measure Do We Use?

We've seen that both GDP and GNP are measures of a nation's aggregate income. But GDP discloses aggregate income solely from domestic production, while GNP discloses aggregate income from both domestic production and foreign sources. Which measure will we be using in our study of macroeconomics? The answer is both—for two reasons:

1. Most of macroeconomics is concerned with analyzing and interpreting relationships between variables. Some key variables involve the use of net foreign factor income. For such purposes, GNP serves as the appropriate measure.

2. To examine the domestic economic performance of nations, and to compare their performance either at a given time or over a period of years, either GDP or GNP may be the appropriate measure. The choice depends on the relative importance of net foreign factor income to the countries being compared, and on the availability of the needed GDP and/or GNP data. Because many countries don't prepare such figures, they are often estimated by United Nations and other official sources.

EXHIBIT
1

International Comparisons of Gross National Product and Gross Domestic Product, 1990
(latest comparable data)

In any given year, a nation's GNP may be greater than, equal to, or less than its GDP. This is because GNP includes both domestic income and net foreign factor income, while GDP includes only domestic income. For some countries annual net foreign factor income fluctuates widely, so the difference between GNP and GDP from one year to the next may be considerable.

The nations shown here, commonly called the Group of Seven, or simply G-7, account for more than two-thirds of the world's total output.

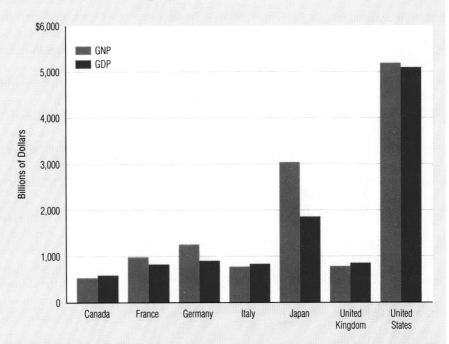

Source: World Bank; U.S. Central Intelligence Agency; and Organization for Economic Cooperation and Development (OECD). Data reflect foreign exchange-rate conversions and adjustments for purchasing power parity by OECD.

Both GDP and GNP are at the heart of macroeconomics. Attempts to influence these measures are often the goal of government economic policies. For purposes of macroeconomic analysis, however, it usually proves useful to ignore the distinction between GDP and GNP and to express both simply as "aggregate output" (or "aggregate income"). This practice will be adopted in later chapters.

The main reason for studying macroeconomics is to learn how to analyze and interpret relationships between variables that affect aggregate output. An understanding of the relationships helps us to evaluate government policies aimed at altering the level of aggregate output.

Distinguishing Between Nominal and Real Data

The items that make up aggregate output range from apples and automobiles to zinc and zippers. However, because we can't add these diverse items, they must first be stated in terms of their monetary values. Then, when we add x dollars' worth of automobiles to y dollars' worth of oranges to z dollars' worth of doctors' services, and so on, we arrive at a total dollar figure. If we do this for all final goods and services produced in the economy during any given year, the result is GDP. And if we repeat this process for several years, the different GDPs can be compared. In that way, we may be

EXHIBIT
2

Gross Domestic Product

(in current and constant dollars)

GDP is shown in both current and constant dollars. Nominal GDP is measured in current dollars, which represent actual prices as they existed each year. Real GDP is measured in constant dollars, which represent the actual prices of a base year.

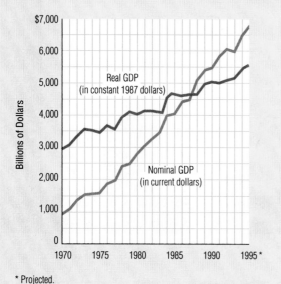

* Projected.

able to tell whether there has been a long-run growth or decline in the economy.

However, we must first determine whether prices have increased or decreased. If the prices of goods and services change from one year to the next, GDP may also change—even if there has been no change in physical output. For instance, if apples cost 20 cents each this year, five apples will have a market value of $1.00. But next year, if the price rises to 30 cents each, five apples will have a market value of $1.50.

This poses a problem: How can we tell whether the variations in GDP are due to differences in prices or to differences in *real output*—that is, output unaffected by price changes? The answer is shown in Exhibit 2. Observe that GDP is expressed in two ways. One is in *current dollars,* reflecting actual prices as they existed each year. This is often referred to as *nominal* GDP. The other is in *constant dollars,* reflecting the actual prices of a previous year, or the average of actual prices in some previous period. The previous year or period is called the *base*. GDP expressed in constant dollars is referred to as *real* GDP.

The use of constant dollars is a way of compensating for the distorting effects of *inflation*—the long-run upward trend of prices. This is accomplished by a statistical process called *deflation,* which "reverses" the ef-

EXHIBIT
3

Deflating with a Price Index

How values expressed in *current* dollars are converted into values expressed in *constant* dollars of another year

Index numbers are percentages of some base period. They are widely used by government and private sources in reporting business and economic data. Column (4) expresses the prices of column (3) in the form of index numbers. Ordinarily, the base period chosen is assumed to be fairly "normal." In this illustration, Year 2 has been arbitrarily selected as the base period.

When the values in *current dollars* [column (5)] are divided by the *index numbers* [column (4)], the result is a new set of values in *constant dollars* of the base year [column (6)]. The two value series are plotted for comparison in the accompanying chart.

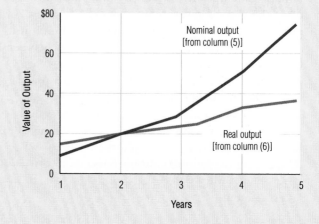

fect of the price increase.* You can get an idea of how this is done by studying Exhibit 3.

National Income Accounting†

GDP and other aggregate income figures are estimated by economists in the National Income Division of the U.S. Department of Commerce. For this task, the economists must organize and interpret nationwide economic data pertaining to the economy's four sectors. This activity is called "national income accounting."

National income accounting involves extraordinary complexities. This is one reason why the Commerce Department continually revises its estimates of GDP and related macroeconomic data. Each year the figures are revised for the previous year and every prior year several decades back. As a result, the current numbers and most of the past ones that you see today in government publications will be somewhat

---

*Deflation should not be confused with *disinflation,* which is a slowing down of the rate of inflation.

†*Note to instructors:* This section is optional. It may be omitted without affecting continuity.

different next year. Many numbers will also be different the following year and each year after that for many years to come.* However, the revisions are generally relatively moderate. As a result, the existing numbers are always useful in analyzing and interpreting aggregate economic developments, which are the chief concerns of macroeconomics.

Imagine that you're a recent college graduate employed as a junior economist in the U.S. Department of Commerce. Your job is to help develop estimates of GDP and related aggregate income measures. In order to arrive at the best estimates, there's a number of pitfalls you'll have to guard against. First, you'll have to be careful to avoid the tendency to double-count. Second, you'll have to be sure to include all productive activities and exclude all nonproductive ones.

Avoid Double Counting

Recall that the definition of GDP covers only *final* goods and services purchased. These are distinguished from *intermediate* goods and services, which enter into the production of final commodities. For example, if you purchase a new automobile this year, it

---

*Data going back to the 1950s are still being revised today.

(1) Year	(2) Units of output	(3) Price per unit of output	(4) Price index Each price in column (3) as a percent of the price in base period (Year 2)	(5) Nominal output Value in *current dollars* of each year (2) × (3)	(6) Real output Value in *constant dollars* of base period (Year 2) (5) ÷ (4)
1	3	$2	2/4 = 0.50 or 50%	$ 6	6/0.50 = $12
2 = base period	5	4	4/4 = 1.00 or 100%	20	20/1.00 = 20
3	6	5	5/4 = 1.25 or 125%	30	30/1.25 = 24
4	8	6	6/4 = 1.50 or 150%	48	48/1.50 = 32
5	9	8	8/4 = 2.00 or 200%	72	72/2.00 = 36

EXHIBIT
4

Sales Values and Value Added at Each Stage of Producing a Loaf of Bread

Stages of production	(1) Sales values (dollars per loaf)	(3) Value added (= income payments: wages, rent, interest, profit) (dollars per loaf)
Stage 1: Fertilizer and seed	$ .04	$ .04
Stage 2: Wheat growing	.28	.24
Stage 3: Flour milling	.48	.20
Stage 4: Bread baking	.88	.40
Stage 5: Bread retailer, final value	1.20	.32
Total sales values	$2.88	
Total value added (= total income)		$ 1.20

Stage 1 A farmer purchases 4 cents worth of seed and fertilizer, which he applies to his land.

Stage 2 The farmer grows wheat, harvests it, and sells it to a miller for 28 cents. The farmer has thereby added 24 cents worth of value. His factors of production then receive this 24 cents in the form of income: wages, rent, interest, and profit. (Remember that profit is the payment for entrepreneurship—one of the factors of production.)

Stage 3 The miller, after purchasing the wheat for 28 cents, adds 20 cents worth of value by milling the wheat into flour. The miller's factors of production receive this 20 cents as income: wages, rent, interest, and profit.

Stage 4 The baking company buys the flour from the miller for 48 cents, then adds 40 cents worth of value to it by baking it into bread. This 40 cents becomes factor incomes in the form of wages, rent, interest, and profit.

Stage 5 The retailer buys the bread from the baker for 88 cents and sells it to you, the final user, for $1.20. The retailer has thus added 32 cents in value, which, again, shows up as factor incomes in the form of wages, rent, interest, and profit.

Note that the value of the final product, $1.20, equals the sum of the values added.

is a final good. However, the materials of which the automobile was made, such as steel, engine, tires, and paint, are intermediate goods. Because the values of final goods include the values of all intermediate goods, only final goods are included in calculating GDP. If you allow intermediate goods to enter the picture, you will commit the cardinal sin of *double counting*—or perhaps even triple and quadruple counting.

Exhibit 4 illustrates the effect of double counting with an example of the production of a loaf of bread. As you can see, the "total sales values" at the bottom of column (2) include the sales values at all the intermediate stages. This, of course, is an incorrect statement of the actual value of the product. However, the sales value of the final product, or the total *value added* for all the stages of production, given in column (3),

shows the true value of the total output. It also shows the total income—the sum of wages, rent, interest, and profit—derived from the production process.

We can summarize with an important principle:

GDP may be calculated by totaling either the market values of all final goods and services or the values added at all stages of production. The values added are equal to the sum of all incomes—wages, rent, interest, and profit—generated from production.

Include Productive Activities, Exclude Nonproductive Ones

The purpose of deriving GDP is to develop a measure of the economy's total output, based on the market values of final goods and services produced. However, even if all these market values are estimated, some *productive* activities do not show up in the market. The value of these productive nonmarket activities should nevertheless be included in GDP. Likewise, there are also some *nonproductive* activities that do appear in the market. These nonproductive market activities should be excluded from GDP.

Here are some examples of productive nonmarket activities:

■ **"Rent" of Owner-Occupied Homes** The rent that people pay to landlords enters into GDP. However, the majority of dwellings in the United States are owner-occupied. The rental value of this housing—the rent that people "save" by living in their own homes—may be thought of as the value of shelter produced. This value is assumed to be the same amount that individual homeowners would receive if they became landlords and rented out their homes to others. Hence, this amount is included in GDP.

■ **Farm Consumption of Home-Grown Food** The value of food that people buy is included in GDP. But the value of food that farmers grow and consume themselves is also a part of the nation's productive output and is therefore included in GDP.

Some productive nonmarket activities never enter into GDP because their values either are too difficult to estimate or involve complex definitional issues. These include such activities as the labor of a do-it-yourselfer who handles his or her own repairs and maintenance around the house. Some other unpaid-for activities not included in GDP are the services of homemakers in their capacities as cooks, housekeepers, tutors, dietitians, chauffeurs, and so on.

Here are some examples of nonproductive market activities:

■ **Transfer Payments** Government and businesses often shift funds within or between sectors of the economy with no corresponding contribution to current production. Such shifts of funds are called **transfer payments**. Because these payments are not made for current output, they are excluded from GDP. Some examples of government transfer payments are social security benefits, unemployment compensation, and welfare payments. Some examples of business transfer payments are charitable contributions, allowances for bad debts, and interest payments from one firm to another.

■ **Securities Transactions** When you buy or sell stocks or bonds, you exchange one form of asset for another—either money for securities or securities for money. These financial transfers add nothing to current production and therefore are excluded from GDP. (However, broker commissions on security transactions are included in GDP, because brokers perform a productive service by bringing buyers and sellers together.)

■ **Sales of Used Goods** Billions of dollars are paid each year for used automobiles, houses, machines, factory buildings, and so on. But these goods are omitted from the calculation of current GDP because each was counted as part of the GDP in the year in which it was sold new. (As with brokers, however, the value added by dealers in used-merchandise transactions is included in current GDP.)

Is GDP a Measure of Society's Well-Being?

GDP is a comprehensive indicator of the economy's output. However, it's an imperfect measure of society's well-being. To begin with, GDP reveals nothing about these important developments that have occurred since the early twentieth century:

■ The growth of leisure time—that is, the substantial reduction in the workweek that has taken place

■ The improved quality and variety of goods and services that the economy produces

■ The growth of total output relative to the population

The long-run trends of these variables have been upward. Based on them, one could argue that GDP *understates* our material well-being. That is, our society is much better off materially than GDP figures indicate.

One could also argue that GDP *overstates* our material well-being. This is because GDP figures make no distinction between what is useful and what many people regard as frivolous. GDP embraces everything from the cost of hospital care to the wages of belly dancers. It includes cloth coats for people and mink coats for dogs, lifesaving antibiotics, and useless or even harmful dietary supplements.

Gross Domestic "Disproduct"

There are also problems with trying to use GDP as a measure of *social* well-being. This is because GDP doesn't reflect the amount of *spillover* cost that results from production. We refer to spillover cost as "disproduct" when we want to emphasize its negative effect on the interpretation of gross national product. To illustrate:

- The cost of air and water pollution is a disproduct of the nation's factories.

- The cost of treating lung-cancer victims is a disproduct of cigarette production.

- The cost of geriatric medicine is a disproduct of good medical care in the earlier years, which results in increased longevity.

- The cost of commuter transportation is a disproduct of living in the suburbs.

- The cost of aspirin for headaches resulting from TV commercials is a disproduct of advertising.

Can you suggest some more examples?

If this process were carried through our whole product list, the sum would be *gross domestic disproduct*. And if the total were then subtracted from the aggregate of production as measured by GDP, we would find that our society is not as well off as the GDP figures indicate.

Other Exclusions from GDP

Even if disproduct were subtracted from GDP, the resulting estimate would still be far from complete as a "social indicator," or index of social well-being. Because GDP measures the market value of final goods and services, it can reflect only the amount of money that society exchanges for goods and services. Many productive activities that affect our standard of living are not compensated in money. Such activities are excluded from the calculation of GDP, while similar activities that are compensated in money are included in GDP. For example:

- Homemakers' services are excluded from GDP, while the services of paid housekeepers are included.

- The benefits received from public goods are excluded from GDP, while the costs of providing these goods are included.

- Environmental pollution arising from production is excluded from GDP, while the clean-up costs are included.

- The value of education is excluded from GDP, while the costs incurred to acquire education are included.

- The effects of crime are excluded from GDP, while the funds allocated to fight crime are included.

Conclusion: GDP and Social Welfare

Because of the many inclusions and exclusions involved in calculating GDP, some economists have expressed interest in devising a better measure of the economy's true output. Such a measure would indicate society's well-being or *social welfare* rather than just the market value of final goods and services.

Would it be possible to transform GDP into a general measure of social welfare? Probably not:

"Social welfare" is a multidimensional concept. It involves many economic and psychological interpretations and implications. This makes precise definition, let alone measurement, impossible.

Something to Think About

1. Would it be better to produce wool suits and scholarly treatises than mink coats and romance novels? Would the nation thereby move closer to "worthwhile" national goals? Worthwhile according to whom?

2. Instead of doing all their own cooking, cleaning, and maintenance, many heads of households are buying more convenience foods and hiring out more domestic services than they did in the past. The prices paid for these goods and services are reflected in GDP. This trend means either (a) actual production is increasing, or (b) there is a tendency for GDP to overstate the extent to which actual production is increasing. What do you think?

EXHIBIT 5

Gross Domestic Product = Gross Domestic Income
(a two-sector model—without a government or foreign sector)

A simplified circular-flow model can be used to illustrate the fundamental principle that gross domestic product and gross domestic income are actually two sides of the same coin. *The nation's flow of output in the upper pipeline equals the nation's flow of income in the lower pipeline.* As explained in the text, profit is the residual or "balancing item" that brings this equality about. Can you explain why? For example, how is the model affected if profits are positive? Zero? Negative (that is, if there are losses instead of profits)?

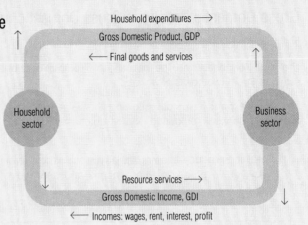

Two Ways of Looking at GDP

You now know that GDP is the market value of all final goods and services produced during the year. You also know that GDP is equivalent to gross domestic income, GDI. Let's use the familiar circular-flow model to illustrate this equality.

Exhibit 5 is a circular-flow model that depicts a simple economy consisting of only two sectors—households and businesses. The upper pipeline shows GDP as the sum of household-sector expenditures on business-sector output. The lower pipeline shows GDI as the sum of business-sector income payments for household-sector resource services provided.

The chief lesson of this diagram is that the total amount spent on production equals the total amount realized from production. This concept can be represented by the following equation:

$$\left.\begin{array}{l}\text{Total flow of}\\\text{expenditures}\\\text{on final output}\end{array}\right\}\text{GDP} = \text{GDI}\left\{\begin{array}{l}\text{Total flow of}\\\text{income from}\\\text{final output}\end{array}\right.$$

Why do GDP and GDI always balance out? The answer is profit. In Exhibit 5, the lower pipeline shows that GDI consists of wages, rent, interest, and profit.

Of these, only profit is not fixed by contract. Therefore, profit is the "balancing item" that brings about the equality of GDP to GDI. Profit may thus be positive, negative, or zero in a given year.[*]

This model contains only two sectors in order to provide a "first look" at the relationship between an economy's output and its income. A complete model, consisting of four sectors, is necessary for understanding all of the forces at work. Such a model is presented in the form of a table in Exhibit 6.

GDP from the Expenditure Viewpoint: A Flow-of-Product Approach

On the left side of the table in Exhibit 6, the economy is divided into four major sectors: household, government, business, and foreign. These are the major markets for the output of the economy. In any one year, the total expenditures of these sectors constitute the nation's GDP. A historical record of these expendi-

---

[*]In modern history, the business sector's profit has never been zero. The only year in which it was negative was 1933—the bottom of the Great Depression. In that year, the sum of wages, rent, and interest exceeded GDP. But because profit was negative, the identity GDP = GDI was maintained.

EXHIBIT
6

Gross Domestic Product = Gross Domestic Income (1991 estimates)

(a four-sector model, in billions of dollars)

The data for measuring the nation's total output can be estimated from two points of view:

- The expenditure side—showing the value of goods and services produced and/or purchased by each sector

- The income side—showing the payments made and/or received in producing those goods and services

The expenditure side is divided into four sectors—household, government, business, and foreign. These represent the major markets for the output of the economy. The sum of the four sectors' expenditures on final products (output) constitutes GDP. The income side summarizes the costs incurred or payments made by business firms to produce final products. They are wages, rent, interest, profit, indirect business taxes, and capital consumption allowances or depreciation. Their sum less net foreign factor income equals GDI.

Expenditure viewpoint: flow of product	Output
Household sector	
Personal consumption expenditures	$3,887
+	
Business sector	
Gross private domestic investment	725
+	
Government sector	
Government purchases of goods and services	1,087
+	
Foreign sector	
Net exports of goods and services	–27
Gross Domestic Product, GDP	**$5,672**

Income viewpoint: flow of costs	Income
National income (including net foreign factor income)	
Wages	$3,768
Rent	–13
Interest	481
Profit	305
+	
Nonincome (expense) items	
Indirect business taxes	471
Capital consumption allowance (depreciation)	624
Gross National Income (= GNP)	5,709
Less: Net foreign factor income	37
Gross Domestic Income, GDI	**$5,672**

tures is presented in the first several columns of the table on the inside front cover of this book. Note that the sum of the four expenditure columns for any given year equals GDP. Let's see what can be said about the meaning of these four categories.

Personal Consumption Expenditures

Frequently referred to as "consumption expenditures" or simply "consumption," this category consists of expenditures on consumer goods and services. Some examples are food, clothing, appliances, automobiles, medical care, and recreation.

Government Purchases of Goods and Services

The items in this category are purchased by all levels of government. They include guided missiles, school

buildings, fire engines, pencils, and the services of clerks, administrators, and all other government employees. However, recall that transfer payments, which are a significant portion of government expenditures, are omitted because they don't represent part of current output of goods and services.

Gross Private Domestic Investment

This category includes total investment spending by business firms. The term "investment" has a special meaning in economics. In everyday language, a person makes an investment when buying stocks, bonds, or other assets with the intention of receiving an income or making a profit. In economics, *investment* means additions to, or replacement of, physical productive assets. Thus, investment represents spending by business firms on new job-creating and income-producing goods. Because such expenditures contribute significantly to GDP, they are of major concern in economics.

Investment goods fall into two broad classes:

1. New capital goods, such as machines, factories, offices, and residences, including apartment houses and owner-occupied homes. (Owner-occupied homes are included because they could just as well be rented out to yield incomes to their owners, as do apartment houses.) When a firm buys a used machine or an existing factory, it merely exchanges money assets for physical assets. The purchase itself creates no additional GDP. But, when a firm buys *new* machines or *new* buildings, it creates jobs and incomes for steelworkers, carpenters, bricklayers, and other workers, thereby contributing to the nation's GDP.

2. Increases in *inventories*—stocks of goods that a firm keeps on hand. They include raw materials, supplies, and finished goods. For GDP accounting purposes, increases in inventories are as much a part of a business firm's physical capital as are plant and equipment. Thus, the market values of any additions to inventories are part of the current flow of investment spending that makes up GDP. In contrast, any declines in inventories are reductions in the flow of investment spending that makes up GDP.

In the process of producing goods during any given year, some existing plant and equipment is used up. Economists at the U.S. Department of Commerce call this "consumption of fixed capital." For brevity, we will refer to it simply as "capital consumption," or *depreciation.* Because of depreciation, a part of the year's gross private domestic investment goes to replace the used up portion. Any amount left over, called *net private domestic investment,* represents a *net addition* to the total stock of capital. For example, suppose:

> Gross private domestic investment = $400 billion
> Replacement for depreciation = $300 billion

then:

> *Net* private domestic investment = $100 billion

You can see from this that an economy will tend to grow, remain static, or decline according to one of three possibilities:

1. **Gross Investment Exceeds Depreciation** When this happens, net investment is positive. The economy is thus adding to its capital stock and expanding its productive base.

2. **Gross Investment Equals Depreciation** In this case, net investment is zero. The economy is merely replacing its capital stock and is neither expanding nor contracting its productive base.

3. **Gross Investment Is Less Than Depreciation** If this occurs, net investment is negative. The economy is thus diminishing, or *disinvesting,* its capital stock and is thereby contracting its productive base.

To summarize:

The term *investment* **refers to** *gross private domestic investment* **spending by business firms on job-creating and income-producing goods. It consists of replacements or additions to the nation's stock of capital, including its plant, equipment, and inventories—that is, its nonhuman productive assets.**

Net Exports of Goods and Services

Some domestic expenditures are made to purchase foreign goods and services. These are imports. Some foreign expenditures are made to purchase domestic goods and services. These are exports. To measure GDP in terms of total expenditures, we must include the value of *exported goods and services.* This is because the value of our exports represents the amount that foreign buyers spent on purchasing some of our total output. Then we subtract the value of *imported goods and services* from our total expenditures. The reason is that part of our consumption was for imported goods, and we're interested only in measuring the value of domestic output.

The simplest way to perform these adjustments is to combine the separate figures for exports and imports into a single figure called *net exports.* Thus:

> **Net exports = total exports – total imports**

For example, if a nation's total exports in any given year amount to $350 billion, and its total imports are $330 billion, its net exports of $20 billion are part of that year's GDP. (Look back at Exhibit 6.) Of course, the country's imports may exceed its exports in any particular year. In that case, net exports will be negative and will reduce GDP. If you have any doubts about this, look again at Exhibit 6 and note the effect on GDP if net exports are negative.

GDP from the Income Viewpoint: A Flow-of-Costs Approach

Now turn your attention to the right side of the table in Exhibit 6. This shows a second method of calculating GDP. It is expressed in terms of the flow of costs or payments that businesses incur as a result of production. The first four items—wages, rent, interest, and profit—represent incomes (including net foreign factor incomes) paid to the owners of the factors of production. Hence they are classified as national income. The remaining two types of payments—indirect business taxes and capital consumption allowance (depreciation)—are categorized as nonincome (expense) items. Let's examine the reasons for these classifications.

Wages

The broad category of *wages* embraces all forms of remuneration for work. Thus, it includes not only wages but also executive salaries and bonuses, commissions, payments in kind, incentive payments, tips, and fringe benefits. It also includes earnings received by owners of unincorporated businesses, such as proprietorships and partnerships.

Rent

Income earned by persons for the use of their real property, such as a house, store, or farm, is *rent.* This category also includes the estimated rental value of owner-occupied nonfarm dwellings and royalties received by persons from patents, copyrights, and rights to natural resources.

Interest

Interest is expressed in net rather than gross terms. It represents the business sector's total interest payments to other sectors minus their total interest payments to the business sector. All other types of interest payments are considered "unproductive." Some examples of unproductive interest payments for purposes of GDP accounting are interest payments between individuals, between businesses, and between government and individuals. Therefore, such payments are omitted from this classification.

Profit

Profit consists of corporate profits before payments of corporate income taxes or disbursements of dividends to stockholders. Profits of unincorporated businesses are not counted here because they were already included as part of wages.

The sum of wages, rent, interest, and profit is called *national income* . It consists of the payments that business firms make to the owners of the factors of production in return for the services provided by those factors. Hence the term "national income" means national income at factor cost.

The next two components to be examined are indirect business taxes and capital consumption allowance (depreciation). Because these two items are not payments to the owners of productive resources, their inclusion in GDI requires some explanation.

Indirect Business Taxes

Indirect business taxes consist primarily of sales, excise, and real property taxes incurred by businesses. You'll recall that an indirect business tax is actually "paid"—that is, turned over to the government—by the business firm on which the tax is imposed. Therefore, the tax is regarded as a business expense—the same as wages and other costs. This is true even though the real burden of the tax may be borne by the firm's customers in the form of higher prices. (Keep in mind that *all* of a firm's costs are ultimately borne by its customers in the form of prices paid.) Because the tax is viewed as a business expense, it is included in GDI as a cost item.

To put it somewhat differently, indirect business taxes tend to be passed on or shifted "forward" by business firms to buyers. (This is why they are called "indirect," in contrast to *direct* taxes, such as personal income taxes, which are not shifted.) Sales taxes are typical. If you live in a state or city that has a 5 percent general sales tax and you buy a product whose price is $1, your total *expenditure* is actually $1.05. Of this, $1 goes to pay incomes—the wages, rent, interest, and profit—earned for making the product. The remaining 5 cents goes to the local government, which has not contributed directly to production. It follows, therefore, that indirect business taxes cause the expenditure side of GDP to be greater than the income side. In view of this, indirect business taxes must be added to total incomes (or subtracted from GDP) in order to represent correctly the total value of payments made to produce GDP.

Capital Consumption Allowance (Depreciation)

In the process of producing GDP, some decline in the value of existing physical capital occurs as a result of wear and tear, obsolescence, and accidental loss. To reflect this decline, firms count as part of their costs a *capital consumption allowance*—or simply "depreciation." The allowance consists primarily of depreciation on business plant and equipment and on owner-occupied dwellings. For purposes of national income accounting, depreciation may be thought of as the portion of the current year's GDP that goes to replace the physical capital "consumed" or used up in production.

Depreciation is thus the difference between gross and net private domestic investment, as already explained. *If there were no such thing as depreciation, and if the government returned all indirect business taxes to households, the nation's income from production would be identical to its output.* However, because depreciation is a reality, it causes the income side of GDP to be less than the expenditure side. Therefore, depreciation must be added to total incomes (or subtracted from GDP) if GDI is to equal GDP.

Net Foreign Factor Income

When we add national income—the sum of wages, rent, interest, and profit—to the nonincome items, we get *gross national income*, which is the same as GNP. The difference between this and GDP, as you learned earlier in the chapter, is *net foreign factor income*. Therefore, when we subtract net foreign factor income from GNP, the result obtained is GDI.

To summarize:

The nation's aggregate output, GDP, equals the nation's aggregate income, GDI. This is true because the total flow of expenditures on final output equals the total flow of income from final output. GDP is the sum of expenditures by the economy's four sectors—household, business, government, and foreign. GDI is the sum of the incomes earned from production and the nonincome expenses incurred, less net foreign factor income.

Examining the Nation's Income Statement

You've seen that gross domestic product equals gross domestic income. But gross domestic income isn't the money that households actually have available for spending. Let's see why, by examining the items listed in the nation's income statement shown in Exhibit 7. As you'll see, there are several different components of a nation's income. The income statement shows these components *for a given period* (such as a year), and how income was allocated between consumption and saving.

EXHIBIT
7

The Nation's Income Statement: Gross Domestic Product and Related Accounts
(billions of dollars)

There are several different components of a nation's income. Can you fill in the figures for the most recent year? See the table on the inside front cover of the book.

	19__
Gross domestic product (GDP)	$____
Minus:	
Capital consumption allowance (depreciation)	____
Equals: Net domestic product (*NDP*)	____
Plus: Net foreign factor income	____
Minus:	
Indirect business taxes	____
Equals: National income (*NI*)	____
Minus: Income earned but not received	
Corporate income taxes	____
Undistributed corporate profits	____
Social insurance contributions	____
Plus: Income received but not earned	
Transfer payments	____
Equals: Personal income (*PI*)	____
Minus:	
Personal taxes	____
Equals: Disposable personal income (*DPI*)	____
Out of which come:	
Personal consumption expenditures	____
Personal savings	____

Gross Domestic Product to Net Domestic Product

We begin with gross domestic product. In order to arrive at a closer measure of the dollars received by individuals, we must subtract the portion that was spent to replace used-up capital goods. This is the *capital consumption allowance* (or depreciation) figure. The number that results is net domestic product, or simply *NDP.* As shown in Exhibit 7:

GDP − capital consumption allowance = *NDP*

Net Domestic Product to National Income

Net Domestic Product (NDP) measures the total sales value of goods and services available for society's consumption and for adding to its stock of capital equipment. But *NDP* still doesn't represent the dollars people actually have available to spend. One reason is that *NDP* includes only income that Americans receive from U.S. production while it excludes income that Americans receive from foreign production. Another reason is that *NDP* includes indirect business taxes—such as sales taxes. Therefore, to arrive at a closer estimate of the dollars people actually receive, we have to do two things to *NDP*:

1. *Add* net foreign factor income. This reflects the income that Americans earned abroad. By adding it to *NDP*, we are recognizing that income consists of foreign earnings as well as domestic earnings.

2. *Subtract* indirect business taxes. These taxes, for purposes of national income accounting, are assumed to be shifted forward by sellers to consumers in the form of higher prices. Therefore, the sum of all indirect business taxes must be deducted from *NDP* in order to arrive at a more accurate estimate of the dollars available to people for actual spending.

The addition of net foreign factor income and the deduction of indirect business taxes result in national income. Thus, as Exhibit 7 shows:

> *NDP* + net foreign factor income
> – indirect business taxes
> = *NI*   ↙GDP–Deprec.
>
> $NI = NDP - IBT + NFFI$

National Income to Personal Income

National income (NI) is the total of all incomes earned by the factors of production *both at home and abroad*. *NI* thus includes net foreign factor income. As you learned earlier, *NI* is the sum of wages, rent, interest, and profit earned by the suppliers of labor, land, capital, and entrepreneurship. Does *NI* represent the dollars that people actually had available for spending? Once again, the answer is no. Some people earned income they did not receive; others received income they did not earn.

For example, the stockholders in a corporation are its owners and hence earn the corporation's profits. However, stockholders don't receive all the profits,

for two reasons. Some profits are paid to the government in the form of corporate income taxes. Some profits are retained in the business for future expansion instead of being distributed to stockholders as dividends. Likewise, social security *contributions* are taken out of workers' current earnings, and thus they are also part of income earned but not received.

As for income received but not earned, the major items are transfer payments. These are merely shifts of funds within the economy—primarily from the government sector to households—for reasons other than current production. Examples include welfare payments, social security *benefits,* and tax refunds.

To measure the dollars people actually had available for spending, we therefore adjust the *NI* in two ways:

1. *Subtract* income earned but not received.

2. *Add* income received but not earned.

These two steps result in a figure called personal income. As shown in Exhibit 7:

> *NI* – income earned but not received
> + income received but not earned
> = *PI*
>
> $PI = NI - IENR + RINE$

Personal Income to Disposable Personal Income

Personal income (PI) is the total received by persons from all sources. It is the dollars that you and I receive for the various ways in which we contribute to the nation's output. Does *PI* measure the dollars actually available to people for spending? The answer is still no, because out of personal income people must first pay their personal taxes. This amount must therefore be deducted from *PI*, leaving a figure called ***disposable personal income (DPI)***. It is this amount that people actually have available for spending. How much do they spend? The data in the inside front cover of the book show that the great bulk of *DPI* goes for personal consumption, while the rest is saved. Summarizing with an equation, Exhibit 7 shows:

> *PI* – personal taxes = *DPI*

Putting the foregoing ideas together, we've seen that there are five measures of income and output for the economy:

$DPI = PI - pers tax$

EXHIBIT
8

The Flow of Aggregate Income and Related Concepts

Can you fill in the data for the most recent year? See the table on the inside front cover of the book.

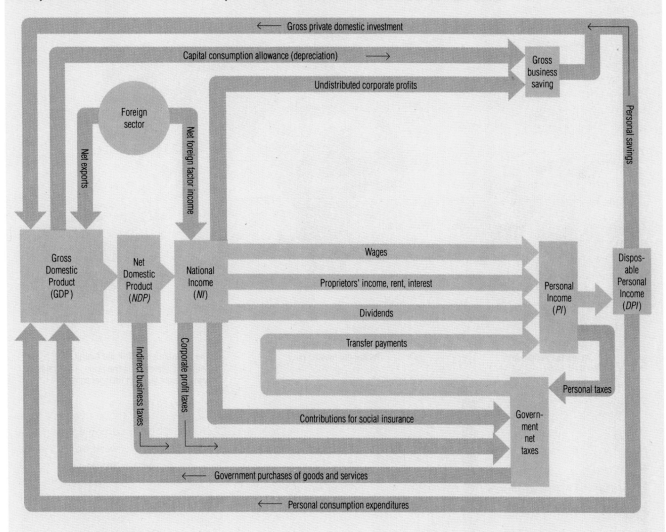

- Gross domestic product

- Net domestic product

- National income

- Personal income

- Disposable personal income—or, simply, disposable income

These measures are closely interrelated. They can be derived from one another, and tend approximately to parallel one another over time. In many macroeconomic discussions (except those involving specific accounting practices as described in this chapter), *economists loosely use the term "national income" or "aggregate income" to represent all five terms.* To help you visualize the various concepts, a comprehensive aggregate-income flow model is shown in Exhibit 8.

EXHIBIT
9

GNP per Capita, 1991

A country's gross national product divided by its population

Norway Sweden Finland
Germany
United Kingdom
Ireland
France
Spain
Portugal
Italy
Canada
United States
Mexico
Brazil
SOUTH
AMERICA
Algeria Libya
AFRICA
Iran
Iraq
Saudi
Arabia
Egypt
Former Soviet Union
China
India
Korea
Japan
Australia
New Zealand

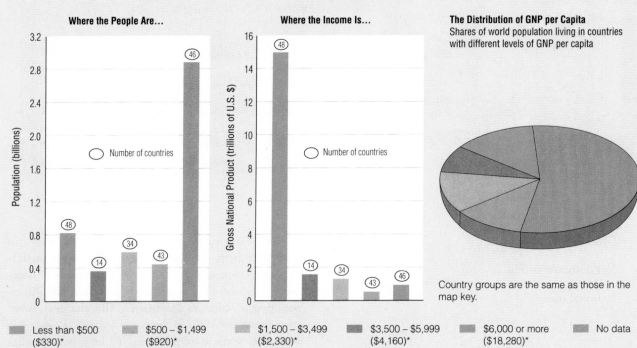

Where the People Are...

Population (billions)

○ Number of countries

48
14
34
43
46

Where the Income Is...

Gross National Product (trillions of U.S. $)

○ Number of countries

48
14
34
43
46

The Distribution of GNP per Capita
Shares of world population living in countries with different levels of GNP per capita

Country groups are the same as those in the map key.

| ■ | Less than $500 ($330)* | ■ | $500 – $1,499 ($920)* | ■ | $1,500 – $3,499 ($2,330)* | ■ | $3,500 – $5,999 ($4,160)* | ■ | $6,000 or more ($18,280)* | ■ | No data |

*Average GNP per capita in U.S. dollars shown in parentheses.

Source: World Bank; Organization for Economic Cooperation and Development.

Global Perspective: International Comparisons of Aggregate Income

How does U.S. aggregate income compare with that of other nations? Exhibit 9 shows GNP per capita throughout the world in the latest year for which comparable data are available. GDP data were not available for these comparisons.

There are several things you should know about GNP per capita in order to interpret this information correctly. The same principles apply to GDP per capita.

First, GNP per capita is obtained by dividing a country's GNP by its population:

$$\text{GNP per capita} = \frac{\text{GNP}}{\text{population}}$$

The result tells you the share of GNP that each person would have *if* GNP were divided equally.

Second, GNP per capita doesn't tell you anything about the way GNP is actually distributed among people and places. This is shown in the separate charts. You should take a few minutes to study them because they provide valuable insights about today's world. Note particularly those countries and regions that are the richest, those that are the poorest, and those that are most heavily populated. Does there appear to be a relationship between these characteristics?

Third, to increase GNP per capita, some countries try to slow their population expansion, but most countries try to raise their rate of economic growth. They do this by improving the quality of human and material resources—the factors of production. Several approaches are often employed simultaneously:

The quality of human resources is enhanced by providing people with more and better education, health, and work skills. The quality of material resources is improved by developing efficient communication, energy, and transportation systems, and by providing better factories, machines, and technology.

The policies that nations adopt to achieve these goals are at the heart of macroeconomics.

Origins: How National Income Accounting Came About

Today, such widely employed concepts as gross national product and disposable personal income are essential yardsticks of economic performance. But they

Simon Kuznets
(1901–1985)

Sir Richard Stone
(1913–   )

came into extensive use only a few decades ago, largely as a result of the efforts of two economists. One was Simon Kuznets, at that time an economist at the National Bureau of Economic Research, a prominent private research organization. The other was Richard Stone, who was serving as a research assistant in economics at England's Cambridge University.

Kuznets: Father of National Income Accounting

More than anyone else, Kuznets pioneered the development of national-income data. When the United States plunged into the Great Depression of the early 1930s, the lack of appropriate information was, said Kuznets, "a scandal. No one knew what was happening. The data available then were neither fish nor flesh nor even red herring."

It remained for Kuznets to point out the kind of information that was needed. When the Senate ordered official GNP and other national-income estimates, the Department of Commerce turned to the National Bureau of Economic Research for assistance. The young Kuznets went to Washington as a consultant, lecturing government economists and statisticians on his concepts. On January 4, 1934, a Senate document was published that contained the country's first national-income figures. They covered the period 1929 to 1932. This was the beginning of one of the most significant advances in the history of economics. The measurement of GNP and related concepts were not fully developed by the Department of Commerce until the 1940s. (GDP was developed decades later, and the U.S government officially shifted emphasis from GNP to GDP as recently as 1992.) Although the technical structure of GNP is quite different from that of Kuznets's original conception, he is still recognized as the person most responsible for its statistical formulation.

Stone: International Systematizer

It remained for another young scholar to provide a national-income accounting system that other countries could adopt. That person was Richard Stone. During the early 1940s (the World War II period), Stone worked as a research assistant to an eminent British economist, John Maynard · Keynes (pronounced "canes"). Keynes's ideas were revolutionizing the way people thought about economic problems. Stone helped prepare a statistically based profile of the British economy that enabled the country's leaders to assess its resources with far greater accuracy than had been possible before.

After the war, Stone headed a United Nations project that developed a standard national-income accounting model for other countries. Today most countries follow these guidelines, making international comparisons possible.

Many Honors

To a degree rarely equaled by other economists, both Kuznets and Stone have demonstrated an ability to analyze and structure huge masses of data. From these, they were able to draw many provocative hypotheses about long-term economic change.

Kuznets's and Stone's lifeworks have been crowned with honors. Among them have been the Nobel prize. It was awarded to Kuznets in 1971 when he was 70, and to Stone in 1984 when he was 71.

Summary of Important Ideas

1. A nation's aggregate output equals its aggregate income. These are measured by gross domestic product and by gross national product. Gross domestic product equals income earned from domestic production. Gross national product equals income earned from domestic production plus net foreign factor income. Nominal data, such as nominal GDP, represent dollar values before the effects of inflation are removed. Real data, such as real GDP, represent dollar values after the effects of inflation are removed.

2. GDP data are calculated by the U.S. Department of Commerce. Some pitfalls that must be avoided in making the calculations are (a) failing to take the effects of price changes into account, (b) double (actually, multiple) counting, and (c) the inclusion of nonproductive transactions.

3. From the expenditure standpoint, GDP is the sum of personal consumption expenditures, government purchases of goods and services, investment, and net exports. GDP can be viewed from the income standpoint as gross domestic income (GDI). This is the sum of wages, rent, interest, and profit, plus two nonincome business expense items: indirect business taxes and depreciation, less net foreign factor income.

4. The items that make up the nation's income accounts are GDP, *NDP, NI, PI,* and *DPI.* All five measures are closely related and can be derived from one another. They are among the most important measures of our economy's performance. In economic discussions (except those involving accounting practices) we often refer to all five measures as "national income" or "aggregate income."

5. The financial status of a nation is reflected by its income statement. This shows gross domestic product and related accounts.

6. GNP per capita reveals the share of aggregate income that would be received by each person if GNP were distributed equally. International comparisons of GNP per capita enable us to see which countries are relatively poor and which are relatively affluent. Nations can raise their income levels by adopting policies designed to improve the quality of human and material resources—the factors of production.

7. The measurement of gross domestic product and its related variables is called "national income accounting." Its underlying concepts were formulated in terms of GNP by an American economist, Simon Kuznets, during the Great Depression, which occurred in the 1930s. Kuznets's main ideas subsequently became the basis of national income accounting by the U.S. Department of Commerce. During the 1940s, a British economist, Richard Stone, led a worldwide team of economists in formulating international standards of national income accounting. Today, due to the efforts of Kuznets and Stone, comparisons of economic performance among most nations is possible.

Terms and Concepts to Review

gross domestic product	*interest*
gross national product	*profit*
real output	*national income*
current dollars	*(at factor cost)*
constant dollars	*capital consumption*
inflation	*allowance*
deflation	*net domestic product*
index numbers	*personal income*
value added	*disposable personal*
transfer payments	*income*
investment	
inventory	
depreciation	
disinvestment	
wages	
rent	

Questions and Problems

1. Annual differences between GDP and GNP are normally less for most large countries than for most small ones. The United States, for example, usually experiences some of the smallest annual differences of any major country. What does this indicate?

2. Suppose that a nation's GDP increased from $100 billion to $200 billion. What has happened to its *real* GDP during that period if:

a. prices remained the same   *doubled, 100% up*

b. prices doubled   *same.*

c. prices tripled from their constant level in (a)   *33% down*

d. prices fell by 50 percent of their constant level in (a)   *4 X higher?*

3. What happens when you "deflate" a *rising* current-dollar series, as in Exhibit 2? Obviously, the constant-dollar series lies below the current-dollar series for all years after the base year, and above it for all years prior to the base year. What would happen if you deflated a current-dollar series that was *declining* rather than one that was rising? Explain your answer.

4. Why is "value added" a logically correct method of measuring the nation's output?

5. The level of inventories serves as a "balancing" item between sales to final users and current production. True or false? Can sales to final users exceed current production? Can sales be less than current production? Explain your answers in terms of changes in inventories and their effects on GDP.

6. How is the growth or decline of an economy related to its net investment? Do you think an economy's percentage growth or decline is related to its percentage change in net investment? Explain.

7. What is the effect on national income if you (a) marry your housekeeper; (b) take an unpaid vacation? Is there any effect on social welfare (that is, society's well-being) from either act?

8. Which of the following are included, and which are not included, in calculating GDP?

a. One hundred shares of General Motors stock purchased this week on the New York Stock Exchange

b. Wages paid to teachers

c. A student's income from a part-time job

d. A student's income from a full-time summer job

e. The value of a bookcase built by a do-it-your-selfer

f. The purchase of a used car

g. A monthly rent of $1,800 that a homeowner "saves" by living in his or her own home instead of renting it out to a tenant

9. Each year the total amount of dollar payments by checks and cash far exceeds—by many billions of dollars—GDP. If GDP is the market value of the economy's final output, how can this huge difference exist?

10. Gross business saving represents that part of business income that is available for various forms of investment. Examine the following hypothetical data (in billions of dollars):

Corporate profits	$90
Corporate income taxes	43
Dividends to stockholders	25
Retained profits	22
Depreciation	75

a. How much is gross business saving? Show your method of calculation.

b. Of what significance is depreciation in your calculation?

c. Can gross business saving be larger than corporate profits *before* taxes and dividends? Can it be smaller? Explain.

11. Examine the following hypothetical data (all in billions of dollars) for a particular year:

(1) Gross private domestic investment	$180
(2) Contributions for social insurance	25
(3) Interest paid by consumers	9
(4) Personal consumption expenditures	600

(5) Transfer payments	60
(6) Undistributed corporate profits	45
(7) Indirect business taxes	75
(8) Net exports of goods and services	5
(9) Capital consumption allowance	60
(10) Government purchases of goods and services	175
(11) Corporate income taxes	70
(12) Personal tax and nontax payments	90
(13) Net foreign factor income	5

On the basis of these data, calculate (a) gross domestic product, (b) net domestic product, (c) domestic income, (d) personal income, (e) disposable income. (*Suggestion:* You will find the table on the inside front cover of the book a helpful guide.)

12. Examine the following hypothetical data (all in billions of dollars) for a particular year:

(1) Indirect business taxes	$ 90
(2) Corporate profits before taxes	150
(3) Capital consumption allowance	90
(4) Compensation of employees	675
(5) Undistributed corporate profits	60
(6) Proprietors' income	120
(7) Contributions for social insurance	40
(8) Corporate income taxes	70
(9) Net interest	15
(10) Transfer payments	80
(11) Personal tax and nontax payments	105
(12) Rental incomes	45
(13) Personal consumption expenditures	750
(14) *Net* foreign factor income	10

On the basis of these data, calculate the five types of national income discussed in this chapter. (*Hint:* Do not try to calculate GDP first.)

13. A country's gross domestic product rose from $285 billion in 1980 to $504 billion in 1990. During the same period, the country's general price level (1992 = 100) rose from 72.1 to 88.7.

a. What was the percentage increase of nominal GDP over the decade?

b. By how much did average prices, measured by the general price level, rise over the decade?

c. How would you calculate GDP for 1980 and for 1990, expressed in 1992 dollars?

d. Is the percentage change of GDP in constant dollars greater of less than the percentage change in current dollars? Show your calculations.

14. Personal consumption expenditures differ between regions of the country. Convert personal consumption expenditures for the midwest region into 1982–1984 dollars for the years shown in the following table. What is the economic significance of your calculations?

Year	Personal consumption expenditures (midwest region, billions of dollars)	Consumer Price Index (1982–1984)
1975	$432.8	53.8
1980	500.3	82.4
1985	532.2	107.6
1990	697.3	130.7

15. Which measure of national income best tells you:

a. the amount by which the economy's production exceeds the capital equipment used up in producing it

b. the amount of income available to consumers for spending

c. the market value of commodities produced for final use

d. the amount of income available to people for government taxation

e. the incomes earned by resource owners engaged in production

Which measure of national income is best?

16. (a) List several productive activities you do regularly that aren't counted in GDP. (b) What would their market value be if they were included in GDP accounts? (c) How might a system be established that would include the value of such activities? (d) What would be the advantages of such a system? The disadvantages?

17. (a) Suppose that people start baking their own bread, sewing their own clothes, repairing their own cars, and growing their own vegetables to a much greater extent than has been the case before. How would GDP be affected? How would social welfare be affected? (b) Over the long run, some nonmarket activities have become market activities. Child care is one example. Can you name some others? How is GDP affected? Is the effect "real" or "artificial"?

18. Some countries, such as Iceland, Saudi Arabia, and Brunei in Southeast Asia, have a relatively low GDP, yet they are among the more affluent nations in the world. In the United States, the *gross state product* (how would you define it?) of Montana and Wyoming are among the lowest in the country. But these states are about as well off as California and New York, which have the highest gross state product (GSP) in the country. How can this be?

T A K E   A   S T A N D

Gross Domestic Product: Does It Measure Economic Welfare?

Gross domestic product (GDP) is a key measure of economic performance, and one of the most closely watched economic statistics. GDP measures the overall production of goods and services in the economy. A growing GDP is a sign of a healthy economy. Shrinking GDP means that the economy is in recession.

For the most part, commentators uncritically regard growing GDP as good and shrinking GDP as bad. But is this association of GDP with overall national welfare justified? Governing the measurement of GDP are complicated rules known as national income accounting. These rules may draw overly fine and perhaps arbitrary distinctions between the types of production activity to be included in and excluded from GDP. The statistic may therefore be misleading, at best, as a basis for considering the overall good of the nation. *Does gross domestic product measure economic welfare?*

No: GDP Has Nothing to Do with Economic Welfare

Rises in GDP say that the income of the nation is increasing, but may not say much about the national welfare. Consider a few examples:

■   Mr. Smith and Ms. Jones are neighbors who clean their own houses. Then each starts a housecleaning business and hires the other to clean house. GDP rises.

■   An auto mechanic repairs cars privately for cash. Then she takes a job with an auto repair shop and is put on the payroll. GDP rises.

■   Declines in working conditions lead to greater on-the-job injuries. More workers are hospitalized, so the output of hospitals increases. GDP rises.

■   Increased pollution causes deterioration of air quality and greater incidence of respiratory diseases, leading again to increased medical expenditures. GDP rises.

■   Increased pollution of rivers, land, and groundwater leads to costly clean-up efforts. GDP rises.

■   Worldwide political instability leads to large increases in defense expenditures. GDP rises.

■   Increasing crime rates force policymakers to increase the size of the police force and to build more prisons. GDP rises.

In the housecleaning and auto-mechanic examples, GDP rises although no additional goods or services have been produced. The other examples show GDP rising as a result of measures taken to counteract a social ill or a harmful byproduct of industry. Where, then, is the net gain in the national welfare? There is none.

Yes: It's the Best Measure We Have

GDP statistics are not intended as a direct measure of economic welfare, and no economist would argue that they are perfect for that purpose. Nevertheless, data on GDP do provide us with useful information on economic welfare, probably the best information we have.

The reason is simple. Individuals derive satisfaction from consuming goods and services. This undisputed notion is at the heart of economic analysis. Other things equal, therefore, an increase in our output means that there are more goods and services available for consumption, and so the people are better off. To put the point another way, remember that GDP is also a measure of overall income earned in the economy. If income rises, people are better off, but if income falls, people are worse off.

The usefulness of GDP as a measure of economic welfare is apparent from comparisons across time and across countries. Few would deny that economic welfare is higher now than it was one hundred years ago, or that U.S. standards of living are higher than those in, say, Mexico. Such differences are captured in the GDP statistics.

Finally, expenditures on national defense, or the police, or health care certainly do contribute to economic welfare. If our country is safer, or our streets are safer, or we are healthier, then we are all better off. It is misguided to suggest that the inclusion of such expenditures makes GDP an inadequate measure of welfare.

The Question: Does Gross Domestic Product Measure Economic Welfare?

■   Some argue that GDP often rises simply as a result of national income accounting. They also observe that GDP may rise as a byproduct of events associated with declines in national welfare. These problems make GDP a highly misleading statistic for measuring economic welfare.

■   Others concede that the GDP statistics are not perfect as measures of welfare, but argue that they are useful nonetheless. Since GDP is a measure of overall output, and since people in society derive satisfaction from consuming that output, increases in GDP can, in general, be associated with rising welfare.

Where Do You Stand?

1. The *No* argument cited a number of different events, such as increases in pollution, crime, or political instability, that might cause a rise in measured GDP. In what way might the causes of these events influence your opinion of how accurately GDP measures the nation's welfare?

2. Focusing narrowly on GDP undoubtedly causes us to ignore much that contributes to our overall quality of life. Can you think of some examples? Do these examples suggest that GDP statistics are irrelevant for measuring welfare?

3. Has GDP become a more reliable or less reliable measure of economic welfare as the economy has grown?

4. Is GDP a useful measure of economic welfare? Justify your stand.

Monitoring the Economy: Business Cycles, Unemployment, and Inflation

Learning Guide

Watch for answers to these important questions

What is the nature of the fluctuations in general economic activity that are commonly referred to as "business cycles"? Why do these fluctuations occur? Can they be forecast?

Why is unemployment a problem of continuous concern in our economy? What are some of the causes of unemployment?

What is inflation? How does it affect each of us? Why is it important for our economy to achieve greater price stability?

Are business cycles only of domestic concern, or are their effects often felt in other countries?

What is econometrics? How is it used by some governments and by many corporations to analyze business cycles?

Fluctuations in economic activity—or "business cycles," as they are frequently called—are a recurrent plague for mixed economies such as ours. Inflation and unemployment are the negative results of that plague—the costs we've paid throughout much of our history.

EXHIBIT
1

What Do Business Cycles Look Like?

An Historical Picture of American Business Cycles

Fluctuations are recurrent but not periodic. That is, the peaks and troughs of business activity do not occur at regular intervals.

Fluctuations may occur in production, prices, income, employment, or in any other

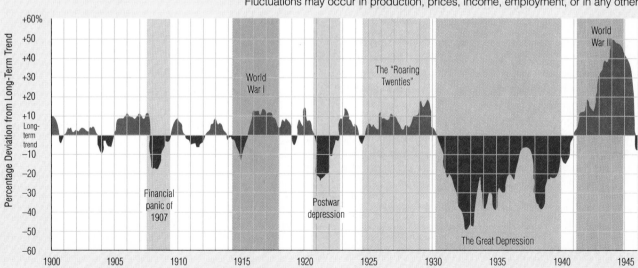

This chapter examines the nature and interrelations of business cycles. Once we understand their costs, we'll look at ways of trying to reduce them.

The federal government tries to keep all the adverse consequences of business cycles at bay simultaneously. However, our nation's policymakers aren't consistently successful. Both the problems and their solutions will occupy much of our attention in the study of macroeconomics.

Business Cycles: A Long History of Fluctuations

You can get an idea of the course of business cycles by looking at the historical picture in Exhibit 1. Notice that, although we haven't had the frequent booms and busts that characterized the economy prior to World War II, we still have fluctuations in business activity. This suggests the following definition of business cycles:

Business cycles **are fluctuations in general economic activity. The fluctuations are recurrent but nonperiodic (that is, irregular). They occur in aggregate variables, such as real GDP, employment, and prices, that move at about the same time and in the same direction but at different rates.**

It's important to note what the definition *excludes:*

■ Business cycles aren't *seasonal fluctuations*—short-run changes such as the upswing in retail sales that occurs each year during the Christmas and Easter periods.

■ Business cycles aren't *secular trends*—long-run growth or decline that characterizes practically all economic data over a period of many years.

Prior to the mid-twentieth century, business cycles were often quite pronounced. Economists used the terms "prosperity" and "depression" to identify strong cyclical upswings and downswings. Since then, fluctuations in economic activity have tended to become more moderate. Consequently, the terms "recovery"

chronological series of economic data. Such series are called *time series*. In order to measure business cycles for the economy as a whole it's first necessary to combine many different time series into a single index of business activity. The value of the index for each year is then expressed as a percentage of its long-term "average" or trend. When the resulting data are graphed, they resemble the fluctuations in the chart.

Source: 1900 to 1988 by Ameritrust; adapted with changes. Data since 1988 are author's estimates.

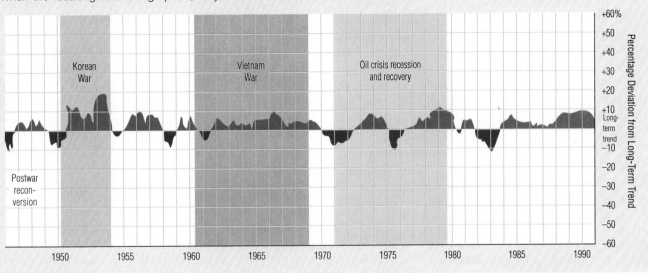

and "recession" are customarily employed to describe economic expansions and contractions.

Output, Employment, and Price Fluctuations During Business Cycles

One striking set of observations about business cycles concerns the different behavior of durable-goods and nondurable-goods industries. *Durable goods* are those that have a long life span. Businesses purchase durable capital goods such as iron and steel, cement, and machine tools. Consumers purchase durable goods such as automobiles, furniture, and appliances. *Nondurable goods* are goods that usually have a shorter life span than most durable goods. Examples of nondurable goods, which are primarily purchased by consumers, include fresh food, clothing, and cosmetics.

Over the course of a business cycle, durable-goods (or hard-goods) industries tend to experience relatively wide fluctuations in output and employment, and relatively small fluctuations in prices. Nondurable-goods (or soft-goods) industries, tend to experience relatively small fluctuations in output and employment, and relatively wide fluctuations in prices. Let's see why this happens, by examining the reasons for fluctuations in output, employment, and prices.

Fluctuations in Output and Employment

Durable goods—precisely because they're durable—don't usually have to be replaced at a particular time. If necessary, they can be repaired in order to last longer. What does this fact about durable goods mean to businesses and consumers who purchase them?

In a recession, total demand for an economy's output decreases. This causes a decline in employment, because *fluctuations in output and employment tend to be related*. Business managers thus find themselves with excess production capacity. Therefore, they see little chance for profiting from investment in capital goods. Likewise, consumers find that they can get along with their existing cars and other durable goods, and so they decide to postpone buying new ones. As a result, the durable-goods industries experience relatively sharp decreases in total, or aggregate, demand.

During recovery, aggregate demand for the economy's output rises. Business executives and consumers are ready to replace as well as add to their existing stocks of capital and durable goods. The durable-goods industries, therefore, experience relatively sharp increases in aggregate demand.

The purchase of nondurable goods isn't as readily postponable as it is for durable goods. Therefore, the change in demand for nondurable goods over the course of a business cycle tends to be much less pronounced.

Some comparisons between income and consumer spending are shown in Exhibit 2. Note the relatively wider fluctuations for durable goods than for nondurable goods.

Fluctuations in Prices

The degree of competition in an industry is often influenced by the number of its sellers. This usually affects the way in which the industry adjusts its prices and outputs in response to changes in demand.

Many durable-goods industries tend to have relatively small numbers of dominant sellers. The aluminum, locomotive, aircraft-engine, and telecommunications-equipment industries are typical. The "big three" or "big four" producers in these industries control a large proportion of the total output of their product. Consequently, the largest producers can influence the prices charged by firms in the industry, and can often follow relatively stable pricing policies despite fluctuations in sales. As a result, when the producers are confronted with a substantial decline in sales, they try to reduce costs and maintain profit margins by cutting back on production and jobs. Eventually, if market sluggishness continues, some hard-pressed firms may seek to reduce their inventories by cutting prices. But even then, price decreases are likely to be small in relation to declines in output and employment.

The opposite tends to occur in industries that produce nondurable goods. In these industries, a considerable number of sellers are usually competing in the same market. Each firm, therefore, is likely to have too small a share of the market to ignore the importance of price reduction as a means of countering a decrease in sales. Consequently, when sales fall substantially, firms that produce nondurable goods tend to reduce their prices while holding output and employment relatively steady.

To summarize:

EXHIBIT
2

Consumer Spending Relative to Income

Consumer spending fluctuates with income over the years. But expenditures for durable goods fluctuate much more widely relative to income than expenditures for nondurable goods.

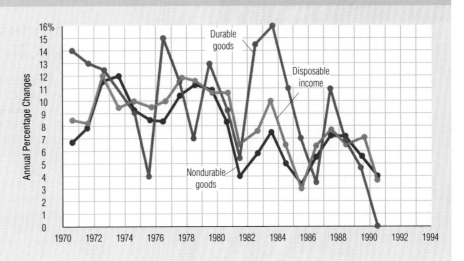

The type of goods produced by an industry helps account for different degrees of price, output, and employment changes when sales decline. During a recession, for example, we first hear about production cutbacks and layoffs in durable-goods industries such as automobiles and construction—not in nondurable-goods industries such as food processing and textiles. The latter industries may also reduce their output and employment, but for them the *percentage* decreases are usually much smaller.

Tracking the Economy

Which way is the economy heading? Are business conditions going to improve during the coming months? Or will production and employment continue at their present levels?

These are the kinds of questions that economists (and other people) frequently ask. The answers are often obtained from certain statistical indexes, called *time series*, because they're expressed chronologically. Among those time series that are used to monitor the nation's health are gross national product, employment, housing starts, consumer prices, and retail sales. Hundreds of other indexes are also closely watched.

Some of the more important ones are shown on the inside front and back covers of this book.

The time series that are continuously scrutinized are obviously too numerous to list. However, a number of them can be classified in one of three categories:

Coincident Indicators These time series tend to move approximately in phase with changes in real GDP and therefore are measures of current economic activity. *Examples:* nonagricultural employment, industrial production, manufacturing and trade sales.

Leading Indicators These time series tend to move ahead of changes in real GDP, producing peaks and troughs before the economy as a whole. *Examples:* new orders for plant and equipment, new building permits, stock-market prices.

Lagging Indicators These time series tend to trail behind changes in real GDP. *Examples:* business loans outstanding, manufacturing and trade inventories, unit labor costs.

The trouble with all three types of indicators (especially with leading indicators) is that they often give false signals by temporarily reversing their upward or downward direction. This, of course, impairs their use-

Why Economists Miss the Mark

by Rob Norton

"Has Macro-Forecasting Failed?" That's the title of a timely National Bureau of Economic Research paper by economist Victor Zarnowitz of the University of Chicago. The answer is—what else?—yes and no. Forecasters have gotten steadily better at anticipating growth rates during an expansion, Zarnowitz finds. But downturns are their downfall.

Don't shoot your macroeconomist, Zarnowitz urges. While the failure to call downturns is a major problem—and one that should be at the top of the forecasters' agendas for fixing—the discipline has come a long way. On the whole, forecasters provide decision-makers in business and government with essential and reasonably accurate information about the direction of the economy, and they are a good bet to keep improving.

Source: *Fortune,* January 27, 1992, p. 25.

EXHIBIT 3

Forecasting with Economic Indicators: Computer, Crystal Ball, or Tea Leaves?

The U.S. Department of Commerce publishes monthly composite indexes of leading, coincident, and lagging indicators. The leading indicators are widely used as forecasting tools by economists in business and government.

Ideally, the three types of indicators behave like those in the graph. Their leads and lags either predict, parallel, or follow the peaks and troughs of the economy. The shaded area covers a downturn (recession) for the economy as a whole, represented by the coincident indicator.

In reality, the leads are not always so definite or consistent. If they were, forecasting would be a simple task. History shows that the leading indicators frequently fail to predict changes in real GDP with reasonable accuracy. Because of this, the use of leading indicators is only one of several tools used by economists to forecast changes in economic activity.

Indicators
(shaded area denotes recession)

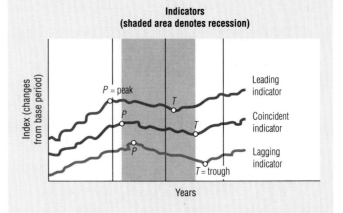

fulness for interpreting and forecasting economic trends. You can appreciate this by examining the explanation in Exhibit 3.

The Challenge: Reduce Instability

Some people contend that the business cycle could be eliminated if only certain adjustments were made. This belief is especially popular during economic recessions. "Find a proper balance between wages and prices." "Improve labor-management relations." "Reform our tax system." If these and other measures were adopted, it is said, economic instability would be eliminated.

Unfortunately, such beliefs are false. Even if these desirable objectives could be achieved, we would still experience economic fluctuations. The reasons aren't difficult to see:

Business cycles are an inherent characteristic of mixed economies. This is because households, which express their demands for goods and services in the marketplace, aren't the same as the businesses that seek to fulfill those demands. *Each group is composed of different people with different motivations.* **Consequently, the economic actions of the two groups—their decisions to spend or not to spend—generally differ. The result is that waves of economic activity are always being created.**

In view of this, you'll find that eliminating all instability is *not* one of the goals of macroeconomics. That would be impossible in our type of economy—a free society in which people make their own economic decisions. Instead, a chief goal is to *reduce* instability by formulating appropriate government policies. This task, as you'll see in your remaining study of macroeconomics, poses a never-ending challenge to economists and political leaders.

Unemployment

Business cycles and the level of employment in the economy are related. During periods of economic expansion, people find it easier to get jobs, so unemployment declines. During periods of economic contraction, many people lose their jobs, so unemployment rises. Unemployment is thus an economic variable that fluctuates over time. To understand why, we must first learn how the variable is defined and measured.

Fundamental to the idea of unemployment is the *labor force.* It consists of all people 16 years of age or older who are employed, plus all those unemployed who are actively seeking work. The *total* labor force includes those in the armed services as well as those in the civilian labor force. However, only the *civilian labor force* is of interest to us here, because this is the segment that experiences unemployment.

The number of unemployed who are actively seeking work is determined by a monthly survey of approximately 60,000 households reported by the U.S. Department of Labor. (In the survey, a person is defined as "actively seeking work" if he or she claims to be looking for a job and is available to accept one if it is offered.) This unemployment figure divided by the number of those in the civilian labor force is the government's *official **unemployment rate.*** Thus:

$$\text{Unemployment rate} = \frac{\text{number of unemployed people actively seeking work}}{\text{number of people in the civilian labor force}}$$

The Department of Labor reports seven measures of unemployment to accommodate different definitions of the concept. The *official* measure is the one that government uses and the one commonly cited in news reports. Exhibit 4 identifies all seven measures.

EXHIBIT
4

Measuring Unemployment: Seven Different Concepts

How should unemployment be measured? The answer depends on how the concept is defined. The U.S. Department of Commerce, which compiles the unemployment data, publishes seven different measures, ranging from the narrowest to the broadest. In the accompanying chart, the narrowest, U_1, consists of those people unemployed for 15 weeks or more. The broadest, U_7, includes *all* types of unemployed—full-time, part-time, and so on.

There is thus no single "true" measure of unemploy- There are different measures, reflecting different judgments about the economic and psychological hardship caused by unemployment. However, U_5, the government's *official unemployment rate*, is the most familiar measure and the one that is commonly cited in the news media.

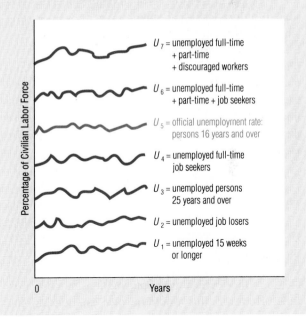

U_7 = unemployed full-time + part-time + discouraged workers

U_6 = unemployed full-time + part-time + job seekers

U_5 = official unemployment rate: persons 16 years and over

U_4 = unemployed full-time job seekers

U_3 = unemployed persons 25 years and over

U_2 = unemployed job losers

U_1 = unemployed 15 weeks or longer

Types of Unemployment

When conducting the survey, certain difficulties are encountered in trying to measure unemployment. This is because the circumstances and conditions of unemployment vary widely among individuals. Accordingly, distinctions are made between different kinds of unemployment.

Frictional (Transitional) Unemployment

A certain amount of unemployment, which is of a short-run nature and is characteristic of a dynamic economy, may be called *frictional unemployment.* It exists because of "frictions" in the economic system resulting from imperfect labor mobility, imperfect knowledge of job opportunities, and the economy's inability to match people with jobs instantly and smoothly. Typically, frictional unemployment consists of people temporarily out of work because they are between jobs or in the process of changing jobs. It is possible to reduce frictional unemployment by improving labor mobility and knowledge of job opportunities. But in a society that values freedom, frictional unemployment cannot and should not be completely eliminated. Efforts to do so would greatly reduce people's freedom to change jobs. In view of the nature of frictional unemployment, an equally suitable and more descriptive name for it might be *transitional unemployment.*

Cyclical Unemployment

The type of unemployment that results when workers are laid off because of business recessions is called *cyclical unemployment.* It is a result of business recessions because producers try to reduce costs by cutting back on production and jobs. Obviously, society would like to reduce cyclical unemployment as much as possible. However, this would involve conquering the business cycle. Although substantial progress in this direction has been made, cyclical unemployment continues to be a frequently recurring problem. Therefore, it is a topic of major importance in subsequent chapters.

Structural (Mismatch) Unemployment

Unlike cyclical unemployment, which results from economic instability, *structural unemployment* arises from deep-rooted conditions and changes in the economy. Two major groups of people make up the structurally unemployed.

One group consists of the *hard-core unemployed.* These are people who lack the education and skills needed in today's complex economy and who are often the victims of discrimination.

The other group consists of skilled workers, college graduates, and professionals whose talents have been made obsolete by changes in technology, markets, or national defense priorities. Thus, mathematicians, physicists, chemists, artists, musicians, and other people whose specialized skills or training are not always in strong demand frequently find themselves unemployed.

Structural unemployment thus exists because the location and skill requirements of job openings do not always match the location and skills of unemployed workers. Therefore, a more descriptive name for structural unemployment is *mismatch unemployment.*

Unemployment or Underemployment : Are They the Same?

If you get a college degree and end up working as an office clerk, are you unemployed? The answer, of course, is no. However, you may be "underemployed."

Underemployment (also called disguised employment) is a condition that exists when employed resources are not being used in their most efficient ways. This may happen when individuals are employed below their training or capabilities.

Underemployment is an interesting problem that raises some thought-provoking questions. For example:

1. If a scientist who is unable to find work in the field of science takes a job as a taxi driver, should his or her unused scientific skills be counted as unemployed? If so, then the taxi-driving skills should not be counted as employed. Otherwise, the same individual would be counted as two people—an unemployed scientist and an employed taxi driver.

2. Is a taxi-driving scientist an economic loss to society? Apparently not—from a *social* viewpoint. The fact that the scientist was able to get a job as a taxi driver rather than as a scientist indicates that society valued the services of an additional taxi driver more highly than the services of an additional scientist.

In view of this, perhaps the taxi-driving scientist should not be classified as underemployed.

What do you think? Can underemployment exist in a market economy? Is underemployment separate and distinct from frictional, cyclical, and structural unemployment? (*Suggestion:* To answer the questions, it helps to distinguish between the short run and the long run.)

Measuring Unemployment: Who Are the Unemployed?

The accuracy of unemployment figures is always subject to attack, especially when the figures are high. Critics point out that the overall unemployment rate may at times be either overstated or understated because of the inclusion or exclusion of three categories of workers:

1. The Marginally Employed The jobless total is swollen by the inclusion of many people, among them some homemakers and students, who may be only marginally dependent on regular paychecks.

2. Discouraged Workers The unemployment total is understated by the failure to include "the hidden unemployed"—discouraged people who have given up trying to find work.

3. The Partially Employed The published unemployment statistics do not reflect the fact that many jobholders work only part-time because they cannot find full-time jobs. Those workers are still counted as employed, understating actual employment.

With overstatement here and understatement there, unemployment data are always somewhat ambiguous. Because of this, perhaps the chief value of such data lies in what they reveal about the *direction* in which unemployment is changing.

Employment Ratio: A Different Measure

The shortcomings of the unemployment rate have led to the development of a measure called the *employment ratio.* This is the percentage of the working-age population (persons 16 years and over) that is employed. Thus:

$$\text{Employment ratio} = \frac{\text{number of employed people}}{\text{working-age population}}$$

The advantage of the employment ratio (compared to the unemployment rate) is that it focuses on the number of jobs actually held by people while ignoring those people who are entering and leaving the labor force. Thus, if businesses hire more workers, the employment ratio goes up. Meanwhile, the unemployment rate may remain constant or even rise, because it's dependent on the size of the labor force rather than on the size of the working-age population.

Of course, the employment ratio is affected by the number of part-time workers. This also influences the unemployment rate. But, when the proper statistical adjustments are made, economists agree that the employment ratio is a much better indicator of the economy's health.

Despite its advantages, the employment ratio cannot serve as the government's official measure unless Congress decides to legislate the change.

Full Employment and "Natural" Unemployment

Ideally, the economy should maintain a high level of employment. But how high is high? There is no simple answer. Transitional employment is unavoidable and generally desirable. Cyclical and structural unemployment stem from different causes. Therefore, government measures aimed at reducing one kind of unemployment may not work very effectively at reducing the other. In addition, as you'll discover in later chapters, some government policies that seek to raise the level of employment can create serious inflationary pressures, causing the average price level to rise.

To help deal with these problems, economists use a concept called *full employment.* It is the level of employment at which two conditions prevail:

1. Everyone who wants to work is working, except for those who are frictionally and structurally unemployed.

2. The rate of change of the average price level (that is, the rate of inflation) is stable—neither accelerating nor decelerating.

You can see from this definition that, when the economy is operating at full employment, there is no cyclical unemployment. However, frictional and structural unemployment exist. Together these constitute *natural unemployment.* It follows that the expression *natural employment* may be used as another name for full employment.

EXHIBIT
5

Estimating the Economic Cost of Unemployment: The GDP Gap

How much output does society lose from unemployment? You can obtain a rough estimate by calculating the GDP gap. This is the difference, in any given year, between potential GDP and actual GDP. *Potential GDP is the output that would occur at full employment.* For example, suppose that full employment exists when 94 percent of the civilian labor force is working. Then potential GDP can be derived from the following formula:

$$\text{Potential GDP} = \frac{\substack{\text{hours worked} \\ \text{by all persons} \\ \text{at full employment}}}{\substack{\text{actual hours worked} \\ \text{by all persons}}} \times \left(\substack{\text{actual} \\ \text{GDP}}\right)$$

$$= \frac{\left(\substack{\text{94\% of} \\ \text{civilian} \\ \text{labor force}}\right)\left(\substack{\text{average} \\ \text{weekly} \\ \text{hours} \times 52}\right)}{\left(\substack{\text{actual} \\ \text{employment}}\right)\left(\substack{\text{average} \\ \text{weekly} \\ \text{hours} \times 52}\right)} \times \left(\substack{\text{actual} \\ \text{GDP}}\right)$$

Notice that two of the factors, *average weekly hours times 52*, cancel out. This leaves the formula:

$$\text{Potential GDP} = \frac{\substack{\text{94\% of civilian} \\ \text{labor force}}}{\text{actual employment}} \times \left(\substack{\text{actual} \\ \text{GDP}}\right)$$

Here is an illustration of the calculation:

Suppose that in a given year, the civilian labor force was 100 million, actual employment was 92 million, and actual GDP was $2,100 billion.

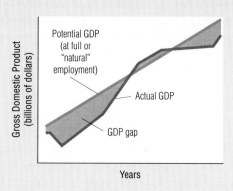

Applying the formula,

$$\text{Potential GDP} = \frac{94 \text{ million}}{92 \text{ million}} \times (\$2{,}100 \text{ billion})$$
$$= 1.02 \times (\$2{,}100 \text{ billion})$$
$$= \$2{,}146 \text{ billion}$$

The GDP gap in any given year is then the difference between potential GDP and actual GDP:

GDP gap = potential GDP – actual GDP

Using the above example,

$$\text{GDP gap} = \$2{,}146 \text{ billion} - \$2{,}100 \text{ billion}$$
$$= \$46 \text{ billion}$$

The graph provides a hypothetical illustration of the GDP gap over a period of years. Can you construct a graph from actual data covering the most recent 10 years? All the information you need is available in the tables inside the front and back covers of this book.

QUESTION How might actual GDP sometimes exceed potential GDP? (*Hint*: Remember the meaning of *natural unemployment*.)

Costs of Unemployment

Unemployment is a problem of continuing concern because it imposes costs on all of us.

Our nation bears a social cost of unemployment. This cost includes the consumer goods and capital goods that society fails to produce, and the deterioration of human capital resulting from the loss of skills. The cost also includes the human misery and depriva-

tion and the social and political unrest brought on by high levels of unemployment.

All of the costs of unemployment cannot be measured. However, it is possible to estimate the resulting loss of output. This estimate, known as the GDP *gap, is widely used as a guide for establishing government policies aimed at reducing unemployment.* Exhibit 5 shows how to calculate the GDP gap.

Inflation

If you were asked to define business cycles in ten words or less, you would be correct to say that they are essentially fluctuations in output, employment, and prices. Because the first two of these variables have thus far been our main concern in this chapter, we can now turn our attention to the third.

What is it that erodes the purchasing power of the dollar, acts as a hidden tax, and contributes to economic instability? Answer: Inflation. **Inflation** is a rise in the general price level (or the average level of prices) of all goods and services over a prolonged period. The purchasing power of a unit of money (such as the dollar) varies inversely with the general price level. For example, if prices double, purchasing power decreases by one-half; if prices halve, purchasing power doubles. Therefore, inflation is also a reduction in the purchasing power of a unit of money.

Does inflation mean that all prices rise? Clearly not. In almost any period of inflation, some prices rise, some are fairly constant, and some even fall. However, the "average" level of prices—the **general price level—**rises.

Types of Inflation: Is Our Nation Inflation-Prone?

Different explanations for inflation have been given from time to time. Here are the more common types you're likely to encounter in the news media and should know something about. Note that some of them may overlap in their causes and effects.

Demand-Pull Inflation

The traditional type of inflation is known as **demand-pull inflation.** It takes place when total expenditures for goods are rising while the available quantity of goods is not growing fast enough to meet the demand. Goods may be in short supply because resources are already fully utilized or because production cannot be increased rapidly. As a result, the general level of prices begins to rise. This is the market's way of responding to a situation sometimes described as "too much money chasing too few goods."

Cost-Push (Market-Power) Inflation

A second type of inflation is **cost-push inflation.** It occurs when prices increase because payments to one or more groups of resource owners rise faster than pro-

ductivity. This may happen because the resource owners are able to exert enough market power to achieve their objectives. Typical forms of cost-push inflation are wage-push inflation and commodity inflation.

Wage-Push Inflation This occurs when strong labor unions manage to press for wage increases in excess of productivity gains. Unit costs of production are thereby raised, exerting pressure on sellers to increase prices in order to maintain profit margins.

Commodity Inflation This occurs when prices of material inputs rise sufficiently to cause significant increases in costs of production. Firms are prompted to respond by raising the prices of finished goods. Since the 1970s, for example, inflation in the United States and abroad has sometimes been worsened by commodity inflation resulting from rising costs of oil and certain other raw materials.

Expectations Inflation

Inflation can result from simultaneous demand-pull and cost-push forces. Suppose the public believes that the inflation rate is about to accelerate. The expectation that prices are going up will lead many people to increase their spending, many workers to press for higher wages, and many firms to raise their prices. The expectation of an increase in inflation can, therefore, be self-fulfilling. Expectations play a critical role in economics.

Who Loses from Inflation? Who Gains?

Does inflation impose the same burden on all of us? Not necessarily. The effects of inflation are not distributed equally. Most people suffer from it, but others sometimes benefit. To see why this is so, we must understand the difference between two kinds of income:

1. **Nominal income** This is the amount of money received for work done. It is also referred to as *money income.*

2. **Real income** This is the purchasing power of nominal income as measured by the quantity of goods and services that it can buy.

Clearly, your nominal income may be quite different from your real income. The latter is determined not only by your nominal income but also by the prices of the things you purchase. In view of this, let's see how inflation can affect people in *real* terms.

If the rate of inflation were fairly steady, it would be easier for people to plan for it. They could do this by *anticipating* future increases in the average prices of goods and services. Then they could adjust their *present* earning, buying, borrowing, and lending activities in such ways as to offset the expected depreciation of the dollar. However, if they failed to forecast the rate of inflation correctly, they might inadvertently transfer some of their wealth to other groups in society.

As an illustration, suppose that you lend a friend $100 for 1 year. If you expect the general price level to remain stable, and if you want to earn a real return (in terms of constant purchasing power) of 5 percent, you will charge 5 percent interest on the loan. Assume, however, that you expect the average level of prices to rise by 10 percent. In that case, you should charge about 15 percent interest on the loan. Of this, 5 percent represents a real return and 10 percent represents compensation for your loss in purchasing power due to inflation.

Suppose that a year elapses and your friend pays you what is owed, but the rise in prices has been greater than you anticipated. Are you better or worse off? Obviously, the repaid loan plus interest has not provided full compensation for your decreased purchasing power. Hence, your change in real wealth is less than you anticipated. You have suffered a loss from inflation. Your friend, on the other hand, has repaid the loan with less purchasing power than was orginally borrowed. Your friend has thus experienced an increase in wealth—a gain from inflation. On the whole, therefore, there has been a redistribution of wealth—in this case, from you to your friend—because of your failure to predict inflation correctly.

Conversely, if the rise in prices has been less than you anticipated, you are better off. You will experience an increase in wealth—a redistribution from your friend to you. Can you explain why?

To generalize:

People who don't predict inflation correctly are unable to adjust their economic behavior to compensate for it. As a result, some people experience gains while others experience losses. *The net outcome is a redistribution of wealth between debtors and creditors.* **The redistribution isn't on the basis of income levels, number of dependents, or other socially acceptable economic criteria. Instead,** *it is haphazard and inequitable in a manner unrelated to society's objectives.*

Measuring Inflation: The Declining Value of Money

Everyone is aware that many things cost more today than they did a few years ago. It's plain enough that the trend of prices has been upward. By how much? You can gain some idea from the graph in Exhibit 6, which shows important price indexes.

The **Consumer Price Index** (CPI) is an average of the prices of various goods and services commonly purchased by families in urban areas. Generally referred to as a "cost-of-living index," the CPI is published monthly by the Bureau of Labor Statistics of the U.S. Department of Labor.

What Is Hyperinflation?

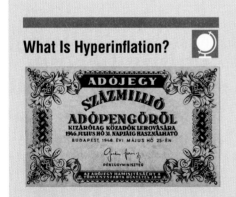

Hungarian inflation currency. A 100 quintillion pengo note, 1946—the highest denomination note issued in the history of currency (100,000,000,000,000,000,000).

The 100 Quintillion Note

The governments of certain countries, especially some Latin American nations, often turn out paper money as if it were confetti. The result is that their economies frequently experience annual inflationary rates of several hundred, and often more than a thousand, percent. That, as far as anyone is concerned, is hyperinflation.

But these are not the worst hyperinflations in history. That distinction belongs to the financial debacles that took place in Germany in the 1920s and in Hungary after World War II (1945).

Germany in 1923 suffered 4 *trillion* percent inflation. During that hectic period, Germans literally took their weekly wages home in wheelbarrows full of money. And the wheelbarrows were often worth more than all the currency inside.

Hungary holds the all-time inflation record. In 1946 that country suffered a 5 *quadrillion* percent inflation. It was brought on by the issuance of 100 quintillion pengo notes. That's 100 followed by 18 zeros.

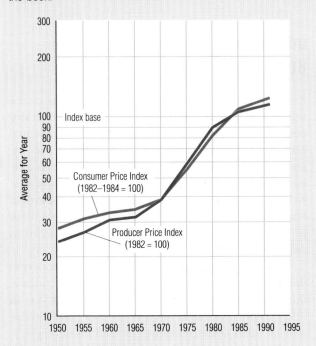

EXHIBIT
6

Price Indexes

The Consumer Price Index and the Producer Price Index are prepared by the U.S. Department of Labor. They are the most widely used measures of inflationary price trends in our economy. Can you project the indexes for the next several years? What are you assuming when you make such projections?

TECHNICAL NOTE The vertical axis of this figure is scaled logarithmically. This facilitates comparison of relative (percentage) changes in the graphs. To understand why, look up the meaning of *logarithmic scale* in the Dictionary at the back of the book.

Source: U.S. Department of Labor.

The *Producer Price Index* (PPI) is an average of selected items priced in wholesale markets. The items whose prices go into the index include raw materials, semifinished products, and finished goods. The PPI, like the CPI, is also published monthly by the Department of Labor.

You've probably heard it said that the dollar today is worth only 60 cents, or 50 cents, or perhaps even

less. Such statements try to convey the idea that today's dollar buys only a fraction of what a dollar bought during some period in the past. What fraction? It depends on which past period you choose as a reference point. The decline in the purchasing power of the dollar is much greater during high inflationary years than during lower ones.

The most widely used measure of the general price level is the Consumer Price Index. It tells you the average level of prices in a given year as a percentage of the average level of prices in some other year, called the "base year." For the base year, of course, the average is 100 percent of itself. In any other year, the average may be greater than, equal to, or less than 100 percent. Whichever it is will depend upon whether the average level of prices has risen, remained constant, or fallen in relation to the base year.

Exhibit 7 illustrates how the CPI is interpreted. Look at the hypothetical data shown in the first two columns. Suppose we arbitrarily select Year 1 as the base year. This means that the CPI for that year equals 100.

Note that the CPI in Year 2 was 125 percent of its value in Year 1. This tells you that the average level of prices was 25 percent higher in Year 2 than in the base year. In Year 3, the CPI was 87 percent of its value in Year 1. That is, the average level of prices was 13 percent lower in Year 3 than in the base year.

With the use of this information, the value or purchasing power of the dollar is calculated in the third column. You do this by expressing the CPI in decimal form and taking its reciprocal. (The reciprocal of a number is 1 divided by that number.) The result for each year is given in the fourth column.

EXHIBIT
7

Measuring the Value of the Dollar

(1) Year	(2) CPI	(3) Reciprocal		(4) Value of dollar
1(base)	100	1 ÷ 1.00	=	$1.00
2	125	1 ÷ 1.25	=	0.80
3	87	1 ÷ 0.87	=	1.15

EXHIBIT
8

Tracking Inflation: Consumer Prices and the Value of Money

The Consumer Price Index (CPI) is an average of the prices of various goods and services commonly purchased by families in urban areas. The reciprocal of the CPI thus provides a measure of the value, or purchasing power, of the dollar.

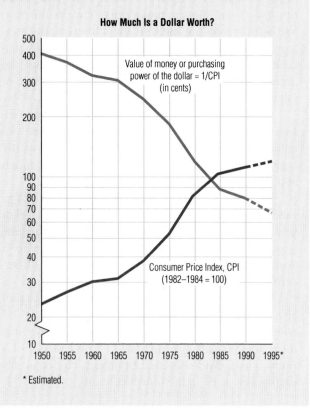

How Much Is a Dollar Worth?

* Estimated.

The actual CPI is shown in the table on the inside back covers of this book. From these data, the linked performances of the CPI and the value of money are graphed in Exhibit 8.

Conclusion: The Need for Price Stability

The term "inflation" means persistently rising prices. However, it's important to remember that not *all* prices rise at the same rate. Nor does the average price level rise at a steady pace. As a result, inflation tends to be erratic and incorrectly anticipated. Among those households that underestimate inflation, it creates

more losers than winners. But even if households could anticipate inflation correctly, they would still lose wealth to the extent that they held money during periods of rising prices. Of course, most households do. Consequently, a point mentioned earlier is worth emphasizing:

Inflation results in inequities caused by haphazard redistributions of wealth.

As you'll learn in later chapters, inflation also has adverse effects on the economy's efficiency and growth. And history shows that our own and other mixed economies may be inflation-prone. For these reasons, much of macroeconomics is concerned with understanding the causes of inflation and with formulating policies for achieving price stability.

International Transmissions of Business Cycles

As you learned earlier in the chapter, business cycles, unemployment, and inflation are not unique to our country. They occur in all capitalistically oriented economies because *households and businesses are composed of different people with different motivations.* As a result, decisions by the two groups to spend or not to spend generally differ. The differences create waves of economic activity that may be high or low, long-lived or short-lived, but which never repeat themselves in any systematic way.

An interesting aspect of business cycles concerns their impact on other nations. Are economic fluctuations in our own country a cause of fluctuations in other countries? And is the reverse true—that fluctuations in other countries cause fluctuations here?

The answers haven't always been clear. Since the nineteenth century, our nation has experienced frequent economic expansions as well as economic contractions. In some periods the fluctuations tended to occur at about the same time in all major nations. At other times the fluctuations appeared to be unrelated, or even inversely related, to those in other countries. There are thus very few long-run patterns on which to base a definitive answer.

But the trends have been changing in recent decades. Some evidence of this can be seen in Exhibit 9. International comparisons of output, employment, and prices—which are among the major economic variables that compose business cycles—are presented for the world's leading industrial nations. The com-

EXHIBIT
9

International Transmissions of Business Cycles: Output, Prices, and Unemployment in Major Industrial Countries

National economies are linked by international trade and investment. Therefore, changes in economic variables that comprise business cycles are experienced by most nations at about the same time. Because of the growing integration of the world's economies, the international transmission of business cycles is becoming more pronounced.

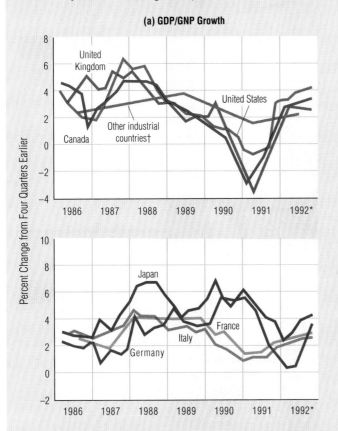

(a) GDP/GNP Growth

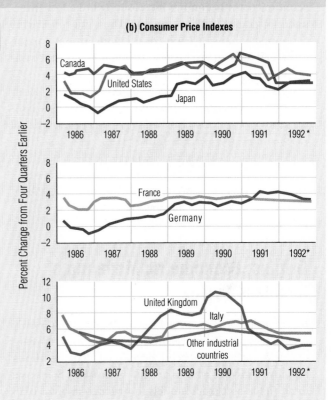

(b) Consumer Price Indexes

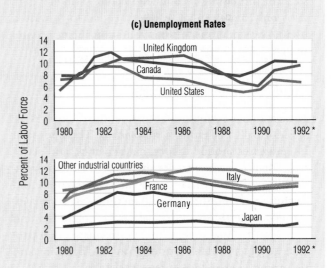

(c) Unemployment Rates

*Projections by International Monetary Fund.

Source: International Monetary Fund.

parisons indicate that the variables often tend to move more or less together. This is because national economies are becoming increasingly linked by international trade and investment. Thus, the effects of economic expansions and contractions in some major industrial nations are likely to be felt in many other nations as well.

As countries become economically integrated, there is a greater tendency for economic developments in one nation to affect those in others. Because of this, the international transmission of business cycles is a matter of substantial importance to all countries. To deal with the problem, representatives of leading industrial nations meet from time to time to discuss ways of reducing the international impact of business cycles.

Origins: Econometric Modeling of Business Cycles

Business cycles have existed for centuries. But it is only relatively recently that scientific methods for analyzing business cycles have been developed. The methods employed involve what is known as *modeling*. Scientists in all fields construct models in order to analyze real-world conditions or phenomena. However, a model is an abstraction of the reality it depicts. Therefore, instead of presenting a complete picture, a model contains only the essential features needed to provide a useful explanation of the condition being represented.

The Econometric Approach

Models that are employed in the study of business cycles normally make use of **econometrics**. This approach integrates economic theory, mathematics, and statistics. That is, econometrics expresses economic relationships in the form of mathematical equations and verifies the results by statistical methods. By constructing econometric models that can be quantified and tested with actual data, econometricians seek to provide rigorous explanations of economic behavior and to forecast aggregate economic variables.

Large-scale econometric models may consist of hundreds, or even thousands, of equations. To a great extent, the size and complexity of models is limited only by the availability of appropriate data required to construct them.

Ragnar Frisch
(1895–1973)

Jan Tinbergen
(1903–   )

Lawrence Klein
(1920–   )

In the 1930s, economists Ragnar Frisch of Norway and Jan Tinbergen of the Netherlands pioneered the use of econometric models. Economists ever since have been constructing large-scale econometric models to help make predictions and policy recommendations. In 1969, Frisch and Tinbergen became the first recipients of the Alfred Nobel Memorial Prize in Economic Science.

In the United States, econometric modeling came into its own during the 1950s. The person chiefly responsible was a professor at the University of Pennsylvania—Lawrence Klein. He, and subsequently other economists, constructed econometric models of the American economy and of other economies. An important feature of Klein's research was his incorporation of international influences into business-cycle models. In recognition of his contributions to the advancement of economic science, Klein was awarded the Nobel Prize in economics in 1980.

Forecasting and Simulating

Econometric models are utilized by some national governments and by a number of major corporations. In general, users can employ the models for two purposes—*forecasting* and *simulating*.

When utilized for forecasting, econometric models provide predictions of the short-term and long-term course of economic variables. Examples of such variables are consumption expenditures, investment expenditures, prices, interest rates, and gross national product. The predictions serve users as a guide for judging future directions and trends in the economy.

When utilized for simulating, econometric models replicate operations within the economy and the outcomes of different policies. A national government, for example, may want to know what the effects will be on such variables as GDP, housing construction, employment, and interest rates if personal income taxes are increased or decreased by specific percentages. To arrive at answers, the alternative tax rates are fed into the model, and the resulting estimated outcomes are computed.

Econometric models can thus serve as powerful tools for economic analysis and as guides for government policymaking. This explains why they have gained considerable acceptance both in the private and public sectors. But economists know that econometric models are of limited usefulness—for an obvious reason:

Economic conditions are always changing. As a result, even the most comprehensive econometric models often fail to anticipate accurately new levels of production, employment, prices, interest rates, or other measures of activity. Because of this, econometric models undergo continuous revision and refinement in an effort to reflect current relationships between key variables in the economy.

Business Cycles or Business Chaos?

In their attempts to predict business cycles, economists have suggested many different causes. One is instability in business investment. Another is recurrent expansions and contractions of money and credit by the nation's banking system. A third is uncontrollable random events, such as wars or political instability in foreign nations.

Thanks to the work of a few meteorologists, mathematicians, physicists, and biologists, another explanation of business cycles is being explored—*chaos*. Chaos theory holds that large, complex systems containing many different competing forces exhibit unpredictable fluctuations.

Chaos theory was first proposed by meteorologists attempting to predict the weather. They concluded that long-term predictions were impossible because complex interactions of air masses, storm fronts, and temperatures around the world cause the weather to change in unpredictable ways. Theoretically, the flap of a butterfly's wing in Asia could lead to a thunderstorm in North America. Because the actions of butterflies can never be fully known, weather is ultimately unpredictable.

With millions of buyers, sellers, commodities, and markets interacting in complex ways, the economy may be as chaotic a system as the weather. Indeed, some economists suggest that business expansions and contractions are chaotic and unpredictable changes in economic activity. Economic fluctuations that occur in a seemingly regular, and even periodic, manner one moment swing wildly out of control the next. So economists are now beginning to ask the question, *Are business fluctuations predictable cycles or unpredictable chaos?*

Summary of Important Ideas

1. Mixed economies suffer from recurrent but nonperiodic fluctuations in economic activity known as business cycles. The major phases of such cycles are recession and recovery.

2. Industries react to business cycles in different ways. Most durable-goods industries tend to experience relatively wide fluctuations in output and employment and relatively small fluctuations in prices. The opposite is likely to occur in many nondurable-goods industries. In these industries, prices fluctuate relatively more than output and employment.

3. The economy's health, or illness, is reflected by economic indicators. Hundreds of these are published each month by government and private sources. Many of the indicators are closely monitored by economists and business executives who are interested in interpreting and forecasting business activity.

4. The unemployment rate is commonly expressed as a percentage of the labor force. However, because there are different concepts of unemployment, this commonly used measure is subject to criticism. A much better measure is the *employment ratio,* which is the percentage of the working-age population that is employed.

5. Inflation is a persistent rise in the general price level. Looked at another way, it is a persistent reduction in the purchasing power of a unit of money, such as the dollar. Inflation is commonly attributed to demand-pull or cost-push forces. In general, inflation tends to redistribute wealth haphazardly without regard to social goals. It also impairs a nation's efficiency and growth.

6. In recent decades, there has been an increased tendency for fluctuations in economic activity to be transmitted from one country to another. This tendency will gain in importance as the world's economies become more economically integrated.

7. Several national governments and a number of major corporations make use of econometric models. The models, which in most cases are extraordinarily comprehensive, are employed to forecast and simulate business cycles. But even the most comprehensive econometric models often forecast incorrectly because they are unable to capture all of the key variables and changing relationships that affect economic activity.

Terms and Concepts to Review

business cycles

seasonal fluctuations

secular trends

time series

labor force

unemployment rate

frictional unemployment

cyclical unemployment

structural unemployment

underemployment

employment ratio

full employment

natural unemployment

natural employment

inflation

general price level

demand-pull inflation

cost-push inflation

nominal income

real income

Consumer Price Index

Producer Price Index

econometrics

Questions and Problems

1. If business cycles were recurrent and periodic, would they be easily predictable? Why? What, precisely, would you be able to predict about them?

2. Suppose you were to compare two industries, automobiles and agricultural products, over the course of a business cycle. Which would be more stable with respect to (a) output and employment, and (b) prices? Explain why.

3. It is customary to remove both the seasonal and long-term trend influences from time series data before undertaking an analysis of cyclical forces. Although there are no unusual controversies concerning removal of the seasonal factor, there is considerable disagreement among economists over removal of the trend. Can you suggest why?

4. Can you explain how the interaction of changes in consumption spending and investment spending may cause business cycles?

5. What do you suppose are some of the chief difficulties in using leading indicators for forecasting purposes?

6. Is a rising level of total spending likely to cure the problems of cyclical unemployment and structural unemployment—without encouraging inflation? Explain.

7. Is it preferable to have full employment with mild inflation or moderate unemployment with no inflation? Explain.

8. "Because of the changing composition of the labor force, a single measure of full employment proves to be an inadequate goal." In view of this statement, what alternatives can you suggest? Discuss.

9. It is often said that our economy has a built-in inflationary bias and is inflation-prone. Can you give reasons to account for this statement?

10. Minimum-wage legislation, despite its good intention, has been called "the most racially discriminating law on the books." Can you explain why? Can you show, with supply and demand curves, how minimum-wage legislation results in unemployment? What market solution can you suggest to increase employment among low-skilled members of the labor force?

11. "Reduce working hours. Spread the work. That's the way to solve the unemployment problem." So say many critics, union leaders, and social reformers. They argue for a reduction in working time—with *no loss of pay*—as a cure for unemployment. Do you agree with them?

12. Graphing Exercise It is important to become familiar with the kinds of economic data that are reported in newspapers and business magazines. The data are used to evaluate business and economic activity. Therefore, examine the tables on the inside front and back covers of the book. To help you understand how the columns are grouped, notice the names of the column headings as well as the names of the main categories above them.

Objective: To graph changes in GDP and in two other variables over a 10-year period in order to decide whether all three are related.

Procedure: (You may use a computer if you wish.)

Step (a) On a sheet of paper (preferably graph paper), copy the most recent 10 years of GDP figures from the inside front cover. Label your column "Column 1."

Step (b) Calculate the annual percentage changes of GDP in a new column. Label the column "Column 2."

Step (c) Select at least two of the following variables from the inside back cover:

- Average Weekly Hours of Work
- Unemployment
- Total New Construction
- Business Expenditures for New Plant and Equipment
- Manufacturers' New Orders

Copy the most recent 10 years of data for the variables you selected, and calculate the annual percentage changes. Enter the columns of figures in your table as you did for GDP in Steps (a) and (b).

Step (d) On a sheet of graph paper, sketch the graphs of the *percentage changes* that you calculated in Steps (b) and (c). Draw all three graphs on the same grids so you can compare them. Use colored pencils or ink to distinguish the graphs, and label them correctly. *Do a neat, professional job.* Refer back to the graphs in the chapter if you need help.

Interpretation: Do the graphs appear to be related? That is, do they seem to increase or decrease at about the same time? Can you suggest some reasons for your answers?

TAKE A STAND

Unemployment: Should We Care?

The unemployment rate is not a remote and lifeless statistic. A rise of a single percentage point means that over a million additional workers are out of work and seeking jobs.

Workers cannot produce output if they are unemployed. Therefore, a change in the unemployment rate signals a change in GDP. The unemployment rate is thus one of the most-watched indicators of an economy's overall health. Over the course of the business cycle, unemployment rises as the economy dips into recession, and falls as the economy recovers. In the recessions of the late 1970s and early 1980s, the unemployment rate reached 10 percent. In the relatively mild recession of the early 1990s, the unemployment rate was 7 percent.

At any given time, about half of all unemployment workers are in that state not because they were fired and not because they quit, but because they were laid off. Many have families to support and mortgages or other debts to pay; they must find work if they are to meet their financial obligations. To make matters worse, the unemployment rate is not even an adequate measure of those out of work. Some people who would like to work may be so discouraged by their failure to find employment that they drop out of the labor force entirely, in which case they are no longer officially counted as unemployed.

Our society's interest in and concern for the unemployed is reflected both by the close attention we pay to unemployment statistics and by the fact that we have social programs to alleviate the hardships of unemployment. The most important of these programs is federal unemployment insurance, which provides payments to temporarily unemployed workers while they seek new jobs. Forecasters who try to predict economic performance pay close attention to new claims for unemployment insurance benefits, since an increase in such claims often warns of a recession ahead. Yet unemployment may simply be part of the natural and normal functioning of a market economy and so perhaps need not be a great source of concern, especially since unemployment insurance provides workers with a safety net. So, *should we really care about unemployment?*

No: Some Unemployment Is Desirable

The economy is dynamic. Young adults enter the labor force and look for jobs. Workers dissatisfied with their current employment quit and look for other opportunities. Individuals relo-

cate because their spouses or partners find employment in a different part of the country. Mothers and fathers withdraw temporarily from the labor force to rear children, and then return to seek new employment. People grow old and retire. The labor requirements of businesses change with evolving economic circumstances. Advances in technology, changes in consumers' tastes, or changes in the cost of raw materials cause some industries to flourish and hire more workers while other industries go into decline and lay off workers. All of these changes are normal, natural, and desirable. All affect the unemployment rate.

Put simply, unemployment is (primarily) frictional: It is a consequence of workers searching for desirable jobs and firms' searching for competent workers to fill available positions.

Achieving good matches between workers and jobs necessitates such search. If firms always accepted the first applicant for a position and workers always accepted their first job offer, then the unemployment rate would be lower, but the economy would be operating much less efficiently. The unemployment insurance that protects workers from financial hardship allows them some selectivity—they need not take the first job that comes their way. Most unemployed workers find a suitable new job in a month or so—long before their unemployment benefits expire.

Yes: Unemployment Is Costly

It is true that much unemployment is frictional. However, much is not. If we measure unemployment by the total number of person-weeks spent unemployed, most are actually suffered by the *long-term unemployed*—those who go many months without finding a job. Some are workers with specialized skills that are no longer needed because of structural changes in the economy. Often, these are older workers who cannot easily acquire new skills, are reluctant to seek work in a new location because of family obligations, or face discrimination in hiring.

Extended periods of unemployment make all workers less and less employable. Unemployed workers cannot keep their skills polished and cannot gain additional on-the-job experience. Firms may be reluctant to hire workers who have been unemployed for a protracted period. To make matters worse, the long-term unemployed eventually use up their unemployment insurance benefits.

Unemployment often brings more than financial hardship. Studies reveal that the unemployed often suffer a loss of self-esteem and experience depression and anxiety, and there is strong evidence linking increases in unemployment to increased suicides. Unemployment may also be associated with social ills such as crime, delinquency, divorce, and strained race relations. In addition, studies have shown that workers who are laid off from their jobs are less loyal and less committed when they find new employment. So while the main burden of unemployment is of course borne by those actually out of work, society suffers as well.

Finally, we should care about unemployment because, at least at high levels, it indicates poor economic performance. Much of the variation in the unemployment rate is attributable to the fluctuations of the business cycle. When the economy is in recession, one of our most important resources is being wasted: People who would like to work and produce goods and services are instead forced to be idle.

The Question: Should We Care About Unemployment?

■   Some economists argue that unemployment is primarily frictional: It is a consequence of the continuous dynamic matching of workers and jobs. Therefore, unemployment helps the economy to function efficiently. When people are unemployed, it is usually because they choose to continue searching for a desirable job rather than accept one that doesn't measure up to their expectations.

■   Others argue that much unemployment is structural or cyclical, and is a source of considerable hardship to those out of work—especially those who spend many months unable to find employment. In addition, unemployment imposes significant costs on society as a whole.

Where Do You Stand?

1. The *No* argument pointed out that most unemployed workers are re-employed within a month or two, but the *Yes* argument stated that most person-weeks of unemployment are suffered by the long-term unemployed. At first glance, the two arguments appear contradictory. Can you explain why they are consistent?

2. Why might you care if your neighbor were unemployed?

3. Some economists draw a distinction between voluntary and involuntary unemployment. Others argue that the distinction is meaningless. If a laid-off engineer cannot find another engineering job, but could find a job delivering newspapers, is that person voluntarily or involuntarily unemployed? Do you think that most unemployment is voluntary or involuntary?

4. Should we care about unemployment? Justify your stand.

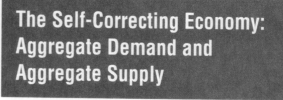

Chapter 7

The Self-Correcting Economy: Aggregate Demand and Aggregate Supply

Demand and Supply: Micro Foundations of
   Macroeconomics

Early Classical Macroeconomics

Today's Macroeconomics

Shifts of the Curves

Inflationary and Recessionary Gaps

Origins: Early Classical Economists

Learning Guide

Watch for answers to these important questions

What does market clearing mean? What conditions are necessary for markets to clear?

How does price flexibility ensure that the economy is self-correcting? Why is the notion of price stickiness so important?

What is the meaning of aggregate demand? Of aggregate supply? What factors may cause the aggregate demand and aggregate supply curves to shift?

How does an economy adjust by itself to full employment? Why does the process take time?

Who were some of the early classical economists? What were their contributions to economics?

Sir Isaac Newton, seventeenth-century English knight and one of the greatest mathematicians and physicists of all time, never studied much economics. If he had, he would have concluded that business cycles obey his basic law of physics: What goes up must come down. But he would have added the proviso that what comes down also goes up.

You've already seen evidence of this. Major macroeconomic indicators such as GDP, unemployment rates, and the price level rarely remain constant. They almost always are either rising or falling. These fluctuations affect all of us. They influence our ability to get jobs, to buy the things we want, and to save for things we would like to buy in the future. In a broader sense, they affect the goals of our economy: efficiency, equity, stability, and growth.

Why do fluctuations in economic variables occur? Should measures be undertaken to reduce them? If so, what should those measures be? These questions are at the heart of many macroeconomic problems you read and hear about every day. The issues that result from them constitute much of the driving force behind major political campaigns. Because the questions are of fundamental importance, they require our continuing concern. Consequently, they will occupy much of our attention throughout the rest of our study of macroeconomics.

Demand and Supply: Micro Foundations of Macroeconomics

When you studied demand and supply near the beginning of this course, you saw how the equilibrium price of a good is determined in a particular market. One of the principles learned from that study is this:

An individual market in which numerous buyers and sellers deal in a standardized good is self-correcting. That is, when a change occurs in demand or in supply, the price and quantity of the product adjust automatically to their new equilibrium levels. As a result, the market clears, leaving no surpluses or shortages.

This, of course, is a microeconomic principle because it refers to an individual market and a specific product. But the principle oversimplifies the situation. For one thing, it doesn't say *how long* the market clearing process may take.

Market Clearing: Flexible Versus Sticky Prices

When a change occurs in demand or in supply of a product, the price must adjust to a new equilibrium level in order for the market to clear. This means that the price must be *flexible*. If it isn't—if the price happens to be relatively inflexible—the market will not clear. Economists refer to prices that are relatively inflexible as "sticky." Thus, if the price of a product is sticky, a change in its demand or supply will cause either a surplus or a shortage of the product.

To refresh your understanding of this concept, look at Figure (a) of Exhibit 1, which provides a model of the market for steak. Notice first that, as in all demand and supply models, quantity is measured on the horizontal axis and price on the vertical.

The downward-sloping demand curve *D* tells you that buyers are willing to purchase more steak at lower prices than at higher ones. The upward-sloping supply curve *S* means that sellers are willing to offer more steak at higher prices than at lower ones. The intersection of the two curves determines an equilibrium point *E*. This corresponds to an equilibrium quantity of 6 million pounds and an equilibrium price of $4 per pound.

EXHIBIT
1

Self-Correcting Markets and Price Flexibility

A self-correcting market is one that clears when there are changes in supply or demand. As a result, there are no surpluses or shortages. The rate at which a market clears depends on the degree of price flexibility.

FIGURE (a) A decrease in demand for steak shifts the demand curve to the left from *D* to *D'*. If the price is flexible, it will drop from $4 to $3 and the market will clear. If the price is sticky, it will remain at $4. This will create a *surplus* of 2 million pounds.

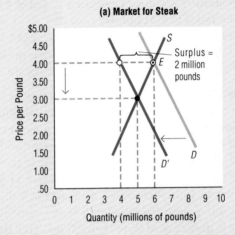

(a) Market for Steak

FIGURE (b) A decrease in supply of gasoline shifts the supply curve to the left from *S* to *S'*. If the price is flexible, it will rise from $1 to $1.20 and the market will clear. If the price is sticky, it will remain at $1. This will create a *shortage* of 2 million gallons.

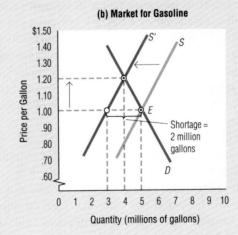

(b) Market for Gasoline

Now suppose that many consumers of beef decide to change their diet, substituting fish and chicken for steak. The demand for steak will decrease—the demand curve will shift to the left from D to D'. Will the market clear? That depends on whether the price is flexible or sticky:

- If the price is *flexible* in a downward direction, it will decline quickly. The result will be a new equilibrium price of $3 per pound and a new equilibrium of 5 million pounds.

- If the price is *sticky* in a downward direction, it will tend to adjust slowly. As long as it remains at $4 per pound, the quantity supplied of 6 million pounds *exceeds* the quantity demanded of 4 million pounds. The result is a *surplus* of 2 million pounds. The speed at which this surplus diminishes depends on how fast the price declines to the market-clearing level of $3 per pound.

What happens if the price of the product is sticky in an upward direction? This possibility is illustrated by a model of the market for gasoline, shown in Figure (b) of Exhibit 1. Suppose there's a decrease in the supply of gasoline—a shift of the supply curve to the left from S to S'. As long as the price remains at $1 per gallon, the quantity demanded of 5 million gallons exceeds the quantity supplied of 3 million gallons. The result is a *shortage* of 2 million gallons. This shortage will diminish as the price rises to the equilibrium or market-clearing level of $1.20 per gallon.

Price Flexibility and Market Competition

A sticky price, in contrast to a flexible price, is thus one that adjusts slowly (if at all) to changes in supply or demand. What causes a price to be sticky? As will be explained in this and in later chapters, there are several major causes. One that can be mentioned at this time is the degree of competition in the market. This is determined in part by the number of buyers and sellers in the market.

The organized exchange markets such as the stock market and the commodity market have numerous buyers and sellers. This helps make them among the most competitive markets in existence. As a result, prices in the organized exchange markets adjust almost instantly to changes in demand and supply. These markets clear within seconds, leaving no surpluses or shortages.

In many other markets, competition is substantially less pronounced. Such markets include those for

aircraft, cigarettes, industrial chemicals, photographic equipment, and tires. Although there are many buyers of these products, there are relatively few producers of each. Because of lower competitive pressures, producers are less inclined to reduce prices when demands for their products decrease, and more inclined to raise prices when demands increase. Prices of these goods are therefore much more *sticky downward* than upward. When surpluses occur, the markets tend to clear relatively slowly.

To summarize:

When prices are flexible, markets clear quickly, leaving no surpluses or shortages of goods or services. When prices are relatively inflexible or sticky, markets tend to clear slowly because surpluses or shortages may last for prolonged periods. In general, all freely competitive markets are eventually self-correcting. But the speed with which they clear depends on the price flexibility in each market.

These principles have been illustrated in terms of microeconomic models of demand and supply. Is it possible to formulate a general *macroeconomic* model of demand and supply that explains similar ideas? The answer, as you'll discover in this chapter, is yes. However, you can best appreciate the model by seeing it developed from the classical foundations on which it rests.

The foundations were laid by Adam Smith in his masterwork, *The Wealth of Nations* (1776), which marked the beginning of **classical economics**. This body of thought emphasized human self-interest and the operation of universal economic laws. These laws, like an "invisible hand," guide the economy automatically toward full-employment equilibrium if the government adheres to a policy of *laissez-faire* or noninterventionism. These ideas, which have endured to the present day as part of a larger system of classical thinking, constitute what may be called "classical macroeconomics."

Early Classical Macroeconomics

A fundamental proposition of classical macroeconomics was expressed by an early nineteenth-century French economist and journalist, Jean Baptiste Say. In 1803, he wrote:

A product is no sooner created than it, from that instant, offers a market for other products to the full extent of its own value. Thus, the mere circumstance of the creation of one product immediately opens a market for other products.

According to Say, therefore, each product generates demand in the economy equal to its own value. As a result, *total* demand must equal *total* supply.

This conclusion came to be known as "Say's law." But the idea was expressed more pointedly by David Ricardo, a British contemporary of Say, a member of Parliament, and a great pioneer in economic thought:

> No man produces but with a view to consume or sell, and he never sells but with an intention to purchase some other commodity which may be immediately useful to him or which may contribute to future production. By producing, then, he necessarily becomes either the consumer of his own goods, or the purchaser and consumer of the goods of some other person.

Thus, producing a dollar's worth of bread, for example, generates a dollar's worth of purchasing power consisting of wages, rent, interest, and profit. This can be used to buy the bread—or other goods produced.

Say's law means that *supply creates its own demand.* **The income a person receives from production is spent to purchase goods and services produced by others. For the economy as a whole, therefore, total production equals total income. In modern economics, as you'll see shortly, this is expressed as** *aggregate supply equals aggregate demand.* **It follows that any addition to output generates an equal addition to income, which in turn is spent on the added output.**

Notice that Ricardo and Say weren't claiming that the oversupply of some particular items couldn't occur. Unprofitable overproduction of specific goods can and does happen when business managers misjudge consumer demands. A producer of garlic-flavored breath mints will generate income sufficient to buy the mints, but that doesn't mean that anyone will want them. Errors such as this, however, are temporary, and are corrected as business managers shift resources out of the production of less profitable goods and services and into the production of more profitable ones. What is impossible, according to the classical view expressed by Ricardo and Say, is *general* overproduction, or a deficiency in aggregate expenditure. Supply cannot, in the aggregate, exceed demand.*

---

*It proves helpful to review the circular-flow model described in Chapter 1. Can you see why that model is actually a graphic depiction of Say's law?

An obvious conclusion that can be drawn from Say's law is that firms will always find it profitable to hire unemployed resources up to the point of full employment. This is true provided that the owners of unemployed resources are willing to be paid no more than their physical productivities justify. If this condition is met, there can be no prolonged periods of unemployment—for two reasons:

1. Workers and other resource suppliers will be receiving what they're worth, as measured by the market value of their physical productivities—their contribution to production.

2. The additional income earned from increased production will be spent on purchasing the additional output.

Therefore:

The economy is self-correcting—its markets always clear. Because of this, the economy adjusts *automatically* **to full employment as if guided by Adam Smith's "invisible hand."**

Let's now examine some of the implications of these ideas.

Aggregate Expenditure = Aggregate Income or Output

In an individual market, a surplus occurs if, at a particular price, the quantity supplied of an item exceeds the quantity demanded. The early classical economists gave particular attention to the question of whether the macroeconomic equivalent of a surplus could exist. If the total supply of goods and services exceeded the total demand, it would force firms to cut back on output, thereby putting workers out of jobs. Incomes earned by households would thus fall, causing total demand to decrease. With rising unemployment and declining income, the economy would go into a recession.

Could this happen? The answer given by classical economists was an emphatic *no.* For a surplus to exist in the first place, they contended, the public's total demand for output must be insufficient to purchase the total supply. But this is impossible because, as Say's law implies, people earn income in order to spend it. Thus, a basic premise of early classical economics is this:

Aggregate expenditure on goods and services always equals aggregate income or output.

This premise is best understood by expressing it in the familiar language of national income accounting. What the statement means is that *gross domestic expenditure equals gross domestic income* (GDI), *which as you know always equals gross domestic product* (GDP).

All Savings Are Invested

There's a possible flaw in the idea that aggregate expenditure always equals aggregate income. Though it seems clear that firms, in producing goods and services, generate income sufficient to purchase those goods and services, it doesn't necessarily mean that all of this income will be spent. What if people choose to *save* a portion of their income rather than spend it? Will these savings represent a withdrawal or "leakage" of funds from the economy's circular flow of income and expenditure? Will aggregate expenditure then fall below aggregate income or output, resulting in excess production, increasing unemployment, and decreasing incomes? In short, will the economy enter a recession?

The early classicists' answer was no. When people save (by putting their money in a bank, for example), businesses borrow those savings and pay a price for them called *interest*. The businesses will invest this borrowed money in capital goods in order to carry on profitable production. Saving by households, therefore, leads directly to spending by businesses on capital or investment goods. Thus, aggregate income is always spent. Part of it is spent by households for consumption, and part of it is spent by businesses for investment.

What mechanism ensures that all money saved is invested? The classicists' answer is interest, which they view as a reward for saving. That is, **interest** is the price that businesses pay households to persuade them to consume less in the present so that they can consume more at a later date. Current interest rates are determined in the economy's money and capital markets, collectively called the "loanable funds" market. In this market, households' supply of savings interacts with businesses' demand for them.

This is illustrated in Figure (a) of Exhibit 2. Notice that the quantity of loanable funds is measured on the horizontal axis and the interest rate, *which is always ex-* *pressed as a percentage*, is measured on the vertical. As in any market, price serves as the mechanism that balances quantity demanded and quantity supplied.

The downward-sloping demand curve means that businesses will desire more credit at lower interest rates than at higher ones. (For example, businesses would be willing to borrow more money at a 10 percent interest rate than at 15 percent.) The upward-sloping supply curve means that households will provide more savings at higher interest rates than at lower ones. (For instance, households would be willing to save more money at a 15 percent interest rate than at 10 percent.)

Thus, early classical economists based their theories about saving on three assumptions:

1. No business will borrow (and thereby pay interest) unless it plans to invest in profitable production.

2. No household will save (and thereby forgo the pleasure of spending) unless it's offered interest in return.

3. The interest rate is flexible (not sticky), thus ensuring that the market for loanable funds always clears quickly.

These assumptions suggest another premise of early classical economics:

Every dollar saved by households is borrowed and invested by businesses.

The early classicists believed that this helped to ensure the maintenance of a full-employment level of aggregate spending.

All Prices Are Flexible

But what would happen if some unemployment of resources did develop? The result would, of course, be a decline in aggregate income or purchasing power. Would such a condition prevail for very long? The early classical economists' answer was no. The reason, they said, is that *prices in all markets are flexible*. Therefore, markets clear quickly, leaving no surpluses or shortages because prices adjust rapidly to their equilibrium levels.

These ideas are illustrated in Exhibit 2. Here's how the graphs are interpreted:

EXHIBIT
2

Markets in Classical Theory

In classical theory, all markets are assumed to be competitive and all resources mobile. Therefore, prices and quantities are flexible, adjusting *automatically* to their equilibrium levels through the free play of market forces.

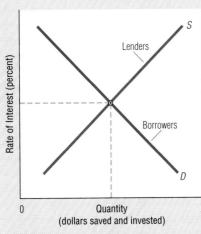

(a) Loanable Funds Market (dollars)

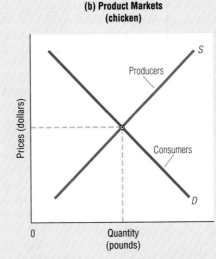

(b) Product Markets (chicken)

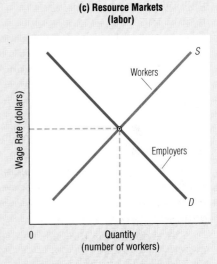

(c) Resource Markets (labor)

FIGURE (a) In the loanable funds market, a flexible interest rate ensures that all funds saved by households will be borrowed for investment by businesses. Therefore, there can be no surplus or shortage.

FIGURE (b) In the product markets, a flexible price ensures that the quantity of a good consumers want to buy equals the quantity producers want to sell. Therefore, there can be no surplus or shortage.

FIGURE (c) In the resource markets, a flexible wage rate ensures that the quantity of labor employers want to hire equals the quantity workers want to sell. Therefore, there can be no surplus or shortage.

In Figure (a)—the loanable funds market—the interest rate can be thought of as the *price* that borrowers pay lenders for loanable funds. This price equates the quantity demanded of loanable funds and the quantity supplied.

In Figure (b)—the product markets—chicken is used as an example. The dollar price of this good equates the quantity demanded and the quantity supplied.

In Figure (c)—the resource markets—labor is used as an example. The downward-sloping demand curve means that employers will hire more labor at a lower wage rate than at a higher one. The upward-sloping supply curve means that workers will offer more labor at a higher wage rate than at a lower one. The wage rate, which can be thought of as the *price* of labor, equates the quantity demanded of labor and the quantity supplied.

The early classicists believed that the economy's resources are mobile and its markets, composed of numerous buyers and sellers, are highly competitive. Therefore:

Prices in all markets adjust quickly to change in demand and supply, ensuring that the economy is rapidly self-correcting.

Today's Macroeconomics

The dictionary tells us that the word "classical" means standard or authoritative rather than new or experimental. This explains why classical architecture, art, literature, and music have endured for centuries. The same is true of classical economics. Although it has undergone many extensions and refinements since its founding by Adam Smith, most of its early ideas are an integral part of today's economic thinking. Particularly important in early classical as well as in modern macroeconomics is the notion of a self-correcting economy, the meaning of which might best be appreciated with an analogy.

In the modern macro view, the economy behaves somewhat like a ship at sea. When the water is calm, the ship remains upright—in "equilibrium"—and the passengers experience a smooth trip. When the water is turbulent, the ship may rock violently, causing many passengers to become seasick. But even in rough seas the ship is self-correcting: It tends *automatically* toward its upright or equilibrium position.

The economy has the same tendency. At any given time it may be operating at a level other than full employment. But this is a *short-run* phenomenon. In the *long-run*, because the economy is self-correcting, it always tends to move toward full-employment equilibrium. Let's see why, by constructing a model that will serve us throughout the rest of our study of macroeconomics. As you'll see, this model, and a precise distinction between the short run and the long run, are some of the features that distinguish modern macroeconomics from its early version.

The model to be constructed will relate two variables—the economy's real output and the average price level. Because real output is the same as the economy's real income, the model is called an **income-price model.** But the relationship between the variables will consist of two curves—an aggregate demand curve and an aggregate supply curve. Therefore, the income-price model may also be called an *aggregate demand/aggregate supply* model. Economists use both names interchangeably. The model, it may be noted, was conjectured in the early 1950s and developed in the 1970s.

The Aggregate Demand Curve

The first step in developing an income-price model, or aggregate demand/aggregate supply model, is to for-

The Aggregate Demand Curve

The aggregate demand *(AD)* curve is downward sloping. This means that the public will spend more on real output at a lower average price level than at a higher one. The reason for this inverse relation is explained by three effects:

1. **Real-Balance Effect** At lower average prices, the purchasing power or *real* value of people's cash balances is greater. This enables people to spend more.
2. **Interest-Rate Effect** When prices decline, interest rates tend to decline, too. This stimulates total spending.
3. **Net-Export Effect** A decline in the price level makes domestic goods cheaper for foreigners to buy. This stimulates exports relative to imports, thereby increasing net exports.

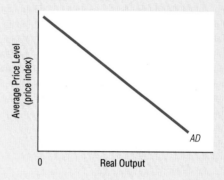

mulate an *aggregate demand (AD)* curve. Exhibit 3 shows a typical aggregate demand curve. Note that real output is measured on the horizontal axis. The average price level, expressed as a price index, is measured on the vertical.

How is the *AD* curve interpreted? **Aggregate demand** may be defined as the *total value of real aggregate output that all sectors of the economy are willing to purchase at various average price levels.* The downward slope of the *AD* curve tells you that the public will spend more on real output at a lower average price level than at a higher one. There are three reasons for this: the real-balance effect, the interest-rate effect, and the net-export effect.

Real-Balance Effect

At any given time you may be holding a cash balance, such as in a savings account, with which to buy goods and services. The *real* value or purchasing power of this balance varies inversely with the average price level. That is, at lower prices your cash balance can buy more; at higher prices your cash balance can buy less. The same is true for everyone else. Therefore, changes in the average price level affect people's *real* cash balances, and hence total spending. This idea is called the **real-balance effect**. (It's also sometimes called the *Pigou effect*, after Arthur Pigou, an early twentieth-century British economist who formulated the concept.)

Interest-Rate Effect

The public borrows money to finance its purchases of houses, cars, factories, machines, and many other goods. Interest rates, which may be viewed as the costs of borrowing money, tend to vary directly with the average price level. There are two reasons for this:

- When prices decline, people's *real* cash balances increase. This reduces the public's demand for credit—which causes interest rates to decline. Spending thus becomes less costly, thereby increasing the amount of consumption and investment demand by households and businesses.

- When prices rise, the opposite occurs. People's *real* cash balances decline, so the public borrows more funds in order to finance purchases. This increases the public's demand for credit, causing interest rates to rise. Spending thus becomes more costly, and the demand by households and businesses for consumption and investment goods decreases.

The ways in which changes in the price level affect interest rates, which in turn affect total spending, is called the **interest-rate effect**. (It's also sometimes called the *Keynes effect*, after John Maynard Keynes, a distinguished British economist of the first half of the twentieth century.)

Net-Export Effect

Some of our GDP is sold to other countries. These are our exports. Some of other countries' GDP is bought by us. These are our imports. The difference between the value of the economy's total exports and the value of its total imports is called **net exports**. Thus, for any given year:

Net exports = total exports − total imports

A decrease in the domestic price level relative to foreign prices encourages foreign spending on domestic goods. Therefore, exports increase relative to imports. The result is an increase in net exports and, therefore, an increase in the amount of aggregate demand. This is called the **net-export effect**. It also works in reverse. If the domestic price level rises relative to foreign prices, net exports and hence the amount of aggregate demand decrease.

The Constant Money-Supply Assumption

Like most relationships in economics, the real-balance effect, the interest-rate effect, and the net-export effect assume that all other things remain the same. One of the most important of the "all other things" is the public's nominal cash balance. That is, the amount of money held by the public—the supply of money in the economy—is assumed to remain constant. An increase in the quantity of money relative to income would leave the public with larger real cash balances to spend, and the aggregate demand curve would shift to the right. A decrease would leave the public with smaller real cash balances to spend, and the aggregate demand curve would shift to the left. The sources of a change in aggregate demand will be explored shortly. For now, you should be able to sketch and interpret the changes in a graph of aggregate demand.

The Long-Run Aggregate Supply Curve

The aggregate demand curve is only half the income-price model. The other half is an *aggregate supply* curve. **Aggregate supply** may be defined as *the amount of real aggregate output that will be made available at various average price levels.* One type of aggregate supply curve—a long-run curve—is illustrated in Exhibit 4. (A short-run aggregate supply curve will be illustrated shortly.)

You can't help but notice that the curve is a vertical line. It characterizes two fundamental ideas of classical economics:

1. *In the long run, the economy operates at the full- or natural-employment level.* The curve is thus labeled *LRAS* to stand for **long-run aggregate supply**. The volume of output produced at this level is the economy's potential output, called **potential real output**.

EXHIBIT
4

The Long-Run Aggregate Supply (*LRAS*) Curve

The long-run aggregate supply curve is a vertical line at the full- or natural-employment level of output. The curve tells you that, in the long run, firms will produce the same real output at higher price levels as at lower ones.

Notice this fact from the horizontal axis: Because of the existence of some natural (frictional and structural) unemployment, the full- or natural-employment output is *smaller* than the output produced if 100 percent of the labor force is employed. This, you'll recall, accords with the definition of full employment.

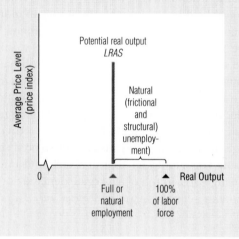

2. *In the long run, output is independent of prices.* The same real output may be produced at a relatively low price level as at a relatively high one. This, as you'll soon see, follows logically from the classical assumption that prices are flexible.

Notice that, on the horizontal axis, the output at full or natural employment is smaller than the output produced if 100 percent of the labor force is employed. This is consistent with the meaning of full employment explained in the previous chapter. The difference in output is due to the existence of some natural (frictional and structural) unemployment.

Combining the Curves

The aggregate demand curve and the long-run aggregate supply curve can now be shown on the same graph. This is done in Exhibit 5. As you can see, the intersection of the two curves determines an equilibrium at the full- or natural-employment level of real output and a corresponding average price level at *P*.

Suppose aggregate demand should now increase—shift to the right—from *AD* to *AD'*. This might happen, for example, if the quantity of money in the economy were to rise, leaving people with larger cash balances to spend. Because resources are already fully employed, the increased spending would bid up wages and other resource costs without raising real output. The impact would therefore be entirely on prices. The average price level would rise from *P* to *P'* without having any effect on output and employment.

The reverse, of course, would occur if the quantity of money in the economy were to decline. People would have smaller cash balances available to spend, so aggregate demand would decrease and the curve would shift to the left. The average price level would therefore fall without affecting output and employment.

Thus, by examining the relationship of the relevant variables, the income-price model permits interpretation of a fundamental classical belief:

In the long run, the economy is self-correcting because *prices are flexible.*

What About the Short Run?

As you learned early in the chapter, when prices are sticky, markets take longer to self-correct. The economy, therefore, can experience prolonged contractions and expansions in output and employment. You saw the evidence of this in the previous chapter, in a chart depicting the long-run history of U.S. business cycles.

To help explain business cycles, economists distinguish between the short run and the long run:

The *short run* is a period in which most prices are sticky. This results in market surpluses and shortages that may delay the economy's tendency to self-correct. The *long run* is a period long enough for all prices to be flexible. Consequently, there are no surpluses and shortages—that is, the economy self-corrects. Thus: *In the short run, the economy may or may not operate at full em-*

EXHIBIT
5

Aggregate Demand and Long-Run Aggregate Supply

In the long run, the economy operates at its full- or natural-employment level of output. Therefore, any change in aggregate demand, such as a change from *AD* to *AD'*, would cause the average price level to change from *P* to *P'*. However, production and employment would remain unaffected. Thus, *in the long run, the price level fluctuates while the full-employment level of real output tends to remain stable.*

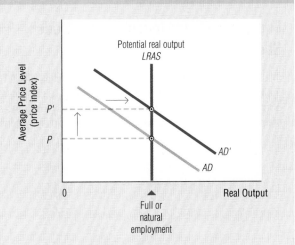

ployment. In the long run, the economy always operates at full employment.

The distinction between the short run and the long run makes it possible to use a separate model for each. The difference between the models is reflected by the shape of the aggregate supply curve. This provides a practical means of interpreting changes in the economy's production, employment, and prices.

The two models are illustrated in Exhibit 6. Three features of the graphs should be pointed out:

First, observe that both diagrams are relating the same two variables—real output measured on the horizontal axis and the average price level measured on the vertical axis. Second, because of the existence of some natural (frictional and structural) unemployment, the full- or natural-employment output is *smaller* than the output produced if 100 percent of the labor force is employed. Third, in contrast with the vertical *LRAS* curve in Figure (b), the short-run *AS* curve in Figure (a) has three distinct properties:

1.   It Is Upward Sloping.   The curve tells you that, up to a point, businesses will supply larger volumes of output at higher prices than at lower ones. This is because most wages and certain other production costs are set by contracts and hence don't increase immediately in response to rising prices. Therefore, higher prices

mean the opportunity for wider profit margins, which gives producers incentive to increase output.

2.   It Rises More Quickly as the Full-Employment Level of Real Output Is Approached.   The curve becomes steeper because, as increasing quantities of the economy's resources are utilized, labor and other inputs become scarcer. Less efficient resources are thus brought into use. Therefore, greater increases in prices relative to costs are needed to bring forth additional increments of output. Otherwise it wouldn't be profitable for firms to hire the additional resources.

3.   It Continues Rising After the Full-Employment Level of Real Output Is Reached.   The curve extends beyond the vertical line representing the economy's potential real output. This, you'll recall, is the level of output that exists at full employment. For example, if full employment is assumed to exist when 95 percent of the labor force is employed, then the remaining 5 percent constitutes natural unemployment. As explained in the previous paragraph, steeper increases in prices are therefore necessary to call forth the additional output needed to absorb this remaining pool of less efficient unemployed resources.

In concluding, let's review what the short-run and long-run curves show us:

EXHIBIT
6

Equilibrium in the Income-Price Model: Short Run and Long Run

FIGURE (a) Short Run The *AS* curve is upward-sloping. This means that rising prices bring forth higher levels of real output and employment. (Note: In the short run, as explained later, the *AD* and *AS* curves may or may not intersect at full employment.)

FIGURE (b) Long Run The *LRAS* curve is vertical. This means that only the price level can fluctuate with changes in aggregate demand while real output and employment remain stable at their full or natural levels.

In both diagrams, the equilibrium price level at P is determined by the inter-section of the aggregate demand section of the aggregate demand.

(a) Short Run

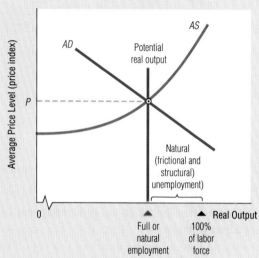

(b) Long Run

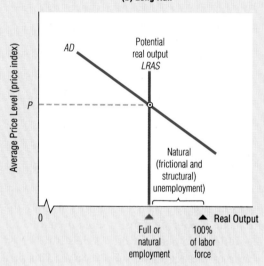

In the short run, rising prices bring forth higher levels of real output and employment. Therefore, the upward-sloping aggregate supply curve in Figure (a) is a *short-run aggregate supply curve.*

In the long run, the economy produces its potential real output regardless of the average price level. Therefore, the vertical aggregate supply curve in Figure (b) is a *long-run aggregate supply curve.*

Summary Thus Far

1. The speed with which markets clear, leaving no surpluses or shortages, depends on whether prices are flexible or sticky. In any market, the degree of competition is an important factor affecting price flexibility.

2. Much of early classical macroeconomics was rooted in the concept of *Say's law*—the proposition that supply creates its own demand. This led the classicists to conclude that, because prices are flexible, the economy is self-correcting: It adjusts automatically to full-employment equilibrium. These ideas were formulated without the use of models, and with no clear distinction between the short run and long run.

3. Today's macroeconomics revises and extends early classical thinking. Through the use of an *income-price model*, real output and the average price level are related by means of an aggregate demand curve and an aggregate supply curve. The aggregate supply curve is upward-sloping in the short run because prices are sticky, and vertical in the long run because prices are flexible. Today's macroeconomic ideas are thus more refined and precise than those of the early classicists.

Shifts of the Curves

You don't have to have studied economics to be aware that real output and the average price level are always fluctuating. That kind of information is reported frequently in the news. But you do have to know some economics to understand why the fluctuations occur. You've already learned that real output and the average price level are both determined by the intersection of the aggregate demand and aggregate supply curves. It follows that any changes, or shifts, in these curves will cause fluctuations in the two variables.

Why do the curves change? Shifts occur as a result of changes in any underlying conditions that are assumed to be constant when the curves are drawn. Some of these changes may affect only the *AD* curve, some only the *AS* curve, and some both.

Changes in Aggregate Demand

You can best understand the conditions that will shift the aggregate demand curve by recalling that expenditures by all four sectors of the economy are the sources of aggregate demand. These are:

- *consumption expenditures*—by the household sector

- *investment expenditures*—by the business sector

- *government expenditures*—by the public sector

- *net exports*—by the foreign sector

If you refer to the first four columns of the table on the inside front cover of the book, you can verify that the sum of these expenditures equals GDP in the fifth column. Therefore, anything that changes one of the four expenditure values will shift the aggregate demand curve—the total amount spent on real GDP at each average price level. The aggregate demand curve will shift to the right as a result of an increase in any of the expenditure components, as illustrated in Exhibit 7. It will shift to the left if there is a decrease in any of these components. Here are some examples of changes that will shift the curve.

Changes in Inflationary Expectations

What would you do if you expected a substantial rise in prices during the coming months? If you were planning to make a relatively large purchase—perhaps

EXHIBIT
7

Changes in Aggregate Demand

An increase in aggregate demand means that there is a shift of the curve to the right—from *AD* to *AD'*. The result is a rise in the average price level from *P* to *P'* and an increase in real output from *Q* to *Q'*.

A decrease in aggregate demand—a shift to the left—has the opposite effects.

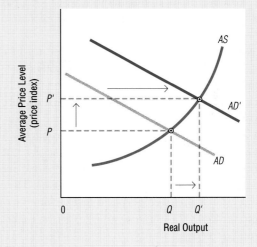

some new clothes, a video recorder, or a personal computer—you would try to buy these goods now instead of waiting.

The same behavior can be assumed for the public. If consumers expect a significant rise in prices in the near future, household-sector spending will increase as potential buyers seek to fulfill some of their purchase intentions now. If business executives expect prices to rise, business-sector spending will increase as firms place new orders for plant, equipment, and inventories.

The public's decision to buy will bring about an *increase in aggregate demand*—a rightward shift of the *AD* curve to *AD'*—as in Exhibit 7. Because of this, the equilibrium average price level will rise from *P* to *P'*. Correspondingly, the equilibrium level of real output will increase from *Q* to *Q'*

The opposite will occur if a significant decline in prices is expected. Households and businesses will postpone some purchases, especially major ones, in order to wait for lower prices. This will cause a *decrease in aggregate demand*—a shift of the curve to the left. The result will be a lower equilibrium average price level and a lower equilibrium level of real output.

Changes in Cash Balances

Imagine winning $1,000 in a lottery. Because the amount of money you now have in relation to your income is larger than it normally is, you'll probably spend much of the excess cash balance. Your demand for goods and services will thus increase.

From time to time, the amount of money in the economy increases substantially—for reasons that will be explained in several later chapters. When this happens, the public finds itself holding significantly larger cash balances in relation to its income than it normally holds. As a result, it spends much of the excess balances on goods and services. This causes an *increase in aggregate demand*—a rightward shift of the curve from *AD* to *AD'*—as shown previously in Exhibit 7. The effect is a rise in the average price level from *P* to *P'*. Correspondingly, there is also an increase in real output from *Q* to *Q'*.

The opposite effects will be seen if there is a substantial decrease in the amount of money in the economy. The public finds itself holding significantly smaller cash balances in relation to its income than it normally holds. This brings about a *decrease in aggregate demand*—a shift of the curve to the left. As a result, both the average price and real output decline to new equilibrium levels.

Changes in Tax Rates

If the amount of taxes you pay declines, you'll be left with more income to spend. This enables you to buy more of the things you want, thereby increasing your demand for goods and services.

Most consumers tend to react in the same way. When government reduces tax rates, people are left with more disposable income. To the extent that they spend it, there is an *increase in aggregate demand*—a shift of the curve to the right, as you saw in Exhibit 7. Conversely, when tax rates are increased, people are left with less disposable income. To the extent that this causes a reduction in spending, there is a *decrease in aggregate demand*—a shift of the curve to the left. You should be able to determine the effects on price and output in each of these cases.

Changes in Government Spending

In order to provide goods and services such as national defense, public education, and health and welfare benefits, the government must purchase the inputs it needs in the marketplace. These purchases, which are commonly referred to simply as government spending, are an important part of aggregate demand. An increase in government spending will shift the aggregate demand curve to the right; a decrease will shift it to the left. As before, you should be able to determine the effects on price and output for each case.

Changes in Net Exports

The economy's net exports, you'll recall, can be expressed as an equation. Thus, for any given year:

Net exports = total exports − total imports

Many things can affect net exports. One key determinant is the income level in countries with which we trade. If our trading partners are enjoying increased income, they will buy more of our goods. Total exports will rise relative to total imports, causing net exports to increase. Our aggregate demand curve will thus shift *to the right*.

On the other hand, declining income abroad can translate into declining income here. If our trading partners have less income, they will purchase fewer goods from us. Net exports will decrease, shifting our aggregate demand curve *to the left*.

You can thus see that, in a world of global interdependence, economic fluctuations in one country may well induce similar fluctuations in another.

Changes in Aggregate Supply

Like the aggregate demand curve, the aggregate supply curve can also shift. The shifts are due to changes in firms' costs of doing business. These changes can result from a variety of causes. Let's examine some of them.

Changes in Business Costs

Suppose the average price level has been rising significantly for some time. If unions, expecting the inflationary trend to continue, succeed in negotiating wage increases, business costs will rise. Increases in prices of raw materials, such as oil or certain other important basic commodities, will also raise business costs. So too will increases in corporate taxes, or government regulations that impose heavy expenses on companies.

EXHIBIT
8

Changes in Aggregate Supply

A decrease in aggregate supply means that there is a shift of the curve to the left—from *AS* to *AS'*. The result is a rise in the equilibrium average price level from *P* to *P'* and a decrease in the equilibrium real output level from *Q* to *Q'*.

An increase in aggregate supply—a shift to the right—has the opposite effects.

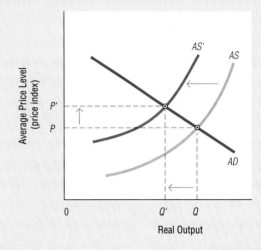

The result of increased business costs will be a *decrease* in aggregate supply. The *AS* curve will shift to the left, as shown in Exhibit 8. This means that a *higher* average price level is now needed to call forth any *given* volume of real output. The effect on the equilibrium average price level is a rise from *P* to *P'*. The effect on the equilibrium volume of real output is a decline from *Q* to *Q'*. Of course, if there are *reductions* in business costs, the result will be an *increase* in aggregate supply. The *AS* curve will shift to the right. Prices will thus decline and real output will rise.

Summing Up

In our dynamic economy, changes in aggregate demand and aggregate supply are always occurring. These give rise to economic fluctuations, commonly called business cycles. Summarizing what we've learned:

The average price level and real output (i.e., real GDP) fluctuate because of shifts in the aggregate demand and aggregate supply curves. Shifts in the aggregate demand curve are caused by changes in such conditions as inflationary expectations, cash balances, tax rates, government spending, and net exports. Shifts in the aggregate supply curve are caused by changes in business costs. These costs include wages, raw materials costs, business taxes, and the expenses of complying with government regulations.

Inflationary and Recessionary Gaps

The basic income-price model, which is fundamental to the study of macroeconomics, is now complete. To see one of its more important applications, let's use the model to interpret a recurring problem of our economy—inflations and recessions.

As you learned earlier in this chapter, short-run real output is determined by the intersection of the aggregate demand and aggregate supply curves. Long-run real output, on the other hand, is determined by the economy's potential output—represented by a vertical long-run aggregate supply curve at the full- or natural-employment level. These differences result in the fact that short-run real output can be less than, equal to, or greater than long-run real output.

Some implications of this can be understood by examining the three graphs in Exhibit 9.

Inflationary Gap In Figure (a), actual real output exceeds potential real output (both are measured on the horizontal axis). This is because the *AD* and *AS* curves intersect at point *E*—to the right of the vertical *LRAS* curve. The economy is thus experiencing a condition of overfull employment. That is, resources are being overutilized at the equilibrium price level, thereby putting upward pressure on prices. The difference between actual and potential real output is referred to as an ***inflationary gap***.

Inflationary and Recessionary Gaps

Inflationary and recessionary gaps are measured in terms of real output. They occur when, at the equilibrium price level, the corresponding actual output is either greater or less than the economy's potential output.

FIGURE (a) Inflationary Gap At the equilibrium price level, the corresponding actual output is greater than the economy's potential output.

FIGURE (b) No Gap At the equilibrium price level, the corresponding actual output is the same as the economy's potential output.

FIGURE (c) Recessionary Gap At the equilibrium price level, the corresponding actual output is less than the economy's potential output.

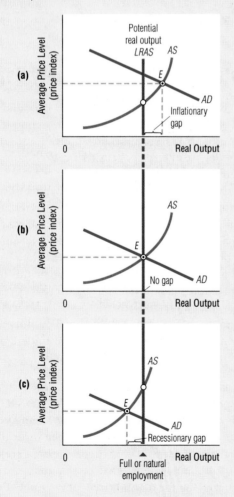

No Gap In Figure (b), actual real output is the same as potential real output. Because the *AD* and *AS* curves intersect at point *E* along the vertical *LRAS* curve, there is no gap between actual and potential output.

Recessionary Gap In Figure (c), actual real output is less than potential real output. This is because the *AD* and *AS* curves intersect at point *E*—to the left of the vertical *LRAS* curve. The economy is thus underutilizing its available resources at the equilibrium price level, resulting in a ***recessionary gap***.

Conclusion: Closing the Gaps; Self-Correcting Adjustments

Our economy often experiences inflationary and recessionary gaps. This is to be expected because many prices are sticky rather than flexible. But because the economy is self-correcting, the gaps eventually close by themselves. How does this happen? The answer is best understood in terms of the nature of the adjustment process:

In a self-correcting economy, inflationary and recessionary gaps eventually close automatically through *changes in aggregate supply.*

Let's see how the adjustments occur by looking at Exhibit 10. In Figure (a), suppose the economy is in short-run equilibrium at point *E*. Because this represents overfull employment, the economy is experiencing an inflationary gap. Tight labor markets will push wages upward as workers try to "catch up" with rising prices. Resource costs will thus increase, causing the aggregate supply curve to shift leftward from *AS* to *AS′*. The economy moves *automatically* to full-employment equilibrium and to a *higher* price level as it travels along the adjustment path from *E* to *E′*.

In Figure (b), suppose the economy is at point *E*. Because this represents less than full employment, the economy is experiencing a recessionary gap. The existence of unemployed resources will put downward pressure on wages. After some period of resistance, workers will agree to accept wage cuts as a condition of employment. Reduced wages will result in lower resource costs, causing the aggregate supply curve to shift rightward from *AS* to *AS′*. The economy thus moves *automatically* to full-employment equilibrium and to a *lower* price level as it travels along the adjustment path from *E* to *E′*.

EXHIBIT 10

Closing Inflationary and Recessionary Gaps: Self-Correcting Adjustments

FIGURE (a) Inflationary Gap The short-run equilibrium point at *E* occurs at overfull employment. This puts upward pressure on wages and other resource costs, causing the *AS* curve to shift to *AS'*. The inflationary gap thus closes as the economy moves along the adjustment path from *E* to *E'*.

FIGURE (b) Recessionary Gap The short-run equilibrium point at *E* occurs at less than full employment. This puts downward pressure on wages. Despite initial resistance by unemployed workers, they eventually accept wage cuts in order to get jobs. Reduced wages result in lower resource costs, causing the *AS* curve to shift to *AS'*. The recessionary gap thus closes as the economy moves along the adjustment path from *E* to *E'*.

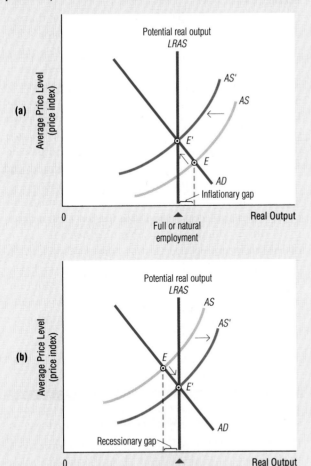

What about changes in aggregate demand? Can shifts of the *AD* curve succeed in closing inflationary and recessionary gaps, just as shifts of the *AS* curve do? The answer is that they can, but the shifts don't occur *automatically* in the same sense as shifts in aggregate supply. Instead, they may be brought about by changes in government policies, public expectations, or other causes. The nature of these causes will occupy much of our attention in several later chapters.

The income-price model, represented by *AD* and *AS* curves, demonstrates that the economy is self-correcting in the long run. However, the long run is defined *operationally* in terms of price flexibility, not in terms of calendar time. As a result, the model doesn't predict how many months or years it may take for the self-correcting forces to operate. Despite this weakness, *AD/AS* analysis provides an extremely useful way of depicting the overall behavior of the economy. Therefore, the income-price model will be used frequently throughout your remaining study of macroeconomics.

Origins: Early Classical Economists

"I am a beau only to my books," remarked Adam Smith. Little did the shy, absent-minded scholar suspect that the extraordinary power of his ideas would (as you learned in Chapter 1) spawn a discipline capable of attracting not only its fair share of crackpots and cranks, but also many of the world's greatest minds.

Smith's masterwork, *The Wealth of Nations* (1776), marked the beginning of *classical economics*. Much of its ideas have dominated the Western world since then. Classical economists typically emphasized people's self-interest and the operation of universal economic laws. These laws tend automatically to guide the economy toward full-employment equilibrium if the government adheres to a policy of laissez-faire.

During the nineteenth century, these ideas, initiated by Adam Smith, were refined and expanded by his many disciples. Almost all were English, and their ranks included philosophers, historians, clerics, bankers, scientists, lawyers, school teachers, and politicians. Two are especially worthy of mention because of their views on ideas expressed and implied in this chapter.

Jean Baptiste Say
(1767–1832)

David Ricardo
(1772–1823)

Jean Baptiste Say

"Supply creates its own demand." This was the famous Law of Markets expounded by the French economist Jean Baptiste Say in his *Treatise on Political Economy* (1803). This work was the first popular and systematic presentation of Adam Smith's ideas. As a result, it established Say as one of the leading economists of the early nineteenth century.

Say's law became central to classical economic thinking. In modern language, the law meant that the level of aggregate output (GDP) always equaled the level of aggregate income (GDI). This income enabled society to buy the output produced. Therefore, general overproduction of goods (due to a deficiency in aggregate spending) was impossible.

But what if businesses misjudged the markets for their goods? In that case, the classicists contended, unprofitable overproduction of specific commodities could and would occur. But such errors would be temporary and would be corrected as entrepreneurs strove to fulfill consumers' preferences by shifting resources out of the production of unprofitable goods and into the production of profitable ones.

David Ricardo

Generally considered to be the greatest of the early classical economists, David Ricardo was the first to view the economy as an analytical model. That is, he saw the economic system as an elaborate mechanism with interrelated parts. His task was to study the system and to discover the laws that determine its behavior. In so doing, Ricardo formulated theories of value, wages, rent, and profit. These theories, although not entirely original, were for the first time stated completely, au-

thoritatively, and systematically. Portions of them became the basis of many subsequent writings by later scholars. Some of Ricardo's ideas remain pillars of economics to this day.

Ricardo, an English businessman rather than an academician, wrote a number of brilliant papers. His ideas were largely incorporated in his work *Principles of Political Economy and Taxation* (1817). The book was an immediate success, and it attracted many disciples. As a result, Ricardo's influence became pervasive and lasting. Indeed, Ricardian economics became a synonym for classical political economy, or "classical economics," as we call it today. Fifty years were to pass before that influence began to be greatly refined and extended by new generations of classical scholars.

Like most other early classical economists, Ricardo was mainly concerned with the forces that determine the production of an economy's wealth and its distribution among the various classes of society. He also made major policy recommendations to Parliament concerning the dominant social and economic problems of his day. As a result of his wide-ranging contributions, Ricardo ranks as a major figure in the development of economic thought.

Summary of Important Ideas

1. When prices are flexible, markets clear quickly. As a result, changes in demand or supply leave no surpluses or shortages. When prices are sticky, markets clear slowly. Changes in demand or supply thus cause surpluses or shortages, some of which may exist for relatively long periods.

2. Early classical macroeconomics rested on the belief that *all* prices (including interest rates and wages) are flexible. This enables markets to clear quickly—and the economy to be rapidly self-correcting.

3. Modern macroeconomics has revised and extended some of the early classical beliefs. Today's economy, for example, can be represented by an income-price, or aggregate demand/aggregate supply, model. The *short-run* version of this model consists of a downward-sloping aggregate demand curve and an upward-sloping aggregate supply curve. The intersection of the curves determines an equilibrium average price level and an equilibrium level of real output.

4. The *long-run* version of the income-price model consists of a downward-sloping aggregate demand curve and a vertical aggregate supply curve at the economy's potential output level. This means that, in the long run, fluctuations in aggregate demand cause fluctuations in the average price level. However, potential output and employment remain stable at the full- or natural-employment level.

5. Shifts of the aggregate demand curve and of the aggregate supply curve occur frequently. These shifts cause fluctuations in the average price level and in real output. Among the conditions responsible for shifting the *AD* curve are changes in inflationary expectations, cash balances held by the public, tax rates, government spending, and net exports. Conditions that shift the *AS* curve are those that cause changes in business costs. These include wages, raw materials costs, business taxes, and government regulations.

6. Inflationary or recessionary gaps occur when, at the equilibrium price level, the corresponding real output is either greater or less than potential real output. Such gaps eventually close automatically through changes in aggregate supply, thus ensuring that the economy is self-correcting. However, the time required for the adjustment is unknown. The gaps can also close through changes in aggregate demand, but the changes aren't automatic. Instead they may be initiated by certain government policies or other factors that are studied in later chapters.

7. The early classical economists, almost all of whom were British subjects, wrote during the late eighteenth and early nineteenth centuries. Among the classicists who achieved lasting fame were: Adam Smith, a Scottish philosopher; Jean Baptiste Say, a French popular writer; and David Ricardo, an English businessman.

Much of today's economic thinking is rooted in ideas expressed by these and other prominent figures.

Terms and Concepts to Review

classical economics	*net-export effect*
Say's law	*aggregate supply*
interest	*long-run aggregate supply*
income-price model	*potential real output*
aggregate demand	*short run*
real-balance effect	*long-run*
interest-rate effect	*inflationary gap*
net exports	*recessionary gap*

Questions and Problems

1. Does Say's law apply to *individual* goods or markets? Explain.

2. Why do people save? Why do businesses invest?

3. During a recession, a firm will probably increase its sales if it cuts its prices, and it will reduce its costs if it cuts its wages. True or false? Why?

4. What is *aggregate demand*? Assuming that all other things remain the same, how would each of the following cause the aggregate demand curve to shift?
 a. Increase in household-sector spending
 b. Decrease in personal income taxes
 c. Decrease in interest rates
 d. Decrease in business-sector investment spending

5. How do the conditions listed in question 4 affect the average price level?

6. Early classical economists believed that markets clear very quickly. What do you think this means?

7. How does an upward-sloping aggregate supply curve affect the conclusions of the long-run income-price model?

8. In reality, is it possible for both output and employment to differ from their natural levels? What does this suggest about the slope of the aggregate supply curve?

TAKE A STAND

Economic Recessions: Are They Inevitable?

The U.S. economy currently produces more than $5 trillion worth of goods and services each year—over three times as much as forty years ago, even after correcting for inflation. History teaches us that overall output in developed economies grows substantially over time. As a result, succeeding generations enjoy higher and higher standards of living. But this economic growth is not smooth, and the long-run tendency for economies to grow is frequently interrupted by periods in which output falls rather than rises. During these *recessions*, workers are laid off from their jobs, unemployment rises, and consumption falls.

While recessions are normally fairly short-lived, they can occasionally be protracted and severe. The Great Depression of the 1930s lasted for much of the decade and, at its worst, saw almost one quarter of the labor force out of work. The memory of bread lines still haunts many of our parents and grandparents. Since World War II, the U.S. economy has suffered eight recessions of differing lengths and severity, the most recent of which began in July 1990. None of these recessions caused anything like the despair of the 1930s. Nevertheless, they are frightening reminders that continued increases in prosperity are not guaranteed, that some day we again may suffer a severe economic contraction. For example, on October 19, 1987, when the stock market fell by over 500 points, some commentators recalled the market crash of 1929 that preceded the Great Depression, and wondered if another were on the way.

Not all economists share that foreboding. Some think that the Depression was a special case, a recession that accelerated out of control because adequate safeguards did not yet exist, and because policy responses were ill-advised. They believe that recessions are, like the common cold, simply an unpleasant and inconvenient fact of life that we cannot do too much about. Others hold that recessions are not necessarily bad for the economy. Still others believe that intelligently formulated government policies can eliminate or at least lessen such downturns. There is no consensus, and the question remains. *Are recessions inevitable?*

Yes: Recessions Are a Fact of Life

Economies grow for two reasons. First, over time, we build up our stocks of resources—factories, machines, and trained and experienced workers—used to produce goods and services. Second, we develop new inventions and innovations that improve our ability to produce. Resource increases and technical advances ensure that potential output increases over time. But technical advances are likely to be erratic and so need not lead to smooth economic growth. Moreover, the economy is continually affected by events beyond our control that alter our ability to produce. For example, the Organization of Petroleum Exporting Countries (OPEC) dramatically raised oil prices twice during the 1970s. On each occasion, the resulting increase in energy prices raised the cost of producing goods and services, and led to two recessions. Because such adverse shocks to aggregate supply are bound to arise from time to time, the occasional recession is inevitable.

The low output and high unemployment we observe during a recession may even be desirable. Adverse shocks that cause recessions may also cut worker productivity. It makes sense for employers to lay workers off when their labor is relatively unproductive. Favorable shocks, such as advances in technology, cause economic booms. It then makes sense for employers to rehire workers and even engage new ones when their labor is relatively productive. The fluctuations in output and employment that arises over the course of the business cycle may simply reflect the normal and efficient adjustment of a well-functioning economy to different shocks. If so, it is then undesirable to eliminate recessions, even if it is possible.

Economists sometimes suggest, in addition, that recessions have another benefit: Managers may make the hard decisions required to streamline production and improve efficiency only if forced to do so by hard economic times.

No: **Recessions Are Avoidable**

If wages and prices were perfectly flexible, so that markets always cleared, then recessions might be nothing more than an efficient response to adverse shocks. While downturns can indeed be caused by adverse shocks to aggregate supply, many economists believe that these downturns sketch into costly and persistent recessions because prices and wages are sticky. Slow adjustment of prices and wages means that it takes time for the economy to return to potential output following a shock.

The costs of economic recessions can be severe—as much as five percent of a year's GDP, or about $1,000 for every person in the country, may be lost forever in a typical recession. Perhaps worse, the costs are borne very unevenly, with those who are laid off being the biggest losers.

By judicious use of government policy, however, policymakers can act to offset such shocks and prevent the consequent economic problems. (They do so by changing aggregate demand, as explained in more detail in later chapters.) If a decline in consumption spending threatened to push the economy into recession, economic policymakers could respond by stimulating the economy in a number of ways. For example, the federal government could increase its spending or cut taxes in order to increase the demand for goods. Alternatively, the country's central bank (the *Federal Reserve*) could push interest rates down in order to encourage firms to spend more on new factories and machines.

It is true that designing policies to prevent recession is more complicated than simply shifting lines on a graph. Inaccuracies in economic data mean that policymakers may not be sure the economy is in recession until the downturn is well under way, and the policies they enact can take time to have their impact on the economy. Policymakers may not even be exactly sure of the size of potential GDP, and so may not know the size of the recessionary gap. Nevertheless, carefully designed government polices can reduce or eliminate recessions and their substantial costs.

The Question: **Are Recessions Inevitable?**

■   Some economists argue that recessions are a natural and inevitable consequence of adverse shocks to the economy. Flexible wages and prices ensure that GDP stays at or close to potential. Declines in economic activity reflect temporary decreases in potential output. Therefore, such declines are to be expected and may even be healthy.

■   Others argue that recessions are costly periods in which resources are wasted—factories lie idle and workers are unemployed. It is both possible and desirable to eliminate or at least minimize recessions through well-chosen policies.

Where Do You Stand?

1. Do you think it makes sense that managers of firms are more likely to eliminate inefficiency in bad economic times than in good? Explain.

2. Economists pay considerable attention to consumer confidence. How might declining consumer confidence cause a recession? If consumers believe that a recession is temporary, does that make it more likely to be temporary? If consumers fear depression, does that make depression more likely?

3. How might you use the income-price model to explain a protracted recession or depression?

4. Are recessions inevitable? Justify your stand.

Chapter 8

Productivity and Economic Growth: Increases in Long-Run Aggregate Supply

What Is Productivity?

What Is Economic Growth?

What Determines Economic Growth?

International Comparisons and Growth Targets

The Classical Explanation of Growth: How Economics Became the "Dismal Science"

Origins: The Ghost of Malthus

Learning Guide

Watch for answers to these important questions

What is productivity? How is it measured? Why is it important? How can it be encouraged?

What is economic growth? How is it measured? What factors determine it?

How do the growth rates of the world's major economies compare with one another? What economic policies are likely to encourage growth?

How did early classical economists explain economic growth? What roles did population and capital play in the classical theory? Is the theory correct for nations today?

The greater thing in this world is not so much where we stand as in what direction we are going.

OLIVER WENDELL HOLMES

Whenever the economy experiences prolonged periods of steep inflation, high taxes, sluggish economic growth, or weak international competitiveness, many observers conclude that the nation must somehow achieve a massive gain in efficiency. It must seek to increase its output from existing labor and capital, and it must look for ways to offset rising wage and materials costs with new and better production methods.

Many things can be done to help the country realize these goals. Revising the tax system to instill more production incentives is one approach. Increasing the quantity of physical capital that labor can work with is another. And improving the quality of labor as well as the efficiency with which labor and capital are combined is still another. These and related measures enhance the nation's *productivity* and, therefore, its *economic growth*. Hence, the meanings and implications of these concepts are important to understand.

What Is Productivity?

How many miles does your car get to a gallon of gasoline? What is the average amount of wheat produced per acre of land? Does the Japanese steel industry produce more tons of steel per dollar of investment than the American steel industry does? Which word-processing application enables a secretary to produce the largest number of letters per hour?

These and similar questions concern problems of productivity. What is *productivity?* It is the relationship between output of goods or services and one or more of the inputs used to produce the output. Productivity is thus measured by a ratio of output to input:

$$\text{Productivity} = \frac{\text{output}}{\text{input}}$$

In order to understand productivity (and to avoid common misconceptions about it), it's important to note what is *not* included in the concept.

First, productivity is not a measure of the total volume of output. Neither does it disclose how hard anyone works. Therefore, measures of actual productivity neither imply nor support judgments about what is "good" or "bad" (unless they are judgments of performance relative to established productivity goals).

Second, a measure of productivity is not necessarily a measure of efficiency. For example, a lawyer may be able to type more letters per day than a typist. But is typing letters the most efficient use of the lawyer's time? Probably not. Therefore, the lawyer hires a typist to do the typing. The lawyer is then able to be more efficient by devoting full time to the practice of law. Of course, it might be possible to increase the typist's productivity by providing better equipment, such as a larger desk or a faster computer and word processing application. But it might be more *efficient* (that is, more profitable) for the lawyer to send fewer letters per day, which would require less of the typist's time.

Thus:

Measures of productivity are measures of the use of resources or of the degree of their use. Consequently, measures of productivity may or may not serve as indicators of the volume of output or of efficiency. Whether or not they do depends on how the measures are constructed and employed.

Two Measures of Productivity

Because productivity is a ratio of output to input, higher productivity can be attained by either (a) getting more output with the same amount of input or (b) getting the same output with less input.

Although many different measures of productivity can be formulated, the two that have gained the widest use are *partial productivity* and *total-factor productivity*.

Partial Productivity

The measure of *partial productivity* uses only one input in its denominator. Labor is the input most commonly used, but land and capital are also frequently employed. Such ratios as output per worker, yield per acre, and production per machine are examples of partial-productivity measures.

The most familiar measure of labor productivity in the United States is the index of output per hour of all persons employed in the business sector. Published by the U.S. Department of Labor, the index is shown on the inside back cover of this book. The index is calculated by dividing real GDP (that is, GDP in constant dollars) originating in the business sector by labor-hours employed in that sector.

Why are the contributions of government to GDP excluded from the measure? Because, unlike the private sector, which sells readily identifiable products to individuals at market prices, most of the products of the public sector consist of hard-to-measure services. These goods are given away "free" or at below-market prices. Some examples include national defense, police and fire protection, and subsidized health care. These, unlike the products produced by the private sector, are provided in order to fulfill collective rather than individual wants.

Total-Factor Productivity

A second measure of productivity is called *total-factor productivity*. The denominator of this index is the sum of all the measurable inputs (labor, land, capital) used in production. However, because some inputs may be more important than others in a particular production process, it is necessary to "weight" the inputs according to their relative significance.

For example, certain heavy industries, such as the automobile and steel industries, have become increasingly capital-intensive. They are using more machines and fewer workers. Therefore, greater numerical weight must be given to the importance of capital relative to labor when measuring such industries' total-factor productivity. In such high-technology fields as the biomedical and microelectronics industries, improvements in productivity depend heavily on research and development. Therefore, the time and money spent on these activities must be given relatively greater weight than other inputs when estimating the gains in total-factor productivity of these industries.

Searching for the Right Measure

It's usually easier to define a concept than it is to measure it. Productivity is no exception. Efforts to quantify it have been the subject of much controversy, leading to the conclusion that any measure is at best a tolerable compromise between conflicting objectives.

For instance, if your car gets 25 miles to a gallon of gasoline and your friend's car gets 20, then your car is more productive than your friend's with respect to gasoline consumption. However, if your friend's car uses a quart of oil per thousand miles while yours uses the same amount in 500 miles, then your friend's car is more productive than yours with respect to oil consumption.

Which car is more productive overall? There's no simple answer. To understand why, it is necessary to clarify certain practical problems associated with the measurement of three components of productivity—output, input, and level of coverage.

Output Measurement and Its Problems

Of the two figures from which a productivity ratio is derived, output is usually the more difficult one to determine. There are three major reasons for this:

1. Dissimilar Products Some products are sufficiently uniform that their outputs can be measured in physical units. Examples are tons of steel or bushels of wheat. But most products are dissimilar. Therefore, to derive a measure of total output, the outputs of these goods must be combined into a composite number. The most common procedure is to use the money value of products as the measure of output. But then the figures must be deflated by an appropriate price index in order to eliminate the effects of inflation. The results obtained are a measure of real output— that is, output expressed in constant dollars of a past period.

An example in terms of GDP, presented in Exhibit 1, serves as an illustration. Notice that each year's *nominal* GDP, shown in column (1), is divided by a general price index, shown in column (2). The base period for column (2) is assumed to be Year 2. As a result, a measure of *real* GDP, expressed in constant dollars of Year 2, is derived in column (3).

An important point to understand is that the general price index is an average. It expresses each year's average price level as a percentage of the average price level in the base period. For example, in Exhibit 1, Year 2 was chosen as the base from which inflation will be measured. Therefore, the average

EXHIBIT
1

Deflating Output with a Price Index
(hypothetical data)

When the outputs of dissimilar products are combined to form a composite number, that measure is commonly expressed in terms of money value. Gross domestic product (GDP) provides a typical example.

Years	(1) Nominal GDP (billions of current dollars)	(2) General price index	(3) Real GDP (billions of constant dollars of year 2) (1) ÷ (2)†
1	$ 982.4	91.4	$1,075
2*	1,171.1	100.0	1,171
3	1,412.9	116.0	1,218
4	1,702.2	133.7	1,273
5	2,127.6	152.1	1,399

*Base period. The general price index [column (2)] is assigned a value of 100 for this period.

†Before dividing, move decimal place in column (2) two places to the left.

price level is assigned a value of 100 percent. In Year 1, the average was 91.4 percent of what it was in Year 2. In Year 3, the average was 116 percent of what it was in Year 2, and so on.

2. Changes in Quality The quality of most goods does not remain constant. Because of advances in technology, the durability, design, and appearance of many products tend to improve over time. These improvements are not always reflected in the price indexes used as deflators of value figures. As a result, measures of productivity often understate such actual gains in productivity.

3. Nonquantifiable Services The provision of many types of services cannot be divided into well-defined units. Consequently, their production is often extremely difficult, if not impossible, to measure. How, for example, can the outputs of teachers, musicians, scientists, and numerous other producers of services be quantified in order to provide a basis for estimating their productivities? The answer is that usually they cannot. Because of this, useful productivity measures have been developed for only a few industries in the service sector.

Input Measurement and Its Problems

"Input" constitutes the denominator of the productivity equation. Although a variety of specific inputs may be used, they generally fall into one of three categories—labor, capital, and land.

1. Labor Productivity The improvement of human resources has always been a fundamental concern of economics. Consequently, the most common types of productivity ratios are those that measure labor productivity. Labor productivity may be expressed alternatively as (a) output per hour of employed persons, and (b) output per worker-hour. Both measures are widely used, mainly because they utilize data that are relatively easy to obtain when compared to other types of inputs. However, the data don't reflect differences in workers' skills, abilities, or other qualitative characteristics.

2. Capital Productivity Another measure of productivity is output per unit of capital. In terms of tangible capital, some common formulations of productivity include output per plant, output per machine, and output per square foot of factory space. In terms of intangible capital, expressions such as output per dollar of current assets (that is, cash and near-liquid assets) or output per dollar of inventory serve as measures of capital productivity. As you can see, the concept of capital is complex. Consequently, there's no single measure that serves all purposes.

3. Land Productivity A third measure of productivity is output per unit of land. Agriculture provides the most common examples. Data expressing yield per acre for wheat, corn, oats, and other grains are published regularly by the U.S. Department of Agriculture. So, too, are figures reporting the value per acre of land and the value of buildings per acre of land. These and similar measures provide indicators of the intensity of land use. That is, they reveal the extent to which a unit of land is fulfilling the purposes to which it is being put. However, as with labor and capital, there are qualitative differences in land. This makes a single measure of land productivity difficult to establish.

Level of Coverage

In addition to the problems of measuring output and input, the scope or comprehensiveness of any measure of productivity must also be considered. This is because measures of productivity can be prepared for almost any level of activity.

For example, at the lowest (that is, the simplest) level, many firms prepare productivity measures for their own operations. These are compared with industry averages and trends to reveal how well the company is performing relative to the industry. Among the more familiar measures of productivity at this level are output per worker, output per worker-hour, and output per department or division of the firm.

At the next higher level, trade associations consisting of groups of firms in the same industry often publish productivity data for their entire industry. (The measures are typically expressed in the form of index numbers.) Industry productivity data thus reflect the productivity gains of all firms within the industry. These gains can occur when firms improve their efficiency or when they increase their utilization rates of specific inputs.

Finally, the highest level or most general measures of productivity are those made at the national level. No perfect indicator of national productivity exists—for at least three reasons:

1. A comprehensive measure of the economy's output, such as GDP, excludes certain productive activities like homemakers' services. (Can you recall others?)

2. Government productivity cannot be measured completely. This is because many of the services government provides, such as national defense, public safety, education, and cultural opportunities, are given away "free" rather than sold in a market.

3. Some of the factors used in production cannot be classified and combined with other quantifiable resources to produce a comprehensive, unambiguous measure of input. Capital, as you've seen, is one example. Can you think of others?

Because of these and other difficulties, there exist relatively few measures of productivity at the national level. The most widely quoted are (a) output per hour of all persons in the private business sector, and (b) output per worker-hour. Both sets of data are published regularly by the U.S. Department of Labor. The figures, along with other statistics, are widely used as guidelines for wage and salary negotiations by unions and management.

Decreases in Productivity

If everyone produces more, the economy's productivity increases and the nation as a whole grows richer. Yet the economy has gone through long periods when it has experienced declines in productivity relative to some other major industrial countries. What are the reasons for this? There are many, but among the more important are these:

Growth of Service Industries The banking, entertainment, retailing, health-care, insurance, and other service industries have expanded rapidly. Productivity in the service sector is difficult to measure because outputs and inputs are not usually as easy to identify as they are in manufacturing.

Inefficient Labor and Management Practices Over the long run, many unions have been able to negotiate shorter workweeks, longer vacations, and more paid holidays. These actions may have contributed to reducing productivity. In addition, the managements of many firms have been remiss in eliminating outmoded business practices and procedures, thereby failing to fulfill their functions as efficient coordinators of their firms' resources. These actions have also been important contributors to declines in productivity.

Restrictive Government Policies Through such selective measures as tariffs, subsidies, regulations, and controls, government has promoted certain industries while hampering others. Through tax legislation favoring consumption over capital formation, government at times has reduced incentives to work, save, and invest. Taken together, these policies have often had dampening effects on the economy, reducing productivity and causing resources to be misallocated.

Stimulating Productivity for Economic Growth

It's easy to understand why today's most thoughtful business, labor, and political leaders are seeking ways to increase the economy's productivity. They realize that rising levels of output relative to input is a key to improving living standards. Therefore, if productivity doesn't increase, workers will have to put in more hours, or a larger number of workers will be needed, to provide a rising volume of output per person.

An increase in productivity means that the economy is producing more goods and services with its existing factors of production. The nation's real GDP therefore rises. A decrease in productivity means the opposite—and, consequently, leads to a decline in the nation's real GDP.

The most common measures of productivity are partial measures based usually on one factor of production, labor. For example, labor productivity is measured by output per employed person or output per worker-hour. However, a more comprehensive view of how well the economy is utilizing its productive resources is provided by a different index, *total-factor*

productivity. This is a measure of output relative to non-human resources as well as human ones.

Unfortunately, total-factor productivity is more difficult to quantify because it combines in its denominator a weighted sum of *all* inputs used in production. Thus, partial-productivity measures, based mainly on labor inputs because they are typically the largest and easiest to quantify, remain the most widely used indexes of productivity.

What can be done to step up gains in productivity? The greatest single need is for more investment in new plant and equipment. Over the long run, the largest increases in productivity come from the adoption of improved technology. This requires that economic policies be formulated to encourage more rapid advances in technology, thereby stimulating productivity, which in turn leads to faster economic growth.

International Trends and Comparisons of Productivity

In the long run, the single most important determinant of a nation's standard of living is the rate of productivity growth. Rising productivity translates into an expanding economic pie—a growing GDP—and therefore greater wealth. This is significant for social as well as economic reasons. Only wealthy nations are able to accumulate enough savings to help finance the attainment of most social goals. These include reductions in poverty and improvements in education, transportation, health care, and the environment. Poor nations spend practically all of their income on basic consumption goods, leaving little or no savings with which to pay for social betterment.

Over time, industrial nations experience changes in productivity, and these occur at different rates. As a result, nations' living standards vary. Some international trends and comparisons of productivity and living standards are shown in Exhibit 2. Here is what the graphs tell you:

Figure (a): Rising Productivity Since 1900, the United States has had the highest productivity growth rate of the major industrial nations. The sharpest increases occurred during and after World War II. During the war, American farms and factories operated at full capacity to provide food, fiber, and manufactured goods (planes, guns, tanks, and ships) for the nation and its allies. Since the war, rapid advances in technology have continued almost unabated, enabling all of the industrial nations to experience steady gains in output per worker.

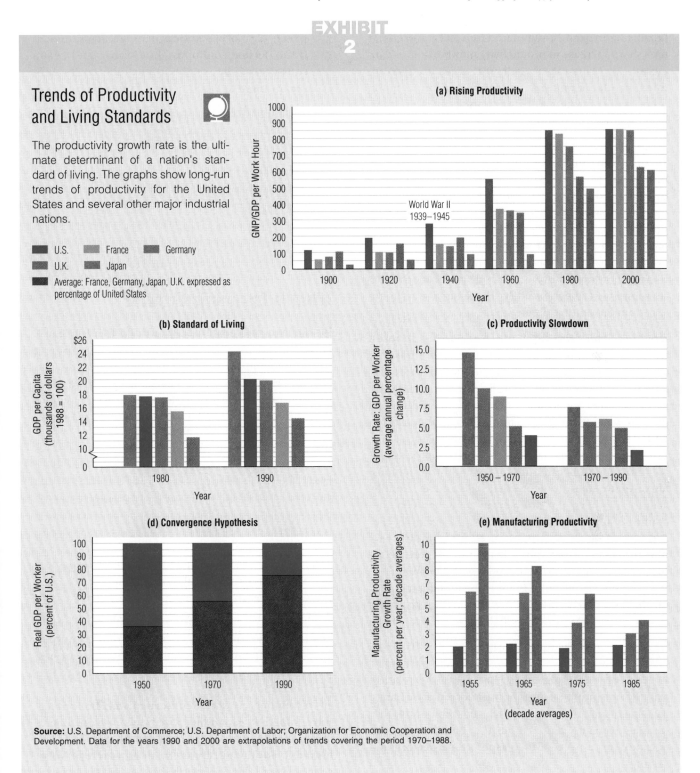

EXHIBIT 2

Trends of Productivity and Living Standards

The productivity growth rate is the ultimate determinant of a nation's standard of living. The graphs show long-run trends of productivity for the United States and several other major industrial nations.

- U.S.
- France
- Germany
- U.K.
- Japan
- Average: France, Germany, Japan, U.K. expressed as percentage of United States

(a) Rising Productivity

(b) Standard of Living

(c) Productivity Slowdown

(d) Convergence Hypothesis

(e) Manufacturing Productivity

Source: U.S. Department of Commerce; U.S. Department of Labor; Organization for Economic Cooperation and Development. Data for the years 1990 and 2000 are extrapolations of trends covering the period 1970–1988.

Figure (b): Standard of Living Gains in productivity lead to improvements in living standards. The improvements, measured by increases in real output per capita, consist of the goods we use frequently. They include automobiles, cameras, and computers as well as TV sets, video recorders, and washing machines. They also include the services of teachers, doctors, and lawyers as well as those of barbers, waiters, and mechanics. In other words, they include all of the goods and services that comprise GDP. During the 1980s,

Japan's standard of living soared, reflecting the country's sharp increase in productivity shown previously in Figure (a). Many experts believe that Japan's gain in living standards will slow dramatically in the coming years, reducing the gap between itself and the other leading industrial nations.

Figure (c): Productivity Slowdown Between 1970 and 1990, major industrial countries experienced a decline in the total productivity growth rate per worker. That is, total productivity in the industrial nations continued to increase during this period, as suggested in Figure (a), but the *rate of increase* slowed down. In relative terms, the largest slowdown was experienced by the United States, partly because in the 1970s and 1980s its growth rate was already relatively low. The smallest slowdown was experienced by the United Kingdom, which underwent hardly any change.

Figure (d): Convergence Hypothesis Reasons for the productivity slowdown have baffled experts and government officials in all of the leading industrial countries. Perhaps the best explanation is that the slowdown should be interpreted as a convergence of productivity growth rates. According to the *convergence hypothesis,* most technological advances are available to all nations that possess the labor and entrepreneurial skills to utilize them. Because the major industrial nations already have most of the needed skills and are rapidly acquiring others, the productivity gaps between the countries are closing. Thus in 1950, for example, the average productivity of the four major industrial nations other than the United States was 35 percent of U.S. productivity. In 1970 the figure was 55 percent; in 1990 it was 75 percent. If the trend continues, the productivity gap between all five industrial nations will be largely closed by the year 2010.

Figure (e): Manufacturing Productivity Since the 1950s, the average growth rate of U.S. manufacturing productivity has been remarkably stable. Because of this relative stability, the graph neglects annual percentage changes (which may fluctuate widely) and shows only the decade averages centered at the middle of each decade. Two aspects of the graph are particularly revealing:

1. Contrary to widespread popular belief, the growth rate of U.S. manufacturing productivity has not declined. Instead it has consistently averaged approximately 2 percent.

2. The relatively high growth rates in manufacturing productivity once experienced by Germany and

Japan, the world's leaders, have greatly subsided. If the decline continues, the German and Japanese rates will be roughly comparable to the U.S. rate by the year 2010.

To summarize:

Increases in productivity are necessary for nations to achieve higher living standards, as measured by real GDP per capita. Evidence suggest that, over the long run, productivity gaps between major industrial nations are closing. Assuming the long-run trends continue, the leading industrial countries will attain similar living standards during the first decade of the 21st century.

What Is Economic Growth?

Productivity and economic growth go hand in hand. However, there is often confusion about the meaning of economic growth. This is because politicians and economists are fond of hurling statistics at each other showing growth rates of various countries or regions over different periods. Hence, an accurate definition is needed.

Economic growth is the rate of increase in an economy's full-employment real output or income over time. That is, economic growth is the rise in an economy's full-employment output in constant prices. Economic growth may be expressed in either of two ways:

1. As the increase in total full-employment real GDP over time

2. As the increase in per-capita full-employment real GDP over time

The first of these measures is usually employed to describe the expansion of a nation's economic output. The second is used to express the development of a nation's standard of living and to compare it with that of other nations.

Economic growth is concerned with policy measures aimed at expanding a nation's *capacity* to produce. The concept of economic growth can thus be illustrated in two ways. One is by an outward shift of an economy's production-possibilities curve. The other is by a rightward shift of an economy's long-run aggregate supply curve. Recall that *both curves assume that the economy is producing at its full-employment level of output.*

The first case, utilizing a production-possibilities curve, is shown in Exhibit 3. In this model, as you learned early in the course, the economy is assumed to

EXHIBIT
3

Economic Growth Can Be Seen As an Outward Shift of an Economy's Production-Possibilities Curve

Economic growth is not a movement along a given curve, such as from *S* to *T*, because this is merely a change in the composition of total output. Nor is economic growth a movement from a point of unemployment, such as *U*, to a point on the production-possibilities curve, such as *S, V,* or *T.* Economic growth is an *outward shift* of the curve.

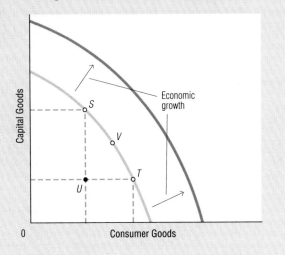

EXHIBIT
4

Economic Growth Can Be Seen As a Rightward Shift of an Economy's Potential Real Output Curve

At any given time, actual real output is determined by the intersection of the *AD* and *AS* curves. Potential real output, portrayed by the vertical *LRAS* curve at full employment, can be estimated from the formula given in the text. Economic growth can be depicted as a rightward shift of the curve. The inflationary and recessionary gaps, which aren't needed to illustrate economic growth, are nevertheless of interest because they show the state of the economy before and after the shift of the *LRAS* curve.

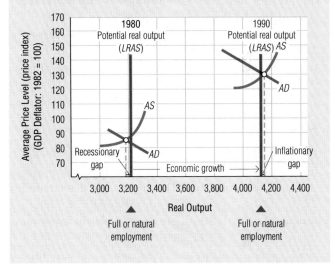

be producing only two classes of goods. For convenience, we'll call them consumer goods and capital goods, and identify them as such on the axes of the graph. Suppose the inner curve depicts the economy's current *capacity* to produce. It follows that economic growth isn't a movement along the curve from one point to another. Such a move reflects only a change in the combinations of goods produced, not a change in the capacity to produce. Nor is economic growth a movement from a point of unemployment, such as *U,* to a point on the curve, such as *S, V,* or *T.* Such a move reflects only increased utilization of the existing capacity to produce. Instead, economic growth is an outward shift of the production-possibilities curve. The new curve, compared to the previous one, depicts a greater *capacity* to produce.

Economic growth can also be illustrated by increases in an economy's long-run aggregate supply (*LRAS*) curve. Because it identifies the economy's potential real output, the curve is a vertical line at the full employment level of output. In Exhibit 4, actual and potential real output are shown graphically for different years. For any given year, actual real output is determined by the intersection of the *AD* and *AS* curves. Potential real output may be calculated from the following formula used in an earlier chapter to estimate the GDP gap.*

Let's assume that full or natural employment exists when 94 percent of the labor force is employed. Be-

*See Exhibit 5 in Chapter 6.

cause we want the results to be in real rather than nominal dollar figures, the formula uses real GDP:

$$\text{Potential real GDP} = \frac{94\% \text{ of civilian labor force}}{\text{actual employment}} \times \text{actual real GDP}$$

The data needed to perform the calculations from any specific year are given on the inside front and back covers of the book. To assist you, the above formula expressed in terms of the column numbers is, for any given year:

$$\text{Potential real GDP} = \frac{.94 \text{ (col. 30)}}{\text{col. 30} - \text{col. 31}} \times \text{col. 26}$$

Economic growth—the increase in potential real output over the years—is illustrated by the rightward shift of the *LRAS* curve. As a point of interest, recessionary and inflationary GDP gaps are also shown. This enables you to see how actual real output compared to potential real output in each of the given years.

Measuring Economic Growth

Is the economy of the United States growing, declining, or stagnating? How does its growth compare with that of other economies? The answers are determined by the way we measure growth. Although the definition seems clear-cut, experts do not always agree on the results, because the methods of calculation can involve some controversial procedures. Economists, therefore, simply use past measures of output or income, as suggested by the definition of economic growth, and derive long-term growth trends from these historical records. Frequently, the trends are projected into the future at various assumed compound rates of growth—like money growing at compound interest in a savings account.

What Determines Economic Growth?

Suppose we assume that the economy is operating at full employment. The growth of real GDP will then be determined by improvements in the nation's resources and the ways in which they are used. These major growth-determinants include:

1. Quantity and quality of human resources

2. Quantity and quality of "natural" resources

3. Accumulation of capital

4. Specialization and scale of production

5. Rate of technological progress

6. Environmental factors

These are also the kinds of growth determinants that influence an economy's production-possibilities curve, as you'll see over the next several pages.

Quantity and Quality of Human Resources

Recall that economic growth can be expressed in terms of real GDP per capita. We can derive real GDP per capita with the following simple formula:

$$\text{Real GDP per capita} = \frac{\text{total real GDP}}{\text{population}}$$

The rate of economic growth is measured by the rate at which the left side of this equation, at full employment, increases over time. This in turn will depend on the rate at which the numerator of the right side of the equation, at full employment, increases relative to the denominator.

The faster the rate of increase in total real GDP at full employment as compared to the rate of increase in population, the faster the rise in real GDP per capita. Hence, the rate of economic growth will be faster also.

The formula for real GDP per capita uses the measure of population only in quantitative terms. But qualitative considerations also affect economic growth. While an increase in population will increase the size of the labor force, it is the *productivity* of the labor force that will determine the rate of increase (or decrease) in real GDP. The chief factors determining labor productivity include:

- Time spent at work, such as the average length of the workweek

- Education, health, and skills of workers

- Quantity and quality of the tools and capital equipment used by workers

Over the past several decades, modern industrial nations have experienced a steady decline in the first of these determinants along with a continuous increase in the last two. This suggests that the *quality* of a country's human resources (as well as their quantity) influences the country's economic growth.

Quantity and Quality of "Natural" Resources (Land)

An economy's output and economic growth also depend on the quantity and quality of its soil, minerals, water, timber, and so on. These are commonly referred to as natural resources. In economics, however, they are classified under the general heading of "land" as a factor of production.

Some economists contend that there is no such thing as a "natural" resource. They argue that resources provided by nature are of no value to society unless people are able to put them to use. When that happens, the resources are no longer natural. A nation may be rich in resources, but its material well-being or rate of economic growth will not be influenced in the slightest if these resources remain "natural," or untapped. Demand and cost conditions must be favorable if a resource is to be converted from a natural (or "neutral") to a positive state. This means that there must be a high enough level of demand for the products that the resource will help to produce. There must also be an adequate supply and low enough cost of capital, labor, and technical skills to transform the resource by putting it to a profitable use.

Of course, the quantity and quality of a nation's natural resources aren't necessarily fixed. By diverting some of its *existing* labor and capital into research, a society may be able to discover or develop *new* natural resources within its own borders that will enhance its future rate of economic growth. In terms of the production-possibilities curve, this means that some consumer goods must be sacrificed in the present to enable the economy to reach a higher curve in the future.

Accumulation of Capital

A society must also forgo some current consumption in order to build capital goods such as factories, machines, transportation facilities, dams, and educational institutions. These add to the nation's stock of capital. The rate at which a nation can accumulate capital will influence its economic growth.

Why is the rate of capital accumulation, or investment by businesses, greater in some countries than in others? Two reasons are fundamental: (1) profit expectations of business executives and (2) government policies toward investment. Although the influence of these conditions differs among nations, one aspect of the process of capital accumulation is relevant to all—the necessity for *sacrifice.*

Thus, capital accumulation is closely related to the volume of savings. This is the portion of a society's income that is not spent for consumption. In order to add to their long-run stock of capital goods, the people of a country must refrain from consuming a portion of their current output (or income) so that a larger proportion of it can be devoted to new investment. This principle helps to explain why poor countries, like poor families, are ordinarily unable to save as much as rich ones and, hence, experience little or no economic growth. In general:

The cost of economic growth to a society is the consumption that it must sacrifice in order to save for the purpose of accumulating capital.

Specialization and Scale of Production

The greatest improvement in the productive powers of labor and the greater part of the skill, dexterity, and judgment with which it is anywhere directed, or applied, seem to have been the effects of the division of labor.

So said Adam Smith in *The Wealth of Nations.* Smith then gave the celebrated example of a pin factory: "One man draws out the wire, another straights it, a third cuts it, a fourth points it, a fifth grinds it . . ." and, as a result, there is a far greater output than if each man were to make the entire pin himself.

Smith also made the interesting point that the division of labor is limited by the "extent of the market." He observed that, in a small isolated economy, there will be less division of labor and a smaller scale of operations to satisfy local needs than in a large exchange economy such as London's.

These comments on specialization and scale of production provide significant insights into the process of economic growth. In the early stages of a nation's economic development, production is relatively non-specialized and the scale of operations is small. In such circumstances, businesses often produce only to supply the needs of the surrounding community, without advancing to the factory stage of production.

This situation prevailed in the United States until the end of the eighteenth century. But with the expansion of the market and advances in the technology of production, more specialization and a greater scale of

ECONOMICS IN THE NEWS

How Well Off Are We?

Data on Incomes, Living Standards Don't Square with Current Pessimism

By Clare Ansbetty and Thomas F. O'Boyle

As pessimistic as some of its people seem to be, by many measures America remains a land of prosperity and opportunity.

Consider this:

—The poor aren't necessarily poorer. As a group, the poorest 20 percent of housholds saw their mean household income—adjusted for inflation—increase 5 percent from 1980 to 1990, according to Census data.

—Whatever they might think, many of today's middle-aged adults are better off than their parents. Today, one in four women has a college degree, compared with one in ten of their mothers. The average income of a young family of 25- to 35-year-olds, adjusted for inflation, if 40 percent higher than 30 years ago, when their parents were their age.

—The United States retains the highest standard of living in the world. Per capita income is still 17 percent higher than in Japan. The Japanese. who work an average 6 percent more hours each year than Americans, pay twice as much rent as residents of New York City and 28 percent more for basic staples from apples to appliances.

—Many Americans can and do improve their lot. One study by the Urban Institute found that nearly half the people in the lowest income level moved up in each of the past two decades. In fact, in all but the highest income level, more people stayed the same or moved up than fell behind.

Of course, studies can be drummed up to support almost any proposition. Lately those getting the most attention suggest that things have been getting worse.

Fabian Linden, an economist with the Conference Board, says the general malaise is so great that if you dare suggest things aren't terrible, "people become enraged."

"To say real disposable income has increased," Mr. Linden adds, "doesn't mean we don't have profound social problems." He is especially troubled by the roughly 25 percent of households with incomes below $15,000. "But we've tended to paint the world with black paint, ignoring people who are making it," Mr. Linden says. "Not tycoons, but ordinary folk, who generation after generation improve their lot."

A better measure of income is inflation-adjusted family income, which has risen 0.57 percent annually on average since 1973. That's a total real gain for the period of 5.4 percent.

Still, the good news isn't as good as it might be—or as it used to be. Higher family incomes have come about in large part because so many more wives now work. Annual productivity gains have slowed to 1 percent from 3 percent in the 1940s through the 1970s. And while the United States is still ahead of Japan, that country has closed the gap since 1960, when America's standard of living was 70 percent higher. Wages in the United States are rising, but not as fast as they once did. And today's adults can't expect the same leaps as their grandparents, who worked themselves into the middle class on the backs of a grade-school education and sometimes saw their children earn six-figure incomes by the time they reached 30.

Source: *The Wall Street Journal*, August 11, 1992, p. A11.

operations became possible. Larger volumes of output and lower unit costs were thus realized. This has become a continuing process in the economic growth of nations and regions.

Economic growth is not just an increase in the quantity of the factors of production. Economic growth also involves fundamental changes in the organization and techniques of production. These include changes in the *structure* of production as represented by the input-output relationships that characterize an economy's firms and industries.

A nation's economic growth, therefore, will be determined in part by the potential it has for increasing the specialization of its resources and the scale of its production. Thus, there are qualitative as well as quantitative considerations°that determine economic growth.

Rate of Technological Progress

One of the most important qualitative determinants of economic growth is the rate of technological progress. This is the speed at which new knowledge is both developed and applied to raising the standard of living.

If you remember your study of American history, you will recall that the early nineteenth century was a period of rapid technological advancement. The invention of the cotton gin, the steamboat, the milling machine, the locomotive, and numerous other devices contributed enormously to the young nation's economic progress.

It must be kept in mind, however, that these technological advances were accompanied by legal and economic innovations that also had important consequences for the nation's development. Two particularly spectacular advances that occurred during the early 1800s were critical:

1. *The rapid growth of banking, including the creation of a government bank as well as several dozen state-chartered banks.* These provided new and important sources of credit for business transactions.

2. *The rapid adoption of the corporate form of business organization.* This provided opportunities for accumulating large amounts of finance capital (money) with limited liability on the part of owners.

In an expanding economy where risk taking was a vital element of growth, these features made possible the financing and adoption of the technical innovations mentioned above. Clearly, therefore:

Technological progress involves more than just invention. Technological progress embraces an effort on the part of society as a whole to get the most out of existing resources and to discover new and better resources through continuous improvements in education, engineering, management, and marketing.

Environmental Factors

All of the points considered thus far lead to an important conclusion: *The political, social, cultural, and economic environment must be favorable if significant growth is to occur.* This means, among other things, that there must be a *banking and credit system* capable of financing growth. There must be a *legal system* that establishes the ground rules of business behavior. There must be a *tax system* that doesn't discourage new investment and risk taking. And there must be a *stable government* that is sympathetic to economic expansion.

It is no accident that such countries as the United States, Canada, the United Kingdom, and Japan have experienced periods of rapid economic growth despite their different political systems. Some African, Latin American, and Asian countries have had little or no significant economic growth for many years—and in some cases even for many decades.

Conclusion: The Problem of Measurement

Of the six determinants of growth discussed here, how important is each in affecting a country's economic growth? Can we measure their separate influences? These questions are extremely difficult to answer, because some causes of growth are qualitative rather than quantitative. Consequently, there is a tendency among economists to reduce the causes of growth to three sets of "measurable" determinants:

1. Growth of the labor force

2. Growth of capital (the rising value of the nation's stock of capital—plant, equipment, and the like)

3. Technological progress (that is, "all other things")

The first two determinants can be measured reasonably well. The third cannot. Therefore, in measuring the causes of an economy's growth, the contributions of the first two determinants of total economic growth are estimated quantitatively. Then the contribution of the third determinant is viewed as a "residual" or catchall for all determinants other than labor and capital.

Technological Progress: Classic Examples in America's Early Development

A remarkable series of events took place in the United States within the short space of 13 years, between 1790 and 1803. It demonstrates how the rate of technological progress can influence the evolution of a national economy.

In 1790, a brilliant young Englishman, Samuel Slater, employed by a merchant firm in Rhode Island, began spinning cotton thread by machine, thus marking the first effective introduction of the factory system in this country. In the same year, John Fitch constructed and operated successfully the world's first regularly scheduled steamboat. When this was later employed on Western waters, it cut the costs of transportation remarkably and enabled the West to become part of the national economy.

In 1793, Eli Whitney invented the cotton gin, which made possible the extensive cultivation of cotton and subsequently transformed the economy of the South. In 1800, this same young graduate of Yale College contracted to manufacture 10,000 rifles for the government. He succeeded in producing them with precisely made interchangeable parts—the first step toward assembly-line production.

In 1803, a Philadelphia inventor named Oliver Evans achieved almost complete automation in the milling of wheat into flour by an ingenious system of machines that weighed, cleaned, ground, and packed the flour with virtually no human assistance.

These and other inventions of the era played a key role in the nation's economic growth during the nineteenth century.

(a) Carding, drawing, roving, and spinning in Slater's Mill, 1790.

(b) John Fitch's first steamboat, Philadelphia, 1790.

(c) Eli Whitney's first cotton gin, 1793.

(d) Oliver Evans's automated mill, Philadelphia, 1803.

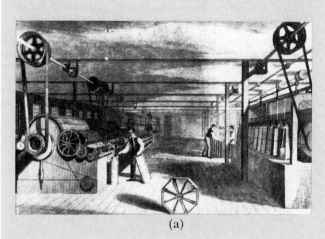

(a)

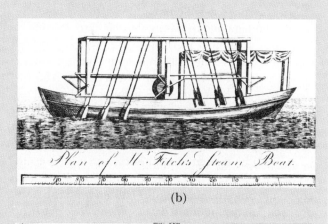

(b)

(c)

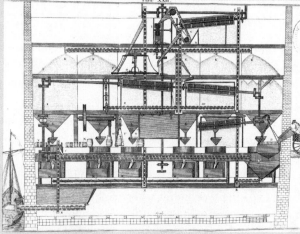

(d)

As a simple example, suppose an economy grows at the rate of 5 percent annually over a given period. If 3 percent is estimated to have been due to the growth of labor and capital combined, the remaining 2 percent might be attributed to technological progress. For purposes of measurement, therefore, "technological progress" includes such things as better machinery and technology, better management, and greater labor skills.

How important is technological progress?

It has been estimated that, in the United States, more than 80 percent of the increase in output per capita since the early part of the twentieth century has been due to technological progress. This leaves less than 20 percent to be explained by the other two determinants. In terms of *total* output (as distinct from output per capita), technological progress has accounted for somewhat more than 50 percent of the growth of production in the United States and various other industrial nations.

This suggests that economic growth is best envisioned as a continuous development and discovery of new and better ways of doing things. Economic growth is thus *more* than just a quantitative expansion of existing inputs or outputs.

Summary Thus Far

1. The largest long-run gains in productivity—the ratio of output to input—come from increased capital investment and from the adoption of new technology. Productivity is the fundamental determinant of living standards. These are becoming more equal among major industrial nations as the productivity gaps between them close.

2. Economic growth is the rate of increase in an economy's full-employment real output or income over time. Graphically, a nation's economic growth can be depicted by an outward shift of its production possibilities curve or by a rightward shift of its potential real output (*LRAS*) curve.

3. Economic growth rates and productivity are closely linked by three measurable determinants: growth of the labor force, growth of capital, and technological progress (or "all other things"). Among the advanced nations, technological progress has accounted for more than 50 percent of the growth of production since 1900.

International Comparisons and Growth Targets

How do the growth rates of nations compare with one another? Can growth policies be adopted to ensure that America remains competitive with other major countries? These are the kinds of questions that always arise in public-policy discussions concerning economic growth. The answers, as we'll see, can be quite complex.

Comparative Growth Rates

Comparisons of growth rates for a number of countries are presented in Exhibit 5. A nation's growth rate may change significantly over a period of a few years. Therefore, in order for growth comparisons to be meaningful, it's best to use average data covering a relatively large number of years, usually several decades.

The graphs show the growth rates of mixed economies and command economies. The mixed economies are market-oriented economies in which resources are allocated predominantly by the forces of demand and supply. The command economies are centrally planned economies in which resources are allocated predominantly by government authority. In both types of economies, growth rates have varied considerably over the years.*

The growth estimates for command economies are made by Western Intelligence sources, particularly the U.S. Central Intelligence Agency (CIA). Before 1990, CIA estimates were generally accepted without reservation by interested observers. In 1990, however, the CIA reported that its methods of estimating growth contained some serious faults, and that the figures may have been overstated by as much as one-third.

Keeping this in mind, China's apparently high economic growth rate in the 1980s resulted from that country's experimentation with free-market policies. But due to political turmoil that occurred in 1989, the policies were largely rescinded for several years. This caused China's economy to lose much of the gain it made during that decade.

*Since 1990, the command economies of Eastern Europe and the former U.S.S.R. have moved increasingly toward becoming market economies. China has also moved in that direction, but much more hesitantly.

EXHIBIT
5

Comparative Growth Rates

In order for comparisons to be meaningful, growth rates must be compared over a period of many years. (Data for mixed economies are published by their respective governments.

Data for command economies are estimated by Western intelligence sources and may reflect considerable error.)

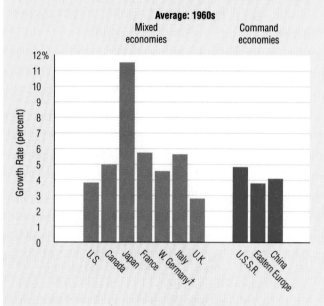

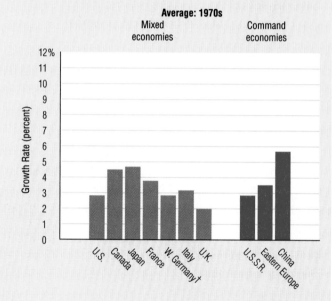

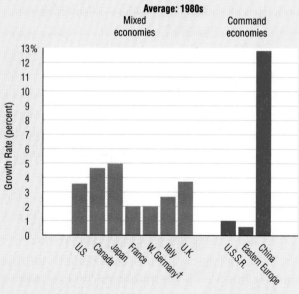

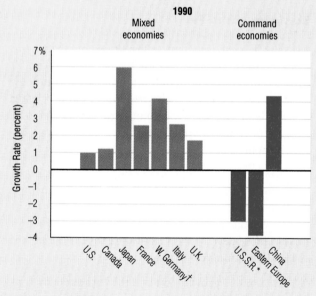

* The U.S.S.R. was disunited in 1991 and became the Commonwealth of Independent States in 1992.

† West Germany, a market economy, was reunited with East Germany, a command economy, in 1991. The new Germany is a market economy.

Source: U.S. Department of Commerce; Organization for Economic Cooperation and Development; U.S. Central Intelligence Agency.

Targeting Growth

One of the greatest economic challenges a nation can face is to set a productivity growth-rate goal for some specified time period and to design policies aimed at attaining that goal. This task, which amounts to targeting growth, is a formidable one that involves three major decisions. They are:

1. Choosing a growth-rate goal

2. Choosing a target year

3. Choosing appropriate policies

Choosing a Growth-Rate Goal

Selecting a desired growth rate is based in part on historical experience. If the nation's average annual growth in output per worker has averaged 2 percent, raising the figure by 1 percentage point would amount to a 50 percent increase in the labor productivity growth rate. However, if the nation's average annual growth in output per worker has averaged 3 percent, raising the figure by 1 percentage point would amount to a $33\frac{1}{3}$ percent increase in the labor productivity growth rate. In reality, America's average annual growth in output per worker has, since the beginning of the twentieth century, averaged approximately 2.3 percent. Therefore, raising the figure by 1 percentage point would amount to an increase of about 43 percent in the labor productivity growth rate.

Thus, because seemingly small percentage *amounts* of change can equate to much larger percentage *changes,* care must be taken to choose a growth-rate goal that's realistically attainable.

As stated above, nations that plan for growth are likely to rely on past growth rates as their primary guide.

Choosing a Target Year

The second decision in targeting growth involves the selection of a target year. Before making the selection, it must be remembered that economic growth is not a temporary spurt in real output that may arise from fortuitous circumstances. Rather, economic growth is a sustained expansion in real output over a decade or more. Therefore, the year chosen should be far enough in the future to allow time for fundamental

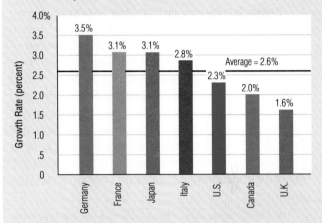

Labor Productivity Growth Rates Needed for U.S. Parity

Rates of labor productivity growth that the United States must maintain to the year 2020 in order to stay abreast of other major industrial nations.

Source: Adapted from data in William J. Baumol, Sue Anne Batey Blackman, and Edward N. Wolff, *Productivity and American Leadership: The Long View,* Cambridge and London, The MIT Press, 1989.

long-run changes in resource use to occur. However, the year chosen should also be close enough for the benefits to be realized by most of today's population.

For now, the year 2020 can serve as a suitable target year. The nature of the problem can then be appreciated by examining Exhibit 6. The graph shows the *labor productivity growth rate that the United States must maintain to the year 2020 in order to stay abreast of its major industrial competitors.* For example, to keep up with Germany, American labor productivity would have to grow at an average rate of 3.5 percent annually. To keep up with Japan, American labor productivity would have to grow at an average rate of 3.1 percent annually. The remainder of the graph is interpreted similarly. As you can see, the growth rate for United States labor productivity is below the average of seven major industrial nations. As you can also see:

In order to stay abreast of its top four industrial competitors, the United States must increase its labor productivity growth rate by approximately 1 percentage point and maintain the increase to the year 2020.

Choosing Appropriate Policies

The third decision in targeting growth involves the adoption of policies needed to attain the goal. Policies were suggested earlier in the chapter on the determinants of economic growth. The policies required are those that will increase the rate of capital investment and the quality of labor. Two broad guidelines can thus be recommended:

1.   Revise Tax Policies to Encourage Investment   Investment in plant and equipment—that is, *real* investment—is undertaken by businesses in anticipation of profits. Companies finance real investment with their own savings (called retained earnings) and by selling financial claims such as stocks and bonds. The purchase of financial claims—that is, *financial* investment—is undertaken by the private sector in anticipation of profitable returns. Therefore, tax policies designed to encourage both real and financial investment are of paramount importance. Such policies may include:

a. *Accelerated depreciation allowances for business.* These permit firms to "write off" (depreciate) expenditures on plant and equipment at faster rates. The tax savings that firms realize can help them finance the purchase of new plant and equipment.

b. *Permanent elimination of taxes on interest income and capital gains.* This would leave the private sector with more savings. The increased savings could be used to help finance both real and financial investment.

c. *Sharp reductions in the national debt and in military spending.* This would permit further decreases in income taxes, thus enlarging the volume of savings. Increased savings could help finance investment spending.

d. *Replacement of all or part of the income tax with a national sales tax (such as a value-added tax).* People earn income by working and investing, thereby adding to the nation's wealth and GDP. An income tax thus penalizes people for what they put into the economy, while a national sales tax penalizes people for what they take out of the economy. (Can you see why?) An income tax therefore inhibits growth while a national sales tax promotes it. Further, a national sales tax, which would normally be regressive, can be made approximately proportional by exempting such essentials as food, prescription drugs, and some percentage of utilities. The benefits of replacing all or part of the income tax with a national sales tax, in conjunction with the other measures that have been proposed, can thus be considerable.

2.   Promote Investment in Knowledge   During most of the twentieth century, education per worker and advances in knowledge were the largest contributors to economic growth. The two together accounted for 39 percent of potential national income.* This suggests what economists have known for decades: The scarcest resource for our society is not land or muscle power, but brain power. In view of this, what guidelines can be suggested for promoting investment in knowledge? Two chief ones are these:

a. *Encouragement of research and development (R&D).* Research studies have estimated that the private returns to investment in R&D are relatively high—more than 20 percent—and that the returns to society are even higher. Several government policies that encourage greater involvement in R&D can therefore be recommended:

- Favorable tax write-offs on R&D expenditures
- Subsidies and grants for projects expected to produce rapid growth
- Exemptions from the antitrust (antimonopoly) laws for companies collaborating on large-scale projects

b. *Encouragement of human-capital investment.* Those members of the labor force whose services are in demand constitute the nation's human capital. America's greatest challenge is to find ways of improving the quantity and quality of human capital. A knowledge of economics can be helpful in designing incentive programs for states and cities to adopt. The incentives should accomplish two objectives: (1) encourage competition among schools, and (2) provide rewards to students and teachers based on performance levels. There is a vast amount of room for research and experimentation in designing creative incentive programs. To finance such programs, a system of government and business grants could be established. If appropriate tax write-offs for business were provided, many firms would undoubtedly be willing to provide the necessary funding.

---

*Edward F. Denison, *Trends in American Economic Growth*, 1929–1982, Washington, DC, The Brookings Institution, 1985, Chap. 2 and Tables 8–1 to 8–7.

Successful targeting of economic growth requires policies that will shift the economy's *LRAS* curve to the right. The tax system can play an important role in this respect. Structuring it to provide sufficient incentives can encourage investment in physical and human capital. This raises productivity, which is the wellspring of a steadily rising level of living.

The Classical Explanation of Growth: How Economics Became the "Dismal Science"

In the late eighteenth and early nineteenth centuries, certain English classical economists formulated theories that dealt in large part with economic development. These economists included Adam Smith, David Ricardo, and Thomas Malthus. Ricardo and Malthus were basically pessimistic. They argued that a country's economic growth must end in decline and stagnation. The ideas of these men compose what may appropriately be called the "classical" theory of economic growth. Their views are interesting and can help us to understand modern economic problems of growth.

The Subsistence Theory and Diminishing Returns

The early classical economists contended that there was some standard of living at which the population—especially the working population—would just maintain itself, with no tendency to increase or decrease. They called this the "subsistence level." Although determined primarily by physical or biological requirements, this level is also influenced by social and customary needs, which in turn affect the decision to have children.

Thus, the classicists argued that if wages per worker fell below the subsistence level, people would tend to stop having children. The decline in population would cause an increase in real aggregate income—that is, real GDP—per capita. Conversely, if wages per worker rose above the subsistence level, people would tend to start having more children. The increase in population would cause a decrease in real GDP per capita. This early-nineteenth-century classical theory is known as the **subsistence theory of wages** (also called the *iron,* or *brazen, law of wages*).

The classical model of economic growth is based on a *subsistence theory.* In its simplest form the classical model can be expressed in terms of two basic propositions:

1. The population of a country tends to adjust to a subsistence level of living.

2. Increases in population, with technology and natural resources (land) held constant, result *eventually* in decreasing incomes per capita as a result of the operation of the "law of diminishing returns" (explained below).

These concepts are illustrated in Exhibit 7. The population of a country is scaled on the horizontal axis, and its material standard of living (as measured by real GDP per capita) is scaled on the vertical. The curve labeled *L* shows the actual level of living that the society can maintain for various levels of population applied to the fixed quantity of other resources. The *L* curve may therefore be thought of as an *average product curve* representing the average output per person (or per worker). It results from adding more and more people to a given amount of land while production techniques are held constant.

The average product or actual level-of-living curve (*L*) rises to a maximum at *Y* and then declines. This represents the eventual tendency for "diminishing returns" to set in as a growing population is applied to a fixed amount of resources. The ideal or o*ptimum population* is therefore at *N*, because this yields a level of living equal to the distance *NY*. This is the highest level attainable on the curve. Any other combination of population and fixed resources is less than optimal because it yields a lower output per person.

Although the early classical economists didn't use graphs, their ideas can be expressed as shown in Exhibit 7. Thus, suppose the standard of living at *S* represents the subsistence level of living. Then the equilibrium size of the population, according to the classicists, is 0*M* (=*SR*). The reason is that if the population is larger than 0*M*, the actual level of living will be below the subsistence level. Hence, the population will decline and real GDP per capita will therefore increase. However, if the population is less than 0*M*, the actual level of living will be above the subsistence level. Consequently, the population will increase and real GDP per capita will therefore decrease. Thus, the "subsistence level" in the classical model is a long-run equilibrium level of living for the population as a whole.

Economics—The "Dismal Science"

Because of this pessimistic theory, economics (or political economy, as it used to be called) came to be known as the "dismal science." Clearly, if the subsistence level of living is a long-run equilibrium toward which society is always tending, there's no hope of ever improving the future of humankind. Even the discovery of new natural resources or the implementation of new production techniques would at best provide only temporary benefits until the population had time to adjust to these new developments. Then a larger number of people would be left living in the same minimal circumstances as before.

For example, suppose that new natural resources are discovered, or more land becomes available, or new production techniques are developed. The effect, as shown in the graph in Exhibit 7, is to raise the average product curve from L to L'. The reason for the increase is that the same population now has more or better fixed resources with which to work. However, the increase in benefits per person from MR to MR' will be of limited duration. Because average product is now above the subsistence level, the population will increase until it reaches a new equilibrium at K. At this point, more people will be living at the same subsistence level $0S$ ($=KT$) than before.

The Malthusian Specter

Among the early English classical economists, there was one whose theory of population (illustrated by the above model) is especially well known. His name was Thomas R. Malthus, and his famous theory is often encountered in various social-science courses.

The Malthusian theory of population (first published by Malthus in 1798 and revised in 1803) stated that population increases faster than the means of subsistence. That is, population tends to increase as a geometric progression (1, 2, 4, 8, 16, 32, and so on) while the means of subsistence increase at most only as an arithmetic progression (1, 2, 3, 4, 5, 6, and so on). This is because a growing population applied to a fixed amount of land results in eventually diminishing returns to workers. Human beings are therefore destined to misery and poverty unless the rate of population growth is retarded. This may be accomplished either by preventive checks, such as moral restraint, late marriages, and celibacy; or, if these fail, by positive checks, such as wars, famines, and disease.

EXHIBIT 7

The Subsistence Theory and Diminishing Returns

In the classical model of Ricardo and Malthus, the actual level-of-living curve L depends on the size of the population (or number of workers) applied to a fixed amount of land. The population tends toward an equilibrium level at M. This corresponds to the subsistence level represented by the distance MR. Even the effect of an upward shift of the actual level-of-living curve from L to L', due to the development of new resources or new production techniques, is of short-run duration. The population simply expands to the new size at K, leaving the average output per person, KT, at the same subsistence level as before.

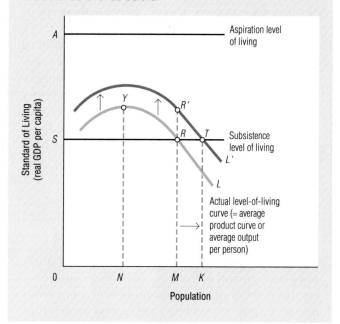

Has the prediction of Malthus been realized? There is no doubt that it has in certain crowded, underdeveloped areas of Asia, Africa, and Latin America. Here, industrialization and economic growth are impeded because agriculture is inefficient and unable to feed both the people on farms and those who live and work in the cities. In many of these areas, war, famine, and disease are the main curbs on population, even though major efforts are being made to encourage use of contraception.

Some Proposed Solutions

Can the underdeveloped, overpopulated countries escape from the "Malthusian trap"? Three ways out may be suggested.

One solution would be to shift millions of people from overpopulated to underpopulated regions—from the small farms in some parts of Africa and Asia, for example, to the vast jungles of South America that await development. But the many obvious political and social obstacles make this policy unrealistic.

A second possibility would be to develop new resources and production techniques. This would need to be done at a sufficiently rapid rate so that the upward shifts of the average product curve would more than offset the growth in population. In this way, the population would never catch up with the rising level of output per person, and the level of living would continually increase.

A third approach would be to seek ways of raising the "subsistence level" to where it becomes an *aspiration level*—a target or a goal for which to strive. In the graph in Exhibit 7, for example, the standard of living might be raised from the level at *S* to the level at *A*. Note that this new level is above the maximum possible level of living that is attainable with any present combination of population and resources. Therefore, there might be continual pressure on people to reduce the existing population in order to rise higher on the average product curve. Alternatively, there might be sufficient pressure on people to discover and develop new resources and production techniques so that the entire average product curve is shifted upward. It's more likely, however, that some combination of both possibilities would occur.

The "Hot-Baths" Hypothesis

The second and third solutions, resource development and a raised subsistence level, have occurred and are continuing to occur in some of today's rapidly developing nations. The third approach, that of raising the subsistence level to an aspiration level, is based on a fascinating assumption. It suggests that a relationship may exist between population growth and living standards in many overpopulated, underdeveloped countries. This relationship has been called—facetiously—the *hot-baths hypothesis:*

There may be a significant relationship between human fertility rates and "hot baths." Suppose a soci-ety reaches a certain minimum level of living at which it has a reasonable abundance of the creature comforts of life—adequate food, clothing, housing, sanitation, and so on. From then on, its desire for more and better material things, as measured by its aspiration level, may continually rise. If this happens, then the society's population will tend automatically to seek its economically optimum size through the practice of birth control. But this assumes that the society's living conditions can first be brought (probably with outside help from other nations) to the minimum threshold level.

To repeat, this is only an hypothesis—a tentative proposition that has never been explored and tested in different nations under varying cultural and social conditions. Nevertheless, it is an interesting and important concept. Indeed, foreign aid to poor, overpopulated nations has sought, in large part, to raise living conditions in those countries to some minimum level. Hopefully their economies can then break out of their stationary states and enter a new phase of more self-sustaining and self-propelling economic growth.

Capital Deepening and Diminishing Returns

The subsistence theory of wages in the classical model implies the existence of a *subsistence theory of profits* as well.

For example, the model of population growth that was developed in Exhibit 7 may be adapted to serve as a model of the growth of nonhuman capital. This includes buildings, machines, inventories, and so on. This can be done by measuring the total stock of capital—capital investment—along the horizontal axis and the percentage rate of return on capital investment along the vertical axis. The curve *L* is then the "profitability" curve of capital, which results from applying different amounts of capital to a fixed quantity of other resources.

When looked at in this way, the model indicates that capital is accumulated in anticipation of future interest returns or profits. Thus, when the stock of capital in the economy is relatively low, the anticipated return on capital is high, thereby encouraging further accumulation. As capital is accumulated, however, the law of diminishing returns eventually sets in. If we suppose that $0S$ represents the minimally acceptable or "subsistence rate" of profits, capital accumulation will proceed to the level at *M*. Improvements in any of the fixed resources or in production techniques will, of course, shift the profit curve upward from L to L', thereby bringing about a further accumulation of capital to the amount at K.

An increase in the stock of capital relative to other resources, especially labor, is called *capital deepening*. What are the effects of such a deepening, assuming that there are no changes in technology? Clearly, the operation of the inexorable law of diminishing returns will determine the answer. The interest or profit rate on capital must *decline* as the stock of capital becomes more plentiful relative to the stock of other resources. Simultaneously, the real wages of labor must *rise* as this resource becomes more scarce relative to the growing stock of capital.

Conclusion: The Classical View of Growth

These ideas led the early English classical economists—especially David Ricardo—to the conclusion that the development of an economy depends on the relative growth of two critical variables: *population* and *capital.* If population grows faster than capital, wages fall and profits rise. Conversely, if capital grows faster than population, profits fall and wages rise. From time to time, one of these variables may grow faster than the other, thereby causing an upward shift in the level-of-living curve of population or in the profit curve of capital. Eventually, however, both wages per worker and profits per unit of capital must tend toward a long-run level of subsistence. Land, however, remains fixed in supply, according to the classical theory. Therefore, landlords stand to benefit over the long run as rents continue to rise with increases in population and in output per worker.

What Are the Long-Run Trends?

Have the predictions of the early English classical economists been confirmed by history? For most of the advanced or developed economies of the world, the answer is no. For those economies, three very long-run patterns have been evident:

1. The trends of real wages and of output per worker have been sharply upward, not downward. These trends result mainly from rapid expansion in the growth of the capital stock at a rate faster than the growth of population, thus resulting in a *deepening* of capital.

2. Interest rates, or the profit rate on capital, have fluctuated in the business cycle, with no particular upward or downward trend.

3. Land rents have, in most of the advanced countries, moved upward relatively slowly, and actually declined in relation to other factor prices.

In general terms, the average product curve in each of the advanced countries has shifted upward over time at a pace rapid enough to more than offset tendencies toward diminishing returns and Malthusian subsistence equilibrium. This upward shift can be attributed to changes in the conditions that are assumed to remain "fixed" when the curve is drawn. In broad terms, these include:

- Improvements in the quantity and quality of labor

- Increased specialization and the scale of production

- Advances in technology

- Government policies conducive to growth

These "fixed" determinants, as you learned earlier, are the ones that determine a nation's economic growth. Each nation possesses these determinants in different degrees. This is why countries with very high population densities, that is, number of people per square mile, often experience widely varying rates of growth. For example, Hong Kong, Singapore, and several other Asian nations have some of the highest population densities in the world. Yet these countries often sustain vigorous growth rates. Egypt, India, and some African and Latin American nations also have very high population densities. However, these countries usually experience little or no growth. The classical theory of growth, therefore, is limited as an explanation of economic development.

The classical theory of growth holds that a rising number of people laboring with existing capital results in a declining level of output per person. Evidence suggests that this theory serves best as a short-run explanation of growth. In the long run, even in countries with relatively high population densities, the presence of sufficient growth-determining conditions can more than offset the dampening effects of population expansion. However, the absence of sufficient growth-determining conditions can leave these countries in a subsistence state of Malthusian equilibrium.

Thomas R. Malthus
(1776–1834)

Origins: The Ghost of Malthus

In the last third of the eighteenth century, two great problems occupied the attention of most thinking people in England. One of the problems was widespread poverty; the other was how many English residents there were. Socialists called attention to the poverty problem with a promise of a Utopian world—a paradise—in which the needs of all would be satisfied. The population problem had prompted Adam Smith to remark in *The Wealth of Nations* (1776), "No society can surely be flourishing and happy, of which the far greater part of the members are poor and miserable."

Were England's resources adequate to bring about a fulfillment of the socialists' dreams? A hitherto unknown English clergyman, Thomas Robert Malthus, thought not. In 1798, he published a treatise of 50,000 words entitled *An Essay on the Principle of Population, as It Affects the Future Improvement of Society*. Based on his observations in various countries, the essay proposed Malthus's now-famous rule that "population, when unchecked, goes on doubling every twenty-five years or increases in a geometric ratio," while the means of subsistence can only increase in an arithmetic ratio.

Wide Influence

Malthus became a professor of history and published a revision of his essay in 1803. In this he moderated his rigid "formula" and spoke more of a tendency of pop-

ulation to outrun the supply of food. Human beings, he concluded, were destined to misery and poverty unless the rate of population growth is slowed. The slowdown could be attained by preventive checks such as moral restraint, late marriages, and celibacy. If these fail, then positive checks such as wars, famine, and disease would occur.

Malthus and his population theory were severely criticized by people in nearly every walk of life. Politicians, clergymen, philosophers, and journalists raised cries of heresy. Some, like the editor of England's leading literary journal, *The Quarterly Review* (July, 1817), admitted that it was easier simply "to disbelieve Mr. Malthus than to refute him." Others, notably Ricardo and other classical economists, made Malthus's theory the basis of their own theories of wages and rent.

The generalizations expressed by Malthus have been recognized by governments throughout the world, and by the United Nations in its efforts to assist the over-populated, underdeveloped countries. Although there may be a tendency to dismiss the gloomy forebodings of the Malthusian theory, its warnings cannot be pushed aside. They are a stark reality for millions of people in many nations today.

Effective Demand

In addition to his population theory, Malthus made other outstanding contributions to economics, notably in his *Principles of Political Economy* (1820). He was an intimate friend of the great English classical economist, David Ricardo. It is impossible to disassociate their economic views, even though the two men were often in substantial disagreement. For one thing, Ricardo was as incapable of grasping the pragmatic and empirical approach of Malthus as Malthus was incapable of appreciating the rigor and subtle deductive reasoning of Ricardo.

Among the notable contributions that Malthus made to economic thought was the concept of "effective demand." He defined it as the level of aggregate demand necessary to maintain continuous production and to sustain economic growth. More than a century was to pass before the problem of effective demand would rise again to public notice. In the 1930s, John Maynard Keynes, a British economist and founder of modern macroeconomics, paid tribute to the pioneering work of Malthus on this subject.

Summary of Important Ideas

1. Productivity is the ratio of output to input. Although there are different indexes of productivity, all seek to measure the ways in which resources are used and the extent of their use.

2. Economists are interested in measuring partial-factor productivity as well as total-factor productivity. The former is usually based on one input, whereas the latter is based on all inputs. Because of the difficulty of measuring *all* inputs used in production, partial-factor productivity indexes are much more widely employed than total-factor productivity indexes.

3. Productivity is the key to economic growth—a rising level of real GDP per person. A major step toward improving productivity is the promotion of new investment in plant and equipment. This requires the adoption of economic policies aimed at encouraging rapid advances in technology.

4. International trends in productivity suggest that living standards in advanced industrial nations are coming closer together. If the present trends continue, the major industrial countries will attain similar standards of living during the first decade of the twenty-first century.

5. There are many determinants of a nation's economic growth. Among them are the quantity and quality of human and natural resources, the rate of capital accumulation, the degree of specialization and scale of production, the rate of technological progress, and the nature of the socioeconomic and political environment. For measurement purposes, however, these are usually reduced to three sets of determinants: (a) growth of the labor force, (b) growth of capital, and (c) technological progress (or "all other things" not represented by the previous two measurable causes).

6. International comparisons of economic growth rates show that they vary widely over long periods of time. Because economic growth is a rightward shift of an economy's *LRAS* curve, policies intended to stimulate growth must succeed in raising productivity and aggregate output. Such policies, therefore, must focus on ways of encouraging investment in physical and human capital. Tax policies can play a chief role in this respect.

7. The classical theory of economic growth concluded that both wages per worker and profits per unit of capital must eventually tend toward a level of subsistence. Empirical evidence, however, has not borne out this conclusion. Instead, the evidence shows that the conditions determining economic growth can more than offset a nation's population growth rate and lead to higher levels of real output per person. But in countries where the growth-determining conditions are inadequate to offset population expansion, subsistence levels of equilibrium can and do occur.

8. Near the beginning of the nineteenth century, an English classical economist, Thomas Malthus, formulated the theory that population growth would outrun the food supply. People were therefore condemned to living in poverty unless population growth were restrained. This theory, which served as a basis for classical growth theory, has become a stark reality in many parts of the world.

Terms and Concepts to Review

productivity
partial productivity
total-factor productivity
economic growth
subsistence theory of wages
Malthusian theory of population
capital deepening

Questions and Problems

1. It is often contended that increased government spending, as a percentage of GDP, slows down productivity and, therefore, the rate of growth of real output. Can you suggest at least three reasons why?

2. It is often said that pollution controls hurt productivity. Can you explain why this may be true?

3. Is our economic definition of growth "better" than the biological definition? The latter expresses growth as an *organic process*—a transference of material from one part of an organism (such as a part of the human body) to another. Explain.

4. What are the shortcomings of the economic definition of growth? That is, what sort of "amenities" does the definition omit as far as the growth of a society is concerned?

5. The conditions that determine an economy's growth are both quantitative and qualitative. The quantitative conditions are susceptible to measurement and can be incorporated in a growth model. Does this mean that such models are incomplete to the extent that qualitative conditions are omitted? What can be done about correcting the situation? Explain your answer.

6. It has been suggested that the income tax system, which provides equal deductions for each dependent, might be revised with the objective of regulating family size by taxation. How might this be done? Develop a specific example.

7. What do you think of a population-control plan that parallels several decades of American agricultural policy, giving subsidies for "fallow acres" and penalties for "overcropping?"

8. History shows that predominantly agricultural market economies may experience an agricultural revolution before an industrial revolution. For example, the proportion of workers employed in agriculture may decrease before the proportion employed in manufacturing increases. Can you suggest reasons for this?

9. In most of the world's advanced market economies, the service sectors have been expanding relatively faster than the manufacturing sectors. As a result, the percentage of workers employed in services has increased relative to the percentage employed in manufacturing. Can you explain why?

10. How may U.S. immigration policies affect America's economic growth? (a) Does an inflow of foreigners depress American wages and retard economic expansion? (b) Should the United States prohibit all immigration, or should it have a restrictive policy that admits immigrants on the basis of their skills?

11. If Ricardo and Malthus had been living in the United States rather than England during the early nineteenth century, do you think they would have developed the same theory of economic growth? Explain your answer. (*Hint:* Think in terms of the subsistence theory and the supply of relatively scarce resources as compared to fairly plentiful ones.)

12. What is meant by an "optimum population?" Do you believe there really is such a thing? Is it as applicable to the United States as it is to India? Why or why not?

TAKE A STAND

The Productivity Slowdown: Need We Worry?

Our current way of life could scarcely have been imagined by our great-grandparents when they were young. Technological advances over the past century have brought us airplanes, automobiles, computers, smart bombs, television, plastic sandwich bags, chocolate-flavored breakfast cereals, and so on. For all the concern sometimes expressed about our economy, we also live in a period of unparalleled prosperity, with more goods and services available than ever before. If such advances continue for the next century, then the world our great-grandchildren will inhabit may be equally difficult for us to imagine.

Increases in our standard of living over time reflect improvements in the productivity of labor—that is, the average amount of output produced by each worker. Productivity increases when we acquire more physical capital or human capital, or when technological improvements allow us to produce more goods with existing resources. Sustained improvements in our standard of living ultimately rest on continuing improvements in productivity.

That is why economists and others were particularly concerned when they noticed that, starting in the early 1970s, there has been a marked decrease in the rate of productivity growth. In contrast to, say, the 1960s, when U.S. GDP per person grew at about 2.5 percent per year on average, the rate of growth in the 1970s and 1980s was almost a full percentage point lower. With similar declines occurring in other developed economies, slowdown in productivity growth is a worldwide problem.

Economists are unsure of the causes of the slowdown. Demographic factors, increases in oil prices, changes in the composition of output, and new government regulations are among the potential culprits. Very probably, the slowdown is the result not of one single cause, but of a combination of factors. How concerned we should be depends largely on which causes we believe to be most important. The primary causes may, after all, be only temporary. *Need we worry about the slowdown in productivity growth?*

Yes: Small Declines Compound Fast

A decline of less than one percentage point in the rate of productivity growth may not sound like much. But the phenome-

non of exponential growth, which is exactly the same as the principle of compound interest, means that small differences in growth rates rapidly accumulate into large overall changes. For example, U.S. GDP per capita in 1970, measured in 1987 dollars, was $14,024. In 1990, U.S. GDP per capita in 1987 dollars was $19,421, implying that the annual growth rate was 1.6 percent. If GDP per capita had instead grown at the 1960s rate of 2.5 percent per year, then the 1990 GDP would have been over $23,000, or 19 percent higher than it actually was. On average, had the growth rate been nine-tenths of a percentage point higher, we would all have been almost one-fifth richer. As the example shows, even a small change in the rate of productivity growth should be a matter of great concern.

A second reason for worry about the productivity slowdown is that it may reflect a decline in educational quality and inventiveness. History teaches that technological progress has been the key determinant of long-run improvements in our standard of living. If, as a society, we neglect to develop the know-how or we run out of ideas for producing new and better goods more and more efficiently, then we can no longer look forward to the rising standards of living that we have previously enjoyed. Joel Mokyr, an economic historian who has studied technological progress, emphasizes that we cannot take such progress for granted. According to Mokyr, the long-run history of different societies reveals that developments in technology are the rare exception, not the rule:

> The unprecedented prosperity enjoyed today by a substantial proportion of humanity stems from accidental factors to a greater degree than is commonly supposed. Moreover, technological progress is like a fragile and vulnerable plant, whose flourishing is not only dependent on the appropriate surroundings and climate, but whose life is almost always short. It is highly sensitive to the social and economic environment and can easily be arrested by relatively small external changes.*

No: Beware the Hasty Judgment

Another lesson of history is that concern about the productivity slowdown may be premature. Current growth rates do look slow when they are compared to those of the 1950s and 1960s. But it is those two decades that are exceptional by historical standards. In the late nineteenth and early twentieth centuries, U.S. productivity grew by about 2 percent per year on average. Current growth rates are not all that much lower. Moreover, it is too early to tell whether the current slowdown is a temporary change or growth rates are permanently lower.

Many of the most plausible explanations of the productivity slowdown are short-run in nature. For one, the baby-boom generation began to enter the labor force in the 1970s. The large influx of young and inexperienced workers would naturally have contributed to the slowdown. We should then expect to see higher productivity growth again as this generation becomes more experienced and more productive. For another, oil prices increased dramatically in the 1970s. Firms were forced to shift to more energy-efficient means of production and to scrap their energy-intensive machinery. For a time, then, capital goods depreciated much more quickly than usual, but this is not a cause for long-run concern.

Third, the slowdown may reflect the shifting composition of output away from manufacturing and into services. In manufacturing, productivity increases frequently involve introducing machines to replace manual labor. The extra capital allows output per worker to increase. But it is harder to introduce machines to replace dentists, lawyers, hairdressers, or economists; hence, it is harder to increase productivity in the service sector. The growing importance of the service sector in our economy is therefore likely to cause slower productivity growth.

Finally, the slowdown may be due in part to increased government regulations that make firms less productive. For example, environmental regulations might force a firm to collect, treat, and properly dispose of its waste rather than simply dump it into a nearby river. Measured economic growth is then lower, but national welfare is not. The problem is just that GDP statistics do not fully capture our overall standard of living.

The Question: Need We Be Concerned About the Productivity Slowdown?

- The principle of compound interest means that a small decline in the productivity growth rate rapidly accumulates into a large relative fall in our standard of living. Further, the productivity slowdown may reflect a decline in our inventiveness that bodes ill for our long-term prosperity. The slowdown should be a source of great concern.

- The slowdown may be simply a return to normal long-run levels of growth following the anomalous experience of the 1950s and 1960s. Also, the most likely causes of the slowdown are short-run phenomena. Therefore, worries about the productivity slowdown are premature.

Where Do You Stand?

1. Some economists have noted that the United States is experiencing a productivity decline relative to other countries. Suppose that U.S. productivity grows at 3 percent a year. Do you think that it is better for the United States if productivity in other countries grows at 2 percent or at 4 percent, or does it make no difference? Explain.

2. Some economists have argued that the productivity slowdown may be due in part to misallocation of talent. The economists Kevin Murphy, Andrei Shleifer, and Robert Vishny have suggested that perhaps "lawyers are indeed bad, and engineers good, for growth."* Do you think it is damaging to the economy if young people choose careers that do not directly create wealth?

3. What features of the social and economic climate might cause technological progress to wither or to flourish?

4. Need we worry about the productivity slowdown? Justify your stand.

---

*Joel Mokyr, *The Lever of Riches* (New York: Oxford University Press, 1990), p. 16.

*K. Murphy, A. Shleifer, and R. Vishny, "The Allocation of Talent: Implications for Growth," *Quarterly Journal of Economics,* May 1991, p. 529.

Part 3

Monetary Economics: Money, Banking, and Monetary Policy

Chapter 9

Money, Financial Markets, and the Banking System

Meaning and Functions of Money
Measuring Money
Financial Markets
Financial Intermediaries
The Federal Reserve System
Organization of the Banking System

Learning Guide

Watch for answers to these important questions

What is money? What forms does it take? How is it defined and measured?

How are some debt (or credit) instruments used as money? In what markets are these instruments exchanged? What economic functions do these markets perform?

What are foreign exchange markets and the foreign exchange rate?

What are financial intermediaries? Why do they exist? What economic functions do they perform?

What is the Federal Reserve System? Why was it created? What are its objectives?

How is the banking system organized? How are depositors protected? What is the "new" banking?

If you ask most people what economics is about, they're likely to say that it has something to do with money. That answer is not incorrect. Economics, especially macroeconomics, has a great deal to do with money. We'll see why by examining the meaning of money and the functions—or needs—that it fulfills in every society.

Meaning and Functions of Money

What is money? Most people would probably say, "It's *currency*—paper money and coins." But that definition is only partially correct. Throughout the history of civilization many different things have served as money. Among them are: various metals (such as gold, silver, copper), rice, wheat, seeds, salt, cattle, sheep, wool, stones, seashells, tobacco, and wampum (Indian beads). There is no limit to the things that can serve as money if enough people are willing to agree on them. Clearly, therefore, a practical definition of money is needed—one that explains how it "works" and what it does in our society:

Money is anything that is widely used and freely accepted as payment for goods and services. Money functions as a (1) medium of exchange, (2) measure of value, (3) standard of deferred payments, and (4) store of value.

204

Medium of Exchange

The function of money as a medium of exchange is the one that is most widely understood. It means simply that money is used to pay for goods and services. As a result, money facilitates transactions between buyers and sellers. Imagine what it would be like to live in a society in which there was no money. All transactions would have to be conducted by barter—an exchange of one good for another.

For example, if you wanted to acquire this book, you would first have to locate someone who had it. Then you'd have to find out if that person wanted to exchange it for the good or service you were offering in return. If so, you'd have realized a *double coincidence of wants.* If not, you'd have had to keep searching until you found the person who met your needs.

The same would be true for everyone else. Any individual or firm that wanted to engage in a transaction would have to find another party whose preferences were precisely complementary. Thus, barter is obviously a very inefficient way of doing business because it involves considerable *transaction costs*—the time, effort, and expense that go into the purchase or sale of a good. You can understand, therefore, why the medium-of-exchange function of money improves *transaction efficiency.* Money makes it unnecessary for buyers or sellers to establish a double coincidence of wants.

Measure of Value

An inch is a measure of distance, an ounce is a measure of weight, a degree is a measure of temperature. Similarly, a dollar is a measure of value. It tells you how much things are worth in terms of money. It therefore allows us to compare the value of one item with that of another. For example, if the price of a motorcycle is $3,000 and the price of a car is $15,000, the value of the car is five times that of the motorcycle. Stated differently, five motorcycles together have the same value as one car.

Money thus serves as a "common denominator," or *unit of account,* in terms of which the value of goods is quoted. A barter economy is one with no unit of account. Prices of goods must be quoted in terms of one another. A pizza, for example, might cost a paperback book, a T-shirt, four pairs of socks, three cans of tuna fish, two pounds of tomatoes, or any number of other things. And each of these goods, of course, would have a price in terms of the others. Buying and selling, therefore, would be extremely inefficient because the number of prices would quickly become mind-boggling.

For example, in a barter economy in which there were only 10 goods, 45 prices would be needed to express the values of all of the goods. If there were 100 goods, nearly 5,000 prices would be necessary. And if there were 1,000 goods, approximately half a million prices would have to exist! In a money economy, the number of prices equals the number of goods because each good has its own price. The measure-of-value function of money, like the medium-of-exchange function, greatly improves transaction efficiency.

Standard of Deferred Payments

If you use a credit card to purchase something, you are buying now and paying later. When the bank sends you your bill, it will, of course, be expressed in dollars—the unit of account used for money. Both you and the bank are thus utilizing money as a standard of deferred payments.

Suppose that you choose not to pay your bill by the due date. In that case the bank will add a finance charge to the amount you owe. The finance charge is determined by an *interest rate*—a percentage figure representing the price to be paid for the use of credit. The interest rate is thus a link between the present and the future—between "buying now and paying later." It is closely related to the function of money as a standard of deferred payments.

Store of Value

The final function of money is to serve as an accumulation of purchasing power, that is, a store of value. This function of money enables us to earn income in the present and spend it in the future. Money is not unique as a store of value. Land, buildings, stocks, bonds, jewelry, and many other assets are also accumulations of purchasing power, in that they can be sold to acquire other goods.

The ability of money to function as a store of value depends on the behavior of the general price level. If the price level rises, the value of a unit of money, such as the dollar, falls. If the price level falls, the value of a unit of money—the dollar—rises. The price level and the value of a unit of money are thus *inversely* related. *Inflation,* which is usually described simply as rising prices, contributes directly to the decline in the value of a unit of money.

This brief description of the nature and functions of money provides a background for understanding its important and complex role in today's economy. You may find it helpful to remember the functions of money with a simple rhyme:

> Money is a matter of functioning four,
> a medium, a measure, a standard, a store.

Measuring Money

Now that you think you know exactly what money is, you're in for a bit of a surprise. No one—neither the authors of this book, nor your professor in this course, nor the experts in Washington—has a precise understanding of money. This explains why economists are always searching for "*M*"—an ideal measure of the quantity of money available in the nation.

Several different measures of the quantity of money are currently in use. They are designated by the symbols *M*1, *M*2, *M*3, and *L*. Of these four measures, *M*1 is the narrowest, or least inclusive, and *L* is the broadest, or most inclusive. Let's turn to Exhibit 1 to understand why there's much more to the concept of money than you may have thought.

*M*1: Narrow Transactions Money—The Basic Money Supply

The most familiar form of money is that used by people for routine spending. This classification of money is *M*1. It may be thought of as "narrow transactions money," which means simply that it's readily spendable. The main components of *M*1 are the currency and coin in circulation plus **checkable deposits**—those on which checks can be written. *M*1 is often referred to simply as the "basic money supply."

As you can see from Exhibit 1, substantially less than one-third of the basic money supply consists of currency. This includes coins as well as $1 bills, $5 bills, etc. Traveler's checks, which are simply another form of currency, are a very small percentage of *M*1.

The largest component of *M*1 is *checkable deposits,*

including demand deposits of commercial banks and "other" types. If you write checks to pay for some of the things you buy, you may have one of several kinds of checkable deposits. It's helpful to distinguish between them. The most common kinds are demand deposits and savings-type checking accounts.

If you have a **demand deposit** with a bank, the bank promises to pay immediately an amount of money specified by you, the owner of the deposit. A demand deposit is thus a type of "checkbook money," because it permits transactions to be paid for by check rather than with currency. But unlike other checkable deposits, a demand deposit doesn't pay interest to its owner. Demand deposits are used by individuals and primarily by business firms.

Other types of checkable deposits are savings-type checking accounts. There are two major types. **Negotiable-order-of-withdrawal (NOW)** accounts are essentially interest-bearing checking accounts available to individuals and to nonprofit organizations. They are offered by most banks, savings and loan associations, and other depository institutions. **Share-draft** accounts are basically the same as NOW accounts, but they are provided by credit unions. Some other minor types of checking accounts exist in some states.

The main components of *M*1 are currency and checkable deposits. Because checkable deposits are readily convertible into cash, *M*1 is frequently referred to as the "basic money supply."

*M*2: Medium-Range Money

*M*2 is a broader measure of money than *M*1. *M*2 encompasses *M*1 and certain other assets. This enlarged category may be regarded as medium-range money. Among the components of *M*2 are savings deposits and certain short-term debt instruments, or IOUs. A short-term debt instrument is a contract between a borrower and a lender, the borrower agreeing to repay a loan with interest by a specified date within a year. (In contrast, a long-term debt instrument specifies a date of repayment beyond a year.)

Savings Deposits

Savings deposits come in different forms, such as passbook accounts, savings certificates, and certificates of deposit. All, however, are simply different kinds of time deposits issued by certain depository institutions such as banks.

A **time deposit** is money held in a depository-insti-

EXHIBIT
1

Counting Up the Money Supply

"*M*1 is up 3 percent. *M*2 is up 1 percent. *M*3 is unchanged." This is the kind of information that most banks in the country telecommunicate weekly to the Federal Reserve System in Washington, D.C. There the nation's central bank, commonly referred to as the "Fed," makes the adjustments necessary to report the week's supply of money. Each classification is made up of various components, as the table shows.

Note from the percentage figures that the proportions constituting *M*1 have changed considerably over the years. In particular, demand deposits, which don't pay interest to their holders, have declined in relative importance whereas other checkable deposits, which do pay interest, have gained. The proportions in the remaining categories, on the other hand, have remained relatively more stable.

	Money Supply							
	1980		1985		1990		1991	
	Amount (billions)	Percent of total	Amount (billions)	Percent of total	Amount (billions)	Percent of total	Amount (billions)	Percent of total
*M*1 = Narrow transactions money, the basic money supply	$ 412	100%	$ 620	100%	$ 825	100%	$ 897	100%
Currency	115	28	168	27	246	30	267	30
Checkable deposits	292	71	446	72	571	69	622	69
Demand deposits	261	63	267	43	277	34	289	32
NOW, share-draft, and other accounts	31	8	179	29	294	36	333	37
Traveler's checks	4	1	6	1	8	1	8	1
*M*2 = Medium-range money	$ 1,633	100%	$ 2,563	100%	$ 3,328	100%	$ 3,425	100%
*M*1	412	25	620	24	825	25	897	26
+[small-denomination savings (time) deposits; (overnight) repurchase agreements; money-market mutual-fund shares; (overnight) Eurodollars]	1,221	75	1,943	76	2,503	75	2,528	74
*M*3 = Wide-range money	$ 1,991	100%	$ 3,196	100%	$ 4,111	100%	$ 4,172	100%
*M*2	1,633	82	2,563	80	3,328	81	3,425	82
+[large-denomination time deposits; term repurchase agreements; term Eurodollars]	358	18	633	20	783	19	747	18
L = Liquid and near-liquid assets	$ 2,328	100%	$ 3,826	100%	$ 4,967	100%	$ 4,993	100%
*M*3	1,991	86	3,196	84	4,111	83	4,172	84
+[short-term Treasury securities; high-grade commercial paper; banker's acceptances]	337	14	630	16	856	17	821	16

Source: Board of Governors of the Federal Reserve System.

tution account of an individual or firm. Several types of time deposits have specified maturity dates, at which times the principal with accumulated interest becomes payable to the owner. For other kinds of time deposits, the depository institution may require advance notice of withdrawal. Only "small-denomination" time deposits, defined as those under $100,000, are counted in *M*2.

Repurchase Agreements

Certain borrowers and lenders often make contracts involving the sale and buyback of short-term debt instruments. Such contracts are called *repurchase agreements* (RPs or "repos"). The borrower sells the securities to the lender and agrees to repurchase them on a later date at the same price plus interest.

RPs frequently arise when a borrower, such as a bank, is temporarily in need of funds. It may borrow from a corporation that has idle cash balances to lend. The bank borrows by contracting to sell to the corporation and subsequently repurchase some of its short-term government securities, such as U.S. Treasury bills. All banks hold government securities, including Treasury bills and bonds, in their portfolios as part of their income-earning assets. By selling some of these assets to the lending corporation, the bank acquires the temporary funds it needs. The corporation, of course, earns a return on what amounts to a secured loan to the bank. The term of RPs may range from one day to several months. Those included in $M2$ are overnight RPs held up to 24 hours by commercial banks.

Money-Market Mutual-Fund Shares

Also counted as part of $M2$ are shares in money-market mutual funds. The *money market* is where short-term credit instruments, such as U.S. Treasury bills, corporations' commercial paper or promissory notes, and other types of financial claims described later are bought and sold. A *mutual fund* is an organization that pools people's money and uses it to buy securities, such as short-term debt instruments, stocks, and bonds. Putting the two terms together, a *money-market mutual fund* is one that buys money-market securities exclusively.

If you own shares (that is, a deposit account) in a money-market mutual fund, as do millions of individuals and corporations, you can write checks against your account. The minimum amount of the check must usually be $500. Therefore, an account of this type is like a checkable deposit included in $M1$, but it's somewhat more restrictive. Because of this, it is counted as part of $M2$.

Overnight Eurodollars

The remaining component of $M2$ is dollar deposits held in banks outside the United States, mostly in Europe. These deposits are called *Eurodollars*. They are owned by American and foreign banks, corporations, and individuals. Eurodollars represent dollar obligations that are constantly being shifted from one country to another in search of the highest return. Because of their growing importance in our financial system, overnight Eurodollars held by residents of the United States are included in $M2$.

$M3$: Wide-Range Money

A still broader classification of money is called $M3$. It includes $M2$ plus these additional components:

- Large-denomination time deposits at all depository institutions. A large-denomination time deposit is defined as one of $100,000 or more.

- Term repurchase agreements and term Eurodollars. These instruments are arranged for terms as little as 2 days to as long as several months.

L: Liquid and Near-Liquid Assets

The *liquidity* of an asset is the ease with which it can be converted into cash quickly without loss of value relative to its purchase price. The most liquid asset is cash itself. You can always exchange a dollar for a dollar.

The broadest classification of money is L. It consists of cash and the assets represented by $M3$, plus other near-liquid assets. These include:

- U.S. Treasury debt instruments—IOUs—that are approaching maturity, as well as U.S. savings bonds because they're readily cashable.

- Certain short-term business obligations, such as commercial paper (promissory notes or IOUs) issued by major corporations and banker's acceptances issued by banks.

This classification of money is as instructive for what it leaves out as for what it contains. For example, why do you suppose that stocks and long-term bonds have been excluded? Can you think of other assets that might have been included?

Conclusion: Money Is a Spectrum of Assets

Against this background, let's look again at the deceptively simple questions, "What is money?" and "How is it measured?"

Currency and checkable deposits are readily convertible into one another. Together, they constitute money in the *narrow* sense.

In a broader sense, some other assets are also "money." But they are often called *near-monies.* Their values are known in terms of money, and they can easily be converted into money, if this is desired. Some important examples are time deposits, such as savings certificates, and U.S. government short-term securities held by individuals and businesses. Other examples include the cash value of insurance policies, high-grade commercial paper, and similar near-liquid assets.

So the answers to the questions, "What is money?" and "How is it measured?" are by no means simple. Because there are different concepts of money, its definition and measurement are subject to controversy. The issues are examined in later chapters. Meanwhile, you'll find it helpful to think about money in the following way:

Money is more than just paper currency and coins. *Money is a spectrum of assets. The spectrum ranges from currency and checkable deposits through various types of time deposits to financial claims against government and some businesses.*

Financial Markets

Who goeth a borrowing goeth a sorrowing.

Benjamin Franklin

Let us all be happy and live within our means, even if we have to borrow the money to do it.

Anonymous

One of the reasons money is a complex concept is that it is closely related to credit (and debt). This relationship is what you'd expect, because credit replaces money, supplements money, and, in the final analysis, provides the base of the nation's money supply.

Credit and debt are the same thing looked at from two different sides. If I lend you money, my credit to you is the same as your debt to me. We can say, therefore, that the term *credit* implies a promise by one party to pay another for money borrowed or for goods or services received. Credit may be regarded as an extension of money.

A significant part of credit is that part represented by credit instruments. Because credit and debt are the

same thing looked at from two different sides, credit instruments are also known as debt instruments. *Both terms are used interchangeably.* However, "debt instrument" is the more commonly used term. **Debt** or **credit instruments** are financial documents that serve either as promises to pay or as orders to pay. They provide the means by which funds are transferred from one party to another.

The most familiar example of a debt instrument is an ordinary **promissory note,** or simply a **note.** It's an "IOU"—a promise made by one party to pay another a specified sum of money by a given date, usually within a year. Such notes are issued by individuals, corporations, and government agencies. Firms make heavy use of notes to borrow working capital from banks at certain busy times of the year. The interest on such loans is a chief source of income for banks and certain other lending institutions.

Other types of debt instruments are in use. The most important ones are traded in the nation's **financial markets**. Two major components of the financial markets are the money market and the capital market. These markets perform the important economic function of exchanging claims for liquidity (cash). It is *in the financial markets that organizations with surplus funds purchase claims against organizations in need of funds.*

The Money Market

Markets exist for many types of debt instruments. A *money market* is a center where short-term debt instruments issued by banks, corporations, and governmental entities are bought and sold. A variety of debt instruments are traded in the money market. Among the most important are the following:

Treasury Bills

Each week, in order to help finance its operations, the U.S. Treasury issues marketable obligations known as **Treasury bills**. They come in minimum denominations of $10,000, and they mature in 3 months, 6 months, or 1 year. The bills are sold at weekly auctions. The Treasury sells 3-month bills most often, and 6-month and 1-year bills less frequently as needed, at a discount from face value. This means that if you buy a 1-year Treasury bill today for $9,500, you will receive $10,000 at maturity—a rate of return of 5.3 percent.

The money that the Treasury raises from the sale of its bills helps the federal government meet its operating expenses. These include the salaries of civil service employees and armed forces personnel, the costs of supplies for government offices, and numerous other things for which the government disburses money.

Other Instruments

Government agencies, banks, and corporations sell a variety of other interest-earning money-market securities. Some of them were mentioned briefly earlier in the chapter. The more important instruments are described in Exhibit 2.

EXHIBIT 2

Money-Market Instruments

In addition to Treasury bills, the following money-market instruments are traded extensively by banks. As you'll learn in subsequent chapters, the buying and selling of money-market instruments have important effects not only on the banking system but on the economy as a whole.

Federal agency discount notes are sold by certain government agencies. Among them are the Federal Home Loan Bank, the Federal National Mortgage Association, the Government National Mortgage Association, and the Federal Farm Credit Bank System. The money raised by these agencies is used to provide mortgages and other types of loans.

Negotiable certificates of deposit (NCDs) are large-denomination notes ($100,000 or more) issued by major banks. The banks sell these securities to corporations and large individual investors, who buy them for their interest payments. (As you may know, most banks also sell deposit or savings certificates for smaller investors. However, these are merely special types of time deposits. They are smaller in size and are not resalable, unlike negotiable CDs.)

Commercial paper consists of promissory notes, mostly in minimum denominations of $10,000, sold by about 1,000 major corporations. The most familiar example is GMAC paper, issued by General Motors Acceptance Corporation, to finance the purchase of General Motors cars.

Banker's acceptances arise both in domestic trade and in international trade. In effect, a banker's acceptance (BA) is a bank-guaranteed "postdated check" written by one of its customers. If the bank stamps the check "accepted," it becomes a BA. This means that the bank assumes the customer's debt and guarantees payment on the postdated day. (The customer, of course, must eventually repay the

bank the full amount plus interest.) In the interim, if the bank should need short-term funds, it can sell the check in the money market at a discount from face value.

Repurchase agreements, popularly known as RPs or "repos," constitute a kind of collateralized loan. As mentioned earlier in the chapter, in a repurchase agreement the borrower sells the lender a credit instrument, usually a government security. In addition, the borrower simultaneously agrees to buy the instrument back on a later date at the same price plus interest at a specified rate. The lender (investor) thus holds a security as collateral for a loan with a fixed maturity and a fixed interest rate. Banks, often in need of short-term funds, are major users of RPs. The RPs are sold to corporations and large individual customers who have surplus cash balances to lend.

Tax-exempt money-market instruments are short-term obligations sold by some state and local governments and by local housing and urban renewal agencies. They are issued in anticipation of future tax revenues. Banks are among the major purchasers of these instruments. One reason is that they are considered safer from default than some other money-market instruments. A second reason is that their interest payments are exempt from federal income tax.

Federal funds, unlike the credit instruments described so far, are not represented by paper claims that change hands in the money market. Instead, they are unsecured loans that banks and certain other depository institutions make to one another, usually overnight, out of their excess reserves. Federal funds are an integral part of the money market. The purchase and sale of such funds is limited to banks, savings institutions, and certain government agencies in need of very short-term liquidity.

The Capital Market

Besides the money market, another important financial market is the *capital market.* This is where long-term financial instruments that mature in more than one year from the date of issue are bought and sold.

Bonds of various types are among the major debt instruments traded in the capital market. A *bond* is an agreement to pay a specified sum of money (called the principal) either at a future date or periodically over the course of a loan. During this time, interest at a fixed rate may be paid on certain dates. Bonds are issued by corporations (corporate bonds), state and local governments (municipal bonds), and the federal government (government bonds). Bonds are used for long-term financing, which is financing that extends beyond 1 year—sometimes as long as 30 years.*

Five major types of instruments are bought and sold in the capital market:

- U.S. government bonds—issued by the Treasury and by certain government agencies, such as the Federal National Mortgage Association and the Federal Home Loan Bank

- Municipal bonds—issued by state and local governments

- Corporate bonds

- Mortgages

- Corporate stock

Bonds and mortgages are debt instruments. Corporate stock is an equity (ownership) instrument. The yields on some major types of debt instruments are shown in Exhibit 3. Notice that the yields normally differ from one another at any given time. The differences reflect maturity dates, the stated interest rates on the securities, risk of default, tax treatment, marketability, and other conditions.

In general, municipal bonds normally have the lowest yields because the interest received by purchasers of such bonds is exempt from federal income taxes. In contrast, interest earned on Treasury bonds and corporate bonds is not exempt from federal income taxes. Therefore, municipal bonds can be sold at

lower yields than comparable bonds issued by the Treasury or by corporations.

Long-term Treasury bonds generally have a lower yield than comparable corporate bonds. The reason is that Treasury bonds carry no risk of default. Yields on high-quality corporate bonds, in turn, are lower than those on mortgages, which cost more to administer and are less easily marketed.

Economic Functions of Money and Capital Markets

The business, government, and foreign sectors are continually seeking funds to finance capital expenditures as well as the production of goods and services. The acquisition of these funds is made possible through financial markets, particularly the money market and the capital market. Taken together, these markets perform the task of transferring funds from lenders to borrowers. More specifically:

The money market primarily enables firms and government entities (federal, state, and local) to obtain liquidity. This happens when these organizations borrow funds by selling short-term claims against themselves.

The capital market primarily facilitates the transfer of funds from savers to borrowers. This occurs when borrowing institutions acquire funds by selling long-term claims against themselves.

To some extent, these functions overlap. In general, however, *the money and capital markets allocate financial resources between borrowers and lenders and between short-term and long-term uses.*

The Foreign Exchange Market

Other financial markets also play a role in allocating financial resources. One of them is the *foreign exchange market.* It is a world market in which instruments used for international payments are bought and sold. The instruments include national currencies such as U.S. dollars, Japanese yen, British pounds, French francs, Canadian dollars, and Mexican pesos. The foreign exchange market makes it possible for these and other national currencies to be traded for one another. Trading is conducted by major banks and dealers for their own accounts and on behalf of their clients.

Why are currencies traded? One of the chief reasons is to pay for imports. For example, suppose Germans want to purchase American-made blue jeans.

---

*Debt instruments that are like bonds but mature in more than 1 year and less than 10 years from the date of issue are often called "notes." For consistency, we'll use the term "bonds" to refer to such debt instruments. Some bonds, called consols, issued by the British government have no maturity date. They are perpetual bonds that live forever.

EXHIBIT
3

Capital-Market Yields

Yields on debt securities normally differ from one another at any given time. The differences depend on risk of default, maturity dates, tax considerations, and several other conditions. But notice that although the yields differ, they tend to rise and fall at about the same time.

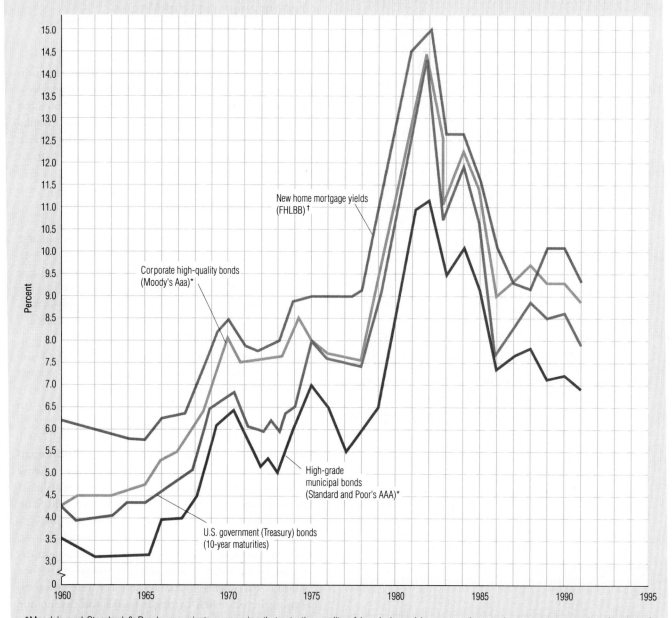

*Moody's and Standard & Poor's are private companies that rate the quality of bonds issued by corporations and government agencies. A rating of Aaa by Moody's or AAA by Standard & Poor's represents the highest quality—that is, the lowest risk of default.

†FHLBB stands for the Federal Home Loan Bank Board, a government agency.

The German consumers are willing to pay for the jeans with German marks, but American producers want to be paid in U.S. dollars. To purchase the blue jeans, therefore, German importers must convert their marks to U.S. dollars. This conversion takes place in the foreign exchange market.

The foreign exchange market works like many other markets. At any given time there are people holding marks who want to sell them for dollars. There are also people holding dollars who want to sell them for marks. The price of one currency in terms of another is determined by competitive forces of demand and supply. Competition between buyers and sellers results in an equilibrium price of marks in terms of dollars. It follows that competition also results in an equilibrium price of dollars in terms of marks. The same is true for other currencies. The price of one currency expressed in terms of another currency is called the *foreign exchange rate.*

Exhibit 4 shows a few major countries and curren-cies. Column (1) states the name of the country and its currency. Column (2) gives the amount you would have to pay in U.S. dollars to get one unit of the currency. Column (3) shows the currency per U.S. dollar: the amount of the currency you can get for one dollar. Note that column (3) is simply the reciprocal of column (2).

The foreign exchange market is a mechanism for making international payments. Because of the growing significance of world trade and investment, the foreign exchange market is playing an increasingly important role in allocating financial resources between nations.

The world's largest financial markets are in New York City and Tokyo. Other major markets are in London, Paris, and Hong Kong. These markets attract funds from numerous countries and perform a vital function in meeting the financing needs of businesses and governments.

Financial Intermediaries

The institutions that serve the money and capital markets are known as *financial intermediaries.* These organizations constitute a connecting link between lenders and borrowers. How? By creating and issuing financial obligations or claims ("IOUs") against themselves in order to obtain funds with which to acquire profitable financial claims against others. In this and the next few chapters, you will learn how financial intermediaries do this.

A chief function of financial intermediaries, therefore, is to provide liquidity. This refers to the ease with which an asset can be converted into cash quickly without loss of value relative to its purchase price. Financial intermediaries also perform other important economic functions. They provide the economy with the money supply and with near-liquid assets. Financial intermediaries thus facilitate investment in plant, equipment, and inventories.

For our purposes, financial intermediaries may be divided into two broad classes: (1) commercial banks, and (2) all other financial institutions. The latter includes mutual savings banks, savings and loan associations, credit unions, insurance companies, private pension funds, finance companies, mortgage companies, and so on. Because these institutions deal in financial claims, *most of the activity of financial intermediaries consists of the wholesaling and/or retailing of funds.*

EXHIBIT 4

Foreign Exchange Rates

Friday, February 7, 1992

If you know the U.S. dollar price of a foreign currency, its reciprocal will give you the foreign currency price of the U.S. dollar. The U.S. dollar price of currencies is given in column (2). The corresponding foreign-currency prices of the U.S. dollar, shown in column (3), are the reciprocals.

(1) Country (currency)	(2) U.S. dollar per unit of foreign currency	(3) Foreign currency per U.S. dollar 1÷(2)
United Kingdom (pound)	$1.8370	.5444
Canada (dollar)	.8489	1.1780
France (franc)	.18665	5.3576
Germany (mark)	.6410	1.5601
Italy (lira)	.0008514	1174.54
Japan (yen)	.007979	125.33

Commercial Banks

All banks deal in money and credit instruments. However, a **commercial bank** is the major type of bank engaged in making business loans by creating demand deposits. (Remember that a demand deposit is the technical term for a checkable deposit that doesn't pay interest to its owner.) In addition, a commercial bank may engage in many of the same activities carried on by other financial institutions. These activities include buying and selling money-market instruments, taking savings accounts or time deposits, providing mortgages, and selling financial services. However, the handling of demand deposits is a fundamental part of a commercial bank's business.

When you establish a demand-deposit account with a commercial bank, the bank creates and issues a financial obligation or claim against itself. It does this by agreeing to honor your checks on demand up to the amount of the deposit.

However, when a bank accepts your savings or time deposit, it creates a claim against itself that is legally payable after a specified time. For example, although a bank rarely does so, it can legally require notice of intended withdrawal from a savings deposit— usually 30 days or more. Hence, any time deposit, of which a savings deposit is perhaps the most familiar type, may be thought of as a claim that carries a stipulated maturity date.

Other instruments representing time-deposit claims are savings certificates and special types of savings accounts offered by banks and some non-bank financial institutions. However, none of these are as liquid as demand deposits.

Demand deposits are among the most liquid of all claims created and issued by financial intermediaries. Checks written against them are acceptable in exchange for currency.

The role played by commercial banks in expanding and contracting demand deposits is of enormous importance in understanding how the economy works. Therefore, commercial banking will occupy a considerable part of our attention in subsequent chapters.

Other Financial Intermediaries

Of course, other kinds of financial intermediaries seek to accommodate the particular needs and preferences of borrowers. Like commercial banks, these institutions create and issue claims against themselves in order to obtain funds with which to acquire profitable claims against others.

For example, mutual savings banks and savings and loan associations issue time-deposit claims. These claims are very much like time-deposit claims provided by commercial banks—except, in some cases, for differences in maturities and yields. The assets or claims against others that the issuing institutions acquire with the funds consist primarily of real estate mortgages, corporate bonds, and government securities.

Likewise, credit unions issue savings deposit claims to their members. The funds obtained are primarily to provide consumer loans. Insurance companies issue claims in the form of policies against themselves. Then they use most of the funds collected in premiums to purchase real estate mortgages, corporate securities, and government bonds. In like manner, other financial intermediaries generate obligations against themselves in order to acquire funds with which to purchase profitable, but often less liquid, obligations against others.

Providing Liquidity

Because the claims acquired by financial intermediaries are frequently less liquid than the claims they issue, it seems plausible that these intermediaries may sometimes find themselves temporarily illiquid. This means that they are unable to meet unexpected demands for payment out of their own assets. Situations of this type occurred frequently in American history. Sometimes they gave rise to financial crises or panics.

To help avoid financial crises, legislation designed to protect the public has been passed. It has provided insurance for bank deposits and set minimum financial requirements for banks, insurance companies, and certain other financial intermediaries. In addition, federally sponsored institutions have been created to provide liquidity to some financial intermediaries by lending to them or by purchasing assets from them. Notable among these have been special federal banks that supply funds to savings and loan associations and make intermediate-term loans to farmers. Most important for our purposes, however, have been the Federal Reserve Banks. They supply funds to depository institutions as one of the functions of the Federal Reserve System.

The Federal Reserve System

On December 23, 1913, President Woodrow Wilson signed the Federal Reserve Act. This created the Federal Reserve System and marked the beginning of a new era in American banking. Periodic money panics—"runs" on banks by depositors fearing that the banks were failing—had plagued the country since the early nineteenth century. Based on what was learned from the great panic of 1907, one of the worst in American history, the Act was designed to end extreme variations in the money supply and thus avoid panics. It did contribute (along with other legislation) to improving the stability of the banking system.

Objectives, Organization, and Functions

The *Federal Reserve System*—usually referred to as the Fed—is the nation's central bank. Like other central banks throughout the world, the Federal Reserve regulates the flow of money and credit. That is its chief responsibility. It also performs many service functions for depository institutions, the Treasury, and the public. Broadly speaking, the Federal Reserve System seeks to provide monetary conditions favorable to the realization of four national objectives: high employment, stable prices, steady economic growth, and a sound international financial position.

The Fed's form of organization is something like a pyramid, as illustrated in Exhibit 5. It consists of:

1. Member banks
2. Federal Reserve Banks
3. The Board of Governors
4. The Federal Open Market Committee
5. Other committees

Member Banks

At the base of the Federal Reserve pyramid are the System's *member banks.* All national banks (chartered by the federal government) must be members, and state banks (chartered by their respective states) may join if they meet certain requirements. Of some 12,000 commercial banks, fewer than 5,000 are members. However, these member banks are for the most part the larger banks in the country, holding the great bulk of all demand deposits.

Today the number of member banks relative to nonmember banks is not particularly significant. This is because legislation enacted in 1980 requires *all* depository institutions, members as well as nonmembers, to meet the same sets of standards with respect to reserve requirements. In addition, all institutions can purchase, on equal terms, the System's services, such as check clearing and electronic transfer of funds, and deliveries of currency when needed. Therefore, although more than half the banks in the nation do not belong to the Federal Reserve System, this doesn't affect the System's ability to influence the economy by controlling the money supply.

Federal Reserve Banks

The country is divided into twelve Federal Reserve districts, each with a *Federal Reserve Bank.* There are also more than two dozen Federal Reserve Bank branches serving areas within the districts. (See the map in Exhibit 5.)

Technically, each Federal Reserve Bank is owned by its member banks, which are the stockholders. But, unlike most private institutions, the Reserve Banks are operated in the public interest rather than for profit. However, they are, in fact, highly profitable because of the interest income they earn on the government securities that they own. After meeting their expenses, they pay a relatively small part of their earnings to the member banks as dividends, and return the major portion to the U.S. Treasury. Note that the district Federal Reserve Banks (and branches) constitute the second level of the pyramid.

Board of Governors

At the peak of the pyramid is the *Board of Governors* in Washington. It consists of seven members appointed by the President and confirmed by the Senate. Members are appointed for 14 years, one term expiring every 2 years. This pattern reduces political influences on the Board—members do not come and go with every presidential election. The chairperson of the Board, who is also a member of the Board, is appointed by the President for a 4-year term.

The Board of Governors supervises the Federal Reserve System and tries to see that it performs effectively. However, the Board's primary function is to influence the amount of money and credit in the economy.

EXHIBIT
5

Organization and Map of the Federal Reserve System

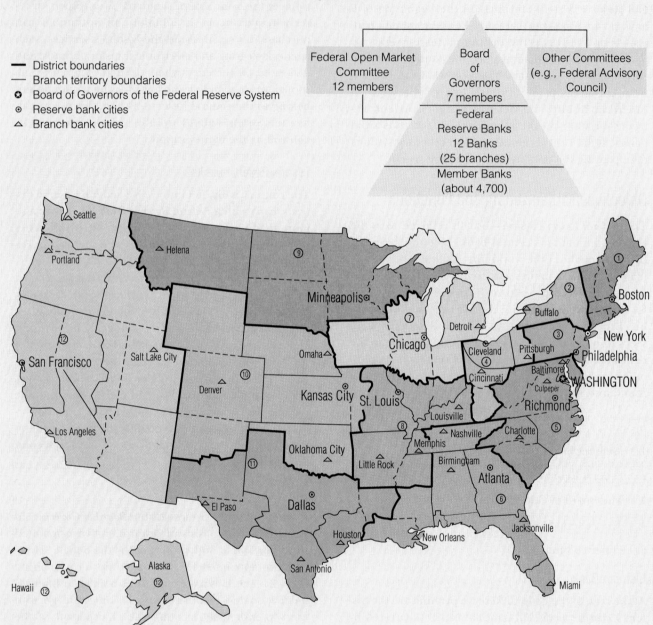

Federal Open Market Committee and Other Committees

The most important policymaking body within the System is the *Federal Open Market Committee.* This committee consists of twelve members. They include the seven members of the Board of Governors plus five presidents of the Federal Reserve Banks who serve in rotating order (except for the president of the Federal Reserve Bank of New York, who is a permanent member). The committee's chief function is to make policy for the System's purchase and sale of government and other securities in the open market in New York. Actual transactions are carried out by the Trading Desk of the Federal Reserve Bank of New York.

Several other committees play a less significant role in the Federal Reserve System's operations. The most important one is the *Federal Advisory Council,* which advises the Board of Governors on major current developments.

Summing Up: Functions of a Central Bank

Every nation has a central bank. Some of the world's leading central banks are the Federal Reserve System, the Bank of England, the Bank of France, the Bank of Japan, and the Bundesbank of Germany. The central banks of America's two neighboring countries are the Bank of Canada and the Bank of Mexico.*

Unlike the central banks of some countries, the Federal Reserve System is relatively new. Shortly after America's founding and a few times during the nineteenth century, several systems of government banks were established. But they were not true central banks and they proved inadequate to fulfill the chief goal of a central bank—the provision of liquidity.

The primary function of a central bank is to regulate the flow of money and credit in order to promote efficiency, stability, and growth. This function is common to all central banks. However, a central bank may also perform other financial functions for government, businesses, and households.

In addition to regulating the flow of money and credit in the economy, the Fed provides important services to the Treasury, the public, and depository institutions. These services include:

- Acting as a fiscal agent for the Treasury
- Operating a nationwide check clearinghouse
- Providing for the electronic transfer of funds among depository institutions
- Supplying currency for circulation
- Publishing statistics and reports on banking and related financial matters

Looking Abroad: What Will Europe Learn from the Fed?

During the first decade of the twentieth century, a major financial crisis known as the Panic of 1907 created a run on the nation's banks. In response, President Theodore Roosevelt initiated a thorough study of the banking system. The congressional commission charged with this study visited the central banks of leading European countries and presented a report suggesting the creation of an American central bank. Based on the commission's recommendations, legislation was passed in 1913 establishing the Federal Reserve System.

During the last decade of the twentieth century, major changes involving international trade and finance in Europe are greatly affecting the Continent's banks. In response, representatives of the European Community, an association of nations for mutual economic betterment, have visited the Fed to learn about its organization and operation. What the representatives sought were ideas for creating a European central bank—or more precisely, a "central bank of central banks." Known as the European System of Central Banks, the still-tentative ESCB may be modeled partly after the Fed and partly after Germany's Bundesbank.

Will a true European central bank be established? Probably not. It's doubtful that nations will give up a fundamental part of their sovereignty by allowing an international organization to regulate the flow of money and credit. History provides few examples of nations that have sacrificed any form of sovereignty voluntarily. What may come about, therefore, is not a unified central bank like the Fed but an association of central banks that provides some of the same services

*Except in the United States and Germany, practically all central banks are named after their countries. In 1913, when Congress was considering the establishment of a central bank, most of the legislators wanted to call it the Bank of the United States. This is undoubtedly the name that would have been adopted. However, there was at that time a large private bank in New York with a similar name. To avoid confusion, Congress decided to call the new central bank the Federal Reserve System.

as the Fed. These include the operation of a system-wide check clearinghouse, provisions for electronic transfers of funds among banks, and the publication of reports on banking and related matters.

If the ESCB is ever established, it is likely to be more of a service institution than a true central bank. It will not regulate the flow of money and credit in the European Community, but it will perform some services similar to those provided by the Fed.

Organization of the Banking System

The banking system in the United States has an unusual structure, one not found in any other country. Known as a *dual banking system,* this organization grew out of legislation passed during the 1860s for the purpose of creating federally chartered banks. As a result, our banking system consists of two classes of commercial banks—national banks and state banks.

National Banks   These are commercial banks chartered by the federal government. Such banks are required to belong to the Federal Reserve System. About one-third of all commercial banks today are national banks; the rest are state banks. Although fewer in number, national banks hold considerably more than half the deposits of the banking system and are larger than most state banks. In case you're wondering how to tell the difference between a national bank and a state bank, the method is simple. A national bank is required to have either the word "national" in its title or the letters "N.A." (for *national association*) after its name. If it has neither, it's a state bank.

State Banks   These are commercial banks chartered by state governments. State banks may or may not be members of the Federal Reserve System. Today, only about 10 percent of state banks are members.

Banking Supervision: A Regulatory Thicket

Partly because of our dual banking system, which is rooted in U.S. political history, the nation's banks are regulated by several government agencies:

Comptroller of the Currency   This federal entity, which is part of the Treasury Department, charters all national banks. It also oversees the operations both of national banks and of those state banks that are members of the Federal Reserve System.

Federal Reserve System   The Fed exercises some degree of regulation over all banks, national as well as state. In addition, it exerts some control over thrift institutions, such as savings banks and savings and loan associations.

Federal Deposit Insurance Corporation (FDIC)   This agency supervises the operations of all insured banks. These include national banks, state banks that belong to the Fed, and insured banks that do not. Only a small number of banks are uninsured. The FDIC, therefore, has regulatory authority over almost all banks.

State Banking Commissions   All fifty states exercise varying degrees of control over their state-chartered banks (as well as other depository institutions). The only banks not subject to state regulations are national banks. This is because they are federally chartered and hence subject to federal regulations.

All banks in the United States are regulated by at least two government agencies, most are regulated by three, and many are regulated by four. As a result, there is considerable overlapping and conflicting supervisory responsibility among the regulatory agencies. This leads to much waste of resources and duplication of effort.

A partial illustration of the complex network of regulation is shown in Exhibit 6.

Deposit Insurance: Protecting Your Money

What happens to your money if a bank in which you have a deposit fails? Chances are you will be protected by insurance, provided by the *Federal Deposit Insurance Corporation* (FDIC). This government agency came into existence in 1934 when the country was in the throes of a major depression. More than 9,000 banks had failed during the years 1930–1933, leaving depositors unprotected. The FDIC was created to protect depositors and thereby help improve bank stability.

The main function of the FDIC is to insure deposits at commercial and savings banks. Each insured bank pays an annual premium equal to a fraction of 1 percent of its total deposits. In return, the FDIC insures each account up to $100,000 against loss due to bank failure. The FDIC also supervises insured banks and presides over the liquidation of banks that do fail.

All national banks must be insured by the Federal Deposit Insurance Corporation, and state banks may apply to the FDIC for insurance coverage if they wish.

EXHIBIT
6

The Bank-Regulation Thicket

Bank regulatory agencies exchange some of their information and accept one another's audits for certain purposes. Nevertheless, duplication of efforts in the regulation of banking leads to significant inefficiency and waste of resources.

This diagram illustrates only part of the regulatory maze. It includes only commercial banks and no other types of depository institutions, such as credit unions and savings and loan associations. These are regulated by the Fed and by agencies not shown.

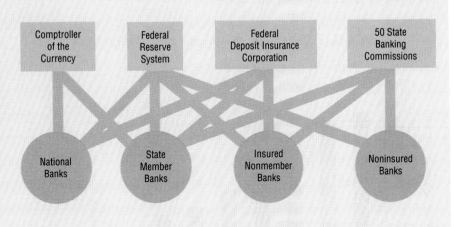

Since the late 1930s, practically all banks in the United States (more than 98 percent of them) have been covered by this insurance. Banks have therefore become much more stable than they were before the creation of government insurance. As a result, widespread runs on banks by panicky depositors seeking to withdraw their funds are no longer common. Nevertheless, a run will sometimes occur when a particular bank is believed to be in trouble.

While federal deposit insurance helps maintain the stability of the banking industry, the viability of the present insurance system has come into question. Does the existence of insurance encourage banks to take greater risks because the losses to depositors will be protected? Many experts think so. This has sparked controversy over whether the insurance system should be revised and how large losses can be forestalled in the future.

"Nonbank Banks": Do We Need Banks Anymore?

Most Americans would find it difficult to conceive of a bankless society. But that may very well be a reality in the not-too-distant future. Today consumers and businesses can meet practically all of their banking needs without ever setting foot in a bank. All they need do is use the services of a "nonbank bank."

Want to open an insured savings account or government-guaranteed checking account? Brokerage firms such as Merrill Lynch & Co. or Prudential Securities will gladly accommodate you. Need a mortgage loan to finance the purchase of a house? Call an insurance company or even some Wall Street securities firms. Thinking of financing the purchase of a car? Your dealer can arrange an auto loan through the credit division of one of the big automakers—Ford, General Motors, or Chrysler. These, and the financing arms of many other major corporations such as General Electric, Exxon Corporation, and Sears, Roebuck and Co., are among the largest financial institutions in the nation. Many of them make loans to businesses as well as to households. And a growing number are providing additional services such as consumer financial counseling, securities brokerage, personal property appraisals, credit and collection assistance, and tax preparation.

The rapid growth of these "nonbank banks" has contributed to a major transformation of the banking industry, resulting in what is called the *new banking*. What accounts for this evolution? One of the main factors has been the movement toward bank deregulation that began gathering momentum in the late 1970s. (But alarming numbers of bank failures in some years since then occasionally prompt Congress to consider re-regulating certain banking activities.)

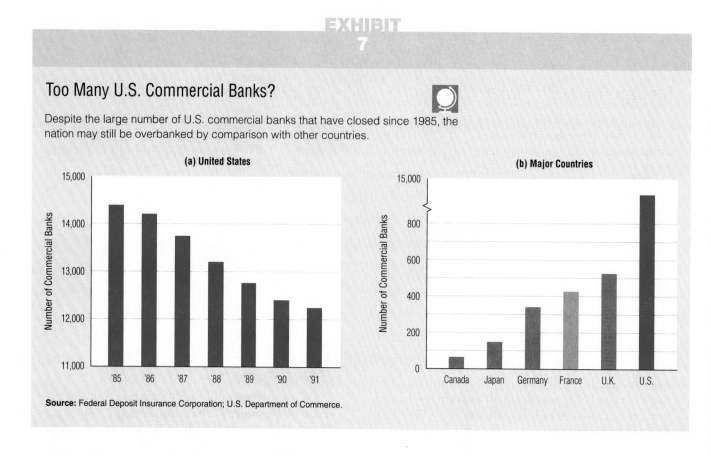

**EXHIBIT
7**

Too Many U.S. Commercial Banks?

Despite the large number of U.S. commercial banks that have closed since 1985, the nation may still be overbanked by comparison with other countries.

Source: Federal Deposit Insurance Corporation; U.S. Department of Commerce.

Another factor has been the development of telecommunications and computerized information systems that permit the rapid and low-cost transfer of funds worldwide.

Does this mean that banks are obsolete? Perhaps not completely. But their role will continue to shrink in the face of new challenges from competitors that were nonexistent until relatively recently. The industry's downsizing, however, still has a way to go. As Exhibit 7 shows, despite the large numbers of bank closings since 1985, the United States still has far more banks than other major countries.

Summary of Important Ideas

1. Money is a medium of exchange, a measure of value, a standard of deferred payments, and a store of value. These functions of money are fundamental to understanding our monetary and banking system.

2. Money should be thought of as a spectrum of assets. "Narrow transactions money," $M1$, is readily

spendable money. It constitutes the basic money supply and consists primarily of currency and checkable deposits.

3. Broader measures than $M1$ are also in use. They incorporate savings deposits, money-market mutual-fund shares, and various kinds of highly liquid assets referred to as near-monies.

4. National currencies are exchanged through the foreign exchange market. The price of a currency, termed the "foreign exchange rate," affects a country's purchases of imports and sales of exports.

5. The money market and the capital market are major financial markets. Short-term debt instruments are bought and sold in the former, long-term instruments in the latter. These markets thus perform the economic function of allocating financial resources between borrowers and lenders and between short-term and long-term uses.

6. The foreign exchange market is another important financial market. The foreign exchange market allocates financial resources between nations.

7. Financial intermediaries, such as banks, insurance companies, credit unions, and other financial institutions, are connecting links between lenders and borrowers. They create and issue financial claims against themselves in order to acquire proceeds with which to purchase profitable financial claims against others. A large part of financial intermediaries' activities thus consist of the wholesaling and/or retailing of funds.

8. The Federal Reserve System is the central bank of the United States. It consists of about 4,700 member (commercial) banks scattered throughout the nation, twelve Federal Reserve Banks (plus more than two dozen branches) located in various cities, and a seven-member Board of Governors appointed by the President and confirmed by the Senate. The function of the System is to foster a flow of money and credit that provides for stable prices, orderly economic growth, and strong international financial relationships.

9. The United States has a dual banking system consisting of national banks and state banks. All banks are supervised by several government agencies. Almost all bank deposits (demand and time) are insured by the FDIC.

10. The banking industry is undergoing dramatic changes. Today many so-called nonbank banks are performing functions previously done only by traditional banks.

Terms and Concepts to Review

currency	promissory note
money	financial markets
double coincidence of wants	Treasury bills
transaction costs	negotiable certificate of deposit (NCD)
unit of account	federal funds
interest rate	capital market
checkable deposits	bond
demand deposit	foreign exchange market
time deposit	foreign exchange rate
repurchase agreement	financial intermediaries
money market	commercial bank
Eurodollars	Federal Reserve System
liquidity	member banks
near-monies	dual banking system
debt instrument	national banks
state banks	Federal Deposit Insurance Corporation

Questions and Problems

1. Which function of money is most important in today's society? Explain.

2. Which function does money perform least efficiently?

3. How would the functions of money be affected if the value of the dollar increased from year to year?

4. The more money you have, the richer you are. Similarly, the more money a nation has, the richer it is. Therefore, nations can become rich simply by printing more money. Do you agree?

5. If the price of the dollar in terms of Japanese yen declines from 150 yen to 100 yen, what happens to the price of yen (in dollars)? Explain why this happens.

6. (a) How would an increase in the interest rate in the United States, relative to Japan, affect the sale of U.S. bonds to Japanese investors? (b) How would an increase in the U.S. price level, relative to Japan's, alter international trade between the United States and Japan? (*Suggestion*: Think in terms of Americans buying Japanese goods and Japanese buying American goods.)

7. What economic reasons can you give for the existence of money markets?

8. Money-market instruments must possess certain characteristics in order to function *efficiently*. Can you think of three? What does "efficiently" mean in this case?

9. What economic reasons can you give for the existence of capital markets?

10. Capital markets have played an important role in our nation's growth. Can you explain why?

11. Financial intermediaries play a much more important role in today's economy than they did several decades ago. They are also more significant in the United States than in most African, Asian, or Latin American countries. Why?

12. Every nation has its own central bank. Why? What minimum functions does a central bank perform that a commercial bank does not?

TAKE A STAND

Electronic Funds Transfer: Will We Become a Cashless Society?

Over the past few years, cash transactions have been replaced in growing numbers by electronic funds transfers. Wages, for example, are frequently transferred directly from the employer's bank account to the employee's. There is no paycheck, only electronic signals shooting through the banking system's network of computers. Increasing numbers of consumers have been making their monthly telephone, electricity, credit card, mortgage, and car loan payments by electronic funds transfer instead of by cash or check. And some consumers pay for purchases by presenting a debit card that authorizes a direct transfer of funds from the buyer's bank to the seller's.

Due to major technological advances in the development of computers, communications equipment, and information processing, electronic funds transfer is becoming easier and cheaper. Billions of dollars can be sent almost anywhere in the world with a few computer keystrokes. The likelihood of continued advances in technology suggests that the electronic transfer of funds will become even easier in the future.

While banks and large corporations are the heaviest users of electronic funds transfer, so many consumers are taking advantage of the system that it could conceivably replace checks and cash as the preferred medium of exchange. *Will we become a cashless society?*

Yes: Electronic Transfers Are a More Convenient Medium of Exchange

The items used as media of exchange have evolved over the years. In primitive societies, certain commodities, such as live-

stock and animal skins, performed the medium-of-exchange function of money. Even someone with no immediate need for those commodities would be willing to accept them as payment because they could readily be traded for other goods. As societies progressed to more convenient ways of conducting trans-

actions, metals, especially gold and silver, replaced other commodities as the medium of exchange. Metal coins gave way to paper currency. Paper currency, in turn, has been largely replaced by checks. Soon, electronic funds transfer will replace checks and cash as the primary medium of exchange.

Electronic funds transfer is the easiest, safest, and quickest method available for conducting transactions. Cash has to be carried around and guarded, and lost or stolen cash is gone forever. Although a lost or stolen check might not be cashed by the depositor's bank, stopping payment on it is troublesome and costly. With electronic funds transfer, there is no need to put checks in the mail for monthly mortgage, car loan, and utility payments. Purchases from retail stores or even vending machines can be made merely by passing a debit card through a scanner.

Eventually, the need for cash will disappear. In the same way that they have replaced other commodities as money, cash and checks will soon be replaced by electronic funds transfer.

No: Cash Is More Convenient

Electronic funds transfer is unquestionably becoming an important part of the banking system. Yet even as technological changes have made electronic funds transfer an increasingly efficient method of payment, the use of cash has grown. There are at least three reasons.

First, for buyers and sellers it is often easiest and most convenient to conduct transactions with cash. Checks take time for buyers to write, for sellers to deposit, and for banks to clear. Credit and debit cards require access codes, authorization numbers, and collection procedures.

Second, cash transactions are anonymous. This quality makes cash ideal for buyers and sellers who want to keep their transactions confidential. Illegal transactions are conducted almost exclusively in cash because cash is difficult to trace.

Third, the same technology that gave rise to electronic funds transfer also created the automated teller machine, which allows depositors convenient access to the exact amount of cash they want when they want it. Depositors need no longer make large, periodic withdrawals of cash and then risk losing it.

The use of electronic funds transfer will undoubtedly continue to increase. But it won't replace cash. At most, electronic funds transfer may one day replace checking accounts. Cash has been, and continues to be, the most convenient medium of exchange.

The Question: Will We Become a Cashless Society?

■ Advances in computer, communications, and information-processing technology lead many to speculate that we will become a cashless society in the near future. In the same way that cash and checking accounts have replaced other types of money, electronic funds transfer will replace cash and checks.

■ Others disagree. Cash remains the most convenient and the most confidential means of payment. In comparison, checks, credit cards, and debit cards are cumbersome to use and require detailed record-keeping. There is no reason to believe that we will soon be a cashless society.

Where Do You Stand?

1. Which do you view as more convenient—cash or electronic funds transfer? Explain.

2. If people demand cash for illegal transactions, could criminal activities be controlled by eliminating the use of cash? Explain.

3. Many people are concerned that government, banks, and businesses already know too much about our private life. Total reliance on electronic funds transfer means that a record would exist of every transaction a person makes. How might this affect privacy?

4. Will we become a cashless society? Justify your stand.

Banking Institutions: Money Creation and Portfolio Management

The Fundamental Principle of Deposit Banking

Banks' Balance Sheets and Reserves

Deposit Expansion by a Single Bank

Deposit Expansion by the Banking System

Managing a Bank's Portfolio

Bank Failures: When Fractional Reserve Banking Goes Bad

Origins: Portfolio Management

Learning Guide
Watch for answers to these important questions

How do we define money? What is the goldsmith's principle and how does it relate to fractional-reserve banking?

Why is an individual bank in a banking system unable to lend more than the amount of its excess reserves? What would happen if it tried to do so?

Can the banking system as a whole lend more than its excess reserves? What is the deposit multiplier? What is the money multiplier? What do these multipliers tell you?

What objectives do banks seek in the management of their portfolios? How do these objectives impinge on one another?

How do banks allocate their funds among different classes of reserves? Which types of securities are likely to be found in a typical bank's portfolio?

What caused bank failures during the 1980s? What were the consequences of those failures?

How does portfolio management relate to security diversification?

The average person probably thinks of a bank as an institution in which to deposit money and from which to withdraw money. But banks are a good deal more than that. They play a fundamental role in the financial and monetary structure of our economy.

Banks engage in a varied assortment of financial activities. These activities include:

- Dealing in money and credit instruments

- Making business loans by creating checking deposits, and retiring those deposits when the loans are repaid

- Providing other financial services and functions such as making available time and savings deposits, granting long-term mortgage loans, operating a trust department, and renting safe-deposit boxes

The ways in which banks conduct most of these activities can have important effects on our economy. Therefore, in this chapter we'll examine the basic economic functions of today's banking institutions.

The Fundamental Principle of Deposit Banking

You've already learned that there are different measures of money, depending on what is included in its definition. For example, you'll remember from the previous chapter that $M1$, the basic money supply, consists mainly of currency and checkable deposits. Thus we may say that for practical purposes

Money = currency + checkable deposits

Checkable deposits, you'll recall, consist primarily of demand deposits, NOW accounts, and credit union share accounts. All of these are used to carry on day-to-day business activities. Therefore, checkable deposits are also called *transaction deposits.*

Proportions of Currency and Checkable Deposits

Most of us are more familiar with currency than with checkable deposits. The amount of currency in circulation at any time is determined by the public—you and everyone else. This is because currency and checkable deposits are basically interchangeable. You'll generally cash a check when you need currency and deposit currency in your checking account when you have more cash than you need.

Everyone behaves in much the same way. As a result, the public always holds the exact amount of cash that it wants by shifting its holdings back and forth between currency and checkable deposits. Over the course of a year, the public holds a smaller proportion of $M1$ in currency than in checkable deposits. But at certain times of the year, such as Christmas and Easter, the proportion of currency in circulation increases significantly because people desire more cash for spending. After the holidays, the proportion of currency in circulation decreases significantly as businesses deposit their cash receipts in checking accounts.

The Goldsmith's Principle and Fractional Bank Reserves

Because checkable deposits are by far the largest part of our money supply, it's important to know how they come into existence and what role they play.

Our system of deposit banking is based on a modernized version of what may be called the **goldsmith's principle.** This principle was discovered centuries ago by English precious-metal artisans, who were called goldsmiths. People deposited gold with these artisans for safekeeping. The goldsmiths quickly discovered that not many people would want to withdraw their gold at any given time. Therefore, it wasn't usually necessary to keep all of the gold on hand. Instead, only a portion of it needed to be kept in reserve for those individuals who might want to withdraw their gold. The rest could be "put to work" earning interest by being loaned to others in return for a promise of repayment.

Following the lead of the goldsmiths, banks today keep only a fractional—as opposed to 100 percent—reserve against deposits. Thus, we have what is called a *fractional-reserve banking system.* Its fundamental principle is this:

Not all of the customers of a bank will withdraw their funds at the same time. On any given day, some customers will decrease their deposits by withdrawing funds in the form of cash and checks drawn on the bank. On the same day, other customers will increase their deposits by depositing funds in the form of cash and checks drawn on other banks. Under normal conditions, the volume of deposits and withdrawals will tend to be equal over a period of time.

In a bank, of course, there is always the possibility that, during some periods, withdrawals will exceed deposits. To meet such contingencies, reserves equal to less than 5 percent of deposits are usually more than adequate. However, to give the Federal Reserve greater control over the supply of currency and deposits, the law requires banks to maintain higher fractional reserves of liquid assets against their deposit liabilities. The percentage of reserves that the banking system actually keeps on hand averages roughly 10 percent.

Banks' Balance Sheets and Reserves

The ways in which checkable deposits are expanded and contracted can best be illustrated in terms of changes in a bank's assets, liabilities, and net worth. These terms have special meanings:

For any economic entity such as an individual, household, or firm:

Assets are things of value that are owned—cash, property, and the rights to property.

Liabilities are monetary debts or things of value that are owed to creditors.

Net worth, or owners' equity, is the difference between assets and liabilities.

Thus, for any individual, household, or firm,

Assets – liabilities = net worth

Therefore, it's also true that

Assets = liabilities + net worth

The second equation is the one we'll use.

When these data are grouped together for analysis and interpretation, the financial statement on which they appear is called a **balance sheet.** Exhibit 1 shows a condensed balance sheet for all U.S. commercial banks. Notice that the balance sheet is arranged according to the second equation: The amount of assets is shown to be equal to the amount of liabilities and net worth.

On a bank's balance sheet, the principal assets are reserves, loans, and government securities; the principal liabilities are deposits.

Legal Reserves

Assets that a bank or other depository institution (such as a savings and loan association or a credit union) may lawfully use as reserves against deposit liabilities are called **legal reserves.** Legal reserves consist of currency held in the vaults of the bank—called *vault cash*—plus deposits held with the district Federal Reserve Bank. Any other financial reserves, even government securities (which were once acceptable up to certain limits as legal reserves), are classified as *nonlegal reserves.* This definition of legal reserves applies to *all* depository institutions. They all are subject to uniform reserve requirements on similar classes of deposits.*

There are two categories of legal reserves—required and excess.

Required Reserves These are the minimum amount of legal reserves that a bank is required by law to keep against its deposit liabilities. For example, if the required-reserve ratio is equal to 20 percent, a bank with checkable deposits of $1 million must hold at least $200,000 (= $1 million × .2) of required reserves.

Excess Reserves These are the amount of a bank's legal reserves over and above its required reserves. Excess reserves, you'll see, determine a bank's lending power.

It follows from these definitions that

Legal reserves = required reserves + excess reserves

and therefore

Excess reserves = legal reserves – required reserves

---

*Banking laws and practices identify many different kinds of reserves. Among them are legal reserves, nonlegal reserves, required reserves, excess reserves, primary reserves, secondary reserves, tertiary reserves, borrowed reserves, nonborrowed reserves, free reserves, and idle reserves. However, *there are no such things as "total reserves" or "reserves."* These terms are ambiguous and should not be used, even though some writers employ them as synonyms for legal reserves. The term "legal reserves" was first defined in the Louisiana Bank Act of 1842 and has since been used in state and federal bank legislation including the Federal Reserve Act of 1913.

Consolidated Balance Sheet of All Commercial Banks
December 31, 1991 (in billions)

(1)	**ASSETS**	
(2)	Vault cash (currency and coin)	$ 30.7
(3)	Reserves with Federal Reserve Banks	29.2
(4)	**Legal reserves: (2) + (3)**	**59.9**
	These are assets that banks may lawfully use as reserves against their deposit liabilities.	
(5)	Loans	2,283.9
	Consists of the value of claims (or IOUs) held by banks against borrowers.	
(6)	Investment securities	704.9
	Includes mostly Treasury bills, Treasury notes, Treasury bonds, federal agency securities, municipal securities, and bankers' acceptances.	
(7)	Other assets	33.2
	Includes cash items in process of collection, the value of bank premises, and other items.	
(8)	**Total assets: (4) + (5) + (6) + (7)**	**$ 3,081.9**
(9)	**LIABILITIES AND NET WORTH**	
(10)	Transaction (checkable) deposits	$ 672.6
(11)	Other liabilities	2,163.6
	Includes savings deposits, time deposits, borrowings such as negotiable CDs issued by banks, and other items.	
(12)	**Total liabilities: (10) + (11)**	**2,836.2**
(13)	**Net worth: (8) – (12)**	**245.7**
	This is the ownership interest of banks' stockholders.	
(14)	**Total liabilities and net worth: (12) + (13)**	**$ 3,081.9**

Source: Board of Governors of the Federal Reserve System.

It further follows that any changes in either a bank's legal reserves or its required reserves will change its excess reserves. As you study the processes by which banks expand and contract checkable deposits, you should keep these simple equations in mind.

Deposit Expansion by a Single Bank

Let's begin with an illustration of how a single bank seeks to expand its checkable deposits. To keep the explanation from becoming unnecessarily complicated, we will make two simplifying assumptions:

- **Uniform Transaction Deposits**   We will assume that depository institutions offer only one type of checkable deposit. (In reality, several types of checkable deposits, also known as transaction deposits, are available.)

- **Fixed Required-Reserve Ratio**   We will also assume a reserve requirement of 20 percent against deposits. (In reality, the average requirement for depository institutions as a whole is closer to 10 percent. This figure will be used for some of the problems at the end of the chapter.)

Stage 1   Let's begin by assuming that Bank *A* has the following simplified balance sheet:

Bank *A*: Balance Sheet
Stage 1: Initial Position

Assets			Liabilities and Net Worth	
Legal reserves		$ 5,000	Deposits	$20,000
Required	$4,000		Net worth	1,000
Excess	1,000			
Loans (claims)		16,000		
		$21,000		$21,000

The first thing to notice is that the balance sheet "balances." That is, the totals always conform to the equation: assets = liabilities + net worth.

The left side shows that the bank's assets consist of legal reserves and loans. The legal reserves (which consist of vault cash plus deposits with the district Federal Reserve Bank) are made up of required reserves and excess reserves. Loans are classified as assets because they represent financial claims held by the bank against borrowers. These claims (or accounts receivable) are usually in the form of promissory notes.

The right side of the balance sheet shows that deposits are liabilities. This is because the bank is obligated to honor checks drawn by its depositors up to the amount shown.

Also on the right side of the balance sheet, observe that net worth is the difference between total assets and total liabilities. It is thus a "balancing item" representing stockholders' ownership in the bank.

Note that, with $20,000 of deposits and a reserve requirement of 20 percent, required reserves (on the left side) are $4,000. Because legal reserves are $5,000, excess reserves are equal to $1,000.

Stage 2   Because Bank *A* has $1,000 in excess reserves, it can make loans equal to this amount. Suppose you, a businessperson, borrow the funds and give the bank your promissory note in exchange. The bank then credits your account for $1,000. *Before* you write any checks, how does the bank's balance sheet look?

Bank *A*: Balance Sheet
Stage 2: After the bank grants a loan of $1,000 but before checks are written against it

Assets		Liabilities and Net Worth	
Legal reserves	$ 5,000	Deposits	$21,000
Loans (claims)	17,000	Net worth	1,000
	$22,000		$22,000

As the balance sheet now shows, deposits have risen to $21,000. This $1,000 increase reflects the bank's commitment (a liability) to honor your checks up to $1,000. In addition, loans have increased to $17,000, reflecting the promissory note (an asset) you gave the bank for $1,000. As a result of this transaction, *the bank has created $1,000 of new money.*

Stage 3   Of course, you can take your $1,000 out in currency if you wish. However, you will probably find it more convenient to write checks in order to pay your bills.

Suppose that you write a check for the full $1,000 and give it to a supplier from whom you've purchased materials. The supplying company then deposits the check in its own bank, Bank *B*, which in turn presents it to Bank *A* for payment. The effect on Bank *A* is shown in the following balance sheet. The bank's deposits are reduced to $20,000 and its legal reserves to $4,000. Note that required reserves are 20 percent of deposits, or $4,000—which equals the bank's legal reserves. The bank, in other words, no longer has excess reserves. Therefore, it can no longer make loans.

Bank *A*: Balance Sheet
Stage 3: Final Position

Assets			Liabilities and Net Worth	
Legal reserves		$ 4,000	Deposits	$20,000
Required	$4,000		Net worth	1,000
Excess	0			
Loans (claims)		17,000		
		$21,000		$21,000

This analysis leads to an important conclusion:

No individual bank in a banking system can lend more than its excess reserves. In other words, when a bank's excess reserves are zero, it has no unused lending power. The bank, therefore, is *fully loaned up.**

Of course, the supplier to whom you gave your $1,000 check might have had an account in Bank *A* instead of in Bank *B*. In that case, the *total* deposits of Bank *A* would have been unaffected. The bank, when processing the check, would simply have reduced your account by $1,000 and increased the supplier's account by the same amount. In the great majority of cases, however, this situation does not exist. Instead:

As a borrower writes checks against a deposit, the borrower's bank loses reserves and deposits to other banks within the banking system. Hence, a bank cannot afford to make loans in an amount greater than its excess reserves.

Deposit Expansion by the Banking System

Although a single bank can't make loans totaling more than its excess reserves, the banking system can lend several times that amount. Let's examine the reasons for this by continuing with our illustration. To keep matters simple, we'll focus our attention on the relevant *changes* to the balance sheet and disregard all other items. As before, the reserve requirement is assumed to be 20 percent.

Stage 4 The $1,000 check you paid your supplier is deposited in the supplier's account in Bank *B*. Bank *B*'s deposits increase by $1,000 and its legal reserves (after the check clears) increase by $1,000. Let's assume that Bank *B* was fully loaned up prior to this transaction. The bank sets aside 20 percent or $200 of the new deposit in required reserves. That leaves 80 percent, or $800, in excess reserves.

Bank *B*: Partial Balance Sheet
Stage 4: Bank *B* receives the $1,000 deposit lost by Bank *A*

Assets			Liabilities	
Legal reserves		+$1,000	Deposits	+$1,000
Required	+$200			
Excess	+ 800			
		+$1,000		+$1,000

Stage 5 Bank *B*, of course, will try to lend $800—an amount equal to its excess reserves. Assuming it grants such a loan, its balance sheet *before* any checks are written will show that deposits have risen from $1,000 to $1,800. Loans have increased by a corresponding amount. Thus:

Bank *B*: Partial Balance Sheet
Stage 5: After Bank *B* grants a loan for $800 but before checks are written against it

Assets			Liabilities	
Legal reserves		+$1,000	Deposits	+$1,800
Loans (claims)		+ 800		
		+$1,800		+$1,800

Stage 6 Let's assume that the borrower writes a check for the entire amount of the loan and that the check is deposited by its recipient in Bank *C*. This will cause Bank *B* to lose $800 in deposits and (after the check clears) $800 in legal reserves to Bank *C*. This will leave Bank B with the following net changes:

Bank *B*: Partial Balance Sheet
Stage 6: After a check for $800 is written against Bank *B*

Assets			Liabilities	
Legal reserves			Deposits	
(net change			(net change	
=+$1,000			=+$1,800	
−$800)		+$ 200	−$800)	+$1,000
Loans (claims)		+ 800		
		+$1,000		+$1,000

---

*To understand how banks create money, it helps to assume that they lend their excess reserves. In reality, banks don't lend their excess reserves. Banks lend dollar for dollar an amount equal to their excess reserves.

Notice that the change in Bank B's legal reserves is equal to 20 percent of the change in its deposits. Therefore, its excess reserves are now zero. Hence, Bank B is said to be fully loaned up.

Stage 7 Bank C receives the $800 deposit that was lost by Bank B in Stage 6. Bank C thus gains (after the check clears) $800 in legal reserves. Assuming that Bank C had been fully loaned up, it then sets aside 20 percent of the deposit, or $160, as required reserves. Therefore, it has 80 percent, or $640, in excess reserves.

Bank C: Partial Balance Sheet
Stage 7: Bank C receives the $800 deposit lost by Bank B

Assets			Liabilities	
Legal reserves		+$800	Deposits	+$800
Required	+$160			
Excess	+ 640			
		+$800		+$800

Stage 8 Suppose that Bank C now grants a loan equal to the amount of its excess reserves. *Before* any checks are written, both its deposits and loans will have risen by $640.

Bank C: Partial Balance Sheet
Stage 8: After Bank C grants a loan for $640 but before checks are written against it

Assets		Liabilities	
Legal reserves	+$ 800	Deposits	+$1,440
Loans (claims)	+ 640		
	+$1,440		+$1,440

Stage 9 The borrower writes a check against the loan and deposits the check in Bank D. Deposits and legal reserves in Bank C go down by $640 (once the check clears). This leaves Bank C with the following net changes:

Bank C: Partial Balance Sheet
Stage 9: After a check for $640 is written against Bank C

Assets		Liabilities	
Legal reserves		Deposits	
(net change		(net change	
=+$800		=+$1,440	
−$640)	+$160	−$640)	+$800
Loans (claims)	+ 640		
	+$800		+$800

Because the increase in Bank C's legal reserves is equal to 20 percent of the total increase in its deposits, its excess reserves are zero. The bank is therefore fully loaned up.

Stage 10 and Beyond You can see by now that a logical expansionary process is taking place. It's sufficient, therefore, to illustrate briefly a few further steps in the sequence. Note the changes experienced by Banks D, E, and F on their partial balance sheets. As before, it's assumed that each bank is initially fully loaned up. (All data are rounded to the nearest dollar.)

Bank D: Partial Balance Sheet

Assets		Liabilities	
Legal reserves	+$128	Deposits	+$640
Loans (claims)	+ 512		
	+$640		+$640

Bank E: Partial Balance Sheet

Assets		Liabilities	
Legal reserves	+$102	Deposits	+$512
Loans (claims)	+ 410		
	+$512		+$512

Bank F: Partial Balance Sheet

Assets		Liabilities	
Legal reserves	+$ 82	Deposits	+$410
Loans (claims)	+ 328		
	+$410		+$410

And so on.

The deposit-creation process continues until all excess reserves in the system are "used up"—that is, until all legal reserves have become required reserves.

The process of deposit expansion is illustrated in Exhibit 2. As you can see, both the table and the graph depict the same ideas that were demonstrated above in terms of changes in banks' balance sheets.

The Deposit Multiplier

You may have noticed that the expansion in deposits by the banking system as a whole is influenced by the required-reserve ratio. The reciprocal of the required-reserve ratio—that is, the number 1 divided by the required-reserve ratio—gives what may be called the

EXHIBIT
2

Multiple Expansion of Checkable Deposits Through the Banking System

The table shows the cumulative expansion of checkable deposits in the banking system as a whole. An initial deposit of $1,000 and a required reserve of 20 percent are assumed. Data are rounded to the nearest dollar.

Note in column (2) that new deposits, which are banks' liabilities, are also equal to banks' new legal reserve assets. These increases are allocated partly to new required reserves in column (3) and partly to new excess reserves in column (4).

New excess reserves become new loans in the form of newly created money, which is deposited in banks. Thus, the total of $4,000 created in column (4) is the same as the new deposit expansion created in column (2). The deposit multiplier, therefore, based on the initial increase in excess reserves of $800, shown in column (4), is 5. This is because 5 × $800 = $4,000.

If all banks in the system are arranged in decreasing order of new deposits created, the multiple-expansion process illustrated in the table can be depicted clearly in the form of a bar graph.

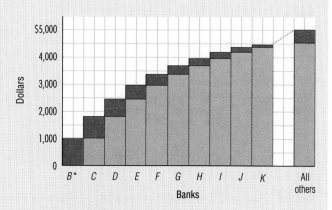

* This deposit came from Bank *A* in Stage 4.

The Increase in a Bank's Deposit Liabilities Equals the Increase in Its Legal Reserve Assets

(1) Banks	(2) New checkable deposits (= new legal reserves)	=	(3) New required reserves at 20%	+	(4) New excess reserves (= new loans) or newly created money	(5) Cumulative new deposits [from col. (2)]
B	$ 1,000 (initial*)		$ 200		$ 800	$1,000
C	800		160		640	1,800
D	640		128		512	2,440
E	512		102		410	2,952
F	410	new	82		328	3,362
G	328	deposit	66		262	3,690
H	262	expansion	52		210	3,952
I	210	= $4,000	42		168	4,162
J	168		34		134	4,330
K	134		27		107	4,464
All other banks	536		107		429	5,000
Totals	$ 5,000		$1,000		$4,000	

* This deposit came from Bank *A* in Stage 4.

"deposit multiplier." Thus, letting r represent the required-reserve ratio,

$$\text{Deposit multiplier} = \frac{1}{\textbf{required-reserve ratio}} = \frac{1}{r}$$

Hence, if you know the required-reserve ratio, you can determine the deposit multiplier. For instance, in our example, the required-reserve ratio was 20 percent, or ⅕. Therefore,

$$\text{Deposit multiplier} = \frac{1}{\frac{1}{5}} = 5$$

What does this mean? You'll recall that *the increase in a bank's deposit liabilities is also equal to the increase in its legal reserve assets.* Thus, in the table of Exhibit 2, the new deposits (and new legal reserves) in column (2) are allocated to two components. One is new required reserves in column (3). The other is new excess reserves in column (4). When the new excess reserves are lent, they become newly created money that ends up as new deposits in column (2). The table thus illustrates two fundamental ideas:

If the deposit multiplier is 5:

- An initial excess reserve of $800, shown in column (4), results in a total of newly created money for the banking system as a whole of 5 × $800 = $4,000.

- The newly created money is in the form of a *net gain* in checkable deposits.

These ideas can be expressed by a simple formula. Let D represent the change in checkable deposits for the banking system as a whole. Also, let E be the amount of initial excess reserves and r the required-reserve ratio. Then,

$$D = \text{deposit multiplier} \times E$$

That is,

$$D = \frac{1}{r} \times E$$

To illustrate, if r = 10 percent, or 1/10, the deposit multiplier is 10. Therefore, initial excess reserves E of $1,000 can result in a net increase in newly created money, in the form of checkable deposits, of as much as 10 × $1,000 = $10,000.

The following definition helps summarize the basic concept:

The *deposit multiplier* **is the reciprocal of the required-reserve ratio. Its value determines the maximum** *multiple* **by which the banking system's deposits can expand as a result of an initial amount of excess reserves.**

Conditions That Modify the Expansion of Deposits

In our discussion of the multiple expansion of bank deposits, we've made two assumptions:

1. Banks will make loans equal to the full amount of their excess reserves.

2. All newly created money will become checkable deposits.

In the real world, these assumptions usually don't hold precisely. Two major conditions affect the expansion of checkable deposits:

Leakage of Cash into Circulation It's unlikely that all newly created money will become checkable deposits. A business borrowing money from a bank may take part of it in cash. Or, someone who is paid a debt by check may "cash" some or all of it rather than deposit the entire amount. For these reasons, some money that would otherwise serve as excess reserves will leak out of the banking system. This leakage will leave less new reserves available for banks to lend.

Idle Excess Reserves Banks don't always make loans equal to the full amount of their excess reserves. They may sometimes maintain idle excess reserves because they are pessimistic about economic conditions and desire a "safety margin." Thus, if the reserve requirement were 20 percent, banks might at times choose to have available an average reserve of 25 percent. This, of course, would reduce the deposit-creating ability of the banking system from 5 : 1 to 4 : 1. It may also happen that businesses are not willing to borrow the banking system's entire excess reserves. That may be the case during a recession, for example, when business executives are gloomy about the future.

The Money Multiplier

Because the deposit-multiplier formula provides a rough approximation, we should use a more precise formula that expresses the money supply, $M1$, in relation to the **monetary base.** This is simply the sum of currency held by the public plus legal reserves. The monetary base may thus be thought of as "high-powered" money. It supports the money supply ($M1$) because our fractional-reserve banking system enables the system to *create* more money (through checkable deposits) than it holds in required reserves. Therefore, $M1$ is always some *multiple m* of the monetary base B:

$$M1 = mB$$

In this formula, *m* may be called the *money multiplier.* It has several important aspects:

The Money Multiplier *m* Can Be Derived from Regularly Published Data for *M*1 and *B* Thus, for example, if in a given year $M1$ is \$700 billion and B is \$300 billion, then $m = M1/B = \$700$ billion$/\$300$ billion $= 2.3$. Over the long run, the value of *m* has ranged between 2 and 3.

The Money Multiplier *m* for *M*2 Is Larger Than That for *M*1 This is because $M2$ includes $M1$ plus time deposits, overnight repurchase agreements, Eurodollar deposits, and money-market mutual-fund shares. Consequently, $M2$ is bound to be a larger multiple of the monetary base than $M1$ is. Over the long run, the $M2$ money multiplier has usually ranged between 9 and 11. This makes it about four times the size of the $M1$ money multiplier.

The Money Multiplier *m* Is Not a Constant but a Variable It is affected by the same conditions that modify the expansion of checkable deposits. However, it's important to note that these conditions affect B as well as *m*. That is:

> The conditions that influence the multiplier *m* also influence the monetary base B. This means that *m* and B are *not* independent of each other. Changes in one can cause changes in the other, and changes in either can affect $M1$ and $M2$.

Because of these and other determinants of *m*, *the money multiplier is not precisely predictable.* It's also influenced by various banking practices. These include:

1. The different percentages of reserves that the law requires banks to hold against checkable deposits

2. The ways in which banks manage their portfolios of income-earning securities

Despite the difficulties of predicting changes in $M1$ and $M2$ with the money multiplier, it's a tool that the Fed relies on heavily for regulating the flow of money and credit.

Managing a Bank's Portfolio

As a bank expands and contracts its deposits, its excess reserves change. In order to earn the largest possible profit on these changing volumes of reserves, the bank continually acquires and disposes of income-earning (or interest-earning) assets. These assets, which con-

sist of securities and loans, make up what is known as the bank's *portfolio*.

A bank's securities are primarily of two types:

- *Public-sector debt securities* issued by the U.S. Treasury, federal agencies (such as the Federal National Mortgage Association, among others), and municipal governments

- *Private-sector debt securities* including promissory notes, other short-term debt instruments, and corporate bonds

The manner in which banks as a whole manage their portfolios can have important impacts throughout the financial markets and on the borrowing and expenditure practices of households and businesses. Let's see why.

Objectives: Liquidity, Profitability, and Safety

Imagine that you're responsible for managing a bank's portfolio. Obviously, one of your major tasks is to acquire and dispose of earning assets. A problem you must continually face, therefore, is maintaining a proper balance among liquidity, profitability, and safety. Let's look at what these terms mean.

Liquidity

Liquidity may be defined as the ease with which an asset can be converted into cash quickly without loss of value in relation to its purchase price.

Liquidity is a matter of degree. Money (that is, cash) is an asset that is perfectly liquid because it always retains the same value in terms of itself. (You can always exchange a dollar for a dollar.) A government obligation that is near maturity is almost as liquid as money because it's highly marketable and its current price is relatively close to its redemption value. However, a building is normally a relatively illiquid asset. It cannot easily be sold, and it may yield a substantial loss when it is.*

Profitability

Earning profits is a second goal in portfolio management. Profits consist of two parts. One is the difference

---

Caution: Don't confuse liquidity with marketability. They're not the same. An asset may be marketable but not necessarily liquid. Your car is an example. You may be able to sell it quite easily, but you probably won't get back anywhere near what you paid for it. United States Treasury bonds are another example. They're extremely marketable but they aren't necessarily liquid—as explained in the next chapter. On the other hand, U.S. Treasury bills are both highly marketable and near-liquid.

between what you pay for an asset and what you realize when you redeem or sell it. The other is any returns you receive from the asset before you sell it.

In the case of government bonds, which are an important form of earning assets for banks, profit is expressed by a single percentage figure called *yield to maturity*. A bond's yield to maturity may be 10 percent, 15 percent, or some other amount—and it will fluctuate according to market conditions. Portfolio managers, therefore, are continually changing the compositions of their earning assets. They do this by selling bonds and other securities that have lower yields in order to purchase those that have higher yields.

Safety

Maintaining safety is a third goal in portfolio management. Safety refers to the probability that a borrower will fulfill the contractual terms of an investment. In the case of a bond, for example, the main contractual terms are that the interest and principal payments will be made when due. Safety is a matter of degree. The safest of all financial obligations are Treasury securities—bills, notes, and bonds. This is because they are backed by the good faith and taxing power of the federal government. Bonds issued by many municipal governments also rank very high on the safety scale.

Safety and liquidity don't always go together. Market prices of U.S. Treasury bonds, for example, may fluctuate substantially, thereby impairing their liquidity. But the safety of Treasury securities—that is, payment of interest and principal—is never in doubt.

The Conflict Between Liquidity and Profitability

The ideal bank portfolio is liquid, profitable, and safe. But it's impossible to maximize all three objectives at the same time.

A bank's most immediate obligation is to pay cash on demand. The moment it is unable to make payment on a check, the bank must close its doors. Holding a certain portion of its assets in the form of vault cash helps a bank meet its liquidity needs. But, because a bank's vault cash yields no return, there's a conflict between liquidity and profitability:

- Too large a proportion of a bank's assets in the form of cash provides greater liquidity but an undesirable and unnecessary loss of income. (Recall the concept of *opportunity cost*.)

- Too small a proportion of a bank's assets in cash permits higher income from investment in earning assets, but at the risk of illiquidity and failure.

A portfolio manager has to strike a compromise between these two extremes. Moreover, the compromise must be achieved with a relatively high degree of safety. This is because banks are subject to many legal and conventional constraints that limit the types of earning assets they may acquire.

The conflict between liquidity and profitability is illustrated in Exhibit 3. The axes of the graph represent the two extreme alternatives. Keeping all the bank's funds in cash is represented by the vertical distance $0M$. Investing all the bank's funds in earning assets is represented by the horizontal distance $0N$. Neither of these extreme alternatives is acceptable. The former would leave the bank in too liquid a position to earn income. The latter would leave the bank completely illiquid and unable to pay cash on demand.

EXHIBIT 3

Investment-Possibilities Line

Each point along the line MN denotes a different combination of cash and earning assets. Thus, point A denotes G dollars of cash and H dollars of earning assets. Point B denotes J dollars of cash and K dollars of earning assets. The portfolio manager of a bank seeks to maintain an optimum combination of cash and earning assets (or liquidity and profitability). However, this objective is subject to various legal constraints designed to assure a high degree of safety,

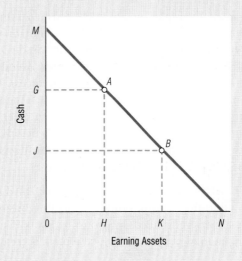

Suppose we now connect the two points *M* and *N*. The resulting line *MN* shows all the combinations of cash and earning assets in which it is possible to invest the bank's funds. Therefore, it may be called an "investment-possibilities line." There is some point along the line—some combination of cash and earning assets—that is the optimum for a particular bank at a particular time. The challenge faced by every bank's portfolio manager is to find that point. It will provide the bank with the highest possible level of earnings consistent with liquidity and safety.

Asset Management: Priorities for Allocating Bank Funds

Because of the conflict among liquidity, profitability, and safety, priorities for allocating a bank's funds must be established. That is, criteria are needed for deciding how banks are to utilize their limited funds. In practice, banks distinguish among four classes of uses:

Primary Reserves: Liquid Assets This category of assets has the highest priority because the bank must be able to pay cash to depositors on demand. Primary reserves consist of a bank's legal reserves (vault cash and deposits with the Fed) and the demand deposits it may have with other banks. In other words, a bank's primary reserves consist of *liquid assets*. They are instantly available to meet depositors' needs. However, they are "dead" assets because they yield no return to the bank.

Secondary Reserves: Near-Liquid Assets This category of assets, which has the second highest priority, provides "protective investment." It is made up of *near-liquid earning assets*. Examples include such short-term financial obligations as Treasury bills, investment-quality bonds that are approaching maturity, high-grade commercial paper (such as promissory notes issued by large corporations), and banker's acceptances. The main purpose of secondary reserves is to earn income while ensuring that the bank will be able to meet expected and more or less regular seasonal demands for liquidity. These demands typically occur during peak business periods such as Christmas and Easter.

Tertiary Reserves: Customer Loan Demands The third priority in allocating a bank's funds is meeting business and consumer credit needs by providing loans. This is the fundamental purpose for which a bank is created.

By fulfilling this objective, a bank enhances its profits because *interest rates on loans are usually higher than those on securities.* However, to the extent that desirable loans are not always available, this priority gives way to the following one.

Residual Reserves: Investments for Income The fourth priority concerns the remainder of a bank's funds after the three previous priorities have been satisfied. These residual funds are invested in long-term debt securities aimed at providing additional income. These investments, of course, are also subject to the constraints of safety. Therefore, they consist primarily of notes and bonds issued by the federal government, and of investment-grade debt securities issued by state governments, local governments, and corporations.

This order of priorities applies to all banks. However, the actual distribution of funds among the four categories differs somewhat for individual banks. In general, these differences reflect varying legal requirements, local business needs, and ways banks choose to balance the objectives of liquidity, profitability, and safety.

Conclusion: Types of Bank Investments

The types of securities in which banks can invest are regulated by law. Therefore, three types of debt securities are likely to be found in a typical bank's portfolio:

1. **U.S. Government Securities** These consist of *Treasury bills, Treasury notes,* and *Treasury bonds.* All are readily marketable if the bank should wish to sell them, and they differ from each other in their periods of maturity. Those approaching maturity thus contribute greatly to satisfying the *near-*liquidity requirements of banks.

2. **"Quasi-governmental" Securities** These consist of notes and bonds issued by various agencies of the federal government. As mentioned earlier, examples are the Federal Home Loan Bank and the Federal National Mortgage Association.

3. **Municipal and Corporate Debt Securities** Municipal securities are marketable bonds and notes issued by state and local governments. Called simply *municipals,* they provide holders with interest income that is exempt from all federal income taxes. Banks also purchase corporate debt securities consisting of bonds and

notes. While there is some default risk attached to municipal and corporate debt securities, banks limit the risk by purchasing only *investment grade* securities (as determined by bond rating companies). Such securities have a low default risk.

In general:

Banks manage their portfolios by buying and selling earning assets in order to enhance profits. These actions influence both legal reserves and currency in circulation. Therefore, they affect the components of the money-multiplier formula and hence the level of economic activity.

Bank Failures: When Fractional-Reserve Banking Goes Bad

The FDIC has helped prevent bank failures for most of its history. From 1940 to 1980, the FDIC closed an average of only 6 banks per year. However, in the 1980s the FDIC closed an average of over 100 banks per year. Exhibit 4 presents the trend in bank failures since 1934.

Banks were not the only financial institutions to suffer in the 1980s. By the following decade, over half of the nation's 3,000 S&Ls either had failed or had been operating for several years at a loss. Why?

Causes of Bank and S&L Failures

The bank and S&L failures of the 1980s cannot be attributed to a single cause. The troubles started in the 1970s when institutions making long-term, low-interest mortgage loans were suddenly faced with rising inflation and rising interest rates. To pay their depositors competitive interest rates, many institutions began operating at a loss.

These institutions suffered further from legislation in the early 1980s that deregulated the banking sector. This legislation removed interest-rate limitations, reduced regulatory oversight, and raised deposit insurance to $100,000. The increased insurance encouraged depositors to shop around for the best interest rate rather than the most reliable institution. Interest rates soared as financial institutions competed for depositors. To pay the higher rates, many institutions made high-risk loans in anticipation of correspondingly high yields.

Bank Failures in the United States, 1934–1990

Two periods during this century have seen a significant number of bank failures in the United States. Between 1930 and 1932, more than 9,000 banks failed. This exhibit shows bank failures only after the FDIC was created in 1933, which was after the worst problems had passed. The second period of numerous bank failures occurred in the 1980s, when more than 1,000 banks closed their doors.

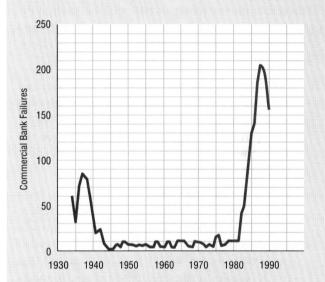

Source: Federal Deposit Insurance Corporation, *Annual Reports*.

Many of these loans were mortgages made to finance speculative purchases of commercial real estate. As a result, by the mid-1980s commercial real estate was overinvested. Office complexes and shopping centers stood empty, property values fell, and speculators went bankrupt and defaulted on their mortgage loans. Meantime, the banks that had made these risky loans were left with overpriced real estate, lost principal, and little interest income.

At the same time, the economy in general had begun to falter. For example, Texas, Oklahoma, and Kansas were hard hit by declines in energy and agriculture. Businesses in or affected by those industries defaulted on their bank loans. Workers who were laid off or forced to accept pay cuts reduced their deposits and either postponed applying for loans and mortgages or defaulted on the ones they already had.

White-collar crime dealt another blow to troubled S&Ls. With regulation either lax or absent, some bank officers made questionable or illegal loans to themselves, to relatives, to friends. Without regulatory scrutiny, these abuses often went undetected until a significant share of the bank's assets had been lost.

Consequences of Bank and S&L Failures

The cost to the taxpayers of covering the insured deposits of failed institutions has been estimated at hundreds of billions of dollars. What are the lasting effects of the "S&L mess"?

- **Few Deposits Were Lost** Although approximately 1,000 banks failed during the 1980s and early 1990s, thanks to FDIC insurance few deposits were lost. This is in sharp contrast to events of the 1930s, when some 9,000 banks failed and many depositors lost their life savings.

- **Asset Sales Depressed Prices** The Resolution Trust Corporation (RTC)—the agency established to address the problem of bank failures—began selling off much of the real estate held by the failed institutions in the late 1980s. Critics contend that the RTC sales further depressed property values that were already low because of poor economic conditions.

- **Bank Regulations Have Changed** Most states now allow banks to have statewide branches, and many states allow interstate branches.

- **Many Banks Merged** The new regulations contributed to a wave of bank mergers that has resulted in stronger institutions with more diversity in their loans and assets.

Origins: Portfolio Management

"Don't put all your eggs in one basket."

This familiar proverb has been passed down through the ages. But most of those who heard it never realized

Harry Markowitz
(1927–   )

that it has profound scientific implications. Three who did, and received lasting recognition for their efforts, are Harry Markowitz, James Tobin, and William Sharpe. Their work has been largely responsible for spurring the explosion of investment products and techniques that are part of today's complex and sophisticated financial markets.

Traditionally, financial investment focused on approaches to beating the stock market by picking undervalued securities. Thousands of books and articles written since the 1940s have offered ad hoc procedures and rules for doing this. The best known treatise was a comprehensive volume by Benjamin Graham and David Dodd entitled *Security Analysis*. This work became the bible of Wall Street—the heart of the nation's investment community, located in New York City. The book went through several editions and spawned other books which, for decades, served as standard texts in business-school courses on finance and investments.

Diversification Principle

Many people still follow the prescriptions offered in the conventional works. But most of the prescriptions, which are today regarded as folklore, have been swept away by modern portfolio theory. The theory was initially formulated in the early 1950s by Harry Markowitz, a mathematical statistician at Baruch Col-

James Tobin
(1918–   )

William Sharpe
(1934–   )

lege, the business school of the City University of New York. Markowitz used the theory to show how separate investments within a portfolio work together to produce desired returns.

Markowitz's approach was to set up a menu of risks and returns. Risk is defined as the variability of returns, and is measured by the standard deviation, a concept that every student learns in a first course in statistics. Using sophisticated mathematical methods, Markowitz showed how securities with higher risks yield higher returns, and securities with lower risks yield lower returns. By adding and subtracting individual securities from a portfolio, risk and return are affected. And, by diversifying securities within a portfolio, risks can be reduced substantially with little or no sacrifice of return. This finding may be called the *diversification principle.*

In practical terms, Markowitz's main conclusion is that the key to investing in securities successfully is to spread the risk—to avoid putting all your eggs in one basket. If you're going to invest in stocks, it's better to buy Coca-Cola and Ford, for example, rather than Coca-Cola and Pepsi Cola or Ford and General Motors. To many of today's investors, this insight seems obvious. But like many scientific discoveries, it flew in the face of conventional wisdom when Markowitz first demonstrated it. This is because the diversification principle was diametrically opposite to the standard investment practice of trying to pick individual stocks

that were believed to be undervalued and therefore destined to rise.

The thrust of Markowitz's contribution was the demonstration that failure to diversify is extremely risky. This conclusion helped spark the growth of mutual funds, which today are major participants in financial markets. For his role in changing the theory and practice of financial investing, Markowitz was awarded the Nobel Prize in 1990.

Drawing on some of Markowitz's pioneering ideas was James Tobin, an eminent economist at Yale University and adviser to President Kennedy during the early 1960s. Among Tobin's many contributions, his best-known work—and probably his most significant achievement—was his development of portfolio selection theory. The theory attempts to explain how people and institutions seek to obtain optimum combinations of risk, yield, and liquidity in their investment portfolios. In contrast to Markowitz, who is primarily a mathematician, Tobin provided highly original insights into the economic theory and implications of portfolio management. Despite the complex mathematics involved in Tobin's work, he summarizes his theory simply as "not putting all your eggs in one basket."

The Swedish Royal Academy of Science, however, hasn't allowed Tobin's modesty to obscure his accomplishments. In 1981, the Academy awarded Tobin the Nobel Prize for his extraordinary research leading to the advancement of economic science.

Capital Asset Pricing Model

It remained for yet another scholar to elaborate the concepts developed by Markowitz. That person was William Sharpe. In the early 1960s, fresh out of graduate school, he published an article whose ideas are known today by every college student in finance as the *capital asset pricing model*. The model seeks to determine how the prices of individual securities would reflect their risk in a "Markowitz world."

Sharpe's method was to develop a way of measuring the risk of a stock. The measure—known by the Greek letter *beta*—reflects the relationship between a stock's returns and the returns on stocks in the market as a whole. Based on historical data, a stock whose returns fluctuate about as much as the market as a whole gets a beta of 1. A stock with a beta of 2 is twice as volatile as the market, while a stock whose beta is less than 1 is more stable than the market. Sharpe's model shows that the higher the market risk, the higher the beta, and therefore the higher the return that can be expected over the long run.

Studies have found that betas for individual stocks are highly unstable over time. Therefore, there's no assurance that a stock's beta will be the same next year as it is this year. However, studies have also shown that the betas of well-diversified portfolios are quite stable over time. As a result, the concept of beta is now a standard tool used by many individual investors in stocks and by practically all managers of multi-million-dollar portfolios.

Sharpe's research findings have spawned thousands of studies and greatly influenced the evolution of global financial markets. The Swedish government awarded Sharpe the 1990 Nobel Prize in recognition of his accomplishments in the area of finance.

Implications for Investment Practices

Markowitz, Tobin, and Sharpe created a revolution in the study of financial economics that continues to this day. The insights they provided into the operation of financial markets have changed dramatically the way banks, insurance companies, pension funds, mutual funds, and other financial institutions manage their investment portfolios. Theories about diversification and its many implications are at the heart of today's investment management practices. The modern study of investment management is due in large part to the accomplishments of Markowitz, Tobin, and Sharpe.

Summary of Important Ideas

1. Commercial banking rests on the goldsmith's principle. This enables banks to maintain fractional reserves—rather than 100 percent reserves—against deposits, because not all customers will withdraw their funds at the same time. Banks can earn interest by making loans that equal the amount of their excess reserves.

2. A single bank in a banking system cannot lend an amount that exceeds its excess reserves. When a bank's excess reserves are zero, the bank is fully loaned up.

3. The banking system as a whole can expand deposits by a multiple of its excess reserves. This process is known as the principle of multiple expansion of bank deposits.

4. The amount by which the banking system as a whole can expand deposits depends on the required-reserve ratio and the initial amount of excess reserves. The required-reserve ratio determines the deposit multiplier. This number, when multiplied by initial excess reserves, reveals the maximum amount of expansion that can take place.

5. The deposit multiplier can be replaced by a broader measure—the money multiplier. This expresses the money supply ($M1$) as some multiple m of the monetary base B. Thus: $M1 = mB$. A similar concept exists for $M2$.

6. The objectives of banks' portfolios are liquidity, profitability, and safety. Banks seek an optimum combination of cash and earning assets consistent with a high level of safety. Hence, they are largely limited to three major classes of investments: U.S. government securities, federal agency securities, and investment grade municipal and corporate securities. The way in which banks manage their portfolios of these securities affects the money multiplier and, therefore, the level of economic activity.

7. The 1980s had an unusually high number of bank failures. Although these failures ended in relatively few lost deposits, they did lead to depressed property values, changes in banking regulations, and a wave of bank mergers.

8. Modern portfolio theory was developed by Harry Markowitz, James Tobin, and William Sharpe. This theory indicates how banks, businesses, and households can manage their asset portfolios to obtain optimum combinations of risk, income, and liquidity.

Terms and Concepts to Review

goldsmith's principle	*monetary base*
fractional-reserve banking system	*money multiplier*
	liquidity
assets	*yield to maturity*
liabilities	*primary reserves*
net worth	*secondary reserves*
balance sheet	*Treasury bills*
legal reserves	*Treasury notes*
required reserves	*Treasury bonds*
excess reserves	*municipals*
deposit multiplier	

Questions and Problems

1. What is meant by "fractional-reserve banking"? How did it come into existence? Is it relevant today?

2. An individual bank cannot lend more than the amount of its excess reserves. Let us see why by observing what would happen if it tried to do so.

Suppose that the reserve requirement is 20 percent, and Bank Z is holding:

Assets		Liabilities	
Vault cash	$ 50,000	Deposits	$200,000
Loans and other assets	160,000	Net worth	10,000
	$210,000		$210,000

a. How much are Bank Z's excess reserves?

b. The reserve requirement is assumed to be 20 percent, or one-fifth. Show the effect on Bank Z's balance sheet after it expands its loans in a 5 : 1 ratio. What is the percentage of reserves to deposits?

c. Suppose that borrowers write checks against their new deposits and the checks are deposited in other banks. Show the effect on Bank Z's balance sheet after all the checks are presented to it for payment.

What has happened to the bank's reserves against deposits?

d. What can Bank Z do to correct the situation? If it succeeds, how would its balance sheet look?

e. What do you conclude from this exercise?

3. Suppose you borrow $1,000 in currency from Midwest Bank and give the bank your promissory note in return.

a. Show the effects on the following balance sheets:

Your Balance Sheet

Change in Assets	Change in Liabilities and Net Worth

Midwest Bank's Balance Sheet

Change in Assets	Change in Liabilities and Net Worth

b. Complete Balance Sheet 2 below.

Balance Sheet 1—Midwest Bank
Before making $1,000 loan

Assets		Liabilities and Net Worth	
Cash	$ 3,000	Deposits	$20,000
Reserves	4,000	Other liabilities	25,000
Loans	15,000		
Other assets	50,000	Net worth	27,000
	$72,000		$72,000

Balance Sheet 2—Midwest Bank
After $1,000 in cash is withdrawn by borrower

Assets		Liabilities and Net Worth	
Cash	_____	Deposits	_____
Reserves	_____	Other liabilities	_____
Loans	_____		
Other assets	_____	Net worth	_____

c. How would Balance Sheet 2 be affected if you had written $1,000 in checks against your deposit instead of withdrawing the money in cash?

4. Some people argue that "loans create deposits," whereas others contend that "deposits permit loans." Which statement is correct? Which is likely to be defended by economists? By bankers? Explain.

5. Assume that the reserve requirement is 10 percent. There are no currency withdrawals. Bank *A*'s partial balance sheet is as follows:

Bank A

Assets		Liabilities	
Legal reserves	$ 16	Deposits	$100
Loans	84		
	$100		$100

a. How much can Bank *A* expand deposits? Explain.

b. If all other banks are loaned up, how much can Bank *B* lend? How much can Bank *C* lend? What is the maximum for the whole banking system? Explain.

6. What is the deposit multiplier when (a) required reserves are 1 percent; (b) required reserves are 10 percent; (c) required reserves are 100 percent?

7. For Bank *A,* legal reserves are $1,000, required reserves are $800, and deposits are $8,000. All other banks are loaned up. By how much can the banking system expand its deposits?

8. Will the *actual* amount of deposit expansion by the banking system equal the *predicted* amount? Explain.

9. Fill in the blanks and the gaps for the omitted banks in the following table. Assume a 15 percent reserve requirement against deposits. What basic principle does the table illustrate?

	Amount Added to Checking Accounts (= legal reserves)	Excess Reserves (= amount lent)	Required Reserves
Bank 1	—	$10,000	—
Bank 2	$10,000	8,500	$____
. . .	. . .	. . .	
Bank 11	2,315	1,968	347
. . .	. . .	. . .	. . .
. . .	. . .	. . .	. . .
. . .	. . .	. . .	. . .
. . .		. . .	. . .
Bank 20	537	457	80
All other banks	____	____	____
Total—all banks	$____	$____	$____

10. Why is the money-multiplier formula a better guide for judging deposit expansion than the deposit-multiplier formula?

11. According to modern portfolio theory, households and banks face similar choices in portfolio management. Discuss how you would manage your own portfolio of assets in order to balance the goals of liquidity, profitability, and safety. Do you think portfolio management used by banks also applies to households?

12. Portfolio Management by Linear Programming One of the most challenging tasks faced by banks is the management of their portfolios. These consist of cash and earning assets. The latter include various types of financial claims—such as government securities, debt instruments issued by businesses, and other obligations. Banks continually change the composition of their portfolios, striving to achieve the best balance among three conflicting objectives: liquidity, profitability, and safety.

The method that many banks use to attain an optimally balanced portfolio involves a scientific technique known as linear programming.

Investment-Possibilities Line Northfield Bank and Trust Company has $100 million to allocate between two classes of earning assets—loans and securities. This task is represented in Figure (a) by the line AB, which is called an "investment-possibilities line." Each point along this line denotes a different possible combination of loans and securities totaling $100 million.

For example, at point A, the bank allocates $100 million to securities and nothing to loans. At point B, the bank allocates $100 million to loans and nothing to securities. At any point between A and B, the bank allocates some money to loans and some money to securities, with the allocations to both totaling $100 million.

Of course, line AB represents the maximum attainable combinations of loans and securities totaling $100 million. If the bank decides to invest less than that amount, the combination chosen will be represented by a point to the left of, or "inside," line AB.

Security/Loan Line The bank is seeking the most profitable combination of loans and securities. At the same time, it doesn't want to risk investing too much in one of these alternatives relative to the other. From experience the bank has found that a minimum of $30 in negotiable securities for every $100 in loans, a ratio of 30 percent, provides a satisfactory balance. Therefore, line $0E$ represents what may be called a "security/loan line." Each point along this line denotes a different combination of loans and securities for which the volume of securities is always 30 percent of the volume of loans. For example, point H denotes $20 million in loans and $6 million in securities. Point E denotes $100 million in loans and $30 million in securities.

Minimum-Loan Line Although banks also earn income from other sources, lending is their most important

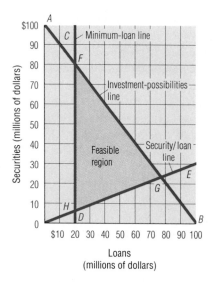

FIGURE (a) **Constraints and Feasibility** Three intersecting straight lines establish the constraints on the bank's portfolio. The problem is to select the most profitable combination of loans and securities. This combination is represented by a point somewhere in the feasible region.

activity. Every bank therefore seeks to accommodate its principal customers by fulfilling their requests for loans. Northfield Bank and Trust has estimated that its customers' aggregate demand for loans will total at least $20 million for the period under consideration. This is shown by line CD, which is called a "minimum-loan line." Note that this line is vertical, intersecting the horizontal axis of the chart at $20 million. This means that the bank's portfolio cannot contain less than that amount in loans, irrespective of the amount allocated to securities.

The Feasible Region The three lines just discussed represent constraints. That is, they impose limiting conditions on the bank's portfolio decisions. For example, the investment-possibilities line tells you that the size of the portfolio is limited to a maximum of $100 million. The security/loan line tells you that the amount allocated to securities must be at least 30 percent of the amount allocated to loans. And the minimum-loan line tells you that the amount allocated to loans must be at least $20 million.

The three constraint lines define the shaded area *FGH*. This area may be called the "feasible region" because it designates the field within which portfolio decisions can be made. Thus, any portfolio represented by a point outside the feasible region violates one or more of the constraints. Conversely, any portfolio represented by a point within the feasible region or on its boundaries satisfies all the constraints. Therefore, the bank's portfolio must consist of some combination of loans and securities that can be represented by a point within the feasible region.

Income Line To select the most profitable portfolio, the bank has to know the rate of return on loans and securities. These returns will vary. However, suppose that the bank is currently earning a 10 percent return on its loans and a 5 percent return on its securities. The level of income that can be earned from the portfolio will depend on the amounts allocated to loans and securities.

In Figure (b), each line, which is called an "income line," shows the amount of funds that must be allocated to loans and securities to earn a given income based on the known rates of return. At point *J*, for example, the bank allocates $20 million to securities. Assuming a 5 percent rate of return, this produces an income of $1 million. At point *K*, the bank allocates $10 million to loans. Assuming a 10 percent rate of return, this also yields an income of $1 million. If we connect the two points, we get the income line *JK*. Each point along line *JK* denotes a different allocation of funds to securities and to loans for which the combined income totals $1 million.

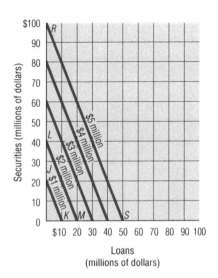

FIGURE (b) Income Lines Each downward-sloping income line shows the amount of funds that must be allocated to loans and securities to earn a given income. The lines are based on a 10 percent return on loans and a 5 percent return on securities.

Line *LM* is a $2 million income line, and line *RS* is a $5 million income line. As you can see, the bank's income increases as the income lines move outward from the origin of the graph.

The Optimum Portfolio We can now determine the bank's optimum portfolio by combining the ideas portrayed in Figures (a) and (b), as shown in Figure (c).

The bank's goal is to select an optimum portfolio—a combination of loans and securities that yields the highest income obtainable while meeting the identified constraints. There are two considerations: (1) The optimum portfolio will be represented by a point located somewhere within the feasible region. (2) The highest income obtainable will be represented by an income line that lies as far as possible to the right while still touching the feasible region.

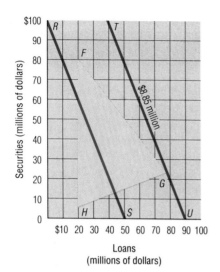

FIGURE (c) **The Optimum Portfolio** With the given constraints, the most profitable portfolio is determined by an income line *TU* that lies as far as possible to the right while still touching the feasible region. This occurs at point *G*. The optimum portfolio thus consists of $77 million in loans and $23 million in securities.

Notice that although the income line *RS* contains points that are in the feasible region, none of these points represents the most profitable portfolio.

The income line *TU*, however, just touches the feasible region at point *G*. Therefore, the most profitable portfolio is the one indicated by this point. It denotes a portfolio consisting of $77 million in loans and $23 million in securities.

What will be the bank's income from this portfolio? The bank earns 10 percent on loans and 5 percent on securities. Therefore, earnings will be $7.7 million on loans and $1.15 million on securities for a total of $8.85 million on the entire portfolio.

Conclusion: A Practical Tool Northfield Bank and Trust is one of many banks that utilize linear programming as a management tool. In practice, banks' assets are broken down into detailed categories and grouped in various ways to achieve a balance among three conflicting objectives: liquidity, profitability, and safety. Numerous constraints are then introduced that set limits on the ways in which the variables may be combined to attain the optimum result. With a computer, answers can be obtained to complex problems that would otherwise be impossible to solve.

Questions

1. Formulate a definition of linear programming. Can you suggest how a business firm might use linear programming to improve efficiency in production?

2. (a) What constraints face Northfield in its efforts to attain an optimum portfolio? (b) Would the portfolio be affected by a change in any of the constraints? Explain.

TAKE A STAND

Banks: Can They Be "Too Big to Fail"?

In the early 1980s, Continental Illinois was one of the largest banks in the United States. It was also in trouble. The high oil prices of the 1970s had led the bank to extend many loans to energy producers in the belief that such loans would be highly profitable. But in 1981, oil prices started to fall sharply, and Continental Illinois began to lose money on these loans. Most of the bank's deposits were not covered by the Federal Deposit Insurance Corporation (FDIC), which covers deposits only up to $100,000 per depositor per bank. Depositors, fearing that their funds were at risk, began a run on the bank.

Policymakers could have chosen not to intervene, in which case Continental Illinois would almost surely have collapsed. But the Federal Reserve and the FDIC feared that the failure of such a large bank could have severe repercussions for the entire banking system, so they put together a multibillion dollar bailout that protected the funds of all depositors. Continental Illinois, it seemed, was a bank that was too big to be permitted to fail.

Although the FDIC technically does not insure deposits above $100,000, the experience of Continental Illinois and other bailouts has led investors to believe that, in practice, all deposits at large banks are safe. There have, indeed, been further bailouts that have proved costly to the FDIC, which is now itself in financial trouble. Banking legislation passed by Congress in November 1991 apparently signals a retreat from the "too big to fail" doctrine, however. The legislation limits the ability of the FDIC to protect uninsured deposits after 1994. Yet the debate over the potential dangers of bank failures is still unresolved. *Are some banks so big that they should not be permitted to fail?*

No: Banks Are Just Like Any Other Business

It is certainly unfortunate for stockholders and holders of uninsured deposits if a bank fails, just as it is unfortunate for stockholders and creditors of a company if that company goes bankrupt. But failure as well as success is an integral part of

capitalism. Under capitalism, enterprises that can efficiently supply a good or a service that people want will be successful and rewarded with high profits. Conversely, businesses that are inefficient or fail to provide something that people want will be unable to compete in the marketplace. The market rewards skill and good management and penalizes ineptitude and bad management. Banks are just like any other business, and should be subject to the same discipline of the market.

If bank managers know that their institution will not be permitted to fail no matter how much it loses, then their incentive to do an effective and responsible job disappears. In particular,

they may not be properly concerned about the riskiness of their portfolio of assets, and may choose to invest in high-risk assets that promise the possibility of a high return. After all, they might reason, if these prove to be bad investments, the government will step in. Economists call this type of behavior a *moral hazard*.

The policy of protecting large banks is also inherently unfair because it discriminates against small banks. How can small banks compete on equal terms with large banks that can earn high returns on high-risk loans but never suffer failure if the loans go bad? Finally, the FDIC does provide protection of up to $100,000 to each depositor, so the decision to permit a bank failure does not mean that poor individuals are going to lose their life savings.

Yes: Banks Are Different

Banks are not just like any other business. Banks and other financial institutions play a special role in our economy. They are the link between savers and investors, taking deposits from those who wish to save and extending loans to those who wish to invest. The smooth functioning of financial markets is essential to the overall health of the economy. Many economists believe that major banking failures during the 1930s contributed to the length and severity of the Great Depression.

The simple fact of its size means if a large bank is permitted to fail, many savers and borrowers are affected. But the biggest fear of policymakers is that the collapse of a large bank may reverberate throughout the entire financial system. If one large bank fails, then savers and investors may begin to have doubts about the stability of other banks. Bank runs may be contagious. If depositors see that one bank is having difficulty meeting its obligations, they may withdraw their funds from other banks, and thereby put those banks at risk.

No one knows for sure what the consequences of the collapse of a large bank would actually be. But the worst-case scenario is that the failure of one bank could precipitate a crisis in the entire financial system, with catastrophic consequences for the economy as a whole. Policymakers cannot afford to take this chance.

The Question: Are Some Banks Too Big to Fail?

▪ Some believe that banks should be treated no differently from any other business. Banks that make bad investments should be permitted to fail, with the FDIC providing protection to small depositors.

▪ Others argue that banks should be treated differently because of the special role of financial institutions in our economy. A modern economy can function successfully only if it has a healthy financial sector. The failure of a large bank could create a crisis in the entire financial system with serious repercussions for the entire economy.

Where Do You Stand?

1. In the early 1980s, the federal government also bailed out the financially ailing Chrysler Corporation. Why might some companies be too big to fail?

2. Suppose depositors at a failing bank start a run on that bank. Do the repercussions for the economy depend in part on what those depositors do with their funds? Discuss.

3. Can you imagine a modern economy without banks? How might it differ from the U.S. economy?

4. Are some banks too big to be permitted to fail? Justify your stand.

Source: George G. Kaufman, "Are Some Banks Too Large to Fail? Myth and Reality," *Contemporary Policy Issues*, Vol. 8, Number 4, pp. 1–14, October 1990.

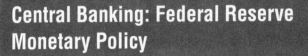

Chapter 11

Central Banking: Federal Reserve Monetary Policy

Major Controls

Minor Controls

How Monetary Policy Affects Interest Rates and
 Business Investment

Evaluating Monetary Policy

Learning Guide

Watch for answers to these important questions

What is the meaning of monetary policy? What institution is responsible for conducting monetary policy?

How does the Federal Reserve influence economic activity? What tools are available to the Fed for controlling the money supply?

Which monetary policies are likely to result in higher, and which in lower, interest rates? How do changes in interest rates affect business investment?

How does monetary policy affect interest rates and business investment?

How does monetary policy affect exchange rates and net exports?

What are the advantages and limitations of monetary policy?

FED EASES, BOND PRICES SOAR

DISCOUNT RATE INCREASED BY FED

FED TO SELL U.S. SECURITIES

Newspapers often contain headlines like these. They reflect the two roles of the *Federal Reserve System*.

First, it is a "banker's bank." It performs for depository institutions some of the same services that these institutions perform for the public.

Second, the Fed is the nation's monetary authority. In this role, it exercises an important influence on economic and monetary policy.

We have already learned about the Fed's banking role. In this chapter we will look at the Fed's part in making and implementing monetary decisions.

Essentially, the Fed has six instruments or tools of monetary policy that can be used to modify or in some cases reverse the direction of the economy. They are:

1. Reserve ratios

2. The discount rate

3. Open-market operations

4. Foreign exchange market intervention

5. Margin regulations

6. Moral suasion

The first three instruments are extremely important controls because they affect the nation's money growth rate and the overall availability of credit. They can therefore be classified as "major controls."

246

The fourth instrument seeks to influence the flow of international financial payments into or out of the country. The fifth is specifically for regulating the purchase of stocks on the nation's securities exchanges. The sixth is a psychological technique that relies on personal communication and public opinion. These three instruments of monetary policy can be classified as "minor controls."

Now let's see what is meant by monetary policy.

Monetary policy is the deliberate exercise of the monetary authority's (the Fed's) power to induce expansions or contractions in the money supply. The principal purposes of monetary policy are to achieve price stability, to help dampen the swings of business cycles, and to help bring the nation's output and employment to desired levels.

We have learned that the economy is self-correcting. This means that it *eventually* adjusts automatically to its full- or natural-employment level. Why, then, does the Fed engage in monetary policy? The answer, as you might guess, is to hasten the economy's adjustment to full employment and/or to maintain full employment and stable prices. The extent to which the Fed does or does not succeed in attaining these goals is a subject of continual debate.

It helps to begin with an understanding of the overall asset-and-liability structure of the institutions we will be discussing. Exhibit 1 therefore provides a self-explanatory consolidated balance sheet for the nation's twelve Federal Reserve Banks. One of the chief concerns of this chapter is to show the way in which Federal Reserve monetary policy affects certain items on the balance sheet.

Major Controls

Recall that the three primary controls for influencing the level of economic activity available to the Federal Reserve are (1) changes in bank reserve ratios, (2) changes in the discount rate, and (3) open-market operations. Let's see how each helps to shape the nation's monetary policy.

Changing Reserve Ratios

You already know that banks must maintain required reserves equal to a minimum percentage of their deposit liabilities. Why? As you will see momentarily, it is primarily to provide the Fed with one of its mechanisms for controlling the money supply.

EXHIBIT
1

Consolidated Balance Sheet of Twelve Federal Reserve Banks

December 31, 1991 (in billions)

(1) ASSETS

(2) Loans	$ 2.2
Money on loan to depository institutions.	
(3) U.S. government securities	281.8
Includes Treasury bills, Treasury notes, and Treasury bonds.	
(4) Other securities	4.6
Includes bankers' acceptances and debt instruments issued by federal agencies.	
(5) Total loans and securities:	
(2) + (3) + (4)	**288.6**
(6) Other assets	64.5
Includes cash items in process of collection, the value of bank premises, and other items.	
(7) Total assets: (5) + (6)	**$ 353.1**

(8) LIABILITIES AND NET WORTH

(9) Federal Reserve notes	$ 287.9
Paper money issued by the Federal Reserve System and used by the public.	
(10) Depository institutions' reserves	29.4
That part of legal reserves that depository institutions maintain with their Federal Reserve Banks.	
(11) Other liabilities	30.5
Deposits held by the U.S. Treasury, foreign central banks, and other claims.	
(12) Total liabilities: (9) + (10) + (11)	**347.8**
(13) Net worth	**5.3**
The ownership interest of the member banks because they are the stockholders of the Federal Reserve Banks.	
(14) Total liabilities and net worth:	**$ 353.1**
(12) + (13)	

Source: Board of Governors of the Federal Reserve System.

Banks' required reserves may be held in the form of vault cash or as deposits with the local Federal Reserve Bank. The actual percentage requirements are graduated according to the size of banks' deposits. For the banking system as a whole, the average reserve requirement is approximately 10 percent of checkable deposits.

The following partial balance sheets show the effects of different reserve-ratio requirements. (All data are in billions of dollars.) If the average required-reserve ratio for all banks were 15 percent, $15 billion of reserves would be needed to support $100 billion of deposits:

All Banks: Partial Balance Sheet

Assets		Liabilities	
Required reserves	$15	Deposits	$100
Excess reserves	0		
Legal reserves	$15		

But if the average required-reserve ratio for all banks were reduced to 10 percent, required reserves would decline from $15 billion to $10 billion. This would make $5 billion of excess reserves available for lending.

All Banks: Partial Balance Sheet

Assets		Liabilities	
Required reserves	$10	Deposits	$100
Excess reserves	5		
Legal reserves	$15		

As you already know, excess reserves can support a *multiple expansion* of deposits for the banking system as a whole.

The process can also be reversed, however. For example, suppose there were an increase in the average required-reserve ratio. If banks were fully loaned up before the increase and had no excess reserves, they might have to sell some of their earning assets to raise the necessary funds to cover their reserve deficiency. This would cause a *multiple contraction* of deposits for the banking system as a whole.

Thus, changes in the required-reserve ratio can affect the economy as a whole in the following ways:

A *decrease* in the required-reserve ratio tends to be expansionary because it permits banks to lend more money and thereby enlarge the money supply. An *increase* is contractionary because it requires banks to reduce the money supply if their excess reserves are insufficient to support the higher reserve requirement, which is usually the case. The Federal Reserve System can thus affect the supply of money and the availability of bank credit. It can do this through its control over reserve ratios and, therefore, over the volume of bank reserves.

A diagram depicting the economic effects of the Federal Reserve's influence on banks' reserves is presented in Exhibit 2.

The ability to alter the required-reserve ratio is the Federal Reserve System's most powerful monetary tool. But it is a fairly blunt tool and is employed infrequently. Other instruments of control, as will be seen shortly, can be applied with greater flexibility and more refinement.

Changing the Discount Rate

Federal Reserve Banks can lend money at interest to depository institutions just as these depository institutions can lend money at interest to the public. Thus, it may be said that the Federal Reserve Banks are credit wholesalers, whereas depository institutions are credit retailers. (Keep in mind that depository institutions and banks are essentially the same, for our purposes.)

No Federal Reserve policy tool is as well-known or as poorly understood as the **discount rate.** In reality, it's simply the interest rate depository institutions are charged for their loans from the Reserve Banks. It is called a "discount rate" for historical reasons. The interest on the loans used to be deducted—or discounted—from the loan when it was made, rather than added on when the loan was repaid. But this practice hasn't existed for decades.

Today when a bank borrows, it gives its own secured promissory note to the Federal Reserve Bank. The Reserve Bank then increases the borrowing bank's reserves by the appropriate amount. Why would a bank want to borrow from the Fed? Usually, the bank wants to replenish its reserves, which may have been "used up" as the bank granted loans and purchased investments.

The Federal Reserve's lending policy at the "dis-

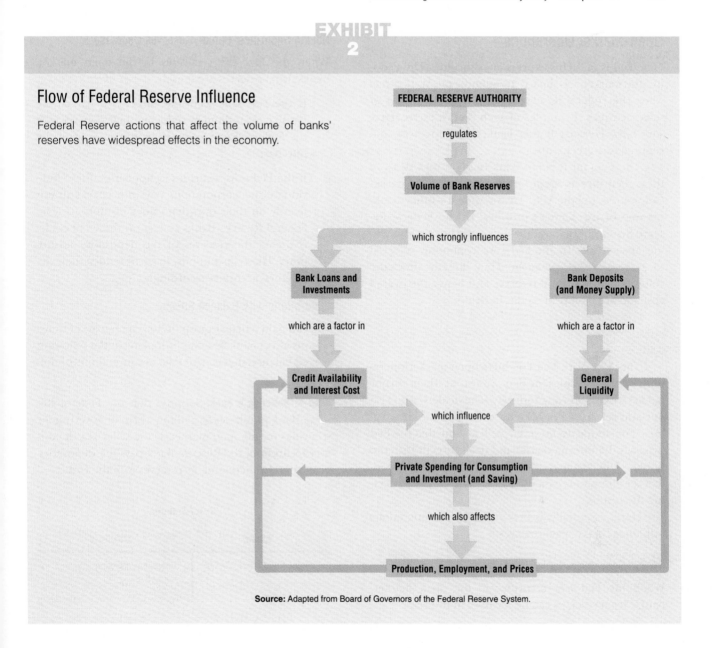

EXHIBIT 2

Flow of Federal Reserve Influence

Federal Reserve actions that affect the volume of banks' reserves have widespread effects in the economy.

FEDERAL RESERVE AUTHORITY

regulates

Volume of Bank Reserves

which strongly influences

Bank Loans and Investments

Bank Deposits (and Money Supply)

which are a factor in

which are a factor in

Credit Availability and Interest Cost

General Liquidity

which influence

Private Spending for Consumption and Investment (and Saving)

which also affects

Production, Employment, and Prices

Source: Adapted from Board of Governors of the Federal Reserve System.

count window" (an expression commonly used in banking circles) can have significant influences. It can affect not only banks' reserves but also credit conditions in the economy as a whole.

The direct effect of changes in the discount rate is to raise or lower the price of admission to the discount window. An increase in the discount rate makes it more expensive for banks to borrow; a reduction has the opposite effect. Indirectly, increases in the discount rate are usually associated with a rise in market interest rates and a general tightening of credit. De-

creases in the discount rate tend to be associated with a reduction in market interest rates and an overall easing of credit.

The discount rate was the preeminent tool of monetary policy in the early years of the Federal Reserve System. This has long since ceased to be the case. The major reason is that banks have alternative ways of replenishing their reserves. For example, a bank may sell earning assets such as securities or notes, or borrow from other sources (including other banks), rather than seek loans from the Federal Reserve.

Open-Market Operations

"The Fed is in." This expression, short for "The Fed is in the market," is heard frequently on Wall Street when the Federal Reserve Bank of New York buys or sells securities. Examples of such securities are Treasury bills, Treasury bonds, banker's acceptances, and repurchase agreements.

The Federal Reserve Bank of New York deals in these securities as agent for the Federal Open Market Committee, for the U.S. Treasury, or for other banks (as one of the services provided by the Federal Reserve System). Such transactions—the buying and selling of securities by the Fed—are commonly referred to as **open-market operations**. They directly affect the volume of banks' legal reserves and hence the overall cost and availability of credit. In fact:

Open-market operations are the Fed's most important monetary tool for achieving economic stabilization.

The New York Fed conducts open-market operations with securities dealers (most of them major banks) located in New York City. The dealers, who also buy and sell to the public, are thus *financial intermediaries*. For simplicity, however, we'll assume that the Fed bypasses the intermediaries and deals directly with the public. This assumption makes the process of open-market operations easier to understand without affecting the results.

Here, essentially, is how open-market operations influence banks' legal reserves:

Buying Securities: Banks' Reserves Increase

When the Fed *buys* securities in the open market, banks' legal reserves can be *increased* in two ways:

- If the Fed buys securities directly from banks, it pays for them by increasing the banks' reserves with the Federal Reserve Banks by the amount of the purchase.

- If the Fed buys securities from nonbanks, such as individuals or corporations, it pays for them with checks drawn on itself. The recipients of the checks then deposit them in their own banks, which, in turn, send the checks to the Federal Reserve Banks for collection. The Reserve Banks honor the checks by increasing the reserves of the banks.

Selling Securities: Banks' Reserves Decrease

When the Fed *sells* securities in the open market, banks' legal reserves are thereby *decreased:*

- If the Fed sells securities directly to banks, the banks pay for them by reducing their reserves with the Federal Reserve Banks by the amount of the purchase.

- If the Fed sells securities to nonbanks, these individuals and corporations pay with checks drawn mainly on their own depository institutions. The Federal Reserve Banks collect on these checks by reducing the reserves of the depository institutions. These institutions, in turn, reduce their depositors' accounts accordingly.

Illustrations with Balance Sheets

You can gain a firmer grasp of how open-market transactions affect bank reserves by looking at the following partial balance sheets. (All data are in millions of dollars.)

Case 1: Seller Is a Bank Suppose that the Federal Reserve Bank purchases $1 million worth of government securities in the open market. If the seller is a depository institution, the Reserve Bank pays the depository institution by increasing its reserves with the Fed.

Reserve Bank

Assets		Liabilities	
Government securities	+ $1	Depository institution reserves	+ $1

Depository Institution (Bank)

Assets		Liabilities
Government securities	− $1	
Reserves with Federal Reserve Bank	+ $1	

Case 2: Seller Is a Nonbank If the seller is a nonbank, such as an individual or corporation, the check received in payment from the Federal Reserve Bank will most likely be deposited at the seller's depository in-

stitution. That bank, in turn, sends the check to the Reserve Bank for credit to its reserve account:

Reserve Bank

Assets	Liabilities
Government securities + $1	Depository institution reserves + $1

Depository Institution (Bank)

Assets	Liabilities
Reserves with Federal Reserve Bank + $1	Deposit + $1

Note that the effect on the depository institution's reserves is the same in Case 1 and in Case 2. That is:

When the Fed purchases securities in the open market, the legal reserves of the depository institution are *increased* **by the value of the securities.**

Case 3: Buyer Is a Bank The effects are opposite when the Federal Reserve Bank sells $1 million of government securities in the open market. If the buyer is a depository institution, it acquires $1 million in government securities and loses $1 million of reserves:

Reserve Bank

Assets	Liabilities
Government securities – $1	Depository institution reserves – $1

Depository Institution (Bank)

Assets	Liabilities
Government Securities + $1 Reserves with Federal Reserve Bank – $1	

Case 4: Buyer Is a Nonbank If the buyer of the securities is a nonbank, the Federal Reserve Bank receives payment with a check drawn on the buyer's depository institution. When the check clears, the depository institution's reserves at the Reserve Bank and the buyer's

deposit at the depository institution are both reduced by the value of the check.

Reserve Bank

Assets	Liabilities
Government securities – $1	Depository institution reserves – $1

Depository Institution (Bank)

Assets	Liabilities
Reserves with Federal Reserve Bank – $1	Deposits – $1

Note that the ultimate effect is the same in Cases 3 and 4. Thus:

When the Fed *sells* **securities in the open market, the legal reserves of the bank are** *reduced* **by the value of the securities.**

Although these open-market operations have been illustrated for only one depository institution, the same ideas apply to all such institutions, that is, to *all banks* within the banking system. The overall economic effects of such transactions can therefore be summarized:

Open-market purchases of government securities are expansionary. They increase bank reserves and therefore permit a multiple growth of deposits. Conversely, open-market sales of government securities are contractionary. They reduce bank reserves and force a multiple decline of deposits.

Policy Effects: Aggregate Demand and Aggregate Supply

The effects of open-market operations can be analyzed in terms of the familiar aggregate demand/aggregate supply model. This is done in Exhibit 3. Notice that, as always, real output is measured on the horizontal axis and the average price level is measured on the vertical axis. The aggregate demand and aggregate supply curves are *AD* and *AS,* respectively. They determine the corresponding price level *P* and output quantity *Q.*

Now let's see what happens when the Fed decides to pursue either expansionary or contractionary open-market operations.

EXHIBIT
3

Expansionary and Contractionary Open-Market Operations

The *AD* and *AS* curves determine the full-employment output level at *Q* and the corresponding price level at *P*.

Suppose the economy is in a recession, with output at *Q'* and the price level at *P'*. The Fed tries to bring the economy to the full- or natural-employment level by *buying* securities in the open market. This expansionary monetary policy increases banks' reserves and the public's liquidity. The aggregate demand curve thus shifts to the right from *AD'* to *AD*. Consequently, output increases from *Q'* to *Q*, and the average price level rises from *P'* to *P*.

Conversely, if the economy is at an overfull employment and production level such as *Q''*, the Fed will *sell* securities in the open market. This contractionary policy shifts the aggregate demand curve to the left from *AD''* to *AD*. As a result, output decreases from *Q''* to *Q*, and the average price level declines from *P''* to *P*.

Note that this analysis assumes no changes in aggregate supply.

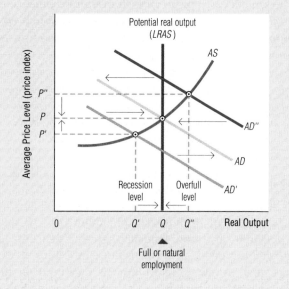

Expansionary Policy Suppose the economy is at a recession level of production such as *Q'*. The Fed may try to increase output and employment by *buying* securities in the open market. This adds to banks' reserves. If lending increases, putting more money in the hands of the public, the aggregate demand curve shifts to the right from *AD'* toward *AD*. Output and employment thus move to their full- or natural-employment level. Simultaneously, the average price level rises from *P'* toward *P*.

Contractionary Policy Now suppose the economy is at an overfull employment and production level such as *Q''*. The Fed may decide to *sell* securities in the open market to dampen economic activity. Banks' reserves and the public's liquidity are thereby reduced. This shifts the aggregate demand curve to the left from *AD''* toward *AD*. At the full- or natural-employment level, output has declined from *Q''* toward *Q*, and the average price level has declined from *P''* toward *P*.

In reality, the Fed doesn't have the ability to make precise enough adjustments in the money supply to "fine-tune" the economy. Consequently, when it pursues activist monetary policies, evidence shows that the Fed often overshoots or undershoots its targets—sometimes by a wide margin. This can result in either too much or too little liquidity in the economy, causing undesirable fluctuations in production, employment, and prices.

Because of the Fed's inability to adjust the money supply precisely, the ways in which the Fed conducts its policies is a frequent subject of debate.

Minor Controls

In addition to its major instruments or tools, the Federal Reserve has some relatively minor ones it can use to influence economic activity. The more important of these minor controls are foreign exchange market intervention, margin regulations, and moral suasion.

Foreign Exchange Market Intervention

The Federal Reserve holds inventories of U.S. dollars and other major currencies. The same is true of the other leading central banks—those of Britain, Canada, France, Germany, Italy, and Japan. Because widely fluctuating foreign-exchange rates can cause global economic instability, the central banks try to reduce excessive swings in the prices of their currencies. The banks do this by buying or selling their own currencies against others.

For example, suppose the price of the U.S. dollar in terms of other major currencies is rising on the world market. The Fed may sell dollars for those currencies in an effort to drive down the price of the dollar. The lower price of the dollar has two effects:

1. American goods become less expensive for foreigners to buy, causing U.S. exports to increase.

2. Foreign goods become more expensive for Americans to buy, causing U.S. imports to decrease.

Because exports increase and imports decrease, net exports (= exports – imports) rise. This can have an expansionary effect on the economy.

The opposite results occur if the Fed decides to buy U.S. dollars in order to reverse a decline in their price on the world market. The Fed pays for the dollars with British pounds, German marks, Japanese yen, or other major currencies. A higher price of dollars makes American goods more expensive for foreigners to buy. This causes U.S. exports to decrease. A higher price of dollars also makes foreign goods less expensive for Americans to buy. This causes U.S. imports to increase. The decrease in exports and increase in imports cause net exports to decline. This can have a contractionary effect on the economy.

The Fed can participate continuously in the foreign exchange market if it wishes to influence net exports. However, it seldom does so. Instead:

The Fed intervenes intermittently in the foreign exchange market and usually coordinates intervention with the other leading central banks. Intervention is not normally undertaken to influence net exports. A major purpose of intervention is to help reduce wide fluctuations in exchange rates in order to encourage fairly stable levels of international trade and investment.

Margin Regulations

The Federal Reserve Board is empowered to set the so-called *margin requirement.* This is the percentage down payment that must be made when someone borrows from a brokerage firm to finance purchases of stock. This power was granted by Congress during the early 1930s. In that era, it was widely believed that the excessive use of credit during the 1920s to purchase stocks was a major cause of the great stock market crash of 1929.

Of course, the higher the margin requirement, the larger the proportion of stock purchases that must be paid for in cash. Therefore:

An increase in margin requirements discourages stock market speculation with borrowed funds. Conversely, a decrease in margin requirements may encourage purchases of stocks.

The margin requirement is altered infrequently because it is not as important as it once was. Indeed, the Fed has urged Congress to end its role in setting margin rules. Nevertheless, the margin requirement remains a device for dampening or stimulating activity in the stock market. This, in turn, can affect the ability of firms to sell stocks in order to finance new investment.

Moral Suasion

Of course, by using written and oral appeals, the Federal Reserve's Board of Governors can always exert pressure on bankers to expand or restrict credit. This process, called *moral suasion,* does not compel compliance, and hence is believed to be the least effective means of control available to the Fed. Nevertheless, it has been successful on some occasions. During recessions, it has sometimes stimulated the expansion of credit by encouraging banks to lend more. During times of inflation, it has sometimes discouraged lending and restricted the expansion of credit. In a more general sense, the Federal Reserve exercises moral suasion every day when it deals with individual member banks on matters of ordinary loan policy.

Summarizing:

To be effective, all the major and minor monetary controls must be coordinated by the Federal Reserve. Its goal is to promote economic growth and stability through management of the money supply.

How Monetary Policy Affects Interest Rates and Business Investment

The tools of monetary policy are exceedingly important. Through the proper use of its monetary controls, the Fed can strongly influence the nation's level of economic activity.

Two of the Fed's tools—the discount rate and open-market operations—are especially significant because they are actively used and are closely connected with interest rates. Before we examine this connection, we need to understand the relationship between the prices of bonds and their yields.

Bond Prices and Bond Yields

Bonds are a type of debt instrument—a financial claim that pays interest to its owner. If you buy a bond, the annual percentage rate of return on the instrument is the **yield.** Exhibit 4 shows the relationship between the market price and yield of a $100 bond. In Figure (a), the bond matures in one year and has a nominal interest rate of 10 percent. This means that the bond pays its holder an interest of $10 yearly. Thus, if you could buy the bond for around $99, you would receive $100 upon maturity plus $10 in interest. The chart shows that this is an *effective* yield of about 11 percent. But if you could buy the bond today at a market price of $101, you would still get only $100 back at maturity

EXHIBIT
4

Bond Prices and Bond Yields Vary Inversely

A bond pays its owner a fixed amount of dollars annually. Therefore, the lower the price at which you can buy the bond, the higher the percentage return—or yield—you'll receive, and vice versa.

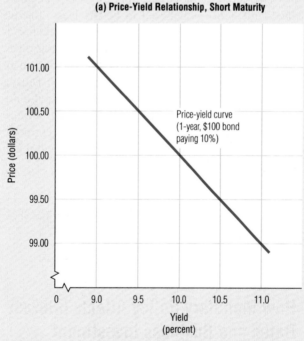

(a) Price-Yield Relationship, Short Maturity

Price-yield curve
(1-year, $100 bond
paying 10%)

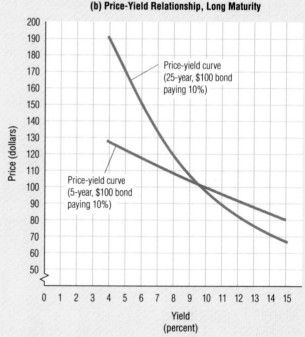

(b) Price-Yield Relationship, Long Maturity

Price-yield curve
(25-year, $100 bond
paying 10%)

Price-yield curve
(5-year, $100 bond
paying 10%)

FIGURE (a) The graph shows the price-yield relationship for a 1-year, $100 bond paying 10 percent (that is, $10 annually) to its owner. If you can buy the bond for $99, the yield to you at maturity will be approximately 11 percent. At a price of $101, the yield at maturity will be approximately 9 percent. The price-yield curve appears to be a straight line because the bond has a relatively short maturity.

FIGURE (b) As the number of years to maturity increases, the price-yield relationship becomes more noticeably curved. This chart shows how the price-yield curve looks if the bond in Figure (a) matures in 5 years or in 25 years.

(thereby losing $1 from your purchase price) plus $10 in interest. This is an *effective* yield of about 9 percent.

In Figure (a), the price-yield relationship appears to be a straight line. This is because the bond has a relatively short maturity of 1 year. As the term to maturity gets longer, the price-yield relationship becomes more noticeably curved. Figure (b), for example, shows the price-yield curves for the bond if it matures in 5 years or in 25 years.

The curves in both diagrams illustrate the same principle:

The price of a bond varies inversely with its yield. **This is because the annual interest payments received on a bond are a fixed amount. Therefore, the higher the market price of a bond, the lower its yield, and vice versa. This principle applies to all debt instruments, not just to bonds.**

Open-Market Operations and Interest Rates

You've already seen how open-market operations affect the money supply. We now need to establish more clearly just how open-market operations affect yields, and therefore interest rates, on debt instruments.*

Suppose the Fed seeks to change the money supply. It does this by buying or selling debt instruments such as Treasury bills and Treasury bonds. All debt instruments compete with one another for investors' dollars. As a result, yields on existing debt instruments and interest rates on newly issued debt instruments move up and down together. Therefore, just as bond prices and bond yields vary inversely, so too do bond prices and interest rates vary inversely.

When the Fed buys securities, such as Treasury bonds, it injects new reserves into the banking system. Because the Fed is such a huge participant in the market, its actions can influence the prices, and therefore the yields, of debt instruments. This in turn affects interest rates in the market. By buying bonds the Fed can shift the demand curve for bonds to the right. The increase in demand drives up the price of bonds. The higher price of bonds implies lower bond yields, and hence lower interest rates in the market. This is illustrated in Figure (a) of Exhibit 5.

---

*Recall that a debt instrument is also a credit instrument. It's a liability of the party that issues it and an asset of the party that owns it. Although the two concepts have the same meaning, the term "debt instrument" is supplanting the term "credit instrument" (which used to be widely employed) as the preferred expression.

EXHIBIT 5

Open-Market Operations and Bond Prices

The demand for and supply of bonds determines their market price. Because yields are reflected by interest rates, a higher price results in lower yields and interest rates; a lower price has the opposite effect.

FIGURE (a) If the Fed buys bonds in the open market, it shifts the total demand for them to the right from *D* to *D'*. The increase in demand drives bond prices up from *P* to *P'*. This causes yields and interest rates (not shown on the graph) to decline.

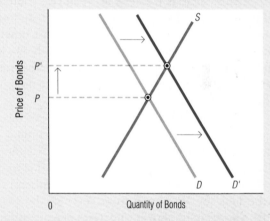

(a) The Fed Buys Bonds: Increase in Demand

FIGURE (b) If the Fed sells bonds in the open market, it shifts the total supply of them to the right from *S* to *S'*. The increase in supply pushes bond prices down from *P* to *P'*. This causes yields and interest rates (not shown on the graph) to rise.

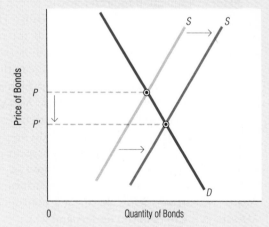

(b) The Fed Sells Bonds: Increase in Supply

Alternatively, if the Fed sells Treasury bonds it drains reserves from the banking system. By selling bonds, the Fed can shift the supply curve of bonds to the right. The price of bonds will fall, causing their yields, and therefore interest rates in the market, to go up. This is shown in Figure (b) of Exhibit 5.

When the Fed buys Treasury bonds, their prices are driven up. This forces market interest rates down. When the Fed sells Treasury bonds, their prices are pushed down. This forces market interest rates up.

Interest Rates and Investment

Changes in interest rates on Treasury securities affect interest rates on other short- and long-term financial instruments, such as banker's acceptances, commercial paper, negotiable certificates of deposit, and corporate bonds. The reason is that the debt instruments traded in the financial markets compete with one another for investors' dollars. Therefore, interest rates on financial instruments tend more or less to move up and down together.

Changes in interest rates, in turn, affect investment spending. Recall from the study of national income accounting that the Department of Commerce calls investment spending *gross private domestic investment* (GPDI). Annual figures are shown in column (2) of the table on the inside front cover of the book. GPDI consists of two broad categories of expenditure: (1) spending on new capital goods—plant, equipment, and increases in inventory; and (2) spending on residential construction.

Spending on New Capital Goods Firms typically turn to the financial markets to acquire the funds they need for investment. If interest rates decline, it becomes cheaper for businesses to borrow. This tends to encourage more investment. If interest rates rise, businesses find it more costly to borrow, so investment is discouraged. Does this mean that, if a firm has its own retained earnings (which are a source of new investment) to invest, management doesn't have to be concerned about the cost of borrowing? Or, to put it differently, do interest rates in the financial markets affect management's decision to buy new capital goods as opposed to buying income-earning securities instead? The answer is yes. Recall the concept of *opportunity cost* to help you understand why.

Spending on Residential Construction Nearly all housing is purchased through mortgage loans. Because mortgages, like bonds, are long-term debt instruments, their interest rates tend to follow interest rates on bonds. In general, lower interest rates on home mortgages tend to encourage housing purchases, while higher interest rates tend to discourage them.

There is thus an *inverse* relationship between total investment spending and the interest rate. This is illustrated in Exhibit 6. The downward-sloping demand curve for investment, D_I, shows the total amount of investment that will be undertaken at various interest rates, all other things remaining the same. What are these "all other" things? With respect to business investment, which is by far the largest component of total investment, four major conditions are assumed constant when the D_I curve is drawn:

EXHIBIT 6

The Business Sector's Demand Curve for Investment (hypothetical data)

The interest rate is the cost of funds. Other things remaining the same, investment expenditures will be greater at a lower interest rate than at a higher one. Therefore, the business sector's demand curve for investment, D_I, is downward sloping.

In this example, investment expenditures will be $300 billion at an interest rate of 20 percent and $900 billion at an interest rate of 5 percent.

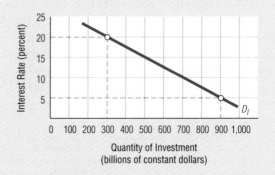

Profit Expectations If business executives are optimistic about economic conditions, they will tend to increase investment spending in anticipation of greater profits. This will shift the investment demand curve to the right. If executives are pessimistic, they will decrease investment spending, thereby shifting the curve to the left. Expectations, of course, are psychological and subjective. In order to judge them, government and private sources conduct frequent surveys of executives to determine how much they intend to spend on capital goods.

Changes in Technology The development of new and more efficient methods of production often requires the construction of new plants and the installation of new equipment. This increases the demand for investment, causing the demand curve to shift to the right.

Costs of New Capital Goods Changes in the prices that businesses must pay for new plant and equipment affect their decisions to buy those goods. A decrease in the price of new capital goods shifts the demand curve for investment to the right; an increase in price shifts the curve to the left.

Corporate Income Tax Rates Business decisions to invest in new capital goods are based on expected profits *after* taxes. Because a reduction in corporate income tax rates makes firms more profitable, it is likely to shift the demand curve for investment to the right. On the other hand, a rise in corporate tax rates reduces profitability and, therefore, is likely to shift the curve to the left.

The relationship between the interest rate and business-sector investment spending is *inverse*. A decline in the interest rate increases the amount of investment spending, while a rise in the interest rate decreases the amount of investment spending. Changes in demand for investment—that is, shifts of the investment demand curve—are caused by changes in such factors as profit expectations, technology, costs of new capital goods, and corporate income tax rates.

International Effects of Monetary Policy

Investment by the domestic business sector is not the only expenditure affected by changes in the interest rate. Because ours is an open economy, changes in the interest rate also influence net exports.

The reason is easy to see. If interest rates in the United States rise, foreign investors will want to purchase more interest-earning debt securities, such as bonds. To do so, the investors must first buy U.S. dollars. The resulting increase in the demand for dollars causes their price to rise in the foreign exchange market.

The opposite occurs if interest rates in the U.S. fall. Foreign investors will be inclined to reduce their investment in American interest-earning assets. The resulting decrease in the demand for dollars causes their price to fall in the foreign exchange market.

The level of our nation's interest rates thus affects foreign investment as well as the exchange rate. Changes in the exchange rate, in turn, influence the country's imports and exports. The reason was explained earlier in the chapter. Recall that an increase in the world price of the dollar causes U.S. exports to decline and U.S. imports to rise. Therefore, the difference between them, net exports, falls. A decrease in the world price of the dollar has the opposite effect. The volume of U.S. exports increases and the volume of U.S. imports decreases. Therefore, net exports rise.

Changes in the Fed's monetary policy can thus have international consequences. The easiest way to understand the consequences is to view them as a chain of events. Exhibit 7 diagrams the chain of events caused by a contractionary policy:

The international effects of a contractionary monetary policy by the Fed can be thought of as passing through five stages: (1) Interest rates increase. This causes (2) foreign investment in the U.S. to increase, which in turn (3) raises the world price of U.S. dollars. As a result, (4) U.S. exports decrease, U.S. imports increase, and (5) net exports decline.

The international effects of an expansionary monetary policy are the opposite of these. Can you explain them without referring to the diagram?

Monetary policies of other major countries can have similar international consequences. Because of this, representatives of the seven largest industrial nations—Britain, Canada, France, Germany, Italy, Japan, and the United States—meet regularly. Their organization, called the Group of Seven (or G-7), seeks to coordinate monetary policies in efforts to minimize disruptions in international economic relations.

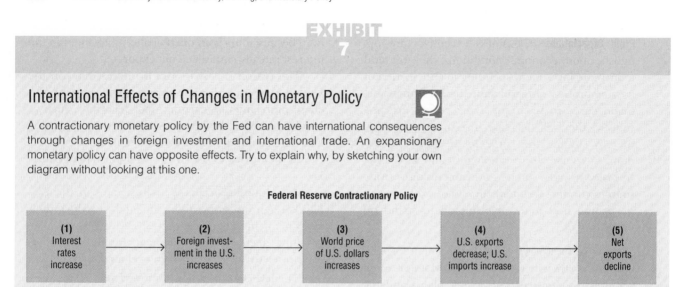

EXHIBIT
7

International Effects of Changes in Monetary Policy

A contractionary monetary policy by the Fed can have international consequences through changes in foreign investment and international trade. An expansionary monetary policy can have opposite effects. Try to explain why, by sketching your own diagram without looking at this one.

Federal Reserve Contractionary Policy

| (1) Interest rates increase | → | (2) Foreign invest-ment in the U.S. increases | → | (3) World price of U.S. dollars increases | → | (4) U.S. exports decrease; U.S. imports increase | → | (5) Net exports decline |

Evaluating Monetary Policy

How effective is monetary policy in influencing economic activity? More specifically, how well do the three major tools of monetary policy—changes in reserve requirements, changes in the discount rate, and open-market operations—work in achieving their objectives? As with many other policy areas in economics, this is a subject of continuing debate. However, most analysts agree that monetary policy has several limitations.

Reserve Requirements

The ability to change reserve requirements is the Fed's most powerful means of controlling the money supply. However, the Fed rarely uses this method—for two major reasons. One of these is that changing reserve requirements has unpredictable effects on the economy's supply of money. The other is that it causes bank liquidity problems. Let's see why.

Unpredictable Effects

Altering reserve requirements is a blunt tool of monetary control. This is because small changes in the reserve ratio can produce considerably larger changes in the money supply than might be desirable. You can best understand the reason by thinking in terms of the money-multiplier formula. As you learned in the previous chapter, our nation's depository institutions con-stitute what is called a *fractional reserve banking system.* Therefore, M1 is always some multiple *m* of the monetary base *B*. Thus:

$$M1 = mB$$

where M1 is currency plus checkable deposits, *m* is the money multiplier, and *B* is the monetary base consisting of currency held by the public plus legal reserves. (A similar formula with a different-sized multiplier exists for M2.)

As you also learned in the previous chapter, *m is not precisely predictable, though historically it has averaged between 2 and 3.* (The multiplier for M2 has averaged between 9 and 11.) Therefore, with today's checkable deposits amounting to hundreds of billions of dollars, even a one-percentage-point increase in the required-reserve ratio will produce a decrease in excess reserves of several billion dollars. This in turn will cause a multiple contraction of deposits and, hence, an even larger, unpredictable decline in the money supply.

The reverse, of course, is also true. A one-percentage-point decrease in required reserves is likely to generate a multiple expansion of deposits and therefore a relatively large and unpredictable increase in the money supply. Thus:

Altering reserve requirements is not a means of "fine-tuning" the money supply (nor is any other monetary control available to the Fed). The Fed can never be sure that a given change in reserve requirements will result in the "right" quantity of money for the economy.

Bank Liquidity Problems

A second reason the Fed rarely alters reserve requirements is that such actions may adversely affect the ways banks manage their liquidity. At any given time, there are usually many banks that are either in, or close to, "equilibrium." That is, they are fully loaned up and invested and so hold little or no excess reserves. For these banks an increase in reserve requirements creates liquidity problems. The banks must then seek ways to restore their equilibrium positions. They often do this by entering the financial markets to acquire the funds they need. They thus engage in asset or in liability management.

Banks engage in **asset management** when they sell some of their income-earning securities, such as Treasury bills, Treasury bonds, and municipal bonds. If the prices of these instruments thereby decline, interest rates rise. (Remember that the prices of debt instruments and interest rates are inversely related.)

Banks engage in **liability management** when they borrow. They may borrow from the Fed, from the public (by selling debt instruments such as repurchase agreements, banker's acceptances, and negotiable CDs), and from other banks. The increase in demand for funds that results from this increase in borrowing may also exert upward pressure on interest rates.

If conducted on a large enough scale, asset and/or liability management can thus have an impact on interest rates. This consideration is always of concern to the Fed.

The Fed can exercise monetary control by changing reserve requirements. However, such changes can create uncertainty by causing unpredictable fluctuations in the economy's supply of money and in banks' liquidity. Because these are conditions that the Fed tries to avoid, reserve requirements are rarely changed.

Discount Rate

When depository institutions are in need of funds, they may try to attain liquidity by borrowing at their Federal Reserve Bank's "discount window." As you've already learned, the interest rate that borrowing institutions pay for these loans is called the *discount rate*. But the Fed usually tries to employ the discount rate as a tool of monetary policy. The Fed doesn't see itself primarily as a convenient source of short-term loans for borrowers. Therefore, the Fed regards borrowing at the discount window to be a privilege, not a right.

One of the important aspects of discount-rate policy is its effects on household and business spending. Changes in the discount rate are always reported in the news media. Because the announced changes are sometimes perceived as signals that the Fed is altering its policies, these changes have been known to trigger responses by the public. For example:

- An announced decrease in the discount rate can be interpreted by the public to mean that the Fed is trying to stimulate the economy. This may encourage business activity because the public *expects* economic expansion to occur and therefore increases its consumption and investment spending.

- An increase in the discount rate can be interpreted in the opposite way. The Fed is presumed to be trying to dampen the economy. The public *expects* economic contraction to occur and therefore curbs its spending.

These types of public responses to reported changes in the discount rate illustrate what is known as the **announcement effect.** In reality, however, the announcement may sometimes be a "false signal." This is because changes in the discount rate are not always undertaken by the Fed in the pursuit of monetary policy. From time to time the discount rate is adjusted simply to bring it into line with short-term interest rates in the financial markets. When this happens, the announcement can cause confusion and instability.

Open-Market Operations

Of the various monetary policy tools available to the Fed, open-market operations are by far the most used. When it buys securities in the open market, the Fed adds to banks' legal reserves and thereby enlarges the monetary base. Depending on the size of the money multipliers, M1 and M2 expand by their respective multiples of the increase in the base. Conversely, when the Fed sells securities, it reduces the monetary base and causes multiple contractions of M1 and M2.

The credit instruments bought and sold by the Fed consist primarily of Treasury securities—especially Treasury bills. Treasury notes and Treasury bonds are also used extensively. In addition, the Fed deals to a significant but less important extent in several other types of instruments. They include banker's acceptances, repurchase agreements, and federal agency obligations (such as those issued by the Federal National Mortgage Association, the Government National Mortgage Asociation, and the Federal Home Loan Bank). All of these instruments are highly marketable, as evidenced by the fact that their prices and yields are quoted daily in major financial newspapers.

The main advantage of open-market operations is *flexibility.* **The Fed can vary its purchases and sales of securities quickly and smoothly to attain a desired volume of legal reserves or size of monetary base. Because of this, the Fed relies much more heavily on open-market operations than on its other monetary-policy tools.**

Limitations of Monetary Policy

Monetary policy also has some limitations. Most of them arise out of specific situations and circumstances.

Incomplete Countercyclical Effectiveness

Monetary policy is a *countercyclical* weapon. It's used in order to reduce the peaks and troughs of business fluctuations. Unfortunately, it may have limited results.

For example, during an inflation, the Federal Reserve can use its instruments of control to choke off borrowing and to establish an effective tight-money (high-interest-rate) policy. But during a recession, the reverse is not necessarily true. An easy-money (low-interest-rate) policy can't ensure that businesspeople will want to borrow. If they regard the economic outlook as poor, their increases in loans and spending won't be as large as needed to attain high employment. Further, during such periods banks may become more conservative in their lending policies.

Thus, monetary policy is more effective and more predictable as an anti-inflation instrument than as an antirecession instrument.

Can't Correct Cost-Push Inflation

There have been periods when inflation has resulted from upward pressure on wages or other costs. This pressure has typically arisen from the monopolistic power that some large unions, oil-producing countries, or other important suppliers of resources have at times been able to exert in the market. Monetary policy can do little to correct such situations. At most, contractionary actions taken by the Fed may help dampen a cost-push inflation, but they aren't likely to eliminate it. Further, the Fed often hesitates to step too hard on the monetary brakes in such circumstances for fear of pushing the economy into a recessionary inflation. This condition—a combination of stagnation and inflation—is often called "stagflation."

May Be Offset by Changes in the Velocity of Money

An activist monetary policy, as you've seen, requires that the Federal Reserve authorities follow one of two approaches:

- Decrease the money supply, or more precisely the money growth rate, to curb inflationary pressures.

- Increase the money supply, or money growth rate, to stimulate economic activity.

Unfortunately, the effectiveness of these actions may sometimes be at least partially offset by opposite changes in the *velocity*, or *turnover rate, of money.* This is simply the average number of times per year that a dollar is spent.

The velocity of money is affected by the public's expectations of, or confidence in, the future course of the economy. In periods of high employment, when people are optimistic, they tend to spend more freely. Hence, velocity may increase at a time when the Fed is trying to contract the money growth rate. In recessionary periods, when people are pessimistic, they tend to curb their spending. Hence, velocity may decrease at a time when the Fed is trying to expand the money growth rate.

Significant changes in the velocity of money can exert a substantial effect on the price level. How? By causing aggregate demand, and therefore prices, to rise when velocity increases and to decline when velocity decreases. As a result:

Changes in velocity may offset, to some extent, expansionary or contractionary monetary policies. This impairs the Fed's efforts to achieve its objectives.

Limited Fed Control over Lending

It's difficult for the Federal Reserve authorities to exercise as much control over the total volume of lending as it would like. There are two reasons:

1. **Nonbank Financial Intermediaries** Nonbank lenders, such as insurance companies and finance companies, exercise an important influence in the financial markets. They hold large amounts of funds, which they're continually trying to "put to work" by investing them or lending them to the public.

Is the Fed Too Independent? A Recurring Question

If asked to name Washington's most powerful agency, most people would probably say the FBI or the CIA. In reality, the Federal Reserve Board has more influence.

The Fed's actions directly affect such things as the interest rate charged on a bank loan, the ability of a potential home buyer to obtain a mortgage, and many other conditions affecting people's lives. Because the Fed is so powerful and its influence is so extensive, critics keep asking whether it's too powerful and too independent. Indeed, the question has been raised, and in several instances seriously debated, by economists, legislators, and Federal Reserve officials in almost every presidential administration since Harry S Truman's (1945–1952).

The power and independence of the Fed is resented by many political leaders. Some of them contend that the term of office of Reserve Board officials should be changed to coincide with the President's. Each President could then choose a Board whose policies would be consistent with the Administration's goals.

The accompanying chart shows a relationship between central-bank independence and the rate of inflation. The chart indicates that inflation rates tend to be lower in those countries that have the most independent central banks. Can you suggest why?

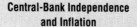

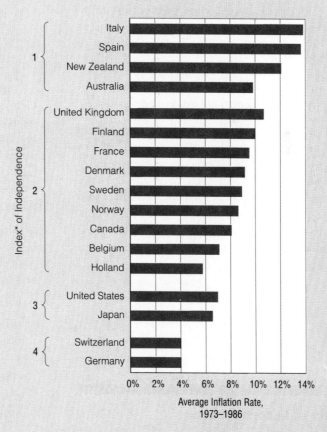

Central-Bank Independence and Inflation

Index* of Independence

Average Inflation Rate, 1973–1986

* 1 is least independent central bank, 4 is most independent.

Source: *The Economist*, February 2, 1991, p. 77.

2.　**Money-Market Securities** Substantial holdings of money-market instruments are in the hands of banks and business corporations. These organizations can sell the securities as needed to obtain additional cash.

Because lending by nonbank financial intermediaries and the sale of money-market securities are largely outside the Fed's control, the liquidity they provide can offset the Fed's restrictive monetary policies.

Forecasting and Timing Difficulties

Assuming the Fed takes an active role in managing the money growth rate, at what stages in the business cycle should specific expansionary or contractionary monetary policies be instituted? This question concerns economic forecasting and the proper timing of interventions. Unfortunately, the Fed is unable to do either with sufficient accuracy. As a result, many experts believe that the Fed's monetary policies have often been either overly expansionary or overly contractionary and have therefore caused even greater instability. This has led to frequent criticisms of the Fed and to proposed solutions ranging from its nationalization to its elimination.

Conclusion: Continuing Importance

Through monetary policy, the Federal Reserve System seeks to provide the economy with the "right" rate of money growth—enough to encourage high employment, steady prices, and rising real GDP. These are the basic economic goals of efficiency, stability, and growth. (Equity, the fourth economic goal, isn't significantly affected by monetary policy.) The Fed finds it difficult to attain these goals because of the limitations of monetary policy. Nevertheless:

Monetary policy is a fundamental tool used for achieving macroeconomic objectives. Despite the shortcomings of monetary policy, it plays a key role in the economy.

Summary of Important Ideas

1. The chief responsibility of the central banking system is to regulate the supply of money and credit so as to promote economic stability and growth. The ways in which this responsibility is fulfilled determine our monetary policy.

2. The major instruments or tools of monetary policy available to the Federal Reserve System are changes in reserve requirements, changes in the discount rate, and open-market operations. The minor ones are foreign exchange market intervention, margin regulations, and moral suasion.

3. Monetary policy has important effects on interest rates and business investment. Through open-market operations and the discount rate, the Fed affects the prices of debt instruments. These prices, in turn, affect interest rates. Changes in interest rates, in turn, influence business investment decisions.

4. The effects of monetary policy are reinforced through net exports. Expansionary monetary policy, by lowering the interest rate, decreases the foreign exchange rate and increases net exports. Contractionary monetary policy has the opposite effect. The Fed also occasionally undertakes direct intervention to influence the foreign exchange rate. The increasing importance of foreign trade means that the Federal Reserve System needs to consider the monetary policies of other countries.

5. Changes in reserve requirements can have unpredictable effects on the money supply and can create bank liquidity problems. Changes in the discount rate may have limited effects because banks can acquire funds in ways other than borrowing from the Fed. As a result, open-market operations, although they also have some limitations, are the chief tool of monetary policy used by the Reserve authorities.

6. Monetary policy has advantages and limitations as a method of economic stabilization. Its chief advantage is flexibility. Its main limitations are these:

a. It is an incomplete countercyclical weapon.

b. It is relatively weak in combating cost-push inflation.

c. It may be offset by changes in the velocity (rate of turnover) of money.

d. It has limited control over nonbank lending and credit operations.

e. It suffers somewhat from forecasting and timing difficulties.

Despite these shortcomings, monetary policy will continue to play an integral role in the economy.

Terms and Concepts to Review

monetary policy

discount rate

open-market operations

margin requirement

moral suasion

yield

fractional-reserve banking
     system

asset management

liability management

announcement effect

Questions and Problems

1. How do changes in reserve requirements, the discount rate, and margin requirements affect economic activity? Explain.

2. How do open-market operations work? When do they tend to be expansionary? Contractionary?

3. Suppose that the reserve-ratio requirement is 15 percent. If the Federal Reserve Bank purchases $1 million of government securities in the open market, a bank increases both its legal reserves and deposits by that amount. (Do you remember why?) Construct a "cumulative expansion" bar graph similar to the one in this chapter. The graph should show the initial net new deposit and the *potential* cumulative expansion of bank deposits that may take place at each "round" of deposit creation. (*Suggestion*: You may find it helpful to construct a table showing the multiple expansion of bank deposits. The table can then be used to sketch the graph.)

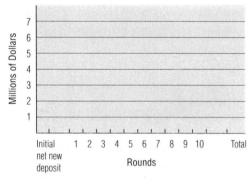

4. Suppose that the Federal Reserve issues more paper currency than people want. (a) What will happen to bank reserves? (b) What can the Reserve authorities do to offset the consequences?

5. Using two long "T-accounts" arranged side by side as shown, depict the positive (+) or negative (−) changes represented by each of the following transac-

tions. To help you identify transactions, label each one with its corresponding letter (a, b, c, etc.).

Federal Reserve Banks		Depository Institutions (Banks)	
Assets	**Liabilities**	**Assets**	**Liabilities**

a. The Federal Reserve buys $100 of government securities from a dealer and pays the dealer with a check drawn on itself, which the dealer deposits in the bank.

b. The bank sends the $100 check to the Federal Reserve, which credits the bank's reserve deposit.

c. The Fed buys $100 of government securities from a bank and pays with a check on itself.

d. The bank sends the $100 check to the Federal Reserve for credit to its account.

e. The Federal Reserve lends $100 to a bank.

f. A depositor writes a check for $100 against a deposit and cashes it at her bank.

g. A depositor adds $100 in currency to a deposit.

h. The Treasury sells $100 of securities to the non-banking public and deposits the checks it receives in its accounts at various banks. (*Note*: To facilitate tax collections and revenue disbursements, the Treasury maintains a checking account in almost every bank in the country.)

i. The Treasury transfers $100 of deposits from depository institutions (banks) in which it holds accounts to Federal Reserve Banks.

j. The Treasury pays $100 for services by writing a check against its deposit at the Federal Reserve. (*Note*: To facilitate the disbursement of government funds, the Treasury maintains a checking account at each of the Federal Reserve Banks.)

k. The party to whom the check was paid deposits it. The bank sends the $100 check to the Federal Reserve for collection.

6. Suppose that, in country *A*, half of gross domestic product is due to international trade. In country *B*, the proportion is only 10 percent. Which country is better able to control its economy through monetary policy? Explain.

7. Sometimes, Washington urges other nations to lower their interest rates through expansionary monetary policy. Why would the U.S. government do this?

Chapter 12

Monetary Theory: Relationships Among Money, Interest Rates, and Prices

The Money Supply Affects Output and Prices
Determination of the Interest Rate
The Propositions of Monetarism
The Monetarist View of Monetary Policy
Origins: How Monetarism Evolved

Learning Guide

Watch for answers to these important questions

What relationship exists between the money supply and the price level? How is this relationship expressed? What theory exists to explain it?

How are interest rates determined? What relationship exists between interest rates and prices?

What ideas underlie the concept of monetarism? What role does monetarism play in today's macroeconomic thinking?

What were the contributions of Irving Fisher and Milton Friedman to monetary policy?

Money is a matter of functioning four,
A medium, a measure, a standard, a store

You first encountered this rhyme when you began the study of money several chapters ago. The rhyme describes the various functions that money fulfills in every society. Recall that the four functions of money are:

1. *A medium of exchange*—money is used as a means of payment for things.

2. *A measure of value*—money is used to express the prices of things.

3. *A standard of deferred payments*—money is borrowed or loaned, and is repaid in the future with interest.

4. *A store of value*—money is saved so that it can be spent in the future.

Some of the ramifications of these functions of money were pointed out in previous chapters. More will be explained in this chapter and in some subsequent chapters. However, from now on we will focus our attention on the third and fourth functions. They involve complex relationships among such variables as the quantity of money in circulation, interest rates, and the potential purchasing power of money—that is, the rate of inflation. As a result, they give rise to issues and problems that affect all of us in our daily lives.

The Money Supply Affects Output and Prices

There is a direct relationship between the money supply and the level of economic activity. The relationship is such that changes in the former can produce similar changes in the latter. In this chapter we'll examine the reasons for this relationship.

You've already learned how the Federal Reserve, through its discretionary actions, can influence the money supply and thereby the level of economic activity. For example, to encourage economic expansion, the Fed can increase the supply of money by engaging in open-market purchases of government securities. To initiate economic contraction, the Fed can decrease the supply of money by undertaking open-market sales of government securities. (You'll recall that the Fed can also vary reserve requirements and the discount rate to help achieve its goals. However, it relies most heavily on open-market operations.)

Changes in the money supply may lead not only to changes in output but also to changes in the price level. This cause-and-effect relationship between changes in the money supply and changes in the price level was fundamental to the thinking of classical economists of the nineteenth and early twentieth centuries. But the relationship was not stated with precision until the early 1900s. At that time, a distinguished American economist at Yale University, Irving Fisher (1867–1947), expressed the link between money and prices by means of an equation. The modernized version of that equation is called the "equation of exchange." It is also sometimes called the "Fisher equation."

Equation of Exchange

You may not be able to determine how fast individual dollars are spent. However, you can measure the average speed of money movements in the economy as a whole by using a simple formula.

Let V stand for the *income velocity of money*. This is the average number of times per year each dollar is spent on purchasing the economy's annual output of final goods and services—its GDP. Further, let M denote the nation's money supply. This is the amount of money in the hands of the public. The income velocity of money can then be expressed as

$$V = \frac{GDP}{M}$$

For example, suppose that in a certain year the GDP was $800 billion and the money supply was $200 billion. Then V = $800/$200 = 4 per year for that year. In other words, each dollar must have been used an average of four times to purchase the economy's GDP.

The M in the equation can, of course, be "transposed" to the left side. The equation then becomes

$$MV = GDP$$

As you'll recall, gross domestic income (GDI) is equal to GDP. Therefore, MV is also equal to GDI.

Now suppose that we refine the equation by expressing GDP in terms of its component prices and quantities. Let P stand for the average price of final goods and services produced during the year, and let Q stand for the physical quantity of those goods and services. The *value* of final output is then price times quantity. That is, GDP = $P \times Q$. For example, GDP = the average price of apples times the number of apples, plus the average price of haircuts times the number of haircuts, plus . . . and so on for all final goods and services produced. The equation can therefore be written

$$MV = PQ$$

This is known as the *equation of exchange*. As mentioned above, it's a modernized version of the equation that Fisher formulated in the early 1900s. Fisher developed the equation about 30 years before the concepts of aggregate income and aggregate output were introduced into economics.

To see how the equation of exchange works, imagine a highly simplified case in which the students in your class constitute an economy whose total supply of money, M, is $80. Further, assume that the class produces a quantity of output, Q, equal to 60 units of a good and that the average price, P, of this output is $4 per unit. Since $MV = PQ$, we can solve for V in terms of P, Q, and M:

$$V = \frac{PQ}{M} = \frac{(\$4)(60)}{\$80} = 3$$

Thus, each dollar is spent an average of three times per year to purchase the class's output.

The equation of exchange is actually an identity. It states that the total amount of society's income, MV, *spent* on final goods and services is equal to the total amount of money *received*, PQ, for society's final goods and services.

The equation $MV = PQ$ also tells us that the flow of money can be looked at from either the buyers' or the sellers' point of view. The flow is the same in either case. As in the study of market demand and supply, the quantity of a commodity purchased is equal to the quantity sold.

The Quantity Theory of Money

What does the equation of exchange tell us about the influence of the money supply on national income and expenditure? We can best answer this question by making a couple of assumptions.

1. Assume That *V* Remains Constant This assumption means that by controlling *M* we would control GDP. If *M* is increased, either *P* or *Q* or both will have to increase in order to maintain equality between the right and left sides of the equation. The changes in *P* or *Q* will depend on the state of the economy. In a period of recession, *Q* will tend to rise relatively more than *P* as unemployed resources are reemployed. In a period of relatively high employment, *P* will tend to rise more than *Q* as full utilization of resources is approached. What do you suppose would happen in a period of full employment?

2. Assume That Both *V* and *Q* Remain Constant This assumption is, in fact, what the early classical economists believed. They assumed that *V* was constant over time because it was determined by the long-run money-holding and money-spending habits of the public. These habits, the classicists argued, were fairly stable. Further, they assumed that *Q* was constant because the economy was self-correcting. That is, the economy was always at, or was at least rapidly tending toward, full employment. The classical economists thus concluded that *P depends directly on M*. Because of this, their theory has come to be known as the "quantity theory of money."

Quantity Theory of Money The level of prices in the economy is directly proportional to the quantity of money in circulation. As a result, *changes* in the price level are directly proportional to *changes* in the money supply. That is, a given percentage change in the money supply will cause an equal percentage change in the price level in the same direction.

The quantity theory of money states, for example, that a 10 percent increase in *M* will cause a 10 percent increase in *P*. Likewise, a 5 percent decrease in *M* will cause a 5 percent decrease in *P*.

What the Evidence Shows

How well does the quantity theory of money correspond with the facts? Can changes in *M* really be used to predict changes in *P*?

In evaluating the theory using historical evidence, it is necessary to distinguish between long-term and short-term changes.

In the long run, history shows, changes in *P* have appeared to be strongly influenced by changes in *M*. For example, in the late sixteenth century, the Spanish importation of gold and silver from the New World caused major price increases in Europe. Likewise, the discovery of gold in the United States, Canada, and South Africa during the latter half of the nineteenth century brought sudden expansions in the money supply and rapidly rising prices in these countries. During more recent history, the excessive printing of money by most countries has resulted in periods of upward-spiraling prices. In these and various other cases, prices have risen directly with increases in the quantity of money, without corresponding increasing in output.

In the short run, changes in *M* have been a relatively weak predictor of changes in *P*. This is because *V* and *Q* aren't as stable as the classical quantity theory of money assumes. As you can see in Exhibit 1, *V*1 and *V*2, which are the velocities of *M*1 and *M*2, respectively, usually vary widely from one year to the next. And annual changes in the economy's output, *Q*, as you've seen in previous chapters, may also sometimes be substantial. The instability of both variables, *V* and *Q*, contributes to the difficulty of forecasting short-term changes in the price level.

In addition, what might occur if *P* increases as a result of an increase in *M*? In that case, the rise in prices might encourage an increase in *V* as people spend money more quickly for fear of future price increases. If this happens, *P* is no longer merely a passive variable dependent on *M*. It's also a *causal* variable that can contribute to changes in other factors.

Thus:

Because of the complex interrelations among the variables in the equation of exchange, the classical quantity theory of money hasn't proved suitable for predicting changes in *P* from changes in *M*. But evidence shows that the theory provides a useful guide for judging the *influence* of monetary forces on changes in the general price level.

EXHIBIT
1

Income Velocity of Money

The income velocity of money (*V*) may fluctuate considerably from year to year. These graphs show the velocities of *M*1 (= currency + checkable deposits) and *M*2 (= *M*1 + small-denomination savings deposits). Observe that both graphs are derived from the equation of exchange, *V* = GDP/*M*.

(a) Income Velocity of *M*1

*M*1 velocity

$$V1 = \frac{GDP}{M1}$$

(b) Income Velocity of *M*2

*M*2 velocity

$$V2 = \frac{GDP}{M2}$$

Note: The vertical scales are different.

Modernizing the Quantity Theory: The Importance of Velocity

Because of its obvious inadequacies, the classical quantity theory of money has undergone substantial revision by various economists in recent decades. Notable among them is Nobel laureate Milton Friedman of the Hoover Institution and Professor Emeritus of the University of Chicago.

The revised or "modern" quantity theory retains much of the traditional doctrine but reorients it to allow *V* to vary. Thus, *V* is now believed to be influenced by certain conditions that undergo frequent change. One of these conditions is the public's *expectations* about the economy's aggregate income and employment.

For example, if people fear unemployment or are pessimistic about the future, they will tend to refrain from spending. This means that money will turn over more slowly. That is, its velocity will decline.

Conversely, if people are optimistic about the future, they will increase their spending. Money will thus turn over more quickly. That is, its velocity will rise.

Clearly, then:

Expectations affect velocity. But because they respond to ever-changing political and economic conditions, expectations are primarily short-run phenomena. As a result, short-run fluctuations in the velocity of money are difficult to predict. Modern quantity theorists believe, however, that given sufficient economic knowledge, *fluctuations in V are reasonably predictable in the long run.* **Therefore, in the opinion of modern quantity theorists, the underlying determinant of GDP (or** *PQ* **in the equation of exchange) is still the quantity of money.**

Determination of the Interest Rate

Any study of money must inevitably lead to a discussion of the rate of interest and to an analysis of the forces that determine it. This is a matter of great importance. If there were no such thing as interest, there wouldn't be any incentive for those who have money to make it available to those who want it. **Interest,** therefore, is a *price* that brings lenders and borrowers together. It may be thought of as the price for the use of credit or loanable funds, as will be explained shortly.

What determines the rate of interest? This question was asked as far back as biblical times and has always been of fundamental concern in economics. The answer, as we know it today, was initially developed by classical economists of the nineteenth century.

Classical Explanation of Interest

People usually think of interest as a payment for the use of money. This interpretation is adequate for most purposes. To the early classical economists, however, interest had a more specific meaning.

You'll recall that, in the simplified circular-flow model, the total economy is divided into two parts—a household sector and a business sector. The household sector supplies the savings that the business sector borrows. The business sector uses the borrowed funds to invest in capital goods for the purpose of carrying on profitable production. Interest, therefore, is a price that businesses pay households to persuade them to consume less in the present. Households are willing to accept this arrangement because it allows them to consume more at a later date.

In other words:

Interest is a payment for saving, for "abstinence" from consumption. It is the price for overcoming people's preference for present as opposed to future consumption.

Saving, in classical theory, therefore leads *automatically* to spending on capital or investment goods. A flexible interest rate in the competitive financial markets (the money and capital markets) assures this. That is, the interest rate, determined by the free play of supply and demand, adjusts to the level where every dollar saved by households is borrowed and invested by businesses.

The determination of the market rate of interest is illustrated in Exhibit 2. The upward-sloping saving-supply curve *S* of households intersects the downward-sloping investment demand curve *D* of businesses. This intersection determines the equilibrium interest rate *r* on the vertical axis. As explained in the exhibit, the household sector *lends* loanable funds, or savings, and the business sector *borrows* them.

Fisher's Modernization: The Real Interest Rate and the Market (Nominal) Interest Rate

These ideas of classical economics were further developed near the beginning of this century by economist

EXHIBIT 2

The Market Rate of Interest in Classical Theory

In the classical theory, the interest rate is the price paid for the use of *loanable funds*. These consist mainly of the amount of savings that the household sector will make available to the business sector at various rates of interest.

Like any other price, the interest rate rations the supply of a good—in this case, loanable funds—among those who want to use it. Only those business borrowers who are willing and able to pay the market interest rate *r* can acquire the funds they want. In numerical terms, *r* might be 6 percent, 10 percent, or some other percentage.

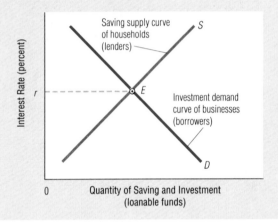

Irving Fisher. Therefore, the classical explanation of interest is also sometimes called the Fisher theory of interest. It makes an important distinction between two interest rates: the real rate and the market (or nominal) rate.

The *real rate of interest* is the interest rate measured in terms of goods. That is, it is the rate that would prevail in the market if the general price level remained stable. Suppose you lend a friend $100 today with the understanding that you will be repaid $105 one year from today. In that case, you're giving up $100 worth of goods now for what you expect will be $105 worth of goods a year from now. The *real* rate of interest is therefore 5 percent.

According to the classicists, this rate is established by *real*, as distinguished from nominal, economic forces of demand and supply. The "real demand" for funds by businesses is determined by the productivity (and therefore the efficiency) of physical capital. The greater the productivity of capital, the greater its profitability, and therefore the larger the amount of funds that businesses will want to borrow to purchase it. The "real supply" of funds by households is determined by the willingness of consumers to abstain from present consumption. The greater their willingness, the larger the amount of funds that they will want to lend.

The *market rate of interest* is the actual or money rate that prevails in the market at any given time. (The market rate is thus another name for the nominal rate.) Unlike the real rate, which is not directly observable, the market rate is the one we actually see in the markets. This is because the market rate reflects the quantity of loans measured in units of money, not in goods. Hence, it is the rate people ordinarily have in mind when they talk about "the" interest rate.

A crucial point in classical theory is that the real rate and the market rate usually are not equal. Only if borrowers and lenders expect the general price level (that is, the value of a unit of money) to remain constant will both rates be the same. This doesn't ordinarily happen. People are always expecting prices either to rise or to fall. Therefore, the market rate of interest will depart from the real rate, depending on either of two conditions:

Expectations of Inflation Suppose people believe that prices will rise—and hence that the purchasing power of a unit of money will decline. In that case, the market rate of interest will be higher than the real rate. For example, if lenders and borrowers expect the price level to rise 5 percent per year, the market rate of interest will tend to be the real rate plus 5 percent. This *inflation premium* is necessary to compensate lenders for their loss in purchasing power. At the same time, borrowers will be willing to pay the premium because they will be repaying their loans with money worth 5 percent less per year than the money they borrowed.

Expectations of Deflation Suppose people believe that prices will fall—and therefore that the purchasing power of a unit of money will rise. In that case, the market rate of interest will be below the real rate. The difference is a "deflation discount" (or *negative inflation premium*). This discount is necessary to compensate borrowers for their loss in purchasing power. Lenders will be willing to grant the discount because

they will be repaid with money worth 5 percent more per year than the money they initially lent.

These ideas can be summarized briefly:

The market rate of interest may be greater than, equal to, or less than the real rate. The difference depends on whether households and businesses expect the general price level to rise, remain constant, or decline. Any difference between the market rate and the real rate is reflected by either a positive or a negative inflation premium. The premium is the amount necessary to compensate lenders or borrowers for adverse changes in purchasing power resulting from anticipated inflation or deflation.

Broadening the Explanation: The Loanable-Funds Theory of Interest

This classical explanation of interest can be enlarged to include all sectors of the economy, not just the household and business sectors. The more comprehensive version is known as the "loanable-funds theory of interest." It's used extensively by banks, the Federal Reserve, and other financial institutions as a basis for forecasting changes in interest rates. If you take certain courses in finance, you'll make frequent use of this theory.[*]

Loanable funds, as the name implies, are sums of money available for lending. Therefore, loanable funds can be thought of as money used to purchase financial claims. For example, if you lend a friend $100 and receive in return an IOU, you've exchanged money for a financial claim of equal value. When your friend repays the loan, you will exchange the claim for money. All sectors of the economy continually exchange money and financial claims by buying and selling one for the other. Therefore, the economy's sectors are the sources of demand and supply of loanable funds. As shown by the diagrams in Exhibit 3, the interaction of these various sources determines the rate of interest in the financial markets. Let's see how, by interpreting the diagrams briefly.

---

[*]Formulated by a British economist, Dennis Robertson, in 1933, the loanable-funds theory of interest may be considered an extension of the classical theory. Another theory of interest, called the *liquidity-preference* (or *Keynesian*) *theory,* is useful for showing how interest rates change as a result of increases or decreases in the money supply by the central bank. This theory is explained in a later chapter. Meanwhile, it may be noted that the loanable-funds theory and the liquidity-preference theory are mutually consistent—that is, *logically equivalent.*

EXHIBIT
3

The Loanable-Funds Market

The sum of the separate demand and supply curves from all sources gives the total market demand and supply curves. The interaction of the total market curves determines the equilibrium interest rate and the equilibrium quantity of loanable funds.

(a) Sources of Demand for Loanable Funds

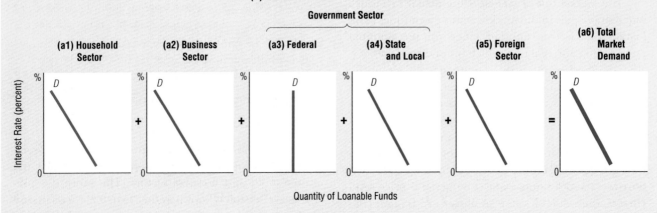

(b) Sources of Supply for Loanable Funds

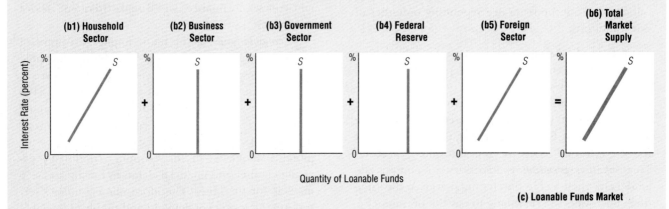

FIGURE (c) The intersection of the total market demand and supply curves from Figures (a6) and (b6) determines the equilibrium interest rate r and the equilibrium quantity Q.

(c) Loanable Funds Market

Demand for Loanable Funds

The sources of demand for loanable funds are the four sectors of the economy—household, business, government, and foreign. The sum of their separate demands comprise the total market demand for loanable funds.

Figure (a1) The household sector desires loanable funds to help finance credit purchases. Its demand curve is downward-sloping because consumers will borrow more money at lower interest rates than at higher ones.

Figure (a2) The business sector desires loanable funds to help finance the purchase of investment goods—plant, equipment, and increases in inventories. Its demand curve is also downward-sloping because businesses are likely to borrow more at lower interest rates than at higher ones.

Figures (a3) and (a4) Like the household and business sectors, the government sector borrows when its expenditures exceed its revenues. Evidence shows that the federal government's demand for loanable funds is independent of interest rates. That is, the government borrows what it needs to finance its annual budget deficits, regardless of the level of interest rates. Therefore, the federal government's demand curve for loanable funds is a vertical line. State and local government demand, however, is sensitive to interest rates and is represented by a downward-sloping curve.

Figure (a5) The foreign sector is also sensitive to interest rates. Foreign corporations and governments seek to borrow more loanable funds in the United States (by selling bonds and other debt instruments) at lower interest rates than at higher rates.

Figure (a6) When the quantity of loanable funds demanded by all sectors at each interest rate is summed, the result obtained is the total market demand curve for loanable funds. This curve is downward-sloping because the curves that compose it are either vertical or downward-sloping.

Supply of Loanable Funds

The total market supply curve of loanable funds is derived in a similar way. But notice the following distinctions among the sources of supply:

Figure (b1) The household sector's savings—the difference between income and spending—are the economy's chief source of loanable funds. The supply curve is upward-sloping, indicating that households will save more at higher interest rates than at lower interest rates.

Figure (b2) The business sector's savings consist of retained earnings and depreciation. Economists believe that the supply curve is vertical (or nearly so) because the amount of business savings isn't affected significantly by a change in the level of interest rates.

Figure (b3) Government budget surpluses, which may be thought of as government savings, are a source of supply of loanable funds. But there's no evidence that such savings, either at the federal level or at the state and local levels, are related to interest rates. As a result, the savings for all levels of government are lumped together and their supply curve is graphed as a vertical line.

Figure (b4) The Federal Reserve has the ability to increase or decrease the amount of money in the economy by altering reserve requirements, conducting open-market operations, and changing the discount rate. This ability makes the Fed (through the banking system) an important source of supply of loanable funds. However, there is evidence that the quantity of money supplied by the Fed at any given time is independent of the interest rate. Therefore, the supply curve is graphed as a vertical line.

Figure (b5) The foreign sector is a growing source of supply of loanable funds. Many foreign investors, including households, businesses, financial institutions, and some governments, use their savings to acquire financial claims against American borrowers—especially American corporations and the U.S. Treasury. Because foreign lenders are sensitive to interest rates, the foreign sector's supply curve is upward-sloping.

Figure (b6) When the quantities supplied by all sectors at each interest rate are summed, the result is the total market supply curve of loanable funds. Because the curves that compose it are either vertical or upward-sloping, this curve is upward-sloping.

Interest-Rate Determination

When the total market demand and supply curves from Figures a6 and b6 are combined, as they are in Figure (c), their intersection determines the equilibrium point. Thus, in Figure (c) the equilibrium interest rate is r and the equilibrium quantity is Q.

Summarizing:

The *loanable-funds theory of interest* holds that the interest rate is determined by the demand for and the supply of money (loanable funds) used to purchase financial claims.

The sources of demand for loanable funds are (1) household-sector borrowing (credit purchases) to finance consumption; (2) business-sector borrowing to finance purchases of capital goods; (3) government-sector borrowing to finance budget deficits; and (4) foreign-sector borrowing.

The sources of supply of loanable funds are (1) household-sector savings—the difference between households' income and spending; (2) business-sector savings in the form of retained earnings and depreciation; (3) government-sector savings (budget surpluses); (4) Federal Reserve increases in the money supply; and (5) foreign-sector savings in the form of loans to American borrowers.

The demanders and suppliers of loanable funds are continually formulating new expectations about economic conditions. Their expectations affect their borrowing and lending decisions. As a result, the total market demand and supply curves are always shifting. These shifts cause interest rates in the economy to fluctuate.

Deriving the Real Interest Rate: A Modern View

The loanable-funds (or extended classical) theory of interest is held today by practically all economists. The theory is used extensively in the world of finance. Like their early twentieth-century predecessor, Irving Fisher, today's economists believe that the interest rates you see quoted in the market contain an *inflation premium*. This premium reflects the public's expectations about future prices. Therefore, market interest rates and prices tend to move together, as shown in Exhibit 4.

You can use Fisher's ideas to estimate the real interest rate from the following equation:

Market interest rate

= real interest rate + inflation premium

This equation, and the classical theory underlying it, is called the *Fisher effect.* Conversely, the real interest rate is equal to the market interest rate *minus* the inflation premium:

Real interest rate

= market interest rate – inflation premium

To illustrate, here's how the real interest rate might be estimated.

EXHIBIT 4

Price Level and the Interest Rate

Interest rates respond to inflation. Higher rates of inflation generally lead to higher interest rates. This is because lenders want to be compensated for the purchasing power they expect to lose due to inflation. And borrowers are willing to pay higher interest rates because they expect to be repaying their loans with cheaper dollars.

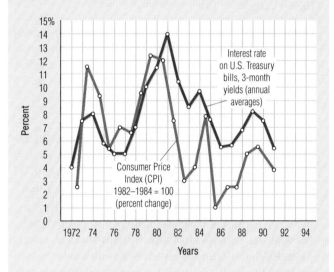

First, as your measure of the market interest rate, you should use the yield on 3-month Treasury bills. The reason is that these financial instruments provide a better combination of high marketability, short maturities, and zero default risk than any other securities. Their yield represents a "pure" rate of interest—the rate on a short-term riskless loan. (All other interest rates are affected by length of loan, risk of default, and other factors that make them less than "pure.") The average annual yield on 3-month Treasury bills is shown on the inside back cover of this book.

Second, in order to obtain a measure of the inflation premium, you should estimate borrowers' and lenders' *expectations* of future prices. But expectations are subjective and changeable, so any estimate will be at best a reasonable guess based on recent trends. Exhibit 5 illustrates a rather simple two-step procedure for estimating the inflation premium:

Step 1 Choose a measure of the overall level of prices. One such measure, as you know, is the Consumer

Price Index (CPI). However, there is an even broader indicator called the **GDP deflator,** which is also sometimes called the **Implicit Price Index (IPI).** Constructed by the U.S. Department of Commerce, the GDP deflator, or IPI, is an average of the various price indexes used to deflate the components of GDP. Therefore, the GDP deflator is the most comprehensive measure of the general price level available. The index, which for convenience will be referred to here as IPI, is shown in the table on the inside back cover of the book under the name "GDP deflator."

Step 2 Calculate the most recent percentage change in the IPI to obtain the inflation premium for the current period. For example, suppose the IPI increased from 120 in Year 1 to 126 in Year 2, the current year. This is shown in column (2) of the table in Exhibit 5. Then, as shown in column (3), the percentage change or inflation premium for the current year is $(126 - 120)/120 = 0.05$, or 5%. This procedure *assumes* that the inflation premium in the current year is best estimated by the percentage change in the general price level from the previous year. Of course, other assumptions could also be made. In fact, the inflation premium normally depends on a number of conditions, not just on the most recent percentage change in the general price level.

EXHIBIT 5

Calculating the Inflation Premium

One possible estimate of the inflation premium is the *percentage change* in the general price level from the previous year to the current year. The real interest rate in column (5) will then reflect the observed market interest rate in column (4) *minus* the estimated inflation premium in column (3).

(1) Year	(2) General price level (IPI)*	(3) Estimated inflation premium (% change in IPI)	(4) Market interest rate (observed)	(5) Real interest rate (4) – (3)
1 (previous)	120	5%		
2 (current)	126		9%	4%

* The Implicit Price Index is another name for the GDP deflator.

Example Suppose that, in the current year, the market interest rate is 9 percent, as shown in column (4). Then, if the inflation premium for the year (calculated in step 2) is 5 percent, the real interest rate in the current year is 4 percent. This is shown in column (5).

Conclusion: Prices and Interest Rates Move Together

Is the connection between prices and interest rates valid? There is strong evidence for believing that it is. Historically, market interest rates have risen when prices have increased over a period and have declined when prices have decreased for some time. This pattern indicates that high market interest rates reflect current as well as expected inflation. Evidence of this pattern can be seen in many nations. Countries that traditionally experience steep inflations generally have much higher market interest rates than countries whose price levels are relatively more stable.

This inflation-premium link between prices and interest rates suggests a way for the monetary authority (the Federal Reserve) to reduce interest rates:

Excessive increases in the quantity of money result in "too much money chasing too few goods." Consequently, prices and interest rates rise. By reducing the money supply, or more precisely, the rate of growth of the money supply, the monetary authority can retard inflation. Slowed inflation helps bring about eventual reductions in the market rate of interest.

It's significant that practically all economists today concur on the relationship between prices and interest rates. What they disagree about is the *speed* and *extent* of adjustment of prices and interest rates to changes in the money supply.

The Propositions of Monetarism

The foregoing ideas about the money supply, prices, and interest rates have, with some modifications, been part of the main body of economic thinking since the late 1800s. In other words, for more than a century, economists have believed that a relationship exists among these three fundamental economic variables:

■ The supply of money in the economy

■ The average price level

■ The rate of interest

Unfortunately, the precise nature of the relationship among these variables has been difficult to determine. Further, even when the relationships have been established, they've often proved to be transitory rather than long lasting. Nevertheless, efforts to discover the relationship continue, not only in the United States but in some other countries as well. These efforts have resulted in a body of ideas known as "monetarism." Its chief protagonist has been an eminent American economist, Milton Friedman.

As suggested by its name, monetarism assigns a strategic role to the influence of money in the economy. Therefore, *monetarism looks to the monetary policy of the Federal Reserve System as the chief factor that affects inflation.*

You can best understand the implications of monetarism by examining its main propositions—the pillars on which it rests.

The Quantity Theory of Money Revisited

The beliefs of monetarism stem from the ideas of Irving Fisher. These include the familiar quantity theory of money and the equation of exchange:

$$MV = PQ \quad \text{or equivalently} \quad MV = \text{GDP}$$

You'll recall how Fisher and other early classical economists interpreted the first equation. They believed that the velocity (V) of money was constant over time because V depended on the long-run spending habits of the public. These habits, the classicists contended, were fairly stable. They also assumed that the quantity (Q) of final output was constant because the economy was always either at full employment or at least rapidly tending toward it. Therefore, the early classicists concluded, a given percentage change in the quantity of money (M) will cause an equal percentage change in the average level of prices (P) in the same direction.

From the second equation, $MV = \text{GDP}$, it follows that changes in the quantity of money will also cause changes in society's aggregate income. For example, because V is assumed to be constant, a 10 percent increase in M will cause a 10 percent increase in *nominal* GDP. This relationship suggests the first proposition of monetarism:

Monetarists (like their early classical predecessors) believe that changes in the quantity of money exert a dominant influence on changes in the price level and in nominal GDP.

Some evidence used by monetarists to support this cause-and-effect relationship between money and prices is shown in Exhibit 6. There are three things to notice from this graph:

1. On the average, changes in the money growth rate usually cause changes in the price level in the same direction about 2 years later. In the words of monetarists, the effects of changes in the money growth rate on the rate of inflation are *"long and variable."* This fundamental generalization is one that monetarists have derived from statistical studies going back to the late nineteenth century. (Monetarists have also found that a similar relationship, not shown in the chart, exists between the money growth rate and nominal GDP. This relationship follows from the second equation above: $MV = \text{GDP}$.)

2. The causal variable used is money per unit of output. This is simply $M2$ divided by real GDP. Because $M2$ includes $M1$ plus small-denomination time deposits, monetarist studies have found $M2$ to be the most suitable comprehensive variable available for tracking the relationship between money and prices. Year-to-year percentage changes in the causal variable are compared to year-to-year percentage changes in the effect variable—the price level measured by the GDP deflator.

3. The relationship between money and prices for the period 1900 to 1980 (not shown in the graph) was considerably stronger than the relationship since 1980. This change occurred largely because legislation passed in 1980 and 1982 partially deregulated the banking system. Interest-earning checkable deposits (NOW accounts), which are a substantial component of the money supply, were introduced in that period. These deposits compete with other short-term interest-earning investments such as money-market mutual funds. As a result, the velocity of money has become more volatile. The increased volatility has weakened the relationship between the two variables (money and prices) in the graph.[*]

---

[*]Regardless of the strength or weakness of the relationship, an important principle should be kept in mind. When two variables move together, whether directly or inversely, they are said to be correlated (from the word "co-related"). But this correlation doesn't necessarily mean that one variable is a cause of the other. *Correlation doesn't establish causation.* If causation exists, it must be explained by a *theory,* which is what monetarism is. These principles of correlation and causation apply to *all* branches of science, not just to economics.

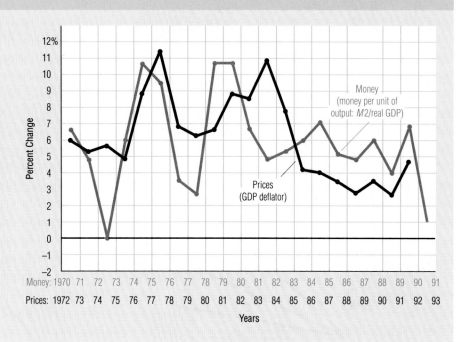

EXHIBIT 6

Changes in Money Growth and the Price Level

Monetarists believe that the relationship between the monetary growth rate and the rate of inflation is "long and variable." On average, it takes about 2 years for a change in money growth to affect the price level. As explained in the text, partial deregulation of the banking system that occurred in the early 1980s made the velocity of money more unstable. This instability weakened the relationship between the two variables in the graph (money and prices).

Demand for Money

Although monetarism is rooted in the classical quantity theory of money and in the equation of exchange, it differs from them in certain important ways.

First, monetarists point out that people want money for what it will buy—for its *real* purchasing power. Therefore, monetarists *redefine* M as the amount of money people want to hold in the form of real cash balances. (The new M is thus a demand variable, not a supply variable as in the original quantity theory of money.) This demand, they say, depends in a predictable way on two key variables:

1. Expected average long-run income

2. Expected returns on money and competing assets (stocks, bonds, and goods) as reflected by interest rates

Let's see how the public's demand for money is affected by these two variables—income and interest rates.

Money and Aggregate Income: A Direct Relation

Monetarists believe that the public's demand for money—that is, for *real cash balances*—varies *directly* with society's income, GDP. This relation between

money and income is easy to see when it's expressed in terms of an equation. For example, we can take the equation of exchange

$$MV = PQ$$

and rewrite it in terms of M:

$$M = \frac{PQ}{V} \quad \text{or equivalently} \quad M = \frac{1}{V}PQ$$

Expressed in this form, the equation on the right emphasizes the relation between the demand for money M and the nation's income. To see why, suppose we let k stand for the ratio $1/V$. Then the right-hand equation becomes

$$M = kPQ$$

Of course, because PQ is the same as GDP, this equation can also be written

$$M = k\text{GDP}$$

What does the equation tell us? The answer can be expressed in words:

People want to hold *real purchasing power,* **that is, an amount of money (M) equal to a specific fraction (k) of society's income (PQ, or GDP). This is simply another way of saying that the public's demand for** *real cash balances* **varies directly with society's** *income.*

EXHIBIT
7

The Public's Demand for Money Depends on Aggregate Income (GDP)

At any given time, the public wishes to hold some fraction of its aggregate income (GDP) in the form of money. For example, it may wish to hold 10 percent, 20 percent, 50 percent, or some other percent of GDP as money. The public wants money (that is, cash balances) mainly for transaction purposes—that is, to buy the GDP.

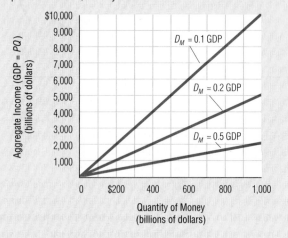

EXHIBIT
8

Money and Aggregate Income (GDP)

The public's demand for money (D_M) is equal to some fraction (k) of society's aggregate income (GDP). The supply of money (S_M) is determined by the Federal Reserve. Therefore, an increase in the supply of money from S_M to S_M' provides people with excess cash balances. These balances are then spent, which causes the equilibrium level of aggregate income to rise from GDP_1 to GDP_2.

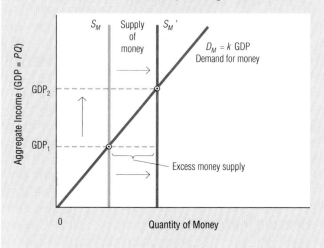

This proposition is illustrated graphically in Exhibit 7. Note that the quantity of money is measured on the horizontal axis and society's aggregate income, GDP, is measured on the vertical axis. The figure conveys the following points:

1. At any given time, the public's demand for money, D_M, is equal to some fraction of GDP. For example, suppose the public's demand-for-money curve is D_M = 0.1GDP. This means that people will want to hold 10 percent of GDP as money. Thus they will desire to hold $100 when GDP is $1,000, and $1,000 when GDP is $10,000.

Suppose instead that the public's demand-for-money curve is D_M = 0.5GDP. In this case people will desire to hold $500 when GDP is $1,000, and $1,000 when GDP is $2,000.

As you can see, any other upward-sloping D_M curve, such as D_M = 0.2GDP, can be interpreted in a similar way.

2. The fraction of its income that the public wants to hold in the form of money is indicated by the *relative*

steepness (slope) of the D_M curve. In general, the smaller the percentage of its income that the public will desire to hold as money, the greater the relative steepness of the curve.

What are the implications of the relationship between the demand for money and GDP? The answer is illustrated in Exhibit 8. Note that the quantity of money is again measured on the horizontal axis and society's aggregate income, GDP, on the vertical. As in the previous diagram, two important points are conveyed by this graph:

1. The public's demand-for-money curve, D_M, represents some fraction, k, of society's aggregate income, GDP. Thus, D_M = kGDP. The supply-of-money curve, S_M, is a vertical line. This indicates that, at any given time, the quantity of money (which is determined by the Fed) is a fixed amount and is unresponsive to changes in aggregate income.

2. The equilibrium income is determined by the intersection of the D_M and S_M curves. Initially, it's GDP_1. Suppose the Federal Reserve decides to increase the supply of money from S_M to $S_M{}'$. This increase will produce an excess money supply in relation to what people want. They will therefore spend away the excess, which causes aggregate income to rise to the new equilibrium at GDP_2.

Money and Interest Rates: An Inverse Relation

As you learned earlier, monetarists believe that a second major variable affecting the public's demand for money is the expected return on assets. These include money, stocks, bonds, and goods. Because they compete with one another for the public's dollars, the returns on assets are reflected by interest rates in the economy's financial markets. The nature of the relationship between the demand for money and interest rates, monetarists contend, is *inverse*. That is, people want to hold smaller cash balances when interest rates are high and larger cash balances when interest rates are low.

The reason for this preference isn't hard to see. The economy is composed of decision-making units—individuals, households, and firms. These economic entities hold their wealth (that is, things of value they own) in *portfolios of assets*. The assets might be both financial and nonfinancial in nature. Examples of some of the things you might own are money, stocks, bonds, a car, a house, furnishings, and perhaps a business. Because all of these items constitute wealth, each is, according to monetarists, a part of your portfolio of assets.

How much of its portfolio will the public hold in the form of cash balances? The answer depends on how profitable it is to hold other assets, such as securities, property, and so on. For example, suppose there is a rise in the interest rate that can be earned on other assets relative to the interest rate that can be earned on cash balances. This rise in the interest rate increases the *opportunity cost* of holding money. People therefore reduce their holdings of cash balances—their demand for money—in order to take advantage of the higher interest returns available elsewhere. The reverse, of course, occurs when the interest returns on other assets decline. People increase their holdings of cash balances. In general, therefore, the public's demand for cash balances varies *inversely* with interest rates.

This relationship affecting the public's demand for money emphasizes the influence of two factors—aggregate income and interest rates. Summarizing the key ideas:

Monetarists believe that the public's demand for real cash balances varies *directly* with aggregate income and *inversely* **with interest rates. Under normal conditions the public's demand for real cash balances tends to be stable in relation to those variables.**

The Stability of Velocity

You now know that, according to monetarist thinking, the amount of money people want to hold is equal to a constant fraction (k) of GDP. You've also learned that $k = 1/V$. Therefore, because k is constant, V must also be constant in order for the equation to hold true. Further, if $k = 1/V$, then $V = 1/k$.

To illustrate these ideas, suppose that people want to hold 25 percent of their income in the form of cash balances. Then, $k = \frac{1}{4}$. And, since $V = 1/k$, $V = 4$. This means that each dollar is spent an average of four times during the year to purchase the economy's GDP.

Similarly, if people want to hold 20 percent of their income as cash, then $k = \frac{1}{5}$. Hence, $V = 5$. Each dollar is thus spent an average of five times per year.

But what determines V? We've seen that the velocity of money can and does fluctuate over the years. Nevertheless, monetarists believe that V bears a stable relationship to the variables that determine it. One of the chief variables, as we saw earlier, is the public's *expectations of inflation*. If people expect prices to rise, they will be inclined to spend more of their cash balances now. This will cause V to increase. Conversely, if people expect prices to decline, they will delay spending some of their cash balances. This will cause V to decrease. Thus:

Monetarists believe that changes in V vary in a direct way with the public's inflationary expectations. That is, V increases when the public expects prices to rise, and decreases when the public expects prices to fall. (In contrast, the early classical economists, you'll recall, assumed that V was stable over time.)

The Transmission Mechanism: Portfolio Adjustments

Monetarists' ideas concerning the demand for money and its velocity of circulation can now be brought together. The linkage is what may be called the **transmission mechanism for monetary policy,** or simply the **transmission mechanism.** This is the process by which changes in the rate of growth of the money supply, or simply the monetary growth rate, bring about changes in people's spending behavior. Spending behavior, in turn, affects prices, interest rates, and other economic variables.

The transmission mechanism, as the monetarists see it, may be thought of as a sequence of events:

First, decisions to increase or decrease the monetary growth rate are frequently made by the Fed. These monetary-policy actions are aimed at achieving the basic economic goals of efficiency, stability, and growth. One of the most fundamental tenets of monetarism is the belief that the Fed fails to achieve these goals because its expansions and contractions of the monetary growth rate are *erratic*. As a result, monetarists argue, the Fed's actions often turn out to cause inefficiency, instability, and inadequate growth.

Second, erratic changes in the monetary growth rate cause discrepancies between people's actual and desired real cash balances. To restore equilibrium, individuals adjust the composition of the assets in their portfolios. For example, if a disequilibrium is caused by unexpected increases in the monetary growth rate, people reduce their excess cash balances by buying any of a wide range of other assets.

Third, individuals are always shifting their holdings of wealth among different assets. They do this in an effort to obtain the highest possible rates of return on their portfolio of assets. For example, if returns in the securities market are higher than returns in the real-estate market, people will shift some of their funds out of buildings and land and into stocks and bonds. These reallocations of wealth are reflected by changes in the relative prices of assets as spending patterns shift over a wide range of goods and services.

Thus:

Monetarists believe that the transmission mechanism by which changes in the monetary growth rate cause changes in total spending is essentially a *portfolio-adjustment process*. Individuals are seen as disposing of their excess money balances over a broad spectrum of assets. These include stocks, bonds, consumer goods, and producer (capital) goods. As a result, the relative prices of these goods are always changing in response to shifts in people's spending patterns caused by fluctuations in monetary growth rates. The changes in prices, in turn, affect people's inflationary expectations, and thereby influence interest rates and the velocity of money.

This explanation is summarized by the diagram in Exhibit 9. It provides a simplified illustration of how most of today's monetarists would describe the transmission mechanism.

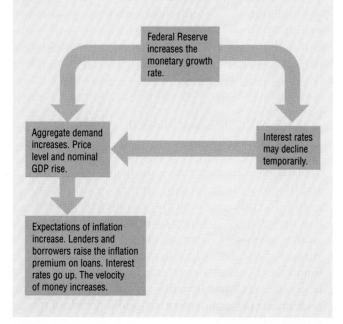

EXHIBIT 9

The Transmission Mechanism: The Monetarists' View

There are several different monetarist explanations of the transmission process. This simplified composite description fits most monetarists' views. However, differences of opinion exist over the speed and extent of adjustment of some of the variables in the boxes to changes in the monetary growth rate.

Federal Reserve increases the monetary growth rate.

Interest rates may decline temporarily.

Aggregate demand increases. Price level and nominal GDP rise.

Expectations of inflation increase. Lenders and borrowers raise the inflation premium on loans. Interest rates go up. The velocity of money increases.

The Monetarist View of Monetary Policy

Monetarists have always maintained that inflation is the result of "too much money chasing too few goods." Therefore, they conclude, *an acceleration in the monetary growth rate will produce an acceleration in the inflation rate at some later time.*

You can gain a better appreciation of this idea by thinking about it in terms of an aggregate demand/aggregate supply model. To begin with, remember that one of the causes of an increase in aggregate demand—a shift of the *AD* curve to the right—is a *rapid increase in the money supply*. When this happens, the public finds itself holding significantly more purchasing power—more real cash balances relative to its aggregate income—than it desires. It therefore spends the excess balances. Prices and output then rise as the economy adjusts to a new equilibrium position.

The nature of the adjustment is illustrated in Exhibit 10. Note that, as in all previous *AD/AS* models, real output is measured on the horizontal axis and the average price level is measured on the vertical axis. The adjustment process can best be explained in several "stages":

Stage 1 Suppose the economy is in a recession. This occurs, for example, if the *AD* and *AS* curves intersect at point *a*. The resulting levels of output and employment are at *Q*, and the corresponding average price level is at *P*.

Stage 2 With employment below its natural level, the economy has excess resources available. The excess creates downward pressure on resource costs, especially wages. The *AS* curve therefore shifts slowly rightward to *AS'*, where it intersects the *AD* curve at *b*. That is, the economy adjusts *automatically*. It reaches its full- or natural-employment level, with the corresponding price level at *P'*, *without special monetary stimulation by the Fed*. Therefore, because the economy is self-correcting, monetarists believe that the Fed should take a nonactivist stance.

Stage 3 But what happens if the adjustment doesn't occur as rapidly as the monetary authorities desire? In that case the Fed may try to hasten the process by taking an *activist* stance. It does this by increasing the money supply. This increase causes the *AD* curve to shift to the right—to *AD'*. But the *AS* curve is also shifting rightward, as explained in Step 2. Both the *AD* and *AS* curves thus shift simultaneously but at different rates. The price level, or rate of inflation, may therefore fluctuate as the economy moves along a wavering path toward the short-run equilibrium point *c*.

Stage 4 By the time point *c* is reached, two conditions exist:

Scarcities in the form of shortages of labor and materials have developed in various resource markets. These shortages arise because aggregate output and employment have reached "overfull" levels at *Q'*. That is, the economy is operating in the frictional and structural unemployment range. Therefore, fewer factors of production are available for firms to acquire.

Real wages have declined. The reason is that most money wages are frozen by 2- or 3-year contracts and hence have not risen as fast as prices.

How Monetarists View an Activist Monetary Policy

Suppose the economy is in a recession with the level of output at *Q*. Excess capacity in the economy automatically causes the *AS* curve to shift to *AS'* as resource costs decline. The economy moves along the path from *a* to *b*, reaching full employment at the average price level *P'*.

However, if the Fed simultaneously pursues an activist policy by rapidly increasing the money supply, the *AD* curve shifts rightward to *AD'*. With both the *AS* and *AD* curves shifting at different rates, the equilibrium point may move waveringly from *a* to *c* without necessarily going through *b*. At *c*, overfull employment creates upward pressure on resource costs, causing the aggregate supply curve to shift back to *AS*. As a result, the equilibrium point moves from its short-run position at *c* to its long-run position at *d*. Thus, because of the Fed's intervention, the economy has adjusted to full employment at the price level *P''*.

This type of analysis leads monetarists to conclude that an activist monetary policy causes instability and inflation.

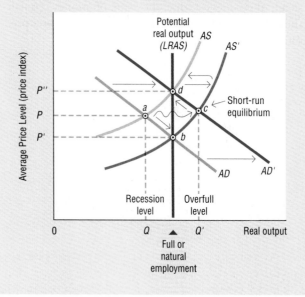

Both of these conditions create upward pressure on resource costs as unions negotiate for higher wages. The aggregate supply curve thus shifts back from *AS'* to *AS*, moving the equilibrium point from its short-run position at *c* to its long-run position at *d*. At this point real output and employment have declined to their natural levels while the corresponding price level has risen to *P''*.

Thus:

Monetarists contend that an activist monetary policy, compared with a nonactivist one, has adverse effects in both the short run and the long run. In the short run it causes instability of prices, output, and employment. In the long run it results in higher prices while attaining the same levels of output and employment that would have been realized *automatically* with a nonactivist policy.

Policy Recommendation: Rules, Not Discretion

You can now see that, according to monetarist thinking, the Fed's efforts to "fine-tune" the economy by manipulating the money supply, or more accurately the rate of growth of the money supply, may actually be *destabilizing*. That is, these steps may help cause the very fluctuations in output, employment, and prices that the Fed, in its well-intentioned efforts, is trying to reduce. Therefore, monetarists believe that monetary policy shouldn't be left to the discretion of the Fed. Instead, they suggest that the rate of money growth should be governed by *rules*. The following two prescriptions have received the widest attention:

1. ***Money-Supply Rule*** The Fed should adhere to a policy of steady monetary expansion at a rate that is consistent with the economy's long-run growth of real GDP—about 3 to 4 percent annually. This steady expansion would promote stability. A faster rate of money growth would cause inflation by resulting in "too much money chasing too few goods." A slower rate could cause a recession by failing to meet the expanding needs of business.

2. ***Monetary Targeting*** The monetary growth rate should be linked to quarterly or semiannual changes in some comprehensive economic indicator. Hundreds of indicators, some of which appear on the inside covers of this book, exist. By tying money growth to the appropriate indicator, the Fed would have a clear guide for conducting monetary policy.

Although the money-supply rule is the most frequently championed prescription, many monetarists (as well as nonmonetarists) have also advocated monetary targeting.

Has the Fed adopted either of these rules? The answer is no. Monetary policy, the Fed contends, can't be determined by following a few simple guidelines. The economy is extremely complex, and conditions both at home and abroad are continually changing. There-fore, the Fed maintains that *discretionary policies, not fixed rules,* are necessary to achieve desired levels of efficiency, stability, and growth. However:

Exercising discretion doesn't mean that the Fed's monetary-policy decisions are arbitrary. The Board of Governors continually monitors numerous economic indicators to help it decide whether the rate of money growth should be increased, decreased, or held fairly constant.

Targets and Indicators

Several indicators receive particular attention because of their overall importance. Among the major ones are these:

Gross Domestic Product

Changes in both nominal and real GDP are of continual concern to the Fed. As you've learned, excessive monetary growth normally causes the price level to rise. Nominal GDP thus increases but real GDP may not. This difference is most easily seen in terms of the familiar equation GDP = PQ. If monetary expansion causes P to rise while Q remains constant, nominal GDP will increase while real GDP stays the same. And if both P and Q rise but P rises faster, nominal GDP will increase more than real GDP. When conducting monetary policy, the Fed is never sure of the extent to which changes in money growth may affect both nominal and real GDP. Consequently, the Fed must also look at other indicators for guidance.

Index of Commodity Prices

One of the indicators that receives the Fed's particular attention is commodity prices. Corn, barley, oats, soybeans, wheat, flaxseed, canola, and rye are examples of commodities. So are copper, gold, silver, platinum, palladium, lumber, crude oil, and gasoline. These and other raw materials, which are bought and sold in world markets, are inputs used by industry. Their prices thus affect the prices of finished goods several months later. Therefore, the Fed monitors an index (average) of commodity prices to help decide the course of monetary policy. Unfortunately, the index is an imperfect guide for forecasting price-level changes because commodity prices fluctuate widely in world markets. As a result, the index often sends false signals of changing inflation rates.

Yield Curve

Interest rates on debt instruments are another important indicator watched by the Fed. Suppose you draw a

EXHIBIT
11

Yield Curves: Loanable Funds Market

A yield curve is a graph of short- and long-term interest rates on debt instruments—such as U.S. Treasury securities. It reveals borrowers' and lenders' *expectations* of future interest rates. The Federal Reserve Board and financial institutions employ yield curves to forecast interest rates. Three basic types of yield curves are ascending, descending (inverted), and flat. A humped yield curve may combine elements of all three. Although the curves shift and change shape frequently, the ascending yield curve is the one that is normally expected.

Technical note: The horizontal axis of this figure is scaled logarithmically. This facilitates comparison of relative (percentage) changes in the graphs. To understand why, look up the meaning of *logarithmic scale* in the Dictionary at the back of the book.

Source: Federal Reserve Bank of Cleveland.

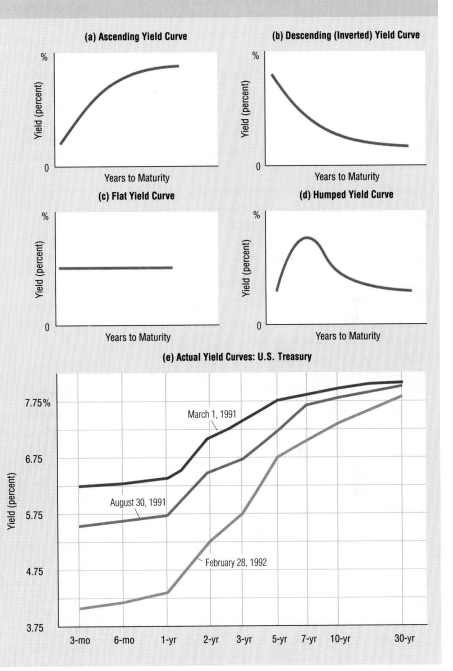

graph of the relationship between short- and long-term interest rates (yields) on debt instruments that are alike in all respects except term to maturity. The resulting curve is called a *yield curve.* You can visualize it best by examining yields on U.S. Treasury securities because they're alike in three important respects: zero default risk, equal tax treatment, and high marketabil-

ity. Several types of yield curves, any one of which may exist at a particular time, are illustrated in Exhibit 11. Here's what the curves tell you:

Figure (a) An ascending yield curve means that lenders and borrowers in the market expect interest rates to rise in the long run. This curve is the one that's normally expected and the one that usually occurs. In behavioral terms, its upward-sloping shape means that lenders require, and borrowers are willing to pay, higher interest rates in order to tie up money for longer periods.

Figure (b) A descending curve, also called an inverted curve, means that the market (that is, lenders and borrowers) expects interest rates to decline in the long run.

Figure (c) A flat or horizontal curve means that the market expects interest rates to remain the same in both the short and the long run.

Figure (d) A humped curve combines elements of the others. This one, the most common type, means that the market expects interest rates to rise in the short run and to decline in the long run. The curve may or may not flatten out at its right end.

Figure (e) The actual yield curve is based on recent experiences. A different type may exist on any given date.

A yield curve provides a forecast of future interest-rate levels. (For example, an ascending curve indicates higher long-term rates and foretells higher inflation.) Therefore, yield curves are one of several forecasting tools used by the Fed. However, the curves often shift and change their shape because they reflect lenders' and borrowers' *expectations* of future interest rates. As a result, they have significant shortcomings as guides for monetary policy.

Monetary Base

Most people who keep up with the business news have heard of *M*1 and *M*2. These are the most widely known measures of money. But there are other measures that are not well-known. One that the Fed watches closely is called the **monetary base**. As you've already learned, it consists of the sum of legal reserves and currency in circulation. The monetary base is often called "high-powered" money because it supports the money supply (currency + checkable deposits). Because of our fractional-reserve banking system, the money supply is a multiple of the monetary base.* Therefore, to the extent that the Reserve authorities "manage" the monetary base through open-market operations and other tools of monetary policy, they exercise a strong influence over the total monetary assets of the public.

---
*For example, *M*1 = *mB*. Recall that this is the money-multiplier concept studied in Chapter 10.

Federal Funds Rate

A bank, as you know, must maintain required reserves against deposits. However, it doesn't have to maintain the required amount every day. It can avoid penalty fees by keeping its *average* daily reserve balances relative to its *average* daily deposits over a 2-week period equal to or above the required level. One way it can do this is to borrow other banks' excess reserves that are on deposit with the Fed. (Other ways include asset and/or liability management, such as selling Treasury securities, issuing negotiable CDs, or perhaps borrowing from the Fed.) The loans, which are usually on an overnight basis, are called "federal funds" because they are simply bookkeeping transactions arranged through the Federal Reserve's electronic transfer system. The interest rate that the borrowing bank pays the lending bank is called the **federal funds rate.** The Fed pays close attention to this interest rate. It's a basic indicator of what's happening to other short-term interest rates because they tend to move in the same direction as the federal funds rate.

Long-Run Expected Price Level (*P**)

It should be apparent by now that the Fed is eclectic. It selects from the many available indicators those that it considers best for its purposes. One indicator that gets considerable attention is the familiar *equation of exchange*. To best understand how it's used by the Fed, keep in mind that the equation may be expressed in these equivalent forms:

$$[1] \ PQ = MV \qquad [2] \ V = \frac{PQ}{M} = \frac{GDP}{M} \qquad [3] \ P = \frac{MV}{Q}$$

In order to utilize the equation of exchange, the Fed modifies it in four ways:

First, the Fed uses *M*2 as a measure of money. (*M*2, you'll recall, includes mainly currency and checkable deposits plus small-denomination time deposits under $100,000). The Fed employs *M*2 because it has been found to be a more suitable variable than *M*1 for relating money growth to the price level.

Second, the Fed introduces a new symbol called "*V*2-star," written *V*2*. This symbol represents the long-run average value of *V*. For example, look at equation [2]. Because *PQ* is the same as GDP, the average value of *V* (represented by *V*2*) is calculated for each year by dividing the annual value of GDP by the correspond-

EXHIBIT
12

Estimating the Long-Run Expected Price Level with the *P*-Star Equation

Using the *P*-star equation, you can estimate *P** as shown in the illustrative calculation below. The hardest part is choosing a value for average velocity, *V2**. This has usually ranged from 1.55 to 1.71, depending on the number of years used to calculate the average.

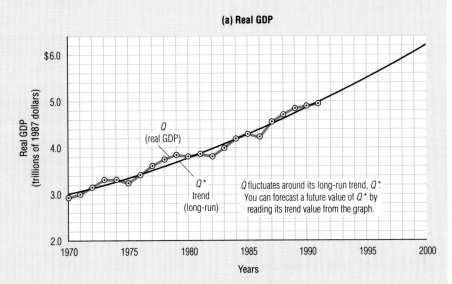

(a) Real GDP

Q (real GDP)

Q* trend (long-run)

Q fluctuates around its long-run trend, *Q**. You can forecast a future value of *Q** by reading its trend value from the graph.

ILLUSTRATIVE CALCULATION: For 1990, M2 = \$3.33 trillion (which you can look up in the inside back cover of the book). Suppose that *V2** = 1.69 (the assumed average value of V2), and that *Q** = \$4.9 trillion [estimated from Figure (a)]. Then:

$$P^* = \frac{M2 \times V2^*}{Q^*} = \frac{\$3.33 \times 1.69}{\$4.9}$$

$$= 1.15, \text{ or } 115 \text{ in Figure (b)}$$

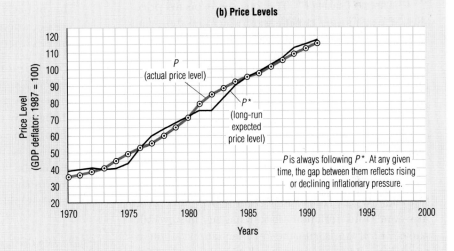

(b) Price Levels

P (actual price level)

P* (long-run expected price level)

P is always following *P**. At any given time, the gap between them reflects rising or declining inflationary pressure.

ing annual value of *M* (represented by *M2*). The resulting ratios are then averaged to obtain a single value for *V* (called *V2**).

Third, the Fed introduces a new symbol called "*Q*-star," written Q^*. This symbol represents the long-run trend value of *Q*—the economy's real GDP. The long-run trend value can be estimated for any year by reading it off the graph in Figure (a) of Exhibit 12.

Fourth, the Fed uses *M2*, V^*, and Q^* to define a new variable called "*P*-star," written P^*. This symbol represents the long-run expected price level. Its graph is shown in Figure (b) of Exhibit 12.

Based on these modifications, the Fed provides a

revised equation of exchange called the ***P-star equation***:

$$P^* = \frac{M2 \times V2^*}{Q^*} \quad \text{or} \quad P^* = M2\left(\frac{V2^*}{Q^*}\right)$$

The equation links the long-run expected price level P^* to the money growth rate *M2*. This is emphasized by the equation on the right. The reason for the linkage is that the velocity of money (*V2*) is always tending toward its average value $V2^*$, and real GDP (or *Q*) is always tending toward its long-run trend value Q^*. Therefore, changes in P^* depend on the remaining variable, *M2*, which is strongly influenced by monetary policy.

Forecasting With P^*

The P-star equation is easy to use. All it requires is a substitution of values for $M2$, V^*, and Q^*, and some simple arithmetic. The equation is a convenient tool for the Fed to use in forecasting how changes in the rate of money growth will affect inflation. However, the Fed interprets the equation in light of the gap between the actual and expected price levels that you saw in Figure (b) of Exhibit 12. The Fed keeps two facts in mind:

1.   Changes in Determinants Cause Price Gaps   The long-run expected price level, P^*, is a function of $M2$. The short-run or actual price level, P, is determined by the intersection of the economy's aggregate demand and aggregate supply curves. Both sets of determinants change frequently. Consequently, there's usually a *price gap*, or difference, between P^* and P. The size of the gap normally varies from year to year.

2.   *P* is Always Chasing *P**   The long-run expected price level, P^*, is a moving target toward which the short-run or actual price level, P, is always tending. If P^* is per-sistently greater than P, it means that the current mon-ey supply $M2$ is growing too fast relative to potential real output. Therefore, inflation will increase *after a time lag* as P rises toward P^*. Conversely, if P^* is persistently less than P, the money supply is growing too slowly relative to potential real output. Therefore, inflation will de-crease *after a time lag* as P declines toward P^*.

These interpretations of P and P^* suggest that the Fed can exercise substantial control over the price gap—and thus inflation—by managing the growth rate of $M2$. If this is true, the P-star equation can serve as a sole guide for monetary policy. Is this in fact the case? Here's what the evidence shows:

The chief strength of the P-star equation is that it helps the Fed assess long-term consequences of policy actions by suggesting the direction in which inflation will be moving. The chief weakness of the equation is that it often fails to predict short- or even intermedi-ate-term changes in the actual price level (P). The fail-ure to predict these changes occurs mainly because the velocity of $M2$ fluctuates relatively widely from year to year. Therefore, because of the equation's forecasting limitations, the Fed uses it in conjunction with various other indicators mentioned above as a guide for mone-tary policy.

Summing Up: Monetarism Today

We have analyzed the propositions of monetarism and the reasons that monetarists reject policy activism. We can now combine these ideas to summarize the mean-ing of monetarism.

Monetarism is a theory of the relationship between changes in the monetary growth rate and changes in the price level. Among the main propositions of mon-etarism are these:

1.   People want money for what it will buy—for its purchasing power. The public's demand for money is thus a demand for *real cash balances*.

2.   The amount of money, or real cash balances, peo-ple want to hold varies *directly* with expected aver-age long-run aggregate income (GDP) and *in-versely* with expected interest rates.

3.   The velocity of money is influenced strongly by the public's *expectations of inflation*. Velocity in-creases when people expect prices to rise, and de-creases when people expect prices to fall.

4.   The economy is always tending toward *full-employment equilibrium*. Therefore, changes in the monetary growth rate are the primary cause of changes in the price level, which in turn cause changes in *nominal* GDP. Because monetary-policy activism is thus a chief source of instability, it should be avoided. Instead, the rate of money growth should be governed by rules (such as the money-supply rule), not by central bank discretion.

Monetarists believe that the consequences of changes in the monetary growth rate on the price level are often *long and variable*. **They also agree that politi-cal and economic shocks, such as wars or sharp in-creases in world oil prices, can be important factors contributing to inflation. However,** *monetarists contend that, over the long run, the rate of growth of the money supply has been the most significant determinant of inflation.*

How do these monetarist ideas accord with today's economic thinking? During the 1970s when there was a significant correlation between money growth and inflation, monetarist theory was in its heyday. But in the 1980s the relationship weakened: Money growth fluctuated widely while inflation was down. Many crit-ics thus concluded that monetarism was a dead the-ory—an idea whose time had gone.

But the critics were exaggerating. To say that monetarism is dead is to say that its origin as well as one of the most fundamental concepts of economics—the quantity theory of money—is dead. Few if any economists would make that contention. Monetarism has given economists and government policymakers an increased awareness of the role of money in the economy. Consequently, their views, even if not strictly monetarist, are often "monetaresque." Thus:

Instead of being adopted in their entirety, selected monetarist ideas have been added to the collection of theories that compete for the attention of policymakers in Washington. These theories, along with what seems politically expedient at the time, constitute today's mixed bag of economic policy.

Origins: How Monetarism Evolved

Monetarism expresses a relationship between money and prices. Belief in such a relationship goes back hundreds of years. In the seventeenth century, the great English physicist, Isaac Newton, hypothesized a connection between domestic prices and international gold movements. A century later, David Hume, an eminent English philosopher and a close friend of Adam Smith, attributed rapid price increases to "new gold importations and coinage thereof." During the nineteenth century, many economic and political writers accounted for the occurrence of steep inflations by explaining them in terms of excessive money growth.

Despite the long-held belief in a link between money and prices, it was not until the twentieth century that economists began to understand the link. Two scholars responsible for providing that understanding were Irving Fisher and Milton Friedman.

Fisher: The First Monetarist

Irving Fisher, a professor of economics at Yale University, was one of America's foremost economists of the early twentieth century. A mathematician as well as economist, he wrote twenty-eight books and dozens of articles in professional journals. Of his books, eighteen were on diverse areas of economics and statistics. The remainder consisted of some widely used mathematics textbooks and several volumes on diet and

Irving Fisher
(1867–1947)

health—subjects that interested him because he contracted tuberculosis at the age of 31.

During his youth, Fisher was strongly influenced by one of his father's closest friends, a physician named John Kellogg. A strict vegetarian, Dr. Kellogg founded the famous breakfast cereal company that bears his name. The association with Kellogg made Fisher a fanatical believer in proper nutrition. After recovering from tuberculosis, Fisher wrote his most widely read book, *How to Live: Rules for Healthful Living Based on Modern Science*. The book was an astounding success, and it went through more than ninety editions. But despite its subtitle, the book revealed a side of Fisher's thinking that was more zealotry than science. In the book, Fisher offered such prescriptions as correct posture, comfortable shoes, and thorough chewing of food as essential conditions for good health and long life.

Fisher was also an inventor. He created new scientific mapping methods, power-driven mechanisms, and mechanical devices. Only one of his inventions achieved wide commercial acceptance—a card index system mounted on a rotary stand. Fisher established a company to market the product. The company subsequently merged with other firms to become, in 1926, the nation's largest typewriter manufacturer, the Remington Rand Corporation. Before selling his rights to the invention, Fisher earned more than $1 million in royalties, which he parlayed into $9 million in the stock market. He lost it all in the crash of 1929. But his invention, which has since been owned and sold by several businesses, is still in wide use. Today it is marketed in both mechanical and electronic versions under the name Rolodex.

Equation of Exchange

As an economist, Fisher is renowned for his contributions to the theory of money, interest, and prices. One of these contributions is his famous equation of exchange, $MV = PQ$. Formulated in the early 1900s, almost three decades before national-income concepts and data became available, the equation states an identity between aggregate income and aggregate output.

Fisher used his equation to explain a cause-and-effect relationship between the quantity of money (M) and the price level (P). He assumed that the velocity of circulation (V) and the quantity of the economy's final output (Q) were constant—or at least that they always tended rapidly toward equilibrium. Therefore, he concluded, if there is "a doubling in the quantity of money . . . it follows necessarily and mathematically that the level of prices must double." Or, in general, *"one of the normal effects of an increase in the quantity of money is an exactly proportional increase in the general level of prices."* From this it is evident, according to Fisher, that business cycles are not inherent in the economy but are due almost entirely to excessive expansions and contractions in the money supply—"especially in the form of bank loans."

Today the belief that a link exists between money growth and prices is universally held. However, because Fisher was the first to propose the nature of the link, he has sometimes been referred to as "the first monetarist."

Friedman: America's Best-Known Monetarist

Fisher completed his major work in economics during the 1930s. Picking up where Fisher left off, Milton Friedman helped carry the torch of classical monetary theory during the latter half of the twentieth century. Through his professorship at the University of Chicago and his publications both scientific and popular, Friedman became one of the most influential economists of our time. He was awarded the Nobel Prize for economics in 1976. Today he is at the Hoover Institution at Stanford University.

Since Adam Smith's formulation of classical economic theory more than two centuries ago, the free market has held widespread credence among economists. But Friedman goes further. He holds the unshakable conviction that the free market is the best mechanism ever conceived for allocating society's resources and for ordering human affairs.

Milton Friedman
(1912–   )

Much of Friedman's reputation is based on his approach to money and his founding of modern monetarist theory during the 1960s. Using carefully documented research going back to the late nineteenth century, he argued that the crucial factor affecting economic trends has been the quantity of money in circulation. As a fervent believer in free markets, Friedman opposes the use of discretionary monetary policy by the Federal Reserve to achieve economic stability. Instead he advocates a *money supply rule*—an expansion of the nation's money supply at a steady rate in accordance with the economy's growth and capacity to produce. Friedman gives four major reasons for this view:

1. Past Performance of the Fed Throughout its history, the Fed has proclaimed that it was using its monetary powers to promote economic stability. But the record often shows the opposite. Despite its good intentions, the Fed has often permitted the quantity of money to expand and contract erratically. Therefore, the urgent need is to prevent the Fed from being a source of economic disturbance.

2. Limitation of Our Knowledge Economic research has established two propositions:

a. There are close, regular, and predictable relationships among the quantity of money, national income, and prices over a number of years. Therefore, a stable price level over the long run requires that the quantity of money grow at a fairly steady rate roughly equal to the average rate of growth of the nation's output—its real GDP.

b. The relationship between the quantity of money and economic activity is much looser in the short run (from month to month or from quarter to quarter) than it is over a number of years. Therefore, any attempt to use monetary policy for fine-tuning the economy is bound to create economic instability because not enough is known about short-run relationships between money and prices.

3. Promotion of Confidence An announced, and adhered to, policy of steady monetary growth would provide the business sector with a firm basis for confidence in monetary stability. No discretionary policy could produce such confidence even if it happened to produce roughly steady monetary growth.

4. Neutralization of the Fed An independent Fed is at times too removed from political pressures and at other times unduly affected by them. A money-supply rule would insulate monetary policy from the arbitrary power of a small group of people (the Fed's appointed officials) not subject to control by the electorate, and from the short-run pressures of partisan politics.

Feasible Policy

Is the adoption of a money-supply rule technically feasible? Friedman claims that it is. Although he admits that the Fed could not achieve a precise rate of growth in the money supply from day to day or from week to week, it could come very close from month to month and quarter to quarter. If and when it does, he says, it will provide a monetary climate favorable to economic stability and orderly growth. And that, Friedman concludes, is the most we can ask from monetary policy at our present state of knowledge.

Summary of Important Ideas

1. The equation of exchange is $MV = PQ$. It states, in effect, that the economy's gross domestic income (which is the same as MV) is spent on purchasing the economy's gross domestic product (which is the same as PQ). The equation is thus a truism or identity because it tells us that the same flow of money can be looked at either from the buyer's or the seller's point of view.

2. The quantity theory of money assumes that the velocity of money and the volume of output are constant. Therefore, in terms of the equation of exchange, changes in the general price level are directly proportional to changes in the quantity of money.

3. Modern quantity theorists take into account the fact that the velocity of money varies. But they believe that fluctuations in V are determined by the public's expectations. Therefore, modern quantity theorists focus much of their attention on the conditions that influence the public's expectations and on the changes in the money supply as a determinant of GDP.

4. The interest rate affects the business sector's decision to invest. The rate of interest, as explained by the loanable-funds theory of interest, is determined by market forces of supply and demand between lenders and borrowers.

5. In classical theory, the market, or nominal, rate of interest is not necessarily the same as the real rate. The market rate will depart from the real rate if the public expects the general price level to rise or decline. Any differential between the market rate and the real rate represents an "inflation premium." This may be either positive or negative. It is the amount necessary to compensate lenders or borrowers for anticipated changes in purchasing power resulting from inflation or deflation.

6. Monetary policy consists of changes in the rate of growth of the money supply. Such changes can affect interest rates, business investment, and, consequently, the level of aggregate expenditure. Monetary policy can thus be a mechanism for causing inflations and recessions.

7. Monetarist beliefs are rooted in the classical quantity theory of money and the equation of exchange, $MV = PQ$. However, monetarists reinterpret the quantity theory as a theory of the demand for *real* cash balances.

8. Monetarism contends that the demand for money—that is, the demand for real cash balances—depends mainly on aggregate income and on interest rates. The relationship between this demand and aggregate income is *direct;* the relationship between this demand and interest rates is *inverse.* Under normal conditions both relationships tend to be stable.

9. The velocity of money is strongly influenced by the public's expectations. It increases when the public expects prices to rise, and decreases when the public expects prices to fall.

10. The transmission mechanism is viewed by monetarists as a portfolio-adjustment process. That is, people spend their excess money balances on a wide range of both consumer and investment goods.

11. Monetarists believe that the economy is inherently self-correcting. They also believe that an activist monetary policy impedes the self-correction process and causes instability. They therefore conclude that monetary policy should be based on rules and not left to the discretion of the Fed. Although the money-supply rule has received the widest attention, monetary targeting has also been strongly advocated.

12. The Fed contends that the economy is too complex to be guided by simple rules. Reserve officials monitor many economic indicators and base monetary policies on judgments of economic trends.

13. Monetarism is rooted in the work of Irving Fisher, an early twentieth-century scholar and leading American economist. Monetarist theory was developed during the 1960s, largely by Milton Friedman. The theory criticizes the Fed as a chief source of instability, and concludes that a stable money growth rate is the best means of promoting steady economic expansion.

Terms and Concepts to Review

income velocity of money	*Fisher effect*
equation of exchange	*GDP deflator*
quantity theory of money	*transmission mechanism*
interest	*money-supply rule*
real rate of interest	*monetary targeting*
market rate of interest	*yield curve*
inflation premium	*monetary base*
loanable funds	*federal funds rate*
loanable funds theory of interest	*P-star equation*
	monetarism

Questions and Problems

1. Suppose that the Federal Reserve buys securities in the open market and that the securities are sold by nonbanks, such as individuals and corporations. As a result of this transaction alone, what will be the *initial* directions of change, if any, of *M, P, Q,* and *V* (in that order) and *MV* in the equation *MV = PQ?* Explain.

2. In terms of the equation *MV = PQ,* what are likely to be the effects on *P, Q,* and *PQ* if there is a large increase in the money supply under conditions of (a) substantial unemployment, or (b) high or full employment? Explain your answer.

3. Suppose the interest rate on short-term loans is the same as that on long-term loans. What are the advantages and disadvantages to lenders of being in short-term as opposed to long-term investments?

Answer questions 4 and 5 together.

4. "Increases in aggregate demand have a greater effect on real output than on the price level." Construct an aggregate demand/aggregate supply graph that illustrates this proposition. For convenience, *assume that the* AS *curve is a straight line.* On the basis of your graph, is monetary expansion more effective for combatting recessions or inflations?

5. "Increases in aggregate demand have a greater effect on the price level than on real output." As in the previous question, construct an *AD/AS* graph that illustrates this proposition. Assume that the *AS* curve is a straight line. What does your graph imply about monetary expansion aimed at eliminating recession? What about monetary contraction aimed at reducing inflation?

6. Assuming that all other things remain the same, state whether the interest rate is likely to rise or fall as a result of each of the following. Explain why. *Suggestion*: Sketch supply-and-demand diagrams to help you arrive at your answers.

a. An increase in credit purchases by the household sector

b. Expectations of a recession by the business sector

c. The incurrence of a large budget deficit by the government sector

d. Expectations of a recession in Europe and Japan

e. An increase in profits by the business sector

f. An increase in individual income taxes

g. The incurrence of a large budget surplus by the government sector

h. Efforts by the Fed to curb inflationary pressures

7. The velocity of money varies directly with interest rates. Can you explain why? (Think in terms of opportunity cost and the effects of inflation.)

8. Erratic growth of the money supply may cause more instability than rapid but steady growth. Can you explain why?

9. If the money supply increased at a steady rate of 3 to 4 percent a year, would business cycles still occur? How would monetarists answer this question?

10. There is a close relationship between nominal GDP and the money supply. Can you offer an explanation as to why either one may be the cause of the other?

11. "The Fed cannot simultaneously control both the money supply and interest rates." Is this statement true? Explain.

12. How does Fisher's original equation of exchange compare to the P* equation?

13. Is the Fed's P* equation consistent with monetarist theory? Why or why not?

14. Forecasting P* (*Refer to the graphs, formula, and illustrative calculation in Exhibit 12.*) Can you forecast P* for a future year? To do so, you must first forecast M2 so that you can use it in the formula. *Suggestion:* On a sheet of graph paper, make a freehand graphic projection of the long-run trend of M2. (If you have access to a computer with a graphing program, it may be able to make the projection for you.) Use the last 10 years of figures from the inside back cover of the book as a basis for your projection. Using the P* formula, make a high, medium, and low forecast of P* by assuming three widely different average values of V2* between 1.55 and 1.71. Show the results of the forecasts on a graph of P* covering the same 10-year period as M2.

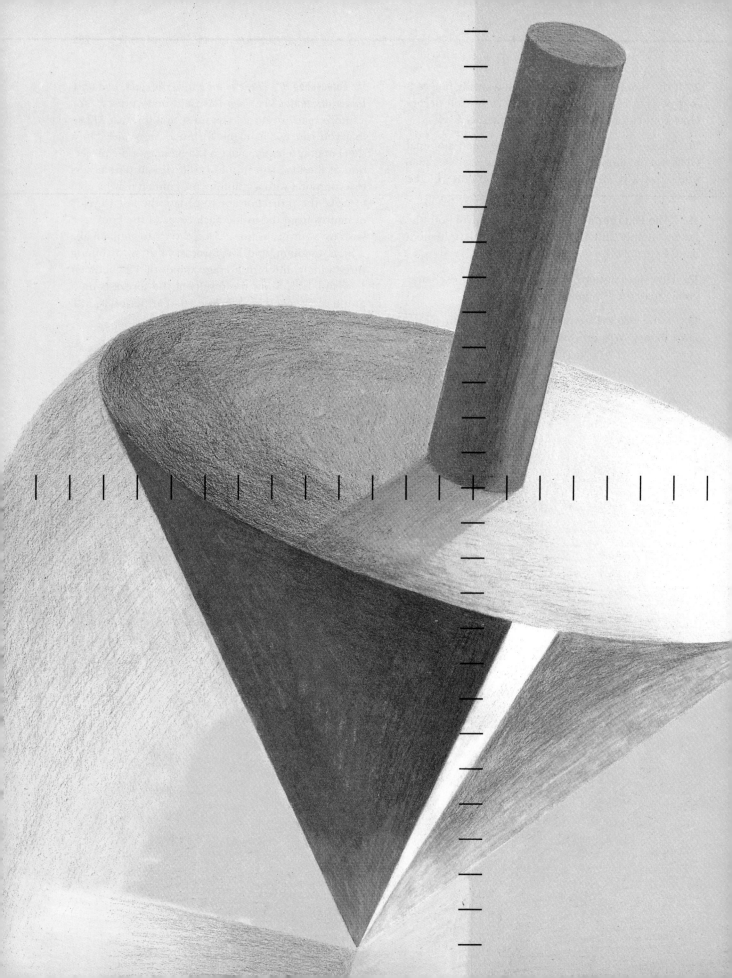

Part 4

Unemployment, Fiscal Policy, and Macroeconomic Equilibrium

Chapter 13

Lapses from Full Employment: The Basic Keynesian Model

The Keynesian Response to Classical Theory
Consumption Expenditure
Private Investment Expenditure
Government Expenditure and Net Foreign Expenditure
The Income-Expenditure Model
Origins: Keynesian Economics

Learning Guide

Watch for answers to these important questions

What are the basic beliefs of early classical macroeconomics? How does Keynesian economics respond to these beliefs?

What relationships exist between consumption and income? Between saving and income? How do changes in income affect consumption and saving?

What is investment? How is investment expenditure related to the interest rate?

How are imports related to aggregate income?

What contributions did John Maynard Keynes make to the study of macroeconomics? Why were they considered revolutionary?

With perfectly free competition . . . there will always be a strong tendency toward full employment. The implication is that such unemployment as exists at any time is due wholly to the fact that frictional resistances (caused by monopolistic unions and firms maintaining rigid wages and prices) prevent the appropriate wage and price adjustments from being made instantaneously.

So wrote the early twentieth-century English classical economist Arthur C. Pigou, in a book entitled *The Theory of Unemployment* (1933). Pigou was interpreting economic conditions of the 1930s—a decade in which the world was caught in the throes of a deep depression. Commonly referred to as the Great Depression, it was the longest and most painful economic setback of modern history.

For example, at the bottom of the business cycle in 1933, approximately 25 percent of the labor force was unemployed. For the remainder of the decade, unemployment never dropped below 14 percent of the labor force. Comparable rates of unemployment existed in the United Kingdom and other European countries during this period.

Such severe and prolonged unemployment obviously contradicted classical (traditional) thinking, which held that *the economy is rapidly self-correcting*. As a result, many economists of that era were inclined to explain away the inconsistency between theory and reality by saying that it was the "world" and not the theory that was at fault. A flexible wage and price policy, Pigou and other classical economists contended, "would abolish fluctuations of employment entirely." In America, many prominent economists added the specific proviso that the government under President Franklin Delano Roosevelt's administration should stop interfering with the free operation of the markets through extensive regulatory legislation and activities.

In response, an eminent British scholar named John Maynard Keynes (pronounced "canes") published a treatise entitled *The General Theory of Employment, Interest and Money* (1936). In this landmark book, Keynes strongly criticized the classical theory and formulated a theory of his own. This new theory soon revolutionized economic thinking and became, for several decades, a major foundation for the study of macroeconomics.

Much of modern macroeconomic theory is still rooted in the work done by Keynes. But in addition, a good deal of non-Keynesian thinking has been integrated into today's macroeconomics. The remainder of this chapter deals with the basic macroeconomic relationships that Keynes and later economists developed. Subsequent chapters will bring the relationship together and build on them with certain non-Keynesian ideas. The result will be a comprehensive view of macroeconomics as it exists today.

The Keynesian Response to Classical Theory

At the heart of early classical macroeconomics is the belief that the economy is rapidly self-correcting. This belief, as you have learned, is based on three major assumptions:

- **Say's Law: Supply Creates Its Own Demand** This proposition means that for the economy as a whole, total income earned from production is spent to buy the goods and services produced.

- **All Savings Are Invested** Because the interest rate is flexible, it adjusts quickly to ensure that the household sector's savings become the business sector's borrowing for investment.

- **Prices and Wages Are Flexible** This results in the prices and quantities of goods and labor adjusting automatically to their equilibrium levels through the free play of market forces.

These classical assumptions lead to the conclusion that the economy's markets always clear quickly, leaving no surpluses or shortages.

Exhibit 1 reviews the reasoning behind the classicists' belief that the independent operation of demand and supply causes markets to reach full, or natural, employment.

How does Keynesian macroeconomic theory contrast with classical theory? We can best answer this question by formulating the arguments Keynes used to attack the classicists' reasoning. As you read these arguments, keep in mind that they were developed during the Great Depression of the 1930s.

Aggregate Expenditure May Not Equal Full-Employment Aggregate Income

Keynesian theory rejects the classical contention that aggregate expenditure (total spending) always equals *full-employment* aggregate income. It also rejects the contention that the economic system is always rapidly self-correcting. Indeed, Keynesian theory demonstrates that the economic system may be in equilibrium at less than full employment for prolonged periods of time.

Changes in aggregate expenditure play a critical role in Keynesian theory. An economy may be operating at a level equal to or below full employment. If the economy experiences a drop in aggregate expenditure, there will be a consequent decline in real output and resource use. If the economy experiences an increase in aggregate expenditure, there will be a consequent rise in real output and resource use. And if aggregate expenditure continues to increase above full-employment levels, the result will be rising prices without any corresponding increase in real output and resource use.

Savers and Investors Are Different People with Different Motivations

Keynesian theory also rejects the classical view of saving and investment.

Keynes pointed out that in an advanced economy, *saving and investing are undertaken by different groups for different reasons.*

In our own economy, for example, households such as yours and mine may save for any of several reasons: to purchase a new car, to finance an education, to make a down payment on a house, or to pay for a vacation. Households may also save to provide for future security, to amass an estate that can be passed on to fu-

EXHIBIT
1

Reviewing Some Microeconomic Foundations of Macroeconomics

Among the microeconomic foundations of macroeconomics is the idea that prices and quantities in specific markets adjust by themselves. For example, suppose the price in any market happens to be either at P' or at P''. The interaction of demand-and-supply forces in that market will cause the price to move automatically and relatively rapidly to its equilibrium level at P. At the same time the quantity in that market will change as the price changes. When the adjustments are completed in all markets, all quantities and all prices will be at their equilibrium levels, determined by the equilibrium point E. There will be no shortages or surpluses. This means that there will be full, or natural, employment. Thus, the economy is self-correcting.

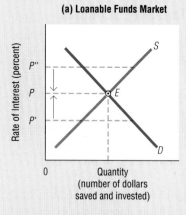

(a) Loanable Funds Market

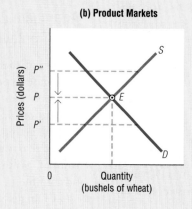

(b) Product Markets

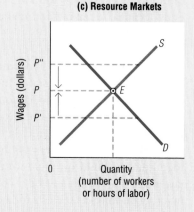

(c) Resource Markets

ture generations, or to buy stocks and bonds for income or future profit. And, of course, many households may save simply to accumulate funds without a specific purpose in mind.

Business firms save when they retain part of their net profits rather than distribute them to stockholders. A firm's reasons for saving, however, are different from those of a household. Businesses usually save in order to invest in factories, equipment, and inventories; they may also borrow for the same purposes. In any case, they invest primarily on the basis of the rate of profit they anticipate. Summarizing:

Both households and businesses save. However, their motivations are different. Households save in order to accumulate funds for a variety of purposes. Businesses save in order to invest in factories, equipment, and inventories. The amount that businesses want to save for investment fluctuates widely from year to year and is not likely to equal the amount households choose to save. The interest rate, therefore, is not a mechanism that brings about the equality of saving and investment at *full employment*, as the classicists assumed.

Many Prices and Wages Are Sticky

Finally, Keynes argued that prices and wages do not always exhibit the flexibility that the classicists assumed. In a variety of important industries, prices are established by firms that have considerable monopoly power in their respective markets. In addition, wage rates in numerous industries are established by contracts between employees and employers. As a result, many prices and wages tend to be "sticky" rather than flexible.[*]

Sticky prices and wages cause output and employment to bear the brunt of changes in total spending. For example, in the early stages of a recession when total spending is declining, we often hear of production being cut and workers being laid off. But we seldom hear of prices and wages going down. If they went down sufficiently, the recession would be mild and short-lived because output and employment would remain close to their full-employment levels.

---

[*]Recall from Chapter 7 that economists customarily use the term "sticky" when referring to prices, wages, or other variables that are relatively inflexible.

Nevertheless, let's assume for the moment that wages and prices are flexible and that the fall in wages during a period of unemployment is greater than the fall in prices. This is what the classical economists postulated. If the wage decreases (relative to prices) are experienced by one firm only, the firm's profits will increase and it will be encouraged to expand its production and employment. But, Keynes pointed out, suppose wage decreases (in relation to prices) are experienced by *all* firms in the economy. In that case, *real wages* (that is, money wages relative to the general price level) or general purchasing power will decline. The result is likely to be a further reduction in output and employment instead of the reverse. To summarize:

A reduction in *real* wages within a single firm isn't likely to affect buyers' expenditures for that firm's product. However, it can't be assumed that a general reduction in *real* wages of *all* workers throughout the economy will have no effect on *aggregate* expenditures.

Modern Keynesian Conclusion: Self-Correction May Take a Long Time

In contrast to classical and early Keynesian belief, today's Keynesian theory puts forward these ideas:

A modern capitalistic economy provides no assurance of a rapid adjustment toward full employment. The decade-long Great Depression of the 1930s, a number of long recessions since then, and the many years in which the unemployment rate has exceeded its natural rate have demonstrated this. Therefore, even if the classical argument that the economy self-corrects—that is, adjusts to full employment—is true, history shows that it may take a relatively long time to do so.

In this and the next several chapters we'll be examining the implications of these views. Before doing so, it helps to emphasize two Keynesian concepts that were implied above and will be demonstrated later.

1. The level of aggregate output is determined by the level of aggregate expenditure.

2. The level of aggregate expenditure may not always be high enough to ensure a full-employment level of aggregate output.

Aggregate expenditure thus plays a critical role in Keynesian theory. What is aggregate expenditure? It

can often be thought of simply as total spending. But now a more precise definition is needed. **Aggregate expenditure** is the sum of desired or planned spending that will be undertaken at each aggregate-income level by all sectors of the economy. Aggregate expenditure is thus made up of spending by the household, business, government, and foreign sectors. Let's see what these expenditures entail.

Consumption Expenditure

The household sector spends its income on consumer goods and services. Such spending, called simply **consumption,** is by far the largest component of aggregate expenditure. What factors determine consumption?

Take your own case. What determines the amount your family spends on goods and services? You can probably think of many determinants. First and foremost is your family's disposable income—the amount it has left after paying personal taxes. The situation is much the same for other families.

Disposable income is usually the single most important determinant of a family's consumption expenditures.

Other determinants will also have some influence on a family's consumption. These include the family's previous income levels, its expectations of future income, its expectations of future prices, the size of the family, and the ages of its members.

The Propensity to Consume

No two families spend their incomes in exactly the same way. However, the relationship between a family's disposable income and its consumption expenditures is illustrated by the schedule in the first two columns of Exhibit 2. In this table, *prices are assumed to be constant.* This assumption enables you to compare the family's spending with its real (rather than its nominal) income. The difference between disposable income and consumption is the family's saving, which is shown in column (3). Notice that, as disposable income increases, consumption increases and so does saving.

The consumption and saving data are graphed in Exhibit 3. Let's consider the upper figure first. Note that consumption expenditures are measured on the vertical axis and disposable income is measured on the horizontal. Observe also that both axes are drawn to

EXHIBIT
2

Schedule of a Family's Consumption and Saving in Relation to Income
(annual data in constant dollars, that is, prices are assumed to be constant)

This table illustrates the relationship between consumption and income. The figures show that, as the family's disposable income increases, the amount it spends on consumption and the amount it saves also increase. The meanings of the various columns are explained in the text.

(1) Disposable income (after taxes), *DI*	(2) Consumption *C*	(3) Saving, *S* (1) – (2)	(4) Average propensity to consume, *APC* (2) ÷ (1)	(5) Average propensity to save, *APS* (3) ÷ (1)	(6) Marginal propensity to consume, *MPC* Change in (2) / Change in (1)	(7) Marginal propensity to save, *MPS* Change in (3) / Change in (1)
$16,000	$18,400	–$2,400	1.15	–0.15		
20,000	21,200	–1,200	1.06	–0.06	0.70	0.30
24,000	24,000	0	1.00	0.00	0.70	0.30
28,000	26,800	1,200	0.96	0.04	0.70	0.30
32,000	29,600	2,400	0.93	0.07	0.70	0.30
36,000	32,400	3,600	0.90	0.10	0.70	0.30
40,000	35,200	4,800	0.88	0.12	0.70	0.30
44,000	38,000	6,000	0.86	0.14	0.70	0.30
48,000	40,800	7,200	0.85	0.15	0.70	0.30

* The *consumption function* is assumed to be expressed by the equation $C = \$7,200 + 0.7\,DI$. Thus, if disposable income (*DI*) is zero, the family's consumption expenditures (*C*) is $7,200. This amount, as explained in the text, can be financed by dissaving, borrowing, or by being subsidized.

the same scale. Therefore, the 45 degree diagonal is the line along which consumption *C* is 100 percent of disposable income *DI*. That is, the ratio *C/DI* = 1.

The consumption curve *C* is the graph of the data in columns (1) and (2) of the table in Exhibit 2. The intersection of this curve with the diagonal line is the "break-even point." This is the point at which a family's consumption exactly equals its disposable income. At this level the family is just getting by, neither borrowing nor saving.

To the right of the break-even point, the family is consuming less than its income. The vertical distance between the consumption line and the diagonal represents *saving*. It is that part of income not spent on consumption. To the left of the break-even point, the family is consuming more than its disposable income. The difference is called *dissaving*. It is the amount by which consumption exceeds income. How does a family dissave or live beyond its means? By spending its previous savings, by borrowing, or by receiving gifts from others (that is, by being subsidized).

Here are some important ideas to remember:
The level of consumption depends on the level of disposable income. As income increases, consumption increases, but not as fast as income. This relationship between consumption and income is called the *propensity to consume*, or the *consumption function*. The word "function" is thus used here in its mathematical sense. It means a quantity whose value depends on the value of another quantity. (For example, we say that the amount of consumption depends on, or is a function of, the level of income).

EXHIBIT
3

A Family's Consumption and Saving in Relation to Income

(annual data in constant dollars)

The vertical distances show how much will be consumed and saved at each income level, according to the figures in Exhibit 2. For example, at an income of $44,000, the amount spent on consumption is $38,000 and the amount saved is $6,000.

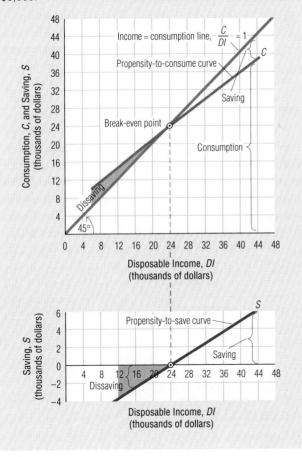

The Propensity to Save

You know that saving is the difference between income and consumption. You also know that consumption depends on income. Therefore, you may correctly conclude that saving depends on income. (Keep in mind that the term "income" as used here means *disposable income*.)

The data on saving from column (3) of the table in Exhibit 2, taken together with the data in column (1), are shown in the graph in the lower panel of Exhibit 3. Here, disposable income is again measured on the horizontal axis, but saving alone is now measured vertically. The saving curve S depicts the vertical differences between the diagonal line and the consumption curve in the upper chart. As you can see:

The level of saving depends on the level of income. This relationship between saving and income is called the *propensity to save* **or the** *saving function.*

Thus, the saving curve S is the propensity-to-save curve.

Average Propensities to Consume and to Save

On the average, how much of each dollar of its disposable income will the family spend on consumption? How much will it save? The answers to these questions are given in columns (4) and (5) of Exhibit 2.

The *average propensity to consume (APC)* is the proportion of its disposable income the family will spend on consumption at each income level. It's simply the ratio of consumption to income:

$$APC = \frac{\text{consumption}}{\text{income}}$$

Similarly, the *average propensity to save (APS)* is the proportion of its disposable income the family will save at each income level. It's the ratio of saving to income:

$$APS = \frac{\text{saving}}{\text{income}}$$

For example, at an income level of $40,000, the family will spend 88 cents of each dollar or a total of $35,200. It will save 12 cents of each dollar, or a total of $4,800. In other words, the family will spend 88 percent of its income and save 12 percent.

Note that as income increases, *APC* decreases. Therefore, *APS* increases because both must total 1 (or 100 percent) at each income level. What can you learn from the fact the *APC* declines with rising in-

Note that the consumption curve C is the family's propensity-to-consume curve. It assumes that, apart from income, *all other conditions that may affect consumption remain constant.* What are these "other" conditions? The most important are (1) the family's previous income levels, (2) its expectations of future income, and (3) its expectations of future prices. These conditions are assumed constant because they are the ones that change most often in the relatively short run.

comes? Basically, this tendency confirms the everyday observation that the rich save a larger proportion of their incomes than the poor.

Marginal Propensities to Consume and to Save

It usually isn't enough to know the proportion of its income that a family will spend on consumption and the proportion it will save. For government policymaking purposes, it may be even more important to know how much of each extra dollar of income a family will spend on consumption and how much of that dollar the family will save. These amounts are called the *marginal propensity to consume* and *the marginal propensity to save*. They are shown in columns (6) and (7) of Exhibit 2.

In column (6), the **marginal propensity to consume (MPC)** is the change in consumption resulting from a unit change in income. The *MPC* tells you the *fraction of each extra dollar of income that will go into consumption*. As you can see from the table, the formula for calculating *MPC* is

$$MPC = \frac{\text{change in consumption}}{\text{change in income}}$$

As shown in the table, an *MPC* of 0.70 means that 70 percent of any *increase* in income will be spent on consumption.

Referring to column (7) the **marginal propensity to save (MPS)** is the change in saving resulting from a unit change in income. The *MPS* tells you the *fraction of each extra dollar of income that will go into saving*.

$$MPS = \frac{\text{change in saving}}{\text{change in income}}$$

As shown in the table, an *MPS* of 0.30 means that 30 percent of any *increase* in income will be saved.

What is the difference between *APC* and *MPC*? What is the difference between *APS* and *MPS*? At any given level of income, the *APC* relates *total* consumption to *total* income, while the *MPC* relates a *change* in the amount of consumption to a *change* in the amount of income. The "average" may thus be quite different from the "marginal," as you can see from the table in Exhibit 2. The same kind of reasoning applies to the difference between *APS* and *MPS*. The "average" tells you about totals while the "marginal" tells you about changes. Note from the table, however, that just as *APC* plus *APS* must always total 1 (or 100 percent) at any *level* of income, *MPC* plus *MPS* must always total 1 (or 100 percent) for each *change* in income.

The *MPC* and *MPS* are of great practical value. They can tell you, for instance, the amount by which disposable income must increase in order to bring about a desired increase in spending. For example, suppose that the nation is in recession and the *MPC* for the economy as a whole is 0.70. This means that to increase the volume of consumption by $700 million in order to move the economy closer to full employment, the level of aggregate disposable income must be raised by $1 billion. As you'll see in later chapters, government often adopts various economic measures in an effort to achieve such a goal.

"Marginals" Are Slopes

By now you may have recognized an important feature of *MPC*. Because it's the change in total consumption resulting from a unit change in income, it measures the **slope** of the consumption function or line. Similarly, the *MPS* measures the slope of the saving line. Let's recall what you learned about slope in the Introduction to the book. The slope of any straight line is defined as the number of units it changes vertically for each unit it changes horizontally. This is shown in Exhibit 4. Observe that the line rises 4 units on the vertical axis for a run of 6 units on the horizontal. Therefore, the slope, which is the rise over the run, is 2/3.

You should be able to verify that the slope of a straight line is the same at every point. This is why the table in Exhibit 2 shows all values of *MPC* as equal and all values of *MPS* as equal. That is, the consumption and saving functions in this example are each straight lines.

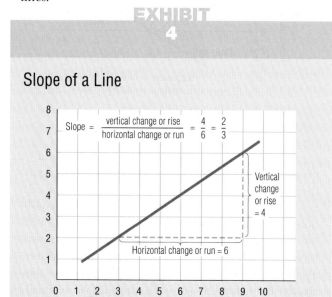

EXHIBIT 4

Slope of a Line

Two Kinds of Changes Involving Consumption

The consumption function (the propensity-to-consume curve) expresses a relationship between consumption expenditures and income. Your understanding of this concept can serve as a basis for distinguishing between two kinds of variations in consumption. One is a change in the amount consumed. The other is a change in consumption.

Change in the Amount Consumed

Examine the graphs in Exhibit 5. In the upper graph, any movement along the consumption curve represents a *change in amount consumed.* The change will consist of an increase in the amount consumed if income rises and a decrease in the amount consumed if income falls. This is indicated by the vertical dashed lines. Thus:

- A movement to the right always signifies an increase in income and hence a movement upward along the existing C curve.

- A movement to the left indicates a decrease in income and therefore a movement downward along the existing C curve.

Note also in the lower figure that saving, like consumption, varies directly with income. Therefore, a change in the amount saved—either an increase or a decrease—occurs for the same reason as a change in the amount consumed. The reason, of course, is a *change in income.*

Change in Consumption

A second type of variation in consumption, shown in Exhibit 6, is a *change in consumption.* This may take the form of an increase in consumption, shown by a shift of the curve to a higher level. Or it may take the form of a decrease in consumption, shown by a shift of the curve to a lower level. An increase in consumption from curve C to curve C' means that, at any given level of income, people are now willing to consume more and save less than before. What does a decrease from curve C to curve C'' mean?

The consumption curve may shift as a result of a change in any one of the other consumption determinants that were assumed to remain constant when the curve was initially drawn. What are these determinants? Some of the more important ones are:

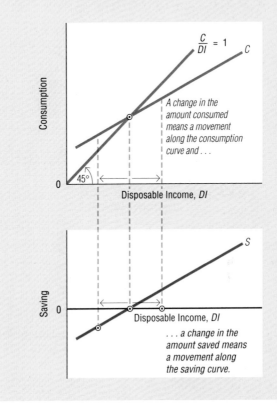

EXHIBIT 5

Changes in the Amounts Consumed and Saved
(variables are in constant dollars)

A change in the amount consumed means a movement along the consumption curve and . . .

. . . a change in the amount saved means a movement along the saving curve.

1. Expectations of future prices and incomes

2. The volume of liquid and financial assets (for example, cash, stocks, or bonds) owned by a household

3. Credit conditions—ease of borrowing money

4. Anticipation of product shortages (resulting, for example, from a war or a strike)

An increase in any one of these consumption determinants (and several others that you may be able to think of) can cause an increase in consumption that will shift the curve upward. Likewise, a decrease in any one can cause a decrease in consumption that will shift the curve downward. Because these determinants do not usually remain constant for very long, the *true* consumption function for the economy is likely to vary over a period of time.

EXHIBIT
6

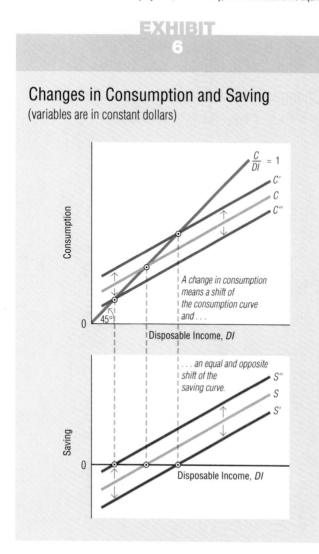

Changes in Consumption and Saving
(variables are in constant dollars)

A change in consumption means a shift of the consumption curve and . . .

. . . an equal and opposite shift of the saving curve.

Private Investment Expenditure

"The economy turns on capital investment; capital investment turns on confidence; confidence turns on certainty; and certainty turns on predictability." These words, spoken by the president of a major corporation, suggest that investment is of critical importance to our economy.

Investment, in this context, means spending by business firms on physical capital, such as additions to plant, equipment, inventories, and residential construction. As you know, the private sector's consumption expenditure and investment expenditure are the two major components of aggregate expenditure. Therefore, having studied consumption, we must now turn our attention to understanding investment.

If you were in business, what would determine your decision to invest? The fundamental answer, of course, is your profit expectation. If you think a new

machine will add sufficiently to your profit, you'll try to purchase it. If you believe that an extension to your factory will yield greater profits, you'll try to build it.

In the business world, the money you get back each year from an investment, in relation to the dollars invested, is called the *rate of return.* It's always expressed as a percentage. Thus, if you buy land for $1,000 and rent it out for $100 a year, the annual rate of return on your investment is 10 percent.

$$\text{Rate of return} = \frac{\text{annual receipts}}{\text{investment}}$$

$$= \frac{\$100}{\$1,000} = 0.10, \text{ or } 10\%$$

Understanding the *MEI*

The rate of return measures the profitability of an existing investment. More often, we want to know whether an *additional* (or "marginal") investment should be undertaken. The measure that businesses use for determining this is called, by economists, the "marginal efficiency of investment."

The *marginal efficiency of investment (MEI)* is the expected annual rate of return on an *additional* unit of a capital good. Thus, you might have an *MEI* or expected rate of return of 25 percent for one type of investment, 15 percent for another, and so on.

You can gain a better understanding of the *MEI* by studying the graph in Figure (a) of Exhibit 7. At any given time, a business firm is faced with a number of investment opportunities. These may include renovating its existing plant, purchasing new machines, acquiring additional power facilities, or installing a computer system. Each project competes for a firm's limited funds. However, some projects are expected to be more profitable—that is, to have a higher rate of return (or *MEI*)—than others. In view of this, which projects should management select? Or, to put it differently, how much investment expenditure should management undertake?

The first step in answering this question is to imagine that the managers of a firm *rank* alternative investment projects in decreasing order of their *MEI*s. Figure (a) graphs the costs and corresponding *MEI* for five investment projects being considered by Darcy Manufacturing, Inc. The most profitable investment open to the firm is the renovation of its plant at a cost of $2 million. For this, the firm anticipates a rate of return, or *MEI*, of 27 percent, which is read from the vertical axis. The next most profitable investment is the addition of a new wing to its factory at a cost of $1 mil-

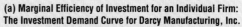

Investment Demand in the Private Sector

FIGURE (a) The stepped curve is the *MEI* (or rate-of-return) curve for one firm: Darcy Manufacturing Inc. The curve shows the amount of investment that Darcy Manufacturing will make at various interest rates or costs of funds at any given time. *This MEI curve is thus the firm's demand curve for investment.* In the economy as a whole, there are many such stepped curves at any given time, one for each firm.

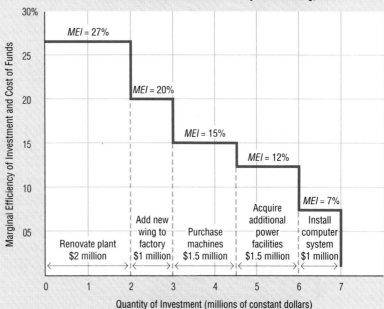

(a) Marginal Efficiency of Investment for an Individual Firm: The Investment Demand Curve for Darcy Manufacturing, Inc.

FIGURE (b) The *MEI* curve for all firms is a smooth line obtained by summing individual *MEI* curves. It shows the total amount of private-sector investment that will be made at various interest rates or costs of funds. Thus, *this MEI curve is the economy's aggregate demand curve D_I for investment.* Note that because this is the *MEI* curve for *all firms* in the economy, the horizontal axis in this figure measures *billions* of constant dollars.

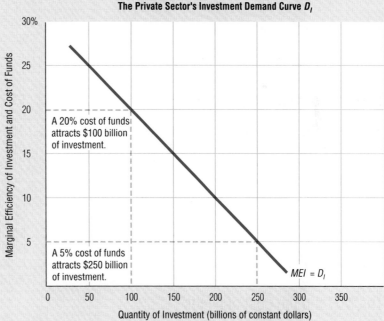

(b) Marginal Efficiency of Investment for All Firms: The Private Sector's Investment Demand Curve D_I

lion, for which the *MEI* is 20 percent. Each remaining investment project is interpreted in a similar manner. Let's assume that the risks of loss associated with these investments are the same. Then the descending order of *MEI*s can be used to interpret two principles that are very familiar to people in business:

1. Fewer investment opportunities are available to a firm at higher rates of return than at lower ones. For example, it's harder to find investments yielding 27 percent than to find investments yielding 7 percent.

2. A firm will tend to choose the most profitable investment projects. Therefore, a project with a higher *MEI* or anticipated rate of return is likely to be selected over a project with a lower one. Thus, Darcy Manufacturing will be more likely to purchase machines, which have an *MEI* of 15 percent, than to acquire additional power facilities, which have an *MEI* of 12 percent.

Cost of Funds: The Rate of Interest

Once the *MEI* (or rate of return) on an investment is estimated, the next step is to establish the cost of funds needed to finance the investment. Only then can the firm decide whether the investment is worth undertaking.

If a firm borrows money for an investment, it must pay the market interest rate. This annual interest rate is the firm's cost of funds. (If you take courses in finance, you'll find that the cost of funds is also called the *cost of capital*.) Alternatively, the firm may decide to use its retained earnings instead of borrowing. Does this mean that the money is "free"? Obviously not. The interest return the firm sacrifices by not lending the money in the financial markets (through the purchase of bonds or other securities) is its cost of funds. Because this cost reflects the benefit that the firm is forgoing, it's the **opportunity cost** of the firm's investment.

Like the *MEI*, the cost of funds is expressed as a percentage. Thus, the *MEI* and the cost of funds can be easily compared.

The *MEI* and the Cost of Funds

How much investment will the firm undertake? First, let's assume that the market interest rate represents the cost of funds to the firm. Therefore, the cost of funds will be the same whether the firm borrows the money or uses its own. Now, by comparing the *MEI*

and the cost of funds, we can determine how large an investment the firm will make.

A firm will invest in those projects for which the *MEI* exceeds the cost of funds.

For example, look again at Figure (a) of Exhibit 7. At a cost of funds (shown on the vertical axis) of, say 13 percent, Darcy Manufacturing would demand $4.5 million for investment. Of this amount, $2 million would be spent on renovating its plant in anticipation of a return or *MEI* of 27 percent. In addition, $1 million would be allocated to a new wing for its factory for an expected *MEI* of 20 percent. Finally, $1.5 million would be used to buy new machines in anticipation of an *MEI* of 15 percent. If the cost of funds should fall to 6 percent, Darcy will demand an *additional* $2.5 million, or a *total* of $7 million. The firm would invest the extra amount in the next two projects—the acquisition of power facilities and a computer system. In general, therefore, *the total amount of investment funds demanded by the firm depends on its MEI relative to the interest rate or cost of funds.*

This analysis leads to two important principles:

-   A demand curve relates the quantities that buyers will purchase at various prices. For business investments, the prices are interest rates (costs of funds) to firms. Hence, the *MEI* curve shows the amounts of investment that a firm will undertake at various interest rates. This is illustrated by the solid irregular or step-shaped line in Figure (a) of Exhibit 7. It follows that *a firm's MEI curve is its demand curve for investment.*

-   Each firm's *MEI* curve is based on its investment requirements and expectations. If the individual *MEI* curves of businesses are summed, we get the *MEI* curve for all firms in the economy. Because there are many firms, the steps disappear, giving a smooth line like the one in Figure (b) of Exhibit 7. The *aggregate MEI curve depicts total private investment demand at different rates of interest.* For example, at an interest rate of 20 percent, the amount of private-sector investment would be $100 billion. If the interest rate fell to 5 percent, the investment would increase to $250 billion.

Determinants of the *MEI*: Shifts of the Curve

The *MEI* curve, or D_I, curve, is an investment demand curve. Like any demand curve, it may shift as the result of a change in one or more of its determinants. Four are particularly important.

1. **Expected Demand** To businesses, the *expected* return on an investment will depend largely on the demand anticipated for the product produced by the investment. If you're a shoe manufacturer, your expected *MEI* for shoe machinery will be influenced by the demand you anticipate for your shoes. Similarly, for the economy as a whole, the expected return on a new investment will be influenced by businesses' anticipations of total spending on their products.

2. **Technology and Innovation** Advances in technology and the introduction of new products often require new plants or new equipment. This stimulates the demand for additional capital.

3. **Cost of New Capital Goods** Changes in the cost of new goods affect firms' demand for them. A rise in the cost of new capital goods shifts the *MEI* curve to the left (a decrease in demand). A fall in cost shifts the curve to the right (an increase in demand).

4. **Corporate Income Tax Rates** Businesses are interested in expected rates of return on investment expenditures *after* allowances for corporation income taxes. Therefore, an increase in the tax rates, other things being equal, shifts the *MEI* curve to the left (a decrease in demand). A decrease in the tax rates shifts the curve to the right (an increase in demand).

These and other determinants of the *MEI* affect businesses' *expected* rates of return on investment. Because one or more of the determinants is always changing, the *MEI* curve is continually shifting right or left. As a result, the level of private investment in the economy fluctuates widely over the years, as shown in Exhibit 8.

In Keynesian theory, fluctuation in private investment is the most important cause of fluctuations in income and employment. And income and employment fluctuations are the major reasons for periods of prosperity and recession.

EXHIBIT
8

The Instability of Private Investment (in constant dollars)

The *MEI* curve for all firms, shown previously, is continually shifting, owing to constant changes in the conditions that determine it. As a result, private investment spending, shown here, fluctuates widely over the years. Note that changes in GDP are closely related to changes in investment. Notice also that the data measure year-to-year changes, so the data points are plotted between the years.

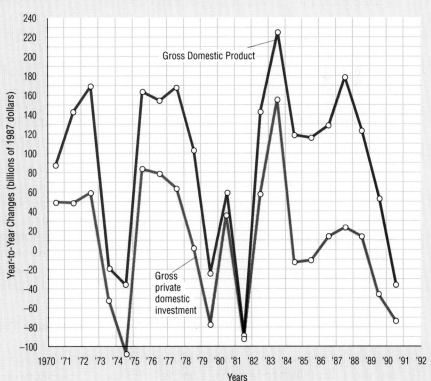

Government Expenditure and Net Foreign Expenditure

The remaining domestic component of aggregate expenditures stems from the government.

Government expenditure, which consists of public investment spending, depends to a large extent on public needs. These include such things as highways, schools, welfare benefits, and defense requirements. The volume of government expenditure is independent of profit expectations and, beyond the minimum levels required by society, is determined at will by government. No scientific law or guiding set of principles exists to predict changes in the level of public investment.

Finally, an open economy must include net foreign expenditure in the calculation of aggregate expenditure.

Net foreign expenditure is the difference between total foreign expenditures on domestic output and total domestic expenditures on foreign output. Put another way, a nation's net foreign expenditure is the difference between a country's total exports and its total imports. Therefore, a nation's net foreign expenditure is the same as its net exports:

Net exports = total exports – total imports

Because many different kinds of goods and services are exchanged in international trade, a country's exports and imports are always measured in terms of their monetary values.

As you can see from the above equation, the size of a nation's net exports will depend on the determinants of total exports and total imports. There are several such determinants. One of the most important is a country's relative real income (or purchasing power) compared to that of the rest of the world. Assuming that all other determinants of imports and exports remain the same, let's consider what happens when a nation's relative real income increases and what happens when it decreases.

1. **Increase in Real Income** Suppose the level of real income in the United States rises in relation to the rest of the world. As a result, Americans now have more purchasing power and can buy more goods—including more products from other countries. Among additional foreign goods that Americans might purchase are Japanese cars, German steel, British woolens, French perfumes, Italian shoes, and foreign scenery (that is, trips

abroad). In terms of the above equation, America's total imports will increase relative to total exports and cause net exports to decrease.

2. **Decrease in Real Income** Conversely, suppose the level of real income in the United States declines in relation to the rest of the world. The opposite effects will occur. Americans will purchase fewer products from abroad. Therefore, total imports will decrease relative to total exports. As a result, net exports will increase.

A nation's imports and aggregate income are thus directly related. Other things remaining the same, as aggregate income increases, the volume of imports increases. As aggregate income decreases, the volume of imports decreases. This relationship leads to a concept called the **marginal propensity to import (MPM).** It may be defined as the change in imports resulting from a unit change in income. The marginal propensity to import tells you the *fraction of each extra dollar of income that will be spent on imports.* The *MPM* may therefore be calculated from the formula:

$$MPM = \frac{\text{change in imports}}{\text{change in income}}$$

An *MPM* of 0.10, for example, means that 10 percent of any *increase* in income will be spent on imports.

Of course, changes in imports can affect net exports—or net foreign expenditure. Therefore:

Because net foreign expenditure (along with consumption expenditure, investment expenditure, and government expenditure) is part of total expenditure, fluctuations in net exports are a cause of instability.

Conclusion: Reviewing the Basic Relationships

You now have many of the building blocks necessary for understanding much of Keynesian macroeconomic theory. This theory, along with the main ideas of modern classical theory, will be developed in greater detail in the following chapters. You can review the fundamental concepts explained thus far by making sure that you understand the relationships presented in Exhibit 9.

Summary Thus Far

1. Keynesian economics was born during the Great Depression of the 1930s. During that decade, the

Some Key Relationships in Keynesian Macroeconomic Theory

These diagrams help you visualize important relationships in simple geometric terms. Notice the differences between the measurement of the average propensities and the measurement of the marginal propensities.

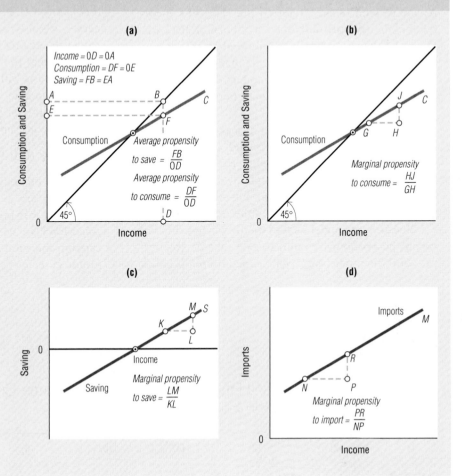

United States and other advanced countries experienced their highest unemployment rates in modern history.

2. Classical economists during the 1930s contended that the economy would self-correct quickly if government adopted a laissez-faire policy. Keynes disagreed with the classicists' belief, offering three major reasons:

   a. Total spending may not always equal full-employment aggregate income, as the classicists assumed. Instead total spending may fall below full-employment aggregate income and lead to recession and increased saving.

   b. The increased saving will not necessarily be borrowed by businesses and used for investment, as the classicists assumed. Instead, businesses may re-

frain from investing because profit expectations during recessions are gloomy.

   c. Markets for goods and resources don't always clear quickly, as the classicists assumed. Instead, there is a tendency for surpluses to prevail for long periods because many prices and wages are sticky.

3. Aggregate expenditure by the economy's four sectors consists of consumption expenditure, investment expenditure, government expenditure, and net foreign expenditure. Aggregate expenditure is affected by three "marginal" relationships. They are the household sector's marginal propensity to consume, the business sector's marginal efficiency of investment, and the foreign sector's marginal propensity to import.

The Income-Expenditure Model

As you've seen, Keynes rejected the classical self-correction theory and developed a theory of his own. Keynes's followers subsequently refined his theory and expressed it in the form of a model that could be used to explain the workings of the modern economy. Our objective at this time is to become familiar with this basic model.

The model is "basic" in that it deals only with the household and business sectors and omits, for the time being, the public and foreign sectors. With this model you can learn how a simple, two-sector system works before the other sectors are introduced to make the model more representative of the real world.

Because the model focuses on the relationship between the economy's real aggregate income (or output) and the public's aggregate expenditure on goods and services, it's called the *income-expenditure model.* And because the model uses two curves—an *aggregate expenditure* (*AE*) curve and an *aggregate output* (*AO*) curve—it's also called an *aggregate expenditure/aggregate output* or *AE/AO* model. An essential feature of this model is that the *average price level remains constant.* It thus contrasts with the income-price or aggregate demand/aggregate supply (*AD/AS*) model studied in earlier chapters. That model, you'll recall, assumed that the *average price level can vary.*

Structure of the Model

The table in Exhibit 10 shows the values of the variables that are relevant to the income-expenditure model for a hypothetical economy. Because a stable price level, or constant dollars, is assumed (as indicated in the subtitle), all dollar figures are in *real*, not nominal, terms.

EXHIBIT 10

Determination of Income and Employment Equilibrium: Income-Expenditure Model
(hypothetical economy, billions of constant dollars)

(1) Real output (aggregate output = aggregate income)	(2) Level of employment (in millions)	(3) Consumption, C (planned)*	(4) Saving, S (planned) (1) – (3)	(5) Investment, I (planned)	(6) Aggregate expenditure, AE (planned) (3) + (5)	(7) Inventory accumulation (+) or depletion (−) (1) – (6) or (4) – (5)	(8) Direction of income and employment
$100	30	$140	−$40	$40	$180	−$80	increase
200	35	220	−20	40	260	−60	increase
300	40	300	0	40	340	−40	increase
400	45	380	20	40	420	−20	increase
500	**50**	**460**	**40**	**40**	**500**	**0**	**equilibrium**
600	55	540	60	40	580	+20	decrease
700	60	620	80	40	660	+40	decrease
800	65	700	100	40	740	+60	decrease
900	70	780	120	40	820	+80	decrease

* The consumption function is assumed to be $C = \$60 + 0.8$ (real output). Thus, if real output is zero, the economy's consumption spending is $60 billion. As you learned earlier in the chapter, the economy can consume this amount by dissaving, borrowing from other countries, or by receiving subsidies (gifts and grants) from other countries.

Note from columns (1) and (2) that the amount of employment depends on real output. Higher levels of real output result in higher levels of employment because more people are employed to produce the increased output.

Consumption and saving, shown in columns (3) and (4), vary directly with real output—which is the same as aggregate income. (Remember from your study of national income accounting that aggregate output equals aggregate income.) Note from the column headings that consumption and saving are the amounts that households *plan* (or *intend*) to consume and save at each income level.

The amount of investment spending by the business sector, column (5), is also planned. Although investment spending fluctuates widely over time, it is assumed in this "basic" model to be *independent* of real output. Therefore, this table shows planned investment spending (=$40 billion) as constant in relation to real output.

Column (6), aggregate expenditure, is simply the total amount of spending on consumption and investment planned by all sectors of the economy.

The difference between aggregate output and aggregate expenditure is the economy's change in inventory, shown in column (7). (Note that the change in inventory is also the difference between saving and investment.) As will be explained, the inventory level tends toward *zero unplanned* or undesired accumulation or depletion. When this level of inventory is reached, income and employment have no tendency to change. As shown in column (8), zero unplanned changes to inventory means that income and employment are in equilibrium.

With this background, you can now turn your attention to Exhibit 11. It displays graphically the data from the table in Exhibit 10. Some important features of the graphs in Exhibit 11 should be noted:

Figure (a) depicts both aggregate expenditure and aggregate output. The aggregate expenditure curve, *AE*, shows the amount that households and businesses *plan* to spend for consumption and investment (measured on the vertical axis) at each level of aggregate output or income measured on the horizontal axis.

Because the scales of both axes are the same, the 45 degree line serves as a reference line. At each point along this line, aggregate expenditure equals aggregate output, *AO*. That is, $AE/AO = 1$ (or 100 percent).

EXHIBIT
11

Determination of Income and Employment Equilibrium: Income-Expenditure Model
(based on data in Exhibit 10)

FIGURE (a)   FIGURE (b)

At the equilibrium point *E*:

| Aggregate output equals aggregate expenditure ($AO = AE$) | *and* | Saving equals investment ($S = I$) |

To the right of *E*:

Aggregate output is greater than aggregate expenditure ($AO > AE$)   *and*   Saving is greater than investment ($S > I$)

To the left of *E*:

Aggregate expenditure is greater than aggregate output ($AE > AO$)   *and*   Investment is greater than saving ($I > S$)

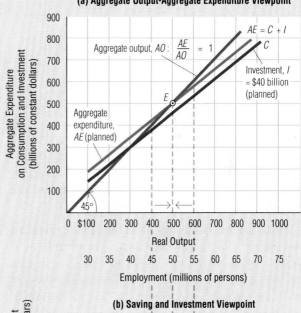

(a) Aggregate Output-Aggregate Expenditure Viewpoint

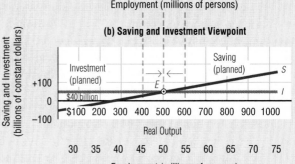

(b) Saving and Investment Viewpoint

Therefore, the line is labeled *aggregate output*, AO, and used below as a basis for comparison with the planned *AE* line.

In addition to the *AE* and *AO* curves, Figure (a) shows the consumption curve, *C*. If you compare *C* with the saving curve, *S*, depicted in Figure (b) you'll see that consumption and saving vary directly with income. This is what you would expect from your knowledge of the propensities to consume and to save.

Figure (b) also depicts the investment curve, *I*. Because planned investment is constant ($40 billion), *I* is a horizontal line. Why is investment the same at all levels of aggregate output? As emphasized in an earlier chapter:

The investment plans of businesses depend on the marginal efficiency of investment (*MEI*) relative to the interest rate. The *MEI* is affected by such determinants as expected product demand, the rate of technological change and innovation, the cost of new capital goods, and corporate income tax rates. Therefore, the level of investment that businesses *plan* or intend to undertake can be assumed to remain constant in relation to aggregate output. (The level of investment varies widely from year to year, however, as you've already learned.)

The Equilibrium Level of Income and Employment

You now have the information needed to interpret the income-expenditure model. The question to be answered is: What will be the equilibrium levels of aggregate income and employment—and why? As you can see, there are two parts to the question.

1. What are the equilibrium levels of aggregate income and employment? Look again at the table in Exhibit 10. It shows that the equilibrium level of aggregate output (=$500 billion) in column (1) equals the sum of consumption spending in column (3) and investment spending in column (5). That is, *in equilibrium, aggregate output equals aggregate expenditure*. This means that businesses are able to hold the precise level of inventory they desire. They are neither accumulating goods nor depleting their stock of goods and therefore have no incentive to change their level of production. As a result, there are no changes in inventory in column (7). Thus, the difference between aggregate output and aggregate expenditure (or between planned saving and planned investment) is zero.

The equilibrium points *E* in the two figures in Exhibit 11 depict these notions graphically. Note the vertical dashed line connecting the equilibrium points. It shows that, in this hypothetical economy, equilibrium occurs at an aggregate output level of $500 billion and an employment level of 50 million persons.

2. Why do aggregate income and employment tend toward equilibrium? As a start toward an answer, ask yourself what happens when they are not in equilibrium. There are two possibilities:

a. Suppose that real output is greater than $500 billion—say $600 billion. This means that businesses are paying $600 billion in the form of wages, rent, interest, and profit, which are incomes to owners. (Remember that aggregate output = aggregate income.) At the same time, the corresponding level of planned expenditures, *C* + *I*, is $580 billion. The consequences can be seen both from the table in Exhibit 10 and from the graphs in Exhibit 11. Thus:

In Figure (a), the amount that businesses produce ($600 billion) is greater than the amount that households and businesses together want to buy ($580 billion).

In Figure (b), the amount that households plan to save ($60 billion) is greater than the amount that businesses plan to invest ($40 billion).

For both these reasons, businesses find their sales to be less than anticipated. Inventories accumulate beyond desired levels, so managers cut back on production and lay off workers. As a result, aggregate output, income, and employment decrease toward their equilibrium levels as shown by the arrows in the figures.

b. Conversely, suppose that real output is less than $500 billion—say $400 billion. In this case, the reverse process occurs. Stated briefly: In Figure (a) households' and businesses' planned aggregate expenditure *exceeds* aggregate output; in Figure (b) businesses' planned investment *exceeds* households' planned saving. Households and businesses together are buying goods at a faster rate than firms are producing them. As a result, business inventories are being depleted—that is, they are falling below desired levels. Managers therefore expand production and hire more workers. This causes aggregate output, income, and employment to increase toward their equilibrium levels, as indicated by the arrows in the figures.

Thus, three fundamental conclusions may be drawn from the income-expenditure model:

1. **Income and employment tend toward an equilibrium level at which aggregate output equals aggregate expenditure and planned saving equals planned investment.**

2. **The movement toward equilibrium takes place as businesses seek to adjust their inventories to desired levels.**

3. **Equilibrium can occur at *any* level of employment, depending on the level of real output at which aggregate expenditure happens to equal aggregate output.**

Injections and Withdrawals: The "Bathtub Theorem"

You can gain further understanding of why equilibrium can occur at any level of employment by considering a physical analogy.

Suppose that we use the notions of "injections" and "withdrawals" to account for expansions and contractions in the economy's circular flow of income. These terms can be defined in the following way:

- **Injections** These are expenditures that are not dependent on income. Investment expenditures are an example. So too are government expenditures and exports. The effect of injections is to increase aggregate expenditure and thus to raise the economy's level of income and employment.

- **Withdrawals** These are "leakages" from total income. Saving is an example. Other examples you'll be learning about are taxes and imports. The effect of withdrawals is to decrease aggregate expenditure and thus to reduce the economy's level of income and employment.

You can visualize the impact of injections and withdrawals by looking back at Figure (b) in Exhibit 11. Injections may be represented by investment *(I)*, and withdrawals or leakages may be represented by saving *(S)*. As you've already learned, equilibrium will occur where *I = S*. This is the level of income and employment at which injections and withdrawals are equal.

The *"bathtub theorem"* illustrated in Exhibit 12 shows how investment and saving affect the economy's level of real output.

- Injections, represented by investment spending, are inflows that raise the level of water in the tub. Withdrawals, represented by saving, are outflows that lower the level.

EXHIBIT
12

Injections and Withdrawals: The "Bathtub Theorem"

You can visualize the effects of investment and saving on the economy's real output. The level of water in the tub can rise, remain the same, or fall. Whichever it does depends on whether the investment injections are greater than, equal to, or less than the saving withdrawals. But at any *given* level of real output (or water in the tub), investment equals saving.

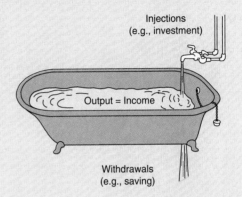

Injections
(e.g., investment)

Output = Income

Withdrawals
(e.g., saving)

- If the investment injections exceed the saving withdrawals, the level in the tub will rise. If the saving withdrawals exceed the investment injections, the level in the tub will fall.

- The water in the tub can be in equilibrium at *any* level provided the investment injections equal the saving withdrawals. Or, to put it differently:

At any *given* level of real output or of real income, investment equals saving.

Origins: Keynesian Economics

"You have to know that I believe myself to be writing a book on economic theory which will largely revolutionize . . . the way the world thinks about economic problems." So wrote John Maynard Keynes to the Irish wit and author George Bernard Shaw in 1935.

Keynes was right. He did indeed write a book that revolutionized economic thinking. As a result, he became recognized as one of the most brilliant and influential economists of all time. In fact, as one who helped shape the thinking of future generations of scholars, Keynes ranks with Adam Smith and Karl Marx.

Keynes was born in Cambridge, England, the son of a noted economist, John Neville Keynes. The younger Keynes was educated at Eton and Cambridge, where he first majored in mathematics but later turned his attention to philosophy and economics. After college, he took a civil service post in the British government's India Office. Later, he returned to England and served as a teaching fellow at Cambridge, where his talents were quickly recognized. He became editor of the *Economic Journal,* Britain's most distinguished economic publication—a position that he held for 33 years.

Many-Sided Genius

To say that Keynes was brilliant is an understatement. He was a genius with diverse talents who combined teaching with an active and highly successful business

John Maynard Keynes
(1883–1946)

life in the fields of insurance, investments, and publishing. In addition to his many publications in economics, he wrote a highly regarded book on the philosophical foundations of probability. The book served for decades as required reading by graduate students in mathematical logic and philosophy. He also amassed a fortune of more than $2 million by speculating in the international currency and commodities markets. Perhaps most impressive, however, is the fact that Keynes accomplished these feats in his "spare time". He wrote his mathematics book while employed in government service, and he accumulated his fortune by analyzing financial reports and phoning orders to his broker for a half hour each morning before breakfast.

Unconventional Ideas

Keynes's most celebrated work, *The General Theory of Employment, Interest and Money* (1936), is one of the most influential books ever written in economics. Here Keynes made it clear that he was departing significantly from traditional economic theory. This theory held that there is a natural tendency for the economy to reach equilibrium at full employment. Indeed, Keynes showed that equilibrium can be reached and maintained at a level of output less than full employment.

Because of this, Keynes advocated reduction in the central bank interest rate (the discount rate) to stimulate investment. He also believed in progressive income taxation to make incomes more equal and thereby increase the percentage of aggregate income that people spend on consumption. And he argued for government investment through public works as a "pump-priming" process when private investment expenditures fall off. Today, these and several related ideas are part of a larger family of concepts that make up modern macroeconomic theory and policy.

Summary of Important Ideas

1. The Keynesian theory of income and employment is rooted in several fundamental ideas. Among them:

Aggregate expenditure may be greater than, equal to, or less than full-employment aggregate income.

The interest rate may fail to equate households' intended saving and businesses' intended investment. This is because saving and investment are done by different people for different purposes.

Many prices and wages are *sticky,* not flexible. The reason is that, in many important industries:

a. Larger firms have sufficient market power to resist price decreases.

b. Wage rates are often established by contracts.

2. The propensity to consume, or the consumption function, expresses a relationship between consumption and disposable income. The relationship is that as income increases, consumption increases, but not as fast as income.

3. At any given level of income, the average propensity to consume (*APC*) is the proportion of income spent on consumption. Similarly, the average propensity to save (*APS*) is the proportion of income saved. Therefore, $APC + APS = 1$ (or 100 percent). Out of any given increase in income, the marginal propensity to consume (*MPC*) is the proportion of the increase spent on consumption. Similarly, the marginal propensity to save (*MPS*) is the proportion of the increase saved. Hence, $MPC + MPS = 1$ (or 100 percent).

4. A *change in the amount consumed* means a movement along the consumption curve as a result of a change in income. A *change in consumption* means a shift of the entire consumption curve to a new level. This occurs because of a change in one or more of the "other" things that are assumed to be constant when the curve is initially drawn. These factors include expectations of future prices and income, the volume of liquid and financial assets owned by households, credit conditions (ease of borrowing money), and anticipation of product shortages.

5. Investment expenditure, like consumption and saving, is a variable in income and employment determination. The expected rate of return on an additional unit of investment is called *the marginal efficiency of investment (MEI)*. Investment occurs when the *MEI* exceeds the rate of interest or cost of funds incurred in making the investment.

6. Private investment spending depends on the profit expectations of businesses. These expectations are determined by such conditions as expected product demand, the rate of technology and innovation, cost of new capital goods, and corporate income-tax rates. Because most of these conditions are always changing, private investment tends to be highly volatile over the years and is the major cause of fluctuations in economic activity.

7. Expenditures by the public sector and the foreign sector are part of aggregate expenditure. Government expenditure is unrelated to profit expectations. Imports, like consumption expenditures, are related to aggregate income. This relationship is expressed by the marginal propensity to import.

8. The income-expenditure model provides a Keynesian depiction of the macroeconomy. It demonstrates that real output and employment can be in equilibrium at *any* level, not necessarily at the full-employment level. In equilibrium, two conditions exist:

a. Aggregate expenditure equals aggregate output, as represented by the intersection of the *AE* and *AO* curves.

b. Planned saving equals planned investment, as represented by the intersection of the *S* and *I* curves.

9. Real output and the level of employment tend toward equilibrium. In the income-expenditure model, equilibrium occurs where aggregate output equals aggregate expenditure and planned saving equals planned investment. The movement toward equilibrium occurs as businesses adjust for unplanned inventory accumulations or depletions. At any given time, the location of the equilibrium point may or may not correspond to full (natural) employment.

10. Keynesian theory argues that the economy may operate at less than full employment for prolonged periods. Evidence of this is seen in the Great Depression of the 1930s and in a number of subsequent recessions.

11. Investment spending may be thought of as an injection into the economy's circular flow of income; saving may be thought of as a withdrawal. Disparities between the "inflow" of investment and the "outflow" of saving will cause the economy's level of income to rise or fall. However, at any *given* level of income, the investment inflow equals the saving outflow.

12. Economics in the twentieth century was revolutionized by the work of John Maynard Keynes. His book, *The General Theory of Employment, Interest and Money* (1936) presented a theory that contradicted the classical belief that the economy is rapidly self-correcting. Keynes's ideas have provided much of the basis of modern macroeconomic theory and policy.

Terms and Concepts to Review

Say's law	*slope*
real wages	*change in amount consumed*
aggregate expenditure	
consumption	*change in consumption*
saving	*investment*
dissaving	*marginal efficiency of investment*
propensity to consume	
propensity to save	*opportunity cost*
average propensity to consume	*marginal propensity to import*
average propensity to save	*income-expenditure model*
marginal propensity to consume	*aggregate output*
marginal propensity to save	*"bathtub theorem"*

Questions and Problems

1. In the field of marketing, a set of concepts called *Engel's laws* is often used. Look up the meaning of this idea in the Dictionary at the back of the book. Then express Engel's laws in terms of the average propensity to consume (*APC*).

2. Why does the *APC* differ from the *MPC*? Why does the *APS* differ from the *MPS*?

3. What conditions other than income are likely to be important in determining consumption?

4. Complete the following table using the assumption that 50 percent of any increase in income is spent on consumption. Sketch the graphs of consumption and saving. Label all the curves.

DI	C	S	APC	APS	MPC	MPS
$100	$150	___	___	___	___	___
200	___	___	___	___	___	___
300	___	___	___	___	___	___
400	___	___	___	___	___	___
500	___	___	___	___	___	___
600	___	___	___	___	___	___

5. Would you expect expenditures on consumer durable goods to fluctuate more widely than expenditures on consumer nondurable goods? Explain your answer.

6. What would be the effect on aggregate consumption if social-welfare expenditures on public hospitals, parks, medical care, and so on were financed entirely by our progressive income tax system? Does it make any difference if there are tax loopholes?

7. How would you distinguish between a "change in amount invested" and a "change in investment"?

8. What kinds of changes in the tax law might be used to stimulate investment demand? To discourage it?

9. Suppose most business executives expect an economic slowdown. How might this affect their investment decisions and hence the business cycle?

10. How would an increase in the incomes of foreign countries affect aggregate expenditures in the United States?

11. Using the income-expenditure model, illustrate why Keynes advocated a reduction in the central bank interest rate to stimulate the economy.

TAKE A STAND

IRAs: Do They Promote Household Saving?

Households have two basic uses for disposable income—consumption and saving. Changes in households' decisions about how much income to consume and how much to save have profound short-run and long-run macroeconomic effects.

In the short run, increases in saving and corresponding decreases in consumption can harm economic performance. For example, if consumers become fearful or uncertain about the future, they may choose to decrease their consumption and increase their saving. Because consumption accounts for about two-thirds of aggregate expenditures, such a decrease can push the economy into recession.

In the long run, however, increases in saving are helpful to the economy because they encourage growth. Saving by households makes funds available for businesses to borrow and invest. Investment builds up the economy's capital stock, which allows for the production of more goods in the future.

If the economy is in recession, therefore, policymakers often look for ways to persuade consumers to spend more and save less. But in good economic times, the opposite is true—policymakers and economists advocate measures to encourage household saving and promote growth. One such measure is the Individual Retirement Account (IRA), first offered in 1974. IRAs provide tax incentives to encourage saving for retirement.

When IRAs were introduced, they were available only to those not covered by an employee pension plan. The 1981 Economic Recovery Tax Act made IRAs widely available, and they soon became a significant component of saving. Between 1982 and 1986, IRA contributions represented about 30 percent of total personal saving. The popularity of IRAs stemmed from the favorable tax treatment they received. Specifically, contributions up to $2,000 were tax-deductible, and the interest earnings were untaxed. (Withdrawals were taxed, and there was a penalty for early withdrawal.)

The 1986 Tax Reform Act restricted the preferential treatment of IRAs, and the interest they earn is no longer tax-free. Instead, the tax is deferred until the interest is withdrawn. There

has since ensued much argument about the desirability of tax breaks on IRAs. For the most part, the debate can be reduced to one question: *Do IRAs promote household saving?*

Yes: **A Lower Price Increases the Quantity Demanded**

The demand for IRAs is like the demand for any product. If the price comes down, people buy more. When IRAs are given favorable tax treatment, they make saving cheaper, and so encourage people to save more. The effect is substantial. Suppose, for example, that an individual saves $2,000 a year between ages 25 and 65. At an interest rate of 10 percent and a marginal tax rate of 30 percent, these funds kept in a conventional savings account would have an after-tax value of $320,000. Were the funds deposited instead in tax-exempt IRAs, they would yield $789,000.

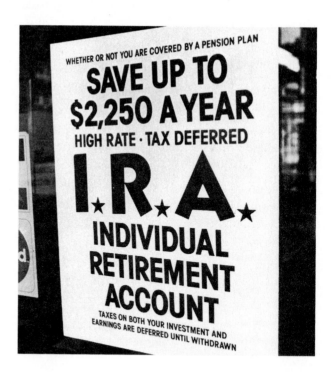

A study by economists Steven Venti of Dartmouth College and David Wise of Harvard University suggests that IRAs do promote saving. Venti and Wise examined data on individual households and concluded that if IRAs continued to receive favorable tax treatment, an increase in the limit on IRA contributions would lead to a substantial increase in IRA saving. More important, their findings suggest that about two-thirds of this increase would represent new saving. There is also some evidence that IRA-type plans, introduced in Canada in the mid-1970s, generated a significant increase in saving in that country.

Finally, IRAs may promote saving for other reasons. Venti and Wise suggest that the penalties on early withdrawals from IRA accounts make them a desirable form of saving for those who lack self-control. And the publicity surrounding IRAs may have caused people to think more about their plans for retirement.

No: IRA s Only Reallocate Saving

There is no doubt that a significant percentage of saving in the 1980s was deposited in IRAs. The key macroeconomic question, however, is: Did IRA contributions represent new saving, or did individuals simply reallocate their saving in order to obtain the tax advantages of IRAs?

The study by Venti and Wise does suggest that favorable tax treatment of IRAs encourages substantial new saving. Other economists, however, have questioned their methods and their findings. A study of household expenditures by John Scholz of the University of Wisconsin and William Gale of the University of California at Los Angeles concluded that only a small percentage of IRA contributions in the mid-1980s represented new saving.

It is possible that the preferential tax treatment given to IRAs could lead to a *decrease* in total saving. Suppose that an individual has targeted a level of wealth to be achieved at retirement. Using IRAs rather than conventional forms of saving, this person can save less and still attain the target.

Circumstantial evidence suggests that IRAs do not promote saving. In the mid-1980s, when IRAs were widely available, the personal saving rate dropped—from about 8 percent in the mid-1970s to about 4 percent in 1986. In the late 1980s, conversely, the personal saving rate rose even though IRAs became less popular.

Reinstating tax breaks for IRAs is therefore unlikely to have a notable effect on total private saving. It would, however, benefit the rich. According to one estimate, 95 percent of the benefits of such tax incentives would go to the wealthiest 20 percent of the population. The wealthy would not save more, but they

would reduce their taxes by switching from other forms of saving to IRAs. Low-income households, by contrast, don't have that option; they cannot afford to set aside funds for retirement.

Finally, remember that the tax incentives offered on IRAs represent lost revenue for the government. Less tax revenue means in turn that the government deficit is higher, which reduces total national saving.

The Question: Do IRAs Promote Household Saving?

■ Some believe that if the government reduces the price of IRAs by according them more favorable tax treatment, households will increase their demand. That is, they will put more of their funds into IRAs and save more than they would have otherwise.

■ Others believe that tax breaks for IRAs do not inspire a significant increase in new saving. Instead, the tax breaks induce households to switch to IRAs from other forms of saving.

Where Do You Stand?

1. If tax breaks on IRAs encourage a reallocation of saving rather than an increase in the total amount, are they likely to have a short-run effect on aggregate expenditures or a long-run effect on economic growth? Explain.

2. Could other determinants of household consumption and saving overwhelm the "price" effect of tax breaks on IRAs?

3. What considerations are most likely to motivate you to save? Would these change if you were among the poorest 10 percent or the richest 10 percent of the population? Explain.

4. Do IRAs promote household saving? Justify your stand.

Source: "IRAs' Sponsors Are Inflating Plans' Benefits," *The Wall Street Journal,* October 28, 1991, pages A2, A4; Jane Gravelle, "Do Individual Retirement Accounts Increase Savings?," *Journal of Economic Perspectives,* Spring, 1991, pp. 133–148; Steven Venti and David Wise, "Have IRAs Increased U. S. Saving? Evidence from Consumer Expenditure Surveys," *Quarterly Journal of Economics,* August, 1990, pp. 661–698.

Chapter 14

Income and Employment Determination: Extending Macroeconomic Principles

The Multiplier Principle
Completing the Income-Expenditure Model
The Income-Price Model: Accommodating Two Views
Implications of a Varying Price Level

Learning Guide

Watch for answers to these important questions

What is the multiplier principle? How does it affect changes in real output?

How is the complete income-expenditure model illustrated graphically? What variables in the model "come together" to determine macroeconomic equilibrium? How does the model depict inflationary and recessionary gaps?

Using the income-price model, how can we distinguish between the original and modern views of Keynesian equilibrium?

How can the income-expenditure model be linked to the income-price model? What are the multiplier effects of a varying price level? What is the open-economy multiplier?

Economics is both a science and an art. As a science, economics identifies relevant variables and the relationships between them. The relationships serve as principles, or rules, that govern economic processes. You've already learned a number of principles in previous chapters.

As an art, economics applies the principles to the solution of real-world problems. This is usually the responsibility of policymakers.

At the government level, policymakers are our elected representatives and their appointees. Therefore, economic policies are usually inseparable from politics. As a result, policymakers in all democratic countries face two challenges. One is to understand the economic principles on which policies are based. The other is to design policies that are acceptable to voters. This challenge exists because almost every economic policy involves short-run and long-run trade-offs that benefit some groups while harming others.

The purpose of this chapter is to extend your knowledge of economic principles—the science of economics. The chapter begins by building on the simplified two-sector income-expenditure model developed in the previous chapter. As you'll recall, the model is based on the assumption of a *constant price level*. When the model is completed, it will be used to analyze two basic business-cycle problems—inflation and recession. You'll then see how the ideas underlying the model can be revised to incorporate the effects of a changing price level, and you'll learn some of the implications of that revision. When the analysis is completed, you'll be better able to appreciate some of the challenges that policymakers face in implementing economic principles—the art of economics.

The Multiplier Principle

One of the most significant variables affecting aggregate expenditure, and therefore the economy's level of income, is the amount of investment. You already know that an increase in investment can cause an increase in income. Likewise, a decrease in investment can cause a decrease in income. What you may not know is that the effect on income of changes in investment spending may be amplified.

An increase in investment may cause a magnified increase in aggregate income (and therefore in aggregate output, too). A decrease in investment may cause a magnified decrease in aggregate income. The amount by which a change in investment is multiplied to give the ultimate change in income is called the *multiplier.*

For example, if an increase in investment of $5 billion per year causes an increase in income of $10 billion, the multiplier is 2. If, instead, the increase in income is $15 billion, the multiplier is 3.

In order to understand the multiplier principle, you must recall two important concepts learned in the previous chapter:

1. *The marginal propensity to consume (MPC)* is the fraction of each additional dollar of income that is spent on consumption.

2. *The marginal propensity to save (MPS)* is the fraction of each additional dollar of income that is saved.

How does the multiplier work? It can be illustrated in three ways: numerically, in the form of a table; graphically, in the form of a diagram; and algebraically, in the form of an equation. Keep in mind that, in each of these illustrations, the price level is assumed to be constant. That is, the illustrations apply to the income-expenditure model.

Numerical Illustration

Suppose that businesses decide to spend $5 billion more per year on construction of new plants and equipment. This means that unemployed workers, suppliers of raw materials, and so on will be hired for the construction. If we assume that they have an *MPC* of 4/5 and hence an *MPS* of 1/5, they will tend to

EXHIBIT 1

The Multiplier Illustrated Numerically
(all data in billions of constant dollars)

$MPC = 4/5$ $MPS = 1/5$ multiplier = 5

Expenditure rounds	Increase in aggregate income	Increase in consumption $MPC = 4/5$	Increase in saving $MPS = 1/5$
1 Increase in investment = $5 billion	$ 5.00 → $ 4.00		$1.00
2	4.00 → 3.20		0.80
3	3.20 → 2.56		0.64
4	2.56 → 2.05		0.51
5	2.05 → 1.64		0.41
6	1.64 → 1.31		0.33
All other rounds	6.55	5.24	1.31
Total	$25.00	$20.00	$5.00

spend four-fifths and save one-fifth of any additional income they receive. The four-fifths they spend will provide additional income for more unemployed workers and suppliers. These workers will, in turn, spend four-fifths of the income they receive, thereby providing income for still more workers and suppliers, and so on.

The ultimate effect of the $5 billion increase in investment on income is illustrated in Exhibit 1. In the first round of expenditures, the increase in investment becomes increased income to the owners of the newly hired resources. Because their *MPC* is 4/5 and their *MPS* is 1/5, they utilize 80 percent, or $4 billion, for increased consumption and 20 percent, or $1 billion, for increased saving.

In round 2, when the four-fifths is spent on consumption, firms find their sales increasing and their inventories decreasing. Therefore, firms hire more resources in order to increase their production. This creates $4 billion of income for the owners of the resources. These income recipients then utilize four-fifths, or $3.2 billion, for increased consumption and one-fifth, or $0.8 billion, for increased saving.

In round 3 and in each subsequent round, the process is repeated. Four-fifths of each increase in income is spent in the following round and is thereby added to the economy's previous gain in income.

Thus, a permanent increase in investment of $5 billion in round 1 has brought about an ultimate increase in income of $25 billion. The multiplier is therefore 5. This overall increase in aggregate income consists of a $20 billion increase in consumption plus a $5 billion increase in saving. The total saving increase is always the amount of the original investment, as you can verify from the table.

Note from the table that the greatest increases in income occur during the first few rounds. In the subsequent rounds, the income effects tend to fade away gradually—like the ripples produced by a stone dropped into a pond.

Graphic Illustration

Exhibit 2 depicts the same multiplier concept graphically. It shows how an increase in investment, represented by an upward shift of the $C + I$ curve in Figure (a), or by an upward shift of the I curve in Figure (b), causes a magnified increase in real output. As before, the diagrams are based on the assumption that the MPC is 4/5 and the MPS is 1/5. That is, the aggregate expenditure curve has a slope of 4/5, and the saving curve has a slope of 1/5.

Point E in both diagrams represents the initial equilibrium level at which aggregate expenditure equals aggregate output and saving equals investment. Point E' in both diagrams identifies a new equilibrium resulting from an increase in investment. Note from the description accompanying the diagrams that the increase in real output is a *multiple* of the increase in investment. The multiplier, as you can see, is 5.

Can you also see that the multiplier works in reverse? For example, what happens to real output if investment falls back to its initial level? What happens if investment falls below its initial level?

Algebraic Illustration

The numerical and graphic illustrations of the multiplier demonstrate that the increase in aggregate income, or aggregate output, is related to the marginal propensities to consume and to save. For example, you have already learned from the study of the consumption function that

$$MPC + MPS = 1$$

Therefore,

$$MPS = 1 - MPC$$

From the previous illustrations, you know that MPC is 4/5 and MPS is 1/5.

Therefore, you can easily verify that

$$\text{Multiplier} = \frac{1}{1/5} = \frac{1}{1 - 4/5} = 5$$

This is the same value of the multiplier obtained previously in the numerical and graphic illustrations.

These ideas have been stated in the form of a specific example. They can now be expressed in a general formula:

$$\text{Multiplier} = \frac{1}{MPS} = \frac{1}{1 - MPC}$$

This means that, if you know either the MPC or the MPS, you can determine the multiplier immediately. (This is what was done above to determine a multiplier of 5.) Then, once you know the value of the multiplier, you can predict the ultimate change in income that may result from a change in investment by the formula:

$$\text{Multiplier} \times \frac{\text{change in}}{\text{investment}} = \frac{\text{change}}{\text{in income}}$$

The same formula applies to a decrease as well as an increase in investment. Go back and check it out in the illustrations above, just to make sure that you see how it works.

Notice that the *multiplier is the reciprocal of the MPS*. (The reciprocal of a number is 1 divided by that number.) Thus, the lower the MPS, the less withdrawal or "leakage" into extra saving that occurs at each round of income and the greater the MPC. Therefore, the lower the MPS, the greater the value of the multiplier. Conversely, the greater the MPS, the lower the MPC. Therefore, the lower the value of the multiplier.

To summarize:

The *multiplier* principle states that changes in investment can bring about magnified changes in income. This idea is expressed by the equation: multiplier × change in investment = change in income. The formula for the multiplier is thus

$$\text{Multiplier} = \frac{\frac{\text{change in}}{\text{income}}}{\frac{\text{change in}}{\text{investment}}} = \frac{1}{MPS} = \frac{1}{1 - MPC}$$

where *MPS* is the marginal propensity to save and *MPC*

EXHIBIT
2

The Multiplier Effect When the Price Level Is Constant: Income-Expenditure Model

MPC = 4/5
MPS = 1/5
Multiplier = 5

FIGURE (a) An increase in the level of investment of $5 billion causes an increase in the level of real output of $25 billion. Hence, the multiplier is 5.

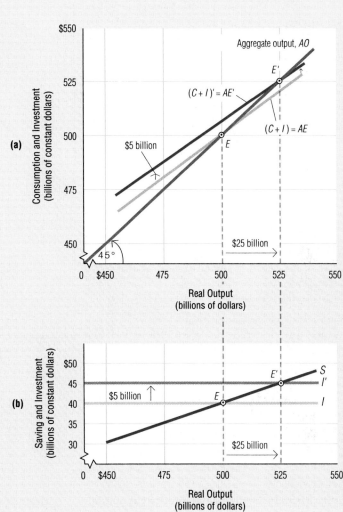

(a)

FIGURE (b) The multiplier effect can also be seen in terms of a savings-investment diagram. What happens to real output if investment falls back to $40 billion? To $35 billion?

(b)

is the marginal propensity to consume. (*Note:* This multiplier is also sometimes called the *simple multiplier,* the *expenditure multiplier,* or the *investment multiplier.* These names are used to distinguish it from other multipliers in economics.)

As stated at the outset, we've assumed that the price level is constant. Later in the chapter you'll see that the size of the multiplier is affected when the price level is allowed to vary.

Completing the Income-Expenditure Model

You may be thinking that the income-expenditure model you have studied is too limited: It includes only the household and business sectors. To be more realistic, the model should incorporate the two remaining sectors of the economy—the government and the foreign sector.

EXHIBIT
3

The Complete Income-Expenditure Model

The income-expenditure model shows how the components of total spending by all sectors of the economy, as well as injections and withdrawals, are related to real aggregate income.

(a)

FIGURE (a) As real output increases, consumption increases. However, investment and government spending are assumed to be independent of aggregate income, so they remain constant in relation to it. Net exports (= exports – imports) decrease because imports rise while exports remain the same.

FIGURE (b) *Withdrawals*: Saving, taxes, and imports, which rise as real output increases, have the effect of reducing aggregate expenditure and therefore the levels of income and employment.

(b)

Injections: Investment, government spending, and exports, which are assumed to be independent of real output, increase aggregate expenditure and thus raise the economy's income and employment.

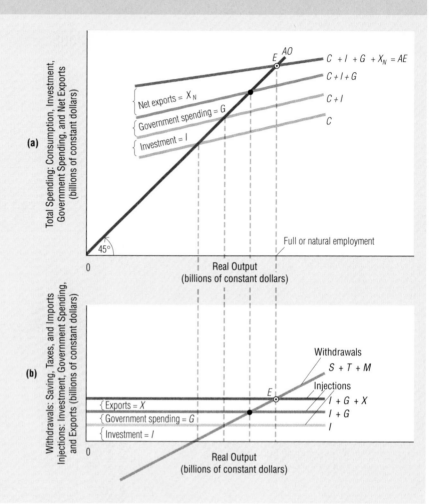

Exhibit 3 shows how the enlarged final model looks. In Figure (a), notice first that as in the two-sector model, the horizontal axis measures real output. However, the vertical axis measures total spending by *all* sectors of the economy. Observe also that these variables are expressed in constant dollars.

In the lower diagram, Figure (b), which can be thought of as the "foundation" of the model, the horizontal axis again measures real output. However, the vertical axis measures *withdrawals* and *injections*. As you learned from the bathtub theorem illustrated in the previous chapter, withdrawals are "leakages" from total income. They have the effect of decreasing aggregate expenditure and thereby reducing the economy's income and employment. Notice from Figure (b) that, as the economy's real income rises, three types of with-

drawals consisting of saving (S), taxes (T), and imports (M) occur.

1. S increases because the household sector saves a larger amount of its income.

2. T increases because the government collects more taxes from household and business incomes.

3. M increases because the household and business sectors import more goods—cars, electronics products, machinery, steel, and so on.

All three types of withdrawals vary directly with income. Therefore, they could be graphed separately as three upward-sloping curves. However, doing so would make the diagram unnecessarily complicated. To avoid this complication, the three withdrawals are simply added together and graphed as a single curve labeled $S + T + M$.

Also in Figure (b), notice the injections, which represent expenditures. As you learned from the bathtub theorem, the effect of investment I, government spending G, and exports X is to increase aggregate expenditure and thus raise the economy's income and employment. To keep the diagram simple so it conveys the essential ideas, *all three expenditures are assumed to be autonomous—independent of real output. Consequently, they remain constant as the nation's real output increases.* As you will see momentarily, the conclusions drawn from the model are not affected by this simplifying assumption.

Components of Aggregate Expenditure

Now let's turn to the upper diagram, Figure (a). This diagram may be thought of as the "superstructure" of the model. It's by far the more important diagram, and the one that's almost always employed in income-expenditure analysis.

To begin with, you know from the study of the consumption function that consumption varies directly with income. Therefore, the curve C is upward sloping. You also know that investment I is assumed to be independent of income, so it's simply "added on" to consumption to obtain the $C + I$ curve. Similarly, government spending G is assumed to be independent of income. Therefore, it too is simply "added on" to consumption and investment to obtain the $C + I + G$ curve.

What about net exports X_N? Net exports are the difference between the dollar value of exports X and the dollar value of imports M. That is: $X_N = X - M$. But you saw above that, as domestic income increases, X remains constant. This is because it depends on other countries' incomes, not on ours. M, however, increases because it depends on our nation's income, not on other countries'. As a result, net exports, shown in the diagram, are smaller at higher levels of domestic income than at lower levels. These concepts explain the following essential ideas illustrated in the model:

Aggregate expenditure [Figure (a)] is the sum of consumption spending by the household sector, investment spending by the business sector, government spending by the government sector, and net-export spending by the foreign sector. Thus: $C + I + G + X_N = AE$. The equilibrium point occurs where $AE = AO$. This point determines the equilibrium levels of real output and of total spending. [Notice that, in Figure (b), the equilibrium point occurs where $S + T + M = I + G + X$. This point also determines the equilibrium level of real output.]

Based on what you've already learned, two conclusions should now be apparent from Figure (a):

1. If the economy is at full employment, a decrease in any of the variables comprising aggregate expenditure will cause the AE curve to decline. After the decline, the economy will be in equilibrium at a lower level of real output and a correspondingly lower level of total spending.

2. If the economy is in a recession, the opposite can occur. An increase in any of the variables comprising aggregate expenditure will cause the AE curve to rise to a higher equilibrium level of real output and a correspondingly higher level of total spending.

The level of total spending is thus of fundamental importance in the income-expenditure model. Increases or decreases in total spending shift the aggregate expenditure curve, causing changes in the economy's output and employment.

Inflationary and Recessionary Gaps

In any field of science, the value of a theory or model depends to a large extent on its ability to explain a particular real-world phenomenon. How, then, can the income-expenditure model be used to explain two fundamental and recurring problems of macroeconomics—inflation and recession?

To answer the question, the first step is to recognize a fundamental proposition of the income-expenditure model:

At the full- or natural-employment level of real output, aggregate expenditure may be greater than, equal to, or less than aggregate output.

These three possibilities determine the condition or "state" of the economy at any given time. To see why, let's examine the scenarios depicted in Exhibit 4:

Inflationary Gap   This is shown in Figure (a). The *inflationary gap* (measured on the vertical axis) occurs because aggregate expenditure AE exceeds aggregate output AO at the full- or natural-employment level. As a result, the excess in total spending when resources are already fully employed pulls up prices. This causes the *nominal* (rather than *real*) value of output to rise.

EXHIBIT
4

Inflationary and Recessionary Gaps: Income-Expenditure Model

In the income-expenditure model, inflationary and recessionary gaps are measured in terms of total spending (in constant dollars). The gaps occur when, at the full- or natural-employment level, aggregate expenditure is either greater than or less than the economy's aggregate output.

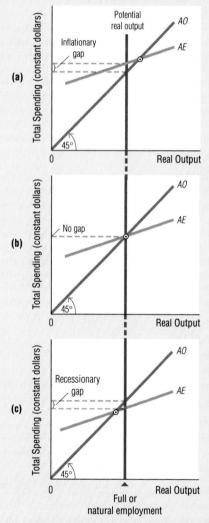

FIGURE (a) **Inflationary Gap**   Aggregate expenditure AE exceeds aggregate output AO at full employment.

FIGURE (b) **No Gap**   Aggregate expenditure AE equals aggregate output AO at full employment.

FIGURE (c) **Recessionary Gap**   Aggregate expenditure AE is less than aggregate output AO at full employment.

No Gap   This is illustrated in Figure (b). Aggregate expenditure AE equals aggregate output AO at the full- or natural-employment level. Therefore, there's neither too much nor too little total spending.

Recessionary Gap   This is seen in Figure (c). Aggregate expenditure AE falls short of aggregate output AO at the full- or natural-employment level. The *recessionary gap* (measured on the vertical axis) occurs because the deficiency of total spending pulls down the value of real output.

Conclusion: Understanding Business Cycles

When we began the study of macroeconomics, we learned that it has two objectives. The first is to explain why business cycles occur. The second is to explain what policies, if any, can be adopted to reduce their severity.

In our study thus far of the income-expenditure model, we have been concerned with the first objective. The model has helped us to understand how business cycles—fluctuations in output and employment—arise and how they create inflationary and recessionary gaps. As we've seen, the gaps are always defined with reference to full employment, and they are explained in terms of aggregate expenditure and aggregate output. Thus:

At the economy's full- or natural-employment level, an inflationary gap occurs when aggregate expenditure is greater than aggregate output, that is, when $AE > AO$. Conversely, a recessionary gap occurs when aggregate expenditure is less than aggregate output, that is, when $AE < AO$. Total spending is thus a critical variable in the income-expenditure model. The level of total spending in relation to total output is the engine that drives the economy.

The income-expenditure model is now completed. In order to make the best use of it, we must see how it relates to the other macroeconomic model learned in earlier chapters—the income-price model. Before doing so, a brief summary will prove helpful.

Summary Thus Far

1.   The multiplier principle expresses the idea that a change in investment can bring about a larger change in real output. The amount of change in real output depends on the size of the multiplier, which varies inversely with the marginal propensity to save.

2. In the income-expenditure model, the level of aggregate expenditure is determined by withdrawals and injections. Withdrawals, consisting of saving, taxes, and imports, reduce aggregate expenditure. Injections, consisting of investment, government spending, and exports, increase aggregate expenditure.

3. At the economy's full- or natural-employment level, aggregate expenditure may be greater than, equal to, or less than aggregate output. Changes in aggregate expenditure cause business cycles that create inflationary and recessionary gaps.

The Income-Price Model: Accommodating Two Views

Much of today's macroeconomics was born during the Great Depression of the 1930s. Its originator was British economist John Maynard Keynes (pronounced "canes"). During many periods of history, including the 1930s, the *general price level was relatively constant*. Inflation normally averaged less than 1 percent annually. As a result, it was reasonable for Keynes to assume the existence of a constant price level when he developed his theory of the macroeconomy.

Experiences since the mid-twentieth century have taught us that inflationary rates can vary widely. There are periods when average year-to-year increases in prices can be relatively small and other periods when the increases can be relatively substantial. How can we understand the consequences of these changes? The best way is to examine them in terms of the *income-price* model.

You're already familiar with the income-price model from several earlier chapters. To brush up on its main ideas, refer to Exhibit 5 and the review that follows. Then you'll be able to see how the model can accommodate both the "old" assumption of a constant price level and the modern assumption of a varying price level.

Reviewing the Basic Concepts

Exhibit 5 consists of two graphs—a short-run model in Figure (a) and a long-run model in Figure (b). Observe that the average price level in the two graphs is measured on the vertical axis and real output is measured on the horizontal axis. (The horizontal axis also measures the level of employment, but it's *implied* rather than explicitly indicated.)

EXHIBIT 5

The Income-Price Model: Short-Run and Long-Run Equilibrium

The difference between the short-run and long-run income-price models lies in the shape of the aggregate supply curve.

(a) Short Run

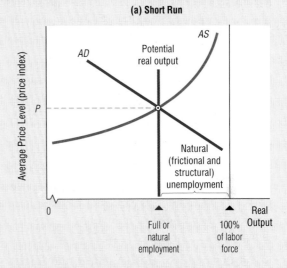

FIGURE (a) In the short run, many production costs (especially wages) are fixed by contract. Firms therefore find it profitable to increase output and employment as the average price level rises. As a result, the short-run *AS* curve is upward sloping.

(b) Long Run

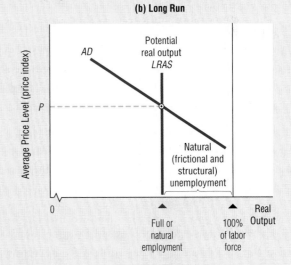

FIGURE (b) In the long run, the economy is self-correcting. This means that the average price level can fluctuate (due to shifts in the *AD* curve) while output and employment remain stable at their full or natural levels. As a result, the long-run aggregate supply (*LRAS*) curve is vertical.

In analyzing the two graphs, the first important feature to note is the ***aggregate demand* (*AD*)** curve. It tells you the amount of real aggregate output that will be purchased by all sectors of the economy at various average price levels. The downward slope of the curve means that the public will buy more real output at a lower average price level than at a higher one. Let's review the reasons briefly:

- **Real-Balance Effect** At lower average prices, the purchasing power or the *real* value of people's cash balances is greater. Therefore, people can buy more goods with their cash balances.

- **Interest-Rate Effect** When prices decline, interest rates tend to decline, too. Therefore, people can buy more goods because borrowing costs are lower.

- **Net-Export Effect** A decline in the price level reduces the price of domestic goods relative to the price of foreign goods. The resulting rise in exports relative to imports causes an increase in net exports, which adds to the amount of aggregate demand.

Recall that the real-balance effect, the interest-rate effect, and the net-export effect assume that all other conditions—particularly the rate of money growth in the economy—remain constant. Do you remember why? *Hint:* How might rapid increases or decreases in money growth influence these effects?

The second important feature of the graphs is the ***aggregate supply* (*AS*)** curve. It shows the total value of real aggregate output that will be made available at various average price levels. An important property of the *AS* curve in Figure (a) is that it's upward sloping. This tells you that, up to a point, businesses will supply larger volumes of output at a higher average price level than at a lower one. The reason is easy to understand. Many wages as well as certain other production costs are set by contracts and, hence, do not increase immediately in response to a rising price level. Therefore, in the short run higher prices mean wider profit margins, which give producers incentive to increase output. This points up an important distinction between the short-run and long-run aggregate supply curves in the two figures:

In the short run [Figure (a)], a rising average price level calls forth higher volumes of real output and employment. Therefore, the short-run aggregate supply (*AS*) curve is upward sloping.

In the long run [Figure (b)], the economy produces its potential (full-employment) real output regardless of the average price level. Therefore, the *LRAS* curve is vertical.

Interpreting Keynes with an Income-Price Model

When the *AD* and *AS* curves are combined, their intersection determines both the equilibrium output and the equilibrium price level. In the short run, the equilibrium output *may* occur at the full- or natural-employment level, as shown in Figure (a). However, it *may* also occur at a lower or a higher employment level and, hence, at a correspondingly lower or higher price level than *P*.

In general, the equilibrium output and price levels will be determined by where the *AD* and *AS* curves happen to intersect. But as you've learned, the income-price model assumes that both real output and the average price level are self-correcting. Therefore, any equilibrium that isn't at the natural level is a short-run situation. Depending on the stickiness of prices and wages, real output and the price level will ultimately adjust automatically to their long-run values.

This poses a challenge:

Can the Keynesian assumption of a constant price level and the possibility of prolonged unemployment be expressed in terms of the income-price model?

The answer is yes. But the income-price model has to be modified in order to do it. This is because Keynes didn't use graphs when he constructed his theory. Graphic models were formulated in later years by other economists. The two income-price models in Exhibit 6 thus depict both strict and modified Keynesian views. The models therefore allow us to interpret Keynesian ideas both from a traditional and a modern vantage point.

Strict Keynesian View

Had Keynes used graphs, he would have assumed that the aggregate supply curve could be depicted as a reverse *L*-shaped curve. This is the situation shown in Figure (a) of Exhibit 6. The reason for this shape is based on Keynes's assumption of a *constant price level*. Thus, at any output short of full employment, the economy has unemployed resources. Therefore, as aggregate demand increases from AD_0 to AD_1, producers can expand real output to the full-employment level

EXHIBIT
6

Keynesian Equilibrium in the Income-Price Model

Keynes didn't use graphs when he formulated his theory of macroeconomics more than half a century ago. However, these Keynesian interpretations of equilibrium illustrate some of his ideas.

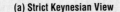

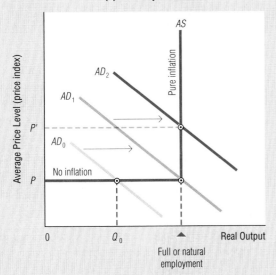

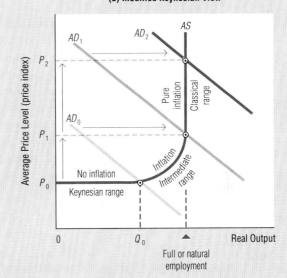

FIGURE (a) Strict Keynesian View Keynes would have viewed the *AS* curve in terms of a horizontal and a vertical range—a reverse *L*-shape. Increases in aggregate demand from AD_0 to AD_1 result in *noninflationary* expansions in real output and employment because there are unemployed resources available. Once full employment is reached, an increase in aggregate demand to AD_2 results in pure inflation because prices rise without any expansion in real output or in employment. This reverse *L*-shaped *AS* curve represents the original Keynesian view.

FIGURE (b) Modified Keynesian View This revised version introduces an "intermediate range" for the *AS* curve. Although the economy's aggregate demand and aggregate supply curves have shifted frequently over the long run, they have generally intersected in this middle range. This helps explain why our nation has often experienced irregular rates of inflation along with expansions in real output while employment has remained less than "full." The intermediate range of the *AS* curve represents the modern Keynesian view.

without bidding up the prices of resources. This is because, within this range of output, competition among unemployed resources remains strong enough to keep the average price level at *P*.

But what happens if the aggregate demand curve increases beyond AD_1, say, to AD_2? The result will be pure inflation—an increase in the price level to *P'* without any increase in output. Keynes reasoned that, once the economy is operating at full employment, further increases in aggregate demand can result only

in higher prices, not in additional production and jobs. This view of the nature of inflation accorded with that held by the classical economists in Keynes's time.

Modified Keynesian View

One of the shortcomings of this strict Keynesian view is its failure to deal with the simultaneous occurrence of inflation and high (but not necessarily full) employment. This is a condition that our economy has often experienced in the last several decades. Accordingly,

Figure (b) provides a modified version of the Keynesian view by incorporating two new features:

- **Revised Aggregate Supply Curve** The *AS* curve is divided into three "ranges." The Keynesian range (no inflation) and the classical range (pure inflation) are based on Figure (a) and have already been explained.

- **Intermediate Range** In this range, increases in aggregate demand from AD_0 to AD_1 will stimulate increases in output. The reason is the same as that for the upward-sloping *AS* curve. That is, in this range prices are rising faster than firms' production costs because much of the latter (especially wages) are fixed periodically by contractual agreements. As less efficient resources are brought into use, the *AS* curve becomes steeper. Therefore, further increases in aggregate demand cause the average price level to rise faster than real output. *This is a modern version of the Keynesian view.*

Conclusion: Short-Run Determinants Are Important

From our analysis, you can see that unemployment and inflation are related problems. They arise from conditions that determine the relative positions of the economy's *AD* and *AS* curves. Depending on the shapes of the curves and the point at which they intersect, the economy will experience some combination of unemployment and inflation. The outcome can be a misallocation of resources, resulting in losses of efficiency, stability, and growth. Because of this, it is important to be aware of the determinants of aggregate demand and aggregate supply. Once these determinants are understood, we can better evaluate government policies aimed at reducing unemployment and inflation.

We've already seen that most of the determinants of aggregate demand and aggregate supply are short run, not long run, in nature. This accounts for the following quotation, which was written about three-quarters of a century ago:

> But the long run is a misleading guide to current affairs. *In the long run we are all dead.* Economists set themselves too easy, too useless a task if in tempestuous seasons they can only tell us that when the storm is long past the ocean is flat again.
>
> –John Maynard Keynes

Summing Up: Traditional and Modern Keynesian Views

As you have seen, Keynes's original interpretation of equilibrium was based on the assumption of a *constant price level*. The newer view of equilibrium is based on the assumption of a *varying price level*. One of the appealing features of the income-price model is that it can accommodate both views.

Thus, traditional and modern Keynesian beliefs can be illustrated with an income-price model like the one in Figure (b) of Exhibit 6. In this model, the *AS* curve has a modified, reverse *L*-shape covering three ranges:

1. **Noninflationary Range** This is the horizontal segment of the curve. In this range, increases in aggregate demand bring about increases in real output and employment while the average price level remains stable.

2. **Inflationary Range** This is the upward-sloping segment of the curve. In this range, increases in aggregate demand bring about increases in real output, employment, *and* the average price level.

3. **Pure-Inflationary Range** This is the vertical segment of the curve. In this range, increases in aggregate demand bring about rising prices without any increases in real output and employment.

The inflationary or upward-sloping range of the *AS* curve is the one in which the economy usually operates. Therefore, modern Keynesians focus primary attention on this segment. One of their chief goals is to explain the magnitude of changes in real output, employment, and inflation that result from shifts in aggregate demand.

Implications of a Varying Price Level

To say that the economy usually operates in the inflationary or upward-sloping range of the *AS* curve is just another way of stating that the average price level varies. We know this to be true from personal experience. The price of food, clothing, books, transportation, and most of the other things we buy changes frequently. In view of this, what implications does a varying price level have for the income-expenditure model? How does a varying price level affect the operation of the multiplier, which was explained near the beginning of the chapter?

EXHIBIT
7

How the Income-Expenditure and Income-Price Models Are Related Through the *AE* and *AD* Curves

The income-expenditure model and the income-price model can be linked by their aggregate expenditure and aggregate demand curves. Keep in mind that the income-expenditure model assumes prices remain the same. Therefore, *a given aggregate expenditure curve is associated with its own constant price level.* Thus, as explained in the text, the vertical dashed lines connect the equilibrium point on an *AE* curve with its associated price level on the *AD* curve.

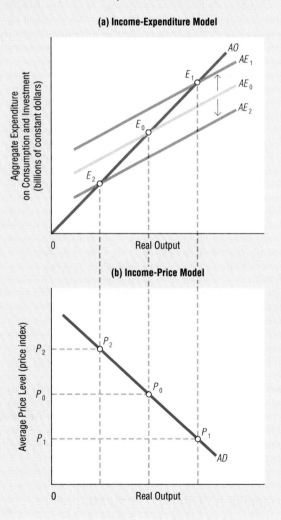

(a) Income-Expenditure Model

(b) Income-Price Model

Linking the Income-Expenditure and Income-Price Models

We've seen that the macroeconomy can be represented by two models: the income-expenditure model, and the income-price model. Although the two appear to be independent, there actually is a relationship between them.

The diagrams in Exhibit 7 enable you to see how the models are linked. Figure (a) shows the income-expenditure model with aggregate expenditures measured on the vertical axis. Figure (b) presents the aggregate demand portion of the income-price model with the average price level measured on the vertical axis. In both diagrams, real output is measured on the horizontal axis. As a result, the two models can be linked by their aggregate expenditure and aggregate demand curves. The linkage is based on the fact that, in the income-expenditure model, the average price level is assumed to be constant. Therefore, *a given aggregate expenditure curve is associated with its own average price level.*

Thus:

1. The AE_0 curve in Figure (a) is associated with the price level at P_0 in Figure (b). A vertical dashed line connects the equilibrium point E_0 with P_0.

2. If the price level decreases, people have more purchasing power, so total spending increases. (Recall the real-balance effect, the interest-rate effect, and the net-export effect). Therefore, the aggregate expenditure curve in Figure (a) rises to AE_1. This curve is associated with the lower price level at P_1 in Figure (b). A vertical dashed line connects the equilibrium point E_1 with the price level P_1.

3. If the price level increases, people have less purchasing power, so total spending decreases. The aggregate expenditure curve in Figure (a) thus declines to AE_2. This curve is associated with the higher price level at P_2 in Figure (b). A vertical dashed line connects the equilibrium point E_2 with P_2.

The income-expenditure and income-price models can be related through their aggregate expenditure and aggregate demand curves. Linking the two models enables us to see how changes in the average price level cause changes in aggregate expenditure, which in turn cause changes in the equilibrium level of real output.

Multiplier Effects

Near the beginning of the chapter, you learned how the operation of the *multiplier principle* could cause a change in investment to create a magnified change in real output. You'll recall that the explanation of the principle was based on the assumption of a constant price level, and that a graphic analysis of the concept was done in terms of the income-expenditure model of Exhibit 2. (You should refer back to Exhibit 2 to refresh your understanding of the model.)

What happens to the multiplier effect if the price level is assumed to be variable? To answer the question, we must use an income-price model. This is done in Exhibit 8. Note that the equilibrium point at E_0 results from the intersection of the aggregate supply curve AS and the initial aggregate demand curve AD_0. This equilibrium point denotes an income level of $500 billion and a price level of P_0.

Now, let's assume the same $5 billion increase in investment, and therefore in aggregate expenditure, that was employed in the income-expenditure model in Exhibit 2. Because investment spending is part of aggregate demand, the effect of this increased expenditure is to shift the aggregate demand curve to the right from AD_0 to AD_1. The equilibrium point, therefore, changes from E_0 to E_1. This new equilibrium point denotes an income level of $520 billion and a price level of P_1. The gain in real income is thus $20 billion, and hence the multiplier is 4.

What would have happened if the price level had remained constant at P_0? In that case, the new equilibrium point would have been at E'_0. (In other words, the aggregate supply curve, as in the strict Keynesian view presented earlier, would have been the horizontal dashed line extending from P_0 to E'_0.) Therefore, the equilibrium income would have been $525 billion. Thus, an increase in aggregate expenditure of $5 billion would have resulted in an increase in real income of $25 billion. The multiplier, therefore, would have been 5—the same as in the income-expenditure model of Exhibit 2.

This example has assumed that the increase in the price level from P_0 to P_1 was 20 percent. (In reality, if the slope of the AD curve is given, the amount of the increase will depend on the *slope* of the AS curve.) Because of this, the size of the multiplier was 20 percent less (4 instead of 5) than it would have been if the price level had remained constant (that is, if the AS curve had been a horizontal line with a slope of zero).

EXHIBIT
8

The Multiplier Effect When the Price Level Varies: Income-Price Model

Investment spending by businesses is part of the economy's aggregate demand. Therefore, an increase in investment of $5 billion shifts the aggregate demand curve to the right from AD_0 to AD_1. This increases real income by $20 billion—a multiplier of 4—and the price level by an assumed 20 percent. If the price level had remained constant at P_0, the AS curve would have been the horizontal dashed line from P_0 to E'_0. The increase in real income would have been $25 billion, a multiplier of 5.

Thus, when the price level rises, part of the multiplier's effect is lost through higher prices, and only part is left to increase real income. In this example, a 20 percent increase in prices resulted in a 20 percent smaller multiplier (4 instead of 5). It also resulted in a 20 percent smaller increase in real output (to $520 billion instead of $525 billion).

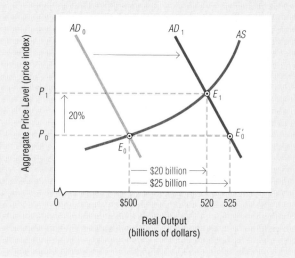

Similarly, the increase in real income was 20 percent less (to $520 billion as compared with $525 billion) than would have been realized if the price level had remained constant.

Conclusion: Different-Sized Multipliers

The multiplier principle is of fundamental importance in macroeconomics. The larger the multiplier, the greater the amount by which an increase in investment results in an increase in aggregate income. However, the size of the multiplier will be affected by the *change* in the average price level. Thus:

If the aggregate supply curve is upward-sloping, an increase in investment, and therefore in aggregate demand, causes the average price level to rise. As a result, the size of the multiplier is smaller than it would be if the average price level remained constant. This is because part of the multiplier's effect is lost through higher prices, and only part is left to increase real income.

International Aspects: The Open-Economy Multiplier

Even if the price level remained constant, the size of the multiplier would still be reduced due to the influence of other factors. One of these is imports—the goods we buy from abroad. If ours were a "closed economy"—one that isn't engaged in international trade—we wouldn't have any imports. Therefore, part of the increased income resulting from the higher level of investment would be spent on domestic goods, and the rest of the increase would be saved. This means that, as you saw earlier, $MPC + MPS = 1$.

But ours is an "open economy"—one that engages in international trade. As a result, *given the level of exports, changes in imports can affect the size of the multiplier.* Let's see why.

When aggregate income goes up, we buy not only more domestically produced goods but also more foreign-made goods. Among the goods we purchase from other countries are cars, electronic products, steel, textiles, and trips abroad (which may be thought of as "scenery imported"). Thus, just as the nation's propensity to consume is directly related to aggregate income, so too is the nation's propensity to import.

As a result, when the economy's aggregate income increases, part of the increase is spent on domestic goods, part of it is saved, and part of it is spent on foreign goods. The fraction that's spent on domestic goods is the *MPC*. The fraction that "leaks" into saving is the *MPS*. And the fraction that might have been used to purchase domestic goods but instead "leaks" into the purchase of foreign goods may be called the marginal propensity to import (*MPM*).

As you'll recall, the **marginal propensity to import** is the change in imports resulting from a unit change in income:

$$MPM = \frac{\text{change in imports}}{\text{change in income}}$$

It follows that, in an open economy, $MPC + MPS + MPM = 1$. This suggests that the multiplier for an open economy, like the multiplier for a closed economy, is the *reciprocal of the leakage.* But the leakage now includes imports as well as saving. Thus, the multiplier for an open economy can be expressed by the formula:

$$\text{Open-economy multiplier} = \frac{1}{MPS + MPM} = \frac{1}{\text{leakage}}$$

It's easy to see what this means in terms of some numbers. Suppose, for example, that the *MPS* is 0.20 and the *MPM* is 0.05. The total leakage is 0.25. Therefore, *even if the price level remains constant,* the open-economy multiplier is $1/0.25 = 4$. This means that an increase in investment of $5 billion will increase real output by 4 times that amount, or $20 billion. In a closed economy, on the other hand, the multiplier is $1/0.20 = 5$. The same change in investment would have resulted in a change in real output of $25 billion. The difference, obviously, is due to the size of the leakage, which is larger in an open economy than in a closed one. It follows that, if the price level were to rise, the size of the open-economy multiplier would be reduced still further.

An increase in investment causes aggregate income to rise by an amplified amount. But the increase in aggregate income induces some imports, or "leakages." As a result, the full multiplier effect on income is smaller than would exist if imports remained constant. The size of the multiplier is further reduced by any rise in the price level that results when aggregate demand increases.

The open-economy multiplier is more commonly known as the "foreign-trade multiplier." It is an important concept in the study of international trade.

Summary of Important Ideas

1. The multiplier principle explains how a change in investment (or in total spending) can cause a magnified change in real output. The multiplier is equal to the reciprocal of the marginal propensity to save. Therefore, the larger the *MPS*, the smaller the multiplier.

2. In the complete income-expenditure model, aggregate expenditure AE is the sum of consumption expenditure C by the household sector, investment expenditure I by the business sector, government expenditure G by the government sector, and net exports X_N by the foreign sector. The equality of AE and aggregate output AO determines the equilibrium levels of real output and of total spending. (The equilibrium level of real output can also be explained in terms of injections and withdrawals. When these two flows are equal, the corresponding level of real output is determined.)

3. Changes in aggregate expenditure cause fluctuations in real output. The fluctuations create inflationary and recessionary gaps. The size of the gaps is measured in terms of disparities between aggregate expenditure and aggregate output at full employment.

4. In the income-price model, the downward-sloping aggregate demand curve and upward-sloping aggregate supply curve determine an equilibrium output and price level. At any given time, the location of the equilibrium point may or may not correspond to full (natural) employment.

5. The original version of Keynesian equilibrium can be illustrated with a modified income-price model. In the model, the AS curve has a reverse L-shape. In the horizontal range, increases in aggregate demand bring about increases in real output and employment while the average price level remains constant. In the vertical portion, which occurs at full employment, increases in aggregate demand are purely inflationary. If an upward-sloping segment is "inserted" between the horizontal and vertical portions, a modern Keynesian view of the AS curve is obtained. Along this segment, increases in aggregate demand bring about increases in real output, employment, *and* the average price level.

6. The income-expenditure and income-price models can be linked through the aggregate expenditure and aggregate demand curves. This linkage associates each AE curve with a particular price level on an AD curve. As a result, it can be seen how changes in the average price level cause changes in aggregate expenditure, which in turn cause changes in real output.

7. The multiplier will be smaller if prices vary than if they are constant. This is because a rising price level dissipates part of the multiplier's effect through higher prices. As a result, only a portion of the multiplier is left to increase real income.

8. The multiplier will also be smaller in an open economy—one that engages in international trade. This is because part of any increase in aggregate income will be spent on imports rather than on domestically produced goods. Imports, like savings, are a "leakage" from the economy's circular flow of income.

Terms and Concepts to Review

multiplier	*net-export effect*
inflationary gap	*aggregate supply*
recessionary gap	*marginal propensity to*
aggregate demand	*import*
real-balance effect	*open-economy multiplier*
interest-rate effect	

Questions and Problems

1. To help reinforce your understanding of the income-expenditure model, complete the following table for a hypothetical economy. Assume that the consumption function is a straight line and that investment is constant at all levels of income. (All figures are in billions of constant dollars.)

Real Output	C	S	I	APC	APS	MPC	MPS
$100	$125	___	$25	___	___		
200	200	___	___	___	___	___	___
300	___	___	___	___	___	___	___
400	___	___	___	___	___	___	___
500	___	___	___	___	___	___	___

a. From the data in the table, draw a graph of the consumption function and of the consumption-plus-investment function. Underneath this graph, draw a graph of the saving and investment curves. Then connect the two sets of break-even points with vertical dashed lines.

b. Has there been a multiplier effect as a result of the inclusion of investment? If yes, by how much does it change income? What is the numerical value of the multiplier?

c. What is the equilibrium level of income and output before and after the inclusion of investment?

d. What will income be if investment increases by $10 billion?

e. What will happen to your answer for (d) if the price level rises by 25 percent? Explain the reason for your answer.

2. How does the size of the multiplier vary with *MPC*? How does it vary with *MPS*? Explain why, without using any equations. How does the size of the multiplier vary with changes in the price level?

3. Suppose consumption spending remained the same for all levels of income. What would be the value of the *MPC*? Would the value of the *MPS* be positive, zero, or negative?

4. Suppose your consumption *C* is related to your disposable income *DI* by the equation

$$C = 120 + 0.60\ DI$$

a. What will be your consumption at an income level of 100?

b. How much income do you require to support a consumption level of 420?

c. What will be your consumption if your income is taxed at 100 percent? How can your consumption be financed under such circumstances?

d. What is the value of your *MPC*? What is the value of your *MPS*?

e. Prepare your personal consumption and saving schedule, and graph the consumption and saving functions for income levels from *DI* = 100 to *DI* = 500. What is your equilibrium level of income?

5. If the previous problem were for an entire economy, and if planned investment were 50, what would be the equation for aggregate expenditure? Draw the aggregate expenditure curve and investment curve on your graphs. Estimate the equilibrium level of income from your graphs.

6. (Advanced Problem) Refer to your graphs from the previous problem.

a. At a realized income of 500, how much is unplanned investment? How much is realized investment? Is this an equilibrium situation? Explain.

b. At a realized income of 400, how much is unplanned investment? How much is realized investment? Is this an equilibrium situation? Explain.

c. At the realized-income levels in (a) and (b), does saving equal investment? Explain.

7. Can you suggest at least one method that government might employ in an effort to close inflationary and recessionary gaps?

8. Suppose the investment multiplier in an economy is 4, real output is 1,000, and the full-employment real output is 1,200. If prices remain constant, how much would aggregate expenditure have to rise in order for real output to reach full employment?

9. Suppose the investment multiplier is 5, real output is 2,500, and the full-employment real output is 2,000. How much would aggregate expenditure have to fall to return the economy to full employment?

10. How do modern Keynesians view equilibrium in terms of the income-price model?

11. The average price level may be called an "aggregate-expenditure shifter." What does this expression mean?

12. In the original Keynesian view, if the *AS* curve were a vertical line, would an increase in aggregate demand have a multiplier effect?

13. What are "leakages?" Of what importance are they in terms of the multiplier concepts studied in this chapter? *Hint*: Recall the bathtub theorem and what it explains.

TAKE A STAND

Just-in-Time Inventory Management: Will It Reduce Recessions?

The instability of business investment is often cited as a chief reason for business cycle fluctuations. A firm's capital investments in factories, office buildings, equipment, and the like usually follow a long-term plan, but its investment in inventories may be highly variable. Inventories are stocks of raw materials, intermediate goods, and final products that businesses keep on hand to avoid problems caused by input shortages or sudden sales increases. Firms in the United States usually maintain inventories equal to approximately 4 months of sales.

During a recession, firms reduce their investment in inventories. While inventory investment amounts to perhaps 1 percent of GDP, 70 to 80 percent of the decline in GDP during recessions is typically attributed to the decline in inventory investment. Even in nonrecessionary periods, inventory investment is the most volatile component of GDP. On average, it accounts for 50 percent of the change in GDP in any given year.

This situation may be changing. In the 1980s, many manufacturing firms began adopting just-in-time (JIT) inventory management techniques, which were being used with notable success in Japan. Rather than purchase large amounts of inputs on an infrequent basis and store the resulting inventory, firms using JIT purchase smaller amounts of inputs on a more frequent basis to match consumer demand more closely. For example, computer manufacturers often order only 2 to 3 *hours'* worth of inputs several times a day, just in time to fill orders. By holding less inventory, these firms reduce their costs.

With JIT inventory management, firms keep relatively small inventories and restock them often. Widespread adoption of this strategy could virtually eliminate the large, infrequent inventory purchases that are believed to affect economic stability. *But will just-in-time inventory management reduce recessions?*

Yes: JIT Keeps Inventories Low

Evidence is beginning to mount that JIT inventory management has already lessened the severity of business cycle fluctuations. In the 1970s only about 5 percent of the firms in the United States used JIT inventory management. Many of these were food producers and retailers dealing with perishable products. By 1990, the proportion of firms using JIT had reached over 15 percent. Most of these were manufacturers of automobiles, computers, and office machinery that chose to adopt JIT in order to keep pace with their successful Japanese competitors.

Many firms that did not explicitly adopt JIT practices did reduce the average amount of time between ordering inputs and using them in production. In 1975, this "lead" time between purchase and use averaged 80 days for the economy as a whole. By 1990, average lead time had dropped to 45 days.

As a recession approaches and sales decline, firms experience a buildup of inventory. But when sales fall, firms generally wish to hold less inventory. Over the course of the recession, therefore, firms reduce production and concentrate on selling off existing inventory. Economists attribute the length and severity of recessions in part to this inventory effect. JIT techniques allow firms to manage their operations so as to reduce inventory fluctuation.

During the 1980s, inventory stockpiles declined from 3.5 months' sales to slightly more than 3 months' sales. Even with the approach of the recession of 1990, inventories did not increase relative to sales. The reason is that firms using JIT management were able to adjust purchases and production rapidly enough to prevent a buildup of inventory. When the recession hit, these firms did not have to lay workers off, cancel planned purchases, or leave facilities idle. This made the recession less severe and less lengthy than it otherwise might have been.

No: The Effect Is Weak

Changes in inventory investment are one of several consequences of business cycles, not a cause. New inventory management techniques such as JIT may change the character of recessions, but cannot eliminate business cycles entirely. In fact, JIT is likely to have only a minimal effect on business cycles.

JIT may serve merely to redistribute inventory rather than reduce it. Suppose a large firm decides to cut its inventories and buy materials only as needed. Its suppliers may decide to increase their inventories in order to be confident of meeting the firm's demand for frequent, irregular deliveries. One report speculates that the decline and subsequent revival of Detroit's warehouse district may reflect precisely this scenario. The decline began as U.S. automakers adopted JIT and reduced their inventories. The upturn may be attributable to inventory increases on the part of the automakers' suppliers.

Even if JIT were to cause real reductions in inventory, so few firms have adopted the technique that its effect on recessions is likely to be negligible. Despite the increase in popularity of JIT during the 1980s, over 80 percent of U.S. firms still do not use the technique.

Any tendency of JIT to dampen recession may disappear in a protracted downturn. True, in the early stages of recession, firms that use JIT experience a smaller buildup and subsequent reduction of inventory than firms that do not. Non-JIT firms have a more difficult adjustment period, but all firms eventually attain an inventory-to-sales ratio consistent with their lower sales. While JIT eases a firm's transition into a recessionary period, neither JIT nor any other inventory management technique can bring about a recovery.

Finally, some economists have suggested that the primary cause of business cycles is the pursuit of political self-interest. Elected officials, including the president and members of Congress, recognize that voters are more likely to re-elect incumbents during prosperous periods than during recessions. Before an election, therefore, politicians may seek to stimulate the economy by changing government spending and taxation, or by persuading the Federal Reserve to increase the money supply. If inventory management techniques were to make the economy more stable in the face of such shocks, self-interested politicians would simply engineer bigger shocks.

The Question: Will Just-in-Time Inventory Management Reduce Recessions?

■   Some believe that JIT inventory management practices in the 1980s were responsible for reducing the amount of inventories that firms maintained. With little inventory buildup, these firms were able to continue operations despite the approach of a recession at the decade's end. JIT management thus helped to control the length and severity of the recession.

■   Others maintain that inventory changes do not cause business cycles. The effects of JIT inventory management on a recession, therefore, are likely to be negligible. The effects of political manipulation should not be overlooked.

Where Do You Stand?

1. Could reductions in average holdings of inventories make the economy less stable? Explain.

2. Name two industries, other than those listed here, that could effectively use JIT inventory management, and two that would have difficulty using JIT. Explain why.

3. JIT inventory techniques are an offshoot of an innovative management philosophy developed in the 1940s by an American expert in quality control, W. Edwards Deming. Effectively rejected by American businesses, Deming's recommendations were subsequently adopted in Japan. Why do you suppose that JIT management was initially ignored in the United States but is now being adopted by a growing number of companies?

4. Will just-in-time inventory management reduce recessions? Justify your stand.

Source: Donald P. Morgan, "Will Just-In-Time Inventory Techniques Dampen Recessions?" *Economic Review*, Federal Reserve Bank of Kansas City, March/April 1991, pp. 21-33.

Chapter 15

Taxing, Government Spending, and the New Fiscal Policy

Federal Budget Management: Sources and Uses of Funds

The Theory of Fiscal Policy

Problems of Fiscal Policy

Fiscal Policy and Supply-Side Economics

Learning Guide

Watch for answers to these important questions

From what sources does the federal government receive its funds? To what uses are the funds put?

When and why did fiscal policy come into existence? What are the differences between nondiscretionary and discretionary fiscal policy?

Why is discretionary fiscal policy difficult to implement? What problems does implementation pose?

How does demand-side economics differ from supply-side economics? What are the main principles of supply-side economics? In what ways have modern fiscal policy beliefs been affected by supply-side thinking?

Perhaps nowhere is the use of economics more evident than in efforts pursued by Washington to close inflationary and recessionary gaps. These efforts can take a number of different forms. One of them that you learned about earlier, is called *monetary policy*. It consists, you'll recall, of deliberate actions by the Federal Reserve System (the Fed) to manage the money growth rate in order to encourage full employment at stable prices. These goals, of course, correspond to the familiar economic goals of efficiency and stability.

Another type of effort is called *fiscal policy*. Originally formulated as a method for attaining efficiency only, it has evolved into a means of achieving that goal by promoting economic growth. In this modern form, therefore, it's sometimes called *new* fiscal policy.

The word "fiscal" comes from the Latin *fiscus*, meaning treasury. The U.S. Department of Treasury is the money-raising and money-spending agent of the federal government. The Treasury raises money for the government by collecting taxes from households and businesses. (When you pay your income tax, you send a check to the Internal Revenue Service, which is a division of the Treasury.) The Treasury spends money for the government by writing checks to pay for government purchases and programs. *Fiscal policy is thus concerned with taxing and government spending.*

Note to Instructors: As explained in the preface, this chapter provides the Keynesian background relevant to fiscal policy and uses the income-price model exclusively. Therefore, instructors who are omitting the income-expenditure model can cover this chapter independently of the two previous chapters on Keynesian economics.

Federal Budget Management: Sources and Uses of Funds

The principal issues of fiscal policy focus on how the federal government, *represented by the Treasury*, manages its budget. Therefore, let's examine the ways in which the government raises and spends money, and the economic consequences of these activities.

To begin with, taxation and spending can affect the government's budget. The government's **budget,** like a household's budget, is an itemized estimate of expected revenues and expenditures for the year. Of course, expectations may not be realized. Consequently, like a household's budget, the government's annual budget may end up in one of three states:

- **Budget Balance** The budget will balance if total revenues equal total expenditures. History shows that this is unlikely to happen unless the government commits itself to matching its spending with tax revenues.

- **Budget Deficit** The budget will show a deficit if total expenditures exceed total revenues—as has happened in almost every year for well over half a century. As you learned when you studied monetary economics, the Treasury finances a budget deficit by selling debt instruments—bills and bonds—to the public.

- **Budget Surplus** The budget will show a surplus if total revenues exceed total expenditures. Although an annual budget surplus has been realized only a few times since the 1930s, it raises significant questions that are an important part of fiscal policy.

Where the Money Comes From

In order to manage its budget, the government raises money in two ways—taxing and borrowing. Taxing brings revenue into the government. Borrowing brings in additional funds that have to be paid back. Each has different effects on the economy.

Taxing

For purposes of fiscal policy, income taxes (rather than sales taxes, property taxes, or other kinds of taxes) are the most important by far. Changes in the rate structure of income taxes can affect both government revenues and the level of economic activity.

For instance, suppose that, during a recession, government decides to stimulate the economy with a

decrease in tax rates. What are some of the potential outcomes?

A reduction in tax rates *may* result in a short-term reduction in government revenues. But it will also leave people with more disposable income. The increase in disposable income will likely be allocated partly to increased consumption and partly to increased saving. The increased consumption will stimulate aggregate demand. The increased saving, to the extent that it's borrowed by businesses for investment in plant, equipment, and inventories, will also stimulate aggregate demand. In response to increased demand, output and employment will increase. The overall effect of the tax rate reduction will thus be expansionary. In the long run, therefore, because of the higher level of economic activity, government tax revenues will rise—perhaps even more than enough to offset their short-term decline.

This is only one of several possible scenarios. Can you evaluate the possible effects of an *increase* in tax rates undertaken to curb an inflation?

Borrowing

A second method by which the government can raise money is by borrowing. Government borrows money when tax revenues aren't sufficient to cover expenditures. In other words, borrowing is the means by which the government finances a deficit. Borrowing consists of selling Treasury debt instruments—bills and bonds—to the public. These sales *may* have two consequences:

1. **Higher Interest Rates** Treasury bills and bonds compete with business debt instruments, such as corporate promissory notes and bonds, for investors' dollars. As a result, if all other things remain the same, heavy sales of Treasury debt instruments may drive up interest rates. This is because both the Treasury and business borrowers may find that they must offer higher interest rates to lenders in order to persuade them to purchase additional securities.

2. **Crowding Out** Higher interest rates mean higher borrowing costs. Many businesses, of course, aren't willing to pay the higher costs. Consequently, private investment is reduced because numerous business firms are "crowded out" of the financial markets by government deficit spending.

It should be emphasized that government borrowing *doesn't necessarily* cause higher interest rates and crowding out. Their occurrence depends on the amount of borrowing undertaken. In today's global financial markets, even the federal government, the world's largest single borrower, can often borrow substantial volumes of funds without affecting interest rates significantly.

Where the Money Goes

How does the government spend its tax revenues and borrowed funds? There are two broad forms that government spending may take—transfer payments and social-goods expenditures.

Transfer Payments

When you first studied gross domestic product and the other national income accounts earlier in this course, you were introduced to the concept of **transfer payments.** They were defined as expenditures within or between sectors of the economy for which there are no corresponding contributions to current production.

Certain types of transfer payments, such as unemployment compensation and welfare benefits, rise automatically during a recession. As a result, they help to cushion a decline in the nation's income. Other transfer payments, such as old-age, disability, and veterans' benefits, are independent of aggregate income and therefore unaffected by changes in it.

Social-Goods Expenditures

The second broad form of government spending is undertaken to provide **social goods.** These were defined earlier as products provided by the public sector because society believes that such goods aren't provided in sufficient quantity by the private sector. Examples of social goods include national defense, public health, highways, parks, public buildings, slum-clearance projects, and regional development. Social-goods expenditures include money spent to create temporary public-service employment in government agencies. The jobs may range from lawn mowing to special types of social work, but the purpose is to provide short-term employment for people until they can find jobs in the private sector.

Conclusion: Budget Management and Fiscal Policy

The ways in which the federal government raises and spends money influence whether the federal budget will show a surplus or a deficit. These can have an effect on inflation:

The occurrence of a budget surplus means that the government has taken more money out of the economy in taxes than it has put back via spending. An increase in the surplus is therefore anti-inflationary. The occurrence of a budget deficit means that the government has put more money into the economy via spending than it has taken out in taxes. An increase in the deficit *may* therefore be inflationary. Whether it is or not depends on how the deficit is financed and the use to which the money spent by the government is put.

The Theory of Fiscal Policy

The problem posed by fiscal policy can be expressed in the form of a question. If at any time the economy is experiencing either an inflationary or a recessionary gap, can government adopt taxing and spending measures that will close the gap? This is the problem that fiscal policy has long tried to solve. Let's see why, by examining the way in which the theory of fiscal policy evolved.

Historical Background: Keynesian Foundations

The question whether government can formulate policies to help stabilize the economy isn't new. It began to receive serious consideration at the end of World War II (1945), when the nation was converting from wartime to peacetime status. In that era there was widespread concern that the removal of wartime price controls and the conversion to peacetime production would cause substantial inflation and unemployment. To reduce the chances of these happening, the federal government in the late 1940s assumed a new economic role. Adopting a philosophy known as *Keynesian economics,* Washington during the next several decades made substantial use of fiscal actions in efforts to achieve and maintain full employment.

Keynesian economics is a body of economic thought that originated with the British economist John Maynard Keynes (pronounced "canes") in the late 1930s. It was a critique of prevailing classical economics, which held that the economy is rapidly self-correcting. According to Keynesian theory, prices and wages in many industries are relatively rigid, not flexible. Because of this, markets may not self-correct quickly. Instead the economy may depart from its full-employment level for prolonged periods. Therefore, appropriate fiscal and monetary policies are needed to achieve and maintain a high level of resource utilization. In other words:

The Keynesian view holds that a market economy is unable to sustain full employment without policy activism by government.

Quickly dubbed the *new economics,* Keynesian economics became a revolution in economic thinking and political action. It encouraged economists and legislators to believe that the government could stabilize the economy at full employment. With respect to fiscal policy, all that Washington had to do was manipulate correctly government spending and tax rates. This manipulation would greatly reduce the peaks and troughs of business cycles and thus fine-tune the economy. Exhibit 1 shows that policy activism in the form of fiscal actions seeks to make the fluctuations in real GDP (and therefore employment) less severe.

Keynesian economics was in its heyday from the late 1940s until the early 1970s. But in the mid- and late 1970s, the United States experienced its worst recession in 30 years and one of its worst inflations in modern history. As a result, the Keynesian belief that government could successfully "manage" the economy came to be regarded as somewhat naive. Keynesian economics thus declined in relative importance. However, it by no means disappeared. Even though parts of the theory have come to be considered obsolete even by modern Keynesians, much of it continues to play a significant role in the thinking of many economists and policymakers.

What actions can government take to help stabilize economic fluctuations? There are two categories of fiscal action: nondiscretionary controls and discretionary manipulation.

Nondiscretionary Controls: Self-Correction

Significant changes in government spending and taxes occur automatically over the business cycle without any explicit action being taken by the president or Congress. Such changes occur as a result of *nondiscretionary* fiscal activities. These are neither deliberate nor planned responses by government to specific economic conditions. Rather, they are controls that are "built" into the economy and are called *automatic fiscal stabilizers.* They help cushion the economy against a recession by retarding a decline in aggregate income. They also help curb an inflation by retarding an in-

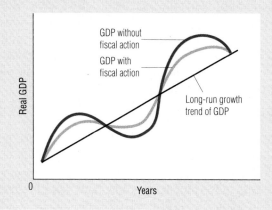

EXHIBIT 1

The Goal of Fiscal-Policy Activism

The growth of GDP has fluctuated around a rising long-run trend. Fiscal-policy activism seeks to reduce the severity of those fluctuations.

crease in aggregate income. *Automatic fiscal stabilizers* thereby contribute to keeping the economic system in balance without human intervention or control, much as a thermostat helps to maintain an even temperature in a house.

Three Important Stabilizers

The most influential automatic fiscal stabilizer is the progressive income tax. Also important are unemployment provisions and corporate dividends.

Progressive Income Tax   Personal income taxes are the largest source of revenue to the federal government. When the economy's income rises, aggregate demand increases—the *AD* curve shifts to the right. However, the tax rate that individuals pay on their rising incomes is progressive, so the increase in income available for spending—disposable income—is restrained. This reduces the extent of the rightward shift of aggregate demand, and thereby curbs an economic boom. The same principle also works in reverse. When people's disposable incomes decline, the *AD* curve shifts to the left. But the tax rate also declines. This decline tends to moderate the leftward shift of the *AD* curve, and thus curb an economic recession.

Unemployment Taxes and Welfare Benefits   During times of prosperity and high employment, tax collections to support the jobless and the poor increase while the benefits paid to these groups decrease. This tax increase has a dampening effect on the economy. During periods of recession and unemployment, the reverse occurs: Collections decrease while benefits paid increase. This has a stimulative effect on the economy.

Corporate Dividend Policies   The chief nongovernmental source of economic stability is corporate dividends. Corporations generally maintain fairly stable dividends for several years at a time. That is, their dividend payouts to stockholders don't fluctuate with each reported increase or decrease in profits. Steady dividend policies tend to have a stabilizing influence over the course of a business cycle.

How Income Tax Receipts Limit Fluctuations

Exhibit 2 illustrates the effects of income tax receipts on the peaks and troughs of business cycles. The diagram relates real GDP (measured on the horizontal axis) with government spending and tax revenues (measured on the vertical axis). To simplify the analysis, it helps to keep two points in mind.

1. The line G is horizontal because government expenditures are assumed to remain constant at all levels of GDP. That is, G is independent of income. You can think of an increase in G as an *injection* into the economy's circular flow of income. The injection increases aggregate demand and thereby raises the economy's real GDP. It thus *expands* the circular flow of income.

2. The line T slopes upward because tax revenues increase as GDP rises. That is, T is dependent on income. An increase in T can be thought of as a *withdrawal* from the economy's circular flow of income. The withdrawal decreases aggregate demand and thereby reduces the economy's real GDP. It thus *contracts* the circular flow of income.

Exhibit 2 shows a balanced budget at an output of GDP_0. Here's what happens when GDP changes:

■ An increase in output from GDP_0 to GDP_1 causes tax revenues to rise. The increase in revenue *automatically* creates a budget surplus. But because T exceeds G, withdrawals from the circular flow exceed injections. The net effect is a contraction of the circular flow. This contraction tends to curb an economic boom.

■ A decrease in output from GDP_0 to GDP_2 causes tax revenues to decline. The decrease in revenue *automatically* creates a budget deficit. But because

EXHIBIT
2

Income Tax Receipts as Automatic Stabilizers

If the level of government expenditures (G) is given, budget surpluses and deficits will depend on tax revenues (T). These vary directly with GDP. Thus, beginning with a balanced budget at GDP_0:

■ An increase in GDP results in a budget surplus—a withdrawal from the circular flow that tends to restrain an economic expansion.

■ A decrease in GDP results in a budget deficit—an injection into the circular flow that tends to soften an economic contraction.

The steeper the line T, the larger will be the budget surpluses and deficits and the greater will be the automatic stabilizing effect. The steepness (slope) of T varies directly with the progressivity of the tax structure.

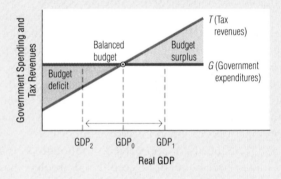

G exceeds T, injections exceed withdrawals. The net effect is an expansion of the circular flow. This expansion tends to soften an economic recession.

As you can see, the size of the budget surplus or deficit will depend on the steepness (slope) of line T. The slope, in turn, is determined by the progressivity of the tax structure. A more progressive structure will result in a steeper line, and therefore larger surpluses and deficits. The more progressive the tax structure, the greater the automatic stabilizing effect of the income tax. A less progressive structure will have the opposite effect. It will cause T to be less steep, thereby reducing the size of the surpluses and deficits. Hence the automatic stabilizing effect will also be reduced.

On the whole, the automatic stabilizers tend to moderate the severity of business cycles. Some studies have suggested that all the automatic stabilizers acting together may reduce the amplitudes (highs and lows) of cyclical swings by as much as one-third.

Discretionary Fiscal Policy

Not all fiscal activity occurs automatically. Some of it is *discretionary*, meaning that it's undertaken intentionally by Washington in response to particular economic conditions. Such conscious actions suggest the need for a modern explanation of *fiscal policy.* It may be defined as deliberate spending and taxing decisions by the government to achieve efficiency and growth. Efficiency is attained by stabilizing the economy at full employment, thus reducing the severity of business cycles. Growth is realized by providing incentives to work, save, and invest, thus achieving a steady increase in real GDP per capita. The two goals reinforce one another.

Historically, fiscal policy has proceeded along two lines. The older one may be called demand-side fiscal policy. The newer one is referred to as supply-side fiscal policy.

Demand-Side Fiscal Policy

Demand-side fiscal policy originated as a direct result of Keynesian beliefs. Specifically, recessionary gaps occur because of insufficient aggregate demand, and inflationary gaps occur because of excessive aggregate demand. The occurrence of these gaps suggests that fiscal policy should differ over the course of a business cycle. The government spending and taxing policies needed to cure recession aren't the same as those needed to curb inflation. For example:

- During a recession, the goal is to raise aggregate demand to the full-employment level. Thus, an *expansionary* fiscal policy is needed to close the recessionary gap. The policy may require an increase in government spending (G), a decrease in tax revenues (T) brought about by a reduction in tax rates, or some combination of both.

- During a period of rapid inflation, the goal is to lower aggregate demand to the full-employment level. Therefore, a *contractionary* fiscal policy is needed to close the inflationary gap. The policy may necessitate a decrease in G, an increase in T, or some combination of both.

Exhibit 3 shows how government spending and taxing policies can be used to close inflationary and recessionary gaps. The diagrams illustrate what happens when fiscal policies are used to shift *aggregate de-*

EXHIBIT
3

Demand-Side Fiscal Policies for Closing Recessionary and Inflationary Gaps

To close a recessionary or an inflationary gap, government can use fiscal policies to shift the *AD* curve.

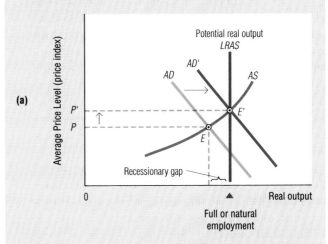

FIGURE (a) Closing a Recessionary Gap An increase in government demand, a decrease in individual or corporate income taxes, or some combination of both will shift aggregate demand rightward from *AD* to *AD'.* The average price level will rise from P to P'.

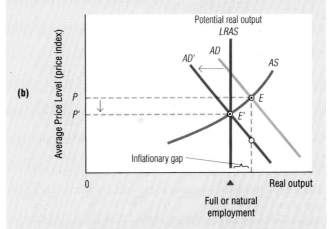

FIGURE (b) Closing an Inflationary Gap A decrease in government demand, an increase in individual or corporate income taxes, or some combination of both will shift aggregate demand leftward from *AD* to *AD'.* The average price level will decline from P to P'.

mand. This, as you'll recall, is the value of real total output that will be purchased by all sectors of the economy at each average price level:

$$AD = C + I + G + X_N$$

Recall, too, that *aggregate supply* is the value of real total output that will be made available at each average price level.

Figure (a) shows that, in trying to close a recessionary gap, government can adopt fiscal policies aimed at increasing aggregate demand. These efforts would shift the curve from *AD* to *AD'*. Examples of such policies are increases in government demand (that is, government spending), decreases in individual and corporate income taxes (in order to raise consumption and investment demand), or some combination of both. With the closing of the gap, the average price level would rise from *P* to *P'*.

Figure (b) shows how fiscal policies can be used to close an inflationary gap. The policies involve measures designed to decrease aggregate demand. For example, reductions in government demand, increases in individual and corporate income taxes, or some combination of both, would shift the aggregate demand curve from *AD* to *AD'*. This shift would be accompanied by a decrease in the average price level from *P* to *P'*.

The diagrams thus provide an extremely useful way of understanding and interpreting demand-side fiscal policy.

Supply-Side Fiscal Policy

A newer approach to fiscal policy utilizes changes in corporate income-tax rates (as well as some other measures) to influence aggregate supply. Studies have shown that in setting profit goals, many businesses *plan* for taxes by estimating expected tax payments and treating them as part of current costs. As a result, increases in taxes, like increases in wages, material prices, or other business expenses, shift the economy's aggregate supply curve to the left. Conversely, decreases in taxes, like decreases in other business costs, shift the curve to the right.

These shifts are the basis of supply-side fiscal policy. Such policy can be either expansionary or contractionary. For example, suppose that firms experience an increase in resource costs due to a sharp rise in the world price of a major raw material such as oil. The higher costs cause a decrease in aggregate supply. That is, the aggregate supply curve shifts to the left, creating a recessionary gap. Therefore, an *expansionary* fis-

cal policy in the form of reduced corporate tax rates helps close the gap by shifting the curve to the right.

The process is illustrated in Figure (a) of Exhibit 4. An increase in business costs causes a recessionary gap. Therefore, a decrease in corporate tax rates will reduce business costs and shift the aggregate supply curve rightward from *AS* to *AS'*. This shift closes the recessionary gap and lowers the price level.

The reverse condition resulting from a decrease in resource costs may also occur. The lower costs cause an increase in aggregate supply. That is, the aggregate supply curve shifts to the right, creating an inflationary gap. Therefore, a *contractionary* fiscal policy consisting of increased corporate tax rates helps close the gap by shifting the curve to the left.

This process can be seen in Figure (b) of Exhibit 4. A decline in business costs causes an inflationary gap. An increase in corporate tax rates will raise business costs and shift the aggregate supply curve leftward from *AS* to *AS'*. This shift closes the inflationary gap and raises the price level.

As you can see, the diagrams are extremely important in helping to explain the workings of supply-side fiscal policy.

Conclusion: Mixed Effects

In reality, it's usually difficult to separate demand-side fiscal policies from supply-side fiscal policies. The reason is that some government policies influence aggregate demand and aggregate supply simultaneously, which creates mixed effects. For example, changes in corporate tax rates can affect the business sector's demand for investment as well as its planned costs of production. Nevertheless, when analyzing fiscal actions you'll find it useful to consider their demand-side and supply-side effects on price and output. This procedure helps reduce a complex problem to simpler terms.

Summarizing:

Fiscal-policy ideas began to develop in the late 1940s as an outgrowth of Keynesian economics. This body of thought contends that because prices and wages in many industries are relatively rigid rather than flexible, the economy may fail to self-correct rapidly. To encourage correction to full employment, therefore, specific government spending and taxing policies are needed. By reducing the swings of business cycles, such policies promote efficiency, stability, and economic growth.

EXHIBIT
4

Supply-Side Fiscal Policies for Closing Recessionary and Inflationary Gaps

To close a recessionary or an inflationary gap, government can use fiscal policies to shift the *AS* curve.

(a)

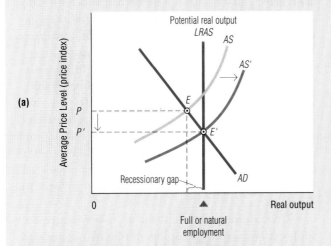

(b)

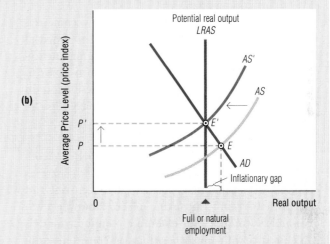

FIGURE (a) **Closing a Recessionary Gap** A decrease in corporate tax rates reduces business costs. This cost reduction will stimulate production and shift the aggregate supply curve rightward from *AS* to *AS'*. The average price level will decline from *P* to *P'*.

FIGURE (b) **Closing an Inflationary Gap** An increase in corporate tax rates raises business costs. This cost increase will slow production and shift the aggregate supply curve leftward from *AS* to *AS'*. The average price level will rise from *P* to *P'*.

Problems of Fiscal Policy

The foregoing principles of discretionary fiscal policy provide two simple prescriptions:

1. To close a recessionary gap, increase (shift to the right) aggregate demand and/or aggregate supply. This shift is accomplished by decreasing individual and corporate income taxes, increasing government expenditures, or both.

2. To close an inflationary gap, decrease (shift to the left) aggregate demand and/or aggregate supply. This shift is accomplished by increasing individual and corporate income taxes, decreasing government expenditures, or both.

How well do these prescriptions for fiscal policy actually work? In practice, many complicated economic and political difficulties are involved in determining and carrying out an effective fiscal policy. Several classes of difficulties are particularly noteworthy.

Making Policy Decisions: Choices, Forecasting, and Timing

Because fiscal policy deals with government spending and taxing, fiscal-policy decisions require legislative approval by Congress and the president. The chief difficulties these policymakers face involve (1) the selection of appropriate policies, (2) the forecasting of cyclical turning points, and (3) the timing of counter-cyclical policies.

Selecting Appropriate Policies

An increase in government spending and a decrease in taxes can achieve the same expansionary effect on real output. A decrease in government spending and an increase in taxes can achieve the same contractionary effect on real output. If you were a member of Congress, which of these policies would you be inclined to support? The question is typical of the choices that legislators and policymakers often must make.

Your answer is likely to depend on your opinion about the relative size of government in the economy. If you believe that the government should play a larger role than it does, you'll support measures that tend to enlarge the public sector. You will therefore favor increased government spending on social goods to close a recessionary gap, and you'll favor increased taxes to close an inflationary gap.

Alternatively, if you believe that the government is already too large, you'll advocate measures aimed at reducing the public sector and promoting private initiative. You'll therefore favor reductions in taxes to close a recessionary gap, and you'll favor reductions in government spending to close an inflationary gap.

Forecasting Cyclical Turning Points

Business-cycle forecasting is an inexact science. Economists can usually explain reasonably well why past recessionary or inflationary trends have occurred and why present trends are taking place. However, even economists working with elaborate computer models can't predict with much accuracy or consistency the future turning points—the peaks and troughs—of business cycles. Yet these turning points must be identified before attempts can be made to moderate their impact with appropriate fiscal policies.

Timing Countercyclical Policies

Appropriate timing of countercyclical fiscal policies is complicated by a variety of delays. Three types of delays are especially important:

Identification Lag It generally takes many months before a cyclical turning point can be identified. By that time a recession or inflation, or perhaps both, may be far advanced.

Action Lag Even after a cyclical turning point has been identified, it takes many more months before Washington decides on what action is to be taken. The president, the president's advisers, and Congress all typically become involved in the time-consuming debates and compromises that major fiscal-policy decisions entail.

Effects Lag After countercyclical policies are implemented, additional months must pass for their effects to be realized. In fact, it may take a year or more for the full economic impact to be felt.

What is the overall result of these lags? Various studies have concluded that all three together usually delay the main impact of countercyclical fiscal policies by 2 to 3 years.

Predicting Price-Level Effects

A second source of difficulty with fiscal policy arises from the uncertain inflationary consequences of demand-side stimulation. As you've already seen, an expansionary fiscal action aimed at closing a recessionary gap results in a rightward shift of the economy's aggregate demand curve. The demand increase also causes an increase in the average price level. The extent of the increase depends on the *relative steepness* (*slope*) of the economy's aggregate supply curve.

Let's see why by looking at Exhibit 5. In both diagrams, an expansionary demand-side fiscal policy shifts the aggregate demand curve from *AD* to *AD'*. This shift closes the recessionary gap. But in the recessionary range, which lies to the left of the vertical full-employment line, the *AS* curve is relatively flatter in Figure (a) than in Figure (b). As a result, the average price level rises by 5 percent in Figure (a) and by 10 percent in Figure (b).

Thus, although in reality the economy's aggregate supply curve is upward-sloping, its relative steepness at any given point is unknown. Consequently, it is impossible to predict with much accuracy the potential price-level effects of a particular fiscal action. Therefore, the inflationary consequences of expansionary demand-side fiscal policies are always in question.

Restrictive Effect: Crowding Out

Some critics contend that one of the most serious consequences of fiscal policy is the ***crowding out*** of private borrowers. Crowding out can occur when the federal government pursues an expansionary policy by borrowing heavily to finance expenditures.

For example, in order to cover its budget deficits, the Treasury borrows in the financial markets by selling debt securities such as bonds. The Treasury thus competes with private borrowers in bidding for available funds. This competition may cause interest rates—the prices of the borrowed funds—to rise. Private borrowers who are unwilling to pay the higher interest rates find themselves crowded out of the market. As private investment decreases, the circular flow of income contracts. This contraction will work against the expansionary effect of the government's spending and taxing policies.

Does crowding out actually occur? In other words, is there a *positive* relationship between deficits and interest rates? The evidence is by no means clear. Since the early 1960s, there have been some periods when

EXHIBIT 5

Inflationary Effects of an Expansionary Demand-Side Fiscal Policy

The economy's aggregate supply curve is upward sloping. However, the *relative steepness* (*slope*) of the curve at any point is unknown. As a result, an expansionary demand-side fiscal policy aimed at closing a recessionary gap can have unpredictable inflationary effects. Thus, in Figure (a) the inflationary effect of closing the gap is 5 percent; while in Figure (b) it's 10 percent. The reason for the difference is that, in the recessionary range, the *AS* curve in Figure (a) is relatively flatter than in Figure (b).

Relatively Flat *AS* Curve in the Recessionary Range

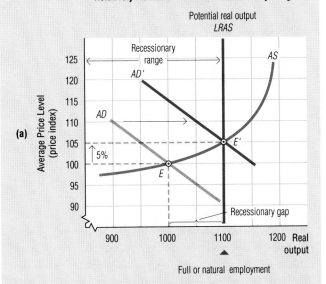

(a)

Relatively Steep *AS* Curve in the Recessionary Range

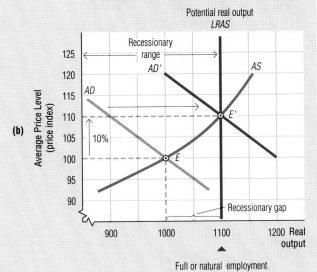

(b)

deficits and interest rates increased and decreased together, and other periods when one of the variables increased while the other decreased. Although several reasons can be given to explain these mixed results, one of the most persuasive is the *globalization of financial markets*. Governments can borrow large quantities of funds just as readily in London, Tokyo, and other major financial centers as they can in New York. As a result, the Treasury's deficit in any given year is likely to represent a relatively small percentage of the total demand for credit in the world's financial markets.

Coordinating Fiscal and Monetary Policy

Another problem with fiscal policy is the need to coordinate it with monetary policy in order to achieve the goals of efficiency, stability, and growth. What roles should fiscal and monetary policies play? The answer depends on whether the policies are designed to be "easy" or "tight." An easy policy is one that encourages expansionary effects. A tight policy is one that encourages contractionary effects. Two examples illustrate some of the possible consequences of easy and tight policies.

Easy Fiscal Policy and Tight Monetary Policy

An easy fiscal policy consisting of increased government spending and reduced taxes may create serious inflationary pressures. To compensate, the Fed may adopt a tight monetary policy consisting of slower money growth in order to raise interest rates. Rising interest rates will cause business investment, and therefore real output, to decline. If the contractionary effects of a tight monetary policy outweigh the expansionary effects of an easy fiscal policy, the economy could go into a recession.

Tight Fiscal Policy and Easy Monetary Policy

A tight fiscal policy consisting of reduced government spending and higher taxes may retard the economy too much. To compensate, the Fed may adopt an easy monetary policy consisting of faster money growth in order to lower interest rates. If the Fed succeeds, the lower rates will encourage increased business investment and cause real output to rise.

But suppose the Fed mistakenly overcompensates with the money growth rate—as has often happened. The rate of inflation will increase because of the familiar monetary phenomenon of "too much money chasing too few goods." In addition, the rising inflation will be accompanied by rising interest rates because creditors will want to be compensated for their loss in purchasing power.* With the economy experiencing both higher prices and higher interest rates, business investment may stagnate, and cause the rate of growth of real output to decline.

These are only two of several possible policy scenarios that can be formulated. They indicate that coordinating fiscal and monetary policies is a difficult and risky task. Most economists doubt the ability of policymakers to do it successfully.

Public-Choice Problem: Political Business Cycles

In addition to the economic difficulties of implementing discretionary fiscal policies, there are political problems to overcome. These arise mainly from what is known in both economics and political science as "public choice."

One of the most significant public-choice problems concerns the way elected officials cater to their constituents. Political leaders know that voters are concerned with the *personal, short-term effects* of economic policies. Therefore, legislators seeking reelection will often adopt policies designed to achieve favorable short-term results, regardless of what the unfavorable long-term consequences may be.

For example, it's not unusual for the government to follow conservative spending policies (aimed at curbing inflation) during the early years of an administration and liberal spending policies (intended to stimulate employment) in the later years, as election time draws closer. This periodic alternation has resulted in what economists and political scientists call a "political business cycle."

Conclusion: Some Successes and Failures

The effectiveness of fiscal policy has been the subject of many critical evaluations. Three main conclusions, based on studies of recessions and inflations since the 1950s, may be summarized briefly.

First, attempts to curb recessions through expansionary demand-side fiscal policies have had only lim-

ited success. Government taxation and spending programs designed to increase aggregate demand have generally been adopted too late—usually after the worst of a recession was over—to be very effective. Nor have government spending programs succeeded in achieving sustained full employment. However, over the long run, transfer payments (particularly unemployment insurance, welfare assistance, and social security benefits) have contributed to reducing the severity of business recessions. This moderating effect occurs because transfer payments enable recipients to maintain higher levels of consumption expenditures than would be possible otherwise. As a result, the economy's aggregate demand curve is also higher.

Second, attempts to restrain inflation through contractionary demand-side fiscal policies have been even less successful than measures aimed at curbing recession. A major reason is that inflation usually results primarily from *excessive monetary expansion—too much money chasing too few goods*. In addition, because of their concerns about reelection, political leaders are generally reluctant to increase income taxes sufficiently to pay for rising levels of government spending. For both reasons, the economy's aggregate demand curve has often shifted to the right at a faster rate than its aggregate supply curve. This excess of demand has resulted in frequent increases in the average price level.

Third, attempts to increase real output and employment through expansionary supply-side fiscal policies have been relatively successful. Evidence of this success, based on several major studies of the United States and other countries, will be presented later in the chapter. Meanwhile, a chief finding of the studies may be noted briefly. The studies conclude that reductions in tax rates and improvements in the efficiency of the tax system encourage risk taking, investment, and economic growth. Therefore, supply-side fiscal policies warrant serious consideration in any government fiscal program.

Demand-side fiscal policies have generally placed greater emphasis on promoting short-term stability than on promoting long-term growth. History shows that the policies have been moderately better at limiting recessions than at curbing inflations. However, many experts believe that the economy's automatic fiscal stabilizers have played a more important role than demand-side fiscal policies in helping to encourage stability.

In contrast with demand-side fiscal thinking, which originated with Keynesian policy in the late

---

*This is the familiar *Fisher effect* that you learned about in an earlier chapter. To refresh your understanding, look up the term in the Dictionary at the back of the book.

1940s, supply-side fiscal ideas are of more recent origin. They focus on aggregate supply rather than aggregate demand. Therefore, they look to production rather than consumption for the means of sustaining steady economic expansion. Supply-siders are thus more concerned than demand-siders with the lasting consequences of fiscal policy.

Supply-side fiscal policies have placed greater emphasis on promoting long-term growth than on promoting short-term stability. Major research studies based on domestic and foreign experiences have concluded that these policies have been successful. As a result, the modern or "new" view of fiscal policy focuses on government spending and tax policies as effective means of encouraging a rising trend of real output per person.

Fiscal Policy and Supply-Side Economics

The encouragement of mere consumption is no benefit to commerce, for production alone furnishes the means for consumption. Thus, it is the aim of good government to stimulate production, of bad government to encourage consumption.

—Jean Baptiste Say (1803)

Say was a popular French journalist, an adviser to government officials, and an early classical economist of considerable repute. If he were alive today, he would be offering the same advice to political leaders that he dispensed in his own day. His and other economists' classical beliefs, which have undergone substantial extension and refinement in recent decades, have replaced much of Keynesian thinking since the 1970s. As a result, modern classical ideas are at the heart of today's economic thought. Some of the ideas emphasize a distinction between demand-side and supply-side economics.

Demand-side economics prescribes measures and policies to regulate purchasing power. Because traditional Keynesian economics places major emphasis on fiscal and monetary policies to control aggregate demand, it has been characterized as demand-side economics.

Supply-side economics reflects a renewed emphasis on the ramifications of **Say's law**—the proposition that "supply creates its own demand." Thus, supply-side economics prescribes measures and policies to stimulate production. Some of the most fundamental supply-side policies are those that make use of *incentives*. For example, reductions in marginal tax rates—the taxes paid on the last increment of wages, interest, and dividends—provide people and businesses with incentives to work, save, and invest. The result is increased output, or supply. Let's now examine three key features of supply-side economics:

1. Rejection of Keynesian demand-management policies

2. Tax reduction to stimulate production

3. Nonmonetization of government deficits

Before beginning, it helps to keep an important fact in mind:

Although supply-side economics is largely concerned with taxes, it prescribes an *integrated* set of fiscal and monetary guidelines for the government to follow. Therefore, supply-side views are most meaningful when they're related not only to fiscal policy but, where appropriate, to monetary policy as well.

Rejection of Keynesian Demand-Management Policies

Supply-side economists point out that Keynesian theory provides an underconsumption explanation of recessions. That is, Keynesian economics attributes unemployment to insufficient aggregate demand, which results in a recession. Therefore, to restore full employment, government policy should aim at stimulating aggregate demand. Keynesian demand-management policies are implemented mainly through changes in taxes, government spending, and the monetary growth rate.

Supply-siders reject such policies because:

1. Experience shows that the Fed is unable to achieve economic stability by manipulating the monetary growth rate. Therefore, the Fed should give up trying to do so. Instead it should adopt measures that will ensure a steady monetary growth rate and, as a result, stable prices.

2. Whenever incentives to produce are stifled, any form of demand stimulation will lead to inflation. Policies should therefore be formulated to increase the supply of goods by encouraging increases in *productivity*.

3. Contrary to traditional Keynesian belief, not all income tax cuts are the same. Only reductions in

marginal tax rates (rather than in average or total tax rates) provide people and businesses with strong incentives to undertake additional work, saving, and investment.

4. Traditional Keynesian belief holds that an increase in government spending has the same objective as a reduction in taxes: to increase aggregate demand. Supply-siders argue strongly against increased government spending. They hold that a reduction in taxes, if properly designed, can exert a substantial impact on *incentives* to produce, and result in increased supply. An increase in government spending, supply-siders argue, absorbs resources from the private sector and thus expands the size of the government relative to business. The government operates less efficiently than the private sector because government has fewer incentives to produce. Thus, increasing the size of the government results in lower output.

Summarizing these ideas:

Supply-side macroeconomic policies stand in sharp contrast to Keynesian demand-side macroeconomic policies. The goal of supply-side economics is to stimulate aggregate *supply* rather than aggregate demand. Thus, the principal supply-side prescription is (1) strict monetary controls to curb inflation, and (2) tax reductions to encourage greater output. It's especially important to reduce marginal tax rates on income in order to encourage work, saving, and investment.

Tax Cuts to Stimulate Production

The belief that high taxes can create *disincentives* to produce is by no means new, as the following quotations show:

Exorbitant taxes destroy industry by producing despair. An attentive legislature will observe the point when the revenue decreases and the prejudice begins.

—DAVID HUME (1756)

High taxes, sometimes by diminishing the consumption of the taxed commodities and sometimes by encouraging smuggling, afford a smaller revenue to government than what might be drawn from more moderate taxes.

—ADAM SMITH (1776)

David Hume was an eminent Scottish philosopher and a close friend of Adam Smith. Smith, as we've learned, was the founder of modern economics. As their words indicate, both understood human nature as it relates to taxation.

For instance, they would have agreed with the idea underlying Figure (a) of Exhibit 6. The diagram, called a *Laffer curve,* expresses a relationship between tax revenues and the marginal tax rate—the tax rate on the last increment of income. The relationship shows that, as the tax rate increases from zero to 100 percent, government revenues from taxation correspondingly rise from zero to some maximum and then decline to zero. The optimum tax rate—the one that produces the largest revenue—is somewhere between the two extremes.

An important feature of the curve, as shown in Figure (a) of Exhibit 6, is that it has both a "normal" range and a "prohibitive" range. In the normal range, a higher tax rate brings higher revenues. In the prohibitive range, the tax rate is so high that it impairs incentives. Therefore, a tax cut would actually increase revenues by spurring the incentive to work and invest.

Supply-siders contend that, if *marginal* tax rates are in the prohibitive range, they should be cut. This action would make working, saving, and investing more rewarding, thereby stimulating economic activity. The result would be greater economic growth and employment, leading to higher, not lower, tax revenues.

The Laffer curve depicts an interesting idea. The problem with it, however, is that no one knows where the optimum point is located or even what the true shape of the curve is. This uncertainty can pose difficulties for public policy.

For example, let's look at Figure (b) of Exhibit 6. The actual Laffer curve might be either curve *A* or curve *B*. Suppose that the present tax rate is *r* and that the goal is to maximize revenues. Tax rates should be *decreased* if *A* is the correct curve and *increased* if *B* is correct. Alternatively, revising the tax laws to reduce deductions and close loopholes could shift the entire curve to a higher level—say, *C*. Along curve *C*, revenues would be greater over the entire range of tax rates (except, of course, at zero and 100 percent).

Because of such uncertainties, it's easy to see why the Laffer curve, a fundamental concept of supply-side economics, is nevertheless highly controversial.

EXHIBIT
6

Dr. Laffer's Famous Curve

"Except for the optimum rate, there are always two tax rates that yield the same revenues." So says economic consultant and former professor Arthur W. Laffer, whose Laffer curve has received a great deal of attention from many legislators and economists.

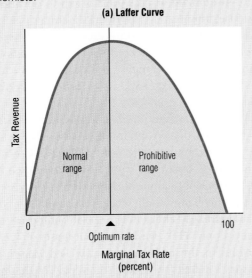

(a) Laffer Curve

FIGURE (a) The Laffer curve is a fundamental concept of supply-side economics. Basically, it says that, if marginal tax rates are in the "normal" range, increases in the rates will yield more tax revenues. But if marginal tax rates are in the "prohibitive" range, *decreases* in the rates will actually produce more revenues by stimulating incentives to work, save, and invest.

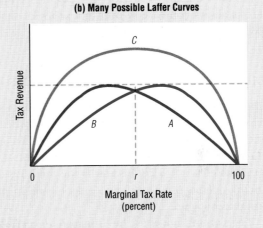

(b) Many Possible Laffer Curves

FIGURE (b) In reality a Laffer curve of some kind may exist. However, neither the optimum tax rate nor the true shape of the curve is known. For instance, curve A and curve B are two of many possible shapes. Depending on whether curve A or curve B is correct, the present tax rate r must be either decreased or increased to maximize revenues. However, reducing tax deductions and closing tax loopholes could shift the curve upward to curve C. This curve yields higher revenues at *all* tax rates between the extremes of zero and 100 percent.

Depreciation Reform

Depreciation is the decline in the value of a fixed asset, such as plant or equipment, due either to wear and tear or to obsolescence resulting from technological advances. Depreciation policies are an aspect of tax policies.

Companies treat depreciation as a cost. The tax laws allow firms to "write off," or deduct from their income each year, a certain amount of depreciation on buildings, machines, vehicles, and other capital goods as a cost of doing business. The tax laws can vary the amount of time over which a good can be depreciated.

For example, suppose a firm owns a building that cost $1 million. If the tax laws require the firm to write off the building over 20 years, the firm can deduct $50,000 a year from its income as a depreciation expense. If the tax laws allow a building to be depreciated over 10 years, however, the firm can deduct $100,000 a year.

Obviously, the more a firm can deduct each year for depreciation, the smaller its profit will be and the less it will pay in income taxes.

Therefore:

Laws permitting rapid depreciation—that is, faster write-offs of capital goods—can be an important part of a tax-reduction policy.

By lowering their taxes, depreciation reform can give firms a greater incentive to undertake new investment to replace existing capital equipment. However, faster write-offs also (1) reduce tax revenues to the Treasury, and (2) benefit capital-intensive firms but not labor-intensive ones. (Examples of labor-intensive firms are those that specialize in high technology, research, and development.) Because the benefits of depreciation aren't the same for all types of businesses, there is always controversy over any proposal that involves changes in depreciation rates.

Nonmonetization of Government Deficits

A third major feature of supply-side fiscal policy concerns deficit financing. Budget deficits occur when expenditures exceed revenues. The means of paying for deficits are taxation and borrowing—matters of primary concern to us all. This is why the methods of financing deficits often become a major issue in presidential campaigns.

Legislation known as the *Gramm-Rudman-Hollings Act* requires that the federal budget be balanced each year. However, in the event of a recession, Congress can suspend the law for up to two years. Do the president and Congress have the resolve to live within the strict interpretation of the law? Evidently not. When the federal budget is in deficit, it can be brought into balance either by cutting spending, by raising taxes, or by some combination of both. But because such actions are unpopular, elected officials can try to satisfy their constituents by looking for painless ways to reduce a budget deficit. One method, which has been employed several times, is to amend the law by making it more flexible. Another, which has been used for decades, is simply to exclude some categories of spending from the budget. By employing such accounting devices, the official budget can be made to appear balanced even if it isn't.

Thus, although legislation exists that requires a balanced budget, it seems doubtful that the legislation will eliminate deficits in the true sense. Therefore, let's see how supply-side fiscal policy views the financing of deficits.

Managing Deficits

Supply-siders recognize that, in the short run, a reduction in marginal tax rates may result in increased budget deficits until the positive effects of the tax cuts take hold. Are rising budget deficits likely to be inflation-

ary? The answer, say the supply-siders, depends on how the Federal Reserve reacts.

The Treasury, as you know, incurs a budget deficit by spending more than it collects in taxes. It finances the excess spending (that is, it gets funds to cover it) by selling debt instruments such as Treasury bills and Treasury bonds to the public. The increased supply of debt instruments on the market, unless offset by an increase in demand, causes their prices to decline and, therefore, interest rates to rise. (Remember that prices of debt instruments and interest rates are *inversely* related.) As a result, many would-be borrowers who can't afford to borrow at higher interest rates may be forced out of the financial markets—a process referred to earlier as *crowding out*.

What can the Fed do when it sees interest rates rising and fears the possibility of recession? It may engage in open-market purchases of Treasury securities in an effort to bid up their prices so as to bring interest rates down. This action, of course, enlarges banks' reserves. The banks then seek to expand their loans, which increases checkable deposits and hence the money supply. Thus, through its purchases of Treasury securities in the open market, the Fed *monetizes* the Treasury's deficits by making them part of the money supply. (As you'll recall from earlier chapters, the term "monetize" means to convert into money.)

Supply-siders argue that rising deficits aren't by themselves inflationary. This is because they represent transfers of purchasing power from the public to the Treasury with no net increase in total spending. However, if the Fed monetizes the Treasury's deficits, the results will be inflationary because *monetization transforms the deficits into money.*

Supply-side ideas thus provide an interesting contrast to Keynesian ideas:

- According to Keynesian policy, a budget deficit resulting from a tax cut without a spending cut creates a fiscal stimulus. The stimulus becomes even more pronounced when the Fed monetizes the deficit.

- According to supply-side thinking, a deficit isn't inflationary unless monetized by the Fed. *The purpose of a tax cut is to improve production incentives, not to provide a fiscal stimulus. Therefore, a deficit resulting from a tax cut shouldn't be monetized.*

Does this mean that mounting deficits are harmless as long as they aren't monetized? Supply-siders answer no, emphasizing an important point:

A tax reduction enables people to save a larger portion of their incomes. If the tax reduction is accompanied by a curtailment of government spending, the increased savings will be encouraged to flow into private investment. But if the tax reduction isn't accompanied by a curtailment of government spending, the increased savings may be used to purchase Treasury securities, thus helping to finance the growth of government spending. To reduce the chances of this happening, *tax reductions should be accompanied by cutbacks in government spending.**

Conclusion: The New Fiscal Policy

These supply-side beliefs are an integral part of what some modern economists—including Keynesians as well as classicists—call the *new* fiscal policy. Before continuing, it helps to summarize the main ideas:

- Experience shows that fiscal policy cannot be used to "fine-tune" the economy—that is, maintain it at full employment. Therefore, the primary goal of fiscal policy should be to *stimulate economic growth.* All other benefits are assumed to flow from this.

- Economic growth is stimulated by using tax policies that promote incentives to work, save, and invest. Therefore, *marginal* rather than average tax rates are important because taxes paid on the last increment of income influence people's decisions to undertake economic activity.

- Increases in savings that result from revised tax policies should be available to finance business investment, not the growth of government. Therefore, government spending should be curbed.

Have supply-side tax policies lived up to expectations? To answer this question, we must look back at a period in recent history—the Reagan presidential administration of the 1980s.

The Legacy of Reaganomics

Proclaiming a belief in supply-side economics when he began his first term in 1981, President Reagan initiated a plan for implementing its main ideas. In partic-

ular, he sought to slash tax rates and cut government spending. These measures, he contended, would create jobs and stimulate production in the private sector, thereby promoting efficiency, equity, stability, and growth. The news media quickly dubbed Reagan's economic policies "Reaganomics."

Reaganomics began with the intention of attaining *equal reductions in taxes and government spending.* But this was not to be. Dramatic tax-cutting legislation went into effect in 1982, and the president pressed Congress to cut total expenditures accordingly. However, he also wanted huge increases in defense spending, which accounted for about a third of the budget, while social security payments were to be left untouched. Recognizing that these goals were incompatible, Congress refused to match the tax cuts with spending cuts. As a result, the principles of supply-side economics were never fully implemented. Nevertheless, much can be learned from examining the effects of the steep reductions that were made in marginal tax rates. Here are the chief findings and consequences based on comprehensive studies.*

1. People respond more rationally to changes in marginal tax rates than is commonly believed. An increase in the tax rates reduces people's economic incentives. Consequently, the government is likely to collect less revenue than anticipated. Conversely, a decrease in the tax rates improves people's economic incentives. Therefore, even if the lower rates bring in smaller tax revenues, the decline will probably be temporary and less than predicted. These lessons have been learned not only in the United States but in numerous other countries that have experimented with marginal tax-rate reductions since the early 1980s.

2. High marginal tax rates encourage financial decisions aimed at lowering taxable income rather than raising economic returns. Taxpayers find it rewarding to shelter income by purchasing tax-exempt bonds rather than taxable ones, and pressuring employers for fringe benefits such as health insurance and company cars instead of higher

---

*In the early 1980s, some of President Reagan's supply-side advisers predicted that tax reductions would generate revenues faster than the growth of government spending, thus reducing the deficit. By the mid-1980s it became apparent that these predictions were incorrect. As a result, most supply-siders revised their views, arguing that tax reductions should at least be accompanied by a freeze, if not by cutbacks, in government spending.

*The most extensive study of the effects of tax cuts was done by former Harvard University economist Lawrence Lindsey, *The Growth Experiment* (Basic Books, 1990). The book is based on the author's prize-winning doctoral dissertation done at Harvard. Lindsey is now a member of the Federal Reserve System's Board of Governors. See also Michael J. Boskin and Charles E. McClure Jr., eds., *Worldwide Tax Reform: Case Studies of Developed and Developing Countries* (San Francisco: ICS Press, under the auspices of the International Center for Economic Growth, 1990).

salaries. Conversely, sharp cuts in the tax rates encourage investments based on economic potential—those likely to maximize returns rather than minimize taxes. Scarce capital is thus allocated to its highest valued uses, and so maximizes the nation's economic efficiency and tax revenues.

3. The older Keynesian demand-side view assumes that tax reductions will stimulate only aggregate demand. Although the demand stimulus will lead to increased output, it will also generate higher rates of inflation. (Think in terms of the *AD/AS* model.) But this belief neglects the newer supply-side view, which holds that reductions in marginal tax rates, if properly designed, can stimulate aggregate supply by encouraging greater work effort, risk taking, and capital investment. The result will be increased output accompanied by disinflation.

4. Gains in economic efficiency are greatest when top marginal tax rates are reduced substantially from relatively high levels. During President Kennedy's administration (1964), tax rates were cut from 91 percent to 70 percent, and in President Reagan's term (1981) from 54 percent to 28 percent. Gains in efficiency are much smaller when the top marginal rates are reduced from relatively moderate levels—those in the vicinity of 35 percent.

5. If top marginal rates are already at relatively moderate levels, further gains are best attained not by revising the rate structure but by improving the efficiency of the tax system. Therefore, attention should be focused on closing tax loopholes. By eliminating many of the special deductions currently allowed, tax collections will increase and equity will be enhanced.

Fiscal Policy Today

These findings gleaned from studies of Reaganomics have led to dramatic changes in fiscal thinking.

For example, before the adoption of supply-side fiscal policies during the Reagan era, the Keynesian belief that taxes affected only the ability of private individuals to spend held sway. It was generally thought that the government could maintain aggregate demand by transferring spending power from the private sector to the public sector. Because every tax dollar collected from individuals would be spent by government, taxes didn't matter insofar as total spending was concerned.

Supply-side economists responded to this argument by contending that increased public-sector spending doesn't simply offset decreased private-sector spending. Instead, it outweighs private-sector spending and produces *negative* net effects. Transfers of spending power from individuals to government increase the size of the public sector relative to the private sector. As government grows, incentives to produce decline, and the economy stagnates. To reverse this course, decreases in marginal tax rates—the taxes paid on the last increment of income earned—are needed. As you've seen, supply-side economics contends that reductions in marginal tax rates and improvements in the efficiency of the tax system stimulate the private sector by increasing incentives to work, save, and invest.

Most of today's economists, including many Keynesians, agree with these views. They also believe that the difficulties of predicting the impacts of government spending and tax-rate changes on the economy are usually insurmountable. Consequently, discretionary fiscal policy should not rely on such predictions.

In conclusion, a fundamental precept of modern fiscal policy bears emphasizing:

Evidence shows that high marginal tax rates reduce incentives and distort resource allocation, which, in turn, impair economic growth. Government spending and tax policies, if properly designed, can enhance the economy's capacity to produce, and thereby encourage economic growth. Therefore, tax legislation should seek to attain low marginal rates and the fewest deductions possible so that all assets, incomes, and resources are taxed similarly.

Summary of Important Ideas

1. Fiscal policy concerns the ways in which the federal government acquires and allocates funds. Funds are acquired from taxes and borrowing, and are allocated to transfer payments and social-goods expenditures. A surplus in the federal budget occurs if acquisitions exceed allocations. A deficit occurs if acquisitions are less than allocations. If acquisitions equal allocations, the budget is balanced.

2. Fiscal policy came into existence in the late 1940s as part of Keynesian economics. This body of thought contends that, because prices and wages in many industries are relatively rigid rather than flexible, the

economy may not self-correct rapidly. Therefore, policy activism by government is needed to help stabilize business cycles.

3. Automatic fiscal stabilizers such as income taxes, welfare benefits, and corporate dividends tend to moderate the severity of business cycles. Fiscal-policy activism is also called discretionary fiscal policy. It seeks to reduce the severity of business cycles by manipulating government spending and taxing. These manipulations, its advocates contend, are needed in order to supplement the economy's automatic fiscal stabilizers.

4. Discretionary fiscal policy may be demand-side or supply-side in nature. Both types seek to close recessionary and inflationary gaps through government spending and taxing measures. Demand-side policies attempt to shift the economy's aggregate demand curve, while supply-side policies attempt to shift the aggregate supply curve. In reality, fiscal policy measures usually affect both aggregate demand and aggregate supply simultaneously, so it's impossible to estimate the separate results.

5. The implementation of fiscal policy faces many obstacles. Among the more important are the difficulties of forecasting, timing, and coordination. Because these pose largely unsolvable problems, fiscal policy is no longer viewed as a means of fine-tuning the economy—that is, achieving short-term adjustments to full employment.

6. The modern view holds that fiscal policy should seek to stimulate economic growth. Growth is achieved through tax policies that promote incentives to work, save, and invest. By increasing the economy's capacity to produce, such policies increase the likelihood that the economy's other three goals—efficiency, equity, and stability—will be achieved.

Terms and Concepts to Review

budget	*fiscal policy*
budget balance	*crowding out*
budget deficit	*demand-side economics*
budget surplus	*supply-side economics*
transfer payments	*Say's law*
social goods	*Laffer curve*
Keynesian economics	*Gramm-Rudman-Hollings*
automatic fiscal stabilizers	*Act*

Questions and Problems

1. Some experts contend that there is a relationship between budget deficits and interest rates. Can you suggest what the relationship is?

2. "The Treasury's influence on interest rates depends on the 'extent' of the market." What does this mean?

3. From the late 1940s until the mid-1960s, the achievement of price stability was rarely mentioned as an objective of fiscal policy. Why? What was the objective?

4. The more progressive our tax structure, the greater the dampening effect on fluctuations in real output. Therefore, a tax structure that is highly progressive is good for the economy. Do you agree?

5. "If business-cycle turning points could be forecast with reasonable accuracy, fiscal policy would be a reliable means of maintaining continuous full employment." Do you agree?

6. "The effect on the price level of a supply-side fiscal policy designed to close a *recessionary gap* will depend on the relative steepness of the aggregate demand curve." Do you agree? Use graphs to support your answer.

7. "The effect on the price level of a supply-side fiscal policy designed to close an *inflationary gap* will depend on the relative steepness of the aggregate demand curve." Do you agree? Use graphs to support your answer.

8. Why does supply-side fiscal theory place particular emphasis on changes in *marginal* tax rates rather than changes in average tax rates?

9. How would a supply-side advocate respond to the argument that deficits cause both inflation and higher interest rates?

10. How do you suppose most of today's economists view the short-run and long-run goals of fiscal policy and monetary policy?

TAKE A STAND

A Balanced Budget Amendment: Is It a Good Idea?

The federal budget deficit in 1992 is estimated at between $300 and $400 billion, or $1,200 to $1,600 for every adult and child in the country. For most of our country's history, the federal budget has been approximately in balance, meaning that government expenditures and transfer payments were approximately matched by government receipts from taxation. In the 1980s, this pattern abruptly changed. Tax cuts and defense buildups under President Reagan caused the deficit to rise to over $200 billion in 1983; the deficit has exceeded $150 billion every year since then. Such deficits are unprecedented in peacetime.

The total federal debt, which is the accumulated sum of past deficits, is approximately $4 trillion. The interest payments on this debt are now around $200 billion, or roughly the size of the deficit in many recent years. In other words, the government borrows enough funds each year to pay the costs of funds borrowed in the past. This is a little like using your Visa credit card to pay the interest on your MasterCard.

There has been much talk of deficit reduction, but little has been achieved. In 1985, Congress passed the Gramm-Rudman-Hollings Act, which set guidelines for the reduction of the deficit. The act was subsequently amended to make it more "flexible." As yet, Congress and the President have been unable to agree on a package of spending cuts and tax increases large enough to pay off the deficit.

Frustration over the size of the deficit has led to a number of calls for a balanced budget amendment to the constitution, which would force the federal government to get rid of the deficit. In 1992, a proposal for a balanced budget amendment was endorsed by President Bush but narrowly defeated in Congress. This proposal was not the first, and is almost certainly not the last. *Should we adopt a balanced budget amendment to the constitution?*

Yes: A Balanced Budget Amendment Would Eliminate Harmful Deficits

In deciding whether or not to advocate a balanced budget amendment, we should explore two related issues: Are deficits harmful? And is an amendment to the constitution the most effective way to eliminate them?

Deficits are harmful because they lead to a crowding-out of investment. When federal expenditures exceed revenues, the government borrows to finance the ensuing deficit. At the same time, firms routinely borrow to finance investment. Since only a limited pool of funds is available, borrowing by the government means that there are fewer funds available for the private sector. Private-sector investment is therefore lower than it would be in the absence of the government deficit. Less investment means a slower buildup of capital, which results in slower economic growth and a lower standard of living in the future.

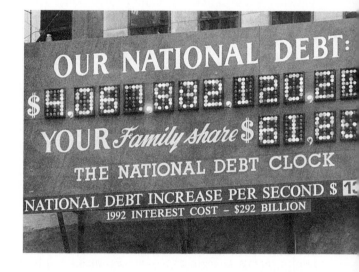

Imagine our society as being like a single individual. Our total income is our GDP. Some of our income goes to private consumption, and some goes to consumption by the government. The remainder is our national saving, which is set aside to finance consumption in the future. If the budget deficit increases because government spending increases, then, other things equal, national saving falls. If the budget deficit increases because taxes are cut, then the lower taxes will stimulate private consumption, which again causes national saving to fall. Either way, increases in the budget deficit reduce the amount that the country as a whole saves and so reduces our future standard of living.

Although persistent budget deficits threaten the long-term health of our economy, neither President Reagan nor President Bush, both Republicans, could come to any agreement with the Democratic-led Congress on how to achieve deficit reductions. The Republican party tends to favor reducing the deficit by cutting spending, while the Democratic party tends to favor increasing taxes. The resulting political deadlock has contributed to the increasing deficit. In any case, realizing that neither spending cuts nor tax increases are likely to be welcomed by voters, politicians of both parties find little incentive to take serious action. A balanced budget amendment is the best way to force policymakers to be fiscally responsible.

No: A Balanced Budget Amendment Would Make the Economy Less Stable

Not all economists agree that the deficit is particularly harmful. Some argue that the true deficit is smaller than the measured deficit. Others observe that we should distinguish between government expenditures on consumption (for example, payments to government employees) and on investment (for example, the building of roads and schools) before passing judgment on the deficit. Still others argue that changes in private saving may offset changes in the government deficit.

Nevertheless, a large number of economists—probably a majority—agree that deficits are harmful but disagree strongly with the idea of a balanced budget amendment. The reason is that such an amendment is likely to make the economy much less stable because it would remove automatic fiscal stabilizers.

Suppose that the economy goes into a recession. Because income falls, tax revenues decrease. Because some people lose their jobs, unemployment insurance and other transfer payments increase. By lessening the drop in disposable income, these stabilizers keep consumption from falling as far as it would otherwise, and lessen the severity of the recession. Contrast this scenario with a balanced budget world. If the economy went into recession, decreases in tax revenues and increases in welfare payments would lead to an increase in the deficit. The government would be forced to balance the budget again, by cutting spending, raising taxes, or both. These changes would tend to decrease aggregate demand and widen the recessionary gap.

The deficit may threaten the long-run health of the economy, but the balanced budget amendment is a cure with side-effects that are worse than the disease.

The Question: Is A Balanced Budget Amendment Desirable?

■   Some economists argue that deficits cause crowding out of private investment, leading to slower economic growth. Political considerations make it unlikely that Congress and the President will agree on measures to reduce the deficit, which suggests that a balanced budget amendment is the only possible cure.

■   Others argue that the harmful effects of the deficit may be overstated. Moreover, a balanced budget amendment would make the economy much less stable because it would eliminate automatic stabilizers.

Where Do You Stand?

1.   If a balanced budget amendment were to be passed by Congress, ratification by the states would be a lengthy process. Some commentators have suggested that politicians who support a balanced budget amendment are actually trying to avoid dealing with the deficit now. What is your opinion?

2.   One effect of a balanced budget amendment would be to involve the courts in matters of economic policy. Do you think that this is desirable?

3.   A balanced budget amendment is an example of a *policy rule:* It specifies how policy should be conducted and thus limits the discretion of policymakers to change fiscal policy. What advantages and disadvantages are there in limiting the discretionary power of policymakers?

4.   Should we pass a balanced budget amendment? Justify your stand.

Fiscal-Policy Multipliers in the Keynesian Income-Expenditure Model

The Expenditure Multiplier

The Tax Multiplier

Simultaneous Changes

The Balanced Budget Multiplier

Summarizing with Three Simple Formulas

Does the Balanced Budget Multiplier Work?

Fiscal policy is concerned with government spending and taxing. The economic consequences of fiscal policy are best evaluated by using the income-price model. This is because the model assumes that the price level may vary. However, some of the consequences of government spending and taxing can also be evaluated by using the income-expenditure model. This is because the model permits the formulation of several useful fiscal policy multiplier concepts.*

The Expenditure Multiplier

Let's assume for the moment that taxes remain constant. Then an increase in government spending can be viewed as an *injection* of purchasing power into the economy's circular flow of income. That is, the increased spending becomes a net addition to total spending, which raises the aggregate expenditure (*AE*) curve in the income-expenditure model.

The rise in government expenditure has a multiplier effect on real output. (So, too, does a rise in any of the other variables that comprise the *AE* curve—consumption expenditure, investment expenditure, and net exports.) The reason is that a rise in govern-

---

*The multiplier principle and the complete income-expenditure model were illustrated and explained in Chapter 14. You'll find it helpful to review those topics at this time.

ment expenditure increases the sales and profits of firms that sell to the government. This leads to further expansions in output throughout the economy. This magnifying effect of an increase in expenditures is expressed as an *expenditure multiplier.* Thus:

Increased government spending can raise the level of aggregate expenditure from an unemployment to a full-employment level. However, any additional spending that raises aggregate expenditure above full-employment levels will be inflationary.

Important: To convince yourself that you understand this idea, make sure you can illustrate it by sketching an income-expenditure diagram. Refer to Chapter 14 if you need help.

The Tax Multiplier

What happens to the equilibrium level of real output when spending remains constant and taxes vary? As you would probably guess, an increase in taxes can be viewed as a *withdrawal* of purchasing power from the economy's circular flow of income. For example, an increase in individual income taxes leaves households with less disposable income to spend. This decrease in

income causes a decrease (downward shift) in the aggregate expenditure curve. The result is a lower equilibrium level of real output .

It probably comes as a surprise to learn that the decrease in real output won't be the same numerical amount as the increase in taxes. Instead the decrease will be a *multiple* of the increase in taxes. To see why, let's look at the familiar consumption-function diagram in Exhibit 1. The diagram rests on three assumptions:

1. The *C* curve assumes that consumption expenditures depend on aggregate income while *all other factors that may affect consumption remain constant.* Therefore, a change in any of these "other" factors will cause the *C* curve to shift.

2. The marginal propensity to consume (*MPC*)—the fraction of each additional dollar of income spent on consumption—is assumed to be 4/5. It follows that the marginal propensity to save (*MPS*)—the fraction of each additional dollar of income saved—is 1/5. Therefore, the expenditure multiplier, which equals 1/*MPS*, is 5.

3. The net increase in individual income taxes imposed on consumers is assumed to be $20 billion.

EXHIBIT 1

Effect of Increased Taxes on Consumption and on GDP
(hypothetical economy)

MPC = 4/5

MPS = 1/5

Expenditure multiplier = 5

T = tax increase of $20 billion

As a result of the tax increase, the consumption curve shifts downward from *C* to *C'*. Hence, the equilibrium point changes from *E* to *E'*. The amount of change equals *MPC* × *T*. Thus, because *MPC* = 4/5 and the tax increase is $20 billion, the *C* curve shifts downward by 4/5 × $20 billion = $16 billion.

However, because the expenditure multiplier is 5, real output on the horizontal axis decreases by a multiple of the decrease in spending—by 5 × $16 billion = $80 billion. Note too that, although the decrease in real output is equal to 5

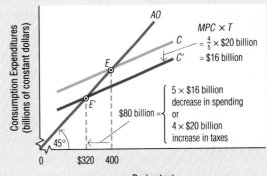

times the $16 billion decrease in spending, it is equal to 4 times the $20 billion increase in taxes. The number 4 may therefore be called the *tax multiplier.*

With these assumptions in mind, we may analyze the results of the increase in taxes in two steps:

Step 1 The first effect of the $20 billion increase in taxes is to reduce people's disposable income by $20 billion. Therefore, the consumption curve in Exhibit 1 shifts downward from *C* to *C'*. However, because *consumption depends on income* and the *MPC* is 4/5, consumption expenditures decrease by 4/5 of $20 billion = $16 billion. Thus, as you can see, the *decrease in consumption, measured by the amount of downward shift of the C curve, equals MPC × T.*

Step 2 What will be the effect of the increased taxes on real output? Because the expenditure multiplier is 5, a decrease in consumption expenditures of $16 billion will reduce real output by 5 × $16 billion = $80 billion. Equivalently, because taxes have increased by $20 billion, real output will be reduced by a multiple of that amount, namely, 4 × $20 billion = $80 billion. This is shown in the diagram, where the equilibrium real output changes from $400 billion at *E* to $320 billion at *E'*, a decrease of $80 billion.

As you might expect, a decrease in taxes of $20 billion would have had the opposite effect. Such a decrease would have stimulated consumer spending, raised aggregate expenditure, and thereby—according to theory—increased real output by $80 billion.

Simultaneous Changes

Suppose that we now allow government spending, *G*, and taxes, *T*, to vary simultaneously. For instance, what will be the effect if *G* and *T* are both increased simultaneously by the same amount—in our example, by $20 billion?

- By itself, the increase in *G* would raise real output by 5 × $20 billion = $100 billion. In general, the factor by which an increase in total spending, by raising aggregate expenditure, may be expected to expand real output is called the *expenditure multiplier* (M_E). In this example, M_E has a numerical value of 5.

- By itself, the increase in *T* would lower real output by 4 × $20 billion = $80 billion. In general, the

factor by which an increase in personal income taxes, by lowering aggregate expenditure, may be expected to contract real output is called the *tax multiplier* (M_T). In this example, M_T has a numerical value of 4.

The Balanced Budget Multiplier

It follows that the net effect of *equal* increases of $20 billion in *G* and *T* will be to increase real output by 1 × $20 billion = $20 billion. In general, the multiple by which equal changes in government spending and taxes affect changes in real output is called the *balanced budget multiplier* (M_B). As you can see, M_B has a numerical value of 1.

The reason for this result is that the $20 billion increases in *G* and *T* are precisely equal, but their effects are opposite. The two multiplier processes thus cancel each other out—except on the first round, when the full amount of *G* ($20 billion) is added to real output. This is why the *net* multiplier effect of equal increases in *G* and *T* is 5 – 4 = **1**.

In summary:

If *G* and *T* are increased (or decreased) simultaneously by equal amounts, real output will be increased (or decreased) by the same amount. For example, a simultaneous increase in *G* and *T* by $20 billion will raise real output by 1 × $20 billion = $20 billion. Similarly, a simultaneous decrease by $20 billion will lower real output by 1 × $20 billion = $20 billion. Thus, the numerical value of the expenditure multiplier, M_E, minus the numerical value of the tax multiplier, M_T, is called the *balanced budget multiplier, M_B. In general, if prices remain constant, $M_B = M_E - M_T = 1$.*

Summarizing with Three Simple Formulas

Economic concepts can often be expressed concisely as formulas, or equations. Here are three simple ones that summarize the balanced budget multiplier concept.

The Expenditure Multiplier If the economy is in a recession, an increase in spending can cause a magnified expansion of real output. The amount of the expansion will depend on the size of the expenditure multiplier. Symbolized M_E, the expenditure multiplier equals the reciprocal of the *MPS*. Thus:

$$M_E = \frac{1}{MPS} \qquad (1)$$

The Tax Multiplier An increase in taxes on consumers reduces their incomes. This in turn reduces their consumption expenditures because consumption depends on income. The decrease in consumption is determined by the *MPC*. Therefore, the tax multiplier, symbolized M_T, is simply a fraction (equal to *MPC*) of the expenditure multiplier. That is, $M_T = MPC \times M_E$. Substituting from (1), this equation can be written:

$$M_T = MPC \times \frac{1}{MPS} \quad \text{or simply} \quad \frac{MPC}{MPS} \qquad (2)$$

The Balanced Budget Multiplier Because expenditures are injections of purchasing power, they have an expansionary effect on the economy's circular flow of income. And because taxes are withdrawals of purchasing power, they have a contractionary effect on the economy's circular flow of income. Therefore, the net effect of equal and simultaneous increases in government spending G and taxes T is determined by the difference between the expenditure and tax multipliers. This difference is the balanced budget multiplier, M_B. Thus:

$$M_B = M_E - M_T \qquad (3)$$

It's now just a short step to see why the numerical value of M_B is 1. First we substitute in (3):

$$M_B = M_E - M_T$$
$$= \frac{1}{MPS} - \frac{MPC}{MPS}$$
$$= \frac{1 - MPC}{MPS}$$

But you already know that *MPS* is the same as $1 - MPC$. Therefore, substituting in the last equation,

$$M_B = \frac{1 - MPC}{1 - MPC} = \frac{MPS}{MPS} = 1$$

Does the Balanced Budget Multiplier Work?

If the government would raise taxes and use the additional revenues to pay for additional expenditures, it would balance the budget while still adhering to an expansionary policy. Therefore, the effect on the economy would be stimulative—not neutral as is often believed.

Is this statement correct? The answer is yes—according to the balanced budget multiplier theory.

But does the theory always work as expected? In other words, is the balanced budget multiplier always equal to 1, or can it be larger or smaller? The answer depends on the theory's underlying assumptions. Among them:

1. The Average Price Level Must Be Constant This is perhaps the most obvious assumption. The balanced budget multiplier principle was formulated in the 1950s. In that era, when Keynesian economics was in its heyday, the annual inflation rate averaged less than 2 percent. As a result, the various multipliers remained fairly stable and it was possible to estimate them with reasonable confidence. But in periods of fluctuating inflation rates such as the United States has often experienced since the mid-1960s, the multipliers are much less stable. Consequently, their usefulness as a guide for policy-makers has declined in relative importance.

2. Government Spending Must Be Noncompetitive The increase in government spending shouldn't compete with private spending. But in reality, it often does. Consequently, if government spends more on education, transportation, health, and so on, the private sector may spend less on these. In that case, private-sector consumption expenditures will decrease, saving will increase, and hence the expansionary effect of government spending will be reduced.

3. Taxes Must Not Create Disincentives The increased taxes needed to pay for enlarged government spending shouldn't be counterproductive. In reality, however, they may be. For example, if people feel that taxes are already high, further increases may reduce households' incentives to work and save, and businesses' incentives to invest. Some critics believe that this has happened at various times. The resulting decrease in production would reduce the expansionary effect of the balanced budget multiplier.

4. *MPC*s Must Be the Same The group that receives the benefits of increased government spending must have the same *MPC* as the group that pays the increased taxes. In reality, however, this is not likely. Therefore, the tax multiplier may actually be greater than, equal to, or less than the expenditure multiplier. These possibilities alter the expansionary effect.

Dubious Assumptions

The balanced budget multiplier theory is an integral part of fiscal-policy analysis. However, because of some questionable premises on which the theory is based, it hasn't gone without criticism. In general:

The balanced budget multiplier theory rests on some dubious assumptions. Therefore, although it is logically correct *within the income-expenditure model,* it may not always work as expected. For example, fluctuating inflation rates and increased government spending and taxes may at times impede rather than stimulate the private sector's growth. The effect of these impediments will be to increase rather than to decrease unemployment and inflation.

Summary of Important Ideas

1. In the income-expenditure model, real output and employment are affected by the interaction of three types of multipliers. They are the expenditure multiplier, the tax multiplier, and the balanced budget multiplier.

2. An increase in government spending, with individual income taxes held constant, will raise aggregate expenditure. An increase in those taxes, with govern-

ment spending held constant, will reduce aggregate expenditure. And a simultaneous and equal change in government expenditure and individual income taxes will alter real output by the amount of the change. The alteration of real output occurs because of the operation of the balanced budget multiplier principle.

3. The balanced budget multiplier concept is based on several assumptions. Perhaps the most important is a constant price level. If the price level fluctuates significantly, as it has often done for the past several decades, the various multipliers become unstable and lose

Terms and Concepts to Review

expenditure multiplier   *balanced budget multiplier*
tax multiplier

Questions and Problems

1. Assume that the economy is in recession, the *MPC* is 1/2, and an increase of $100 billion in output is needed to achieve full employment. Then, using diagrams if necessary, and assuming that private investment is constant, answer the following questions:

a. How much should government spending be increased to achieve full employment?

b. What would happen if taxes were reduced by $10 billion? Is this enough to restore full employment? If not, how large a tax reduction is needed?

2. In Problem 1, what would be the effect of a simultaneous increase in government spending and taxes of $50 billion? What would be the effect of a simultaneous decrease of $50 billion? Explain why. Would the situation be different in the case of a simultaneous increase in *G* and *T* under full employment? Explain.

ECONOMICS IN THE NEWS.

Keynes's Legacy: Fiscal-Policy Alternatives

As the Economy Sags, Washington Scrambles for Ways to Fix It

By Alan Murray

WASHINGTON—A quarter century ago, economists were in the ascendancy. *Time* magazine ran a cover photo of British economist John Maynard Keynes in 1965 and declared that his followers "had descended in force from their ivory towers and now sit confidently at the elbow of almost every important leader in government and business."

Today, that easy confidence has evaporated. The nation has learned that the tools for combating recessions are far less potent than once thought. Here's a look at some of the antirecessionary fiscal-policy options the government has.

Middle-Class Tax Cuts

This is the clear favorite of the politicans, but wins little praise from the experts. If a tax cut for the middle class is permanent, it could indeed stimulate consumer spending and boost the economy. But because the middle class is so big, the cost will be immense, swelling an already swollen deficit.

Another proposal would give a permanent tax cut for the middle class while paying for it by raising taxes on high-income Americans. There may be an argument for this on social equity grounds, but it would do little to stimulate the economy, since it simply shifts income from one group to another.

Investment Tax Credit

Economic evidence suggests the credit—a tax break for companies that invest in new equipment—has in the past provided a short-term boost to investment spending. And unlike middle-class tax cuts, this tax break is even *more* potent if it's temporary. If companies know the credit is going to expire after two years, they are likely to speed up investment spending they had planned for the future—giving a boost to the economy.

The credit has its drawbacks. It only encourages certain types of traditional equipment investments, and does little, for instance, to boost investment in research or new technologies. Moreover, it is expensive. The one eliminated in 1986 cost more than $25 billion a year in lost tax revenue.

Capital Gains Tax Cut

The virtue of a capital gains tax cut is that it provides an investment incentive at little—if any—costs to the government. Indeed, administration calculations suggest the tax cut actually *raises* money in the first few years it's in effect. That's because in the United States, the capital gains tax—which is the tax on the increase in the value of an investment—is essentially voluntary. Wealthy people can choose, if they wish, to hold their assets until they die, and thereby pass them along to heirs without paying any tax on the gain. The wealthy are less likely to sell those assets and pay the tax if the tax rate is high. Thus, a lower tax rate can result in more sales and perhaps more tax revenue for the government.

The main argument against the tax cut, however, is an egalitarian one. The greatest benefit from a cut in capital gains taxes goes to the wealthy.

Increased Spending

The government could choose simply to increase its own spending, thus stimulating the economy.

Critics say, however, that government bureaucracies tend to be a slow and inefficient means of channeling increased spending to the economy. Moreover, in Washington, "temporary" spending increases—as well as "temporary" tax cuts—have a way of becoming permanent, and thus increasing the budget deficit.

No Quick Fix

In the end, of course, any rescue package should be greeted with only modest expectations. Many of the problems the U.S. economy faces—overbuilt commercial real estate markets, overextended banks, debt-burdened consumers—are ones that must be worked out over time.

Source: *The Wall Street Journal,* December 9, 1991, p. A1.

Chapter 16

Money, Interest, and Macroeconomic Equilibrium

Determination of the Interest Rate

Keynesian Macroeconomic Theory: Putting
the Pieces Together

Origins: How the Keynesian Revolution Came to America

Learning Guide

Watch for answers to these important questions

What is meant by "the" interest rate? How does the classical, or loanable-funds, explanation of the interest rate differ from the Keynesian, or liquidity preference, explanation?

How do changes in interest rates come about? How do these changes affect the volume of investment spending by businesses?

What basic relationships exist among the variables constituting the income-expenditure, or Keynesian, model? How do changes in the money supply affect interest rates and investment, and hence aggregate demand?

How did John R. Hicks and Alvin Hansen contribute to the Keynesian revolution?

The importance of money essentially flows from its being a link between the present and the future. . . . The possession of actual money lulls our disquietude; and the premium which we require to make us part with money is the measure of the degree of disquietude.

—JOHN MAYNARD KEYNES

The "link between the present and the future"—the "premium" to which Keynes referred in the above quotation—is the rate of interest. This variable plays a strategic role in the Keynesian explanation of how the economy works. It's also a key factor in the use of money as a *standard of deferred payments,* one of the four functions of money you've already learned about.

Any discussion of the rate of interest almost always involves a discussion of money. The two are closely related, as you saw in the earlier chapters on money, banking, and monetary policy.* Once the relationship is reviewed, as will be done in this chapter, your understanding of the basic Keynesian income-expenditure model will be complete. You'll then see how the strategic variables in the model fit together within the macroeconomy.

Determination of the Interest Rate

To begin with, why is the study of interest important? The answer is easy to see. Businesses invest in plant and equipment because they expect to earn profits.

*See especially Chapters 11 and 12.

That is, they acquire capital goods as long as the anticipated rate of return on an additional unit of investment—called the **marginal efficiency of investment**—exceeds the cost of funds. (To refresh your understanding of this concept, look up the definition of "marginal efficiency of investment" in the Dictionary at the back of the book.) The cost of funds is the rate of interest—the price a borrower pays a lender to acquire money.

What's Meant by "the" Interest Rate?

When you studied our monetary and banking system, you learned that there is no such thing as "the" interest rate. That is, there is no single rate of interest for all the various debt instruments that are traded in the money and capital markets. Instead, there are many different rates on the different types of commercial paper, Treasury bills, Treasury bonds, corporate bonds, and so on.

The interest rates for debt instruments depend on a number of conditions. Among them are the risk of default by borrowers, maturity dates (that is, when the instruments become due for payment), marketability (the ease with which the instruments can be sold), and the tax consequences. Each of these differs among debt instruments. Despite the differences, however, interest rates are interrelated. That is, they tend to increase or decrease together, although they may do so by different amounts. Therefore, it often proves convenient to talk about "the" interest rate rising or declining, as long as we remember that we're actually referring to the *whole structure of interest rates*.

With this background, the question to be addressed is, *What determines the rate of interest?* The answer can be given in terms of two closely related explanations—the classical or loanable-funds theory and the Keynesian or liquidity preference theory.

Classical Explanation: Loanable-Funds Theory of Interest

The classical explanation of saving and investment provides a basis for the *loanable-funds theory of interest*. The theory is familiar from your earlier study of money and interest. A review of what you've already learned about combined with some additional aspects will provide you with a more comprehensive understanding of the theory's main features.

The Market Rate of Interest in Classical Theory

In the classical theory, the interest rate is the price paid for the use of *loanable funds*. These funds consist mainly of the amount of income that is saved by households, and thereby made available for investment, mainly to businesses, at various rates of interest.

As any other price acts to ration the supply of a commodity, so does the interest rate act to ration loanable funds. Only those borrowers who are willing and able to pay the market interest rate can acquire the funds. This rate is at *r*. In numerical terms, *r* might be 6 percent, 10 percent, or some other percentage.

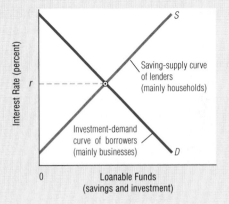

Household Saving and Business Investment

According to classical thinking, people work to earn income so that they can spend it on consumption. Moreover, they want to spend their income when they receive it, not save it to spend at a later date. Therefore, if they are to be persuaded to save some of their income, they must be rewarded for their sacrifice. The reward they receive is interest. Interest is thus a payment for *saving*, for abstaining from spending. That is, *interest is the price that must be paid to overcome people's preference for present as opposed to future consumption.*

Who pays interest? One answer, of course, is businesses. They borrow households' savings in order to invest in plant, equipment, and inventories. Thus:

Classical theory contends that household-sector saving *automatically* equals business-sector investment. The equality is brought about by a flexible interest rate. This rate is determined by the free play of demand and supply forces in the economy's competitive financial (money and capital) markets.

These ideas are illustrated by the demand and supply curves in Exhibit 1. Notice that the interest rate is measured on the vertical axis and the quantity of loanable funds is measured on the horizontal axis. The upward-sloping supply curve tells you that households are willing to save more—that is, make more loanable funds available—at higher interest rates than at lower ones. The downward-sloping demand curve shows that businesses are willing to borrow a larger quantity of loanable funds at lower interest rates than at higher ones. The equilibrium interest rate, r, is determined by the intersection of the two curves.

Other Sources of Saving and Investment

In reality, households aren't the only source of supply of loanable funds, nor are businesses the only source of demand for loanable funds. Several other economic entities that you learned about when you studied monetary economics are also demanders and suppliers of loanable funds. They are listed in Exhibit 2.*

Summarizing:

The *loanable-funds theory of interest* holds that the interest rate is determined by the demand for and the supply of money available for lending—called "loanable funds." The sources of demand for loanable funds are (1) business investment, (2) household consumption, (3) government deficit financing, and (4) net borrowing by the foreign sector. The sources of supply of loanable funds are (1) household savings, (2) retained earnings of businesses, (3) budget surpluses of government entities, (4) net lending by the foreign sector, and (5) Federal Reserve increases in the money supply.

Keynesian Explanation: Liquidity Preference Theory of Interest

What did Keynes have to say about the role of the interest rate and the conditions that determine it? We already know part of the answer. In the Keynesian income-expenditure model:

- Fluctuations in capital spending (or investment) by businesses are the main cause of fluctuations in real output.

- Businesses spend on capital goods when the interest rate is less than the marginal efficiency of investment.

*Refer to Chapter 12 for graphic illustrations of how the four sectors of the economy interact to determine the interest rate in the loanable-funds theory.

EXHIBIT 2

Major Sources of Demand and Supply for Loanable Funds

Sources of Demand for Loanable Funds*

- Business-sector investment
- Household-sector credit purchases
- Government-sector budget deficits
- Foreign-sector borrowing, net[†]

Sources of Supply of Loanable Funds*

- Household-sector savings (the difference between households' income and spending)
- Business-sector savings (undistributed profits, or retained earnings, and depreciation)
- Government-sector budget surpluses (including federal, state, and local governments)
- Foreign-sector lending, net[†]
- Federal Reserve increases in the money supply

*At any given time, some households, businesses, and government entities may be suppliers and some may be demanders of loanable funds. But during most years the household sector is a net supplier of funds, while the business sector (excluding banks) and the federal government are net demanders of funds.

[†]The term "net" (N) represents foreign-sector lending (L) to the United States *minus* foreign-sector borrowing (B) from the United States. That is, $N = L - B$. Thus, if N is positive, the foreign sector is a net supplier of loanable funds to the United States. If N is negative, the foreign sector is a net demander of loanable funds from the United States.

Therefore, the interest rate affects investment spending.

As for the conditions determining the rate of interest, Keynes argued that the classical theory is correct for an economy that's always at, or at least rapidly tending toward, full employment. His own theory of interest, he contended, *though logically equivalent to the classical loanable-funds theory,* is a more suitable guide for interpreting central-bank monetary policy.

Keynes and the Classicists

You can best understand Keynes's theory of interest by comparing his thinking with that of the classicists. For example, look again at the investment-demand curve illustrated earlier in Exhibit 1. This classical view shows the amount of capital spending that businesses are willing to undertake at each rate of interest (or cost of funds). The investment-demand curve, *D*, therefore, is the same as the marginal efficiency of investment (*MEI*) curve that Keynes used when he formulated his theory.

Although the investment-demand curve is the same as the *MEI* curve, there's an important difference in the way a change in investment is viewed by classical economists and by Keynesians. This difference can be seen by comparing the two figures in Exhibit 3:

Classical View [Figure (a)] The classicists regarded interest as the price that equates the demand for investment with the supply of saving *at full employment*. It follows that a change in the business sector's demand for investment will shift the demand curve and bring about a new equilibrium rate of interest. Thus, for example, a decrease in investment from *D* to *D'* will cause the rate of interest to drop from *r* to *r'*. However, *the economy will remain at full employment at this new interest rate.*

Keynesian View [Figure (b)] In the Keynesian income-expenditure model, investment spending is one of the components of aggregate expenditure. As a result, a decrease in investment spending causes *AE* to decline to *AE'*. But aggregate expenditure varies directly with real output. Therefore, the decrease in aggregate expenditure causes a drop in real output from *N* to *N'*. And, because employment depends on real output, the level of employment also declines.

According to Keynes, the classicists were wrong in assuming that a change in investment would affect only the interest rate and not the levels of real output and employment.

Because he disagreed with the classicists' assumptions, Keynes found it necessary to develop an alternative (though logically equivalent) theory of interest—one that would fit his income-expenditure model. This alternative formulation is called the "liquidity preference theory."

Statement of the Liquidity Preference Theory

In classical theory, as you've learned, interest is a reward for "waiting"—for "abstinence" from consumption. *In Keynes's theory, interest is a reward for "parting" with liquidity, for not hoarding money.* Because of this, the rate of interest is determined entirely by the demand

EXHIBIT 3

Effect of a Change in Investment

Investment spending on plant, equipment, and increases in inventory is undertaken by the business sector in anticipation of profits. The classical theory and the Keynesian theory predict different outcomes from a change in investment.

(a) Classical View

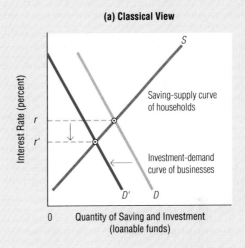

FIGURE (a) Classical View A decrease in investment from *D* to *D'* will cause the equilibrium rate of interest to decline from *r* to *r'*. The economy remains at full employment at this new rate of interest.

(b) Keynesian View

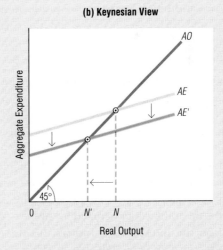

FIGURE (b) Keynesian View Investment spending is one of the components of aggregate expenditure, *AE*. Therefore, a decrease in investment will cause *AE* to decline to *AE'*. Hence, real output will decline from *N* to *N'*. And, because employment depends on output, the level of employment will also decline.

for and the supply of money. But two factors underlying demand and supply must be understood; liquidity preference and the quantity of money.

On the demand side, in Keynes's view, money is wanted because it's the only perfectly liquid asset. People would rather hold some of their assets in money than in any other form. The public's desire to hold some assets in liquid form is called *liquidity preference*. Therefore, to persuade you to give up some of your perfectly liquid assets, you must be offered a reward. *Interest is the price you must be paid to give up liquidity preference.* If you hold money, that is, if you hoard it by withholding it from circulation, you sacrifice interest. Therefore, *interest is the opportunity cost of holding money.*

On the supply side, according to Keynes, the quantity of money is the important factor. As you already know, the quantity of money is determined by the central bank (the Fed) through its control over reserve requirements, open-market operations, and the discount rate. (Look back at Exhibit 2 and note that the Fed is one of the sources of supply of loanable funds.) *In Keynes's view, therefore, expansions and contractions of the money supply play a key role in the determination of the interest rate.*

Determinants of Demand and Supply

The demand for money is a demand for liquidity. Why should you and I and everyone else prefer to hold assets in liquid form? Keynes provided three reasons, which he called the transactions, precautionary, and speculative motives.

1. Transactions Motive Households and many businesses must hold some of their assets in the form of money (currency and checkable deposits). This is because they purchase goods and services more or less continuously from day to day, while they receive income only at intervals, such as weekly or monthly. Therefore, they must hold a certain amount of money to bridge the gap between pay periods. The amount required—the transactions demand for money—doesn't depend on the interest rate. Instead, it's directly related to the level of economic activity. Thus, as aggregate income rises, so does the need for money for transactions.

2. Precautionary Motive A second reason households and businesses want to hold part of their assets in liquid form is to meet unforeseen developments. Examples are illnesses, accidents, losses of employment,

strikes, or market fluctuations. Although individuals and firms may be able to convert other assets into money at such times, the possibility of loss due to forced liquidation under unfavorable market conditions prompts them to reserve money for these contingencies. Like the transactions demand for money, the precautionary demand for money is influenced by aggregate-income levels, not by changes in the interest rate.

3. Speculative Motive Finally, households and businesses may prefer to hold part of their assets in the form of money to enable them to take advantage of changes in interest rates. Individuals and firms tend to hold more securities—especially bonds—and less money when the interest rate is high, to take advantage of high returns. Conversely, individuals and firms tend to hold more money and fewer securities when the interest rate is low. This is because the risk of holding bonds—the possible fall in their prices—more than offsets the interest returns.

The Fed The transactions, precautionary, and speculative motives determine the total demand for money. What determines the supply? The answer, of course, is the monetary authority—the Fed. As stated earlier, the Fed controls the quantity of money in the economy through its open-market operations, reserve requirements, and discount-rate policy.

Determining the Interest Rate

The determinants of the interest rate can be summarized and illustrated with the demand and supply model in Exhibit 4.

Observe that the quantity of money is measured on the horizontal axis and the interest rate is measured on the vertical. Observe also, from the subtitle of the diagram, that *the level of aggregate income is assumed to be constant.* This condition is needed because the total demand for money includes transactions and precautionary demands. Both of these, you've learned, tend to vary directly with aggregate income. Therefore, by holding aggregate income constant, transactions and precautionary demands are also held constant. This enables you to examine the relationship between the demand for money and the interest rate.

In the diagram, the demand curve D_M for money is downward sloping. This is because holding money entails an *opportunity cost* in terms of interest income forgone. Therefore, the public prefers to hold a

EXHIBIT
4

Determination of the Interest Rate in the Keynesian Model
(assuming a constant level of aggregate income)

The demand for money varies *inversely* with the interest rate. The reason is that, at higher interest rates, people want to hold less money and more interest-earning securities (such as bonds and other debt instruments). At lower interest rates, the reverse is true. Therefore, the D_M curve is downward sloping.

The supply of money is determined by the Fed through its reserve requirements, open-market operations, and discount-rate policy. At any given time the quantity of money in the economy is unrelated to the interest rate. Therefore, the S_M curve is a vertical line.

The intersection of the D_M and S_M curves determines the equilibrium rate of interest r.

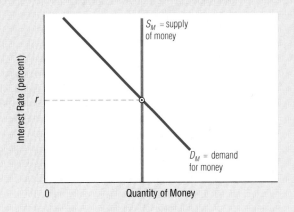

smaller proportion of its assets in money (and hence a larger proportion in interest-earning securities) when interest rates are high. This preference is reversed when interest rates are low. The public then prefers to hold a larger proportion in money (and hence a smaller proportion in interest-earning securities). As you have learned, the public's desire to hold some of its assets in liquid form (that is, money) is called *liquidity preference.*

Since the supply of money is determined by the Fed, it is simply the stock of money available at any given time. Therefore, the supply-of-money curve S_M is a vertical line. It tells you that the quantity of money is unresponsive to changes in the interest rate.

You can now see what happens in the market when the demand for money interacts with the supply of money. A specific interest rate emerges: the equilibrium rate of interest r is determined by the intersection of the D_M and S_M curves.

Summarizing:

The *liquidity preference theory of interest* was formulated by J. M. Keynes. The theory contends that households and businesses want to hold some of their assets in the most liquid form, namely, in cash (or demand deposits). The reason is to satisfy three motives: (1) the transactions motive, (2) the precautionary motive, and (3) the speculative motive. These motives determine the demand for money, while the monetary au-

thority—the Fed—determines its supply. The demand for and supply of money together determine the equilibrium rate of interest.

Why Interest Rates Change

Like other demand and supply curves, those in Exhibit 4 assume that all the other conditions affecting demand and supply remain constant. If one of these conditions changes, the relevant demand or supply curve will shift. This shift will bring about a new equilibrium rate of interest, as illustrated by the diagrams in Exhibit 5.

Changes in Demand   If aggregate income rises, the quantity of money demanded for transactions and precautionary purposes also rises. Therefore, the public's *liquidity preference,* or demand for money, increases. As Figure (a) shows, the money-demand curve thus shifts to the right from D_M to $D_M{'}$. Therefore, the interest rate rises from r to $r{'}$. The opposite occurs if there is a decline in aggregate income. The public's liquidity preference decreases. Therefore, the money-demand curve shifts to the left, which causes the interest rate to decline.

Changes in Supply   Actions taken by the Fed increase the supply of money. For example, by buying securities in the open market, by lowering reserve requirements, or by reducing the discount rate, the Fed can "inject"

EXHIBIT 5

Changes in Interest Rates

Changes in the demand for, or in the supply of, money cause changes in interest rates.

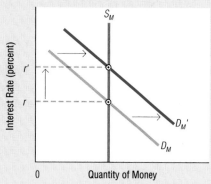

(a) Change in Demand for Money

FIGURE (a) An increase in the public's *liquidity preference* will increase its demand for money. The money-demand curve shifts to the right from D_M to D_M'. This causes the interest rate to rise from r to r'. A decrease in the demand for money will have the opposite effect, and cause the interest rate to decline.

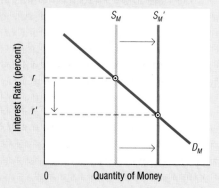

(b) Change in Supply of Money

FIGURE (b) An increase in the supply of money by the Fed will shift the money-supply curve to the right from S_M to S_M'. This shift causes the interest rate to decline from r to r'. A decrease in the supply of money will have the opposite effect, and cause the interest rate to rise.

reserves into the banking system. As Figure (b) shows, the money-supply curve shifts to the right from S_M to S_M'. This shift lowers the interest rate from r to r'. The reverse occurs if the Fed decreases the supply of money. The money-supply curve shifts to the left, which causes the interest rate to rise.

Practical Implications: Interest Rates and Business Investment

You can now appreciate two practical differences between the loanable funds and liquidity preference theories:

1. In the loanable-funds (LF) theory, as you saw earlier in Exhibit 2, the sources of demand and supply of funds are identified. The interaction of all the sources of demand with all the sources of supply determines the equilibrium interest rate. This interaction suggests how financial economists and analysts working in the securities markets use the LF theory to forecast interest rates. They estimate the quantities of funds that will be demanded and supplied by each sector, and then combine the estimates to arrive at a forecast. (If you take certain courses in finance, you'll use this method to make such forecasts yourself.)

2. In the liquidity preference (LP) theory, attention is focused on the stock of money. The source of the supply of money is the central bank and the source of demand is the public. This theory is thus narrower than the LF theory. However, the chief purpose of the LP theory is not to forecast interest rates but to *interpret the effects of changes in monetary policy on interest rates.* Such interpretations help explain why interest rates sometimes change when the Fed announces its weekly estimate of the money supply.

The loanable-funds theory of interest is more comprehensive than the liquidity preference theory. Despite their apparent differences, however, the two theories are logically equivalent.

Of course, a theory that explains how interest rates are determined tells only half the story. The other half concerns the practical matter of how changes in interest rates affect business investment decisions. Before we move on to that important topic, let's review three fundamental concepts that you learned when you first studied the Keynesian income-expenditure model:

EXHIBIT
6

The Interest Rate and Investment

FIGURE (a) Financial Market A shift in the money-supply curve from S_M to S_M' increases the quantity of money from Q to Q'. Therefore, the rate of interest drops from r to r'.

FIGURE (b) Business Sector The drop in the interest rate from r to r' causes the amount of investment to increase from I to I'. This is because businesses invest to the point where the MEI equals the interest rate (or cost of funds).

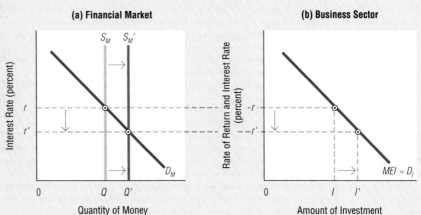

(a) Financial Market

(b) Business Sector

- Businesses base their investment decisions on anticipated profitability. Profitability is measured by the percentage rate of return on investment. The anticipated rate of return on an additional unit of investment is called the *marginal efficiency of investment* (*MEI*).

- At any given time, each firm's *MEI* curve is its *demand curve for investment*. Like any demand curve, the *MEI* curve is downward-sloping. This tells you that the amount of investment spending a firm will undertake is greater at lower interest rates (costs of funds) than at higher rates.

- When anticipated rates of return of all the firms in the economy are summed, the result is an *MEI* curve for the business sector as a whole. This curve, like each firm's individual *MEI* curve, is downward sloping. It may be thought of as the *business sector's demand curve for investment*.

As you already know, *both the rate of return on investment and the interest rate are measured in percentage terms*. As a result, we can link the financial market, where interest rates are determined, with the business sector, where investment decisions are made.

Exhibit 6 illustrates this linkage. In Figure (a), the equilibrium rate of interest r is determined by the intersection of the demand and supply curves of money. This rate is the cost of funds to firms. Therefore, in Figure (b), the amount of investment undertaken by the business sector at this rate of interest is I.

What happens if the volume of investment at I is

insufficient to achieve full employment? In that case, according to the Keynesian model, the monetary authority can lower the rate of interest in Figure (a) by increasing the money supply—say, from Q to Q'. If the D_M curve remains fixed, the equilibrium rate of interest will decline from r to r'. Accordingly, the amount of investment in Figure (b) will increase from I to I'. This increase in the amount of investment, as you know, will have a magnified effect on income, owing to the operation of the investment multiplier.

You can now see how monetary policy can stimulate economic activity. For example:

- To what extent will the interest rate fall as a result of an increase in the money supply? The answer depends on the *relative steepness* of the D_M curve.

- To what extent will the amount of investment increase as a result of a decline in the interest rate? The answer depends on the *relative steepness* of the D_I (or *MEI*) curve.

- To what extent will income rise as a result of an increase in investment? The answer depends on the size of the *multiplier*—that is, the investment multiplier.

You can verify these answers yourself by sketching some flatter and steeper curves and then noting the differences. As for the size of the (investment) multiplier, you'll recall that it depends on the marginal propensity to consume or to save. That is, it equals $1/(1-MPC)$ or $1/MPS$.

Conclusion: Interest Rates— A Continuing Concern

In the real world, fluctuations in interest rates occur frequently. These fluctuations can affect the payments that businesses must make on loans to purchase investment goods. The fluctuations can also affect the payments that households must make on loans to purchase cars, major appliances, and houses. Therefore, the role of interest rates in the economy is never taken lightly. Indeed, it's a topic of continuing concern to everyone.

The mechanism that establishes equilibrium in the financial market is the rate of interest. The rate is affected by changes in the money supply, which are controlled by the Federal Reserve. Because of their impact on interest rates and economic activity, the Fed's monetary policies are watched closely and are reported almost daily in the news media.

Keynesian Macroeconomic Theory: Putting the Pieces Together

The main ideas of Keynesian macroeconomic theory that we set out to develop are now completed. To un-

derstand the overall structure of the theory, it helps to diagram it. A diagram will permit you to see how the variables are linked, and will provide a basis for integrating some important relationships.

Outline of the Keynesian Theory

A diagrammatical outline of the Keynesian theory is provided in Exhibit 7. To begin with, the diagram shows that *the level of aggregate income (or output) depends on the level of aggregate spending.* (Hence the expression "income-expenditure model.") Aggregate spending, in turn, has four components: consumption spending, investment spending, government spending, and net exports.

Consumption Spending (C)

Consumption spending depends on the propensity to consume. It's expressed by a mathematical relationship between consumption and income called the *consumption function.*

The consumption function determines both the average propensity to consume and the marginal propensity to consume. The latter, in turn, determines the investment multiplier, which is the reciprocal of the marginal propensity to invest.

EXHIBIT 7

Outline of the Keynesian Theory of Income Determination

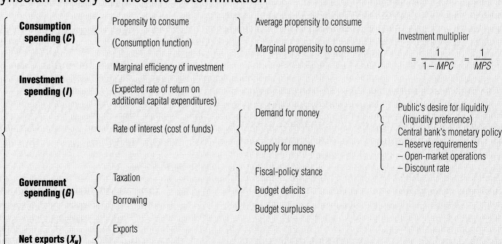

Investment Spending (I)

Investment spending depends on the marginal efficiency of investment relative to the rate of interest. The marginal efficiency of investment is the expected rate of return on additional capital expenditures. The rate of interest is the cost of funds for financing those expenditures.

The rate of interest is determined by the demand for money and the supply of money. The demand for money is a demand for liquidity. The supply of money is determined by the Fed's monetary policy. It depends on reserve requirements, open-market operations, and the discount rate.

Government Spending (G)

Government spending is financed by taxation and borrowing. The ways in which these are combined determine the government's fiscal-policy stance. This stance is reflected in the size of budget deficits or surpluses.

Net Exports (X_N)

Exports are goods and services sold abroad. The dollar value of our exports is the amount foreigners spend to purchase some of our GDP. Imports are goods and services that we buy from abroad. The dollar value of our imports is the amount we spend to purchase some of the rest of the world's GDP. With respect to aggregate expenditure, we're interested only in the effects of imports and exports on the value of our own GDP. Therefore, total imports are subtracted from total exports to obtain net exports:

Net exports = total exports − total imports

Integrating Some Basic Relationships

The Keynesian model can also be expressed as a set of integrated relationships. This is done graphically in Exhibit 8. Although the graphs are highly simplified, they contain many of the essential ideas of Keynesian macroeconomic theory.

EXHIBIT 8

Simplified Keynesian Theory: Income-Expenditure Model

FIGURE (a) In the financial market, the interest rate r is determined by the demand for money D_M and the supply of money S_M.

FIGURE (b) In the business sector, the amount of investment spending I is determined by the marginal efficiency of investment $MEI (= D_I)$ and the interest rate r.

FIGURE (c) In the total economy, investment spending I is added to consumption spending C. So too are government spending G and net exports X_N. The sum of expenditures of all four sectors of the economy constitute aggregate expenditures AE. As shown by the vertical dashed line, the intersection of AE and AO (aggregate output) determines real output.

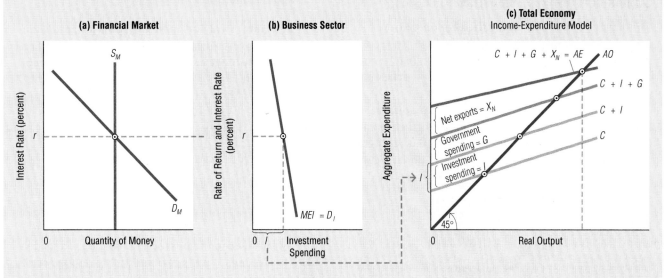

First, look at the financial market in Figure (a). This is where the rate of interest is determined. The intersection of the supply-of-money curve S_M and the demand-for-money curve D_M establishes the market rate of interest r.

Second, look at the business-sector diagram in Figure (b). The interest rate that is determined in the financial market becomes the cost of funds to businesses. As a result, the business sector undertakes investment up to the point at which the marginal efficiency of investment MEI (the expected rate of return on additional investment) equals the interest rate. The MEI curve is thus the business sector's demand curve for investment, D_I. Note that the amount of investment spending corresponding to r is I.

Finally, look at the diagram for the total economy in Figure (c). Observe that investment spending I by the business sector is added to consumption spending C by the household sector. The combined spending of both sectors is thus shown by the line $C + I$. If government spending G is added to $C + I$, total spending by the household, business, and government sectors is represented by the line $C + I + G$. And if net exports are added to this total, the resulting line, $C + I + G + X_N$, is the aggregate expenditure AE curve for the total economy.* Notice from the vertical dashed line that the intersection AE and AO (aggregate output) determines real output.

For any given level of real output, $AE = C + I + G + X_N$. You can verify this formula with actual numbers by looking at the first five columns of data in the inside front cover of the book.

Conclusion: Policy-Activism Choices

The Keynesian model of how the economy works has important implications for public policy. Let's consider some of them with regard to the two great, recurring problems of national economic policy—recession and inflation.

What happens if the equilibrium level of output in Figure (c) of Exhibit 8 is either above or below the full- or natural-employment level? Obviously, there will be either a recessionary or an inflationary gap. What can be done to close the gap? In terms of the

Keynesian model, the answer depends on your beliefs concerning policy activism. For example:

If you advocate *fiscal-policy* activism, you'll offer one of two policy prescriptions for government:

1. To close a recessionary gap, raise the AE curve by reducing individual and corporate taxes and/or increasing government expenditures. These actions will stimulate the economy by increasing consumption spending C, investment spending I, and/or government spending G.

2. To close an inflationary gap, lower the AE curve by raising individual and corporate taxes and/or reducing government expenditures. These actions will dampen the economy by decreasing consumption, investment, and/or government spending.

In contrast, if you advocate *monetary-policy* activism, you'll offer one of these two policy prescriptions to the Fed:

1. To close a recessionary gap, stimulate the economy by increasing the money supply. In Figure (a) of Exhibit 8, the increase will shift the S_M curve to the right. The interest rate r will thus decline and cause the amount of investment spending in Figure (b) to increase. This increase will raise the AE curve in Figure (c).

2. To close an inflationary gap, dampen the economy by decreasing the money supply. This will shift the S_M curve to the left. The interest rate r will thus rise, causing the amount of investment spending to decline. As a result, the AE curve will also decline.

In reality, fiscal and monetary policies aren't mutually exclusive—they aren't adopted on an "either-or" basis. Washington is always utilizing some combination of both.

Can a single "best" combination of fiscal and monetary policies—an ideal fiscal-monetary mix—be established? Probably not. Different combinations of policies can exert different and unpredictable influences on real output, employment, and the average price level. Therefore, the actual fiscal-monetary mix undergoes frequent changes as policymakers search for ways to guide the economy along a desired growth path.

As you'll see in the next several chapters, considerable disagreement exists over the ability of policymakers to achieve this goal.

*Observe from the diagram that net exports (= total exports − total imports) decline with larger values of real output (or income). The reason is that, as real income rises in relation to the rest of the world's, the volume of goods and services we buy from abroad increases relative to the volume of goods and services we sell abroad.

Origins: How the Keynesian Revolution Came to America

The decade of the 1930s is known in history as the Great Depression. It was an era in which unemployment rates reached 25 percent of the labor force, stock-market prices plunged more than 50 percent, nearly 9,500 banks failed, and businesses numbering many times that amount went bankrupt. It was an era in which everyone searched desperately for explanations of how such cataclysmic economic events could occur, and for steps that could be taken to correct them.

The most promising explanation, in the opinion of most experts at the time, came from British economist John Maynard Keynes. In a book entitled *The General Theory of Employment, Interest and Money* (1936), he launched a new way of thinking about economics. The new view was accepted so quickly and so widely by most economists and political leaders that it was dubbed the *Keynesian Revolution*. In less than a decade, the terms "economics" and "Keynesian economics" became almost synonymous, and the systematic study of Keynesian economics came to be known as "macroeconomics."

When Keynes's *General Theory* was published, it was recognized immediately as a work of major importance. But it was also extremely difficult to comprehend. As a result, within the first year of its publication relatively few people had read the entire book, and only a fraction of those who read it claimed to understand it. But within the next several years, some economists who grasped Keynes's message wrote articles and books to explain it. These scholars thus became the catalysts that sparked the Keynesian Revolution. Two of the most prominent catalysts were John R. Hicks and Alvin H. Hansen.

Hicks: The Other Keynes

Hicks, a British economist and friend of Keynes, was among the leading economic theorists of the twentieth century. He was the author of dozens of major books and articles dealing with many aspects of economics. Among his best-known works was an article entitled, "Mr. Keynes and the 'Classics'", *Econometrica,* April 1937, published a year after Keynes's *General Theory.* The article, which has been reprinted in hundreds of books, turned a ray of light on Keynesian theory making it accessible to professors and graduate stu-

John R. Hicks
(1904–1989)

dents. As a result, economists soon began referring to Hicks as "the other Keynes."

Hicks explained the Keynesian system by pointing out that much of it involves a relationship between two markets—a market for goods and a market for money. Using separate pairs of curves to explain the two markets, Hicks showed how both markets must be in equilibrium in order for the economy's income and employment levels to be stable. The genius of Hicks's graphic device was its demonstration that Keynes and his classical contemporaries each saw the economy from a different point of view. As a result, Keynes was able to come up with novel solutions to problems that classical economists had long thought were settled.

Hicks's graphic model has proved to be amazingly durable and versatile. It has become a standard analytical tool taught in intermediate macroeconomics courses, and is used to analyze and interpret a wide variety of concepts. But Hicks made many other major contributions to economics as well. These were recognized by some of the world's leading universities, which granted Hicks more than a dozen honorary degrees. But Hicks's crowning award came in 1972, a few years after his retirement from England's distinguished Oxford University. In that year the King of Sweden bestowed one of his government's highest honors upon Hicks—the Alfred Nobel Memorial Prize in Economic Science.

Hansen: The American Keynes

Hicks's graphic model of Keynesian theory proved extremely helpful, but the model was still abstract. What was needed was an explanation of how the theory could serve as a basis for government policymaking.

Alvin H. Hansen
(1887–1975)

The task of providing that explanation fell to a professor at Harvard University, Alvin Hansen. He made extensive use of Hicks's graphic device. However, Hansen broadened the concept by employing it as a vehicle for formulating government macroeconomic policies. As a result, the graphic model and its interpretation came to be known as the "Hicks-Hansen synthesis."

Hansen did more than any other economist to bring Keynes's ideas to America. In a series of books that began in 1941, Hansen provided lucid explanations of Keynesian theory and policy. The first book, *Fiscal Policy and Business Cycles* (1941), served as a standard text in graduate macroeconomics courses for more than a decade. That book was followed during the 1950s and early 1960s by three others. All of them clarified further the new macroeconomics and applied it to policies aimed at maintaining full employment.

One of Hansen's books was particularly welcomed by students. In *A Guide to Keynes* (1953), Hansen provided a chapter-by-chapter, and sometimes page-by-page, explanation of every concept in Keynes's *General Theory*. The *Guide* thus did for Keynes's book what Cliffs Notes (which was not yet in existence) have done for literature. But the *Guide* was only one of Hansen's many publications, all of which were welcomed both by students and professors. During the 1950s, in recognition of his steady outpouring of articles and books extolling Keynesian economics, Hansen's colleagues gave him the nickname of "the American Keynes."

As an educator, Hansen's enthusiasm was infectious. Through his teaching and writings, he inspired and helped train an entire generation of economists.

Many of them went on to achieve international recognition for their scholarship. Hansen also contributed greatly to the teaching of the new macroeconomics by inventing an ingenious graphic model to illustrate Keynes's main ideas. The popular name given to the model, which resembles the letter *X* tipped on its side, is the "Keynesian cross." Its more formal name, expressed in terms of the two variables that it relates, is the income-expenditure model.

Summary of Important Ideas

1. The classical theory of interest is the *loanable-funds theory*. It holds that the interest rate is determined by the demand for and supply of loanable funds. The main sources of demand for loanable funds are business-sector investment, household-sector credit purchases, the financing of government-sector deficits, and the net foreign-sector borrowing. The sources of supply of loanable funds are household-sector savings, business-sector retained earnings, government-sector budget surpluses, the Fed's increases in the money supply, and net foreign-sector lending.

2. The Keynesian theory of interest is the *liquidity preference theory*. Although it seems different from the loanable-funds theory, the two theories are logically equivalent. The liquidity preference theory holds that the interest rate is determined by the demand for and supply of money. Interest is the opportunity cost of holding liquid assets—money. People want to hold money to satisfy their transactions, precautionary, and speculative motives. These constitute the demand for money. The supply of money is determined by the Fed through its reserve requirements, open-market operations, and discount rate.

3. Keynesian macroeconomic theory states that the level of aggregate income equals aggregate expenditures. This consists of consumption spending, investment spending, government spending, and net exports. Each of these is determined by and helps to determine other variables. The relationships among these variables constitute the income-expenditure model of Keynesian economics.

4. Keynesian economics provides a guide for policy activism. This may consist of alterations in fiscal policy, monetary policy, or combinations of both. There's probably no ideal balance because different combinations of taxing, government spending, and money-supply growth rates have different and unpredictable impacts on the economy. Thus, in their efforts to guide the economy along a desired growth path, policymakers frequently vary the fiscal-monetary mix.

5. Two economists who played major roles in advancing Keynesian ideas were John R. Hicks and Alvin H. Hansen. Hicks, a British professor at Oxford University, was the first to present many essentials of Keynes's theory in terms of a graphical model. Hansen, an American professor at Harvard University, applied Hicks's model extensively, developed the income-expenditure model (also known as the "Keynesian cross"), and made many original contributions as well. Together, Hicks and Hansen were the first scholars to make Keynesian economics accessible to most economists and policymakers.

Terms and Concepts to Review

marginal efficiency of investment

loanable-funds theory of interest

transactions motive

precautionary motive

speculative motive

liquidity preference theory of interest

Questions and Problems

1. "In the classical theory, the change in the interest rate resulting from a change in the demand or supply of loanable funds will depend on the *relative slopes* of the demand and supply curves." Demonstrate this proposition graphically.

2. Will the interest rate rise or fall as a result of each of the following changes? Explain the reason for your answer. Assume that *all other things remain the same.*

  a. Increase in household savings

  b. Increase in corporate income taxes

  c. Increase in government spending

  d. Increase in the monetary growth rate

  e. Decrease in business investment

  f. Decrease in credit purchases by consumers

  g. Decrease in the federal budget deficit

3. "In the income-expenditure model, the changes in real output and employment resulting from a change in aggregate expenditure will be determined by the *relative slope* of the *AE* curve." Demonstrate this proposition graphically.

4. Suppose the interest rate on short-term loans is the same as that on long-term loans. What are the advantages and disadvantages to lenders of being in short-term as opposed to long-term investments?

5. The classical theory holds that the equilibrium rate of interest equates the demand for and supply of *loanable funds*. The Keynesian theory holds that the equilibrium rate of interest equates the demand for and supply of *money*. What is the difference between these ideas? (*Suggestion:* Look up the meanings of *loanable-funds theory of interest* and *liquidity preference theory of interest* in the Dictionary at the back of the book.)

6. Does the interest rate affect people's liquidity preferences? Explain.

7. If a reduction in an already relatively low interest rate does not result in an expansion of investment, what might this suggest in terms of the Keynesian theory of interest?

8. Assume that the economy is in macroeconomic equilibrium. What effect would each of the following changes, considered separately and without regard to secondary results, have on income? Explain why.

  a. Increase in the money supply

  b. Increase in liquidity preference

  c. Increase in the marginal efficiency of investment

  d. Decrease in consumption

In general terms, how would secondary effects have influenced your answers?

9. There is much concern about our large national debt. Why doesn't government allay the concern by simply printing enough money to pay off the debt?

Part 5

Macroeconomics Today:
Ideas, Issues, and Policies

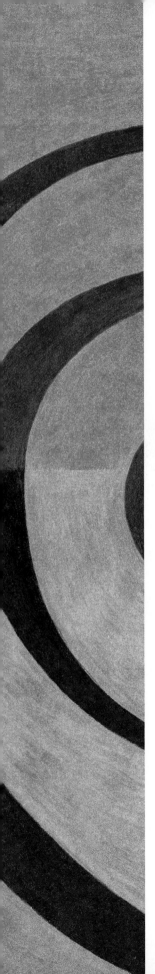

Chapter 17

Today's Macroeconomic Theories: Explaining Business Cycles

Keynesian Economics

Monetarism

Rational Expectations Theory

Real Business Cycle Theory

Basic Questions

Learning Guide

Watch for answers to these important questions

How are the concepts of inflationary and recessionary gaps interpreted in terms of the income-price model?

Why is Keynesian economics referred to as a theory of unemployment? What role does government policy play in this theory?

What is monetarism? How do its views on the transmission mechanism, the velocity of money, and the assumption of a self-correcting economy compare with those of Keynesianism?

What is meant by rational expectations? Why do they neutralize the effects of systematic policy changes?

What is real business cycle theory? Why does the theory view monetary policy as a result of the business cycle, not a cause of it?

How do the various macroeconomic theories view the issue of policy activism versus nonactivism?

What do macroeconomic theories try to do? The answer, as you've learned, is that they seek to explain why business cycles occur and what, if anything, can or should be done to lessen their severity.

Business cycles result in inflations and recessions. These, as you've seen many times in previous chapters, are best analyzed with a macroeconomic model. The one that's usually employed because it relates the economy's real aggregate income to the average price level is the familiar *income-price model*. This model is also called the *aggregate demand/aggregate supply* or *AD/AS model*. One of its chief uses is to help interpret inflationary and recessionary gaps. Let's see how, by reviewing the diagrams in Exhibit 1.

In the income-price model, inflationary and recessionary gaps are defined in terms of real output, which is measured on the horizontal axis. Notice from the vertical line connecting all three graphs that the gaps are defined with reference to potential real output, which corresponds to the full (natural)-employment level.

The diagrams illustrate three possible conditions.

1. **Inflationary Gap [Figure (a)]**   This occurs when, at the equilibrium price level, actual output exceeds potential (real) output. Because the amount of employment corresponding to actual output is greater than the amount that would exist at full employment, an inflationary gap results in a condition of overfull employment.

EXHIBIT
1

Inflationary and Recessionary Gaps

Inflationary and recessionary gaps are always measured with reference either to potential (real) output or to full (natural) employment. These are corresponding concepts, as you can see from the graphs.

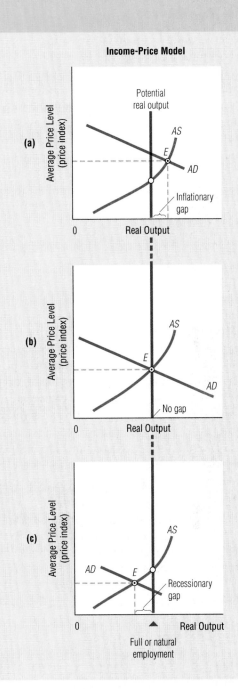

Income-Price Model

FIGURE (a) Inflationary Gap At the equilibrium-price level, actual output exceeds potential output.

FIGURE (b) No Gap At the equilibrium-price level, actual output equals potential output.

FIGURE (c) Recessionary Gap At the equilibrium-price level, actual output is less than potential output.

2. **No Gap [Figure (b)]**   This desirable state of affairs is realized when, at the equilibrium price level, actual output equals potential output, and the economy's actual employment is equal to full employment.

3. **Recessionary Gap [Figure (c)]**   This occurs when, at the equilibrium price level, actual output is less than potential output. Because the amount of employment at the actual output level is less than the amount that would exist at full employment, a re-

cessionary gap results in a condition of "under-full" employment.

Macroeconomic theories explaining inflationary and recessionary gaps are the foundations on which economic policies are built. Therefore, an understanding of the theories provides a basis for evaluating policies. At present, several different theories compete for the attention of policymakers in Washington. Some of the theories were explained in earlier chapters. In this chapter we'll review those theories and set forth several others as well. Because each theory is largely a reaction and challenge to its predecessor, it is useful to examine the theories in the order in which they were developed.

Keynesian Economics

The theory we refer to by the name of its originator, John Maynard Keynes, was conceived during the Great Depression of the 1930s. Keynesian theory was a response to the prevailing classical theory that the economy is self-correcting. This means that if excessive unemployment occurs, market forces automatically restore the economy to its full- or natural-employment level.

The reason for self-correction, classical economists said, is that the economy's markets are highly competitive. This ensures that prices, wages, unemployment levels, and interest rates will adjust quickly to changing conditions of demand and supply. Until these adjustments are completed, some surpluses or shortages will arise in specific markets. But in the long run, *which classical economists took to mean quite promptly*, the markets will clear and the economy will return to full-employment equilibrium.

A Theory of Unemployment

Unfortunately, classical economists never specified how much time it would take for the economy to achieve equilibrium. The deep and prolonged Depression of the 1930s led Keynes to his famous lament, "In the long run we are all dead." He believed that the costs of large-scale unemployment are so high that policymakers should not wait for their nations' economies to self-correct. Instead, Keynes argued, a new theory was needed that would "largely revolutionize the way the world thinks about economic problems."

The new theory that Keynes formulated attempted to accomplish two things.

First, it tried to explain why an economy may experience extended periods of substantial unemployment.

Second, it tried to provide guidelines to help policymakers speed up the economy's return to full-employment equilibrium.

To understand the implications of these goals, let's review some of the highlights of Keynesian theory as it's seen by today's economists.

Demand-Side Shocks and the Modern (Neo-) Keynesian Response

Keynesian theory is based on a demand-side explanation of business cycles. At the heart of Keynesian thinking is the belief that a recession is created by a decrease in aggregate demand. A demand-side shock, such as a sharp cutback by the Fed of the monetary growth rate, can throw the economy into a tailspin. A reduction in money growth decreases consumption and investment spending. These decreases in spending cause the economy's aggregate demand curve to shift to the left. Hence, production and employment decline.

The evidence of these effects, Keynesians point out, can be seen from a study of business cycles. Modern Keynesians, called neo-Keynesians, argue that many wages and prices are "sticky." That is, they tend not to respond quickly to market pressures. Why? Because in most major industries wages are fixed by employment contracts and prices are set to yield planned profit margins. Consequently, when aggregate demand declines, companies try to reduce costs by laying off workers and cutting back on production. Unemployment thus rises, causing neo-Keynesians to conclude that markets don't clear as quickly as the classicists claim.*

These ideas can be expressed in terms of an income-price model like the one shown earlier in Exhibit 1.

---

*Keynes addressed his book, *The General Theory of Employment, Interest and Money* (1936) to his friend, colleague, and leading British classical economist, Arthur C. Pigou. In a book entitled *The Theory of Unemployment* (1933), Pigou readily acknowledged that labor-market surpluses were due to "frictional resistances [that] prevent the appropriate wage and price adjustments from being made instantaneously." However, Pigou and other classicists believed that market pressures would quickly overcome the resistances (which they called "stickiness"), thus eliminating the surpluses. Keynes disagreed, arguing that the continued high unemployment proved that market pressures weren't strong enough to do the job.

If wages and prices were perfectly flexible, the economy's aggregate supply curve would be a vertical line corresponding to the potential output line at the full-employment level of real output. A decrease in aggregate demand would thus cause a decline in the price level without affecting employment. But because prices and wages are sticky, the economy's aggregate supply curve is upward sloping (like the *AS* curve in the diagrams) rather than vertical. Hence a decrease in aggregate demand causes unemployment to rise.

Experience shows that, when aggregate demand declines, the first and hardest hit industries are usually those that produce consumer durable and capital goods. Some examples are the automotive, construction, and machinery industries. Because they also employ relatively large numbers of workers, unemployment in these key industries causes unemployment to spread to other segments of the economy. As a result, the recession worsens, or, in terms of the income-price model, the recessionary gap widens.

Efficiency, Stability, and Growth

In a recession, the economy's efficiency declines. That is, the economy fails to make full use of available resources. As the recession deepens, the expected profitability of new investment (called the marginal efficiency of investment) decreases. The business sector responds with cuts in investment spending. These cuts cause aggregate demand to contract further, driving the economy deeper into recession. Fluctuations in investment spending are thus an important contributor to instability—or business cycles.

If available resources aren't being fully used, they're being wasted. This is inefficient. Unemployment, reflected in the income-price model by the size of a recessionary gap, is a measure of the economy's inefficiency. The reduction of unemployment—or the maintenance of a high level of employment—is the primary concern of Keynesian analysis. This explains why Keynesianism has traditionally focused *relatively* greater attention on improving efficiency than on promoting price stability and economic growth. (Equity, a fourth goal of economics, is addressed primarily by microeconomic rather than macroeconomic theories and policies.)

Policy Activism

Keynes's ideas led many economists and political leaders to believe that the economy could be "fine-tuned."

That is, government could select a target rate of employment and, through judicious use of fiscal and monetary policies, maintain that rate without experiencing significant recessions or inflations. Fiscal and monetary policies could thus serve as *countercyclical tools.* They could reduce the size of recessionary and inflationary gaps and thereby make business cycles smoother.

These beliefs evolved during the 1950s and were adopted wholeheartedly by Presidents Kennedy and Johnson during the 1960s.* But in the early 1970s, the U.S. economy caught a new illness called *stagflation.* Defined by a Washington economist who coined the term as a combination of stagnation and inflation, its symptoms are slow economic growth, high unemployment, and rising prices. Stagflation thus combines some of the features of recession and inflation. Economists believe that the stagflation of the early 1970s was due primarily to excessive expansions in the money supply and sharp increases in resource costs, especially world oil prices. The higher resource costs led producers to cut back on employment. As the combination of unemployment and inflation reached unprecedented heights, many economists concluded that Keynesian economics was unable to cope with stagflation. As a result, Keynesianism began to decline in relative importance.

Keynesian economics **dominated economic thinking for nearly four decades—from the late 1930s until the early 1970s. Indeed, as late as 1971, Republican President Richard Nixon announced that "now I am a Keynesian." In doing so, Nixon was expressing a broad consensus that government, by assuming the role of policy activist, can fine-tune the economy through its fiscal and monetary policies.**

Monetarism

By the time Nixon declared himself a Keynesian, a major challenge of Keynesian economics had already begun. Under the leadership of Milton Friedman, then at the University of Chicago, a body of ideas known as *monetarism* was rapidly gaining acceptance

---

*At a press conference early in 1963, President Kennedy was asked by a reporter to explain the reason for advocating tax reduction. He replied, "To stimulate the economy. Don't you remember your Economics 101?"

among economists and political leaders throughout the United States, Japan, and Western Europe.

Monetarism, you'll recall, is a theory of the relationship between changes in the monetary growth rate and changes in the price level.* Monetarism, like classical theory, is based on the belief that the economy is always at, or at least is rapidly tending toward, full-employment equilibrium. Therefore, changes in the monetary growth rate are disruptive. They are a primary cause of changes in the price level, and hence in the economy's nominal output. Monetarists contend that discretionary monetary policy—as often practiced by the Federal Reserve—tends to be erratic and is thus a cause of instability. To promote stability, the central banking system should abandon discretionary monetary policy and adopt a constant money-growth-rate rule.

These ideas suggest some important points of comparison between monetarism and Keynesianism. Three that are especially important are (1) the transmission mechanism, (2) the velocity of money, and (3) the economy's self-corrective tendency.

The Transmission Mechanism

How does a change in the money growth rate affect interest rates, the price level, aggregate demand, GDP, and other important macroeconomic variables? In more general terms, what are the channels through which a change in money growth influences economic activity? The answer involves what is known as the *transmission mechanism for monetary policy,* or simply the transmission mechanism. Although there are several different models of monetarist and Keynesian transmission mechanisms, a brief description of the main ideas of each helps to emphasize the distinctions between them.

In the monetarist view, an increase in money growth may cause interest rates to decline temporarily, and make borrowing cheaper. But the increased availability of money leaves people with more liquidity—that is, more real cash balances than they wish to hold. This creates the familiar condition of "too much money chasing too few goods." As people spend the excess cash balances on goods and services, aggregate demand increases. Consequently, the price level, nominal GDP, interest rates, and expectations of inflation rise.

How does this monetarist explanation of the transmission mechanism compare with the Keynesian version? Recall that the interest rate is determined by the demand for and supply of loanable funds. Therefore, an increase in money growth—the supply of money—causes interest rates to decline. This decline makes interest-earning debt instruments (such as bonds) less attractive than stocks as alternative investments. The demand for stocks therefore increases, raising their price. Modern research shows that the decline in interest rates and the rise in stock prices stimulate both investment and consumption spending—for two reasons:

1. **Decreased Cost of Money Capital** Firms find it cheaper to obtain investment funds because they can borrow at lower costs and because they can issue less stock to acquire the money they want. Consumers also find it cheaper to finance the purchase of durable goods (such as cars and major appliances) and residential housing.

2. **Increased Consumer Wealth** Stocks are an important part of the household sector's assets. Rising stock prices, therefore, increase consumers' wealth and encourage greater consumption. This relationship, called the "wealth effect," has been found to be an important factor affecting consumption.

Both monetarist and modern Keynesian theory agree that monetary stimulation increases aggregate demand. But monetarist theory contends that the economy's self-correcting mechanism tends to work relatively rapidly, so stimulation is inflationary. Modern Keynesian theory contends that the economy's self-corrective mechanism may work relatively slowly, so stimulating the economy can hasten the adjustment to full employment.

Velocity of Money

A second point of comparison between monetarism and Keynesianism concerns the velocity of money. This, you'll recall, represents the turnover of money—the average number of times per year that a dollar is spent to purchase the GDP. (Remember the equation of exchange $MV = PQ = $ GDP.)

Today's monetarists view V not as a stable *number,* but as a stable *function* of a key variable—aggregate income. However, in the monetarist model, aggregate income is not simply GDP (although it may be depicted as such for purposes of explaining the basic concepts of monetarism). Aggregate income is de-

---

*Monetarism was explained in detail in Chapter 12.

fined instead as a complex mathematical expression that combines both current GDP and the public's *expectations* of long-run average GDP. Therefore, because monetarists believe that *V*—the connecting link between money and prices—is a stable function, they conclude that money is the primary determinant of prices and hence of nominal GDP.

Research findings since the early 1980s have somewhat altered monetarists' views concerning the stability of *V*. The relationship between money and prices has turned out to be looser than the monetarists expected. As a result, *V* has proven to be quite difficult to predict. Nevertheless, monetarists still believe that *V* is *relatively* stable, although they agree that it may not be as stable as was once thought. Monetarists have thus moved somewhat closer to the Keynesian view, which has always held that *V* is unstable. *To the extent that V is unstable, it's possible for changes in the money growth rate to be offset, at least in part, by opposite changes in V.*

Self-Correction

A convergence of monetarist and Keynesian beliefs has not occurred in all areas. Two examples help illustrate some important differences:

1. Monetarists argue that the economy is inherently stable at a high level of employment unless it is disturbed by erratic monetary growth rates. Keynesians contend that, even with fairly steady monetary growth rates, inadequate business investment can cause the economy to become bogged down in a prolonged period of unemployment.

2. Keynesians don't deny the importance of monetary policy, but they contend that fiscal policy (government spending and taxing) also plays an important role in helping to maintain full employment. Monetarists argue that expansionary fiscal policy is largely ineffectual because government borrowing creates upward pressure on interest rates, thereby crowding out private investment.

How do these differences of opinion affect judgments about the kinds of policies that should be emanating from Washington? As we answer this question, keep in mind the following summary of monetarist and Keynesian attitudes toward public policy:

- **Monetarists believe that, if the money supply is expanded at a steady rate, the economy will rapidly absorb the adverse effects of normal economic disturbances. This will enable real GDP to resume**

its normal growth path. Therefore, no active stabilization policies should be undertaken. Indeed, such policies actually turn out to be *destabilizing.*

- **Modern Keynesians contend that the economy doesn't necessarily revert quickly to its normal growth path when subjected to disturbances. Therefore, stabilization actions, consisting of appropriate fiscal-monetary policies, are needed to maintain high levels of employment.**

Rational Expectations Theory

During the 1970s, while monetarism was gaining international recognition, several young free-market economists were launching an intellectual revolution. Notable among these were Robert Lucas at the University of Chicago, Thomas Sargent and Neil Wallace at the University of Minnesota, and Robert Barro (currently at Harvard University) at the University of Rochester. Their views, known as *rational expectations theory,* represent a major advance in economic thinking.

Expectations play an important role in all areas of human activity. Your decision to drive to work or to campus is influenced by your expectation of arriving safely. A company's decision to increase production or to hire more workers is based on its expectation of profit. A bank's decision about which assets to hold is influenced by its expectations concerning returns, liquidity, and risk. The Fed's decision to increase or decrease the monetary growth rate is influenced by its expectations about inflation, employment, and production. In light of these and many other examples that can be given, it's necessary to see what is meant—and not meant—by the theory of rational expectations.

What Are Rational Expectations?

The dictionary tells us that the word "rational" means having or using the ability to reason logically. The word "expectation" means the act of looking forward to the probable occurrence of something. These definitions suggest that a rational expectation is a logically reasoned forecast or prediction that a certain event is likely to occur in the future. Thus, if the U.S. Weather Service forecasts that the temperature tomorrow will be 60° F and there will be a 40 percent chance of rain, that's an example of a rational expectation. Let's see why by considering a more detailed example.

Suppose you're an economist working for a food processing company like General Mills or Pillsbury. Because the company buys wheat for milling into flour, part of your job is to forecast the price of wheat several months before it's harvested. To prepare a forecast, you make use of past and current information. The failure to do so could be costly. For example, ignoring the news of a drought in the farm belt could cause the company to pay more for wheat at harvest time than if it had been stocked up beforehand.

The information you examine includes current and past wheat prices, rainfall data, yield-per-acre figures, and other facts published by the U.S. Department of Agriculture and other government sources. You then analyze the data, perhaps construct a statistical equation or model, and arrive at what you believe is the best estimate of what the price of wheat is likely to be. Because it is based on a logical, appropriate analysis of relevant data, your estimate is a rational expectation.

You can best understand rational expectations theory by examining some of its assumptions and implications.

Four Propositions of Rational Expectations Theory

Expectations are forecasts of future occurrences. Rational expectations theory is concerned with the way in which forecasts are made. Although the theory is quite complex, a concise explanation of its main ideas can be given within a framework of four propositions.

1. Optimal Forecasts

People form expectations based on existing information and experiences. But some of the information that could be helpful for forming expectations may not be available, and some information that is available may be too costly to obtain. Economists in the automobile industry, for example, are able to forecast total annual automobile sales much more easily than the sales of specific models and colors. This is because the economic information needed to forecast total sales, such as disposable income, automobile prices, and financing terms, is more readily available than the detailed economic and psychological information needed to forecast consumers' preferences for specific models and colors. Because individuals rarely have complete knowledge of *all* the facts that may be relevant to a particular outcome, expectations are almost always formed from limited information. Thus:

Rational expectations needn't be based on *all* relevant information. They need only be based on a reasoned analysis of available information. When this is done, the resulting expectations are the *best possible* forecasts—called *optimal* forecasts—given the available facts.

2. Forecasting Accuracy

Does this mean that, even if expectations turn out to be wrong, they may still be rational? The answer is yes. Individuals don't make the same expectational errors indefinitely; they learn from their experiences. Consequently, when they find themselves making *systematic* expectational errors, they modify the ways in which they form expectations so that the only errors that occur are *random* errors—those due to chance. For example, when people learn that rapid increases in money growth cause inflation, they include this information in forming their expectations of future prices in order to avoid *systematic* underestimation of the average inflation rate. Deviations from this expected rate will then be due to random errors. So:

Rational expectations need not always be accurate; they need only be correct *on average*.

3. Limited Knowledge

In view of the fact that most people have little or no understanding of economics, how can they formulate expectations of GDP, employment, prices, interest rates, and other economic variables? The answer is that they can't. However, it's done for them indirectly by others. A considerable number of government departments, universities, and private organizations use elaborate models to formulate periodic forecasts. The forecasts are reported in newspapers, magazines, and radio and television broadcasts. These reports condition, *consciously or otherwise,* the expectations of the public. As a result:

Rational expectations don't require everyone to be knowledgeable about economics. Those who lack economic understanding are always forming expectations from current information and are learning from experience to correct systematic errors.

4. Effect on Policy

If people formulate expectations rationally, the likelihood that discretionary fiscal and monetary policies employed by the government will create *systematic* expectational errors is eliminated. The reason for this is easy to see. If government pursues *consistent* counter-cyclical policies (based, for example, on economic in-

EXHIBIT
2

Effects of an Increase in Aggregate Demand

An expansionary economic policy shifts the aggregate demand curve to the right—from AD to AD'. The effects on the price level, real output, and employment are viewed differently by each theory.

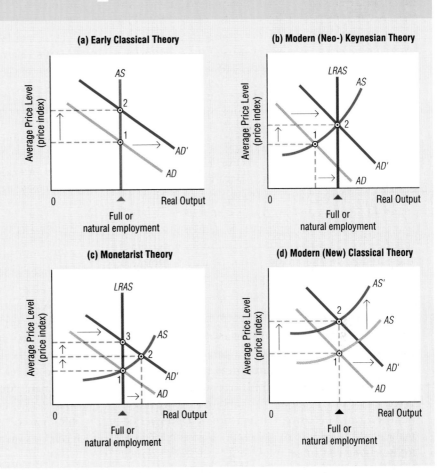

(a) Early Classical Theory

(b) Modern (Neo-) Keynesian Theory

(c) Monetarist Theory

(d) Modern (New) Classical Theory

dicators such as unemployment rates), individuals will recognize those policies as systematic and will anticipate them. People will thus forecast future inflation rates correctly, and will change their behavior so as to counteract any systematic influence on production and employment levels. Thus:

Rational expectations neutralize the effects of systematic policy changes on real (as distinguished from nominal) economic variables. As a result, a *consistent* **countercyclical policy has no effect on real output and employment (although it may affect prices and costs).**

Comparing Rational Expectations to Other Theories

If some of the ideas of rational expectations theory seem familiar, this is no accident. The theory bears a close relationship to classical economics, which dominated economic thinking before Keynes. As a result, rational expectations theory is often called *new classical* or *modern classical economics.* The terms are used interchangeably, and economists who subscribe to rational expectations theory are called new classical or modern classical economists.

Let's look again at the fourth proposition. It implies that, because macroeconomic stabilization measures don't work, *no economic policy matters* insofar as real economic variables are concerned. This is a rather startling conclusion. It contradicts much of what we've learned in this course; namely, that policy *can* affect real output and employment. Apparently, therefore, today's classical economists have some explaining to do. The explanation can best be appreciated in light of the four theories studied thus far. These theories are illustrated in Exhibit 2. The four diagrams show the effects on output, employment, and the price level when an expansionary economic policy causes an increase in aggregate demand from *AD* to *AD'*. The numbers at the intersections of the aggregate demand and aggregate supply curves identify the equilibrium points before and after a shift of either curve or both.

Early Classical Theory [Figure (a)]   In the early classicists' view, the economy is always at full employment, so the aggregate supply curve *AS* is a vertical line at that level of output. (There is no *LRAS* curve because early classical economists made no distinction between the short run and the long run). Because workers know that higher prices result in lower *real* wages, they demand higher nominal wages to compensate. The effect of the increase in aggregate demand is thus purely inflationary. The rise in the equilibrium price level (determined by the change from point 1 to point 2) causes *nominal* output to increase, while *real* output and employment are unaffected. Thus, the effect on real variables is neutral.

Modern (Neo-) Keynesian Theory [Figure (b)]   According to this belief, the economy may be operating at less than full-employment equilibrium (determined by point 1). Modern Keynesians agree that sticky wages and prices cause the *AS* curve to be upward-sloping, rather than vertical. Therefore, the increase in aggregate demand hastens the rise of *real* output and employment to their long-run full-employment levels (determined by point 2). This, according to much Keynesian thinking, is the most important goal of expansionary economic policy. The fact that prices and therefore nominal output also rise is significant but of *relatively* less importance.

Monetarist Theory [Figure (c)]   In the monetarists' view, the economy is either at, or rapidly tending toward, full-employment equilibrium (determined by point 1). Therefore, an increase in aggregate demand can raise *real* output and employment only in the short run (point 2). Workers soon realize that their real wages have decreased because prices have risen faster than wages. Unions respond by pressing for higher wages, which then cause real output and employment to decline and the price level to rise further. In long-run equilibrium (determined by point 3), which occurs relatively quickly, the effect is purely inflationary because the impact on real variables is neutral.

Modern (New) Classical Theory [Figure (d)]   This view holds that, because workers are rational, they know immediately that the perceived increase in aggregate demand

reduces their real wage. The *AS* curve thus adjusts instantly, so *the results of new classical theory are realized in the short run.* (Therefore, there's no need to show an *LRAS* curve, although it would be permissible to do so if you wanted to emphasize the concept.) That is, the price level rises, but the effect on real variables is neutral because real output is always at its natural level. This conclusion obviously contradicts reality, however, because real output is always fluctuating. Modern classical economists thus have to modify their conclusion to allow for this fact. The way in which they do so is best appreciated in terms of the policy implications of the theory.

Policy Implications

A chief purpose of economic theory is to serve as a guide for policymakers. What do the theories conclude about the role of policy activism?

Neo-Keynesianism contends that, because information is costly to obtain and expectations vary widely, it takes time for people to learn about and adjust to new conditions. Therefore, policy activism is warranted because expectations are rational only in the long run. Monetarism and new classicism, on the other hand, stem from the classical tradition. As a result, they end up rejecting policy activism—but for different reasons:

- Monetarist theory contends that we don't know enough about the workings of the economy to stabilize it with discretionary fiscal-monetary policy.

- New classical theory holds that the public defeats discretionary policies because everyone expects them, and therefore acts in ways that thwart their effectiveness.

Do new classical economists conclude that the only correct public policy should be no public policy? Not really. They make two points:

1. Only *systematic* countercyclical economic policy is impotent. Nonsystematic policies—those that are unpredictable because they come as surprises—can and do affect real output and employment. Erratic monetary policies are an example. They cause households and businesses to forecast economic outcomes incorrectly (even though the forecasts are rational) and hence to make mistakes in formulating decisions based on those forecasts. These misperceptions and mistakes account for the upward-sloping *AS* curve and its fail-

ure to adjust instantly, thus causing fluctuations in real output and employment (business cycles).*

2. To reduce uncertainty and promote stability, predictable fiscal-monetary policies consisting of balanced budgets and steady monetary expansion are needed. These will keep the economy on a stable, long-run growth path.

The belief that systematic countercyclical policies don't achieve their desired results because they're widely anticipated is called the **policy ineffectiveness proposition.** In the words of a leading new classical economist, the University of Chicago's Robert Lucas:

> The proposition is not that economic policies do not matter. The question is whether the government can use monetary and fiscal policy to achieve higher levels of employment. The answer turns out to be no.

The essential points underlying the foregoing ideas can be summarizsed briefly:

Rational expectations theory (or *new classical economics*) contends that people learn to anticipate recurring or *systematic* fiscal and monetary policies. Consequently, when the government initiates such policies, they affect only nominal variables such as prices, not real variables such as employment and output. The only policy moves that alter real variables are the ones that aren't expected—the surprise moves. But these cause uncertainty and instability. Therefore, to reduce the severity of business cycles, government should adhere to predictable macroeconomic policies—namely, balanced budgets and a steady monetary growth rate.

Real Business Cycle Theory

Keynesians look at business cycles and say that government should adopt policies to correct them. Monetarists look at business cycles and attribute them to misguided Keynesian policies that should be discarded. New classicists look at business cycles and conclude that they're caused by random policy actions that should be eliminated. Although the three groups have distinct differences of opinions, they also share the belief that business cycles are "bad" and that instability can be cured by economic policy.

Now come other economists who turn these ideas upside down. Their theory, called *real business cycle theory,* contends that instability may not be bad and that countercyclical policies are harmful if they cause the economy to become "overstabilized." These beliefs run counter to more than half a century of economic thinking. Let's see what they involve, by sketching the main features of the theory in terms of three key propositions.

1. Business Cycles Are Caused by Supply-Side Shocks

Real business cycle theory attributes economic fluctuations to shifts in aggregate *supply*—not in aggregate demand. The shifts are caused by supply-side shocks that affect productivity and output, which cause changes in resource costs. Examples of such shocks are changes in technology, government regulations, and the prices of basic commodities (such as oil and other raw materials) that are widely used in production.

Supply-side shocks occur frequently in the world's economies. For instance, our economy has undergone dramatic changes due to the computerization of production and information systems, unexpected fluctuations in the world price of oil, and the deregulation of several major industries. The effects of these developments on firms' labor and material costs cause shifts in aggregate supply, and hence, changes in production and employment.

2. Business Cycles Are Random Walks

What makes such changes dramatic, and what makes them "shocks," is that they're unexpected. Fluctuations in real GDP are thus chance events—or a "random walk" as economists call it. This means that, like any chance event, fluctuations in real GDP are unpredictable.

The reason is easy to see. Like a wheel of fortune or a pair of dice, GDP has no memory. Although it fluctuates from quarter to quarter and from year to year, the ups and downs aren't systematic. To the casual observer, the fluctuations may exhibit what appear to be "patterns." However, these don't occur any more frequently than the run-of-luck patterns you might experience in games of chance such as craps, coin tossing, or roulette. Because of this unpredictability, the Keynesian practice of forecasting changes in

---

*In new classical terminology, business cycles are caused by *expectational errors* resulting from *imperfect information* and *uncertainty* in the economy. If these didn't exist, the *AS* curve would be vertical, as depicted in the early classical theory.

real GDP as a basis for policymaking is regarded by real business cycle theorists as naive.

3. Business Cycles Drive Money Growth

Real business cycle theory is also critical of monetarism for its contention that changes in the money growth rate are a cause of economic instability. According to real business cycle theory, monetary changes are a *result* of the business cycle, not a cause of it. To understand why, let's suppose that a business cycle downturn starts with a supply-side shock that reduces the economy's capacity to produce. If prices and wages are flexible, the economy's aggregate supply curve is a vertical line. The reduction in output is reflected by a shift of the curve to the left. Thus, as shown in Exhibit 3, the aggregate supply curve moves from *AS* to *AS'*. Consequently, real output decreases from *Q* to *Q'*.

The decreased output leads to reduced business investment demand and therefore to reduced demand for credit. The Fed, in order to hold interest rates steady, responds to the decreased demand for credit by reducing the money growth rate. That causes consumption and investment spending to fall. The aggregate demand curve, therefore, moves to the left from *AD* to *AD'*. Proponents of real business cycle theory thus contend that the business cycle drives money growth, rather than the other way around. As a result, monetary policy does not affect real variables such as output and employment, but it does affect nominal variables such as prices and wages. Hence, it's an important determinant of inflation.

There are other aspects of real business cycle theory that distinguish it from the theories examined thus far.* The following definition summarizes some of its main concepts:

---

*Three propositions are especially significant: (1) *Unemployment is entirely voluntary.* In other words, unemployed people can always get jobs, but choose not to do so because they prefer unemployment to the jobs available to them. (2) *Business cycles exist without expectational errors.* That is, business cycles aren't caused by imperfect information and uncertainty, as new classicists claim. Therefore, the aggregate supply curve is vertical, as explained in the previous footnote. (3) *Business cycles are socially optimal.* Society's welfare is maximized by allowing fluctuations in economic activity. Countercyclical policies may therefore *overstabilize* the economy.

It's easy to see why real business cycle theory is quite controversial. Nevertheless, it has attracted wide interest among economists and is the subject of considerable research.

Real Business Cycle Theory: The Effect of a Supply-Side Shock

A recession starts with a supply-side shock. Because prices are assumed to be flexible, the aggregate supply curve is vertical. The shock shifts the *AS* curve to the left to *AS'*, causing a decrease in real output. In order to maintain stable interest rates, the Fed responds to businesses' reduced demand for credit by cutting back on the money growth rate. The resulting decline in consumption and investment demand causes aggregate demand to decrease from *AD* to *AD'*.

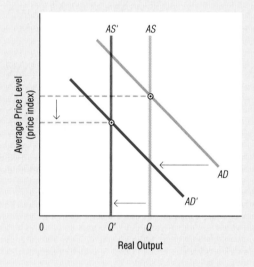

Real business cycle theory contends that economic fluctuations are due to shifts in aggregate supply that are caused by random (and therefore unpredictable) supply-side shocks. Examples of such random shocks are changes in technology, government regulations, and prices of basic commodities such as oil and other raw materials that are widely used in production. Because the Fed alters the money growth rate in response to these real forces at work in the economy, monetary policy is a result of the business cycle, not a cause of it. Therefore, although monetary policy has no effect on real output and employment, it is nevertheless an important determinant of inflation.

Basic Questions

In all branches of science, advances usually occur in essentially the same way. A theory prevails until a better one comes along to replace it. Economics is no exception. Macroeconomists have found fault with prevailing theories and have developed new ones to explain why output and employment fluctuate and what the correct policy responses should be. Since the 1970s, however, there has been more agreement on the shortcomings of existing theories than on what is to replace them. Despite the apparent diversity of opinion, the practical issues can be reduced to a few basic questions and answers.

Are Expectations Rational?

Virtually all economists acknowledge that people assess available information and make decisions based on the best possible forecasts. On the one hand, monetarists, new classicists, and real business cycle theorists believe that people evaluate information relatively quickly, so expectations are rational at least in the short run if not immediately. Modern Keynesians, on the other hand, believe that people need time to assess new information, so expectations are rational only in the long run.

Does the Economy Self-Correct?

Disturbances or shocks of various kinds throw markets into disequilibrium. Aggregate demand curves and aggregate supply curves shift, causing business cycles. Monetarists, new classicists, and real business cycle theorists believe that markets self-correct rapidly, enabling the economy to return quickly to its normal long-run growth path. Modern Keynesians believe that markets may take a long time to self-correct, leaving the economy in a prolonged state of recession.

Should Government Intervene?

Because monetarists, new classicists, and real business cycle theorists share a common faith in the inherent stability of markets, they oppose government interventionist policies. At best, the critics argue, the economic effects of such policies are neutral; at worst they're inflationary. Modern Keynesians, on the other hand,

point to evidence showing that market failures of a macroeconomic nature do occur. Neo-Keynesians contend, therefore, that government has a role to play in adopting the appropriate corrective measures.

Which Theory Should You Believe?

By now, if you're like most students, you hope your professor will tell you which theory is correct. That, fortunately or unfortunately, is impossible. All the theories are "correct" in the sense that their conclusions are derived by logical reasoning from given assumptions. Your preference for a particular theory, therefore, is likely to depend as much on your personal philosophy as on economic considerations. The two are often hard to separate. For example:

- If you're an ideological liberal at heart, you'll tend to side with the neo-Keynesians. In their view, markets aren't always as efficient as they might be. Therefore, although activist fiscal and monetary policies can't be used to fine-tune the economy, government can nevertheless employ them to help improve the situation.

- If you lean toward a conservative philosophy, you'll tend to be in the same camp with monetarists, new classicists, and real business cycle theorists. Despite their differences on theoretical issues, their views on policy matters are fundamentally the same. They agree that *any* activist policy is likely to be harmful.

The overarching policy issue in today's macroeconomics is whether or not government should play an activist role in the economy. The "liberal" view sees market failures and contends that government can do something about them. The "conservative" view sees market stability and argues that government can only disrupt it. Because of these differences in beliefs, the controversy over the role of government in the economy continues.*

---

*The terms "liberal" and "conservative" are political, not economic. Nevertheless, they help to convey the idea that politics and economics are related. In fact, from the time of Adam Smith until the early part of this century, economics was usually called political economy.

Summary of Important Ideas

1. Fluctuations in economic activity are called business cycles. They create recessions and inflations, which result in inefficiency, instability, and slow economic growth. Macroeconomics is fundamentally concerned with explaining why these fluctuations occur and what policies, if any, can be employed to reduce them.

2. The economy's potential output is the value of real output that occurs at full or natural employment. Inflationary and recessionary gaps are measured by the difference between actual and potential output.

3. Keynesian economics was born during the Great Depression and dominated macroeconomic thinking for nearly four decades—from the late 1930s until the early 1970s. While *relatively* less significant than they once were, some Keynesian ideas still play an important role in the thinking of many economists and policymakers.

4. Keynesian theory attributes economic instability—inflations and recessions—to fluctuations in aggregate demand. These fluctuations are caused by demand shocks. Examples are significant changes in taxation, government spending, money growth, inflationary expectations, and international economic conditions. Keynesian economics contends that, because market instability can be prolonged and substantial, government activist policies may be warranted to help bring the economy to its full-employment equilibrium level.

5. Monetarism is a body of ideas that emerged in the late 1960s. It was a reaction to the Fed's erratic money-growth practices of earlier years. Monetarism's main contention is that *inflation is caused mainly by too much money chasing too few goods.* Therefore, monetary policy should be based on rules that limit the central bank's ability to manage money expansion.

6. Rational expectations theory, or new classical economics, came into existence in the early 1970s. It argues that government policies to achieve full employment are ultimately ineffectual. This is because people learn to *expect* the policies and to respond *rationally* in such a way as to thwart them. Therefore, the only policy moves that cause changes in people's behavior are the ones that aren't expected—the *surprise* moves.

This doesn't mean, however, that surprise moves are a desirable way to conduct policies, because unexpected actions cause uncertainty and instability.

7. Real business cycle theory, which emerged in the early 1980s, is based on the premise that fluctuations are caused by shocks to aggregate supply. The shocks are brought about by changes in resource costs. Some examples of supply-side shocks are changes in technology, government regulations, and prices of basic commodities widely used in production, such as oil and primary metals. Because money growth is a *response* to these forces at work in the economy, monetary policy is a result of the business cycle, not a cause of it. Therefore, although monetary policy has no effect on real output and employment, it is an important determinant of inflation.

8. For practical policymaking purposes, the various macroeconomic theories can be reduced to two points of view:

   a. Neo-Keynesians believe that market failures occur and that government, through the use of appropriate fiscal/monetary policies, should play an activist role in helping to correct them.

   b. Monetarists, new classicists, and real business cycle theorists believe that markets self-correct rapidly, and that government therefore should play a nonactivist role in the economy.

Terms and Concepts to Review

stagflation	*policy ineffectiveness*
Keynesian economics	*proposition*
monetarism	*rational expectations theory*
transmission mechanism	*real business cycle theory*
for monetary policy	

Questions and Problems

This chapter has reviewed macroeconomic theories learned in earlier chapters and has added new ones. Therefore, some of the following questions draw on concepts covered in previous chapters. In order to answer these questions to the best of your ability, make use of this book's Index and Dictionary.

1. In dollar terms, is a recessionary or an inflationary gap in the income-price model the same size as a corresponding recessionary or inflationary gap in the income-expenditure model? (*Hint:* What is assumed about the average price level in the two models? How does this affect the size of the gap?)

2. How would Keynesian economics be affected if wages and prices were flexible enough to respond quickly to changes in aggregate demand?

3. Economists have known since the early part of this century that rapid money growth is a cause of inflation. Nevertheless the rate of money growth doesn't provide a reliable basis for predicting inflation. Why? (*Hint:* Refresh your understanding of the *equation of exchange* that you learned about earlier in the course.)

4. Why do numerous economists (including many neo-Keynesians) advocate some sort of money-supply rule? Does it matter whether the rule provides for a slow or a fast rate of money growth—say, 3 percent versus 10 percent?

5. In Keynesian theory, discretionary fiscal policy influences aggregate demand. By manipulating taxing and spending, government can increase or decrease the budget deficit and thereby exert an expansionary or contractionary effect on the economy. But according to rational expectations theory, people aren't so easily deceived. They understand that the principal and interest payments on the national debt will eventually have to be paid with higher taxes. Therefore, when the deficit increases, the public alters its spending behavior by saving more (and consuming less) of its income. Conversely, when the deficit decreases, the public saves less (and consumes more) of its income. *Rational expectations theory thus concludes that the effects of changes in the national debt are neutral.* This is called the **debt neutrality proposition.** Can you think of at least two criticisms of it? (*Hint:* In your role as a consumer, how might you respond to an announced tax change?)

6. You can fool some of the people all of the time, and all of the people some of the time, but you cannot fool all the people all of the time.

—ABRAHAM LINCOLN (1863)

Inflation does give a stimulus . . . when it starts from a condition that is noninflationary. But if the inflation continues, people get adjusted to it. Then, when they *expect* rising prices, the mere occurrence of what has been expected is no longer stimulating.

—SIR JOHN R. HICKS (1967)

These statements, the first by the sixteenth president of the United States and the second by a British economist and Nobel laureate, were made more than 100 years apart. Yet they share the common recognition of a concept explored in this chapter. What is the concept? How would you apply it to each of the following situations?

a. The economy is in a recession, and businesses expect the Fed to take steps toward reducing interest rates.

b. The President and leading members of Congress announce intentions of reducing corporate income taxes in order to spur business investment.

7. Critics of Keynesian economics say that it has often resulted in stop-and-go government policies. What do you suppose this means? What's wrong with such policies?

8. "According to rational expectations theory, government economic policies have no effect." Is this a correct statement? If not, revise it as necessary to make it correct.

9. State whether each of the following is *primarily* a demand-side or a supply-side shock.

a. Change in individual income tax rates
b. Change in net exports
c. Change in the minimum-wage rate
d. Change in the minimum working-age level

10. Why do many critics of Keynesianism advocate policy *rules* rather than policy discretion?

TAKE A STAND

Activist Monetary Policy: Does It Work?

In principle, monetary policy is one of the key tools available to Washington for stabilizing business-cycle fluctuations. The Federal Reserve has undertaken expansionary and contractionary policies on numerous occasions. In the early 1980s, the Fed used contractionary monetary policy to reduce the inflation rate from its high levels of the 1970s. In the recession of the early 1990s, the Fed conducted expansionary monetary policy in an attempt to get the economy out of recession.

Expansionary monetary policy stimulates the economy by increasing aggregate demand. An increase in the money supply reduces interest rates, which in turn stimulates consumption and investment spending. Increased aggregate demand leads to greater production and an expansion of the economy. Contractionary policy has the opposite effect.

Most economists agree in general on this mechanism. Some economists, however, contend that any expansion or contraction due to monetary policy is very short-lived. Others argue that an activist monetary policy is essential if the economy is to avoid prolonged periods of unemployment or inflation. *Does an activist monetary policy really work?*

Yes: Monetary Policy Works in a World of Sticky Prices

Modern Keynesians support an activist monetary policy. These economists have resurrected some principles of Keynesian theory, which dominated economic thinking from the 1930s to the mid-1970s, but fell somewhat out of favor in the late 1970s and 1980s. Modern Keynesians contend that the economy may be subject to extended periods of unemployment or inflation that can be corrected through activist monetary policy.

Contrary to the classical view, modern Keynesians argue that prices are not flexible and markets need not be efficient. In particular, they point out that we do not live in a pure market economy. Many markets are dominated by small numbers of suppliers who have the power to charge higher prices and produce less output than they would in a competitive market with a large number of suppliers. Less output means the employment of fewer inputs, including labor. Thus the economy is likely to suffer from unemployment.

The market power of suppliers also tends to make prices inflexible. In a competitive market, the price of a good is determined by demand and supply. Changes in demand will change this price, but suppliers simply take it as given. A supplier with market power, by contrast, may decide to respond to a change in demand by keeping the price constant and increasing or decreasing production. Part of this price rigidity is due to "menu costs," which is a metaphor for any costs associated with changing prices, such as printing new menus or catalogues, or changing sticker prices. In many cases, it it less costly to change output quantities than to change prices.

In a world of sticky prices, activist monetary policy can affect the employment of resources. An expansion of the money supply increases aggregate demand and so increases the demand for goods and services. Firms respond to increases in demand by supplying more goods. Output and employment increase. An expansionary monetary policy can thus offset a decline in aggregate demand and soften a recession. A contractionary policy can offset an increase in aggregate demand and thereby reduce inflationary pressures. In a pure market economy with flexible prices, activist monetary policy would be unnecessary. In the real world of sticky prices and market power, activist monetary policy can help to stabilize the economy.

No: Only Surprises Matter

Another group, the modern classical economists, contend that an activist monetary policy has no effect on output. This group believes that markets are competitive and efficient enough to move quickly to equilibrium. Prices are flexible, and no individual supplier is able to exert influence over a market. The allocation of all resources, including labor, is efficient.

Modern classical economists also believe that market participants react rationally to policy changes by the Federal Reserve. If the Fed adopts an expansionary policy, the public knows that this will cause inflation. The public thus adjusts its expectations about the inflation rate and acts accordingly: workers demand higher wages and suppliers charge higher prices. All wages and prices will increase in proportion to the change in the money supply, and there will be no change in real output and employment.

The only way that monetary policy can affect aggregate production is through surprise changes in the money supply. In that case, the public may be fooled, but only for a short period of time. For example, more money would generate an increase in aggregate demand. Producers would increase production and workers would spend more hours on the job. As soon as producers and workers recognize the source of the increased demand, however, wages and prices will increase and the economy will move back to its normal or natural level of output.

In the modern classical view, monetary policy is ineffective. If the public is aware of the Fed's actions, changes in the money supply affect prices, not quantities. The public may be fooled, but only temporarily. Modern classical economists contend that the best monetary policy is adherence to a steady rate of monetary expansion sufficient to accomodate the economy's long-run growth rate.

The Question: Does an Activist Monetary Policy Really Work?

■   Modern Keynesians contend that an activist monetary policy is needed to achieve the economy's goals of full employment and price stability. Because suppliers have market power, prices are sticky and the allocation of resources is not efficient. The Fed should play an active role in manipulating aggregate demand to ensure that the economy maintains a stable path of economic growth.

■   Modern classical economists argue that markets are competitive and efficient. Any policies announced by the Fed imme-

diately affect the public's expectations of inflation, so that anticipated changes in the money supply have no effect on output. Only unanticipated changes can affect output, and then only temporarily.

Where Do You Stand?

1. Do you believe that markets in the real world correspond more closely to the modern classical view or to the modern Keynesian view? Explain.

2. How aware is the public of the monetary policies undertaken by the Federal Reserve System? What actions would you take if you read in the newspaper that the Fed is following an expansionary policy?

3. Conservatives tend to favor limited government intervention in the economy and greater reliance on markets, while liberals tend to favor more government control of markets. Which of these two groups is likely to agree with the modern classical view and which is likely to agree with the modern Keynesian view? Explain.

4. Does an activist monetary policy really work? Justify your stand.

Source: Tom Stark and Herb Taylor, "Activist Monetary Policy for Good or Evil?: The New Keynesians vs. the New Classicals," *Business Review*, Federal Reserve Bank of Philadelphia, March/April 1991, pp. 17–25.

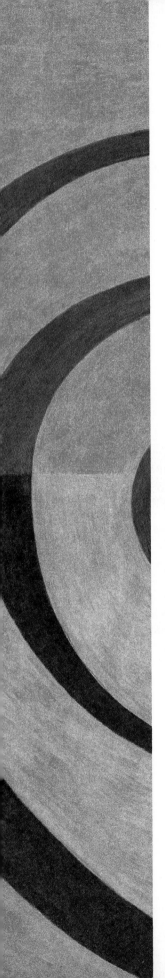

Dynamics of Inflation, Output, and Unemployment

Tracking Inflation and Output

Dynamics of Business Cycles

Inflation and Unemployment: Phillips Curve Analysis

Learning Guide

Watch for answers to these important questions

How does dynamic analysis differ from static analysis? Which type of analysis is most common in economics?

How are demand-side and supply-side inflations initiated? How do their adjustment paths differ?

What role does *time* play in a dynamic model of the business cycle?

What is a Phillips curve? How can it help us interpret today's relationship between unemployment and inflation?

Near the beginning of our study of macroeconomics we learned that the two major problems facing mixed economies have been *unemployment* and *inflation*. Evidence showing that they have been major problems in the United States can be seen from the data on the inside back cover of this book and in Exhibit 1. For the past several decades, unemployment has usually exceeded 5 percent of the labor force, and the price level has often advanced at rates ranging from 3 percent to 10 percent annually.

Fluctuations in the rates of unemployment and inflation are at the heart of business cycles. The cycles occur because of changes in the conditions that cause shifts in the economy's aggregate demand and aggregate supply curves. At any given time the aggregate demand curve is shifting because of changes in the public's demand for goods and services or because of changes in fiscal and/or monetary policies. At the same time, the aggregate supply curve is shifting because of changes in resource costs such as wages and raw-materials prices.

We've already seen how shifts in aggregate demand and aggregate supply can cause the equilibrium values of real output and the price level to change. Once the changes occur, we can determine the differences between the old and new equilibrium positions. This method of investigation is called "static analysis" because it compares "snapshots" of equilibrium positions before and after a change has occurred. Most of

EXHIBIT
1

Unemployment and Inflation: Can We Maintain Efficiency and Stability?

Fluctuations in the unemployment rate mean that the economy fails to maintain *efficiency*—full utilization of resources. Fluctuations in the inflation rate mean that the economy fails to maintain *stability*—a steady average price level.

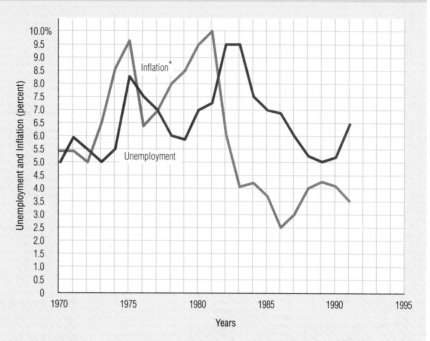

*Inflation is measured by the annual percentage change in the GDP deflator (1987 = 100).

the models we've examined thus far, and indeed most models in economics, employ static analysis. Hence, they're often referred to as **static models.**

In many practical situations, however, we want to study the *time paths* of economic variables rather than just their equilibrium states. That is, we want to see a "motion picture" of the variables as they move over time from one equilibrium position to another. This method of investigation is called "dynamic analysis," and the models it employs are called **dynamic models.** This chapter introduces you to some dynamic models in macroeconomics.

Tracking Inflation and Output

At the heart of macroeconomics is the belief that the economy is self-correcting. But because the self-correcting process may often take longer than policy-makers desire, government often institutes policies aimed at hastening the adjustment to full-employment equilibrium. These actions, however, can cause serious *instability,* as the following analyses of demand-side and supply-side inflation demonstrate.

Demand-Side Inflation: Counterclockwise Adjustment Path

The effect of demand-side inflation (also known as demand-pull inflation) can be seen in Exhibit 2. To begin with, the economy is assumed to be operating at less than full employment. Thus, the intersection of the *AD* and *AS* curves occurs at point *a*. This results in a recessionary gap—an equilibrium price level at *P* and an equilibrium output and employment level at *Q.*

What happens if government adopts an expansionary monetary policy aimed at closing the recessionary gap? The answer can be seen by tracing the adjustment path in the diagram through four stages.

Stage 1: Increased Money Growth The first effect of the government's expansionary policy is to provide people with more money to spend. Assuming the amount of monetary stimulus is "just right," the aggregate demand curve shifts to the right from *AD* to *AD'*. A new equilibrium point is thus established at *b*. Along the adjustment path from *a* to *b*, the price level increases from *P* to *P'*. Simultaneously, output and employment rise from Q to the full- or natural-employment level.

EXHIBIT
2

Demand-Side Inflation: Counterclockwise Adjustment Path

An expansionary monetary policy can increase aggregate demand from *AD* to *AD'*. This will close the recessionary gap by raising the price level from *P* to *P'* and the output-employment level from *Q* to full (or natural) employment. The adjustment path thus goes from *a* to *b*.

Further monetary stimulus will shift aggregate demand to *AD''*. Prices, output, and employment will increase along the path from *b* to *c*, creating an inflationary gap. But with rising prices, resource costs also rise, causing aggregate supply to shift from *AS* to *AS'*. The adjustment path thus goes from *c* to *d*. The result is a new equilibrium at the same full-employment level but at a higher price level *P''*.

Note that the adjustment path runs *counterclockwise* from *a* to *b* to *c* to *d*.

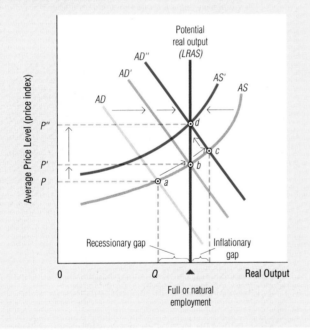

Thus, the *gain in production and employment is achieved at the cost of higher prices.*

Stage 2: Increase in Aggregate Demand If additional monetary stimulus is provided, the aggregate demand curve will shift farther to the right—to *AD''*. This creates an inflationary gap. A new short-run equilibrium point is then established at *c*. Along the adjustment path from *b* to *c*, prices are pulled up faster than production costs, especially wages. Business profits therefore rise, and encourage firms to increase production

and to hire more workers. At point *c*, the employment rate reaches its highest level.

Stage 3: Decrease in Aggregate Supply Workers now begin to realize that prices have been increasing faster than money wages, which means that *real* wages are declining. Unions, therefore, negotiate higher money wages and this leads to higher resource costs for firms. The aggregate supply curve thus shifts from *AS* to *AS'*, which results in a new equilibrium at *d*. Along the adjustment path from *c* to *d*, production costs rise while business profitability and investment incentives decline. The employment rate thus starts decreasing while prices continue rising. At the equilibrium point *d*, the inflationary gap is closed and the economy is back to full or natural employment. At this point, the economy has also adjusted fully to the higher price level at *P''*. This means, for example, that money wages have "caught up" with prices so that real wages are constant.

Stage 4 and Beyond: Stability Until the Next Stimulus It's interesting to note that the equilibrium at *d* is stable—that is, it has no tendency to change. However, it *can* change if government adopts policies and programs financed by increased money growth. (An example would be a program aimed at reducing structural unemployment or a program designed to encourage urban renewal.) The economy would then follow a new inflation-employment adjustment path. But if people come to *expect* inflation, the adjustment path will be shortened. In the extreme, it will even be completely short-circuited. For example, if the inflation is fully anticipated, the price level would simply move "up" the potential real-output line to a new and higher rate of inflation than exists at *P''*. The result would thus be a classical pure inflation, meaning that the price level would rise without any increase in output and employment.

As a final observation, note that the adjustment path from *a* to *b* to *c* to *d* proceeds in a *counterclockwise* direction. This is a characteristic of demand-side inflation.

Supply-Side Inflation: Clockwise Adjustment Path

The adjustment path under supply-side inflation (also known as cost-push inflation) follows a different route from that of demand-side inflation. You can readily see this by examining the following stages, illustrated in Exhibit 3.

EXHIBIT 3

Supply-Side Inflation: Clockwise Adjustment Path

An increase in resource costs can shift the aggregate supply curve leftward from *AS* to *AS'*. The adjustment path from *a* to *b* leads to a higher price level and a decline in output and employment—a recessionary gap.

The higher level of unemployment creates downward pressure on wages. This eventually causes the aggregate supply curve to shift back to *AS*, thereby closing the recessionary gap. But before that happens, government may try to hasten the process with expansionary fiscal-monetary policies. This will shift the aggregate demand curve rightward from *AD* to *AD'*, and the increase in aggregate demand will result in the higher price level at *P'*.

Note that the adjustment path runs *clockwise* from *a* to *b* (and from *b* to *c* if expansionary policies are employed).

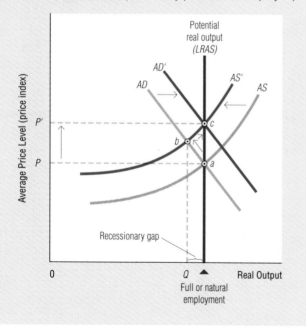

Stage 1: Decrease in Aggregate Supply Suppose that an increase in resource costs (such as the cost of energy or of raw materials) shifts the supply curve to the left from *AS* to *AS'*. The short-run effect is a rise in prices accompanied by a reduction in real output and employment along the adjustment path from *a* to *b*. At this point the economy is in equilibrium. If government does not try to stimulate the economy by adopting expansionary monetary policies, the aggregate demand curve will remain where it is.

Stage 1': Aggregate Supply Restored The higher level of unemployment will put downward pressure on wages, thereby reducing business costs. This causes the aggregate supply curve to shift rightward to its original position, *AS*. In the process, prices decline while output and employment increase as the economy moves back along the adjustment path from *b* to *a*.

Stage 2: Stimulative Measures Of course, this reverse adjustment to full-employment equilibrium may occur very slowly. Workers do not accept wage reductions without resistance. Therefore, in order to hasten the closing of the recessionary gap, government may undertake expansionary monetary policies while the aggregate supply curve is still at *AS'*. If government adopts such stimulative measures, the aggregate demand curve will shift from *AD* to *AD'*. This will create a new adjustment path from *b* to *c*. At point *c*, the economy is again at full-employment equilibrium, but the price level has risen to *P'*.

Stage 3 and Beyond: Stability Until the Next Event It should be noted that the equilibrium at *c* is stable. However, a new event may occur that again shifts the aggregate supply curve to the left. If that happens, and government tries to close the recessionary gap with expansionary policies, the inflation scenario will repeat itself. Such policies will again cause the aggregate demand curve to shift to the right. This will lead to a new equilibrium at some higher point along the vertical potential real-output line. Note, therefore, that the adjustment path from *a* to *b* (and from *b* to *c* if expansionary policies are employed) is *clockwise* in direction. This is a characteristic of supply-side inflation.

Dynamics of Business Cycles

Business cycles are caused by changes in aggregate demand and aggregate supply. The changes produce fluctuations in the average price level and in real output. By studying the fluctuations over time, we can see how business cycles come about.

Exhibit 4 illustrates how business cycles can occur. In Figure (a), the initial *AD* and *AS* curves intersect at the equilibrium point E_0. This denotes an average price level of P_0 and a corresponding output level of Q_0. The Fed may try to maintain this output level by expanding the money growth rate.[*] If the Fed in-

---

[*]The money growth rate is rarely zero. The Fed is almost always increasing it, sometimes relatively quickly and sometimes relatively slowly.

EXHIBIT
4

How Business Cycles Come About

Business cycles are caused by changes in conditions that cause shifts in aggregate demand and aggregate supply. The process can be illustrated in two steps:

1. In Figure (a), excessive monetary stimulation causes an increase in aggregate demand—a shift of the curve from *AD* to *AD'*. Price and output thus rise from their initial equilibrium levels at E_0 to their new equilibrium levels at E_1. These increases, which are assumed to occur at time t_0, are shown in Figures (b) and (c).

2. The higher price level leads workers to press for higher wages, causing the AS curve in Figure (a) to move leftward toward *AS'*. The final equilibrium is thus at E_2. In Figures (b) and (c), therefore, price and output converge on their corresponding equilibrium levels at P_2 and Q_0, respectively. These equilibrium levels are reached at time t_1.

In reality, aggregate demand and aggregate supply are always changing. Thus, business cycles are continually being generated.

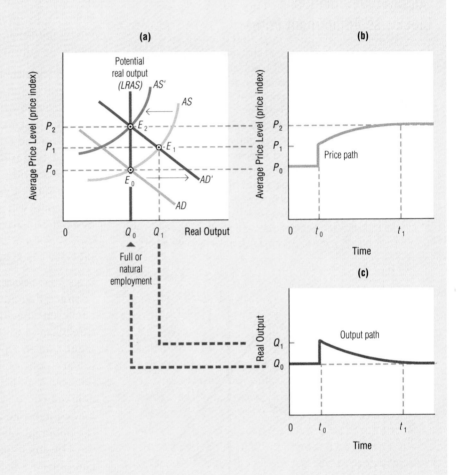

(a)

(b)

(c)

creases the money growth rate too quickly, the result will be an increase in aggregate demand—a shift of the curve to *AD'*. The equilibrium point thus moves from E_0 to E_1.

At this new equilibrium point, the price level has risen to P_1, and the output level to Q_1. These changes are shown as a function of time in Figures (b) and (c). They are assumed to have occurred at time t_0. Notice that price and output each have increased by the amounts shown in Figure (a).

You've already learned that the price level P_1 is

temporary. At this higher price level, resource costs will rise as unions press for wage increases in order to "catch up" with inflation. Therefore, the *AS* curve in Figure (a) will begin moving to the left until it eventually ends up at *AS'*. The final equilibrium point will thus be at E_2. Accordingly, in Figures (b) and (c), price and output will move toward their corresponding equilibrium levels at P_2 and Q_0, respectively. These levels are reached at time t_1. Thereafter, a change in either aggregate demand or aggregate supply will generate a new business cycle.

Inflation and Unemployment: Phillips Curve Analysis

Fluctuations in price and output, of course, don't occur in isolation. They cause changes in other variables, especially inflation and unemployment. To gain a better understanding of macroeconomic dynamics, therefore, let's examine the interaction of these variables.

Many economists believe that there is a relationship between inflation and unemployment and that it can be expressed by a *Phillips curve.* Named for A. W. Phillips, a British economist who proposed it several decades ago, this relationship is illustrated in Exhibit 5. It emphasizes the idea that there can be only one Phillips curve for the economy at any given time. Let's see why.

Observed Phillips Curves

In Exhibit 5, the percentage of unemployment is measured on the horizontal axis. The rate of inflation—the annual percentage change in the price level—is measured on the vertical. The Phillips curve labeled PC_1 depicts the statistical relationship between unemployment and inflation that existed in the 1960s. The curve can be thought of as an "average" of the cluster of dots that it represents. Each point on the curve designates a specific *combination* of unemployment and inflation. The point labeled *A*, for instance, represents an unemployment rate of 5 percent and an inflation rate of 3 percent.

What happens if there is a shift—for reasons to be explained shortly—from PC_1 to PC_2? This, in fact, is what happened in the early 1970s. Any given point on this higher curve when compared to a corresponding point on the lower curve denotes *at least* as much of one variable plus more of the other. For example, point *B* represents the same unemployment rate as point *A* (5 percent), but a higher inflation rate (6 percent). Point *D,* on the other hand, represents the same inflation rate as point *A*(3 percent), but a higher unemployment rate (6.5 percent). The same notion applies to any other point you may choose. Any point on curve PC_2 between *B* and *D,* however, represents a higher rate of both unemployment and inflation as compared with point *A* on curve PC_1. These ideas suggest that lower Phillips curves are "better" and higher ones are "poorer" for the economy as a whole.

EXHIBIT 5

A Curve Named Phillips: Different Ones at Different Times

A Phillips curve (*PC*) depicts a statistical relationship between unemployment and inflation. Each curve is an "average" of the cluster of dots that it represents. Points (such as *A*) along a lower curve denote smaller combinations of unemployment and inflation than corresponding points (such as *B* and *D*) along a higher curve. Therefore, lower curves are better for the economy than higher ones.

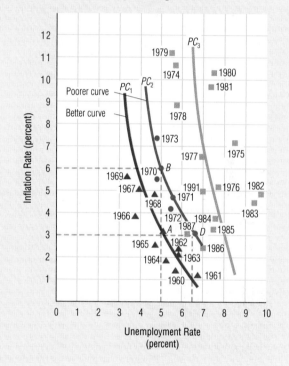

The Phillips curve, of course, hasn't stood still. It shifted again to PC_3 in the late 1970s and the 1980s, to reflect a different statistical relationship between unemployment and inflation.

You can now see why a Phillips curve can be defined in the following way:

A *Phillips curve* represents a statistical relationship between unemployment and inflation. Every point on the curve denotes a different combination of unemployment and inflation. A movement along the curve measures the change in one of these variables associated with a change in the other.

Why has the Phillips curve shifted over time? The answer can be given in terms of two sets of explanations—changes in aggregate demand and changes in aggregate supply.

Changes in Aggregate Demand

As you'll recall, Keynesian economics was born during the Great Depression of the 1930s. Keynes' ideas led most economists and political leaders to believe that the economy could be fine-tuned. That is, government could select a target rate of employment and, with the appropriate combinations of fiscal and monetary policies, achieve it. Of course, if the target chosen was too high, the economy might experience moderate inflation. But some Keynesians thought that even this undesirable effect could be reduced if the government adopted legislation designed to restrain increases in prices and wages.

These beliefs dominated economic thinking until the 1970s. In that period, Keynesian ideas became the subject of increasing criticism as the combination of inflation and unemployment reached unprecedented heights. Many economists at the time argued that the practice of setting a numerical target for employment (or unemployment) should be discarded. Instead the Fed should stabilize the price level by maintaining a steady rate of money growth, and the market should be allowed to determine the *"natural"* or lowest percentage of unemployment sustainable.

The basic idea is illustrated in the Phillips curve model of Exhibit 6. The model rests on the assumption that *a separate Phillips curve is associated with each expected rate of inflation.* Because the economy always tends toward the natural rate of unemployment, the vertical line is simply a long-run Phillips curve *(LRPC).* To understand why, we can examine the inflation-unemployment adjustment path that results from an increase in aggregate demand. This might occur, for example, because of an *unexpected* increase in the money growth rate.

Stage 1: More Money Causes Inflation The economy is assumed to be at point *a*, representing a hypothetical natural unemployment rate of 5 percent and an inflation rate of 6 percent. The Phillips curve associated with this inflation rate is *PC.* As you know from your study of the income-price model, an unexpected expansion in the money growth rate causes the aggregate demand curve to shift to the right. (You should

EXHIBIT 6

Moving Along the Long-Run Phillips Curve

Expansionary monetary policies can result in an increase in aggregate demand. This causes the Phillips curve to shift upward as the public comes to expect higher rates of inflation.

In the short run, there may be a limited trade-off between unemployment and inflation as the economy moves along an adjustment path, such as the path from *a* to *b*. Along this path, unemployment declines as inflation increases. But in the long run the economy is self-correcting. It returns to its natural rate of unemployment and a higher inflation rate, along a path such as the path from *b* to *c*.

It follows that, to reduce the inflation rate, the Fed would have to contract the money growth rate (thus reducing aggregate demand) in order to lower the Phillips curve. The economy would then move *down* an adjustment path (such as *cfa*).

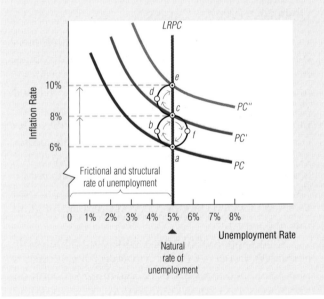

sketch your own income-price diagram with *AD* and *AS* curves to illustrate this.) In Exhibit 6, therefore, the unemployment rate decreases and the inflation rate rises as these variables move along the adjustment path from *a* to *b*. At point *b*, the unemployment rate reaches its lowest level. Meanwhile, the public's *expectation* of higher inflation causes the Phillips curve to shift to *PC'*.

Stage 2: Costs Adjust to Inflation Wages and other resource costs, which have been lagging behind inflation, are now adjusted upward. This causes the aggregate supply curve in the income-price model (which you sketched in Stage 1 above) to shift to the left. In the diagram, therefore, the unemployment rate and the inflation rate move from point *b* to point *c*. At this point, unemployment is back to its natural rate of 5 percent, and inflation, now fully anticipated by the public, is at the higher rate of 8 percent. With respect to workers, nominal wages have "caught up" with prices so that real wages are constant. In general, the equilibrium at *c* is stable—that is, it has no tendency to change.

Stage 3: Stability Until the Next Stimulus Of course, the equilibrium *can* change if new government policies or programs (as described earlier) lead the Fed to employ further stimulative monetary measures. The economy would then follow the inflation-unemployment path shown by the curved line *cde*. This would shift the curve to *PC''*.

Moving Back to Stage 1 Levels How does the economy get back to point *a*? Let's assume that the economy is at *c*. If the Fed ends monetary stimulation, aggregate demand (in the income-price model that you sketched in Stage 1 above) declines relative to aggregate supply. As a result, the inflation rate declines and the unemployment rate at first increases, then decreases, following the path *cfa*. At point *a*, the economy is again in stable equilibrium, this time at the same 5 percent natural rate of unemployment and at a 6 percent inflation rate.

Against this background, you can now appreciate more fully the meaning of the natural rate of unemployment. To begin with, let's *assume* that full employment exists when 95 percent of the labor force is employed. Therefore, 95 percent is the natural rate of employment. Looking again at Exhibit 6:

The *natural rate of unemployment* is the percentage of unemployment (including frictional and structural) that's consistent with full employment and a stable rate of inflation. (A stable rate of inflation is one that's neither accelerating nor decelerating, such as 6 percent, 8 percent, or 10 percent in the diagram.)

You can now see why the vertical line *LRPC* in the figure is a *long-run Phillips curve*. It relates different rates of inflation to a constant natural rate of unemployment. This concept suggests two ideas illustrated in Exhibit 6:

- In the short run, expansionary monetary policies aimed at reducing unemployment may be successful, but they're likely to create inflationary pressures. These occur as the economy moves along an adjustment path (such as *abc*) from one point on the *LRPC* curve to a higher one.

- In the long run, the economy is already at full employment. Therefore, increases in the money growth rate can lead only to more inflation. Thus, *there is at best only a short-run trade-off between unemployment and inflation.*

Summarizing:

Shifts of the Phillips curve may be caused by fluctuations in aggregate demand. These can result from changes in monetary policies. The fluctuations in aggregate demand cause changes in *inflationary expectations.* Because the economy is self-correcting, it adjusts in the long run to its natural rate of unemployment and to some stable rate of inflation. However, the inflation rate may change if the Fed's policies result in significant changes in the monetary growth rate.

Changes in Aggregate Supply

Fluctuations in aggregate demand aren't the only cause of shifts in the Phillips curve. Fluctuations in aggregate supply can also shift the curve. These fluctuations result from changes in three sets of factors: resource costs, the economy's competitive structure, and government fiscal policies.

Changes in resource costs occur when raw-materials prices, wage rates, and other conditions affecting the production expenses of the business sector are altered. A notable example of this occurred during the late 1970s, when world oil prices escalated, causing the aggregate supply curve to shift to the left. This resulted both in a higher inflation rate and in a higher Phillips curve, as you saw earlier in Exhibits 5 and 6.

Similarly, changes in the economy's competitive structure have a direct effect on the aggregate supply curve. In general, an increase in competition leads to improvements in efficiency. The aggregate supply curve shifts to the right, thereby lowering prices, inflationary expectations, and the Phillips curve. A decrease in competition has the opposite effects, and raises the Phillips curve. There is evidence that, since the early 1980s, greater pressure from foreign competition has often contributed significantly to lowering both inflationary expectations and the Phillips curve.

Finally, changes in components of fiscal policy, including tax rates, business subsidies, and transfer payments, can cause the aggregate supply curve to shift. For example, executives view most business taxes as costs. Therefore, an increase in corporate income-tax (or other business tax) rates may shift the aggregate supply curve to the left, and a decrease may shift it to the right. Such shifts affect inflation rates and, therefore, inflationary expectations and the Phillips curve.

It's important to note that, although economists don't deny the importance of these arguments, they agree that excessive monetary growth rates perpetuate inflationary expectations. Most economists conclude that, *because monetary policies are ongoing and often over-stimulative, such policies tend to be the main cause of inflation and instability in the long run.*

Stop-Go Policy Cycles

Shifts in aggregate demand and aggregate supply can create alternating cycles of unemployment and inflation. To the extent that government policies are responsible for the shifts, they contribute to economic instability. Let's see why, by considering two examples:

1. **Increasing Employment Level**   If the Fed is more concerned with increasing the level of employment than with curbing inflation, it will try to stimulate the economy by adopting an expansionary monetary policy. This can create upward pressure on prices and impose an inflationary bias on the economy.

2. **Curbing Inflation**   If the Fed is more concerned with curbing inflation than with increasing the level of employment, it will dampen the economy by adopting a contractionary monetary policy. This can create downward pressure on prices and impose a deflationary bias on the economy.

Inflationary and deflationary biases occur within each business cycle. These are shown in the two graphs in Exhibit 7. Notice that the familiar Phillips curve variables—the unemployment rate and the inflation rate—are measured on the horizontal and vertical axes, respectively. The graphs, which appear to be clockwise loops, illustrate what may be called *stop-go policy cycles.* Each loop shows the "path" of inflation and unemployment that results at least partly from alternating expansionary and contractionary economic policies during a business cycle.

EXHIBIT 7

"Paths" of Inflation and Unemployment: Stop-Go Policy Cycles

Each loop shows the "path" of inflation and unemployment over a period of years. The loops are due in part to expansionary and contractionary economic policies during a business cycle.

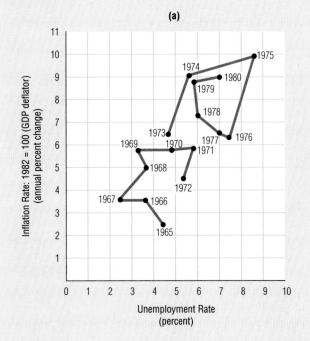

(a)

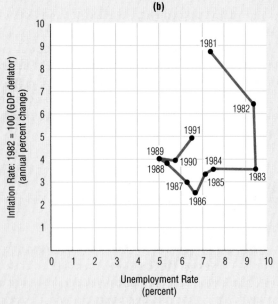

(b)

Inflationary Bias

Let's look at Figure (a). During the 1960s and 1970s the Fed was more concerned with reducing the unemployment rate than with the effects of its policies on the inflation rate. The Fed's monetary policy thus tended to be more expansionary than contractionary. This helped impose a cumulative inflationary bias on the economy. Therefore, the loop covering the period 1973–1980 is higher than the loop covering the period 1965–1972.

However, the higher loop wasn't due entirely to Federal Reserve policy. In the 1970s a series of rapid jumps in resource costs occurred. These resulted partly from sharp increases in oil prices by major oil-producing countries and partly from several poor agricultural harvests in other parts of the world. Exports of American food and fiber rose substantially, and resulted in higher domestic prices.

Deflationary Bias

A third loop exhibiting a cumulative deflationary bias occurred during the 1980s. This is shown in Figure (b). Between 1981 and 1983, the economy experienced a *deflationary recession*—a sharp decline in the inflation rate and a substantial increase in the unemployment rate. Although a number of reasons may account for this, the following are especially important:

Credibility of Government Policy   Between 1979 and 1981 the inflation rate was at its peak. Many policymakers believed that the Fed could cool the economy by reducing the rate of money growth. But doing so could cause a substantial increase in unemployment and perhaps even a major depression. Despite these fears, the Reagan administration decided to take the chance. Both the White House and the Fed issued pronouncements declaring a "war against inflation." The public soon realized that the administration meant what it said and that it wouldn't relent on reducing the money growth rate in the face of rising unemployment. With the credibility of government policy thus established, the public's *expectations* of inflation declined rapidly, and caused the short-run Phillips curve to fall.

Decline in Resource Costs   During the early 1980s, world prices of oil and certain other raw materials fell sharply. Wage-rate increases also slowed down, partly because of high unemployment and partly because of President Reagan's decision in 1981 to fire several thousand air traffic controllers for illegally striking against the government. The latter incident intimidated many union leaders and weakened their bargaining strength in labor-management negotiations.

Supply-Side Policies   Early in the Reagan administration, actions were taken to stimulate production in order to increase real output and reduce inflation and unemployment. Called "supply-side policies," they included the following measures:

1. **Tax Cuts and Accelerated Depreciation**   In order to stimulate increased saving by households and the flow of those savings into business investment, reductions in marginal tax rates were implemented. In addition, businesses were permitted to depreciate their factories, machines, and other capital assets more quickly in order to encourage new investment to replace existing equipment.

2. **Reductions in the Monetary Growth Rate**   To further stimulate increased saving relative to consumption, the Fed helped curb inflation by reducing the rate of money growth. This, of course, wasn't necessarily a supply-side policy, but supply-side advocates viewed it as such. They pointed out that if the public expected the rate of price increases to slow down (that is, if the public expected disinflation instead of inflation), it would reduce consumption and increase saving.

3. **Business Deregulation**   Several major industries and markets were deregulated during the late 1970s and early 1980s. Among them were airlines, the banking system, securities markets, telecommunications, and trucking. In addition, some governmental requirements pertaining to environmental protection and occupational health and safety were relaxed. The effects of these changes were to reduce costs and promote competition in the deregulated industries. These effects, in turn, helped to bring about lower prices of the goods and services provided by these industries.

Rising Value of the Dollar   From 1980 to 1981, the average price of the dollar in terms of the world's other major currencies increased approximately 18 percent, and continued to increase for the next several years. (In addition to the U.S. dollar, the world's major currencies include the British pound, the Canadian dollar, the French franc, the Japanese yen, and the German mark.) The rising value of the U.S. dollar made Japanese cars, British woolens, German steel, and other imports cheaper for Americans to buy. As a result, large-scale competition from imports not only checked the rise in some domestic prices but in many cases forced them down.

Conclusion: Today's Trade-Off

The Phillips curve was initially conceived in the 1960s, and encouraged the widely held belief that a reasonable trade-off existed between unemployment and inflation. This meant that fiscal and monetary policies could be used to bring about substantial reductions in unemployment, but only at the expense of somewhat higher rates of inflation. Conversely, reductions in inflation could be achieved only at the cost of substantial increases in unemployment.

Subsequent experiences have shown these beliefs to be in need of revising. This is best accomplished by expressing the key ideas in terms of short-run and long-run aggregate demand and aggregate supply. To make sure you understand the revision, *try illustrating the following propositions by sketching them graphically:*

1. In the short run, the steepness of the economy's aggregate supply curve increases as output approaches full employment. Therefore, the higher the level of real output, the more likely that expansionary economic policies that increase aggregate demand will affect prices much more than output and employment.

2. In the long run, the economy is already at full employment—the aggregate supply curve is a vertical line. Therefore, expansionary policies that increase aggregate demand cause only prices, not output and employment, to rise.

Thus:

The closer the economy is to full employment, the greater the trade-off between unemployment and inflation. This principle is especially relevant if the economy is operating at a high- but not full-employment level of real GDP, as the U.S. economy has often done in the past. *Evidence shows that, under such circumstances, strong expansionary economic policies are likely to create major inflationary pressures without achieving substantial gains in production and jobs.*

Summary of Important Ideas

1. *Dynamic analysis* traces the paths of the economic variables over time as they move from one equilibrium position to another.

2. Expansionary economic policies can cause a demand-side inflation by shifting the aggregate demand curve to the right. An increase in resource costs can cause a supply-side inflation by shifting the aggregate supply curve to the left.

3. Business cycles are generated by changes in aggregate demand and aggregate supply. The changes cause fluctuations in the average price level and in real output. These fluctuations can be graphed over time to show how business cycles come about.

4. Economists have observed a statistical relationship between unemployment and inflation. The relationship, expressed by a Phillips curve, is inverse. This suggests that a trade-off exists between the two variables.

5. In the short run, the steepness of the economy's aggregate supply curve increases as output approaches full employment. Therefore, at high levels of real output, economic policies that stimulate aggregate demand have a relatively greater impact on inflation than on employment and output. In other words, the trade-off between unemployment and inflation is greater at higher levels of production than at lower ones.

6. In the long run, the economy is already at full employment. Therefore, economic policies that stimulate aggregate demand can result only in higher rates of inflation, not in higher levels of employment and output.

Terms and Concepts to Review

static models

dynamic models

Phillips curve

natural rate of unemployment

long-run Phillips curve

Questions and Problems

1. Look up the meaning of *stagflation* in the Dictionary at the back of the book. Using the concepts of aggregate demand and aggregate supply, explain how stagflation can occur both in a static and in a dynamic sense.

2. How does the degree of wage flexibility affect the responsiveness of employment and prices to short-run changes in aggregate demand?

3. If prices and wages were fairly flexible, would changes in aggregate demand be able to produce business cycles? Explain.

4. "Phillips curves are Phillips curves, regardless of whether they are short run or long run." Do you agree?

5. What legislative and fiscal actions can you recommend to *improve* the economy's Phillips curve? Before answering, explain precisely what is meant by "improve."

6. If everyone had complete knowledge of market prices and if labor were perfectly mobile, what would the short-run Phillips curve look like?

7. How would the position or location of our economy's short-run Phillips curve be affected by each of the following? Explain your answers.

   a. A reduction in tariffs

   b. A decrease in import quotas

   c. A new law making labor unions illegal

   d. A merger of the largest firm in each major industry (for example, automobiles, oil refining, and so on) with the second largest firm in its industry

   e. A new law prohibiting any firm's sales from exceeding 50 percent of its industry's sales

   f. Significant advances made in automation throughout most of industry

8. Some people contend: "Inflation promotes growth and diminishes unemployment. We must recognize that the costs of inflation are much less than the costs of avoiding it. Therefore, we should accept inflation and learn to live with it. This can be done by recognizing that it is easier to compensate the victims of inflation than the casualties of recession." What specific compensatory measures can you propose to make inflation less painful and less inequitable? Discuss.

TAKE A STAND

Zero Inflation: Should the Fed Pursue It?

During the 1970s, inflation was considered "public enemy number one." It was over 6 percent for most of the decade and reached double-digit levels in the late 1970s and early 1980s. Contractionary monetary policies pursued by the Federal Reserve in the 1980s brought inflation back to about 4 percent by the end of the decade. Should the Fed be satisfied with this disinflation and stop at 4 percent, or should it act to lower inflation even further? Some have suggested that zero inflation should be the goal of monetary policy.

The U.S. economy has seldom seen zero inflation, certainly not for any extended period. The lowest inflation experienced in recent decades was between 1 and 2 percent in the early 1960s. Since then, the inflation rate has generally been at least 4 percent.

In principle, zero inflation is easy to attain. Inflation is possible in the long run only if an economy's money supply increases faster than its productive capacity. For example, if output expands by 3 percent each year but the money supply increases by 7 percent, then the economy experiences 4 percent inflation. In theory at least, the Federal Reserve can achieve zero inflation by matching the money growth rate to the long-run growth of real GDP. Disinflation can cause considerable short-run hardship, however. The debate over whether or not to aim for zero inflation therefore centers on the long-run benefits and the short-run costs to the economy. *Should zero inflation be the goal of monetary policy?*

Yes: The Benefits Are Large and Last Forever

When the general price level is rising, a dollar buys fewer and fewer goods. The decline in real value makes people reluctant to hold cash; they would rather keep their wealth in an interest-bearing asset. Such assets pay a return equal to the market interest rate, which includes an inflation premium. Cash pays a return of zero. Thus, the higher the rate of inflation, the greater the incentive to limit holdings of cash. People will expend time and effort in order to economize on their cash holdings. Rather than visit the bank once a month and withdraw $400, in a period of high inflation an individual might go to the bank once a week and withdraw $100. The additional three trips to the bank are, in

effect, transaction costs imposed by inflation, and as such are a source of inefficiency.

Since inflation is rarely predictable, it also generates unanticipated and arbitrary redistributions of income among individuals. Those who fail to anticipate a decline in the purchasing power of the dollar unwittingly transfer some of their wealth to other members of society. The ones who suffer most are those on fixed incomes and those who have made fixed-interest loans. Creditors who underestimate future inflation when setting an interest rate unwillingly transfer some of their wealth to their debtors. The unpredictability of inflation may thus interfere with the efficient functioning of financial markets.

Inflation also interferes with the unit-of-account function of money. If its value changes from year to year, the dollar loses reliability, and thus usefulness, as a unit of measurement. It is as if the mile were to change in length from one day to the next. Not only are these changes inconvenient, they also inhibit the efficient functioning of the price system. The market information that prices convey becomes distorted, and the role of prices in achieving an efficient allocation of resources is compromised.

The opportunity to wipe out these costs provides a compelling reason to strive for zero inflation. Moreover, provided that the public understands the ultimate source of inflation, the costs of achieving this goal will be small. If the Fed credibly commits itself to achieving zero inflation, then people will rapidly adjust their expectations to this level. That is, they will not demand higher payments for the same level of output. The economy's adjustment to zero inflation will thus have little, if any, detrimental effect on output and unemployment.

Finally, and significantly, any costs of attaining zero inflation need be incurred once only, but the benefits of a stable price level, once achieved, persist forever.

No: The Benefits Are Overstated and the Costs Are Significant

Those more skeptical about the desirability of achieving zero inflation argue that its benefits are not that great. For example, the reduction in transaction costs achieved by cutting inflation from 4 percent to zero would probably amount to a fraction of a percent of GDP per year. Many of the other costs of inflation, at least at low levels, can be eliminated by linking wages and prices to an index of the general price level. Workers and firms sometimes sign employment contracts that link dollar wages to the Consumer Price Index.

The costs of attaining zero inflation, by contrast, may be significant, because reductions in inflation can touch off a recession. Witness the recession of 1981–1982. The reduction in inflation achieved by the Fed was obtained at the cost of a severe recession during which unemployment soared to 10 percent, the highest rate since the Great Depression. Declines in output occur because reductions in the money supply decrease aggregate demand.

Zero inflation can be achieved at little cost only if two conditions prevail. Wages and prices must be highly flexible, and the public must believe that the Fed will carry out its intention to curb money-supply growth. But prices and wages are fixed by both explicit long-term contracts and informal agreements, and so cannot adjust rapidly enough to prevent recession when inflation is reduced. An announced goal of zero inflation might be greeted with skepticism. Doubters, suspecting that instead the Fed will increase the money supply to stimulate the economy, would continue to demand wage and price increases that anticipate inflation.

Experience suggests that reducing inflation is very costly. The reduction of 4 percentage points currently needed to bring inflation down to zero would probably cost between 10 and 20 percent of one year's GDP. It would take decades of reduced transactions costs to offset this loss.

Finally, there are benefits to inflation. For example, it provides a means of taxing illegal activity. Over 80 percent of U.S. currency is held either by those in the underground economy or by residents of other countries. Criminals find cash a convenient way to store their wealth because cash is anonymous and difficult to trace. Inflation reduces the real purchasing power of currency and so serves as a hidden tax on activities that are beyond the reach of the IRS.

The Question: Should the Fed Pursue Zero Inflation?

■ Proponents of zero inflation argue that inflation is a source of unnecessary transactions costs, arbitrary redistributions of income, and substantial inconvenience. The costs of eliminating inflation are relatively low and are incurred only once, while the benefits persist indefinitely.

■ Others argue that the transactions costs due to inflation are negligible but the adjustment costs are substantial. Reducing inflation entails a costly recession.

Where Do You Stand?

1. Suppose that the mile and all other units of length became 5 percent shorter every year, so that the measured distance between any two points increased every year. How might society adapt to such an inconvenience? How might society adapt if the changes were unpredictable from year to year?

2. Residents of other countries who hold some of their wealth in the form of dollars are effectively taxed by U.S. inflation. It might seem, then, that we could get a lot of revenue from other countries by generating substantial inflation. Why is such a strategy unlikely to be successful?

3. Advocates of Keynesian theory, monetarism, rational expectations, and real business cycles have differing views of the macroeconomy. Which would support zero inflation and which would not? Why?

4. Should the Federal Reserve pursue zero inflation? Justify your stand.

Sources: S. Rao Aiyagari, "Deflating the Case for Zero Inflation," *Quarterly Review*, Federal Reserve Bank of Minneapolis, Summer 1990, pp. 2–11; W. Lee Hoskins, "Defending Zero Inflation: All for Naught," *Quarterly Review*, Federal Reserve Bank of Minneapolis, Spring 1991, pp. 16–20; and S. Rao Aiyagari, "Response to a Defense for Zero Inflation," *Quarterly Review*, Federal Reserve Bank of Minneapolis, Spring 1991, pp. 21–24.

Chapter 19

Deficits and Debt: Domestic and International Perspectives

Government Budget Deficits

The Public Debt: Today's Issues

Understanding Trade Deficits

Understanding International Indebtedness

Conclusion: Policy Options for Reducing Trade Deficits and Debt

Learning Guide
Watch for answers to these important questions

What is the full-employment (or structural) budget? Why is it favored over the actual budget by many policymakers?

How do traditional views of budget deficits differ from modern classical views? What are the chief criticisms leveled against large budget deficits? How do modern classical economists respond to these criticisms?

Why is the size of the public debt a matter of concern? What's wrong with a large public debt? What practical guidelines exist for public-debt management?

What is meant by the trade balance? How is it related to real output? What does the J-curve explain?

What is a debtor nation? Does international indebtedness worsen a nation's future living standards? Does it cause inflation?

What policy options exist for reducing trade deficits and foreign debt?

For economists, controversy is a fact of life. One reason they often disagree about important issues is that, unlike physical scientists, economists have no laboratory in which to test their theories. Economists must rely instead on the laboratory of historical experience. One result is that economic problems that at one time are thought to be of paramount importance may, at a later time, be considered inconsequential. Perhaps history, by affording us the opportunity to view old problems differently, has a way of changing our understanding of how the world works.

Nowhere is this more evident than in economics. Within the lifetime of today's adults, views concerning deficits and debt, at both the domestic and the international level, have undergone dramatic change. How do the sizes of the government's budget deficits and the national debt affect the economy? What are the economic consequences of international-trade deficits and foreign indebtedness? The answers to these questions have always been controversial, but in many respects the alternatives offered today are different from those offered as recently as a decade or two ago.

If you keep up with the news, you know that four topics concerning deficits and debt are the subject of much controversy. They are:

1. Government budget deficits
2. The national debt
3. International trade deficits
4. International indebtedness

Let's examine these topics and the issues surrounding them.

Government Budget Deficits

The federal government, like many households and businesses, maintains an annual budget. Like households and businesses, the federal government incurs a budget deficit when it spends more than its income during a year. Similarly, it realizes a budget surplus when it spends less than its income during a year. And when its expenditure and its income are equal for the year, the federal government has a balanced budget. But unlike households and businesses, the federal government's "income" is derived almost entirely from taxes.

Budget deficits have been a common occurrence for most of this century. They reached unprecedented levels during the 1980s, as you can see in Exhibit 1. These large annual deficits led Congress to pass the ***Gramm-Rudman-Hollings Act*** (1985) requiring that the federal budget be balanced annually beginning in 1993. The Act also provides that, in the event of a recession or emergency, Congress can suspend the law for up to 2 years.

A budget deficit can be eliminated by a reduction in expenditures or by an increase in taxes. But these

choices are politically unpopular. Lawmakers, therefore, have either ignored the Act or have devised ways to avoid strict adherence to it. Congress, for example, has modified the law several times, removed certain expenditure items from the official budget, and employed various accounting devices in efforts to reduce apparent deficits. However, because these are only cosmetic features, *effective* budget deficits will continue to occur frequently even if the actual (official) budget is ever balanced.

What conditions contribute to budget deficits? Why are they a subject of considerable controversy? These are the questions to which we now turn our attention.

Full-Employment (Structural) Budget

Despite hysterical claims sometimes made in the news media, budget deficits, by themselves, don't necessarily tell us very much. To be meaningful, they must be viewed within the context of business cycles. Logically, the same is true of budget surpluses, even though they have been a rare occurrence during most of this century.

For example, during recession the government's tax receipts fall while the amount paid out in unemployment benefits rises. This helps generate a federal budget deficit. Conversely, during recovery the government's tax receipts increase while the amount paid out in unemployment benefits declines. This helps generate a federal-budget surplus.

The relationship between deficits or surpluses in the actual budget and the business cycle is illustrated in Exhibit 2. Government spending and tax revenues, measured on the vertical axis, are related to real GDP, measured on the horizontal axis. The level of government spending (G) is assumed constant at 200. Increases in real GDP raise the government's tax receipts, so the tax-revenue line (T) is upward sloping.

Suppose the economy goes into a recession. If real GDP declines to 500, the actual budget deficit will increase to 100. This increase might suggest that the existing fiscal policy of taxing and spending is expansionary. In fact, however, *the deficit exists because real output is too low to generate the tax revenues needed to cover government expenditures.* If the economy had been producing at its potential-output level, where real GDP equals 1,500, the *same fiscal policy* would have generated a full-employment-budget surplus of 100.

The ***full-employment budget*** (also called the ***structural budget***) is an estimate of annual government ex-

EXHIBIT 1

Federal Budget Deficit
(as a percentage of GDP)

The magnitude of a budget deficit is more readily appreciated when the deficit is expressed as a percentage of the nation's income (GDP).

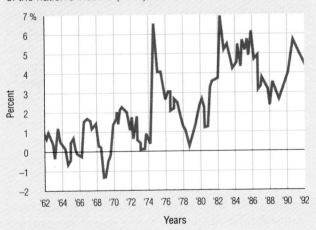

Years

EXHIBIT
2

Budget Deficits and Surpluses

At the recession output of 500, the actual budget *deficit* is 100. But if the economy had been at its potential output of 1,500, the same fiscal (taxation and spending) policy would have produced a full-employment-budget *surplus* of 100. Thus the deficit *doesn't exist because of an expansionary fiscal policy. The deficit exists because, at the recession output, tax revenues shown by the T line aren't high enough to cover government expenditures shown by the G line.* Therefore, the full-employment budget, not the actual budget, is the relevant one for judging the effects of discretionary fiscal policy.

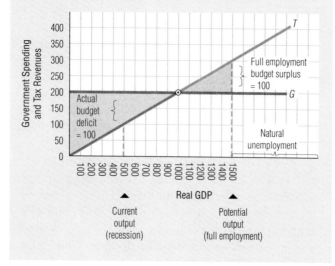

smaller full-employment-budget surplus (or possibly even a full-employment-budget deficit) than figures of 4 or 5 percent. The latter are what some other economists and legislators prefer to define as the natural rate of unemployment.

Expansionary Effects Versus Neutral Effects

Over the years, many different opinions have been voiced about the consequences of budget deficits. Two conflicting beliefs have gained widespread attention. One of them contends that the effects of increases in budget deficits are expansionary. The other belief holds that the effects are neutral.

Expansionary Effects: Increase in Aggregate Demand

According to the traditional view, a budget deficit, brought about, for example, by a reduction in individual income taxes, is expansionary. This is because the tax reduction leaves consumers with more income to spend. The economy's aggregate demand curve, therefore, shifts to the right. This shift can have several effects, depending on whether the economy is in a recession or at full employment, and whether it's "open" or "closed." Let's interpret the effects of changes in aggregate demand with the help of Exhibit 3.

Recession Versus Full Employment Suppose the economy is in a recession. If the Federal Reserve expands the rate of money growth (by monetizing some of the deficit), employment, output, and the price level will rise. However, the extent of the increases will depend on the *relative steepness* of the economy's aggregate supply curve. Thus:

1. If the economy is in a deep recession, resources are underutilized, so there's considerable excess capacity in the economy. Therefore, the leftward portion of the *AS* curve in Exhibit 3 is relatively flat. As a result, an increase in aggregate demand causes a relatively larger increase in output and employment than in the price level. For example, a shift in aggregate demand from AD_1 to AD_2 causes output and employment to rise from Q_1 to Q_2 and the price level from P_1 to P_2.

2. If the economy is in a moderate recession, there is less excess capacity than in a deep recession, so the *AS* curve becomes steeper. Consequently, an increase in aggregate demand causes a relatively large increase in the price level compared to the increase in output and employment. For instance, the increase in aggregate demand from AD_2 to AD_3 causes output and employment to rise from Q_2 to Q_3 and the price level from P_2

penditures and revenues that would occur at the level of potential real GDP—that is, at full employment. Any resulting surplus (or deficit) is called a full-employment surplus (or deficit).

The advantage of the full-employment budget is that it eliminates changes in government revenues and expenditures that are due to cyclical forces. It therefore gives a truer picture of the direction of fiscal policy—that is, whether it is expansionary or contractionary. The full-employment budget also has political utility. In some years when the actual budget is running a deficit, the full-employment budget will show a surplus. This is one reason many legislators favor it.

However, there's a catch. As you can see from the graph in Exhibit 2, *G* and *T* are given. Therefore, any estimate of the full-employment budget depends on the assumed rate of "natural" unemployment. A figure of about 6 percent is believed by many economists and legislators to be realistic. This rate produces a much

Expansionary Effects: Increases in Aggregate Demand

Suppose there's an increase in the government's budget deficit due, say, to a tax reduction. If this causes the aggregate demand curve to shift to the right, the results will be expansionary. The effects on the price level and on output and employment will depend on the *relative steepness* of the aggregate supply curve.

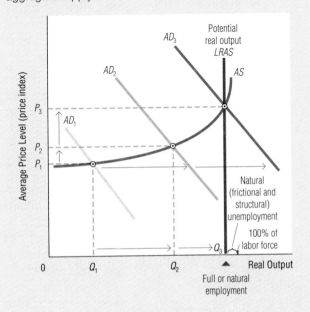

1. In a "closed" economy—one that isn't open to international trade and investment—domestic savings are the chief source of supply of loanable funds. Therefore, when the government runs a budget deficit by borrowing from the private sector, the increased demand for loanable funds creates upward pressure on interest rates. This raises business' costs of borrowing, thereby causing a *crowding out* of private investment.

2. In an "open" economy such as ours, international trade and investment flow freely. The foreign sector can therefore provide the loanable funds needed to fulfill the government's increased demand. Foreign funds thus help to prevent rising interest rates and crowding out. To the extent that this occurs, the budget deficit will be financed by foreign lenders—those who buy the Treasury's debt securities.

3. The inflow of foreign-sector funds, such as British pounds, German marks, and Japanese yen, must be converted into dollars in order to purchase the Treasury's debt securities. This causes an increased demand for dollars and hence a rise in their price in terms of the other currencies. Because the dollar becomes more expensive for foreigners to buy with their currencies, American exports decline. And because the other currencies become cheaper for Americans to buy with their dollars, American imports rise. The decline in exports and the rise in imports encourage a deficit in the U.S. balance of trade.

In summary:

According to the traditional view, an increase in the government's budget deficit has three major effects:

1. **It raises the proportion of GDP spent on consumption (including imports) and reduces the proportion saved.**

2. **It encourages borrowing from abroad to help finance the deficit, and thus helps substitute foreign debt for domestic debt.**

3. **It encourages a trade deficit in the nation's international transactions.**

to P_3. As you can see, if the *AS* curve were steeper, the increase in the price level would be even greater compared to the increase in output and employment.

3. If the economy is at full employment, there is little excess capacity. (The only excess capacity consists of frictional and structural unemployment.) Therefore, the effects of an increase in aggregate demand beyond AD_3 are primarily inflationary. That is, prices rise sharply while output and employment increase relatively little.

Closed Economy Versus Open Economy The government incurs a deficit by spending more than it collects in taxes. The difference is made up by borrowing, that is, by selling government debt securities. How will these sales affect interest rates and the value of the dollar on the world's financial markets?

Neutral Effects: Ricardian Equivalence

A different view of the effects of government budget deficits was first conjectured in 1810 by the great English classical economist, David Ricardo. Called the "Ricardian equivalence theorem," the concept remained largely neglected for more than 170 years. Then, in the 1980s, it was resurrected by Harvard University's Robert Barro, one of the nation's leading modern classical economists.

The Ricardian equivalence theorem contends that *an increase in deficit spending cannot shift the aggregate demand curve.* In other words, the increase in households' income resulting from tax cuts has no effect on consumption spending. This is because people know that the government eventually must repay what it borrows. The government obtains the funds for repayment from taxes, which are collected from the public. Individuals believe that they or their heirs will eventually have to pay taxes equal to the deficit. Therefore, to prepare for the tax payments, *the public increases its saving by an amount equal to the increase in the deficit.**

The Ricardian equivalence theorem implies that the effects of government debt on the economy are not expansionary, as in the previous traditional view, but *neutral.* To understand why, it helps to realize that the government debt—also called the national debt and the public debt—is simply the accumulation of the government's previous budget deficits. Therefore, the Ricardian equivalence theorem may more aptly be called the "debt neutrality proposition."

The *debt neutrality proposition* states that deficits do not cause changes in aggregate demand. Therefore, deficits don't affect consumption, interest rates, GDP, employment, investment, or inflation. Nor do deficits crowd out borrowers. Changes in the national debt have no influence on economic variables because the changes are automatically offset by corresponding changes in savings. Thus *debt is neutral.*

What Does the Evidence Show?   The debt neutrality proposition has been highly controversial and a subject of many research investigations. As with most complex economic issues, the same research findings can be interpreted in different ways. For instance:

- Traditionalists see the evidence as indicating that federal-budget deficits absorb private-sector savings. (Recall that the government finances a

deficit by borrowing from the private sector.) The savings borrowed could better be used by businesses to finance new investment. Such investment would increase the nation's productivity, output, and employment. Therefore, budget deficits divert resources from their most efficient use.

- Modern Ricardians believe the evidence shows that the public is indifferent between financing budget deficits now with current taxes or financing them later with future taxes. The evidence also shows that budget deficits don't affect aggregate demand. Therefore, budget deficits have no consistent effect on interest rates, inflation, investment spending, or other economic variables.

Both points of view are persuasive. Indeed, economists continue to debate the economic impacts of deficits. The arguments on both sides center on two basic questions:

1. How might an increase in the federal deficit affect the economy's aggregate demand curve?

2. How might an increase in the aggregate demand curve affect such key variables as consumption, saving, interest rates, investment, and GDP?

Today's Issues: What's Wrong with Large Budget Deficits?

A substantial number of economists believe that deficits do not affect the direction of interest rates or the rate of inflation. The economy has experienced deficits of all sizes during all phases of the business cycle, without any consistent influence on interest rates or the price level. Why, then, are deficits an ongoing concern to policymakers and the public? The answer depends on whom you ask. All the opinions can be reduced to two types of criticisms: the traditionalist argument and the debt-neutrality argument.

Traditionalist Argument: Deficit Financing Reduces Economic Efficiency

Some economists contend that deficits do affect the economy, but in more subtle ways than was once believed. Because few people care much about small deficits, here are the chief traditional objections to large ones—those in excess of about 1 percent of GDP.

1.   Deficits Curtail Private-Sector Investment   Government deficits are financed by borrowing, that is, by selling

---

*If you find this argument hard to believe, you're among the majority. That's because most people think of saving as that part of income not spent on consumption. However, modern classical economists broaden the meaning of saving by defining it to include the following:

Social Security taxes—because these come out of everyone's paycheck and are like money put in a retirement account.

Purchase of consumer durables—because they provide a steady stream of services for years, like the return on an investment.

Outlays for military hardware and for education, research, and development—because, like consumer durables, they are investments that provide future returns.

The inclusion of these items greatly increases the nation's saving.

Treasury securities to the public. The public buys securities with its savings. Of course, the money borrowed is spent by the government on goods and services. However, if deficits were smaller, more savings could be available to the private sector for investment in modern plant and equipment. Private-sector investment is the key to creating new jobs, enhancing productivity, and raising the standard of living.

2. Deficits Keep the Dollar Strong and Interest Rates High
The government finances deficits by borrowing abroad as well as at home. Borrowing the huge amounts of money needed to finance large deficits creates upward pressure on interest rates. Foreigners wanting to purchase Treasury securities in order to take advantage of the higher interest rates bid up the price of the dollar on world financial markets. This has a direct effect on our daily life:

■ **Crowding Out** High interest rates crowd out some business investment. They also crowd out some consumer spending on interest-sensitive goods—particularly housing, cars, and major appliances. Both types of crowding out can cause unemployment and, therefore, a lower level of real GDP.

■ **Trade Deficit** The strong dollar reduces America's exports by making them more expensive for foreigners to buy. It also increases America's imports by making them cheaper for Americans to buy. A declining volume of exports and an expanding volume of imports can cause a substantial deficit in the nation's balance of trade with other countries. This may also cause domestic unemployment and a lower level of real GDP.

3. Deficits Limit Antirecessionary Options During a recession, the deficit climbs as unemployment-insurance payments rise and tax revenues fall. Policy activists fear that the onset of a recession when the deficit is relatively large and growing makes it that much harder to increase government spending. In their opinion, a large deficit thus limits the use of a major antirecessionary tool of fiscal policy.

4. Deficits May Encourage Monetary Stimulation Deficits are a concern of both fiscal and monetary policy. Heavy borrowing by the Treasury to finance large deficits can cause interest rates to go up. To reduce the chances of a recession, the Fed may increase the money supply in an effort to keep interest rates from rising. This action creates inflationary pressures, and eventually higher, not lower, interest rates. It thus causes a misallocation of resources through its effect on capital markets and private incentives.

5. Deficits Discourage Productive Social Investment Government (like individuals) incurs a deficit by borrowing to pay for current goods and services. The deficit itself isn't either good or bad. What matters is how the money is used. There are two possibilities:

■ Suppose the government uses the borrowed funds to pay for increased welfare benefits, national defense, or interest on the national debt. In that case the borrowing is more necessary than useful and does little to enhance future living standards. (The same is true of an individual who borrows to pay for increased consumption.) Since the early 1980s, a relatively large proportion of the borrowed funds has often been used to finance these types of expenditures. The nation has thus "consumed" much of the deficit.

■ Suppose the government uses the borrowed funds to pay for productive social investment. Examples include education, infrastructure (such as airports, highways, bridges, and port facilities), environmental improvement, and other goods that promise a substantial payoff. In that case the investment can actually improve future living standards. (The same is true of an individual who borrows to pay for college or professional school.) Since the early 1980s, a relatively small proportion of the borrowed funds has typically been used to finance these types of expenditures. The nation has thus failed to "invest" much of the deficit.

Debt-Neutrality Argument: Size of Government, Not Deficit Financing, Affects Economic Efficiency

The traditionalist arguments against budget deficits are by no means universally accepted. The chief opponents of the traditionalist view subscribe to the Ricardian equivalence theorem, or *debt-neutrality proposition*. As explained earlier, this proposition states that *deficit spending has no long-run effect on the economy.*

If the effects of budget deficits, even large ones, are neutral, what fiscal "creed" do debt-neutralists hold? To begin with, they contend that the public is indifferent between financing a balanced budget with current taxes or a budget deficit with future taxes. Therefore, contrary to traditional views, the main fiscal decision affecting economic efficiency—that is, resource allocation—is not how government expenditures should be financed. Instead:

The main fiscal decision affecting economic efficiency is to determine the desired amount of government expenditures as a percentage of GDP. The reason is that government expenditures absorb resources that could be used more productively in the private sector. Therefore, the ratio of government expenditures to GDP provides an indication of the size of government relative to the rest of the economy.

You can calculate government expenditures as a percentage of GDP from the data in the inside front cover of the book—columns (3) and (5). Try calculating the percentage for each year going back at least a decade. Has the trend been rising or falling? According to the debt-neutrality argument, what does the trend suggest?

The Public Debt: Today's Issues

For more than a half-century, the number of budget deficits has far exceeded the number of surpluses. As a result, the government has accumulated a substantial national debt. It consists of Treasury securities—bills, notes, and bonds. The size of the national debt has been the subject of a good deal of controversy and criticism. Before exploring the issues that are involved, you should examine the basic facts by studying the figures and the accompanying comments in Exhibit 4.

Is our present public debt too large? What are its economic consequences? These are the kinds of questions that thoughtful people ask. Some of the answers, as you'll see, are contrary to what is widely believed.

Burdens on Future Generations

> Blessed are the young for they shall inherit the national debt.
>
> —HERBERT HOOVER
> 31st President of the United States, 1929–1933

Many people argue that, when the government incurs long-term debt, it burdens future generations with the cost of today's policies. There is some merit to this argument, but three aspects of it concerning the *benefits* and *costs* of debt need to be examined.

1. To begin with, we must consider the uses to which the borrowed funds are put. Suppose the government spends the money for socially productive purposes such as improving the nation's infrastructure, educational system, and environment. The benefits of these expenditures will be realized by both the present and future generations. But suppose the money is spent for unproductive purposes such as paying for welfare programs and interest on the debt.* In that case, most of the benefits will be realized by the present generation and few will be available to future generations.

2. Suppose the debt is increased by deficit spending during a period of unemployment. To the extent that resources that would otherwise have remained idle are thereby put to work, the increase in debt levies no real cost. That is, no added burden results, either on the generation that incurs the debt or on future generations. Society has benefited from the increased output, and some of the output has added to the nation's capital stock that will be inherited by later generations.

3. Suppose instead that the debt is increased during a period of full employment. There are two cases to consider:

a. Suppose the increased debt is incurred to finance activities that draw resources from the private sector. Examples of such activities are the construction of highways, health-care facilities, transportation systems, and so on. These social-goods expenditures benefit both present and future generations. However, because the costs are incurred during a period of full employment, they are borne primarily by people living during the period. Those people are the ones who experience a decline in current output of private-sector goods as a result of the transfer of resources to the public sector. (To help understand this concept, try sketching a production-possibilities curve to illustrate it.)

b. Suppose the increased debt is incurred in order to finance welfare programs and to pay interest on the existing debt. As you'll recall, these types of expenditures are *transfer payments*—exchanges of funds between sectors of the economy without corresponding contributions to current production. Will such payments provide benefits and costs to present and future generations? You can deduce the answer yourself.

External-Debt Burden: Do We "Owe It to Ourselves"?

In 1960, only about 5 percent of the national debt was owed to foreign creditors. In 1970, the figure was still less than 10 percent. In those days, therefore, it was generally accepted that the debt posed no particular burden because we "owed it to ourselves." That is, the debt was largely owed by the people of the United States to the people of the United States.

---

*Some economists argue that some expenditures on national defense are unproductive.

EXHIBIT
4

The Public (National) Debt and Interest Payments

(a) Public Debt

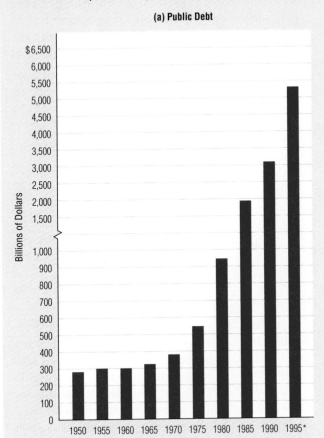

FIGURE (a) Sharp increases in the national debt have occurred at different times and for different reasons. The main causes of the increases have been the need to pay for national defense, other social goods, and income security benefits to the poor and the disabled.

(b) Public Debt as a Percentage of GDP

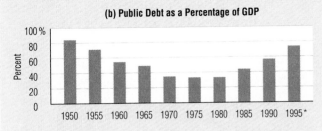

FIGURE (b) A nation's debt as a percentage of GDP is a good indicator of the relative size of that debt.

(c) Interest Payments

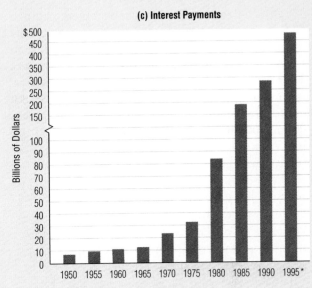

FIGURE (c) The chief burdens of a public debt are the annual interest payments. The long-run trend of these payments has been upward in recent decades.

(d) Interest Payments as a Percentage of GDP

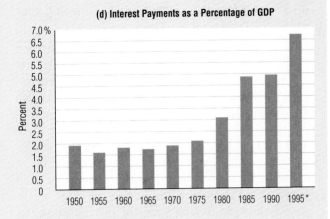

FIGURE (d) The long-run trend of interest payments as a percentage of GDP has risen since the 1960s.

Source: U.S. Department of Treasury.   *Estimated.

Since 1980, there have been years in which about 15 percent of the national debt has been owed to foreign creditors. Because of this relatively high proportion of foreign-held debt, the assertion that we "owe it to ourselves" has become less valid than it once was.

Does a debt owed to foreigners impose a burden on our own and future generations? The answer is that it can. This is because we must pay interest without necessarily receiving corresponding benefits in return. The foreign bondholders may well spend their interest income in their own countries rather than here. But even if they spend it on the purchase of our goods, those goods are the *real* interest (the sacrifice) we are paying for the loans. However, an exception can occur if the sums originally borrowed were spent here to buy capital goods and to create jobs.* In that case, the resulting gains in current output can help cover much of the interest and principal payments of the debt.

Inflationary Burden: Do Deficits Cause Rising Prices and Interest Rates?

A rising public debt results from the tendency of the government to spend more money than it collects in tax revenues. Is this inflationary? The answer is not a clear yes or no. It depends on, among other things, the rate at which the Fed "monetizes" debt. Let's see what this means.

Debt Monetization

The Treasury borrows money to pay for its expenditures in excess of tax revenues by selling Treasury securities—bills, notes, and bonds—to the public. While the Treasury is selling these debt instruments, the Fed may simultaneously be buying Treasury securities in the open market to stimulate the economy. The Fed's purchases, of course, increase banks' reserves. This, in turn, increases checkable deposits, and causes the money supply to rise. By buying Treasury securities, the Fed thus *monetizes* Treasury debt—that is, converts the debt into money. When this happens the inflationary impact is direct. The situation, as you've learned a number of times, becomes one of *too much money chasing too few goods.*

Whether the inflation rate is rapid or slow depends on the volume and speed of the Fed's monetization. This determines the rate at which the money sup-

ply grows. *Thus, the Fed's policies, not the debt, are the direct cause of inflation.*

Deficits Have No Inflationary Influence

Do the deficits that result from government borrowing cause interest rates to rise? Is there a relationship between deficits and inflation? Despite conflicting opinions, widespread agreement exists on two key points:

- **Deficits are simply the accounting result of comparing revenues with expenditures. Therefore, deficits by themselves play no active role in the economy**—*they are not fiscal agents. Government spending and taxing are fiscal agents.*

- *No relationship has yet been established between deficits and the direction of interest rates or the rate of inflation.* **The economy has experienced deficits of all sizes during all phases of the business cycle, yet never have these deficits shown any consistent influence on interest rates or on the price level.**

Conclusion: Practical Debt-Management Guidelines

On the basis of the preceding arguments, should the public debt be allowed to grow without limit? Once again there's no simple answer. However, certain principles of debt management have been proposed by various authorities. These principles assume that the government's ability to meet its payments of interest and principal is determined by the taxpaying capacity of the nation. This, in turn, depends on the growth of real aggregate income, that is, real GDP. Therefore:

According to some experts, there need be no adverse consequences of a large public debt, provided that:

1. **The debt doesn't, over the long run, grow faster than GDP. That is, the public debt as a percentage of GDP shouldn't rise for a prolonged period.**

2. **Interest payments on the debt are a relatively small percentage of GDP.**

3. **The debt is financed by noninflationary means. That is, to avoid a situation of "too much money chasing too few goods," the Fed shouldn't monetize the debt at a significantly faster rate than the growth of long-run real GDP.**

Looking back at Exhibit 4, and recalling what you've learned about inflation in previous chapters, what is your judgment of the extent to which these guidelines have been followed?

---

*British, Canadian, Dutch, and Japanese creditors, for example, have held a substantial proportion of U.S. foreign debt since the early 1980s. As lenders, they have helped finance the construction of American factories, office buildings, hotels, and other investment projects.

Summary Thus Far

1.   The traditional view of budget deficits holds that they are expansionary because they shift the economy's aggregate demand curve to the right. The modern classical view contends that deficits are neutral because the public automatically offsets them by changes in saving. Available evidence suggests that further research is needed because there appears to be some truth in both points of view.

2.   Two major arguments against large budget deficits are that they keep interest rates high and the international value of the dollar strong. As a result, they crowd out private investment and encourage trade deficits. Critics of these arguments contend that deficits have no long-run effect. Instead, the main fiscal problem is to decide on the desired amount of government expenditures as a percent of GDP. This indicates the size of the government sector relative to the rest of the economy.

3.   The benefits and costs to present and future generations of increases in the national debt depend on several factors. The most important are (a) the uses to which the debt is put and (b) the phase of the business cycle in which the debt is incurred. Whether inflation will result depends on whether increases in the debt are monetized by the Fed.

Understanding Trade Deficits

Since the late 1970s, the United States has undergone striking changes in its economic relationships with the rest of the world. As shown in Exhibit 5, America's annual trade balance, measured on the vertical axis by net exports of goods and services, entered a long period of deficits.

A negative trade balance is often interpreted from two different perspectives—one unfavorable and one favorable:

- The unfavorable view holds that, when the trade balance is in deficit, Americans are living beyond their means. That is, the United States is importing more than it is exporting, and is borrowing from other countries to finance its purchases.

- The favorable view holds that incurring international debt to pay for imports represents nothing more than future export sales for American companies. That's because the nation's foreign debt can be repaid only with the money earned from exporting American goods.

EXHIBIT
5

U.S. Trade Balance

The nation's trade balance is the value of exports minus the value of imports:

Trade balance = exports – imports

For the country as a whole, exports result in an inflow of money and imports result in an outflow of money. When the difference is positive, the trade balance is in surplus; when the difference is negative, the trade balance is in deficit.

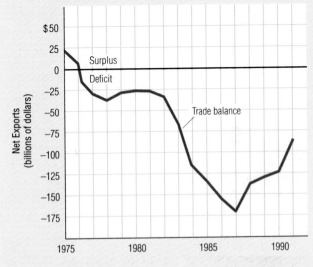

Source: U.S. Department of Commerce.

Which view is correct? Actually, both. But they involve complex implications that are best understood by examining the foundations on which the opinions rest.

The Trade Balance

To begin with, let's review the four categories of expenditures that make up the nation's gross domestic product. As you'll recall, GDP consists of the sum of consumption expenditures C, investment expenditures I, government expenditures G, and net exports of goods and services X_N:

$$GDP = C + I + G + X_N \qquad (1)$$

You can verify this formula by checking the data in the first four columns of the table on the inside front cover of the book.

Suppose we let X stand for total exports and M stand for total imports. Then net exports $X_N = X - M$. Therefore, equation (1) can be written:

$$GDP = C + I + G + (X - M) \qquad (2)$$

It helps to think of this equation as consisting of two parts. One part is $C + I + G$, which represents *gross domestic purchases* by the household, business, and government sectors. The other part is $X - M$, which represents the nation's *trade balance*. Thus, expressed in words, equation (2) says:

GDP = gross domestic purchases + trade balance (3)

By rearranging this equation, the *trade balance* can be stated in terms of the other two variables:

Trade balance = GDP – gross domestic purchases (4)

Changes in the trade balance are thus due to changes in either or both of the other two variables, GDP and gross domestic purchases.

In any given period, the trade balance (or net exports) can be positive, zero, or negative, depending on whether GDP is greater than, equal to, or less than gross domestic purchases.

Let's examine the main factors affecting the size of a nation's trade balance:

1. Real aggregate incomes at home and abroad

2. Relative price levels at home and abroad

3. Foreign exchange rates

4. Macroeconomic policies

Real Aggregate Income and the Trade Balance

As you've already seen in Exhibit 5, the trade balance worsened—became more negative—throughout most of the 1980s. Equation (4) can help you see how this happened. Although GDP increased during this period, gross domestic purchases by the household, business, and government sectors increased even more. As a result, the trade balance declined.

What were the reasons for these developments? The answer depends on the determinants of the nation's imports and exports. One of these determinants is the level of real GDP, that is, real aggregate income, at home and abroad. Imports and exports are related to real GDP in two ways:

1. **Imports Depend on Domestic Real GDP** When our na-

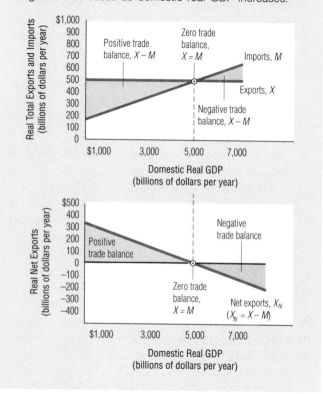

EXHIBIT 6

Net Exports Vary Inversely with Real GDP

In the upper graph, imports increase as domestic real GDP increases. Exports, however, are assumed to remain constant because they depend on other countries' GDPs.

In the lower diagram, the trade balance (net exports)—the difference between exports and imports in the upper diagram—decreases as domestic real GDP increases.

tion's real aggregate income rises, we tend to purchase more goods from other countries. Among the foreign goods we buy are cars, electronics products, clothing, steel, and trips abroad. The dollar volume of our imports thus increases.

2. **Exports Depend on Foreign Real GDP** When other nations' real aggregate incomes rise, they tend to purchase more goods from us. Among the goods we sell them are industrial chemicals, medical equipment, machinery, aircraft, and trips here. The dollar volume of our exports thus increases.

These relationships are illustrated by the graphs in Exhibit 6. In both graphs, domestic real GDP is measured on the horizontal axis. In the upper graph, real *total* exports and imports are measured on the vertical axis; in the lower graph, real *net* exports are measured on the vertical axis.

- In the upper graph, the dollar volume of imports is assumed to depend on domestic real GDP. Therefore, imports increase as domestic real GDP increases. The dollar volume of exports, however, is assumed to be independent of domestic real GDP because it's determined by the GDPs of the countries that buy our exports. Consequently, exports remain constant—in this case at an assumed $500 billion. Note that, at any given level of domestic real GDP, the difference between the export and import curves, $X - M$, is the trade balance (which equals net exports). It may be positive, zero, or negative.

- In the lower graph, net exports are related to domestic real GDP. The curve slopes downward because it reflects the difference between the export and import curves shown in the upper graph.

Relative Price Levels and the Trade Balance

Real aggregate incomes at home and abroad aren't the only conditions that affect net exports. Relative prices at home and abroad also play an important role. The reasons are easy to see in an example:

Suppose the average price level in the United States rises relative to that in Japan. Other things remaining the same, many American goods are now more costly for Japanese to buy. Therefore, *American exports to Japan decline.*

What about American imports from Japan? You can probably deduce the answer yourself. If American goods are relatively more expensive for the Japanese to buy, then Japanese goods are relatively cheaper for Americans to buy. Therefore, *American imports from Japan rise.*

Such changes, of course, directly affect America's net exports—the trade balance. And, as you've just learned, the trade balance is part of the nation's GDP.

Other things remaining the same:

- **Higher prices in the United States relative to those in Japan cause American exports to Japan to decrease and American imports from Japan to increase. Therefore, the U.S. trade balance with Japan worsens, and America's real GDP declines.**

- **Lower prices in the United States relative to those in Japan have the reverse effects. They cause**

American exports to increase and American imports to decrease. This improves the U.S. trade balance with Japan, and America's real GDP rises.

As you'll see, however, "other things" seldom remain the same. Changes in foreign exchange rates alter the results expected from higher or lower price levels in the United States.

Foreign Exchange Rates and the Trade Balance

American companies and individuals who do business with Japan, such as importers buying goods and tourists buying trips, own dollars and need to purchase Japanese yen. Similarly, Japanese companies and individuals doing business with America own yen and need to purchase U.S. dollars. To meet these needs there exists an international financial market called the *foreign exchange market,* in which nations' currencies are bought and sold. The currencies traded there, such as U.S. dollars, Japanese yen, British pounds, French francs, German marks, Canadian dollars, and Swiss francs, are called *foreign exchange.*

The foreign exchange market is a world market consisting of numerous buyers and sellers. Among them are large banks, currency dealers, and individuals. In this market, the price of any one currency in terms of another, such as the price of Japanese yen in terms of the U.S. dollar, is known as the *foreign exchange rate.* At any given time there exists a foreign exchange rate for each currency. The rates are determined by demand and supply. In other words, *foreign exchange rates fluctuate in response to buyers' and sellers' interactions in the foreign exchange market.*

Some of the implications of foreign-exchange-rate fluctuations can be seen in Exhibit 7. The left vertical axis measures the average value of the dollar relative to a group of major currencies. As you can see, the dollar's value peaked in 1985 and then headed downward. What about the trade balance, whose values are measured on the right vertical axis? For reasons explained next, the shape of the curve hasn't always conformed to expectations. This has raised problems of considerable practical concern among the nation's policymakers.

The J-Curve

As you saw in the example involving Japan, when the dollar *appreciates* relative to other currencies, two things are expected to happen:

Value of the Dollar and the Trade Deficit

The value of the dollar relative to other major currencies rose during the first half of the 1980s and then started declining. The trade balance, on the other hand, remained on a steady downward course before reversing direction after 1987.

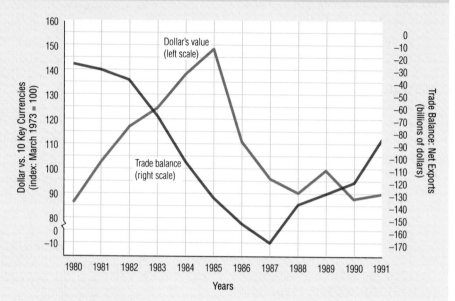

Source: U.S. Department of Commerce; Board of Governors of the Federal Reserve System.

1. American goods become more expensive for foreigners to buy. Therefore, American exports decrease.

2. Foreign goods become cheaper for Americans to buy. Therefore, American imports increase.

As a result of these developments, America's trade balance should worsen. This in fact is what occurred during the first half of the 1980s, as you can see in Exhibit 7.

After 1985, the dollar's value continued to decline. What happens when the dollar *depreciates* relative to other currencies?

1. American goods become cheaper for foreigners to buy. Therefore, American exports increase.

2. Foreign goods become more expensive for Americans to buy. Therefore, American imports decrease.

As a result of these developments, America's trade balance should have improved relatively quickly. This *did not* occur, as you can see by looking again at Exhibit 7. After the dollar peaked in 1985, the trade balance continued its downward course before reversing direction after 1987. If the trade balance had behaved as expected, the curve would have turned upward after 1985. The reason it didn't requires an explanation.

Experience shows that, in the short run, a nation's trade balance may at first vary *directly* rather than inversely with its foreign exchange rate. The reason isn't hard to see. Suppose the U.S. dollar depreciates against the currencies of America's major trading partners. Because people don't change their buying habits quickly, the quantity of goods imported and exported will remain about the same for a while. However, the depreciated dollar makes other currencies more expensive. Americans will therefore have to pay more dollars to purchase the same foreign goods as before. The dollar cost of imports will thus rise, causing America's trade balance to decline. After some months, however, buyers will adjust to the price changes. Imports will then decrease and, because the dollar is cheaper for foreigners to buy, exports will increase. As a result, the trade balance will rise.

A graphic illustration of this concept is presented in Figure (a) of Exhibit 8. Called a *J-curve,* it shows the "path" of a nation's trade balance following a depreciation of the currency. The descending portion of the curve depicts the worsening trade balance that occurs in the short run after the depreciation occurs. Evidence from various countries shows that this phase may last anywhere from 6 months to 30 months. When the short-run phase ends, the curve turns upward.

What happens if the dollar *appreciates* rather than depreciates? As you might guess, the effects on Amer-

EXHIBIT
8

The *J*-Curve

The *J*-curve depicts the short-run and long-run course of a nation's trade balance resulting from currency fluctuations in the foreign exchange market. The short-run phase occurs during the time lag (usually 6 to 30 months) before buyers adjust to changed prices. Until then, the trade balance moves in the opposite direction from its long-run path.

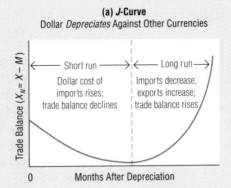

(a) J-Curve
Dollar *Depreciates* Against Other Currencies

Trade Balance ($X_N = X - M$)

←——— Short run ———→←——— Long run ———→

Dollar cost of imports rises; trade balance declines

Imports decrease, exports increase; trade balance rises

0   Months After Depreciation

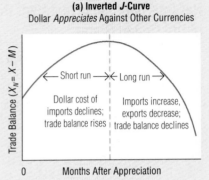

(a) Inverted J-Curve
Dollar *Appreciates* Against Other Currencies

Trade Balance ($X_N = X - M$)

←——— Short run ———→←— Long run —→

Dollar cost of imports declines; trade balance rises

Imports increase, exports decrease; trade balance declines

0   Months After Appreciation

ica's trade balance are the opposite. In the short run the quantities of imports and exports remain about the same, because buying habits change slowly. But because other currencies are now cheaper for Americans to buy, the dollar cost of imports declines and causes the trade balance to rise. After a while, however, American buyers adjust to the price changes and start importing more goods. The curve then enters its long-run phase in which imports increase and exports decrease, causing the trade balance to decline. The "path" of the trade balance can thus be depicted by an inverted *J*-curve—like the one in Figure (b) of Exhibit 8.

In reality, policymakers find it difficult to use the *J*-curve relationship for predicting short-run changes in trade balances. The reason is that a currency usually depreciates (or appreciates) gradually, and at different rates, against most other currencies. This gives rise to many small, often indistinguishable, *J*-curves (or inverted *J*-curves) instead of a single large one. Nevertheless, the *J*-curve concept helps explain why, in the short run, a nation's trade balance often responds slowly and unpredictably to changes in the international value of its currency.

Understanding International Indebtedness

As you've already learned, the United States has been undergoing dramatic changes in its economic relationships with the rest of the world. One of these changes, illustrated earlier in Exhibit 5, was the sharp increase in the nation's trade deficits that began in the early 1980s. Another change, which you will see in Exhibit 9, was the swift drop in America's international financial position from creditor to debtor that began in the late 1980s.

There is considerable misunderstanding about the meaning of international indebtedness. To help correct this, some clarifications are needed.

What Does It Mean to Be a Debtor Nation?

In today's global economy, numerous economic entities within a country own assets in other countries. For example, many American individuals and firms own land, buildings, companies, and securities in other nations. Likewise, many foreigners own similar assets in America. The value of foreign assets owned by Americans is called "U.S. assets abroad," and the value of American assets owned by foreigners is called "foreign assets in the U.S." The difference between them, reported annually by the U.S. Department of Commerce, is called "net international investment position of the United States." However, to help you remember the concept, a simpler and more descriptive name for it is *net foreign investment in the U.S.* Expressed as a formula:

Net foreign investment in the U.S. =
        U.S. assets abroad − foreign assets in the U.S.

As the formula indicates, in order to determine America's net foreign investment, the Department of Commerce includes in its calculations *all* American-owned assets abroad and *all* foreign-owned assets in the United States. Thus, investments in financial instruments such as stocks and bonds are just as important as investments in land and buildings.

EXHIBIT
9

Net International Investment Position of the United States

The value of U.S. assets abroad minus the value of foreign assets in the United States discloses what is formally known as the "net international investment position of the United States." This is simply the value of *net foreign investment in the U.S.* Thus:

Net foreign investment in the U.S. =
    U.S. assets abroad – foreign assets in the U.S.

If the equation for any given year results in a positive number, the United States is a net *creditor* nation. This means that its claims on foreigners are greater than foreign claims on the United States.

If the result is a negative number, the United States is a net *debtor* nation. That is, foreign claims on the United States are greater than U.S. claims on foreigners.

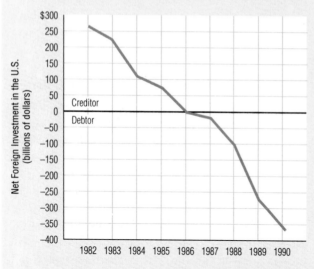

Source: U.S. Department of Commerce. Direct investment is valued at market, not at cost.

The formula thus provides an indication of the international financial position of the country. For example:

If net foreign investment in the U.S. is positive, the value of U.S. assets abroad exceeds the value of foreign assets in the U.S. This means that U.S. claims on foreigners are greater than foreign claims on the United States. Therefore, the United States is a net *creditor* nation.

If net foreign investment in the U.S. is negative, the reverse is true. The value of foreign assets in the United States exceeds the value of U.S. assets abroad. That is, foreign claims on the United States are greater than U.S. claims on foreigners. Therefore, the United States is a net *debtor* nation.

Contrary to popular belief, the United States has been a net debtor nation throughout most of its history. For example, it was a net debtor almost every year from the time of its founding under the Constitution (1789) until the end of World War I (1918). During that period, the nation financed the development of most of its steel manufacturing, railroads, and other major industries with funds obtained primarily from European investors. They were willing to acquire American assets because the United States provided political stability, long periods of steady economic growth, and high rates of return.

In 1919 the United States became a net creditor nation, and it retained that status until nearly 1987. Since then, as shown in Exhibit 9, the nation may have entered a new era in which periods of indebtedness will occur more frequently than in the past.

Changes in Debtor and Creditor Status

Why, as history shows, might the United States (or any other nation) be an international debtor in some years and an international creditor in other years? The answer is easy to see when you think in terms of the familiar trade-balance equation that you learned earlier in the chapter:

Trade balance = GDP – gross domestic purchases

Looking at the equation, suppose the United States imports more than it exports. This means that, in terms of the left side of the equation, the trade balance is negative. It also means that, in terms of the right side of the equation, the United States is spending more than its income because gross domestic purchases exceed GDP.

With the trade balance negative, America's receipts from abroad fall short of its payments to foreigners. America thus experiences an *international deficit*. To finance the deficit, the United States must borrow from other countries or sell assets to them. In either case, financial capital (money) equal to the deficit flows into the United States, causing its liabilities to foreigners to increase by the amount of the deficit. Because the United States is thus a net international borrower, it is a *debtor* nation.

The opposite conditions occur when the United States exports more than it imports. In terms of the above equation, the trade balance is positive. Therefore, GDP exceeds gross domestic purchases. America thus experiences an *international surplus*. This surplus, which is the nation's saving, is used to finance the international deficits of America's trading partners. Because the United States is thus a net international lender, it is a *creditor* nation.

Questions Concerning International Indebtedness

A nation's debt is the accumulation of its previous deficits. This is true whether the debt is domestic or foreign. Many nations have experienced periods of prolonged indebtedness. What are the economic consequences of a large foreign debt? Specifically:

1. Does international indebtedness worsen future living standards?

2. Does international indebtedness cause inflation?

These are the questions most frequently asked about foreign debt.

Does International Indebtedness Worsen Future Living Standards?

As you've learned, a nation experiencing an international deficit is a net international debtor. A debtor nation must use part of its future income to make interest and dividend payments to foreigners. Will this transfer of income reduce the debtor nation's future standard of living? The answer depends on whether the capital inflows (described above) to finance the deficit are used to pay for additional investment or additional consumption. To understand why, it helps to think in terms of production-possibilities curves as you study these two alternatives:

1. **Financing Investment** Suppose the capital inflows are used to pay for additional investment. This includes productive social investment in education, highways, bridges, airports, and other government projects that are likely to encourage further business spending on new plant and equipment. The increased investment will generate future increases in real GDP and employment. This is basically what happened to the United States during the nineteenth and early twentieth centuries. The country was a debtor nation during almost all of that period. However, America's gains in real GDP, financed in large part by borrowing from abroad, were more than enough to repay foreign creditors.

2. **Financing Consumption** Alternatively, suppose the capital inflows are used to pay for additional consumption. This includes government consumption such as payments for increased welfare benefits, national defense, or interest on the national debt. The additional consumption is likely to result in little if any gain in future income. Therefore, to maintain living standards, the debtor nation's domestic savings must rise. Moreover, they must rise sufficiently to finance not only interest and dividend payments to foreigners but new domestic investment as well. Otherwise, the debtor nation's future living standards will decline.

The future living standard of a nation is thus influenced by the burden of its current international indebtedness. How is that burden measured? In the same way as any other debt burden—by the ratio of the debt's size to the debtor's income. Thus, for a nation:

$$\text{Burden of international indebtedness} = \frac{\text{foreign debt}}{\text{GDP}}$$

Exhibit 10 shows a graph of this ratio over recent years in which the United States has been a debtor nation. In conjunction with the formula, the chart conveys some important ideas:

A rising ratio of foreign debt to GDP means that foreign debt is growing relative to GDP. The share of the nation's income accruing to foreigners is thus increasing, causing the burden of international indebtedness to expand. Conversely, a falling ratio of foreign debt to GDP means that foreign debt is declining relative to GDP. The share of the nation's income owed to foreigners is thus decreasing, causing the debt burden to contract.

Does International Indebtedness Cause Inflation?

History shows that many countries with large foreign debts have also experienced high rates of inflation. This coincidence has led some observers to infer that heavy international indebtedness is a cause of inflation. Neither economic theory nor empirical evidence supports this view. As you've already seen, when a nation's gross domestic purchases exceed GDP, the difference is financed by borrowing from other countries. But the borrowing can continue only as long as foreigners are willing to lend. When foreigners reduce their lending, many governments often respond by creating large amounts of new money to pay for the

EXHIBIT
10

America's Burden of International Indebtedness

The burden of any debt can be measured by the ratio of the debt's size to the debtor's income. For a nation, therefore, the burden of international indebtedness may be measured by the ratio of foreign debt to GDP. Foreign debt occurs when net foreign investment in the United States is a negative value. If the trend is rising, it means that the burden is expanding. That is, the country is paying an increasing share of income in the form of interest and dividends to foreigners. If the trend is declining, it means that the burden is contracting. That is, the share of income paid to foreigners is decreasing.

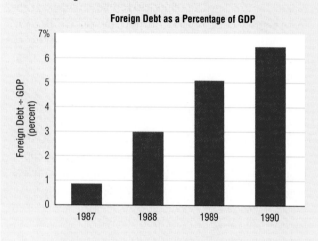

Foreign Debt as a Percentage of GDP

additional spending. This produces high rates of inflation—a condition that would not occur if money growth were restrained.

Illustrations abound in some Latin American countries. Argentina, Bolivia, Brazil, and Peru, among others, have historically been high-debt countries. They have also been high-inflation countries, with prices often rising by several *thousand* percent a year. This is because their governments rarely hesitate to pay for increased spending by simply printing money.

In contrast, some Asian countries, notably Singapore, South Korea, Taiwan, and Thailand have, at various times, also been high-debt countries relative to their GDPs. However, their annual inflation rates in these periods have been relatively moderate—frequently less than 5 percent. The reason is that their governments have resisted the temptation of "easy" fi-

nancing by keeping tight control over the rate of money growth.

These experiences of debtor countries emphasize the importance of maintaining tight monetary policies, especially in the face of mounting foreign indebtedness.

There is little or no connection between a country's rate of inflation and the size of its foreign debt. Debtor countries that experience high rates of inflation do so because of their monetary policies, not because of their levels of international indebtedness.

Conclusion: Policy Options for Reducing Trade Deficits and Foreign Debt

Most people think that trade deficits and international indebtedness are "bad," and should therefore be avoided. In reality, the problem isn't that simple. As we've seen, there are ways in which nations can utilize foreign deficits and debt to increase real GDP. Assuming, however, that this is not what is being done, what macroeconomic policies can countries adopt to reduce foreign deficits and debt? The measures employed are the two policy tools of macroeconomics—fiscal policy and monetary policy.

Tight Fiscal Policy

Look again at the trade-balance equation: $X_N = GDP - (C + I + G)$. Note that a nation will experience a trade deficit if gross domestic purchases (equal to $C + I + G$) exceed GDP. For example, the United States experienced trade deficits in the 1980s because lower tax rates encouraged higher C and I, while G also increased.

In the language of economics, lower taxes and rising government spending are known as an "easy" fiscal policy. One way of shrinking the trade deficit would therefore be to impose a "tight" fiscal policy. This could be done by raising taxes on households and businesses, thereby reducing $C + I$ in the trade balance equation. Increases in G could also be slowed down, perhaps by eliminating some defense spending, curbing the expansion of social security and other entitlement programs, and improving efficiency in government.

Such a fiscal policy would reduce gross domestic purchases and should thus help to improve the trade balance. But from a business-cycle standpoint, the changes could also prove to be contractionary if they decrease aggregate demand and induce a recession. Because of this, the option of reducing the trade deficit through a tight fiscal policy has usually been met with considerable resistance by policymakers.

Easy Monetary Policy

A second way to improve the trade balance is for the Fed to pursue more rapid money growth. This is called an "easy" monetary policy. (In contrast, adherence to a slow rate of money growth is called a "tight" monetary policy.) With an increase in the money growth rate, interest rates are likely to decline—at least temporarily. Lower interest rates would reduce foreign demand for the U.S. dollar, causing its price in terms of other currencies to *depreciate* in the foreign exchange market. American goods would thus become cheaper for foreigners to purchase, so U.S. exports would increase. Foreign goods would become more expensive for Americans to purchase, so U.S. imports would decrease. America's trade balance would therefore improve.

But this result may be only temporary. In the long run, an easy monetary policy creates inflationary pressures if it results in too much money chasing too few goods. Inflationary expectations and interest rates thus rise—in line with the familiar *Fisher effect.** As a result, imports would increase and exports would decrease. Hence, the trade balance would worsen.

Easy Foreign Fiscal-Monetary Policies

A third way for a country to reduce a negative trade balance is for its major trading partners to stimulate their own economies. The resulting increase in the trading partners' demand for the exports of the deficit country would increase, thus helping to close the deficit.

For example, America's major trading partners include Japan and Germany. These countries often have large trade surpluses with the United States. By pursuing easy fiscal and monetary policies, these nations could raise their real outputs, employment levels, and interest rates. The effects on the U.S. trade deficit are easy to see:

---

* This concept was explained in some detail in Chapter 12. For a brief review, look up its meaning in the Dictionary at the back of the book.

First, the Japanese yen and the German mark become more attractive to investors. These currencies therefore *appreciate* in terms of the dollar in the foreign exchange market. Consequently, the dollar *depreciates* in terms of the yen and the mark.

Second, because the yen and the mark are now more expensive in terms of the dollar, Japan and Germany's trade surpluses decline. And because the dollar is now cheaper in terms of the mark and the yen, America's trade deficit also declines.

Unfortunately, these benefits entail a cost. Easy macroeconomic policies are likely to create inflationary pressures in the countries employing them. Therefore, the major industrial nations have resisted adopting easy policies simply to reduce a trade deficit for America (or any other country). They have recognized instead that, in a world whose economies are interdependent, there is a need for policy coordination.

To coordinate economic policies, high-level representatives from the United States, Britain, Canada, France, Germany, Italy, and Japan—known as the Group of Seven (G-7)—meet periodically to propose guidelines for international cooperation. Unfortunately, most of the results of the meetings are kept secret, so it's impossible to assess the effects of G-7's efforts. However, many experts believe that, because each country is more concerned with its own interests than with the common good, G-7 has made only modest progress in achieving the compromises needed to coordinate economic policies.

Summary of Important Ideas

1. Government spending and taxing determine whether the federal government shows a budget deficit, a balanced budget, or a budget surplus. A budget deficit can be eliminated by reducing spending, or by increasing taxes, or by doing some of both. Conversely, a budget surplus can be eliminated by doing the opposite.

2. The full-employment (or structural) budget is an estimate of annual government expenditures and revenues that would occur at the level of potential real GDP—that is, at full employment. This budget thus eliminates changes in government expenditures and revenues that are due to cyclical forces. Because of this, economists use the full-employment budget to determine whether a particular fiscal-policy stance is expansionary or contractionary. However, the budget is criticized for relying on the assumed rate of natural unemployment.

3. There are two competing beliefs concerning the consequences of budget deficits:

a. The traditional view holds that the effects of budget deficits are *expansionary* because they result in a rightward shift of the economy's aggregate demand curve. This increase in demand raises the proportion of GDP spent on consumption (including imports) and reduces the proportion saved. It also encourages borrowing from abroad to help finance the deficit, and it encourages the creation of a trade deficit in the nation's international transactions.

b. The modern classical view holds that the effects of budget deficits are *neutral* because they have no influence on the economy's aggregate demand curve. Therefore, they don't affect consumption, interest rates, GDP, employment, investment, or inflation. This is because the public is indifferent between financing budget deficits in the present with current taxes or financing them later with future taxes. As a result, the public responds rationally to changes in the national debt by offsetting them with changes in savings.

The evidence on this issue is mixed. The debate over the consequences of budget deficits continues.

4. Traditionalists' criticisms of large budget deficits (those in excess of about 1 percent of GDP) are many. Among the chief ones are these: They curtail private-sector investment. By helping to keep the dollar strong, they encourage a trade deficit. By helping to keep interest rates high, they lead to unemployment and decreased GDP. They encourage monetary stimulation. And they discourage productive social investment.

Modern classical economists, believing that debt is neutral, contend that deficits have no long-run effect. What is important, they say, is the amount of government expenditures as a percentage of GDP, because that determines the relative size of government in the economy.

5. The national debt, also called the public debt and the government debt, is the accumulation of past deficits. Because of its large size, the debt has been criticized as (a) a burden on future generations and (b) a cause of inflation.

a. To analyze the benefits and costs of an increase in debt on present and future generations, we must know two things. One is the use to which the money is put. The other is the stage of the business cycle—such as recession or full employment—in which the increased debt is incurred.

b. To determine whether an increase in debt causes inflation, we must know whether the increase is monetized by the Fed. Inflationary pressures may result to the extent that monetization occurs.

6. A nation experiences a trade deficit when its gross domestic purchases, consisting of $C + I + G$, exceed GDP. The difference, which represents net exports, varies inversely with real GDP. That is, as real GDP rises, the nation's trade balance declines, and ultimately changes from positive to negative. The trade balance is also affected by fluctuations of the nation's currency in the foreign exchange market. The *J*-curve (and the inverted *J*-curve) depict the course of a nation's trade balance that results from these fluctuations.

7. A creditor nation is one whose claims on foreigners are greater than their claims on it. The net foreign investment of such a nation is positive. The reverse is true of a debtor nation. Foreigners' claims against it exceed the debtor nation's claims on them. The debtor nation's net foreign investment is therefore negative.

The burden of a nation's international indebtedness varies directly with the ratio of its foreign debt to GDP. There is no significant relationship between a country's rate of inflation and the size of its foreign debt. A country's rate of inflation is normally the result of its monetary policies, not the size of its foreign debt.

8. In order to reduce a trade deficit, methods are needed to minimize the difference between GDP and gross domestic purchases. Approaches to accomplish this include: (a) tighter fiscal policy in the form of increased taxes, (b) easier monetary policy that reduces interest rates, and (c) easier foreign fiscal and monetary policies that boost incomes and lower interest rates among the major industrial nations.

9. Each method of reducing a trade deficit has favorable and unfavorable consequences. These can have impacts not only domestically but internationally. As a result, and because of the increasing economic interdependency of nations, there is a continuing desire among major countries to develop means of coordinating economic policies.

Terms and Concepts to Review

Gramm-Rudman-Hollings Act

full-employment (structural) budget

crowding out

debt-neutrality proposition

transfer payments

foreign exchange market

foreign exchange

J-curve

infrastructure

Fisher effect

Questions and Problems

1. Why do many legislators advocate the use of the full-employment budget rather than the actual budget as a guide for fiscal policy? What risk is involved in using this concept?

2. Suppose the economy is in a recession. If the government reduces tax rates and the aggregate demand curve shifts to the right, how will the *relative steepness* of the aggregate supply curve affect the resulting changes in output, employment, and the price level? Illustrate your answer with diagrams. *Suggestion:* For simplicity, assume that the aggregate supply curve is a straight line.

3. From a "traditionalist" point of view, why might an increase in the government's budget deficit help create a deficit in the nation's trade balance?

4. From a "traditionalist" point of view, is crowding out more likely to occur in a closed economy or in an open economy? *Hint:* In which type of economy are interest rates likely to rise more sharply as a result of an increase in the budget deficit?

5. Many economists and policymakers do not accept the debt-neutrality proposition. This would be true even if there were substantial evidence to support it. Can you suggest why?

6. "Some increases in government expenditures, such as those for health, education, and welfare, are infla-

tionary, whereas other government expenditures, such as those incurred for national defense and public works, are not." Do you agree? What central questions must be considered to determine whether some government expenditures are more inflationary than others?

7. Evaluate the following argument about the public debt: "No individual or family would be wise to continue accumulating indebtedness indefinitely, for eventually all debts must either be paid or repudiated. It follows that this fundamental principle applies equally well to nations. As Adam Smith himself said, 'What is prudence in the conduct of every private family can scarce be folly in that of a great kingdom.'"

8. "A federal deficit crowds out private investment." Is this statement likely to be true during a deep recession? During a period of full employment?

9. "The size of the *externally held* national debt as a percentage of GDP is a more meaningful statistic than the size of the *domestically held* national debt as a percentage of GDP. The same is true of interest payments on the national debt." Do you agree?

10. If the economies of America's major trading partners grow faster than the U.S. economy, how will this affect America's trade balance?

11. Suppose that, on the foreign exchange market, the U.S. dollar *depreciates* 10 percent relative to the currencies of America's major trading partners. Thinking in terms of the *J*-curve, what's likely to happen to America's trade balance in the long run if: (a) the U.S. price level remains constant? (b) the U.S. price level rises more than 10 percent? (c) the U.S. price level rises less than 10 percent?

12. During the nineteenth century, the United States borrowed heavily from abroad. By the early twentieth century, the United States was the richest country in the world. How can a nation become rich by borrowing from other countries?

13. Can a nation have negative trade balances without incurring international debt?

14. How might a tight monetary policy affect the nation's trade balance? Would the effect on the domestic economy be expansionary or contractionary?

T A K E   A   S T A N D

The Trade Deficit: Is It the Result of the Budget Deficit?

The 1980s was a remarkable decade for the U.S. economy. The recession of 1982 was the most severe economic downturn since the Great Depression. But over most of the rest of the decade, the economy recovered slowly and steadily, and enjoyed the longest uninterrupted peacetime expansion ever recorded. Meanwhile, inflation fell from over 10 percent at the start of the decade to about 4 percent by 1990.

One of the most notable features of the U.S. economy in the 1980s was the parallel growth of the budget and trade deficits. Both accounts had been in approximate balance since the end of World War II. In the early to mid-1980s, however, the federal government began to run substantial budget deficits. Since 1983, the federal deficit has exceeded $150 billion per year, and is currently over twice that. About the same time that the federal budget went into such substantial deficit, the trade account also ran a deficit of about the same magnitude. The similar behavior of the two accounts led some to refer to them as "twin deficits," and to speculate that one may cause the other.

More recently, however, the federal deficit has continued to rise, while the trade deficit has improved. At the end of the 1980s and the start of the 1990s, the budget deficit was about 4 percent of GDP while the trade deficit had fallen to less than 1 percent of GDP. The current dissimilarity in the behavior of the two accounts has led some to question the relationship between them. *Is the trade deficit caused by the budget deficit?*

Yes: We Lived Beyond Our Means

When the U.S. economy buys more than it produces, the additional goods must come from other countries. Such was the situation during the 1980s. The government increased its own spending, and encouraged consumption spending by decreasing income taxes. Thus, the conditions that caused the budget deficit also raised demand above domestic production. Foreign producers met this demand, and the U.S. trade account ran a deficit.

The economic links between the two deficits are subtle. Increases in the budget deficit increase the demand for domestic funds and so tend to push up the interest rate. Higher U.S. interest rates make U.S. financial assets more attractive to investors in other countries. In order to purchase U.S. assets, these investors need U.S. dollars, so the demand for the dollar increases. An increase in demand for dollars causes the exchange rate to rise. This appreciation of the exchange rate means that U.S. goods and services are more expensive for foreigners, while foreign goods and services are now cheaper for U.S. consumers. Hence U.S. exports fall and imports rise; that is, the trade deficit increases.

What about the more recent divergence in the behavior of the two deficits? Other things equal, increases in the budget deficit do increase the trade deficit. Other events, however, can also cause the trade balance to change. For example, recent capitalist reforms in Eastern Europe may have opened up promising investment opportunities. With fewer investors competing for U.S. assets, the exchange rate for dollars falls, foreign goods cost more dollars, and the balance of trade improves.

And if investors expect that the dollar is going to depreciate against foreign currencies, U.S. assets again become less attractive and purchases of foreign goods decline.

No: It Was Coincidence, Not Cause

The similar behavior of the two deficits is coincidental. According to the debt-neutrality proposition, budget deficits caused by tax reductions do not expand the economy because they do not spur an increase in aggregate demand. Rather, such deficits encourage household saving. Why? A balanced budget means that current government expenditures are paid with current taxes. A budget deficit means that some current government expenditures are paid with borrowed funds. Rational taxpayers recognize that these borrowed funds will eventually have to be repaid, with interest, from future taxes. Therefore, rather than increase their spending in response to a tax cut, individuals will increase their saving in order to be prepared for the tax increase when it comes.

If the debt-neutrality proposition holds, the suggested link between the two deficits breaks down right at the start: A rise in the deficit should not raise the interest rate. Instead, the increased demand for funds by the government should be offset by an increased supply of funds by individuals, and the interest rate should remain the same.

Remember, however, that the debt-neutrality proposition applies only when an increase in the budget deficit is due to a reduction in taxes. When the deficit rises as a result of increased government spending, there may be an associated rise in interest rates.

Supporters of the debt-neutrality proposition believe that the trade deficit of the mid-1980s was actually the result of a healthy, productive economy. Productivity increased because of deregulation, tax cuts, and other policies conducive to business activity. Higher interest rates were caused by greater productivity, not by the budget deficit. The favorable rates attracted foreign funds, caused the dollar to appreciate, and led to the trade deficit.

The Question: Is the Trade Deficit Caused by the Budget Deficit?

■   The budget deficits in the 1980s arose as a result of increased government spending and decreased tax revenues. Higher government spending, and higher consumer spending fueled by the tax cuts, caused domestic demand to exceed domestic production. Imports increased, and so did the U.S. trade deficit.

■   The debt neutrality proposition holds that tax cuts do not affect domestic spending because they are offset by an increase in household saving. Since they do not affect domestic spending, they do not alter the trade deficit. The resemblance between the two deficits is coincidental.

Where Do You Stand?

1. Commentators often blame the trade deficit on the trade practices of other countries, particularly Japan. This means that foreigners' trade practices must be causing us to consume in excess of our production. Do you think the argument makes sense? What economic adjustment mechanisms might it be ignoring?

2. Why might a budget deficit not be bad? Why might a trade deficit not be bad?

3. Why might the debt-neutrality proposition break down?

4. Is the trade deficit the result of the budget deficit? Justify your stand.

Source: John P. Judd, "Deficits: Twins or Distant Cousins," *Weekly Letter,* Federal Reserve Bank of San Francisco, October 6, 1989.

Chapter 20

International Macroeconomics: Recent Developments in the Global Economy

Economic Integration

The United States of Europe?

International Banking and Financial Markets

Today's International Macroeconomic Policy Issues

Learning Guide

Watch for answers to these important questions

What is economic integration? Why does it occur? What forms or stages may it take?

What are the obstacles to economic integration experienced by the European Community? What effects will the integration have? Are major trading blocs emerging in the global economy?

How are international financial markets and institutions affected by economic integration? Who are the chief participants in international financial markets?

Why does economic integration create macroeconomic policy issues? How do these issues relate to international trade and to international finance? What are America's foreign economic policy objectives?

One of the most remarkable developments in recent decades has been the extraordinary growth of world trade among industrial countries. America's experience serves as a fairly typical example of the pattern of growth that has occurred. Between 1950 and 1970, the annual sum of U.S. exports and imports averaged about 7 percent of GDP. By 1980, the figure had soared to 17 percent. Since then it has been rising at a more modest rate, but some experts predict that it will average between 25 percent and 30 percent after the year 2000.

Of course, the sum of exports and imports—the volume of trade—as a percentage of GDP differs among countries. However, all industrial nations have experienced rapidly rising percentages since 1970. As with the United States, the sum of exports and imports among the industrial nations more than doubled during the 1980s.

The rising international flow of goods and services means that countries are becoming more economically interdependent. Consequently, policy changes that affect conditions in one nation or region of the world can have substantial repercussions on other countries and regions. Understanding some of the major developments in today's global economy will show us how government policies at home and abroad can influence inflation, interest rates, and economic growth in much of the world.

Economic Integration

In our own and most other advanced economies, international trade is almost entirely a private-sector activity. That is, importing and exporting are conducted by companies in response to consumer preferences. This doesn't mean that governments maintain a hands-off policy toward international trade. On the contrary, they have often sought to protect domestic industry by passing legislation designed to discourage trade in some products and to encourage it in others.

Trade Protection

Governments often restrict imports of certain goods in order to protect a domestic industry from foreign competition. Thus, nations with an agricultural industry usually impose restrictions on the importation of foods and fibers that compete with products grown by domestic producers. For example, Asian countries limit the importation of rice, and Japan and the United States limit the importation of beef. Similarly, every country that has an automobile manufacturing industry has at one time or another established restrictions on the importation of cars. All such restrictions have the same purpose—to provide *trade protection* to domestic producers.

Trade protection takes two major forms. One type consists of tariffs; the other includes a variety of nontariff barriers. Each type warrants a separate explanation.

Tariff and Nontariff Barriers

Tariffs are customs duties or taxes imposed by a government on the importation of a good. A tax of $100 on the price of each imported computer would be an illustration of a tariff. So too would a tax of 10 percent on the price of each imported car. The tax is imposed on the importer and is normally passed on to the consumer.

Nontariff barriers are laws or regulations, other than tariffs, used by nations to restrict imports. The most familiar type of nontariff barrier is an **import quota**. Frequently referred to simply as a "quota," it's a law that limits the number of units of a good that may be imported during a given period. An example would be a quota on the number of foreign-made tractors that can be brought into the United States each year.

Other types of nontariff barriers are equally direct but usually more subtle methods of restricting imports. For instance, in order to "protect" the health and safety of their citizens, many countries establish much higher standards of quality for various kinds of imported goods—both food and manufactured products—than for similar goods produced domestically. In addition, governments often subsidize inefficient domestic industries in order to strengthen their competitive positions in world markets and to promote exports. Normally, because most nontariff trade barriers are disguised as health and safety regulations, they provoke little political reaction. Therefore, they have become major forms of trade protection used by all countries.

Since the mid-twentieth century, tariffs have declined and nontariff barriers have gained in relative importance among advanced countries. In developing countries, both tariff barriers and, to a greater extent, nontariff barriers, have risen and remain relatively high. On the whole, therefore, nontariff barriers are today the main impediments to world trade.

Adverse Consequences of Trade Protection

If some domestic industries benefit from trade protection, should import restrictions be imposed? Economists since the time of Adam Smith have been virtually unanimous in their opposition to all forms of protection—for a number of reasons:

1. **It Raises Prices to Consumers** Trade protection enables sheltered firms to become less efficient. Prices rise and quality often suffers because protected firms have less to fear from foreign competition.

2. **It Reduces Consumer Choice** Trade protection narrows the selection of goods available to consumers. They are denied the opportunity to become familiar with alternative goods and to buy what they believe is the best product for their money.

3. **It Decreases Exports** Trade protection makes it harder for foreigners to export their goods, and thus reduces their income. Their ability to import goods is therefore also reduced, and this decreases exports from other countries including the protected country.

These are only a few of the chief criticisms of trade protection. For the most part, such criticisms arise for the same reason:

Protectionist policies of all kinds lead to a misallocation of scarce resources. Political leaders everywhere recognize that removing restrictive practices would increase the volume of trade and raise real incomes worldwide. Nevertheless, some industries and labor groups promote the belief that they are made worse off by free trade. Legislators often succumb to the pressures these groups exert on them for protection.

Trade Liberalization and Regional Integration

If a foreign country can supply us with a commodity cheaper than we ourselves can make it, better buy it of them with some of our own industry, employed in a way in which we have some advantage.

—Adam Smith

Since the late eighteenth century economists have argued that *free trade*—the absence of trade restrictions—leads to the lowest prices and the greatest variety of goods for all. The reason isn't hard to see. Free trade promotes competition because it forces domestic firms to perform at least as well as their foreign rivals. As a result, free trade encourages the most efficient allocation of world resources and the highest rate of economic growth.

By the mid-twentieth century, several decades of high tariffs led many of the world's political leaders to conclude that a new multilateral trading system was needed. The new system would provide for liberalization and economic integration of world trade. Toward this end, several dozen nations adopted specific measures designed to strengthen world commerce.

General Agreement on Tariffs and Trade

The first major step toward liberalization of world trade was the *General Agreement on Tariffs and Trade (GATT)*. This is an international agreement signed in 1947 by twenty-three countries, including the United States. GATT is dedicated to four goals:

1. Nondiscrimination in trade through adherence to unconditional equal treatment for all trading partners
2. Reduction of tariffs by negotiation
3. Elimination of import quotas (with some exceptions permitted)
4. Resolution of differences through consultation

The first goal, nondiscrimination in trade, is embodied in a trade treaty containing a special provision called a *most-favored-nation clause.* This clause requires each signatory country to extend to the others the same low tariff and special trade concessions that it gives to any preferred country. That is, each country treats all signatory countries the same as its "most favored nation." Since the formation of GATT, the number of participating nations has increased to approximately 100. On the whole, GATT has experienced many more successes than failures in reducing trade barriers. As a result, it has been a substantial force for the liberalization of world trade.

Steps Toward Regional Integration

Although worldwide free trade is much desired for economic reasons, political obstacles prevent it from becoming a reality. Nevertheless, regional free-trade agreements among two or more nations are becoming increasingly common. Such agreements promote economic efficiency among participants by enabling them to attain a fuller or more integrated use of resources.

Regional free-trade agreements can thus be viewed as steps toward regional integration. The steps can take four major forms: free-trade areas, customs unions, common markets, and economic unions. Before examining their meanings, notice how they are summarized in Exhibit 1.

1. A *free-trade area* is an association of trading nations that agree to impose no restrictive devices, such as tariffs or quotas, on one another. However, each country is free to impose whatever restrictions it wishes on nonparticipants. The first major example was the European Free Trade Association (EFTA), established in 1960. Its membership, which has varied over the years, has included most of Scandinavia and a few other countries. A more recent example is the U.S.-Canadian Free Trade Agreement signed in 1988. The agreement is being phased in over a 10-year period, with Mexico joining as a third participant in 1993.

2. A *customs union* is an agreement among trading nations to comply with two conditions:

   a. Impose no trade restrictions on one another

   b. Adhere to common external trade barriers against other nations.

The most familiar example of a customs union is Benelux, whose members are Belgium, the Netherlands, and Luxembourg. Similar plans have been adopted in some other geographic areas.

EXHIBIT
1

Four Levels of Economic Integration

Type of economic integration	Eliminate tariffs and quotas among members	Establish a common tariff and quota system	Eliminate restrictions on factor movements	Establish a unified monetary and fiscal system
1. Free-trade area	Yes	No	No	No
2. Customs union	Yes	Yes	No	No
3. Common market	Yes	Yes	Yes	No
4. Economic union	Yes	Yes	Yes	Yes

Source: Adapted from Franklin R. Root, *International Trade and Investment,* 6th ed., Southwestern Publishing Co., 1990, p. 254.

3. A *common market* is an association of trading nations that agree to three conditions:

a. Impose no trade restrictions on one another

b. Adhere to common external trade barriers against other nations

c. Impose no national restrictions on the movement of labor and capital among members

A major example of a common market is the European Community (EC). Established by six countries in 1958, its membership, as shown in Exhibit 2, has grown considerably since then. Because of various administrative and policy differences, the EC is not actually a "pure" common market. Nevertheless, its members are working at achieving that goal.

4. An *economic union* is a fully integrated association of trading nations that agree to four conditions:

a. Impose no trade restrictions on one another

b. Adhere to common external trade barriers against other nations

c. Impose no national restrictions on the movement of labor and capital among members

d. Adopt a single monetary system and central bank, create a unified fiscal system with respect to tax coverage and rates, and adhere to a mutually established foreign economic policy

As you can see, the first three conditions, which are the same as those for a common market, permit the free flow of goods, services, and resources between member countries. The fourth condition goes a giant step further by requiring participants to transfer some economic independence to specially created higher authorities. Because this means that members must surrender some sovereignty, there is considerable doubt that any group of major nations will ever establish a "pure" economic union.

A free-trade area, a customs union, a common market, and an economic union (in that order) represent increasing degrees of economic integration. What can be said about its effects?

On the favorable side:

- It encourages a more efficient allocation of member nations' resources.

- It expands the size of the market for member nations. Their industries thus gain the economies (lower unit costs) of large-scale production.

On the unfavorable side:

- Economic integration places a trade barrier—typically a tariff wall—between the member countries as a whole and all nonmember nations. The result is a restriction of trade by members against nonmembers, causing an economic loss for both groups.

EXHIBIT
2

Europe's New Math: EC + EFTA = EEA

European countries are moving increasingly toward economic integration. Two groups of trading nations—the European Community (EC) and the European Free Trade Association (EFTA)—have been dominant. In the early 1990s, both groups announced their intention to merge and form a new organization called the European Economic Area (EEA).

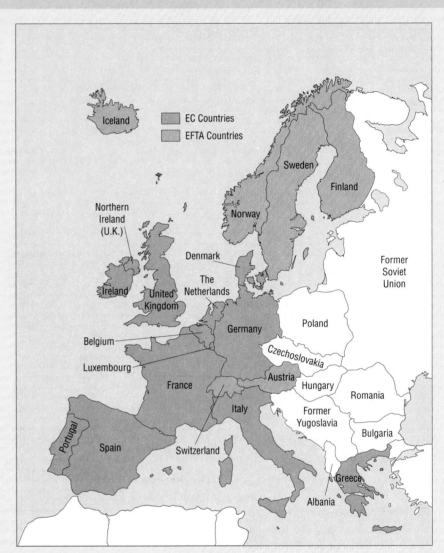

The United States of Europe?

Efforts by major European countries to achieve economic integration were begun in the early 1950s. The efforts were often impeded by political changes and business recessions. Nevertheless, many tariff and quota restrictions were gradually removed. Lifting these restrictions helped to improve the efficiency of European markets and raise the potential for economic growth.

In 1985, Europe's political leaders reconfirmed their belief in economic integration by adopting the Single European Act. Frequently referred to as "Europe 1992," the agreement was designed to establish a complete or pure *common market* by 1992. This was to be accomplished by eliminating all restrictions on the movement of goods, services, capital, and people between member countries. At a later date, *economic union* would be achieved through the creation of a common monetary and fiscal system.

Obstacles to Integration

Despite progress toward integration of the EC, many barriers to trade still exist. The timetable for achieving integration could be extended for years because member nations continue to operate with their own laws and regulations.

Diverse National Standards

In many EC countries, international trade is hampered by the existence of numerous product-safety standards and environmental regulations. Britain, France, and Germany, for example, each have over 10,000 product-safety standards. Sweeping many of them away and replacing them with a single set of "Euronorms," as they are called, is an enormous and evolving task. There are many products for which national standards are so diverse that no solution short of "mutual recognition" is possible. According to this concept, countries accept one another's standards as long as they meet certain minimum requirements of health and safety. Although this approach is gaining increasing use, the process of approving products for mutual recognition has often been agonizingly slow.

Differences in Legal Systems

The member countries of the EC are sovereign nations with their own laws. Many of these laws have served as impediments to trade within the Community. Unlike the United States whose fifty states comprise an economic union, the EC has no uniform code governing transactions in goods, financial instruments, and other assets. The creation of EC-wide corporations, multinational businesses, and international joint ventures is thus much more complicated than if the EC were fully integrated. Further complications arise because property rights in the form of patents and trademarks are issued by each nation rather than by a central EC agency. On the whole, much progress has been achieved in reducing some of these obstacles. However, very little headway has been made in lessening others.

Restrictions on Factor Mobility

With certain exceptions, individuals are free to move between member countries for work. But the exceptions are important. In a number of vocations, some nations have refused to grant mutual recognition to licensed practitioners—among them electricians, plumbers, engineers, doctors, and lawyers. Countries have also maintained selective barriers to capital mobility—the movement of financial assets across national boundaries. This has impeded the integration of financial markets, thereby limiting the efficient channeling of savings into new investment. But these practices may be changing. All member nations are aware of the advantages of permitting factor mobility. Reports from Europe suggest that any remaining barriers to human and capital movements will be eliminated by the end of this decade.

Government Subsidies

A single European market requires that all companies operate in response to competitive market forces *without government aid*. This means that governments must privatize companies they own and refrain from granting special subsidies to selected private firms. Direct subsidies, which are simply cash payments, have long been common. Because of their visibility, however, many governments have replaced them with indirect subsidies such as tax exemptions, low-interest loans, faster debt write-offs, and other subtle means of government assistance. EC countries have generally been reducing these anticompetitive practices. But Italy, Germany, and France, which are the most heavily involved in government ownership and subsidization, have been slow to give up their interventionist policies.

Government Procurement Policies

On the whole, the EC's private sector is becoming more competitive. Meanwhile, the public sector is lagging far behind. For example, because of efforts to support inefficient domestic firms, relatively few government contracts are awarded to lower-cost foreign producers. This has resulted in misallocations of resources. Steps are therefore being taken to open government procurement policies to nondiscriminatory competitive bidding. But because of the politics involved, unrestricted open-market bidding may never become a reality.

Summarizing:

Europe is moving toward economic integration. Currently five major obstacles stand in the way. They are: (1) diverse national standards, (2) differences in legal systems, (3) restrictions on factor mobility, (4) government subsidies, and (5) government procurement policies. Because these obstacles are being gradually reduced, it is impossible to predict when complete economic integration will actually occur.

Analyzing the Effects of Integration

The movement toward European economic integration is continuing. When it is completed, members of the EC will enjoy significant benefits:

1. Firms in the EC will be allowed to ship goods anywhere in the Community without facing numerous nontariff barriers in the form of safety and environmental standards.

2. EC laws will be standardized in many industries. Firms will be able to invest and expand in other member countries and gain access to their markets and resources.

3. EC citizens, from unskilled workers to those in licensed trades and professions, will be able to work and practice in any member country.

4. Government-owned firms within the EC will be privatized, and subsidies designed to protect firms from foreign competition will be eliminated.

5. Procurement procedures by member governments will allow competitive bidding by all EC firms.

Economic integration will thus promote efficiency within the EC by helping to allocate scarce resources to their highest valued uses. How will these developments affect world trade and global economic welfare? The answer requires a distinction between two concepts—trade creation and trade diversion.

Trade Creation Integration will encourage greater competition, increased investment, higher employment, and lower prices. The resulting increase in trade among member countries is known as *trade creation*. If the EC doesn't raise trade barriers against other countries, the gains in real output from increased trade will cause global economic welfare to rise.

Trade Diversion What will happen if the EC, acting as a trading bloc, does impose trade barriers against nonmember countries? Trade between the bloc and the nonmember nations that are the most efficient producers will decline. To help make up for this decline, trade will increase among some member nations that are less efficient producers. The shift of trade from efficiently producing nonmember nations to less efficiently producing member nations is known as *trade diver-*

sion. If the losses in real output from decreased trade with the rest of the world exceed the gains in real output from increased trade within the EC, global economic welfare will decline.

Graphic Analysis

Economic integration of countries within a region thus affects the region's aggregate output. You can see this in terms of the familiar aggregate demand/aggregate supply model in Exhibit 3. As always, real output is measured on the horizontal axis and the average

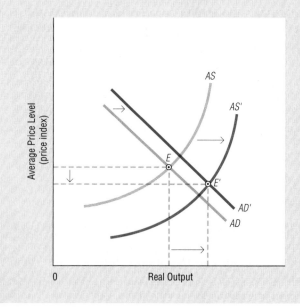

EXHIBIT 3

Effects of Integration on Output and the Price Level

Before integration, the region's equilibrium output and price level are determined by the intersection of *AD* and *AS* at *E*. When integration begins, removal of trade barriers has favorable effects on the region. Investment and productivity increase and cause the *AS* curve to shift rightward to *AS'*. Real income and markets expand and cause the *AD* curve to shift rightward to *AD'*. At the new equilibrium point *E'*, output is larger and the price level is (likely to be) lower than before integration began.

price level is measured on the vertical axis. Before integration, the region's *AD* and *AS* curves intersect at the equilibrium point *E*. After integration begins, trade barriers among member countries are reduced. This economic stimulation exerts both supply-side and demand-side effects:

1. On the supply side, because materials and other production costs decline, profits rise. More funds thus become available for firms to spend on improving productivity and efficiency. As a result, the aggregate supply curve shifts rightward to *AS'*.

2. On the demand side, as firms reach beyond national borders, markets expand and become more competitive. The average price level declines and real income rises. The aggregate demand curve thus shifts rightward to *AD'*.

The overall effects of economic integration can be seen by comparing the new equilibrium level at *E'* to the old one at *E*. At the new level, real output is higher and the average price level is lower than before integration occurred. Thus, the region has gained by becoming an integrated market.

Although member nations benefit from regional integration, the benefits are not shared equally. Some countries in the region gain industries and jobs and others lose them as firms relocate in search of higher profits and workers move in search of higher wages.

Monetary and Fiscal Unification

As you saw earlier in Exhibit 1, *economic union* requires the existence of a common market and a unified monetary and fiscal system. In a unified monetary system, all member economies use a single currency and have a single central bank. In a unified fiscal system, member economies abide by a common set of rules governing tax policies and the size and financing of government budget deficits. The benefits of economic union are easy to see. By coordinating monetary and fiscal policies, member economies can encourage higher levels of employment and production while reducing inflationary pressures.

As the EC has discovered, efforts to attain monetary and fiscal unification are fraught with difficulties. Nevertheless, the EC is working to resolve them. Here are some of the major goals that the member nations are striving to attain.

European Central Bank

High on the list of EC objectives is the establishment of a "central bank of central banks." Called the European System of Central Banks, the ESCB is modeled after Germany's central bank, the Bundesbank, and the U.S. Federal Reserve System. However, the ESCB will be an association of national central banks of member nations. It will operate independently of any national government, and will submit periodic reports of its activities and policies to the EC. The ESCB will have four primary functions:

1. Conducting monetary policy to maintain price stability

2. Managing member nations' central-bank reserves

3. Maintaining member nations' payments systems (including check clearing and related activities)

4. Stabilizing member nations' foreign-exchange rates (the prices of currencies in terms of one another) in order to encourage trade.

In order to assure effective coordination of monetary policy, the EC deems the first function to be the most important by far.

European Currency Unit

The creation of a European central bank will also entail the creation of a single European currency. Called the European currency unit, the ECU (pronounced "ek-coo") will replace existing members' currencies. Combined with checkable deposits, ECUs will become part of the EC's basic money supply—*M1*—and will serve as a medium of exchange. Residents of member countries will thus spend ECUs instead of British pounds, French francs, Spanish pesetas, and such, to pay for goods and services purchased. The new ECU will be issued by the European central bank, which will use the currency to help fulfill monetary policy objectives.*

Unified Fiscal System

Another goal of the EC is to achieve fiscal uniformity. This goal is to be accomplished in two ways—by harmonizing taxes and by eliminating excessive government budget deficits.

---

*The new ECU should not be confused with the current ECU. The current ECU is a trade-weighted average of members' currencies used for accounting purposes in international transactions.

1.   Tax harmonization was largely achieved in 1991 when member countries agreed to replace their widely disparate consumption taxes with a uniform *value-added tax.* This is a type of national sales tax paid by manufacturers and merchants on the value contributed to a product at each stage of its production and distribution. The tax is a rich source of revenue to national governments. In addition, because the tax is refunded on exports, it has no adverse effects on any country's trade with other nations.

2.   Government budget deficits are viewed by the member nations as a potential source of inflation and a cause of high interest rates. The EC's Council of Finance Ministers, therefore, monitors government spending and recommends changes aimed at reducing "excessive" budget deficits. The Council doesn't set binding rules. However, it prohibits the financing of budget deficits with increased money growth, and it can impose sanctions or withhold financial assistance when countries fail to comply with recommendations.

In Europe, discussions are in progress toward achieving monetary and fiscal union. Among the chief issues to be resolved are the creation of a European central bank, the introduction of a single currency, and the transfer of selected powers from national governments to a central EC authority.

Conclusion: Regional Trading Blocs

Nations within a region have much to gain from economic integration. Removal of trade barriers promotes competition. This leads to declining costs, falling prices, and increasing demand. Businesses become more profitable and invest more. Rising investment stimulates economic growth and generates higher levels of real aggregate income and employment.

However, while economic integration creates greater efficiencies in some markets, it may cause new inefficiencies in other markets. This will happen if the nations composing a trading bloc divert trade from the most efficient producers outside the bloc to less efficient producers inside the bloc. World trade and international efficiency will suffer.

At present, three giant trading blocs—call them

the United States of North America, the United States of Europe, and the United States of Asia—are evolving. As shown in Exhibit 4, the North American bloc embraces Canada, the United States, and Mexico. The European bloc consists of the EC member countries identified earlier in Exhibit 2. The Asian block includes the market economies on the continent's western rim, which extends along an arc from Japan and South Korea in the north to Indonesia in the south.

Will the emergence of the world's three major trading blocs encourage a trend toward protectionism within each bloc, or will it lead to increased global efficiency? There are two points of view:

1.   Opponents of regional integration contend that regional trade agreements discriminate against nonparticipants. Protectionism within each bloc largely explains why, since the late 1980s, annual trade volume within each of the three major trading regions has increased about twice as fast as trade between them.

2.   Proponents of regional integration argue that increased protectionism resulting from a regional trade agreement is unlikely—because of two deterrents:

   a. Loss of Efficiencies   The higher costs experienced from raising trade barriers would offset if not exceed the gains achieved from market integration.

   b. Retaliation by Outsiders   A trading bloc that raises trade barriers invites the rest of the world to respond with similar measures.

Both points of view sound plausible. And because trading blocs are an emerging phenomenon in the world economy, it will be some years before their effects are known.

To summarize:

Regional agreements may encourage nondiscriminatory trade among member nations. If that happens, the growth of a worldwide free-trade system will be encouraged and global efficiency will improve. However, regionalism may lead to preferential, and hence discriminatory, exchange between regions. In that case, the trend toward universal free trade that the world has experienced for the past half century will be reversed, and global efficiency will worsen.

EXHIBIT
4

Three World Trading Blocs

Three great trading blocs are emerging as a result of regional economic integration. Within each bloc, the reduction of trade barriers will encourage multilateral trade among members. This will improve world economic welfare. But if the blocs raise protectionist barriers against each other, trade between them will decline and world economic welfare will worsen. The European bloc does not yet include the countries of Eastern Europe, and the Asian bloc does not yet include China.

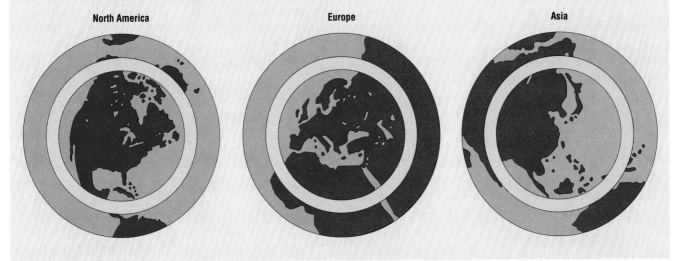

North America   Europe   Asia

International Banking and Financial Markets

As global trading relationships become increasingly integrated, so too do the world's money and capital markets. Witness the extraordinary changes that have occurred in these markets in recent decades:

- The flow of funds across national boundaries has increased sharply.

- Foreign investors have greatly expanded their ownership of stocks, bonds, land, buildings, and other financial and real assets.

- Banks and other financial institutions have enlarged their holdings in the world's financial centers.

These developments are having dramatic macroeconomic effects on the global financial system. To un-

derstand the nature of the effects, it helps to examine the structure of international financial markets in terms of the activities of their major participants.

Structure of International Financial Markets

Financial markets are where financial claims, or instruments, are traded. As you'll recall from an earlier chapter dealing with monetary economics,* financial markets include the short-term *money market* and the long-term *capital market*.

The **money market** is one in which debt instruments maturing in a year or less from the date of issue are bought and sold. Examples include U.S. Treasury bills, corporations' commercial paper or promissory notes, and bankers' acceptances. The **capital market** is

---

*See Chapter 9.

one in which debt instruments maturing in more than a year from the date of issue are bought and sold. Examples are bonds, mortgages, and stock. Money and capital markets collectively help comprise *financial markets.* The economic function of financial markets is to allocate funds between borrowers and lenders and between short-term and long-term uses.

The chief participants in international financial markets are financial institutions, governments, and corporations.

Commercial Banks

Through their lending, payments, and underwriting operations, commercial banks provide credit, facilitate transactions, and finance new issues of corporate stocks and bonds. Commercial banks that perform these activities in more than one country are called international banks. In most cases, international banks are subject to substantially fewer restrictions on their foreign operations than on their domestic ones. As a result, international banking has been growing at a rapid rate. Today, hardly a commercial bank exists that is not to some degree an international bank.

Nonbank Financial Institutions

Nonbank financial institutions include insurance companies, mutual funds, and pension funds. These institutions invest in securities, real estate, and other assets both at home and abroad. The portfolios of assets that nonbank financial institutions maintain undergo considerable turnover because managers frequently shift investments from country to country in search of the highest returns.

Central Banks

The Federal Reserve System, the Bank of Japan, the Bank of England, and some other central banks play important roles in international financial markets. A central bank will often intervene in the world foreign exchange market by buying or selling its own currency against the currencies of its major trading partners. If the bank's intervention is successful, it will help stabilize the price of its currency relative to the others. A stable currency price promotes trade.

Governments

An increasing number of countries are financing part of their spending by borrowing abroad. Nations borrow by obtaining loans from international banks and by selling bonds. In order to enhance the sale of their bonds, governments usually denominate them in the currency of the country in which they are sold. Americans, for example, considering German government bonds, are more likely to buy those denominated in dollars than those denominated in marks. Conversely, Germans would prefer U.S. government bonds denominated in marks to those denominated in dollars. Because of a growing interest in foreign government bonds, business newspapers and magazines often display large advertisements announcing such bond issues.

Corporations

Like some governments, many firms finance at least part of their operations with funds obtained from foreign sources. The funds may be acquired by selling securities—short-term instruments, stocks, and bonds—in other countries, or by borrowing from international banks. Because corporations borrowing abroad want to achieve the widest possible investor appeal, they frequently agree to pay dividends and interest in U.S. dollars, Japanese yen, British pounds, or other internationally accepted currencies.

The activities of these participants in the world's money and capital markets exert powerful financial effects on the global economy. As a result, international banking is an activity of major economic significance. This was not the case a few decades ago:

Before the 1960s, international banking was of relatively limited importance as a global economic activity. Since then it has undergone dramatic expansion—for three major reasons:

1. **The need to finance the rapid growth of world trade**

2. **The need to finance expansion of multinational corporations**

3. **The desire of many banks to escape domestic regulations and taxes by undertaking foreign operations**

Eurocurrencies

If you were to come into some extra money, you might want to open a Eurodollar account. *Eurodollars* are dollar deposits in banks outside the United States, mostly in Europe. Eurodollar deposits are held by U.S. and foreign banks, corporations, and individuals. The deposits represent dollar obligations that are constantly being shifted from one country to another in search of the highest return.

Residents of many nations own deposits in banks outside their country. American, British, Canadian, French, Japanese, and Swiss banks are leading recipients of such deposits. In general, any bank deposits denominated in currencies other than that of the country in which the bank is located are called *Eurocurrencies.* Thus a resident of Japan who holds a yen deposit in a British bank is an owner of Eurocurrencies. So too is a resident of the United States who holds a dollar deposit in a Japanese bank. The prefix "Euro" is therefore a misnomer because Eurocurrencies are held in many banks on several continents.

With the growth of Eurocurrencies, a world Eurocurrency market has emerged whose chief function is to accommodate the international transfer of funds. The financial intermediaries in these markets are commercial banks. They receive deposits in major international currencies and then use these funds to provide loans—mainly to corporations in the major industrialized countries. The volume of Eurocurrency transactions in a particular part of the world depends largely on the amount of international trade for that region. Because of the rapid expansion of trade across the Pacific, much of the growth in the Eurocurrency market has occurred in Asian markets.

Macroeconomic Effects of Eurocurrency Growth

The governments of European and Asian countries regulate domestic deposits in the home currency very closely. However, almost all of these governments exempt domestic banks from holding reserves against Eurocurrency deposits. This enables those banks—called *Eurobanks*—to put all their Eurocurrency deposits to work. As a result, interest rates on Eurocurrency time deposits are higher, and the terms of Eurocurrency loans are usually better, than comparable deposits and loans in the home currency. This has been the major factor contributing to the rapid expansion of the Eurocurrency market.

For purposes of macroeconomic policy, two problems regarding Eurocurrency growth are (1) its impact on worldwide inflation and (2) its effect on central-bank monetary control.

Does Rapid Eurocurrency Growth Cause Inflation?

Some Eurodollar accounts are overnight deposits. However, because they are not quite as liquid as $M1$—currency and checkable deposits—the Federal Reserve classifies overnight Eurodollars as $M2$. Many Eurodollar accounts are for a specified term. Because they are similar to time deposits, the Fed classifies term Eurodollars as $M3$. Of course, all Eurocurrency deposits are *near-monies.* This means they are easily converted into money because their monetary values are known. As a result, their rapid growth contributes (just as does the rapid growth of $M1$) to countries' inflation rates. In general, Eurocurrency growth is a significantly greater cause of inflation in Europe than in the United States. However, the extent of the inflationary effects is unknown.

Does Eurocurrency Growth Impair Monetary Control?

The Eurocurrency system enables people to shift their money rapidly from domestic deposits that are subject to reserve requirements into Eurocurrency deposits that are not. This "shiftability" has both negative and positive consequences:

- On the negative side, depositors' ability to shift funds reduces central-bank control over the monetary aggregates—$M1$, $M2$, and $M3$. It also causes some instability in the aggregates. But experience shows that the reduction in control is relatively small and any instability that occurs is largely short run.

- On the positive side, shiftability encourages efficiency in worldwide financial markets by allowing financial assets to be allocated to their highest-valued uses. As a result, consumers enjoy lower borrowing and investment costs, and greater choice of financial opportunities.

Today's International Macroeconomic Policy Issues

The challenges and opportunities presented by today's global economy give rise to policy issues that you read and hear about almost daily in the news media. The issues fall into two broad categories. One category is international trade, or the commerce of nations. The other is international investment, or the payments of nations.

International Trade

International trade, as we know, consists of importing and exporting. Most international trade is conducted by private firms and individuals, not by governments. Nonetheless, it is governments that institute trade protection policies restricting imports in order to shelter particular domestic industries from foreign competition.

As we have seen, free trade promotes global economic growth and efficiency by fostering competition. When nations import, they obtain goods that might otherwise be either more costly or unavailable. When nations export, they earn the foreign currency needed to pay for imports. Therefore, protectionist policies reduce both the volume of trade and real incomes worldwide.

In recent decades, most of the industrial countries have made dramatic reductions in the most blatant form of protectionism, tariffs. During the past half-century, for example, the United States has cut tariffs from approximately 50 percent on dutiable items to less than 5 percent. Many other nations have decreased their tariffs similarly. Despite this trend, however, industries in many nations, and a number of governments, continue to push hard for trade protection.

America's Position on Trade Protection

Where does the United States stand with respect to trade protection? Washington has long held that America's trade policy rests on a firm belief in free markets. Documents published with some frequency by the U.S. Department of State emphasize eliminating trade barriers wherever possible so that market forces can guide resources into their most productive uses. Despite these pronouncements, dozens of restrictive trade bills are considered annually for enactment, and Congress continues to exhibit reluctance at repealing certain protectionist laws. As a result, although the United States has achieved progress toward promoting open global markets, it still falls significantly short of being a model of free trade.

Trade with Japan

The United States and Japan are the world's two largest economies. Their combined output exceeds more than one-third of global GDP. Japan is one of the world's largest importers of U.S. goods and the United States is one of the world's largest recipients of Japanese goods. Major U.S. exports to Japan are office equipment, wood, cereal grains, electrical machinery, and aircraft. Chief U.S. imports from Japan are motor vehicles, electronic goods, and machinery. Japan is also a major supplier of loanable funds to the United States and some other advanced nations. This money helps to finance borrowing countries' private-sector investment in plant and equipment and public-sector budget deficits.

Every nation strives, as we've seen many times in previous chapters, for four economic goals—efficiency, equity, stability, and growth. In most of the advanced countries, economic policies have traditionally placed relatively greater emphasis on achieving efficiency, equity, and stability than on attaining economic growth. This is because it is generally assumed that successful realization of the first three goals will automatically assure the fourth.

Japan has been an exception to this belief. Beginning in the 1950s, Japanese leaders embraced a growth-oriented philosophy. To encourage sustained expansion, they adopted measures aimed at rapid modernization of manufacturing. The measures included government assistance to selected industries in the form of tax preferences, subsidies, protectionist legislation, and other special favors. These policies helped provide much of the funds needed for financing product research and development and enabled Japan's manufacturers to expand sufficiently to become major exporters. In response to continuous pressure from its major trading partners, Tokyo in 1990 began encouraging imports. But the Japanese people are extremely nationalistic and often prefer to buy higher-priced domestic goods rather than lower-priced imports. As a result, even though Tokyo imposes few tariffs or explicit restrictions on imports of manufactured goods, most exporters find it difficult to penetrate significantly the Japanese market.

The problem has been particularly important for American-Japanese relations—for two reasons. First, both economies are linked closely by their large volume of trade with each other. Second, Japan has usually had huge trade surpluses with the United States. To help achieve a more balanced two-way trade relationship, current U.S. policy toward Japan includes several elements:

- **Macroeconomic Policy Coordination** Both nations have agreed to work toward achieving closer alignments of monetary and fiscal policies. This will help reduce some of the international financial instability (discussed below) that occurs when the public expects differences in inflation and interest rates between the two countries to vary significantly.

- **Structural Changes** As a result of U.S. pleas, Japan has agreed to slow the growth of its industrial sector and to encourage the growth of its service sector. The goals are to be achieved by allocating fewer resources to manufacturing and more resources to the provision of finance, marketing, information, and other services. It's expected that this reallocation will enable Japan to reduce its reliance on exports and to increase its propensity to import.

- **Trade Negotiations** Efforts to improve access to specific Japanese markets are the subject of frequent U.S.-led trade negotiations with Japan. Among the major American-made products discussed in the negotiations are pharmaceuticals, medical equipment, auto parts, construction equipment, telecommunications, and electronics.

A chief purpose of the negotiations is to reduce Japan's nontariff trade barriers in order to relieve trade imbalances with the United States.

The United States has made it clear that it wants comprehensive trade reforms not only with Japan but with all countries. As a result, a top U.S. priority is to reduce both domestic and foreign government measures that distort world trade. These are to be replaced by international agreements that permit *freely functioning world markets* to allocate global resources efficiently.

International Finance

Freely functioning world markets are the primary goal of today's U.S. foreign economic policy. A freely functioning finance market allows the flow of private investment between nations to be determined by global market forces, unimpeded by government measures that distort international capital movements.

America's economic policy toward other countries acknowledges the essential contribution that direct foreign investment makes to efficiency and growth. Benefits accrue to home and host country alike. Therefore, the U.S. government welcomes foreign investment and extends to it the same treatment that it seeks for American investors abroad. To carry out its

policy, the United States has signed bilateral investment treaties with a number of countries and is negotiating with others.

U.S. foreign economic policy rests on the belief that international investment is best encouraged by adhering to several principles:

- **Equal Domestic Treatment** Governments of host countries must agree to accord foreign enterprises the same rights and privileges in like situations as are accorded to domestic enterprises. Exceptions, if any, should be limited to those involving national security.

- **Most-Favored-Nation Treatment** Governments of host countries must agree to accord foreign enterprises the same rights and privileges as the most favorable ones granted to like foreign enterprises from any other nation. By treating all nations as if they were its most favored nation, a host country will be unable to discriminate against foreign investment on the basis of national origin.

- **Protection of Property** Governments of host countries must agree to uphold international law pertaining to property rights. The most common issues that arise concern violation of contracts, expropriation of assets, methods of settling grievances, and prompt and adequate compensation for recovery of damages. Additional issues of importance concern recognition of intellectual property rights such as patents, copyrights, and proprietary claims to technology.

Providing Financial Assistance

America's ability to implement its foreign economic policy is affected by the policies of financial institutions. Two global ones that are especially important are the International Monetary Fund and the World Bank. Both organizations work together closely. Their responsibility is to help provide the financial assistance that some countries need to strengthen their economies and promote steady growth.

The *International Monetary Fund (IMF)* was created by the United Nations in 1944. Its membership includes more than 150 countries. The chief purpose of the IMF is to provide short- and medium-term loans to member nations suffering from serious deficits (net money outflows) resulting from foreign trade and investment. However, the IMF, like any lender, doesn't grant loans without conditions. Borrowing nations must generally agree to adopt (1) fiscal and monetary policies to cut inflation, (2) commitments and measures to repay foreign debts, and (3) domestic legislation and practices to promote competitive markets. Since the late 1980s, the IMF has monitored these conditions more closely than before. As a result, its policies are helping to improve borrowing countries' saving and investment, and to encourage capital inflows from foreign private-sector sources.

The **World Bank** was established by the United Nations in 1945. Initially called the International Bank for Reconstruction and Development, it has evolved into a group of funding sources of which the IBRD is by far the largest. As a result, the organization is sometimes referred to by both names. In general, its main purpose is to help improve productivity in poor countries by financing development projects such as dams, communications and transportation facilities, and health programs. After many years of experience, however, the World Bank learned that costly development projects won't raise productivity so long as governments control market prices. Since the late 1980s, therefore, the World Bank has been requiring a growing number of borrowing nations to adopt market reforms as a condition for receiving financial assistance. Countries that do so find ample funding available; those that do not find it difficult to get loans.

What Future for Global Financing?

The chief goal of America's foreign economic policy is to promote the development of an open and growing world economy. Both the International Monetary Fund and the World Bank can contribute toward this end. By providing the financial support that nations need to correct large trade and capital imbalances and to support sustainable economic growth, the two institutions supplement each other. At the same time they help reinforce the U.S. objective.

With the growth of market economies throughout most of the world, the IMF and the World Bank may become relatively less important as public-funding agencies. Experiences in Asia and Latin America bear this out. When governments privatize firms and eliminate regulations, they improve their domestic economic climate. Private investment surges, and dependency on public funding ebbs. This suggests a prediction:

The global trend toward market reform will continue to cause significant changes in the international

financial system. Private lending organizations such as major banks, insurance companies, and other such institutions, seeing the promise of profitable returns, will play an increasingly important role in financing growing economies. Private lending to growing economies will leave public lending agencies to deal primarily with the weakest economies. Most of these are in Africa, where growth prospects for some countries are so bleak that loans amount to giveaways.

Summary of Important Ideas

1. Since the mid-twentieth century, a new type of world trading system has been emerging. One part of it consists of a growing number of nations—now in excess of 100—that have committed themselves to the liberalization of world trade. The commitment has been implemented by creating international agreements providing for nondiscrimination in importing and exporting among trading nations.

2. A second and more recent part of the new trading system has been a movement among many nations toward regional economic integration. The chief purpose of regional integration is to enable member nations to allocate resources more efficiently. By expanding the size of the market, member nations' allow their industries to gain the economies (lower unit costs) of large-scale production.

3. Europe, North America, and Asia are three major regions where economic integration is occurring. The member nations of the EC have made the greatest progress toward integration thus far. But the EC still faces many obstacles to economic union. These exist because member nations have different laws and regulations governing product safety, environmental standards, business transactions, and professional licensing. Member nations also have different policies concerning government ownership of businesses and subsidization of private businesses. These differences must be eliminated in order for full economic integration to become a reality.

4. Economic integration of countries within a region reduces trade barriers among member nations. As a result, investment and productivity increase, trade expands, and the region's aggregate output and employment rise. But if the regional group, acting as a trading bloc, imposes trade barriers against nonmember countries, it may cause losses in real global output and a decline in global economic welfare.

5. Financial integration goes hand in hand with economic integration. By globalizing money and capital markets, financial integration enables funds to flow across national boundaries, and foreign investors to buy and sell stocks, bonds, land, buildings, and other assets. It also enables large banks, insurance companies, and other major financial institutions to become significant lenders in foreign markets. These institutions help finance the growth of world trade and the expansion of multinational corporations.

6. With the expansion of global trade and investment, the world Eurocurrency market is playing an increasingly important role in accommodating the international transfer of funds. Eurocurrency bank deposits are near-monies and are easily convertible into $M1$. As a result, their rapid growth contributes to inflationary pressures. However, because Eurocurrencies can be readily shifted between nations to garner the highest possible returns, they facilitate the global allocation of assets to their highest-valued uses. This helps improve the long-run efficiency of the world's financial system.

7. The United States has been the world leader in striving for freely functioning global markets. To that end, it has adopted a foreign economic policy with specific objectives. The chief one is to replace both domestic and foreign government measures that misallocate global resources with international agreements that promote unrestricted world trade and finance. Several international agencies, particularly the International Monetary Fund and the World Bank, may be able to contribute to this objective. If their lending policies are properly designed, they can help complement and supplement measures adopted by the United States to promote an open and growing world economy.

Terms and Concepts to Review

tariff
nontariff barriers
import quota
General Agreement on
    Tariffs and Trade
    (GATT)
most-favored nation
    clause
free-trade area
customs union
common market
economic union
value-added tax
money market
capital market
financial markets
Eurodollars
Eurocurrencies
Eurobanks
near-monies
International Monetary
    Fund (IMF)
World Bank

Questions and Problems

1. Why do nations tend to impose nontariff barriers rather than tariffs as a means of restricting trade?

2. Most legislators know that unrestricted trade promotes efficiency and leads to higher real incomes worldwide. Why, then, don't political leaders remove all protective barriers to trade?

3. The fifty states of the United States comprise an *economic union*—the highest level of economic integration. Why? Is it likely that any group of nations will form an economic union?

4. Economic integration can promote trade and enhance global economic welfare. But under some circumstances it may lead to the opposite effect by causing a reduction in global economic welfare. How might this happen?

5. If economic integration leads to the establishment of a central bank, what would be its functions?

6. Why is fiscal unification an ultimate goal of economic integration?

7. Will the emergence of regional trading blocs necessarily lead to a rise in protectionism?

8. A newspaper editor wrote: "The globalization of financial markets is an inevitable accompaniment of growing economic interdependency." What does this mean? Could economic interdependency continue to grow without globalization of financial markets?

9. The central banks of the United States, Canada, Britain, France, Japan, and other major countries are concerned about the growth of Eurocurrency deposits. Can you suggest why?

10. Why is it desirable for major trading nations to coordinate, if possible, their macroeconomic policies?

TAKE A STAND

Regional Trading Groups: Do They Promote Global Integration?

Since its formation in 1958, the European Community (EC) has been moving toward ever greater economic and political union in Europe. The number of nations in the EC has doubled to twelve and still more are seeking membership. The Single European Act of 1985 committed the member countries to allow free movement of goods and people across national boundaries. The Maastricht treaty, which most member nations have already signed, is intended to lead Europe to complete monetary union with a single European currency. We may some day see a United States of Europe competing as a single force in the global economy.

The EC's global competitors have not remained idle. The United States has moved toward developing a North American trading region by jointly agreeing to reduce trade barriers with Canada and Mexico. Japan, through investment and trading ties to other countries in southeast Asia, has created a less formal but equally effective regional trading group in its part of the world. Argentina, Brazil, Paraguay, and Uruguay have established their own common market in South America. Australia and New Zealand have reached a similar agreement.

At the same time that regional trading groups are being formed, many nations are also seeking to foster worldwide economic integration. Negotiations over the General Agreement on Tariffs and Trade (GATT) have sought to promote unrestricted trade, cooperation, and economic integration among all 100-plus members.

On the surface, regional trading groups are generating increased global cooperation and integration. Each country is reaching beyond its own national boundaries to cooperate with others in economic, political, and social matters. This appears to be consistent with the goal of global cooperation pursued by GATT. But is it? Are regional trading groups a step toward global cooperation or a step toward the formation of rival regional trading blocs? *Or do regional trading groups promote global economic integration?*

Yes: Regional Trading Groups Are a Necessary Step

Reaching agreement among over one hundred sovereign nations is a difficult task. Each country has its own special concerns and goals. GATT negotiations, which have been conducted since 1947 to promote free trade among nations, have had both successes and setbacks.

While the general consensus is that free trade benefits the world, it is also acknowledged that the benefits are not shared equally and some individuals may lose out. For example, a major sticking point in the recent Uruguay round of GATT negotiations was the issue of subsidies to farmers. An across-the-board elimination of farm subsidies would promote global efficiency. But individual farmers would suffer.

It takes an enormous sacrifice of time and effort for 100 or more diverse nations to reach an agreement on such issues. It's much easier for 12 countries in Europe with relatively similar goals, cultures, and interests to find mutually acceptable solutions to economic problems. Regional trading groups such as the 12-nation European Community (EC) represent smaller steps than GATT toward global integration, but are more manageable. Trading groups that foster regional economic integration represent a major step toward global integration. If all countries joined regional trading groups, global negotiations such as the GATT conferences could be conducted by a relatively small number of groups instead of by dozens of separate nations. With significantly fewer individual participants, the negotiation process is streamlined, decisions can be made faster, and global economic integration can be achieved sooner.

The advantages of belonging to a regional trading group are recognized by nations outside the EC. Nonmember European nations, including the formerly communist nations of eastern Europe, are currently seeking membership. Proponents of a North American trading group anticipate that it will eventually extend to Central America, South America, and perhaps nations on the Asian side of the Pacific rim. Some economists foresee a time when the pockets of free trade and economic integration that have been created in various parts of the world will merge into a fully integrated global economy.

Global integration is a goal so vast that it might never be achieved. Regional integration is more readily attained, and can lay the groundwork for eventual global cooperation. Regional trading groups are therefore not merely a way station, but a necessary stage in the evolution toward worldwide economic integration.

No: Regional Trading Groups Will Become Rival Trading Blocs

Regional trading groups do not lead to global integration. On the contrary, they inhibit it.

The underlying goal of regional trading groups is to establish a limited number of very powerful, rival trading blocs. These blocs would foster an "us versus them" approach to trade, so that barriers to trade would crumble within a trading bloc, but be strengthened and made more numerous among the various blocs.

We can see this approach at work among regional trading groups that currently exist. The EC, for example, promotes trade among its member nations but restricts imports from non-members. Japan and its trading partners do the same. The United States, while officially seeking global cooperation, has entered into agreements with Canada and Mexico that promote U.S. investment in North America. The United States also hopes to encourage a flow of trade within North America that can take the place of imports from Europe and Japan.

Regional trade agreements such as these only promote antagonism. Each regional trading group, like a medieval ruler, is building a fortress of trade barriers around itself as protection against global competitors. If regional trading blocs develop, the rivalry among them would preclude cooperation and could erupt into destructive trade wars.

The Question: Do Regional Trading Groups Promote Global Integration?

■ One view is that regional trading groups are a necessary step toward global integration. Diversity of national interests means that global cooperation could take decades to achieve. Regional integration should therefore be encouraged.

■ Another view is that regional trading groups are an undesirable alternative to global integration because they foster an "us versus them" view of the world. Ultimately, a few powerful, antagonistic trading blocs will dominate the global economy.

Where Do You Stand?

1. Some analysts have suggested that regional trading blocs are emerging because the costs of transportation and communication have declined. If this is true, is it possible to *prevent* the formation of regional trading blocs? Would lower transportation and communication costs also facilitate global integration? Explain.

2. If the world becomes dominated by regional trading blocs centered on major industrialized nations, what is likely to happen to the less developed countries that are not trading bloc members?

3. Some have argued that international trade, by making nations interdependent, fosters world peace. Do you think that trading groups or trading blocs will make the world a safer place?

4. Do trading blocs promote global integration? Justify your stand.

Sources: Heng-Sheng Cheng, "Toward Trade Blocs," *Weekly Letter,* Federal Reserve Bank of San Francisco, August 5, 1988; Robert Kuttner, "A Vote for Free Trade with Mexico Is a Vote Against Free Trade," *Business Week;* May 6, 1991, p. 18; and Peter Truell, "Free Trade May Suffer From Regional Blocs," *The Wall Street Journal,* July 1, 1991, p. A1.

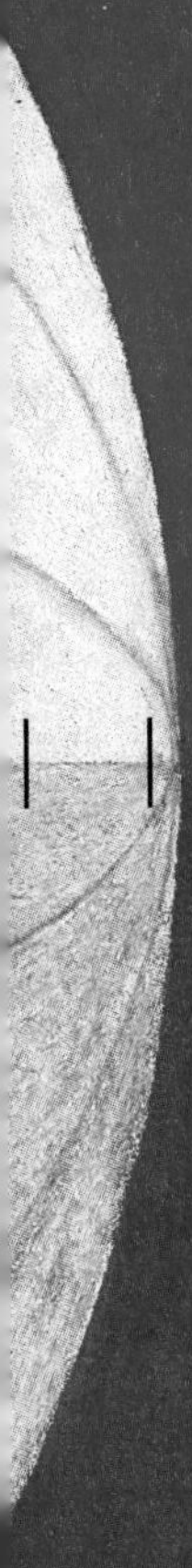

Part 6

International Economics and the World's Economies

447

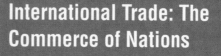

Chapter 21

International Trade: The Commerce of Nations

Why Trade?

The Case for Free Trade

Free Trade Versus Import Protection

Arguments for Protection

Strategic Trade Policy: A Case for Protection?

GATT and Multilateral Trade Negotiations

Learning Guide
Watch for answers to these important questions

Why do nations trade?

What is meant by "comparative advantage"? How do a country's terms of trade differ from its gains from trade?

How are import quotas and tariffs used to restrain trade? What are their consequences?

What arguments are commonly heard in defense of import protection? Are these arguments valid?

What is "strategic trade policy"? Does it provide a valid argument for trade protection?

What is GATT? Has it succeeded in achieving its goals?

Our nation is an integral part of the world economy. You have already seen how some of the economic policies we adopt affect and are often affected by other countries. To understand the reasons for this interaction, we must learn some basic principles that underlie the workings of the world economy.

The study of the world economy is known as "international economics." It's one of the oldest branches of economics. As you'll recall from your study of history, many wars have been fought over international economic issues.

International economics embraces two broad areas of interest:

1. International trade—the commerce of nations

2. International finance—the payments of nations

This chapter surveys the major economic principles and ideas underlying international trade. It then shows how to apply these concepts in order to analyze many practical international economic problems. These problems, you'll find, are the kinds you read and hear about almost every day in the news media.

Why Trade?

World trade has been gaining increasing significance among nations. You can see the growing importance of trade for the United States by noting the trend shown in Exhibit 1.

EXHIBIT
1

The U.S. Economy and Foreign Trade

International trade has assumed an increasingly important role in the economy of the United States in recent decades. The sum of imports and exports of merchandise and services as a percentage of GDP will probably continue to grow in future years.

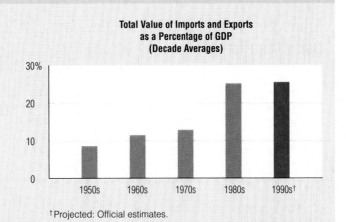

Total Value of Imports and Exports as a Percentage of GDP (Decade Averages)

†Projected: Official estimates.

Major product groups and their chief components*	U.S. Exports: 1991 What was sold (billions of dollars)	U.S. Imports: 1991 What was bought (billions of dollars)
Food products Meat, dairy, grains, fruits, vegetables	$ 29.3	$ 22.0
Beverages and tobacco	6.8	4.8
Crude materials Soybeans, wood, textiles, ores	25.3	13.2
Mineral fuels Coal, petroleum, natural gas	12.0	52.2
Chemical products Chemical elements, medicinals, pharmaceuticals, fertilizers, plastics	43.3	24.5
Machinery and transport equipment Power machinery, electronics, telecommunications, motor vehicles and parts, aircraft and parts	187.1	211.2
Other manufactured goods Paper products, metal and nonmetal goods, fabrics, scientific instruments	70.2	133.6
Total	$374.0	$461.5

Source: U.S. Department of Commerce. Preliminary data.
* Includes merchandise only. Services, which total many billions of dollars, are not included.

The graph shows, for each decade since the 1950s, the average dollar sum of U.S. imports and exports, including services, as a percentage of gross domestic product (GDP). The average rose from less than 10 percent in the 1950s to more than 20 percent in the 1980s. According to some predictions, the proportion will average nearly 30 percent for the 1990s. These trends reflect the growing economic interdependence between the United States and other countries.

Why do nations trade? Why, for example, doesn't the United States produce all of the cars, motorcycles, electronic goods, and cameras that it wants so that Americans wouldn't have to buy these products from Japan? In return, why doesn't Japan produce all of the food, machinery, transportation equipment, and chemicals that it wants so that the Japanese wouldn't have to buy these goods from the United States?

EXHIBIT
2

Production and Trading Possibilities: Terms of Trade and Gains from Trade

For each country, the opportunity cost (or domestic-exchange equation) for meat and wine is represented by the slope of the production-possibilities curve. The **terms of trade**, or units given up per unit received in trade, are represented by the slope of the trade-possibilities curve. Each country, by specializing in production of the good with the lowest opportunity cost and then trading, can end up with more of both goods than it would if it produced them both itself.

For example, suppose that each country tried to be self-sufficient. In Figure (a), the United States might produce

a combination of meat and wine represented by point C. In Figure (b), France might produce a combination shown by point F. By specializing and trading, however, the United States could end up with the products at point I, and France with those at point J. The net benefit or increase in consumption for each country are its **gains from trade**. These are shown by the shaded areas. Thus, for the United States, the gains are 10 units of meat and 10 units of wine. For France, the gains are 10 units of meat and 30 units of wine.

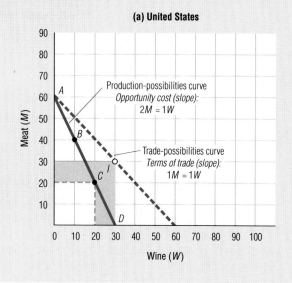

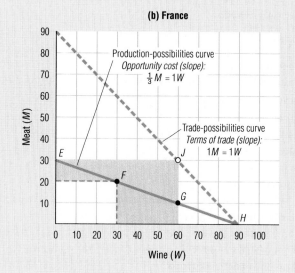

The answer is that nations have different quantities and qualities of human and nonhuman resources and different ways of combining them. As a result, each country can produce certain goods more efficiently, or at relatively lower costs, than others.

This idea can be stated somewhat differently. Imagine a world consisting of only two countries, each producing the same two goods. Under such circumstances, the alternative or **opportunity cost** to each country of producing more of one good is the amount of the second good that must be sacrificed. In view of this, which of the two goods should the countries produce?

The answer is that each should **specialize**. How? By producing the good with the lower opportunity cost and trading with the other country for the good with the higher opportunity cost. In that way, the combined output of both goods will actually be larger, and each country will get more of them than it would if it tried to be self-sufficient by producing both.

Specialization and Trade

These concepts can be illustrated by an example. Exhibit 2 shows hypothetical production-possibilities curves (the solid lines) for meat (M) and wine (W) for the United States and France. To simplify the analysis, the production-possibilities curves are drawn as straight lines instead of being bowed outward. This means that *constant* rather than increasing opportunity costs of production are assumed. Note that opportunity cost is measured by the *slope* of the line—the change in the vertical distance per unit of change in the horizontal.

Domestic-Exchange Equations

What does the assumption of constant opportunity costs imply?

In Figure (a), any point along the United States production-possibilities curve reveals a different output combination of meat and wine. For instance, point *A* denotes an output of $60M$ and $0W$; point *B*, an output of $40M$ and $10W$; point *C*, an output of $20M$ and $20W$; and point *D*, an output of $0M$ and $30W$. In general, at any point along its production-possibilities curve, the United States must sacrifice meat for wine at a rate of $20M$ to $10W$. This is equivalent to a rate of $2M$ to $1W$. The opportunity cost of the two products is therefore $2M = 1W$, or $1M = \frac{1}{2}W$.

In Figure (b), on the other hand, France's production-possibilities curve reveals a different opportunity cost for the two products. For example, in order to go from point *E* to point *F*, France must sacrifice 10 units of meat to gain 30 units of wine. Similarly, a movement from *F* to *G* entails sacrificing another $10M$ for an additional $30W$. In order to go from *G* to *H*, the sacrifice is again the same. Therefore, the rate of sacrifice in France is $10M$ to $30W$. This is the same, of course, as a rate of $1M$ to $3W$, or $\frac{1}{3}M$ to $1W$. The opportunity cost of the two products is therefore $\frac{1}{3}M = 1W$.

Opportunity costs in the United States and France thus determine each country's domestic-exchange equation. The equation expresses each country's opportunity costs—the rate at which either commodity can be "exchanged" for the other. The two equations are therefore:

United States:
$$2M = 1W \quad \text{or equivalently} \quad 1M = \tfrac{1}{2}W$$

France:
$$\tfrac{1}{3}M = 1W \quad \text{or equivalently} \quad 1M = 3W$$

You can now see two facts that are evident from these equations:

1. Wine is more expensive to produce in the United States than in France. In the United States, it costs $2M$ to produce $1W$ whereas in France it costs only $\frac{1}{3}M$ to produce $1W$.

2. Meat is less expensive to produce in the United States than in France. In the United States, $1M$ can be produced for only $\frac{1}{2}W$, whereas in France $1M$ can be produced only at the higher cost of $3W$.

Because of these cost relationships, it can be said that France has a comparative advantage in wine production and that the United States has a comparative advantage in meat production. That is:

Given any two products, a country has a *comparative advantage* in the product with the lower opportunity cost.

Specialization and the Gains from Trade

If the two countries in Exhibit 2 were self-sufficient, each would produce its own meat and wine. The amounts produced in each country would depend on consumer preferences as reflected through the price system. For example, the United States might produce at point *C*, representing 20 units of meat and 20 units of wine. France, on the other hand, might produce at point *F*, representing 20 units of meat and 30 units of wine.

Suppose, however, that each country were to specialize by producing the product in which it has a comparative advantage and then were to trade with the other. In that case, the United States would allocate all of its resources to meat and none to wine, producing at point *A* ($60M$ and $0W$). Likewise, France would allocate all of its resources to wine and none to meat, producing at point *H* ($90W$ and $0M$). By trading, each country could then end up with more meat and more wine, as represented perhaps by points *I* and *J*. Thus:

- At point *I*, the United States consumes 30 units of meat and 30 units of wine. This is greater than the consumption level at point *C* (20 units of meat and 20 units of wine), which existed before trade was undertaken. For the United States, therefore, the *gains from trade* are 10 units of meat and 10 units of wine.

- At point *J*, France consumes 30 units of meat and 60 units of wine. This is greater than the consumption level at point *F* (20 units of meat and 30 units of wine), which existed before trading began. For France, the *gains from trade* amount to 10 units of meat and 30 units of wine.

In other words, through specialization and trade, the United States produces 60 units of meat and France produces 90 units of wine. The United States then exports 30 units of meat to France, and France exports 30 units of wine to the United States. As a result, both countries end up with more meat and more wine than they would if each tried to be self-sufficient in both products.

To summarize:

By specializing in the good in which it has a comparative advantage, each nation is able to produce enough of the good so that it can exchange some of it for the other. Both nations thus obtain *gains from trade*. These are the net benefits or increases in goods that a country receives as a result of trading with others.

Comparative Advantage

You can now appreciate the meaning of the familiar expression "It pays to specialize." This idea refers to the *relative* benefit of producing one good instead of another. The concept can be expressed as a law—one of the oldest in economics.

Law of Comparative Advantage **A basis for trade exists when each of two nations, both capable of producing the same two goods, specializes in producing the one that is *relatively* cheaper for it to produce. This is the good in which the country has a lower opportunity cost—a comparative advantage. The two countries can then have more of both goods by engaging in trade. This is a general principle applicable not only to nations but also to regions and even to individuals.**

The law of comparative advantage accounts for the benefits that nations receive from engaging in trade. Therefore, the law also accounts for the costs that nations incur when they erect barriers to trade.

Terms of Trade

When two parties engage in a transaction, the sacrifice that each makes to obtain something from the other is called the "terms of trade." For example, in order to buy this textbook, you might have had to give up five visits to the movies. Your terms of trade, therefore, are 5 movies = 1 book. If you bought four fewer pizzas in order to accumulate enough money to purchase this book, your terms of trade are 4 pizzas = 1 book. The ***terms of trade*** for a given transaction equal the number of units of goods that must be given up for one unit of goods received by each party to the transaction.

According to Exhibit 2, what are the terms of trade for meat and wine between the United States and France? To begin with, you have already learned that the domestic-exchange equations are:

$$\text{United States:}\quad 2M = 1W$$
$$\text{France:}\quad \tfrac{1}{3}M = 1W$$

In Exhibit 2, of course, these equations simply represent the *slopes* of the production-possibilities curves (solid lines). They express the sacrifice of one good for the other that each country incurs if it chooses to produce both goods.

However, the terms of trade (slopes of the dashed lines) express the actual exchange rates between the two countries' goods. The *slopes* of the lines for both countries, as you can see from the figures, are given by $1M = 1W$. These lines may therefore be called *trade-possibilities curves*. A ***trade-possibilities curve*** depicts the amounts of goods that countries may exchange with each other.

Limits of the Terms of Trade

What determines the exchange ratio under which both countries will find it beneficial to trade?

The terms of trade must fall somewhere between the two domestic-exchange equations, or slopes, in order for both countries to experience gains from trade. Otherwise, one of the countries will not find it advantageous to trade.

Two examples illustrate why this is true.

Example 1 Suppose the terms of trade are $3M = 1W$. Trade would then be advantageous to France but not to the United States. Why? Because, by specializing and trading, France could import 3 units of meat in return for exporting 1 unit of wine. This is a better value than obtaining only $\tfrac{1}{3}$ unit of meat for 1 unit of wine by producing both commodities domestically.

The United States, however, would have to export 3 units of meat in order to import 1 unit of wine. This is more expensive than producing both commodities domestically at a cost of only 2 units of meat for 1 unit of wine.

Example 2 Suppose the terms of trade are $\tfrac{1}{5}M = 1W$. In that case, trade would be advantageous to the United States but not to France. The United States, by specializing and trading, could export $\tfrac{1}{5}$ unit of meat in order to import 1 unit of wine. This is cheaper than producing both products domestically at a cost of 2 units of meat for 1 unit of wine.

France, however, would have to export 1 unit of wine in order to import $\frac{1}{5}$ unit of meat. This is not as good a value as producing both commodities domestically at a cost of 1 unit of wine for $\frac{1}{3}$ unit of meat.

Thus, international trade will not occur in either of these examples because only one country would experience gains from trade. However, if the terms of trade fall *between* the two domestic-exchange equations, as does $1M = 1W$, trade will occur because both countries will be able to realize gains.

What determines the terms of trade? In general:

The terms of trade for nations' goods are determined in world markets by international forces of demand and supply. The larger the overall global demand for a product relative to its supply, the higher its price—or terms of trade—in relation to other goods. Conversely, the smaller the overall global demand for a good, the lower its price—or terms of trade—relative to other goods. However, *the terms of trade must lie within the range of the nations' domestic-exchange equations in order for trade to occur.*

Increasing Costs and Incomplete Specialization

You can see why nations find it profitable to trade. *A basis for trade exists when there are differences in opportunity costs between countries.* Thus, with respect to the United States and France, the difference in the opportunity costs of producing meat and wine reflects the different slopes of their production-possibilities curves.

What would happen if the curves bowed outward? This, as you will recall from your first study of production-possibilities curves near the beginning of the book, is the typical situation. It means that costs are *increasing* rather than remaining constant because resources are not perfectly substitutable between alternative uses.

In other words, as each country expands production of its specialty, its opportunity cost (sacrifice) in terms of the alternative good rises. A point can eventually be reached at which the two opportunity costs are equal. When that happens, the basis for trade, and hence the need for further specialization, is eliminated.

Thus:

When increasing costs result in equal opportunity costs between countries, there are two effects:

1. **Incomplete Specialization** Both countries stop

short of complete specialization because further increases in specialization cease to be beneficial.

2. **Reduced Trade** Each country continues to produce both products—its specialty as well as some of its nonspecialty. Although trade is still carried on, its total volume is less than it would be if costs were constant.

The Case for Free Trade

The study of international trade is one of the oldest branches of economics. Adam Smith, in *The Wealth of Nations*, devoted considerable attention to the subject.

Among the concepts Adam Smith emphasized was that each country has different quantities and qualities of resources. These differences enable each country to produce at least one low-cost product it can sell to others. It therefore behooves nations to specialize in what they can produce most efficiently, and to engage in free (that is, unrestricted) trade. In that way, all countries can share in the gains from trade.

Absolute Advantage

This principle subsequently became known as the ***law of absolute advantage.*** It states that a basis for trade exists when one nation is more efficient (that is, uses fewer resources) than another in producing a good that the other wants. Each country can then specialize in producing the good it can produce most efficiently. By trading, nations can acquire one another's goods more cheaply than they can if they produce the same goods at home.

This law accounts for much of the world's trade. For example, Brazil has an absolute advantage over the United States in the production of coffee. However, the United States has an absolute advantage over Brazil in the production of chemical products (pharmaceuticals, medicines, fertilizer, plastics, and so on). Therefore, Brazil finds it advantageous to specialize in coffee and the United States finds it advantageous to specialize in chemicals. By trading, Brazil gets chemical products more cheaply and the United States gets coffee more cheaply than if each produces both types of products itself.

Similar illustrations can be given with many other goods. For instance: French perfume and Arabian oil; Bolivian tin and Peruvian cotton; Florida oranges and Nebraska wheat. Can you think of other examples?

Comparative Advantage

But what if a country can produce *two* goods, such as meat and wine, more cheaply than another country? Is there still a basis for trade in those goods between the two countries? This question was asked by the English economist David Ricardo in *The Principles of Political Economy and Taxation* (1817). Ricardo's answer was yes, and his brilliant reasoning helped to establish him as the greatest of the classical economists.

Ricardo showed that, even if one country has an absolute advantage in the production of two products, it is the *relative* advantage—the *comparative* rather than absolute advantage—that counts. Ricardo proved this by demonstrating that it pays for each country to specialize in producing the good in which it has the greatest "degree" of advantage. The two countries can then trade for the alternative good.

The law of comparative advantage accounts for the logic of international trade, and it underlies the meat-and-wine example used earlier. Thus, because the United States had a comparative advantage in meat and France had one in wine, it paid for them to specialize and trade. More meat and wine were thereby consumed by the two countries than if each tried to produce both goods.

Can you think of similar illustrations for individuals? For example, if you were a doctor as well as an expert gardener, you might nevertheless employ a gardener who is less competent than yourself. Why? Because you could be more productive (and thus earn more income) as a doctor than as a gardener. Similarly, if you were a lawyer as well as a good typist, you would probably find it more profitable to hire a typist—even one who is less proficient than you.

Conclusion: The Argument for Free Trade

However, suppose a law prohibited you from hiring a gardener (or a typist), so that you were compelled to do the gardening (or typing) yourself. In that case, you would be less efficient in your own occupation.

The same principle applies to countries. Through specialization and free or unrestricted trade, nations achieve a more efficient allocation of world resources. As a result, all nations end up with more goods, and hence with a higher standard of living, than if they imposed legislation restricting free trade.

The effect of free trade on nations is the same as the effect of increases in resources or improvements in technology. That is, the effect on nations is the same as if they experienced outward shifts of their production-possibilities curves. Thus, legislation that restricts free trade also reduces nations' standards of living.

Free Trade Versus Import Protection

The law of comparative advantage demonstrates a fundamental principle. *By engaging in free trade, nations make more efficient use of the world's scarce resources, thereby raising standards of living.*

This principle is universally acknowledged. Nevertheless, all nations impose import restrictions of one form or another to protect some of their domestic industries. The restrictions may be of several types:

Tariffs   These are customs duties or taxes imposed by a government on the importation of a good. Tariffs may be (1) specific, in the form of a tax per unit of the commodity, or (2) ad valorem, based on the value of the commodity.

Import Quotas   These are laws that limit the number of units of a good that may be imported during a specified period. An import quota (often simply referred to as a "quota") is thus an example of a nontariff barrier to free trade.

Nontariff Barriers   These are any laws or regulations, other than tariffs, that nations impose in order to restrict imports. For instance, to "protect the health and safety" of their citizens, many countries establish higher standards of quality for various kinds of imported goods than for similar goods produced domestically. Food products and automobiles provide typical examples. Nontariff barriers (other than import quotas) are direct but subtle protective devices that are never publicly stated as such. Hence, they have become a major form of trade protection and are used to different degrees by all countries.

Analyzing Quotas and Tariffs

The economic effects of quotas and tariffs can be examined more closely within the framework of a demand and supply model. Such a model is presented in Exhibit 3. To simplify the analysis, the model is based on two assumptions:

ECONOMICS IN THE NEWS

"Us" Is "Them"

Protecting Whom from What?

By Bjorn Ahlstrom

I have a problem with the word "foreign." Every few years, someone urges us to protect American commerce by erecting trade barriers against "foreign" products. But what does foreign really mean?

Sony televisions are made in San Diego. Harley-Davidson motorcycles are 50 percent made in Japan. Which one is foreign?

For that matter, what is domestic? Some 335,000 of the "American" cars sold here each year are made in Japan or Korea—more than the number of cars imported by Mazda, Mitsubishi, and Isuzu combined. Chrysler Corp. annually sells in the United States more than 120,000 Chryslers imported from the Far East, representing more than 11 percent of its total sales, while Honda builds more than 320,000 cars here. Which of these are domestic and which foreign?

The Volvo 780 that we sell in the United States has a French engine, a Japanese transmission, an American air conditioner, a German electronic system, Singaporean control valves, a Canadian exhaust system, a Taiwanese power antenna, South Korean electrical components, Swedish axles, and Irish tires. It is designed and assembled in Italy. Is this a Swedish car?

Volvo North America sells the 780. We directly or indirectly (through our dealers) employ 25,000 American citizens—including me. The other cars and trucks we sell are made in Nova Scotia, Virginia, Ohio, Utah, Belgium, and Sweden. Our parent company, AB Volvo, is owned by 162,000 shareholders in 50 countries, quite a few of them in the United States. Is this a foreign company?

I think "international" is a better word. International, just like Ford. Or Coca-Cola. Or IBM.

Companies like these—and there are thousands of us—buy raw materials and components all over the world, wherever the price and the quality are right. We make our products all over the world, wherever it makes the most business sense.

Now let's make this more complicated. AB Volvo is a Swedish company. Our Volvo Penta division makes marine engines in Virginia. Most are sold here, but some are exported, even to Sweden. What's foreign in this case? Are we dealing with imports or exports?

This is not a minor curiosity. Why is Taiwan's trade surplus with the United States so large? One-third of the surplus results from American corporations making or buying things in Taiwan and shipping them back to the United States—at a profit. The same thing is true of Singapore, South Korea, and Mexico: their trade surpluses are heavily dependent on American/international corporations that have based themselves there.

Today, "us" is "them." Except for quite small businesses, there's no such thing as a domestic or foreign company. We're all international. And that means we're all American.

So, when you talk about trade barriers, remember this: You cannot write a trade-restriction law that will not cost American jobs. Or one that will not raise what we pay for American-made products. Or one that will not reduce the value of American savings invested in American and international securities.

The way the world works now, if anyone imposes trade barriers, everyone loses.

Source: Bjorn Ahlstrom is president and chief executive officer of Volvo North America Corporation. This article is adapted from one that appeared in *The Detroit News*, July 14, 1988.

EXHIBIT
3

Quotas and Tariffs at Work

If there were no trade between the two countries, the market price of a sweater would be $90 in the United States and $30 in England.

But if unrestricted trade is permitted, the U.S. and English markets will automatically adjust to a *single* "world" price of $50 per sweater. At this price, the United States will import, and England will export, 400,000 sweaters. The two markets will be in equilibrium because there will be no excess quantities demanded or supplied—no "shortages" or "surpluses."

If the United States imposes an import quota of 200,000 sweaters, the price will rise to $70. Correspondingly, the price in England will decline to $40 in order that English exports of 200,000 sweaters precisely equal American imports. Thus, the two markets will again be in equilibrium, but not at a single world price.

The United States could achieve the same results by imposing a tariff of $30 per sweater. The U.S. price would then rise by $20 and the English price would decline by $10, resulting in a *price differential* of $30.

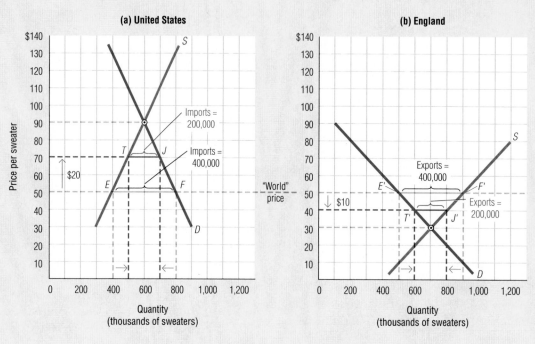

(a) United States

(b) England

1. There are only two countries in the world, the United States and England.

2. Each country produces and consumes wool sweaters.

Therefore, each country's supply and demand for the good is reflected by its own supply and demand curves.

What will be the "world" equilibrium price of wool sweaters under these circumstances? The answer is best understood if we conduct the analysis first under conditions of free trade and then under restricted trade.

Free Trade

If we assume that trade is unrestricted between the two countries, as Exhibit 3 shows, the world equilibrium price will settle at $50. The reason is that, *only* at this price, the United States' excess quantity demanded, *EF* (a "shortage") precisely equals England's excess quantity supplied, *E′F′* (a "surplus"). To make up these differences, the United States imports, and England exports, 400,000 sweaters. The world market is thus in equilibrium. At any other *single* world price, as you can easily verify, there can be no equilibrium, because a shortage in one country is not offset by a surplus in the other.

It is important to note how the $50 world price compares with the domestic price that would exist in each country if there were no trade. In the United States the domestic price would have been $90; in England it would have been $30.

Restricted Trade

Suppose the United States imposes a quota that limits the importation of sweaters to a maximum of 200,000. This will make the excess quantity demanded in the United States equal to *TJ*, at a price of $70 per sweater. The corresponding excess quantity supplied in England will be *T'J'*, at a price of $40 per sweater. This means that the United States will import, and England will export, 200,000 sweaters. The two markets will thus be in equilibrium but at different prices.

What are the economic consequences of the quota? Some of the more important results may be noted:

1. The equilibrium price in the importing country is higher, and the equilibrium price in the exporting country is lower, than the single world equilibrium price that would result in the absence of quotas.

2. Both countries experience a decline in trade—in this example, 200,000 sweaters.

3. American producers benefit from the quota by increasing their production from 400,000 sweaters to 500,000. English consumers also benefit by increasing their consumption from 500,000 sweaters to 600,000. Conversely, the quota penalizes American consumers by reducing their consumption from 800,000 sweaters to 700,000. It also penalizes English producers by reducing their production from 900,000 sweaters to 800,000.

4. The same results could have been achieved if the United States imposed a tariff of $30 per sweater. In order for American imports to equal English exports, the market price in the United States would rise to $70 and the market price in England would decline to $40. The *price differential* of $30, the amount of the tariff, would thus be shared by both countries.

These results suggest a surprising conclusion:

The economic consequences of import restrictions are to a large extent the same as those resulting from an *increase in shipping costs.* **Such costs raise prices in the importing country and reduce the volume of goods consumed. Therefore, anyone who argues in** favor of imposing a quota or tariff on a good in order to protect it from foreign competition should, in order to be logically consistent, also argue in favor of *increasing the cost of transporting the good.*

Visible and Invisible Effects of Protection

If the world's political leaders know that free trade leads to greater efficiency, why do they impose protective trade restrictions? The most common reason among most countries is obvious: *In the industries affected, imports cause unemployment.* For example, the American automobile and steel industries, as well as their suppliers, have suffered substantial increases in unemployment at various times due partly to the importation of foreign cars and steel.

But these are the visible effects. There are also invisible effects that rational policymaking must take into account.

1. **Imports Create Jobs** It is not usually obvious that imports provide a significant source of new jobs. These occur in those industries producing the exports that foreigners buy with the money earned from our imports. Some major American exporting industries include those producing various kinds of agricultural, mineral, fuel, chemical, and manufactured goods.

2. **Protection Reduces Exports** It follows that the volume of our exports suffers from import restrictions. By making it harder for foreigners to sell to us, we reduce their income and therefore their ability to buy our goods. As a result, although we may be reducing unemployment in our protected industries, we may also be increasing it in our exporting industries.

3. **Protection Reduces Consumer Choice** Import restrictions narrow the range of choices available to consumers. They are denied the privilege of purchasing what they believe is the best product for their money. Instead, they are required to pay higher prices either for similar products or for what they regard as less desirable products.

4. **Protection Reduces Competition** Import restrictions limit competition from foreign producers. This permits protected domestic industries to become less efficient and perhaps to gain more monopolistic control over their markets. It is interesting to note that, in the opinion of many experts, unrestricted trade is a far more effective means of promoting competition and efficiency than the federal antitrust (antimonopoly) laws designed for those purposes.

Unemployment and Trade-Adjustment Assistance

It is logical to conclude, therefore, that nations will experience the greatest gains from trade by engaging in free trade. In that way, countries will produce and exchange those goods in which they have the greatest comparative advantage.

But what happens to American workers who become unemployed due to increased foreign competition? In most cases they become eligible for government-financed trade-adjustment assistance. This consists of extended unemployment compensation, job-retraining programs, and moving allowances to help cover the costs of reemployment in distant locations. Unfortunately, the various assistance programs have often been poorly managed and inadequately funded. However, this is a criticism of governmental administrative failures, not of free trade.

Conclusion: Tariffs Preferred to Quotas

Despite the universally acknowledged benefits of unrestricted trade, it is likely that nations will always employ certain forms of protection. This is done for political as well as economic reasons. In democratic countries, it is also done because of enormous pressures exerted by special interest groups that benefit from protection. That being the case, which type of protection is economically preferable—quotas or tariffs?

With respect to quotas, there are two facts to consider:

1. A quota limits the domestic availability of a good. This drives up its price, thus enhancing profits for domestic and foreign producers.

2. A quota requires importers to apply for government licenses. These are usually granted in proportion to the applicant's past sales (not to mention political connections) or some other arbitrary standard unrelated to costs, efficiency, or any other meaningful economic criterion.

With respect to tariffs, there are also two facts to consider:

1. A tariff is a tax on imports. This raises the price of a good and reduces quantity demanded. But a tariff does not discriminate against exporters, so the more efficient ones may still be able to penetrate the protected market.

2. A tariff yields tax revenues to the government.

The benefits of these revenues are distributed in one form or another to various groups in society.

Because of these considerations, quotas are a more harmful form of import protection than tariffs.

Import quotas and tariffs both entail economic costs. Quotas stifle competition, create vested interests in quota allocation, and are discriminatory in their effects. Tariffs distort relative prices but permit market forces to allocate society's resources. Thus, if some degree of trade protection is desired for whatever reason, the country would be better off with tariffs than with import quotas.

Arguments for Protection

The law of comparative advantage and the economic benefits of free trade have never been successfully refuted, despite many heroic attempts to do so. Nevertheless, efforts by special interest groups to obtain import protection are common. American history is replete with long and eloquent pleas by business executives, union representatives, and political leaders contending that theirs is a "different" situation requiring special consideration. Most of these arguments for protection can be grouped into one of the following categories:

1. Infant industry argument
2. National security argument
3. Wage protection argument
4. Employment protection argument

You'll see below that there are flaws in all these arguments. But before you read on, you should understand the following fundamental point:

We can sell abroad only if we buy abroad. When the United States imports from foreign countries, those countries earn thereby most of the dollars they need to purchase American exports. In general, *exports are the cost of trade, and imports are the return from trade,* **not the other way around. Over the long run, a nation must export (sacrifice goods) in order to import (acquire goods).**

Infant Industry Argument

Should a nation pass legislation to protect its growing "infant industries" from foreign competition?

In Defense of Protection

Petition of the Candlemakers

Frederic Bastiat

This article, written in 1847, is an amusing satire upon the popular arguments for protective tariffs. The author was a staunch free trader and French expositor of the classical school of economics.

Petition from The Manufacturers of Candles, Wax Lights, Lamps, Chandeliers, Reflectors, Snuffers, Extinguishers; and from the Producers of Tallow, Oil, Resin, Alcohol, and generally of everything used for lights.

To the Honorable Members of the Chamber of Deputies:

GENTLEMEN—

We are subjected to the intolerable competition of a foreign rival, who enjoys, it would seem, such superior facilities for the production of light, that he is enabled to inundate our national market at so exceedingly reduced a price, that he draws off all custom for us. Thus an important branch of French industry, with all its innumerable ramifications, is suddenly reduced to a state of complete stagnation. This rival is none other than the sun.

If, by shutting out as much as possible all access to natural light, you thus create the necessity for artificial light, is there in France an industrial pursuit which will not, through some connection with this important object, be benefited by it?

If more tallow be consumed, there will arise a necessity for an increase of cattle and sheep. Thus artificial meadows must be in greater demand; and meat, wool, leather, and above all, manure, this basis of agricultural riches, must become more abundant.

If more oil be consumed, it will cause an increase in the cultivation of the olive tree. This plant, luxuriant and exhausting to the soil, will come in good time to profit by the increased fertility which the raising of cattle will have communicated to our fields.

Our heaths will become covered with resinous trees. Numerous swarms of bees will gather upon our mountains the perfumed treasures which are now cast upon the winds.

Navigation would equally profit. Thousands of vessels would soon be employed in the whale fisheries.

There is, in short, no market which would not be greatly developed by the granting of our petitions.

Our petition is, *to pass a law directing the shutting up of windows, dormers, skylights, shutters, curtains, in a word, all openings and holes through which the sun is used to penetrate into our dwellings.*

Gentlemen, you cannot fail to be convinced that there is perhaps not one Frenchman, from the opulent stockholder down to the poorest vendor, who is not interested in the success of our petition.

The question is, whether you wish for France the benefit of gratuitous consumption, or the supposed advantages of laborious production. Choose, but be consistent. And does it not show the greatest inconsistency to check as you do the importation of coal, iron, cheese, and goods of foreign manufacture, in proportion as their price approaches *zero*, while at the same time you freely admit the light of the sun, whose price is during the whole day at *zero*?

An *infant industry* is an underdeveloped industry that may not be able to survive competition from abroad. The infant industry argument for protection says that such industries should be shielded temporarily with high tariffs or quotas. The protection is needed until the industries develop technological efficiency and economies of scale that will enable them to compete with foreign industries.

This type of plea was the basis on which tariffs were established for a number of industries during the nineteenth and twentieth centuries. But economists have come to recognize three major points regarding this argument:

1. Tariffs or other protective devices become the vested interests of particular business and political groups. When that happens, protective measures become extremely difficult to eliminate.

2. Some protected industries never grow out of the "infant" stage. That is, they never become able to compete effectively with more mature industries in other countries.

3. An increase in tariffs or quotas results in higher prices to domestic consumers. Therefore, if an industry must be shielded from foreign competition, a subsidy would be more desirable because it tends to increase output as well as to reduce costs and prices. Moreover, a subsidy is visible and must be voted periodically by Congress. This makes it easier to eliminate when it has outlived its intended function.

National Security Argument

Can we be assured of the strong industrial base in steel we need for modern defense if much of the steel we require were imported from distant countries?

This question provides an illustration of the "national security argument" for protection. The argument is based on the assumption that a nation should be as self-sufficient as possible in the production of goods needed for war and defense.

On the face of it, this plea for protection seems persuasive. On closer examination, however, the following criticisms become apparent:

1. It is primarily a military argument rather than an economic one. Therefore, it should be decided by the proper military experts without the distorting

influence of people who have a direct business interest in the outcome. Those with a knowledge of economics can help by pointing out the costs of protection in terms of resource misallocation and a reduced standard of living.

2. Many industries are important, in one way or another, to defense or national security and could qualify equally well for increased protection.

3. As pointed out in the discussion of the infant industry argument, a subsidy is preferable to a tariff or quota if some form of shielding is necessary.

Wage Protection Argument

Because wages in the United States are among the highest in the world, some people argue that tariffs or quotas are needed to protect American workers from the products of cheap labor abroad. Three criticisms and qualifications of the wage protection argument are particularly important:

1. Labor isn't the only resource entering into production. It's a resource that is combined with varying quantities of capital and land. Because of this, products may often be characterized as *labor-intensive, capital-intensive,* or *land-intensive,* depending on the relative proportions of resources that are employed in production.

2. Other things being equal, low-wage countries will have an advantage over high-wage countries *only* in trading products that are labor-intensive. These are goods for which wages are a relatively large proportion of total costs. In such cases, high-wage countries may be better off not competing with low-wage countries in trading these products.

3. Even where labor-intensive products are concerned, however, high-wage countries may be able to compete effectively with low-wage countries if labor productivity in the former is high enough to compensate for lower wage levels in the latter.

Employment Protection Argument

Supporters of trade protection often argue that tariffs or quotas are desirable because they reduce imports. This leads to higher levels of production, employment, and income in domestic industries.

Is this a valid plea for protection? Like the previous arguments, it may seem persuasive, but the following considerations should be kept in mind:

1. Any benefits in the form of higher income and employment, if they occur, are not likely to last long. The history of tariffs and quotas shows that nations tend to retaliate with their own protective measures, leaving all sides worse off than before.

2. Tariffs and quotas tend to result in higher prices, thus penalizing domestic consumers while benefiting inefficient domestic producers. This encourages a movement of resources out of more efficient industries into less efficient (protected) ones, thereby raising costs and reducing comparative advantage.

3. In international trade, goods pay for goods. Hence, a nation that exports must also import. Protective measures tend to impede this and, therefore, to limit rather than to encourage higher real income and employment in the long run.

Conclusion: Fundamental Principle

The most frequently heard argument for quotas and tariffs is that they *"protect American workers from the products of cheap labor abroad."* Is the argument valid?

If foreign countries can sell textiles, or steel, or computer memory chips, or any other products more cheaply than U.S. manufacturers can, that will mean fewer jobs in those American industries. But it will also mean more jobs in other industries. Which ones? Those that can now export goods to the countries that are spending their dollar earnings to buy American products. Therefore, quotas and tariffs do not protect American jobs. They only protect *some* jobs by preventing the growth of others that would emerge in a free (unprotected) market.

In view of these arguments, you can see why the following principle of international trade is fundamental:

You and I sell ("export") our labor in order to earn income with which to buy ("import") the goods we want. Similarly, nations export in order to earn income with which to buy the imports they want. Thus, just as you and I work in order to consume, nations export in order to import—*not the other way around!*

Strategic Trade Policy: A Case for Protection?

Economists may disagree on many issues. But for more than 200 years they have been almost unanimous in their belief that free trade makes the best use of scarce resources and maximizes consumers' satisfactions. Therefore, whenever pleas in defense of protection have been advanced, economists have been quick to attack them with arguments based on the law of comparative advantage.

Since the early 1980s, however, a new theory in defense of protection has evolved—one that may constitute a "special" case. Recall from the "infant industry" argument for protection that some protected industries never mature. Therefore, if government is to shield a firm or industry from foreign competitors, subsidies are preferable to tariffs and quotas. The new theory says that, under certain circumstances, protective subsidies may actually be beneficial. By introducing certain "exception principles," the theory makes the following argument:

In world markets dominated by a few large firms, a strategic trade policy can be superior to free trade. A *strategic trade policy (STP)* is one in which government alters the terms of competition to favor certain domestic firms over foreign firms. For example, a protective subsidy granted to high-technology firms that have substantial economies of scale may enable the firms to capture significantly larger shares of foreign competitors' markets.

Notice that the example of *STP* theory refers to firms producing high-tech products. Firms involved in supercomputers, optical fibers, microchips, telecommunications, and commercial jet aircraft are examples. Because these firms have extremely high research and development (R&D) costs, they need long production runs to recoup those costs. *STP* emphasizes economies of scale as a major source of comparative advantage for such companies.

Why should government want to protect and promote selected firms within particular industries? Advocates of *STP* offer two reasons:

Increase GDP and Employment Protection enables manufacturers to develop new technologies through increased R&D spending. New technologies can create barriers that help keep potential foreign competitors out of the market. Protected firms may thus be able to

"A Banana into a Cage of Monkeys"

Henry George, a late-nineteenth-century popular writer on economic issues, is best remembered for his advocacy of a "single tax" on land. But he was also an ardent propagandist for free trade, as the following pithy remarks from his work, Protection or Free Trade *(1886), point out.*

Free trade consists simply in letting people buy and sell as they want to buy and sell. Protection consists in preventing people from doing what they want to do. Protective tariffs are as much applications of force as are blockades, and their objective is the same—to prevent trade. The difference between the two is that blockades are a means whereby nations seek to prevent their enemies from trading; protective tariffs are a means whereby nations attempt to prevent their own people from trading. *What protection teaches us is to do to ourselves in time of peace what enemies seek to do to us in time of war.*

* * *

It might be to the interests of lighting companies to restrict the number and size of windows, but hardly to the interests of a community. Broken limbs bring fees to surgeons, but would it profit a municipality to prohibit the removal of ice from sidewalks in order to encourage surgery? Economically, what difference is there between restricting the importation of iron to benefit iron-producers and restricting sanitary improvements to benefit undertakers?

* * *

To introduce a tariff bill into congress or parliament is like throwing a banana into a cage of monkeys. No sooner is it proposed to protect one industry than all the industries that are capable of protection begin to screech and scramble for it.

* * *

All experience shows that the policy of encouragement, once begun, leads to a scramble in which it is the strong, not the weak; the unscrupulous, not the deserving, that succeed. What are really infant industries have no more chance in the struggle for governmental encouragement than infant pigs have with full grown swine about a meal tub.

* * *

To have all the ships that left each country sunk before they could reach any other country would, upon protectionist principles, be the quickest means of enriching the whole world, since all countries could then enjoy the maximum of exports with the minimum of imports.

* * *

Who Will Be The Sacrificial Lamb?

Despite all the economic arguments that can be presented in favor of free trade, many prominent people, including some business executives, labor leaders, and politicians, continue to plead for protection. For example:

"Are we now to tell the typical shoe worker, aged 50, that he must cheerfully surrender his job to a 12-year-old girl in Taiwan or a peasant working behind his cottage in Spain? Can we make him whole by offering him a course in bricklaying or bus driving? He will not buy it. And neither, we think, will the nation."

> George O. Fecteau, Former President
> United Shoe Workers of America

"Thousands of our members have become sacrificial lambs on the altar of foreign trade. The flood of foreign-made tires is being felt by our members in that segment of the rubber industry. If nothing is done to check this trend, thousands of tire plant jobs will be eliminated. We cannot and will not stand still for this. Our people don't want to hear ideological phrases of the learned economists' theories on free trade. What all our members really want is a steady job."

> Peter Bommarito, Former President
> United Rubber Workers

"South African ferrochrome producers, using predatory prices, are destroying producers in a drive to control the U.S. supply of this critical material. Without import relief, there would then be nothing to prevent a South African ferrochrome cartel from extracting monopoly prices or withholding supply from U.S. steel producers and thus substantially disrupting this essential industry."

> A. D. Gate
> Committee of Producers of High Carbon
> Ferrochrome, Washington, D.C.

"Comparative advantage [says] let each country produce what they make best and we have unlimited free trade and the end result is prices are cheaper and everybody's life is better. There is one catch. If the comparative advantage is such that in some countries children work, have no minimum wage, no 40-hour workweek, no other protections, no free unions, then obviously they have an advantage of exploitation and it should not be subsidized by the workers of this country. In fact, it ought to be opposed."

> Edmund G. Brown, Jr.
> Former Governor, State of California

grab larger shares of world markets and eventually earn higher profits. To the extent that the increased profits are spent on new investment, domestic output, wages, and employment will rise.

Provide External Economies Protection may create valuable benefits for other firms and industries in the domestic economy. Such benefits are called *external economies*. The computer and microchip industries, for example, have spawned numerous innovations in the production of other products ranging from automobiles and electronic goods to machine tools and steel. Import protection, *STP* advocates contend, would give domestic firms an incentive to invest more heavily in R&D, thus reducing the chance of their being preempted by foreign competitors.

ECONOMICS IN THE NEWS

Airbus: Predatory Pricing?

Boeing Considers Stretch Version of 737 to Better Vie with Airbus

SEATTLE (Reuter)—Boeing Co. said it was talking with customers about a stretch version of its popular 737 medium-range aircraft, which some analysts said may compete more aggressively with Airbus Industrie's A320 jetliner.

UAL Corp.'s United Airlines, which had been headed toward an all-Boeing fleet, agreed instead to lease 50 A320s from Airbus and took an option for 50 more.

United said in choosing Airbus that the A320 met the airline's performance criteria. Industry analysts noted that Airbus was promoting the jet as having greater range and thrust than Boeing's competing 737-400 jets.

Boeing representatives insist the 737-400 has performance and cost-of-operation advantages over its competition, saying that Airbus simply beat Boeing's offer.

Source: *Investor's Business Daily,* July 22, 1992, p. 3.

The Airbus Example

Because of these advantages, *STP* theory concludes that it isn't necessarily correct to think of a nation's comparative advantage as relatively fixed. Governments can sometimes create their own comparative advantage. Examples of government actions that are capable of altering trade patterns include the launchings of the European Airbus consortium, the Japanese semiconductor industry, and the U.S. space program. Of these, the Airbus project has received the widest attention from both American and European economists.

Airbus Industrie, created in the early 1970s, is a major multinational aircraft manufacturer headquartered in Paris. The company is subsidized by the governments of France and several other European nations because they all have firms that build component parts for Airbus planes. The subsidization scheme has enabled Airbus to gain a significant share of the world aircraft market at the expense of American firms such as Boeing, Lockheed, and McDonnell Douglas.

Several government studies published in Europe have concluded that the Airbus project has been a success. Airbus and its supplying firms in England, France, Holland, and Germany have experienced substantial direct and external benefits in the form of increased employment, advancements in research, and gains in technology. Because of this, the reports conclude, benefits of the program to the participating nations have exceeded its costs.

Critiques of *STP*

This conclusion, as well as the net gains of strategic trade policies claimed by other nations, have been questioned by a number of economists. Some of their chief criticisms have been these:

- Virtually every protected firm in Europe and Japan (including Airbus) has, in almost every year since its creation, been heavily dependent on subsidies. Few of these firms have earned even average profits in most of their years of operation.

- Despite large R&D subsidies and import protection, the English and French computer and semiconductor industries have had only moderate success in expanding their shares of world markets. However, the cost of protection to taxpayers has been substantial.

- There is evidence that protected firms in some countries have engaged in predatory (below-cost) pricing in efforts to gain greater shares of world markets. This has created the potential for retaliatory responses by foreign competitors.

- Protection of high-tech firms may have harmed other industries as well as benefited them. For example, protecting computer companies has probably raised the costs of microchips, other electronic components, and the salaries of engineers. Because of the higher costs, other industries that use the same inputs find it harder to compete in world markets.

The potential *net* benefits obtainable from a strategic trade policy are thus questionable. At best they're likely to be relatively small. At worst they may even be negative.

Conclusion: Free Trade Still Is Preferred

The law of comparative advantage holds that because countries differ from one another in resources and skills, free trade enables nations to gain the benefits of specialization.

STP theory suggests that the law of comparative advantage isn't absolutely rigid. Through the use of a strategic trade policy consisting of subsidization and protection of certain types of industries, nations may be able to make their own comparative advantage. However, this assumes an extraordinary level of knowledge and ability on the part of government officials. The reason is easy to see:

The success of a strategic trade policy depends on many conditions. Among them:

- **The economies of scale of the firms and industries involved**

- **The ability of government to identify a strategic firm or industry**

- **The need for firms to compete rather than collude in their price and output decisions**

- **The knowledge that foreign competitors and their governments will not retaliate, even where substantial profits are at stake**

If these conditions are unknown, as they almost always are, the adoption of a strategic trade policy may turn out to do more harm than good. Because of this, practically all economists continue to favor free trade and to condemn protection.

GATT and Multilateral Trade Negotiations

When World War II ended in 1945, most countries declared their intention to promote international trade and to remove restrictive trade barriers. Under United Nations auspices, a document known as the *General Agreement on Tariffs and Trade* (GATT) was signed in 1947 by the United States and many other countries. The Agreement provides both a code of rules and a forum in which negotiations and other trade discussions take place. The GATT's overall function is to serve as the governing body for international trade relations. Today the great majority of nations are members of the GATT and almost all the nonmembers subscribe to its principles. As a result, the GATT has often played a major role in the settlement of trade disputes between countries.

The GATT seeks to achieve four long-run objectives:

- Nondiscrimination in trade

- Reduction of tariffs

- Elimination of import quotas

- Resolution of differences through consultation

Nondiscrimination in Trade

The GATT requires member nations to treat each other equally by adopting unconditional most-favored-nation clauses in trade agreements. A *most-favored-nation clause* is a provision in a trade treaty by which each signatory agrees to extend to the others the same preferential tariff and trade concessions that it extends to nonsignatories (that is, the same treatment that it gives to its "most favored nation"). Virtually all trading nations have adhered to this principle.

Reduction of Tariffs

Since it went into effect in 1948, GATT has negotiated worldwide reductions in tariffs. In the United States, for example, the average tariff rate on manufactured goods has declined from 16 percent of their value in the late 1940s to less than 5 percent today.

Elimination of Import Quotas

When GATT was established, quantitative restrictions on imports posed the single greatest obstacle to international trade. Today, import quotas are less widespread. However, in the United States and a number of other countries, import quotas have been replaced to some extent by "voluntary" export restraints. These are informal agreements between nations to limit exports of certain products in order to allow time for domestic producers to adjust to changing market conditions. The products usually subjected to export limits include agricultural goods, automobiles, steel, and textiles. Although voluntary export restraints are simply disguised protective quotas, they operate outside the GATT system and hence are not subject to its rules.

Resolution of Differences Through Consultation

Member-nation representatives of the GATT meet periodically to iron out agreements aimed at reducing barriers to trade. The meetings, called "rounds," usually last for several years. At the Tokyo Round, completed in 1979, consultations on export subsidies, import licensing, dumping practices, and other trade issues led to extensive new agreements. The Uruguay Round, which began in 1986 and has continued in several phases, is the most comprehensive thus far. It seeks to achieve long-term, market-oriented reforms by dismantling most remaining trade-distorting practices, setting new standards of trade policies, and integrating developing countries into the GATT system.

Most nations express a commitment to free trade. Through the efforts of the GATT, nations have reduced obstacles to trade. Despite the efforts, however, all nations continue to maintain various trade impediments, disguised as nontariff barriers, in order to protect domestic industries from foreign competition.

some goods in order to receive others. These sacrifices are the terms of trade, and they are measured by the slope of a trade-possibilities curve.

3. A basis for trade exists when there are differences in opportunity costs between countries. Therefore, when few differences exist, there will be incomplete international specialization and hence a reduced volume of world trade.

4. The law of comparative advantage is among the oldest principles of economics. The law shows why it pays for each nation to specialize in producing the goods in which it has the greatest *relative* advantage. Then, by trading with others, nations can have more goods than if each nation tried to be self-sufficient.

5. Despite the mutual benefits of free trade, nations have instituted various forms of protection. Common instruments of protection consist of tariffs, import quotas, and other nontariff barriers.

6. Many arguments may be advanced in favor of protection. Most, however, involve serious flaws. In general, if some form of protection is to be imposed, a tariff is less objectionable on economic grounds than an import quota. However, a subsidy, which is a form of direct assistance, is less objectionable than either.

7. Some experts believe that, in world markets dominated by a few large firms, a strategic trade policy can lead to results that are superior to those realized with free trade. But the conditions needed to implement a successful strategic trade policy are difficult to attain. Consequently, economists continue to contend that the costs of protectionist policies to consumers outweigh the benefits to producers and government.

8. The General Agreement on Tariffs and Trade (GATT) is a system of rules aimed at promoting free trade. Almost all nations subscribe to the rules. As a result, the GATT has succeeded in reducing many trade barriers.

Summary of Important Ideas

1. By engaging in free or unrestricted trade, nations receive the greatest gains from trade. These gains are measured by the increases in goods that a country receives as a result of trading with others.

2. Trade involves sacrifice. A nation must give up

Terms and Concepts to Review

opportunity cost

specialization

gains from trade

law of comparative advantage

terms of trade

trade-possibilities curve

marginal propensity to import

law of absolute advantage

tariff

import quota

nontariff barrier

infant industry

strategic trade policy

General Agreement on Tariffs and Trade (GATT)

Questions and Problems

1. Suppose that, with the same resources, the United States can produce either 40 cars or 40 tons of food per unit of time. With the same resources, Japan can produce either 60 cars or 20 tons of food in the same time. Assume that both countries have constant costs of production (their production-possibilities curves are straight lines).

a. Using graph paper, plot the production-possibilities curves on separate graphs. To facilitate uniformity for classroom discussion, use the vertical axes for cars and the horizontal axes for food. Label the axes and curves.

b. What is each country's domestic-exchange ratio? Are there any comparative advantages? Explain.

c. Suppose that each country is self-sufficient. Then the United States might produce, say, 30 cars and 10 tons of food. Japan, on the other hand, might produce, say, 15 cars and 15 tons of food. On your respective graphs, label these points A and A'.

d. If the United States and Japan each specialize and trade, what combinations of goods will each produce? Label the points B and B', respectively.

e. Suppose the United States and Japan trade 20 tons of food for 40 cars. What combinations of goods will each country consume? Label these points E and E' on the countries' trade-possibilities curves. What are the gains from trade for each country and for the two countries together?

f. Explain the gains from trade in terms of the *slopes* of the production-possibilities curves and the trade-possibilities curves. Label these curves along with their slopes.

2. The Constitution of the United States (Article 1, Sec. 10) states: "No State shall, without the consent of the Congress, lay any imposts or duties on imports or exports, except what may be absolutely necessary for executing its inspection laws." Do you think the Founding Fathers were wise to pass this law? What would happen to the American standard of living if each state were allowed to impose protective barriers to trade with other states and countries?

3. "If you believe in the free movement of goods between nations, you should logically believe in the free movement of people, too. This means that cheap foreign labor should be admitted to the United States, even if it results in the displacement of American labor." Do you agree? Explain your answer.

4. An editorial in a leading newspaper stated: "The United States should develop a large shipbuilding industry. Such an industry would provide more jobs and higher incomes for workers. Moreover, the ships could be used for passenger and cargo service in peacetime, and could be quickly converted for military purposes in case of war. In view of these advantages, it would be wise for the U.S. government to protect the domestic shipbuilding industry from foreign competition until it can grow to a stronger competitive position." Do you agree with this editorial? Explain.

5. Abraham Lincoln is reputed to have remarked: "I don't know much about the tariff. But I do know that when I buy a coat from England, I have the coat and England has the money. But when I buy a coat in America, I have the coat and America has the money." Can you show that Lincoln was correct only in the first sentence of his remark?

TAKE A STAND

Japanese Trade Practices: Are They Unfair?

As the U.S. trade deficit has grown, so has concern over the "fairness" of trade with other nations. Some analysts contend that the trade deficit is largely the result of unfair trade practices by foreign countries. These practices include selling exports at prices below the cost of production and limiting certain imports or forbidding them entirely.

Some see the trade practices of Japan, in particular, as a threat to the U.S. economy. These critics cite the troubled consumer electronics and automobile industries as cases in point, and call for countermeasures. If Japan subsidizes its exports or sells its products below cost, the United States should impose strict tariffs, quotas, or other barriers to Japanese goods. And the United States should not import Japanese goods freely unless Japan agrees to import more American goods.

Others argue that a retaliatory course of action could hurt more than it helps. Restricting Japanese imports would reduce the number of goods available to consumers and cause prices to rise. Domestic importing firms would lose business and employ fewer workers. Furthermore, increasing the trade barriers against Japanese goods is likely to provoke a similar response from Japan. U.S. producers and exporters would then lose business and employ fewer workers. The United States has nothing to gain from restricting trade, but may have a good deal to lose.

Restrictive trade practices have been cited as one of the causes of the Great Depression. The Smoot-Hawley Tariff Act of 1930 raised tariffs to more than 60 percent of an import's price—the highest they have ever been. The intention was to encourage domestic production by discouraging imports and increasing net exports. The result, however, was to provoke other countries to retaliate with a set of restrictions that crippled international trade. Everyone suffered. Similar results could be expected if the United States and Japan—two of the world's economic powers—were to engage in a trade battle.

Any response by the United States to Japan's trade practices must be governed by a rational assessment of their intentions and their effects. It is possible that protective legislation is warranted. It is also possible that the complaints of unfairness are coming from less efficient domestic industries trying to avert competition from more efficient foreign industries. *Are Japanese trade practices unfair?*

Yes: Japan Inhibits Imports and Subsidizes Exports

The real world does not conform to the ideal of free trade. Nations have always protected their industries in order to promote progress. If the United States had not protected its infant textile industry in the early 1800s, the machinery and skilled labor needed to keep pace with the industrial revolution a few decades later might have been lost. Germany, France, and Italy also nurtured and protected their domestic industry in the nineteenth century, and emerged as economic powers. Similarly, Japan's rise to economic prominence is attributable in part to protectionist policies. South Korea, following the same strategy, has achieved a high rate of growth. Many nations restrict trade. Not all, however, gain an unfair advantage from doing so.

Those who accuse Japan of seeking an unfair trade advantage point to the restrictions its government imposes on imports. To protect domestic rice producers, for example, Japan will not allow any foreign rice into the country even though its agricultural capabilities are limited and importing rice would cost less than growing it. Japan also restricts automobile imports. The country exports over $51 billion worth of cars each year but imports $6 billion worth. In addition, Japan's *keiretsu*, groups of mutually owned companies that do business primarily with each other, effectively block foreign firms from gaining more than superficial access to Japan's domestic markets.

Japan's trade practices regarding exports are even more unfair than its policies regarding imports. Over the last three decades, Japan has subsidized its consumer electronics, steel, and automobile industries. The subsidies allow producers to sell those goods at artificially low prices. Japan has also been accused of "dumping"—flooding foreign markets with goods priced below cost. These tactics have been interpreted as an attempt to force out American industries from world markets.

As the world's largest economy, the United States has felt the brunt of unfair Japanese trade practices. Japan's artificially induced advantage has hurt U.S. producers and eliminated U.S. jobs.

No: Japan Has Comparative Advantage in Producing Technologically Advanced Goods

Japan's success in U.S. markets is the result of comparative advantage. Since World War II, Japan has developed the technology and expertise to become the world's most efficient producer of automobiles, consumer electronics, and other products. This has occurred because, compared to the United States, Japan spends proportionally more on education, undertakes more technological research and development, and invests a larger share of gross output in new capital.

Accusations of unfair Japanese trade practices aren't supported by the facts. Per capita, Japan spends almost as much ($1,900) on imported goods as the United States ($2,050). Japan's tariff rate (8 percent) is not much more than that of the United States (6 percent) and other industrialized nations (7 percent). Like other countries, Japan exports more of the goods that it specializes in producing and imports more of the goods in which it does not specialize. For example, Japan exports more cars than it imports, but imports more food, raw materials, and fuels than it exports. In general, goods that Japan cannot produce as efficiently at home, it imports from other countries. Rice is an exception because of its religious and cultural significance.

Cries of unfair trade are a smokescreen to hide special benefits sought by U.S. producers. It is easier to restrict imports than to reduce costs or improve product quality. U.S. cars, for example, are priced to cover executive salaries two to three times higher than those of Japanese auto executives. To keep U.S. cars competitively priced, the government imposes import restrictions that raise the prices of Japanese cars. Still, U.S. consumers continue to buy Japanese cars.

Domestic producers and the federal government attempt to justify protectionist legislation by accusing foreign producers of unfair trade practices. For example, if a foreign producer's

price is 0.5 percent higher in foreign markets than in U.S. markets, American producers immediately complain. Yet the difference is easily explained by changes in the value of U.S. currency relative to other currencies. Unfair trade is also invoked if U.S. profits on exports run less than 8 percent of sales, yet this is a level frequently missed by U.S. firms. These accusations have contributed to the imposition of over 8,000 different taxes and tariffs on imports into the United States.

The Question: Are Japanese Trade Practices Unfair?

■ Some argue that trade restrictions and the *keiretsu* business system block foreign access to Japan's markets. At the same time, industries such as U.S. consumer electronics, steel, and automobile industries suffer when Japanese manufacturers sell such goods at artificially low prices.

■ Others argue that Japan has developed a comparative advantage in producing technologically advanced goods such as consumer electronics and automobiles. Japan naturally exports relatively more of those goods, and imports relatively more agricultural products and other goods that it does not specialize in producing.

Where Do You Stand?

1. Should U.S. consumers care whether low-priced, high-quality Japanese imports are the result of a natural comparative advantage or an artificial advantage? Explain.

2. The United States imposes many trade restrictions on goods imported from less developed countries, such as Mexico, Brazil, and Poland. Discuss whether these restrictions are prompted by unfair trade practices against the United States or have some other cause.

3. Do you think the loss of jobs in an industry that faces competition from foreign imports is a sign of unfair trade? Is the loss of jobs in this type of industry good or bad for the economy? Explain.

4. Are Japanese trade practices unfair? Justify your stand.

Sources: Arthur MacEwan, "The New Evangelists: Preaching That Old-Time Religion," *Dollars and Sense*, November 1991, pp. 6–20; "Beams and Motes," *The Economist*, December 7, 1991, p. 30; "Japan's Troublesome Imports," *The Economist*, January 11, 1992, p. 61.

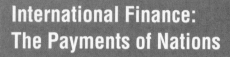

International Finance: The Payments of Nations

The Balance of Payments

The Foreign Exchange Market

Flexible Versus Fixed Exchange Rates

Today's Problems and Policies

Origins: International Economics

Learning Guide

Watch for answers to these important questions

What is the balance of payments? Why do nations prepare balance-of-payments statements?

Where is foreign exchange bought and sold? What determines the exchange rate?

Why must fixed exchange rates result in either overvalued or undervalued currencies? Why do nations today engage in managed floating?

What contributions did David Ricardo, James Meade, and Bertil Ohlin make to the study of international economics?

Lord Baron Rothschild, a famous nineteenth-century British financier, was once asked by a friend to explain the international financial system. He replied, "My dear chap, there are only two men in the world who understand the international financial system—a young department manager in the U.S. Treasury and a rather junior man in the Bank of England. Unfortunately, they disagree."

What do we mean by "international finance"? In the most general sense it deals with the monetary side of international trade. It's therefore concerned with the nature of international transactions. This includes their forms of payment, the ways in which they are recorded for purposes of analysis and interpretation, and their economic effects on the nations that are involved.

These statements may seem somewhat vague at this point. But they suggest that international finance is a vast and complex subject. You can gain some appreciation of its nature by examining two of its main components—the balance of payments and the foreign exchange market.

The Balance of Payments

Many countries publish a periodic financial report called the *balance of payments*. This is a statement of the money value of all transactions between a nation and the rest of the world during a given period, such as a year. These transactions may consist of imports and exports of goods and services and movements of short-term and long-term investments, gifts, currency, and gold. The transactions can be classified into several categories, of which the two broadest are the current account and the capital account.

The balance of payments for the United States is shown in Exhibit 1. Note that the monetary results of transactions are recorded either as debits or as credits. A *debit* to a balance of payments account is any transaction that results in a flow of money out of the country. The outflow is represented by a minus sign (−). A *credit* to a balance-of-payments account is any transaction that results in a flow of money into the country. The inflow is represented by a plus sign (+). Thus, an import is recorded as a debit and an export is recorded as a credit to a balance-of-payments account.

The balance-of-payments statement is easy to comprehend. By reading each line and the accompanying explanations, you will understand how the various items are obtained. If you do that now, the following additional comments will prove helpful.

■ **Line (4)** This discloses what is popularly known as the *balance of trade*. It is that part of a nation's balance of payments dealing with merchandise imports and exports. You will sometimes hear it said that a nation has either a "favorable" or an "unfavorable" balance of trade. Such a statement depends on whether the value of the country's merchandise exports is greater or less than the value of its merchandise imports. In reality, however, as you will discover shortly, the statement is misleading. It neglects the fact that other items in a nation's balance of payments will necessarily offset a surplus or deficit in the balance of trade.

■ **Line (10)** This reflects the net effect of all short-term transactions. A positive number discloses how much money the United States received from the rest of the world. A negative number shows how much the United States paid the rest of the world.

■ **Line (19)** This reflects the net effect of all long-term transactions. Here, too, the number can be either positive or negative.

■ **Line (20)** This is where the current and capital accounts are combined into a single number. If the number is positive, it means that the value of what the nation sold to the rest of the world, such as goods, services, securities, or other assets, exceeded

the value of what it purchased. If the number is negative, the value of what the nation bought from abroad exceeded the value of what it sold.

■ **Lines (21) and (22)** Finally, these entries show you why the balance of payments always balances *in an accounting sense*. That is, the sum of debits equals the sum of credits because of the principle of double-entry bookkeeping. As you can see from the explanation accompanying line (21), the statistical discrepancy assures that the overall balance on line (22) is zero.

The Foreign Exchange Market

It is impossible to use the information provided in the balance-of-payments statement without understanding *foreign exchange.* This consists of instruments used for making international payments. Examples of these instruments include currency, checks, drafts, and bills of exchange (which are orders to pay currency). Foreign exchange is bought and sold in a world market called the "foreign exchange market." The price of one currency in terms of another is the *foreign exchange rate,* or simply the *exchange rate.*

Thus, if you take a trip to France, you will have to sell some dollars to buy French francs. The francs are needed in order to pay for lodging, food, and anything else you purchase while you are in France. If you travel from France to Italy, you can buy Italian lire with any francs or dollars you may have. And if you go from Italy to Britain, you can purchase British pounds with francs, lire, or dollars.

The same principle applies to most other countries you visit. You can generally buy one currency with another.

Graphic Illustration

The market for a currency, like the market for wheat, copper, and other raw material commodities, can be represented by an ordinary demand and supply model. The reasons are easy to see.

1. There are numerous participants in the market for each currency. Most of the participants are banks and other dealers who buy and sell currencies on their own behalf as well as for their customers: importers, exporters, multinational corporations, tourists, and so forth.

EXHIBIT
1

U.S. Balance of Payments, 1990—Summary of International Transactions (billions of dollars)

Debits (–), money outflows.
Credits (+), money inflows.

(1)	CURRENT-ACCOUNT TRANSACTIONS	
(2)	Merchandise exported	$389.6
(3)	Merchandise imported	–497.7
(4)	**Balance on merchandise trade: (2) + (3)**	**–108.1**
(5)	Services exported	133.3
(6)	Services imported	–106.9
(7)	**Balance on services: (5) + (6)**	**26.4**

Services exported (+) include: travel expenditures by foreigners here (which is the same as "scenery exported by the U.S."), interest and dividends received from abroad, banking and insurance services rendered to foreigners by domestic financial institutions, and expenditures by foreign governments here.

Services imported (–) include the opposite, such as travel expenditures by Americans abroad (that is, "scenery imported by the U.S."), interest and dividends paid to foreigners, and so on.

(8)	**Balance on goods and services: (4) + (7)**	**–81.7**
(9)	**Unilateral transfers, net**	**22.3**

These are "one-way" gifts and grants involving no return commitments or claims. Money outflows (–) consist of U.S. private remittances sent abroad plus U.S. government military and nonmilitary grants to other countries. Money inflows (+) are the opposite. The net result (i.e., balance) has generally been negative.

(10)	Balance on current account: (8) + (9)	–59.4
(11)	CAPITAL-ACCOUNT TRANSACTIONS	
(12)	U.S. official reserve assets abroad, net	–2.2

Includes major currencies, gold, and other internationally accepted reserve assets. They are held at the International Monetary Fund, an arm of the United Nations. The assets are owned by the central bank of the United States, the Federal Reserve System. They are used for settling accounts with the central banks of other countries, such as the Bank of England and the Bank of Japan.

(13)	U.S. government assets abroad, other than (12), net	3.0

Includes U.S. government loans and other long-term claims, less repayments.

(14)	U.S. private assets abroad, net	–58.5

Includes direct investment by U.S. individuals and companies in foreign property and securities, plus other financial claims.

(15)	**U.S. assets abroad, net: (12) + (13) + (14)**	**–57.7**

Note: Increases in U.S. assets abroad are money outflows (–). Decreases are money inflows (+).

(16)	Foreign official assets in the U.S., net	32.4

Includes U.S. Treasury securities and other official claims against the U.S. government held by foreigners.

(17)	Other foreign assets in the U.S., net	53.9

Includes direct investment by foreigners in U.S. property and securities, plus other financial claims.

(18)	**Foreign assets in the U.S., net: (16) + (17)**	**86.3**

Note: Increases in foreign assets in the U.S. are money inflows (+). Decreases are money outflows (–).

(19)	Balance on capital account: (15) + (18)	28.6
(20)	Balance on current and capital accounts: (10) + (19)	–30.8

This line would equal zero if there were no omissions in the data, as explained below for line (21).

(21)	Statistical discrepancy	30.8

Includes omissions (which may be quite large) that arise because the balance of payments summarizes millions of individual recorded international transactions only—not unrecorded ones. Hence, complete accuracy is impossible. The statistical discrepancy, which is simply the number on line (20) with the sign reversed, serves as a balancing item. It assures that the balance shown on line (22) below is zero—that is, that the balance of payments balances.

(22)	Overall balance (20) + (21)	0.0

Source: U.S. Department of Commerce.

EXHIBIT
2

The Foreign Exchange Market: Dollar Prices of Japanese Yen

Equilibrium prices and quantities are determined by the interactions of demand and supply.

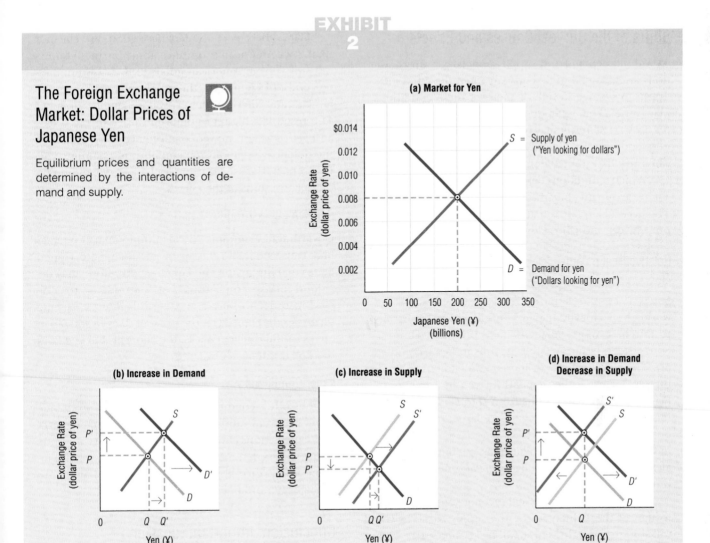

(a) Market for Yen

S = Supply of yen ("Yen looking for dollars")

D = Demand for yen ("Dollars looking for yen")

Japanese Yen (¥) (billions)

(b) Increase in Demand

(c) Increase in Supply

(d) Increase in Demand Decrease in Supply

2. The product, whether it be dollars, francs, lire, or pounds, is standardized. Therefore, like buyers and sellers of raw-material commodities, buyers and sellers of currencies are concerned only with their prices or exchange rates.

3. The market participants' knowledge of currency exchange rates is "perfect." This means that buyers and sellers are completely informed about bids and offers throughout the world, because information is transmitted immediately by computerized information networks.

Because of these conditions, the determination of a currency's price, such as the U.S. dollar price of Japanese yen (¥), can be illustrated as in Exhibit 2. Thus, in Figure (a), the demand curve for yen is down-

ward sloping, indicating that buyers will purchase more yen at lower prices than at higher ones. The supply curve is upward sloping, signifying that sellers will offer more yen at higher prices than at lower ones.

At any given time, the demand curve for yen represents *"dollars looking for yen"* and the supply curve of yen represents *"yen looking for dollars."* The equilibrium price and quantity of yen are determined by the intersection of the two curves. In the figure, the equilibrium price is $0.008 per yen and the equilibrium quantity is ¥200 billion.*

---

*A yen is worth only a fraction of a cent. So if you want to express the price of yen in terms of whole dollars, move the decimal point the correct number of places to the right. Thus a price of $0.008 = ¥1 is equivalent to a price of $8 = ¥1,000. This is also equivalent to a price of $1 = ¥125.

Shifts of the Curves: Causes and Effects

As with all demand and supply models, certain conditions are assumed to be constant when the curves are drawn. A change in one or more of these conditions may cause a change in demand or in supply—*a shift of the curves*. The result may be a new equilibrium price, a new equilibrium quantity, or both, as you learned when you first studied demand and supply.

Which conditions are assumed to be constant? There are many, but three are especially important. They are (1) relative real income levels, (2) relative price levels, and (3) relative interest rates.

Relative Real Income Levels

Suppose that the level of real income in the United States rises in relation to that of the "rest of the world"—specifically, Japan. This enables Americans to purchase more Japanese-made products: Hondas, Sonys, steel, "scenery" (that is, trips to Japan), and so on. The result will be an increase in "dollars looking for yen," causing the demand for yen to increase. In Figure (b), the curve shifts from *D* to *D'*, leading to a higher equilibrium price and a larger equilibrium quantity of yen. The yen thus *appreciates*, or increases in value, relative to the dollar. This, of course, is equivalent to saying that the dollar *depreciates* relative to the yen.

Conversely, if Japan's real income rises in relation to that of the United States, the supply curve of yen will shift to the right. There will be an increase in "yen looking for dollars" as Japanese seek to buy more American goods. In Figure (c), the supply curve shifts from *S* to *S'*, causing the equilibrium price of yen to decline and the equilibrium quantity to increase. The yen thus *depreciates* relative to the dollar, which means the dollar *appreciates* relative to the yen.

Relative Price Levels

How do changes in each country's general price level affect foreign exchange rates? Because the effects are slightly more complicated, it helps to analyze them in two steps.

■ **Step 1**   If inflation in the United States is higher than it is in Japan, many Japanese products (such as cars and electronic goods) will be cheaper than similar American products. In Figure (d), therefore, the demand for yen increases from *D* to *D'* as Americans substitute more of these Japanese goods for American goods.

■ **Step 2**   Because these Japanese goods are cheaper than their American substitutes, some Japanese buyers will switch from American goods to their own domestic goods. In Figure (d), the supply curve shifts from *S* to *S'* because there are fewer "yen looking for dollars." The result is a higher equilibrium price of the yen— an *appreciation* of the yen—and hence a *depreciation* of the dollar. What about the equilibrium quantity? This may remain the same or it may change, depending on the relative shifts of the curves.

Relative Interest Rates

Government economic (fiscal and monetary) policies may cause interest rates to be higher in the United States than in Japan. The Japanese, therefore, may decide to increase their supply of "yen looking for dollars" in order to purchase American interest-earning securities. In Figure (c), the price of the yen will fall in terms of the dollar. That is, the yen will *depreciate* and the dollar will *appreciate*.

Other Conditions

Various other conditions can affect foreign exchange rates. Economic and political policies in each country and expectations about future developments are some of the factors that may play a role. However, relative income level, price level, and interest-rate changes are of major importance, as you will see shortly.

Conclusion: Important Ideas and Potential Problems

In the world of international finance, two concepts are of fundamental importance. One of these is the balance of payments; the other is the foreign exchange market.

The balance of payments discloses the inflows and outflows of money that a nation experiences during a given period. These flows result from the purchase and sale of goods, services, securities, and other assets and from gifts and grants. In general, a nation's balance of payments is affected by the price of its currency relative to others in the foreign exchange market.

The foreign exchange market is a world market in which various nations' currencies (and certain other financial claims) are bought and sold. In an unregulated foreign exchange market—one in which governments do not interfere—equilibrium prices and quantities are determined by the forces of demand and supply. When the price of one currency rises relative to the price of another, the more valuable currency is said to *appreciate* and the less valuable one is said to *depreciate*. It follows that changes in exchange rates affect the prices that domestic buyers pay for foreign goods as well as the prices that foreign buyers pay for domestic goods.

In general:

An *appreciation* **of a nation's currency makes its exports dearer and its imports cheaper. A** *depreciation* **does the opposite: It makes a country's exports cheaper and its imports dearer. Thus, changes in exchange rates may substantially influence a country's balance of payments. This can create fundamental policy problems of deep concern to the community of nations.**

Flexible Versus Fixed Exchange Rates

One of the fundamental financial problems facing an economy concerns its balance-of-payments adjustments to surpluses and deficits. How do adjustments in the balance of payments take place? The answer depends on whether exchange rates are flexible or fixed.

To understand why this is true, recall that a country's balance of payments can be expressed as the sum of its balances on current account and capital account:

$$\text{Balance of payments} = \text{current account} + \text{capital account}$$

This means that, in order for a nation's balance of payments to be zero in any given year, a change in the current account must be offset by an equal and opposite change in the capital account. Otherwise, the balance of payments won't be in equilibrium. That is, the balance of payments won't balance in an *economic* sense (although it will balance in an accounting sense, as explained earlier).

As you'll now see, a nation's balance of payments will always tend toward equilibrium if its currency is flexible—free to fluctuate on the foreign exchange market. But if the nation's central bank intervenes in the foreign exchange market by buying or selling its currency "against the market," the nation's balance of payments may experience prolonged disequilibrium or economic imbalance.

EXHIBIT **3**

The Foreign Exchange Market: Undervaluing the British Pound; Overvaluing the American Dollar

An increase in the demand for pounds from *D* to *D'* raises their free-market equilibrium price from $2 = £1 to $3 = £1.

In order to hold down (undervalue) the price of a pound to $2, the Bank of England can increase the supply of pounds. The Bank does this by printing and selling the amount *EF* (= £200 million) in the foreign exchange market, thus shifting the supply curve from *S* to *S'*. Britain will thereby receive $400 million, calculated at the exchange rate of $2 × £200 million.

D = Demand for pounds: "Dollars looking for pounds"
S = Supply of pounds: "Pounds looking for dollars"

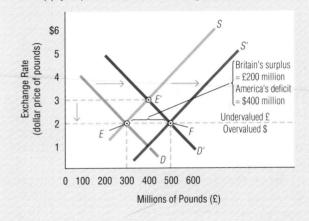

Flexible (Floating) Exchange Rates

Flexible exchange rates are also called floating exchange rates. They are simply exchange rates that are free to fluctuate in response to market forces of demand and supply.

Exhibit 3 provides an illustration in terms of U.S. dollars and British pounds (£). Suppose that the equilibrium exchange rate is $2 = £1 and the equilibrium quantity is £300 million. If U.S. imports from Britain now increase, the demand curve for pounds will shift to the right from *D* to *D'*. The pound will thus *appreciate* to $3 = £1, and the dollar will *depreciate*.

What will be the economic effects? Because the pound is now more expensive, American imports of British goods, as well as American investments in

Britain, will decline. Also, because the dollar is now cheaper, British imports of American goods, and British investments in the United States, will rise. Therefore, at the new equilibrium price of $3 per pound, any disequilibrium (either a deficit or a surplus) in either country's balance of payments will be *automatically* corrected. This automatic correction, it should be emphasized, will always occur under a system of flexible exchange rates.

Fixed Exchange Rates

Despite the advantage of automatic balance-of-payments adjustment under a system of flexible exchange rates, many countries have often maintained fixed exchange rates. Under a system of fixed exchange rates, a country's currency may be either undervalued or overvalued in relation to its free-market price. This can result in a prolonged *economic* disequilibrium in a country's balance of payments even though the statement always balances in an accounting sense.

Undervaluation

An undervalued currency is one whose price is held *below* the price that would exist in a free market. This makes the currency cheaper, thereby encouraging exports. It also makes other currencies dearer, thereby discouraging imports.

For example, look again at Exhibit 3. Suppose Britain wants to offset the increase in demand by keeping the price of the pound at $2. This is easily done. Britain's central bank, the Bank of England, can increase the supply of pounds in the foreign exchange market simply by printing and selling an amount equal to the excess demand EF (= £200 million). This action will have several effects:

1. Exports and Imports Because the pound is now undervalued in terms of the dollar, British goods will be cheaper for Americans to buy. However, the dollar is now overvalued in terms of the pound. Therefore, American goods will be more costly for Britons to buy. Thus, undervaluation of the pound relative to the dollar encourages British exports and discourages British imports.

2. Terms of Trade Britain's terms of trade with the United States will worsen. That is, Britain will have to export more units of goods (such as textiles) for each unit of goods imported (such as food). However, the United States' terms of trade with Britain will improve.

This is because the United States will have to export fewer units of goods for each unit of goods imported.*

3. Balance of Payments Because of the undervalued pound, Britain will experience a surplus in its balance of payments with the United States. And because of the overvalued dollar, the United States will experience a deficit in its balance of payments with Britain. As shown in Exhibit 3, the amount of the surplus or deficit is EF = £200 million = $400 million.

Overvaluation

An overvalued currency is one whose price is held *above* the price that would exist in a free market. This makes the currency dearer, thereby discouraging exports. It also makes other currencies cheaper, thereby encouraging imports.

Intentional overvaluation may be as common as intentional undervaluation. For example, some of the less developed oil-exporting nations have at various times overvalued their currencies. The purpose was to use the money (such as dollars, yen, and marks) earned from oil exports to more developed countries, where demand for oil was relatively strong, to pay for imports of technology, capital, and other goods from those countries.

How does overvaluation work? For illustrative purposes, look at Exhibit 4. It shows the free-market equilibrium price of pounds in terms of dollars at $3 = £1. What would happen if Britain were to fix the exchange rate at $4 = £1? The Bank of England would then have to buy up the excess supply of pounds—equal to the amount GH = £200 million = $800 million. This would shift the demand curve to the right from D to D'. The Bank could make these purchases only as long as it had enough dollars, yen, gold, or other internationally acceptable reserve assets with which to buy the pounds. Once the assets were spent, the demand curve would shift back. The price of pounds would thus fall to the free-market level of $3 per pound, unless other countries were willing to lend additional reserves to the Bank in order to sustain the demand curve at D'.

What would be the results of an overvalued pound? The effects would be the opposite of those for

---

*Remember: The ultimate goal of economic activity is consumption, not production. Therefore, nations export in order to import, *not the other way around!* A country's terms of trade reflect the sacrifice it makes in the form of exports in order to earn income with which to purchase imports.

EXHIBIT 4

The Foreign Exchange Market: Overvaluing the British Pound; Undervaluing the American Dollar

Suppose the free-market equilibrium price of British pounds is $3 = £1. In order to raise (overvalue) the price of a pound to $4, the Bank of England can increase the demand for pounds. The Bank does this by buying up the amount GH (= £200 million) in the foreign exchange market, thus shifting the demand curve from D to D'. Britain will thereby spend $800 million (= $4 x £200 million).

D = Demand for pounds: "Dollars looking for pounds"
S = Supply of pounds: "Pounds looking for dollars"

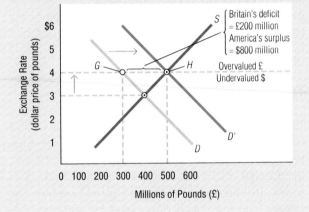

an undervalued one. Try listing the various effects to make sure you understand them.

Managed or "Dirty" Floating

It is obviously easier for a country to maintain an undervalued currency than an overvalued one. Undervaluation requires the nation's central bank simply to continue printing and selling its own currency. Overvaluation, however, requires the central bank to continue receiving an inflow of internationally acceptable reserve assets (such as dollars, marks, yen, and so on) sufficient to buy its own excess currency in the foreign exchange market.

Are today's foreign exchange rates flexible or are they fixed? The answer is that they are some of both. Many nations' central banks intervene in the foreign exchange market to prevent unwanted fluctuations be-

yond a few percentage points. This is called "managed" or "dirty" floating. Both terms are commonly used.

To see how managed floating works, suppose the U.S. central bank wants to keep the exchange rate with the French franc at approximately $1 = Fr 5. If the exchange rate remains at around this level, no intervention by the U.S. central bank—the Fed (or Federal Reserve System)—is undertaken. But if the price of the dollar rises to, say, $1 = Fr 5.3, the Fed would increase the supply of dollars by selling dollars for francs. This would make dollars cheaper and francs dearer. Conversely, if the price of the dollar declines to, say, $1 = Fr 4.7, the Fed would increase the demand for dollars by buying dollars for francs. This would make dollars dearer and francs cheaper.

Countries engaged in managed floating may thus enjoy, at least partially, a major benefit of flexible rates—namely, automatic balance-of-payments adjustments. But more important, keeping foreign exchange-rate fluctuations within a relatively narrow range enables these countries to realize, at least partially, two chief advantages of fixed exchange rates. These are (1) reduced uncertainty and (2) stable terms of trade.

Reduced Uncertainty Fixed exchange rates can encourage international trade and investment. If you are an importer or an exporter, for example, you like to know that the prices at which you do business today will yield an anticipated rate of profit in the coming months. If exchange rates fluctuate, you may realize unexpected losses (as well as gains) when merchandise is paid for upon delivery—say, 30 or 60 days later. The same principle applies whether you are a long-term foreign investor or the president of a multinational corporation. Your objective is to earn future profits on your investment abroad. You do not want to incur the *additional* risk of fluctuations in the foreign exchange rate when you eventually convert your foreign profits into dollars in order to "bring them home."

Stable Terms of Trade A nation's terms of trade tend to vary directly with the international value of its currency. For example, a decrease in the value of the pound will encourage British exports while discouraging imports. Britain will thus give up more units of goods to other countries for each unit of goods imported from them. Of course, an increase in the value of the pound will have the opposite effect. Managed floating, therefore, helps countries to stabilize their terms of trade rather than allowing them to vary substantially.

Thus:

In the opinion of many experts, a system of managed exchange rates combines the advantages of flexible and fixed rates. However, the validity of this conclusion depends on (1) the range of exchange rate fluctuations that countries permit and (2) the frequency of their intervention.

The Group of Seven

In 1986, leaders of seven major industrial nations—Britain, Canada, France, Germany, Italy, Japan, and the United States—agreed to work together to coordinate economic policy. Known as the Group of Seven or G-7, the organization's reason for existence is the belief that floating exchange rates and fixed exchange rates each have advantages and disadvantages. Through international economic cooperation, member nations build on the strengths of both while avoiding the weaknesses of each.

A chief goal of G-7 is to keep the exchange rates of major trading currencies within acceptable ranges in terms of one another. For example, if world market forces cause the price of the U.S. dollar to be "too high" relative to the Japanese yen or the German mark, G-7's central banks in the seven countries sell dollars in an effort to drive down the price. If the dollar's price is deemed to be "too low," the central banks buy dollars in an effort to raise the price. The allowable price range of each country's currency is somewhat flexible, and is reviewed from time to time to see how it accords with its nation's volume of trade. All the price ranges are kept secret in order to reduce chances of speculation.

Several advantages result from G-7's coordinative effort:

- **Sovereignty** It respects the rights of nations to adopt their own corrective fiscal and monetary policies in efforts to adjust their exchange rates.

- **Flexibility** It relies on economic indicators (such as major commodity prices and interest rates) and peer pressure by central bankers rather than on rigid formulas and requirements.

- **Symmetry** It focuses on surplus as well as deficit countries and isn't biased toward or away from domestic policies or exchange rates.

To what extent do G-7's members succeed in achieving greater stability of exchange rates? The an-

swer is unknown. All major industrial nations use stimulative fiscal/monetary policies in efforts to maintain high levels of employment. But history shows that these nations are often unwilling to alter their policies significantly for the sake of improving exchange rate stability.

Exhibit 5 illustrates how the foreign exchange rates of major currencies can vary over a short-run period. Critics of G-7 use such graphs as evidence that coordinative efforts to achieve exchange-rate stability are largely ineffectual. Supporters of G-7 use the same graphs as evidence that the fluctuations might have been more severe if coordinative efforts hadn't been undertaken. In reality, there's probably some truth in both beliefs, but we can't really be sure. Even when it's sometimes announced that G-7 has intervened in the foreign exchange market during a given period, there's never any official pronouncement about the extent of its intervention.

Today's Problems and Policies

Today's international economic system is often characterized by varying degrees of managed exchange rates. However, like all demand and supply curves, those in the foreign exchange market frequently shift. As a result, the currencies of some countries become overvalued, causing balance-of-payments deficits. The currencies of other countries become undervalued, causing balance-of-payments surpluses. Eventually, realignments of exchange rates take place in one of two ways: *devaluation* or *revaluation.*

Devaluation This is an official (government) act that makes the price of a country's currency cheaper in terms of other currencies. History shows that a country whose currency is intentionally significantly overvalued will eventually be forced to devalue it in order to reduce a persistent balance-of-payments deficit.

Revaluation This, the opposite of devaluation, serves to appreciate (rather than depreciate) a country's currency in the foreign exchange market. History shows that a country whose currency is intentionally undervalued is not particularly prone to revalue it in order to reduce a persistent balance-of-payments surplus.

Evidently, devaluation and revaluation are not *lasting* corrective measures. To achieve such corrections, nations must adopt appropriate long-term policies. Three that can be employed are (1) fiscal and mone-

EXHIBIT
5

Foreign Exchange Rates for the U.S. Dollar

Do the Group of Seven's coordinative policies bring greater stability to exchange rates? We can't answer the question because the extent to which G-7 intervenes in the foreign exchange market isn't known.

(a) Trade-Weighted Average Value of the Dollar*

(b) Values of the U.S. Dollar†

* Averages of monthly data.   † Weekly averages, weeks ending at Friday.

Sources: Board of Governors of the Federal Reserve System; Federal Reserve Bank of Cleveland.

tary policies, (2) trade controls, and (3) exchange controls.

Fiscal and Monetary Policies

Government actions pertaining to taxing, spending, and growth of the money supply are known as fiscal and monetary policies. Depending on the ways in which these policies are used, they can have either contractionary or expansionary effects on the nation's economy. How might a nation employ fiscal and monetary policies to correct either a deficit or a surplus in its balance of payments?

Deficit Nation: Contractionary Policies

A *deficit* nation can lower the price of its overvalued currency by pursuing contractionary fiscal and monetary policies. By reducing its prices at home relative to those in surplus nations, the deficit nation will discourage imports and encourage exports. However, contractionary fiscal and monetary policies can also cause increased unemployment at home. The deficit nation may thus be sacrificing domestic employment stability for balance-of-payments equilibrium. This was the case for developing nations such as Mexico and Brazil, which implemented contractionary policies in the early 1990s to lower the prices of their currencies.

The Big Mac Index: A Guide to Currency Values

Economists have long used a concept called *purchasing power parity* to compare prices in one currency in terms of another. The idea makes sense. If you can buy an item for $1 in the United States, you'd expect to be able to buy it for about the same price in other countries. Of course, short-term factors may cause disparities in exchange rates. But in the long run, purchasing power between nations should be about the same everywhere.

How can purchasing power be measured? Economists do it by compiling a representative "basket" of goods and services. They then determine its price, in terms of U.S. dollars or some other currency.

Unfortunately, deciding on what's "representative" is a lot harder than it seems. In Asian countries, rice is much more important than bread as a staple in most people's diets. In many Latin American and European countries, consumers sip far more wine than soft drinks. In the United States, homes with central heating—and, to a growing extent, even air-conditioning—are commonplace, but in many other nations, including some advanced ones, they're rarities. Numerous other differences exist in the quality of goods and in people's preferences for them. This makes it extremely difficult to compare purchasing power between countries.

Enter McDonald's

One possible solution, although a primitive one, is based entirely on the price of McDonald's hamburgers. Available in numerous countries, the Big Mac is known to virtually everyone. So the Big Mac Index (BMI)—the price of a Big Mac in each country expressed in terms of a single currency such as the U.S. dollar—would be understandable to children and to central bankers alike.

Of course, the BMI has faults as well as merits. On the one hand, it's hard to imagine the Bank of Japan intervening in the foreign-exchange market, buying or selling billions of *Biggu Makus* in order to influence the price of the yen. Such transactions can involve substantial losses for the bank. But on the other hand, the BMI is easy to use and interpret. Instead of measuring international trade flows, balance-of-payments imbalances, and other complicated ideas, it simply looks at worldwide prices of hamburgers at today's exchange rates and reveals whether currencies are overvalued or undervalued.

If the BMI ever gains universal acceptance among central bankers, will it affect the way in which they respond to international crises? Probably. One possibility is that if the index plummets, central bankers who guessed incorrectly might find their vaults stuffed with depreciating Big Macs. That lesson might be enough to discourage any further intervention.

A Big Mac Guide to Currency Values: 1992

(1) Country and city	(2) Exchange rate (currency units per U.S. dollar)	(3) Big Mac price	(4) U.S. equivalent price (3) ÷ (2)	(5) Overvaluation (+) or undervaluation (−) relative to U.S. dollar (4) ÷ U.S. Price: $1.95
United States (Chicago)	1.00 dollar	1.95 dollars	$1.95	—
Argentina (Buenos Aires)	0.99 pesos	3.30 pesos	3.33	+71%
Australia (Sydney)	1.31 A. dollars	2.50 A. dollars	1.91	− 2
Brazil (Rio de Janeiro)	4275 cruzeiros	7600 cruzeiros	1.78	− 9
Canada (Toronto)	1.19 C. dollars	2.80 C. dollars	2.35	+21
Britain (London)	0.56 pounds	1.67 pounds	2.98	+53
France (Paris)	5.15 francs	18.0 francs	3.50	+79
Italy (Rome)	1239 lire	3600 lire	2.91	+49
Japan (Tokyo)	125 yen	380 yen	3.04	+56
Germany (Berlin)	1.67 marks	4.30 marks	2.57	+32

Surplus Nation: Expansionary Policies

A *surplus* nation can raise the price of its undervalued currency by pursuing expansionary fiscal and monetary policies. If prices in the surplus nation rise faster than those in deficit nations, imports will be encouraged and exports will be discouraged. However, the surplus nation will then be sacrificing domestic price stability and employment in order to reduce other countries' deficits. This, of course, is not something that the surplus nation is likely to do. This was an unintended but persistent problem for many developing countries, including Mexico and Brazil, in the early 1980s.

A nation's balance of payments is affected by its fiscal and monetary policies. The use of these policies to achieve balance-of-payments equilibrium usually entails a sacrifice of some domestic stability. This is a trade-off that countries are usually reluctant to make.

Trade Controls

A second approach to reducing payments imbalances is through trade controls. A deficit nation can contract imports by imposing tariffs, quotas, and other trade barriers. It can also try to expand exports by subsidizing the industries it wants to encourage and by providing them with special tax benefits.

All countries, to varying degrees, engage in such policies. Their effects are obvious. Because they impede the operation of the law of comparative advantage, they misallocate resources. As a result, efficiency is impaired and the volume of world trade is reduced.

Exchange Controls

Finally, nations can reduce imbalances, or at least manage them more effectively, through exchange controls. These are commonly utilized by command economies. They require exporters to sell their foreign exchange to the government, which then uses the scarce funds to purchase needed imports. These may include such staple goods as foods, raw materials, and capital goods deemed necessary for economic growth. As a general rule, the scarce funds aren't likely to be used for such luxury goods as imported sports cars, audio and video equipment, and liquors.

As with trade controls, exchange controls misallocate resources and therefore contract the volume of world trade. In addition, they severely reduce consumer choice and hence are likely to encourage the growth of black (illegal) markets. For these reasons, exchange controls are not commonly employed by market-oriented economies, except perhaps in wartime emergencies.

In conclusion:

International economic policies are strongly influenced by economic and noneconomic (including political and military) considerations. Because of this, all nations, in varying degrees, impose trade restrictions and engage in managed floating. As a result, most political leaders are continually seeking to establish a set of workable rules for improving the efficiency of the international economic system.

Origins: International Economics

Economists have always been concerned with commercial and financial relationships between nations. Even before the time of Adam Smith, some writers showed a keen awareness of the role that international trade and payments can play in affecting the material well-being of nations. As a result, the study of international economics is as old as the study of economics. In *The Wealth of Nations* (1776), Adam Smith, with acute perception and extraordinary insight, defends free trade and condemns protection:

> It is the highest impertinence of kings and ministers, to pretend to watch over the economy of private people and to restrain their expense, either by sumptuary laws, or by prohibiting the importation of foreign luxuries. They are themselves always, and without any exception, the greatest spend-thrifts in the society. Let them look well after their own expense, and they may safely trust private people with theirs. If their own extravagance does not ruin the state, that of their subjects never will.
>
> To give the monopoly of the home market to the produce of domestic industry must in almost all cases be either a useless or a hurtful regulation. If the produce of domestic industry can be bought there as cheap as that of foreign industry, the regulation is evidently useless. If it cannot, it must generally be hurtful.
>
> It is the maxim of every prudent master of a family, never to attempt to make at home what it will cost him more to make than to buy. The tailor does not attempt to make his own shoes, but buys them of a shoe-

maker. The shoemaker does not attempt to make his own clothes, but employs a tailor; the farmer attempts to make neither the one nor the other, but employs those different artificers. All of them find it in their interests to employ their whole industry in a way in which they will have some advantage over their neighbors, and to purchase with a part of its produce, or what is the same thing, with the price of a part of it, whatever else they have occasion for. What is prudence in the conduct of every private family, can scarce be folly in that of a great kingdom.

That it was the spirit of monopoly which originally both invented and propagated protectionist doctrine cannot be doubted; and they who first taught it were by no means such fools as they who believed it. In every country it always is and must be the interest of the great body of the people to buy whatever they want of those who sell it cheapest. The proposition is so very manifest, that it seems ridiculous to take any pains to prove it; nor could it ever have been called in question had not the interested sophistry of merchants and manufacturers confounded the common sense of mankind.

David Ricardo: Comparative Advantage

Smith's defense of free trade was intuitive and philosophical. A retired English businessman, David Ricardo, provided a scientific defense, formulated in precise analytical fashion and illustrated with numerical examples.

Born four years before the appearance of Smith's masterwork, *The Wealth of Nations,* and writing 40 years after its publication, Ricardo developed rigorously and completely the theory of *comparative advantage.* Expounded in *The Principles of Political Economy and Taxation* (1817), the theory's universality and practicality were recognized almost immediately. This, along with Ricardo's other writings, established him as the greatest of the early classical economists. By the 1820s, a school of Ricardian disciples had formed whose ideas were to influence England's economic policies for decades to come. And by the 1830s, English economists as well as some members of Parliament were no longer referring to comparative advantage as a theory, but as a "law."

Approximately 100 years were to pass before the next major advances in international economics occurred. These were made by England's James Meade and Sweden's Bertil Ohlin.

James Meade: Modern International-Trade Theory

During the early 1930s, James Meade became involved with a renowned British scholar, John Maynard Keynes. Keynes was developing a theoretical structure that was to establish him as the founder of modern macroeconomics. Adopting Keynesian concepts, Meade developed his own ideas in several complex treatises written over a period of nearly two decades. For our purposes the ideas can be viewed as resting on relationships among four fundamental variables:

1. Employment

2. Balance of payments

3. Aggregate demand (or total spending)

4. Exchange rates

The first two variables determine efficiency. The second two variables are tools for attaining efficiency. Thus, suppose employment (the first variable) is too low because the economy is in recession. An increase in government spending will raise aggregate demand (the third variable) and help bring the economy to full employment. But the rise in aggregate demand will affect exchange rates (the fourth variable) and the balance of payments (the second variable). Alternatively, a government policy that leads to a decrease in the exchange rate can raise both aggregate demand and employment. But the lower exchange rate will also affect the balance of payments.

All four variables are thus interrelated. Policies cannot be adopted to deal with some of them without affecting all of them. Therefore, in order for policymakers to judge the impact of their measures on the economy's welfare, the relationships among the variables must be understood.

Meade's major works were written in the 1950s.* During that post-World War II era, foreign exchange rates were held fixed by national governments in order to encourage stable trade among nations recovering from the war. Although much of Meade's contribution was couched within the framework of fixed exchange rates, he nevertheless pointed out fundamental microeconomic and macroeconomic complexities that underlie modern international-trade theory.

---

*Meade published his *Theory of International Policy* in two volumes: *The Balance of Payments* (1951) and *Trade and Welfare* (1955).

James Meade
(1907–   )

Bertil Ohlin
(1899–1979)

After World War II, Meade was appointed part of a joint British and United Nations delegation for the promotion of free trade. This led to the creation of the General Agreement on Tariffs and Trade and to the subsequent trend toward tariff reductions that has continued to this day. In recognition of Meade's many contributions to international economic theory and policy, he was awarded the Nobel Prize in Economics in 1977.

Bertil Ohlin: General Global Equilibrium

By the late-nineteenth century, some economists in France, Switzerland, and England had begun to view the economy as a system of interrelated parts. The parts consisted of goods and prices, and the relationships between them were formed by the interaction of demand and supply in the economy's markets. Resources were assumed to be mobile, always moving to their highest valued uses. This mobility ensured that the economy was always in, or at least tending rapidly toward, a state of so-called "general" equilibrium.

These ideas, especially the assumption of resource mobility, seemed plausible to most economists. But resource mobility was a plausible assumption only within the domestic economy. In the global economy, some factors of production do not move readily across national borders in pursuit of the highest returns. In view of this, can the global economy achieve a state of general equilibrium? Bertil Ohlin, an eminent Swedish economist, theorized that it could.

Writing in the 1930s, Ohlin demonstrated the effect of international trade on wages and other factor payments. The essence of his theory can be stated in one sentence: *Under free trade, the international exchange of goods (rather than resources) will tend to ensure the equalization of similar types of factor payments.*

This tendency, Ohlin said, occurs because of the inexorable operation of the law of comparative advantage. In open world markets, businesses everywhere compete for consumers' expenditures. Consequently, producers in all nations are under pressure to improve efficiency by substituting lower-cost inputs for higher-cost inputs. The increased demand for lower-cost resources causes their prices to rise. Simultaneously, the decreased demand for higher-cost resources causes their prices to decline. Over the long run, therefore, prices of similar types of resources between nations tend to become equal.

Ohlin had little opportunity to see his theory verified. During the Great Depression of the 1930s, the United States and Western European countries adopted high tariffs and other protectionist policies. With the end of World War II in 1945, these trade barriers began a slow but steady decline. As a result, there has been a long-run trend among the major industrial nations toward price equalization of similar types of resources. However, the trend was relatively moderate until about the time of Ohlin's death in 1979. Since then, the trend has become more noticeable as trade barriers have continued to fall.

Ohlin made other major advances in economics. Some, unfortunately, were not translated from Swedish into English for more than a decade. Among them was a theory of macroeconomics that was largely the same as Keynes's but predated the Keynesian theory by several years. This alone would have been sufficient to ensure Ohlin's place in twentieth-century economic thought. Somewhat belatedly, the Swedish Royal Academy of Science acknowledged the importance of Ohlin's highly original work. In 1977, the King of Sweden awarded one of his nation's most respected scholars the Nobel Prize in Economics.

Summary of Important Ideas

1. The study of international finance is concerned with the payments of nations. Such payments are reported in a country's balance of payments, a periodic financial report.

2. The balance of payments summarizes all of a country's recorded money inflows and outflows resulting from international transactions, public and private.

3. Adjustments in the balance of payments take place through the foreign exchange market, where currencies are bought and sold. The prices of currencies are determined by international forces of demand and supply. Consequently, the currencies of nations may appreciate or depreciate relative to one another in the foreign exchange market.

4. Flexible exchange rates permit automatic adjustments to balance-of-payments equilibrium. Nevertheless, most countries today adhere to managed exchange rates in order to keep currency fluctuations within a fairly narrow range. Under such circumstances, balance-of-payments adjustments to equilibrium may not occur automatically.

5. Because of trade restrictions and managed exchange rates, resources are misallocated and world trade is reduced. Consequently, most political leaders are continually seeking workable rules for improving the efficiency of the international economic system.

6. International economics had its formal beginning with the development of the law of comparative advantage by the English classical economist David Ricardo. This law was rooted in Adam Smith's defense of free trade in *The Wealth of Nations.* In 1977, the Nobel Prize for economics was awarded to James Meade and Bertil Ohlin for their contributions to international economics. By blending Keynesian macroeconomic theory with international economic theory, Meade analyzed the mutual effects of full employment and balance of payments through changes in exchange rates and aggregate demand. Ohlin helped modernize

international economics by explaining how comparative advantage would tend to equalize factor payments through the exchange of goods rather than through the movement of factors.

Terms and Concepts to Review

balance of payments	*foreign exchange*
debit	*devalution*
credit	*revaluation*
balance of trade	

Questions and Problems

1. What are the sources of demand for foreign exchange? What are the sources of supply?

2. State whether each of the following transactions is a debit or a credit on the U.S. balance of payments.

a. An American firm imports $100,000 worth of French perfume.

b. An American tourist flies via British Airways from New York to London.

c. A British tourist flies via American Airlines from London to New York.

d. A British tourist flies via American Airlines from New York to London.

e. An American buys stock in a Swiss corporation.

f. An American sells stock in a German corporation.

g. The Federal Reserve Bank of New York reduces its debt to the Bank of Japan.

3. In a free market, if the dollar rate of exchange for French francs rises, what happens to the French rate of exchange for dollars? Explain.

4. How does each of the following transactions affect the supply of money in the United States?

a. The United States sells Chevrolets to England.

b. France sells perfume to the United States.

c. An American tourist visits Japan.

d. A Japanese tourist visits the United States.

5. From an *accounting* point of view, can there be a net positive or net negative balance in the balance of payments? What about an "economic" point of view?

6. Why do nations engage in managed floating?

7. "If a foreign exchange market did not exist, it would be necessary to create one."

On the basis of the following article, discuss why you agree or disagree with this statement.

How Does "the" Foreign Exchange Market Operate?

It is generally not possible to go to a specific building and "see" the market where prices of foreign exchange are determined. With few exceptions, the vast bulk of foreign exchange business is done over the telephone between specialist divisions of major banks. Foreign exchange dealers in each bank usually operate from one room; each dealer has several telephones and is surrounded by video screens and news tapes. Typically, each dealer specializes in one or a small number of markets (such as sterling/dollar or deutschemark/dollar). Trades are conducted with other dealers who represent banks around the world. These dealers typically deal regularly with one another and are thus able to make firm commitments by word of mouth.

Only the head or regional offices of the larger banks actively deal in foreign exchange. The largest of these banks are known as "market makers" because they stand ready to buy or sell any of the major currencies on a more or less continuous basis. Unusually large transactions, however, will be accommodated only by market makers on more favorable terms. In such cases, foreign exchange brokers may be used as middlemen to find a taker or takers for the deal. Brokers (of which there are several major firms and a handful of smaller ones) do not trade on their own account, but specialize in setting up large foreign exchange transactions in return for a commission (typically 0.03 cents or less on the sterling spread).

Most small banks and local offices of major banks do not deal directly in the interbank foreign exchange market. Rather they typically will have a credit line with a large bank or their head office. Transactions will thus involve an extra step. The customer deals with a local bank, which in turn deals with a major bank or head office. The interbank foreign exchange market exists between the major banks either directly or indirectly via a broker.*

8. Suppose the foreign exchange market consists of two currencies, Canadian dollars and British pounds.

a. In the market for pounds, the equilibrium exchange rate is 2 Canadian dollars per pound, and 5 million pounds are exchanged. What are the equilibrium exchange rate and the equilibrium quantity in the market for Canadian dollars?

b. If the equilibrium exchange rate changes to 2.5 Canadian dollars per pound, and 5 million pounds are exchanged, what are the equilibrium exchange rate and the equilibrium quantity in the market for Canadian dollars?

9. Suppose you have the following demands and supplies in the market for German marks:

Price (in U.S. dollars)	Quantity demanded	Quantity supplied
	(in millions of marks)	
$0.54	700	100
0.55	600	200
0.56	500	300
0.57	400	400
0.58	300	500
0.59	200	600
0.60	100	700

a. What is the equilibrium price and quantity?

b. If Germany attempts to fix the exchange rate at $0.59 per mark, what is the extent of the surplus or deficit of marks? What is the extent of the surplus or deficit of U.S. dollars?

c. If Germany attempts to fix the exchange rate at $0.55 per mark, what is the extent of the surplus or deficit of marks? What is the extent of the surplus

*Source: K. Alec Chrystal, "A Guide to Foreign Exchange Markets," *Review*, Federal Reserve Bank of St. Louis, March 1984.

TAKE A STAND

The European Community: Should It Adopt a Single Currency?

Travelers to Europe presently need a different currency for every country they visit: British pounds, Belgian francs, German marks, Italian lire, Greek drachmas, and so on. Soon, however, they may be able to use one currency throughout the European Community (EC). The twelve countries of the EC are moving toward the adoption of the European Currency Unit (ECU) as the single currency of the Community.

The ECU already exists, but you cannot yet obtain one in any bank. At present it is not a physical unit of currency, but purely a bookkeeping device used by the twelve members of the European Community for certain international transactions, such as payments from one nation's central bank to another's. The value of the ECU is the weighted average of the currencies of the members of the EC. These currencies are in turn integrated through a system of managed exchange rates (the European Monetary System), under which the relative value of the currencies can fluctuate only within narrow bands.

Adoption of a single currency within the EC would be one of the most important stages in the process of increasing economic and political union within Europe. The EC was originally established to promote trade among its member nations by eliminating tariffs on goods. In 1985 the EC ratified the Single European Act, which looks toward further removal of impediments to trade by providing for completely free movement of workers, goods, and financial capital across national borders by the end of 1992. In 1989, a European Council "Report on Economic and Monetary Union in the European Community" proposed complete monetary union and the adoption (at a later date) of a single currency. In December 1991, this proposal was ratified by the leaders of the European Community in Maastricht, Holland.

The move toward monetary union was set back by a Danish referendum in 1992 that rejected the Maastricht treaty. Also in 1992, speculative attacks on the pound and the lira precipitated a currency crisis that forced Britain and Italy to withdraw from the system. The future of European monetary union is now uncertain. Some economists and politicians have also become increasingly skeptical about the desirability of such union. *Should the European Community adopt a single currency?*

Yes: Monetary Union Reduces Costs, Promotes Trade, and Helps to Control Inflation

Monetary union is desirable in Europe for the same reasons that it is desirable in the United States. Suppose that each state in the United States decided to adopt its own individual currency. The cost and inconvenience would be immense. Travelers from New York to New Jersey would have to exchange "NYdollars" for "NJdollars." A business in North Dakota that exported goods to South Dakota would have to worry about changes in the relative values of the "SDdollar" and "NDdollar." Resources would be wasted in converting currencies and writing contracts to deal with the risk of exchange rate changes. Businesses would be reluctant to trade across state lines because of the extra costs.

Exactly the same arguments apply in Europe. At present, businesses that trade across European boundaries must expend resources on the exchange of currencies, and must face uncertainty about exchange rate fluctuations. With the adoption of a single currency, these costs would vanish and trade would increase. The argument for monetary union has become more and more compelling as increased economic union has made Europe, economically speaking, more and more like the United States.

Monetary union in Europe entails the establishment of a European Central Bank, much like the Federal Reserve in the United States. Because this bank would possess greater independence than the central banks of member countries, it would be in a better position to resist political pressures to expand the European money supply. Monetary union would therefore reduce the risk of inflation in Europe.

The EC has demonstrated that it can function without exchange-rate changes. While realignments of currency bands within the European Monetary System were initially commonplace, European exchange rates remained stable from 1987 until the currency crisis of 1992. The European Community can operate as a monetary union, and should reap the benefits of a single currency.

No: The EC Is Too Diverse

The twelve members of the European Community are struggling against centuries of political, cultural, and economic differences. Each nation has its own interests and its own problems, and most have their own language. Such differences mean that the economy of the EC is very different from that of the United States.

Different currencies in different countries are desirable if the countries face very different economic problems or have varying goals. The reason is that countries can adopt different monetary policies in order to affect exchange rates and interest rates. For example, bad weather would affect Portugal more adversely than Germany because Portugal is more dependent on agriculture. An increase in oil prices would affect Germany more adversely than Portugal because Germany is more industrial. Germany and Portugal may therefore wish to pursue different monetary policies at different times. Portugal might want to expand its money supply to stimulate its economy in the face of adverse weather shocks. Germany might wish to expand its money supply to help offset the adverse effects of a sharp increase in oil prices. Different countries may also wish to pursue different monetary policies because their relative tolerance for inflation and unemployment varies.

If labor is very mobile, there is less need for exchange rate adjustment and different monetary policies. In the United States, workers can move freely from state to state. If the Texas economy is hurt by a fall in oil prices, Texan workers facing lower wages or unemployment can move to other, more prosperous, states relatively easily. But language and cultural barriers still greatly inhibit the mobility of labor in Europe.

Economic theory suggests that a single currency is desirable in a region where the economic environment is similar and labor is mobile. Economists call this an "optimum currency area." The United States comes reasonably close to this ideal, but Europe does not. And if, as seems likely, the EC expands further to include countries from Eastern Europe or Scandinavia, the argument against a single European currency will become stronger still.

The Question: Should the European Community Adopt a Single Currency?

■   The benefits of a single currency in Europe include reduced costs of doing business and greater convenience, both of which are likely to increase trade. An independent European Central Bank will also help control inflation.

■   If the EC countries adopt a single currency, they lose the ability to conduct independent monetary policies, and hence to respond to shocks that do not affect all countries equally. Cultural and language barriers, meanwhile, impede the mobility of labor. The EC is not an optimum currency area.

Where Do You Stand?

1. The United States is perceived as an "optimum currency area." There are, however, dramatic differences among the various states of the union. Can you think of circumstances under which individual states would have benefited from being able to conduct independent monetary policy? *Hint:* Consider the effect of a fall in oil prices on the economies of Texas and Michigan.

2. Should all nations of the world follow the European Community's lead and adopt a single global currency? Explain.

3. Do you think that the European Community will eventually become a federal system like the United States?

4. Should the European Community adopt a single currency? Justify your stand.

Sources: Martin Feldstein, "Europe's Monetary Union," *The Economist,* June 13, 1992; and Paul de Grauwe, Daniel Gros, Alfred Steinherr, and Niels Thygesen, "In Reply to Feldstein," *The Economist,* July 4, 1992.

Chapter 23

Economic Development: The Less Developed and Newly Industrializing Countries

The Meaning of Economic Development
Low-Income LDCs: Stagnant Growth
Investment and Aid in LDCs
Newly Industrializing Countries: The Pacific Rim
A Market-Based Development Strategy
Origins: An Architect of Economic Development

Learning Guide
Watch for answers to these important questions

What is meant by "economic development"? Why is the concept difficult to apply?

Are there any fundamental principles of economic development? What must be known about agriculture, population, and capital in order to understand their roles as broad determinants of development?

How do international considerations affect economic development? What roles are played by foreign investment and foreign aid?

What are the elements of a market-based development strategy?

What contributions did Sir Arthur Lewis make to development policy?

While millions of inhabitants of advanced industrial nations worry about eating too much, hundreds of millions of people in dozens of poverty-stricken countries worry about starving. The poverty-stricken countries constitute much of Latin America, Africa, and Asia. It is here that most of the 4 billion citizens of the underdeveloped world live, the majority of them ill fed, poorly housed, and illiterate. Because the poor nations contain more than three-fourths of the world's population, it's important to understand the problems they face and the measures that can be taken to help solve these problems.

Some countries, such as South Korea and Taiwan, which were considered poor only a few decades ago, have economies today that are thriving. Contrary to popular myth, their success isn't due to a sophisticated combination of governmental wisdom and economic planning, supplemented by loans and foreign aid from advanced countries. It's due, as we'll see in this chapter, to individual self-interest and to government policies that allow people to engage in economic activities for the purpose of bettering their condition. This is perhaps the fundamental lesson to be learned from the study of economic development.

The Meaning of Economic Development

Poor nations are usually referred to as *less developed countries (LDCs),* underdeveloped countries, or devel-

488

oping countries. They are usually characterized by the following conditions:

- Poverty levels of income and hence little or no saving.

- High rates of population growth.

- Substantial majorities of the labor force employed in agriculture.

- Low rates of adult literacy.

- Extensive *disguised unemployment.* This is a condition in which employed resources (usually labor resources) are not being used in their most efficient ways. The concept is also known as *underemployment.*

- Heavy reliance on one or a few items (mainly agricultural) for export.

- Government control by a wealthy elite, which often opposes any changes that would harm its economic interests.

Among underdeveloped countries, these characteristics are tendencies rather than certainties. Exceptions can be found to all of them.

How many countries of the world are considered "less developed"? Which ones are they? The World Bank divides countries into three groups based on per-capita income—low, middle, and high. The dividing line between low and middle is $600 per person, and between middle and high it is $6,000 per person. The map in Exhibit 1 indicates countries falling into each group. Low-income countries have the worst development problems. These problems are shared in varying degrees by countries in the middle-income group. Yet some middle-income countries, especially in Asia, have achieved remarkable success in recent years.

This chapter examines low- and middle-income LDCs in Asia, Africa, and Latin America to identify successful and unsuccessful economic development strategies.

What Is Economic Development?

Economic development entails the transformation of a country's entire socioeconomic system. This means that there are improvements in the quality of resources as well as changes in attitudes, institutions, and values of the society.

Economic development **is the process by which a nation's real per-capita output or income (its gross do-**mestic product, or GDP) **increases over a long period of time. A nation's rate of economic development is thus measured by its long-run per-capita rate of economic growth.**

The statement that economic development is a long-run process requires emphasis. A short-run spurt in economic growth may be the result of luck. A long-run expansion in production is generally the result of fundamental change. Thus, it is one thing for a society to experience an increase in real per-capita output or income over a period of a few years. It is quite another for that society to sustain the increase for perhaps a decade or more.

In addition to increases in real income per capita, there are other objectives of economic development. Among these are greater equality in the distribution of income, a rising minimum level of income, and reduction of disguised unemployment. However, these are generally regarded as secondary goals—mainly because they are strongly influenced in each country by existing social structures and institutions. Therefore, in a developing country, there is some likelihood that these secondary goals will be at least partially attained if the primary goal of a sustained increase in real income per capita is realized.

Economic and "Environmental" Differences

It is useful to compare the gap, at different points in time, between per-capita incomes in the less developed countries and those in the advanced countries. This comparison enables us to see whether the gulf has widened, narrowed, or remained the same. Economists frequently make such comparisons, and the findings point up a serious problem:

Over the long run, the income gap between the richest countries and the poorest ones has been widening. As a result, an increasing proportion of all goods and services—now more than 80 percent—is produced in countries in which less than 25 percent of the world's people live.

To see clearly why these differences in the economic progress of nations occur, we must first understand the determinants of a nation's economic development. These determinants include the quantity and quality of human resources and natural resources, the rate of capital accumulation, the degree of specialization and scale of production, and the rate of technological progress. They also include environmental considerations—namely, the political, social, cultural, and economic framework within which growth and devel-

EXHIBIT
1

The Developed and Less Developed Countries

Most of the less developed countries are in the tropics—that is, between the Tropic of Cancer and the Tropic of Capricorn.

These countries show various degrees of underdevelopment, ranging from severe to relatively moderate.

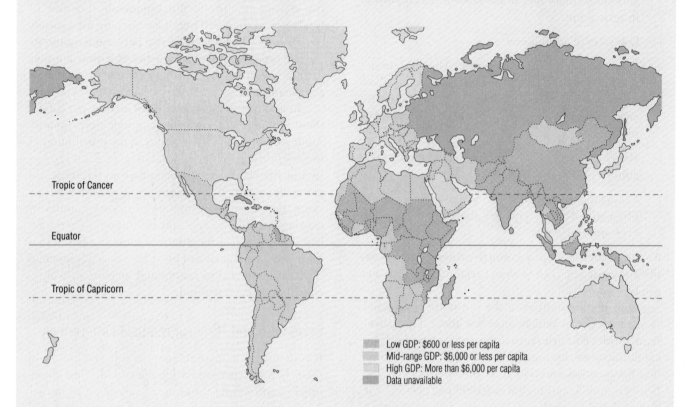

Tropic of Cancer

Equator

Tropic of Capricorn

Low GDP: $600 or less per capita
Mid-range GDP: $6,000 or less per capita
High GDP: More than $6,000 per capita
Data unavailable

Average Annual Growth Rates of Real Output

	Average 1970–1979		Average 1980–1989		Projected Average 1990–1999	
	Total	Per capita	Total	Per capita	Total	Per capita
Developing countries by selected regions	5.7%	3.1%	3.1%	0.8%	2.7%	1.8%
Africa	4.4	0.9	1.6	1.1	1.8	1.4
Asia	5.4	3.4	6.5	4.3	6.9	4.6
Middle East	7.3	2.9	−3.6	−3.9	−1.8	−2.2
Small low-income countries	3.5	1.2	3.6	1.1	3.5	1.8
Sub-Saharan Africa	3.0	0.1	2.5	−0.9	1.5	0.8

Source: International Monetary Fund and the World Bank, Annual Reports.

opment take place. A comparison of these economic determinants explains why the rich nations are getting richer while the poor ones are getting relatively poorer.

Compare the United States, for example, with most underdeveloped countries. The United States has a large labor force with a relatively high proportion of skilled workers. The country has many business leaders who are experienced and disciplined. It has a substantial and diversified endowment of natural resources, an extensive system of transportation and power, and an efficient and productive technology financed by an adequate supply of savings. It also has a stable and comparatively uncorrupt government. And, not to be overlooked, it has a culture in which the drive for profit and material gain is generally accepted. These conditions in combination have stimulated America's economic development.

In the less developed countries, such as India, Colombia, and Ethiopia, many of these conditions are absent. The people in the labor force are largely unskilled and inefficient, and many of them are chronically ill or undernourished. Saving is small or even negative, resulting in low rates of investment and capital accumulation. Further, government is often either unstable or, if not, dictatorial, corrupt, and inefficient. Paradoxically, many poor countries are rich in natural resources. However, because most of these countries lack the other ingredients, they cannot sustain economic development.

Low-Income LDCs: Stagnant Growth

The most serious development problems are experienced by LDCs in Africa, Asia, and Latin America. Many of these countries have experienced little or no growth for decades, despite efforts by the leading industrialized nations to stimulate development. Examining the primary characteristics of LDCs will help us to consider why these countries have remained underdeveloped.

Physical Capital

The great majority of LDCs lack substantial physical capital. There are three chief reasons:

- **Limited Saving** The per-person income level of LDCs is low, often at or near the subsistence level. Because most income is used for necessary consumption, there is little left over for saving and capital investment.

- **Unproductive Uses of Funds** The limited saving that exists in LDCs may be used by government officials for personal benefit or for excessive military expenditures. These provide few economic development benefits.

- **Inappropriate Investment Decisions** Funds used for investment may purchase capital goods that are unsuited to LDCs. A hydroelectric dam, for example, may prove less valuable than sturdy plows and efficient irrigation pumps.

Many economists and government officials used to believe that massive infusions of capital were alone sufficient to induce economic development. Where did this assumption come from? It was based on the microeconomic concept of *marginal productivity*. This is defined as the increase in output resulting from a unit change in a variable input while all other inputs are held fixed.

Because most LDCs have an excess of labor, the marginal productivity of labor (relative to capital) in such countries is low or close to zero. And because most underdeveloped countries have an insufficient amount of capital, the marginal productivity of capital is high. Consequently, the infusion of large doses of capital would appear to be the most effective means of raising real GDP per capita. However, developed countries have been pumping capital into LDCs for decades, with apparently little effect.

Therefore, this tactic has been greatly modified over the years. Research studies and experiences in LDCs have revealed that there are limits to the amount of new capital that LDCs can "absorb" or utilize effectively in any given period. These limits are set by such conditions as the availability of related skilled labor and the level of effective demand for the output of the new capital. It does little good, for example, to build a railroad if there isn't enough skilled labor to operate and maintain it or enough demand for goods transported by the railroad to support it.

Agricultural Development

In most underdeveloped countries, the great bulk of human resources is devoted to agriculture. The share of agriculture in GDP around the world is presented

EXHIBIT
2

The Share of Agriculture in GDP

Industrialized countries such as the United States, Canada, and members of the European Community obtain a relatively small share of gross domestic product from agriculture. LDCs, in contrast, devote a much larger share of their resources to agricultural production. As this map shows, in several African countries and a few Asian countries over 40 percent of gross domestic production comes from agriculture. A comparison with Exhibit 1 indicates that less developed countries tend to have a greater share of GDP in agriculture.

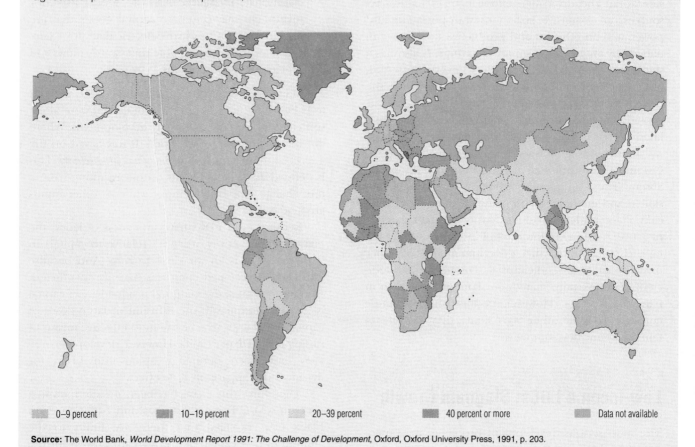

| 0–9 percent | 10–19 percent | 20–39 percent | 40 percent or more | Data not available |

Source: The World Bank, *World Development Report 1991: The Challenge of Development*, Oxford, Oxford University Press, 1991, p. 203.

in Exhibit 2. These human resources tend to be inefficiently employed. As a result, there is a great deal of disguised unemployment or "underemployment."

Agriculture, for the most part, produces the nation's food and raw materials. Therefore, in order for economic development to take place *out of domestic resources,* agricultural efficiency must improve. This is necessary in order to produce a surplus of output over and above what the agricultural sector itself consumes. As this happens, human and material resources are spared from farming to work in manufacturing. This helps expand the industrial sector while consuming the surplus of the agricultural sector. This suggests a proposition of fundamental importance in economic development:

In most LDCs there is a close relationship between the agricultural sector and the industrial sector. The growth of the industrial sector is strongly influenced by prior or simultaneous technical progress in the agricultural sector.

The operation of this important principle has been amply demonstrated in economic history. For example, the development of towns during the Middle Ages was accompanied by, and to a significant extent preceded by, improved methods of agricultural production. The industrial revolution of the eighteenth and nineteenth centuries in Europe and the United States was strongly influenced by an agricultural revolution. This was marked by a number of major innovations, including the introduction of root crops, horse-hoeing husbandry, four-crop rotation, and scientific animal breeding. These developments were of such great importance that they actually overshadowed in certain respects the accompanying industrial revolutions.

Population Growth

Although not all LDCs are "overpopulated," most of them are. In poor regions in Asia, parts of Latin America, and Africa, population presses heavily on physical resources. Accumulation, or saving, is therefore difficult. Why? Because the level of production is low and resources are committed primarily to agriculture in order to produce the bare necessities of consumption. As long as the pressure on food supplies continues, large numbers of people must subsist at the barest survival level. This makes it extremely difficult if not impossible for the nation to benefit from development.

Studies have shown that it isn't so much the absolute *size* of the population as the population *growth rate* that holds back improvements in real income per capita. Because of this, a number of developing countries, including China, Indonesia, India, and Pakistan, have instituted family-planning programs. These have ranged from simple counseling services to large-scale voluntary sterilization schemes (usually vasectomies). A chief difficulty is that any population-control scheme may conflict with local religious traditions, which often impede if not prevent the development of effective programs. In China, it took the power of a totalitarian government to overrule tradition in order to curb population growth. Couples face severe financial penalties if they have more than one child.

An interesting *economic* approach to the problem of overpopulation is proposed in Exhibit 3. After studying it, you'll be interested to know that the proposal isn't as unrealistic as it may seem. Several ver-

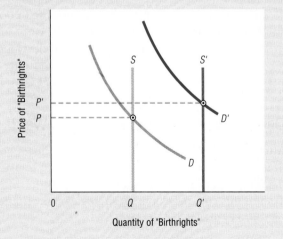

Can Population Be Controlled Through the Price System?

Can the price system be used to help influence the size of a nation's population?

Population control might be exercised through the sale of "birthrights." The government, for example, might decide that each married couple should be entitled to two "free births." Beyond that, a couple would have to pay a price if they wanted to have more children. How much would they have to pay? The answer would depend on the current market price of birthright certificates, each certificate permitting a woman to have one completed pregnancy.

The government would issue a fixed amount of these certificates for a period of time. Hence, the supply curve S would be a vertical line. However, the demand curve D would be normal or downward sloping. Through the free interaction of demand and supply, the equilibrium price would settle at P; the equilibrium quantity would, of course, be Q.

Over a period of time, income (and perhaps population) would grow. Therefore, the demand curve would shift rightward to D'. The government might then decide to issue additional certificates, as shown by the new supply curve S'. This would result in a different equilibrium price P' and an equilibrium quantity Q'. The number of additional certificates the government decided to issue would depend on the degree of control it wished to exercise over the market price and the size of the population.

Question: There are obvious social and economic difficulties in implementing such a system. Can you name them? Can you also suggest ways of overcoming some of the difficulties?

sions of it have either been implemented or are under discussion in such heavily populated countries as China, Hong Kong, Japan, and Singapore.

Human Capital

Human capital as well as physical capital is also limited in LDCs. The "quality" of a population, as measured by its skills, education, and health, is vitally important in influencing a nation's cultural and economic progress. LDCs suffer in four main areas:

1. **Basic Technical Skills** Underdeveloped countries usually suffer from a glut of unskilled workers and a shortage of skilled workers. Most workers lack the skills that could be obtained through appropriate primary-school and secondary-school curricula. Such curricula should be oriented toward technical education and on-the-job training in such fields as agriculture, commerce, industry, and construction.

2. **Middle-Level Skills** Most LDCs also suffer from a shortage of people with middle-level skills. For example, LDCs usually have a much greater need for technicians than for scientists and engineers.

3. **Brain Drain** Human capital is further limited because LDCs have long suffered from a serious "brain drain." This results when their talented younger people going to universities in advanced nations remain there instead of returning to their home countries.

4. **Public Health** Health programs, financed by advanced nations, have reduced disease and mortality rates in LDCs, and resulted in increased population growth. Nevertheless, health care and nutrition are far below the standard in developed countries. Disease and starvation thus continue to limit the quality of the human capital of LDCs.

Development Strategies After World War II

After the end of World War II (1945), the primary goal of many LDCs was to achieve rapid structural transformation of agrarian economies into industrial ones. Toward this end, development strategies concentrated on four key areas:

1. **Physical Capital** LDCs suffered from a lack of productive capital. Many of them therefore sought rapid capital accumulation, in particular by increasing saving as a share of domestic income.

2. **Agriculture** LDCs attempted to use underemployed resources in agriculture, their largest sector, as the source of resources for industrial investment. To achieve this, governments of most LDCs taxed and discouraged agricultural production while they subsidized and encouraged industrial production.

3. **Foreign Trade** LDCs generally sought to remain independent of the global economy and to promote domestic activity. Accordingly, imports were discouraged through high tariffs and nontariff barriers, and exports were discouraged to promote self-sufficiency.

4. **Market Failure** Because most LDCs were primitive economies with limited market activity, development strategies were based on the assumption that markets could not allocate resources as efficiently as government. In most LDCs, the government intervened extensively in production and consumption decisions. In some others, such as China, the government pursued the rigid route of centralized planning offered by communism.

In the 1950s and 1960s, economists, scientists, and technicians from advanced countries met with government leaders of LDCs to help them implement development strategies pertaining to these key areas. Yet the billions of foreign-aid dollars contributed by industrialized nations to help carry out development plans had little effect. Many LDCs remained stagnant.

What Went Wrong?

Most development analysts now feel that this course of action was counterproductive. In many cases, economic development was retarded rather than promoted. Analysts point to several common problems:

- **Human Capital Shortages** Studies have shown that the quality of labor and capital is as important as the quantity in promoting economic development. LDCs expanded their stock of physical capital but made little investment in human capital. An undereducated work force was unable to make efficient use of the physical capital, and economic development stagnated.

- **Urban Unemployment** Restrictions on agriculture encouraged the migration of labor from farms to

ECONOMICS IN THE NEWS

Who Eats How Much?

Nutrition

The World Bank's *World Development Report* says that daily food intake in low-income economies rose from 1,990 calories in 1965 to 2,330 in 1988. But while the poorest still eat too little, rich countries gorge themselves. The Irish munched the most in 1988, with 3,700 calories a day, just ahead of America's 3,670. Of the rich countries, Japan has the healthiest-looking diet, of 2,850 calories per day. The average person in Mozambique tries to survive on a meager 1,630 calories a day, the world's lowest intake. People in disaster-prone Ethiopia, Bangladesh, and Sudan do little better on 1,660, 1,930, and 2,000 calories, respectively. These are just averages; wars, floods, famines, and local politics mean that many people eat far less.

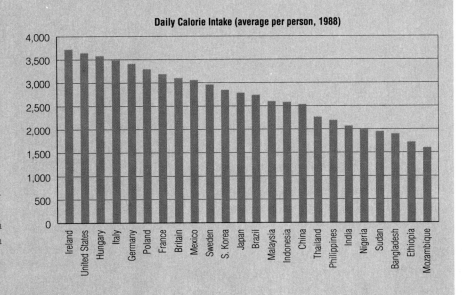

Daily Calorie Intake (average per person, 1988)

Source: *The Economist*, July 13, 1991, p. 107.

cities. Many cities in LDCs grew congested and living conditions became barely tolerable. Urban unemployment was high because job opportunities in the industrial sector did not materialize as planned.

- **Crippled Agriculture** Agricultural restrictions made farming uncompetitive in the global economy compared to subsidized farm production in advanced countries. The agricultural sector was crippled in some LDCs, resulting in frequent food shortages and famines.

- **Uncompetitive Industry** Protection of the industrial sector kept it from competing in world markets.

Firms protected by "infant industry" subsidies never grew up sufficiently to face mature firms from advanced nations.

- **Limited Access to Technology** Trade restrictions and the lack of interaction with other nations delayed the diffusion of technological advances to LDCs. Many studies indicate that technological advances are more important to economic development than increases in the quantity of either labor or capital. Moreover, countries that are isolated from the world economy tend to be unreceptive to new ideas.

- **Limited Government Resources** The administration

of government required resources, especially literate workers, that were usually in short supply. As a result, the public sector was unable to perform many of the basic functions of government.

- **Unstable Macroeconomy** Trade restrictions and extensive government involvement in business created large budget deficits financed by rapid infusions of money into the economy. These contributed to high rates of inflation and an unstable economy.

- **Government Inefficiencies and Corruption** Most LDCs were (and still are) administered by corrupt dictatorships. As a result, many development projects, financed by foreign aid from advanced countries, were undertaken primarily for the benefit of government leaders, their families, and their friends.

Lessons from Selected LDCs

An examination of selected countries illustrates four major types of problems that either were not addressed or were worsened by development strategies after World War II.

Macroeconomic Instability in Argentina In 1900, per-capita income in Argentina was about the same as that in Canada and Australia. Since World War II, Argentina has stagnated economically while Canada and Australia have joined the world's industrial elite. Why? A main cause was macroeconomic instability. Between 1950 and 1990, annual inflation rates averaging several *hundred* percent were not uncommon in Argentina. Decades of instability thus discouraged saving and investment. The lack of investment helps to explain why Argentina's annual growth of per-capita output during most of the period from 1950 to 1990 was close to zero and often negative.

Microeconomic Inefficiency in India In spite of extensive development efforts, India remains one of the least developed countries of the world. There are many reasons. High rates of population growth have prevented increases in total production from raising per-capita output. But more important is the restrictive regulation of the economy. India's government has been heavily involved in almost all facets of investment projects, including size, location, and type of technology. This involvement has enabled government leaders to pursue private interests while restricting the competitiveness of the microeconomy and retarding economic growth.

Trade Restriction in Sri Lanka In 1960, the level of economic development in Sri Lanka and in Malaysia, both in southern Asia, was nearly identical. In 1987, per-capita output in Malaysia was five times that of Sri Lanka. The chief reason is the relative openness of the Malaysian economy. For example, while rubber is an important export in both countries, export taxes on rubber in Sri Lanka are twice as high as those in Malaysia. Trade restrictions have limited the productivity of Sri Lanka's agricultural sector and limited the gains from trade with other nations.

Limited Education in Niger The African country of Niger (not to be confused with Nigeria) is a major exporter of uranium and several other minerals. Most of the population is illiterate. Various studies have indicated that, in any country, education is a key source of economic development. Limited education in Niger helps explain why, despite the country's substantial mineral resources, the annual growth of per-capita output has usually been negative.

Conclusion: Ineffective Development Strategies

LDCs have common characteristics and problems that have prevented development. Past development strategies designed to promote investment in physical capital, reallocate agricultural resources to the industrial sector, restrict trade with other nations, and correct market failures through extensive government planning were misdirected and counterproductive. As will be seen later, the experiences of rapidly industrializing countries in Asia (such as South Korea, Singapore, and Taiwan) since the 1960s suggests more effective development policies.

Investment and Aid in LDCs

Investment in physical capital is no longer viewed as the primary method of promoting economic development. Yet it remains important. Because LDCs are for the most part poor, they do not generate enough savings to finance capital investment. Therefore, they must acquire the needed investment from abroad by obtaining private foreign investment, foreign aid, loans, or a combination of these.

Private Foreign Investment

Capital investment by businesses from advanced industrialized countries accounts for about one-third of external funds received by LDCs. Most of the world's top 100 companies are multinational firms looking for new investment opportunities. Abundant supplies of low-wage labor and raw materials in LDCs make these countries good locations for capital investment. However, investors demand an economic environment that is conducive to investment. To achieve this, LDCs should work toward four objectives:

1. **A Stable Macroeconomy** LDCs must keep inflation rates, taxes, and tariffs low in order to encourage economic stability. Foreign firms seldom undertake long-term investment projects without expectations of reasonably stable levels of cost, revenue, and profit.

2. **An Efficient Microeconomy** LDCs need to promote business development. This is done by reducing restrictive government regulations, monopolies, and other types of market constraints that raise production costs and cause inefficiency.

3. **Infrastructure Investment** LDCs need to provide *infrastructure*—economic and social overhead capital that forms a basis for modern production. Examples of infrastructure include roads, telephone service, energy supplies, schools, and public health services.

4. **A Stable Political System** LDCs must maintain political stability. This is necessary in order to give foreign investors reasonable assurance that their investments will continue to be welcomed by changing political administrations.

Foreign Aid

Even under the best of circumstances, some LDCs may not be able to attract sufficient private foreign investment to meet total capital requirements for sustained growth. In that case, help in the form of foreign aid may be available. *Foreign aid* consists of loans, grants, or assistance by one government to another for the purpose of accelerating economic development in the recipient country.

Among the chief sources of foreign aid are:

- The World Bank, established by a United Nations charter in 1944

- The Agency for International Development (AID), an American organization established in 1961

AID is the U.S. government's main foreign-aid unit. In addition, the European Community, Japan, China, and other nations are sources of assistance to underdeveloped countries. This isn't surprising because, for any country that provides it, foreign aid may be motivated as much by political considerations as by economic considerations.

What are some of the economic issues that arise in the provision of foreign aid? The basic questions involve the amounts, conditions, and forms of aid that should be given.

How Much Aid Should Advanced Countries Give?

Various criteria for granting aid have been proposed. For example:

- Aid should be provided until income per capita in the recipient country has been raised by a certain percentage.

- Sufficient aid should be given to make up a deficit in the recipient country's balance of payments. In simplest terms, this means that, when a nation's outflow of money exceeds the inflow, foreign aid should make up the difference. (This assumes, as is usually the case, that the recipient country tries to maintain a stable world price for its currency, thus preventing its balance of payments from adjusting automatically.)

- Aid should be provided in proportion to a recipient country's needs as measured by its income per capita.

No matter how rational these and other criteria may seem, they ignore the fact that foreign aid is often more a tool of foreign policy than an application of economic logic. Demonstrations outside an American embassy, the destruction of a U.S. government facility, or the thwarting of a military coup can influence appropriations for assistance more than the rational dictates of economic experts.

Should Conditions Be Imposed on Foreign Aid?

Many political leaders believe that assistance should be provided to any poor country that is trying to improve its economic condition. But problems and dilemmas of a political and quasi-political nature tend to cloud this simple criterion. For instance, consider the following questions:

- Should aid be given to communist countries such as China or Cuba?

- Should we see to it that the benefits of aid to a given country are spread throughout the society rather than concentrated in a single socioeconomic class?

- Should aid be given only to countries that accomplish reforms (such as tax, budget, and market reforms), or should it be given without restriction?

Should Foreign Aid Take the Form of Loans or Grants?

The answer to this question involves not only economic considerations but moral, ethical, and social ones as well. In many Muslim countries, for instance, charging interest on loans carries an unfavorable connotation because it implies that the lender is taking unfair advantage of the distress of the borrower.

Nevertheless, some guide for policy decisions is needed. Perhaps the most feasible guide is an "international welfare criterion." This might be a standard that provides grants to countries whose per-capita income is below a specified level, and provides loans to countries above that level. In the past, our foreign-aid policies have often been inconsistent in the use of this or any other standard.

Foreign aid cannot replace private investment as a means of economic development. However, some foreign assistance *in conjunction* **with private investment may be necessary if the LDCs are to make the most effective use of their human and material resources.**

Foreign Loans

Another way in which LDCs have undertaken domestic investment is by borrowing funds from abroad. However, this approach led to some serious debt problems in the 1980s.

During the 1970s, American and other Western banks made extensive loans to many LDCs. Among the most promising borrowers were some of the LDCs in Latin America. Brazil and Mexico, in particular, were on the verge of robust growth, so their governments were eager to acquire the funds needed to finance an industrial revolution. And Western bankers, anticipating steadily rising interest rates in the face of mount-

ing inflation, tripped over themselves to extend the loans.

But a major liquidity shortage occurred in the early 1980s. This impaired the ability of many LDCs to meet payments on their external debts. Chiefly responsible were poorly managed domestic policies in various high-debt countries. These policies resulted in large budget deficits, heavy investment in inefficient public enterprises, excessive government restrictions on business activity, and overvalued exchange rates. By the middle of the decade, as shown in Exhibit 4, the total external debt of all LDCs exceeded $1 trillion. Of this amount, nearly 40 percent was owed by Latin American countries.

Private Western banks weren't the only institutions engaged in lending to LDCs. Two international lending agencies—the *International Monetary Fund* (IMF) and the *World Bank*—have been doing so for decades. Established in 1944, the IMF helps countries overcome short-run financial difficulties, while the World Bank makes loans to aid long-term development. In the late 1980s, in order to restore the creditworthiness of high-debt LDCs, two major IMF–World Bank debt-management plans were undertaken:

1. **Structural Reformation Programs** Debtor countries agreed to restructure their economies to promote faster economic growth. Restructuring consisted of programs undertaken to cut government deficits, encourage greater domestic savings and investment, reduce restrictions on international trade and finance, and allow private enterprise to play a larger role in each country's economy. Commercial banks, the IMF, and the World Bank agreed to increase lending to debtor countries that adopted restructuring programs.

2. **Debt-Reduction Schemes** Banks agreed to refinance their loans to debtor countries by accepting reduced principal and/or interest payments. The payments were backed up by IMF–World Bank guarantees with funds provided by the United States, Japan, and other industrial countries.

While their combined external debt remains in the trillion dollar range, debt management strategies have allowed LDCs to devote more resources to raising their levels of development and fewer to repaying loans. However, the size of the outstanding debt makes the incidence of another debt crisis a distinct possibility.

EXHIBIT
4

External Debt of LDCs

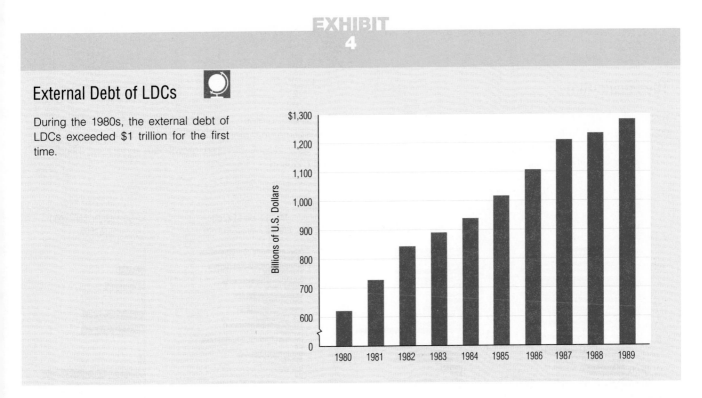

During the 1980s, the external debt of LDCs exceeded $1 trillion for the first time.

Newly Industrializing Countries: The Pacific Rim

Among the LDCs are countries that are undergoing rapid economic growth. They are referred to as the *newly industrializing countries (NICs)*. Notable examples are the Pacific Rim economies of Hong Kong, Singapore, South Korea, and Taiwan. Known collectively by such names as the "four tigers," the "four dragons," and the "gang of four," they have experienced remarkable economic growth rates in comparison with advanced countries, as Exhibit 5 illustrates.

The NICs produce everything from state-of-the-art electronic products to computers, cars, pharmaceuticals, ships, and financial services. Although many conditions help account for their success, several are especially noteworthy:

- Export-oriented growth strategy

- Utilization of modern technology through licensing and joint ventures with foreign firms

- Cooperation between labor and management

- Unbounded commitment to product excellence

- Utilization of large numbers of low-paid but often well-educated workers

These conditions, combined with government attitudes that foster industrialization and growth, have often enabled the NICs to undercut competitors' prices in world markets. The reasons can best be understood by examining the models, or "formulas," for growth that each country adopted.

South Korea: Conglomerate Model

No country has undergone a more rapid economic transformation than South Korea. Beginning in the 1960s, the Korean government adopted the Japanese model of growth by encouraging large conglomerates to spearhead the drive for development. (A "conglomerate" is an amalgamation under one ownership of unlike plants producing unrelated products.)

By "targeting" certain products for their high employment-multiplier potential, and providing leading entrepreneurs with generous financial assistance to produce the products, more than a dozen multinational conglomerates were formed. The four largest, and some of their major exports, are familiar to many Westerners:

- *Samsung:* electronic products, textiles, food processing, insurance

- *Hyundai:* automobiles, industrial machinery

EXHIBIT
5

The Pacific Rim

Along an arc extending from Japan and South Korea in the north to New Zealand in the south is a group of nations that constitute the Pacific Rim. Those that exemplify the newly industrializing countries are South Korea, Taiwan, Hong Kong, and Singapore. These "miracle economies" have experienced extraordinary growth rates since the late 1960s. Other low-income countries of the Pacific Rim that appear to be in the early stages of rapid growth are Indonesia, Malaysia, and Thailand.

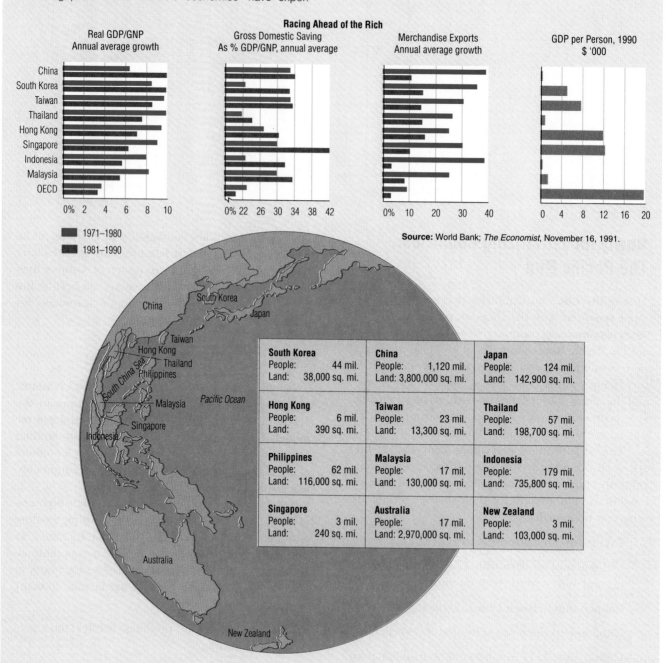

Racing Ahead of the Rich

Real GDP/GNP
Annual average growth

Gross Domestic Saving
As % GDP/GNP, annual average

Merchandise Exports
Annual average growth

GDP per Person, 1990
$ '000

China
South Korea
Taiwan
Thailand
Hong Kong
Singapore
Indonesia
Malaysia
OECD

■ 1971–1980
■ 1981–1990

Source: World Bank; *The Economist*, November 16, 1991.

South Korea	China	Japan
People: 44 mil.	People: 1,120 mil.	People: 124 mil.
Land: 38,000 sq. mi.	Land: 3,800,000 sq. mi.	Land: 142,900 sq. mi.
Hong Kong	**Taiwan**	**Thailand**
People: 6 mil.	People: 23 mil.	People: 57 mil.
Land: 390 sq. mi.	Land: 13,300 sq. mi.	Land: 198,700 sq. mi.
Philippines	**Malaysia**	**Indonesia**
People: 62 mil.	People: 17 mil.	People: 179 mil.
Land: 116,000 sq. mi.	Land: 130,000 sq. mi.	Land: 735,800 sq. mi.
Singapore	**Australia**	**New Zealand**
People: 3 mil.	People: 17 mil.	People: 3 mil.
Land: 240 sq. mi.	Land: 2,970,000 sq. mi.	Land: 103,000 sq. mi.

- *Daewoo:* computer products, automobiles, financial services

- *Lucky–Goldstar:* electronic products, chemicals

These four firms each employ hundreds of thousands of workers and generate annual sales amounting to many billions of dollars. Along with Korea's other major industrial corporations, they are transforming the nation from a pushcart economy to a high-tech economy. But their success will depend on a number of conditions. One of the most important is their ability to export at competitive prices in world markets. This becomes increasingly difficult as government subsidies and tax breaks are withdrawn and transferred to other sectors and industries in order to encourage balanced growth.

Taiwan: Competitive Model

In contrast to Korea's large multinational corporations, Taiwan's companies are mostly small, aggressive, family-owned businesses. Approximately 40,000 firms account for three-fourths of the nation's exports. These enterprises churn out products as diverse as calculators, computers, pharmaceuticals, shoes, and textiles.

Comparisons are often drawn between the economies of Taiwan and South Korea. The argument is made that South Korea's economy is dominated by huge organizations engaged in shipbuilding, steel production, machinery manufacturing, and the like. Therefore, it can compete more effectively in world markets and is less vulnerable to fluctuations in demand for a specific product than is Taiwan's economy.

Does available evidence support this belief? The answer appears to be no. Taiwan's economy is noted for its extraordinary resiliency and competitiveness. Many of its numerous small firms have demonstrated a remarkable ability to shift resources into and out of diverse product lines quickly in response to changing markets overseas. This has enabled Taiwan to maintain higher rates of employment, lower rates of inflation, and an average growth rate of real output comparable to that of South Korea.

Historically, the greatest impediment to Taiwan's economic development has been its archaic financial system. Many of the nation's banks are government controlled and extremely conservative—unwilling to take risks. Financial markets are also relatively undeveloped. As a result, in order to finance business in-

vestment, Taiwan's entrepreneurs must often borrow from family, friends, and private lenders at home and abroad. But this is changing. The conditions that are restraining the nation's growth are well understood by the country's younger leaders, who are striving to liberalize the financial structure.

Singapore: Indicative-Planning Model

Formerly a British colony, Singapore is a small but potent economy specializing in oil refining, drilling-equipment manufacturing, and financial services. After becoming an independent nation in 1965, Singapore entered a clear and well-defined "new-growth era."

The nation's political leaders played an interesting role in guiding Singapore's development. To encourage exports as a means toward rapid growth, government departments published lists and specifications of "pioneer industries" deemed compatible with Singapore's resources. These lists were revised and extended from time to time and became a general set of guidelines for planned development.

In the late 1960s, the highest priority was to reduce the nation's unemployment. Therefore, the industries that were encouraged were those that produce labor-intensive products such as clothing, rubber goods, and toys. During the 1970s, attention turned to capital-intensive goods—petroleum products, drilling equipment, electronic components, and construction materials. Since the early 1980s, the greatest emphasis has been placed on the "brain" industries—electronics, biotechnology, banking, insurance, and other financial services. Throughout its new-growth era that began in the late 1960s, Singapore's overriding goal, as with South Korea and Taiwan, has been the production of products for export.

The method of industrial "rationalization" used by Singapore's leaders is known as *indicative planning.* It consists of the government establishing economic priorities and then providing incentives for firms to meet those priorities. Through tax exemptions, accelerated depreciation of capital expenditures, and financial assistance, entrepreneurs have been encouraged to allocate resources in ways that would achieve the government's stated objectives.

In many cases the government has participated in joint ventures with private firms, but it has done so only to provide assistance. It has almost always left the managerial powers to the private owners. Perhaps what government has done best is to provide the infrastructure. Today Singapore is known throughout the world for its exceptional cleanliness, modern transportation and communication networks, excellent educational system, and *very* strict standards of public safety and health.

Hong Kong: Laissez-Faire Model

When Adam Smith first spoke of the virtues of laissez-faire, Hong Kong was not much more than a barren island. Today, in contrast with South Korea, Taiwan, and Singapore—or virtually any other capitalistic country—Hong Kong is the world's quintessential model of free enterprise.

A British colony since the nineteenth century, Hong Kong is a tiny but vibrant economy. It contains well over 100,000 registered corporations, more than one-quarter million proprietorships and partnerships, some of the lowest individual and corporate income tax rates in the world, and almost no legal restraints on business. No wonder that Hong Kong's economy, with its six million people sharing 391 square miles of land, is one in which "entrepreneuring" is a way of life.

Like Singapore, Hong Kong achieved the status of

NIC during the 1970s. Like Singapore, it was a poor colony that received no help from Britain other than a basic infrastructure. And, like Singapore, it's an eastern gateway to Asia. Therefore, it serves as a major entrepôt—a place where goods are deposited and from which they are distributed.

Because the colony is a huge "warehouse" and trading center with low taxes and few restrictions on commerce, it has become a capitalist safe haven. Hong Kong's network of banks and finance companies handle large amounts of money, much of it unreported. And its cramped factories, many of them in lofts, churn out clothing, plastic goods, textiles, electrical products, and footwear. As with the other NICs, Hong Kong's main business is exporting. The colony is one of the world's largest providers of shipping and financial services, and its total exports per person average more than three times those of Japan.

Despite its glowing success, Hong Kong's political and economic future remains uncertain. Under a 99-year lease signed in 1898, British rule of the colony will cease in 1997. Hong Kong will then become part of the People's Republic of China. Whether Beijing will permit unbridled laissez-faire to continue after that time is anyone's guess.

Thailand—Asia's New Fifth "Tiger"?

To many middle-aged and older Americans and Europeans, Thailand evokes a distant image of the late Hollywood actor Yul Brynner playing his famous role as the King of Siam. But for hundreds of Western and Asian corporate executives, Thailand is the new "in" place to set up shop. Thai workers, many of whom are skilled and industrious, have a literacy rate of about 90 percent and earn a fraction of what their counterparts in South Korea, Taiwan, Singapore, and Hong Kong make. Today more than 1,000 American and Japanese firms have plants in Thailand.

The transformation of the Thai economy began in the early 1980s. Nurtured by political stability and economic conservatism, the country has become the world's leading exporter of canned pineapple and canned tuna, and is moving rapidly into the production of automobiles, electronic components, and various high-tech products. By the year 2000, Thailand's economy may be more diversified—and more resistant to recession—than those of the other "four tigers."

Competition Mounts

Meanwhile, several other low-wage Asian countries are vying for fifth-tiger status. Indonesia is a significant producer of oil, the revenues from which are helping to finance new industries. Malaysia and the Philippines are major exporters of textiles, wood products, and electronic components—products that compete with some of Thailand's important industries. And China, an awakening giant with diverse resources, has shown signs of making a determined effort to become East Asia's largest NIC. All in all, the decade of the 1990s is shaping up as a dynamic one for the nations of the Pacific Rim.

EXHIBIT
6

How the Countries of the Pacific Rim Stack Up

Country	Outlook
At the Top	
Japan	The shift to a more consumer-based economy, just now getting under way, should speed up.
Australia	The lucky country will run out of luck if it can't create internationally competitive industries.
New Zealand	State control of the economy has declined, promising faster growth.
Hong Kong	Look for a slowdown caused by political uncertainty; China takes over from the British in 1997.
Singapore	A tightly controlled press keeps the lid on, and investors often lack timely business information.
Taiwan	Enmity against the mainland is softening, but total reconciliation is still decades off.
South Korea	The region's growth champ must prove it can handle democracy as well as industrialization.
Rising Fast	
Thailand	Exports of manufactured goods and processed food are creating Southeast Asia's next NIC.

Country	Outlook
Potential Stars	
Malaysia	Ethnic tension and bitter political rivalries are putting brakes on a resource-rich economy.
Philippines	The potential is still there. And so are the communist insurgency and political disunity.
Indonesia	Burdened with a huge foreign debt and shrinking petroleum revenues, progress will be slow.
China	Ideology is making the march toward modernization a long one.
At the Bottom	
North Korea	Reliance on exports of arms and terrorism will bring increasing isolation to North Korea.
Burma	Downgraded by the UN from developing status after years of socialism, progress is doubtful.
Vietnam	New foreign investment law is most liberal of any communist country, but no one is rushing in.
Cambodia	Still torn by civil war and Vietnamese occupation, it will be an economic shambles for years.
Laos	Sleepy Laos is at peace, but its economy shows no signs of perking up under communist rule.

Conclusion: Lessons for LDCs

From their development experiences since the late 1960s, it's easy to understand why South Korea, Taiwan, Singapore, and Hong Kong have earned the name "miracle economies." Many efforts have been made to explain why they have often had significantly higher economic growth rates, lower inflation rates, and lower unemployment rates than the advanced countries. Although there are no magic reasons, the more important general ones were listed at the beginning of this section. Summarizing them briefly, they include encouragement of exports, utilization of modern technology, cooperation between labor and management, commitment to product quality, and an effective utilization of capable workers.

These policies can serve as guidelines for growth by less developed countries. What other lessons can the LDCs learn from the experiences of the NICs? Perhaps the most important is the *provision of incentives:*

In almost all of the LDCs, extensive government regulations and controls exist that limit people's economic freedoms and stifle incentives. This results in relatively slow or no economic growth. In the NICs of the Pacific Rim, however, government policies have sought to encourage innovation and enterprise by allowing individuals to respond to incentives. Although government (with the exception of Hong Kong) has often directed development in varying degrees, it has relied on market signals to determine not only *how,* but *for whom,* resources are allocated.

An assessment of the economic outlook for the countries of the Pacific Rim is shown in Exhibit 6.

EXHIBIT
7

A Market-Based Development Strategy

Development policies in the 1990s emphasize the use of competitive markets with selective government intervention. The four elements of this strategy are an efficient microeconomy, a stable macroeconomy, investment in human capital, and global integration. Each reinforces the other three. For example, global integration enhances human capital. Investment in human capital leads to a rapid growth of productivity and a more efficient microeconomy. An efficient microeconomy makes it easier to use financial markets to stabilize the macroeconomy. And a stable macroeconomy is better able to withstand shocks from the global economy and benefit from international trade.

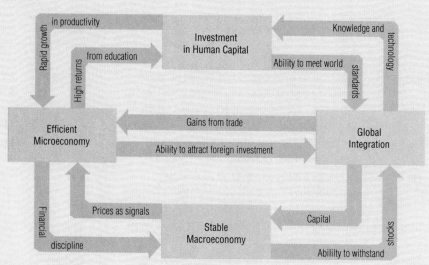

Source: Adapted from *The Economist,* July 13, 1991, p. 77.

Market-Based Development Strategy

Many lessons concerning economic development have been learned during the past several decades. Traditional economic development strategies have proven ineffective, misdirected, and counterproductive. The use of centralized government planning has been discredited. Japan and the four tigers of Asia have achieved remarkable success with market-based economies. Today's development strategy, drawing on experiences of LDCs and NICs, replaces government direction with market competition whenever possible. Exhibit 7 illustrates the four key elements of a market-based development strategy. These elements are:

1. A competitive microeconomy

2. A stable macroeconomy

3. Investment in human capital

4. Integration with the global economy

   As a report by the World Bank states:

   Succeeding in development is indeed the most pressing of all challenges that now confront the human

race. Incomplete though our understanding still is, enough has been learned over the years to point the way. Strategies in which governments support rather than supplant competitive markets offer the best hope for meeting the challenge of development.

Origins: An Architect of Economic Development

When World War II ended in 1945, the European economy was devastated. But the economies of many poverty-stricken nations untouched directly by the war were also dismal. The task of both reconstructing the European economy and providing development assistance to poor countries fell to the newly created United Nations. Under its auspices, several organizations were established that played important roles in helping to build the postwar world economy. One is the United Nations Educational, Scientific, and Cultural Organization (UNESCO), which provides a wide range of services to the less developed regions of the world. Another is the World Bank, which provides loans to promote economic development.

Free Markets Take Hold

A New Discipline in Economics Brings Change to Latin America

By Nathaniel C. Nash

SANTIAGO, Chile—Suddenly, a look at the economic map of Latin America shows a startling change. After a decade of no growth, crippling inflation, rising foreign debt, protectionism, and bloated state payrolls, governments—at least for now—have found a new economic religion.

Balanced budgets are in, as is privatization, the buzzword for selling off government enterprises. Negotiations to reduce foreign debt have been successful in some countries, especially Mexico, and are continuing in others.

Stabilization and discipline have become winning political slogans. The free market, open economies, and deregulation are now part of the vocabulary of taxi drivers and laborers.

Driving this new found optimism and economic activity are profound policy changes. The new consensus says that inflation is bad, particularly for the poor, that governments

Growth Rates of GDP in Major Economies in Latin America		
	1989	1990	1991
Venezuela	−8.3	4.4	10.0
Mexico	3.1	3.9	5.3
Chile	10.0	2.1	4.1
Paraguay	5.8	3.1	3.5
Colombia	3.2	3.8	3.0
Argentina	−4.4	−0.5	3.0
Bolivia	2.8	2.6	n.a.
Uruguay	1.5	0.9	1.6
Ecuador	0.2	1.5	1.5
Brazil	3.3	−4.6	−0.7
Peru	−11.2	−3.9	−4.8

do not know how to run businesses, that printing money is political suicide, and that tax evasion, a time-honored sport here, should be punished severely.

Source: *The New York Times*, November 13, 1991, p. D1.

By the late 1940s, it became clear that the United Nations' agencies would be insufficient to meet postwar reconstruction needs. Accordingly, in 1950 and subsequent years, the United States launched various programs to provide technical and financial assistance to less developed countries. Most of the assistance has been in the areas of agriculture, public health, and education. Many economists, most of them Americans, served as advisers to help recipient governments design, implement, and utilize the programs. But one adviser, who became a leading architect of economic development, was a scholar from the island of Saint Lucia in the British West Indies—William Arthur Lewis.

Lewis's first major contribution to the field was his *Economic Survey 1919–1937*. This 1949 study examined the world economy in the period between the two world wars. In it, Lewis explored the link between "core" industrialized economies and the "periphery," meaning the rest of the world.

Arthur Lewis

(1915–   )

Many economists consider a 1954 journal article by Lewis, "Economic Development with Unlimited Supplies of Labor," to be his most influential work on development. Central to the article is an analysis of human resources in a dual economy—characterized by a traditional farming sector and an urban industrialized sector. Lewis argued that in the early stages of development, human resources are inefficiently utilized by the farming sector. This results in underemployment in that sector. As a country shifts toward industrial activities, labor from the farming sector is available for industry at a low wage. The industrial sector can cheaply and easily draw workers from the surplus pool of farm laborers because of their low opportunity cost. Therefore, workers will shift to the industrial sector at the low wage available to them in the farming sector. As more and more workers shift out of agriculture into industry, however, the supply of surplus labor is exhausted. At some point, the wage in the industrial sector must rise in order to encourage more workers to shift out of farming.

Lewis was president of the American Economic Association and served on the faculties of the London School of Economics, Manchester University, University of the West Indies, and Princeton University. He took frequent trips to advise LDCs in West Africa and the Caribbean. For his contributions, Queen Elizabeth II knighted him in 1963, and he was awarded the Nobel Prize in economics in 1979.

Summary of Important Ideas

1. The per-capita income gap between the richest nations and the poorest nations appears to be widening over the long run. This is due to differences in the determinants of economic development. Among them: the quantity and quality of human and natural resources, the rate of capital accumulation, the degree of specialization and scale of production, the rate of technological progress, and a country's political, social, cultural, and economic framework.

2. Low-income LDCs exhibit four common characteristics—limited physical capital, limited agricultural development, excessive population growth, and limited human capital. Physical capital is limited because of insufficient saving, unproductive use of funds, and inappropriate investment. Limited agricultural development inhibits growth of the industrial sector. Excessive population growth keeps the rate of growth of per-capita output low. Limits on human capital are one of the most serious constraints on development.

3. Development policies after World War II emphasized four areas—investment in physical capital, reallocation of resources from agriculture to industrial production, independence from the global economy, and extensive government control of production and consumption. However, this approach led to several problems, including human capital shortages, an inefficient microeconomy, limited access to new technology, and an unstable macroeconomy.

4. LDCs can acquire funds to invest in physical and human capital in three ways—private foreign investment, foreign aid, and loans. Private foreign investment requires a stable macroeconomy, an efficient microeconomy, infrastructure investment, and a stable political system. Foreign aid from one government to another raises questions concerning the amount, conditions, and forms of aid that should be given. Foreign loans have created a severe debt problem for many LDCs that has been addressed by structural reformation and debt-reduction programs.

5. The NICs of the Pacific Rim have achieved high growth rates under different capitalistic "models." South Korea adopted a conglomerate model; Taiwan, a competitive model; Singapore, an indicative-planning model; and Hong Kong, a laissez-faire model. Despite these differences, a common thread connecting all of the models is the preservation of *incentives*. This has enabled people to realize the rewards of their productive efforts.

6. Today's strategy for increasing living standards in LDCs is market based. It consists of four elements—a competitive microeconomy, a stable macroeconomy, investment in human capital, and integration with the global economy. With this new strategy, the role of government has changed from centralized direction to selective intervention.

7. Arthur Lewis was a major architect of development policies after World War II. His analysis of dual labor markets emphasized the idea that the opportunity costs of transferring resources from agriculture to industry influence the rate of economic growth. His efforts were rewarded with British knighthood in 1963 and the Nobel Prize in 1979.

Terms and Concepts to Review

less developed country (LDC)	*foreign aid*
disguised unemployment	*International Monetary Fund*
economic development	*World Bank*
marginal productivity	*newly industrializing country (NIC)*
infrastructure	

Questions and Problems

1. It is sometimes suggested that underdeveloped nations seeking to industrialize should simply follow the paths taken by the more advanced nations. After all, why not benefit from the experiences of others? Evaluate this argument.

2. In the early years of America's post-World War II aid program (1945–1955), it was argued by many critics that the provision of health and sanitation facilities to LDCs would worsen their situation rather than improve it. The reason is that health and sanitation programs would *reduce* the LDCs' death rates. The argument is still heard today. Can you explain the logic of it?

3. Among the early investments often undertaken by many LDCs are (a) an international airline and (b) a steel mill. Does this make sense? Explain.

4. Rapid economic development requires that a nation save and invest a substantial proportion of its income. What would you advise for the many LDCs whose savings rates are low or virtually zero because the great majority of their population is close to starvation?

5. "Rapid population growth is a serious obstacle to overcome as far as most LDCs are concerned." Can you suggest some *economic* approaches to the solution of this problem?

6. Much foreign aid to LDCs is in the form of military aid. Does this tend to stimulate their economies? If so, why do some critics object to such aid? If not, why is such aid given? Discuss.

7. South Korea, Singapore, and to a lesser extent Taiwan, adopted an economic system sometimes referred to as "state capitalism."

   a. How do you suppose *state capitalism* differs from traditional capitalism? From your knowledge of twentieth-century world history, can you think of two major European countries that adopted state capitalism as their economic system during the 1930s? Why did they do so? (*Hint:* Both countries were enemies of the United States during World War II.)

   b. Why did the above-mentioned three Pacific Rim countries adopt varying degrees of state capitalism? What type of capitalism did Hong Kong adopt?

8. Would a policy that subsidizes exports more effectively promote development than one that restricts imports? Why or why not?

9. Does an unstable macroeconomy keep the microeconomy from being efficient? Explain.

10. Is international trade a panacea for the problems of LDCs? If it is, explain why. If it isn't, are there any panaceas?

11. Would Arthur Lewis support a market-based development strategy? Why or why not?

Transitional Economics: From Central Planning to Free Markets

Understanding Capitalism and Socialism

Why Central Planning Failed

Implementing Market Reforms

Minimizing the Adjustment Period

Origins: Scientific Socialism

Learning Guide

Watch for answers to these important questions

What are the main differences between capitalism and socialism? How does Marxism relate to socialism?

What is central planning? Is it a necessary part of socialism? Why did central planning fail to accomplish its objectives?

What steps do command economies need to take in order to implement a transition to capitalism? What main difficulties are likely to be experienced when these steps are undertaken?

By the year 2000, historians will undoubtedly agree that the last two decades of the twentieth century witnessed the demise of the greatest economic experiment in modern history. In the 1980s, most communist countries, including China, the former Soviet Union, and the nations of eastern Europe, adopted limited market reforms. In the early 1990s, some of these countries went much further and transformed their centrally planned socialistic systems into market-oriented capitalistic economies. These changes have given rise to some of the most pressing economic problems of our time.

The majority of Westerners, taking their economic freedoms for granted, are unable to appreciate the enormous undertaking that a transition from central planning to free markets entails. Not only must attitudes, institutions, and organizations change, but the environment that conditioned people's state of mind must be transformed. This is because socialism and capitalism are more than ideologies reflecting the social needs and aspirations of a society. Over time, the two economic systems produce distinctly different beliefs, expectations, and even ways of life.

Why have most socialist countries chosen to replace central planning with free markets? What difficulties do these countries encounter in their efforts to implement market-oriented structural reforms? Can specific measures be adopted to help achieve a well-functioning market system? These and related questions are the concern of transitional economics.

Transitional economics is the study of how countries convert from a centrally planned (command) economy to a free-market (capitalistic) economy. To appreciate the significance of what the conversion entails, it's necessary to understand the two types of economic systems that affect transitional economies: capitalism and socialism.

Understanding Capitalism and Socialism

During most of the twentieth century, the world's economies could be classified as either capitalistic or socialistic. The chief differences between the two economic systems stem from the way in which they view resource ownership and the role of markets.

Capitalism and Free Markets

Capitalism is an economic system characterized by private ownership of the factors of production and their operation for profit under predominantly competitive conditions. Other names for capitalism are "free enterprise" and "private enterprise." The world's advanced economies and many of the rapidly developing ones are, in varying degrees, capitalistic.

In a capitalistic system, individuals and firms are the main actors on the economic stage. They are the ones who decide *what, how,* and *for whom* scarce resources will be allocated. Because the decisions are made in the marketplace, a capitalistic system enables resources to be allocated to their highest-valued uses.

Like every economic system, capitalism is conditioned by its *institutions.* These are the traditions, beliefs, and practices that are well established and widely held as a fundamental part of a culture. The institutions on which a capitalistic system rests include private property, free markets, the price system, and the role of government as a protector of personal freedoms and rights. These are the institutions that socialist countries must adopt in order to make a successful transition to capitalism.

Socialism and Central Planning

Under socialism, it is not individuals and firms but the government that owns the land and capital used in production. The government is therefore the only actor on the economic stage. Through a central authority, the government uses its own values and objectives instead of the free market to allocate society's scarce resources.

Socialism has always been a movement whose members have divergent viewpoints. At one extreme are those who advocate virtually *total* social ownership of the means of production and distribution. This extreme has existed in nondemocratic (totalitarian) command economies such as the former Soviet Union and present-day China, Cuba, and North Korea. At the other extreme are those who favor government ownership only of "essential" industries (however defined) to "improve the mix" in already mixed economies. This opposite extreme has existed at various times in democratic countries such as Australia, England, France, and New Zealand.

During the latter half of the twentieth century, both viewpoints were, at different times, adopted by a number of nations, implemented as policies, and subsequently modified. In democratic countries, the policies were often discarded because nationalization—that is, government takeovers—of industries turned out unsuccessfully. Indeed, the policies created problems of excessive bureaucratization and inefficiency that were worse than the problems that nationalization had been designed to solve.

These developments prompted many modern socialist thinkers to abandon their traditional opposition to private property. In its place they've adopted the following contemporary view of socialism based on experiences in recent decades:

Socialism is a movement that seeks to improve economic efficiency and equity by establishing public ownership of all important means of production and distribution. Socialism requires some degree of centralized planning to determine *what* goods to produce, *how* to produce them, and *to whom* they should be distributed. The precise extent of public ownership and centralized planning isn't usually specified in today's socialist thinking, and varies widely between countries.

As you can see, the core of both socialism and capitalism is *economic.* The goal of most of today's socialists is to transform capitalism by reducing substantially, though not necessarily eliminating entirely, its most fundamental feature—the existence of private property.

Marxian Roots of Socialism and Communism

The modern concept of socialism evolved mainly since the 1950s. For more than three-quarters of a century prior to that time, socialist thinking was rooted in the writings of a major nineteenth-century German economist and social philosopher, Karl Marx (1818–1883).

Marx expounded his main ideas in two major works, *The Communist Manifesto* (1848) and *Das Kapital* (translated *Capital*) (Vol. 1, 1867). These treatises had incalculable influences on the modern world. With the assistance of his friend and financier, Friedrich Engels (1820–1895), Marx became the founder of so-called scientific socialism. This concept, formulated primarily in *Das Kapital*, consists of five major ideas:

1.   Economic Interpretation of History   All the great political, social, intellectual, and ethical movements of history are determined by the ways in which societies organize their economic systems. The institutions on which these systems rest directly influence the ways in which the basic economic activities of production, exchange, distribution, and consumption of goods are carried on. Thus, economic forces are the prime cause of fundamental historical change.

2.   Theory of Value and Wages   The value of any good is determined by the amount of labor time used in its production. The wages that capitalists pay to labor are held at a subsistence level that is just high enough to enable the working population to sustain itself and to rear children.

3.   Theory of Surplus Value and Capital Accumulation   The value of goods that workers produce is greater than the value, in the form of subsistence wages, that workers are paid. For example, workers may produce $15 worth of goods per hour but be paid a subsistence wage of only $10 per hour. The difference, called "surplus value," rightfully belongs to workers but is literally stolen from them by capitalists. Part of this surplus is used by capitalists for their personal consumption, and part is used to acquire more labor and machines in order to perpetuate and expand the capitalistic system.

4.   Class Struggle   Capitalistic societies are divided into two opposing groups. One of these is the working class, called the "proletariat," which owns nothing but its labor. The other is the capitalist class, called the "bourgeoisie," which owns the means of production and derives its income from exploiting the labor of workers. The capitalists' drive to increase their surplus value and to accumulate capital results in an irreconcilable clash of interests between the oppressed working class and the oppressing capitalist class. This leads to displacement of workers from jobs and to rising unemployment.

5.   Theory of Socialist and Communist Evolution   The proletariat, experiencing increasing misery, will eventually rise and overthrow the capitalistic system by force. The proletariat will then dictate the establishment of a new economic system. The system will pass through two successive stages of economic evolution—socialism and communism:

- **Socialism**   In this first stage, the means of production are owned by the state, and the state is controlled by the workers. Marx called this the "dictatorship of the proletariat." In this stage, society's total output of goods is distributed by the formula: "From each according to his ability, to each according to his labor."

- **Communism**   This second, or mature, stage represents the final, perfect goal of historical development. In Marxian ideology, it means:

  a. A classless society in which all people live by earning and no person lives by owning.

  b. The state is nonexistent, having been relegated to the museum of antiquities "along with the bronze ax and the spinning wheel."

  c. The wage system is abolished and all citizens live and work according to the formula: *"From each according to his ability, to each according to his needs."*

This last quotation describes the ultimate goal of Marxism and the essence of pure communism.

Why Central Planning Failed

In order to implement Marxian principles, communist countries chose to become command economies by adopting central planning. *This device was never suggested or even conceived by Marx.* To a limited extent, communist nations were moderately successful in achieving the economic goals of equity and stability. But all communist countries have suffered frequently—and in some cases almost continuously—from low levels of efficiency and growth.

EXHIBIT
1

Transitional Economies in Europe

Prior to 1990, the nations whose areas are shaded were communist countries with centrally planned economies. After 1990, these nations in varying degrees replaced central planning with free markets, thereby becoming transitional economies. Albania, Bulgaria, and Romania have made the least progress toward market reform.

By the 1980s, the standard of living in communist nations had fallen far below that of the capitalist countries. As a result, many of the world's command economies adopted a movement toward market-oriented reforms. The lightly shaded nations in Exhibit 1 are the European countries that did so. By the early 1990s, all of the shaded countries (least so for Albania, Bulgaria, and Romania) had embarked on a path of abandoning central planning in favor of free markets. They thus became transitional economies.

Why did central planning prove to be a failure? Some reasons are common to all communist nations. These reasons are (1) inadequate market information and (2) insufficient incentives for innovation and economic growth.

Inadequate Market Information

A modern economy consists of many millions of consumers, workers, and firms. Direction and coordination within such an economy require the rapid collection and processing of massive amounts of market information. The information must reveal prices and quantities of goods and resources, preferences of consumers and workers, relative scarcities of human and material resources, and alternative technologies for production. The task is further complicated by the fact that market data are constantly changing. How are the market data needed for allocating society's scarce resources obtained?

In a *market economy*, the price system transmits market information. The operation of demand and supply causes differences in prices of goods. Knowledge of prices enables owners of scarce resources to allocate their resources according to individual preferences. Decisions of *what, how,* and *for whom* to produce are thus determined by interactions of buyers and sellers in the marketplace. For the economy as a whole, scarce resources are thereby allocated to their highest valued uses as if guided by an "invisible hand."

In a *command economy*, there is no price system. Instead, prices are fixed by the central authority. Few free markets exist, and those that do are extremely limited. Therefore, there is very little market information available. As a result, decisions of *what, how,* and *for whom* to produce aren't generally derived from consumer preferences. Instead, a governmentally appointed central planning board makes these decisions based on priorities established by the government. In a few special cases the board may employ surveys or other methods of discovering individual preferences and relative scarcities. But these instances are extremely rare. On the whole, experience shows that no centralized system is capable of collecting market information, much less processing and coordinating it, as efficiently as a decentralized free-market economy.

The informational role of free markets is thus fundamental to economic efficiency. A market economy is a clearinghouse of market information:

- It provides producers with information about consumer preferences.

- It allocates society's resources in accordance with those preferences.

- It provides consumers with information about alternative goods and prices.

- It provides producers with information about the most economical choice of production techniques.

- It processes information by synthesizing the individual buying and selling decisions of millions of households and firms.

This information is necessary for any economy to function. Indeed, had socialism been rigidly enforced, centrally planned economies might not have existed as long as they did. The fact that they lasted for a number of decades can be attributed to the reality faced by socialist leaders. The governments of all communist countries, past and present, have pacified their populaces and reduced public resistance to central planning by tacitly permitting some limited free markets to exist. These serve as economic "safety valves" that contribute in no small way to the survival of socialist governments.

The price system plays a critical informational role in an economy. Therefore, if prices are set by a central planning board instead of by market forces of supply and demand, inefficiency must result. This is because the true values of goods and services to consumers and producers aren't known. Consequently, resources are misallocated. Too many of some goods and too few of others are produced relative to consumer preferences.

Insufficient Incentive Systems

A second reason for the failure of central planning is that it offers no incentives for innovation and productivity. Economic growth therefore suffers. Let's see why, by comparing the role of incentives in free-market economies and in centrally planned ones.

Entrepreneurial Function

The entrepreneurial function consists of organizing and risk taking. Organizing means managing and decision making. Risk taking means bearing the chances of incurring profits and losses.

In free-market economies, the entrepreneurial function is undertaken by private individuals for purposes of gain. This has always been apparent in small businesses where owners and managers are usually the same people. However, private gain is equally applicable, although often less apparent, in large corporations. Although stockholders, as owners of corporations, delegate organizational responsibility, their ultimate goal is personal gain. Of course, gains in

some years may turn into losses in others—and perhaps eventually into failure. These are the risks that entrepreneurs bear.

In centrally planned economies, most of the major means of industrial production—land and capital—are owned by "society," represented by government. Therefore, the entrepreneurial function is performed by government. A central planning board does the organizing and undertakes the risks of business successes or failures. But because the resources are owned by society, the risks are ultimately borne by the people. Therefore, *no individual has anything personal to lose from failure or anything personal to gain from success.*

Wages and Productivity

In free-market economies, relative wages and incomes tend to reflect differences in productivity, or the market value of one's contribution to output. Resources are thus allocated to their highest valued uses. The economy becomes more efficient and experiences growth. Consequently, everyone benefits by sharing proportionately in an expanding economic pie.

In centrally planned economies, relative wages and incomes tend to bear little relationship to productivity. Labor is misallocated and inefficiently used. Workers and managers have substantial job security, giving them little incentive to be productive and innovative. Therefore, economic growth rates are often retarded, leaving the great majority to share more or less equally in a slowly expanding economic pie.

Management and Decision Making

An important feature of centrally planned economies is that their major enterprises are organized as large state-owned monopolies or oligopolies. Socialist leaders have chosen this approach because they find it easier to work with a small number of large firms than with a large number of small ones. The firms are managed by bureaucrats who are appointed to their positions by the ruling political party. The primary qualification for appointment is party loyalty, not managerial expertise.

Managers in centrally planned economies make relatively few decisions on their own. The managers of each enterprise work with the central planning board and with government ministries to establish an output plan and to acquire the resources needed to fulfill the plan. The plan details specific quantities of goods to be produced, resources to be used, and funds to be provided. It may cover any number of years, but usually covers 1 to 5 years. However, it's revised frequently because of planning errors and because of changes in government priorities, consumption preferences, resource availability, and financing needs.

Enterprises in centrally planned economies are characterized by insufficient incentive systems. Managers and workers have little or no motivation to be productive, innovative, develop new products and markets, and improve quality. This has had serious effects on the performance of such economies, causing most of them to take major steps toward reducing or eliminating central planning.

Conclusion: Evaluating Performance of Centrally Planned Economies

How well—or poorly—have centrally planned economies performed? To answer this question, centrally planned economies are judged according to how well they have achieved the four goals of every economy: efficiency, equity, stability, and growth.

Efficiency

Centrally planned (command) economies have been considerably less successful with respect to efficiency than to their other goals. The reasons have been both technical and economic.

Government Protection and Support Enterprises in command economies have traditionally been sheltered from imports and from the entry of domestic rivals. Firms that have failed to cover their costs have normally been subsidized by the state. For both reasons, therefore, enterprise managers have generally been under much less pressure than their capitalistic counterparts to strive for efficiency.

Inadequate Incentives Enterprise managers in command economies haven't been particularly concerned with developing new products and new production methods. Nor have workers found it particularly advantageous to do more than meet their production quotas. The general lack of motivation has been due in large part to inadequate incentive systems. Although piece rates and bonuses have been employed, they have been given limited use. This is because they are viewed by government officials as "temporary but necessary capitalistic evils."

Rigidities and Shortages Central planners lack the free-market prices needed to guide their decisions. As a result, production rigidities and product shortages have been common in command economies. This has led to the creation of "underground" economies or **black markets**—those in which goods are sold illegally. Butter, meat, sugar, jeans, and electronic goods are among the numerous consumer items that have been popular on the black markets of command economies.

Technical and Economic Inefficiency In light of these outcomes, it may be said that command economies have failed to achieve technical efficiency. This, you'll recall, is the maximum ratio of physical outputs to available physical inputs. Instead, the centrally planned economies have suffered from what economists call *X-inefficiency*. This occurs when an organization fails to minimize costs by not making the best use of resources. X-inefficiency is often due to the failures of managers and workers to work as effectively as they can.

Nor have centrally planned economies come close to attaining economic efficiency—maximum production in accordance with consumer preferences. This is because central planning boards, rather than free markets, serve as the chief mechanism for determining what goods will be produced. Historically, central planners in most command economies have given the highest priority to the production of military goods and, to a large extent, capital goods. Consequently, the quantities and qualities of consumer goods have generally been far below the levels prevailing in capitalistic economies.

Equity

Contrary to their stated intentions, in virtually *all* command economies, past and present, the distribution of income is quite uneven. To be sure, practically all citizens in command economies receive heavily government subsidized social goods—especially education, health care, recreation facilities, and housing—at relatively little or no direct costs. To this extent there is apparent equity in the distribution of real income. However, the best social goods are consumed exclusively by the elite groups within society. These are the nation's political and military leaders, who receive the highest incomes.

In addition, enterprise managers earn much higher salaries than ordinary workers, and receive substantial fringe benefits in the form of superior housing, longer vacations, and in some cases a free car. Similarly, scientists, opera singers, athletes, and others in certain preferred occupations (determined by the government) are paid considerably more than semi-skilled and unskilled workers.

The distribution of wealth—the things that people own—is far more uneven than the distribution of income. Since 1990, articles and documents, some published in communist countries and some smuggled out of them, report very high concentrations of wealth among elite groups. This isn't surprising, since their privileged status and higher incomes make possible further accumulations of wealth.

Thus, *contrary to Marxian doctrine, both the distribution of income and the distribution of wealth in communist countries are very unequal and are not generally based on "need."*

Stability

Fluctuations in business investment expenditures, such as expenditures on plant and equipment, are a chief source of business cycles. In a capitalistic economy, investment-expenditure decisions are left up to each firm. In a command system, the decisions are made by central planners. It should be easier, therefore, for a command economy to control and manage aggregate investment expenditures, and thus promote greater stability, than for a capitalistic economy. This has indeed been the case. Over their history, centrally planned economies have usually maintained high employment and stable prices for substantially longer periods than have mixed economies. However, these benefits are deceptive—for two reasons:

1. Because of the considerable inefficiency that exists in command economies, there is a substantial amount of **underemployment**. This condition, also called "disguised unemployment," is one in which employed resources aren't being used in their most efficient ways.

2. By subsidizing the production of many goods and keeping prices below the levels that would exist in free markets, central planners suppress inflation. However, they do so at the cost of creating frequent product shortages, rationing, and black markets.

Thus, command economies are somewhat more stable than capitalistic economies. However, when the costs to society in the form of substantial resource misallocation, suppressed inflation, and product shortages are taken into account, the benefits to society are far less than they appear to be. In fact, the net benefits—the difference between social benefits and social costs—may well be negative.

Growth

Many problems of definition and measurement are encountered when dealing with data about command economies. These difficulties make comparisons with free-market economies much harder. Nevertheless, Exhibit 2 reveals information worth examining. Figure (a) compares the size of the U.S. economy with that of the former Soviet Union, which until 1992 was the world's first and most advanced command economy.* Size is measured by gross national product expressed in constant dollars. Figure (b) compares the growth rates of gross national product of leading free-market economies with those of the major command economies. The data on the command economies are compiled by America's Central Intelligence Agency, and are believed to be overestimated by significantly more than 30 percent.[†]

Two aspects of the graphs are of particular interest:

1. **Figure (a)** The *official* economic data published by the CIA suggest that the former Soviet Union's real gross national product was about one-half that of the United States'. But the figures are known to be overestimated by about one-third—or perhaps significantly more. Therefore, if we assume an error of only one-third, a closer estimate would put the *unofficial* size of the former Soviet economy at about 33 percent of that of the U.S. economy. However, even this figure is probably much too high for recent years. In 1990, the former Soviet Union began experiencing major economic and political turmoil, resulting in dramatic declines in domestic production.

2. **Figure (b)** During the 1980s, the leading market economies experienced higher growth rates than those of all the command economies with the exception of China. The reason for China's remarkable growth rate during the period is explained by extensive market-oriented reforms it initiated after 1979. In large segments of agricultural and industrial sectors, central planning was replaced

---

*The Soviet Union adopted central planning in 1928. Other countries that subsequently became command economies—China, the nations of Eastern Europe, and Cuba—did so in the years between the late 1940s and the early 1960s. In 1992, the Soviet Union dissolved into independent nations determined to pursue capitalistic reforms.

[†]This was first revealed by the CIA in 1990. It was also reported that the former Soviet government compiled relatively little of its own economic data, relying instead on the CIA's published estimates.

EXHIBIT
2

Economic Size and Growth: Centrally Planned Economies and Market Economies

Centrally planned economies publish relatively little information about themselves. Data that they do publish are frequently unreliable and appear irregularly. As a result, estimates of economic size and growth rates are made by intelligence sources in some of the advanced market economies. These estimates are very rough and made in terms of GNP.

FIGURE (a) *Official* estimates published by America's CIA put the size of the Soviet economy (measured in terms of gross national product) at roughly half that of the U.S. economy. However, these figures, according to the CIA's own admissions, may be about one-third or more too high. The *unofficial* size of the former Soviet Union's economy was probably about two-thirds or less of the amount shown in the graph.

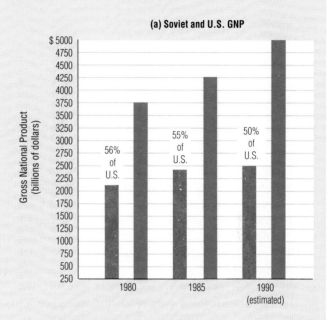

(a) Soviet and U.S. GNP

FIGURE (b) As with Figure (a), *official* economic growth rates of the centrally planned economies, estimated by the CIA, are believed to be substantially overestimated. Therefore, the *unofficial* results are considerably lower than those shown in the graphs. The exact differences are unknown.

Note: Red = centrally planned economy. Green = advanced market economy.

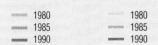

1980	1980
1985	1985
1990	1990

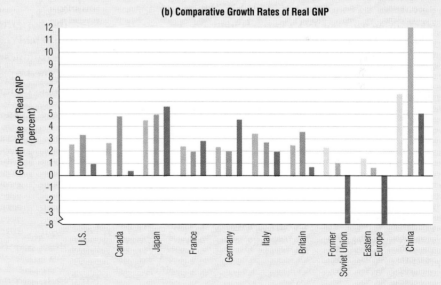

(b) Comparative Growth Rates of Real GNP

Source: Central Intelligence Agency.

with free markets. However, because of internal dissension and a political uprising that occurred in 1989, most reform measures came to a halt by the end of the decade. Since then, there have been some limited easings of controls.

Successes and Failures

The plans of command economies have had multiple goals, based on each country's economic, social, political, and military desires. Because of this, it's extremely difficult to arrive at a single set of conclusions applicable to all of them. Nevertheless, it can be said that all of the command economies have sought to achieve at least two major economic objectives:

1.   Equity   One of the chief goals was to attain substantially greater equality in the distribution of income than exists in capitalistic countries. This was to be accomplished in large part by the provision of universal free health care, education, and other social benefits deemed necessary to further each nation's material and scientific progress. On the whole, the command economies were moderately successful in realizing this social objective. However, with respect to total income distribution, a wide disparity exists between the small, elite upper class and the rest of the population, almost all of whom are poor by Western standards.

2.   Growth   Another chief goal was to achieve continuous rapid expansion of real output at a rate sufficient to attain the highest standard of living in the world. This was to be accomplished by overtaking the advanced capitalistic countries in output per capita as quickly as possible. In general, no command economy succeeded in realizing this objective.

The other two goals of every economic system, *efficiency* and *stability,* were also deemed important by command economies. However, central planners generally gave these goals lower priority. As a result, the relative neglect of them, especially of efficiency, led to serious adverse effects:

The effort to attain rapid growth made it necessary for centrally planned economies to give high priority to the development of heavy industry, such as steel, machinery, and power, and low priority to the production of consumer goods. The consequences turned out to be painful. *Economic efficiency* **suffered because many goods were produced with little regard for buyers' preferences. And** *technical efficiency* **suffered because low worker morale and largely outdated plant and equipment caused poor utilization of production facilities. As a result, levels of living in command economies have generally been inferior to those in advanced market economies.**

Because of these failures, most of the command economies have, since the 1980s, turned to implementing market reforms.

Implementing Market Reforms

In the entire history of human existence, no one has thought of anything more efficient than the free market. By mastering it, we will free ourselves from the abyss and gain the capacity to draw on the achievements of world civilization.

GRIGORY YAVLINSKI
Deputy Prime Minister, former Soviet Union (1990)

When the world entered the last decade of the twentieth century, it was unimaginable that a Soviet official would make such a statement. The former Soviet Union, trying to transform its economy from a centrally planned to a free-market system, was in political and economic chaos. The same was true, more or less, of most of the other command economies that were undergoing similar transitions. Less than two years later, the Soviet economy had collapsed entirely and the Union had ceased to exist.

The troubles experienced by these countries can be attributed to a variety of causes. The major stumbling blocks common to them all include:

1.   An inconsistent legal system

2.   Public ownership of most property

3.   Controlled markets

4.   Absence of financial markets

5.   A nonconvertible currency

Let's explore the measures that can be taken to remove these stumbling blocks.

Revise the Legal System

A chief purpose of law is to ensure the administration of justice. *Justice* is the impartial upholding of actions that society considers reasonable, proper, or deserved. Of course, every society has its own concepts and standards of justice. However, those existing in capitalistic democracies are in certain ways markedly different from those prevailing in socialistic dictatorships.

Principle of Uniformity

In capitalistic democracies, a widely held precept of justice is that the law applies equally to everyone. This may be called the *principle of uniformity*. It ensures that the law will tend to arrive at the same conclusions in essentially similar cases, regardless of the identity of individuals involved. It also explains why judges attach great importance to the doctrine of *precedent*. According to this doctrine, judges in considering new cases should make the same decisions as have judges in previous cases involving similar facts.

The principle of uniformity is an ideal. In practice, it hasn't always been achieved. That's because human beings are less than perfect. And because the law is made, interpreted, and enforced by human beings, perfect justice can probably never be attained. However, only by insisting on maintaining the principle of uniformity can society hope to achieve the highest level of justice humanly possible.

Stability and Flexibility

The principle of uniformity affects two objectives of the law that have major impacts on the economy. These objectives are stability and flexibility.

Stability of the law is particularly important in business transactions. If you wish to buy property or invest money, you want to know that the law pertaining to the transaction will have the same meaning today and tomorrow as it had yesterday. If not—if the law is subject to sudden changes—people will hesitate to make plans. In addition, individuals and businesses will spend excessive amounts of time and money looking for ways to get around the different legal rules. *Stability of the law thus encourages efficiency in transactions.*

Flexibility of the law is also important in business transactions. Economic regulations imposed on enterprises and industries frequently contain provisions that exempt specific actions under certain circumstances. For example, the United States has a law that advertising can't be false or even misleading. However, it is legal to exaggerate the virtues of a product because that is considered harmless "puffery" or "sales talk." As another example, U.S. antitrust laws prohibit firms from engaging in monopolistic practices. But some practices once disallowed are now permitted in order to enable firms to meet growing competition from foreign producers. *Flexibility of the law thus allows it to accommodate changing preferences of society.*

Are the legal goals of uniformity, stability, and flexibility as important to transitional economies as to capitalistic ones? Experts answer yes. They emphasize the following point:

The principle of uniformity hasn't been adhered to in command economies. Laws have typically treated people differently according to their status and power. Legislatures and judges in these countries have changed laws and have often administered them arbitrarily to meet the goals of the state as determined by its leadership. Because of this, legal rules have been neither sufficiently stable nor sufficiently flexible to meet the economic needs of a market economy. Therefore, in order for fundamental long-term economic improvements to occur, the legal systems of transitional economies must be revised to encourage uniformity of treatment as well as stability and flexibility of laws.

Privatize Property

The transition to a market economy requires the adoption of some of its chief traditions, beliefs, and practices. The most fundamental of these is **private property.** This basic institution of capitalism gives each individual the right to acquire economic goods and resources by legitimate means and to use or dispose of them as desired. Of course, society sometimes modifies this right in order to protect public health and safety. For example, laws pertaining to food and drugs are intended to protect public health. Laws regulating automobile traffic and the number of fire exits in buildings protect public safety. Such legislation affects the ways in which some types of property are used. However, they don't alter the fundamental principle of property *rights*.

History shows that private ownership of property provides the strongest incentive to productive effort. History also shows that incentives are necessary to achieve efficiency and economic growth. Unless they provide sufficient incentives, nations cannot achieve substantial and sustained material progress. A major problem of command economies is that most property is owned by the state. Because people are unable to buy, own, use, and sell land and capital as they see fit, the incentive to be productive is absent. Consequently, there is little if any motivation to make the best use of scarce inputs. This leads to serious misallocations of resources, inefficiencies in production and distribution, low productivity rates, and hence slow economic growth.

Methods of Privatization

There are a number of ways in which privatization of land, enterprises, and housing can be achieved. The most feasible approach is to divide the ownership of state-owned properties into claims, such as shares of stock, that can be bought and sold. The claims can then be distributed in either of two ways—by giving them out free or by selling them to the highest bidders.

1.   Distribute Shares for Free   In a socialistic society, state-owned property belongs to the people. Therefore, privatization requires that the property be returned to the people. By giving the people shares in state property, socialistic governments privatize it within a relatively short time. Ownership of property could be transferred to trusts that operate somewhat like mutual funds. The trusts could hold portfolios of assets—land, enterprises, houses—against which they can distribute shares for free to farmers, employees, and tenants. The percentage of shares distributed to each group will undoubtedly be somewhat arbitrary.* However, the initial distribution isn't of primary importance. Because the shares can be traded, markets for them will develop quickly and the assets represented by the shares will tend to be allocated to their highest valued uses.

2.   Sell Shares to the Highest Bidders   A second method of privatization is to sell the shares at auction. In this way the government gains the revenue that it would have lost from giveaways. However, the sale of some state-owned assets will create social inequities. In a command economy, houses, for instance, are owned by the government and are usually rented at very low uniform rates regardless of location. An apartment in the center of a major city, for example, rents for the same price as one in the suburbs that is more than an hour's bus ride away. Political influence and bribery of government officials, rather than a price system, are thus key mechanisms for allocating scarce housing.

---

*For example, 5 percent might go to managers, 20 percent to workers including farmers, and 25 percent to pension funds which would in turn pay everyone's retirement payments. In addition, 25 percent might be used by the government to recapitalize institutions that are intended to remain state owned. These might include, for example, banks, insurance companies, utilities, and hospitals. The remaining 25 percent could be used for miscellaneous purposes. Although many allocation formulas are possible, this is roughly indicative of the privatization method considered in Poland, Russia, and some other East European and former Soviet countries.

The sale of houses at auction would change ownership patterns completely and could produce even worse inequities. Therefore, transitional economies have tended to favor giveaways over auctions as a means of distributing government-owned property.

Giveaways of shares in state-owned assets result in the loss of government revenue that would be realized if the shares were sold. But giveaways have advantages:

1.   They assign property rights to owners quickly, encouraging enterprises to begin functioning efficiently.

2.   They reduce inequities resulting from unanticipated gains and losses in income.

Establish Free Markets

Privatization of property must go hand in hand with free markets. Neither one can function effectively without the other. The belief that they can has turned out to be one of the great delusions of socialism. At various times during the 1980s, China, Hungary, and some other command economies permitted limited experiments with free-market prices without private ownership. Central planners in these countries found that without the ability to buy and sell farms, factories, and equipment, it was impossible to adjust output levels and scales of operation to changing demands and market prices. As a result, enterprise managers were unable to make efficient use of the scarce resources available to them.

These experiments confirmed an essential truth long known to economists:

An economy that permits free markets without private ownership is doomed to fail. Prices set by market forces provide critical information about the relative abundance and scarcity of goods and resources. However, *resources must be free to follow prices.* Otherwise, society will produce too much of some goods and too few of others, thus misallocating resources relative to consumers' preferences.

Institute Financial Reforms

In a centrally planned economy, all financial operations are conducted by the banking system. This consists of a state-owned central bank and a number of its branch banks located throughout the country. The chief purpose of the banking system is to finance the nation's economic plan. Thus, the banking system performs three major functions:

1. It prints money and disburses it to enterprises as specified in the central plan.

2. It collects foreign currencies (called "foreign exchange") and uses them to conduct international transactions. For example, the central bank collects U.S. dollars, Japanese yen, and German marks in payment for the nation's exports and uses the currencies to pay for the nation's imports.

3. It provides savings deposits for the public. This helps reduce inflationary pressures when planning failures cause production shortfalls that result in too much money chasing too few goods.

When a command economy decides to go capitalistic, its chief task is to develop a fully effective private sector. But a robust private sector requires an equally robust financial sector. A transitional economy, therefore, must seek to restructure its financial system.

Restructuring the Financial System

In order to establish a modern financial sector, transitional economies must permit the creation of financial intermediaries, financial instruments, and financial markets. These elements comprise the nation's financial system.

Financial intermediaries are institutions that facilitate the transfer of funds from lenders to borrowers. Financial intermediaries include banks, mortgage companies, pension funds, insurance companies, brokerage firms, and securities dealers. In a transitional economy, financial intermediaries would come into existence to fulfill perceived market demands for their services. With the possible exception of central banks, however, the intermediaries would be privately rather than governmentally owned. Therefore, they would undoubtedly be subject to regulations deemed necessary to permit solvency and profitability while assuring relatively high levels of safety.

Financial instruments are debt and equity claims sold by households, businesses, and governments against themselves in order to acquire funds for conducting operations. The most basic financial instruments are promissory notes, stocks, bonds, and mortgages. Although in modern market economies many other types of instruments exist, they are largely refined and extended versions of the basic ones. Each type of instrument comes into existence to meet the particular desires of investors who purchase them. To encourage economic development, therefore, governments of transitional economies must not limit the private sector's ability to create financial instruments as needed to attract investors' funds.

Financial markets consist largely of a money market and a capital market. Most financial instruments are bought and sold in these markets. Those instruments maturing (coming due) in one year or less are known as short-term instruments and are traded in the **money market**. Those instruments maturing in more than a year are referred to as long-term instruments and are traded in the **capital market**. The chief economic function of a money market is to provide *liquidity*—cash—to households, businesses, and governments desiring it. The chief economic function of a capital market is to channel savings into long-term productive investments. To some extent both of these functions overlap. Nevertheless, the two markets share a common role:

Financial markets facilitate the flow of funds from lenders to borrowers—from savers to investors. In this way, financial markets strongly encourage economic development. Centrally planned economies lack financial markets. Their creation and successful functioning play a key role in the development of transitional economies.

Reforming the Central Banking System

A central bank is at the heart of every nation's financial system. As a result, a central bank's policies have profound effects on the nation's key economic variables. Among them are the price level, interest rates, levels of production and employment, and the international value of its currency.

In market economies, a central bank must perform at least four functions:

1. **Regulate Money Growth**   If the money supply of a nation increases too fast relative to its output of goods and services, there will be too much money chasing too few goods. This will create upward pressure on prices, causing inflation. Conversely, if the money supply increases too slowly relative to the growth of output, production and consumption will be dampened. This may drive the economy into a recession. The central bank, therefore, needs to chart a fairly steady rate of money growth consistent with the economy's long-run capacity to produce. Rates that are substantially

ECONOMICS IN THE NEWS

Coupon Money

Ad Hoc Ukraine Money Drives Out Ruble

By Louis Uchitelle

The Ukrainian Government has given birth to a new national currency.

The new bills, which are the size of Monopoly money and are called coupons, were originally issued as ration tickets that entitled Ukrainians, and not outsiders, to buy the republic's limited supplies of food and other essentials. Actual payment was in Russian rubles. But with Russia's failure to supply Ukraine with enough ruble notes, officials here hastily transformed the coupons into cash.

Here Comes the Hrivnia

"I suppose you have to call the coupons money, although they are not officially a currency," said Leonid G. Steshenko, the First Deputy Prime Minister for Foreign Economic Relations. The new currency, when it comes, will be the hryvnia (pronounced HRIV-nee-uh).

In Moscow, President Boris N. Yeltsin's government raised no objections to the debut of the coupon as a national currency, but Nikolai Domonov, a deputy at Russia's Central Bank, criticized Ukraine's ad hoc procedure.

"If the Ukrainians are going to operate as a separate unit," he said, "then their central bank should draw in the rubles, in exchange for coupons, and send the rubles back to our central bank."

The central bank could then withdraw them from circulation, Mr. Domonov said. Instead, as coupons become more widely used, the rubles they replace are already beginning to flow into Russia.

That happens as Russians sell merchandise in Ukraine for rubles and bring the cash home rather than converting rubles into coupons. One result is higher inflation in Russia as more rubles become available to buy the same quantity of goods, Mr. Domonov said.

Whatever the official status, this nation of 52 million people is now operating with two currencies: the Russian ruble, which is slowly disappearing, and the coupons. Having been printed as ration tickets, the coupon bears neither the national seal nor serial numbers. But half of each Ukrainian's wage is now being paid in coupons and a growing list of products are now priced in coupons.

Source: *The New York Times*, February 13, 1992, p. A1.

faster or slower than this can cause serious economic fluctuations.

2. Act as Fiscal Agent for the Government In market economies, the central bank serves as a government depository. The United States is a fairly typical example. The Federal Reserve System, which is the nation's central bank, acts as fiscal agent for the U.S. Treasury, a department of the federal government. The Treasury deposits any funds it receives in its Federal Reserve accounts and then pays the government's bills by writing checks against the accounts.*

3. Supply Liquidity to the Economy *A central bank should be managed independently of the government and should not be responsible for the direct financing of government deficits.* If a government incurs a budgetary deficit, it should finance the deficit by borrowing from the public, not by ordering its central bank to print more money. Printing money to finance government budgetary deficits creates inflationary strains because it results in too much money chasing too few goods. This phenomenon has been especially common in many Latin American countries. By printing money to pay for their armies, roads, hospitals, schools, and other social goods, these countries have experienced inflations of hundreds and frequently even thousands of percent per year.

4. Operate a Payments System The granting and repayment of loans comprises what the banking industry calls the "payments system." In all market economies, a major function of central banks is to ensure that the payments system works quickly and safely. To help attain this goal, central banks engage in three activities:

- They audit and regulate the affairs of other banks.

- They provide a source of loans to banks in need of short-term liquidity.

- They operate nationwide clearinghouses to provide for rapid collection of funds.

Taken together, these activities contribute to a well-functioning payments system. Therefore, they also enhance the efficiency of banks' operations, thus helping to maintain public confidence in the banking system.

Central banks in transitional economies should play the same role in allocating funds as do central banks in market economies. This requires that the financial sector in transitional economies be reorganized to achieve three goals:

- A well-functioning system of financial intermediaries

- An efficient system of money and capital markets

- A central bank that's managed independently of the government

Establish Currency Convertibility

In market economies, currencies are convertible. By going into any bank, citizens can arrange to buy or sell one currency for another. Americans, for example, can use their dollars to purchase foreign currencies such as British pounds, Canadian dollars, French francs, German marks, and Japanese yen. Americans who own foreign currencies can also sell them to acquire U.S. dollars. The same is true in other market economies. As a result, there exists a world market in foreign currencies. The major participants in the market—the chief buyers and sellers—are banks and currency dealers. The currencies traded are called *foreign exchange,* and the world market in which they're traded is called the *foreign exchange market.*

In market economies, international trade—the flow of goods between nations and the payments for those goods—is governed largely by global market forces of demand and supply. Currency convertibility combined with relatively unrestricted international trade thus yields at least two major benefits:

1. *It permits consumer sovereignty.* Consumers can express their preferences in the marketplace by purchasing the goods they want—domestic or foreign. Because of currency convertibility, importers are able to buy the foreign goods that domestic consumers want to purchase.

2. *It encourages economic efficiency.* Domestic firms find themselves competing with foreign producers to fulfill consumer preferences. Because of currency convertibility, a greater tendency exists for international relative prices to prevail in the domestic economy.

---

*When you pay your income taxes, for example, you send a check to the Internal Revenue Service, which is a division of the Treasury. The money soon ends up in one of the Treasury's deposits at a Federal Reserve Bank. The Treasury then writes checks to pay for the various things on which the government spends money. These include social security, medicare, national defense, health and education, interest on the national debt, and so on. The central banks of other major market economies operate similarly.

In command economies, currencies aren't convertible, and international trade is governed by a central planning board. When preparing its overall plan, the board determines the quantities of goods that will be produced and consumed as well as their prices. It also determines planned surpluses and planned shortages of certain goods. Planned surpluses—defined as goods produced in excess of planned domestic consumption—are exported at prevailing world market prices. Planned shortages—defined as goods consumed in excess of planned domestic production—are imported at prevailing world market prices. Currency convertibility is therefore prohibited because it would subvert planning priorities. It would enable households and enterprises to circumvent the plan by buying abroad those goods that were cheaper on the world market than on the domestic market.

Currency convertibility is necessary to integrate an economy into the world trading system. Convertibility also permits world prices to serve as a guide for developing a domestic price system. Without convertibility, consumer sovereignty is denied and the attainment of economic efficiency is prevented. Therefore, currency convertibility is a necessary condition for successful transition to a market economy.

Minimizing the Adjustment Period

The overall objective of transitional economies is to become well-functioning market economies. This is an extraordinarily difficult task because it requires deep-rooted changes in attitudes, institutions, and organizations. Transitional economies, therefore, are almost certain to encounter numerous problems of conversion.

Experiences in Poland, Hungary, Russia, and other transitional economies of Eastern Europe and the former Soviet Union bear this out. In all of these countries, the chief problems have been high rates of inflation and unemployment accompanied by substantial shortages of food, clothing, fuel, medicine, and other basic goods. But although these are the social costs of adjusting to full capitalism, they need not be prolonged. Governments of transitional economies can minimize the adjustment period by implementing several key measures.

Privatize Property Quickly

A major obstacle facing transitional economies is the privatization of assets. Experience shows that no system can provide proper economic incentives to work, save, invest, and produce unless people believe that they can reap benefits from their sacrifices. And history shows that no system can assure that belief without guaranteeing people the right to buy, own, and sell property as they choose. As China, Cuba, and some other command economies have discovered in recent decades, self-sacrifice doesn't replace self-interest as a motivator when land and capital are owned by the state.

Granted that privatization must occur, how quickly should it be done? A program that permits slow or piecemeal privatization allows time for special interest groups to marshal resistance. Among the chief sources of opposition will be workers and managers who fear loss of jobs, and bureaucrats who expect loss of power. But consumers are also likely to be troublesome. Having observed extensive political cronyism, they feel justified in believing that many assets will be given away cheaply to favored individuals. Therefore:

To minimize the chances of failure, transitional economies should privatize quickly.

Eliminate Monetary Overhang

Transitional economies inherit from planned economies rigidly maintained and strictly enforced price controls. That's because planned economies have too much unspent money—or "monetary overhang." The overhang is due to the quantity of money in the economy exceeding the amount needed to maintain stable prices. As a result, there tends to be too much money chasing too few goods. In market economies, the overhang would be a direct cause of inflation. In planned economies, government prevents inflation by keeping a tight lid on prices.

Monetary overhang arises from three major causes:

1.   Soft Budgets   In planned economies, strict budget requirements aren't usually imposed on large enterprises. Instead they operate on "soft budgets." Major firms, for example, receive government subsidies when expenses exceed revenues. Managers are thus inclined to be somewhat liberal with expenses and to seek favor with workers by granting wage increases in excess of improvements in production efficiency. This leads to inflationary pressures. If enterprises were required to operate on "hard budgets," as is normally the case in market economies, production processes would be more efficient. Firms would go bankrupt if expenses exceeded revenues for prolonged periods, and wage increases would be tied much more closely to gains in productivity.

2. Excessive Enterprise Bank Deposits Virtually all major enterprises in planned economies are state monopolies. Even though they operate on soft budgets, their monopoly status often enables them to accumulate more revenues than are needed to conduct transactions. The excess revenues, which are deposited in state banks, are specially designated for unproductive purposes—such as the payment of retirement and welfare benefits. The money can't normally be used to finance productive investment—the purchase of new plants and equipment—because central planning prohibits enterprises from making independent investment decisions. As a result, enterprise deposits are usually relatively large and continue to grow over the years.

3. Excessive Household Bank Deposits A final major source of monetary overhang in command economies arises because of severe shortages of consumer goods. In allocating scarce resources, central planners typically assign the highest priorities to military spending and to the production of capital goods needed to help achieve substantial economic independence. This results in production inefficiencies and low levels of national income. Consumer goods, many of which are considered unnecessary luxuries, generally receive the lowest priorities. Households, therefore, find themselves with more money than they can spend, and deposit the excess in banks.

Transitional economies are subject to strong inflationary pressure caused by unspent money. What can these countries do to establish economic stability?

A variety of measures can be adopted to eliminate monetary overhang. They include government confiscation of deposits; sale of state-owned property; increased taxation of income and wealth; trade liberalization and currency convertibility; extensive price

decontrol; and removal of subsidies. In addition, the replacement of soft budgets with hard budgets contributes greatly to preventing future overhang.

It's useful to note that these measures, in varying degrees, have been employed by all transitional economies. On the whole, their governments have been quickest at decontrolling prices in large segments of their economies and slowest at privatizing state-owned enterprises. This has encouraged the continuance of inefficiencies, subsidies, and soft budgets, thereby prolonging the adjustment to full capitalism. The resulting high rates of inflation have raised the threat of governments reimposing price controls. But doing so, as officials well know, would eliminate much of the progress already made.

Provide a Safety Net

Transitional economies are bound to experience considerable hardship in their efforts to become market economies. Until stability is achieved, rapid inflation and high rates of unemployment are likely to prevail. To help alleviate the pains of adjustment, transitional governments can institute safety nets for workers and retirees who suffer sharp cuts in their standard of living. Much of the funds needed to finance the safety net can come from the monetary overhang and from the savings realized by eliminating subsidies. This will help maintain citizens' morale and avoid adding to inflationary pressures.

Many deep-rooted changes in beliefs, institutions, and organizations are needed to transform an economy from a planned system to a well-functioning market system. Because of this, both the economic and human costs of transformation are high. Although the costs may not be reducible, the period over which they're borne can be minimized. This will be done, and the benefits of transformation thereby experienced more quickly, if the essential framework of a market system is installed rapidly.

Can Foreign Aid Help?

Should the advanced countries shore up foundering transitional economies with handouts of money and goods? The question has been a subject of frequent debate among the world's political leaders. Failure to provide needed assistance, proponents argue, will weaken reform efforts and encourage political backlashes. These, in turn, may lead to revolutions, the overthrow of transitional governments, and the restoration of communist dictatorships.

In reality, the United States, Britain, France, and other advanced countries have given substantial amounts of aid. So has the International Monetary Fund (IMF) and the World Bank. In general, three types of assistance have been provided:

- Humanitarian aid, consisting of feedgrain, clothing, shelter, fuel, medicine, and other basic goods

- Technical aid, in the form of accounting, financial, legal, and management advisers working with government and industry officials to improve organizational efficiency in the public and private sectors

- Financial aid, including debt relief and loans to help provide the economic support needed to meet reform objectives

Financial assistance is the most costly by far. The bulk of it comes from the IMF and the World Bank. The IMF provides mostly short-term loans to help finance current-account deficits in a nation's balance of payments. The World Bank provides mostly long-term loans to help finance a nation's capital investment for economic growth.

As part of the United Nations, the IMF and the World Bank were created near the end of World War II. During the first few decades of their existence, the two lending agencies often doled out money to needy nations almost for the asking. That is no longer the case. To receive financial backing, the government of a transitional economy must submit a list of reforms and a timetable for adopting them. If the proposal is accepted, the lending agency will grant start-up credit. The borrowing country's economic policies will then be monitored by the lender to determine whether there is sufficient progress to warrant further financing. This, of course, is the way all well-managed banks operate in deciding whether a borrower is a sound credit risk.

To receive financial aid from the IMF and the World Bank, transitional governments must demonstrate determination to make economic reforms work.

But ultimately, success of reforms depends overwhelmingly on what transitional economies do for themselves, without outside help.

Origins: Scientific Socialism

If it is true that people are ultimately judged by the influence of their ideas, then Karl Marx surely ranks as one of the most important people who ever lived. His thoughts have shaped the policies of nations and affected the lives of millions.

Born and educated in Germany, where he studied philosophy, Marx left for France and the prospect of a career in journalism. There he met Friedrich Engels, who became Marx's closest friend and alter ego. Together, while in their late twenties, they wrote *The Communist Manifesto* (1848). This was an inflammatory document urging workers to rise up in revolt against their capitalist exploiters.

Having been expelled from France and later Belgium for his communist activism, Marx spent most of the latter half of his life in England. Here he existed with his wife and children in the depths of poverty, depending for bare survival on two sources. One was the *New York Tribune,* from which he received small and irregular remunerations of $5 to $10 for articles that he submitted. The other was Engels. Engels led a double life. He was fully in accord with Marx's anticapitalistic views, yet he also managed his father's factory in Manchester and even held a seat on the Manchester Stock Exchange.

Major Works

Marx sacrificed everything for his economic and political research, an activity that engaged his full time and effort from morning until night in the great library of the British Museum. The result, after many years of painstaking work, was the publication, in 1867, of Volume I of his enormous treatise, *Das Kapital.* This was not only the "Doomsday Book of Capitalism"—in which Marx predicted the revolutionary overthrow of the capitalistic system and its eventual replacement by communism. The book was also the bible of what Marx called "scientific socialism."

Karl Marx
(1818–1883)

Friedrich Engels
(1820–1895)

munism. Marx predicted its eventual occurrence, but it remained for Lenin to design the structure. This he did in his writings and speeches during the first two decades of the present century, and in his founding of the Soviet Union after the Russian Revolution of 1917.

Failed Expectations

Were Marx's predictions correct? Evidently not. Capitalism, instead of being overthrown, has not only survived but flourished. Nevertheless, during the 75 years following Marx's death, his beliefs gained sufficiently wide appeal to make them acceptable to more than one-third of the inhabited globe.

In the twentieth century, the command economies that adopted Marxian ideology—mainly the former Soviet Union, Eastern European countries, Cuba, China, and North Korea—were called "communistic." But that name was more political than economic. The leaders of these countries actually defined their systems as *socialistic*. This is because, in accordance with Marxian ideology, they viewed their societies as being in the early or *transitory stage* on the road to communism.

Summary of Important Ideas

1. Transitional economics is concerned with the transformation of economies from central planning to free markets. The study of transitional economics is important today because of the interest of many socialist countries in converting to capitalism.

2. Capitalism is characterized by private ownership of land and capital, and by free markets. Socialism is characterized by government ownership of land and capital and by limited, if any, free markets. The goal of most of today's socialists is to transform capitalism by reducing substantially, though not necessarily eliminating entirely, the existence of private ownership.

3. The theories of socialism and communism are rooted in the writings of a nineteenth-century German economist and social philosopher, Karl Marx. In Marxian theory, capitalism is destined to fail and to be replaced first by socialism and then by communism.

Marx's health was never good. In 1883 after a life of extraordinary hardship, intense devotion to family, and a consuming commitment to scholarly research, he died.

Engels labored on Marx's notes for the next several years, and made possible the publication of Volumes II and III of *Das Kapital* (1885, 1894). Four additional volumes under other titles were published in later years from still other notes. On the basis of these and other writings, Marx has come to be regarded as an economist of major significance.

Keep in mind, however, that it was Vladimir Lenin, not Marx, who fashioned the content of com-

Under socialism, the proletariat—the working class as distinct from the capitalist class—will control the state. The state in turn will own the means of production, and workers will be rewarded according to their labor. Under communism, there will be no class distinctions and workers will be rewarded according to need. Socialism is thus an early or transitory stage of economic evolution on the way to communism. Today, however, communism is viewed more often as a political system than an economic system, and communist leaders define their economies as socialistic. In these economies, resources are allocated predominantly by command—that is, by central planning rather than by free markets.

4. Transitional economies seek to correct the failures of central planning by transforming their systems to market economies. Central planning has been a failure for a number of reasons. The chief ones are (a) inadequate market information and (b) insufficient incentive systems.

5. Evidence compiled since 1990 indicates that centrally planned economies have performed much more poorly relative to market economies than was previously believed. Efficiency has been weak due to lack of competition and innovation. Equity, measured by the distribution of income and wealth, has been quite uneven. Stability has been achieved at the costs of underemployment, frequent product shortages, rationing, and black markets. And growth in most years has generally been relatively low, largely because of poor efficiency.

6. In order to achieve a successful transformation, transitional economies must undertake a number of major reforms. Among them: revise the legal system, privatize property, establish free markets, institute financial reforms, and establish currency convertibility. Because several of these changes can be accomplished in different ways, transitional economies will not necessarily use the same methods to attain their goals.

7. The transition process is likely to create many problems. Among them: high rates of inflation and unemployment and shortages of many basic goods. To minimize their magnitude and impact, transitional economies should privatize property quickly, eliminate monetary overhang, and provide an economic safety net. Foreign aid can help reduce the hardships of transition, but ultimately, the success of economic

reforms depends on the transitional government's determination to make them work.

8. Karl Marx founded what he called "scientific socialism." In his chief work, *Das Kapital*, he propounded ideas that subsequently became the basis of modern socialist theory. During much of the twentieth century, Marx's writings influenced the policies of many nations and the lives of hundreds of millions of people. However, contrary to Marx's predictions, capitalism has not only survived but flourished.

Terms and Concepts to Review

transitional economics	*private property*
capitalism	*financial intermediaries*
institutions	*financial instruments*
socialism	*financial markets*
economic interpretation of history	*money market*
surplus value	*capital market*
class struggle	*foreign exchange*
X-inefficiency	*foreign exchange market*

Questions and Problems

1. a. What is meant by an "interpretation of history"? Can you suggest several different types of interpretations? In your previous history courses in high school or college, which interpretations were stressed? Which interpretation did Marx stress?

b. Marx was aware that direct labor was only one of several inputs used in production. He knew that raw materials, machines, and other resources were also necessary. Nevertheless, he argued, labor alone is the basis of value. How do you suppose Marx justified this belief?

c. According to Marx, would surplus value exist if capitalists paid workers what they were "worth"?

d. Do you believe that there is such a thing as a "class struggle" in the Marxian sense? Why or why not? (*Hint:* Can we divide a complex social structure into opposing subclasses? By what criteria?)

e. Referring back to Marx's theory, can you offer at least one brief, critical comment on each of its main ideas? (*Hint:* Try to apply some of the broad concepts you've learned in economics.)

2. In the 1920s, a leading Austrian economist, Ludwig von Mises, advanced the argument that "economic calculation is impossible under socialism." What do you suppose von Mises meant by this statement? Do you agree with it?

3. In a centrally planned economy, is there consumer sovereignty? Is there freedom of consumer choice?

4. Why do leaders in command economies want to engage in the complex and difficult task of planning? Why don't they simply let a free-market system allocate society's resources and distribute the income?

5. Rapid privatization of property is one of the first steps that must be undertaken by a transitional economy. Without it, transition is likely to fail. Why?

6. Command economies often use financial and material incentives, such as bonuses and longer vacations, to spur production. Does this accord with socialistic thinking? If not, why are incentives employed?

7. Why have transitional economies experienced a high rate of inflation after removal of price controls? Give your answer in terms of demand and supply curves.

8. Why is monetary overhang a cause of inflation in transitional economies? Give your answer in terms of demand and supply curves.

9. Why do you suppose that Poland, Russia, and other transitional economies experienced high rates of unemployment after price controls were removed?

10. Privatization of state enterprises is almost certain to cause short-term unemployment. Can you explain why?

TAKE A STAND

After Communism: Free-Market Capitalism?

The transition from communism to a market economy in the former Soviet republics has been turbulent. By the early 1990s, none had reached a full-fledged capitalist economy comparable to that of the United States or the countries of the European Community. Indeed, the economies of the former Soviet republics face extraordinary problems. Their GNP* fell about 2 percent in 1990, and about 13 percent in 1991. Inflation has reached such high levels that prices approximately doubled in 1991. Budget deficits equal to about 10 percent of GNP make inflation difficult to control.

Nevertheless, these nations continue to move toward a market economy. Price controls are being removed, state-owned industries are being privatized, and small-business entrepreneurship is being encouraged. The International Monetary Fund and the World Bank are attempting to provide financial and technical support.

How far down the road to capitalism will the former Soviet republics go? Is it possible that they will create an idealized *laissez-faire* economy that is equally efficient or more so than Western economies? Or will they return to centralized, authoritarian control of the economy? Most analysts view either extreme as unlikely. They believe that some kind of market economy will be adopted. But what kind? *Will free-market capitalism replace communism?*

Yes: Autonomy, Prices, and Rewards

Free-market capitalism is based on individual autonomy, flexible prices, and the chance for rewards. Many analysts argue that the former Soviet republics have already laid this foundation, and that it is not going to crumble any time soon.

---

*In the United States, until 1992 national output was customarily measured in terms of gross national product rather than gross domestic product.

Reforms have given Soviet citizens individual autonomy by allowing them to own land and operate their own small businesses. Privatization efforts are slowly transferring ownership of state-owned enterprises to individuals. With the dismantling of centralized planning agencies, price controls have been eliminated for many products, and prices are being allowed to reflect the relative scarcity of goods. Private ownership and flexible prices have created an environment in which rewards are based on effort. Hard work, entrepreneurial risk taking, and innovation now carry the prospects of greater income.

There have been setbacks in the transition to free-market capitalism. Prices have quadrupled while wages have only doubled. Distribution systems that functioned inefficiently under unified communist rule are barely functioning at all under the conflicting trade policies of the independent republics. Privatization efforts have moved ahead far more slowly than anticipated. Reactionaries have already staged a demonstration in Moscow to demand a socialist restoration. However, the vast majority will not want to barter their new economic and political freedoms for the apparent security of centralized planning. Instead, they will adapt to the major elements of free-market capitalism. Through flexible prices, markets will answer the three fundamental questions of resource allocation: *What* goods are produced? *How* are goods produced? *For whom* are goods produced?

No: Cooperation and Consensus

There is little chance that the former Soviet republics will become free-market economies like those in the West. The people won't allow it. Public unrest over high consumer prices and unemployment caused by market reform will result in a communist backlash. The idealism of *laissez-faire* market economies will be abandoned in favor of more pragmatic means of protecting workers' rights, maintaining job security, preventing large inequities in income, and providing a social safety net.

Three-quarters of a century of comfortably centralized government control will become increasingly attractive during these turbulent times. However, the republics are unlikely to return to an authoritarian government. The future of the republics lies in state-sponsored democratic industrial policy.

This policy will protect infant industries and modernize successful state-owned enterprises. It will also entail cooperation among governments, labor unions, and business associations.

For example, private farmers will negotiate price supports with government and unions will negotiate unemployment benefits and wages with business and government employers.

Free-market capitalism is already creating unacceptable and unnecessary austerity, unemployment, and inflation. The future of the former Soviet republics is cooperation and consensus.

The Question: Will Free-Market Capitalism Replace Communism?

- One view is that the former Soviet republics are well on their way to adopting a Western-style free-market economy. They have already instituted individual autonomy, flexible prices, and the chance for rewards. These reforms will be extremely difficult to undo and will enable the ex-Soviet nations to allocate resources efficiently through free-market capitalism.

- An alternative view is that the former Soviet republics will develop economies based on cooperation and consensus. Through a state-sponsored democratic industrial policy, major industries will remain state owned. Unions, government, and business associations will cooperate in establishing pricing and production decisions.

Where Do You Stand?

1. Should the former Soviet republics—now loosely linked under the Commonwealth of Independent States (CIS)—look to eastern Europe as a model for implementing their own reforms? If not, why not? If so, what insight can they gain and why?

2. Is it likely that one or more of the CIS republics will return to a centrally planned economy? Why or why not?

3. How does the U.S. economy compare to the type of free-market capitalism that may develop in the CIS?

4. Will free-market capitalism replace communism? Justify your stand.

Sources: "A Market: But What Kind: For Views on the Future of the Post-Soviet Economy," *Dollars and Sense,* December, 1991, pp. 6–9; "The Wild East," *The Economist,* January 4, 1992, pp. 40–41; Stanley Fisher and Jacob Frenkel, "Macroeconomic Issues and Soviet Reform," *American Economic Review Papers and Proceedings,* May 1992, Vol. 82, No. 2, pp. 37–42.

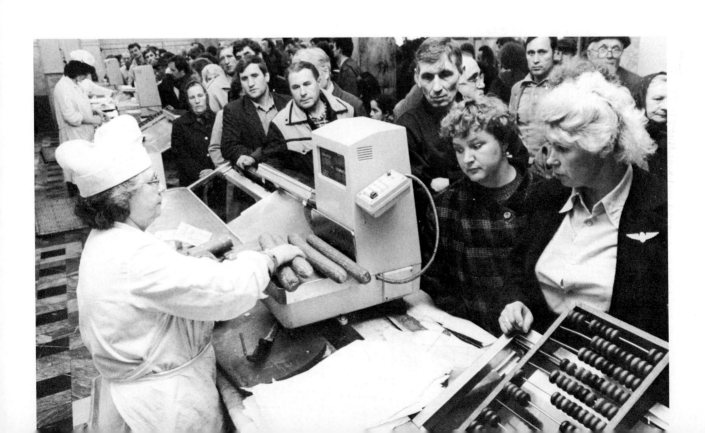

Index

Index

Dictionary of Economic
Terms and Concepts

Dictionary of Economic Terms and Concepts

This Dictionary includes the definitions of every technical word, phrase, and concept given in the text, as well as definitions of many other terms of significance in economics. It also presents cross references and brief examples that explain the significance of important terms. Hence the Dictionary will be a convenient and permanent source of reference—not only for this course, but for future courses you may take in economics, other social sciences, and business.

A

ability-to-pay principle Theory of taxation that holds that the fairest tax is based on the financial means of the taxpayer—regardless of any benefit he or she may receive from the tax. Financial means may be determined by either wealth or income. The U.S. personal income tax is founded on this idea.

absolute advantage, law of Principle that states that a basis for trade exists between nations or regions when each of them, as a result of natural or acquired superiorities, can provide a good or service that the other wants at a lower cost than if each were to provide it for itself. This law accounts for much of the world's trade.

absolute-income hypothesis Proposition that states that a family's propensity to consume (that is, the amount it spends on consumption) depends on its *level* of income—the absolute amount available for spending. This concept of the propensity to consume was the one used by Keynes. *(Contrast with **relative-income hypothesis; permanent-income hypothesis**.)*

acceleration curves Short-run inflation-unemployment relationships showing how the inflation rate speeds up with expansionary fiscal-monetary policies and slows down with contractionary ones. *(See **Phillips curve**.)*

accelerator principle Proposition that net investment in capital goods depends upon changes in the level of output (that is, GDP). This is because capital goods are durable. Therefore, if existing production capacity is adequate, it is possible to produce a constant level of output with existing equipment, replacing it as it wears out. No net investment needs to be undertaken. But if aggregate demand increases, the economy, operating at full capacity, will have to undertake additional investment in order to produce an increase in output. Therefore, net investment is a function of *changes* in the level of output. Thus:

$$\text{Net investment} = \text{accelerator} \times \text{change in GDP}$$

and hence

$$\text{Accelerator} = \frac{\text{net investment}}{\text{change in GDP}}$$

The accelerator itself is a mathematical constant—a number such as 1.0, 1.5, 2.0, and so on—that is estimated by statistical procedures.

accounts payable A company's debts to suppliers of goods or services.

accounts receivable Amounts due to a firm from customers.

accrued expenses payable Obligations, such as wages and salaries, interest on borrowed funds, and pensions.

additional-worker hypothesis Theory which holds that, during a period of rising unemployment, the rate of participation in the labor force increases. The reason is that many of the main income-earners of families lose their jobs. Therefore, people who were not previously in the labor force, such as full-time students and homemakers, are forced to seek employment in order to support the family. *(Contrast with discouraged-worker hypothesis.)*

adjustable peg System that permits governmentally controlled changes in the par rate of foreign exchange after a nation has had long-run disequilibrium in its balance of payments. It allows also for short-run variations within a narrow range of a few percent around the par value.

administered pricing Means by which executives in oligopolistic industries are able to manage ("administer") their firms' prices, instead of permitting them to be determined by the free interactions of market forces. It is based on either of two beliefs about how oligopolies set prices—*cost-plus pricing* and *target-return pricing*.

ad valorem subsidy Fixed percentage subsidy based on the price or value of a commodity.

ad valorem tax Fixed percentage tax on the price or value of a commodity. *Examples:* sales taxes, property taxes, and most import duties.

adverse selection The unfavorable effect of asymmetric information on the outcome of a transaction. With a transaction involving a tangible good, adverse selection tends to restrict the quality of the good exchanged. In a transaction involving insurance, adverse selection is manifested in the tendency of individuals who are above-average risks to seek more insurance protection than other people.

affirmative action Legislation requiring firms working under contracts with the federal government to file numerical equal-opportunity "goals and timetables." These are compliance reports showing that good-faith efforts were made to fill employment quotas with minority group members and women. *(See also equal employment opportunity.)*

agency shop Business firm in which workers are required to pay union dues regardless of whether or not they join the union. It is said to be a "compromise" based on two principles: (1) that workers should not be required to join a union against their wishes, and (2) that all workers in a firm (even those who are not union members) benefit from union representation and should therefore pay for it. Agency shops are legal under the National Labor Relations Act, but they can be specifically outlawed by state right-to-work laws.

aggregate concentration ratio A measure of the relative size of firms within a large segment of the economy. The ratio measures the percentage share of sales, assets, value added, profits, employment (or any other indicator of size) accounted for by the largest firms across entire sectors or subsectors of the economy. The number of "largest firms" may range from a few dozen to several hundred, depending on the size of the sector being measured. *(Contrast with concentration ratio.)*

aggregate demand Total value of real aggregate output that all sectors of the economy are willing to purchase at various average price levels. *(Contrast with aggregate expenditure.)*

aggregate expenditure Total amount of spending on goods and services that all sectors of the economy are willing to undertake at various income levels. Spending and income are usually expressed in real (rather than nominal) terms. *(Contrast with aggregate demand.)*

aggregate output Total value of production of goods and services. It is equivalent in dollars to GDP, and is usually expressed in real (rather than nominal) terms *(Contrast with aggregate supply.)*

aggregate supply Total value of real aggregate output that will be made available at various average price levels. *(Contrast with aggregate output.)*

Agricultural Adjustment Act (1938) Basic farm law (with subsequent amendments) of the United States. It has, at various times, provided for (1) price supports of selected farm products at specified levels; (2) production control through acreage allotments of certain crops; (3) marketing agreements and quotas between the Department of Agriculture and producers in order to control the distribution of selected commodities; (4) payments to farmers and others who follow approved soil conservation practices; and (5) parity payments to farmers for selected agricultural staples.

allocative efficiency *See efficiency.*

Aluminum Company of America (Alcoa) case (1945) Major antitrust case against Alcoa. The company was the dominant firm in aluminum production, accounting for 90 percent of the nation's output. Even though Alcoa did not aggressively seek to attain a monopoly, but rather found that monopoly had been "thrust upon" the company, it was a "passive beneficiary" of monopoly, according to Judge Learned Hand, who therefore found the company in violation of the Sherman Antitrust Act. This stringent interpretation was thus contrary to the traditional *rule of reason* that had prevailed since the Standard Oil case of 1911. As it happened, Judge Hand's rigid interpretation was greatly tempered in subsequent antitrust cases, and has not been strictly applied since 1945.

American Federation of Labor-Congress of Industrial Organizations (AFL-CIO) League of labor unions formed in 1955 by a merger of the AFL and CIO. Its purposes are to improve the wages, hours, and conditions of workers and to realize the benefits of free collective bargaining. It exercises no authority or control over member unions other than requiring them to abide by its constitution and code of ethical practices.

American Tobacco case (1911) Major antitrust case in which the Supreme Court found the "tobacco trust" to be in violation of the Sherman Act. The trust consisted of five major tobacco manufacturers controlling 95 percent of domestic cigarette production. However, the Court did not condemn the trust for that fact. It was the trust's "unreasonable" market behavior, driving competitors out of business, that caused the Court's condemnation.

announcement effect Public's response to reported changes in the Federal Reserve's monetary controls (such as the discount rate). These changes in Fed controls, when announced in the news media, are sometimes interpreted by the public as a distinct change in Federal Reserve *policies*. When this happens, the reaction can be confusion and instability in the private sector.

annually balanced budget Philosophy that holds that total revenues and expenditures in the government's budget should be balanced or brought into equality every year.

antitrust laws Acts passed by Congress since 1890 to prevent monopoly and to maintain competition. The chief ones are (1) the Sherman Antitrust Act (1890); (2) the Clayton Antitrust Act (1914); (3) the Federal Trade Commission Act (1914); (4) the Robinson-Patman Act (1936); (5) the Wheeler-Lea Act (1938); and (6) the Celler-Kefauver Antimerger Act (1950).

Aquinas, St. Thomas (1225–1274) Medieval philosopher who wrote on economic problems during the early stages of modern capitalism. He attempted to harmonize reason with faith by applying principles of Aristotelian philosophy to biblical teaching and canonical dogma. Thus he held that the individual's right to private property accords with natural law; commerce is to be condoned to the extent that it maintains the household and benefits the country; fairness and truthfulness in commercial dealings are essential virtues; and so on. In general, these and other ideas of Aquinas make him one of the important leaders in early economic thought.

arbitrage Act of buying a commodity in one market and simultaneously selling it in another market at a higher price. Arbitrage tends to equalize the price of a commodity in different markets, except for differences in the costs of transportation, risk, and so on.

arbitration Settlement of differences between parties (such as a union and management) by the use of an impartial third party. The two sides select a third party, called an arbitrator, whose decision is legally binding. The arbitrator issues a decision based not on what he or she thinks is wise and fair but on how he or she believes the language of the contract applies to the case. Arbitration in industrial relations almost always deals with the settlement of union-management disputes over the provisions of an existing collective-bargaining contract. *(Contrast with* **mediation***.)*

Arrow, Kenneth Joseph (1921–   ) Leading American economist and Nobel laureate (1972). He is noted for his work in welfare economics, mathematical programming, and growth theory. Arrow served on the President's Council of Economic Advisors in 1962 and has been on the faculties of the University of Chicago, Harvard University, and Stanford University.

Arrow's impossibility theorem Proposition that proves that no voting system is perfect because group decisions cannot be both rational and fair. The reason is that five conditions are needed to meet all requirements of rationality and fairness: (1) the voter must be able to rank alternatives in a consistent manner; (2) the voter must be free to choose any possible ranking of alternatives; (3) the voting outcome must please as many people as possible while displeasing as few as possible; (4) no individual may dictate a decision to the voting group; and (5) the voting system must preserve the ranking of a given set of alternatives if there is added to it another set of alternatives. Arrow's theorem demonstrates that, because of logical inconsistencies, these conditions cannot be applied simultaneously. Thus, it is impossible to construct a "perfect" voting system—one that is completely rational and fair.

asset management Method used by banks to obtain liquidity (raise funds) by selling their income-earning securities such as Treasury bills, Treasury bonds, and municipal bonds.

assets Resources or things of value owned by an economic entity, such as an individual, household, business firm, or government. *Examples:* cash, property, and the rights to property.

automatic fiscal stabilizers Nondiscretionary or "built-in" features that automatically cushion recession by helping to create a budget deficit and curb inflation by helping to create a budget surplus. *Examples:* (1) income tax receipts; (2) unemployment taxes and benefits; and (3) corporate dividend policies.

automatic transfer services (ATS) A combined interest-bearing savings and zero-balance checking account offered by many banks. When a check written against the account is presented for payment, the bank switches the necessary funds from savings to checking. A more apt description, therefore, would be automatic transfer of *savings* (rather than services). ATS accounts are one of several forms of savings-type checkable deposits.

autonomous consumption Consumption that is independent of income. It is the part of total consumption that is unrelated to income. *(Compare* **induced consumption***.)*

autonomous investment Investment that is independent of aggregate income (or output). *(Compare* **induced investment***.)*

autonomous transactions Settlements among nations that arise from factors unrelated to the balance of payments as such. The main classes are merchandise trade and services, long-term capital movements, and unilateral transfers.

average-cost price *See* ***full-cost price***.

average fixed cost Ratio of a firm's total fixed cost to the quantity it produces. Also, the difference between average total cost and average variable cost. Thus,

$$\text{Average fixed cost} = \frac{\text{total fixed cost}}{\text{quantity of output}}$$

Also,

Average fixed cost

= average total cost – average variable cost

average-marginal relationship Mathematical relationship between all corresponding average and marginal curves. The relationship is such that: when an average curve is rising, its corresponding marginal curve is above it; when an average curve is falling, its corresponding marginal curve is below it; and when an average curve is either at a maximum or at a minimum, its corresponding marginal curve intersects (is equal to) it.

average product Ratio of total output or product to the amount of variable input needed to produce that volume of output. Thus,

$$\text{Average product} = \frac{\text{total product}}{\text{variable input}}$$

average propensity to consume (APC) Ratio of consumption to income:

$$\text{Average propensity to consume} = \frac{\text{consumption}}{\text{income}}$$

It thus reveals the proportion of income that is spent on consumption.

average propensity to save (APS) Ratio of saving to income:

$$\text{Average propensity to save} = \frac{\text{saving}}{\text{income}}$$

It thus reveals the proportion of income that is saved (that is, not spent on consumption).

average revenue (AR) Ratio of a firm's total revenue to its quantity of output sold—or, equivalently, its price per unit of quantity sold. Thus,

Average revenue

$$= \frac{\text{total revenue}}{\text{quantity}} = \frac{(\text{price})\ (\text{quantity})}{\text{quantity}} = \text{price}$$

average revenue product (ARP) Ratio of total revenue to the quantity of an input employed. Thus,

$$\text{Average revenue product} = \frac{\text{total revenue}}{\text{quantity of input employed}}$$

average tax rate Ratio or percentage of a total tax to the base on which it is imposed. *Example:*

Average personal income tax rate

$$= \frac{\text{total personal income tax}}{\text{total taxable income}}$$

average total cost Ratio of a firm's total cost to the quantity it produces. Also, the sum of average fixed cost and average variable cost. Thus,

$$\text{Average total cost} = \frac{\text{total cost}}{\text{quantity of output}}$$

Also,

Average total cost

$$= \text{average fixed cost} + \text{average variable cost}$$

average variable cost Ratio of a firm's total variable cost to the quantity it produces. Also, the difference between a firm's average total cost and average fixed cost. Thus,

$$\text{Average variable cost} = \frac{\text{total variable cost}}{\text{quantity of output}}$$

Also,

Average variable cost

$$= \text{average total cost} - \text{average fixed cost}$$

B

backward-bending labor-supply curve Relationship between a worker's real wage rate and the number of labor hours offered. At relatively lower wage levels the relationship is direct: the curve slopes upward over a range of labor hours. However, a point is reached at which the worker is no longer willing to trade additional leisure in return for higher income from working. The relationship then becomes inverse. That is, the curve bends backward, showing that higher real wage rates result in fewer labor hours offered.

Bain index Measure of a firm's monopoly power, based on the divergence between price, *P*, and average total cost, *ATC*. A modified version of the index in which the divergence is expressed as a proportion of price is

$$\text{Bain index} = \frac{P - ATC}{P}$$

The index will be zero (no monopoly power) when the firm is earning only normal profit (that is, $P = ATC$). On the other hand, the index will be greater than zero when the firm is earning an economic or excess profit (that is, $P > ATC$). Basic shortcomings of the index are that (1) large profits do not necessarily indicate the existence of strong monopoly power, since large profits may be the result of greater efficiency or of different accounting methods used for depreciation and asset valuation; (2) it is a static rather than dynamic measure and therefore cannot be applied to firms that experience rapid changes in technology, demand, and so on.

balanced budget Budget with total revenues and total expenditures that are equal.

balanced budget multiplier Hypothesis that asserts that, if government spending and taxes are increased or decreased simultaneously by equal amounts, real output will be increased or decreased by the same amount. *Example:* An equal increase in government spending and taxes of $20 billion will raise real output by 1 × $20 billion = $20 billion. (Similarly, an equal decrease of $20 billion will lower real output by 1 × $20 billion = $20 billion.) The reason for this is that the effects of equal increases in government spending and taxes are opposite. Therefore, the two multiplier processes cancel each other out—except on the first round, when the full amount of government spending is added to real output.

balance of payments Statement of the money value of all transactions between a nation and the rest of the world during a given period, such as a year. These transactions may consist of imports and exports of goods and services, and movements of short-term and long-term investments, gifts, currency, and gold. The transactions may be classified into several categories, of which the two broadest are the current account and the capital account.

balance-of-payments disequilibrium Circumstance that exists when, over a unspecified period lasting several years, a nation's autonomous credits do not equal its autonomous debits. A deficit disequilibrium exists when total autonomous debits exceed total autonomous credits. A surplus disequilibrium occurs when total autonomous credits exceed total autonomous debits.

balance of trade That part of a nation's balance of payments dealing with merchandise imports and exports. A "favorable" balance of trade exists when the value of exports exceeds the value of imports. An "unfavorable" balance exists when the value of imports exceeds the value of exports.

balance sheet Statement of a firm's financial position on a given date. It shows what the firm owns (its assets), what it owes (its liabilities), and the residual or equity of the owners (the net worth).

Bank of the United States Chartered for the period 1791 to 1811, the Bank's function was to assist the Treasury in its fiscal activities and to provide an adequate supply of currency to meet the needs of business. The Bank's performance was generally satisfactory, but its charter was not renewed. Primary opposition came from farmers, who felt that the Bank favored urban commercial interests over rural agricultural ones and that the Bank's financial power was too great.

banker's acceptance Promise by a bank to pay specific bills for one of its customers when the bills become due. It may be thought of as a bank-guaranteed "post-dated" check written by one of its customers and accepted by the bank for payment. The bank thus assumes the customer's debt and guarantees payment on the post-dated day. In the interim, if the bank should need short-term funds, it can sell the check at a discount from face value in the money market. *(See also **bill of exchange; draft**.)*

barter Simple exchange of one good for another without the use of money.

basic wages Payments received by workers for work performed, based on time or output.

basing-point pricing Method of delivered pricing in some industries. Each seller in the industry quotes a given buyer the so-called basing-point price plus the cost of shipping from the basing point to the buyer, regardless of the location from which the product is actually shipped. The basing point is the factory or mill price of the product in a particu-

lar city. *Example:* The steel industry, in the early decades of this century, used a basing-point system known as "Pittsburgh plus." All firms in the industry quoted U.S. Steel's mill price at Pittsburgh plus the cost of rail shipment from Pittsburgh to the buyer, regardless of whether the steel came from Pittsburgh or from some other city closer or farther from the buyer. In this way the industry managed to eliminate competition in price, because all sellers quoted the same delivered price to any given buyer. *(Compare **f.o.b. pricing** and **delivered pricing**.)*

basis In the futures market, the difference between the cash and futures price of a commodity:

$$\text{Basis} = \text{futures price} - \text{cash price}$$

The difference is approximately equal to the carrying costs (including freight, insurance, storage, and so forth of moving the product from local rural markets to major terminal markets, such as Chicago, Omaha, and Kansas City.

"bathtub theorem" A model in the form of a physical analogy—a bathtub. The level of water in the tub represents the economy's output or income. Thus, water flowing into the tub represents "injections." These may consist of investment, government spending, or exports. The effects of these expenditures are to increase aggregate expenditure and thus to raise the water level in the tub (that is, to increase income and employment). Water flowing out of the tub represents "withdrawals." These are "leakages" from total income, which may consist of saving, taxes, and imports. The effects of such leakages are to decrease aggregate expenditure and thus to lower the water level in the tub (that is, to decrease income and employment). Of course, the level of water in the tub remains constant as long as inflows (injections) equal outflows (withdrawals). Also, at any *given* level, inflows equal outflows.

benefit-cost analysis Method of evaluating alternative investment projects by comparing for each the (discounted) present value of all expected benefits or net receipts with the (discounted) present value of all expected costs or sacrifices. Once such comparisons are made, a rational basis exists for choosing one investment project over the other.

benefit-cost (B/C) ratio Ratio of the present value of benefits (net receipts) of an investment to the present value of costs:

$$B/C = \frac{\text{present value of benefits}}{\text{present value of costs}}$$

The *B/C* ratio thus gives the present value of net receipts per dollar of investment cost. The ratio must equal at least 1 in order for the investment to be recovered (that is, repaid by its net receipts).

benefit principle Theory of taxation that holds that a fair tax is one that is levied on people according to the services or benefits they receive from government. The chief difficulties are that: (1) for many goods, benefits cannot be readily determined (for example, national defense, public education, police and fire protection); and (2) those who receive the benefits are not always able to pay for them (for example, recipients of welfare or unemployment compensation).

bilateral monopoly   Market structure in which a monopsonist buys from a monopolist. The equilibrium quantity may be determinate. However, the price level for that quantity is logically indeterminate. That is, the price will end up somewhere between the minimum price preferred by the monopsonist and the maximum price preferred by the monopolist.

bill of exchange   Draft (or type of "check") used between countries. *(See also draft.)*

bimetallic standard   Monetary standard under which the national unit of currency (such as the dollar) is defined in terms of a fixed weight of two metals, usually gold and silver. The United States was on this standard during the nineteenth century, but it usually worked unsatisfactorily because of the operation of Gresham's Law. *(See also Gresham's law; mint ratio.)*

black market   Illegal market in which a good is sold for more that its legal ceiling price. The good may or may not be rationed. If it is, experience indicates that the criteria used for rationing are virtually certain to create skullduggery and inequities. *(Compare white market.)*

Board of Governors   Group of seven people that supervises the Federal Reserve System. Members are appointed by the President and confirmed by the Senate for terms of 14 years each, one term expiring every 2 years.

bond   Agreement to pay a certain sum (called the principal) either at a future date or periodically over the course of a loan. During the period of the loan, a fixed rate of interest may be paid on certain dates. Bonds are issued by corporations and by the federal, state, and local governments. They are typically used for long-term financing.

boycott   Campaign to discourage people from dealing with a particular firm. (Sometimes called a "primary boycott.")

break-even point   Level of output at which a firm's total revenue equals its total cost (or its average revenue equals its average total cost) so that its net revenue is zero. At a break-even point as defined in economics, a firm is normally profitable, since total cost in economics includes normal profit.

Brown Shoe case (1962)   Major antitrust case in which the Supreme Court struck down a merger between Brown Shoe and Kinney Shoe as a violation of the Clayton Antitrust Act. Although both companies were shoe manufacturers and retailers with relatively small market shares, the merger, it was held, would nevertheless "foreclose competition from a substantial share of the market for shoes without producing countervailing economic or social advantages." The Court also held that the merger might increase market concentration in a few cities where both companies had retail stores.

budget   Itemized estimate of expected revenues and expenditures for a given period.

budget deficit   Condition in which total expenditures exceed total revenues.

budget surplus   Condition in which total revenues exceed total expenditures.

Burns, Arthur Frank (1904–)   American economist and expert on business cycles, fiscal policy, and monetary policy. He served as President of the National Bureau of Economic Research, as a professor of economics at Columbia University, and in various high-level government positions, including head of the President's Council of Economic Advisers and Chairman of the Board of Governors of the Federal Reserve System.

business cycles   Recurrent but nonperiodic fluctuations in general business and economic activity that take place over a period of years. They occur in aggregate variables, such as GDP, employment, and prices. The variables move at approximately the same time in the same direction, but *at different rates*. Business cycles are thus accelerations and retardations in the rates of growth of important economic variables.

C

cameralism   A form of mercantilism extensively implemented by German governments during the eighteenth century. Its chief objective was to increase the revenue of the state. (The word comes from *Kammer*, meaning "chamber," the name applied to the royal treasury.)

capital   1. As a factor of production, capital is a manufactured good that is used to produce other goods. That is, capital is a produced means of further production. Examples of capital goods (which are also called *investment goods)* are machines, tools, and factories used for the ultimate purpose of manufacturing consumer goods. In a broad sense, therefore, human resources are also part of an economy's capital. 2. As money, capital represents the funds that business people use to purchase capital goods. 3. In accounting, capital may sometimes represent net worth or the stockholders' equity in a business.

capital consumption allowance   Expression used in national-income accounting to represent the difference between "gross" and "net" private domestic investment. It consists almost entirely of depreciation and is often used as if it were synonymous with it.

capital deepening   An increase in an economy's stock of capital at a faster rate than the increase in its other resources, particularly labor. As the volume of capital per worker rises, the average output per worker rises.

capitalism   Economic system characterized by private ownership of the factors of production and their operation for profit under predominantly competitive conditions.

capital market   A market in which long-term credit and equity instruments, maturing in more than a year from date of issue are bought and sold. Examples are bonds, mortgages, and stock.

capital-output (or capital/output) ratio Concept sometimes used in a "total" sense, and sometimes in a "marginal" sense. Thus: **1.** The "total" capital-output ratio is the ratio of an economy's total stock of real capital to the level of its income or output. **2.** The "marginal" capital-output ratio is the change in an economy's income or output resulting from a unit change in its stock of real capital. Thus a ratio of 3/1 means that three units of additional capital produce one unit of additional output.

capital stock Unit of ownership in a corporation. It represents the stockholder's proprietary interest. Two major classes are common stock and preferred stock.

capital widening Increases in an economy's stock of capital at the same rate as the growth of its labor force, thus maintaining the same volume of capital per worker and hence the same average output per worker.

capture theory of regulation Theory describing how a regulated industry may come to control the agency responsible for its regulation. *Example:* Under regulation of the Civil Aeronautics Board from the 1930s to the 1970s, the airline industry received special benefits, such as higher prices, fewer competitive pressures, and higher profits.

cartel Association of producers in the same industry established to increase the profits of its members by adopting common policies affecting production, market allocation, or prices. A cartel may be domestic or international in scope. In the United States, organizations of independent business enterprises established for mutually beneficial purposes are called *trade associations,* not cartels. The latter term has been reserved exclusively for foreign or international associations. However, when a trade association or similar group fixes prices, restricts output, or allocates markets for its members, it behaves in *effect* like a cartel.

Celler Antimerger Act (1950) Major antitrust law. An extension of Section 7 of the Clayton Antitrust Act, it prohibits a corporation from acquiring the stock or *assets* of another corporation if the effect would be a substantial lessening of competition or a tendency toward monopoly. *Note:* Prior to this law, only the acquisition of *stock* by competing corporations was illegal under the Clayton Antitrust Act.

certificate of deposit (CD) *See negotiable certificate of deposit.*

Chamberlin, Edward Hastings (1899–1967) American economist who was one of the pioneers in developing the theory of monopolistic competition. His doctoral dissertation, *The Theory of Monopolistic Competition* (Harvard, 1933), became a standard work in the field. In this and in subsequent editions and articles, Chamberlin emphasized the role of product differentiation, advertising, and differences in consumer preferences as factors contributing to the existence of "partial" or "competing monopolists." Chamberlin thus identified a new form of market structure, monopolistic competition, the theory of which has become an essential part of microeconomics.

change in amount consumed Increase or decrease in the amount of consumption expenditure due to a change in income. It may be represented by a movement along a consumption-function curve.

change in consumption Increase or decrease in consumption, represented by a shift of the consumption-function curve to a new position. The shift results from a change in any of the factors that were assumed to remain constant when the curve was drawn. These may include (1) expectations of future prices and incomes, (2) the volume of liquid assets owned by households, (3) credit conditions, and (4) anticipations of product shortages.

change in demand Increase or decrease in demand, represented by a shift of the demand curve to a new position. The shift results from a change in any of the factors that were assumed to remain constant when the curve was drawn. These may include (1) buyers' money incomes, (2) the prices of related goods, (3) buyers' tastes or preferences, (4) the number of buyers in the market, and (5) buyers' expectations about future prices and incomes.

change in quantity demanded Increase or decrease in the quantity demanded of a good due to a change in its price. It may be represented by a movement along a demand curve.

change in quantity supplied Increase or decrease in the quantity supplied of a good due to change in its price. It may be represented by a movement along a supply curve.

change in supply Increase or decrease in supply shown by a shift of the supply curve to a new position. The shift results from a change in any of the factors that were assumed to remain constant when the curve was drawn. These may include (1) the state of technology, (2) resource prices or the costs of the factors of production, (3) the prices of other goods, (4) the number of sellers in the market, and (5) sellers' expectations regarding future prices.

checkable deposits Depository-institution accounts that are subject to withdrawals by check. *Examples: demand deposits, negotiable orders of withdrawal* (NOW accounts), and credit-union *share-draft* accounts. Checkable deposits are also called *transaction deposits.*

checkoff Procedure by which an employer, with the written permission of the worker, withholds union dues and other assessments from paychecks and then transfers the funds to the union. This provides an efficient means by which the union can collect dues from its members.

Christian socialism Movement, since the late nineteenth century, by various church groups to preach the "social gospel"—a type of social legislation and reform that seeks to improve the well-being of the working classes by appealing to Christian ethical and humanitarian principles.

circular flow of economic activity Model demonstrating the movement of goods, resources, payments, and expenditures among sectors of the economy. A simple model may include the household and business sectors and the product and resource markets—but other models may be constructed that are more complex.

Clark, John Bates (1847–1938) Leading American economist whose major treatise, *The Distribution of Wealth* (1899), was the first American work in pure economic theory. The book developed what is essentially the modern version of the marginal-productivity theory. This theory demonstrates that a (perfectly competitive) capitalistic society distributes incomes to resource owners in proportion to the market values of their contribution to production. The theory was thus used by others to justify capitalism as a fair (equitable) system. Clark, it should be noted, had much in common with his British contemporary, Alfred Marshall. Both used similar methodologies in analyzing economic problems. Clark, however, tended to be more theoretical and abstract.

classical economics Body of economic thought emphasizing human self-interest and the operation of universal economic laws. These tend automatically to guide the economy toward full-employment, or natural-employment equilibrium, if the government adheres to a policy of laissez-faire or noninterventionism. Among the early chief proponents of classical economics were Adam Smith (1723–1790), Jean Baptiste Say (1767–1832), Jeremy Bentham (1748–1832), Thomas Robert Malthus (1766–1834), David Ricardo (1772–1823), Nassau William Senior (1790–1864), and John Stuart Mill (1806–1873).

class struggle In the theories of Karl Marx, an irreconcilable clash between the bourgeoisie (or capitalist class) and the proletariat (or working class) arising out of the surplus value that capitalists appropriate from workers. The class struggle will eventually be resolved when the proletariat overthrows the bourgeoisie and establishes a new and equitable economic order.

Clayton Antitrust Act (1914) A major antitrust law aimed at preventing unfair, deceptive, dishonest, or injurious methods of competition. It made the following practices and arrangements illegal, where their effect is a substantial lessening of competition or a tendency toward monopoly: (1) price discrimination, except where there are differences in grade, quality, or quantity sold, or where the lower prices make due allowances for cost differences in selling or transportation, or where the lower prices are offered in good faith to meet competition; (2) tying contracts between sellers and purchasers; and (3) intercorporate stockholdings among competing corporations. It also makes illegal, regardless of the effect on competition, (4) interlocking directorates, if the corporations involved are competitive and if any one of them has capital, surplus, and undivided profits in excess of $1 million.

closed shop A firm that agrees that an employee must be a union member before being employed and must remain a union member after becoming employed. It is illegal under the Labor-Management Relations (Taft-Hartley) Act of 1947.

coalition bargaining Method of bargaining by which a federation of unions (such as the AFL-CIO) tries to coordinate and establish common termination dates for contracts with firms that deal with a number of unions at their plants throughout the economy. Its purpose is to enable the federation to strengthen union bargaining positions by threatening to close down all plants simultaneously.

Coase theorem Proposition that demonstrates that, if (1) property rights are clearly defined and (2) the number of affected parties is small, individuals seeking to maximize their well-being will negotiate the internalization of their own externalities. The resulting allocation of resources will be efficient and will have been arrived at by private agreement—without a solution imposed by an outside authority (that is, government). Basically, the parties involved will find that, if transactions costs (the costs including time and effort of negotiating contracts) are low because few people are involved, mutual gains will be realized from voluntary agreements. Thus, for example, a farmer whose crops are damaged by the wandering cattle of a neighboring rancher can pay the rancher to reduce his output of cattle. When all costs and benefits are taken into account, an efficient output of crops as well as of cattle is attained without an externally (governmentally) imposed decision.

cobweb theorem Generic name for a theory of cyclical fluctuations in the prices and quantities of various agricultural commodities—fluctuations that arise because, for certain agricultural products, (1) the quantity demanded of the commodity at any given time depends on its price at that time, whereas (2) the quantity supplied at any given time depends on its price at a previous time when production plans were initially formulated. Hogs and beef cattle have been notable examples.

coefficient of relative effectiveness (CRE) Term used in the former Soviet Union to mean the expected payoff or percentage rate of return on a capital investment; akin to the concept of marginal efficiency of investment in Western economics.

coincident indicators Time series that tend to move approximately "in phase" with the aggregate economy and hence are measures of current economic activity.

collective agreement A collective-bargaining contract worked out between union and management, describing wages, working conditions, and related matters.

collective bargaining Negotiation between a company's management and a union for the purpose of agreeing on mutually acceptable wages and working conditions for employees.

collective farms Agricultural cooperatives consisting of communities of farmers who pool their resources, lease land from the government, and divide the profits among the members according to the amount and kind of work done by each.

collective good See *public good.*

command economy Economic system in which an authoritarian government exercises primary control over decisions concerning what to produce and how much to produce. It may also, but does not necessarily, decide for whom to produce.

commercial bank   Type of financial depository institution, chartered by federal or state governments. It is primarily engaged in buying and selling money-market instruments and in making business loans by creating demand or checking deposits. It may also engage in certain other financial activities, such as holding time or savings deposits, making long-term mortgage loans, and managing investments.

commercial paper   Unsecured promissory notes, usually in minimum denominations of $10,000, sold by several hundred major corporations. The most familiar example is GMAC paper, sold by General Motors Acceptance Corporation, to finance the purchase of General Motors cars.

common market   Association of trading nations that agrees: (1) to impose no trade restrictions, such as tariffs or quotas, on participants; (2) to establish common external barriers (such as a common external tariff) to nonparticipants; and (3) to impose no national restrictions on the movement of labor and capital among participants. *Example:* European Community (EC).

common-property good   Good not subject to private ownership. *Example:* Fish in the ocean represent a renewable resource not owned by any individual.

common stock   Shares that have no fixed rate of dividends and hence may receive higher dividends than the fixed rate on preferred stock, if the corporation's earnings are sufficiently high.

Commonwealth (Mass.) v. Hunt (1842)   The first case in which a (Massachusetts) court held a trade union to be a lawful organization. It declared that workers could form a union to bargain collectively with employers.

communism   **1.** In the theories of Karl Marx, the final and perfect goal of historical development. It is characterized by: (a) a classless society in which all people live by earning and no person lives by owning; (b) the disappearance of the state; and (c) the abolition of the wage system so that all citizens live and work according to the motto: *"From each according to his ability, to each according to his needs."* **2.** An economic system based on (a) social ownership of property, including most of the means of production and distribution. (b) government planning and control of the economy.

company union   A labor union limited to a particular firm. It is usually unaffiliated with any other union.

comparable worth   Argument that asserts that women should be paid as much as men are paid for performing tasks in other occupations requiring comparable (not identical) skills, training, responsibilities, hazards, and effort. The purpose is to reduce sex discrimination in employment by eliminating the pay gap between female-dominated occupations (e.g., elementary-school teaching, nursing, secretarial work) and most other jobs.

comparative advantage, law of   Principle that states that a basis for trade exists when each of two nations, both capable of producing the same two goods, specializes in the one that is relatively cheaper to produce. Each nation can have more of both goods if it produces one and trades for the other. This principle is applicable to individuals and regions as well as to nations.

comparative statics   Method of analysis in which the effects of a change in one or more of the determining conditions in a static model are evaluated by comparing the results after the change with those before the change. *Example:* Comparing the effects on equilibrium prices and quantities (in a demand and supply model) resulting from a shift in demand or supply curves. It is like comparing two "snapshots" of a phenomenon—one taken before the change and one after.

compensatory (accommodating) transactions   Settlements among nations that are a direct response to balance-of-payments considerations. They may be thought of as balancing items that arise to accommodate differences in money inflows and outflows resulting from so-called autonomous transactions. The two main classes are short-term capital movements and shifts in gold holdings.

competition   Rivalry among buyers and sellers of goods or resources. Competition tends to be directly related to the degree of diffusion (as opposed to the concentration) of market power and the freedom with which buyers and sellers can enter or leave particular markets. It is sometimes used to mean perfect (pure) competition, depending on whether it is employed in that context.

complementary goods   Commodities that are related such that at a given level of buyers' incomes, an increase in the price of one good leads to a decrease in the demand for the other, and a decrease in the price of one good leads to an increase in the demand for the other. *Examples:* ham and eggs; hamburgers and buns. *(Compare substitute goods.)*

compounding   Process by which a given amount, expressed in dollars, is adjusted at interest to yield a future value. That is, interest when due is added to a principal amount and thereafter earns interest. *Example:* At 6 percent, a principal of $1, plus interest, amounts to a sum of $1.06 after one year, and to an additional 6 percent, for a sum of $1.124, after two years, and so on. Compounding is thus the opposite of *discounting*.

compound interest   Interest computed on a principal sum and also on all the interest earned by that principal sum as of a given date.

Comptroller of the Currency   Federal agency that charters all national banks. It also oversees the operations of national banks and of those state banks that are members of the Federal Reserve System.

concentration ratio   Percentage of an industry's output accounted for by its largest firms—typically, by its four largest. The percentage (or ratio) is usually based either on sales, value added, or value of shipments. Sometimes, however, other measures of size, such as assets or employment, are used.

conglomerate merger   Amalgamation under one ownership of unlike plants producing unrelated products. It reflects a desire by the acquiring company to spread risks, to find outlets for idle capital funds, to add products that can be sold with the firm's merchandising knowledge and skills, or simply to gain economic power on a broader front.

conscious parallel action   A common course of behavior among competing firms. It can consist of identical price behavior (such as price leadership and followership), the sharing of markets, or the calculation of delivered prices according to a common formula. Conscious parallel action may or may not be the result of collusion or prior agreement. Therefore, it may or may not be held illegal by the courts, depending on the circumstances in each case.

consent decree   A means of settling cases in equity among the parties involved (such as a defendant firm and the Department of Justice). The defendant does not admit guilt, but agrees nevertheless to cease and desist from certain practices and to abide by the rules of behavior set down in the decree. This is the chief instrument employed by the Justice Department and by the Federal Trade Commission in the enforcement of the Sherman and Clayton Acts. The majority of antitrust violations are settled in this manner.

conspicuous consumption   Expression originated by Thorstein Veblen (1857–1929) to mean that those above the subsistence level (that is, the so-called "leisure class") are mainly concerned with impressing others through their standard of living, taste, and dress—in Veblen's words, through "pecuniary emulation." ("Keeping up with the Joneses" is a popular expression of this concept.)

constant-cost industry   Industry that experiences no increases in resource prices or costs of production as new firms enter the industry. This will happen only when the industry's demand for the resources it employs is an insignificant proportion of the total demand for those resources.

constant dollars   Expression reflecting the actual prices of a previous year or the average of actual prices of a previous period of years. Hence economic data are often quoted in constant dollars. These are also called *real dollars. (Compare current dollars.)*

Consumer Price Index (CPI)   Average of prices of goods and services commonly purchased by families in urban areas. Generally referred to as a "cost-of-living index," the CPI is published by the Bureau of Labor Statistics of the U.S. Department of Labor.

consumer sovereignty   Concept of the consumer as "king"— in the sense that the consumer registers his or her preferences for goods by "dollar votes" in the marketplace. In a highly competitive economy, competition among producers will cause them to adjust their production to the changing patterns of consumer demands. In less competitive circumstances, where monopolistic forces and other imperfections exist, resources will not be allocated in accordance with consumer wishes.

consumer's surplus   Difference between what a consumer pays and the maximum amount, called the *demand price*, he or she would be willing to pay for a given quantity of a good. *(Contrast with producer's surplus.)*

consumption   Expenditures on consumer goods and services.

consumption function   Relationship between consumption expenditures and income, expressed as a graph or equation. The relationship is such that, as income increases, consumption increases, but not as fast as income. The expression *propensity to consume* is often used synonymously. (*Note:* The word "function" is employed here in its mathematical sense to mean a variable whose value depends on the value of another variable. Therefore, the expression "consumption function" can also be used to designate *any* type of relationship between consumption and income— not necessarily the type defined above. However, the above type is the most common one.)

contestable market   One that is characterized by ease of entry or exit—the ability to enter or leave the market at little cost. Companies already in such a market are under pressure to maintain a low-price policy. This discourages outsiders from entering, capturing some of the industry's profits, and getting out quickly. Airlines and trucking provide good examples of contestable markets because the principal assets—planes and trucks—though expensive, are both mobile and readily resalable.

contribution margin   That portion of a firm's price, above its direct or average variable cost, that contributes to fixed costs (overhead) and the earning of profit. It may be expressed either as an amount or as a percentage markup on average variable cost.

contributive standard   Criterion of income distribution popularly expressed by the phrase, "To each according to his or her contribution." It means that, if the market value of one person's production is twice that of another's, then the first person should be paid twice as much as the second. This is the predominant criterion of income distribution in market-oriented economies. You will consider the contributive standard a just or equitable one only if you believe that each person is entitled to the fruits of his or her labor. *(Compare equality standard; needs standard.)*

corporation   Association of stockholders created under law but regarded by the courts as an artificial person existing only in the contemplation of the law. The chief characteristics of a corporation are (1) limited liability of its stockholders; (2) stability and permanence; and (3) ability to accumulate large sums of capital through the sale of stocks and bonds.

correspondence principle   Proposition that demonstrates that, in order for comparative statics (the comparison of equilibrium positions in static states) to be meaningful, it is first necessary to develop a dynamic analysis of stability.

cost   Sacrifice that must be made to do or to acquire something. What is sacrificed may be money, goods, leisure time, security, prestige, power, or pleasure.

cost-benefit analysis   See *benefit-cost analysis*.

cost-effectiveness analysis   Technique of selecting from alternative programs the one that attains a given objective at the lowest cost. It is a type of analysis most useful when benefits cannot be measured in money.

cost-plus pricing   Method of pricing whereby the seller's price (P), at a given level of output, is determined by adding a percentage markup to the direct cost (or average variable cost, AVC) of the product. Thus:

$$P = AVC - \% \text{ markup } (AVC)$$

Thus, if a firm's AVC at a given level of output is $100 per unit, a 50 percent markup would result in a price of $150 per unit:

$$P = \$100 + 0.50 \, (\$100) = \$150 \text{ per unit}$$

cost-push inflation   Condition of generally rising prices caused by factor payments to one or more groups of resource owners increasing faster than productivity or efficiency. It is usually attributed to monopolistic market power possessed by some resource owners, unions, or business firms. "Wage-push" and "profit-push" are the most common forms of cost-push inflation.

countervailing power   Proposition that the growth of market power by one group may tend to stimulate the growth of a counterreaction and somewhat offsetting influence by another group. *Examples:* Big labor unions face big corporations at the bargaining table; chain stores deal with large processing and manufacturing firms; and big government faces big business and big unions.

craft union   Labor union composed of workers in a particular trade, such as bakers, carpenters, or teamsters. It is thus a "horizontally" organized union.

crawling peg   System of foreign-exchange rates that permits the par values of a nation's currency to change automatically by small increments, downward or upward, if in actual daily trading on the foreign exchange markets the price in terms of other currencies persists on the "floor" or "ceiling" of the governmentally established range for a specified period.

credit   1. A promise by one party to pay another for money borrowed or for goods and services received. Credit may therefore be regarded as an extension of money. 2. In international economics, any transaction that results in a money inflow or receipt from a foreign country. It may be represented on a balance-of-payments statement by a plus sign.

credit instrument   See *debt instrument*.

creeping inflation   Slow but persistent upward movement in the general level of prices over a long period of years, typically at an average annual rate of up to 3 percent.

Cross elasticity of demand   Percentage change in the quantity purchased of a good resulting from a 1 percent change in the price of another good. Thus:

Cross elasticity of demand

$$= \frac{\text{Percentage change in the quantity purchased of } X}{\text{percentage change in the price of } Y}$$

$$= \frac{(Q_{X2} - Q_{X1})/(Q_{X2} + Q_{X1})}{(P_{Y2} - P_{Y1})/(P_{Y2} + P_{Y1})}$$

in which Q_{X1} and Q_{X2} represent quantities purchased of X before and after the change in the price of Y, and P_{Y1} and P_{Y2} represent the corresponding prices of Y before and after the change. The cross elasticity of demand thus measures the responsiveness of changes in the quantities purchased of a good to changes in the price of another good. In general, the higher the coefficient of elasticity, the greater the degree of substitutability. (For example, competing brands of goods in the same industry, such as competing brands of television sets, have high positive cross elasticities.) A coefficient of zero indicates goods that are nonsubstitutes or are unrelated. (Examples are lettuce and beer, hats and books.) A negative coefficient indicates goods that are complementary. (Examples are watches and watchbands, cameras and film, shirts and ties).

crowding out   Proposition that states that large increases in government spending, whether financed by taxing, borrowing, or printing new money, are likely to reduce business investment spending. There are two reasons: (1) Resources that might otherwise be used by the private sector are diverted to public use. (2) Interest rates tend to be pushed up when government spending is financed by borrowing or by printing money. This increases the costs of business borrowing and forces many firms out of the financial markets. For both reasons, therefore, private incentives to work, save, and invest may be diminished, thus reducing productive capital investment.

currency   Paper money and coins.

current assets   Cash and other assets that can be turned quickly into cash.

current dollars   An expression reflecting actual prices of each year. Hence economic data are often quoted in current dollars. These are also called **nominal dollars**. (*Compare* **constant dollars**.)

current liabilities   Debts that fall due within a year.

current yield   Annual return on an investment expressed as a percentage of its present price.

customs union   Agreement among trading nations to abolish trade barriers, such as tariffs and quotas, among themselves and to adopt a common external policy of trade (such as a common external tariff with all nonmember nations). *Example:* Benelux (Belgium, the Netherlands, and Luxembourg).

cyclically balanced budget Philosophy that holds that total revenues and expenditures in the government's budget should be balanced or brought into equality over the course of a business cycle.

cyclical unemployment Unemployment that results from business recessions or depressions because aggregate demand falls too far below the full-employment level of aggregate output and income.

D

deadweight loss The loss in efficiency, measured by the value of output sacrificed, that society incurs as a result of firms practicing monopoly ($MC = MR$) rather than marginal-cost ($MC = P$) pricing.

death taxes Taxes imposed on the transfer of property after death. They consist of estate and inheritance taxes and are imposed by federal and state governments at progressive rates.

debit In international economics, any transaction that results in a money outflow or payment to a foreign country. It may be represented on a balance-of-payments statement by a minus sign.

debt instrument (credit instrument) A written promise by one party to pay another a stated amount of money on specified dates. Examples of debt instruments are promissory notes, bonds, and other IOUs. A debt instrument is also called a credit instrument because it's a liability of the party that issues it and an asset of the party that owns it.

debt neutrality proposition Theory that deficits do not cause changes in aggregate demand. Therefore, they do not affect real interest rates, GDP, employment, investment, or inflation, nor do they crowd out borrowers. Changes in the national debt have no influence on economic variables because the changes are automatically and exactly offset by corresponding changes in savings. Thus *debt is neutral.* (This proposition is also called the *Ricardian equivalence theorem,* after David Ricardo, the early nineteenth-century English classical economist who formulated the concept.)

decreasing-cost industry Industry that experiences decreases in resource prices or in its costs of production as it expands because of new firms entering the industry. This situation might arise for a while as a result of substantial external economies of scale.

deduction In logical thinking, a process of reasoning from premises to conclusions. The premises are more general than the conclusions, so deduction is often defined as reasoning from the general to the particular. (Opposite of *induction.*)

deflation **1.** Statistical adjustment of data by which an economic time series expressed in current dollars is converted into a series expressed in constant dollars of a previous period. The purpose of the adjustment is to compensate for the distorting effects of inflation (that is, the long-run upward trend of prices) through a reverse process of "deflation." **2.** Decline in the general price level of all goods and services—or, equivalently, a rise in the purchasing power of a unit of money. (*Compare* **inflation.**)

delivered pricing Method of pricing whereby the seller charges the buyer a destination price consisting of both a factory price (called a "mill price") and a shipping charge. However, in order to match the price of a competitor, the factory price may be some other company's mill price rather than the seller's, and the shipping charge may in fact be greater or less than the actual transportation costs that are incurred. When that happens, prices quoted on a delivered basis are discriminatory. They do not reflect the seller's marginal cost of producing and selling the product. (*Compare* **f.o.b. pricing** *and* **basing-point pricing.**)

demand Relation expressing the amounts of a commodity that buyers would be willing and able to purchase at various prices during a given period of time, all other things remaining the same. This relation may be expressed in a table (called a demand schedule), in a graph (called a demand curve), or in a mathematical equation.

demand curve Graph of a demand schedule, showing the number of units of a commodity that buyers would be able and willing to purchase at various prices during a given period of time, all other things remaining the same.

demand deposit Promise by a bank to pay immediately an amount of money specified by the customer who owns the deposit. It is thus "checkbook money" because it permits transactions to be paid for by check rather than with currency. However, unlike other types of checkable deposits, a demand deposit does not pay interest to its owner.

demand, law of Principle that states that the quantity demanded of a good varies inversely with its price, assuming that all other things that may affect demand remain the same. These "all other" things include (1) buyers' money incomes; (2) the prices of related goods in consumption; and (3) tastes and other nonmonetary determinants. Among them: consumer preferences, number of buyers in the market, and characteristics of buyers.

demand price Highest price a buyer is willing to pay for a given quantity of a commodity.

demand-pull inflation Condition of generally rising prices caused by increases in aggregate demand at a time when available supplies of goods are becoming more limited. Goods may go into short supply because resources are fully utilized or because production cannot be increased rapidly enough to meet growing demand.

demand schedule Table showing the number of units of a commodity that buyers would be able and willing to purchase at various possible prices during a given period of time, all other things remaining the same.

demand-side economics Measures aimed at achieving efficiency through policies designed to regulate purchasing power. Keynesian economics, because it tends to focus on fiscal and monetary policies to control aggregate demand, has been characterized as demand-side economics. *(Contrast with **supply-side economics**.)*

deposit multiplier Proposition that states that an increase in the banking system's checkable deposits, D, will be some multiple, m, of the system's excess reserves, E. Thus,

$$D = mE$$

In the formula, m is the reciprocal of the required-reserve ratio, r. Thus: $m = 1/r$. The above deposit-multiplier formula can, therefore, be written

$$D = 1/r \times E$$

Example: If $r = 10$ percent and $E = \$1,000$, then $D = 1/0.10 \times \$1,000 = \$10,000$. Thus, excess reserves of $\$1,000$ can result in as much as a $\$10,000$ increase in checkable deposits. The formula assumes, however, that the banking system is fully loaned up to begin with—that is, before there is any increase in excess reserves. In reality, there are so-called "leakages" that prevent the deposit-multiplier from exerting its full impact. They include (1) the percentage of checkable deposits that the public withdraws as cash; (2) the percentage of checkable deposits that banks, for one reason or another, hold as excess (idle) reserves; and (3) the percentage of checkable deposits that the public transfers into reservable time deposits.

Depository Institutions Acts (1980, 1982) Legislation consisting of the Depository Institutions Deregulation and Monetary Control Act (1980) and the Depository Institutions Act (1982). Taken together, both laws provided for the following: (1) *Uniform reserve standards:* All depository institutions must meet the same reserve requirements on similar types and sizes of deposits. (2) *Transaction accounts:* All depository institutions may hold interest-bearing checkable deposits. These, along with demand deposits at commercial banks, constitute transaction accounts. (3) *Federal Reserve accessibility:* All depository institutions that issue transaction accounts can borrow on equal terms from their Federal Reserve Bank. Depository institutions can also purchase the Fed's services, such as check clearing and electronic transfer of funds, if desired. (4) *Thrift-institution banking powers:* Savings-and-loan associations and savings banks have limited authority to offer demand deposits and to make commercial loans. (5) *Money-market deposit accounts:* Depository institutions can offer higher-yielding deposit accounts with limited checking privileges at money-market interest rates.

depreciation Decline in the value of a fixed asset, such as plant or equipment, due to wear and tear, destruction, or obsolescence resulting from the development of new and better techniques.

depression Lower phase of a business cycle in which the economy is operating with substantial unemployment of its resources and a sluggish rate of capital investment and consumption resulting from little business and consumer optimism.

derivative market One in which claims against financial instruments, such as stocks, bonds, or other assets, are traded. The claims traded are called **derivative securities**.

derivative securities Claims against financial instruments such as stocks, bonds, or other assets. Examples of derivative securities are puts, calls, and other options. They are called "derivatives" because their market value is *derived* from the price behavior of specific underlying financial instuments or other assets.

derived demand Demand for a product or resource based on its contribution to the product for which it is used. *Examples:* The separate demands for bricks, lumber, and so on, are derived partly from the demand for construction; the demand for steel is derived partly from the demand for automobiles.

devaluation Official (government) act that makes a domestic currency cheaper in terms of foreign currencies (or in terms of gold under a gold standard). It is typically designed to reduce a nation's balance-of-payments deficits by increasing exports while reducing imports. *(Contrast with **revaluation**.)*

dialectical materialism Logical method of historical analysis. In particular, it was used by Karl Marx, who employed the philosopher Hegel's idea that historical change is the result of inherently conflicting or opposing forces in society and that the forces are basically economic or materialistic.

"dictatorship of the proletariat" Expression used by Karl Marx to describe a state of Marxian socialism in which the bourgeoisie (or capitalist class) has been toppled from power and, along with its properties, is under the management of the proletariat (or working class), which is also in control of the state.

diminishing marginal utility, law of In a given period of time during which tastes remain constant the consumption of a product *may at first* result in increasing marginal (that is, incremental) satisfactions or utilities per unit of the product consumed. However, a point will eventually be reached beyond which further units of consumption of the product will result in decreasing marginal utilities per additional unit of the product consumed. This is the point of diminishing marginal utility. *Note:* Even though marginal utility may rise at first, *it must eventually fall*. It is the diminishing phase of marginal utility that is relevant and serves as the basis for the law.

diminishing returns (variable proportions), law of In a given state of technology, the addition of a changing or variable factor of production to other fixed factors of production may at first yield increasing marginal (that is, incremental) returns per unit of the variable factor added, but a point will be reached beyond which further additions of the variable factor will yield diminishing marginal returns per unit of the variable factor added. This is the point of diminishing marginal returns. *Note:* Even though marginal returns may rise at first, they must eventually fall. It is the diminishing phase of marginal returns that is relevant and serves as the basis for the law.

direct payments Method of subsidizing sellers while permitting the price of a commodity to be determined in a free market by demand and supply. If the price turns out to be "too low," sellers are compensated by a subsidy from the government for the difference between the market price received and some higher, predetermined target price. If the market price turns out to be equal to or greater than the target price, no subsidized compensation is provided. Under this system, therefore, consumers pay and sellers receive the market price of the commodity, but sellers *may in addition* receive a subsidy. (*Note:* A plan of this type has long existed for certain farm commodities.)

direct tax Tax that is not shifted—that is, its burden is borne by the persons or firms originally taxed. *Examples:* personal income taxes, social security taxes paid by employees, and death taxes.

discounting Process by which a given amount, expressed in dollars, is adjusted at interest to yield a present value. *Example:* At 6 percent, $1.06 one year hence has a present value of $1; $1.124 two years hence has a present value one year hence of $1.06, and a present value today of $1. Discounting is thus the opposite of compounding.

discount rate Interest rate charged to depository institutions on their loans from the Federal Reserve Banks. It is called a "discount rate" because the interest on a loan is discounted when the loan is made, rather than collected when the loan is repaid.

discouraged-worker hypothesis Theory that holds that a rising level of unemployment leads to declining labor-force participation rates. This is because the chances of finding a job diminish during recession. Therefore, many workers stop trying and leave the labor force. (*Contrast with additional-worker hypothesis.*)

disequilibrium State of imbalance or nonequilibrium. *Example:* a situation in which the quantities demanded and supplied of a commodity at a given price are unequal, so there is a tendency for market prices and/or quantities to change. Any economic entity or system, such as a household, a firm, a market, or an economy, that is not in equilibrium is said to be in disequilibrium.

disguised unemployment (underemployment) Condition in which employed resources are not being used in their most efficient ways.

disinvestment Reduction in the total stock of capital goods caused by failure to replace it as it wears out. *Example:* the consumption or using up of factories, machines, and so forth at a faster rate than they are being replaced so that the productive base is diminishing.

disposable personal income Income remaining after payment

of personal taxes; what people have available for spending.

dissaving Expenditure on consumption in excess of income. This may be accomplished by drawing on past savings, borrowing, or receiving help from others.

dividend Earnings that a corporation pays to its stockholders. Payments are usually in cash, but they may also be in property, securities, or other forms.

division of labor Specialization in productive activities among workers, resulting in increased production because it (1) permits development and refinement of skills; (2) avoids the time that is wasted in going from one job to another; and (3) simplifies human tasks, thus permitting the introduction of labor-saving machines.

double coincidence of wants A necessary condition for a barter exchange: each party must have what the other wants and must be willing to trade at the exact quantities and terms suitable to both.

double taxation Taxation of the same base in two different forms. A typical example is the corporate income tax: the corporation pays an income tax on its profits, and the stockholder pays an income tax on the dividends received from those profits.

draft Unconditional written order by one party (the creditor or drawer) on a second party (the debtor or drawee) directing the second party to pay a third party (the bearer or payee) a specified sum of money. An ordinary check, therefore, is an example of a draft.

dual banking system Expression referring to the fact that all commercial banks in the United States are chartered either as national banks or as state banks. This organizational structure, not found in any other country, is a unique outgrowth of American political history.

dual labor market Hypothesis that states that the labor market is segmented into two distinct markets. One is a primary labor market, in which jobs are characterized by relatively high wages, favorable working conditions, and employment stability. The other is a secondary labor market, in which jobs, when they are available, pay relatively low wages, provide poor working conditions, and are highly unstable. White-collar and blue-collar workers, many of whom are union members, account for most of the participants in the primary market. In contrast, the competitively "disadvantaged poor"—the unskilled, the undereducated, and the victims of racial prejudice—are confined to the secondary market.

dumping Sale of the same product in different markets at different prices. *Example:* A monopolist might restrict his output in the domestic market and charge a higher price because demand is relatively inelastic, and "dump" the rest of his output in a foreign market at a lower price because demand there is relatively elastic. He thereby gains the benefit of lower average total costs on his entire output (domestic plus foreign) and earns a larger net profit than if he sold the entire output in the domestic market—which he could do only by charging a lower price per unit on all units sold.

duopoly   Oligopoly consisting of two sellers. Hence it may be either a perfect duopoly or an imperfect one, depending on whether the product is standardized or differentiated.

dynamic model   One in which economic phenomena are studied by relating them to preceding or succeeding events. The influence of time is therefore taken explicitly into account. A dynamic model is thus like a "motion picture" as distinguished from a "snapshot." (*Compare* **static model**.)

E

econometrics   Integration of economic theory, mathematics, and statistics. It consists of expressing economic relationships in the form of mathematical equations and verifying the resulting models by statistical methods.

economic costs   Payments made to the owners of the factors of production to persuade them to supply their resources in a particular activity.

economic development   Process whereby a nation's real per-capita output or income (its GDP) increases over a long period of time. A nation's rate of economic development is thus measured by its long-run per-capita rate of economic growth.

economic efficiency   *See* **efficiency**

economic good   Scarce commodity—that is, any commodity for which the market price is greater than zero at a particular time and place. (*Compare* **free good**.)

economic growth   Rate of increase in an economy's full-employment real output or income over time—that is, the rise in its full-employment output in constant prices. Economic growth may be expressed in either of two ways: (1) as the increase in total full-employment real GDP over time, or (2) as the increase in per-capita full-employment real GDP over time. The "total" measure is employed to describe the expansion of a nation's economic output or potential. The "per-capita" measure is often used to express a nation's material standard of living.

economic indicators   Time series of economic data, classified as leading, lagging, or coincident indicators. They are used in business-cycle analysis and forecasting.

economic interpretation of history   Proposition advanced by Karl Marx (and others) that the great political, social, intellectual, and ethical movements of history are determined by the ways in which societies organize their social institutions to carry on the basic economic activities of production, exchange, distribution, and consumption of goods. Thus, economic forces are the prime cause of fundamental historical change.

economic man   The notion that each individual in a capitalistic society, whether he or she be a worker, businessperson, consumer, or investor, is motivated by economic forces and hence will always act to obtain the greatest satisfaction for the least sacrifice or cost. Satisfaction may take the form of profits to a businessperson, wages or leisure hours to a worker, pleasure to a consumer from the goods that he or she purchases, and so on.

economic plan   Detailed method, formulated beforehand, for achieving specific economic objectives by governing the activities and interrelationships of those economic entities, namely firms, households, and governments, that have an influence on the desired outcome.

economic (pure) profit   Payment to a firm in excess of its economic costs, including normal profit. It is the same as net revenue.

economic rent   Payment made to an owner of a factor of production, in an industry in equilibrium, in excess of the factor's supply price or opportunity cost. The payment is thus above the minimum amount necessary to keep the factor in its present occupation. Economic rent is therefore a surplus to the recipient.

economics   Social science concerned chiefly with the way society chooses to employ its limited resources, which have alternative uses, to produce goods and services for present and future consumption.

economic system   The laws, institutions, customs, and practices that determine the ways in which a society allocates its scarce resources. Capitalism, socialism, and communism provide examples of different types of economic systems.

economic union   A fully-integrated association of trading nations that meets the three conditions of a common market and also agrees to adopt a single monetary system and central bank, create a unified fiscal system, and adhere to a mutually established foreign economic policy.

economies (diseconomies) of scale   The decreases and increases in a firm's long-run average costs as the size of its plant is increased. The factors that give rise to economies of scale are (1) greater specialization of resources; (2) more efficient utilization of equipment; (3) reduced unit costs of inputs; (4) opportunities for economical utilization of byproducts; and (5) growth of auxiliary facilities. Diseconomies of scale may eventually set in, however, due to (1) limitations of (or "diminishing returns" to) management in its decision-making function and (2) competition among firms in bidding up prices of limited resources.

efficiency   The best use of what is available to attain a desired result. Two specific types of efficiency are "technical" and "economic." **1.** *Technical efficiency:* Condition that exists when a production system—a firm, an industry, an economy—is achieving maximum output by making the fullest utilization of available inputs. The system is then producing on its production-possibilities curve. This means that no change in the combination of resources can be made that will increase the output of one product without decreasing the output of another. **2.** *Economic (allocative) efficiency:* Condition that exists when a production system has achieved technical efficiency *and* is fulfilling consumer preferences by producing the combination of goods that people want—are willing and able to buy—with their present incomes. This means that no change in the combination of resources or of output can be implemented that will make someone better off without making someone else worse off—each in his or her own estimation. (*Note:* Economic efficiency is synonymous with *Pareto optimality.*)

elasticity Percentage change in quantity (demanded or supplied) resulting from a 1 percent change in price. Mathematically, it is the ratio of the percentage change in quantity (demanded or supplied) to the percentage change in price:

$$\text{Elasticity, } E = \frac{\text{percentage change in quantity}}{\text{percentage change in price}}$$
$$= \frac{(Q_2 - Q_1)/(Q_2 + Q_1)}{(P_2 - P_1)/(P_2 + P_1)}$$

in which Q_1 and Q_2, and P_1 and P_2, denote the corresponding quantities and prices before and after the change. This coefficient of elasticity (which is usually stated numerically without regard to algebraic sign) may range from zero to infinity. It may take any of five forms:

Perfectly elastic	$(E = \infty)$
Relatively elastic	$(E > 1)$
Unit elastic	$(E = 1)$
Relatively inelastic	$(E < 1)$
Perfectly inelastic	$(E = 0)$

The preceding definition refers to what is known as *price elasticity* of demand or supply. It is one of several types of elasticities that exist in economics and is the one that is commonly understood unless otherwise specified. In general, elasticity may be thought of as the responsiveness of changes in one variable to changes in another, where responsiveness is measured in terms of percentage changes.

Employment Act of 1946 Act of Congress that requires the government to maintain high levels of employment, production, and purchasing power. To assist the President in this task, the act authorizes him to appoint a panel of experts known as the Council of Economic Advisors.

employment ratio Percentage of the working-age population (defined as 16 years of age and older) that is employed:

$$\text{Employment ratio} = \frac{\text{number of employed people}}{\text{working-age population}}$$

employment-training policies Deliberate efforts undertaken in the private and public sectors to develop and use the capacities of human beings as actual or potential members of the labor force. Employment-training policies are also known as *human-resource policies.*

Engel's law Relationship between consumer expenditures and income derived by a nineteenth-century German statistician, Ernst Engel, and based on research into workingmen's purchases in Western Europe during the 1850s. The relationship states that, as a family's income increases: (1) the percentage it spends on food decreases; (2) the percentage it spends on housing and household operations remains about constant (except for the part spent on fuel, light, and refrigeration, which decreases); and (3) the percentage it spends on all other categories and the amount it saves increase (except for medical care and personal care items, which remain fairly constant). In general, the *total* amount spent increases as a family's income increases. *Note:* Strictly speaking, only the first condition above is attributed to Engel; the other two are modernized versions of his early findings, based on more recent research.

entrepreneurship Factor of production that is defined as the function performed by those who assemble the other factors of production, raise the necessary money, organize the management, make the basic business policy decisions, and reap the gains of success or the losses of failure. The entrepreneur is the innovator and the catalyst in a capitalistic system. He need not be exclusively an owner or a manager; the entrepreneurial function may be performed by either or both, depending on the size and complexity of the firm.

equal advantage, law of In a market economy, owners of resources will always transfer them from less desirable to more desirable uses. As this happens, the occupations *out* of which resources are transferred often tend to become more desirable, while the occupations *into* which resources are transferred tend to become less desirable. This transfer process continues until all occupations are equally desirable. At this point, there is no gain to be made by further transfer of resources. Hence the economy is in equilibrium. *Note:* The term "desirable" includes both monetary and nonmonetary considerations. The latter helps explain why permanent differences in monetary rewards may exist between various occupations.

equal employment opportunity Legislation prohibiting discrimination in employment on the basis of race, religion, sex, or national origin. (*See also* **affirmative action.**)

equality standard Criterion of income distribution popularly expressed by the phrase, "To each equally." You will regard the equality standard as a just or equitable one only if you assume that all people are alike in the *added* satisfaction or utility they get from an extra dollar of income. If this assumption is false—if an additional dollar of income actually provides a greater gain in utility to some people than to others—then justice is more properly served by distributing most of any increase in society's income to those who will enjoy it more. In reality, there is no conclusive evidence to suggest that people are either alike or unlike in their capacities to enjoy additional income. Therefore, no scientific basis exists for assuming that an equal distribution of income is more equitable than an unequal one. *(Compare **contributive standard; needs standard**.)*

equation of exchange   Expression of the relation between the quantity of money (M), its velocity of circulation (V), the average price (P) of final goods and services, and the physical quantity (Q) of those goods and services:

$$MV = PQ$$

The equation states that the total amount of money spent on goods and services *(MV)* is equal to the total amount of money received for goods and services *(PQ)*. *(See also **quantity theory of money**.)*

equilibrium   State of balance between opposing forces. An object in equilibrium is in a state of rest and has no tendency to change.

equilibrium conditions   Set of relationships that defines the equilibrium properties of an economic entity such as a household, a firm, or an entire economy.

equilibrium price   **1.** Price of a commodity determined in the market by the intersection of a demand curve and a supply curve. (Also called **normal price**.) **2.** Price (and corresponding equilibrium quantity) that maximizes a firm's profit.

equilibrium quantity   **1.** Quantity of a commodity determined in the market by the intersection of a demand curve and a supply curve. **2.** Quantity (and corresponding equilibrium price) that maximizes a firm's profit.

equity   Justice or fairness. In economics, equity refers to justice with respect to the distribution of income or of wealth within a society. Because justice is subjective rather than objective, equity may be thought of as both a philosophical concept and an economic goal. However, there is no scientific way of concluding that one standard or mechanism for distributing income is just and therefore "good" while another is unjust and therefore "bad." Each society or type of economic system establishes its own standards of distribution. Nevertheless, economics can help to evaluate the material consequences of any standard that a society adopts. *(See also **contributive standard; equality standard; needs standard**.)*

escalator clause   Provision in a contract whereby payments such as wages, insurance or pension benefits, or loan repayments over a stated period are tied to a comprehensive measure of living costs or price-level changes. The consumer price index and the implicit price index (GDP deflator) are the measures most commonly used for this purpose.

estate tax   Progressive (graduated) tax imposed by the federal government and by most state governments on the transfer of all property owned by a decedent at the time of death. Exemptions, deduction, and rates vary widely among the states.

Eurobanks   Financial institutions that hold Eurocurrency deposits and make Eurocurrency loans.

Eurocurrencies   Bank deposits denominated in currencies other than that of the country in which the bank is located.

Eurodollars   Dollar deposits in banks outside the United States, mostly in Europe. They are held by American and foreign banks, corporations, and individuals and represent dollar obligations that are constantly being shifted from one country to another in search of the highest return.

European Recovery Program (ERP)   Commonly known as the "Marshall Plan" (after Secretary of State George C. Marshall, who proposed it in 1947), this was a comprehensive recovery blueprint for European countries, financed by the United States, for the purposes of (1) increasing their productive capacity, (2) stabilizing their financial systems, (3) promoting their mutual economic cooperation, and (4) reducing their dependence on U.S. assistance. The ERP was terminated in 1951 after considerable success, and its functions were absorbed by other government agencies and programs.

excess reserves   Quantity of a bank's legal reserves over and above its required reserves. Thus:

Excess reserves = legal reserves − required reserves

Excess reserves are the key to a bank's lending power.

excise tax   Tax imposed on the manufacture, sale, or consumption of various commodities, such as liquor, tobacco, and gasoline.

exclusion principle   Basis for distinguishing between nonpublic and public goods. A good is nonpublic if anyone who does not pay for it can be excluded from its use; otherwise, it is a public good.

expenditure multiplier   Principle that states that changes in total spending can bring about magnified changes in real aggregate income. The expenditure multiplier (M_E) is thus the same as the investment multiplier, except that the independent variable is broadened to include total spending rather than investment spending only. *(See **multiplier**.)*

explicit costs   Money outlays of a firm recorded in its books of account. *(Compare **implicit costs**.)*

external economies and diseconomies of scale   Conditions that bring about decreases in a firm's long-run average costs as a result of factors that are entirely outside of the firm as a producing unit. They depend on adjustments of the industry and are related to the firm only to the extent that the firm is a part of the industry. *Example:* External economies may result from improvements in public transportation and marketing facilities as an industry develops in a particular geographic area, however, diseconomies may eventually set in as firms bid up the prices of limited resources in the area.

externalities   External benefits or costs for which no compensation is made. (Externalities are also called **spillovers**.)

F

Fabian socialism   Form of socialism founded in England in

1884. It emerged as an outgrowth of utopian socialism by advocating gradual and evolutionary reform within a democratic framework.

factors of production Human and nonhuman productive resources of an economy, usually classified into four groups: labor, entrepreneurship, land, and capital. (Used interchangeably with term "resources.")

Fair Labor Standards Act of 1938 An act, with subsequent amendments, that specifies minimum hourly wages, overtime rates, and prohibitions against child labor for workers producing goods in interstate commerce.

family-allowance plan Plan that provides every family, rich or poor, with a certain amount of money based exclusively on the number and age of its children. Families above certain designated income levels return all or a portion of the money with their income taxes, but those below specified income levels keep it. More than 60 countries have family allowance plans.

Fawcett, Millicent Garrett (1847–1919) English economic educator whose book, *Political Economy for Beginners* (1870), was largely a simplification and abridgement of classical economics as expressed by Mill in 1848. (*See Mill, John Stuart.*) Her book was highly successful, went through ten editions over a period of forty years, and established her as an outstanding popularizer of classical economic ideas.

featherbedding "Make-work" rules designed by unions to restrict output by artificially increasing the labor or labor-time on a particular job. Outlawed by the Labor-Management Relations (Taft-Hartley) Act of 1947.

Federal Advisory Council Committee within the Federal Reserve System that advises the Board of Governors on important current developments.

federal agency discount notes Short-term credit instruments sold (issued) by certain government agencies. Among these are the Federal Home Loan Bank, the Federal National Mortgage Association, and the Federal Farm Credit Bank System. The money raised by these agencies is used to provide mortgages and other types of loans.

Federal Deposit Insurance Corporation (FDIC) Government agency that insures deposits (demand and time) at commercial and savings banks. Each insured bank pays an annual premium equal to a fraction of its total deposits, in return for which the FDIC insures each account up to $100,000 against loss due to bank failure. In addition to its insurance function, the FDIC supervises insured banks and presides over the liquidation of banks that do fail. National banks (chartered by the federal government) are required to be insured by the FDIC, and state-chartered banks may apply if they wish. Two parallel agencies that perform similar functions are the Federal Savings and Loan Insurance Corporation, which insures deposits in savings and loan associations, and the National Credit Union Administration, which provides deposit insurance for federally chartered credit unions. Since the late 1930s, practically all banks have been covered by insurance, thereby eliminating bank runs and permitting greater bank stability.

federal funds Unsecured loans that banks and certain other depository institutions make to one another, usually overnight, out of their excess reserves. The purchase and sale of federal funds is limited to banks, savings institutions, and certain government agencies.

federal funds rate Interest rate at which banks borrow excess reserves from other banks' accounts at the Fed, usually overnight, to keep required reserves from falling below the legal level. In general, the lower the volume of excess reserves, the higher will be the federal funds rate. Therefore, the federal funds rate is an important indicator that the Fed watches to decide whether it should add to banks' reserves or take them away. For short periods of time, the Fed can largely control the federal funds rate. For example, the rate can be raised by selling Treasury bills to the banking system, thereby pulling out reserves. Conversely, the rate can be lowered by buying bills from the system, thereby putting in reserves. As part of its policymaking function, the Fed tries to maintain a federal funds rate that is consistent with other monetary goals.

Federal Open Market Committee The most important policymaking body of the Federal Reserve System. Its chief function is to establish policy for the System's purchase and sale of government and other securities in the open market.

Federal Reserve Bank One of the 12 banks (plus branches) that makes up the Federal Reserve System. Each serves as a "banker's bank" for the member banks in the district by acting as a source of credit and a depository of resources.

Federal Reserve System Central banking system created by Congress in 1913. It consists of (1) 12 Federal Reserve Banks—one located in each of 12 districts in the country; (2) a Board of Governors; (3) a Federal Open Market Committee and various other committees; and (4) several thousand member banks, which hold the great majority of all commercial bank deposits in the nation.

Federal Trade Commission Government agency created in 1914. It is charged with preventing unfair business practices by enforcing the Federal Trade Commission Act and by exercising concurrently with the Justice Department the enforcement of prohibitive provisions of the Clayton Antitrust Act as amended by the Robinson-Patman Act.

Federal Trade Commission Act (1914) A major antitrust law of the United States. Its chief purpose is to prevent unfair (that is, deceptive, dishonest, or injurious) methods of competition and, as amended by the Wheeler-Lea Act (1938), to safeguard the public by preventing the dissemination of false and misleading advertising of food, drugs, cosmetics, and therapeutic devices.

financial instruments Debt and equity paper claims sold by households, businesses, and governments against themselves to acquire funds for conducting operations. *Examples:* promissory notes, stocks, bonds, and mortgages.

financial intermediaries Business firms that serve as middlemen between lenders and borrowers by creating and issuing financial obligations or claims against themselves in order to acquire profitable financial claims against others. Examples of such firms are commercial banks, mutual savings banks, savings and loan associations, credit unions, insurance companies, and all other financial institutions. In general, they are wholesalers and retailers of funds.

financial markets   Markets in which debt, equity, and related instruments or claims are traded. Major financial markets are the *money market*, the *capital market*, the *foreign exchange market*, and the *derivative market*. Financial markets allocate funds between borrowers and lenders, short-term and long-term uses, and domestic and foreign uses.

firm   Business organization that brings together and coordinates the factors of production—capital, land, labor, and entrepreneurship—for the purpose of supplying goods or services.

First Bank of the United States   *See Bank of the United States.*

fiscal drag   Tendency of a high-employment economy to be held back from its full growth potential because it is incurring budgetary surpluses. Such surpluses may arise because, other things being equal, a progressive tax system tends to generate increases in revenues relative to expenditures during periods of high employment.

fiscal policy   Deliberate spending and taxing decisions by the government to achieve efficiency and growth. Efficiency is attained by stabilizing the economy at full employment, thus reducing the swings of business cycles. Growth is realized by providing tax incentives to work, save, and invest. Modern fiscal-policy theory places substantial emphasis on achieving growth.

Fisher effect   Proposition that holds that the nominal or market interest rate equals the real interest rate plus an inflation premium:

$$\text{Market interest rate} = \text{real interest rate} + \text{inflation premium}$$

The *market (or nominal) interest rate* is the one actually observed in the market. The *real interest rate* is the one that would exist if lenders and borrowers expected no inflation. (It is thus the interest rate in terms of goods.) The *inflation premium* is the public's expectation of the percentage change in the price level.

Fisher equation   *See equation of exchange.*

Fisher, Irving (1867–1940)   One of America's foremost economists during the first half of the twentieth century. A professor at Yale University, he authored many books and articles on diverse topics, including statistics and monetary theory. Among his many contributions was the "Fisher equation," which he used to explain the cause-and-effect relationship between the money supply and the price level. (*See equation of exchange and quantity theory of money.*)

fixed assets   Durable assets of an enterprise used to carry on its business, such as land, buildings, machinery, equip-

ment, office furniture, automobiles, and trucks.

fixed costs   Costs that do not vary with a firm's output. *Examples:* rental payments, interest on debt, property taxes.

floating exchange rates   Foreign exchange rates determined in a free market by demand and supply.

f.o.b. pricing   Method of pricing whereby the seller charges a buyer the firm's own mill price and places the product "free on board" (or "freight on board") at a nearby shipping site (such as a truck-loading platform, railway station, or dock), with the buyer actually paying the freight costs to the destination point. For many products priced in this way, the buyer is even permitted to pick them up at the mill, if the buyer so chooses. Prices quoted on a strict f.o.b. basis are not discriminatory because they reflect the seller's marginal cost of producing and selling the product. (*Compare delivered pricing.*)

"forced" saving   Situation in which consumers are prevented from spending part of their income on consumption. Some examples include: (1) prices rising faster than money wages, causing a decrease in real consumption and hence an increase in real (forced) saving; (2) a corporation that plows back some of its profit instead of distributing it as dividend income to stockholders; and (3) a government that taxes its citizens and uses the funds for investment, thereby preventing the public from utilizing a portion of its income for the purchase of consumer goods.

foreign aid   Loans, grants, or assistance from one government to another for the purpose of accelerating economic development in the recipient country.

foreign exchange   Instruments used for making international payments. Such instruments consist not only of currency, but also of checks, drafts, and bills of exchange (which are orders to pay currency).

foreign exchange market   A world financial market in which instruments used for international payments are bought and sold. The instruments include national currencies such as U.S. dollars, Japanese yen, British pounds, French francs, Canadian dollars, and Mexican pesos. (*See foreign exchange.*)

foreign exchange rate   Price of one currency expressed in terms of another.

foreign-trade multiplier   Principle that states that fluctuations in net exports (that is, imports minus exports) may generate magnified variations in national income. It is based on the idea that a change in exports relative to imports has the same multiplier effect on national income as a change in expenditure "injections" into the income stream. Similarly, a change in imports relative to exports has the same multiplier effect on national income as a change in "withdrawals" from the income stream. In general, an increase in exports tends to raise domestic income, but the increased income also encourages some imports, which act as "leakages." These tend to reduce the full multiplier effect that would exist if imports remained constant.

forward exchange   Foreign exchange bought (or sold) at a given time and at a stipulated current or "spot" price, but payable at a future date. By buying or selling forward exchange, importers and exporters can protect themselves against the risks of fluctuations in the current exchange market.

forward prices   Proposed plan for reducing price uncertainty and encouraging greater stability in agriculture through the use of the price system as an adjustment mechanism. Under the plan, a government-appointed board would predict in advance of breeding or seeding time the equilibrium prices of commodities, based on expected demand and supply. The government would then guarantee those predicted or forward prices in two ways: by storage programs and direct payments to farmers, if actual prices should fall below forward prices, and by a direct tax on farmers, if actual prices should rise above forward prices.

four-firm concentration ratio   *See concentration ratio.*

fractional-reserve banking system   One in which required reserves are smaller than (some fraction of) deposits. This means that the supply of money in the economy is always some multiple of the monetary base (currency held by the public plus legal reserves).

free good   One that can be acquired without sacrifice—without giving something up.

free market   One in which buyers and sellers can engage in transactions without restrictions imposed by government or by any external force.

free-rider problem   Tendency of people to avoid paying for a good's benefits when they can be obtained free. Public goods (such as national defense, air-traffic control, and so on) provide examples because the benefits of such goods are indivisible and therefore cannot be denied to individuals, whether they pay or not. Those who do not pay are thus "free riders." If many people become free riders, there might be no way of knowing how much of a public good should be provided. In that case, some form of collective action, usually through government, is taken.

free-trade area   Association of trading nations whose participants agree to impose no restrictive devices, such as tariffs or quotas, on one another but are free to impose whatever restrictive devices they wish on nonparticipants. *Example:* The European Free Trade Association (EFTA).

frictional unemployment   Unemployment due to maladjustments in the economic system resulting from imperfect labor mobility, imperfect knowledge of job opportunities, and a general inability of the economy to match people with jobs instantly and smoothly. A common form of frictional unemployment consists of people who are temporarily out of work because they are between jobs.

Friedman, Milton (1912–)   A leading American economist and Nobel laureate (1976) who did pioneering work in the study of consumption theory, monetary economics, and other fields. Most of his career was spent as a professor at the University of Chicago, where he was the foremost exponent of the "Chicago School" of economic thought. This approach to economics extolls free markets, a minimal role for government, and other libertarian views. Friedman thus follows in the tradition of Adam Smith and most other classical economists.

fringe benefits   Monetary advantages other than basic wages that are provided by employers for their employees. Examples include supplementary pay, time off with pay, insurance benefits, pensions, and income-maintenance payments for economic layoffs or job termination.

full-cost (average-cost) price   Price for a given volume of output that is at least high enough to cover all of a firm's costs of production—that is, its average total cost for that volume of output. If demand is great enough to enable the firm to sell its entire output at that price, the firm will earn a normal profit. If it can sell its output at a still higher price, it will earn an economic (or pure) profit.

full (natural) employment   Level of employment at which (1) everyone who wants to work is working, except for those who are frictionally and structurally unemployed, and (2) the average price level is stable.

Full Employment and Balanced Growth (Humphrey-Hawkins) Act (1978)   Federal law with three major provisions: (1) Requires the President to set long-term and short-term production and employment goals, including an annual unemployment-rate target of 4 percent, and to identify means for attaining the goals through public-employment programs, employment-training policies, and so on. (2) Requires the Federal Reserve to declare semiannually its monetary policies and their relation to the President's goals. (3) Requires the government to undertake actions that will achieve the goal of full employment while striving for a zero-percent inflation rate.

full-employment (structural) budget   Estimate of annual government expenditures and revenues that would occur at the level of potential real GDP—that is, at full employment. Any resulting surplus (or deficit) is called a full-employment surplus (or deficit).

"functional finance"   Philosophy that holds that the government should pursue whatever fiscal measures are needed to achieve noninflationary full employment and economic growth—without regard to budget balancing per se. The federal budget is thus viewed functionally as a flexible fiscal tool for achieving economic objectives rather than as an accounting statement to be balanced periodically.

functional income distribution   Payments in the form of wages, rents, interest, and profits made to the owners of the factors of production in return for supplying their labor, land, capital, and entrepreneurial ability.

futures markets   Financial markets in which futures contracts—legal agreements to exchange a commodity or financial instrument for a fixed price at some designated later date—are bought and sold.

G

gains from trade   Net benefits or increases in goods that a country receives as a result of trading with others. This concept also applies to trading between small economic entities, such as regions and individuals.

gain-sharing plans   Incentive compensation systems that tie pay increases to some measure of company performance. Among the measures commonly used are profit, productivity, value-added in manufacturing, or a ratio of labor costs to sales revenues. Profit-sharing plans, in which businesses distribute a share of net profits to workers, are perhaps the best-known examples of gain-sharing plans.

Galbraith, John Kenneth (1908–)   American economist whose writing, in the tradition of the "institutionalist school," is perhaps closest to that of Thorstein Veblen. Like Veblen, Galbraith criticized America's capitalistic institutions and processes. Among his chief propositions are these: (1) The market system, dominated by big business, does not perform the way the "conventional wisdom" of traditional economics says that it does. (2) Modern industry is run by a "technostructure" of elite specialists who bamboozle consumers through advertising, thereby insulating big business from the free market. (3) A larger public sector is needed, both economically and politically, to reduce the power of large corporations and to "educate" the people to appreciate "the higher things in life."

GDP deflator   Weighted average of the price indexes used to deflate the components of GDP. For any given year,

$$\text{GDP in constant prices} = \frac{\text{GDP in current prices}}{\text{GDP deflator}}$$

Therefore,

$$\text{GDP deflator} = \frac{\text{GDP in current prices}}{\text{GDP in constant prices}}$$

The GDP deflator is also called the ***Implicit Price Index*** .

General Agreement on Tariffs and Trade (GATT)   International commercial agreement signed in 1947 by the United States and 22 other countries for the purpose of achieving four basic long-run objectives: (1) nondiscrimination in trade through adherence to unconditional most-favored-nation treatment, (2) reduction of tariffs by negotiation, (3) elimination of import quotas (with some exceptions), and (4) resolution of differences through consultation.

general-equilibrium theory   Explanation or model of the interrelations between prices and outputs of goods and resources in different markets and the possibility of simultaneous equilibrium among all of them. It is primarily of theoretical interest, but it focuses attention on the fact that, in the real world, markets are often interdependent.

general price level   Expression representing the "average" level of prices in the economy. It is often represented by the ***GDP deflator*** (or ***Implicit Price Index***), although no index can accurately reflect all prices.

George, Henry (1839–1897)   Prominent American economist whose book, *Progress and Poverty* (1879), ranks as one of the most widely read economic treatises of all time. In the book he advocated a *single tax* on land as the source of all government revenue. In support of his proposal, he argued that, unlike other factors of production, land is provided by nature. Therefore, rent to landlords is an unearned surplus that increases as population grows, depriving the landless of their birthright to a share of the surplus. The solution is government taxation of all land rent. If this were done, no other taxes would be needed. (*See single tax.*)

gift tax   Progressive (graduated) tax imposed by the federal government and by some state governments. It is paid by the donor or person who makes the gift, not the donee or recipient of it. Exemptions, deduction, and rates vary widely among the states.

Gini coefficient of inequality   A measure of the degree of inequality in a distribution. On a Lorenz diagram, it equals the numerical value of the area between the Lorenz curve and the diagonal line divided by the entire area beneath the diagonal line. The ratio may vary between 0 (no inequality) and 1 (complete inequality).

gold-bullion standard   Monetary standard under which (1) the national unit of currency (such as the dollar, pound, or mark) is defined in terms of a fixed weight of gold; (2) gold is held by the government in the form of bars rather than coin; (3) there is no circulation of gold in any form within the economy; and (4) gold is available solely to meet the needs of industry (as in jewelry and dentistry) and to settle international transactions among central banks or treasuries. This is the standard that the United States and most advanced nations adopted when they went off the gold-coin standard in the early 1930s.

gold (coin) standard   Monetary standard under which (1) the national unit of currency (such as the dollar, pound, or franc) is defined by law in terms of a fixed weight of gold; (2) there is a free and unrestricted flow of the metal in any form into and out of the country; (3) gold coins are full legal tender for all debts; (4) there is free convertibility between the national currency and gold coins at a defined rate; and (5) there are no restrictions on the coinage of gold. Nearly 50 countries of the world were on this standard in the late nineteenth and early twentieth centuries.

gold-exchange standard   Monetary standard under which a nation's unit of currency is defined in terms of another nation's unit of currency, which in turn is defined in terms of, and is convertible into, gold. This standard prevailed in the noncommunist world from 1944 to 1971 and is primarily of international economic significance. Thus, in this period, the U.S. dollar was defined as equal to 1/35 of an ounce of gold and was convertible to foreign central banks at this rate. Each foreign central bank, in turn, defined the par value of its own currency in terms of the U.S. dollar and maintained it at that level. The entire system operated by international agreement (under the **International Monetary Fund**).

gold points Range within which the foreign exchange rates of gold-standard countries will fluctuate. Thus the gold points are equal to the par rate of exchange plus and minus the cost (including insurance) of shipping gold. The upper and lower gold points for a nation are called its "gold-export point" and its "gold-import point," respectively, because gold will be exported when the foreign exchange rate rises above the upper level and will be imported when the rate falls below the lower level. One nation's gold-export point is thus another nation's gold-import point and vice versa.

goldsmith's principle Banks can maintain a fractional—rather than 100 percent—reserve against deposits, because customers will not ordinarily withdraw their funds at the same time. Hence the banks can earn interest by lending out unused or excess reserves. This principle was discovered centuries ago by the English goldsmiths, who held gold in safekeeping for customers.

government monopoly Monopoly both owned and operated by either a federal or a local government. *Examples:* The U.S. Postal Service, many water and sewer systems, and the central banks of most countries.

Gramm-Rudman-Hollings Act Legislation, passed in 1985, that requires the federal budget to be balanced each year. In the event of a recession or emergency, Congress can suspend the law for up to two years. The law has not been adhered to by Congress.

grants-in-aid Financial aid at the intergovernmental level that consists of (1) revenues received by local governments from their states and from the federal government; and (2) revenues received by state governments from the federal government. These revenues are used mainly to help pay for public welfare assistance, highways, and education.

Great Leap Forward Ambitious economic plan undertaken by China during 1958–1960 to accelerate enormously its rate of economic growth. The plan was unrealistic and forced the country into a major economic crisis.

greenbacks Paper money (officially called United States Notes) issued by the Treasury to help finance the Civil War, 1861–1865. The currency was not redeemable in specie (gold or silver coins) and was the first official legal-tender money issued by the federal government. (*Note:* The U.S. dollar today is sometimes called a "greenback," but this is a colloquial rather than a literal term.)

Gresham's law Principle which asserts that cheap money tends to drive dear money out of circulation. Thus, suppose two kinds of metals, such as gold and silver, circulate with equal legal-tender powers (as happened in the United States under the bimetallic standard during the nineteenth century). Then, the cheaper metal will become the chief circulating medium while the dearer metal will be hoarded, melted down, or exported, thereby disappearing from circulation. The law is named after Sir Thomas Gresham, Master of the Mint under Queen Elizabeth I during the sixteenth century. (*See also* **mint ratio; bimetallic standard.**)

gross domestic disproduct Sum of all social costs or reductions in benefits to society that result from producing the gross domestic product. *Example:* Pollution of the environment is part of gross domestic disproduct, to the extent that it is caused by production of the gross domestic product.

gross domestic income (GDI) The equivalent of gross domestic product from the "income" viewpoint. Thus, GDI is income earned from domestic production. For calculation purposes, GDI = national income (= the sum of wages, rent, interest, and profit) + indirect business taxes + capital consumption allowance – net foreign factor income.

gross domestic product (GDP) The total market value of all final goods and services produced during a year by domestically located resources, regardless of whether the resources are American- or foreign-owned. (*Compare with* **gross national product, GNP.** *GDP and GNP are related by the formula GDP = GNP – net foreign factor income.*)

gross national income (GNI) The equivalent of gross national product from the "income" viewpoint. Thus, GNI is income earned from domestic production and from foreign production. For calculation purposes, GNI = national income (the sum of wages, rent, interest, and profit) + indirect business taxes + capital consumption allowance.

gross national product (GNP) Total market value of all final goods and services produced during a year by domestically owned resources, regardless of where the resources are located. (*Compare with* **gross domestic product, GDP.** *GNP and GDP are related by the formula GNP = GDP + net foreign factor income.*)

growth *See* **economic growth.**

guaranteed annual income Plan that awards all families under a certain "poverty line" level a straight allowance for each parent plus specified amounts for each child according to the size of the family. No family receives less than a designated amount; and, as a family's income rises, the payment from the government is reduced until a break-even level (which is a little higher than the poverty line) is reached.

H

hard-core unemployed People who are unemployed because they lack the education and skills for today's complex economy. (Discrimination may also be a contributing factor.) They consist mainly of certain minority groups, such as blacks, Chicanos, the "too-old," the "too-young," high-school dropouts, and the permanently displaced (who are victims of technological change).

hedging Purchase and sale of a commodity in two different markets at the same time and a corresponding offsetting sale and purchase of the same commodity in the two markets at a later time. The markets involved are the cash or spot market, in which a physical commodity is bought and sold, and the futures or forward market, in which contracts for subsequent delivery of the physical commodity are bought and sold. Hedging helps firms to reduce inventory costs, adjust to changing market conditions, and plan future supplies of goods needed for production. Hence it also leads to lower prices.

Herfindahl index A measure of market concentration. It equals the sum of the squares of the market shares of all the firms in an industry. For example, if an industry has three firms with market shares of 70 percent, 20 percent, and 10 percent, then

$$\text{Herfindahl index} = (0.70)^2 + (0.20)^2 + (0.10)^2 = 0.54$$

The index can range from 0 to 1. An index of 0 denotes pure competition—the absence of monopoly power. An index of 1 denotes pure monopoly—the absence of competition. An index between these limits denotes the degree of monopoly power. If all firms in a market are of equal size, the index equals the reciprocal of the number (N) of firms—that is, $1/N$. Because of the squaring process, the magnitude of the Herfindahl index is affected more by large firms than by small ones. (For example, a 90 percent market share, when squared, equals .081. A 10 percent market share, when squared, equals .01.) Therefore, it is not necessary to know all of the market shares in an industry in order to estimate a Herfindahl index. The index can be closely approximated simply by using the market shares of the industry's largest firms.

Hicks, John R. (1904–1989) Leading British economist and Nobel laureate. He contributed significantly to the reconstruction of demand theory through the development of indifference-curve analysis. His work thus follows in the tradition of general equilibrium theory as formulated by Léon Walras and Vilfredo Pareto in the late nineteenth century. Among Hicks' other leading contributions have been a refinement of the marginal-productivity theory of wages and an integrated analysis of Keynesian with classical theory.

"high-powered money" See *monetary base*.

hog-corn price ratio Number of bushels of corn required to buy 100 pounds of live pork:

$$\text{Hog-corn price ratio} = \frac{\text{price of live hogs per 100 pounds}}{\text{price of corn per bushel}}$$

When the ratio is relatively low, hog production decreases because farmers find it more profitable to sell their corn in the market than to use it for feeding hogs. Conversely, when the ratio is relatively high, hog production increases because farmers use the corn to feed more hogs and to market them at heavier weights.

horizontal equity Doctrine that states that "equals should be treated equally." *Example:* Persons with the same income, wealth, or other taxpaying ability should, in order to bear equal tax burdens (or make equal subjective sacrifices), pay the same amount of tax. (Compare **vertical equity**.)

horizontal merger Amalgamation under one ownership of plants engaged in producing similar products. The products might be close substitutes, such as competing brands of cement, or moderate substitutes, such as tin cans and jars. The objective is to round out a product line that is sold through the same distribution channels, thereby offering joint economies in selling and distribution efforts. The result may be an enhancement of market power.

Hotelling's paradox Proposition that states that monopolistically competitive firms must, in order to attract each other's customers, make their products as similar to existing products as possible without destroying the differences. Therefore, as a type of market structure, monopolistic competition leads to maximum differentiation of products with minimum differences between them. (This proposition was formulated analytically in 1929 by a distinguished economist and statistician, Harold Hotelling. Because the theory of monopolistic competition had not yet been formulated, Hotelling's model was based on what he called "industries composed of many firms and similar goods.")

Hotelling's rule Relationship stating that scarcity rent must increase at a rate equal to the prevailing rate of interest in the economy.

household All persons living in the same home. A household may thus consist of one or more families.

human capital The stock of skills and productive knowledge embodied in people.

human-resource policies Deliberate efforts undertaken in the private and public sectors to develop and use the capacities of human beings as actual or potential members of the labor force. (Human resource policies are also known as *employment-training policies*.)

human resources Productive physical and mental talents of the people who constitute an economy.

Humphrey-Hawkins Act See *Full Employment and Balanced Growth Act (1978)*.

hyperinflation Situation in which prices are rising with little or no increase in output. It is also sometimes called "runaway" or "galloping" inflation, if prices are rising rapidly.

hypothesis A working guess about the behavior of things, or an expression about the relationship between variables in the real world. In economics, the "things" may include consumers, workers, business firms, investors, and so on, and the variables may include prices, wages, consumption, production, or other economic quantities.

I

imperfect competition A classification of market structures that falls between the two extremes of perfect competition and monopoly. It consists of monopolistic competition and oligopoly.

implicit costs Costs of self-owned or self-employed resources that are not recorded in a company's book of accounts. *Example:* the alternative interest return, rental receipts, and wages that a self-employed proprietor forgoes by owning and operating his own business.

*Implicit Price Index See **GDP deflator.***

import quota Law that limits the number of units of a good that may be imported during a given period.

*impossibility theorem See **Arrow's impossibility theorem.***

incidence Range of occurrence or influence of an economic act. It is a term used primarily in the study of taxation and refers to the economic entity (such as a household or a firm) that bears the ultimate burden of a tax.

income Gain derived from the use of human or material resources. A flow of dollars per unit of time. *(Compare **wealth.**)*

income-consumption curve (ICC) In indifference-curve analysis, a line showing the amounts of two goods that a consumer will purchase when his or her income changes while the prices of the goods remain the same. Geometrically, it is a line connecting the tangency points of price lines and indifference curves as income changes while prices remain constant.

income distribution Division of society's output (that is, the income society earns) among people. Income distribution thus concerns the matter of who gets how much, or what proportion, of the economy's total production. *(See **functional income distribution; personal income distribution.**)*

income effect Increased quantity demanded of a good due to a rise in a buyer's real income, resulting from a decrease in the price of a good. *Example:* If you are a consumer of beef, a decrease in its price increases your real income or purchasing power. This enables you to buy more beef, and perhaps more of some other things (such as chicken, pork, and even nonmeat products) as well. The income effect assumes that the consumer's money income, tastes, and the prices of other goods remain constant. It helps explain why a demand curve slopes downward. *(See also **substitution effect.**)*

income elasticity of demand Percentage change in the quantity purchased of a good resulting from a 1 percent change in income. Thus,

Income elasticity of demand

$$= \frac{\text{percentage change in quantity purchased}}{\text{percentage change in income}}$$

$$= \frac{(Q_2 - Q_1)/(Q_2 + Q_1)}{(Y_2 - Y_1)/(Y_2 + Y_1)}$$

in which Q_1 and Q_2 represent the quantities purchased be-

fore and after the change in income and Y_1 and Y_2 represent the corresponding levels of income before and after the change. Thus the income elasticity of demand denotes the responsiveness of changes in quantity purchased to changes in income, where responsiveness is measured in terms of percentage changes.

income-expenditure model This relates the economy's real aggregate income (or output) to the public's total spending on goods and services. The model assumes that the *average price level remains constant.* The income-expenditure model may also be called the *aggregate output/aggregate expenditure* model. It is the model on which Keynesian economics is based.

income-price model This relates the economy's real aggregate income (or output) to the average price level. The model assumes that the average price level varies. The income-price model may also be called the *aggregate demand/aggregate supply* model.

income statement Financial statement of a firm showing its revenues, costs, and profit during a period. Also known as a profit-and-loss statement.

income tax Tax on the net income, or the residual that remains after certain items are subtracted from gross income. The two types of income taxes are the personal income tax and the corporation income tax.

income velocity of money Average number of times per year that a dollar is spent on purchasing a part of the economy's annual flow of final goods and services—its GDP. It equals the ratio of GDP to the quantity of money. *(See also **equation of exchange.**)*

incomes policy Laws aimed at curbing inflation by establishing conditions under which businesses' production costs (especially wages), prices, and profits may be allowed to increase. *Examples:* Wage and price controls.

inconvertible paper standard Monetary standard under which the nation's unit of currency may or may not be defined in terms of any metal or other precious substance; however, there is no free convertibility into these other forms. Historically, this standard has existed on a domestic basis in all countries since the worldwide abandonment of gold in the 1930s.

increasing-cost industry Industry that experiences increases in resource prices or in its costs of production as it expands because of new firms entering it. This will happen when the industry's demand for the resources it employs is a significant proportion of the total demand for those resources.

increasing (opportunity) costs, law of On an economy's production-possibilities curve, the real cost of acquiring either good is the increasing amount of the alternative good that the society must sacrifice or "give up" because it cannot have all it wants of both goods.

Independent Treasury Act (1846) Law that created the Independent Treasury System (1846–1863). During its life, the law enabled the Treasury to act as its own bank, receiving and disbursing its own funds, thus making it independent of the banking system. The Independent Treasury System also engaged in the purchase and sale of government bonds, thus affecting the quantity of money. This procedure, which decades later was called *open-market operations*, became an integral part of the Federal Reserve System after its establishment in 1913.

independent union Labor union not affiliated with any federation of labor organizations. It may be national or international, and it is not limited to workers in any one firm.

indexation Assignment of inflation-adjusting escalator clauses to long-term contracts. Thus wages, rents, interest payments, and even the tax system can be readjusted in proportion to price changes so that people's gains due to inflation are not taxed away, thereby reducing real income. *Example:* If your income goes up by 10 percent when prices go up by 10 percent, you have no more purchasing power than before. Yet your income tax will rise because you will be pushed into a higher tax bracket. This situation can be avoided by indexing the income tax, thereby "correcting" it for inflation. *(See escalator clause.)*

index numbers Figures that disclose the relative changes in a series of numbers, such as prices or production, from a base period. The base period is usually defined as being equal to an index number of 100, and all other numbers in the series both before or after that period are expressed as percentages of that period. Index numbers are widely used in reporting business and economic data.

indifference curve Graph of an indifference schedule. Every point along the curve represents a different combination of two goods, and each combination is equally satisfactory to a recipient because each one yields the same total utility.

indifference schedule Table showing the various combinations of two goods that would be equally satisfactory or yield the same total utility to a recipient at a given time.

indirect tax Tax that can be shifted either partially or entirely to someone other than the individual or firm originally taxed. *Examples:* sales taxes, excise taxes, taxes on business and rental properties.

induced consumption That part of total consumption that is related to income.

induced investment Tendency of changes in aggregate income to stimulate changes in investment. Thus it is that part of total investment that is related to aggregate income (or output). It may also be directly related to induced consumption, which in turn is related to income. (*Compare autonomous investment.*)

induction Process of reasoning from particular observations or cases to general laws or principles. Most human knowledge is inductive or empirical since it is based on the experiences of our senses. (Opposite of **deduction**.)

industrial orga3ization Branch of applied microeconomics concerned with the ways in which firms direct their production and marketing activities to meet consumer demands. The study of industrial organization is divided into three parts: (1) *Market structure*—the types of competitive environments within which firms operate. (2) *Market conduct*—the practices and policies that firms adopt in their pursuit of profits. (3) *Market performance*—the effect of business behavior on the economy's four goals (efficiency, equity, stability, and growth). A fourth area, *market policy*, deals with the legal environment (such as the antitrust laws) within which firms operate. This is sometimes treated separately, and sometimes integrated with the study of industrial organization.

industrial relations Rules and regulations governing the relationship between union and management. It often deals with such matters as union security (for example, the type of recognition that the union is accorded, or its financial arrangement for collecting dues) and methods of controlling the quantity and kind of union membership through apprenticeship requirements, licensing provisions, initiation fees, and seniority rules.

industrial union Labor union consisting solely of workers from a particular industry. Examples are a union of all workers in the automobile industry or a union of all workers in the steel industry. An industrial union is thus a "vertically" organized union.

industry Group of firms producing similar or identical products.

infant industry Underdeveloped industry that in the face of competition from abroad, may not be able to survive the early years of struggle before reaching maturity.

inferior good A good whose consumption varies inversely with money income (prices remaining constant) over a certain range of income. *Examples:* potatoes, used clothing, and other "cheap" commodities bought by poor families. The consumption of these commodities declines in favor of fancier foods, new clothing, and the like as the incomes of low-income families rise.

inflation Rise in the general price level (or average level of prices) of all goods and services over a prolonged period. Equivalently, it is a decline in the purchasing power of a unit of money (such as the dollar) over a prolonged period. The general price level thus varies inversely with the purchasing power of a unit of money. For example, if prices double, purchasing power decreases by one-half; if prices halve, purchasing power doubles.

inflationary gap Amount by which aggregate expenditure exceeds aggregate real output at full employment. Also, the amount by which actual real output, at its corresponding equilibrium price level, exceeds potential real output. Either condition causes inflationary pressures.

inflation premium Differential between the market rate of interest and the real rate of interest. The differential may be positive, negative, or zero. Its size is the amount necessary to compensate lenders or borrowers for adverse changes in purchasing power resulting from anticipated inflation or deflation.

infrastructure A nation's economic and social overhead capital needed as a basis for modern production. *Examples:* roads, telephone lines, power facilities, schools, and public health services.

inheritance tax Tax imposed by most state governments on property received from persons who have died. It is primarily progressive (graduated) in rate structure, but exemptions, deductions, and rates vary widely among the states.

injunction Court order requiring that a defendant refrain from certain practices or that he take a particular action.

innovation Adoption of a new or different product or of a new or different method of production, marketing, financing, and so on. It thus establishes a new relation between the output and the various kinds of inputs (capital, land, labor, and so forth) in a production process. In a more formal sense, it is the setting up of a new production function.

innovation theory Explanation originated by Joseph Schumpeter (1883–1950) that attributes business cycles and economic development to innovations that forward-looking businesspeople adopt in order to reduce costs and increase profits. Once an innovation proves successful, other businesspeople follow with the same or with similar techniques, and these innovations cause fluctuations in investment that result in business cycles. The innovation theory has also been used as a partial explanation of how profits arise in a competitive capitalistic system.

institutions Those traditions, beliefs, and practices which are well established and widely held as a fundamental part of a culture. *Example:* Institutions of capitalism include private property, economic individualism, laissez-faire, and free markets. (*Note:* In sociology, social systems are often characterized by their institutions. Examples of sociological institutions are marriage, the family, and so on. Institutions are thus the pillars or foundations on which a social system rests.)

interest **1.** Return to those who supply the factor of production known as "capital" (that is, the payment for supplying the funds with which businesspeople buy capital goods). **2.** Price paid for the use of credit or loanable funds over a period of time. It is stated as a rate—that is, as a percentage of the amount borrowed. Thus an interest rate of 10 percent annually means that the borrower pays 10 cents interest per $1 borrowed per year, or $10 per $100 borrowed per year, and so on. (*Note:* This definition of interest assumes that borrowers and lenders expect prices to be stable. If they are not, there will be a difference between the actual (or market) rate of interest and the real rate. (*See* **real rate of interest.***)

interest-rate effect Proposition that states that changes in the average price level result in changes in interest rates in the same direction, thereby affecting the public's spending. For example, when the average price level rises, the public's demand for borrowed funds increases in order to help finance consumption and investment purchases. Interest rates thus rise. This makes spending more costly, thereby reducing people's purchases of goods and services. The reverse happens when the average price level falls. The public's demand for credit decreases because people do not need as much borrowed funds to finance their purchases. Therefore, interest rates decline. This makes spending cheaper, thereby expanding people's purchases of goods and services. (*Note:* The interest-rate effect assumes that "all other things," especially the supply of money in the economy, remain constant.)

interlocking directorate Situation in which an individual serves on two or more boards of directors of competing corporations.

internal economies and diseconomies of scale Conditions that bring about decreases or increases in a firm's long-run average costs or scale of operations as a result of size adjustments within the firm as a producing unit. They occur regardless of adjustments within the industry and are due mainly to physical economies or diseconomies. *Example:* Internal economies may result from greater specialization and more efficient utilization of the firm's resources as its scale of operations increases, but internal diseconomies may eventually set in because of the limited decision-making abilities of the top management group.

internal labor market System of procedures and policies that determines the advancement of workers in those firms that adhere to a policy of promotion from within. Each firm's internal market contains its own rules governing job movement within the organization. To the extent that companies rely on such markets, they limit the ability of workers to move from one firm to another. This impedes worker mobility and hence reduces the efficiency of external labor markets.

International Development Cooperation Agency (IDCA) The most important American organization concerned with foreign aid. Created in 1979, it represents a major restructuring and consolidation of previous development programs operated by different U.S. agencies and various multilateral organizations. IDCA has two major functions. The first is to advise government on development policies. The second is to administer funds voted annually by Congress for the purpose of providing economic, technical, and defense assistance to nations that are identified with the free world. (IDCA includes within its organization the Agency for International Development, the government's chief foreign-aid unit, which was previously part of the U.S. State Department.)

International Monetary Fund (IMF) Established by the United Nations in 1944 for the purpose of eliminating exchange restrictions, encouraging exchange-rate stability, and providing the worldwide convertibility of currencies in order to promote multilateral trade based on international specialization. More than 150 nations are members of the Fund.

inventory Stocks of goods that business firms have on hand, including raw materials, supplies, and finished goods.

investment Spending by business firms on new job-creating and income-producing goods, such as plant, equipment, and increases in inventory, and by households on residential construction. Investment thus consists of replacements of, or additions to, the nation's stock of capital and housing.

"invisible hand" Expression coined by Adam Smith in *The Wealth of Nations* to convey the idea that each individual, if left to pursue his self-interest without interference by government, would be led, as if by an invisible hand, to achieve the best good for society.

involuntary unemployment Situation in which people who want work are unable to find jobs at the wage rates prevailing for the skills and experience they have to offer.

isoquant Curve along which each point represents a different combination of two inputs or factors of production (such as capital and labor) and each combination yields the same level of total output.

J

J-curve The short-run and long-run "path" of a nation's trade balance following a *depreciation* of the currency. The descending portion of the curve is realized in the short run after the depreciation occurs, because it takes some time for people to change their buying habits. Thus, the quantities of goods imported and exported remain about the same for a while, but the costs of imports rise because foreign currencies are more expensive to buy. Therefore, the trade balance declines. In the long run, buyers adjust to the price changes, causing the trade balance to rise. The reverse situation, resulting in an inverted *J*-curve, occurs when a nation's currency appreciates in the foreign exchange markets.

Jevons, William Stanley (1835–1882) English neoclassical and mathematical economist who made major contributions to value and distribution theory, capital theory, and to statistical research in economics. He is best known as a leading contributor to marginal utility analysis. "Value," he pointed out, "depends entirely upon utility." In equilibrium, marginal utilities are proportionate to prices. "From this, the ordinary laws of demand and supply are a necessary consequence." Jevon's major work in economics was

his book, *Theory of Political Economy* (1871).

job classification Process of describing the duties, responsibilities, and characteristics of jobs, point-rating them (perhaps by established formulas based on engineering time studies of workers in such jobs), and then grouping the jobs into graduated classifications with corresponding wage rates and wage ranges.

job-competition market Labor market in which the number and types of jobs are determined mainly by prevailing technology. Workers are employed to fill particular job openings associated with existing plant and equipment. (A factory, for example, needs a specific number of workers such as operators, maintenance people, and supervisors to run its machines.) Wages for these jobs are established largely by institutional and legislative conditions—industry custom, union-management contracts, minimum-wage laws, etc.—rather than by market forces. The function of job-competition markets, therefore, is to allocate workers to a given number of vacancies at prevailing relatively fixed, wage rates.

jurisdictional strike Strike caused by a dispute between two or more craft unions over which shall perform a particular job. Outlawed by the Taft-Hartley Act, 1947.

K

Keynes, John Maynard (1883–1946) British economist and founder of macroeconomics as we know it today. His most widely known work was his book *The General Theory of Employment, Interest and Money* (1936), in which he reorganized thinking about macroeconomic problems. The following chief features characterize the so-called Keynesian "system": (1) the dependency of consumption on income, called the *consumption function;* (2) the *multiplier* relationship between investment expenditures and income; (3) the *marginal efficiency of investment* as a measure of businesses' demand for investment; and (4) the use of *fiscal policy* and *monetary policy* to maintain full employment. In contrast to the classical theory, Keynes showed that our economic system could remain in equilibrium at less than full employment. Therefore, he concluded, active fiscal and monetary policies by government are needed to maintain high levels of resource utilization and economic stability. *(See also **Keynesian economics**.)*

Keynesian economics Body of economic thought that originated with the British economist John Maynard Keynes in the 1930s. It has since been extended and modified to the point where many of its basic analytical tools and ideas are now an integral part of general economic theory. In contrast to classical economics, which emphasized the automatic tendency of the economy to achieve full-employment equilibrium under a government policy of laissez-faire, Keynesian economics seeks to demonstrate that an economy may be in equilibrium at less than full employment.

The theory, therefore, concludes that appropriate government fiscal and monetary policies are needed to maintain full employment and steady economic growth with a minimum rate of inflation.

kinked demand curve A "bent" demand curve, and a corresponding discontinuous marginal-revenue curve, facing an oligopolistic seller. The kinked curve signifies that, if the seller raises the price above the kink, sales will fall off rapidly because other sellers are not likely to follow the price upward. If the seller reduces the price below the kink, sales will expand relatively little because other sellers are likely to follow the price downward. The market price, therefore, tends to stabilize at the kink.

Knights of Labor National labor organization founded in 1869. It rejected the traditional organizing of workers by crafts, preferring instead the mass unionization of both unskilled and skilled workers. The Knights championed the cause of workers and achieved many liberal improvements and reforms, but began to decline in the late 1880s due to several factors: (1) opposition by craft leaders who preferred organization along craft lines; (2) internal dissension among leading members and groups; and (3) suspicion—unproved—that it was involved in Chicago's Haymarket riot and bombing of 1886. By 1917, it had ceased to exist.

Kuznets, Simon Smith (1901–1985) Russian-born American economist who made major contributions to the study of national-income accounting, economic growth, productivity, and related areas. He is the "father" of national-income accounting because much of his efforts toward improving the theory and measurement of national income during the 1930s became a foundation for subsequent methods by the U.S. Department of Commerce. In 1971, at the age of 70, Kuznets was awarded the Nobel Prize in Economic Science.

L

labor **1.** Factor of production that represents those hired workers whose human efforts or activities are directed toward production. **2.** All personal services, including the activities of wageworkers, professional people, and independent businesspeople. "Laborers" may thus receive compensation not only in the form of wages but also as salaries, bonuses, commissions, and the like.

labor force The employable population, defined for measurement purposes as all people 16 years of age or older who are employed plus all those who are unemployed but actively seeking work.

labor-force participation rate Percentage of the total population, or of one or more subgroups of the population, that is in the labor force. Subgroups are classified by race, sex, age, marital status, and other demographic characteristics. Thus, some examples of labor-force participation rates are:

(1) the percentage of the nation's total white population that is in the labor force; (2) the percentage of the nation's black women, ages 19 to 24, that is in the labor force; and (3) the percentage of the nation's married men that is in the labor force.

Labor-Management Relations (Taft-Hartley) Act (1947) An amendment to the National Labor Relations (Wagner) Act of 1935. It retains the rights given to labor by the 1935 Act but also: (1) outlaws "unfair labor practices" of unions, such as coercion of workers to join unions, failure to bargain in good faith, jurisdictional strikes, secondary boycotts, and featherbedding; (2) outlaws the closed shop but permits the union shop; (3) requires unions to file financial reports with the NLRB and union officials to sign affidavits to the effect that they are not Communists; (4) prohibits strikes called before the end of a 60-day notice period prior to the expiration of a collective-bargaining agreement; and (5) enables the President to obtain an 80-day court injunction against strikes that endanger national health or safety.

Labor-Management Reporting and Disclosure (Landrum-Griffin) Act (1959) Act that amended the National Labor Relations Act of 1935 by (1) requiring detailed financial reports of all unions and union officers; (2) severely tightening restrictions on secondary boycotting and picketing; (3) requiring periodic secret-ballot elections of union officers; and (4) restricting ex-convicts and Communists from holding positions as union officers.

Laffer curve A hypothetical relationship between tax revenues and the tax rate. The relationship is such that, as the tax rate increases from zero to 100 percent, tax revenues rise correspondingly from zero to some maximum level and then decline to zero. The optimum rate is thus the one that produces the maximum revenue. Rates that are lower than optimum are deemed "normal" because tax revenues can be increased by raising the rate. Rates that are higher than optimum are regarded as prohibitive because they impair personal and business incentives and are thus counterproductive. Therefore, when the tax rate is in the prohibitive range, tax reductions should bring increased economic activity and higher, not lower, tax revenues. (*Note:* There is no concrete evidence to support this assumed relationship between tax revenues and the tax rate.)

lagging indicators Time series that tend to follow or trail aggregate economic activity.

laissez-faire "To let (people) do (as they choose)"—an expression, coined in France during the late seventeenth century, that today is interpreted to mean freedom from government intervention in all economic affairs.

land Factor of production that includes land itself (in the form of real estate) as well as mineral deposits, timber, water, and other nonhuman or "natural" resources.

law Expression of a relationship between variables, based on a high degree of unvarying uniformity under the same conditions. (Often used synonymously with *principle*.)

leading indicators Time series that tend to move ahead of aggregate economic activity, thus reaching peaks and troughs before the economy as a whole.

least-cost principle Principle stating that the least-cost combination of inputs is achieved when a dollar's worth of any input adds as much to total physical output as a dollar's worth of any other input.

legal monopoly Privately owned firm that is granted an exclusive right by government to operate in a particular market. In return, government may impose standards and requirements pertaining to the quantity and quality of output, geographic areas of operation, and the prices or rates that are charged. The justification of legal monopoly is that unrestricted competition in the industry is socially undesirable. Public utilities are typical examples of legal monopolies.

legal reserves Assets that a bank or other depository institution (such as a savings and loan association or credit union) may lawfully use as reserves against its deposit liabilities. For a member bank of the Federal Reserve System, legal reserves consist of deposits held with the district Federal Reserve Bank plus currency held in the vaults of the bank—called "vault cash." Any other highly liquid financial claims, such as government securities, are classified as *nonlegal reserves.*

Lerner index Measure of a firm's monopoly power, based on the divergence between the price, *P*, and marginal cost, *MC*, expressed as a proportion of price. Thus,

$$\text{Lerner index} = \frac{P - MC}{P}$$

When a firm is in equilibrium, the index will range between 0 and 1. It will be zero (no monopoly power) for a firm in perfect competition, since $P = MC$. At the other extreme, the index will be 1 (complete monopoly power) in the rare case of a firm whose marginal costs are zero. Basic shortcomings of the formula are that (1) marginal-cost data for a firm are not generally known and cannot be readily derived; and (2) it is a static rather than dynamic measure.

Lerner's theorem Proposition that states that because individuals' marginal utilities of money are unknown, society will maximize *probable* total utility by establishing and maintaining an equal distribution of income. (Named after Abba P. Lerner, an American economist who developed the theorem in 1944.)

less developed country (LDC) A nation that, in comparison with the more developed countries, tends to exhibit such characteristics as (1) poverty level of income and hence little or no savings, (2) high rate of population growth, (3) substantial majority of its labor force employed in agriculture, (4) low rate of adult literacy, (5) extensive disguised unemployment, (6) heavy reliance on a few items for export, and (7) government control by a wealthy elite.

liabilities Monetary debts or things of value owed to creditors by individuals, households, business firms, or government.

liability management Method used by banks to obtain liquidity (raise funds) by borrowing either from the Fed, from the public (by selling debt instruments such as repurchase agreements, bankers' acceptances, and negotiable CDs) or from other banks.

limited liability Restriction of the liability of an investor, such as a stockholder in a corporation, to the amount of his investment.

liquidity Ease with which an asset can be converted into cash quickly without loss of purchase price. Liquidity is thus a matter of degree. Money is perfectly liquid, whereas any other asset may possess a lower degree of liquidity—depending on how easily it can be sold without loss.

liquidity preference theory of interest Theory formulated by J. M. Keynes (1883–1946). The theory contends that households and businesses would rather hold their assets in the most liquid form—cash or demand deposits. The reason is to satisfy three motives: (1) the "transactions motive," to carry out everyday purchasing needs; (2) the "precautionary motive," to meet possible unforeseen conditions, and (3) the "speculative motive," to take advantage of change in interest rates. These motives determine the demand for money, whereas the monetary authority determines its supply. The demand for, and supply of, money together determine the equilibrium rate of interest.

liquidity trap Condition in which an increase in the supply of money will not further reduce the rate of interest, because the total demand for money at that relatively low interest rate (expressed in terms of a liquidity-preference curve) is infinite. This means that, at the low rate of interest, everyone would rather hold money in idle balances than risk the loss of holding long-term securities offering poor yields. (In geometric terms, the liquidity trap exists at that rate of interest where the liquidity-preference curve becomes perfectly horizontal.)

loanable funds Money available for lending; money used to purchase financial claims. *Example:* If you lend a friend $100 and receive an I.O.U. in return, you have exchanged money for a financial claim of equal value. That is, you have purchased a financial claim. When your friend repays the loan, you will exchange (sell) the claim for the money.

loanable-funds theory of interest The interest rate is determined by the demand for and the supply of money (loanable funds) used to purchase financial claims. The sources of demand for loanable funds are: (1) household sector borrowing (credit purchases) to finance consumption; (2) business-sector borrowing to finance purchases of capital goods; (3) government sector borrowing to finance budget deficits; and (4) foreign-sector borrowing to finance foreign consumption, investment, and government budget deficits. The sources of supply of loanable funds are: (1) household-sector savings—the difference between households' income and spending; (2) business-sector savings in the form of retained earnings and depreciation; (3) government sector savings consisting of budget surpluses; (4) Federal Reserve increases in the money supply; and (5) foreign-sector savings in the form of loans to American borrowers.

lockout   Closing down of a plant by an employer in order to keep workers out of their jobs.

logarithmic scale   Special type of scale used in graphing. The scale is spaced in logarithms. As a result, equal *percentage* changes between numbers are represented by equal distances along the scale. For example, a 100 percent change is always the same distance on the scale whether the change is from 1 to 2, 2 to 4, 3 to 6, 5 to 10, 10 to 20, or 50 to 100. In contrast, a conventional scale is spaced arithmetically. Therefore, equal *amounts* of change between numbers are represented by equal distances along the scale. Thus the changes from 1 to 2, 2 to 3, 6 to 7, 15 to 16, and so on, are all the same distances on an arithmetic scale. A logarithmic scale is useful for comparing *ratios* of change between data. In contrast, an arithmetic scale is used to compare *amounts* of change between data.

long run   1. Macroeconomics. Period that is long enough for all prices to be flexible. As a result, there are no market surpluses or shortages—that is, the economy self-corrects. 2. Microeconomics. Period that is long enough for a firm to enter or leave an industry and to vary its output by varying all its factors of production, including its plant scale. Therefore, all its costs are variable.

long-run aggregate supply (LRAS) curve   Straight line depicting the economy's potential real output. This is the same as the economy's full-employment (or natural-employment) level of real output. The curve indicates that the amount of real output at this level does not vary with changes in the price level.

long-run average cost (LRAC) curve (planning curve)   Curve that is tangent to, or envelops, the various short-run average total cost curves of a firm over a range of output representing different scales or sizes of plants. Thus it shows what the level of average costs would be for alternative outputs of different-sized plants.

long-run industry supply curve   Locus or "path" of a competitive industry's long-run equilibrium points. That is, the long-run industry supply curve connects the stable equilibrium points of the industry's demand and supply curves over a period of time, both before and after these curves have adjusted completely to changed market conditions. The long-run industry supply curve may be either upward-sloping, horizontal, or downward-sloping, depending on whether the industry is an increasing-, constant-, or decreasing-cost industry.

long-run Phillips curve (LRPC)   Relationship between changing rates of inflation and a constant natural rate of unemployment. Geometrically, the curve is a vertical line. It thus emphasizes the idea that there is no long-run trade-off between the rate of unemployment and the rate of inflation.

Lorenz diagram   Graphic device for comparing the actual distribution of a variable with an equal distribution of that variable. It is most often employed to compare a society's actual distribution of income among families with an equal distribution. For example, each axis of the chart is scaled from 0 to 100 percent. Then the cumulative percentage relationships between two variables, such as "percent of income" and "percent of families," are plotted against each other. The resulting (Lorenz) curve of actual income distribution is then compared to a 45° diagonal line representing equal income distribution. The degree of difference between the two curves indicates the extent of income inequality. Similar curves may be constructed to show other types of distributions (such as distribution of wealth or distribution of wages in a factory).

M

macroeconomics   The part of economics that deals with the economy as a whole, or with large subdivisions of it. It analyzes the economic "forest" rather than the "trees."

Malthusian theory of population   First published by Thomas Malthus in 1798 and then revised in 1803, this theory states that population tends to increase as a geometric progression (1, 2, 4, 8, 16, 32, and so forth) while the means of subsistence increase at most only as an arithmetic progression (1, 2, 3, 4, 5, 6 and so forth). This is because a growing population applied to a fixed amount of land results in eventually diminishing returns to workers. Human beings are therefore destined to misery and poverty unless the rate of population growth is retarded. This may be accomplished either by (1) preventive checks, such as moral restraint, late marriages, and celibacy or, if these fail, by (2) positive checks, such as wars, famines, and disease.

Malthus, Thomas Robert (1776–1834)   English classical economist. Best known for his theory that held that population would tend to outrun the food supply. The result would be a bare subsistence level of survival for the laboring class. (See **Malthusian theory of population**.) Malthus, in his book *Principles of Political Economy* (1820), also developed the concept of "effective demand," which he defined as the level of aggregate demand necessary to maintain full employment. If effective demand declined, he said, overpopulation would result. He thus anticipated a fundamental concept in modern macroeconomics.

manpower policies   *See employment-training policies.*

Marcet, Jane Haldimand (1769–1858)   English economic educator whose book, *Conversation on Political Economy* (1816), conveyed in dialogue form the teachings of her classical-economic predecessors and contemporaries—Smith, Say, Malthus, and Ricardo. She thus contributed significantly to the teaching of economics.

marginal cost (MC) Change in total cost resulting from a unit change in output. Marginal cost is thus the additional cost of one more unit of output. It is calculated by a formula:

$$\text{Marginal cost} = \frac{\text{change in total cost}}{\text{change in quantity}}$$

Marginal cost is also the change in total variable cost resulting from a unit change in quantity. The reason is that total cost changes because total variable cost changes, whereas total fixed cost remains constant.

marginal-cost price Price (or production) of output as determined by the point at which a firm's marginal cost equals its average revenue (demand). This is an optimum price for society because the value of the last unit to the marginal user (measured by the price he pays for the last unit, which is equal to the price he pays for any other unit) is equivalent to the value of the resources used to produce that unit. However, this marginal-cost price will leave the firm suffering a loss if it results in a price below the firm's average total cost.

marginal efficiency of investment (MEI) Expected annual percentage rate of return on an addition to investment—that is, on an additional unit of a capital good. It is determined by such factors as (1) the demand for the product that the investment will produce; (2) the level of production costs in the economy; (3) technology and innovation; and (4) the stock of capital available to meet existing and future market demands. An *MEI* curve is thus a demand curve for investment. It shows the amount of investment spending that businesses are willing to undertake at each rate of interest (or cost of funds).

marginal extraction cost The cost of removing (producing) one additional unit of a resource. In other words, it is the cost of producing one more unit of a resource.

marginal product Change in total product resulting from a unit change in the quantity of a variable input employed. It is calculated by a formula:

$$\text{Marginal product} = \frac{\text{change in total product}}{\text{change in variable input}}$$

Marginal product thus measures the gain (or loss) in total product from adding an additional unit of a variable factor of production.

marginal productivity The increase in output resulting from a unit change in a variable input while all other inputs are held fixed.

marginal-productivity theory of income distribution Principle that states that, when there is perfect competition for inputs, a firm will purchase factors of production up to the point at which the price or marginal cost of the factor is equal to its marginal revenue productivity. Therefore, in real terms, each factor of production will be paid a value equal to what it contributes to total output—that is, it will be paid what it is "worth."

marginal propensity to consume (MPC) Change in consumption resulting from a unit change in income. It is calculated by a formula:

Marginal propensity to consume

$$= \frac{\text{change in consumption}}{\text{change in income}}$$

It thus reveals the fraction of each extra dollar of income that is spent on consumption.

marginal propensity to import (MPM) The change in imports resulting from a unit change in income. *MPM* may be calculated from the formula:

$$\text{Marginal propensity to import} = \frac{\text{change in imports}}{\text{change in income}}$$

It thus reveals the fraction of each extra dollar of income that will be spent on imports.

marginal propensity to invest Change in investment resulting from a unit change in aggregate output. It is calculated by a formula:

Marginal propensity to invest

$$= \frac{\text{change in investment}}{\text{change in aggregate output}}$$

marginal propensity to save (MPS) Change in saving resulting from a unit change in income. It is calculated by a formula:

$$\text{Marginal propensity to save} = \frac{\text{change in saving}}{\text{change in income}}$$

It thus reveals the fraction of each extra dollar of income that is saved.

marginal propensity to spend (MPE) Change in total spending on consumption, investment, and imports resulting from a unit change in aggregate income. The marginal propensity to spend, *MPE*, consists of the marginal propensity to consume, *MPC*, the marginal propensity to invest, *MPI*, and the marginal propensity to import, *MPM*. Thus, out of any change in aggregate income,

$$MPE = MPC + MPI + MPM$$

marginal rate of substitution (MRS) **1.** In demand theory, the rate at which a consumer is willing to substitute one commodity for another along an indifference curve. It is the amount of change in the holdings of one good that will just offset a unit change in the holdings of another good, so that the consumer's total utility remains the same. Thus, along an indifference curve,

$$\text{Marginal rate of substitution} = \frac{\text{change in good } Y}{\text{change in good } X}$$

The marginal rate of substitution is always negative because one commodity must be decreased when the other is increased in order to keep total utility the same (that is, to remain on a given indifference curve). **2.** In production theory, the marginal rate of substitution is the change in one type of productive input that will just offset a unit change in another type of productive input, so that the total level of production (along an *isoquant*) remains the same. Some examples of productive inputs are capital and labor, fertilizer and land.

marginal revenue (MR) Change in total revenue resulting from a unit change in quantity. It is calculated by a formula:

$$\text{Marginal revenue} = \frac{\text{change in total revenue}}{\text{change in quantity}}$$

Marginal revenue thus measures the gain (or loss) in total revenue that results from producing and selling an additional unit. It is analogous to marginal cost.

marginal revenue product (MRP) Change in total revenue resulting from a unit change in the quantity of a variable input employed. It is calculated by a formula:

$$\text{Marginal revenue product} = \frac{\text{change in total revenue}}{\text{change in variable input}}$$

Marginal revenue product thus measures the gain (or loss) in total revenue from adding an additional unit of a variable factor of production.

marginal tax rate Ratio, expressed as a percentage, of the change in a total tax resulting from a unit change in the base on which it is imposed. *Example:*

Marginal personal income tax rate

$$= \frac{\text{change in total personal income tax}}{\text{change in total taxable income}}$$

$$= \frac{\text{marginal tax}}{\text{marginal income}}$$

marginal utility Change in total utility resulting from a unit change in the quantity of a commodity consumed. It is calculated by a formula:

$$\text{Marginal utility} = \frac{\text{change in total utility}}{\text{change in quantity consumed}}$$

Marginal utility thus measures the gain (or loss) in satisfaction from an additional unit of a good.

margin requirements 1. Percentage down payment required of a borrower to finance the purchase of stock. This rate is set by the Federal Reserve System's Board of Governors. An increase in margin requirements is designed to dampen security purchases; a decrease, to encourage them. **2.** Percentage down payment required of a borrower to finance the purchase of futures contracts in the futures market. The rate is set by the exchange's regulatory commission.

market-clearing price The price at which there are no surpluses or shortages of a good.

market economy Economic system in which the questions of what, how much, and for whom to produce are decided in an open market through the free operation of demand and supply. There are no "pure" market economies, but several specialized markets (such as the organized commodity exchanges) closely approximate some of the properties of a pure market system. (*Compare* **command economy.**)

market failure Inability of a market, for whatever reason, to allocate resources efficiently. (The term is usually applied to a competitive market, and the cause of the failure is usually an externality.)

market price Actual price that prevails in a market at any particular moment.

market rate of interest Actual or money rate of interest that prevails in the market at any given time. (*Contrast with* **real rate of interest.**)

market share Percentage of an industry's output accounted for by an individual firm. Measures of output usually employed are sales, value added, or value of shipments.

market socialism Economic system with several distinguishing characteristics: (1) Public ownership of all enterprises and means of production and distribution (namely land and capital) deemed essential by the state. (2) Centralized planning combined with decentralized decision making in state-owned enterprises to permit flexibility in carrying out plans. (3) Free markets with limited private ownership of capital, and sometimes of land, in prescribed businesses such as farming, retailing, services, and small manufacturing. (4) Market incentives such as bonuses, profit-sharing, and prizes to encourage greater productivity and efficiency in state-owned enterprises.

Marshall, Alfred (1842–1924) English economist who synthesized neoclassical thinking around the turn of the century and made many pioneering contributions as well. Among these were making a formal distinction between the short run and the long run and describing the equilibrium of price and output resulting from the interaction of demand and supply. He also formulated the concept of elasticity, made the distinction between money cost and real cost, and framed many other economic concepts. Much of modern microeconomics stems from Marshall's work. His best-known book, *Principles of Economics,* went through eight editions and was a standard reference and text in economics from 1890 until the 1930s.

Martineau, Harriet (1802–1876) English economic educator whose book, *Illustrations of Political Economy* (1834), emphasized the teaching of economics through applications and real-life experiences. She was thus a pioneer in the use of the "case method" of teaching—along the lines used today in many business and in some economics courses.

Marx, Karl Heinrich (1818–1883) Prussian-born and German-educated founder, with Friedrich Engels (1820–1895), of so-called "scientific socialism." This consists of a body of ideas that were best expressed in Marx's most important economic work, *Das Kapital* (translated *Capital*), the first volume of which was published in 1867. The main concepts rest on five fundamental doctrines: (1) *Economic interpretation of history:* Economic forces are the prime cause of fundamental historical change. (2) *Theory of value and wages:* The value of any commodity is determined by the amount of labor-time embodied in its production. The wages that capitalists pay to labor are held at a subsistence level that is just high enough to allow the working population to sustain itself and to rear children. (3) *Theory of surplus value and capital accumulation:* The value of goods that workers produce is greater than the value, in the form of subsistence wages, that workers receive. The difference, called "surplus value," rightfully belongs to workers, but it is literally stolen from them by capitalists. Part of this surplus is used by capitalists for their personal consumption and part to acquire more labor and machines in order to perpetuate and expand the capitalistic system. (4) *Class struggle:* The capitalists' drive to increase their surplus value and to accumulate capital results in the displacement of labor and in mounting unemployment. This leads to an irreconcilable clash of interests between the working class and the capitalist class. (5) *Theory of socialist and communist evolution:* The working class (called the "proletariat"), experiencing increasing misery, will eventually rise and overthrow the capitalistic system by force. The proletariat will then dictate the establishment of a new system characterized in its early stage by socialism and in its mature stage by full communism. The motto of socialism will be: "From each according to his ability, to each according to his labor." The motto of communism will be : *"From each according to his ability, to each according to his needs."* The last quotation describes the ultimate goal of Marxism and the essence of pure communism.

materials balance   Methods and means utilized to relate specific inputs (such as raw materials, labor, and machines) to specific outputs in order to attain full utilization of resources. The objective is to produce a certain number of units of a good (such as houses) and to plan the specific quantities and combinations of inputs needed to accomplish the job. Input-output analysis provides a powerful tool for this purpose.

maximum-profit principle   Principle explaining that the most profitable combination of inputs is achieved by employing each factor of production up to the point at which the marginal cost of the factor is equal to its marginal revenue product.

median   Special type of average that divides a distribution of numbers into two equal parts—one half of all cases being equal to or greater than the median value, and one-half being equal to or less.

median voter principle   This principle states that, under the majority voting rule, the median voter—the person whose preferences are in the "middle" of all the voters—determines the outcome of an election because his or her vote ensures a majority.

mediation   Method of settling differences between two parties (such as a union and management) by the use of an impartial third party, called a mediator, who is acceptable to both sides but makes no binding decisions. Mediation in industrial relations is commonly employed to settle labor-management disputes concerning the *negotiation* of a collective-bargaining contract. The mediator tries to maintain constructive discussions, search for common areas of agreement, and suggest compromises. Federal, state, and most large local governments provide mediation services for labor-management disputes. Mediation is also sometimes called "conciliation." *(Contrast with* **arbitration**.*)*

member bank   Bank that belongs to the Federal Reserve System. All national banks (chartered by the federal government) must be members. State banks may join if they meet certain requirements.

mercantilism   Set of doctrines and practices aimed at promoting national prosperity and the power of the state by (1) accumulating precious metals (mainly gold and silver) through the maintenance of favorable trade balances, (2) achieving economic self-sufficiency through imperialism, and (3) exploiting colonies by monopolizing their raw materials and precious metals while reserving them as exclusive markets for exports. Mercantilism reached its peak in the seventeenth century, serving as a political and economic ideology in England, France, Spain, and Germany.

merger   Amalgamation of two or more firms under one ownership. The three common forms are (1) *horizontal,* uniting similar plants and products; (2) *vertical,* uniting dissimilar plants in various stages of production of the same good; and (3) *conglomerate,* uniting dissimilar plants and products.

merit good   Product provided by government because society deems some minimum amount of the commodity worthy (or meritorious) of production. Merit goods share, in different degrees, some of the properties of both public and private goods. Among numerous examples of merit goods are municipal golf courses, public libraries, national parks, public education, and public hospitals. These and other merit goods are subject to the *exclusion principle,* even though it may not always be invoked. *(See* **exclusion principle; public good.**)

microeconomics   The part of economics that is concerned with the study of specific economic units or parts of an economic system, such as its firms, industries, and households, and the relationships between these parts. It analyzes the "trees" of the economy as distinct from the "forest."

Mill, John Stuart (1806–1873)   Last of the major English classical economists. His two-volume treatise, *Principles of Political Economy* (1848), was a masterful synthesis of classical ideas. Mill advocated laissez-faire, but he was also a strong supporter of social reforms. Among them: worker education, democratic producer cooperatives, redistribution of wealth, shorter working days, taxation of unearned gains from land, and social control of monopoly. Mill supported these measures because he mistrusted government and wanted to guarantee to individual workers the benefits of their contributions to production. Therefore, although Mill was often called a socialist, he was in fact a "moderate conservative" by today's standards. He believed too strongly in individual freedom to advocate major government involvement in the economy.

minimum differences, principle of See *Hotelling's paradox.*

minimum efficient scale (MES) The smallest level of output at which a firm incurs its lowest long-run average cost, thus exhausting economies of scale.

mint ratio Under a bimetallic standard, the ratio of the weight of one metal to the other, and their equivalent in terms of the national unit of currency (such as the dollar), as defined by the government. For example, during the nineteenth century, when the United States was on a bimetallic standard, the government defined the mint ratio for many years as

15 grains of silver = 1 grain of gold = $1

The mint ratio was therefore 15:1. Since it remained fixed by law, it resulted in either gold or silver being driven out of circulation, depending on the relative market values of the two metals. *(See also bimetallic standard; Gresham's law.)*

Mitchell, Wesley Clair (1874–1948) Leading American economist during the first half of the twentieth century. Mitchell was a professor of economics at Columbia University and a founder of the National Bureau of Economic Research, one of the world's major centers for quantitative research in aggregative economic activity. Mitchell's lifework was the study of business cycles, their history, nature, and causes. Much of what is known today about economic fluctuations has grown out of the pioneering research done by Mitchell.

mixed economy Economic system in which the questions of what to produce, how much to produce, and for whom to produce are decided for some goods by the free market and for other goods by a central government authority. There are varying forms and degrees of mixed economies.

model Representation of the essential features of a theory or of a real-world situation, expressed in the form of words, diagrams, tables of data, graphs, mathematical equations, or combinations of these.

monetarism A theory of the relationship between changes in the monetary growth rate and changes in the price level. It is based on the belief that the economy is always at, or at least rapidly tending toward, full-employment equilibrium. Therefore, changes in the monetary growth rate are the primary cause of changes in the price level, and hence changes in nominal GDP. Monetarists contend that discretionary monetary policy tends to be erratic and is thus a cause of instability. To promote stability, the Federal

Reserve System should adhere to a policy based on rules, not discretion. *(See money-supply rule and monetary targeting.)*

monetary asset Claim against a fixed quantity of money, the nominal amount of which is unaffected by inflation or deflation. *Examples:* bonds, accounts receivable, savings deposits, promissory notes, and cash. For every monetary asset, there is an equal monetary liability. *(See also monetary liability.)*

monetary base *Net* monetary liabilities of government—the Fed and the Treasury—held by the public. It equals the sum of currency held by the public plus legal reserves. The monetary base may be called "high-powered" money because it supports the money supply (currency plus checkable deposits), which, because of our fractional-reserve banking system, is a *multiple* of the monetary base. The size of the monetary base thus affects the total monetary assets of the public.

Monetary Control Act See *Depository Institutions Acts.*

monetary liability Promise to pay a claim against a fixed quantity of money, the amount of which is unaffected by inflation or deflation. For every monetary liability, there is an equal monetary asset. *(See also monetary asset.)*

monetary policy Deliberate exercise of the monetary authority's (that is, the Federal Reserve's) power to induce expansions or contractions in the money supply in order to achieve price stability, to help dampen the swings of business cycles, and to bring the nation's output and employment to desired levels.

monetary standard Laws and practices that define a nation's currency and establish the conditions, if any, under which it is ultimately redeemable.

monetary targeting Proposal that the Federal Reserve link money growth to quarterly or semiannual changes in some comprehensive economic indicator, such as real GDP or a commodity price index. The purpose is to limit, if not eliminate, the central bank's discretionary power over monetary policy.

monetary theory (of business cycles) Explanation of economic fluctuations in terms of financial factors, such as changes in the quantity of money and credit and changes in interest rates. Upswings occur when credit and borrowing conditions become favorable enough for businesspeople to borrow; downswings occur when the banking system begins to restrict its expansion of money and credit.

money Anything that is widely used and freely accepted in payment for goods and services. In modern society, money has at least these four functions: (1) as a medium of exchange for conducting transactions; (2) as a measure of value for expressing the prices of things; (3) as a standard of deferred payments, which permits borrowing or lending for future repayment; and (4) as a store of value, which permits saving for future spending.

money illusion Situation in which a rise in all prices and incomes by the same proportion leads to an increase in consumption, even though real incomes remain unchanged.

money income Amount of money received for work done. It is thus the same as **nominal income**. *(Compare **real income**.)*

money market A market in which short-term debt instruments maturing in a year or less from date of issue are bought and sold. Examples include U.S. Treasury bills, corporations' commercial paper or promissory notes, and bankers' acceptances.

money multiplier Principle that states that the money supply, such as *M1*, is some multiple, *m*, of the monetary base, *B*. Thus

$$M1 = mB$$

M1 consists of currency plus checkable deposits, *B* consists of currency held by the public plus legal reserves, and *m* is the money multiplier. It should be kept in mind that *m* is not a constant but a variable. It is affected by portfolio decisions of households, financial institutions, and other businesses. These decisions also affect *B*. Therefore, *m* and *B* are *not* independent, and changes in either can influence *M1*. *(See **monetary base**.)*

money-supply rule Guide for economic expansion advanced by some economists, especially by Milton Friedman. The "rule" states that the Federal Reserve should expand the nation's money supply at a steady rate in accordance with the economy's long-term real GDP growth trend and capacity to produce. This rate is 3 to 4 percent per year for the United States. More than this would lead to strong inflationary pressures; less would tend to be stagnating if not deflationary.

money wages Wages received in cash. *(Compare **real wages**.)*

monopolistic competition Industry or market structure characterized by a large number of firms of different sizes producing heterogeneous (similar but not identical) products, with relatively easy entry into the industry.

monopoly Industry or market structure characterized by a single firm producing a product for which there are no close substitutes. The firm thus constitutes the entire industry and is a "pure" monopoly.

monopoly price The profit-maximizing price for an imperfect competitor. It is the price (and the corresponding output) at which *MC = MR* and *M < P*. At this price, the value of the last unit to the marginal user (measured by the price he or she pays for the last unit, which is equal to the price paid for any other unit) is greater than the value of the resources used to produce that unit.

monopsony Market structure characterized by only a single buyer and many sellers of a good or service. It may be thought of as a "buyer's monopoly."

moral hazard Increased risk of loss, or increased cost, incurred by one party to a contract when the other party adopts a less careful attitude. *Example:* A person insured against car theft may be more careless about taking precautions to avoid car theft. This encourages more car theft, thus raising the cost of car insurance. Moral hazard thus results from careless but legal behavior.

moral suasion Oral or written appeals by the Federal Reserve board to banks, urging them to expand or restrict credit but not requiring them to comply.

most-favored-nation clause Provision in a trade treaty by which each signatory country agrees to extend to the others the same preferential tariff and trade concessions that it may in the future extend to nonsignatories (that is, the same treatment that each gives to its "most favored nation"). Most trading countries have adhered to this principle since 1948.

multiple expansion of bank deposits Process by which a loan made by one bank is used to finance business transactions and ends up as a deposit in another bank. Part of this may be used by the second bank as a required reserve, the rest being lent out for business use so that it is eventually deposited in a third bank; and so on. The total amount of credit granted by the banking system as a whole will thus be a multiple of the initial deposit. *(See also **deposit multiplier**.)*

multiplier Principle that states that changes in investment can bring about magnified changes in income, as expressed by the equation: multiplier × change in investment = change in income. (The variables are expressed in *real*, not nominal, terms.) The multiplier coefficient is given by the formula

$$\text{Multiplier} = \frac{\text{change in income}}{\text{change in investment}}$$
$$= \frac{1}{MPS} = \frac{1}{1 - MPC}$$

in which *MPS* stands for the marginal propensity to save and *MPC* the marginal propensity to consume. *(Note:* This multiplier is sometimes called the "simple multiplier," the "investment multiplier," or the "expenditure multiplier." The last expression emphasizes the idea that *any* change in spending, whether by households, businesses, or government, and whether for consumption or for investment, can have a multiplier effect on income. However, the term *investment* is used in this definition because that is the variable that is usually assumed to change.)

multiunit bargaining Collective-bargaining arrangement covering more than one plant. It may occur between one or more forms in an industry and one or more unions, and it may take place on a national, regional, or local level. It is sometimes called "industry-wide bargaining"—usually inaccurately, because it rarely affects an entire industry.

municipals Marketable financial obligations—mostly bonds—issued by state and local government authorities (the latter including cities, towns, school districts, and so on). Interest income paid to their owners is exempt from federal income taxes and usually also from state income taxes of the state in which they are issued.

N

national bank   Commercial bank chartered by the federal government. Such banks are required to belong to the Federal Reserve System. A minority of banks today are national banks, but they hold considerably more than half the deposits of the banking system and are larger than most state-chartered banks.

National Banking Act (1863)   Legislation aimed at standardizing banking practices and reaffirming the existence of our dual banking system. The law contained the following main provisions: (1) Opportunities for banks to be federally chartered, thus making them national banks. (2) Issuance of Treasury currency backed largely by government bonds. (3) Federal taxation of state bank notes, thus forcing them out of existence. (4) Holding of cash reserves against notes and deposits.

national income (at factor cost)   **1.** Total of all net incomes earned by, or ascribed to, the factors of production. National income consists of the sum of wages, rent, interest, and profit that accrues to the suppliers of labor, land, capital, and entrepreneurship. (*Note:* National income should not be confused with the total income received by people from all sources—that is, personal income. The difference between the two is based on various accounting considerations.) **2.** In general terms and in theoretical discussions, the expression "national income" is often used in a generic sense to represent the income or output of an economy.

National Labor Relations (Wagner) Act (1935)   Basic labor relations law of the United States. It (1) guarantees the right of workers to organize and bargain collectively through representatives of their own choosing: (2) forbids employers to engage in unfair labor practices, such as discrimination or interference, and (3) authorizes the National Labor Relations Board to enforce the act and supervise free elections among a company's employees.

National Labor Relations Board (NLRB)   Government agency established under the National Labor Relations Act of 1935 to enforce that act, to investigate violations of it, and to supervise free elections among a company's employees in order to determine which union, if any, is to represent them in collective bargaining.

natural employment   *See full employment and contrast with natural unemployment.*

Natural Gas Act (1938)   Legislation granting the Federal Power Commission (FPC) authority over the interstate transportation of natural gas and empowering the Commission to regulate rates and services.

natural monopoly   Firm that experiences increasing economies of scale (that is, decreasing long-run average costs of production) over a sufficiently wide range of output, enabling it to supply an entire market at a lower unit cost than two or more firms. Electric companies, gas companies, and railroads are classic examples.

natural output level   Amount of real output produced when the economy is operating at the natural level of employment (or unemployment). The natural output level is thus the same as the economy's potential real (or full-employment) output.

natural rate of employment   Percentage of unemployment that is consistent with full (or natural) employment and a stable rate of inflation. (A stable rate of inflation is one that is neither accelerating nor decelerating, such as 6%, 8%, 10%, or any other percentage.)

natural rate of unemployment   Percentage of unemployment (including frictional and structural) that is consistent with full employment and a stable rate of inflation. (A stable rate of inflation is one that is neither accelerating nor decelerating, such as 6%, 8%, 10%, or any other percentage.)

natural unemployment   Level of unemployment (including frictional and structural) that is consistent with full (or natural) employment and a stable price level. In other words, it is the level of unemployment at which (1) there is only frictional and structural unemployment and (2) the rate of inflation is stable. *[Contrast with full (natural) employment.]*

near-monies   Assets that are almost, but not quite, money. They can easily be converted into money because their monetary values are known. *Examples:* time or savings deposits, U.S. government bonds, and cash values of insurance policies.

needs standard   Criterion of income distribution popularly expressed by the phrase, "To each according to his or her needs." This is the distributive principle of pure communism and an approximate criterion for apportioning income in most families. If you regard the needs standard as a just or equitable one, you are assuming that a central authority is capable of determining what constitutes your (and everyone else's) needs. (*Compare* **equality standard; contributive standard.**)

negative income tax   Plan for guaranteeing the poor a minimum income through a type of reverse income tax. A poor family, depending on its size and income, would be paid by the government enough either to reduce or to close the gap between what it earns and an explicit minimum level of income. That level might be equal to or above the government's designated "poverty line." As the family's income increases, the government's payment declines to zero.

negotiable certificate of deposit (CD)   Large-denomination notes (minimum: $100,000) issued by major banks. Banks sell these securities to corporations and large individual investors, who buy them for their interest payments. (*Note:* Most banks also issue deposits or savings certificates for smaller investors. However, these are merely special types of time deposits. They are smaller in size and not marketable, unlike negotiable CDs.)

negotiable order of withdrawal (NOW)   A check written against an interest-bearing account. NOW accounts are offered by most banks and other depository institutions. *(See also* **share-draft.***)*

neoclassical economics   Approach to economics that flourished in Europe and the United States between 1870 and World War I. Among its leaders were William Stanley Jevons in England, Carl Menger in Austria, Léon Walras in Switzerland, Vilfredo Pareto in Switzerland, Alfred Marshall in England, and John Bates Clark and Irving Fisher in the United States. The neoclassicists were primarily concerned with refining the principles of price and allocation theory, "marginalism," the theory of capital, and related aspects of economics. They made early and extensive use of mathematics, especially differential and integral calculus, in the development of their analyses and models. Much of the structure of modern economic science is built on their pioneering work.

net domestic product   Total sales value of goods and services available for society's consumption and for adding to its stock of capital equipment. It represents society's net output for the year and may be obtained by deducting a capital-consumption allowance from gross domestic product.

net-export effect   The change in a country's exports relative to imports resulting from a change in the domestic price level relative to foreign prices. For example, if a country's domestic price level declines relative to foreign prices, exports increase relative to imports. Therefore, net exports rise. Conversely, if the domestic price level rises relative to foreign prices, exports decrease relative to imports. Therefore, net exports decline.

net exports   The difference between the value of the economy's total exports and the value of its total imports.

net foreign factor income (NFFI)   Income received by U.S. owners of resources used abroad *minus* income paid to foreign owners of resources used in the United States. *Example:* Suppose American resource owners earn $1 billion in wages, rent, interest, and profit from foreign operations, and foreign resource owners earn $0.8 billion of similar income from U.S. operations. The difference, $0.2 billion, is *net foreign factor income* to the United States. Because *NFFI* is part of the nation's wages, rent, interest, and profit, it is included in national income. For any given year, a country's net foreign factor income may be positive, zero, or negative.

net-profit ratio   Ratio of a firm's net profit after taxes to its net sales. It is one of several general measures of a company's performance.

net revenue   A firm's "pure" or net profit, which is equal to its total revenue minus its total cost.

net worth   Difference between the total assets or things of value owned by a firm or individual and the liabilities or debts that are owed.

new classical economics   *See* **rational expectations theory.**

newly industrializing country (NIC)   A formerly less developed country that is undergoing rapid economic growth.

nominal dollars   *Same as* **current dollars.**

nominal GDP   GDP expressed in current dollars of each year, thus reflecting the actual prices of each year. *(Compare* **real GDP.***)*

nominal income   Amount of money received for work done. It is also known as **money income.** *(Compare* **real income.***)*

nonprice competition   Methods of competition that do not involve changes in selling price. *Examples:* advertising, product differentiation, and customer service.

nontariff barriers   Laws or regulations, other than tariffs, used by nations to restrict imports. For instance, in order to "protect" the health and safety of their citizens, many countries establish much higher standards of quality for various kinds of imported goods than for similar goods produced domestically. Food products and automobiles provide some typical examples. Actually, nontariff barriers (other than import quotas) are direct but subtle protective devices that are never publicly identified as such. Hence, they have become major forms of trade protection used by many countries.

normal good   A good whose consumption varies directly with money income, prices remaining constant. Most consumer goods are normal goods. *(Same as* **superior good.***)*

normal price   The dynamic equilibrium price toward which the market price is always tending but may never reach.

normal profit   Least payment that the owner of an enterprise will accept as compensation for his entrepreneurial function, including risk taking and management. Normal profit is part of a firm's total economic costs, since it is a payment that the owner must receive in order to keep him from withdrawing his capital and managerial effort and putting them into an alternative enterprise.

normative economics   A subjective approach to economics. Because it deals with "what ought to be" rather than "what is," normative economics is based on value judgments that reflect particular ethical views. Economic policies are often influenced substantially by normative considerations. *(Compare* **positive economics.***)*

Norris-La Guardia Act (1932)   Act of Congress that outlawed the yellow-dog contract and greatly restricted the conditions under which court injunctions against labor unions could be issued.

notes payable   Promises to pay the holder, such as a bank, a sum of money within the year at a stated rate of interest.

O

Okun's law Relationship between changes in unemployment and the rate of economic growth (measured by changes in real output). The law, based on long-run trends, states that unemployment (1) decreases less than 1 percent for each percentage point that the annual growth of real output exceeds its long-term average and (2) increases less than 1 percent for each percentage point that the annual growth of real output falls short of its long-term average. The economy, therefore, must continue to grow considerably faster than its long-term average rate in order to achieve a substantial reduction in the unemployment rate. (The law is attributed to Arthur Okun, chairman of the Council of Economic Advisors under President Lyndon Johnson.)

oligopoly Industry or market structure dominated by a few firms selling either (1) a homogeneous or undifferentiated product—the industry is then called a "perfect" or "pure" oligopoly—or (2) heterogeneous or differentiated products—the industry is then called an "imperfect" oligopoly. Some examples of perfect oligopolies are the copper, steel, and cement industries. Some examples of imperfect oligopolies are the automobile, soap, detergent, and household-appliance industries.

oligopsony Industry or market structure characterized by only a few buyers of a commodity. *Example:* Natural-gas pipeline companies are oligopsonists in that there are only a few of them that purchase gas for transportation from any given field.

open-market operations Purchases and sales of government securities by the Federal Reserve System. Purchases of securities are expansionary because they add to commercial banks' reserves; sales of securities are contractionary because they reduce commercial banks' reserves.

open shop Business firm in which the employer is free to hire either union members or nonmembers.

operating profit ratio Ratio of a firm's operating profit to its net sales.

opportunity cost Value of the benefit that is forgone by choosing one alternative rather than another. It is also called "alternative cost," because it represents the implicit cost of the forgone alternative to the individual, household, firm, or other decision-making entity. The opportunity cost of any decision is thus the value of the sacrificed alternative. Because it may often be subjective, opportunity cost is not entered in a firm's public accounting records. (*Compare* **outlay costs**.)

outlay costs Money expended to carry on a particular activity. They are the explicit costs that are entered in a firm's public accounting records, such as its income statement, to arrive at a measure of profit. *Examples:* wages and salaries, rent, and other money expenditures of a firm.

overinvestment theory (of business cycles) Explanation that holds that economic fluctuations are caused by too much investment in the economy as businesspeople try to anticipate rising demands during an upswing, and by sharp cutbacks in investment during a downswing when businesspeople realize they expanded too much in the previous prosperity.

P

P-star equation A formula used as one of many monetary-policy indicators by the Federal Reserve System. The equation is:

$$P* = \frac{M2 \times V2*}{Q*}$$

The symbol $P*$ represents the long-run price level, $M2$ is the medium-range measure of the money supply, $V2*$ is the long-run average (trend) of $M2$'s velocity, and $Q*$ is the long-run average (trend) of real GDP. The actual price level P at any given time is determined by the intersection of the economy's aggregate demand and aggregate supply curves. P tends to track $P*$, which in turn is linked to the growth rate of $M2$.

paradox of thrift Proposition that demonstrates that, if people as a group try to increase their saving, they may end up by saving less. The conclusion of the paradox is that an increase in saving may be desirable for an individual or family. However, for an entire economy, it will lead to a reduction in income, employment, and output if it is not offset by an increase in investment. The concept was first introduced by Bernard Mandeville in *The Fable of the Bees* (1714) and was later recognized in the writings of several classical economists. It subsequently became an integral part of Keynesian economics. Today it is viewed as a short-run, not long-run, condition.

Pareto optimality Condition that exists in a social organization when no change can be implemented that will make someone better off without making someone else worse off—each in his or her own estimation. Because an economic system is a type of social organization, Pareto optimality is synonymous with *economic efficiency*. (*See also* **efficiency**.)

Pareto, Vilfredo (1848–1923) Italian economist and sociologist who developed many elegant mathematical formulations of economic concepts, especially those pertaining to general equilibrium theory. His work provided a foundation for indifference-curve analysis. He showed that a theory of demand could be developed without dependence on utility, by observing consumer purchases of combinations of goods that are equally acceptable. Heavily influenced by Léon Walras, Pareto succeeded him as Professor of Political Economy at the University of Lausanne, Switzerland. (*See* **Pareto optimality**.)

parity price   Price that yields an equivalence to some defined standard. *Examples:* (1) In agriculture, a price for an agricultural commodity that gives the commodity a purchasing power (in terms of the goods that farmers buy) equivalent to the purchasing power that it had in a previous base period. (2) In international economics, the price or exchange rate between the currencies of two countries that makes the purchasing power of one currency substantially equivalent to the purchasing power of the other.

parity ratio   In agriculture, an index of the prices farmers receive divided by an index of the prices they pay. It is used to measure the economic well-being of agriculture as a whole.

partial-equilibrium theory   Explanation or model of a particular market, assuming that other markets are in balance. It thus ignores the interrelations of prices and quantities that may exist between markets. *Example:* Ordinary demand-and-supply analysis is normally of a partial-equilibrium nature, since it usually focuses on a single market while neglecting others.

participation rate   See *labor-force participation rate.*

partnership   Association of two or more individuals to carry on, as co-owners, a business for profit. The partners are solely responsible for the activities and liabilities of the business.

patent   Exclusive right conferred by government on an inventor, for a limited time. It authorizes the inventor to make, use, transfer, or withhold an invention (which might be done even without a patent), but it also gives the inventor the right to exclude others or to admit them on his or her own terms (which can be done only with a patent). Patents are thus a method of promoting invention by granting temporary monopolies to inventors.

patent monopoly   Firm that exercises a monopoly because the government has conferred upon it the exclusive right—through issuance of a patent—to make, use, or vend its own invention or discovery.

peak-load pricing   A practice that utilizes the fact that demand elasticities for some products differ at certain times. Therefore, instead of charging the same price at all times, the seller charges a higher price during peak-demand periods, when demand is more inelastic, and a lower price at other times. In this way, the selling firm reallocates its limited facilities during periods of high demand, thus reducing consumption and obtaining a more even use of its facilities at all times. *Example:* Telephone companies charge higher long-distance rates during the daytime (a peak period) and lower rates during the night (an off-peak period). Some electric utilities practice peak-load pricing based on different time periods.

perfect competition   Name given to an industry or market structure characterized by a large number of buyers and sellers all engaged in the purchase and sale of a homogeneous commodity, with perfect knowledge of market prices and quantities, no discrimination in buying or selling, and perfect mobility of resources (*Note:* The term is usually employed synonymously with *pure competition,* although there is a technical distinction. Pure competition does not require perfect knowledge or perfect resource mobility, and hence it does not produce as smooth or rapid an adjustment to equilibrium as does perfect competition. However, both types of competition lead to essentially the same results in economic theory.)

permanent-income hypothesis   Proposition that states that a family's propensity to consume (that is, the amount it spends on consumption) depends on its anticipated long-run or permanent income—the average income expected to be received over a number of years. In addition, the theory holds that a family's consumption is approximately proportional to its permanent income. This hypothesis is thus an alternative theory of the consumption function. (*Contrast with* **absolute-income hypothesis; relative-income hypothesis.**)

personal income (**PI**)   In national-income accounting, the total income received by persons from all sources.

personal income distributions   Shares of total income received by people. The shares are often expressed in terms of percentages of aggregate income received by each fifth of all families, or in terms of the percentage of families falling within specific income classes.

Phillips curve   Curve that represents a statistical relationship between unemployment and inflation. Every point on the curve denotes a different combination of unemployment and inflation. A movement along the curve reflects the change in one of these variables associated with a change in the other.

Phillips Petroleum case (1954)   Major regulation case in which the Supreme Court authorized the Federal Power Commission to regulate natural-gas prices that producers charge interstate pipeline companies. This was the first time in the nation's history that the Supreme Court ordered a regulatory commission to expand the scope of its authority.

physiocrats   Group of French economists of the middle eighteenth century led by François Quesnay. In 1758, Quesnay presented a circular-flow diagram to depict what he called the "natural order" of an economic system. This model was a crude forerunner of general-equilibrium theory, which was developed in mathematical precision in the late nineteenth century.

planned economy   Economic system in which the government, according to a preconceived plan, plays a primary role in directing economic resources for the purpose of deciding what to produce, how much, and possibly for whom.

planning-program-budgeting system (**PPBS**)   Method of revenue and expenditure management based on (1) determination of goals, (2) assessment of their relative importance to society, and (3) allocation of resources needed to attain the goals at least cost. In more general terms, PPBS is a budgeting method that relates expenditures to specific goals or programs so that the costs of achieving a particular program can be identified, measured, planned, and controlled.

plant Establishment that produces or distributes goods and services. In economics, a "plant" is usually thought of as a firm, but it may also be one of several plants owned by a firm.

policy analysis Formulation of problems within a conceptual framework so that they can be evaluated by the use of fundamental principles. Policy analysis is thus a scientific approach to the study of public issues. It differs from policy description in that it permits rigorous evaluations of problems rather than mere narrations of them. For example, because the news media address the lay public, they tend to concentrate more on policy description than on policy analysis.

policy ineffectiveness proposition Argument advanced by new-classical economists. It holds that widely expected or *systematic* fiscal-monetary policies have no impact when initiated because they've already been incorporated into people's decisions. The only policies that cause changes in people's behavior are the ones that are not expected—the *surprise* policies. These, however, aren't advisable because they cause uncertainty and instability. Therefore, government should adhere to fiscal-monetary *rules* of balanced budgets and steady monetary growth in order to ensure stability. *(See **rational expectations theory** for a fuller explanation.)*

pollution rights Licenses or permits that give the purchaser the right to release up to a specified amount of pollutants in a given place during a given period of time. These licenses are then bought and sold in an organized market not unlike the stock market.

positive economics An objective approach to economics. Because it deals with empirically verifiable statements—"what is," rather than "what ought to be"—positive economics is based on no particular ethical positions and makes no value judgments. Economic principles are examples of positive economics.

potential real output The level of aggregate output in constant dollars that would exist if the economy were at full or natural employment.

poverty line Measure of poverty among families, defined in terms of a sliding income scale that varies between rural and urban locations according to family size.

precautionary motive Desire on the part of households and businesses to hold part of their assets in liquid form so that they can be prepared for unexpected contingencies. This motive is influenced primarily by income levels rather than by changes in the interest rate, and it is one of the chief sources of demand for loanable funds in the modern theory of interest.

preferred stock Shares of stock that receive priority (that is, preference) over common stock at a fixed rate in the distribution of dividends—or in the distribution of assets, if the company is liquidated.

prepayments Business expenditures made in advance for items that will yield portions of their benefits in the present and in future years. *Examples:* advance premiums on a fire-insurance policy; expenses incurred in marketing a new product.

present value Discounted value of future sums of money. The discount is taken at a specified interest rate for a specified period of time. Present value is thus a sum of money adjusted for interest over time.

price The exchange value of a commodity—that is, the power of a commodity to command some other commodity, usually money, in exchange for itself.

price-consumption curve (PCC) In indifference-curve analysis, a line that connects the tangency points of price lines and indifference curves by showing the amounts of two goods that a consumer will purchase when his or her income and the price of one good remain constant while the price of the other good varies.

price discrimination Practice by a seller of charging different prices to the same or to different buyers for the same good, without corresponding differences in costs. (It may also consist of charging buyers the same price despite corresponding differences in costs.)

price elasticity of demand The ratio of the percentage change in quantity (demanded or supplied) to the percentage change in price.

$$\text{Price elasticity} = \frac{\text{percentage change in quantity}}{\text{percentage change in price}}$$

price leadership Adherence by firms in an oligopolistic industry, often tacitly and without formal agreement, to the pricing policies of one of its members. Frequently, but not always, the price leader will be the largest firm in the industry and other firms will simply go along with the leader by charging the same price.

price line (budget constraint) In indifference-curve analysis, a line representing all the possible combinations of two commodities that a consumer can purchase at a particular time, given the market prices of the commodities and the consumer's money budget or income.

price maker A market participant that has sufficient market power to influence the price of a good.

price system Mechanism that allocates scarce goods or resources by rationing them among those buyers and sellers in the marketplace who are willing and able to trade at the going prices. The term is often used to express the way prices are established through the free play of demand and supply in competitive markets composed of many buyers and sellers. In reality, of course, there may be "noncompetitive" price systems in markets where buyers or sellers are relatively few in number.

price taker A market participant who does not have sufficient market power to influence the price of a good.

primary reserves A bank's legal reserves (consisting of vault cash and demand deposits with the Federal Reserve Bank) and demand deposits with other banks.

prime rate Interest rate charged by banks on loans to their most credit-worthy customers.

principal/agent problem Relationships, which may be conflicting or cooperative, that arise when one party empowers another to act as a representative. *Example:* Stockholders of a corporation are principals who employ managers to act as agents. This may create some opposing as well as mutually beneficial consequences.

principle Fundamental law or general truth. It is often stated as an expression of a relationship between two or more variables. *(See also law.)*

private benefit Utility that accrues to an individual, household, or firm as a result of a particular act. *(Compare social benefit.)*

private cost Disutility (including dollar cost) that accrues to an individual, household, or firm as a result of a particular act. *(Compare social cost.)*

private goods Privately owned and controlled goods and services allocated by markets. Sellers can transfer ownership of private goods to buyers in return for payment.

private property Basic institution of capitalism that gives each individual the right to acquire economic goods and resources by legitimate means and to use or dispose of them as he or she wishes. This right may be modified by society to the extent that it affects public health, safety, or welfare.

private rate of return The business or financial rate of return on an investment—that is, the rate that businesspeople try to anticipate before investing their funds. In financial terms, it is the expected net profit after taxes and all costs, including depreciation, and may typically be expressed as a percentage annual return upon either the total cost of a project or the net worth of the stockholder owners.

private sector That segment of the total economy consisting of households and businesses, and a foreign sector, but excluding government.

"process of creative destruction" An expression coined by the economist Joseph Schumpeter (1883–1950) to describe the growth of a capitalistic economy as a process of replacing the old with the new—that is, old methods of production, old sources of supply, and old skills and resources with new ones.

Producer Price Index (PPI) Average of selected items priced in wholesale markets, including raw materials, semi-finished products, and finished goods. The PPI is published monthly by the Bureau of Labor Statistics of the U.S. Department of Labor.

producer's surplus Difference between what a producer receives and the minimum amount, called the *supply price,* he or she would be willing to accept for a given quantity of a good. *(Contrast with consumer's surplus.)*

production function Relationship between the number of units of inputs that a firm employs and the corresponding units of output produced.

production-possibilities curve Curve that depicts all possible combinations of total output for an economy. The curve assumes (1) a choice between producing either one or both of two kinds or classes of goods; (2) full and efficient employment of all resources (that is, no underemployment); and (3) a fixed supply of resources and a given state of technological knowledge.

productivity Relationship between the output of goods or services and one or more of the inputs used to produce the output. Productivity is calculated from a ratio:

$$\text{Productivity} = \frac{\text{output}}{\text{input}}$$

A distinction is made between two measures of productivity—partial and total-factor. *Partial productivity* uses only one input in the denominator, as in output per worker or yield per acre. *Total-factor productivity* uses a "weighted" sum of all measurable inputs (land, labor, capital) employed in production. Because of the difficulty of measuring *all* inputs in a production process, partial rather than total-factor productivity is the most widely used type of measure.

product markets Markets in which businesses sell outputs that they produce (in contrast with resource markets in which they buy the inputs they need in order to produce).

profit 1. Return to those who perform the entrepreneurial function. The residual (if any) after the payment of wages, rent, and interest to the owners of labor, land, and capital. 2. Difference between total revenue and total cost. It is the same as net revenue, a residual or surplus over and above normal profit that accrues to the entrepreneur/owner after all economic costs, including explicit (outlay) and implicit (opportunity) costs, have been deducted from total revenue.

progressive tax Tax whose percentage rate increases as the tax base increases. The U.S. personal income tax is an example. The tax is graduated so that, other things being equal and assuming no loopholes, a person with a higher income pays a greater percentage of his income and a larger amount of tax than a person with a lower income.

promissory note Commitment by one person to pay another a specified sum of money by a given date, usually within a year. It is thus an "I.O.U." Such notes are used by individuals, corporations, and government agencies.

propensity to consume   Relationship between consumption expenditures and income such that, as income increases, consumption increases, but not as fast as income. A graph or equation that expresses this relationship is called a *consumption function.*

propensity to save   Relationship between saving and income such that, as income increases, saving increases, but faster than income.

property resources   Nonhuman productive resources of an economy, including its natural resources, raw materials, machinery and equipment, and transportation and communication facilities.

property tax   Tax on any kind of property, whether real property (land and buildings) or personal property (such as stocks, bonds, and home furnishings).

proportional tax   Tax whose percentage rate remains constant as the tax base increases; hence, the amount of the tax paid is proportional to the tax base. The property tax is an example. Thus, if the tax rate remains constant at 10 percent, a taxpayer who owns $10,000 worth of property pays $1,000 in taxes, and a taxpayer who owns $100,000 worth of property pays $10,000 in taxes.

proprietorship   Simplest form of business organization, in which the owner or proprietor is solely responsible for the activities and liabilities of the business.

prosperity   Upper phase of a business cycle, in which the economy is operating at or near full employment and a high degree of business and consumer optimism is reflected by a vigorous rate of capital investment and consumption.

psychological theory (of business cycles)   Explanation of economic fluctuations in terms of people's responses to political, social, an economic events. These responses, the theory holds, set off cumulative waves of optimism and pessimism, causing cycles in economic activity.

public choice   Branch of economics concerned with the study of nonmarket collective decision making, or the application of economics to political science. In less formal terms, public choice is an economic approach to the study of politics. The goal of public choice is to develop ways of understanding how government works. Such knowledge enables us to suggest ways of improving efficiency in the public sector.

public good   One that is not subject to the exclusion principle. That is, the good's benefits are indivisible and hence no one can be excluded from its consumption for not paying. Therefore, most public goods, but not all, are produced by the public sector because the private sector is usually unable or unwilling to provide them. Other characteristics of a public good are (1) very low (or even zero) incremental or marginal costs and (2) spillover costs to some groups and spillover benefits to others. *Examples:* national defense, fire protection, air-traffic control, radio broadcasting, and most television transmission.

public sector   That segment of the total economy consisting of all levels of government. It is thus exclusive of the household and business segments, which constitute the private sector.

public works   Government-sponsored construction, defense, or development projects that usually (but not always) entail public investment expenditures that would not ordinarily be undertaken by the private sector of the economy.

pure competition   *See* **perfect competition** *for similarities and differences.*

pure interest rate   Theoretical interest rate on a long-term, riskless loan, where the interest payments are made solely for the use of someone else's money. In practice, this rate is often approximated by the interest rate on long-term negotiable government bonds.

pure market economy   Competitive economic system characterized by many buyers and sellers, so that prices are determined by the free interaction of demand and supply.

Q

quality circles   Committees of a company's workers that meet periodically to discuss ways of improving production methods, job satisfaction, and productivity.

quantity theory of money   Classical theory of the relationship between the price level and the money supply. It holds that the level of prices in the economy is directly proportional to the quantity of money in circulation. The relationship is such that a given percentage change in the stock of money will cause an equal percentage change in the price level in the same direction. The theory assumes that the income velocity of circulation of money remains fairly stable and that the quantity of goods and services is constant because the economy is always at, or is rapidly tending toward, full employment. *(See also* **equation of exchange.***)*

quasi-public good   *Same as* **merit good.**

R

Ramsey pricing   Method of regulatory pricing, especially for a natural monopoly producing several products. In such a firm, marginal costs are less than average total costs. Therefore, a price structure that covers the firm's full costs results in marginal cost being less than price ($MC < P$). This causes a misallocation of resources. Ramsey pricing minimizes the misallocation by setting prices relative to marginal cost in *inverse relation to demand elasticity.* Thus, in a regulated industry, prices of goods that are relatively inelastic in demand would be set to yield a higher ratio of price to marginal cost than prices of goods that are relatively elastic in demand.

rate of return   The interest rate that equates the present value of cash returns on an investment with the present value of the cash expenditures relating to the investment. That is, the rate of return on an investment is the interest rate at which the investment is repaid by its net receipts (that is, the difference between total receipts and total costs).

rate-of-return pricing   Method of pricing designed to yield a profit equal to a specific percent of the value of a firm's physical capital. The percentage, such as 10%, 12%, or some other percent, is called the "rate of return." State regulatory agencies frequently impose this method of pricing on public utilities—electric companies, bus companies, etc. The agency requires a firm to set prices that are expected to yield a certain percentage rate of return on capital. If the expected rate of return isn't realized, the agency allows prices to be adjusted accordingly.

ratio (logarithmic) scale   Scale on a graph on which equal distances represent equal percentage changes. (It is equivalent to plotting the *logarithms* of the same data on an ordinary arithmetic scale.)

rational abstention   Decision by an individual who, after weighing the benefit and cost of voting, decides not to vote. This is because the chance of one vote determining the outcome of an election is practically zero. Therefore, the marginal cost (in time and effort) of voting vastly outweighs the marginal benefit. (*Contrast with* **rational ignorance.**)

rational expectations   Anticipations based on a reasoned analysis of available (but not necessarily *all*) information. They are thus the *best possible* forecasts—called *optimal* forecasts—given the existing facts. Therefore, rational expectations need not always be accurate; they need only be correct *on average*.

rational expectations theory   Belief that people learn to anticipate recurring or systematic fiscal and monetary policies. Consequently, when the government initiates such policies, they affect only nominal variables such as prices, not real variables such as employment and output. The only policy moves that alter real variables are the ones that aren't expected—the surprise moves. But these cause uncertainty and instability. Therefore, to reduce the severity of business cycles, government should adhere to predictable macroeconomic policies—namely, balanced budgets and steady money growth. (Rational expectations theory is the basis of new classical economics.)

rational ignorance   Conscious decision by a voter to remain uninformed about an election issue. The decision is made because the marginal cost (in terms of time and effort) of becoming informed exceeds the marginal benefit—the low probability that the voter's preferred outcome will be realized because that vote is only one of many. (*Contrast with* **rational abstention.**)

rationing   Any method of restricting the purchases or use of a good. Government may, for various reasons, institute a system of rationing when, over an extended period of time, the quantity demanded of a good exceeds the quantity supplied at a given price.

real asset   Claim against a fixed amount of a commodity or the right to a commodity, the money value of which is affected by inflation or deflation. *Examples:* house, car, and most other goods and services. (*See also* **real liability.**)

real-balance effect   Proposition that states that changes in the average price level affect the public's real cash balances and hence people's spending behavior. For example, a decline in the average price level causes the real value or purchasing power of the cash balances held by the public to increase. Therefore, people expand their spending on goods and services. Conversely, a rise in the average price level causes the real value of the public's cash balances to decrease. Therefore, people contract their spending on goods and services. (*Note:* The real balance effect assumes that "all other things," especially the economy's money supply, remain constant.)

real business cycle theory   Doctrine that economic fluctuations are due to shifts in aggregate supply that are caused by random (and therefore unpredictable) supply-side shocks. Examples of such random shocks are changes in technology, government regulations, and prices of basic commodities such as oil and other raw materials that are widely used in production. Because the Fed alters the money growth rate in response to these real forces at work in the economy, monetary policy is a result of the business cycle, not a cause of it. Therefore, although monetary policy has no effect on real output and employment, it's nevertheless an important determinant of inflation. Other aspects of the theory include the propositions that (1) unemployment is entirely voluntary because people can always find work if they want to accept available jobs, (2) business cycles exist without expectational errors, and (3) business cycles are socially optimal.

real dollars   Nominal dollars adjusted for price changes. (*See* **constant dollars.**)

real GDP   GDP expressed in constant dollars of a previous period, thus reflecting the actual prices of that period. (*Compare* **nominal GDP.**)

real income   Purchasing power of money income or the quantity of goods and services that can be bought with money income. (*Compare* **nominal income.**)

realized investment   Actual investment out of any realized level of income. Equal to the sum of planned and unplanned (inventory) investment.

real liability   Promise to pay a fixed amount of a commodity, or right to a commodity, the money value of which is affected by inflation or deflation. (*See also* **real asset.**)

real output   Value of physical output unaffected by price changes.

real rate of interest   The interest rate measured in terms of goods. It is the rate that would prevail in the market if the general price level remained stable. Factors determining it are "real demand" for funds by businesses and "real supply" of funds by households. The former, in turn, is determined by the productivity of borrowed capital, and the latter by the willingness of consumers to abstain from present consumption. (*Contrast with* **market rate of interest**.)

real wages   Quantity of goods that can be bought with money wages. Real wages thus depend on the prices of the goods bought with money wages.

recession   Downward phase of a business cycle, in which the economy's income, output, and employment are decreasing and a falling off of business and consumer optimism is reflected by a declining rate of capital investment and consumption.

recessionary gap   Amount by which aggregate real output exceeds aggregate expenditure at full (natural) employment. Also, the amount by which potential real output exceeds actual real output at the latter's corresponding equilibrium price level. Either condition exerts downward pressure on production, employment, and prices.

Reciprocal Trade Agreements program   Plan for expanding American exports through legislation that authorizes the President to negotiate U.S. tariff reductions with other nations in return for parallel concessions. The program consists of the Trade Agreements Act of 1934, with subsequent amendments, and related legislation.

recovery   Upward phase of a business cycle, in which the economy's income, output, and employment are rising and a growing degree of business and consumer optimism is reflected by an expanding rate of capital investment and consumption.

refunding   Replacement or repayment of outstanding bonds by the issuance of new bonds. It is thus a method of prolonging a debt by paying off old obligations with new obligations.

regressive tax   Tax whose percentage rate decreases as the tax base increases. In this strict sense, there is no regressive tax in the United States. However, if we compare the rate structure of the tax with the taxpayer's net income rather than with its actual base, the term "regressive" applies to any tax that takes a larger share of income from low-income taxpayers than from high-income taxpayers. Most proportional taxes are thus seen to have regression effects. A sales tax, for instance, is the same for rich people as for poor people. But the latter spend a larger percentage of their incomes on the consumer goods. Therefore, the sales taxes they pay—assuming that there are few if any exemptions—are a greater proportion of their incomes.

relative-income hypothesis   Proposition that states that a family's propensity to consume (that is, the amount it spends on consumption) depends on its previous peak level of income or on the relative position that the family occupies along the income scale. A family's spending behavior is thus influenced by the highest past income levels to which it has become accustomed and by the incomes of other families in the same socioeconomic environment. This hy-pothesis is an alternative theory of the propensity to consume. (*Contrast with* **absolute-income hypothesis; permanent-income hypothesis**.)

rent   Return to those who supply the factor of production known as "land."

rent seeking   Effort by individuals or firms to receive benefits, usually by political means, that they would not otherwise receive. *Examples:* An industry that lobbies in Congress for import protection; a labor union that seeks pro-union legislation.

repurchase agreement (RP or "repo")   A type of collateralized loan. The borrower sells the lender a debt instrument, usually a government security, and simultaneously agrees to buy it back on a later date at the same price, plus interest at a specified rate. The lender (investor) thus holds a security as collateral for a loan of fixed maturity at a fixed interest rate. Banks, often in need of short-term funds, are major users of RPs. They are sold to corporations and to large individual customers who have surplus cash balances to lend.

required reserves   Minimum amount of legal reserves that a bank is required by law to keep against deposit liabilities. Thus, if the reserve requirement is 10 percent, a bank with demand deposits of $1 million must hold at least $100,000 of required legal reserves.

resale price maintenance   Practice whereby a manufacturer or distributor of a branded product sets the minimum retail price at which that product can be sold, thereby eliminating price competition at the retail level.

reservation price   Lowest price at which a seller will offer a minimum amount of a good. Graphically, the reservation price is the one that corresponds to the lowest point on a supply curve. This price, therefore, determines the *height* of the curve. (*Contrast with* **supply price**. Note that the supply price is the same as the reservation price *only* at the lowest point on a supply curve.)

reservation wage   Lowest wage rate at which a worker will offer a minimum amount of labor. Graphically, the reservation wage is the one that corresponds to the lowest point on a labor-supply curve. This wage rate, therefore, determines the *height* of the curve.

resource markets   Markets in which businesses buy the inputs or factors of production they need to carry on their operations.

restrictive agreement   Conspiracy of firms that restrains trade among separate companies. It may involve a direct or indirect form of price fixing, output control, market sharing, coercion, exclusion of competitors, and so on. It is illegal under the antitrust laws.

restrictive license   Agreement whereby a patentee permits a licensee to sell a patented product under restricted conditions. The restrictions may include the patentee's limiting the geographic area in which the licensee may operate, level of output, or limiting the price the licensee may charge in selling the patented good.

return on net worth   Ratio of a firm's net profit after taxes to its net worth. It provides a measure of the rate of return on stockholders' investment.

return on total assets   Ratio of a firm's net profit after taxes to its total assets. It measures the rate of return on, or the productivity of, total assets.

revaluation   Official (government) act that makes a domestic currency more expensive in terms of foreign currencies (or in terms of gold under a gold standard). (*Contrast with* ***devaluation***.)

revenue sharing   Plan by which the federal government turns over a portion of its tax revenues to state and local governments each year.

Ricardian equivalence theorem   *See* ***debt neutrality proposition***.

Ricardo, David (1772–1823)   English classical economist, generally regarded as the "greatest of the classical economists." Ricardo was responsible for refining and systematizing much of classical economic thinking. He formulated theories of value, rent, wages, and international trade, some of which have since been modified but many of which have endured to the present. In general, Ricardo held a scientific view of the economy; therefore, the task of economists, he believed, was to discover the laws that determine economic behavior. Among Ricardo's chief contributions that are of major relevance today are the ***law of diminishing returns***—one of the most fundamental laws of economics; the theory of economic rent (studied in microeconomics); and the ***law of comparative advantage*** (studied in international economics).

right-to-work laws   State laws that make it illegal to require membership in a union as a condition of employment. These laws exist mostly in southern and midwestern states; their main effect is to outlaw the union shop, but in practice they have been relatively ineffective.

risk   Quantitative measurement of the mathematical probability (or "odds") that a given outcome (such as a gain or a loss) will occur. Because risk is predictable, losses that arise from risk can be estimated in advance and can be "insured" against—either by the firm itself or by an insurance company. *Examples:* The losses resulting from rejects on an assembly line can be "self-insured" by being built into the firm's cost structure; the possibility of fire damage can be externally insured by an insurance company.

rival consumption, principle of   Principle stating that the use of a good by one person prevents another from receiving its benefits. *Example:* A hamburger is *rival* in consumption because, when it is eaten by one person, it can't be enjoyed by others.

Robinson, Joan (1903–1983)   English economist who is best known for her distinguished treatise *The Economics of Imperfect Competition*, published in 1933. In this book, she identi-fied and developed the new concept of monopolistic competition (which she called "imperfect competition"). This type of market structure, she emphasized, was characterized by "partial monopolies" producing similar products in order to fulfill diversified consumer preferences. Imperfect competition, she said, was thus a realistic market structure. Therefore, its underlying theory must be understood in order to evaluate the market behavior of a major segment of the private sector.

Robinson-Patman Act (1936)   A major antitrust law of the United States, and an amendment to Section 2 of the Clayton Antitrust Act dealing with price discrimination. Commonly referred to as the "Chain Store Act," it was passed to protect independent retailers and wholesalers from "unfair discrimination" by larger sellers who enjoy "tremendous purchasing power." The act declared the following illegal: (1) payment of brokerage fees when no independent broker is employed; (2) granting of discounts and other concessions by sellers (such as manufacturers) to buyers (such as wholesalers and retailers), unless such concessions are made to all buyers on proportionately equal terms; (3) price discrimination, except where the price differences make "due allowances" for differences in cost or are offered "in good faith to meet an equally low price of a competitor"; and (4) charging lower prices in one locality than in another, or selling at "unreasonable low prices," when either of these practices is aimed at "destroying competition or eliminating a competitor."

rule of reason   Interpretation of the courts (first announced in the Standard Oil case of 1911) that the mere size of a corporation, no matter how impressive, is no offense. To be held in violation of antitrust law, a firm must show "unreasonable" exertion of monopoly power. This interpretation, also known as the "good-trust-versus-bad-trust" criterion, was largely reversed in the Aluminum Company of America case in 1945. Nevertheless, the "reasonableness" of market behavior is still a factor that is often considered by the courts in antitrust cases.

rule of 72   Approximate formula for expressing the relationship between the number of years, *n*, required for a quantity to double if it grows at an annual rate of compound interest, *r*. Thus, $nr = 72$. Therefore,

$$n = \frac{72}{r} \quad \text{and} \quad r = \frac{72}{n}$$

Example: At 6 percent interest compounded annually, a quantity will double in $n = 72/6 = 12$ years. Similarly, if a quantity doubles in 12 years, the compounded annual rate of growth is $r = 72/12 = 6$ percent.

S

sales tax   A flat percentage levy imposed on retail prices of selected items. The rates and the items taxed vary from state to state.

Samuelson, Paul Anthony (1915–) Leading American economist and the first American to receive the Nobel Prize in Economic Science. Samuelson's publications are extensive. His first treatise, Foundations of Economic Analysis (1947), based on his doctoral dissertation, explored the notion of equilibrium in many new and provocative ways. It also developed a concept of economic dynamics that was highly original and sophisticated. His hundreds of articles range through numerous areas of economics. Many of these articles, dealing with both macroeconomic and microeconomic topics, have become classics. In addition, Samuelson authored an introductory text that served as the standard work in the field for several decades.

"satisfice" A concept to convey the idea that, in reality, firms seek not to maximize profit but to achieve certain levels of satisfaction. *Example:* Firms try to attain a particular target level or rate of profit, and they try to achieve a specific share of the market or a certain level of sales.

saving That part of income not spent on the consumption of goods and services.

Say, Jean Baptiste (1767–1832) French classical economist. He is best known for his popularization of Adam Smith's *Wealth of Nations* (1776) and for formulating the "Law of Markets"— the classical doctrine that supply creates its own demand. Say's law thus asserted the impossibility of general overproduction. This idea was central to classical economic thought, because it led to the conclusion that markets were "self-correcting" if left free of government intervention.

Say's law An assertion that "supply creates its own demand." That is, the total supply of goods produced must always equal the total demand for them, since goods fundamentally exchange for goods while money serves only as a convenient medium of exchange. Therefore, any general overproduction is impossible. This assertion, named after the French economist Jean Baptiste Say (1767–1832), was fundamental in classical economic thought, for it led to the conclusion that the economy would automatically tend toward full employment equilibrium if the government followed a policy of laissez-faire.

scarcity At any given time and place, economic goods, including resources and finished goods, are limited in the sense that they have alternative uses. These scarce goods can be increased, if at all, only through sacrifice of other resources or goods.

scarcity rent The economic rent earned by an exhaustible resource.

Schumpeter, Joseph Alois (1883–1950) Leading Austrian-American economist. His theories can be expressed in the form of several fundamental propositions. (1) The entrepreneur (that is, the businessperson) is the central actor– the prime mover of capitalism. (2) In striving for profit, the entrepreneur innovates by introducing new production techniques and new organizational methods. (3) Innovations cause economic growth, but they are also responsible

for business cycles, which ultimately lead to the erosion of capitalism. (4) This erosion is already occurring because the capitalistic institutions that encouraged and nurtured entrepreneurship in the nineteenth and early twentieth centuries have either disappeared or undergone substantial change.

scientific method A disciplined mode of inquiry represented by the processes of induction, deduction, and verification. The essential steps of the scientific method consist of (1) recognition and definition of a problem, (2) observation and collection of relevant data, (3) organization and classification of data, (4) formulation of hypotheses, (5) deductions from the hypotheses, and (6) testing and verification of the hypotheses. All scientific laws may be modified or challenged by alternative theoretical formulations, and hence the entire cycle consisting of these six steps is a self-correcting process.

seasonal fluctuations Short-term swings in business and economic activity within the year that are due to weather and custom. *Examples:* upswings in retail sales during holiday periods, such as Christmas and Easter; changes between winter and summer buying patterns.

secondary boycott Attempts by a union, through strikes, picketing, or other methods, to stop one employer from doing business with another employer. Outlawed by the Labor-Management Relations (Taft-Hartley) Act of 1947.

secondary reserves A bank's earnings assets that are near-liquid (that is, readily convertible into cash on short notice without substantial loss). *Examples:* short-term financial obligations, such as U.S. Treasury bills, high-grade commercial paper, bankers' acceptances, and call loans.

Second Bank of the United States Chartered for the period 1816 to 1836, the Bank's functions were to serve as fiscal agent for the Treasury, issue its own notes, and finance both rural and commercial business interests. However, the Bank's generally conservative policies caused periods of financial strain throughout the economy. When Andrew Jackson, a "hard-money" advocate who opposed the issuance of paper money by banks, became the nation's President in 1828, he undertook measures to weaken the Bank's effectiveness. As a result, when the Bank's federal charter expired in 1836, it was not renewed.

selling costs Marketing expenditures aimed at adapting the buyer to the product. *Examples:* advertising, sales promotion, and merchandising.

separation of ownership and control The notion that, in a modern large corporation, there is a distinction between those who own the business (the stockholders) and those who control it (the hired managers). If stock ownership is widely dispersed, the managers may be able to keep themselves in power for their own benefit rather than for the primary benefit of the corporation and its stockholders.

shadow prices Estimates of a commodity's prices that would prevail in a highly competitive market composed of many buyers and sellers. Shadow prices are established for accounting purposes as a means of valuing goods and resources that are not valued in the desired way by the price mechanism.

share draft A check written against an interest-bearing account provided by a credit union. Share draft accounts are one of several forms of savings-type checkable deposits. (*See also **negotiable order of withdrawal**.*)

Sherman Antitrust Act (1890) A major antitrust law of the United States. It prohibits contracts, combinations, and conspiracies in restraint of trade, as well as monopolization or attempts to monopolize in interstate trade or foreign commerce. Violations are punishable by fines, imprisonment, or both.

shortage The amount by which the quantity demanded of a commodity exceeds the quantity supplied at a given price, as when the given price is below the free-market equilibrium price. (*Compare **surplus**.*)

short run **1. Macroeconomics.** Period in which most prices are sticky. This results in market surpluses and shortages that delay the economy's tendency to self-correct. **2. Microeconomics.** Period in which a firm can vary its output through a more or less intensive use of its resources but cannot vary production capacity because it has a fixed plant scale.

simple multiplier *See **multiplier**.*

single tax Proposal advanced by the American economist Henry George (1839–1897). It contended that the *only* tax a society should impose is a tax on land. This is because all rent on land is unearned surplus that increases as a result of natural progress and economic growth. Three major shortcomings have been leveled against this thesis. (1) A single tax on land would not yield enough revenues to meet government's spending needs. (2) A single tax on land would be unjust, because surpluses would accrue to resource owners other than landlords if the owners were to gain some monopolistic control over the sale of their resources in the marketplace. (3) A single tax on land would be difficult to administer because it would not distinguish between land and capital—that is, between the proportion of rent that represents a surplus and the proportion that results from improvements made on the land.

slope Rate of change or steepness of a line as measured by the change (increase or decrease) in its vertical distance per unit of change in its horizontal distance. It may be calculated from a ratio:

$$\text{Slope} = \frac{\text{change in vertical distance}}{\text{change in horizontal distance}}$$

Hence, a horizontal line has a zero slope, and a vertical line has an "infinite" slope. All straight lines that are upward or positively inclined have a slope greater than zero. (Analogously, all straight lines that are downward or negatively in-

clined have a slope less than zero.) Parallel lines have equal slopes. The slope of a straight line is the same at every point, but the slope of a curved line differs at every point. Geometrically, the slope of a curve at a particular point can be found by drawing a straight line tangent to the curve at that point. The slope of the line will then be equal to the slope of the curve at the point of tangency. In economics, all "marginals" are slopes or rates of change of their corresponding "totals." *Examples:* The marginal propensity to consume represents the rate of change or slope of its corresponding total propensity to consume; a marginal-cost curve is the slope of its corresponding total-cost curve; a marginal-revenue curve is the slope of its corresponding total-revenue curve; and so on. The concept of slope or rate of change (that is, "marginality") is unquestionably the most powerful and important analytical tool of economics.

Smith, Adam (1723–1790) Scottish philosopher and author of *The Wealth of Nations* (1776). This was the first comprehensive, systematic study of economics. The treatise earned Smith the appellation "Founder of Economics." In the book, he analyzed such concepts as specialization, division of labor, value and price determination, the distribution of income, the accumulation of capital, and taxation. He argued that, if individuals were left alone to pursue their self-interests, their behavior would, as if guided by an "invisible hand," lead to maximum benefits for society. He thus concluded that laissez-faire (that is, nonintervention of government) was essential to a society's economic efficiency. (*Note:* Smith's ideas became the foundation upon which the whole subsequent tradition of classical economics was constructed.)

social balance Existence of an optimum distribution of society's resources between the private and public sectors. The former is represented by the production of private goods, such as cars, clothing, and television sets. The latter is represented by the production of such social (merit) goods as libraries, public health, and education.

social benefit Utility that accrues to society as a result of a particular act, such as production or consumption of a commodity. It includes both private and external (or spillover) benefits. Thus:

Social benefits = private benefits + spillover benefits

(*Compare **private benefit**.*)

social cost Disutility that accrues to society as a result of a particular act, such as production or consumption of a commodity. In includes private costs and reductions in incomes or benefits (externalities or spillovers) caused by the act. Thus:

Social costs = private costs + spillover costs

(*Compare **private cost**.*)

social goods Products provided by government, usually because society believes that such goods are not adequately provided by the private sector through the free market. Social goods include (1) *public goods,* such as national defense, public safety, and street lighting, and (2) *merit goods,* such as public education, libraries, and museums. *(See **public good; merit good.**)*

socialism **1.** In the theories of Karl Marx, a transitory stage between capitalism and full communism, in which the means of production are owned by the state, the state in turn is controlled by the workers ("dictatorship of the proletariat"), and the economy's social output is distributed by this formula: From each according to his ability, to each according to his labor. **2.** In its contemporary form, a movement that seeks primarily to improve economic efficiency and equity by establishing (a) public ownership of all important means of production and distribution and (b) some degree of centralized planning to determine *what* goods to produce, *how* they should be produced, and *to whom* they should be distributed. (The precise extent of public ownership and centralized planning isn't usually specified in today's socialist thinking and varies widely among countries.)

social rate of return Net value of a project to an economy (that is, of a town, city, state, or country). It is estimated on the basis of the net increase in output that a project such as a new industry may be expected to bring, directly or indirectly, to the area being developed. The industry's contribution is determined by subtracting from the value of what it produces the cost to society of the resources used. Hence the measure is intended to reflect all economic and social benefits as well as costs. *(Compare **private rate of return**.)*

Social Security Act (1935) The basic comprehensive social security law of the United States. Its programs include: (1) *Old Age and Survivors Insurance (OASI)*: This program, which is the largest of the three, is what most people refer to as "social security." It pays benefits to retired workers and their dependents and survivors. (2) *Disability Insurance (DI)*: This program awards benefits to disabled workers and their dependents. (3) *Hospital Insurance (HI)—Medicare*: This is a health-insurance program providing two sets of benefits: (a) hospital services to those over 65 years of age who are covered by social security (that is, by OASDI) and (b) supplementary medical insurance, available on an optional basis to the elderly. These last benefits are financed partly through monthly premium charges paid by participants and partly through the general tax revenues of the Treasury. (4) *Public Assistance (PA)*: This is a *noninsurance* program. It provides public charity in the form of welfare services, institutional care, food, housing, and other forms of assistance to the needy.

social security tax Payroll tax that finances the U.S. compulsory social-insurance program covering old-age and unemployment benefits. The taxes are paid both by employees and by employers, based on the incomes of the former.

Special Drawing Rights (SDRs or "paper gold") Supplementary reserves (established in 1969) in the form of account entries on the books of the International Monetary Fund.

SDRs, which are allocated among participating countries in accordance with their quotas, can be drawn upon by governments to help finance balance-of-payments deficits. They are meant to promote an orderly growth of reserves that will help the long-run expanding needs of world trade.

special interest group Organization that has more to gain, or lose, from specific government actions than the general public. It can influence the political system by lobbying legislators to support its causes.

specialization Division of productive activities among individuals and regions so that no one person or area is self-sufficient. Total production is increased by specialization, thus permitting all participants to share in a greater volume of output through the process of exchange or trade.

specie Money in the form of gold or silver coins. The nominal or stated value of the coin should equal the market value of the metal contained in the coin, but this does not usually happen. The reason is that the market value of the gold or silver in the coin fluctuates according to demand and supply. Therefore, the metallic value of the coin may be greater or less than the nominal value stated on the coin. *(See **mint ratio**.)*

specific subsidy Per-unit subsidy on a commodity. *(See also **subsidy**.)*

specific tax Per-unit tax on a good. *(See also **tax**.)*

speculation **1.** In the popular sense, any business transaction in which a high risk of loss is assumed in exchange for the chance of receiving large gains. **2.** In the futures market, the purchase or sale of a futures contract without having an offsetting interest in the actual commodity. An increase in the price of the futures contract creates a profit for buyers of the contract (who are called "longs") and a corresponding loss for sellers of the contract (who are called "shorts").

speculative motive Desire on the part of households and businesses to hold part of their assets in liquid form so that they can take advantage of changes in the interest rate. This motive is thus tied specifically to the interest rate and is one of the chief sources of demand for loanable funds in the modern theory of interest.

spillovers External benefits or costs for which no compensation is made. (Spillovers are also called ***externalities***.)

spot (cash) markets Markets that involve the immediate exchange of commodities or financial instruments for cash.

stable equilibrium Condition in which an object or system (such as a price, firm, industry, or market) in equilibrium, when subjected to a shock sufficient to disturb its position, returns toward its initial equilibrium as a result of self-restoring forces. (In contrast, an equilibrium that is not stable may be either unstable or neutral.)

stagflation Combination of *stagnation* and *inflation*. It is a condition characterized by slow economic growth, high unemployment, and rising prices. Stagflation thus combines some of the features of recession and inflation.

Standard Oil case (1911) Major antitrust case in which Standard Oil of New Jersey was ordered broken up by the Supreme Court. The Court held Standard Oil to be in violation of the Sherman Antitrust Act because the company had engaged in "unreasonable market practices, including the attempt to drive others from the field and to exclude them from their right to trade." In this case, the Court introduced an important new criterion for judging monopoly behavior. *(See rule of reason.)*

state bank Commercial bank chartered by a state government. Such banks may or may not be members of the Federal Reserve System.

static model One in which economic phenomena are studied without reference to time—that is, without relating them to preceding or succeeding events. Time, in other words, is not permitted to enter the analysis in any manner that will affect the results. A static model is thus like a "snapshot" as distinguished from a "motion picture." *(Compare dynamic model.)*

static multiplier The multiplier without regard to the time required to realize its full effect. *(Compare truncated multiplier.)*

stock Units of ownership interest in a corporation. The kinds of stock include common stock, preferred stock, and capital stock.

strategic-resource monopoly Firm that has a monopoly because it controls an essential input to a production process. *Example:* De Beers of South Africa, which once owned most of the world's diamond mines.

strategic trade policy (STP) One in which government alters the terms of competition to favor domestic over foreign firms. For instance, a protective subsidy granted to a firm with substantial economies of scale may enable the firm to capture all or at least a large share of a foreign competitor's market. In world markets dominated by a few large firms, a strategic trade policy can in theory be superior to free trade. However, there are many difficulties involved in developing the "right" strategy. Most economists, therefore, continue to believe that free trade is preferable to a strategic trade policy.

strike Agreement among workers to stop working, without resigning from their jobs, until their demands are met.

structural budget See *full-employment budget.*

structural inflation Condition of generally rising prices caused by uneven upward demand or cost pressures in some key industries, such as automobiles, construction, or steel. Structural inflation may occur even if aggregate demand is in balance with aggregate supply for the economy as a whole.

structural unemployment Type of unemployment, usually prolonged, existing because the location and skill requirements of job openings do not always match the location and skills of unemployed workers. It arises from changes in technology, markets, or national priorities. Most types of workers—unskilled, skilled, or professional—are subject to structural unemployment as a result of any of these factors.

subsidy Payment (usually by government) to businesses or households that enables them to produce or consume a product in larger quantities or at lower prices than they would otherwise.

subsistence theory of wages Theory developed by some classical economists of the late eighteenth and early nineteenth centuries. It held that wages per worker tend to equal what the worker needs to "subsist"—that is, to maintain himself and to rear children. If wages per worker rose above the subsistence level, people would tend to have more children and the population would increase, thereby lowering real incomes per capita. Similarly, if wages per worker fell below the subsistence level, people would tend to have fewer children and the population would decline, thereby increasing real incomes per capita. Wages per worker would thus tend to remain at the subsistence level over the long run. This theory is also known as the "brazen (or iron) law of wages."

substitute goods Commodities that are related such that, at a given level of buyers' incomes, an increase in the price of one good leads to an increase in the demand for the other and a decrease in the price of one good leads to a decrease in the demand for the other. *Examples:* gin and vodka, beef and pork. *(Compare complementary goods.)*

substitution effect Increased quantity demanded of a good when its price declines, because the good replaces some other goods that the consumer purchases. *Example:* A decrease in the price of beef may result in its being substituted for chicken, pork, veal, and perhaps some nonmeat products. The substitution effect assumes that the consumer's money income, tastes, and the prices of other goods remain constant. It helps explain why a demand curve slopes downward. *(See also income effect.)*

sunspot theory Theory of business cycles proposed in England during the late nineteenth century. It held that sunspot cycles (disturbances on the surface of the sun) exhibited an extremely high correlation with agricultural cycles for a number of years; therefore, sunspots must affect the weather, the weather influences agricultural crops, and the crops affect business conditions. This theory received worldwide popularity when it was first introduced, but then fell into disrepute because the high correlation between sunspots and agricultural cycles did not endure; it was the result of accidental rather than causal factors.

superior good A good whose consumption varies directly with money income, prices remaining constant. Most consumer goods are superior goods. (A superior good is also called a *normal good* because if represents the "normal" relationship between income and demand.)

supermultiplier An enlargement of the simple multiplier, reflecting the inclusion of the marginal propensity to invest, *MPI*. It may be expressed by the formula

$$\text{Supermultiplier} = \frac{1}{1 - (MPC + MPI)} = \frac{1}{1 - MPE}$$

in which *MPE* denotes the marginal propensity to spend.

supplementary (fringe) benefits Forms of compensation to workers other than basic wages, such as bonuses, pension benefits, and holiday and vacation pay.

supply A relation expressing the various amounts of a commodity that sellers would be willing and able to make available for sale at various prices during a given period of time, all other things remaining the same. This relation may be expressed as a table (called a supply schedule), as a graph (called a supply curve), or as a mathematical equation.

supply curve Graph of a supply schedule, showing the number of units of a commodity that sellers would be able and willing to sell at various prices during a given period of time, all other things remaining the same.

supply, law of Principle that states that the quantity supplied of a good usually varies directly with its price, assuming that all other things that may affect supply remain the same. These "all other" things include (1) resource prices, (2) prices of related goods in production, and (3) the state of technology and other nonmonetary determinants, such as the number of sellers in the market.

supply price Least price necessary to bring forth a given output. Hence it is the lowest price a seller is willing to accept to persuade him to supply a given quantity of a commodity.

supply schedule Table showing the number of units of a commodity that sellers would be able and willing to sell at various possible prices during a given period of time, all other things remaining the same.

supply-side economics Measures aimed at achieving efficiency through policies designed to stimulate production. While there are many policies that may encourage increased production, the most fundamental supply-side policies are those that make direct use of *incentives*. For example, reductions in marginal tax rates—the taxes paid on the last few dollars of wages, interest, and dividends—provide direct incentives to work, save, and invest. (*Contrast with* **demand-side economics**.)

surplus The amount by which the quantity supplied of a commodity exceeds the quantity demanded at a given price, as when the given price is above the free-market equilibrium price. (*Compare* **shortage**.)

surplus value In the theories of Karl Marx, the difference between the value that a worker creates (as determined by the labor-time embodied in the commodity that the worker produces) and the value that he or she receives as determined by the subsistence level of wages. This surplus, according to Marx, is appropriated by the capitalist and is the incentive for the development of a capitalist system.

surtax Tax imposed on a tax base in addition to a so-called normal tax. *Example:* a surtax on income in addition to the normal income tax. Note that a surtax is imposed on an existing tax base; it is not a "tax on a tax" as is popularly believed.

switching point Moment when a resource price, after rising far enough, equals the price of a substitute resource.

syndicalism Economic system that demands the abolition of both capitalism and the state as instruments of oppression and, in their place, the reorganization of society into industry-wide associations or syndicates of workers. The syndicates, fundamentally trade unions, would replace the state. Each syndicate would then govern its own members in their activities as producers but leave them free from interference in all other matters. The chief exponent of syndicalism was the French social philosopher Georges Sorel (1847–1922), some of whose views later influenced the growth of fascism.

T

target-return pricing Method of pricing that seeks to attain a desired (targeted) percentage rate of return on stockholders' equity or ownership at a planned level of output. The target-return price (*P*) may be expressed by the equation

$$P = \frac{\% \text{ target return stockholders' equity}}{\text{planned output quantity, } Q} + AVC_Q$$

in which AVC_Q is the direct or average variable cost of production at the planned output, *Q*. *Example:* Suppose that a firm plans to produce 10,000 units of output next year at an average variable cost of $50 per unit. If stockholders' equity is $1 million and the firm targets a 20 percent return, it will charge a price of $70 per unit:

$$P = \frac{0.20 \,(\$1,000,000)}{10,000} = \$50 = \frac{\$200,000}{10,000} + \$50$$
$$= \$70 \text{ per unit}$$

Two implications are apparent from target-return pricing: (1) Price varies directly with average variable cost and inversely with the quantity produced. (2) Target-return pricing disregards demand considerations and assumes that the firm can sell its planned output quantity at the target-return price.

tariff Customs duty or tax imposed by a government on the importation (or exportation) of a good. Tariffs may be (1) specific, in the form of a tax per unit of the commodity, or (2) ad valorem, based on the value of the commodity.

tax A compulsory payment to government. Its purposes may be (1) to influence efficiency through resource allocation (so as to produce more of some commodities and less of others); (2) to influence equity through income and wealth distribution; (3) to influence economic stabilization; and (4) to influence economic growth.

tax avoidance Legal methods or "loopholes" used by taxpayers to reduce their taxes. (*Compare* **tax evasion**.)

tax base An object that is being taxed, such as income (in the case of an income tax), the value of property (in the case of a property tax), or the value of goods sold (in the case of a sales tax.)

tax-based incomes policy (TIP) A proposal for curbing inflation. The program provides tax benefits for those workers and firms that keep wage and price increases within established guidelines and tax penalties for those that do not. The guidelines, based on the economy's productivity and the current rate of inflation—perhaps an average of both— would be announced annually by government. In general, TIP is at best a short-run anti-inflation measure because it deals with the symptoms of inflation, not the cause.

tax evasion Illegal methods of escaping taxes, such as lying about income or expenses. (*Compare* **tax avoidance**.)

tax incidence Burden of a tax—that is, the economic entities, such as households, consumers, or sellers, that ultimately bear the tax.

tax multiplier Relation between a change in personal income taxes and the resulting change in aggregate output. For example, an increase in taxes reduces people's disposable income by that amount. Because consumption depends on income, the level of consumption will decrease by *MPC* multiplied by the change in income (or taxes). This in turn will cause a magnified drop in real output, depending on the size of the expenditure multiplier, M_E. Thus the tax multiplier, M_T may be expressed by the formula

$$M_T = MPC \times M_E$$
$$= MPC \times \frac{1}{MPS}$$

tax rate Amount of tax applied per unit of tax base, expressed as a percentage. *Example:* A tax of $10 on a base of $100 represents a tax rate of 10 percent.

tax shifting Changing of the burden or incidence of a tax from the economic entity upon which it is initially imposed to some other economic entity. *Example:* Sales and excise taxes are imposed on the products of sellers, but these taxes are shifted in whole or in part through higher prices to buyers of the goods.

technical efficiency See *efficiency.*

terms of trade Number of units of goods that must be given up for one unit of goods received by each party (such as a nation) to a transaction. The terms are thus equal to the ratio at which goods are exchanged. In general, the terms of trade are said to move in favor of the party that gives up fewer units of goods for one unit of goods received and

against the party that gives up more units of goods for one unit of goods received. In international economics, the concept of terms of trade plays an important role in evaluating exchange relationships between nations.

theory Set of definitions, assumptions, and hypotheses put together in a manner that expresses apparent relationships or underlying principles of certain observed phenomena in a meaningful way.

time deposit Money held in a depository-institution account of an individual or firm. Certain types of time deposits have specified maturity dates. For other types, the depository institution may require advance notice of withdrawal.

time preference Human desire for a good in the present as opposed to the future. The desire is reflected by the price people are willing to pay for immediate possession of the good as opposed to the price they are willing to pay for future possession.

time series A set of data ordered chronologically. Most of the published data of business and economics are expressed in the form of time series.

time value of money The notion that dollars at different points in time cannot be made directly comparable unless they are first adjusted by a common factor—the interest rate. For example, if your money can earn 6 percent annually, the $1 today is worth $1.06 to you one year from today. Similarly, $1.06 next year is worth an additional 6 percent, or $1.124, two years from today. Conversely, $1.06 one year from today is worth $1 to you today; $1.124 two years from today is worth $1.06 a year from today, and is worth $1 today. (*See also* **compounding; discounting**.)

TIP See *tax-based incomes policy.*

Tobin, James (1918–) Leading American economist and professor emeritus at Yale University. Much of his research involved the integration of Keynesian macroeconomic theory with the ways in which people and institutions behave in the marketplace. His best-known work was on the subject of portfolio-selection theory, for which he was commended when he received the Nobel Prize in 1981.

token money Any object (usually coins) whose value as money is greater than the market value of the materials of which it is composed. *Example:* pennies, nickels, and so on.

total cost Sum of a firm's total fixed costs and total variable costs.

total fixed costs Costs that do not vary with a firm's output. *Examples:* rental payments, interest on debt, property taxes.

total-marginal relationship Relationship between all corresponding total and marginal curves such that, when a total curve is increasing at an increasing rate, its corresponding marginal curve is rising; when a total curve is increasing at a decreasing rate, its corresponding marginal curve is falling; and when a total curve is increasing at a zero rate, as occurs when it is at a maximum, its corresponding marginal curve is zero. (*Note:* The case of decreasing total curves gives rise to negative marginal curves, but these situations are not ordinarily relevant or realistic in an economic sense.)

total revenue (TR)   A firm's total receipts; equal to price per unit times the number of units sold.

total variable costs   Costs that vary directly with a firm's output, rising as output increases over the full range of production. *Examples:* costs of raw materials, fuel, labor, and so on.

trade association   Organization of independent business enterprises (usually but not always in the same industry) established for mutually beneficial purposes. (*Note:* A trade association that behaves illegally by fixing prices, restricting output, or allocating markets for its members is similar to a cartel.) (*See also* **cartel**.)

Trade Expansion Act (1962)   Part of the U.S. Reciprocal Trade Agreements program. This act broadened the powers of the President to (1) negotiate further tariff reductions on broad categories of goods; (2) lower or eliminate tariffs on those goods for which the European Common Market and the United States together account for at least 80 percent of total world exports; (3) lower tariffs by as much as 50 percent on the basis of reciprocal trade agreements, provided that such agreements include most-favored-nation clauses so that the benefits of reduced tariffs are extended to other countries; and (4) grant vocational, technical, and financial assistance to American employees and businesspeople whose industries are adversely affected by tariff reduction.

trade-possibilities curve   Curve that depicts the amounts of goods that countries may exchange with each other. The *slope* of the curve measures the **terms of trade**.

transaction deposits   *See* **checkable deposits**.

transaction costs   The time, effort, and expense that go into the purchase or sale of a good.

transactions motive   Desire on the part of households and businesses to hold some of their assets in liquid form so that they can engage in day-to-day spending activities. This motive is influenced primarily by the level of income rather than by changes in the interest rate, and it is one of the chief sources of demand for loanable funds in the modern theory of interest.

transfer payments   Expenditures within or between sectors of the economy for which there are no corresponding contributions to current production. *Examples:* social security payments, unemployment compensation, relief payments, veterans' bonuses, net interest paid on government bonds and on consumer loans, and business transfers (such as charitable contributions and losses resulting from theft and from debt defaults).

transmission mechanism (for monetary policy)   Process by which changes in the monetary growth rate bring about changes in people's spending behavior, and affect prices,

interest rates, and other economic variables.

Treasury bills   Marketable financial obligations of the U.S. Treasury. They have minimum denominations of $10,000, and they usually mature in 3 months, 6 months, or 1 year.

Treasury bonds   Marketable financial obligations of the U.S. Treasury, maturing in more than 10 years from the date of issue. (These are *not* U.S. Savings Bonds, with which most people are familiar.)

Treasury notes   Marketable financial obligations of the U.S. Treasury, maturing in 1 to 10 years from date of issue.

trend   Long-run growth or decline of an economic time series over a period of years.

truncated multiplier   The multiplier applicable to a finite number of time periods. Its size approaches that of the static multiplier as the number of periods increases. However, it always realizes more than half the effect of the static multiplier within the first few periods. Thus the truncated multiplier for, say, four periods is:

Truncated multiplier for four periods
$$= 1 + MPC + (MPC)^2 = (MPC)^3$$

two-part tariff   Pricing method whereby the buyer pays two different sums: a fixed charge representing an access fee and another charge varying with use. This pricing method is suitable for a product with separable complementary demands. (*Examples:* Public utilities charge a minimum fee and then levy an additional charge based on services rendered. An amusement park may charge an entrance fee and then impose separate charges for individual attractions.) In most cases, the fixed fee is intended to recover installation and maintenance costs, while the variable charges are designed to pay for the operation of specific services actually consumed.

tying contract (tie-in sale)   Practice whereby a seller requires the buyer to purchase one or more additional or "tied" products as a condition for purchasing the desired or "tying" product. *Examples:* block bookings of motion pictures in which movie theaters are required to take "B" films as a condition for obtaining "A" films; the United Shoe Machinery Co., which once required shoemakers to purchase other materials as a condition for purchasing their shoe machinery.

U

uncertainty   State of knowledge in which the probabilities of outcomes resulting from specific actions are not known and cannot be predicted because they are subjective rather than objective phenomena. Uncertainties, therefore, are not insurable and cannot be integrated into the firm's cost structure.

underconsumption theory (of business cycles)   Explanation of economic fluctuations that holds that recessions result from consumer expenditures lagging behind output because too large a proportion of society's income is not spent on consumption. According to the theory, society distributes income too inequitably to enable people to purchase all the goods produced.

underemployment   See *disguised unemployment.*

unemployment   Situation that exists whenever resources are out of work or are not being used efficiently. There are various types of unemployment, such as technological, frictional, structural, disguised, involuntary, and cyclical. (Each of these is defined separately in this Dictionary.) The type most commonly meant, unless otherwise specified, is *involuntary unemployment.*

unemployment benefits   *Wee*kly payments, administered by state governments, to "covered" workers who are involuntarily unemployed.

unemployment rate   Percentage of the civilian labor force that is not working but is actively seeking work. The figure is based on a monthly survey conducted by the U.S. Department of Labor.

$$\text{Unemployment rate} = \frac{\text{number of unemployed people actively seeking work}}{\text{civilian labor force}}$$

unfair competition   Deceptive, dishonest, or injurious methods of competitive behavior. Such practices are illegal under the antitrust laws.

union   Organization of workers that seeks to gain a degree of monopoly power in the sale of its services so that it may be able to secure higher wages, better working conditions, protection from arbitrary treatment by management, and other economic improvements for its members.

union shop   Business firm that permits a union nonmember to be hired on condition that he or she join the union after being employed.

unit of account   A "common denominator" in terms of which the value of goods is quoted. A nation's currency such as the dollar, the pound, the yen, or the franc, are examples. A barter economy is one with no unit of account.

U.S. Steel case (1920)   Major antitrust case against U.S. Steel Corporation. The company, formed from a consolidation of many independent firms in 1901, accounted for nearly half the national output of iron and steel. Nevertheless, the Court found no evidence of wrongdoing and refused to order the breakup of the company. "The law does not make mere size an offense, or the existence of unexerted power an offense," said the Court. This was thus an application of the *rule of reason* by the Court, one of many such applications that have been made.

utility   Ability of a good or service to satisfy a want. Utility is determined by the satisfaction that one receives from consuming something.

utopian socialism   Philosophy advanced by a group of English and French writers in the early nineteenth century that advocated the creation of model communities, largely self-contained, in which the instruments of production were collectively owned and government was primarily on a voluntary and wholly democratic basis. The leading proponents were Robert Owen (1771–1858) in England and Charles Fourier (1772–1837) in France.

V

value   Power of a commodity to command other commodities in exchange for itself, as measured by the proportional quantities in which a commodity exchanges with all other commodities.

value added   Increment in value at each stage in the production of a good. The sum of the increments for all stages of production gives the total income—the aggregate of wages, rent, interest, and profit—derived from the production of the good.

value-added tax   Type of national sales tax paid by manufacturers and merchants on the value contributed to a product at each stage of its production and distribution.

variable costs   Costs that vary directly with a firm's output, rising as output increases over the full range of production. *Examples:* costs of raw materials, fuel, labor, and so on.

variable proportions, law of   See *diminishing returns, law of*

Veblen, Thorstein Bunde (1857–1929)   American institutional economist and critic of neoclassical economics. He emphasized the role of social institutions (that is, customs and practices) as major determinants of economic behavior. Among his many books, his first and best-known one was *The Theory of the Leisure Class* (1899). In this book he coined the famous phrase "Conspicuous consumption" as a characteristic of the "leisure class." (*See conspicuous consumption.*)

verification   Testing of alternative hypotheses or conclusions by means of actual observation or experimentation—that is, by reference to the facts.

vertical equity   Doctrine that states that "unequals should be treated unequally." *Example:* Persons of different income, wealth, or other taxpaying ability should, in order to bear equal tax burdens (or make equal subjective sacrifices), pay different amounts of tax. (*Compare horizontal equity.*)

vertical merger   Amalgamation under one ownership of plants engaged in different stages of production of the same or similar goods, from raw materials to finished products. It may take the form of forward integration into buyer markets or backward integration into supplier markets. The chief objective is to achieve greater economies by combining different production stages and by regularizing supplies, thereby increasing profit margins. *Example:* A shoe manufacturer may merge with a chain of retail shoe stores, and with a leather-processing firm.

W

wages   **1.** Payment to those owners of resources who supply the factor of production known as "labor." This payment includes wages, salaries, commissions, and the like. **2.** The price paid for the use of labor. It is usually expressed as time rates, such as so much per hour, day, or week, or less frequently as rates of so much per unit of work performed.

wages-fund theory   Classical theory of wages best articulated by John Stuart Mill in 1848. It held that producers set aside a portion of their capital funds for the purpose of hiring workers needed for production. The amount of the fund depends on the stock of capital relative to the number of workers. In the long run, however, the accumulation of capital is itself limited or determined by the tendency toward a minimum "subsistence rate" of profits; hence the only effective way to raise real wages is to reduce the number of workers or size of the population (*Note:* This theory was a reformulation of the *subsistence theory of wages.*)

Walras, Léon (1834–1910)   French economist whose major work, *Elements of Pure Economics* (1874), was done at the University of Lausanne, Switzerland. He is regarded as one of the greatest economic theorists of all time. This is due to his mathematical formulations of the theory of general equilibrium "under a system of perfectly free competition." The model links the various markets of the economy through systems of equations, and shows the conditions needed to determine equilibrium prices and quantities. The Walrasian system thus represents the perfection of classical and neoclassical economics.

"wastes" of monopolistic competition   Expression used to denote overcrowded "sick" industries of monopolistic competition; the wastes are characterized by chronic excess capacity and inefficient operations. *Examples:* retail trades; textile manufacturing.

wealth   Anything that has value because it is capable of producing income. A "stock" of value as compared to a "flow" of income. (*Compare income.*)

welfare economics   Branch of economic theory concerned with the development of principles for maximizing social welfare.

Wheeler-Lea Act (1938)   Amendment to the Federal Trade Commission Act. It was passed primarily to protect consumers, rather than just business competitors, from unfair (deceptive, dishonest, or injurious) methods of competition. Thus, injured consumers are given equal protection before the law with injured merchants. The act also pro-

hibits false or misleading advertisements for food, drugs, cosmetics, and therapeutic devices.

white market   Legal market in which ration coupons for a commodity are transferable, permitting people who do not want all their coupons to sell them to those who do. A white market thus reduces, but does not eliminate, the inequities and skullduggery generally associated with rationing and a black market. (*Compare black market.*)

World Bank   An organization established by the United Nations in 1945 to help improve productivity in poor countries by financing development projects, communications and transportation facilities, and health programs.

X

X-inefficiency   Failure of an organization to minimize costs by not making the best use of its resources. X-inefficiency is often due to the failures of managers and/or employees to work as effectively as they can.

Y

yellow-dog contract   Contract that requires an employee to promise as a condition of employment that he will not belong to a labor union. Declared illegal in the Norris-La Guardia Act of 1932.

yield   Effective rate of return on any type of investment. It includes both annual returns and any profit (or loss) that is realized when the investment is terminated. The yield is expressed as a percentage figure.

yield, current   Annual return on an investment expressed as a percentage of its present price.

yield curve   Graph of the relationship between short-term and long-term interest rates (yields) on debt instruments that are alike in all respects except term to maturity. The graph is usually drawn for U.S. Treasury securities because they are alike in three important respects: zero default risk, equal tax treatment, and high marketability. At any given time a yield curve may be ascending, descending (i.e., inverted), flat, or humped (which combines elements of the previous three). The ascending type is the one that is normally expected. In general, a yield curve is a forecast of short- and long-term interest rates by financial market participants—lenders and borrowers.

yield to maturity   Percentage figure reflecting the effective yield on a debt instrument (such as a bond). The figure is based on the difference between its purchase price and its redemption price, taking into account any returns received by the bondholder in the interim.

Population, Employment, Wages, and Productivity | Production, Business Activity | Prices

	29	30	31	32	33	34	35	36	37	38	39	40	41	42	43
	Population	Civilian labor force	Unemployment	Unemployment as percentage of civilian labor force	Average weekly hours of work	Average gross hourly earnings	Output per hour of all persons	Compensation per hour	Index of industrial production	Total new construction — Value put in place	Business expenditures for new plant and equipment	Manufacturers' new orders	Consumer Price Index	Producer Price Index (total finished goods)	GDP deflator (Implicit Price Index)
					Total private nonagricultural sector		Business sector								
Year	Millions of persons			Percent	Hours	Dollars	1982=100		1987 =100	Billions of dollars			1982-84 =100	1982 =100	1987 =100
1960	180.7	69.6	3.9	5.5	38.6	2.09	65.6	21.1	38.1	54.7	39.44	30,232	29.6	33.4	26.0
1961	183.8	70.5	4.7	6.7	38.6	2.14	68.1	21.9	38.4	56.4	38.34	31,112	29.9	33.4	26.3
1962	186.7	70.6	3.9	5.5	38.7	2.22	70.4	22.9	41.6	60.2	40.86	33,440	30.2	33.5	26.8
1963	189.4	71.3	4.1	5.7	38.8	2.28	73.3	23.8	44.0	64.8	43.67	35,511	30.6	33.4	27.2
1964	192.1	73.1	3.8	5.2	38.7	2.36	76.5	25.0	47.0	72.1	51.26	38,240	31.0	33.5	27.7
1965	194.6	74.5	3.4	4.5	38.8	2.45	78.6	26.0	51.7	78.0	59.52	42,137	31.5	34.1	28.4
1966	197.0	75.8	2.9	3.8	38.6	2.56	81.0	27.8	56.3	81.2	70.40	46,420	32.4	35.2	29.4
1967	199.1	77.3	3.0	3.8	38.0	2.68	83.0	29.4	57.5	83.0	72.75	47,067	33.4	35.6	30.3
1968	201.2	78.7	2.8	3.6	37.8	2.85	85.4	31.8	60.7	92.4	76.42	50,657	34.8	36.6	31.7
1969	202.7	80.7	2.8	3.5	37.7	3.04	85.9	34.1	63.5	99.8	85.74	53,990	36.7	38.0	33.3
1970	204.9	82.8	4.1	4.9	37.1	3.23	87.0	36.7	61.4	100.7	91.91	52,022	38.8	39.3	35.1
1971	207.1	84.4	5.0	5.9	36.9	3.45	90.2	39.0	62.2	117.3	92.91	55,921	40.5	40.5	37.0
1972	208.9	87.0	4.8	5.6	37.0	3.70	92.6	41.5	68.3	133.3	103.40	64,182	41.8	41.8	38.8
1973	211.9	89.4	4.3	4.9	36.9	3.94	95.0	45.1	73.8	146.8	120.03	76,003	44.4	45.6	41.3
1974	213.9	91.9	5.2	5.6	36.5	4.24	93.3	49.5	72.7	147.5	139.67	87,327	49.3	52.6	44.9
1975	216.0	93.8	7.9	8.5	36.1	4.53	95.5	54.5	66.3	145.6	142.42	85,139	53.8	58.2	49.2
1976	218.0	96.2	7.4	7.7	36.1	4.86	98.3	59.4	72.4	165.4	158.44	99,513	56.9	60.8	52.3
1977	220.2	99.1	7.0	7.1	36.0	5.25	99.8	64.2	78.2	193.1	184.82	115,109	60.6	64.7	55.9
1978	222.6	102.3	6.2	6.1	35.8	5.69	100.4	69.9	82.6	230.2	216.81	131,629	65.2	69.8	60.3
1979	225.1	104.0	6.1	5.8	35.7	6.16	99.3	76.7	85.7	259.8	255.26	147,604	72.6	77.6	65.5
1980	227.8	106.9	7.6	7.0	35.3	6.66	98.6	85.0	84.1	259.7	286.40	156,359	82.4	88.0	71.7
1981	230.1	108.7	8.3	7.5	35.2	7.25	99.9	93.0	85.7	272.0	324.73	168,025	90.9	96.1	78.9
1982	232.5	110.2	10.7	9.7	34.8	7.68	100.0	100.0	81.9	260.6	326.19	162,140	96.5	100.0	83.8
1983	234.8	111.6	10.7	9.6	35.0	8.02	102.2	103.7	84.9	294.9	321.16	175,451	99.6	101.6	87.2
1984	237.0	113.5	8.5	7.5	35.2	8.32	104.6	108.1	92.8	348.8	373.83	192,879	103.9	103.7	91.0
1985	239.3	115.5	8.3	7.2	34.9	8.57	106.1	113.0	94.4	377.4	410.12	195,706	107.6	104.7	94.4
1986	241.6	117.8	8.2	7.0	34.8	8.76	108.3	118.6	95.3	407.7	399.36	195,204	109.6	103.2	96.9
1987	243.9	119.9	7.4	6.2	34.8	8.98	109.4	122.7	100.0	419.3	410.52	209,389	113.6	105.4	100.0
1988	246.1	121.6	6.7	5.5	34.7	9.25	110.4	128.0	105.4	432.2	455.49	227,025	118.3	108.0	103.9
1989	248.0	123.8	6.5	5.3	34.7	9.66	109.5	132.5	108.1	443.7	507.40	240,758	124.0	113.6	108.4
1990	250.0	124.8	6.9	5.5	34.5	10.02	109.7	139.6	109.2	446.4	532.61	243,643	130.7	119.2	112.9
1991	252.7	125.3	8.4	6.7	34.3	10.34	110.2	140.0	107.1	404.7	529.97	246,751	136.2	121.7	117.0
1992	255.4	126.6	8.0	6.3	34.1	10.38	110.4	140.2	108.1	403.6	558.60	245,012	141.1	125.6	121.0